■ THE RESOURCE FOR THE INDEPENDENT TRAVELER

"The guides are aimed not only at young budget travelers but at the indepedent traveler; a sort of streetwise cookbook for traveling alone."

—The New York Times

"Unbeatable; good sight-seeing advice; up-to-date info on restaurants, hotels, and inns; a commitment to money-saving travel; and a wry style that brightens nearly every page."

—The Washington Post

"Lighthearted and sophisticated, informative and fun to read. [Let's Go] helps the novice traveler navigate like a knowledgeable old hand."

—Atlanta Journal-Constitution

"A world-wise traveling companion—always ready with friendly advice and helpful hints, all sprinkled with a bit of wit."

—The Philadelphia Inquirer

■ THE BEST TRAVEL BARGAINS IN YOUR PRICE RANGE

"All the dirt, dirt cheap."

—People

"Anything you need to know about budget traveling is detailed in this book."

—The Chicago Sun-Times

"Let's Go follows the creed that you don't have to toss your life's savings to the wind to travel—unless you want to."

—The Salt Lake Tribune

■ REAL ADVICE FOR REAL EXPERIENCES

"The writers seem to have experienced every rooster-packed bus and lunar-surfaced mattress about which they write."

—The New York Times

"A guide should tell you what to expect from a destination. Here Let's Go shines."

—The Chicago Tribune

LET'S GO PUBLICATIONS

TRAVEL GUIDES

Alaska & the Pacific Northwest 2003
Australia 2003
Austria & Switzerland 2003
Britain & Ireland 2003
California 2003
Central America 8th edition
Chile 1st edition **NEW TITLE**
China 4th edition
Costa Rica 1st edition **NEW TITLE**
Eastern Europe 2003
Egypt 2nd edition
Europe 2003
France 2003
Germany 2003
Greece 2003
Hawaii 2003 **NEW TITLE**
India & Nepal 7th edition
Ireland 2003
Israel 4th edition
Italy 2003
Mexico 19th edition
Middle East 4th edition
New Zealand 6th edition
Peru, Ecuador & Bolivia 3rd edition
South Africa 5th edition
Southeast Asia 8th edition
Southwest USA 2003
Spain & Portugal 2003
Thailand 1st edition **NEW TITLE**
Turkey 5th edition
USA 2003
Western Europe 2003

CITY GUIDES

Amsterdam 2003
Barcelona 2003
Boston 2003
London 2003
New York City 2003
Paris 2003
Rome 2003
San Francisco 2003
Washington, D.C. 2003

MAP GUIDES

Amsterdam
Berlin
Boston
Chicago
Dublin
Florence
Hong Kong
London
Los Angeles
Madrid
New Orleans
New York City
Paris
Prague
Rome
San Francisco
Seattle
Sydney
Venice
Washington, D.C.

GREECE
INCLUDING CYPRUS
2003

Jonelle Lonergan Editor
Andrew Zaroulis Associate Editor

Researcher-Writers
Kevin Connor
Gary Cooney
Emily Ogden
Geoffrey Reed
Jen Taylor
Scottie Thompson

Avra Van Der Zee Map Editor
Angela Mi Young Hur Managing Editor
Eduardo Montoya Typesetter

Macmillan

HELPING LET'S GO If you want to share your discoveries, suggestions, or corrections, please drop us a line. We read every piece of correspondence, whether a postcard, a 10-page email, or a coconut. Please note that mail received after May 2003 may be too late for the 2004 book, but will be kept for future editions. **Address mail to:**

Let's Go: Greece
67 Mount Auburn Street
Cambridge, MA 02138
USA

Visit Let's Go at **http://www.letsgo.com,** or send email to:

feedback@letsgo.com
Subject: "Let's Go: Greece"

In addition to the invaluable travel advice our readers share with us, many are kind enough to offer their services as researchers or editors. Unfortunately, our charter enables us to employ only currently enrolled Harvard students.

Published in Great Britain 2003 by Macmillan, an imprint of Pan Macmillan Ltd.
20 New Wharf Road, London N1 9RR
Basingstoke and Oxford
Associated companies throughout the world
www.panmacmillan.com

Published in the United States of America by St. Martin's Press.

ISBN: 1-4050-0069 4
First edition
10 9 8 7 6 5 4 3 2 1

Let's Go: Greece is written by Let's Go Publications, 67 Mount Auburn Street, Cambridge, MA 02138, USA.

Printed in the USA on recycled paper with soy ink.

WHO WE ARE

A NEW LET'S GO FOR 2003

With a sleeker look and innovative new content, we have revamped the entire series to reflect more than ever the needs and interests of the independent traveler. Here are just some of the improvements you will notice when traveling with the new *Let's Go*.

MORE PRICE OPTIONS

Still the best resource for budget travelers, *Let's Go* recognizes that everyone needs the occassional indulgence. Our "Big Splurges" indicate establishments that are actually worth those extra pennies (pulas, pesos, or pounds), and price-level symbols (❶ ❷ ❸ ❹ ❺) allow you to quickly determine whether an accommodation or restaurant will break the bank. We may have diversified, but we'll never lose our budget focus—"Hidden Deals" reveal the best-kept travel secrets.

BEYOND THE TOURIST EXPERIENCE

Our Alternatives to Tourism chapter offers ideas on immersing yourself in a new community through study, work, or volunteering.

AN INSIDER'S PERSPECTIVE

As always, every item is written and researched by our on-site writers. This year we have highlighted more viewpoints to help you gain an even more thorough understanding of the places you are visiting.

IN RECENT NEWS. *Let's Go* correspondents around the globe report back on current regional issues that may affect you as a traveler.

CONTRIBUTING WRITERS. Respected scholars and former *Let's Go* writers discuss topics on society and culture, going into greater depth than the usual guidebook summary.

THE LOCAL STORY. From the Parisian monk toting a cell phone to the Russian *babushka* confronting capitalism, *Let's Go* shares its revealing conversations with local personalities—a unique glimpse of what matters to real people.

FROM THE ROAD. Always helpful and sometimes downright hilarious, our researchers share useful insights on the typical (and atypical) travel experience.

SLIMMER SIZE

Don't be fooled by our new, smaller size. *Let's Go* is still packed with invaluable travel advice, but now it's easier to carry with a more compact design.

FORTY-THREE YEARS OF WISDOM

For over four decades *Let's Go* has provided the most up-to-date information on the hippest cafes, the most pristine beaches, and the best routes from border to border. It all started in 1960 when a few well-traveled students at Harvard University handed out a 20-page mimeographed pamphlet of their tips on budget travel to passengers on student charter flights to Europe. From humble beginnings, *Let's Go* has grown to cover six continents and *Let's Go: Europe* still reigns as the world's best-selling travel guide. This year we've beefed up our coverage of Latin America with *Let's Go: Costa Rica* and *Let's Go: Chile;* on the other side of the globe, we've added *Let's Go: Thailand* and *Let's Go: Hawaii.* Our new guides bring the total number of titles to 61, each infused with the spirit of adventure that travelers around the world have come to count on.

CONTENTS

MAPS

HOW TO USE THIS BOOK

ORGANIZATION. Your journey begins in Athens, the country's capital and transportation hub. From there, coverage radiates outward through the Peloponnese, the mainland, and the islands hugging the coast, concluding with Cyprus. The black tabs on the side of the book should help you navigate your way through.

PRICE RANGES AND RANKINGS. Our researchers list establishments in order of value from best to worst. Our absolute favorites are denoted by the Let's Go thumbs-up (☒). Since the best value does not always mean the cheapest price, we have incorporated a system of price ranges in the guide. The table below lists how prices fall within each bracket.

GREECE	❶	❷	❸	❹	❺
ACCOMMODATIONS	€1-10	€10-25	€25-40	€40-70	€70-100
FOOD	€1-5	€5-10	€10-15	€15-25	€25-40
CYPRUS	❶	❷	❸	❹	❺
ACCOMMODATIONS	£1-6	£6-14	£14-24	£24-40	£40-60
FOOD	£1-3	£3-5	£5-10	£10-15	£15-20

PHONE CODES AND TELEPHONE NUMBERS. Phone numbers in text are preceded by the ☎ icon. Since Greek telephone numbers now require the local code regardless of the region you're calling from, all local codes are incorporated into the telephone numbers in the text.

WHEN TO USE IT

TWO MONTHS BEFORE. The first chapter, **Discover Greece,** contains highlights of the region, including Suggested Itineraries (see p. 4) that can help you plan your trip. The **Essentials** (see p. 25) section contains practical information on planning a budget, making reservations, renewing a passport, and has other useful tips.

ONE MONTH BEFORE. Take care of insurance, and write down a list of emergency numbers and hotlines. Make a list of packing essentials (see **Packing,** p. 40) and buy anything you are missing. Read the coverage and make sure you understand the logistics of your itinerary (buying ferry tickets, catching ferries, finding a place to stay when you miss the ferry, etc.). Make hostel and hotel reservations.

2 WEEKS BEFORE. Leave an itinerary and a photocopy of important documents with someone at home. Sip an iced coffee and pretend it's a Greek *frappé* while you peruse the **Life and Times** (see p. 7), which has info on history, culture, recent political events, and more.

ON THE ROAD. The **Appendix** contains a glossary of phrases, the Greek alphabet, a pronunciation guide, and other helpful information that may slip your mind after your eighth ouzo shot. Now, arm yourself with a travel journal and hit the road.

A NOTE TO OUR READERS The information for this book was gathered by *Let's Go* researchers from May through August of 2002. Each listing is based on one researcher's opinion, formed during his or her visit at a particular time. Those traveling at other times may have different experiences since prices, dates, hours, and conditions are always subject to change. You are urged to check the facts presented in this book beforehand to avoid inconvenience and surprises.

RESEARCHER-WRITERS

Kevin Connor *Central Greece, the Sporades, Saronic Gulf, and Northeast Aegean Islands*

Kevin negotiated around ferry strikes and surly bus drivers to complete an epic itinerary that spanned the region. An experienced kayaker, hiker, and marathon runner, the self-proclaimed "palest man in Greece" slathered on sunblock and tackled outdoors coverage on Evia (p. 347) and the mainland, leaving local wildlife and the occasional empty ouzo bottle in his wake.

Gary Cooney *Central and Northern Greece*

After extensive backpacking in Europe and China, Gary was well-prepared for trekking through mainland Greece. The hard-working Dublin native found out the best the country has to offer, from 5-star hotels in Thessaloniki (p. 213) to humble monk's quarters on Mt. Athos (p. 256). Not many RWs would think to ring up their editors from halfway up Mt. Olympus (p. 230), but Gary kept us updated with his exploits and kept us rolling with his dry wit all summer.

Emily Ogden *Cyprus and the Dodecanese*

Having just completed her prize-winning undergraduate thesis in creative writing, Emily took off for Cyprus two days after graduation, where she wowed us with her fluid prose and skillful driving (p. 576). Our own incarnation of Lawrence Durrell and Lord Byron, Emily was so taken with Rhodes (p. 465), Karpathos (p. 496), and the Knights Templar that she stayed on in Greece at the end of the summer, where she plans to continue writing poetry.

Geoffrey Reed *Crete, the Cyclades, and Northeast Aegean Islands*

Facing the Valley of Death (p. 561), a leper colony (p. 551), and the fearsome Mykonosian nightlife (p. 402), Geoff proved himself an intrepid adventurer and, in between, a first-class writer. Wherever he went, he always returned with excellent research and an entertaining yarn. An avid hiker, Geoff's whirlwind itinerary seemed not to faze him at all. He was always on the move, chasing the essence of Greece and, occasionally, a "stolen" rental car.

Jen Taylor *Peloponnese and Ionian Islands*

Jen brought savvy to an itinerary that involved days in charming, dusty villages in the Peloponnese and nights in pulsating clubs on the Ionian Islands. A former editor for *Let's Go: Greece* and a frequent contributer to letsgo.com, she researched her route gleefully and never lost her amazing eye for detail. Jen's experience and good humor have helped this book immensely. She'll be back in Greece soon, if only to ride her beloved Diakofto rack-railway (p. 137).

Scottie Thompson *Athens and the Cyclades*

Only a skilled and patient traveler could have tackled the intimidating city of Athens so thoroughly and still have had the energy to research the bustling Cyclades. Luckily, Scottie had the experience (earned in South Africa, the US, and across Europe) and the mindset needed to do the job. A dancer, actor, and choreographer when not on the road, she struggled through ferry strikes, vicious maelstroms (p. 76), and rude cab drivers in Greece to tell us the tale. She rambled through cities and villages with a constant smile.

CONTRIBUTING WRITERS

Eleni N. Gage, a former researcher-writer and editor of *Let's Go: Greece and Turkey,* is the author of *North of Ithaka,* a travel memoir about Northern Greece to be published by the Free Press in Spring 2004.

Gregory A. Maniatis is the founder of *Odyssey Magazine,* the leading international magazine about Greece and Greeks around the world. He has also contributed to *New York Magazine,* the *Independent,* the *Washington Monthly,* Time-Life Books, and other publications.

Nicholas Papandreou is a writer living in Greece. He is the author of two novels, *A Crowded Heart* (Picador) and *Kleptomnemon: The Thief of Memories.* He is currently an advisor to the Ministry of the Aegean, where a major effort is underway to preserve the architectural integrity of the area. His articles and columns appear in weekly and monthly newspapers and magazines throughout Greece.

ACKNOWLEDGMENTS

Let's Go Greece thanks a pantheon of gods and goddesses for loving Greece as much as we do: The writers, who kept us drooling over their "mmmm"s and marveling at their travel savvy all summer; Angela for her gentle reminders to line edit (or face her wrath); Avra for braving jagged coastlines, tiny islands, and Greek transliteration; Hannah for squeezing us between Germany and Hungary; Amy for the torch icon; Adam and Harriett for keeping the pod so lively; and Erzulie for paving the way.

Jonelle sends gratitude and a bagel sans lox to the unflappable St. Andrew, for his eagle-eyed edits and endless tolerance. Thanks to: Melissa, Harcourt, and the fine folks in B-11a for indulging my hatred of Pagemaker; My litigious Walker St. roommates; Kat, Susan, Jenn, and Loni, living it up on both coasts; Robbie for summer concertgoing and Sugi for summer novel reading; John Mayer for the guitar pick; Mom and Dad for airport pickups, trips to the circus, and everything in between.

Andrew thanks: Jonelle, without you, I would still be staring at the Athens chapter, which would not have made for a very good book. Thank you. Mom and Dad for introducing me to Greece and for far too many things to list in a space this small. Eternal gratitude to Lara, Christina, and Peter for keeping me sane and for caring so much and to Chloe and Sophie for similar reasons. Yasas to Julie, Ellis, and Beth and to my friends around the world (Eliot E33-34, here's to you). And thank you, Lindsey, for constant support and inspiration.

Avra thanks: Andrew and Jonelle for being so amazing to work with. Thanks to the stellar Greece RWs—Emily, Jen, Scottie, Geoff, Kevin, and Gary—for making these maps possible. Thanks to Mapland for turning a room with no doors into a sanctuary of sorts. Thanks to my roommates, Jack, and Charlotte for keeping me afloat.

Editor
Jonelle Lonergan
Associate Editor
Andrew Zaroulis
Managing Editor
Angela Mi Young Hur
Map Editor
Avra Van Der Zee

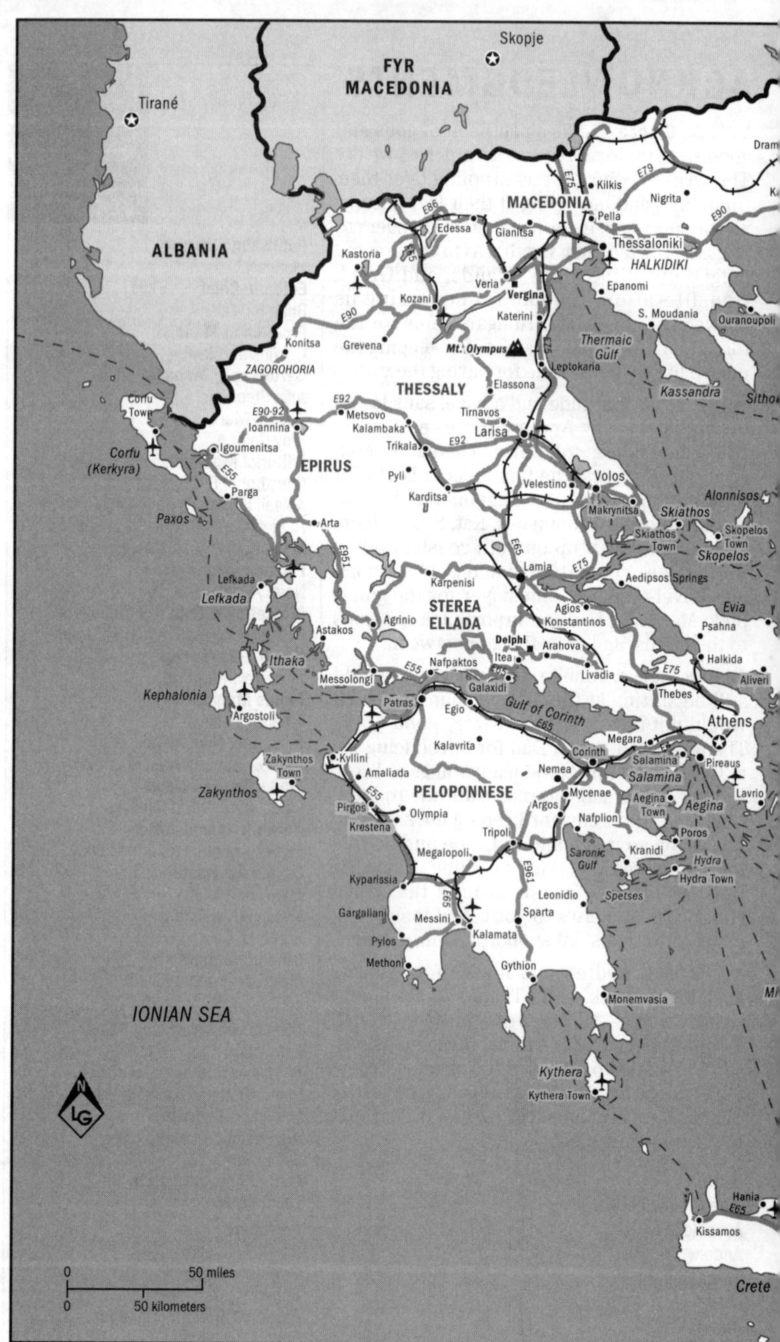

FYR MACEDONIA
Skopje
Tirané
ALBANIA
MACEDONIA
Kilkis
Nigrita
Pella
Edessa
Gianitsa
Thessaloniki
HALKIDIKI
Kastoria
Veria
Vergina
Epanomi
Kozani
Katerini
S. Moudania
Ouranoupoli
Thermaic Gulf
Grevena
Mt. Olympus
Konitsa
ZAGOROHORIA
Leptokaria
THESSALY
Elassona
Kassandra
Corfu Town
Metsovo
Kalambaka
Tirnavos
Ioannina
Larisa
Corfu (Kerkyra)
Igoumenitsa
Trikala
EPIRUS
Pyli
Volos
Velestino
Karditsa
Parga
Makrynitsa
Alonnisos
Skiathos
Paxos
Arta
Skiathos Town
Skopelos Town
Skopelos
Lamia
Lefkada
Karpenisi
Aedipsos Springs
Lefkada
STEREA ELLADA
Agios Konstantinos
Evia
Agrinio
Astakos
Psahna
Delphi
Arahova
Ithaka
Itea
Halkida
Nafpaktos
Messolongi
Livadia
Aliveri
Kephalonia
Galaxidi
Thebes
Patras
Egio
Gulf of Corinth
Argostoli
Athens
Megara
Kalavrita
Corinth
Salamina
Pireaus
Zakynthos Town
Kyllini
Nemea
Salamina
Amaliada
Lavrio
Zakynthos
PELOPONNESE
Mycenae
Aegina Town
Aegina
Pirgos
Argos
Olympia
Nafplion
Krestena
Poros
Tripoli
Saronic Gulf
Kranidi
Megalopoli
Hydra
Hydra Town
Kyparissia
Leonidio
Spetses
Gargaliani
Sparta
Messini
Kalamata
Pylos
Methoni
Gythion
Monemvasia
IONIAN SEA
Kythera
Kythera Town
Hania
Kissamos
Crete
0 50 miles
0 50 kilometers

BULGARIA
TURKEY
BLACK SEA
Orestiada
Didimotho
THRACE
Soufli
Istanbul
Xanthi
Komotini
E85
E90
Alexandroupolis
Sea of Marmara
Limenas
Thasos
Samothraki
Samothraki
Mt. Athos
Limnos
Agia Marina
Mytilini
Lesvos
TURKEY
Skyros Town
AEGEAN SEA
Skyros
Chios
Chios Town
Izmir
Karystos
Andros
Andros
Samos Town
Kea
Tinos
Ikaria
Samos
Syros
Tinos Town
Mykonos Town
Hermoupolis
Mykonos
Kythnos
Delos
Patmos
Leros
Serifos
Kalymnos Town
Sifnos
Paros
Naxos
Naxos
Kalymnos
Kos Town
Paros
Amorgos
Ios
Astypalea
Kos
Symi
Folegandros
Nisyros
Rhodes Town
Anafi
Tilos
Santorini
Halki
Rhodes
SEA OF CRETE
Karpathos
E75
Iraklion
Kassos
Rethymno
Agios Nikolaos
Sitia
Arkalohori
Timbaki
Mires
Ierapetra
Greece

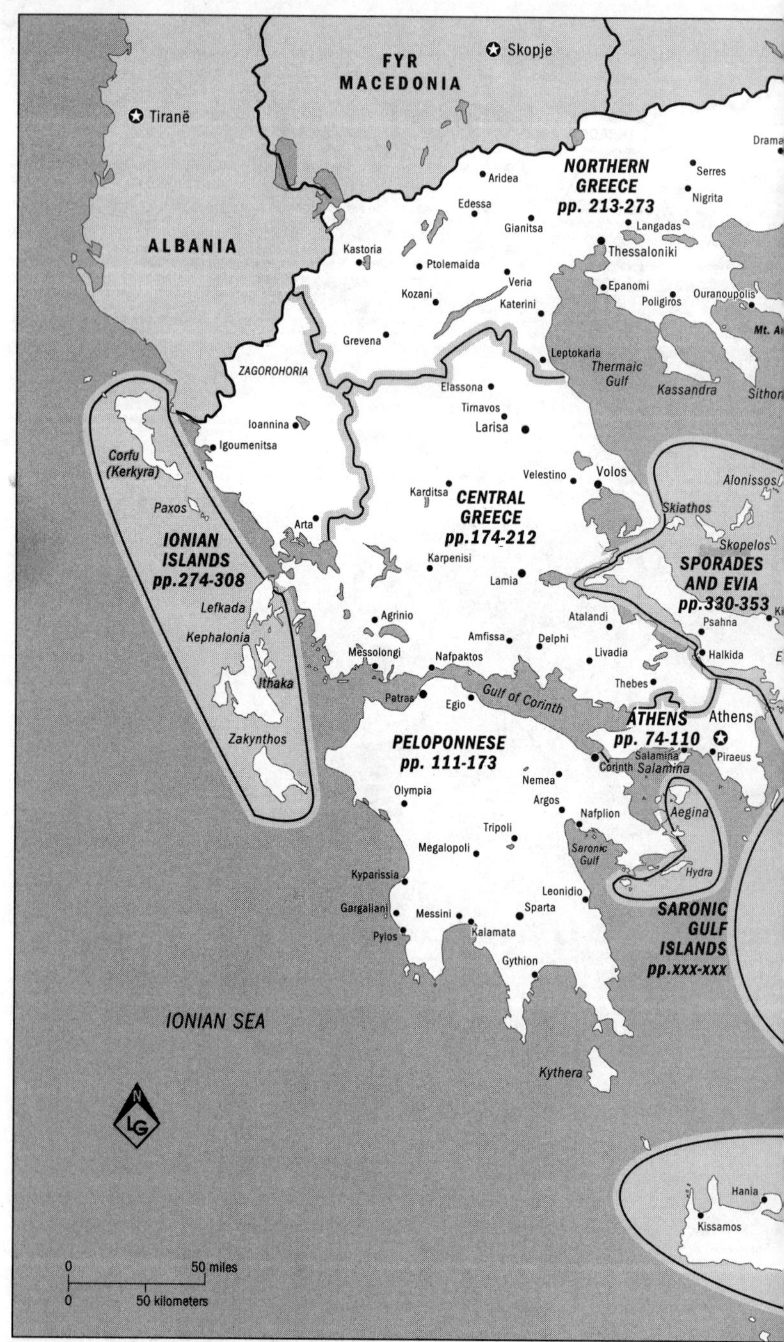

FYR MACEDONIA
Skopje
Tiranë
ALBANIA
NORTHERN GREECE pp. 213-273
Drama
Serres
Nigrita
Aridea
Edessa
Gianitsa
Langadas
Thessaloniki
Kastoria
Ptolemaida
Veria
Kozani
Katerini
Epanomi
Poligiros
Ouranoupolis
Grevena
Leptokaria
Thermaic Gulf
Kassandra
ZAGOROHORIA
Elassona
Tirnavos
Larisa
Ioannina
Igoumenitsa
Corfu (Kerkyra)
Paxos
Velestino
Volos
Karditsa
CENTRAL GREECE pp.174-212
Alonissos
Skiathos
Skopelos
Arta
IONIAN ISLANDS pp.274-308
Karpenisi
Lamia
SPORADES AND EVIA pp.330-353
Psahna
Atalandi
Agrinio
Lefkada
Kephalonia
Amfissa
Delphi
Messolongi
Nafpaktos
Livadia
Halkida
Ithaka
Thebes
Patras
Egio
Gulf of Corinth
ATHENS pp. 74-110
Athens
Zakynthos
PELOPONNESE pp. 111-173
Salamina
Piraeus
Corinth
Nemea
Olympia
Argos
Nafplion
Aegina
Tripoli
Megalopoli
Saronic Gulf
Hydra
Kyparissia
Leonidio
Gargaliani
Messini
Sparta
Pylos
Kalamata
SARONIC GULF ISLANDS pp.xxx-xxx
Gythion
IONIAN SEA
Kythera
Hania
Kissamos
0
50 miles
0
50 kilometers

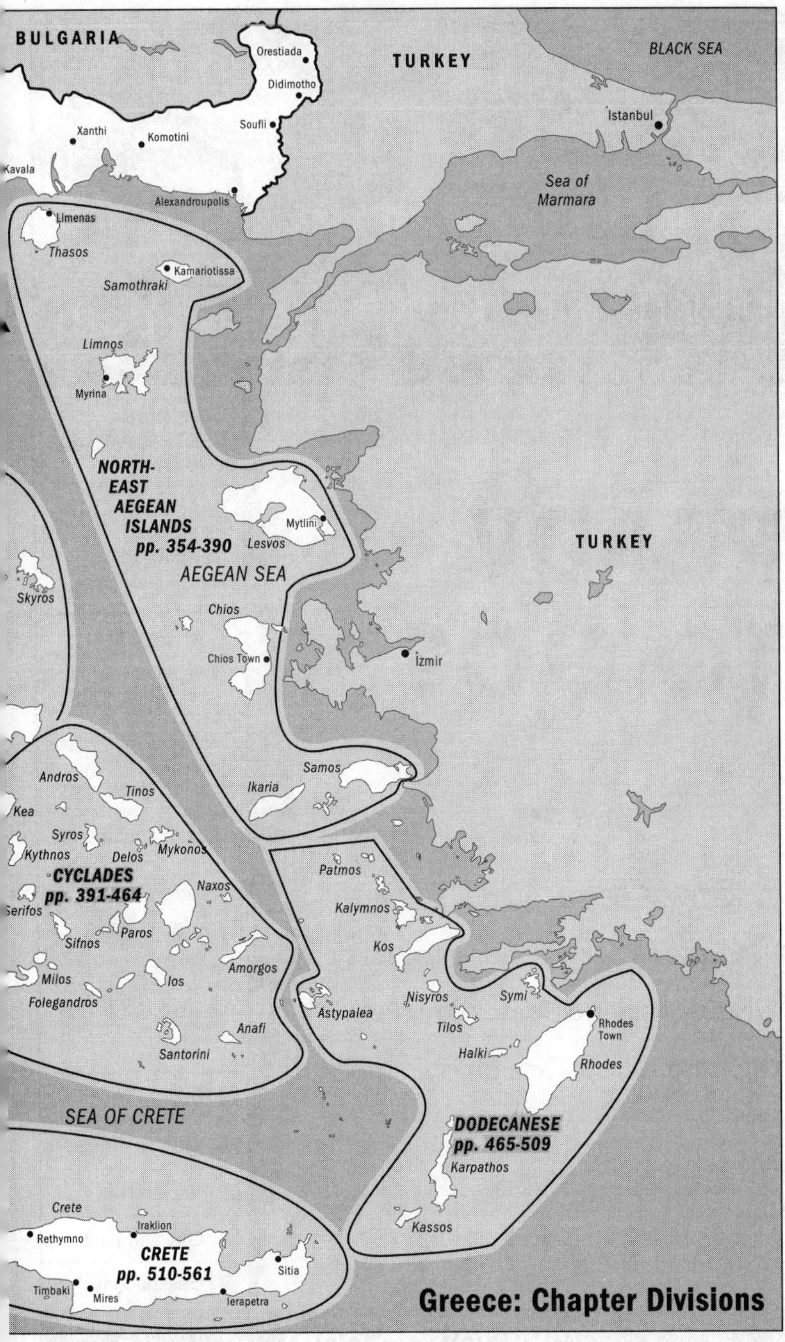

BULGARIA
TURKEY
BLACK SEA
Orestiada
Didimotho
Soufli
Istanbul
Xanthi
Komotini
Kavala
Alexandroupolis
Sea of
Marmara
Limenas
Thasos
Kamariotissa
Samothraki
Limnos
Myrina
NORTH-
EAST
AEGEAN
ISLANDS
pp. 354-390
Mytlini
Lesvos
TURKEY
AEGEAN SEA
Skyros
Chios
Chios Town
İzmir
Samos
Andros
Tinos
Ikaria
Kea
Syros
Mykonos
Kythnos
Delos
CYCLADES
pp. 391-464
Patmos
Naxos
Serifos
Kalymnos
Paros
Sifnos
Kos
Amorgos
Milos
Ios
Folegandros
Nisyros
Symi
Astypalea
Rhodes
Town
Tilos
Anafi
Halki
Santorini
Rhodes
SEA OF CRETE
DODECANESE
pp. 465-509
Karpathos
Crete
Iraklion
Kassos
Rethymno
CRETE
pp. 510-561
Sitia
Timbaki
Mires
Ierapetra
Greece: Chapter Divisions

DISCOVER GREECE

A land where sacred monasteries are mountainside fixtures, three-hour sea-side siestas are standard issue, and dancing on tables until daybreak is a summer rite: Greece's treasures are impossibly varied. Renaissance men long before their time, the ancient Greeks sprung to prominence with their philosophical, literary, artistic, and athletic mastery. Millennia later, schoolkids still dream of Hercules and the Medusa; when those kids grow up, they hanker after Greece's island beaches, free-flowing booze, and the gorgeous natural landscape, which was once the playground of a pantheon of gods. The all-encompassing Greek lifestyle is a frustrating and delicious mix of high speed and sun-inspired lounging, as old men hold lively debates in town plateias, young kids zoom on mopeds around the clock, and unpredictable schedules force a go-with-the-flow take on life.

FACTS AND FIGURES

OFFICIAL NAME Hellenic Republic

POPULATION 10,623,835

CAPITAL Athens

LENGTH OF COASTLINE PER GREEK CITIZEN 1.3m

TOTAL AREA OF GREEK BEACHES 30,000 sq. km

DRINK OF CHOICE Ouzo

PERCENTAGE OF UNINHABITED ISLANDS 88%

RATIO OF FOREIGNERS TO LOCALS 9 tourists to every 10 Greeks

NUMBER OF CALORIES IN THE AVERAGE SOUVLAKI 528

WHEN TO GO

June through August is **high tourist season** in Greece and Cyprus. Bar-studded beaches set the scene for revelry and Dionysian indulgence, as the hundred-degree sun blazes over ancient cities and modern-day sun-worshipers alike. Hotels, domatia, clubs, and sights are, like the nightlife, in full swing. If the crowds or frantic pace of summer travel grate on you, consider visiting during May, early June, or September, when gorgeous weather smiles on thinner crowds. Avid hikers can take advantage of the mellower weather to traverse the unsullied expanses of Northern and Central Greece. In ski areas, winter brings another high season: you can hit the slopes at Mt. Parnassos (p. 177), Mt. Pelion (p. 201), or Metsovo (p. 249). The **low season,** from October through May, generally has cheaper airfares, lodging, and food prices, but many sights and accommodations have shorter hours or close altogether. At this time of year Greece hibernates, resting from summertime farming, fishing, and tourism. Ferries, buses, and trains run considerably less frequently, and life is quieter. For a temperature chart, see **Climate,** p. 601. For a list of Greek festivals, see **Festivals,** p. 22.

THINGS TO DO

Mountain chains, bougainvillea-speckled islands, silver-green olive groves, and the stark contrast of ocher land against the azure Aegean comprise the Greek landscape, the refuge of mythological beasts. This varied land of isolated villages, jasmine-scented islands, and majestic ruins satisfies even the pickiest visitor with its infinite diversions. Don't be afraid to plot out your own route: the famous Greek hospitality will make you feel welcome wherever you go. For more on regional bests, check out the **Highlights of the Region** boxes that begin each chapter.

THE ROAD TO RUIN(S)

As the birthplace of drama, democracy, and western philosophy, Greece's long history has left a wealth of sites in its impressive wake. The mother of all ruins, the **Acropolis** (p. 95), still presides over modern Athens. The gigantic, perfectly proportioned columns of the **Parthenon,** combined with the sun's beating rays and the brilliant gleam of white marble, conjures up the same awe inspired in a millennia of worshipers and pilgrims. A voyage through the **Peloponnese** will transport you back to the era of nymphs, satyrs, and gods in disguise. Take a lap around the well-preserved stadium on the way to the original Olympic fields at **Ancient Olympia** (p. 142), peer into Agamemnon's tomb at **Mycenae** (p. 120), or experience catharsis after watching the performance of an ancient tragedy in the magnificent theater at **Epidavros** (p. 130). Byzantine times stand still at the extensive city-site of **Mystras** (p. 163), the former locus of Constantinople's rule in the Peloponnese. On the mainland, get to "know thyself" at the ancient **Oracle of Delphi** (p. 183). Chase after the floating island of **Delos,** birthplace of Apollo and Artemis, for a peek at the Temple of Apollo and an island-wide archaeological site (p. 408). More archaeological sites include: Heinrich Schliemman's reconstruction of the Minoan palace at **Knossos** (p. 519); an untarnished Minoan site at **Phaistos** (p. 525); Santorini's **Akrotiri,** a city frozen in time by a volcanic eruption (p. 450); onetime cult capital **Paleopolis** on Samothraki (p. 383); and the dual ruins of **Pella** and **Vergina** in Northern Greece, frequented by Philip II and his son Alexander the Great (p. 228). From Rhodes, you can reach the remnants of three of the seven wonders of the ancient world by daytrip. The **Colossus of Rhodes** leaves no trace today, though you can contemplate what its giant leg span must have been (p. 471).

ISLANDS IN THE SUN

In Greece's summertime schedule, beach-side days melt through spectacular sunsets into starry, disco-filled nights, in a continuum of hedonistic delight. Roll out of bed and onto the beach around noon; nap in the late afternoon after strenuous sunbathing; head for a harborside dinner at 11pm; throw back after-dinner drinks, catch a movie, or hit the clubs until 5am, all under the stars; watch the sun rise over the ocean; and hit the hay before another sun-drenched day. It's nearly impossible to resist the allure of Greek sun and sea. The islands have long been a sun-worshiper's paradise, from Apollo's followers to disciples of Coppertone. As soon as you sail from Athens to the **Saronic Gulf Islands** (p. 309), the roasting Greek sun will bronze your (entire) body and release your inhibitions. A favorite of international vacationers, **Skiathos** in the Sporades harbors the piney Biotrope of Koukounaries beach and magical Lalaria (p. 334). In the Aegean Sea, **Santorini's** black-sand beaches soak up the sun's hot rays and stay warm long after the stunning sunsets over the Sea of Crete (p. 442) have faded. Swim below sea caves once ransacked by pirates on the coast of **Skyros** (p. 344) or bask on the Lesvian shore, where beaches stretch out for miles from Sappho's home of **Skala Eressou** (p. 377). Stumble out of all those superfluous clothes at **Mykonos's** wild, nude Super Paradise Beach (p. 402). If your eyes get tired of all those bare backsides, seek solace on a secluded strip of sand. The much-beloved haunt of booze-loving backpackers, **Corfu,** is ringed by fabulous beaches on all sides, in addition to hosting that legendary party haven, the Pink Palace (p. 274). Snorkel, waterski, or just loaf in the sun on **Ios** (p. 421) and **Naxos** (p. 434). Perfect your tan around **Paleohora** in Crete (p. 545) or at castle-crowned Haraki Beach in **Rhodes** (p. 465).

TAKE A HIKE

Greece isn't just Athens, islands, bars, and babes. If you have enough self-discipline to tear yourself away from the fun in the sun, you'll soon realize that a wilderness experience can be just as invigorating. To do so, you'll have to either bust out your walking stick or rev up your engines. Hiking or motorbiking—or a combination of the two—lets you cruise between rural villages independent of constantly changing bus schedules. On foot, you'll cross through foothills draped with olive groves, passing mountain goats and wildflowers along the way. Drowsy **Dimitsana** (p. 148) and cobblestoned **Stemnitsa** (p. 149) distinguish themselves from the tourist bustle of the rest of the Peloponnese. In the Ionian Sea, Odysseus's kingdom of **Ithaka** is an untapped hiker's paradise, where the Cave of the Nymphs—the hiding place for Odysseus's treasure and the conclusion of an enthralling hike—will seduce you (p. 292). Northern **Thassos** (p. 383) is full of secluded ruins, superior hikes, and village-to-village strolls. Rural **Alonnisos,** a largely uninhabited island in the Sporades, is crisscrossed by trails and moped-friendly roads, and hugged by beaches (p. 339) ideal for refueling after a fatiguing hike. Outlying islands are protected as part of the National Marine Park and make for a pleasant daytrip. The untouched traditional Greek villages of the **Zagorohoria** (p. 251) and their surrounding wilderness make walking an adventure. The neighboring **Vikos Gorge** (p. 253), the world's steepest canyon, challenges hikers with a six-hour-long trek. You can explore more gorgeous gorges in Crete: the **Samaria Gorge** (p. 543), Europe's longest gorge, and the quieter **Valley of Death** (p. 561) plunge you below eagles' nests and trees clinging to the steep canyon sides.

Eighty percent of the Greek landscape is mountainous, to the delight of climbers. Clamber to the abode of the gods at **Mt. Olympus** (p. 230), ascending over 2900 steep, stunning meters to one of its eight peaks. During the summer, Dionysus's old watering hole, **Mt. Parnassos,** makes a great hiking and mountain-biking trip (p. 177); in winter, skiers storm the 2400m slopes. The trails around **Zaros** in Crete wind up to mountainside sanctuaries and to Zeus's childhood hiding place, **Kamares Cave** (p. 523).

LET'S GO PICKS

BEST USE OF ANIMAL INSTINCT: Cower before the predatory **raptors** of Dadia National Reserve (p. 271). Pad quietly through the **Valley of the Butterflies** on either Paros (p. 426) or Rhodes (p. 465). Be amazed at animal antics at the **Pink Palace,** Corfu (p. 286).

BEST BEACHES: The famous **black** and **red** sand beaches of Santorini (p. 445) satisfy those bored with golden pebbles. Strip down to the bare essentials on **Paradise** beach on Mykonos (p. 402).

BEST CASTLES: Check out the famous Phaistos disc and sit in the throne room of the **Palace of Phaistos** on Crete (**p. 525**). Get medieval with the **Knights of St. John** in their castle on Kos (**p. 478**).

BEST PLACE TO USE YOUR ILLUSION: Mourn the absence of the **Venus de Milo** while sunning on Milos (p. 454).

MOST GUT-WRENCHING RIDES: Hold on tight if you take the ride from tiny Diakofto to tinier **Kalavrita** (p. 138) on the rattling and rolling rack-railway. Imagine the fear in the eyes of those who were hauled up via rope as you take the easy way up (climbing the stairs) to the monasteries of **Meteora** (p. 211).

WILDEST PARTIES: Visit **Pierro's,** the first gay bar in Greece, on wild Mykonos (**P. 402**). Welcome to **The Jungle,** one of many places to get drunk on Ios (**P. 438**).

BEST PLACE TO FLEX YOUR MUSCLE: Take a lap around the **stadium** at Ancient Olympia (p. 142) and imagine the laurel wreath on your head.

BEST PLACE TO CATCH FIREFLIES: The luminescent critters light up the forests of **Monodendri** (p. 252).

SUGGESTED ITINERARIES

RUINS, RAMBLES, AND RELICS

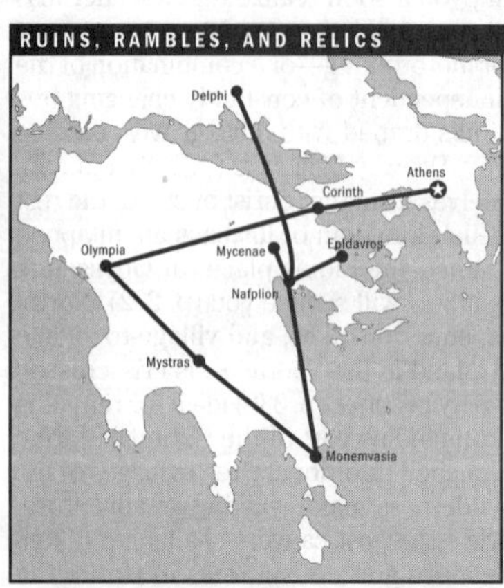

RUINS, RAMBLES, AND RELICS (1 WEEK) Put down that well-worn copy of the *Odyssey:* it's time to see the real deal. Arrive in **Athens** (p. 74) and charge straight to the gleaming **Acropolis,** which still looms over the city (p. 95), and the neighboring **Agora.** Escape the hot sun and lose yourself in the rooms and rooms of ancient treasure and statuary at the **National Archaeological Museum** (p. 103). Then head out from the capital to **Ancient Corinth,** whose fountain once quenched Pegasus's thirst (p. 116). Send up a cheer in the stadium at **Ancient Olympia,** and wonder at the life-like perfection of the Hermes of Praxiteles (p. 142). Clamber over the Byzantine wonderland of **Mystras,** a maze-like ruined city (p. 163), and to the otherworldly pedestrian and donkey-only city of **Monemvasia** (p. 169). Watch the setting sun color Venetian **Nafplion** (p. 124), then stroll the waterfront in the evening. On the way back to Athens, visit **Mycenae** and walk beneath the Lion's Gate (p. 120), then exult in the perfect acoustics of the theater at **Epidavros** (p. 130). End your journey with a pilgrimage to **Delphi,** the ancient oracle that still retains its mystic aura (p. 180).

POST-EURAIL PARTY (1 WEEK) Finish up a Eurail trip by taking the ferry from Brindisi, Italy to **Corfu** (p. 274), home to gorgeous beaches and the infamous Pink Palace. Continue on via Patras to **Athens,** where you can catch an eyeful of the Acropolis before heading out to the islands (p. 74). As soon as you get off the ferry to **Mykonos,** start shedding those inhibitions: nude beaches abound, and nightlife sizzles (p. 402). When you've warmed up for a day, move on to **Ios,** an isle of pure bacchic hedonism (p. 438). Recuperate from the damage on the black sand beaches of **Santorini** (p. 445), then test out the tawny sand outside **Iraklion,** on Crete (p. 511).

POST-EURAIL PARTY

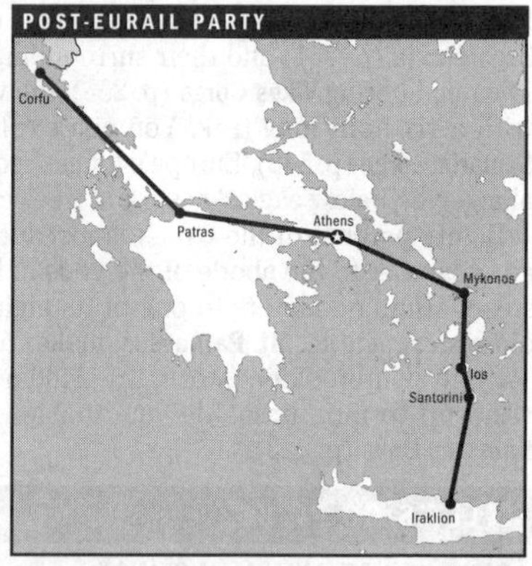

OLYMPIC ADVENTURE (1-2 WEEKS) If you're going to Greece for the **Olympic Games,** save some time between your venue-hopping for a little Hellenic exploration. Although you won't have much time to escape the crowded streets of **Athens** (p. 74), that doesn't mean that you can't enjoy the country. Begin with an morning trek to the top of the brilliant **Acropolis** (p. 95); from up there, even Olympic Athens seems peaceful. Stroll back down to the base of the hill for an amble around the **Agora** (p. 99), the heart of ancient Athens. **Plaka** (p. 81) at midday is a great place to break up a day of athletic events; its narrow streets provide much needed shade and quiet. Keep your eyes peeled for VIPs while strolling in the chic neighborhood of **Kolonaki** (p. 86). After window shopping on its boutique-lined roads, have a cooling coffee *frappé* in the square in late afternoon.

Then head for the top of rocky **Mt. Lycavittos** (p. 102) for a pollution-addled, brilliant red sunset over the city. When the crowds and heat get to be too much, catch the metro to **Piraeus** (p. 106), hop aboard the next ferry to the nearby but charming **Saronic Gulf Islands** (p. 309) and unwind. Little **Hydra** (p. 321) may be the perfect stop for the traffic-weary: no cars are allowed on the island. Back on the mainland, find a day or two for a trip to the site of the great Oracle of Apollo, **Delphi** (p. 183), or a pilgrimage to where it all began, **Olympia** (p. 142)

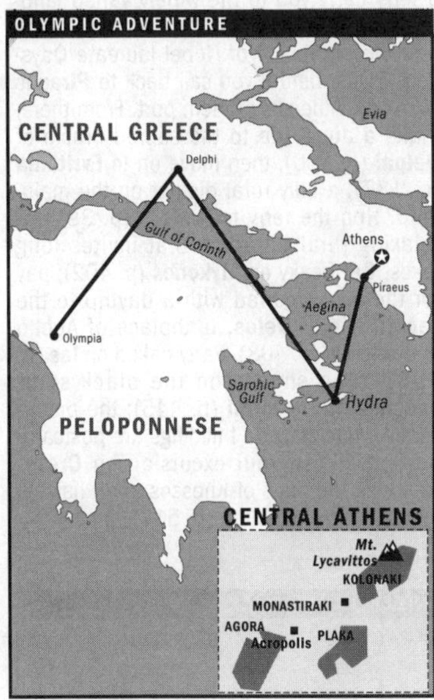

MAINLAND CIRCUIT (2 WEEKS) Set off from **Athens** (p. 74) to trek through undertouristed mainland Greece, home of cliffside Byzantine monasteries, cobblestoned traditional villages, and the buzz of Thessaloniki. You'll probably need rented wheels of some kind. Set off for the oracle at **Delphi,** where you could receive advice about your upcoming travels in the form of a dream (p. 180). Continue on to **Lamia,** to climb the built-and-rebuilt ruins of the town Castro (p. 192). **Karpenisi,** the capital of the mountainous Evritania region, is the next stop (p. 187). From here, hike out among the tiny villages of the neighborhood; **Proussos,** with its spectacular cliffside monastery, is a highlight (p. 191). Pass through Karpenisi again on the way to Volos and the **Mt. Pelion Peninsula,** the onetime haunt of centaurs and present-day hideaway of traditional village life (p. 201). Before you roll out through Larisa and Trikala, head for the frescoed church of Porta Panagia in nearby Pyli, where you can dine beside a Roman footbridge. Avoid the traditional means of ascent to the **Monasteries of Meteora**—a terrifying, free-swinging rope—and save your prayers to give thanks for the fabulous view (p. 211). Pass through Ioannina on the way to the **Zagorohoria** villages, eminently hikeable and extremely friendly (p. 251). Stay in **Thessaloniki** (p. 213) to daytrip to the ancient sites of gold-showered **Vergina** (p. 227) and nearby **Pella** (p. 228); Alexander the Great grew up in the neighborhood. For the greatest hike of them all head straight to the home of the gods on **Mt. Olympus** (p. 230). After the grueling, exultant climb, relax for a day on offshore **Thasos** before heading out (p. 387).

ISLAND ESCAPE (2 WEEKS) For a slower, more relaxed trip, leave from Athens for **Andros,** a beach-lovers' paradise surrounded by small Neoclassical towns (p. 391). Don't miss the sunsets; you certainly won't miss the crowds that jam other beach islands. Try to tear yourself away to **Tinos,** and lie in the sand beside a ruined 4th century BC temple (p. 396). Stay the night with a local family for a truly Greek experience. Shake off your sloth at one of the crazed clubs of **Mykonos** (p. 402), and do penance for the previous night's debauchery during a daytrip to the sacred isle of **Delos,** the birthplace of Apollo and Artemis (p. 408). Next stop is **Naxos,** to snorkel among caves, sea urchins, and crystalline sand (p. 414). If the ferry schedule complies, slip away to one of the **Little Cyclades:** Koufonisia, Donousa, Iraklia, and Schinousa (p. 421). The small-town solitude will saturate your being; ease back into reality with a stopover in western Crete, around **Rethymno** (p. 531).

ISLAND ESCAPE

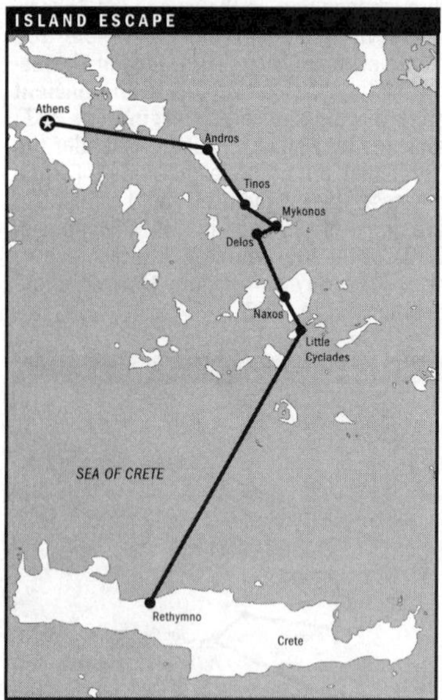

GREEK TO ME (3 WEEKS) To see a large portion of Greece in a few weeks, start in **Athens** (p. 74); the National Archaeological Museum, the Acropolis, and the many smaller museums provide a refresher course in Greek history. Move on to **Nafplion** (p. 124), a gorgeous Venetian city and a perfect base for exploring the neighboring sights of the theater of **Epidavros** (p. 130), the alleged abode of the Atreus clan at **Mycenae** (p. 119), and the original Olympic field at sacred **Olympia** (p. 140). Head to Patras to catch the ferry to **Corfu** (p. 274), island that mixes debaucherous overdevelopment with untouched wilderness. Cross back to the mainland at Igoumenitsa on your way to the **Zagorohoria** (p. 251), a district of petite towns that stick to traditional folkways. The Byzantine sights of **Thessaloniki** beckon (p. 213), with fabulous mosaics and the awesome archaeological sites of **Vergina** (p. 227) and **Pella** (p. 228), a quick jaunt away. The industrious will set out for **Mt. Olympus** (p. 230), to grapple with the gods' abode. Men who plan ahead and collect the proper approvals and forms may visit **Mt. Athos,** the ultratraditional monastic community jutting out of Halkidiki (p. 256). Recline for a few days on the shores of **Thasos** just offshore (p. 387), then loop down to **Limnos** (p. 381) off the Turkish coast. Let a ferry carry you to the widely varied landscapes of **Lesvos** (p. 370), Sappho's home and the birthplace of Nobel laureate Odysseus Elytis, before you sail back to **Piraeus** (p. 106), Athens's modern port. From there, make a quick trip to the sacred oracle of **Delphi** (p. 180), then move on to **Evritania** (p. 187), a hilly rural district on the mainland. Hop the ferry to **Andros** (p. 391), a relaxing rural paradise that invites long hikes. Get freaky on **Mykonos** (p. 402); pay for the sins incurred with a daytrip to the sacred isle of **Delos,** birthplace of Apollo and Artemis (p. 408). Party naked on **Ios** (p. 438), then snooze on the black sand beaches of **Santorini** (p. 445); the picturesque white cliffside buildings are postcard-perfect. Finish your excursion on **Crete,** exploring the ruins of Knossos and Phaistos just outside of **Iraklion** (p. 511).

GREEK TO ME

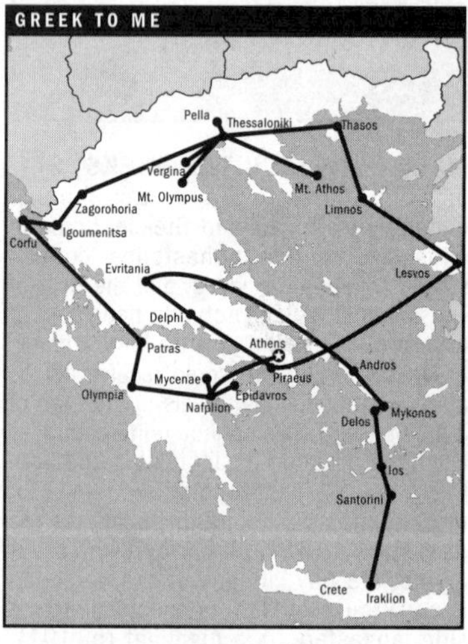

LIFE AND TIMES

The entire world has shared in the intellectual, literary, artistic, and religious majesty of Greece, a land far too small to have achieved so much. Among rocky fields, dusty olive groves, and windswept cliffs, the Greeks have flourished for millennia against all odds. Greece's unique position at the crossroads of Europe and Asia and surrounded by a welcoming sea has defined its times. The relics of Crete's Minoan civilization reveal Egyptian and Babylonian influence, while, in the bushy beards and long black robes of Orthodox priests, the mores of the Eastern Roman Empire have survived through the Byzantine Era to the present time. Four hundred years under the Ottoman Turks left a spice in Greek food, an Eastern twang in its *bouzouki* music, and an occasional skyline of minarets. Greece declared independence in 1821 and now struggles to maintain the glory of Classical Athens, the splendor of Imperial Byzantium, and the religious purity of Ottoman folkways in an increasingly post-industrial nation governed by a reborn democracy.

HISTORY

ANCIENT GREECE (THROUGH AD 324)

The romance of Ancient Greece has transfixed the world, throughout history and to the present day. The influence of the ancient Greeks pervades Western language, philosophy, and literature. Greek culture grew from agricultural and fishing communities: the coastal Aegean fostered prosperity, with its access to the ocean and its nearby olive trees, grapes, forests, and fertile land. Walled towns, constructed around a central high point, or **acropolis,** protected seaside settlements. Immigrants and traders from Anatolia, the Levant, and Egypt added a dash of global chic to the ancient Greek world.

EARLY GREEK CIVILIZATION. The Bronze Age discovery of metalworking kicked off a rapid expansion of Greek influence. Peering over the shoulders of their eastern neighbors, Greeks learned bronze toolmaking and weaponry. Three Aegean cultures built their reputations on bronze: the mainland's Mycenaean, Crete's Minoan, and the islands' Cycladic. Island civilization flourished early on. The wall frescoes and marble figurines of the **Cycladic** culture showed Middle Eastern influence and a strong geometric element. By about 2000 BC, the **Minoans** (named for the step-dad of the Minotaur) busily constructed glorious palaces at Knossos (p. 519), Malia (p. 529), and Phaistos (p. 525) as centers of government, religion, and trade; a strong fleet made the Minoans the lords of the Aegean. Around 1500 BC, a **Mysterious Cataclysm**—tidal waves, volcanoes, and/or alien invasions—wiped the Minoans out of existence. The mainland **Mycenaeans** overtook the Aegean after the Minoans faded. Their impenetrable cities, girded by walls of titanic proportions, accumulated tremendous wealth under the leadership of kings such as Agamemnon (of Homeric fame). The invasion of fierce Dorian tribes into Greece around 1000 BC brought an end to the Mycenaean civilization and pushed the Aegean into an anarchical 300-year Dark Age.

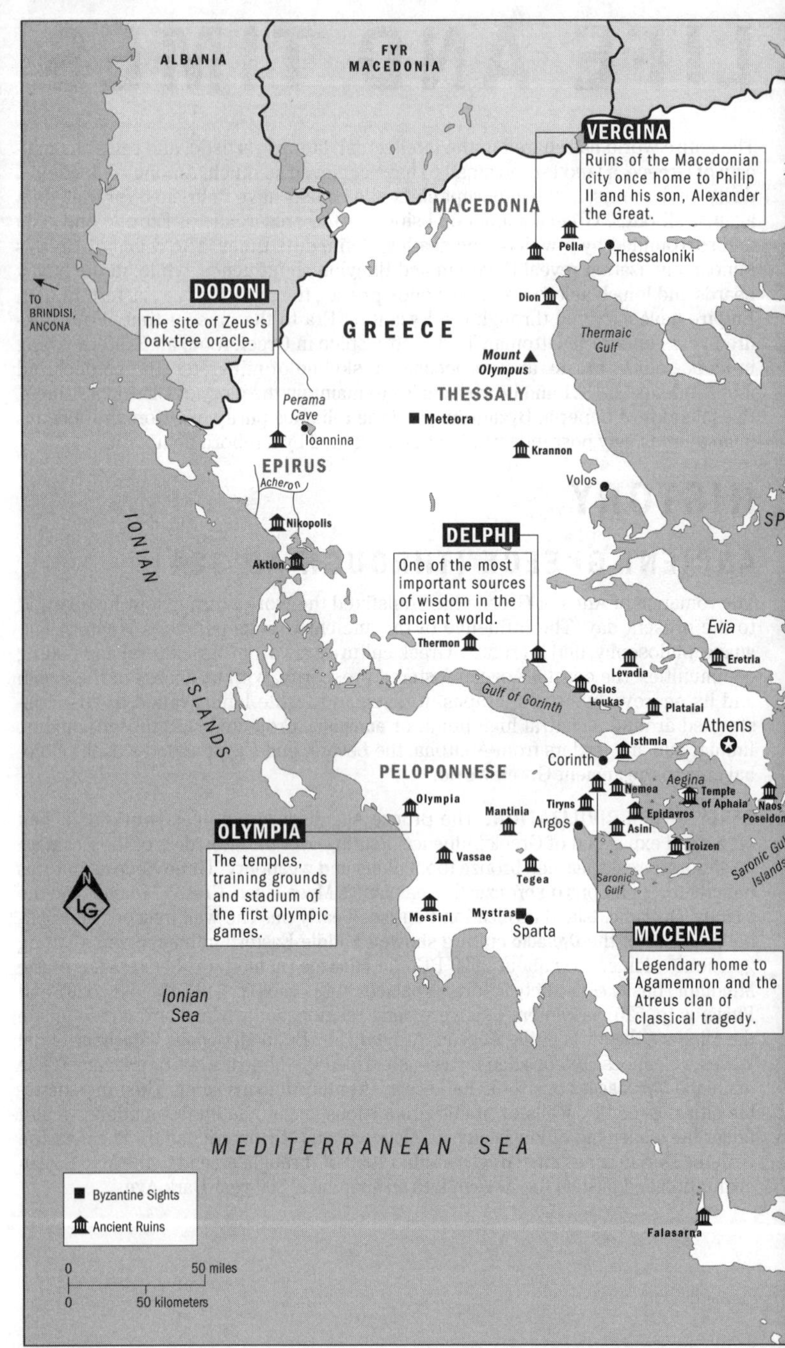

ALBANIA
FYR MACEDONIA
VERGINA
Ruins of the Macedonian city once home to Philip II and his son, Alexander the Great.
MACEDONIA
Pella
Thessaloniki
DODONI
The site of Zeus's oak-tree oracle.
TO BRINDISI, ANCONA
Dion
GREECE
Thermaic Gulf
Mount Olympus
THESSALY
Perama Cave
Meteora
Ioannina
Krannon
EPIRUS
Acheron
Volos
IONIAN
Nikopolis
DELPHI
Aktion
One of the most important sources of wisdom in the ancient world.
Evia
Thermon
Eretria
Levadia
ISLANDS
Osios Loukas
Gulf of Corinth
Plataiai
Athens
Isthmia
Corinth
PELOPONNESE
Aegina
Nemea
Temple of Aphaia
Tiryns
Olympia
Mantinia
Epidavros
Argos
Asini
OLYMPIA
Troizen
The temples, training grounds and stadium of the first Olympic games.
Vassae
Tegea
Saronic Gulf
Messini
Mystras
Sparta
MYCENAE
Legendary home to Agamemnon and the Atreus clan of classical tragedy.
Ionian Sea
MEDITERRANEAN SEA
Byzantine Sights
Ancient Ruins
Falasarna
0
50 miles
0
50 kilometers

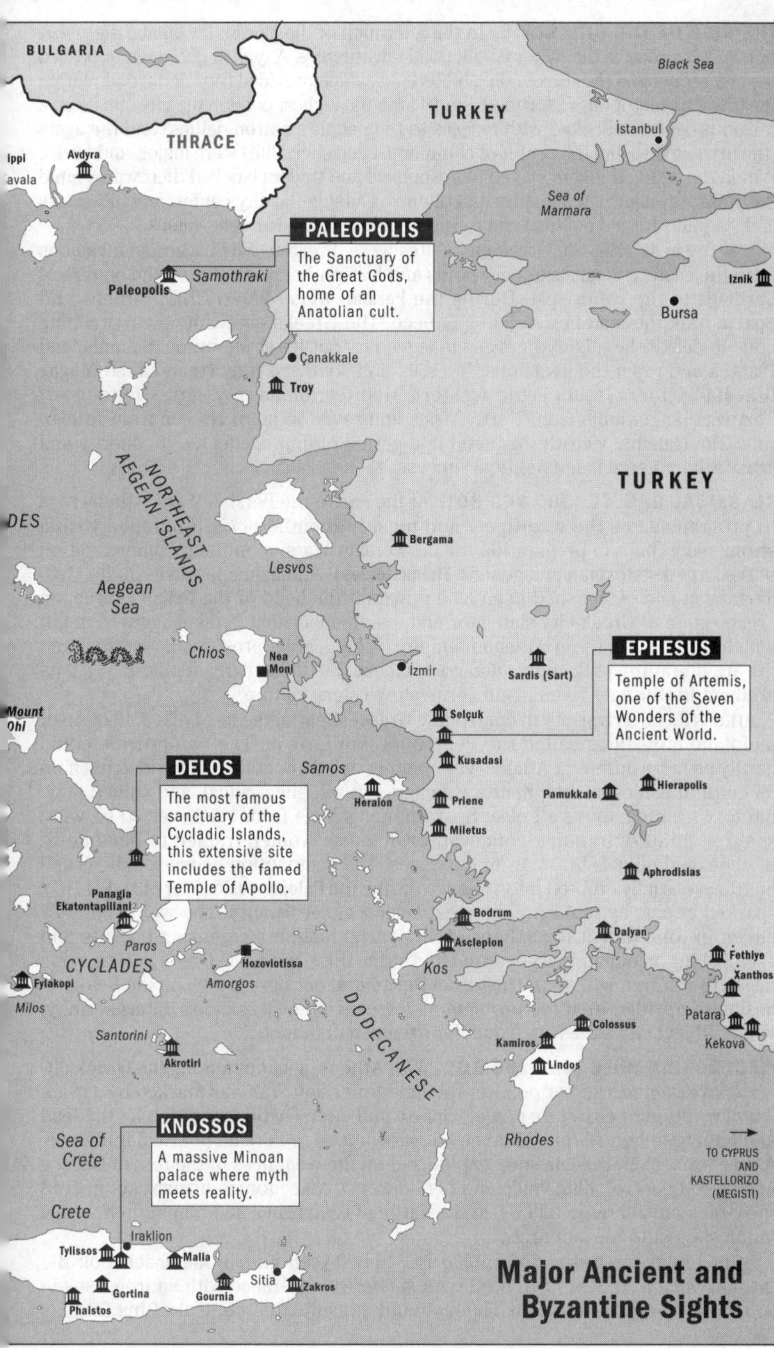
BULGARIA
THRACE
TURKEY
Black Sea
İstanbul
Sea of Marmara
Iznik
Bursa
Avdyra
PALEOPOLIS
The Sanctuary of the Great Gods, home of an Anatolian cult.
Samothraki
Paleopolis
Çanakkale
Troy
NORTHEAST AEGEAN ISLANDS
TURKEY
Bergama
Lesvos
Aegean Sea
Chios
Nea Moni
İzmir
Sardis (Sart)
EPHESUS
Temple of Artemis, one of the Seven Wonders of the Ancient World.
Selçuk
Kusadasi
Samos
Heraion
Priene
Miletus
Pamukkale
Hierapolis
Aphrodisias
DELOS
The most famous sanctuary of the Cycladic Islands, this extensive site includes the famed Temple of Apollo.
Panagia Ekatontapiliani
Paros
CYCLADES
Fylakopi
Milos
Hozoviotissa
Amorgos
Bodrum
Asclepion
Kos
Dalyan
Fethiye
Xanthos
Patara
Kekova
DODECANESE
Colossus
Kamiros
Lindos
Santorini
Akrotiri
KNOSSOS
A massive Minoan palace where myth meets reality.
Sea of Crete
Crete
Iraklion
Tylissos
Malia
Sitia
Zakros
Gortina
Gournia
Phaistos
Rhodes
TO CYPRUS AND KASTELLORIZO (MEGISTI)
Mount Ohi
Major Ancient and Byzantine Sights

THE RISE OF THE CITY STATE. In the aftermath of the Dorian invasions, the *polis*, or city-state, rose as the major Greek political structure. A typical *polis* encompassed the city proper and the surrounding hinterland, which provided food and wood. Within the town, the acropolis (a fortified citadel atop the highest point in the city and often a religious center bedecked with **temples** to the people's patron deities) and the **agora** (the marketplace and the center of commercial and social life) were major landmarks. Within the agora, thinkers waxed philosophical and traders hawked their wares amid the **stoas,** open-air paths lined with columns. Outside the city center, amphitheaters and stadiums hosted political and religious gatherings and athletic games.

Starting in 495 BC, the Greek city-states were threatened by barbarian invasions from the eastern **Persians** under Darius and his son Xerxes and from the empire of **Carthage** to the southwest. During the **Persian Wars** (490-477 BC), Athens and Sparta took the lead in defending Greece. The Greeks overcame overwhelming odds to defeat the mighty Persians in legendary battles at Marathon, Salamis, and Plataea and repel the invasions. In Sicily and southern Italy (then called **Magna Graecia**—wider Greece), the western Mediterranean city-states fended off Carthaginian assaults from North Africa and saved western Greece from foreign rule. The Hellenic victories ushered in a period of unprecedented prosperity and artistic, commercial, and political success.

CLASSICAL GREECE (500-400 BC). At the end of the Persian Wars, Athens rose to prominence as the wealthiest and most influential *polis*. Equipped with a strong navy (built in preparation for the Persian Wars upon the recommendation of the famed statesman and general **Themistokles**), Athens made waves in the Mediterranean and established itself as a power at the head of the **Delian League,** an organization of Greek city-states formed to defend against Persian aggression but which really acted as an Athenian empire. Athens grew prosperous and fostered the art, literature, philosophy, and government (including early democracy, a government for the ages) which still permeate Western culture.

Athens faced a rival city in controlling Greece: Sparta, the head of a collection of mainland city-states called the Peloponnesian League. The two powers could hardly be more different: Athens was commercial, democratic, and prided itself on its cultural achievements; Sparta was agricultural, oligarchical, and valued stoic military training above all else. Spartan men's lives from age seven to 60 were spent in military training, conquest, or defense; women trained to become fit mothers and models for their military sons. The competition between Athens and Sparta eventually erupted into violence during the **Peloponnesian War** (431-404 BC), sparked in part by rapid Athenian expansion under **Pericles.** The war eventually ended in total defeat for Athens, with Spartan soldiers capturing the city and establishing an oligarchial government. During this period, the Greek *polis* system began to rot from within; the historian **Thucydides,** our best source on the Peloponnesian Wars, identified the problem as a *stasis*—the Greeks lost internal unity, while subject city-states chafed under Athenian dominion.

MACEDONIAN RULE (400-200 BC). With Athens, a leader among the Greek cities, so weakened, the period after the Peloponnesian War was marked by a gradual devolution of city-state power. Sparta and later Thebes tried to take the lead and hold together a Greek alliance but succumbed to Persian political influence. A new force in **Macedonia** soon capitalized on the weakness of the rest of Greece and seized control. **King Philip** and his improved Macedonian **phalanx** conquered the Greek city-states in 338 BC at the battle of Chaeronea and bound them into a union subject to his monarchy.

After Philip's assassination in 336 BC, his 20-year-old son **Alexander** took the throne. Once a student of Aristotle, Alexander ruled Greece with an iron fist—in 335 BC he mercilessly razed Thebes—and consolidated control of his father's empire. In control of Greece, Alexander then turned his ambitions east. By the time of his sudden death at 33, he ruled Egypt and the entire Persian Empire; he had spread Greek culture and language throughout the eastern Mediterranean. During the Hellenistic Era that followed, literary and artistic forms diffused throughout the former empire, and Classical learning reached faraway realms.

The Macedonian empire quickly crumbled after the death of Alexander the Great in 323 BC, leaving three powers in its wake: the **Antigonids** in Macedonia, the **Seleucids** in Asia Minor, Syria, and Persia, and the **Ptolemies** in Egypt. The dissolution of Alexander's empire restored a measure of independence to the Greek city-states. Three Greek powers ruled the 3rd century BC: the Peloponnesian **Achaean Confederacy,** the Delphi-based **Aetolian Confederacy,** and the city-state of Sparta. However, Greek self-rule was short-lived. By 27 BC, the upstart Roman Empire had conquered Greece and incorporated it into the province of **Achaea.**

BYZANTINE ERA (AD 324-1453)

Unlike other lands ruined by the fall of the Roman Empire, Greece emerged from Roman rule into a **Byzantine** period of cultural rebirth, prosperity, and power that stretched from the Balkans through Greece to Asia Minor and into Egypt.

ROMAN EMPIRE: EAST SIDE (324-500). As Rome slowly declined, the empire became dominated by competing halves: an eastern half (centered in Anatolia, the Levant, and Greece) and a western half centered at Rome. The unusual political arrangement ended in a scramble for power, finally won by **Constantine** in AD 312. Before his decisive victory, Constantine saw a vision of a cross of light in the sun, bearing the fiery inscription, "In this sign, you will conquer." The newly installed eastern emperor interpreted this as a sign from the Christian God who was winning converts throughout the former Roman Empire. Later, Constantine legalized Christianity within his empire. Founding **Constantinople** (modern Istanbul) in 324, he gave the Roman Empire a new capital, built over the ancient city of Byzantium. While Western Europe was overrun by barbarian invaders, this eastern empire, today known as the Byzantine Empire, became a center of learning, trade, and influence unrivaled in its time.

NETTLESOME NEIGHBORS (500-1453). During the 6th century, **Emperor Justinian's** battles against the Sassanians of Persia and the western Vandals (who had sacked Rome) overstretched the empire's strength. Justinian was more successful in domestic politics as he codified Roman laws and undertook massive building projects such as the church of **Agia Sophia,** an architectural masterpiece that still stands in Istanbul. However, the empire's power waned under the force of constant raids by Slavs, Mongols, and Avars. In many areas of the mainland and Peloponnese, Greek culture was wiped out entirely by barbarian conquest, and the Greek language and script only returned after later missions from Constantinople.

THE CURSE OF CRUSADERS. Even as they protected themselves from invaders, the Byzantine Greeks attempted to spread **Christianity.** Missionaries reached out from the empire's contracted borders into the Slavic kingdoms and Russia, sowing the seeds of Orthodox Christianity throughout Eastern Europe. In 1071, the Byzantines lost control of eastern Anatolia to the Selçuk Turks; Greek monasteries in the Aegean and Black Sea areas converted to armed fortresses to ward off Turkish pirates. From 1200 to 1400, the Byzantine Empire was plagued by Norman and Venetian Crusaders, who conquered and looted Constantinople in 1204 and imposed western Catholic culture upon the city. Despite its strong emperors, Byzantium needed to ally with Latin, Slavic, and even Turkish rulers by marriage in order to survive. At last, the once indomitable Byzantine Empire was reduced to only Constantinople and its environs. Finally, on May 29, 1453 (a day still considered cursed by Greeks), the Ottoman Turks overran the much-reduced city.

THE OTTOMAN OCCUPATION (1453-1829)

TURKISH LORDSHIP. Old Byzantium suffered an undignified name change under the Ottoman Turks, this time renamed **Istanbul**—a Turkish corruption of the Greek *steen Poli* (to the City)—in 1453. The city again became the seat of an empire. For centuries the Ottoman Empire prospered, though eventually its diverse regions grew apart and the empire weakened. The Muslim Turkish rulers treated their Greek subjects as a **millet**—a separate community ruled by its own religious leaders. Greeks paid the *cizye*, a head tax dictated by Islamic law, but were otherwise free to worship as they chose. The Orthodox Greek church became the moderator of culture and tradition and the foundation of Greek autonomy. Though Greeks could choose to integrate into Ottoman society, anti-Turk nationalist sentiments began to build. Encouraged to revolt by Orthodox leaders, Greeks began to chafe under 400 years of Turkish rule. By the 19th century, they were pushing for complete independence from the empire.

THE GREAT IDEA (1821-1900)

GREEK NATIONALIST REVOLT. On March 25, 1821, Bishop Germanos of Patras raised a Greek flag at the monastery of Agia Lavra and sparked an empire-wide rebellion. Middle-class rebels hoped that the Orthodox Russian czar and Greek peasants would join the revolt; when they didn't, the rebels met a crushing defeat. Disorganized but impassioned guerrillas in the Peloponnese and Aegean islands waged sporadic war on the Turkish government for years. Under the leadership of rebel heroes Botsaris, Koundouritis, Miaoulis, Mavrokordatos, and Ypsilanti, the Greeks slowly chipped away at Ottoman control of their homeland. Finally, in 1829, with great support from European powers, Greece won its independence.

Russia, Britain, and France wanted a free Greece but also wanted to restrict its power. The borders of the new Greece were narrow, including only a fraction of the six million Greeks living under Ottoman rule. For the next century, Greek politics centered around achieving the *Megali Idhea*—the Great Idea, freeing Constantinople from the Turks and uniting all Greeks, even those in Asia Minor, into one sovereign state. Although Greece gained much territory over the next century, including the great city of **Thessaloniki** (Salonica) in Macedonia and the island of **Crete,** it never realized this great goal.

TWENTIETH CENTURY

EXPAND AND CONTRACT. In 1833, the European powers declared Greece a **monarchy** and handed the crown to a succession of Germanic princes. However, the 1864 constitution downplayed the power of the king and emphasized the importance of the elected prime minister. In 1920, Prime Minister **Eleftherios Venizelos,** immortalized in street names across Greece, wrangled new Greek territory in the aftermath of the Balkan Wars and World War I. Savvy Balkan alliances nearly doubled Greece's territory. Defying King Constantine's request for neutrality, Venizelos set up an Allied revolutionary government in Thessaloniki. After the First World War, Venizelos realized Greece wouldn't get land in Asia Minor, and in 1919 he ordered an outright invasion of Turkey. However, the young Turkish general (and *de facto* leader of the country) Mustafa Kemal, later to be known as **Atatürk,** crushed the invasion. As the Greek army retreated, the Turkish forces ordered the slaughter of Greek citizens all along the Asia Minor coast. The Treaty of Lausanne, signed in 1923, enacted a massive population exchange that sent a million Greeks who lived in Asia Minor to live in Greece, and sent 400,000 Turkish Muslims from Greece to Turkey. This population exchange ended the *Megali Idhea* but began a series of economic problems for Greece.

THE SECOND WORLD WAR. The 1930s were rocked by political turmoil, as Greeks lived through brief intervals of democracy amid a succession of monarchies and military rule. King George II was overthrown by a series of coups that reinstated a democracy; Venizelos, the former Prime Minister, headed the new government for five years, though royalists eventually forced his exile. The extreme nationalist **General Metaxas** succeeded him as Prime Minister in a fixed election, as George II again took the throne in 1936. Metaxas inaugurated an oppressive military state, yet his leadership during the early stages of World War II earned him lasting respect. Most notably, Metaxas rejected Mussolini's request that Italy occupy Greece during World War II with a resounding "No!" ("Oχι!"). Although the nation defeated the Italian forces, Greece fell to Germany in 1941 and endured four years of bloody and brutal Axis occupation. The communist-led resistance received broad popular support, though many resistance fighters received aid from the Western powers, which were eager to prevent a communist Greece.

FORMING THE MODERN GREEK STATE. Civil war broke out in 1944, in an early Cold War stand-off that the left-wing, Soviet-backed Democratic Army eventually lost to the US-supplied anti-communist coalition government. Through a rather disgraceful American intervention, Greece instituted the Certificate of Political Reliability, which guaranteed that the bearer had politically acceptable views. Keeping a visible hand in Greek politics, the US helped place General Papagos, **Constantine Karamanlis,** and the right-wing Greek Rally Party in power. When Karamanlis resigned after the assassination of a communist official in 1963, left-wing **George Papandreou** came to power, to America's disappointment.

The right-wing respite was short-lived; the army staged a **coup** on April 21, 1967, which resulted in rule by a **military junta** for seven years. Making extensive use of torture, censorship, and arbitrary arrest to repress Communist forces, the junta enjoyed official US support and investment at the height of the Cold War. The junta ultimately fell in 1973 after the government helped provoke a **Turkish invasion of Cyprus** (p. 564) and a nationwide **student uprising.**

Former president Karamanlis returned to take power in 1975, instituting parliamentary elections and organizing a referendum on the form of government. Monarchy was defeated by a two-thirds vote, and a new constitution was drawn up in 1975, calling for parliamentary government with a ceremonial president appointed by the legislature—the system still in use today.

NOVEMBER 17

After 27 years of fruitless investigation, the Athenian government made its first arrest of suspects of the Novemeber 17 (N17) terrorist group in July 2002. The breakthrough came shortly after a failed bombing attempt in Piraeus on June 29, 2002. The testimony of suspected N17 member Savvas Xeros, who was injured in his attempt to plant the bomb, shed new light on the details of the organization. Police finally made progress in their pursuit of N17 after the incident, arresting three members of the group and unveiling a large weapon stash.

The terrorist group, a radical leftist organization, borrows its name from the date of the 1973 student uprising in protest of the military regime ruling Greece. Although the group has occasionally targeted international politicians—the most recent assassination was of a British government worker, Stephen Saunders, in June 2000—the primary targets of the group are Greek public figures. Since 1975, N17 has claimed responsibility for 23 deaths.

The anti-Western group opposes Greek membership in NATO and the EU. Although tourists should be aware of the organization, they need not fear the group as a regular threat. With the Olympics on the horizon, the government is under intense pressure from the international community to bring the organization under control. These latest developments are indeed promising signs.

TODAY

TOWARD EUROPE. Under the guidance of party founder **Andreas Papandreou,** the leftist Panhellenic Socialist Movement (PASOK) won landslide electoral victories in 1981 and 1985. Appealing to voters with the simple campaign slogan **Allaghi** ("Change"), Prime Minister Papandreou promised a radical break with the past. In office, he steered Greece into the European Economic Community (EEC) and pioneered the passage of women's rights legislation, though many of his policies were anti-Western: he spoke against NATO and maintained friendships with Libyan strongman Mohammar Qaddafi and PLO leader Yasser Arafat. When a scandal involving the chair of the Bank of Crete implicated government officials in 1989, Papandreou lost control of Parliament. After three general elections in the space of 10 months, **Constantine Mitsotakis** of the New Democracy party (Nea Demokratia, or ND) became Prime Minister by a slim parliamentary majority.

AUGMENTATION AND AUSTERITY. Attempting to solve Greece's economic and diplomatic problems and align the country with mainstream European politics, Mitsotakis imposed an **austerity program** that limited wage increases and authorized the sale of state enterprises. This policy became tremendously unpopular when it threatened thousands of public sector jobs, and, in 1993, Mitsotakis was defeated by a resurgent Papandreou in an emergency election. Just two years later, poor health forced Papandreou to leave his position.

Fellow socialist **Costas Simitis** took control of the party and has since pursued aggressive economic reforms, privatizing banks and companies despite the opposition of perpetually striking labor unions. The ruling PASOK party has also made strides in international relations by being more NATO-friendly and opening talks with Turkey. The administration has also slashed Greece's budget deficit, brought inflation down, and cut the national debt in an attempt to meet the qualifying standards for entry into the **European Monetary Union (EMU).** Simitis, who was barely reelected in the 2000 election over ND challenger **Costas Karamanlis,** was instrumental in Greece's successful bid to enter the EMU in January 2001.

GREECE AND TURKEY: BREAKING THE ICE. One of Simitis's continuing projects is normalizing relations with nearby Turkey. The two nations have been on less-than-friendly terms in the past (see p. 12), but, in great part through mutual displays of support after both countries suffered devastating earthquakes in 1999, they have recently begun to earn each other's trust. In January 2001 Foreign Minister **George Papandreou**—widely considered a future prime minister candidate—traveled to Turkey, the first such visit in 37 years. While there, he signed four cooperation agreements concerning tourism, the environment, the protection of investments, and terrorism. Talks have even begun concerning the fiery issue of Cyprus, which remains divided into Turkish and Greek Cypriot states. Though the discussions have been fruitless so far, the dialogue has brought the nation's closer together and helped guarantee an extended peace in the Aegean.

THE KKE The Greek Communist Party, or KKE, is the third-strongest political party in Greece, far behind New Democracy and PASOK. Looking askance at NATO, the West, and US influence, KKE members cringe at American cultural dominance. Leave your Union Jack backpacks and Old Glory bathing suits at home, as many KKE supporters harbor strong anti-Western sentiments, particularly the youthful, extremist set. Be prepared for a lot of angry graffiti, equating Americans with Nazis and the US President with Hitler. Noisy Western patriots will probably meet with no more than angry glances or verbal harassment, but it's a good idea to lie low, out of respect and common sense.

HOME GAMES. In the summer of 2004, the **Olympic Games** will return to their national birthplace as Athens plays host to the world's athletes and spectators. At least, that is the hope: in the past seven years since the Olympics were awarded to the capital, the Greek government's tardy and sloppy preparation for such an enormous undertaking has repeatedly earned the wrath of the **International Olympic Committee** (IOC). Complaints have ranged from insufficient hotel beds to slow progress on significant sports arenas to embezzlement and corruption. Finally, it appears the government has finally understood the severity of the IOC's reprimands and has recently whipped the Olympic movement into shape. Headed by the dynamic **Gianna Angelopoulos-Daskalaki,** the organizing committee has spurred the transformation of the city. With the Olympic sports complex finally complete in the Athenian suburbs, the construction of the Olympic Village progressing, the redone subway system earning rave reviews, and the new airport running efficiently, the 2004 Olympics might just work after all. However, don't expect the sort of organizational precision that marked the 2000 Olympics in Sydney. The 2004 Olympics will be frantic but ultimately satisfying in the Greek manner.

PEOPLE

DEMOGRAPHICS

THE MANY... Current estimates put the population at about **10.7 million** people. The population is 98% ethnically Greek and 98% Greek Orthodox (see p. 17), but the extremely homogeneous ethnic and religious population is sometimes overshadowed by the large number of foreign visitors who travel in Greece.

...AND THE FEW. Both the Greek government (which does not recognize official ethnic divisions) and the Greek people generally deny any overt racism. There is a growing concern about widespread prejudice toward a rapidly expanding refugee and migrant population.

Roughly 400,000 ethnic **Albanians,** most in northern Greece, make up the country's largest minority population; recently, reports of violence perpetrated by the Greek border patrol against illegal Albanian immigrants have cropped up.

The **Gypsies,** or **Roma,** make up another significant minority group; they have remained on the fringes of Greek society for centuries and are now concentrated in Athens and Thessaloniki. Plagued by poor health, low literacy rates, and extensive poverty, the Gypsy population is typically viewed by Greeks as one of the country's largest social problems.

The most populous religious minority group is made up of over 130,000 Slavic and Turkish **Muslims** in Thrace who remain separated from the Greeks in both language and culture. **Jewish** communities were present in Greece since the first century AD, but the majority of the Jewish population was deported to concentration camps during the Nazi occupation of World War II (p. 273). Only about 5,000 Jews live in Greece at present. Other official minorities include the **Vlachs** and the **Sarakatsanis,** both nomadic shepherds descended from Latin-speakers who settled in Greece. The Greek region of Macedonia is inhabited by some 60,000 **Slavs** still unrecognized by the Greek government as an ethnic or cultural minority.

LANGUAGE

THE MODERN TONGUE. The Greek language, **ellenika,** is much more than a medium for communication. Greeks use it carefully and treat it adoringly. It is a link to their cherished past and a key to continued Greek success and independence in the future. Because barely 12 million people speak the language around the world, each and every speaker of Greek is essential to the continued life of the tongue. For that reason, the passing of the language through the generations is often portrayed as a solemn duty for parents and a treasured gift for children.

To the non-Greek speaker, the intricate levels of nuance, idiom, irony, and poetry imbued in the language can present a seemingly impenetrable wall to understanding. Indeed, Greek is one of the most difficult languages for English speakers to learn fluently. With complex conjugations for verbs and strict declensions for adjectives and nouns, Greek will bring back bad memories from high school classics class. Although mastering Greek is a truly daunting task, learning enough to order a meal, send a postcard, and get to the airport is surprisingly easy. The Greek language is obsessively phonetic; with a cursory knowledge of the **alphabet** (p. 603), one should have no problem pronouncing any word. Making matters easier still, all multisyllabic Greek words come with handy accents, which mark the syllable to be emphasized. Sentences are usually simple, and sentence structure is very similar to English. Greeks tend to speak quickly, so listen carefully for important, recognizable nouns and you may well get their point. If all else fails, resort to signals and gestures. Greeks constantly use their hands and their bodies when they talk, and body language is sometimes as useful as a dictionary. Using gestures is an easy way to get your point across, too.

PRACTICE MAKES PASSABLE. With a little work, any tourist to Greece should be able to get by easily. Don't be embarrassed to practice your Greek in front of native speakers. Greeks are famously welcoming of foreigners' trying their hand at the language, although they may not be able to repress the occasional giggle when, instead of ordering another bottle of wine, for example, you ask for their hand in marriage. Of course, almost all Greeks, and certainly anyone working in the tourist industry, will understand English, but try to learn a little Greek. Even in the worst case scenario, you'll end up with a couple of new spouses.

RELIGION

ANCIENT GODS. Greek myths bubble with spicy, titillating **scandal** as they tell us how the world got to be the way it is. The adventures of the gods and their long-suffering mortal counterparts have inspired artists, writers, and psychoanalysts.

GREEK GOD	ROMAN NAME	JOB DESCRIPTION
Zeus	Jupiter	King of gods; law maker; kept order with handy thunderbolt.
Hera	Juno	Queen of Olympus; goddess of women and marriage; Zeus's sister and wife.
Ares	Mars	God of war and the spirit of battle; represented the gruesome aspects of fighting.
Hephæstus	Vulcan	Fire god; divine smith and patron of all craftsman; Aphrodite's homely husband.
Demeter	Ceres	Goddess of the Earth and fertility.
Aphrodite	Venus	Love goddess; Cupid's mom and boss; noted philanderer.
Athena	Minerva	Goddess of wisdom and craft; Athens's protectress; born from Zeus's head.
Hades	Pluto	God of the Underworld; Zeus's brother; Motto: Always room for one more.
Poseidon	Neptune	God of the sea and of water; brother of Zeus.
Apollo	Apollo	Sun god; patron of music, song, and poetry; python-slayer; Artemis's twin.
Artemis	Diana	Goddess of the hunt, the moon, wild animals, vegetation, chastity, and childbirth.
Hermes	Mercury	Messenger god; presided over animals, commerce, shrewdness, and persuasion; patron god of travelers.

THE ORTHODOX CHURCH. **Greek Orthodoxy** is the religion of 98% of the Greek population. The Orthodox Church is rigidly hierarchical in structure, with one archbishop of Athens, 85 bishops in 77 dioceses, and 7500 parishes. **Bishops** don't have a lot of contact with their congregations on an everyday basis; **priests,** easily recognizable by their long black robes, beards, and cylindrical hats, interact more closely with the people, but still remain fairly removed from secular life. Orthodox clergy spend most of their time praying, reflecting, and preparing the sacraments, rather than pursuing missions in the secular world at large. Greece's many isolated **monastic communities** (such as **Mt. Athos,** p. 256) have had trouble adapting to the modern world, but many continue to attract young Greek and foreign recruits.

OTHER RELIGIONS. Fortunately for the minority 2%, the constitution guarantees freedom of religion, and the Greek Orthodox Church remains separate from the Greek state. Muslims are Greece's largest religious minority (see **People,** p. 15). The country's small Catholic population is concentrated in the Cyclades, and a few towns in mainland Greece have small Jewish communities.

CULTURE

FOOD & DRINK

Recent medical studies have highlighted the Greek diet as a good model for **healthy** eating; its reliance on unsaturated olive oil and vegetables has prevented high rates of heart disease despite the fairly sedentary lifestyle of the populace. Penny-pinching carnivores will thank Zeus for lamb, chicken, or beef **souvlaki** and hot-off-the-spit **gyros**, pronounced "yiro," stuffed into a pita. Vegetarians can also eat their fill on the cheap. **Tzatziki,** a garlicky cucumber yogurt dip, with bread is a good way to start off a meal (or ripen your breath enough to ward off any overly-amorous overtures). Try the feta-piled **horiatiki** (a.k.a. Greek salad), savory pastries like **tiropita** (cheese pie, a pastry full of feta) and **spanakopita** (spinach and feta pie), and the fresh fruits and vegetables found at markets and vendor stands in most cities. Bottles of **spring water** are dirt cheap, so there's no excuse not to keep hydrated.

Liquid refreshment typically involves a few basic options, including the strong, sweet sludge that is **Greek coffee** or the frothy, iced coffee **frappés** that take an edge off the heat in the summer. Potent **raki** and **tsipouro,** moonshine born of the remnants of wine-making, are especially popular on the mainland and Crete. **Ouzo** (a powerful, licorice-flavored Greek spirit sure to earn your respect) is served with **mezedes,** which are snacks consisting of tidbits of octopus, cheese, and sausage.

Breakfast, served only in the early morning, is generally very simple: a piece of toast with *marmelada* or a pastry. **Lunch,** a hearty and leisurely meal, can begin as early as noon but is more likely eaten sometime between 2 and 5pm. After a few hours' nap, it's time to eat again. **Dinner** is a drawn-out, relaxed affair served late; 7:30pm is *very* unfashionably early for dinner. Eat with the Greeks sometime between 10pm and midnight—then party all night or head home for another nap. A Greek restaurant is known as a **taverna** or **estiatorio;** a grill is a **psistaria.** Many restaurants don't offer printed menus. Waiters will ask you if you want salad, appetizers, or the works, so be careful not to wind up with mountains of food, since Greek portions tend to be large. Restaurants often put bread and water on the table as a matter of course; an added charge for the bread is listed on the menu as the couvert. You may never see ice in the glasses or butter on the table; many restaurants won't have them. Service is always included in the check, but it is customary to leave some change as an extra tip.

CUSTOMS & ETIQUETTE

Greek hospitality is legendary. From your first days in the country, you will be invited to drop by a stranger's home for coffee, share a meal at a local taverna or attend a engagement party or a baptism. The invitations are genuine; it's impossible to spend any length of time in the country and not have some friendly interaction with locals. Greet new acquaintances (along with shopkeepers and waiters) with *kalimera* (good morning) or *kalispera* (good evening).

Personal questions aren't considered rude in Greece, and pointed inquires from locals can be a bit disconcerting. Expect to be asked about family, career, salary, and other personal information by people you've just met. Returning questions in kind is expected and appreciated.

FOOD AND DRINK. As a general rule, when offered food or drink, take it—it's almost always considered rude to refuse. Coffee is usually offered upon arriving at someone's home. Wine drinkers should be aware that glasses are filled only halfway and constantly replenished; it's considered bad manners to empty your glass. When eating dinner with Greeks at a restaurant, the bill is usually paid by the host rather than split amongst the diners. Never offer money in return for an invitation to dine in someone's home. A small gift, such as toys for the host's children, is a welcome token of gratitude.

PHOTOGRAPHY. Take signs forbidding photography seriously, especially in Cyprus. Never photograph anything having to do with the military. Even if photography isn't specifically forbidden in a particular church or monastery, avoid using a flash and taking pictures of the main altar.

THE ARTS

Order, proportion, and symmetry have shaped the tradition of Greek art from its earliest stages. Greek art grew around the belief that "man is the measure of all things." The living human form became artists' favorite subject after years of dabbling with abstract and stylized geometrical shapes. Meanwhile, Greek temples incorporated light and space as integral parts of the place of worship. It is impossible to overestimate how much Western culture owes to the architectural and artistic achievements of the ancient Greeks—Augustus Caesar, Michelangelo, Jacques-Louis David, Thomas Jefferson, Constantine Brancusi, and even Salvador Dalí found inspiration in Greek works.

HISTORY

ARCHAIC PERIOD (700-480 BC). During the Archaic Period, Greek art and architecture morphed from the stylization of earlier times to the curving, human realism of the Classical Period. Sculptors and vase painters produced abstracted images of the human form, and architects fine-tuned temple-building and proportion in construction. The acropolis, agora, amphitheater, and gymnasium were among the structures that were perfected during this period.

The Doric and Ionic architectural orders—whose columns have lined many an art history student's nightmares—departed along their own paths during these years. The **Doric order** breathed new life into the former design of a one-room *cella* (a temple's inner sanctum) and its surrounding area with new columns and classy marble. Around the 6th century BC, Greece's colonies along the coast of Asia Minor branched off into the more exotic **Ionic order.** The curlicued Ionic columns differed from the austere Doric order in the slender, fluted bodies of each column, often topped with twin volutes (scrolled spiral uppers). Ornate Ionic temples boasted forests of columns: the Temple of Hera at Samos (p. 359) sported 134.

In the beginning of the 5th century BC, sculpture turned toward realistic depiction, which would reach its height soon afterward in the Classical Period. The relaxed posture of the free-standing **Kritios Boy** (490 BC), now in the **Acropolis Museum** in Athens (p. 99), broke the stiff, symmetrical mold of the archaic *kouroi* with an individualized personality: the Kritios Boy's weight is shifted onto one leg, and his hips and torso tilt as naturally as the Earth on its axis.

As sculptors focused on the realistic, two-dimensional art remained firmly in the abstract. Athenian **vase painters** depicted humans using Corinth's **black figure technique,** drawing black silhouettes with carved features. Human figures appeared in the half-profile of Egyptian art: moving figures' chests faced forward, and each person stared straight out with both eyes. The figures conveyed emotion with gestures rather than facial expression, and most pulled their hair in grief or flailed their limbs in joy.

CLASSICAL PERIOD (480-323 BC). The arts flourished during the Classical Period, as Athens reached the peak of its political and economic power under Pericles and his successors (p. 10). Perfecting Doric architecture and dabbling in the Ionic style, Classical temples were more spacious and fluid than the stocky temples of the Archaic Period. The peerless Athenian **Acropolis** (p. 95), built during this period, embodied "classic" for the entire Classical world; its star attraction, the **Parthenon,** shows the fullness of the Greek obsession with perfect proportions. *Everything* on the Parthenon—from its floor space to the friezes above the columns—is in a four-to-nine ratio.

Sculptors mastered the natural representation of the human form during the Classical Period. The milestone sculptures of the **Temple of Zeus** at Olympia (p. 144) exhibit an obsessive attention to detail. Indeed, the personal and mood-evoking Classical style fully broke from formulaic Archaic sculpture. Notable sculptures from the Classical Period include the bronze statues of the **Charioteer** (470 BC) at Delphi (p. 183) and the **Poseidon** from the Artemisium wreck (465 BC), now in Athens's **National Archaeological Museum** (p. 103).

By the middle of the 5th century BC, Classical sculptors had loosened the stylized stiffness of the early Archaic Period, favoring a detailed realism that still lacked facial expression. Sculptors pursued a universal perfection of the human form, suppressing the imperfections that make people unique. This impersonal, idealized **severe style** embodied the idealization of Plato's forms and the athletic heroism that Pindar praised in his Olympic odes. It remained in vogue through the start of the 4th century BC.

Classical potters swooned over the **red figure technique** that had been gaining steam since 540 BC. Red figure vase painting featured a black painted background, allowing the naturally reddish clay to show through as the drawn figures. Vase-makers then painted on details with a fine brush. Inspired by the new-found realism in sculpture, anonymous early Classical masters the **Berlin Painter** and the **Kleophrades Painter** lent their subjects an unparalleled level of psychological depth.

HELLENISTIC PERIOD (323-46 BC). After the death of Alexander the Great, a new Hellenistic Period rose out of the ashes of Classical Greece. Eastern Greeks made architecture a flamboyant affair. Scuttling the simpler Doric and Ionic styles, they whipped up ornate, flower-topped **Corinthian-style columns.** Hellenistic architects worked on a monumental scale, building complexes of temples, *stoas* (colonnaded walkways), and palaces. Astoundingly precise **acoustics**

GRIN AND BARE IT While architects were fussing over columns, early Archaic sculptors began to craft large-scale figures called *kouroi*. Each *kouros* was a naked, idealized young man, symmetrically posed, with one leg forward and hands clenched at his sides, smiling goofily under stylized curls. The *kouroi* stood in temples as offerings to deities or as memorials to fallen warriors. An early example dedicated to Poseidon at Sounion (c. 590 BC) now stands in the **National Archaeological Museum** in Athens (p. 103). In the 6th century BC, a new obsession with the natural human form led to more lifelike *kouroi,* such as the stunning Anavissos *kouros*, also in the National Archaeological Museum. The female equivalent of the *kouros,* the *kore*, posed in the latest fashions instead of in her birthday suit; sculptors focused on the drape of a *kore*'s clothing, suggesting the female form through folds and hemlines.

graced the enormous amphitheaters at **Argos** (p. 122) and **Epidavros** (p. 130); a coin dropped onstage is audible in the most distant seat in the theaters, even 2200 years after their construction.

Hellenistic sculpture exuded passion, displaying all the technical mastery and twice the emotion of Classical works. Artists tested the aesthetic value of ugliness, sculpting the grotesque figure of **Laocoön** as snakes writhe around him, dragging him to death; only a Roman copy of the Hellenistic original survives.

With the arrival of the **Roman empire** in Greece, the Hellenistic style shifted to suit Roman tastes. Greek artists created works for Romans in Italy and for the old Hellenistic kingdoms of the east. Architects built mostly Christian churches; even the Parthenon was temporarily converted to a church, though it was (fortunately) left unaltered in its structure. Under the Romans, Greek art and architecture spread throughout the empire, but its innovative glory had passed.

BYZANTINE & OTTOMAN (AD 324-1829). The art and architecture in Greece under Byzantine and Ottoman rule belonged more to these imperial cultures than to native Greek culture. Byzantine artistry developed within a set of religious conventions that limited creative experimentation but still created magnificent mosaics, iconography, and church architecture. Early Byzantine churches show their roots in Roman Christianity: based on the Roman basilica layout, the Byzantine versions were long buildings with a semicircular apse at one end and windows lining a wooden ceiling (forming a clerestory). A column-lined outer courtyard stood on a church's western side; on the eastern side, people entered the vestibule through two doors, often bronze or inlaid with silver. These doors opened onto the *naos*, the church proper. Inside, a central nave reached from the church's inner door to the choir rows, and was separated from two side aisles by arched colonnades. The floor and lower parts of the walls were usually covered in **marble,** while the upper parts were reserved for **mosaics** and occasionally **frescoes.**

Byzantine artists transformed almost any flat surface they encountered into art: they illuminated manuscripts, carved ivory panels, embossed bronze doors, and covered *cloisonée* enamels with jewels. The dazzling mosaics and **icons** of Byzantine churches showed the greatest of Byzantine talent: artists underwent years of spiritual and technical training before gaining permission to portray sacred subjects. Byzantine icons aimed for religious authenticity, intended to transmit—not just represent—the spiritual power of the subject. Each figure stared out with a soul-searing gaze, adding to the power of the images; a determined frontal pose against a gold background in the church's dim light created the illusion of the figure floating between the wall and the viewer.

Brilliant Byzantine mosaics were composed of **tesserae,** small cubes of stone or ceramic covered in glass or metallic foil. A unique shimmering effect was produced by contrasting gold and silver tesserae at sharp angles to reflect light. Sparkling examples of mosaics can be seen in the churches of **Thessaloniki** (p. 213), at the **Monastery of Osios Loukas** (p. 179), on **Mt. Athos** (p. 256), and at **Meteora** (p. 211).

CURRENT SCENE

FINE ARTS. Nationalist sentiment after Greek independence led the government to subsidize Greek art. King Otto encouraged young artists to study their craft in Munich, and the **Polytechneion,** Greece's first modern art school, was established in 1838. The first wave of post-independence Greek painters showed strong evidence of their German training; sculptors looked to Classical Greece for inspiration.

Twentieth century Greek painters have contended with European trends: Impressionism, Expressionism, and Surrealism all made their mark on 19th century Greek artists. Other painters rejected foreign influence, among them the much-adored **Theophilos Chatzimichael** (1873-1934). In the present day, the paintings of **Yiannis Psychopedis** (b. 1945) combine social and aesthetic criticism. Painter **Opy Zouni** (b. 1941) has won international renown for her geometric art.

LITERATURE. Greek independence in 1821 (see p. 12) gave rise to the **Ionian School** of modern literature, which dealt with the political and personal issues of the Greek revolution. **Dionysios Solomos** (1798-1857)—whose *Hymn to Liberty* became the Greek national anthem—is still referred to as the National Poet. Twentieth-century poets would infuse their own odes with Modernism, alternately denouncing and celebrating nationalism and politics. Winner of a 1979 Nobel Prize in Literature, **Odysseas Elytis** (1911-96) looked at politics in a different light and incorporated French Surrealism in an effort toward national redemption.

Nikos Kazantzakis (1883-1957) may be the best known modern Greek author. His many novels include *Odyssey*, a modern sequel to the Homeric epic, *Report to Greco*, **Zorba the Greek** (1946), and **The Last Temptation of Christ** (1951); the last two have been made into successful films. *Freedom or Death*, his homage to Greek revolts against Ottoman rule on his home island of Crete, analyzes the Greek-Turkish conflict and looks into the Greek concept of masculinity.

THEATER. Modern Greek theater labors in the shadow of its classical predecessor. A few contemporary playwrights such as **Iakovos Kambanellis** (b.1922), **Demitris Kehadis** (b.1933), and Symiot writer **Eleni Haviara** have wooed audiences with their portrayals of 20th century Greek life. Taking advantage of the international audience provided by the upcoming Olympic Games, the Greek Playwrights Society (www.eeths.gr) is organizing a festival of modern plays from local writers to take place in May 2003. But classical theater still dominates: the **Athens Festival,** held from June to September, features ancient works at the Theater of Herod Atticus (p. 99) and at the **Epidavros Festival** (p. 130), from July to September, even a language barrier won't diminish the power of plays that have survived for millennia.

MUSIC. *Rembetika*, gutsy blues music with folk influences, first made its appearance in Greece in the late 19th century. After decades of increasingly inauthentic performances, interest in traditional *rembetika* has resurfaced, and musicians strumming *bouzouki* (a traditional Greek instrument similar to a mandolin) can be found in several clubs. Trendier venues offer a playlist saturated with Western music—American hits of the 70s and 80s rear their ugly heads all summer long. Popular local band **Pyx Lax** is gaining something of an international following.

HOLIDAYS & FESTIVALS

Greece celebrates a host of religious and political holidays throughout the year. Dates for 2003 include the following:

GREECE'S FESTIVALS (2003)

DATE	NAME & LOCATION	DESCRIPTION
January 1	Feast of St. Basil/New Year's Day	Carrying on a Byzantine tradition, Greeks cut a New Year's sweet bread (*vassilopita*) baked with a lucky coin inside.
January 6	Epiphany	The Eastern Church's celebration of Jesus's baptism.
February 17	Carnival	Three weeks of feasting and dancing precede Lenten fasting. Patras, Skyros, and Kephalonia host the best celebrations.
March 10	Green Monday	Start of Lent, the 4-week period of fasting before Easter.
March 25	Greek Independence Day/ Feast of the Annunciation	Commemorates the 1821 struggle against the Ottoman Empire and celebrates the Immaculate Conception.
April 23	St. George's Day	Rowdy festivals in Limnos and Hania honor the dragon-slaying knight.
April 27	Easter	The single holiest day in the Greek calendar celebrates Jesus's resurrection from the dead.
May 1	Labor Day	A celebration of workers and a communist demonstration.
June 5	Ascension	Commemorates Jesus's ascension into heaven. Celebrated 40 days after Easter with different rituals in each region.
June 15	Pentecost	The day of the Holy Spirit, celebrated 50 days after Easter.
August 15	Feast of the Assumption of the Virgin Mary	A celebration throughout Greece, particularly on Tinos, that honors Mary's ascent into heaven.
September 8	The Virgin Mary's Birthday	To celebrate Mary's birthday, some villages finance a feast by auctioning off the honor of carrying the Virgin's icon.
October 26	Feast of St. Demetrius	Celebrated enthusiastically in Thessaloniki. The feast coincides with the opening of a new stock of wine.
October 28	Ohi Day	Commemorates Metaxas's cry of "*Οχι!*" (No!) to Mussolini's demand to occupy Greece.
December 25	Christmas	Greeks celebrate both Christmas Eve and Christmas Day. Children make the rounds singing *kalanda* (carols).

ADDITIONAL RESOURCES

GENERAL HISTORY

Paul Cartledge. *Cambridge Illustrated History of Ancient Greece* (Cambridge University Press). A well-written, comprehensive commentary on all aspects of Ancient Greece.

John Julius Norwich. *Byzantium: the Apogee* and *Byzantium: the Decline and Fall* (Knopf). The second and third chapters of Norwich's engaging study of Byzantium.

John Boardman. *Oxford History of Classical Art* (Oxford University Press). A must-read guide, detailing the history of Greek and Roman aesthetic innovation.

Archbishop Timothy (Kallistos) Ware. *The Orthodox Church* (Penguin). An thoughtful introduction to the established religion of Greece, written by the Orthodox Archbishop residing at Oxford.

MYTHOLOGY

Thomas Bulfinch. *The Age of Fable* from *Bulfinch's Mythology* (Modern Library). *The* authority on Greek mythology.

Robert Graves. *The Greek Myths* (Penguin). Meticulously documents sources of the Greek myths and recounts different versions of the tales.

Joseph Campbell. *The Hero with a Thousand Faces* (Princeton University Press). Part of the inspiration for George Lucas's *Star Wars*, Campbell's analysis of myth draws parallels between myth and the journey of life. He postulates that there is a single archetypical mythic hero who reflects man's search for identity.

FICTION AND NON-FICTION

Aristophanes. *Lysistrata*. Athenian women go on a sex strike in an attempt to force their husbands to end the Peloponnesian War. Try Jeffrey Henderson's translation.

Wilis Barnstone. *Sappho and the Greek Lyric Poets* (Penguin). An excellent translation of works by Lesvos's favorite literary daughter.

Louis De Bernieres. *Corelli's Mandolin* (Vintage). An emotional novel about star-crossed lovers—a Kephalonian woman and an Italian officer stationed on the island during WWII.

John Fowles. *The Magus* (Dell). A story of mystery and manipulation inspired by Fowles's years as a teacher on the island of Spetses.

H.A. Lidderdale. *The Memoirs of General Makriyannis, 1797-1864* (Oxford University Press). Though now out of print, Lidderdale's translation of the General's autobiography offers an unflinching portrayal of the Greek uprising.

FILM

Mediterraneo (1991). Eight soldiers find themselves stranded on an anonymous Greek island during World War II in this Italian comedy.

Z (1969). Directed by Costa-Gavras, the thinly veiled depiction of a conspiracy to assassinate a liberal Greek politician won the Academy Award for Best Foreign Film.

Zorba The Greek (1964). An exuberant, sentimental film based on the novel by Nikos Kazantzakis. The most well-known movie about Greece (and rightfully so).

TRAVEL BOOKS

Lawrence Durrell. *Prospero's Cell* and *Reflections on a Marine Venus* (Marlowe & Co). Both books relate to the author's years spent on the island of Corfu (see p. 274).

Patrick Leigh Fermor. *The Mani* (Viking). Fermor, known for rallying Cretan resistance in World War II, writes an account of his adventures in the Mani in the 1950s.

Willard Manus. *This Way to Paradise: Dancing on the Tables* (Lycabettus Press). The hilarious memoirs of an American expat living in pre-tourist Rhodes.

Henry Miller. *Colossus of Marousi* (Norton). Zealous account of Miller's travels in Greece at the start of World War II.

Patricia Storace. *Dinner with Persephone* (Vintage Books). With dry humor and gorgeous detail, the American poet meditates on her travel in Greece in the early 1990s.

THE GREEK DIASPORA

The Greeks are everywhere: 1.5 million in America, over a half million in Germany, at least as many in the former USSR, and hundreds of thousands in Canada, South Africa, Asia, and Australia. All told, five million Greeks live outside Greece. Melbourne, Toronto, New York, and Chicago each calls itself the "biggest Greek city outside Greece."

A disproportionate number of famed Greeks are from the diaspora. Aristotle Onassis (Turkey), Maria Callas (New York), and Spain's Queen Sophia come to mind, as do the poet Constantine Cavafy (Egypt), film director Costa Gavras (France), and actress Jennifer Aniston (California). George Stephanopoulos and Michael Dukakis (both Massachusetts) trail-blazed for the legions of Greek-Americans in politics. Pete Sampras and hockey star Chris Chelios are two of many sports world stars. Nicholas Negroponte (UK), founder of the Media Lab at MIT, is one of the diaspora pioneers in academia.

But in leaving their home, Greeks always looked back—nostalgia, after all, is a Greek word. Rather than fade into their adopted cultures, they maintained *arriktoi desmoi*—unbreakable bonds—with their heritage. The very idea of modern Greece was imported by diaspora Greeks. Before the 1821 Revolution, most Ottoman subjects in the Greek peninsula were uneducated peasants. The Western-educated diaspora taught these Greeks about their history, explaining that they were the inheritors of ancient Greece.

The independence movement began in Paris and Vienna, where the first Greek newspapers and books were published in the 18th century. In Paris, Adamantios Korais revived the classical Greek language; his version of it, katharevousa, remained Greece's official tongue until the 1970s. In London, Alexandros Mavrokordatos used his connections to finance the revolt against the Ottomans. In Odessa on the Black Sea in 1814, Greek merchants founded the society Filiki Etairia, which became the revolution's nexus. Over the following decades, diaspora Greeks built the country's prestigious schools, the National Library, the Archaeological Museum, the University of Athens, and the Athens Observatory. The tradition of using earnings from abroad to finance works at home continues: Until the 1990s, diaspora remittances were Greece's largest source of foreign currency.

The diaspora elite's role in the Revolution was so profound that it sparked conflict with native Greeks—who, having suffered the Ottoman yoke, felt they had a greater claim to the new nation. But the historical vision of a Greece rooted in antiquity and Byzantium ultimately prevailed. Said one rousing orator in 1844 in the Greek parliament: "The Kingdom of Greece is not Greece. It constitutes only one part, the smallest and poorest. A Greek is not only a man who lives within the Kingdom, but also one who lives in Ioannina, Serrai, Adrianople, Constantinople, Smyrna, Trebizond, Crete and in any land associated with Greek history and the Greek race."

This notion of "cultural Greekness" was translated into the Great Idea, which guided Greek foreign policy for almost a century and sought to unite Greece with the capital of Byzantium, Constantinople (now Istanbul), and the Asia Minor coast. The dream ended in 1922, when Kemal Ataturk, the founder of Turkey, led an assault on Smyrna that killed tens of thousands of Greeks. The next year, the Treaty of Lausanne sent over 1 million Greeks from Asia Minor, their home for over 3,000 years, to Greece, a homeland they had never known. A similar fate befell the 100,000 Greeks in Egypt, driven out by Nasser's 1952 revolution. The most recent flood of immigration came in the 1990s, when hundreds of thousands of Greeks liberated from communist rule in Albania and the former USSR made their way home.

Today's diaspora communities are largely the product of two great waves of economic emigration from Greece: the first at the turn of the 20th century, the second after World War II. The Greek-American community has steadily grown in size and influence—it is one of the most prosperous immigrant groups in the US. Similar success stories can be told of the communities in Australia, Canada, and in 70 other countries around the world.

Gregory A. Maniatis is the founder of Odyssey Magazine, *the leading international magazine about Greece and Greeks around the world. He has also contributed to* New York Magazine, *the* Independent, *the* Washington Monthly, *Time-Life Books, and other publications.*

ESSENTIALS

DOCUMENTS AND FORMALITIES

ENTRANCE REQUIREMENTS

Passport (p. 27). Required for citizens of Australia, Canada, Ireland, New Zealand, the UK, and the US.

Visa (p. 27). Required for citizens of South Africa.

Work Permit (p. 27). Required for all foreigners planning to work in Greece.

Driving Permit (p. 60). Required for all those planning to drive.

GREEK CONSULAR SERVICES ABROAD

Australia Embassy: 9 Turrana St., Yarralumla, **Canberra,** ACT 26000 (☎02 6273 3011; fax 6273 2620). **Consulates:** 366 King William St., 1st Fl., **Adelaide,** SA 5000 (☎08 8211 8066; fax 8211 8820); Stanhill House, 34 Queens Rd., **Melbourne,** VIC 3004 (☎03 866 4524; fax 866 4933); 15 Castlereagh St., Level 20, **Sydney,** NSW 2000 (☎02 9221 2388; fax 9221 1423); 16 St. George's Terr., **Perth,** WA 6000 (☎08 9325 6608; fax 9325 2940).

Canada Embassy: 80 MacLaren St., **Ottawa,** ON K2P 0K6 (☎613-238-6271; fax 238-5676; www.greekembassy.ca; embassy@greekembassy.ca). **Consulates:** 1170 Place du Frère André Suite 300, **Montréal,** QC H3B 3C6 (☎514-875-2119; fax 875-8781); 365 Bloor St. E, Suite 1800, **Toronto,** ON M4W 3L4 (☎416-515-0133; fax 515-0209); 500-688 West Hastings St., Suite 500, **Vancouver,** BC V6B 1P1 (☎604-681-1381; fax 681-6656).

Ireland Embassy: 1 Upper Pembroke St., Dublin 2 (☎01 6767 2545; fax 661 88 92).

New Zealand Consulate: 5-7 Willeston St., 10th Fl., Box 24066, Wellington (☎04 473 7775; fax 473 7441).

South Africa Embassy: 1003 Church St., Hatfield, **Pretoria** 0028 (☎12 437 351; fax 434 313). **Consulate:** 11 Wellington Road, 3rd Fl., Parktown, **Johannesburg** 2193 (☎11 484 1794).

UK Embassy: 1a Holland Park, London W113TP (☎0171 229 38 50; fax 229 72 21). **Consulate:** 1a Holland Park, London W113TP (☎0171 221 64 67; fax 243 32 02).

US Embassy: 2221 Massachusetts Ave., NW, **Washington, D.C.** 20008 (☎202-939-5800; fax 939-5824; www.greekembassy.org; greece@greekembassy.org). **Consulates:** 2211 Massachusetts Ave. NW, **Washington, D.C.** 20008 (☎202-939-5818; fax 234-2803); 69 East 79th St., **New York,** NY 10021 (☎212-988-5500; fax 734-8492; nycons@greekembassy.org); 650 North St. Clair St., **Chicago,** IL 60611 (☎312-335-3915; fax 335-3958); 2441 Gough St., **San Francisco,** CA 94123 (☎415-775-2102; fax 776-6815); 12424 Wilshire Building, Suite 800, **Los Angeles,** CA 90025 (☎310-826-5555; fax 826-8670); 86 Beacon St., **Boston,** MA 02108-3304 (☎617-523-0100; fax 523-0511); Tower Place, Suite 1670 3340, Peachtree Rd., NE, **Atlanta,** GA 30326 (☎404-261-3313; fax 262-2798); 520 Post Oak Blvd., Suite 310, **Houston,** TX 77027 (☎713-840-7522; fax 810-0611); World Trade Center, 2 Canal St., Suite 2318, **New Orleans,** LA 70130 (☎504-523-1167; fax 524-5610).

CONSULAR SERVICES IN GREECE

A full listing of embassies is available at the Athens tourist office (see p. 76). Embassies are generally open only in the morning. All embassies, unless noted, are in **Athens.**

Australia: D. Soutsou 37, 115 21 (☎210 645 0404; fax 210 646 6595). Open M-F 8:30am-12:30pm.

Canada: Ioannou Genadiou 4, 115 21 (☎ 210 727 3400; fax 210 727 3480). Open M-F 8:30am-12:30pm. **Consulate:** Tsimiski 17, **Thessaloniki** 546 24 (☎2310 256 350; fax 2310 256 351).

European Community: Vas. Sofias 2 (☎210 727 2100; fax 210 724 4620). Open M-F 8:30am-1pm.

Ireland: Vas. Konstantinou 7, 106 74 (☎210 723 2771; fax 210 724 0217). Open M-F 9am-3pm.

South Africa: Kifissias 60, 151 25 (☎210 610 6645; fax 210 610 6640). Open M-F 8am-1pm.

UK: Ploutarchou 1, 106 75 (☎ 210 727 2600; fax 210 727 2772). Open M-F 8:30am-1pm.

US: Embassy: Vas. Sofias 91, 101 60 (☎210 721 2951; fax 210 645 6282; www.usembassy.gr). Open M-F 8:30am-5pm, for visas 8:30-noon. **Consulate:** Tsimiski 43, 7th Fl., **Thessaloniki** 546 23 (☎2310 242 905; fax 242 927; amcongen@compulink.gr).

TOURIST BOARDS

Tourist info in Greece is available in English 24 hours a day by dialing 171.

Start early when trying to contact tourist offices—like most things Greek, they run on their own relaxed schedule. Polite persistence and genuine excitement about visiting works wonders. Two national organizations oversee tourism: the **Greek National Tourist Organization (GNTO)** and the tourist police *(touristiki astinomia)*. The GNTO can supply general information about sights and accommodations throughout the country. (For additional info and offices abroad, see www.gnto.gr.) The main office is in Athens at Amerikis 2 (☎210 327 1300; info@gnto.gr). Note that the GNTO is known as the **EOT** in Greece. The tourist police deal with more local issues: where to find a room or what the bus schedule is. The offices are open long hours and the staff is often quite willing to help, although their English may be limited. On many islands and in smaller towns, travel agencies will be more helpful (and more likely to exist) than tourist offices; feel free to stop in and ask for advice. *Let's Go* lists tourist agencies and organizations in the **Practical Information** section for most cities.

Australia and New Zealand: 3rd Fl., 51 Pitt St., Sydney, NSW 2000 (☎02 9241 1663; fax 9235 2174; hto@tpg.com.au).

Canada: 91 Scollard St., 2nd Fl., **Toronto,** ON M5R 1G4 (☎416-968-2220; fax 968-6533; grnto.tor@sympatico.ca); 1170 Place du Frére André, Suite 300, **Montréal,** QC H3B 3C6 (☎514-871-1535; fax 871-1498; gntomtl@aei.ca).

UK and Ireland: 4 Conduit St., London W1S 2DJ (☎207 734 5997; fax 287 1369; EOT-greektouristoffice@btinternet.com; www.tourist-offices.org.uk).

US: Head Office, Olympic Tower, 645 Fifth Ave., 9th Fl., New York, NY 10022 (☎212-421-5777; fax 826-6940; www.greektourism.com; gnto@greektourism.com).

PASSPORTS

REQUIREMENTS. Citizens of Australia, Canada, Ireland, New Zealand, South Africa, the UK, and the US need valid passports to enter Greece and to re-enter their own country.

PHOTOCOPIES. Be sure to photocopy the page of your passport with your photo, passport number, and other identifying information, as well as any visas, travel insurance policies, airplane tickets, or traveler's check serial numbers. Carry one set of copies in a safe place, apart from the originals, and leave another set at home. Carry an expired passport or an official copy of your birth certificate in a part of your bag separate from other documents.

LOST PASSPORTS. If you lose your passport, immediately notify the local police and the nearest embassy or consulate of your home government. To expedite its replacement, you will need to know all information previously recorded and show identification and proof of citizenship. In some cases, a replacement may take weeks to process, and it may be valid only for a limited time. Visas stamped in your old passport will be irretrievably lost. In an emergency, ask for immediate temporary traveling papers that will permit you to re-enter your home country. Your passport is a public document belonging to your nation's government. You may have to surrender it to a foreign government official, but if you don't get it back in a reasonable amount of time, inform the nearest mission of your home country.

NEW PASSPORTS. All applications for new passports or renewals should be filed several weeks or months in advance of your planned departure date. Get a passport from your local post office, passport office (available in most major cities), or travel agency. Most passport offices offer emergency passport services for a steep fee. Citizens residing abroad who need a passport or renewal should contact the nearest consular service of their home country.

ONE EUROPE. The idea of European unity has come a long way since 1958, when the European Economic Community (EEC) was created in order to promote solidarity and cooperation. Since then, the EEC has become the European Union (EU), with political, legal, and economic institutions spanning 15 member states: Austria, Belgium, Denmark, Finland, France, Germany, Greece, Ireland, Italy, Luxembourg, the Netherlands, Portugal, Spain, Sweden, and the UK.

What does this have to do with the average non-EU tourist? In 1999, the EU established **freedom of movement** across 14 European countries—the entire EU minus Denmark, Ireland, and the UK, but plus Iceland and Norway. This means that border controls between participating countries have been abolished, and visa policies harmonized. While you're still required to carry a passport (or government-issued ID card for EU citizens) when crossing an internal border, once you've been admitted into one country, you're free to travel to all participating states. Britain and Ireland have also formed a **common travel area,** abolishing passport controls between the UK and the Republic of Ireland. This means that the only times you'll see a border guard within the EU are traveling between the British Isles and the Continent and in and out of Denmark.

VISAS AND WORK PERMITS

VISAS. EU members, as well as citizens of the US, Canada, Australia, and New Zealand are all automatically granted leave for a three-month stay in Greece, though they are not eligible for employment during that time. South Africans need a visa. Apply for visa extensions at least 20 days prior to the three-month expiration date at the **Aliens Bureau,** Alexandras 173, Athens 115 22 (☎210 770 5711), or check with a Greek embassy or consulate.

WORK PERMITS. For long-term employment in Greece, you must first get a **work permit** from a pre-arranged employer. Permits are available at the **Ministry of Labor,** Pireos 40, Athens 104 37. Make all arrangements and negotiations before you leave. (For more information, see p. 67.)

IDENTIFICATION

When you travel, always carry two or more forms of identification on your person, including at least one photo ID. A passport combined with a driver's license or birth certificate is usually adequate. Many establishments, especially banks, require several IDs to cash traveler's checks. Never carry all of your forms of ID together; split them up in case of theft or loss. Bring extra passport-size photos to affix to the various IDs or passes you may acquire on the way.

STUDENT AND TEACHER IDENTIFICATION. The **International Student Identity Card (ISIC),** the most widely accepted form of student ID, provides discounts on sights, accommodations, food, and transport; access to a 24hr. emergency helpline for medical, legal, and financial emergencies (in North America, ☎877-370-ISIC, elsewhere call US collect +1 715-345-0505); and insurance benefits for US cardholders (see **Insurance,** p. 39). In Greece, the card will procure you discounts at many sights and museums, a few hostels, and on the occasional ferry and Olympic Airways flight. If discounts are not listed, make sure to present the card and ask. The ISIC is preferable to an institution-specific card (such as a university ID) because it is more likely to be recognized and honored abroad. Applicants must be degree-seeking students of a secondary or post-secondary school and must be of at least 12 years of age. Because of the proliferation of fake ISICs, some services (particularly airlines) require additional proof of student identity, such as a school ID or a letter attesting to your student status, signed by your registrar and stamped with your school seal.

The **International Teacher Identity Card (ITIC)** offers the same insurance coverage as well as similar but limited discounts. For travelers who are 25 years old or under but are not students, the **International Youth Travel Card (IYTC;** formerly the **GO 25** Card) also offers many of the same benefits as the ISIC.

Each of these identity cards costs US$22 or equivalent. ISIC and ITIC cards are valid for roughly one and a half academic years; IYTC cards are valid for one year from the date of issue. Many student travel agencies (see p. 49) issue the cards, including STA Travel in Australia and New Zealand; Travel CUTS in Canada; usit in the Republic of Ireland and Northern Ireland; SASTS in South Africa; STA Travel in the UK; and Council Travel and STA Travel in the US. For a listing of issuing agencies, or for more information, contact the **International Student Travel Confederation (ISTC),** Herengracht 479, 1017 BS Amsterdam, Netherlands (☎+31 20 421 28 00; fax 421 28 10; istcinfo@istc.org; www.istc.org).

CUSTOMS

Upon entering Greece, you must declare if you've brought currency above US$1000 or if you've brought certain items from abroad. You must pay a duty on the value of those articles if it exceeds the allowance established by Greek customs. Importing biological hazards (agricultural products, raw meat, etc.) is prohibited. Selling anything while abroad is illegal; authorities expect you to return with everything except your money. Upon returning home, you must declare all articles acquired abroad and pay a duty on the value of articles in excess of your home country's allowance. Make a list of valuables brought from home and register them with customs before traveling. Keep receipts for goods acquired abroad.

DUTY-FREE ITEMS. You should also be aware that duty-free was abolished on June 30, 1999 for travel between EU member states; however, travelers between the EU and the rest of the world still get a duty-free allowance when passing through customs. Goods and gifts purchased at duty-free shops abroad are not exempt from duty or sales tax at your point of return and thus must be declared as well; "duty-free" merely means that you need not pay a tax in the country of purchase. Keeping receipts for purchases made in Greece will help establish values when you return. If you will be carrying valuables, you should make a list of their serial numbers and register it with customs. An official customs stamp will ensure that you avoid import duty charges and simplify your return. Be especially careful to document items manufactured abroad.

CUSTOMS IN THE EU. As well as freedom of movement of people within the EU (see p. 27), travelers in the countries that are members of the EU (Austria, Belgium, Denmark, Finland, France, Germany, Greece, Ireland, Italy, Luxembourg, the Netherlands, Portugal, Spain, Sweden, and the UK) can also take advantage of the freedom of movement of goods. This means that there are no customs controls at internal EU borders (i.e., you can take the blue customs channel at the airport), and travelers are free to transport whatever legal substances they like as long as it is for their own personal (non-commercial) use—up to 800 cigarettes, 10L of spirits, 90L of wine (60L of sparkling wine), and 110L of beer. You should also be aware that duty-free was abolished on June 30, 1999 for travel between EU member states; however, travelers between the EU and the rest of the world still get a duty-free allowance when passing through customs.

VALUE ADDED TAX. The European Union imposes a value added tax (VAT) on goods and services purchased within the EU, which is included in the marked price. Non-EU citizens may obtain a refund for taxes paid on retail goods (but not services). In Greece, you must spend over €120 to receive a refund. The percentage of your refund will be about 15.3%. To file for a refund, first obtain a Tax-Free Shopping Cheque, available from shops sporting the blue, white, and silver Europe Tax-Free Shopping logo, and then save the receipts from all of the purchases for which you want to be partially refunded. Upon leaving Greece, you can present your goods, invoices, and Tax-Free Shopping Cheque to customs, which will then validate the Cheque. An immediate cash refund may be available at an ETS cash refund office, or you may have to file for a refund at home. Refunds are available for purchases made by credit card and check. Allow two hours to apply for customs endorsement at your point of departure. There are some **restrictions** on VAT refunds. Goods must be taken out of the country within three months after the end of the month of purchase, and they must be unused. For more information, visit www.globalrefund.com.

MONEY

CURRENCY AND EXCHANGE

The currency chart below is based on August 2002 exchange rates between local currency and Australian dollars (AUS$), Canadian dollars (CDN$), Irish pounds (IR£), New Zealand dollars (NZ$), South African Rand (SAR), British pounds

(UK£), and US dollars (US$). Check the currency converter on websites such as www.bloomberg.com, or a large newspaper for the latest exchange rates.

EUROS (€)	
AUS$1 = €0.54	€1 = AUS$1.85
CDN$1 = €0.63	€1 = CDN$1.57
IR£1 = €1.27	€1 = IR£0.79
NZ$1 = €0.47	€1 = NZ$2.14
ZAR1 = €0.10	€1 = ZAR10.14
US$1 = €1.01	€1 = US$0.99
UK£1 = €1.58	€1 = UK£0.63
1,000,000TL=€0.62	€1 = 1,603,021TL

It's generally cheaper to convert money in Greece and Cyprus than at home. Banks in Greece charge a commission of 2% with a maximum of €6-12 on cashing traveler's checks. However, you should bring enough foreign currency to last for the first 24 to 72 hours of a trip to avoid being penniless should you arrive after banking hours or on a holiday. Travelers from the US can get foreign currency from the comfort of home: **International Currency Express** (☎888-278-6628) deliver foreign currency or traveler's checks overnight (US$15) or second-day (US$12) at competitive exchange rates. When changing money abroad, try to go only to banks or exchange bureaus with at most a 5% margin between their buy and sell prices. Since you lose money with every transaction, **convert large sums** (unless the currency is depreciating rapidly), **but no more than you'll need.** An **ATM card** or a **credit card** (see p. 31) will get you the best possible conversion rates. Most places in Greece now have ATMs that are linked into major international networks.

If you use traveler's checks or bills, carry some in small denominations (the equivalent of US$50 or less) for times when you are forced to exchange money at disadvantageous rates. Bring a range of denominations; charges may be levied per check cashed. Keep money in several forms; ideally, at any given time you will be carrying some cash, some traveler's checks, and an ATM and/or credit card.

THE EURO. The official currency of 12 members of the European Union—all except Denmark, Sweden, and the UK—is now the euro.

The currency has some important—and positive—consequences for travelers hitting more than one euro-zone country. For one thing, money-changers across the euro-zone are obliged to exchange money at the official, fixed rate, and at no commission (though they may still charge a small service fee). Second, euro-denominated travelers cheques allow you to pay for goods and services across the euro-zone, again at the official rate and commission-free.

For information on exchange rates, see below or check a currency converter (such as www.xe.com).

TRAVELER'S CHECKS

Traveler's checks are one of the safest and least troublesome means of carrying funds and are accepted in Greece, generally only at large hotels and chains, but they can be exchanged at almost any bank or exchange kiosk in urban and rural areas alike. **American Express** and **Visa** are the most recognized. Many banks and agencies sell them for a small commission. Check issuers provide refunds if the checks are lost or stolen, and many provide additional services, such as toll-free refund hotlines abroad, emergency message services, and stolen credit card assistance. Ask about toll-free refund hotlines and the location of refund centers when purchasing checks, and always carry emergency cash.

American Express: Checks available with commission at select banks and all AmEx offices. US residents can also purchase checks by phone (☎888-887-8986) or online (www.aexp.com). AAA (see p. 55) offers commission-free checks to its members. Checks available in US, Australian, British, Canadian, Japanese, and Euro currencies. *Cheques for Two* can be signed by either of 2 people traveling together. For purchase locations or more information contact AmEx's service centers: In the US and Canada ☎800-221-7282; in the UK ☎0800 521 313; in Australia ☎800 25 19 02; in New Zealand 0800 441 068; elsewhere US collect ☎+1 801-964-6665. If your checks are lost, call the regional refund number 800 441 27 569.

Travelex/Thomas Cook: In the US and Canada call ☎800-287-7362; in the UK call ☎0800 62 21 01; elsewhere call UK collect ☎+44 1733 31 89 50.

Visa: Checks available (generally with commission) at banks worldwide. For the location of the nearest office, call Visa's service centers: In the US ☎800-227-6811; in the UK ☎0800 89 50 78; elsewhere UK collect ☎+44 020 7937 8091. Checks available in US, British, Canadian, Japanese, and Euro currencies.

ESSENTIALS

CREDIT, DEBIT, AND ATM CARDS

Credit cards are accepted in the more touristed areas of Greece; if you're traveling off the beaten path, be prepared to use other forms of payment. Where they are accepted, credit cards often offer superior exchange rates—up to 5% better than the retail rate used by banks and other currency exchange establishments and are sometimes required to reserve hotel rooms or rental cars. **MasterCard** (a.k.a. EuroCard or Access in Europe) and **Visa** (a.k.a. Carte Bleue or Barclaycard) are most welcomed, with Visa being the most popular by far; **American Express** cards work at some ATMs and at AmEx offices and major airports. Credit cards often offer an array of other services, from insurance to emergency assistance. Check with your company to find out what is covered.

Cash cards—popularly called ATM (Automated Teller Machine) cards—are widespread in larger towns, cities, and ports in Greece; only the smallest towns and remotest areas are without. You can most likely access your home checking account from abroad—savings accounts are harder to access. ATMs get the same wholesale exchange rate as credit cards, but there is often a limit on the amount of money you can withdraw per day (around US$500), and unfortunately computer networks sometimes fail. They typically charge an extra US$1-5 per withdrawal. Memorize your PIN code in numeric form, and if your PIN is longer than four digits, ask your bank for a new number.

Debit cards are a relatively new form of purchasing power that are as convenient as credit cards but have a more immediate impact on your funds. A debit card can be used wherever its associated credit card company (usually Mastercard or Visa) is accepted, yet the money is withdrawn directly from the holder's checking account. Debit cards often also function as ATM cards and can be used to withdraw cash from associated banks and ATMs throughout Greece. Ask your local bank about obtaining one.

The two major international money networks are **Cirrus** (to locate ATMs US ☎800-424-7787 or www.mastercard.com) and **Visa/PLUS** (to locate ATMs US ☎800-843-7587 or www.visa.com).

PIN NUMBERS & ATMS. To use a cash or credit card to withdraw money from a cash machine (ATM) in Europe, you must have a four-digit **Personal Identification Number (PIN).** If your PIN is longer than four digits, ask your bank whether you can just use the first four, or whether you'll need a new one. **Credit cards** don't usually come with PINs, so if you intend to hit up ATMs in Europe with a credit card to get cash advances, call your credit card company before leaving to request one.

People with alphabetic, rather than numerical, PINs may also be thrown off by the lack of letters on European cash machines. The following handy chart gives the corresponding numbers to use: 1=QZ; 2=ABC; 3=DEF; 4=GHI; 5=JKL; 6=MNO; 7=PRS; 8=TUV; and 9=WXY. Note that if you mistakenly punch the wrong code into the machine three times, it will swallow your card for good.

GETTING MONEY FROM HOME

If you run out of money while traveling, the easiest and cheapest solution is to have someone back home make a deposit to your credit card or cash (ATM) card. Failing that, consider one of the following options.

WIRING MONEY. It is possible to arrange a **bank money transfer**, which means asking a bank back home to wire money to a bank in Greece. This is the cheapest way to transfer cash, but it's also the slowest, usually taking several days or more. Money transfer services like **Western Union** are faster and more convenient than bank transfers—but also much pricier. Western Union has many locations worldwide. In the US call ☎800-325-6000, in Canada 800-235-0000, in the UK 800 833 833, throughout Greece call 210 927 1010. The rates for sending cash are generally US$10-11 cheaper than with a credit card, and the money is usually available at the place you're sending it to within an hour. To locate the nearest Western Union location, consult www.westernunion.com or call the national access number listed above. Money transfer services are also available at **American Express** and **Thomas Cook** offices.

US STATE DEPARTMENT (US CITIZENS ONLY). In dire emergencies, the US State Department will forward money within hours to the nearest consular office, which will then disburse it (according to instructions) for a US$15 fee. If you wish to use this service, you must contact the Overseas Citizens Service division of the US Department of State (☎202-647-5225; nights, Sundays, and holidays ☎202-647-4000; http://travel.state.gov).

COSTS

The cost of a trip to Greece will vary considerably, depending on where you go, how you travel, and where you stay. The single biggest cost of your trip will probably be your round-trip **airfare** (see p. 47). If you choose to buy a **Eurail pass** for travel throughout Europe, it will be valid in Greece, but will cost a substantial sum. Before you go, spend some time calculating a reasonable per-day **budget** that will meet your needs.

STAYING ON A BUDGET. To give you a general idea, a bare-bones day in Greece, staying at hostels, campgrounds, or domatia (rooms to let), and buying food at supermarkets or at outdoor food stands, costs about US$35. Note that camping can save a substantial sum of money: about US$10-15 per day. A day with more comforts, with accommodations in a pricier domatia or budget hotel, eating one meal a day in a restaurant, and going out at night, runs US$50. For a luxurious day, the sky's the limit. Also, don't forget to factor in emergency reserve funds (at least US$200) when planning how much money you'll need.

TIPS FOR SAVING MONEY. Saving US$5 per day for a week will fund an entire additional day of travel, so learning to pinch pennies pays off. Take advantage of freebies: hit the **beach,** go **hiking,** tour churches, wander winding streets, and hunt down free open-air **concerts,** traditional **dances,** and outdoor **festivals** (especially in the summer). Do your **laundry** in the sink (where it is allowed). Split **accommodations** costs (in hotels, hostels, and domatia) with trustworthy fellow travelers, since multi-bed rooms are cheaper per person than singles. Buy food in **supermarkets** instead of eating out, split **restaurant** meals, or eat cheap, divine souvlaki from outdoor **food stands.** Don't go overboard with money management. Staying within budget is important, but don't sacrifice your sanity or your health to save a buck.

BARGAINING AND TIPPING

BARGAINING. Bargaining skills are essential in Greece, but you must know when to use them. Paying the asked price for street wares will have the seller marveling at your naïveté, while bargaining at the shop of a master craftsman whose crafts are worth the stated tag will be seen as rude and disrespectful. The more informal the venue, the more flexible the price. If in doubt, hang back and watch someone else buy. Keep the cooperative spirit of bargaining in mind: everyone involved is looking for a fair, agreed-upon price. Merchants with any pride in their wares will refuse to sell to someone who has offended them in the negotiations.

Domatia (rooms to let, see p. 41) prices rise in summer and fall in the winter. Bargain before you get into a **taxi** (be it a boat, car, truck, or guided tour), if your trip won't be metered or ticketed. **Clothing** in general is negotiable. Obvious conveniences like pharmaceutical goods and grocery items are priced as marked, as are street food, taverna fare, and books. **Jewelry** stores usually mark up 10-50%, so shop around to get an idea of what an item is really worth. Then go back to your favorite shop and ask for a lower price. (At a good store, expect 10-20% off, more in cheaper stores; you should also be able to get deals on multiple purchases.)

TIPPING. As with bargaining, when tipping, you should offer enough to show respect, for the goods, but not so much to seem like a show-off. At all but the ritziest restaurants, service is included in the bill; leave an extra euro or two for outstanding service. There is no tipping for any other services (including taxis).

SAFETY AND SECURITY

PERSONAL SAFETY

EXPLORING. Solo travelers may feel quite conspicuous among Greeks, who don't usually travel alone. Westerners in particular may feel nervous around pro-KKE, anti-American, and anti-Western graffiti (see **The KKE,** p. 14). Don't worry about it; if you are heckled by anti-Westerners, just walk away. To stay safe, familiarize yourself with your surroundings before setting out, and carry yourself with confidence. If you must check a map, duck into a shop to do it. If you are traveling alone, be sure someone at home knows your itinerary. **Never admit that you're traveling alone.** When walking at night, stick to busy, well-lit streets and avoid dark alleyways. Do not attempt to cross through parks, parking lots, or other large, deserted areas. Look for children playing, women walking in the open, and other signs of an active community. Find out about unsafe areas from tourist offices, or from the manager of your hotel or hostel. If you feel uncomfortable, leave as quickly as you can, but don't allow fear to turn you into a hermit. Careful, persistent exploration builds confidence and will make your stay even more rewarding.

SELF DEFENSE. There is no sure-fire way to be completely prepared for every threatening situation you might encounter, but a good self-defense course will give you some valuable ways to react to unwanted advances. **Impact, Prepare, and Model Mugging** can refer you to local self-defense courses in the US (☎800-345-5425). Workshops (2-3hr.) start at US$50; full courses run US$350-500.

TRAVEL ADVISORIES. The following government offices provide travel information and advisories by telephone, by fax, or via the web:

Australian Department of Foreign Affairs and Trade: ☎1300 555135; faxback service 02 6261 1299; www.dfat.gov.au.

Canadian Department of Foreign Affairs and International Trade (DFAIT): In Canada and the US call ☎800-267-8376, elsewhere call ☎+1 613 944-4000; www.dfait-maeci.gc.ca. Call for their free booklet, *Bon Voyage...But.*

New Zealand Ministry of Foreign Affairs: ☎(04) 494 8500; fax 494 8506; www.mft.govt.nz/trav.html.

United Kingdom Foreign and Commonwealth Office: ☎020 7008 0232; fax 7008 0155; www.fco.gov.uk.

US Department of State: ☎202-647-5225, faxback service 202-647-3000; http://travel.state.gov. For *A Safe Trip Abroad,* call 202-512-1800.

DRIVING. Driving in Greece requires a fearless temperament and all your attention. Roads, especially on the islands and in rural areas, are narrow and poor. Some lack shoulders, barriers, and gas stations; others are plagued by roaming goats. Although native Greek drivers careen around the roads with astonishingly reckless confidence, visiting drivers should never drive with such abandon. Learn local driving signals and wear a seatbelt in **cars.** Children under 40lbs. should ride only in a specially designed carseat, available for a small fee from most car rental agencies. Always wear a helmet on a **moped** (required by law). Driving any vehicle at night on winding roads is incredibly dangerous and even foolish; plan to take a cab instead if at all possible. Be forewarned that driving a moped is harder than it looks, and countless tourists injure themselves on the bikes. Study route maps before you hit the road, and plan ahead. You may want to bring spare parts. If your car breaks down, wait for police assistance, or locals may help you. **Sleeping in your car** is unsafe and illegal—don't do it. For info on the perils of **hitchhiking,** see p. 60.

TERRORISM. Though certainly not rampant, Greece does have some problems with terrorism, particularly with the high-profile, anti-Western, anti-NATO, anti-US **November 17** (N17) group. In the last 25 years, N17 has claimed responsibility for 23 deaths, including the high-profile assassination of British Defense attaché Stephen Saunders on June 8, 2000. The government has repeatedly pledged to combat terrorism more effectively, especially in the lead up to the 2004 Olympics in Athens. In July 2002, Greek police made their first arrest of a suspected member of the group after a attempted bombing in Piraeus last summer (see sidebar, p. 13). The incident led to four more arrests and the discovery of weapon caches. The group is believed to be small—around 25 members—and officials say they are confident that further arrests will be made in coming months. Tourists are rarely targeted by Greek terrorist groups but should be aware of their existence.

FINANCIAL SECURITY

PROTECTING YOUR VALUABLES. In Greece, you are much more likely to be **ripped off** by a cab driver, restaurant owner, or hotel owner than you are to be outright mugged in the street. **Pickpocketing,** however, is somewhat common, especially at major tourist sites and in Athens (locals warn that Monastiraki market is particularly bad). Be careful in these locations. To avoid being swindled, do your homework. Ask around for prices for hotel rooms, food, and cab rides to find out what a fair price is; don't take a first offer. Always, always, always negotiate cab fare or accommodation price ahead of time, and pay only what you agreed upon, even if they try to change the price on you later. If you're being ripped off, contact the tourist police (listed in the **Practical Information** section for each town). Threatening to go to the police is often enough to convince a taxi driver or pension owner to back off.

Minimize financial risks by leaving expensive watches, jewelry, cameras, and electronics (like your Discman) at home; chances are you'd break them, lose them, or get sick of lugging them around anyway. Second, carry as little cash as possible; instead carry traveler's checks, an ATM card, or credit cards (along with your passport and ID cards) in a **money belt** under your clothes. Third, keep a small cash reserve separate from your primary stash. Keep the equivalent of US$50 sewn into or stored in the depths of your pack, along with your traveler's check numbers and photocopies of your passport, plane ticket, Eurail pass, and any other valuable documents you're carrying. Leave a set of photocopies at home. Don't put a wallet with money in your back pocket. Label every piece of luggage both inside and out. Never count your money in public, and carry only as much as you'll need for the day. If you carry a purse, wear it across your body, away from the street, with the clasp against you. Always have cash stashed away, in case you are robbed.

CON ARTISTS. In larger cities and touristy towns (especially Athens), you may run into **con artists.** They often work in groups. In a classic Athenian scam, you might be invited to a club by a new friend; there you'll meet several of his friends, and everyone will have several drinks. When you get up to go, you'll be stuck with the bill for several dozen *very* expensive drinks. Be wary of such invitations, since they can cost you everything you have.

In a suspicious situation, don't respond or make eye contact, and walk away quickly. Don't ever hand over your passport to someone whose authority you question (ask to accompany them to a police station if they insist), and **don't ever let your passport out of your sight.** Similarly, don't let your bag out of sight; never trust a "station-porter" who insists on carrying your bag or stowing it in the baggage compartment or a "new friend" who offers to guard your bag while you buy a train ticket or use the rest room. Beware of **pickpockets** in city crowds, especially on public transportation. Also, be alert in public telephone booths. If you must say your calling card number, do so very quietly; if you punch it in, make sure no one can look over your shoulder.

ACCOMMODATIONS AND TRANSPORTATION. Never leave your belongings unattended; crime occurs in even the most demure-looking hostel or hotel. Bring your own **padlock** for lockers: don't trust the original locks, and don't store valuables in lockers. If you feel unsafe, look for places with a curfew or night attendant.

Be particularly careful on **buses** and **trains;** some determined thieves wait for travelers to fall asleep. Carry your backpack in front of you where you can see it. When traveling with others, sleep in alternate shifts. When alone, use good judgement in selecting a train compartment: never stay in an empty one, and lock your pack to the luggage rack. In hostels, sleep on top bunks with your luggage above you or in bed with you. Keep important documents and valuables on your person. Don't leave valuables in a **car** while you are away from it; hide tape decks, radios, and baggage in the trunk, or take them with you.

DRUGS AND ALCOHOL. You're subject to the laws of the country in which you travel, so familiarize yourself with those laws before leaving. If you carry **prescription drugs,** it is vital to have both a copy of the prescriptions themselves and a note from a doctor, especially at border crossings. Never try to bring any illegal substances into Greece. Authorities are especially vigilant at the Turkish and Albanian borders and might carefully search your bag for anything you shouldn't have.

HEALTH

Common sense is the simplest prescription for good health while you travel. Drink lots of fluids to prevent dehydration and constipation, and wear sturdy, broken-in shoes and clean socks.

BEFORE YOU GO

Preparation can help minimize the likelihood of contracting a disease and maximize the chances of receiving effective health care in the event of an emergency. For tips on packing a basic **first-aid kit** and other health essentials, see p. 40. In your **passport,** write the names of people you wish to be contacted in case of a medical emergency, and add a list of your **allergies** or medical conditions. Carry up-to-date, legible prescriptions or a statement from your doctor stating the trade name, manufacturer, chemical name, and dosage of any medicine you're carrying. Matching a prescription to a foreign equivalent is not always easy, safe, or possible. While traveling, keep all medication with you in your carry-on luggage.

IMMUNIZATIONS. Travelers over two years old should have the following up-to-date immunizations: MMR (for measles, mumps, and rubella); DTaP or Td (for diptheria, tetanus, and pertussis); OPV (for polio); HbCV (for haemophilus influenza B); and HBV (for hepatitis B). Hepatitis A vaccine and/or immune globulin (IG) are recommended. For recommendations on immunizations and prophylaxis, consult the CDC (see below) in the US or the equivalent in your home country, and be sure to check with a doctor for guidance.

MEDICAL CONDITIONS. Those with diabetes, allergies to antibiotics, epilepsy, heart conditions, or other conditions can obtain a stainless steel **Medic Alert** identification tag (US$35 the first year, $20 annually thereafter), which identifies the wearer's condition and gives a 24hr. collect-call information number. Contact the Medic Alert Foundation, 2323 Colorado Ave., Turlock, CA 95382 (☎888-633-4298; www.medicalert.org). Diabetics can contact the **American Diabetes Association,** 1660 Duke St., Alexandria, VA 22314 (☎800-342-2383; www.diabetes.org), for the article "Travel and Diabetes" and a diabetic ID card, which carries messages in 18 languages explaining the carrier's diabetic status.

USEFUL ORGANIZATIONS AND PUBLICATIONS. The **US Centers for Disease Control and Prevention** (**CDC;** ☎877-FYI-TRIP; www.cdc.gov/travel) maintains an international fax information service and an international travelers hotline. The CDC's comprehensive booklet *Health Information for International Travel,* an annual rundown of disease, immunization, and general health advice, is free online or US$25 via the Public Health Foundation (☎877-252-1200). Consult the appropriate government agency of your home country for consular information sheets on health, entry requirements, and other issues for various countries (see **Consular Services,** p. 25). For quick information on health and other travel warnings, call the **Overseas Citizens Services** (☎202-647-5225; after hours 202-647-4000), contact a passport agency or an embassy or consulate abroad. US citizens can send a self-addressed, stamped envelope to the Overseas Citizens Services, Bureau of Consular Affairs, #4811, US Department of State, Washington, D.C. 20520. For information on medical evacuation services and travel insurance firms, see the US government's website at http://travel.state.gov/medical.html or the **British Foreign and Commonwealth Office** (www.fco.gov.uk).

For detailed information on travel health, including a country-by-country overview of diseases, try the **International Travel Health Guide,** Stuart Rose, MD (Travel Medicine, US$24.95; www.travmed.com). For general health info, contact the **American Red Cross** (☎800-564-1234).

ONCE THERE

MEDICAL ASSISTANCE. In Greece, all EU travelers receive free health care with the presentation of an **E111 form.** There is a doctor on every island and in every town, and emergency treatment is available to travelers of all nationalities in public hospitals. Medical training in Greece is of high quality, but the health care system is vastly underfunded. Public hospitals are overcrowded, and hygiene may not be the best. Private hospitals generally have better care for more money; to use them, you will need good **health insurance.** If your regular policy does not cover travel abroad, you may wish to purchase additional coverage (see p. 39).

Pharmacies *(farmakia)*, labeled by green or red crosses, are on every street corner. In most towns and cities, at least one pharmacy (known as *efimerevon*) is open at all hours—pharmacies post listings of 24hr. pharmacies in their windows.

If you are concerned about being able to access medical support while traveling, there are special support services you may employ. The *MedPass* from **GlobalCare, Inc.,** 6875 Shiloh Rd. East, Alpharetta, GA 30005, USA (☎800-860-1111; fax 678-341-1800; www.globalems.com), provides 24hr. international medical assistance, support, and medical evacuation resources. The **International Association for Medical Assistance to Travelers** (**IAMAT;** US ☎716-754-4883, Canada ☎416-652-0137; www.iamat.org) has free membership, lists English-speaking doctors worldwide, and offers detailed info on immunization requirements and sanitation.

ENVIRONMENTAL HAZARDS. The hot sun beats down on all of Greece all summer long: this may be why you're going to Greece. It's easy to overheat, get sunburned, and forget to drink enough water. Especially on beaches, at outdoor sights, and while hiking, beware of dehydration, sunburn, and heat exhaustion. These conditions can be avoided by drinking enough water, wearing a hat and sunglasses, using sunscreen, and napping during the heat of the day like Greeks do.

Heat exhaustion and dehydration: Heat exhaustion, characterized by dehydration and salt deficiency, can lead to fatigue, headaches, and wooziness. Avoid it by drinking plenty of clear fluids, eating salty foods (like crackers), and avoiding dehydrating beverages (e.g. alcohol, coffee, tea, and caffeinated soda). Continuous heat stress can lead to heatstroke, characterized by a rising temperature, severe headache, and cessation of sweating. Victims should be cooled off with wet towels and taken to a doctor.

Sunburn: Even if you're not prone to sunburn, bring sunscreen with you–though you can buy it in Greece, it's better to have sunscreen on hand as soon as you arrive in this sometimes fiercely hot country. Apply it liberally and often to avoid burns and risk of skin cancer. Even if you don't think you'll be in the sun much, you probably will be, and the sun is merciless, even through clouds. If you get sunburned, drink more fluids than usual and apply an aloe-based lotion.

High altitude: While skiing or hiking in the mountains, allow your body a couple of days to adjust to the reduced oxygen level before doing demanding work. At high elevations alcohol is more potent and UV rays are stronger.

FOOD- AND WATER-BORNE DISEASE. Prevention is the best cure: be sure that everything you eat is cooked properly and that the water is clean. In Greece, the tap water is fairly safe. Bottled water, however, is dirt cheap and widely available, so drink it whenever possible. Always wash your hands before eating, or bring a quick-drying anti-bacterial liquid hand cleaner. Your bowels will thank you.

Traveler's diarrhea results from drinking untreated water or eating uncooked foods. If the nasties hit you, have quick-energy, non-sugary foods with protein and carbohydrates to keep your strength up. Over-the-counter remedies (such as Pepto-Bismol or Immodium) may counteract the problems, but they can complicate serious infections. The most dangerous side effect of diarrhea is dehydration; drink 8 oz. of water with a half teaspoon of sugar or honey and a pinch of salt, try decaffeinated soft drinks, or munch on salted crackers. If you develop a fever or your symptoms don't go away after four or five days, consult a doctor. Consult a doctor for treatment of diarrhea in children.

Microbes, tapeworms, and other **parasites** hide in unsafe water and food. **Giardiasis,** for example, is acquired by drinking untreated water from streams or lakes. Symptoms include swollen glands or lymph nodes, fever, rashes or itchiness, digestive problems, eye problems, and anemia. While camping, boil untreated water, wear shoes, avoid bugs, and eat only cooked food.

OTHER INFECTIOUS DISEASES

Rabies: Transmitted through the saliva of infected animals; fatal if untreated. By the time symptoms appear (thirst and muscle spasms), the disease is in its terminal stage. If you are bitten, wash the wound thoroughly, seek immediate medical care, and try to have the animal located. A rabies vaccine, which consists of 3 shots given over a 21-day period, is available but is only semi-effective.

Hepatitis B: A viral infection of the liver transmitted via bodily fluids or needle-sharing. Symptoms may not surface until years after infection. Vaccinations are recommended for health-care workers, sexually active travelers, and anyone planning to seek medical treatment abroad. The 3-shot vaccination series must begin 6 mo. before traveling.

Hepatitis C: Like Hep B, but the mode of transmission differs. IV drug users, those with occupational exposure to blood, hemodialysis patients, and recipients of blood transfusions are at the highest risk, but the disease can also be spread through sexual contact or sharing items like razors and toothbrushes that may have traces of blood on them.

AIDS, HIV, AND STDS. The World Health Organization estimates that 30 million people have been infected with the **HIV** virus, the virus that causes **AIDS.** The easiest mode of HIV transmission is through direct blood-to-blood contact with an HIV-positive person, usually through shared needles; the most common way to transmit HIV is through sexual intercourse. **Latex condoms** can help prevent transmission; they are available in Greece, but it's a good idea to take a supply with you before you depart for your trip.

For detailed information on **AIDS** in Greece, call the **US Centers for Disease Control**'s 24hr. hotline at 800-342-2437, or contact the **Joint United Nations Programme on HIV/AIDS (UNAIDS),** Appia 20, CH-1211 Geneva 27, Switzerland (☎+41 22 791 36 66; fax 791 41 87). Greece does not require HIV tests for tourists or those with visas. Cyprus tests all foreigners applying for studying, training, or work permits for HIV.

Sexually transmitted diseases (STDs) such as gonorrhea, chlamydia, genital warts, syphilis, and herpes are easier to catch than HIV and can be just as deadly. Hepatitis B and C are also serious STDs (see Other Infectious Diseases, above). Condoms may protect you from some STDs, but oral or tactile contact transmits them, too. Warning signs include swelling, sores, bumps, or blisters on sex organs, the rectum, or the mouth; burning and pain during urination and bowel movements; itching around sex organs; swelling or redness of the throat; and flu-like symptoms. If these symptoms develop, see a doctor immediately.

WOMEN'S HEALTH. Women traveling in unsanitary conditions are vulnerable to urinary tract and bladder infections, which cause a burning sensation as well as painful and frequent urination. To try to avoid these infections, drink plenty of vitamin-C-rich juice and clean water, and urinate frequently, especially right after intercourse. Untreated, these infections can lead to kidney problems, sterility, and even death. If symptoms persist, see a doctor.

Vaginal yeast infections may flare up in hot, humid areas of Greece. Wearing loosely fitting trousers or a skirt and cotton underwear will help, as will over-the-counter remedies like Monistat or Gynelotrimin. Bring supplies from home if you are prone to infection, as they may be difficult to find on the road.

Tampons and **pads** are readily available at pharmacies in cities and large towns; when heading for a remote village, bring your own supply. Although some pharmacies may be able to fill a birth control pill prescription, it is best to bring enough from home to avoid problems. Other methods of contraception, like condoms, are available everywhere.

Women considering an **abortion** should contact the **International Planned Parenthood Federation (IPPF),** Regent's College, Inner Circle, Regent's Park, London NW1 4NS (☎020 7487 7900; fax 7487 7950; www.ippf.org) for more information.

INSURANCE

Travel insurance generally covers four basic areas: medical/health problems, property loss, trip cancellation/interruption, and emergency evacuation. Although your regular insurance policies may extend to travel-related accidents, consider purchasing travel insurance if the cost of potential trip cancellation or interruption is greater than you can absorb. Separately purchased travel insurance generally costs about US$50 per week for full coverage, and trip cancellation or interruption insurance may be purchased separately for about US$5.50 per US$100 of coverage.

Medical insurance (especially university policies) often covers costs incurred abroad; check with your provider. **US Medicare** does not cover foreign travel. **Canadians** are protected by their home province's health insurance plan for up to 90 days after leaving the country; check with the provincial Ministry of Health or Health Plan Headquarters for details. **Homeowners' insurance** (or your family's coverage) often covers theft during travel and loss of travel documents (passport, plane ticket, railpass, etc.) up to US$500.

ISIC and **ITIC** (see p. 28) provide basic insurance benefits, including US$100 per day of in-hospital sickness for up to 60 days, US$3000 of accident-related medical reimbursement, and US$25,000 for emergency medical transport. Cardholders have access to a toll-free 24hr. helpline (run by the insurance provider TravelGuard) for medical, legal, and financial emergencies overseas (US and Canada ☎877-370-4742, elsewhere call collect +1 715-345-0505). **American Express** (US ☎800-528-4800) grants some cardholders car rental insurance (collision and theft, but not liability) and ground travel accident coverage of US$100,000 on flight purchases made with the card. For information on car insurance, see p. 60.

INSURANCE PROVIDERS. **Council** and **STA** (see p. 49) offer a range of plans that can supplement your basic coverage. Other private insurance providers in the US and Canada include: **Access America** (☎800-284-8300); **Globalcare Travel Insurance** (☎800-821-2488; www.globalcare-cocco.com); and **Travel Assistance International** (☎800-821-2828; www.europ-assistance.com). Providers in the **UK** include **Columbus Direct** (☎020 7375 0011). In **Australia,** try **AFTA** (☎02 9375 4955).

PACKING

Pack lightly: lay out only what you absolutely need, then take half the clothes and twice the money. The less you have, the less you have to carry—or lose. For information on hiking, see **Camping and the Outdoors** (p. 42).

LUGGAGE. If you plan to cover most of your itinerary by foot, a sturdy **frame backpack** is unbeatable. (For the basics on buying a pack, see p. 44.) Make sure your luggage is compact and easy to transport: a **suitcase** is a very bad idea if you're going to be moving around a lot. In addition to your main piece of luggage, a **daypack** (a small backpack or courier bag) is a must.

CLOTHES. If you are in Greece at the height of summer, you'll need very little other than **comfortable shoes,** a few changes of **light clothes,** and a **fleece** or sweater. **Flip-flops** are crucial for grubby hostel showers. To visit monasteries or churches, men will need a lightweight pair of pants and women will need a long skirt; both will need covered shoulders. If you plan on taking ferries or hiking, you'll want a warm wool sweater and a windproof jacket.

CONVERTERS AND ADAPTERS. Greek electricity is 220 volts AC, enough to fry any 110V North American appliance. **Americans** and **Canadians** should buy an **adapter** (which changes the shape of the plug) and a **converter** (which changes the voltage; US$20). Don't make the mistake of using only an adapter, unless appliance instructions explicitly state otherwise. **New Zealanders** and **South Africans** (who both use 220V at home) and **Australians** (who use 240/250V) won't need a converter but will need a set of adapters to use anything electrical.

TOILETRIES. Toothbrushes, towels, soap, talcum powder (to keep feet dry), razors, deodorant, tampons, and the all-important sunscreen and aloe vera are readily available at Greek pharmacies. Contact lenses can be expensive and difficult to obtain; bring enough extra pairs and solution for your entire trip. Also bring your **glasses** and a copy of your prescription in case you need emergency replacements.

FIRST-AID KIT. For a basic first-aid kit, pack bandages, aspirin or other painkiller, antibiotic cream, a thermometer, a Swiss army knife, tweezers, sunscreen and aloe, moleskin for foot woes, decongestant, motion sickness remedy, diarrhea and upset-stomach medication, an antihistamine, insect repellent, and burn ointment.

FILM. Film and film developing in Greece can be expensive (about US$10 for a roll of 24 color exposures, though it is more reasonable in some places); try to bring enough film for your entire trip and definitely develop it at home. **Disposable cameras** may be a better option than expensive permanent ones. Airport security **X-rays** *can* fog high-speed film (800IS0 and up), so ask security to hand-inspect it or pack film in your carry-on luggage, since higher-intensity X-rays are used on checked luggage.

OTHER USEFUL ITEMS. For safety purposes, you should bring a **money belt** and a small **padlock.** Basic **outdoors equipment** (plastic water bottle, compass, waterproof matches, pocketknife, sunglasses, hat) may also prove useful. Quick repairs can be done on the road with a **needle and thread** or with **electrical tape** patches. Doing your **laundry** by hand (where it is allowed) is both cheaper and more convenient than doing it at a laundromat—bring detergent, a small rubber ball to stop up the sink, and string for a makeshift clothesline. **Other things** you're liable to forget: an umbrella; sealable **plastic bags** (for damp clothes, soap, food, shampoo, and other spillables); an **alarm clock;** safety pins; rubber bands; a flashlight; earplugs; garbage bags; and a small **calculator.**

ACCOMMODATIONS

Relative to the US and elsewhere in Europe, accommodations in Greece and Cyprus remain a bargain. Budget accommodations in Greece are usually found in domatia (rooms to let), hostels, campgrounds, and budget hotels. **Prices** given in this guide are for the high season. Off-season prices (Oct.-May) are 20-40% cheaper than in high season. Prices may rise on weekends and are usually reduced for extended stays; when renting a room in a domatia, prices are completely negotiable, especially during the week and off season. This guide was researched during summer 2002, and prices may rise 10-20% in 2003. During high season (especially July and August), consider making **reservations**—you may not be able to find a room if you wait until you arrive on an island.

DOMATIA (ROOMS TO LET). Private homes all over Greece put up signs offering domatia (rooms to let). Domatia are perhaps the ideal budget accommodation: they are cheap and as safe as hotels, and allow you to stay in a Greek home and absorb some local culture. At more popular destinations, proprietors with rooms to let will greet your boat or bus, a practice which is theoretically illegal, but common. Always negotiate with domatia owners before settling a price. Before you accept an offer at portside, have a set destination in mind and look for people whose domatia are in the area you want. Many rooms offered at the port or bus stop are inexpensive; since the proprietors are in direct competition with the other domatia owners, good deals abound. Make owners pinpoint the location of their houses to make sure that "ten minutes away" means ten minutes on foot. Don't pay until you've seen the room.

While domatia may be run like small hotels in tourist towns, domatia in out of the way places can provide warm offers of coffee at night and friendly conversation. Prices are quite variable, but you can expect to pay about €12-17 for a single (€25 for a double) in the more remote areas of northern and central Greece, and €15-20 for a single (€25-35 for a double) on heavily traveled islands. Never pay more for domatia than you would for a hotel in town, and remember domatia owners can often be bargained down, especially when the house is not full. If in doubt, ask the tourist police: they may set you up with a room and conduct the negotiations themselves. Most private rooms operate only in high season and are the best option for those arriving without reservations.

HOSTELS. Hostels—typically dorm-style accommodations, sometimes in single-sex large rooms with bunk beds—are not as prevalent in Greece as they are throughout the rest of Europe. Those that exist (usually in the most popular tourist destinations) are almost never affiliated with an international hosteling organization. Thus, a hosteling membership won't do you much good. In Greece, a bed in a hostel will average around €7. You can expect showers and sheets. Hostels are not regulated, so don't be surprised if some are less than clean or don't offer sheets and towels.

Some Greek hostels offer private rooms for families and couples. They sometimes have kitchens and utensils for your use, bike or moped rentals, storage areas, and laundry facilities. Some hostels have a maximum stay of five days. Greek **youth hostels** generally have fewer restrictions than those farther north in Europe. Many are open year-round and a few have midnight or 1am curfews (strictly enforced—you may be left in the streets if you come back too late). In summer, they usually stay open from 6-10am and 1pm-midnight (shorter hours in winter). It's advisable to book in advance in the summer at some of the more popular hostels in Athens, Santorini, Crete, or Nafplion.

HOTELS. The government oversees the construction and (seemingly random) classification of most hotels. Proprietors are permitted to charge 10% extra for stays of less than three nights, and 20% extra overall from July until September 15. Most D- and E-class hotels start at €15 for singles and €25 for doubles. A hotel with no singles may still put you in a room by yourself. More information is available from the **Hellenic Chamber of Hotels,** Stadiou 24, Athens 105 64 (☎210 331 0022; fax 210 322 5449; grhotels@otenet.gr). If a hotel owner solicits you, offering to drive you, make sure you establish the location on a map: it may be miles away.

Late at night, in the off season, or in a large town, it's a buyer's market and bargaining is appropriate. As a security deposit, hotels often ask for your passport and return it when you leave. Don't give it to them—suggest that they take down your passport number or offer to pay up front. You can often leave your luggage in the reception area during the afternoon, though check-out is at 11am or noon.

To charge you more, hotel owners may offer you only their most expensive rooms, compel you to buy breakfast, squeeze three people into a hostel-size triple and charge each for a single, or quote a price for a room that includes breakfast and private shower and then charge extra for both. Don't pay until you've seen the room. If a room seems unreasonably expensive, stress that you don't want luxuries and they may give you a cheaper option. The **tourist police** are on your side. If a hotel flagrantly violates the prices shown by law at the front desk or behind each room's front door, or if you think you've been exploited, threaten to report the hotel to the tourist police. The threat alone often resolves "misunderstandings."

TRADITIONAL SETTLEMENTS. Several traditional villages and buildings have been preserved and restored by the government in an effort to maintain Greece's architectural heritage. The restoration of these Greek villages offers visitors a taste of small town Greek life and improves the regional economy. More than ten settlements host guests: **Makrynitsa** on Mt. Pelion (p. 201) and **Papingo-Zagorohoria** in Epirus (p. 251). There are 12 reconstructed towers in **Vathia** in Mani (p. 164) and an expensive hotel in the Kastro in **Monemvasia** (p. 169). Doubles range €14.67-29.35; tourist offices make reservations and provide information.

CAMPING AND THE OUTDOORS

Camping in Greece releases you from monotonous hotel rooms and hostel regulations and saves you a large amount of money. The Greek National Tourist Organization (GNTO, see p. 28) is primarily responsible for campgrounds; most official GNTO campgrounds have drinking water, lavatories, and electricity. Many campgrounds rent tents for a low fee. The Hellenic Touring Club also runs a number of campgrounds, especially in northern Greece (ask at local tourist offices for more information). In addition, Greece has many private campgrounds, which may include pools, discos, mini-markets, and tavernas. **Prices** depend on the facilities; you'll usually pay roughly €4.50 per person, plus €3 per tent. GNTO campgrounds tend to be ritzier and more expensive (up to €5).

On many islands, some campers choose to bivouac on the beaches. While this is commonplace during July and August, when hotels are booked solid, it is **illegal.** Some police have been known to ignore sleeping bags in the sand, while others charge penalties from stern chastisement to stiff fines. Those who camp on beaches should always clean up after themselves. *Let's Go: Greece* doesn't recommend camping illegally. For more information on camping check out *Soft Paths*, by Bruce Hampton and David Cole (Stackpole Books, US$15) and *Camping Your Way Through Europe*, by Carol Mickelsen (Affordable Press, US$15).

WILDERNESS SAFETY

THE GREAT OUTDOORS. Stay warm, stay dry, and stay hydrated. Most life-threatening wilderness situations can be avoided by following this simple advice. Prepare yourself for an emergency, however, by always packing raingear, a hat and mittens, a first-aid kit, a reflector, a whistle, high energy food, and extra water for any hike. Dress in wool or warm layers of synthetic materials designed for the outdoors; never rely on cotton for warmth, as it is useless when wet.

Check **weather forecasts** and pay attention to the skies when hiking, since weather patterns can change suddenly. Whenever possible, let someone know when and where you are going hiking, either a friend, your hostel, a park ranger, or a local hiking organization. Do not attempt a hike beyond your ability—you may be endangering your life.

CAMPING AND HIKING EQUIPMENT

WHAT TO BUY

Good camping equipment is both sturdy and light. Camping equipment is generally more expensive in Australia, New Zealand, and the UK than in North America.

Sleeping Bag: Most sleeping bags are rated by season ("summer" means 30-40°F at night; "four-season" or "winter" often means below 0°F). They are made either of **down** (warmer and lighter, but more expensive, and miserable when wet) or of **synthetic** material (heavier, more durable, and warmer when wet). Prices range US$80-210 for a summer synthetic to US$250-300 for a good down winter bag. **Sleeping bag pads** include foam pads (US$10-20), air mattresses (US$15-50), and Therm-A-Rest self-inflating pads (US$45-80). Bring a **stuff sack** to store your bag and keep it dry.

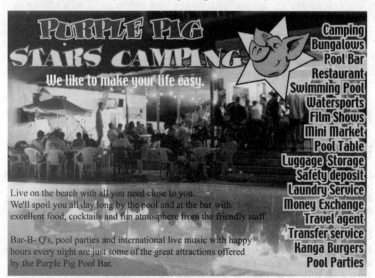

Tent: The best tents are free-standing (with their own frames and suspension systems), set up quickly, and only require staking in high winds. Low-profile dome tents are the best all-around. Good 2-person tents start at US$90, 4-person at US$300. Seal the seams of your tent with waterproofer, and make sure it has a rain fly. Other tent accessories include a **battery-operated lantern,** a **plastic groundcloth,** and a **nylon tarp.**

Backpack: Internal-frame packs mold better to your back, keep a lower center of gravity, and flex adequately to allow you to hike difficult trails. **External-frame packs** are more comfortable for long hikes over even terrain, as they keep weight higher and distribute it more evenly. Make sure your pack has a strong, padded hip-belt to transfer weight to your legs. Sturdy backpacks cost anywhere from US$125-420—this is one area in which it doesn't pay to economize. Fill up any pack with something heavy and walk around the store with it to get a sense of how it distributes weight before buying it. Don't forget a **waterproof backpack cover.**

Boots: Be sure to wear hiking boots with good **ankle support.** They should fit snugly and comfortably over 1-2 pairs of wool socks and thin liner socks. Break in boots over several weeks first in order to spare yourself painful and debilitating blisters.

Other Necessities: Synthetic layered clothes, like polypropylene, and a pile jacket will keep you warm when wet. A **"space blanket"** helps retain body heat and doubles as a groundcloth (US$5-15). Plastic **water bottles** are virtually shatter- and leak-proof. Bring **water-purification tablets** for when you can't boil water. Don't forget a **first-aid kit** (p. 36), **pocketknife, insect repellent, Calamine lotion, sunblock,** and **waterproof matches** or a **lighter.**

ENVIRONMENTALLY RESPONSIBLE TOURISM. The idea behind responsible tourism is to leave no trace of human presence behind. Make sure your campsite is at least 150 ft. (50m) from water supplies or bodies of water. If there are no toilet facilities, bury human waste (but not paper) at least four inches (10cm) deep and above the high-water line, and 150 ft. or more from any water supplies and campsites. Always pack your trash in a plastic bag and carry it with you until you reach the next trash receptacle. For more information on these issues, contact one of the organizations listed below.

Earthwatch, 3 Clock Tower Place #100, Box 75, Maynard, MA 01754, USA (☎800-776-0188 or 978-461-0081; www.earthwatch.org).

International Ecotourism Society, 28 Pine St., Burlington, VT 05402, USA (☎802-651-9818; fax 802-651-9819; www.ecotourism.org).

KEEPING IN TOUCH

BY MAIL

Let's Go lists **post offices** in the **Practical Information** section for each city and most towns. Post offices in Greece are generally open Monday to Friday 7:30am to 2pm, although certain branches may extend their hours into the afternoon and evening, as well as into the weekend.

SENDING MAIL HOME FROM GREECE

Aerogrammes, printed sheets that fold into envelopes and travel via airmail, are available at post offices. You should mark letter both "par avion" and "air mail." Most post offices will charge exorbitant fees or simply refuse to send aerogrammes with enclosures. Airmail from Greece can take anywhere from 1-2 weeks, although times are much more unpredictable from smaller towns. Sending a postcard via airmail to an international destination costs €0.55 within Europe and €0.60 to the US. To send a letter (up to 50g) via airmail to another European country costs €0.85 and to anywhere else in the world, €0.90 (up to 150g). For **express** mail service, ask for *katepeegon;* to **register** a letter, *systemeno;* for **air mail,** *aeroporikos*, and write "air mail" on the envelope.

SENDING MAIL TO GREECE

Mark envelopes "air mail" or "par avion." In addition to the standard postage system whose rates are listed below, **Federal Express** (www.fedex.com; Australia ☎13 26 10; US and Canada ☎800-247-4747; New Zealand ☎0800 73 33 39; UK ☎0800 12 38 00) handles express mail services from most home countries to Greece; for example, they can get a letter from New York to Athens in 2 days for US$31, and from London to Athens in 2 days for UK£28.20.

Australia: Allow 5-7 days for regular **airmail** to Greece. Postcards cost AUS$1; letters up to 50g AUS$1.50; packages up to 0.5kg AUS$13, up to 2kg AUS$46. **EMS** can get a letter to Greece in 2-3 days for AUS$32. www.auspost.com.au/pac.

Canada: Allow 7-10 days for regular **airmail** to Greece. Postcards and letters up to 30g cost CDN$1.25; packages up to 0.5kg CDN$10.20, up to 2kg CDN$34. www.canadapost.ca.

Ireland: Allow 3-4 days for regular **airmail** to Greece. Postcards and letters up to 25g cost IR£0.41. Add IR£3.30 for **Swiftpost International.** www.anpost.ie.

New Zealand: Allow 6-10 days for regular **airmail** to Greece. Postcards NZ$1.50. Letters up to 20g cost NZ$2; small parcels up to 0.5kg NZ$17, up to 2kg NZ$55. www.nzpost.co.nz/nzpost/inrates.

UK: Allow 3 days for **airmail** to Greece. Letters up to 20g cost UK£0.36; packages up to 0.5kg UK£2.67, up to 2kg UK£9.42. **UK Swiftair** delivers letters a day faster for UK£2.85 more. www.royalmail.co.uk/calculator.

US: Allow 4-10 days for regular **airmail** to Greece. Postcards and aerogrammes cost US$0.70; letters under 1 oz. US$1. Packages under 1 lb. cost US$8.70; larger packages cost a variable amount (around US$15). **US Express Mail** takes 2-3 days and costs US$23 for 0.5 lb., US$26 for 1 lb. http://ircalc.usps.gov.

RECEIVING MAIL IN GREECE

There are several ways to arrange pick-up of letters sent to you by friends and relatives while you are abroad. Mail can be sent to Greece through **Poste Restante** (the international phrase for General Delivery) to almost any city or town with a post office. Address Poste Restante letters in the following manner:

Robert SILVERMAN
Aegina Post Office
Aegina, Greece 18010
POSTE RESTANTE

The mail will go to a special desk in the central post office, unless you specify another. As a rule, it is best to use the largest post office in the area, because mail may be sent there regardless of what is written on the envelope. When possible, it is usually safer and quicker (though much pricier) to send mail express or registered. When picking up your mail, bring your passport; If the clerks insist that there is nothing for you, have them check under your first name as well. There is no surcharge for picking up Poste Restante mail in Greece. The **Practical Information** of each city and town contains information for post office listings.

ESSENTIALS

American Express travel offices throughout the world will act as a mail service for cardholders if you contact them in advance. Under this free **Client Letter Service,** they will hold mail for up to 30 days and forward upon request. Address the letter in the same way shown above. Some offices will offer these services to non-cardholders (especially those who have purchased AmEx travelers cheques), but you must call ahead. *Let's Go* lists AmEx office locations in **Practical Information** when available. A complete list is available free from AmEx (US ☎800-528-4800).

BY TELEPHONE

CALLING GREECE FROM HOME

To call Greece direct from home, dial:

1. The **international access code** of your home country. To dial out of **Greece,** the **Republic of Ireland, New Zealand,** or the **UK,** 00; **Australia,** dial 0011; **Canada** or the **US,** 011; **South Africa,** 09.
2. 30 (Greece's country code).
3. The local number.

Thus if a phone number in Greece was listed as 12345 67 890, you would dial the international access code followed by 30 12345 67 890.

Throughout 2002, phone codes in Greece have been changing. In January, most numbers gained an additional "0" at the end of the local code; in November 2002, the leading "0" of most phone numbers will become a "2." In addition, all local calls in Greece must now include the area code. Phone numbers in *Let's Go: Greece* reflect the proposed November changes, but at press time specifics were not available. Contact the Greek National Tourist Organization (GNTO, known as the EOT in Greece, see p. 28) for further information.

CALLING HOME FROM GREECE

A **calling card** is probably your cheapest bet. To **call home with a calling card,** contact the operator for your service provider in Greece by dialing the appropriate toll-free access number. Let's Go has recently partnered with ekit.com to provide a calling card that offers a number of services, including email and voice messaging. Before purchasing any calling card, always be sure to compare rates with other cards, and to make sure it serves your needs (a local phonecard is generally better for local calls, for instance). For more information, visit www.letsgo.ekit.com. All pay phones in Greece are card-operated, and you will need to purchase a card to operate the phone, even if you are going to use your own calling card to place the call (see **Calling Within Greece,** below).

Although incredibly convenient, in-room hotel calls invariably include an arbitrary and sky-high surcharge (as much as US$10). For instructions on dialing direct, see **Placing International Calls.** In an emergency, an expensive alternative to using a calling card is placing a **collect call** through an international operator. An English-speaking operator from your home nation can be reached by dialing the appropriate service provider listed above, and they will typically place a collect call even if you don't possess one of their phone cards.

CALLING WITHIN GREECE

The only way to use the phone in Greece is with a **prepaid phone card.** You can buy the cards at street-side kiosks and *peripteros* in denominations of €3, €12, and €25. The time is measured in minutes or talk units; a €3 card will buy you 100 units, roughly equal to 30min. of local calling within Greece and 5-10min. long-distance within Greece or internationally. The Greek phone service is known as the **OTE** (Organismos Tiliepikinonion tis Elladhos); there are local offices in most towns, and cardphones are often clustered outside.

Type the number slowly; Greece's quirky phones get confused if you type fast. Don't remove the card from the phone until the operator tells you to do so or you will lose your remaining credit.

TIME DIFFERENCES

TIME ZONES					
Seattle San Francisco Los Angeles	Toronto New York Ottawa	London (GMT)	**Athens** Istanbul Nicosia	Hong Kong Manila Singapore	Sydney Canberra Melbourne
4am	7am	noon	2pm	8pm	10pm

BY EMAIL AND INTERNET

The availability of the Internet in Greece is rapidly expanding. In all big cities, in most small cities and large towns, and on many islands, you can find Internet access. Expect to pay between €3-6 per hour. Travelers with laptops can call an Internet service provider via a **modem.** Long-distance phone cards specifically intended for such calls can defray normally high phone charges; check with your long-distance phone provider to see if it offers this option. **Internet cafes** and the occasional free Internet terminal at a public library or university are listed in the **Orientation and Practical Information** sections of major cities. Though in some places it's possible to forge a remote link with your home server, in most cases this is a much slower (and thus more expensive) option than taking advantage of free **web-based e-mail accounts** (e.g., www.hotmail.com and www.yahoo.com).

GETTING TO GREECE

BY PLANE

When it comes to airfare, a little effort can save you a bundle. If your plans are flexible enough to deal with the restrictions, courier fares are the cheapest. Tickets bought from consolidators and standby seating are also good deals, but last-minute specials, airfare wars, and charter flights often beat these fares. The key is to hunt around, to be flexible, and to ask persistently about discounts. Students, seniors, and those under 26 should never pay full price for a ticket.

AIRFARES

Airfares to Greece peak between **June** and **September**; holidays are also expensive. Midweek (M-Th morning) round-trip flights run US$40-50 cheaper than weekend flights, but they are generally more crowded and less likely to permit frequent-flier upgrades. Not fixing a return date ("open return") or arriving in and departing from different cities ("open-jaw") can be pricier than round-trip flights. Patching one-way flights together is the most expensive way to travel. Flights between Greece's regional hubs—Athens and Thessaloniki—tend to be cheaper.

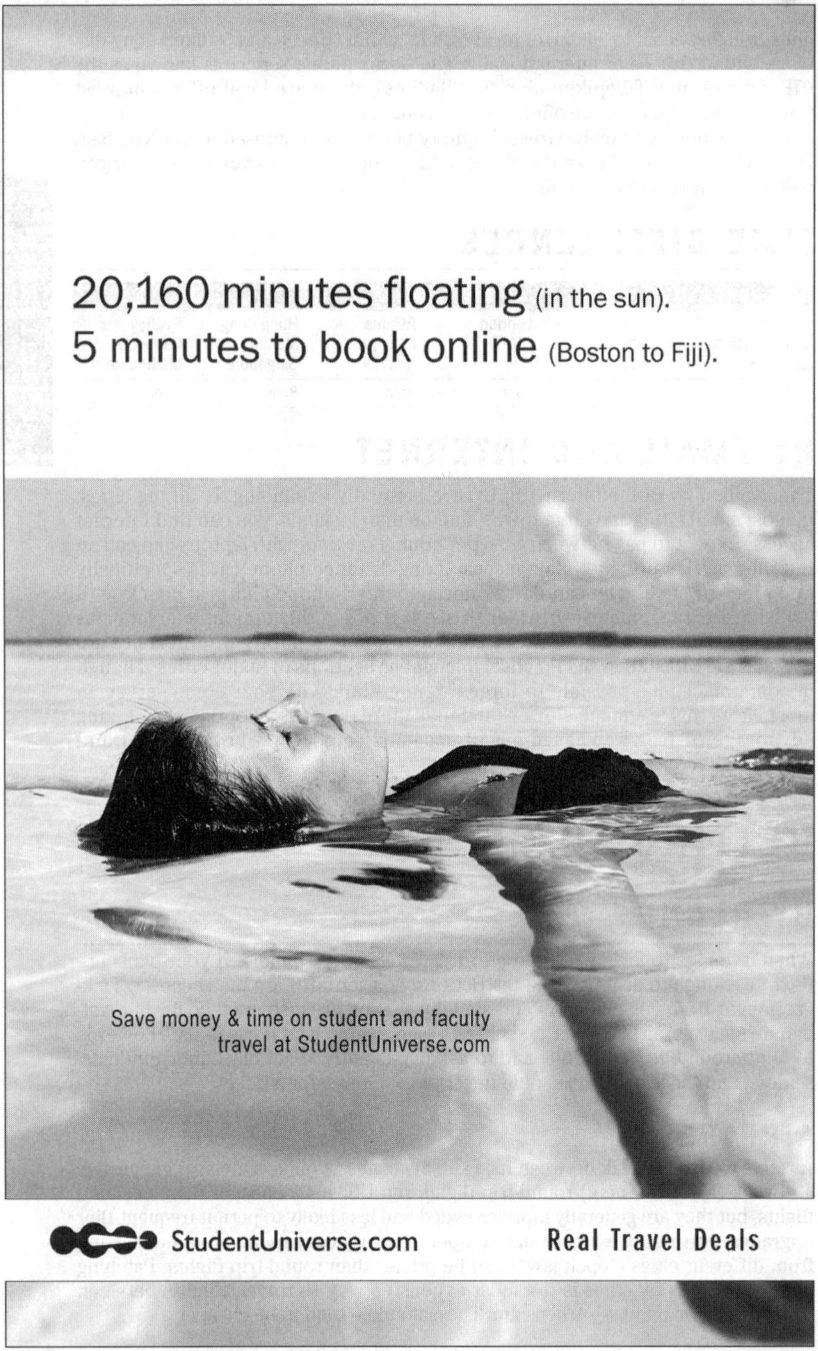

BUDGET AND STUDENT TRAVEL AGENCIES

While knowledgeable agents specializing in flights to Greece can make your life easy and help you save, they may not spend the time to find you the lowest possible fare—they get paid on commission. Travelers holding **ISIC and IYTC cards** (see p. 28) qualify for big discounts from student travel agencies. Most flights from budget agencies are on major airlines, but in peak season some may sell seats on less reliable chartered aircraft.

usit world (www.usitworld.com). Over 50 **usit campus** branches in the UK, including 52 Grosvenor Gardens, **London** SW1W 0AG (☎0870 240 10 10); **Manchester** (☎0161 273 1880); and **Edinburgh** (☎0131 668 3303). Nearly 20 **usit NOW** offices in Ireland, including 19-21 Aston Quay, O'Connell Bridge, **Dublin** 2 (☎01 602 1600; www.usitnow.ie), and **Belfast** (☎02 890 327 111; www.usitnow.com). Offices also in **Thessaloniki** (44 Alexander Svolou, 54621; ☎+30 1 41 32 950; fax 30 1 41 32 901; etospir@usitetos.gr; www.usitetos.gr; open M-F 9am-5pm, SA 10am-2pm) Auckland, Brussels, Frankfurt, Johannesburg, Lisbon, Luxembourg, Madrid, Paris, Sofia, and Warsaw.

Council Travel (www.counciltravel.com). Countless US offices, including branches in Atlanta, Boston, Chicago, L.A., New York, San Francisco, Seattle, and Washington, D.C. Check the website or call 800-2-COUNCIL (226-8624) for the office nearest you. Also an office at 28A Poland St. (Oxford Circus), **London,** W1V 3DB (☎0207 437 77 67). As of May 2002, Council had declared bankruptcy and was subsumed under STA. However, their offices are still in existence and transacting business.

CTS Travel, 44 Goodge St., **London** W1T 2AD, UK (☎0207 636 0031; fax 0207 637 5328; ctsinfo@ctstravel.co.uk).

STA Travel, 7890 S. Hardy Dr., Ste. 110, Tempe AZ 85284, USA (24hr. reservations and info ☎800-781-4040; www.sta-travel.com). A student and youth travel organization with over 150 offices worldwide (check their website for a listing of all their offices), including US offices in Boston, Chicago, L.A., New York, San Francisco, Seattle, and Washington, D.C. Ticket booking, travel insurance, railpasses, and more. In the UK, walk-in office 11 Goodge St., **London** W1T 2PF or call 0207-436-7779. In New Zealand, Shop 2B, 182 Queen St., **Auckland** (☎09 309 0458). In Australia, 366 Lygon St., **Carlton** Vic 3053 (☎03 9349 4344).

Travel CUTS (Canadian Universities Travel Services Limited), 187 College St., **Toronto,** ON M5T 1P7 (☎416-979-2406; fax 979-8167; www.travelcuts.com). 60 offices across Canada. Also in the UK, 295-A Regent St., **London** W1R 7YA (☎0207-255-1944).

COMMERCIAL AIRLINES

TRAVELING FROM NORTH AMERICA

Basic round-trip fares to Athens range from roughly US$600-1100: to Frankfurt US$300-750; London US$200-600; Paris US$250-700. Standard commercial carriers like American (☎800-433-7300; www.aa.com) and United (☎800-241-6522; www.ual.com) will probably offer the most convenient flights, but they may not be the cheapest, unless you manage to grab a special promotion or airfare-war ticket. You might find flying one of the following airlines a better deal, if any of their limited departure points is convenient for you.

Icelandair: ☎800-223-5500; www.icelandair.com. Stopovers in Iceland for no extra cost on most transatlantic flights. New York to Frankfurt May-Sept. US$500-730; Oct.-May US$390-$450. For last-minute offers, subscribe to their email Lucky Fares.

Finnair: ☎800-950-5000; www.us.finnair.com. Cheap round-trips from San Francisco, New York, and Toronto to Helsinki; connections throughout Europe.

FLIGHT PLANNING ON THE INTERNET.

Many airline sites offer special last-minute deals on the Web. **www.greece-flights.com** specializes in discount fares; **www.easyjet.com** lists cheap London-Athens flights. Other sites do the legwork and compile the deals for you—try www.bestfares.com, www.flights.com, www.hotdeals.com, www.lowestfare.com, www.onetravel.com, and www.travelzoo.com.

StudentUniverse (www.studentuniverse.com), **STA** (www.sta-travel.com), **Council** (www.counciltravel.com), and **Orbitz.com** provide quotes on student tickets, while **Expedia** (www.expedia.com) and **Travelocity** (www.travelocity.com) offer full travel services. **Priceline** (www.priceline.com) allows you to specify a price, and obligates you to buy any ticket that meets or beats it; be prepared for antisocial hours and odd routes. **Skyauction** (www.skyauction.com) allows you to bid on both last-minute and advance-purchase tickets.

An indispensable resource on the Internet is the *Air Traveler's Handbook* (www.cs.cmu.edu/afs/cs/user/mkant/Public/Travel/airfare.html), a comprehensive listing of links to everything you need to know before you board a plane.

ESSENTIALS

TRAVELING FROM THE UK & IRELAND

Because of the many carriers flying from the British Isles to the continent, we only include discount airlines or those with cheap specials here. The **Air Travel Advisory Bureau** in London (☎020 7636 5000; www.atab.co.uk) provides referrals to travel agencies and consolidators that offer discounted airfares out of the UK.

easyJet: UK ☎0870 600 00 00; www.easyjet.com. London to Athens (UK£95). Online tickets.

KLM: UK ☎0870 507 40 74; www.klmuk.com. Cheap return tickets from London to Athens (UK£220-280) and other European destinations.

TRAVELING FROM AUSTRALIA & NEW ZEALAND

Singapore Air: Australia ☎13 10 11, New Zealand ☎0800 808 909; www.singaporeair.com. Flies from Auckland, Sydney, Melbourne, and Perth to Athens.

Thai Airways: Australia ☎1300 65 19 60, New Zealand ☎09 377 02 68; www.thai-air.com. Auckland, Sydney, and Melbourne to Athens.

TRAVELING FROM SOUTH AFRICA

Air France: ☎011 770 16 01; www.airfrance.com/za. Johannesburg to Athens; connections throughout Europe.

British Airways: ☎0860 011 747; www.british-airways.com/regional/sa. Cape Town and Johannesburg to the UK from SAR3400 and to Athens from SAR12,175.

Lufthansa: ☎0861 842 538; www.lufthansa.co.za. From Cape Town, Durban, and Johannesburg to Germany and with connections to Athens and elsewhere.

AIR COURIER FLIGHTS

Those who travel light should consider courier flights. Couriers help transport cargo on international flights by using their checked luggage space for freight. Generally, couriers must travel with carry-ons only and deal with complex flight restrictions. Most flights are round-trip only, with short fixed-length stays (usually one week) and a limit of a one ticket per issue. Most of these flights also operate only out of major gateway cities, mostly in North America. Generally, you must be over 21. In summer, the most popular destinations usually require an advance reservation of about two weeks (you can usually book up to two months ahead). Super-discounted fares are common for "last-minute" flights (three to 14 days ahead).

International Association of Air Travel Couriers (IAATC), PO Box 980, Keystone Heights, FL 32656 (☎352-475-1584; fax 475-5326; www.courier.org). From 9 North American cities to Western European cities. One-year membership US$45.

Global Courier Travel, PO Box 3051, Nederland, CO 80466 (www.globalcourier-travel.com). Searchable online database. Six departure points in the US and Canada to Athens. Lifetime membership US$40, 2 people US$55.

STANDBY FLIGHTS

Traveling standby requires considerable flexibility in arrival and departure dates and cities. Companies dealing in standby flights sell vouchers rather than tickets, along with the promise to get to your destination (or near your destination) within a certain window of time (typically 1-5 days). You call in before your specific window of time to hear your flight options and the probability that you will be able to board each flight. You can then decide which flights you want to try to make, show up at the appropriate airport at the appropriate time, present your voucher, and board if space is available. You may receive a monetary refund only if every available flight within your date range is full; if you opt not to take an available (but perhaps less convenient) flight, you can only get credit toward future travel. To check on a company's service record in the US, call the Better Business Bureau (☎212-533-6200). It is difficult to receive refunds, and clients' vouchers will not be honored when an airline fails to receive payment in time. One established standby company in the US is Whole Earth Travel, 325 W. 38th St., New York, NY 10018, USA (☎800-326-2009; fax 212-864-5489) and Los Angeles, CA (☎888-247-4482), which offers one-way flights to Europe from the Northeast (US$169), West Coast and Northwest (US$249), Midwest (US$219), and Southeast (US$199). Intracontinental connecting flights within the US or Europe cost US$79-139.

TICKET CONSOLIDATORS

Ticket consolidators, or **"bucket shops,"** buy unsold tickets in bulk from commercial airlines and sell them at discounted rates. The best place to look is in the Sunday travel section of any major newspaper (such as the *New York Times*), where many bucket shops place tiny ads. Call quickly, as availability is typically extremely limited. Not all bucket shops are reliable, so insist on a receipt that gives full details of restrictions, refunds, and tickets, and pay by credit card (in spite of the 2-5% fee) so you can stop payment if you never receive your tickets. For more info, see www.travel-library.com/air-travel/consolidators.html.

TRAVELING FROM THE US & CANADA

Travel Avenue (☎800-333-3335; www.travelavenue.com) searches for best available published fares and then uses several consolidators to attempt to beat that fare. Consolidators worth trying are **Interworld** (☎305-443-4929; fax 443-0351); **Pennsylvania Travel** (☎800-331-0947); **Rebel** (☎800-227-3235; travel@rebeltours.com; www.rebeltours.com); **Cheap Tickets** (☎800-377-1000; www.cheaptickets.com); and **Travac** (☎800-872-8800; fax 212-714-9063; www.travac.com). Others on the web include the **Internet Travel Network** (www.itn.com); **Travel Information Services** (www.tiss.com); **TravelHUB** (www.travelhub.com); and **The Travel Site** (www.thetravelsite.com). Keep in mind that these are just suggestions to get you started in your research; *Let's Go* does not endorse any of these agencies. As always, be cautious, and research companies before you hand over your credit card number.

TRAVELING FROM THE UK, AUSTRALIA, & NEW ZEALAND

In London, the **Air Travel Advisory Bureau** (☎0207-636-5000; www.atab.co.uk) can provide names of reliable consolidators and discount flight specialists. From Australia and New Zealand, look for consolidator ads in the travel section of the *Sydney Morning Herald* and other papers.

CHARTER FLIGHTS

Charters are flights a tour operator contracts with an airline to fly extra loads of passengers during peak season. Charter flights fly less frequently than major airlines, make refunds particularly difficult, and are almost always fully booked. Schedules and itineraries may also change or be cancelled at the last moment (as late as 48 hours before the trip, and without a full refund), and check-in, boarding, and baggage claim are often much slower. However, they can also be cheaper.

Discount clubs and **fare brokers** offer members savings on last-minute charter and tour deals. Study contracts closely; you don't want to end up with an unwanted overnight layover. **Travelers Advantage,** Trumbull, CT, USA (☎203-365-2000; www.travelersadvantage.com; US$60 annual fee includes discounts and cheap flight directories) specializes in European travel and tour packages.

BY FERRY

Ferry travel is a popular way to get to and travel within Greece and Cyprus; their ports can be reached from a seemingly unlimited number of points, and finding a boat agency to facilitate your trip should not be difficult. Be warned that **ferries run on irregular schedules.** A few websites, like www.ferries.gr, have tried to keep updated schedules online but are often incomplete. You should try to take a look at a schedule as close to your departure as possible; you can usually find one at a tourist office or posted at the dock. That said, you should also make reservations, and check in at *least* 2hr. in advance; late boarders may find their seats gone. If you sleep on deck, bring warm clothes and a sleeping bag. Bicycles travel free, but motorcycles will have an additional charge. Don't forget motion sickness medication, toilet paper, and a hand towel. Bring food to avoid high prices on board.

The major ports of departure from Italy to Greece are Ancona and Brindisi, on the southeast coast of Italy. Bari, Otranto, and Venice also have a few connections. For schedules from Greece to Italy, see Patras (p. 131), Kephalonia (p. 295), Corfu (p. 274), or Igoumenitsa (p. 239). The Brindisi-Patras route (17hr.) is heavily traveled; deck passage to Brindisi is €30-35, including port tax. The travel agency **Manolopoulos** (☎2610 223 621), at Othonos Amalias 35 in Patras, can provide information on ferries to Italy. Ferries also run from Greece to various points on the Turkish coast. Trips from Greek islands that nearly touch the mainland are brief and fairly inexpensive.

BY BUS AND TRAIN

BY BUS. Although trains and railpasses are extremely popular in most of Europe, buses are a sometimes cheaper alternative. Unfortunately, there are almost no buses running directly from any European city to Greece. **Busabout,** 258 Vauxhall Bridge Rd., London SW1V 1BS, is one of the very few European bus lines that also runs to Greece (☎0171 950 1661; fax 0171 950 1662; info@busabout.co.uk; www.busabout.com). Only truly useful if you plan to travel elsewhere in Europe, there are five interconnecting bus circuits covering 60 cities and towns, with **"Add-ons"** that extend to Greece (via Italy) and environs. Standard/student passes are valid for times ranging from 15 days (US$249, UK£169) up to unlimited (US$1089, UK£699). "Add-ons" to **Patras** go through **Venice** (US$45, UK£29) and **Brindisi** (US$30, UK£19).

BY TRAIN. Greece is served by a number of international train routes that connect Athens, Thessaloniki, and Larisa to most European cities. **Eurail** passes are valid in Greece, and may be a useful purchase if you plan to visit one of the 17 other European countries in which they are valid. Fifteen-day youth passes (ages 25 and under) US$401; adults US$572. Eurail passes are available through travel agents, student travel agencies like STA and Council (see p. 49), and **Rail Europe,** 500 Mamaroneck Ave., Harrison, NY 10528 (US ☎888-382-7245, fax 800-432-1329; Canada ☎800-361-7245, fax 905-602-4198; UK ☎08705 84 88 48; www.raileurope.com). Unfortunately, the Greek rail system is one of Europe's most antiquated and least efficient—for example, a trip from Vienna to Athens takes at least 3 days. For information on specific routes see the **OSE** website at www.osenet.gr.

GETTING AROUND

BY FERRY AND HYDROFOIL

Widespread but unpredictable, cheap but slow, ferries will form the backbone of your travel-adventure tales. Be prepared to arrive at the dock 1-2 hours before departure for a decent seat, though a 5min.-early and a 3hr.-late departure are both real possibilities. Bring a good book, a bottle of water, food to last you the trip (snack bars are pricey), and a **windbreaker** (you'll want to wander the deck at sea). For short distances, indoor seats fill up fast; bring a hat to shield you from the sun on upper decks. For longer distances, bring **sleeping bags** or upgrade to a **cabin;** though the latter is usually expensive and disappointing, the former can be paired with insulated mats for starry sea nights on the deck.

MAKING SENSE OF FERRIES. The key to making good use of ferries is understanding ferry routes and planning your trip accordingly. Most ferries, rather than shuffling back and forth between two destinations, trace a four- or five- port route. Most ferry companies will allow you to buy your round-trip ticket **"split,"** meaning that you can ride the Piraeus-Syros-Tinos-Mykonos ferry from Piraeus to Syros, get off, get back on when the same ferry passes Syros several days later, proceed to Tinos, and so on. Remember that geographic proximity is **no guarantee** that you'll be able to get to one island from another. For example, there is no ferry service from Skyros to the rest of the Sporades or to the Northeast Aegean. Also note that there is very little service from the Cyclades to the Dodecanese.

Understanding ferry routes will also help you make sense of discrepancies in ticket prices (going to Hydra from Athens via Poros and Aegina is more expensive than simply going via Poros) and travel times. **Ferry schedules,** generally available for the region from the ferry companies or posted at the port police *(limenarcheio)*, are published weekly and give the departure times, routes, and names of each departing ferry. As particular ferries, even within companies, vary widely in quality, local travelers pay close attention to the names. Ask around or check on the web (www.ferries.gr) for tips, ferry schedules, and prices.

DOLPHIN RIDES. Twice the price and twice the speed, **Flying Dolphins** provide extensive, standardized, and sanitized transport between islands; offices and services are listed in the **Transportation** sections of all towns. However, traveling by Dolphin is like traveling by seaborne airplane: passengers are assigned seats and required to stay in the climate-controlled cabin for the duration of the trip, which may be less than ideal for the easily seasick. If you have the money to spare and want to minimize travel time, Dolphins are convenient enough and they run like clockwork. Otherwise, why sail the Aegean in a craft that won't let you get salt on your fingers and wind in your hair?

BY BUS

Spending time in Greece means traveling by bus. Service is extensive and fares are cheap. On major highways, buses tend to be more modern and efficient than in the mountainous areas of the Peloponnese or northern Greece. The **OSE** (see **By Train,** p. 55) offers limited bus service from a few cities. Unless you're sticking close to train routes, **KTEL** bus service should be sufficient.

Always check with an official source about scheduled departures; posted schedules are often outdated, and all services are curtailed significantly on Saturday and Sunday; major holidays run on Sunday schedules. The English-language weekly newspaper *Athens News* prints Athens bus schedules, and like almost everything else, they are available online (www.ktel.org). Try to arrive at least 10min. ahead of time, as Greek buses have a habit of leaving early. In major cities, KTEL bus lines may have different stations for different destinations, and schedules generally refer to **endpoints** ("the bus leaves Kalloni at three and arrives in Mytilini at four") with no mention of the numerous stops in between. In villages, a cafe or *zaccharoplasteio* (sweet-shop) often serves as the bus station, and you must ask the proprietor for a schedule.

ALL ABOARD! Ask the **conductor** before entering the bus whether it's going to your destination (the signs on the front are often misleading or wrong), and ask to be warned when you get there. If stowing bags underneath the bus, make sure they're in the compartment for your destination (conductors take great pride in packing the bus for easy unloading, and may refuse to open the "final destination" compartment at the "halfway" stop). If the bus passes your stop, stand up and yell **"Stasi!"** (ΣΤΑΣΗ). On the road, stand near a Stasi sign to pick up an intercity bus. KTEL buses are generally **green** or occasionally **orange,** while intercity buses are usually **blue.** For long-distance rides, you should buy your ticket beforehand in the office (if you don't, you may have to stand throughout the journey). For shorter trips, pay the conductor after you have boarded; reasonably close change is expected. Some lines discount round-trip fares by 20%.

BY PLANE OR TRAIN

BY PLANE. In Greece, **Olympic Airways** can be found in **Athens,** Syngrou 96-100, 11741 Athens (☎2801 11 44444), in **Thessaloniki,** Koundouritou 3, Thessaloniki 54101 (☎2310 368 666), and in many large cities and islands. The Olympic Airways website (www.olympic-airways.gr) lists information for every office around the globe. For further flight information within Greece, check regional **Practical Information** listings of airports, destinations, and prices, or get an Olympic Airways brochure at any Olympic office.

In recent years, Olympic's domestic *(esoteriko)* service has increased appreciably; from Athens, an hour's flight (US$60-90) can get you to almost any island in Greece. Even in low season, more remote destinations (Limnos, Hios) are serviced several times weekly, while more developed areas (Thessaloniki, Crete) can have several flights per day. Though somewhat frivolous for short distances, fairly cheap flights seem like more of a deal if they exempt you from overnight ferry rides and potential cost of food and beds on board (e.g., the 22hr. ferry ride from Limnos to Piraeus). Make sure to reserve your tickets one week in advance.

BY TRAIN. Although trains can be cheaper than buses, they run less frequently and take longer: as a rule, Greece has one of Europe's slowest train services. If you're lucky, you may come across a new, air-conditioned, intercity train, which is a different entity altogether: although they are slightly more expensive and rare, they are worth the price. **Eurail** passes are valid on Greek trains. OSE (www.osenet.gr) connects Athens to major Greek cities (like Volos and Thessaloniki). For schedules and prices in Greece, dial 145 or 147. Lines do not go to the west coast, and they are rarely useful for remote areas or archaeological sites. Bring food and a water bottle, because the on-board cafe can be pricey, and the water undrinkable. Lock your compartment and keep valuables on your person.

BY MOPED

BE CAREFUL. A word of caution: **most tourist-related accidents each year occur on mopeds.** Regardless of your experience driving a moped or motorcycle, winding, poorly maintained mountain roads and reckless drivers make using a moped hazardous. Always wear a helmet, and never ride with a backpack.

Motorbiking is a popular way of touring Greece's winding roads. Although renting wheels is the best and most cost efficient way to assert your independence from unreliable or inconvenient public transportation systems, you should be aware that they can be uncomfortable for long distances, dangerous in the rain, and unpredictable on rough roads. On many islands, navigable roads suddenly turn into tiny trails that can only be walked. Furthermore, moped rental shop owners often loosen the front brakes on the bikes to discourage riders from using them (relying on the front brakes makes accidents more likely), so use the back brakes. If you've never driven a moped before, a cliffside road is not the place to learn.

RENTING. Shops renting mopeds are everywhere, and most require only some sort of drivers' license (a Greek license or International Driving Permit is not necessary). Bike quality, speed of service in case of breakdown, and prices for longer periods vary drastically, but you should expect to pay at least €12 per day for a

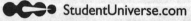

METRO MYSTIQUE UNVEILED. You're not seeing things. Those flashing ghostly images you catch a glimpse of in the Athens Metro are not a figment of your imagination. In preparation for the Olympics, major corporations are pursuing a new method of advertisement in the form of silent movie-like ads played in the subway tunnels in Athens. The high-tech, exorbitantly expensive method of advertisement is controlled by satellite. Lasers in the tunnel, activated when the train is going 50km/hr or more, flash random light sequences that convey the image to the passerby, much like animated flip-books. By 2004, ads from 18 different companies, including Pepsi, Coke, and Nike will be playing throughout the expanded metro system. Due to the archaeological discoveries along planned routes, Athens itself may be little behind schedule with metro preparation. But the corporate world is ready.

50cc scooter, the cheapest bike with the power to tackle steep mountain roads. More powerful bikes cost 20-30% more and usually require a Greek motorcycle license. Many agencies will request your passport as a deposit, but it's wiser just to settle up in advance; if they have your passport and you have an accident or mechanical failure, they may refuse to return it until you pay for repairs. Ask before renting if the price quote includes tax, insurance, and a full tank of gas, or you may pay a few unexpected euros. Information on local moped rentals is in the **Practical Information** section for individual cities and towns.

BY CAR

Cars are a luxury in Greece, a country where public transportation is nonexistent after 7pm. Ferries will take you island-hopping if you pay a transport fee for the car. Drivers must be comfortable with a standard transmission, winding mountain roads, reckless drivers (especially in Athens), and the Greek alphabet—signs in Greek appear roughly 100m before the transliterated versions. Driving can be a cheaper alternative to trains and buses for groups of travelers, and is especially useful for exploring remote villages in northern Greece, though having a car might detract from the traveling experience.

Agencies may quote low daily rates that exclude the 20% tax and **Collision Damage Waiver (CDW)** insurance. Expect to pay €20-40 per day for a rental. Some places quote lower rates but hit you with hidden charges, such as exorbitant refueling bills if you come back with less than a full tank, €0.10-€020 per kilometer drop-off or special charge, or 100km per day minimum mileage. Most companies won't let you drive the car outside Greece.

Foreign drivers are required to have an **International Driving Permit** and an **International Insurance Certificate** to drive in Greece (see below). The **Automobile and Touring Club of Greece (ELPA),** Messogion 395, Athens 11527 (☎210 606 88 00; www.elpa.gr), provides assistance and offers reciprocal membership to foreign auto club members. They also have 24hr. emergency road assistance (☎104) and an information line (☎174 in Athens, 210 60 68 838 elsewhere in Greece; open M-F 7am-3pm). Car rental in Europe is available through the following agencies:

Auto Europe, 39 Commercial St., P.O. Box 7006, Portland, ME 04112 (US and Canada ☎888-223-5555 or 207-842-2000; fax 207-842-2222; www.autoeurope.com).

Avis (US and Canada ☎800-331-1084; UK ☎08705 90 05 00; Australia ☎800 22 55 33; New Zealand ☎0800 65 51 11; www.avis.gr).

Europe by Car, 1 Rockefeller Plaza, New York, NY 10020 (US ☎800-223-1516 or 212-581-3040; fax 246-1458; info@europebycar.com; www.europebycar.com).

Europcar, 145 av. Malekoff, 75016 Paris (☎01 45 00 08 06); US ☎800-227-3876; Canada ☎800-227-7368; www.europcar.com).

Hertz (US ☎800-654-3001; Canada ☎800-263-0600; UK ☎08705 99 66 99; Australia ☎9698 2555; www.hertz.gr).

Kemwel Holiday Autos (US ☎800-576-1590; www.kemwel.com).

INTERNATIONAL DRIVING PERMIT (IDP). If you plan to drive a car while in Greece, you are legally required to have an International Driving Permit (IDP). Although Greek proprietors may ignore the law, get one if you know you plan on driving. Your IDP, valid for one year, must be issued in your own country before you depart; AAA affiliates cannot issue IDPs valid in their own country. You must be 18 years old to receive the IDP. A valid driver's license from your home country must always accompany the IDP.

CAR INSURANCE. Most credit cards cover standard insurance. If you rent, lease, or borrow a car, you will need a **green card,** or **International Insurance Certificate,** to certify that you have liability insurance and that it applies abroad. Green cards can be obtained at car rental agencies, car dealers (for those leasing cars), some travel agents, and some border crossings. Rental agencies may require you to purchase theft insurance in areas that they consider to have a high risk of auto theft. Contact the automobile association in your country for information on obtaining an international driving permit and car insurance.

BY THUMB

Let's Go strongly urges you to consider the risks before you choose to hitch. We do not recommend hitching as a safe means of transportation, and none of the information presented here is intended to do so.

Think before you hitch: those who hitchhike entrust their life to whoever stops beside them on the road, risking theft, assault, sexual harassment, and auto accidents. Safety-minded hitchers avoid getting in the back of a two-door car and never let go of their backpacks. If they feel threatened, they **insist on being let off,** regardless of where they are. They may also act as if they are going to open the car door or vomit on the upholstery to get a driver to stop. Experienced hitchers pick a spot outside of built-up areas, where drivers can stop, return to the road without causing an accident, and have time to inspect potential passengers as they approach; at night, experienced hitchers stand in well-lit places and expect drivers to be leery of nocturnal thumbers. Women should not hitch in Greece.

Greeks are not eager to pick up foreigners, and foreign cars are often filled with other travelers. Sparsely populated areas have little or no traffic—those who hitchhike risk being stuck on the road for hours. Hitchhikers write their destination on a sign in both **Greek and English.** Successful hitchers travel light and stack their belongings in a visible, compact cluster.

SPECIFIC CONCERNS

WOMEN TRAVELERS

Women exploring on their own face additional safety concerns (and **Health Concerns,** p. 36), but you can be **adventurous** without taking undue risks. If you are uneasy about traveling alone, stay in hostels with single rooms that lock from the inside or offer rooms for women only. Check the safety of communal showers in hostels before settling in. Stick to centrally located accommodations and avoid solitary nighttime treks. When traveling, carry extra money for a phone call, bus, or taxi. **Hitching** is never safe for lone women in Greece, or even for two women traveling together. Look as if you know where you're going, even when you don't.

When Greek women travel together, it tends to be to the beach, so Greeks might be curious if they see a woman or group of women traveling in what is not resort territory. **Older Greek women** in villages, towns, and cities can help you if you get in a bind; they're sharp, wise, fearless, and your best allies if you need information, advice, or a respite from persistent amorous attempts by local men.

In **cities,** you may be harassed no matter how you act or what you look like. Your best answer to verbal harassment is no answer at all: ignore catcalls and questioning by sitting motionless and staring straight ahead, or walking away. Wearing a conspicuous **wedding band** or mentioning a "husband" back at the hotel may help ward off unwanted overtures. Note that Orthodox Greeks wear their wedding bands on their right ring fingers. If you do feel threatened, call attention to what is going on: yell **"AHS-se-meh"** (leave me alone), **"vo-EE-thee-ah"** (help) or **"as-te-no-MEE-ah"** (police). Alternatively, you might carry a **whistle** on your key chain to blow in an emergency. *Let's Go: Greece* lists emergency numbers in the **Practical Information** listings of most cities. Memorize the emergency numbers in the places you visit. An **IMPACT Model Mugging** self-defense course prepares people for potential attacks, and raises confidence and awareness about your surroundings (see **Self Defense,** p. 34).

ESSENTIALS

TRAVELING ALONE

There are many benefits to traveling alone, among them greater independence and challenge. Traveling alone in Greece can be a fantastic way to interact with locals and to see less-touristed areas than you might not visit with a group of sightseeing friends. On the other hand, solo travelers are more vulnerable to harassment and street theft. Lone travelers need to be well organized and look confident at all times. Follow **local customs and dress,** and be inconspicuous. **Never admit that you are traveling alone.** Maintain regular contact with someone at home who knows your itinerary. For more tips, pick up *Traveling Solo* by Eleanor Berman (Globe Pequot Press, US$17) or subscribe to **Connecting: Solo Travel Network,** 689 Park Rd., Unit 6, Gibsons, BC V0N 1V7 (☎604-886-9099; www.cstn.org; membership US$25). Alternatively, several services link solo travelers with companions who have similar travel habits and interests; for a bi-monthly newsletter for single travelers seeking a travel partner (subscription US$48), contact the **Travel Companion Exchange,** P.O. Box 833, Amityville, NY 11701 (☎631-454-0880 or 800-392-1256; www.whytravelalone.com; US$48).

There are basic **common sense rules** to follow when traveling alone. Remember that no one knows where you are at all times, so be careful of going anywhere with a newfound friend. Be equally wary when hitting the nightlife, as your defenses may drop as your ouzo consumption increases. To avoid standing out as a tourist in villages, make a *stavros* (a cross: up, down, right, left) in front of all churches as a sign of **respect** for the country's culture and customs; locals are much more likely to accept you once they realize that you respect them in return. In most Greek villages, xenophobia is directed only at rude outsiders; as soon as you show familiarity with Greek customs, people are much more friendly.

OLDER TRAVELERS

Greeks generally have great respect for their elders, so don't expect any problems while traveling. Be aware that many sites are only reachable by strenuous hikes and the hot sun can be dangerous. Senior citizens are eligible for a wide range of discounts on transportation, museums, movies, theaters, concerts, restaurants, and accommodations. If you don't see a senior citizen price listed, ask, and you may be delightfully surprised. See *No Problem! World-wide Tips for Mature Adventurers*, by Janice Kenyon (Orca Book Pub., US$16); *A Senior's Guide to Healthy Travel*, by Donald L. Sullivan (Career Press, US$15); or *Unbelievably Good Deals and Great Adventures That You Absolutely Can't Get Unless You're Over 50*, by Joan Rattner Heilman (Contemporary Books, US$13) for information about trips for older travelers, or consult:

Elderhostel, 11 Avenue de LaFayette Boston, MA 02111, USA (☎877-426-8056; fax 877-426-2166; registration@elderhostel.org; www.elderhostel.org). Outside of the US and Canada call 978-323-4141; fax 617-426-0701. Organizes 1- to 4-week "educational adventures" in Greece on varied subjects for those 55+.

Walking the World, P.O. Box 1186, Fort Collins, CO 80522 (☎800-340-9255; www.walkingtheworld.com), organizes trips for 50+ travelers to Greece.

BISEXUAL, GAY, & LESBIAN TRAVELERS

Though legal in Greece since 1951, homosexuality is still socially frowned upon, especially in more conservative villages. Athens and Thessaloniki offer a slew of gay bars, clubs, and hotels. The islands of **Hydra, Lesvos, Rhodes,** and **Mykonos** (arguably the most gay-friendly destination in Europe) offer gay and lesbian resorts, hotels, bars, and clubs. Gays are not legally protected from discrimination. Consult the following organizations, or pick up *Spartacus International Gay Guide*, by Bruno Gmunder Verlag (US$33); *Damron's Accommodations*, and *The Women's Traveller* (Damron Travel Guides, US$14-19); *Ferrari Guides' Gay Travel A to Z*, *Ferrari Guides' Men's Travel in Your Pocket*, and *Ferrari Guides' Women's Travel in Your Pocket* (Ferrari Guides, US$14-16).

Gay Greek Guide, TΘ 4228, Athens 10210 (☎210 381 5249; English speaker M-F 7-9pm). Call this hotline while in Greece for information on nightlife options.

International Gay and Lesbian Travel Association, 52 W Oakland Park Blvd. #237 Wilton Manors, FL 33311 (☎954-776-2626 or 800-448-8550; fax 776-3303; iglta@iglta.org; www.iglta.com). AUS/NZ/Pacific Rim/ASIA: P.O. Box 1397 Rozelle NSW Australia 2039. Organization of over 1350 companies serving gay and lesbian travelers worldwide. Call for lists of travel agents, accommodations, and events.

Pridenet (www.pridenet.com/europe.html) links to other Greece-specific gay sites, and offers listings and information organized by area and island groupings.

TRAVELERS WITH DISABILITIES

Greece is only slowly beginning to respond to the needs of travelers with disabilities; those with severe physical disabilities won't have it easy. Even the most renowned sights—even the Acropolis—are not wheelchair accessible. Some hotels, train stations, and airports have installed facilities for the disabled, as have some cruise ships that sail to Greek islands. Special air transportation is available aboard Olympic Airways to many of the larger islands.

Those with disabilities should inform airlines and hotels of their disabilities when making arrangements for travel; some time may be needed to prepare special accommodations. Call ahead to restaurants, hotels, parks, and other facilities to find out about ramps, door widths, elevator sizes, and such. **Guide dog owners** should inquire as to the specific quarantine policies ahead of time, and should carry proof of immunization against rabies. Greece's **rail** systems have very limited resources for wheelchair accessibility, but they are probably the best bet for disabled travelers. There are no handicapped-accessible **buses.** Some major **car rental** agencies (Hertz, Avis, and National) offer hand-controlled vehicles. The following organizations offer more information for disabled travelers (see **Other Resources,** p. 64, for useful publications):

Mobility International USA (MIUSA), P.O. Box 10767, Eugene, OR 97440 (☎(541) 343-1284 voice and TDD; fax 343-6812; info@miusa.org; www.miusa.org). Sells *A World of Options: A Guide to International Educational Exchange, Community Service, and Travel for Persons with Disabilities* (US$35).

Moss Rehab Hospital Travel Information Service (☎(215) 456-9600 or (800) CALL-MOSS; netstaff@mossresourcenet.org; www.mossresourcenet.org). An information resource center on travel-related concerns for those with disabilities.

MINORITY TRAVELERS (NON-GREEKS)

Greeks stare, point, whisper, and gossip as a daily pastime. The first thing to notice is that they're not just staring at *you*. Even the larger cities in Greece retain a small-village, island world view, where everyone and everything is gossip material. While Greeks tend to hold stereotypes about every group of people imaginable, they place a great value on **individualism;** you may be asked (out of curiosity, not maliciousness) all manner of questions or referred to continually as "the (insert your nationality here)," "the (insert religion here)," or simply "the foreigner" *(xenos)*. If you deal with individual Greeks for any period of time, they'll treat you as you seem to be (honest, trustworthy, friendly). Still, Greek stereotypes remain global enough to be almost laughable.

Greece presents two strong and entirely different views about foreigners, and travelers should expect to encounter both. One one hand, the Greek tradition of hospitality (**philoxenia**) is unmatched in the Mediterranean. Greeks consider it almost a sacred duty to help travelers, loading them with homemade food and advice. On the other hand, it's important to remember Greece's historical position as the crossroads of empire: most European nations have at one time or another invaded, burned, betrayed, or colonized part of Greece, forging an intense "us-versus-them" Greek nationalism. If you're not obviously Greek, everyone will want to know who you are. **Minority travelers** will have more trouble blending in, and will have to deal with more stares, questions, and comments. While such curiosity may seem in-your-face and invasive by Western standards, think of its roots: 3000 years of experience have taught Greeks to beware foreigners (who could be spies, fugitives, or gods) even when they bear gifts. Once their curiosity is satisfied, they'll be happy to have you in the village, and take pleasure in showing you around.

TRAVELERS WITH CHILDREN

Greeks adore children, and many museums and archeological sites allow children under 18 in for free. Children under two generally fly for 10% of the adult airfare on international flights (this does not necessarily include a seat). International fares are usually discounted 25% for children from two to 11. When deciding where to stay on a family vacation, call ahead to make sure the hotels and pensions allow children; some of hotels and domatia have large rooms for families and roll-away beds for children. If you rent a car, make sure the rental company provides a car seat for younger children. Be sure that your child carries some sort of ID in case of an emergency or in case he or she gets lost.

DIETARY CONCERNS

Greek meals are traditionally organized as follows: bread and olive oil, followed by a lot of largely vegetable or seafood appetizers (fresh vegetables, vegetable pies, fried octopus), followed by a meat or fish dish, followed by fresh fruit. **Vegetarians** (but not vegans, as it is virtually impossible to avoid all animal products in Greek food) can make do if they don't mind occasionally making a meal of appetizers—green beans in oil *(fasolia)*, the omnipresent Greek salad *(horiatiko)*, cooked vegetables *(laderakia)*, spinach-phyllo-feta pastry *(spanakopita)*, greens *(horta)*, flat-beans *(yigandes)*, fresh bread, and wine. In smaller towns, many seemingly vegetarian entrees (like *yemista*, stuffed vegetables) can contain meat, especially in agricultural areas; **ask before you order.** Incidentally, **Lent** is an especially good time for vegetarians and vegans to visit Greece, when meat and meat stock disappear from many dishes. There are almost no Greek vegetarians though, so if questioned your best bet is to argue weather ("It's so hot I only want vegetables") or allergies ("I'm allergic to pork and beef"), as opposed to some kind of ideology: "I don't want to eat meat" will be taken with as much seriousness as "I don't want to eat my vegetables" by well-meaning local grandmothers. As far as actual **allergies** are concerned, the same rule applies: ask before you order, especially at local tavernas that simply serve you whatever is cooking in the kitchen.

Travelers who keep **kosher** should contact synagogues in larger cities for information on kosher restaurants; your own synagogue or college Hillel should have access to lists of Jewish institutions across the nation. If you are strict in your observance, you may have to prepare your own food on the road. **The Jewish Travel Guide,** which lists synagogues, kosher restaurants, and Jewish institutions in over 100 countries, is available in Europe from Vallentine Mitchell Publishers, Newbury House 890-900, Eastern Ave., Newbury Park, Ilford, Essex IG2 7HH, (☎020 8599 8866; fax 8599 0984) and in the US ($16.95 + $4 S&H) from ISBS, 5804 NE Hassallo St., Portland, OR 97213 (☎800-944-6190).

OTHER RESOURCES

Let's Go tries to cover all aspects of budget travel, but we can't put *everything* in our guides. Listed below are websites that can serve as jumping off points for your own research. Almost every aspect of budget travel is accessible via the **web.** Even if you don't have Internet access at home, seeking it out at a public library or at work is well worth it; within 10min. at the keyboard, you can make a reservation at a hostel in Greece, get advice on travel hotspots or experiences from other travelers who have just returned from the Cyclades, or find out exactly how much a ferry from Kephalonia to Corfu costs. Website turnover is high so use search engines (such as www.google.com) to strike out on your own.

THE ART OF BUDGET TRAVEL

How to See the World: www.artoftravel.com. A compendium of great travel tips, from cheap flights to self defense to interacting with local culture.

Rec. Travel Library: www.travel-library.com. A fantastic set of links for general information and personal travelogues.

WWW.LETSGO.COM Our newly designed website now features the full online content of all of our guides. In addition, trial versions of all nine City Guides are available for download on Palm OS™ PDAs. Our website also contains our newsletter, links for photos and streaming video, online ordering of our titles, info about our books, and a travel forum buzzing with stories and tips.

INFORMATION ON GREECE

CIA World Factbook: www.odci.gov/cia/publications/factbook/index.html. Tons of vital statistics on Greece's geography, government, economy, and people.

Foreign Language for Travelers: www.travlang.com will help you brush up on your Greek.

MyTravelGuide: www.mytravelguide.com. Country overviews, with everything from history to transportation.

Geographia: www.geographia.com. Highlights, culture, and people of Greece.

Atevo Travel: www.atevo.com/guides/destinations. Detailed introductions, travel tips, and suggested itineraries.

World Travel Guide: www.travel-guides.com/navigate/world.asp. Helpful practical info.

TravelPage: www.travelpage.com. Links to official tourist office sites in Greece.

PlanetRider: www.planetrider.com. A subjective list of links to the "best" websites covering the culture and tourist attractions of Greece.

GENERAL TRAVEL SITES

Air Traveler's Handbook: www.cs.cmu.edu/afs/cs/user/mkant/Public/Travel/airfare.html. Help finding cheap airfare.

Rec. Travel Library: www.travel-library.com. A fantastic set of links for general information and personal travelogues.

Shoestring Travel: www.stratpub.com. An e-zine focusing on budget travel.

Eurotrip: www.eurotrip.com. This site has information and reviews on budget hostels, as well as info on traveling alone.

GREECE-SPECIFIC SITES

The Internet Guide to Greece: www.gogreece.com features maps, references, discussions, and extensive listings of Greek businesses, schools, news sources, and sports.

Phantis: www.phantis.com. A Greek-specific search engine that accommodates region-specific queries, and contains links to Greek city sites.

Hellenic Federation of Mountaineering and Climbing: www.climbing.org.gr. Learn about great hikes in Greece.

The Perseus Project: www.perseus.tufts.edu. "An evolving digital library," provides a library of classical Greek texts, translations, and an online dictionary.

United Hellas: www.united-hellas.com. A would-be database of all things Greek, from small businesses and folk art sources to places to buy a boat.

The Greek Orthodox Archdiocese of New York: www.goarch.org lists information about the religion of most Greeks.

Greek Ferries: www.ferries.gr claims to maintain a complete and updated list of ferry schedules over all the Greek islands.

The Ministry of Culture: www.culture.gr. Events, history, "cultural maps of Greece," and other fun stuff.

G.S.T. (GREEK STANDARD TIME) Greeks are known the world over for their slow-paced and contemplative enjoyment of life. "Be flexible! Relax! Have fun!" This *philosophia,* unfortunately, doesn't make it particularly easy for travelers accustomed to reliable timetables. Restaurant menus and hours rotate, depending on whim. Train, bus, and ferry schedules are notoriously fickle, and owners of establishments may close up shop at any given moment to pay their respects to the sun god Helios—at the beach. Summer dance clubs return to their city locations in the winter, but will often swap beach locations from year to year. Prices for everything from food to accommodations to that garish head scarf you'll buy for Aunt Barbara are subject to change, depending on various circumstances (season, availability, whether or not you said *"yassou"*). When a proprietor tells you your food will be here "in a minute," be warned that something might get lost in translation.

The Greek Government online: www.government.gr. In Greek with sections in English.

Cyprus homepage: http://kypros.org/Government. Links to most Cypriot government agencies and to the Cyprus virtual tour guide.

Greek poetry: www.webexpert.net/vasilios/gpoetry.htm. An extensive compilation of links to Greek poetry resources, modern and ancient.

ALTERNATIVES TO TOURISM

Traveling from place to place around the world may be a memorable experience. But if you are looking for a more rewarding and complete way to see the world, you may want to consider Alternatives to Tourism. Working, volunteering, or studying for an extended period of time can be a better way to understand life in Greece. This chapter outlines some of the different ways to get to know a new place, whether you want to pay your way through or just get the personal satisfaction that comes from studying and volunteering. In most cases, you will feel that you have a more meaningful and educational experience—something that the average budget traveler often misses out on.

Whatever draws you to Greece, these alternatives will give you an unique perspective on your travels. History buffs can see monuments up close by volunteering for restoration projects and archaeological digs; beach bunnies and club hoppers can pay their way with a few hours of bartending; nature lovers can work with fellow hikers and campers and come face-to-face with local wildlife. Besides giving you a chance to repay the famous Greek *philoxenia*, the opportunities in this chapter will bring you to secluded beaches, hidden ruins and idyllic towns you can't otherwise access.

VISA INFORMATION

Citizens of the US, Canada, Australia, New Zealand and EU member countries are all automatically allowed a three-month stay in Greece, though they are not eligible for employment during that time; South Africans must apply for a visa. Apply for visa extensions at least 20 days prior to the three-month expiration date. If you plan to **study** in Greece for longer than three months, a student visa is necessary. You must first obtain admission into an academic or language program in Greece. Then, as long as you can prove financial support, you need to apply to your embassy for a student visa for however long you want to study (US$20). A tourist visa cannot be changed into a student visa while in Greece, so obtain one well before you leave.

For **legal employment** in Greece, you must first get a work permit from a prearranged employer. Permits are available at the Ministry of Labor, Pireos 40, Athens 104 37. Make all arrangements and negotiations before you leave.

STUDYING ABROAD

Study abroad programs range from basic language and culture courses to college-level classes. In order to choose a program that best fits your needs, you will want to find out what kind of students participate in the program and what sort of accommodations are provided. In programs that have large groups of students who speak the same language, there is a trade-off. You may feel more comfortable in the community, but you will not have the same opportunity to practice a foreign language or to befriend other international students. For accommodations, dorm life provides a better opportunity to mingle with fellow students, but there is less of a chance to experience the local scene. If you live with a family, there is a potential to build lifelong friendships with natives and to experience day-to-day life in more depth, but conditions can vary greatly from family to family.

Those relatively fluent in Greek may find it cheaper to enroll directly in a university abroad, although getting college credit may be more difficult. Some American schools still require students to pay them for credits they obtain elsewhere. Most university-level study abroad programs are meant as language and culture enrichment opportunities, and therefore are conducted in Greek. Still, many programs do offer classes in English and beginner- and lower-level language courses. A good resource for finding programs is www.studyabroad.com, which has links to various semester abroad programs based on a variety of criteria, including desired location and focus of study. The following is a list of organizations that can help place students in university programs abroad or have their own branch in Greece.

AMERICAN PROGRAMS

Arcadia University for Education Abroad, 450 S. Easton Rd., Glenside, PA 19038, USA (☎866-927-2234; www.arcadia.edu/cea). Operates programs in Greece. Costs range from $2550 (summer) to $16,300 (full-year).

International Association for the Exchange of Students for Technical Experience (IAESTE), 10400 Little Patuxent Pkwy. Suite 250, Columbia, MD 21044-3519, USA (☎410-997-2200; www.aipt.org). 8- to 12-week programs in Greece for college students who have completed 2 years of technical study. US$25 application fee.

AHA International, 741 SW Lincoln St., Portland, Oregon 97201-3178, USA (☎800-654-2051; fax 503-295-5969; www.aha-intl.org). 12-week terms in the fall and spring. Costs start at $6,448.

SUNY Brockport, Office of International Education, SUNY Brockport, 350 New Campus Dr., Brockport, NY 14420 (☎716-395-2119/1-800-298-SUNY; fax 716-637-3218; www.brockport.edu/study_abroad). Offers a 2-3 week Mythological Study Tour in Greece, visiting ancient sites and relating ancient myths to Greek life. Basic program starts at $2165, with some extra costs.

PROGRAMS IN GREECE

Several different types of programs are available for studying abroad in Greece: studying directly at a Greek university, studying through an international program, or going to a language school. Most of these programs are located in Greece's most highly traveled areas, especially in Athens, on Crete, and throughout the Cyclades. In addition, aspiring archeologists have a fairly unique opportunity to work on current digs while studying abroad in Greece. Programs vary tremendously in expense, academic quality, living conditions, degree of contact with local students, and exposure to local culture and languages.

College Year in Athens, P.O. Box 390890, Cambridge, MA 02139 (☎617-868-8200 from the US; fax 617-868-8207; ☎210 756 0749 from Greece; info@cyathens.org; www.cyathens.org). Runs a semester-long, full-year, and summer programs for undergraduates (usually juniors), which includes travel as well as classroom instruction (all in English). The program has two tracks, one in Ancient Greek civilization and one in Mediterranean area studies. Scholarships available. Students are housed in apartments in Athens's Kolonaki district. College Year in Athens also offers summer programs, including a 3-week intensive course in modern Greek on Paros, a 6-week study-travel program, and two 3-week modules that cover different subjects every year.

American School of Classical Studies (ASCSA), Souidias 54, Athens (☎210 723 6313; info@ascsa.edu.gr). A highly competitive program open to graduate students. Degrees offered in archaeology, art history, and classical studies.

The Athens Centre, Archimidous 48, Athens 11636 (☎210 701 2268; fax 210 701 8603; info@athens-centre.gr; www.athenscentre.gr). Offers a Modern Greek Language program. Semester and quarter programs on Greek civilization in affiliation with US universities. Offers 4- to 6-week summer Classics programs, a yearly summer theater program, and Modern Greek Language programs in summer on the isle of Spetses.

Deree College, Gravias 6, GR-153 42 Agia Paraskevi, Athens (☎210 60 9 800;deree@acg.edu or info@acg.edu). Part of the American College of Greece. Bachelors offered in a wide variety of subjects; classes taught in English. Open to students of all international backgrounds, including many Greek students.

Art School of the Aegean, P.O. Box 1375, Sarasota, FL 34230-1375 (☎941-351-5597; hera@artschool-aegean.com; www.artschool-aegean.com). Offers 2- to 3-week summer programs in painting and ceramics from $1,700.

LANGUAGE SCHOOLS

Unlike American universities, language schools are frequently independently-run international or local organizations or divisions of foreign universities that rarely offer college credit. Language schools are a good alternative to university study if you desire a deeper focus on the language or a slightly less-rigorous courseload. These programs are also good for younger high school students that might not feel comfortable with older students in a university program. Some programs include:

Languages Abroad, Box 502, 99 Avenue Rd., Toronto, ON M5R 2G5 (☎800-219-9924; www.languagesabroad.com). Runs programs from 3 to 4 weeks long in Athens. Cost varies with length, but 3-week programs start at US$2000; course only $650-750.

School of Modern Greek Language at the Aristotle University of Thessaloniki, Thessaloniki 54006 (☎231 99 7571; fax 231 99 7573; thkaldi@auth.gr; www.auth.gr/smg). Summer, winter and intensive programs offered in conjunction with philosophy classes.

ARCHAEOLOGICAL DIGS

The **Archaeological Institute of America**, 656 Beacon St., Boston, MA 02215-2006 (☎617-353-9361; www.archaeological.org), puts out the *Archaeological Fieldwork Opportunities Bulletin* (US$16 for non-members), which lists field sites in Greece. This can be purchased from Kendall/Hunt Publishing, 4050 Westmark Dr., Dubuque, Iowa 52002 (☎800-228-0810). **The American School of Classical Studies at Athens,** Souidias 54, Athens 10676 (☎210 72 36 313; fax

TEACHING ON THE ROCKS

An interview with Peter Scholtz, a restoration architect and a professor at the Arcadia College (Penn., USA) summer program in Greece, at Cape Sounion, Attica on July 13, 2002.

Q: What is a restoration architect?

A: Well, basically I pull apart ancient sites, obsessing over every stone, and try to reconstruct the image.

Q: Did you study here in Athens?

A: I've been working and studying in Athens for 5 years. I received my masters from Vanderbilt University in Art History and then my Ph.D. from the American School of Classical Studies.

Q: What projects are you undertaking during the rest of the year?

A: I'm currently excavating the Nike Temple on the Acropolis.

Q: Impressive. How did you manage to get that assignment?

A: Well, I was studying here in 1996, and I was on the Acropolis with my advisor, Olga Palagia, one of the most renowned archaeologists and scholars, who teaches at the University of Athens. I kept asking her all of these questions, and she was unable to answer them all because no one knew the answers to them. So she asked me to come back and work with her. It was pretty surreal.

Q: Is the program classroom oriented?

A: No, we travel around Greece and into Turkey to visit the principle archaeological sites and museums. Lectures are given on site.

Q: Is it open to anyone interested?

A: As long as you can speak basic English, you're welcome to enroll.

210 72 50 584; info@ascsa.edu.gr; www.ascsa.org), is a competitive school offering a variety of archaeological and classical studies programs for undergraduates, graduate students, and Ph.D. candidates. Visit the website to find a list of publications and links to other archaeological programs.

WORKING

There are two schools of thought when it comes to working abroad. Some travelers want long-term jobs that allow them to get to know another part of the world in depth (e.g. teaching English, working in the tourist industry). Other travelers seek out short-term jobs to finance their travel. They usually look for employment in the service sector or in agriculture, working for a few weeks at a time to finance the next leg of their journey. This section discusses both short-term and long-term opportunities for working in Greece. Make sure you understand Greece's **visa requirements** for working abroad; See the box on p. 67 for more information.

Those who can teach English find a host of job openings in Greece, and in some sectors (like agricultural work) permit-less workers are rarely bothered by authorities. Students can check with their universities' foreign language departments, which may have connections to jobs abroad. Friends in Greece can expedite work permits or arrange work-for-accommodations swaps.

For US college students, recent graduates, and young adults, the simplest way to get legal permission to work abroad is through **Council Exchanges Work Abroad Programs.** Fees are from US$300-425. Council Exchanges can help you obtain a three- to six-month work permit and also provides assistance finding jobs and housing.

LONG-TERM WORK

If you're planning on spending a substantial amount of time (more than three months) working in Greece, search for a job well in advance. International placement agencies are often the easiest way to find employment abroad, especially for jobs teaching English. **Internships,** usually for college students, are a good introduction to work abroad, though they are often unpaid or poorly paid (many say the experience, however, is well worth it). Be wary of advertisements or companies that claim the ability to get you a job abroad for a fee—often times the same listings are available online or in newspapers or may be out of date. **AIESEC International**, (Various international locations; in the US 127 W 26th St., Floor 10, New York, NY 10001 USA; ☎212-757-4062; www.aiesec.org) offers paid internships in business and technology fields in over 80 countries, including Greece.

TEACHING ENGLISH

Teaching jobs abroad are rarely well-paid, although some elite private American schools pay somewhat competitive salaries. Volunteering as a teacher in lieu of getting paid is also a popular option, and even in those cases, teachers often get some sort of a daily stipend to help with living expenses. In almost all cases, you must have at least a bachelor's degree to be a full-fledged teacher, although often times college undergraduates can get summer positions teaching or tutoring. Those who wish to teach English in Greece should have a university degree (preferably in English literature or history) and a solid command of English. To obtain a teaching license, you must present your diploma and your passport translated into Greek; contact the Hellenic Ministry of Education for more information (Mitropoleos 15, Athens 10185 or call ☎210 323 1656; www.ypepth.gr).

Greek schools rarely require teachers to have a **Teaching English as a Foreign Language (TEFL)** certificate, but certified teachers often find higher paying jobs. Native English speakers working in private schools are most often hired for English-immersion classrooms where no Greek is spoken. Placement agencies or university fellowship programs are the best resources for finding teaching jobs in Greece. The alternative is to make contacts directly with schools or just to try your luck once you get there. If you are going to try the latter, the best time of the year is several weeks before the start of the school year. The following organizations are extremely helpful in placing teachers in Greece.

International Schools Services (ISS), 15 Roszel Rd., Box 5910, Princeton, NJ 08543-5910, USA (☎609-452-0990; fax 609-452-2690; www.iss.edu). Recruits teachers and administrators for American and English schools in Greece. All instruction in English. Candidates should have experience teaching or with international affairs; 2-year commitment expected.

Office of Overseas Schools, US Department of State, Room H328, SA-1, Washington, D.C. 20522 (☎202-261-8200; fax 261-8224; OverseasSchools@state.gov; www.state.gov/www/about_state/schools). Keeps a comprehensive list of schools abroad and agencies that arrange placement for Americans to teach abroad.

Fulbright English Teaching Assistantship, U.S. Student Programs Division, Institute of International Education, 809 United Nations Plaza, New York, NY 10017-3580, USA (☎212-984-5330; www.iie.org). Competitive program sends college graduates to teach a 6-week classics seminar in Greece.

AU PAIR WORK

Au pairs are typically women, aged 18-27, who work as live-in nannies, caring for children and doing light housework in foreign countries in exchange for room, board, and a small spending allowance or stipend. Most former au pairs speak favorably of their experience, and of how it allowed them to experience the country without the high expenses of traveling. Drawbacks, however, often include long hours of constantly being on-duty, and the somewhat mediocre pay. Au pairs in Greece generally work 30-45 hours a week, including a few evenings for €45-70 per week, depending on the number of children, duties, and qualifications. Much of the au pair experience depends on the family you're placed with. The agencies below are a good starting point for looking for employment as an au pair.

Accord Cultural Exchange, 750 La Playa, San Francisco, CA 94121, USA (☎415-386-6203; www.cognitext.com/accord).

Au Pair in Europe, P.O. Box 68056, Blakely Postal Outlet, Hamilton, Ontario, Canada L8M 3M7 (☎905-545-6305; fax 905-544-4121; www.princeent.com).

Athenian Nanny Agency, P.O. Box 51181, Kifissia T.K., 145.10 Athens (☎/fax 301 808 1005; mskinti@groovy.gr).

Luck Locketts & Vanessa Bancroft Nanny and Domestic Agency, 400 Beacon Rd., Wibsey, Bradford, West Yorkshire BD6 3DJ (☎/fax 212 74 402 822; www.lucylocketts.com). Places au pairs and experienced nannies in Greece.

SHORT-TERM WORK

Traveling for long periods of time can get expensive; therefore, many travelers try their hand at odd jobs for a few weeks at a time to make some extra cash to carry them through another month or two of touring around. For citizens of Greece and of EU countries, getting a job in Greece is relatively simple. For all others, finding work in Greece can be difficult. Job opportunities are scarce and the government tries to restrict employment to citizens and visitors from the EU. If your parents were born in an EU country, you may be able to claim dual citizenship or at least the right to a work permit.

THE 2004 GAMES

A GOLDEN OPPORTUNITY

Approximately 16,000 athletes, 20,000 journalists, and seven million spectators will descend on Greece in August 2004—and you could be the one showing them to the stadium.

The Athens 2004 Organizing Committee estimates that a total of 60,000 volunteers are necessary to carry out the Olympic and Paralympic Games, and the volunteer program offers the opportunity to see the world's most prestigious athletic competition from the inside. Positions are largely short term (5-10 days), but volunteers will be needed for various jobs from May through September.

The Greek government is calling for local volunteers in order to rally much-needed support for the Games, and Cyprus has promised to sign up 5,000 of its own citizens. However, foreign volunteers will have to play a large part. Anyone who will be 18 years old by 2004 is welcome to apply. Online applications can be filled out and submitted at www.athens.olympics.org. Candidates will be interviewed, and those selected will be required to attend a training program.

A word to the wise: potential volunteers should secure their accommodations now, as Athens has already expressed concern about the inevitable housing crunch during the Games.

For more information and mail-in applications, call ☎210 200 4000 or e-mail volunteers@athens2004.com.

Arrive in the spring and early summer to search for **hotel jobs** (bartending, cleaning, etc.). Most night spots offer meager pay but don't require much paperwork. Check the bulletin boards of hostels in Athens and the classified ads in the *Athens News*. Most often, these short-term jobs are found by word of mouth, or simply by talking to the owner of a hostel or restaurant. The availability of short-term works varies wildly by region—your best bets are the most touristed areas, especially in the Cyclades. *Let's Go* tries to list temporary jobs like these whenever possible; check the practical information sections in larger cities, or check out the list below for some of the available short-term jobs in popular destinations.

Cafe Extrablatt, Alex. Svolou 46, Thessaloniki (☎2310 256 900), next to the youth hostel. Good level of Greek needed. Contact manager upon arrival. Pay negotiable.

Milos Beach Bar and Cafe, Skala, Kephalonia. (☎26710 83 188; in winter ☎26710 83 231). Hires waitstaff and bartenders for tourist season; summer hiring begins in February and March. Call in advance and ask for Joya Grouzi.

Melissani Restaurant and Snack Bar, Sami, Kephalonia (☎26740 22 395). This large beach bar is one of a few in the Ionian Islands that considers foreign job applicants. Call in advance.

The Pink Palace, Agios Gordios, Corfu (☎26610 53 103). Hires hotel staff, nightclub staff, and DJs. Send a letter of introduction, a resume, and a photo to Dr. George at the above address. Minimum 2 month commitment required.

VOLUNTEERING

Greece is one of the most hospitable countries in Europe; opportunities to return the favor abound in the form of volunteer organizations. Many volunteer services charge you a fee to participate in the program and to do work. These fees can be surprisingly hefty (although they frequently cover airfare and most, if not all, living expenses). Try to do research on a program before committing—talk to people who have previously participated and find out exactly what you're getting into, as living and working conditions can vary greatly. Different programs are geared toward different ages and levels of experience, so be sure to make sure that you are not taking on too much or too little. The more informed you are and the more realistic expectations you have, the more enjoyable the program will be.

Most people choose to go through a parent organization that takes care of logistical details, and frequently provides a group environment and support system. There are two main types of organizations—religious (often Catholic), and non-sectarian—although there are rarely restrictions on participation for either.

Most volunteer opportunities in Greece focus on conservation; there are several Greek non-profits dedicated to preserving local flora and fauna. Cultural organizations and local festivals also require short-term volunteer power; look for posters and flyers around town.

The 2004 Summer Olympics and Paralympic Games (see sidebar, p. 72) are seeking upwards of 60,000 volunteers to assist with the running of the Games between May and September. Placements are available at competition and non-competition venues; knowledge of foreign languages strongly desired.

Archelon Sea Turtle Protection Society, Solomou 57, GR-104 32, Athens (☎/fax 210 523 1342; stps@archelon.gr; www.archelon.gr). Non-profit group devoted to studying and protecting sea turtles on the beaches of Zakynthos, Crete, and the Peloponnese. Opportunities for seasonal field work and year-round work at the rehabilitation center. €70/$65 participation fee includes lodging for work at the center. (Field volunteers are have private campgrounds but must provide their own camping equipment).

Conservation Volunteers Greece, Omirou 15, GR-14562, Kifissia, Greece (☎010 623 1120; cvgpeep@otenet.gr; users.otenet.gr/~cvgpeep). Young volunteers (ages 18-30) participate in 1- to 3-week community programs in remote areas of Greece. Projects range from reforestation to preserving archaeological sites. Lodging provided.

Elderhostel, Inc., 11 Avenue de Lafayette, Boston, MA 92111-1746, USA (☎877-426-8056; fax 877-426-2166; www.elderhostel.org). Sends volunteers age 55 and over around the world to work in construction, research, teaching, and many other projects. Costs average US$100 per day plus airfare.

Service Civil International Voluntary Service (SCI-IVS), SCI USA, 3213 W. Wheeler St., Seattle, WA 98199, USA (☎/fax 206-350-6585; www.sci-ivs.org). Arranges placement in work camps in Greece for those 18+. Registration fee US$65-125.

Volunteers for Peace, 1034 Tiffany Rd., Belmont., VT 05730, USA (☎802-259-2759; www.vfp.org). Arranges placement in work camps in Greece. Membership required for registration. Annual *International Workcamp Directory* US$20. Programs average US$200-500 for 2-3 weeks.

FURTHER READING ON ALTERNATIVES TO TOURISM

Alternatives to the Peace Corps: A Directory of Third World and U.S. Volunteer Opportunities, by Joan Powell. Food First Books, 2000 (US$10).

How to Get a Job in Europe, by Sanborn and Matherly. Surrey Books, 1999 (US$22).

How to Live Your Dream of Volunteering Overseas, by Collins, DeZerega, and Heckscher. Penguin Books, 2002 (US$17).

International Directory of Voluntary Work, by Whetter and Pybus. Peterson's Guides and Vacation Work, 2000 (US$16).

International Jobs, by Kocher and Segal. Perseus Books, 1999 (US$18).

Overseas Summer Jobs 2002, by Collier and Woodworth. Peterson's Guides and Vacation Work, 2002 (US$18).

Work Abroad: The Complete Guide to Finding a Job Overseas, by Hubbs, Griffith, and Nolting. Transitions Abroad Publishing, 2000 (US$16).

Work Your Way Around the World, by Susan Griffith. Worldview Publishing Services, 2001 (US$18).

ATHENS Αθηνα

Athens, the eye of Greece, mother of arts
And eloquence.
—John Milton

One minute of dodging the packs of mopeds in Pl. Syndagma will prove that Athens refuses to become a museum. The city's past and present coexist in a strange yet beautiful harmony. Ancient ruins sit quietly amid the hectic modern streets as quiet testaments to its rich history, and the Acropolis looms larger than life over the city, a perpetual reminder of ancient glory. Hellenistic monuments and Byzantine churches recall an era of foreign invaders, when Athens was ruled from Macedonia, Rome, and Constantinople. The reborn democracy of the past two centuries has revived the city in a wave of madcap construction: the conflicted, oddly adolescent metropolis has gutted its crumbling medieval mansions to become a dense concrete jungle.

Countless vantage points from Athens's seven hills look out over this sprawling work of centuries: Lycavittos, the Acropolis, Pnyx, Strefi, Phillippapou, Hymettus, and the Hill of the Nymphs. Crowded, noisy, polluted, and totally alive, Athens will get you stuck in traffic at 2am on a Tuesday. An efficient new subway system is up and running; it should be completed for the 2004 Olympic Summer Games. Still, civil engineers refuse to destroy the past for the sake of the Metro picking their way among subterranean antiquities, cisterns, and the springs of lost, ancient rivers that sleep beneath the city.

ATHENS

HIGHLIGHTS OF ATHENS

STRUT IT PAST CHIC OUTDOOR CAFES in Kolonaki (p. 86, p. 95), then shake it at the hotspot seaside clubs of Glyfada (p. 95).

LOSE YOURSELF amid ancient relics at the National Archaeological Museum (p. 103).

AMBLE THROUGH THE MEDIEVAL ALLEYWAYS of Plaka (p. 81).

MAKE A PILGRIMAGE to Athena's Parthenon on the Acropolis (p. 98).

HAGGLE with wily merchants at Monastiraki's flea market (p. 86).

SCORE A WINK from the skirted, tasseled *evzones* who guard the Parliament building in Pl. Syndagma (p. 81).

HISTORY

Athens's mythological history began when the Olympian gods got in a tug-of-war over who would be the Attic city's patron and namesake. They decided that whoever gave it the best gift would earn the city. **Poseidon** struck the Acropolis with his trident, and a sea water gushed forth from a well. But **Athena's** wiser gift, an olive tree, won the city's lasting admiration and worship. Rising to political power as early as the 16th century BC, Athens was united as a *polis*, or city-state, by the hero **Theseus** (onetime slayer of the Minotaur). By the 8th century, it had become the artistic center of Greece; initial fame for geometric pottery foreshadowed a shining future. Two centuries later, law-giver and poet **Solon** ended the servitude of native citizens and restored rights to some slaves. Maybe his most important contribution to Athenian government was his codification of the laws, thereby providing the grounding needed for a successful democracy: an informed populace able to take part in ruling. After victories over the Persians at Marathon and Salamis in the 5th century BC, Athens experienced a 70-year **Golden Age** under the democracy of Pericles, the era that produced the Parthenon; the masterpiece tragedies of Aeschylus, Sophocles, and Euripides; and Aristophanes's ribald comedies.

Pericles's Athens fell apart during the bloody, drawn-out **Peloponnesian War** (431-404 BC) against Sparta. Political power shifted north under Philip of Macedon and his son **Alexander the Great,** but Athens remained a cultural center throughout the 5th and 4th centuries BC. In this period, Athens produced three of the most influential philosophers in western history—**Socrates, Plato,** and **Aristotle**—as well as the orator **Demosthenes.** By the 2nd century AD, the **Roman Empire** ruled the city. In AD 324, Emperor Constantine moved the capital of the Roman Empire to Byzantium, ignoring Athens, now an overtaxed backwater. It remained the center of Greek education, but its status (and buildings) lapsed into ruin when the emperor Justinian banned the teaching of philosophy in 529.

Around AD 1000, Byzantine emperor **Basil II** visited Athens. After praying to the Virgin Mary in the Parthenon, Basil ordered craftsmen to restore Athens to its former glory. The city was reborn again and again under successive conquerors—the Franks in 1205, the Catalans in 1311, the Accajioli merchant family in 1387, and the **Ottomans,** whose 400-year rule began in 1456. In 1821, Greek independence brought further waves of renovation and restoration, as well as a spirit of nationalism. Modern Athens's plateias, wide boulevards, and National Garden follow the plan of architects hired by Greece's first king, the German prince Otto (p. 12).

Athens's population and commercial output have skyrocketed in the past century. A 1923 **population exchange** with Turkey brought an influx of ethnic Greeks from Turkish land, swelling the city, and since then rural workers have flocked to industrial jobs here. In the past 100 years, the city's population has exploded from a count of 169 families to almost half of Greece's 10.5 million residents. The preparations for the 2004 Olympic Games have sparked another urban renewal, as the transit authority fights the sinister *nefos* (smog) by banning cars from historic Plaka, limiting driver access downtown, and building a new mass transit subway.

INTERCITY TRANSPORTATION

Flights: El. Venizelou, Greece's new international airport, operates as 1 massive, yet easily navigable terminal (☎210 353 0000). Arrivals are on the ground floor, departures on the 2nd floor. 4 bus lines run to and from El. Venizelou from Athens, Piraeus, and Rafina. To get from Pl. Syndagma in the Athens city center take the **E95** (40min., every 20min., €3). Pick it up on Amalias, to the right of the top right corner of Pl. Syndagma. To get from the Ethniki Amyna subway station, take either the **E94** (every 10min. 7:30am-11:30pm; wait by the subway exit). Take the **E96** from Piraeus (every 30min. 6am-10:55am, every 20min. 11:20am-11pm, every 40min. 11pm-6am; in the square of busy Akti Tzelepi, across from Phillipis Travel). The bus from Rafina leaves every 30min. from the stop midway up the ramp from the waterfront. Buses deposit you at one of the 4 departure entrances; look at the screens to determine which desks are checking in your flight. Buses wait outside the 5 arrivals exits; walk out of the terminal and look for your bus number, or enter the taxi queue. A **taxi** costs €8-10 (€11-13 after midnight), with an extra €0.30 charge for each piece of luggage over 10kg, and a €1.18 surcharge from the airport. Watch drivers carefully; some have been known to rig the meters. Drivers may be unwilling to pick up travelers laden with luggage.

Buses: Terminal A: Kifissou 100 (☎210 512 4910 or 210 513 2601). Take blue bus **#051** from the corner of Zinonos and Menandrou near Pl. Omonia (every 15min. 5am-11:30pm, €0.45). Don't mistake the private travel agency at Terminal A for an information booth. Buses depart for: **Corinth** (1½hr., 1 per hr. 5:50am-10:30pm, €5.70); **Corfu** (10hr., 4 per day 7am-8:30pm,

FROM THE ROAD

METRO MAYHEM

Greece in the summer is notoriously arid. Months go by without a drop of rain, but I learned quickly that, when it does rain, it pours. Having finished my research in Piraeus for the day, I collapsed onto my seat in the Metro. The frenzy of the port was behind me, and I had managed to escape just before the rain started. Smiling at my own good luck, I looked out of the window as we left the station and was surprised that the slight drizzle was beginning to fall faster. Soon the rain was a torrent. I was unprepared for this sort of storm during the summer. It turns out the city was, too. Before we even pulled away from the station, Piraeus was veiled by a sheet of rain.

As the metro moved slowly forward, we came alongside roads completely covered in water. Cars were inching along, hydroplaning across the surface. The metro came to a halt at the Petralona station and didn't budge. A voice come over the loudspeaker, informing us that we would have to wait. A grumble echoed through the car. I pulled out my book and began reading, but the cacophony of cell phone rings and the irritated voices of my fellow metro passengers were impossibly distracting. About 30 minutes later, the PA stirred to life again: the train wasn't going anywhere for awhile. The voice recommended walking home or staying in the train and waiting out the rains. I looked outside at the flooded streets, swallowed hard, and looked at my feet. Flip flops and floods are not a good combination.

€27.90); **Igoumenitsa** (8hr., 5 per day 6:30am-9pm, €28.45); **Patras** (3hr., 30 per day 5:30am-9:45pm, €12.25); **Thessaloniki** (6hr., 11 per day 7am-11pm, €28) via **Larissa.**

Terminal B: Liossion 260 (☎210 831 7153, except Sa-Su). Take blue bus **#024** from Amalias outside the National Gardens or Panepistimiou (45min., every 20min. 5am-midnight, €0.45). Watch the numbers on street signs–Liossion 260 is near several car mechanic shops. Buses depart for: **Delphi** (3hr., 6 per day 7:30am-8pm, €10.20); **Halkida** on **Evia** (1¼hr.; every 30min. 5:30am-9pm, with extra buses on Su; €4.50); **Katerini** (6hr., 3 per day 9:45am-10pm, €24.70).

Mavromateon 29: in Exarhia, between the National Archaeological Museum and Areos Park; take **trolley #18, 11, 5, 2,** or **9.** Buses to: **Marathon** (1½hr., every hr. 6am-10:30pm, €2.40); **Rafina** (1hr., every 30min. 5:40am-10:30pm, €1.55); **Sounion** (2hr., every hr. 5:45am-5:45pm, €4; or 2¼hr., every hr. 6am-6pm, €4).

Pl. Eleftherias: from Pl. Syndagma, go west on Ermou, turn right on Athinas, and turn left on Evripidou. Buses to **Eleusis** and **Daphni.**

Ferries: Check schedules at the tourist office, in the *Athens News,* with the Port Authority of Piraeus (☎210 422 6000), over the phone (☎143), or at any travel agency. Ferry schedules change daily; check close to your departure and be flexible. Most ferries dock at **Piraeus** (p. 106); others at nearby **Rafina** (p. 106). Those headed for the Sporades leave from **Ag. Konstantinos** (p. 196) or **Volos** (p. 197). Those bound for the Ionian Islands leave from **Patras** (p. 131), **Kyllini** (p. 140), and **Igoumenitsa** (p. 239).

Piraeus: Take **Line 1** on the subway south to its end, or take green **bus #40** from Filellinon and Mitropoleos (every 10min.). To: **Iraklion, Hania,** and **Rethymno,** Crete. Also to: **Aegina, Poros, Spetses,** and **Hydra; Chios** and **Lesvos; Ios, Mykonos, Naxos,** and **Paros; Rhodes, Santorini,** and **Sifnos; Kythnos, Serifos,** and **Milos.** International ferries run to **Limassol, Cyprus; Port Said, Egypt;** and **Haifa, Israel.** See **Piraeus** (p. 108) for prices, frequencies, and trip durations.

Rafina: Buses depart from Mavromateon 29, 2 blocks up along Areos Park, or a 15min. walk from Syndagma Square. (1hr., every 30min. 5:40am-10:30pm, €1.55). Ferries to: **Marmari** in Evia, **Andros, Tinos, Mykonos,** and **Naxos.** High-speed **catamarans** (often known as **Flying Dolphins**) sail to: **Andros, Amorgos, Mykonos, Paros, Syros,** and **Tinos. Nel Lines** goes to: **Ag. Efstratios, Limnos, Kavala,** and **Lesvos.** See **Rafina** (p. 110) for prices, frequencies, and trip durations.

Trains: Hellenic Railways (OSE), Sina 6 (☎210 362 4402; www.ose.gr). Call ☎210 529 7777 for reservations or the Greek Railway Organization (☎210 362 4402 or 210 529 7777) for information.☎145 or 147 lists timetables in Greek. Contact the railway offices to confirm schedules before your trip.

Larisis Train Station (☎210 529 8837 or 210 823 7741) serves northern Greece and Europe. Open 24hr. Take **trolley #1** from El. Venizelou (Panepistimiou) in Pl. Syndagma (every 10min. 5am-midnight, €0.45), or take the subway to Sepolia. Trains depart for: **Thessaloniki** (7hr., 4 per day, €14.10; express 5½hr., 6 per day, €27.60); **Bratislava, Slovakia** (€88.40); **Prague, Czech Republic** (€128.60); **Bucharest, Romania**(€53.60); **Budapest, Hungary** (€94.40). To get to Sofia, Istanbul, Bratislava, Prague, Bucharest, and Budapest, take the train from Larisis Station to Thessaloniki and change there; a €24.30 surcharge is included in above prices.

Peloponnese Train Station (☎210 513 1601; 210 529 8739 for buses to Albania, Bulgaria, and Turkey) is in a Victorian building with a silver roof. Open 24hr. From Larisis Station, exit to your right and go over the footbridge; from El. Venizelou (Panepistimiou) in Syndagma, take blue bus **#057** (every 15min. 5:30am-11:30pm, €0.45). Serves **Patras** (4¼hr., €5.30; express 3½hr., €10) and major towns in the Peloponnese.

Luggage Storage: There are lockers at El. Venizelou airport to the left of the Arrivals exits (from €3 per item per day). Open 24hr. Also several offices on Nikis and Filellinon, including **Pacific Ltd.**, Nikis 26 (☎210 324 1007). €2 per day, €7 per week, €30 per month. Open M-Sa 8am-8pm, Su 8am-2pm. Many **hotels** and **hostels** have free or inexpensive luggage storage.

LOCAL TRANSPORTATION

Buses: KTEL (KTEΛ) buses are punctual, so be on time. Buses around Athens and its suburbs are blue or orange and are designated by 3-digit numbers. These buses are good for travel throughout the city and ideal for daytrips to Daphni and Kesariani. Buy blue bus/trolley **tickets** (good for both) at any street **kiosk** and validate it yourself at the orange machine on board. A standard 1-way ticket for a bus or a trolley costs €0.45. Kiosks only sell tickets for Athens and its suburbs; buy several tickets at once if you plan to use buses and trolleys frequently, or buy the "Airport 24hr." ticket (€2.90), which grants unlimited travel on city bus, trolley, and subway within 24hr. of its validation and need not be used to get to the airport. **Hold on to your ticket:** if you drop or don't validate your ticket—even when it seems like nobody is there to make you pay—you can be fined €18-30 on the spot by police. Children under 6 ride free. The tourist office's map of Athens has the most frequented **routes** labeled on it. Buses run M-Sa 5am-11:30pm, Su and public holidays 5:30am-11:30pm. **24hr. service** on the **E95** from Syndagma to El. Venizelou airport, **E96** from Piraeus to El. Venizelou airport, and **040** from Piraeus to Syndagma. Check urban bus schedules (☎185) and domestic bus schedules (☎210 512 4910).

So I turned back to my book. The doors opened and closed sporadically, letting passengers come and go. Most went and returned with food and drink, completely soaked. 2½ hours later (and only 3 pages farther along in my book), the rain stopped. The message on the loudspeaker never changed. I made an executive decision: it was time to hit the road. My neighbor gawked when I told her I was walking to Plaka. 45 minutes of trudging through puddles and wading through small sidewalk lakes led me to a warm, inviting bed. My adventure was over. Still, it was frightening to think that the city had shut down around me. Even in a city as large and important as Athens, a summer rainstorm can grind all action to a halt.

—Scottie Thompson

Trolleys: Yellow, crowded, and sporting 1- or 2-digit numbers, trolleys are distinguished from buses by their electrical antennae. Trolleys don't accept money; buy a trolley/bus **ticket** ahead of time at a **kiosk** (€0.45). Service is frequent and convenient for short hops within town. See the detailed tourist office map for trolley **routes** and stops. Trolleys operate M-Sa 5am-midnight, Su and public holidays 5:30am-midnight.

Subway: In preparation for the 2004 Olympics, Athens is expanding and improving its **Metro.** The underground network consists of 3 lines. **M1,** the green line, runs from northern Kifissia to the port of Piraeus. **M2,** the red line, runs from Ag. Antonios to Dafni. When the planned extensions are completed, M2 will continue from Ag. Antonios to Thivon and from Dafni to Glyfada by the Saronic Gulf. **M3,** the blue line, runs from Ethniki Amyna to Syndagma in central Athens. M3 will continue from Syndagma through Monastiraki to Egaleo and from Ethniki Amyna to Stavros, where a rail line will connect to the airport. There will also be a M3 extension from Panormou to Paradissos. The standard ticket of €0.70 allows for travel along any of the lines (transfer is permitted) in one direction, for up to 90min. after its validation. Buy tickets at Metro stations for €0.60, which permits travel along 1 or 2 subsequent zones of M1. Tell the cashier your destination, and you'll get the right ticket. Trains run 5am-midnight. Remember to **hold on to your ticket** to avoid a fine.

Taxis: Meter **rates** start at €0.74, with an additional €0.24 per km. Everything beyond the start price is €0.44 per km between midnight and 5am. There's a €1.18 surcharge for trips from the airport, and a €0.60 surcharge for trips from port, bus, and railway terminals; add €0.30 extra for each piece of luggage over 10kg. Pay what the meter shows rounded up to the next €0.20 as a **tip.** Hail your taxi by shouting your destination—not the street address, but the area (e.g. "Pangrati"). The driver will pick you up if he feels like heading that way. Get in the cab and tell the driver the exact address or site. Many drivers don't speak English, so write your destination down, in Greek if possible; include the area of the city, since streets in different parts of the city may share the same name. It's common to ride with other passengers going in the same direction. For an extra €1.50, call a radio taxi: **Ikaros** (☎210 515 2800); **Ermis** (☎210 411 5200); **Kosmos** (☎210 801 1300). Get a full list in the *Athens News*.

Car Rental: Try the places on **Syngrou.** €35-50 for a car with 100km mileage (including tax and insurance). Student discounts up to 50%. Prices rise in summer.

ATHENS

PRACTICAL INFORMATION

TOURIST AND FINANCIAL SERVICES

Tourist Office: The **central office** and **information booth** are at Amerikis 2 (☎210 331 0565; fax 210 321 0562. Open M-F 9am-4:30pm), off Stadiou near Pl. Syndagma. Bus, train, and ferry schedules and prices; lists of museums, embassies, and banks; brochures on travel throughout Greece; and an indispensable Athens **map.**

Travel Agencies: STA Travel, Voulis 43. (☎/fax 210 321 1194; cg@robissa.gr. Open M-F 9:30am-5pm, Sa 10am-2pm.) **Consolas Travel,** Aiolou 100 (☎210 321 9228; fax 210 321 0907; info@consolas.gr), next to the post office; a second office is at Filellinon 18 (☎210 322 6657). Other budget travel agencies are along Nikis. **Adrianos Travel, Ltd.,** Pandrossou 28, near Mitropoli Cathedral in Plaka. (☎210 323 1015; fax 210 324 8657; info@adrianostravel.gr. Open M-F 9am-4pm, Sa 10am-1pm.)

Banks: National Bank of Greece, Karageorgi Servias 2 (☎210 334 0015), in Pl. Syndagma. Open M-Th 8am-2pm, F 8am-1:30pm; open for currency exchange only M-Th 3:30-5:20pm, F 3-6:30pm, Sa 9am-3pm, Su 9am-1pm. American Express, the post office, some hotels, and other banks (list available at tourist office) offer **currency exchange.** Commissions of about 5%. 24hr. currency exchange at the airport, but commissions there may be exorbitant.

American Express: Ermou 7 (☎210 322 3380), around the corner from McDonald's in Pl. Syndagma. This air-conditioned office cashes traveler's checks commission-free, exchanges money for small commissions, and provides travel services for AmEx cardholders. Open M-F 8:30am-4pm, Sa 8:30am-1:30pm.

LOCAL SERVICES

International Bookstores: Eleftheroudakis Book Store, Panepistimiou 17 (☎210 331 4180) and Nikis 20 (☎210 322 9388). A browser's delight, with classical and recent literature in Greek, English, French, and German. Open M-F 9am-9pm, Sa 9am-3pm. **Pantelides Books,** Amerikis 11 (☎210 362 3673), overflows with variety in English. Open M and Sa 9am-3pm, Tu-F 9am-8pm. **Compendium Bookshop,** Nikis 28 (☎210 322 1248), has popular new and used books, large fiction and poetry sections, poetry readings in winter, and a **children's book room.** Open M-F 8:30am-4:30pm, Tu and Th-F 4:30-8:30pm, Sa 9am-3pm.

Libraries: The **American Library,** Massalias 22 (☎210 363 8114), on the 4th fl. of the Hellenic American Union behind the university. Open M and Th 3-7pm, Tu-W and F 11am-3pm. The 7th fl. has a **Greek Library** (☎210 362 9886), with English books on Greece. Open M-Th 9am-8pm, F 9am-5pm. The **British Council Library** (☎210 363 3211), Pl. Kolonaki 17, is open Sept.-May M-F 9:30am-1:30pm and Tu-W 5:30-8pm. Open morning hours only in June and July. Closed in August.

Laundromats: Most *plintirios* have signs reading "Laundry." Be sure to specify that you don't mind mixing colors, or you'll end up paying for several loads. At **Angelou Geront 10** in Plaka, a kind Greek grandmother will wash, dry, and fold your laundry for €8. Open M-Sa 8am-7pm, Su 9am-2pm. Syndagma has **National,** a laundromat and dry cleaners, at Apollonos 17 (☎210 323 2266; wash and dry €4.50 per kg; open M-Th 8am-5pm, F 8am-8pm); or go to **Zenith** at Apollonos 12 and Pentelis 1 (☎210 323 8533; wash and dry €4.40 per kg; open M and W 8am-4pm, Tu and Th-F 8am-8pm). Launder one load for €8 near the train stations, at **Psaron 9** (☎210 522 2856; open M-F 8am-9pm, Sa 8am-5pm, Su 8am-2pm), or get the same for €7.50 at **Favierou 3** and **Mager,** near Pl. Vathis. (☎210 524 8580. Open M-F 8am-9pm, Sa 8am-5pm.)

TAXI SMART Beware! Some drivers tinker with their meters, while others may not turn on the meter at all, taking you somewhere and then charging an exorbitant fee. Ask the cost of the fare in advance, and if you don't see the meter running, yell "Meter! Meter!" In addition, if you ask for a hotel, the taxi driver may have another one in mind for you—a hotel that has paid him off. Be firm about where you're going; don't trust a driver who says your hotel is closed or that there are no hostels in town.

EMERGENCY AND COMMUNICATIONS

Telephone Number Information: ☎131.

Emergencies: Police (☎100). **Doctors** (☎105 from Athens, 101 elsewhere; line open 2pm-7am). **Ambulance** (☎161). **Poison control** (☎210 779 3777). **Fire** (☎199). **AIDS Help Line** (☎210 722 2222). *Athens News* lists emergency hospitals. Free emergency health care for tourists.

Tourist Police: Dimitrakopoulou 77 (☎171). Great for information, assistance, and emergencies. English spoken. Open 24hr.

Pharmacies: Marked by a **red** (signifying a doctor) or **green cross** hanging over the street. They're everywhere. Many are open 24hr.; check *Athens News* "Useful Information," which lists the day's emergency pharmacies, or see charts in pharmacy windows.

Hospitals: Emergency hospitals/clinics on duty can be reached at ☎106. **Geniko Kratiko Nosokomio** (Public State Hospital), Mesogion 154 (☎210 777 8901). **Ygeia,** Erithrou Stavrou 4 (☎210 682 7904), is a private hospital in Maroussi. **Aeginitio** state hospital, Vas. Sofias 72 (☎210 722 0811) and Vas. Sofias 80 (☎210 777 0501), is closer to Athens's center. Near Kolonaki is the public hospital **Evangelismos,** Ypsilantou 45-47 (☎210 722 0101). "Hospital" is *nosokomio* in Greek.

Post Offices: Syndagma (☎210 322 6253), on the corner of Mitropoleos; **postal code:** 10300. **Omonia,** Aiolou 100 (☎210 321 6023); **postal code:** 10200. **Exarhia,** at the corner of Zaimi and K. Deligiani; **postal code:** 10691. Open M-F 7:30am-8pm, Sa 7:30am-2pm. An **Acropolis/Plaka** branch (☎210 921 8076) sells stamps and has currency exchange; **postal code:** 11742.

Shipping: To send packages abroad, try parcel post, **Mitropoleos 60** (☎210 324 2489; open M-F 7:30am-7:30pm) and **Nikis 33** (open M-F 7:30am-2pm).

Internet Access:

Berval Internet Access, Voulis 44A (☎ 210 331 1294 or 210 331 1857; berval1@hol.gr). On Voulis St. in **Plaka** and near **Pl. Syndagma,** right next to Berval Travel. Internet services, office support, digital imaging, and games. €5 per hr. Open daily 9am-9pm.

Carousel Cybercafe, Eftihidou 32 (☎210 756 4305), near Pl. Plastira in **Pangrati.** Wood-oven baked pizza after 6pm (€4.50). Internet €4.50 per hr. Open daily 11am-midnight.

Deligrece Internet Cafe, Akadamias 87 (☎210 330 2929; delice@otenet.gr), in **Exharia.** A cool place to hang out even if it didn't have Internet access, Deligrece has big-screen satellite TV broadcasts and cheap espresso (€2). Internet €2.35 per hr. Open daily 7:30am-midnight.

Internet Cafe, Stournari 49, in **Omonia.** Gaze at the city below while checking email (€2 per hr.) amid crowds of Athenian students. Open M-Sa 9am-9pm.

Internet World, Ek. Panolidou (☎210 331 6056), off Imittou. €1 per 15 min. Discount for Athens Center students. Open 11am-11:30pm.

Ivis Internet Services, Mitropoleos 3 (☎210 324 3365 or 210 324 3543; fax 210 322 4205). On the 2nd fl. of the building across the street from the post office in **Syndagma.** Super-fast Internet connection, digital video cameras, word processing, color printing, scanning, and Photoshop for only €3 per hr., €1.40 minimum. Open daily 8:30am-midnight.

Moc@fe Internet Cafe, Marni 49 (☎210 522 7717), in **Omonia** near Karaiskaki Sq. This hip cafe serves up coffee and beer in addition to reasonably priced Internet access. €3.60 per hr. Enjoy Happy Hour at the computer and the bar every evening in August. Open 9am-2am.

Museum Internet Cafe, Patission 46 (☎210 883 3418; museum_net_cafe@yahoo.com), in **Exharia.** After visiting the Archaeological Museum, cherish modern innovations: frothy coffee drinks and email. €4.40 per hr., €1.50 per 20min. Cappuccino €2.35, beer €2-3.55.

Plaka Internet World, Pandrossou 29, 4th fl. (☎210 331 6056; plakaworld@internet.gr) in **Plaka.** €6 per hr.

Rendez-Vous Cafe, Voulis 18 (☎/fax 210 322 3158; cafemeeting@hotmail.com) in **Syndagma.** Sip on coffee or snack on sweets while computing. €3.70 per hr.; €1.20 minimum. Open Tu, Th, F 7:30am-9pm and M,W, Sa 7:30am-6pm.

Sofokleous.com Internet Cafe, Stadiou 5 (☎210 324 8105; sofos1@ath.forthnet.gr), just up Stadiou from Pl. **Syndagma.** Owner Giorgos Kolios is friendly and PC-proficient. Complimentary coffee. €4.40 per hr., €1.47 minimum. Open M-Sa 10am-10pm, Su 11am-7pm.

Skynet Internet Access, 10 Apollonos and 30 Voulis, in Syndagma (☎210 322 7551; fax 210 960 5228; www.skynet.gr). Provides Internet services, printers, quick connection, scanners, CD-Rom burners. €4.40 per hr., €1.47 minimum. Open M-F 9am-8:30pm, Sa 9am-3pm.

OTE: Patission 85 (☎210 821 4449 or 210 823 7040) or Athinas 50 (☎210 321 6699). Offers overseas collect calls, recent phonebooks for most European and Anglophone countries, and **currency exchange** (until 3pm). Open M-F 7am-9pm, Sa 8am-3pm, Su 9am-2pm. For information on **overseas calls** dial ☎161; for **directory assistance** in and outside Athens, dial ☎131. Most phone booths in the city operate by **tele-**

ATHENS

phone cards (€3, €5, or €20 at OTE offices, kiosks, and tourist shops). Push the "i" button on the phones for English instructions. For rate and general info call ☎ 134; for complaints, call ☎ 135; for a domestic English-speaking operator, call ☎ 151.

ORIENTATION

Athenian geography mystifies newcomers and natives alike. When you're trying to figure out the city, don't neglect the detailed **free maps** from the tourist office (p. 78): the city map includes bus, trolley, and subway routes, and the *Now in Athens* magazine has a more exacting street plan. If you lose your bearings, ask for directions back to well-lit **Syndagma** or look for a cab; if you get lost, the **Acropolis** (below which lie Plaka and Monastiraki) provides a reference point, as does **Mt. Lycavittos** (beneath which Kolonaki broods). Athenian streets often have **multiple spellings or names,** so check the map again before you panic about being lost.

Several English-language **publications** can help you navigate Athens. The weekly publication *Athens News* gives addresses, hours, and phone numbers for weekly happenings, as well as listings, news, and ferry information (€1). *Athenorama* lists entertainment information. Athens and its suburbs occupy seven hills in southwest Attica, near the coast. **Syndagma,** the central plateia containing the Parliament building, is encircled by the other major neighborhoods. Clockwise, they are: **Plaka, Monastiraki, Psiri, Omonia, Exarhia, Kolonaki,** and **Pangrati.** To get around, you can walk, take a trolley or bus, or use the efficient subway system (probably the easiest way). A half-hour car, bus, or taxi ride south takes you to the seaside suburb of **Glyfada,** where Bacchantes head to party. **Piraeus** is also to the south of Athens. The new airport is to the southeast.

SYNDAGMA. Pl. Syndagma (Συνταγμα; Constitution Square) stands at the center of Athens. The **Greek Parliament** occupies a pale yellow Neoclassical building on a large plateia uphill from the actual Syndagma square, on the edge of the **National Gardens,** once the royal gardens of Greece's Germanic monarchs. The **Greek National Tourist Office** (EOT), post office, American Express office, transportation terminals, and a number of travel agencies and banks ring the lower end of the Syndagma plateia. The subway stop is located at the upper end of the plateia, and airport buses stop uphill from it, along the road to the right. Budget-friendly travel offices, restaurants, and hotels line **Filellinon** and **Nikis,** parallel thoroughfares that head out from Syndagma toward Plaka. **Ermou** and **Mitropoleos,** which head toward Monastiraki, also cater to travelers on a budget. These streets are just removed enough to provide some nocturnal quiet and safety. The plateia itself buzzes around the clock: car and moped traffic mingles perilously with fearless pedestrians, and people-watchers can spy on lounging kids, mangy dogs, tourists and executives hailing cabs, blank-eyed drug addicts sharing sidewalks with street musicians, and brightly clad panhandlers begging for coins.

PLAKA. Southwest of Syndagma, Plaka (Πλακα) is the center of the old city and the home of most visitors to Athens. Busy at night, Plaka undergoes a daily transformation. Bustling and disorienting by morning, it becomes the perfect place to linger over a coffee and observe the hum of Athenian life after the sun goes down. Bounded by the city's two largest ancient monuments—the **Temple of Olympian Zeus** (p. 100) and the **Acropolis** (p. 95)—the neighborhood also contains the only medieval buildings to survive the double-edged shovel of archaeologists and the frantic building of the past decades. Many of the city's cheap hotels and tourist eateries are here, as are legions of *kamakia* ("octopus spearers," or pick-up artists) who cat-call passing women. Keep walking; harassment is usually only verbal.

National Archaeological Museum
Polytechnic University/School of Fine Arts
EXARHIA
PL. EXARHION
PL. VATHIS
OMONIA
PL. OMONIA
PL. KANINGOS
KARAISKAKI SQUARE
OSE
National Theatre
TO PELOPONNESE STATION (500 m) & LARISSIS STATION (600 m)
Opera House
Theater Museum
University
PL. THEATROU
OTE
PL. ELEFTHERIAS
PL. KLAFTHMONOS
PSIRI
TO KERAMEIKOS MUSEUM (75 m)
TO THISSION (50 m)
National Bank of Greece
MONASTIRAKI
SYNDAGMA
Hephaesteion
Agora
Agora Museum
Mitropoli Cathedral
Agios Eleftherios
American Express
Tomb of the Unknown Soldier
Olympic Airways
Popular Musical Instruments Museum
Agia Apostoli
Hellenic Railways (OSE)
TO PNYX HILL (100 m)
PLAKA
Jewish Museum
Agia Triada
Metamorphosis
Greek Folk Museum
Areopagus
Acropolis
Beulé Gate
Parthenon
Acropolis Museum
Lyssikrates Monument
Odeon of Herodes Atticus
Theatre of Dionysus
Hadrian's Arch
Temple of the Olympian Zeus
PHILOPAPPOU

K. Paleologou, Iliou, Mezonos, Fierou, Favierou, Psaron, Victor Hugo, Karolou, Akominatou, Sonierou, Liossion, Marni, Stournari, Solomou, Kapodistriou, Halkokondili, Veranzerou, Aristotelous, Tritis Septemvriou, Kaningos, Tzortz, Botassi, Bouboulinas, Zaimi, Sp. Trikoupi, Ikonomou, Soultani, Methonis, Eressou, Dervenion, Arahovis, Valtetsiou, A. Metaxa, M. Themistokleous, Em. Benaki, Messolongiou, Zoodochou Pigis, Har. Trikoupi, Mavromichali, Didotou, Asklipiou, Solonos, Skoufa, Massalias, Akadimias, Koumoundourou, Agiou Konstandinou, Satovriandou, Sokratous, Patission (28 Oktovriou), Nikitara, Gamvetta, Fidiou, Zinonos, Leonidou, Keramikou, Kolonou, Deligiorgi, Menandrou, P. Tsaldari, Agissilaou, Sapfous, Geraniou, Likourgou, Klisthenous, Athinas, Stadiou, G. Stavrou, Santaroza, Eleftheriou Venizelou, Arsaki, Ipokratous, Sofokleous, Kratinou, Pesmazoglou, (Panepistimiou), Aristogitonos, Evripidou, Dipilou, Sari, Aristofanous, Eshilou, Agiou Dimitriou, Aidou, Aristidou, Dragatsaniou, Edourard Lo, Sina, Omirou, Amerikis, Nika, Agion Anargiron, Ogigou, Lepenioti, Vissis, Hrissospiliotissass, Agiou Markou, Praxitelous, Hr. Lada, Miaouli, Kolokotroni, Perikleous, Karageorgi Servias, Leka, Voukourestiou, Ermou, Ifestou, Adrianou, Apolonos, Voulis, Nikis, Xenofontos, Diogenous, Kiristou, Lissiou, Nikodimou, Filellinon, Eretheos, Iperidou, Kodrou, Kydathineon, Tripodon, Dedalou, Amalias, Selley, Lyssikrates, Apostolou Pavlou, Dionissiou Areopagitou, Robertou Gali, Frati, Parthenonos, Kariatidon, Mitseon, Makrigianui, Ath. Drakou, Tsami Karatassi, Hatzihristou, Lembessi, Andrea Singrou, Ath. Diakou, Arditou, Markou Mousourou, Missaraliotou, Sofroniskou, Vasilissis Olgas

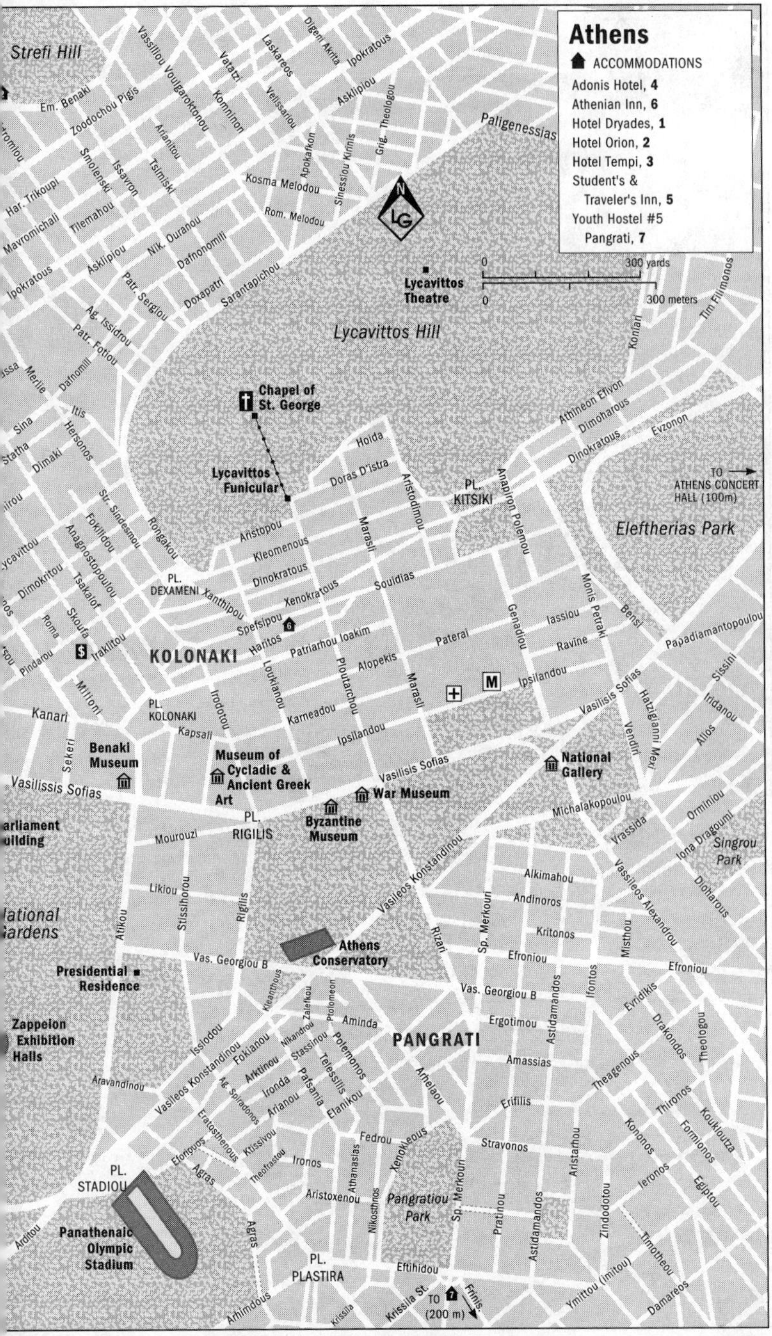

Athens

ACCOMMODATIONS

- Adonis Hotel, **4**
- Athenian Inn, **6**
- Hotel Dryades, **1**
- Hotel Orion, **2**
- Hotel Tempi, **3**
- Student's & Traveler's Inn, **5**
- Youth Hostel #5 Pangrati, **7**

0 300 yards
0 300 meters

Strefi Hill

Lycavittos Theatre

Lycavittos Hill

Chapel of St. George

Lycavittos Funicular

PL. KITSIKI

TO ATHENS CONCERT HALL (100m)

Eleftherias Park

PL. DEXAMENI

KOLONAKI

PL. KOLONAKI

Benaki Museum

Museum of Cycladic & Ancient Greek Art

War Museum

National Gallery

Byzantine Museum

PL. RIGILIS

Parliament Building

National Gardens

Singrou Park

Athens Conservatory

Presidential Residence

Zappeion Exhibition Halls

PANGRATI

PL. STADIOU

Panathenaic Olympic Stadium

Pangratiou Park

PL. PLASTIRA

TO 7 (200 m)

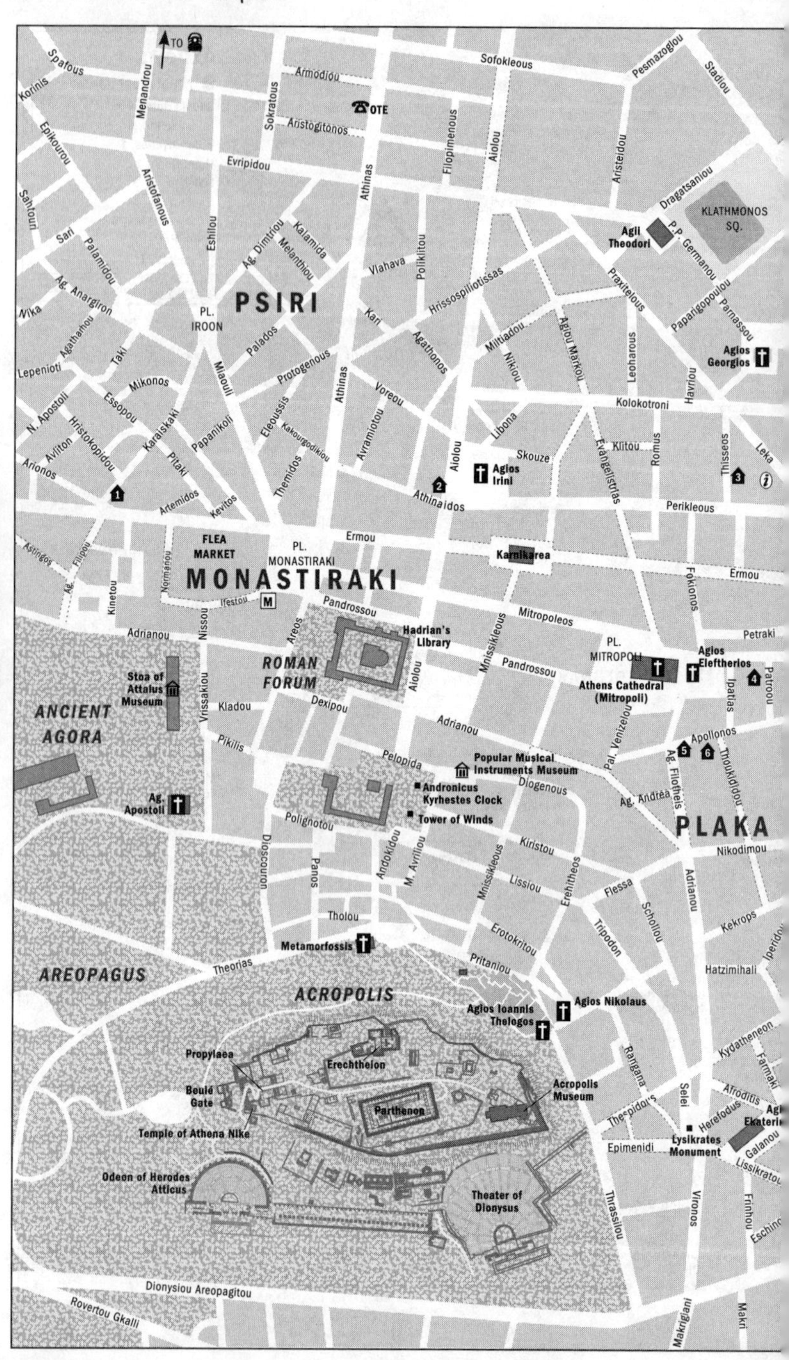
TO
OTE
Sofokleous
Pesmazoglou
Stadiou
Spafous
Korinis
Menandrou
Armodiou
Sokratous
Aristogitonos
Filopimenous
Aiolou
Aristeidou
Epikourou
Evripidou
Athinas
Dragatsaniou
KLATHMONOS SQ.
Agii Theodori
P.P. Germanou
Sahtouri
Aristofanous
Eshilou
Ag. Dimitriou
Kalamida
Melanthiou
Vlahava
Polikitou
Sari
Palamidou
Hrissospiliotissas
Praxitelous
Papanigopoulou
Parnassou
Ag. Anargiron
PSIRI
PL. IROON
Nika
Agatharhou
Paladon
Kari
Agathonos
Miltiadou
Agiou Markou
Leoharous
Lepenioti
Taki
Protogenous
Nikiou
Havriou
Aglos Georglos
Mikonos
Miaouli
Athinas
Voreou
N. Apostoli
Essopou
Kolokotroni
Hristokopidou
Karaiskaki
Eleoussis
Avramiotou
Libona
Aviton
Papanikoli
Kakourgodikiou
Klitou
Romus
Thisseos
Leka
Pitaki
Aiolou
Skouze
Arionos
Themidos
Agios Irini
Evangelistrias
Artemidos
Kevitos
Athinaidos
Perikleous
Astingos
Filipou
FLEA MARKET
PL. MONASTIRAKI
Ermou
Karnikarea
Ermou
Ag.
Normanou
MONASTIRAKI
Fokionos
Kinetou
Ifestou
M
Pandrossou
Mitropoleos
Adrianou
Nissou
Areos
Hadrian's Library
Mnissikleous
Petraki
PL. MITROPOLI
Aglos Eleftherios
Stoa of Attalus Museum
ROMAN FORUM
Aiolou
Pandrossou
Athens Cathedral (Mitropoli)
Patrou
Ipatias
ANCIENT AGORA
Vrissakiou
Kladou
Dexipou
Adrianou
Pal. Venizelou
Apollonos
Pikilis
Pelopida
Popular Musical Instruments Museum
Ag. Filotheis
Thoukididou
Andronicus Kyrhestes Clock
Diogenous
Ag. Apostoli
Ag. Andrea
Polignotou
Tower of Winds
PLAKA
Dioscouron
Andokidou
M. Avriliou
Kiristou
Nikodimou
Panos
Mnissikleous
Erehitheos
Lissiou
Adrianou
Flessa
Tholou
Schollou
Kekrops
Erotokritou
Tripodon
Metamorfossis
Theorias
Pritaniou
Hatzimihali
AREOPAGUS
ACROPOLIS
Agios Nikolaus
Agios Ioannis Thelogos
Kydatheneon
Propylaea
Erechtheion
Rangana
Farmaki
Acropolis Museum
Afroditis
Beulé Gate
Parthenon
Thespidous
Selei
Herefodus
Ekaterini
Temple of Athena Nike
Epimenidi
Lysikrates Monument
Galanou
Lissikratous
Odeon of Herodes Atticus
Theater of Dionysus
Thrassilou
Vironos
Frinhou
Eschinou
Dionysiou Areopagitou
Rovertou Gkalli
Makrigiani
Makri

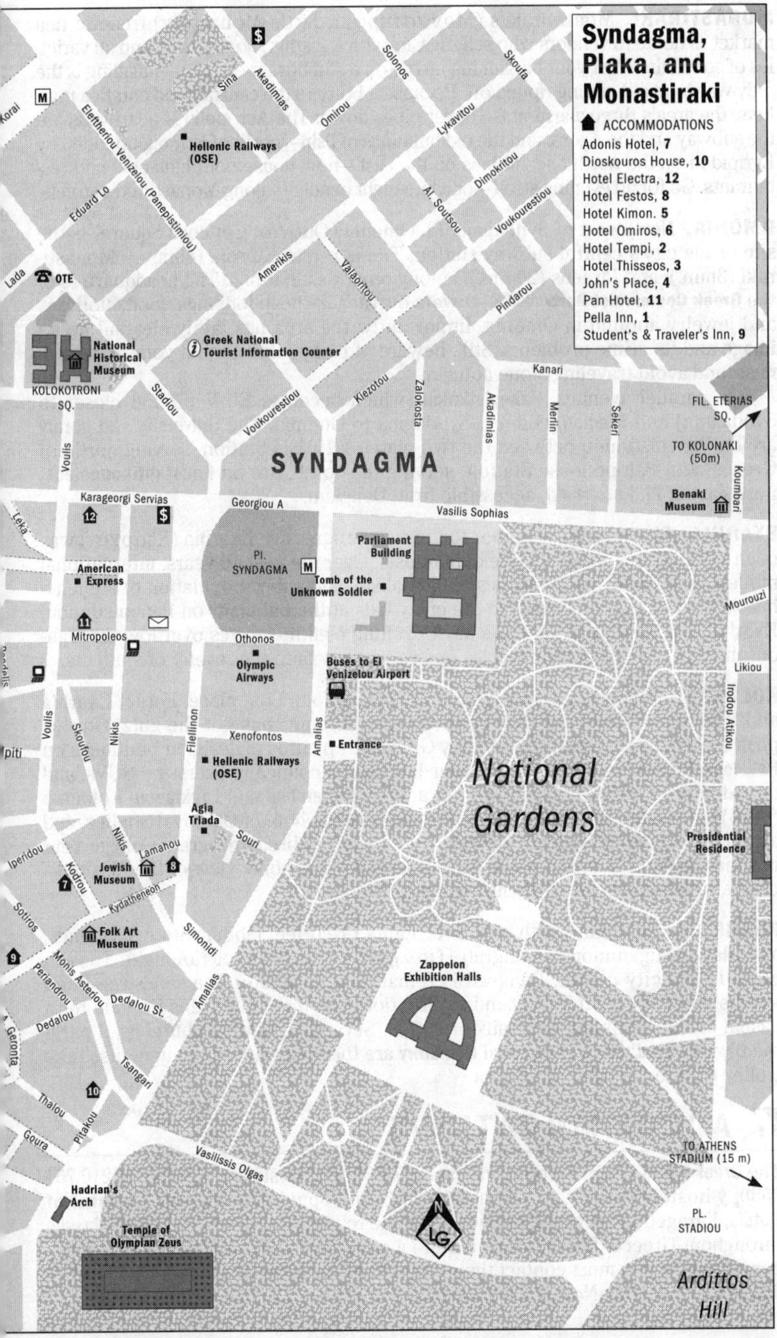

Syndagma, Plaka, and Monastiraki

ACCOMMODATIONS

Adonis Hotel, **7**
Dioskouros House, **10**
Hotel Electra, **12**
Hotel Festos, **8**
Hotel Kimon. **5**
Hotel Omiros, **6**
Hotel Tempi, **2**
Hotel Thisseos, **3**
John's Place, **4**
Pan Hotel, **11**
Pella Inn, **1**
Student's & Traveler's Inn, **9**

SYNDAGMA

National Gardens

Korai
Sina
Akadimias
Solonos
Skoufa
Omirou
Lykavitou
Eleftheriou Venizelou (Panepistimiou)
Hellenic Railways (OSE)
Dimokritou
Eduard Lo
Al. Soutsou
Voukourestiou
Amerikis
Valaoritou
Lada
OTE
Pindarou
National Historical Museum
Greek National Tourist Information Counter
KOLOKOTRONI SQ.
Stadiou
Kriezotou
Zalokosta
Akadimias
Kanari
Merlin
Sekeri
FIL. ETERIAS SQ.
TO KOLONAKI (50m)
Voulis
Koumbari
Benaki Museum
Karageorgi Servias
Georgiou A
Vasilis Sophias
Leka
Parliament Building
PL. SYNDAGMA
American Express
Tomb of the Unknown Soldier
Mourouzi
Mitropoleos
Othonos
Olympic Airways
Buses to El Venizelou Airport
Likiou
Voulis
Skoufou
Nikis
Filellinon
Amalias
Irodou Atikou
Xenofontos
Entrance
Hellenic Railways (OSE)
Agia Triada
Souri
Presidential Residence
Iperidou
Nikis
Lamahou
Kodrou
Jewish Museum
Kydatheneon
Sotiros
Folk Art Museum
Simonidi
Monis Asteriou
Periandrou
Amalias
Zappeion Exhibition Halls
Dedalou St.
Dedalou
Tsangari
Thalou
Pitakou
Goura
Vasilissis Olgas
TO ATHENS STADIUM (15 m)
Hadrian's Arch
PL. STADIOU
Temple of Olympian Zeus
Ardittos Hill

ATHENS

MONASTIRAKI. Monastiraki's (Μοναστηρακι; Little Monastery) frenetic flea market is home to vendors who sell rugs, furniture, leather, *bouzoukis*, and all varieties of souvenirs. Test your bargaining mettle on a stubborn merchant—haggling is the only way to avoid getting ripped off. Because it borders the central food and flea markets, the area's three-alarm noise never pipes down. The Acropolis is nearby, as are the subway and the Agora, and the old buildings of **Psiri**—north of Ermou, bounded by Evripidou on the north and Athinas on the east—now house hot nightspots and restaurants. Go for an evening stroll—or a late-night bender—along Monastiraki's streets.

OMONIA. Northwest of Syndagma, Pl. Omonia (Ομονια; Concord Square) is the site of the city's central subway station. Trains run to Kifissia (40min.), Monastiraki (3min.), and Piraeus (20min.), among other destinations. The headquarters of the **Greek Communist Party** (KKE) towers overhead. Cheap lodgings, food, clothing, and jewelry abound in Omonia. Importantly, the area has lately cleaned up its image and its crime problems. Still, beware of pickpockets, mind your own business, and avoid traveling alone at night.

Two parallel avenues, **Panepistimiou** (which becomes El. Venizelou closer to Syndagma) and **Stadiou,** connect Syndagma to Omonia. The **University** and **library** are on Panepistimiou between the two plateias. Larisis Station, serving northern Greece, and Peloponnese Station, serving the south, are on **Konstantinoupoleos,** northeast of **Pl. Karaiskaki,** accessible from Deligiani.

EXARHIA. Pl. Omonia's neighbor to the east, progressive Exarhia (Εξαρχια) was once the spiritual home of Greek anarchists. Over the past 10 years, international models have imported the values of capitalism, and a new population of students has arrived to match. Thanks to the crazy kids at the **University** on Panepistimiou, Exarhia sports some of Athens's most exciting nightlife. Cafes overflow throughout the night, as the outdoor tables open a window onto the revelry of students.

KOLONAKI. If you've got money to burn, you've found the place. Forget Exarhia and Syndagma: Kolonaki (Κολωνακι; Little Column) has got the glitz. On this posh foothill of **Mt. Lycavittos,** swanky Greeks drop euros in designer boutiques on **Pat. Ioakeim,** jockey for spots for their BMWs and comically oversized SUVs, and crowd into the cafes, bars, and restaurants on **Plutarchou** and **Loukianou.** Kolonaki (p. 95) houses the British Academy, the American School of Classical Studies, and an enclave of expat students, notably from the year-abroad program College Year in Athens. With Plaka just down the hill and an exceptional view of the Acropolis below, Kolonaki shelters Athens's trendiest nightspots.

PANGRATI. Athenian youth chat over Fanta or coffee, jabber into cell phones, and play backgammon in Pangrati (Πανγρατι), southeast of Kolonaki. Though close to the city center, Pangrati is remarkably intimate. The safe, tree-lined streets allow for quiet strolls and exploration, and the many cafes provide for a casual evening, sipping cocktails or coffee. Several Byzantine churches, a park, the **Olympic Stadium,** and **National Cemetery** are the area's major monuments. Take trolley #2, 4, or 11 from Syndagma.

ACCOMMODATIONS

The **Greek Youth Hostel Association,** Damareos 75, lists hostels in Greece. (☎210 751 9530; y-hostels@otenet.gr. Open daily M-F 9am-3pm.) The **Hellenic Chamber of Hotels,** Karageorgi Servias 2, provides info and reservations for hotels of all classes throughout Greece. Reservations require a cash deposit, length of stay, and number of people; you must contact them a month in advance. (☎210 323 7193; fax 210 322 5449. Open May-Nov. M-Th 8:30am-2pm, F 8:30am-1:30pm, Sa 9am-12:30pm.)

SYNDAGMA

Syndagma is at the heart of Athens. Tourist services and cheap accommodations are plentiful. Though it can be a noisy area, it's a good bet for those looking for dirt-cheap hostel rates and close proximity to transportation.

Hotel Festos, Filellinon 18 (☎210 323 2455; consolas@hol.gr). This backpacker-friendly hostel charges rock-bottom prices. Located off a busy street on the border of Plaka, it's a 5min. walk to food, shops, and transport. Breakfast €2, served in a common kitchen/TV room. A/C and common baths. Dorms €15-18; singles €26-30; doubles €36-50; triples €54-75; quads €64-80. Discounted monthly rates for students. ❷

Hotel Thisseos, Thisseos 10 (☎210 324 5960). Take Karageorgi Servias, which becomes Perikleous, and Thisseos is on the right. This home-turned-hostel is close to Syndagma's sights but far from its noise. Friendly staff speaks English. TV in reception area, full kitchen, fans, and common baths. Open 24hr. Towels and sheets upon request. Dorms €15 in high season, €12 in low season. In high season, singles €30; doubles €44. Covered roof available in summer for €8 (bring a sleeping bag). ❶

John's Place, Patroou 5 (☎210 322 9719), near Mitropoleos. Off the major streets, John's has basic amenities. Dim hallways and quiet nights enhance its gothic feel. Singles €20-30; doubles €25-44; triples €30-53. Bargain for a better price. ❸

PLAKA

Student's and Traveler's Inn, Kydatheneon 16 (☎210 324 4808 or 210 324 8802; fax 210 321 0065). An unrivaled location and a lively atmosphere, along with A/C, make this inn a popular place. It courts young backpackers with its large courtyard and balconies, travel services (open 2-8:30pm), and Internet access at the nearby Cyber Cafe (€3 per 30min.; open 8am-11pm). Breakfast 6-11am (€4.50-7). Bring your own sheets, towel, and ask for toilet paper at the desk. 24hr. reception. Lockout at midnight. Call for a reservation and arrive on time. Co-ed dorms €15-20; singles €30-35, with bath €35-40; doubles €30-47/€45-60; triples €45-60/€50-75; quads €75-80/€65-88. Storage available for €15 per month and €7 per week. ❷

Dioskouros House, Pitakou 6 (☎210 324 8165), on the southwest corner of the National Gardens by the Temple of Olympian Zeus. The simple wood-floored rooms are sheltered from the city center; a shaded outdoor bar serves breakfast (€3) and drinks until 11pm. Luggage storage (€1) and book exchange. Singles €25-35; doubles €40-60; triples €60-75; quads €80-100. ❸

Adonis Hotel, Kodrou 3 (☎210 324 9737 or 210 324 9741; fax 210 323 1602). From Filellinon on the way from Syndagma, turn right on Nikodimou and left on Kodrou, which meets Voulis. A family hotel with bath and phones in each plush room, and a delightful rooftop lounge with a view of the Acropolis where you can enjoy continental breakfast from 6:30-9:30am. Rooftop bar open daily 6:30-9:30pm. Singles €39 in high season, €27 in low season; doubles €55.70; triples €74. A/C €10 extra per person. Discounts for stays of more than 2 days. Reserve far in advance. ❸

Hotel Kimon, Apollonos 27 (☎210 331 4658; fax 210 321 4203), 1 block from the Mitropoli Cathedral. Friendly, safe, and close to the sights. Charming roof garden. Breakfast €4. Singles €35, with bath €45; doubles €45; triples €50; quad €70. ❸

Hotel Omiros, Apollonos 15, near Pl. Syndagma (☎210 323 4486; fax 210 323 8059; omiroshotel@hotmail.com). Hotel Omiros is worth the extra money for those looking for a meticulously clean and conveniently located hotel. The relatively spacious rooms are complete with A/C, TV, private baths, and telephones. Breakfast included. Singles €50; doubles €75; triples €93; quads €111. Bargain for 15% student discount, especially during low season. Call ahead to reserve. ❹

MONASTIRAKI

Like Plaka and Syndagma, Monastiraki lies at the center of things. You'll be close to the flea market and nightlife of Psiri. It's noisy fun.

Pella Inn, Karaiskaki 1 (☎210 325 0598; fax 210 325 0598). Walk 10min. down Ermou from Pl. Syndagma; it's 2 blocks from the Monastiraki subway station. Near the hip hangouts of Monastiraki, Pella features a large terrace with impressive views of the Acropolis to complement the comfy rooms. Breakfast €3. Free luggage storage. Common bathrooms. Dorms €10-12; doubles €30-35; triples €36-55; quads €48-60. ❷

Hotel Tempi, Aiolou 29 (☎210 321 3175 or 210 324 2940; fax 210 325 4179; www.travelling.gr/tempihotel). Wedged between an assortment of street vendors, Tempi rents simple rooms with ceiling fans. Rooms facing the rear are much dimmer—ask for a front-facing room. Free luggage storage. Laundry service available. 11am checkout. Singles €30; doubles €40, with bath €48; triples €55. Low-season prices 20% less. ❸

OMONIA

If you're leaving Athens on an early bus or train (or arriving on a late one), you can roll out of bed to your ride from Omonia. The area has been cleaning up its crime problems and gentrifying quickly, but always err on the side of safety and don't travel alone at night.

Hostel Aphrodite, Einardou 12 (☎210 881 0589 or 210 883 9249; fax 210 881 6574; hostel-aphrodite@ath.forthnet.gr). From the Victoria subway station, follow Heiden 2 blocks, then continue along Peioniou 2 more. Turn right on Michail Voda and left on Einardou. From the train station, take Filadelfias to Michail Voda. A staircase with an erotic mural leads to a 24hr. basement bar. Small, comfy rooms with A/C. Breakfast €4.50-7. Safety deposit box, free luggage storage, Internet access, and laundry. 24hr. reception. Dorms €15; doubles €38, with bath €50; triples €48; quads €64. Off-season discount up to €15 per person. Daily bus to the **Pink Palace** in Corfu (round-trip or 1-way, with night stay at Pink Palace included in cost). ❷

Athens International Hostel (HI), Victor Hugo 16 (☎210 523 4170 or 210 523 1095; fax 320 523 4015; athenshostel@interland.gr). Walk down 30 Septemvriou from Pl. Omonia and take a left on Veranzerou, which becomes Victor Hugo after crossing Marni. A few minutes from the Metahourgio subway stop. A continental crowd packs this HI-affiliated youth hostel, the only one in Greece—you'll need to be an HI member or buy a membership (€15) to stay here. Hot water 6-10am and 6-10pm. Laundry (€6) and travel office available. Breakfast and sheets included. Internet access available for €3 per hr. Call or email for reservation. Priority is given to HI members. Dorm-€8.37. ❶

EXARHIA

Home to much of Athens's student population, Exarhia has some of the city's hippest digs. Convenient to the Archaeological Museum, the neighborhood is within walking distance of major public transportation but is quieter and brighter than nearby Pl. Omonia, making it a good choice for young budget travelers.

Hotel Dryades, Dryadon 4 (☎210 382 7116 or 210 330 2387). Elegant Dryades offers some of Athens's nicest budget-conscious accommodations, with large rooms and private baths. Full kitchen and TV lounge. Breakfast €2.50. Internet €2 per 30min. Singles €35-40; doubles €44-53; triples €50-65. ❸

Hotel Orion, Em. Benaki 105 (☎210 382 7362 or 210 382 0191; fax 210 380 5193). From Pl. Omonia, walk up Em. Benaki or take bus #230 from Pl. Syndagma. Filled with hip travelers intent on seeing more than Athens's tourist magnets, Orion rents small rooms with shared baths. Sunbathers relax on the rooftop with music, TV, and board games. Internet €2 per hr. Laundry €3. Breakfast €2.50. Singles €20-30; doubles €30-36; triples €36-40. Bargain for better prices. ❸

The Exarcheion, Themistokleous 55 (☎210 380 0731 or 210 380 1256; fax 210 380 3296). Enjoy the stairway's stylish mural on your way to one of the 50 rooms, each with phone, TV, and a view of Exharia. Private baths and A/C. Breakfast €4. 24hr. bar, Internet for guests, and a roof garden. Make reservations. Singles €30; doubles €36; triples €45. Off-season prices 10% less. 10% discount for *Let's Go* carriers. ❸

KOLONAKI AND PANGRATI

Kolonaki's high prices may scare off budget-wary travelers, but its charming neighborhoods and cozy atmosphere make it a pleasant place to spend the night. Though far from the main attractions, Pangrati offers affordable accommodations.

Youth Hostel #5 Pangrati, Damareos 75 (☎210 751 9530; fax 210 751 0616; y-hostels@otenet.gr). From Omonia or Pl. Syndagma take trolley #2 or 11 to Filolaou (past Imittou), or walk through the National Garden, down Eratosthenous Efthidiou, then 3 blocks to Frinis, and down Frinis until Damareos is on the right. There's no sign for this cheery hostel—just the number 75 and a green door. Bulletin boards spread hosteling wit and wisdom, and the owner speaks English. TV lounge and full kitchen facilities. Hot showers €0.50 for 5min. Sheets €0.75, pillowcases €0.50 each. Laundry token €3 at reception; hang your stuff to dry on the roof. Quiet hours 2-5pm and 11pm-7am. Dorms €7.50. Roof €6; bring a sleeping bag. ❶

Athenian Inn, Haritos 22 (☎ 210 723 8097 or 210 722 9552; fax 210 724 2268). From Pl. Kolonaki, walk one block down Pat. Ioakeim, turn left onto Loukianou, and head right onto Haritos. The hotel will be on your right. The hotel is nicely situated in the fashionable neighborhood of Kolonaki. Rooms are furnished with rustic furniture, A/C, TVs, and phones, and some have balcony views of Mt. Lycavittos. Breakfast included. Singles €60-65; doubles €78-85. ❹

ATHENS

FOOD

SYNDAGMA

Cheap fast food saturates Syndagma like a grease stain on paper. Chains like Goody's, Wendy's, and McDonald's dispense cheeseburgers, french fries, and sodas for €4.50 or traditional *tost* (a grilled sandwich) with feta and lettuce for €1.50. **Everest** and **Delikiosk** make cheap sandwiches like ham and cheese croissants for €2. For more fast food, try the family-owned joints on Nikis: **Makrigianni** (#54), **Mirabelle** (#34), or **To Apollonion** (#10).

Chroma (☎210 331 7793), on Karageorgi Servias and Lekka 8, 100m past the National Bank in Pl. Syndagma. Bright colors abound both inside and outside this chic restaurant and bar. Be adventurous: start with the Moroccan vegetable rolls (€5.50) and move on to ostrich fillet (€10) while you recline on leather couches and listen to the variety of international lounge music. Open 11am-late. Dancing all night. ❸

Old Parliament, Anthimou Gaxi 9 and Karitsi 7, behind the National Historical Museum. Dine on a garden terrace in the shade of the Old Parliament building to the sound of live jazz and Greek music played every night. This gastronomic oasis prepares savory Mediterranean and Italian dishes, from rabbit (€15.50) to seafood spaghetti (€18.50). For dessert try the mango mousse with blackberry coulis (€10). Cocktails €7. Opens at 8am for breakfast. Meals from 12:30pm-2am. Music starts at 10pm. ❹

Nikis Cafe, Nikis 3 (☎210 323 4971), near Ermou. More of a cafe than a restaurant, Nikis serves fresh baguette sandwiches (€3-4) and quiche at all hours. M-F noon-10pm and Sa-Su noon-6pm, you can get a meal, ranging from tangy chicken teriyaki (€6.50)

EDEN VEGETARIAN RESTAURANT

If you're tired of moussaka, souvlaki, gyros, and other meaty dishes and Greece's meager vegetarian selections are getting repetitive, there's hope buried away in Plaka. Take Kydatheneon to Tripidon, turn left onto Lyssiou, and on the first corner you'll find **Eden Vegetarian Restaurant,** the self-proclaimed first of its kind in Greece. This bustling bistro is unassuming but cozy; it's almost always packed with Greeks and foreigners searching for a tasty and wholesome meal. The menu is happy to oblige. Eden seems to be running a mini-totalitarian organic state–vegetables, beer, wine, cheese, and everything else on the extensive menu is fresh, crisp, and delicious.

Best of all, your meal won't cost you an arm and a leg. Fantastic dishes like *boureki* pie (zucchini with feta; €4.90), hummus (€6.50), and flavorful mushroom *stifado* with onions and peppers (€8.80) are cheap and satisfying. Soy is substituted for meat throughout, and the results are very pleasing. Eden reinvigorates your old culinary friends (or foes) like moussaka with soy and organic vegetables and serves up juicy veggie burgers of all kinds. As you step out into Plaka after your meal, your wallet just a little lighter, you'll probably agree that Eden does vegetarian better than any other restaurant in Greece.

Lyssiou 12. ☎210 324 8858. Open M and W-Su noon-midnight.

to sweet or savory crepes (€5-6). Its modern art rivals its frozen margaritas in style (strawberry or banana €6.40). Open Su-Th 8am-2am, F-Sa 8am-5am. ❷

Kentrikon, Kolokotroni 3 (☎210 323 2482 or 210 323 5623), near Stadiou, next to the National Historical Museum. Traditional Greek and foreign dishes served in this cozy niche with indoor A/C and outdoor seating. Branch out with pasta *bolognaise* (€7) or veal with spinach *ragout* (€8.50). Many vegetarian options. Open M-F noon-6pm. ❷

Restaurant Palea Athina, Nikis 48 (☎210 324 5777). Inexpensive elegance pervades the atmosphere; go at night when dim lighting masks the lack of beautiful scenery. Vegetable risotto €5; mussels with bacon €7. Open daily noon-12:30am. ❷

PLAKA

For do-it-yourself meals, **minimarkets** on Nikis sell basic groceries. Most of the tavernas along Kydatheneon, Plaka's main drag, are roughly equivalent; explore quieter streets like **Tripodon** and **Lysiou** for the gems. The restaurants have a traditional feel, many with live Greek music and dancing or stunning views of the Acropolis and Mt. Lycavittos. Check the menus before you sit down—the main tourist area restaurants tend to be expensive.

Jungle Juice, Aiolou 21, under the Acropolis (☎/fax 210 331 6739; athens@junglejuice.it). Snag a turkey sandwich (€1.50) at this fresh-squeezed smoothie and sandwich stand, and wash it down with the "Leone Melone," a blended drink of cantaloupe, mango, and pineapple (€3). Open daily 8am-9pm. ❶

Sissofos, Mnisikleous 31 (☎210 324 6043; www.sissifos.gr). The multi-lingual manager will grab you from the hilly street and set you up on the rooftop patio with dishes like lamb with potatoes in the oven (€9) or swordfish souvlaki (€10.90). The candlelit view and deliciously large portions make the prices worthwhile. Open daily 6:30pm-2am. ❸

T. Stamatopoulos, Lissiou 26 (☎210 322 8722 or 210 321 8549). Family-owned since 1882, the restaurant has an outdoor terrace and–the star attraction–Greek dancing to live music (9:30-11pm). Veal in wine sauce €6.50. Open daily 7pm-2:30am. ❷

MONASTIRAKI

Give up fresh breath in exchange for cheap food by eating some *tzatziki*-smothered gyros at the flea market or explore the chic options that stretch the boundaries of regulation Greek cooking at the markets. Stock up on groceries at **Market Sophos,** Mitropoleos 78 (☎/fax 210 322 6677), near Aiolou.

Savvas, Mitropoleos 86 (☎210 324 5048), tucked in a corner off Ermou. For takeout, this grill is a budget eater's dream, with heavenly, cheap gyros (€1.20); just don't sit down—prices skyrocket if you do. Souvlaki plate €6.50. Open 7:30am-3am. ❶

Attalos Restaurant, Adrianou 9 (☎210 321 9520), near the Thisseon area. Frequented by VIPs from the US Embassy, this traditional Greek taverna serves mussel *saganaki* (€4) and a variety of handmade *croquettes* (a vegetarian plate for 2-4 people costs €8). *Bouzouki* photos adorn the wall. Open 9am-2am. ❷

Dia Tafta, Adrianou 37 (☎210 321 2347), near the Agora. A huge bar lines one wall of the interior, but the streetside tables make it popular. Fresh Greek salad €5.50; variety platters for 4 €10.50-22. Open daily 9:30am-1:30am. ❷

OMONIA

As in Syndagma, the immediate area around Pl. Omonia is filled with fast food joints—busy thoroughfares **30 Septemvriou** and **28 Octovriou** (Pastission) are alive at all hours. For those with kitchen access, pick up ingredients at **Galaxias Discount Market,** 30 Septemvriou 26. To quiet late-night stomach rumblings, stop by the meat market on **Athinas** between Monastiraki and Omonia, where night-owl restaurants are open 3-7am.

Pak Indian Restaurant, 13 Menandrou (☎210 321 9412 or 210 324 2255), from Omonia metro head down P. Tsaldari, turn left on Menandrou, and walk 1½ blocks. Savor spicy and delicious traditional Indian dishes (curry added to taste) in this intimate setting that offers shelter from the bustling street outside. Be sure to order some *naan* (€2) and a veggie *samosa* (€1.50) before moving on to a *tandoori* dish (€7.50-9) and curries (€7-8.50). Vegetarian dishes available. Open daily 11am-2am. ❷

Healthy Food Vegetarian Restaurant, Panepistimiou 57 (☎210 321 0966; fax 210 321 2043). Wholesomeness to make a souvlaki stand blush—everything's made fresh. Muesli (€3.80), carrot apple juice (€1.50). Open daily 8am-10:30pm. ❷

Dafni Taverna, Iolianou 65 (☎210 821 3914). From Pl. Victoria, walk down Aristotelous and turn right on Iolianou. You'll know it's a classic the second you enter the grapevine-shaded courtyard walled by barrels of *retsina*. Traditional Greek appetizers €2-3; entrees €5.50 or less. Open daily noon-1am. ❶

Souvlaki Pitta Pan, Patission 8. Never Never Land jokes aside, this gyro joint is fresh and pleasing. Souvlaki €1.69; fries, pita, and *tzatziki* €5. Open daily 11am-11pm. ❶

DAPHNE'S

To find this wonderful but well hidden bistro, walk down Amalias from the Syndagma metro station to Hadrian's Arch and turn right onto Lyssikratous. **Daphne's** provides sublime flavors in the shelter of a leafy canopy of grape vines within an enclosed rock garden. The rich and famous of Athens and beyond congregate here to enjoy a fine meal. Indeed, former US First Lady Hillary Clinton and daughter Chelsea supped at Daphne's during their 1996 visit.

Daphne's serves some of the best Greek food in the country. The dishes aren't unique, but the preparations certainly are. The superb service and cuisine will undoubtedly satisfy even the most sophisticated connoisseur. Begin your evening with prosciutto and melon (€16.10) or spinach pie (€8.50) before moving onto the mouth-watering rabbit *mavrodaphne* in wine sauce (€16.10). Or order one of the many seafood dishes; they are all superb. Don't forget a bottle of a crisp Chardonnay (€40 and up) or a small bottle of Cabernet Sauvignon (€10). Finish off the evening with homemade ice cream nestled in flaky pastries (€8).

Lyssikratous 4. ☎210 322 7971. Call ahead for reservations. Open daily 6pm-1am.

EXARHIA

Starving twentysomethings demand inexpensive food around Exarhia. Many of the options are basic but tasty: think souvlaki, Greek classics, and a jug of wine. Stop in for a quick souvlaki (€1) on the road at **Souvlaki Kavouras,** Themistokleous 64, or just sit back and enjoy the more authentic atmosphere in this area of Athens.

O Barba Giannis, Em. Benaki 94 (☎210 330 0185). From Syndagma, walk up Stadiou and make a right on Em. Benaki. Athenian students, CEOs, and artists all agree that "Uncle John's" is the place for cheap, delicious food and outstanding service. Lots of fish (around €5), moussaka (€5.30), vegetarian dishes (€3-4), and wine (€1); ask about the day's choices. In off season, open daily noon-1:30am. In summer, open M-F noon-1:30am, Sa noon-6pm. ❶

Yiantes, Valtetsiou 44 (☎210 330 1369), next to the movie theater. Enter this open air blue-walled oasis of snaking vines and little tables for a traditional Greek meal (drinks and all) for €15. Fresh fish €6. Open daily 1pm-1am. ❷

Rosalia, Valtetsiou 58 (☎210 330 2933), by Pl. Exharia. In a hip area of Exharia, this taverna serves appetizing traditional dishes at reasonable prices in the shade of a lovely terrace garden. Try the fried zucchini (€4) or chicken in cream sauce (€5.90). Open daily noon-midnight. ❶

Vergina, Valtetsiou 62 (☎210 330 2136 or 210 380 7992), by Pl. Exarhia. A favorite among locals, the traditional Greek food is pre-prepared at this takeout restaurant; call ahead or walk in. Entrees €3-6. Open daily noon-1am. ❷

KOLONAKI

The surest bargain is the Friday morning **street market** on Xenokratous, where you can grab a week's supply of peanuts, potatoes, and fresh clementines. Otherwise, this is the place to splurge with a super-swanky meal.

Pluto, Plutarchou 38 (☎210 724 4713; www.thepluto.com). Owner and culinary mastermind Constantinos has created a chic restaurant with warm ambience and an international menu. Waves of Greek and international customers line up for seats at the spice-filled glass tables every night. The menu is always evolving, but try the grilled eggplant with feta and tomatoes (€8.50), fillet of sole in saffron and wine sauce (€13.50), or strawberry meringue (€9). Open daily 11am-3am. **Pluto Sushi** is next door. ❸

Food Company, Anagnostopoulou 47 (☎210 361 6619). Anagnostopoulou is two streets below Pl. Dexameni and intersects with Pat. Ioakeim near Pl. Kolonaki. This little bistro is perfect for a tasty takeout meal or a meal at one of the tiny, crowded tables. Pastas, salads, and a revolving mix of warm dishes are the staples here. Top the visit off with a glass of white wine and a fabulous dessert. Entrees €10-15. Open M-Sa 9am-midnight, Su noon-midnight. ❸

PANGRATI

You can pick up fresh food Thursday mornings at the **street market** off Pl. Plastira. Head to Pl. Caravel to relax in cafes and to shop at **Veropoulos,** Formionos 23, a large nearby supermarket. (Open Su-F 8am-9pm, Sa 8am-6pm.)

Dragon Palace, Andinoros 1 (☎210 724 2795 or 210 723 5783). From Syndagma, take Vas. Sofias, turn right onto Rizari at the War Museum, cross the lights and take a left onto Andinoros. Both the restaurant and the Peking duck (€22.10) are large and elegant; the Szechuan chicken (€7.50) packs a spicy punch. Takeout and delivery available. Open daily 6:30pm-midnight; also open noon-1pm in winter. ❷

Kallimarmaron, Eforionos 13 (☎210 701 9727 or 210 701 7234). From the old Olympic Stadium, taken the street on left closest to stadium and walk 1½ blocks. Serves some of the best traditional Greek food in the city. Rabbit with mustard sauce (€9.50) and shrimp baked in salted biscuits (€11) will wow you. ❹

Evdokia, Pl. Plastira 2 (☎210 756 4879), in a small storefront tucked in a corner of the square. Try the cheap vegetable pizza (€1.30) or spanakopita (€1.20). ❶

NIGHTLIFE

Athenian nightlife changes with the seasons. In the winter months, the neighborhoods of **Exharia, Kifissia, Psiri,** and **Syndagma** roar with action. Once summer rolls around, the young and sizzling head to the beachside clubs of **Glyfada, Voula, Vari,** and **Vouliagmeni** to party. Aside from the clubbing hotspots, much of Athens hums with that great Greek hybrid, the cafe-bar, where you can start your day early with a coffee and proceed to a night-time binge at the same place.

PLAKA

For a spellbinding 360° view of Athens at night, go up to **Pnyx Hill,** where in ancient times the Assembly of Athenian citizens met to argue and to deliberate, opposite the Acropolis. The hill now brings natives and tourists together to listen to guitar-strumming by the city lights. Take care when ascending the smooth, slippery steps. Enjoy a film in the night breeze at **Cine Paris,** Kydatheneon 22. (☎210 322 2071. 2nd-run English-language films at 8:50 and 11pm. Tickets €6.)

Bretto's, Kydatheneon 41 (☎210 323 2110). The walls are lit up with colorful bottles of ouzo, brandy, and other liqueurs, all made by friendly Dimitris in his family's 100-year-old distilleries. Buy a bottle for later (5ml-1L), or get an immediate fix at the bar. The homemade wine in the barrels along the back wall is €6.50 per bottle of sweet red, €1.50 per glass. Open daily 10am-midnight.

Lava Bore, Filellinon 25 (☎210 324 5335), on the corner of Simonidi by Amalias, or 200m up Kydatheneon from the Student and Traveller's Inn. This dance club tries hard to live up to its swankier, more crowded Glyfada counterparts. €3 cover includes a drink. Open Su-Th 10pm-4am, F-Sa 10pm-5am.

MONASTIRAKI

The **Psiri** district is the new place to see and be seen in Athens, and Monastiraki's nightlife has revved up to rival Glyfada.

Vibe, Aristophanous 1 (☎210 324 4794), just beyond Plateia Iroön. The blue orbs hanging above the entrance are just a taste of the weird lighting effects in the bar's interior.

Bee (☎210 321 2624), at the corner of Miaoli and Themidos, off Ermou; a few blocks from the heart of Psiri. A red pillar wrapped with 1000 tiny red lights lends an amorous glow to the flirtations below. DJs spin while the friendly staff keeps glasses filled. Drinks €3-9. Open daily 9pm-late.

Revekka, Miaouli 22 (☎210 321 1174). Unassuming by day, this eclectic little cafe-bar blossoms at night, when tables spill out onto the sidewalk and darkness brings youth, music, and flowing drinks. Beer €2. Open 5pm-late.

EXARHIA

Exarhia exudes its funkiness in its many bars, which showcase everything from backgammon to death metal. Check *Athens News* for showtimes of second-run movies at **Cinema Rivera,** Baltetsiou 46 (tickets €6).

Mr. Wired, Valtetsiou 61. The red parachute on the ceiling and thorn bushes painted on the walls give this rock bar an eerie Alice in Wonderland feel. Open daily 10:30pm-late.

Metal Cafe Dionysos, Em. Benaki 96A and Valtetsiou. Superficial conflict (backgammon vs. heavy-metal themed decor and music) leads to ultimate fun. Coffee €1.80; beer €3.25. Open daily 10am-late.

Rock Underground, Metaxa 21 (☎210 382 2019). For a British flavor, try this cafe-bar. Cocktails €5. Open 10am-late.

Korso, Em. Benaki 72 and Metaxa (☎210 384 2077). Artsy and bright. The wine bar in the old house next door opens up when the winter months bring colder weather. Toast €3; *frappé* €2.75. Open daily 10am-2am.

KOLONAKI

Kolonaki is brimming with cafes and bars. **Haritos,** to the right of Plutarchou, is the spot for summertime action—if you're prepared to shell out major euros for drinks. **City, Azul, Baila,** and **Mousa** (Μουσα), all at Haritos 43, spill sophisticated patrons into the street, are open very late, and charge around €5 for a beer, €7 for a cocktail. On **Millioni** by Jackson Hall, smaller crowds chat over drinks and little outdoor tables.

Summertime performances are staged in Lycavittos Theater as part of the **Athens Festival** (p. 21), which has included acts from the Greek Orchestra to Pavarotti to the Talking Heads. The **Festival Office,** Stadiou 4, sells student tickets. An English-language schedule of events is available in mid-June. (☎210 322 1459 or 210 322 7944. Tickets €10-16. Open M-F 9:30am-4pm, Sa-Su 9:30am-2pm.) In summer, open-air cinema in Dexameni square shows current movies. (Nightly shows 8:50 and 11pm. €6.50, students €4.50, children under 5 free.)

Cafe 48, Karneadou 48 (☎210 725 2434), 2 blocks up the hill from Vas. Sofias. Expat classicists and student travelers exchange stories at the bar and practice their dart game in the back room. Cozy and friendly atmosphere makes the bar a perfect place for a low-key evening with friends. With a student ID, a large beer costs €3. A free shot comes with each drink on Tu and Th. Open M-Sa 9am-2am, Su 4pm-2am.

The Daily, Xenokratous 47 (☎210 722 3430). This small cafe-bar is where Kolonaki's chic foreign student populations converge to imbibe, take in Latin music and reggae, and watch soccer and basketball on TV. Fabulous, shaded outdoor seating and open-air bar. Pints of Heineken €3; cocktails €5-6. Open daily 9am-2am.

Jazz in Jazz, Dinokratous 4. From behind the well-worn wooden bar, Kostas can be persuaded to muse about jazz and teach swing lessons. Endless old jazz records draw Athens's faithful. €5 cover includes a drink. Open daily Nov.-May noon-3am.

PANGRATI

The cafes along Imittou let you people-watch in style. A walk between Imittou 128 and 67 resonates with the vitality of the twentysomethings relaxing among friends in the many cafes adorning the street. Most cafes are open daily 9am-2am. Movies show twice nightly at Imittou 107 (€6). **Village Cinemas,** Imittou 10 and Hremonidou, in the Millennium Center, shows the latest blockbusters in state-of-the-art theaters. (☎210 757 2440. Shows at 11pm. Call for listings.)

Sideradiko Cafe, Imittou 128 (☎210 701 8700; www.sideradikocafe.gr). The name ("iron") fits the metal, stone, and mirror interior. Despite the severe decor, it offers a comfy night of Trivial Pursuit, Abalone, Scrabble, or MindTrap. Fresh fruit juices €3.80; beer €4.50. Open daily 9am-3am.

Excite, Imittou 109 (☎210 751 5487), next to the movie theater. This trendy spot with brightly colored leather couches is nestled among several busy cafes. Milkshake €4.70; martini €5.90. Open 9am-late.

Ellas Espresso, Pl. Plastira 8 (☎210 756 2565), is a large cafe with a shaded terrace and 4 TVs suspended above its indoor bar. *Frappé* €3. Open daily 9am-3am.

GLYFADA AND THE COAST

It's hot, you're cool...where to go? Come summertime, join the chic of the Athens club scene as they migrate to the big, swanky, seaside clubs of **Glyfada.** Take the **A3** or the **B3** bus from Vas. Amalias (along the street to the right of the top corner of Pl. Syndagma; €0.75) to Glyfada, and then catch a cab from there to your club. A **taxi** right to Glyfada should cost about €8, but the ride back into the center of Athens in the early morning—due to heavy traffic and higher night-time rates—can cost €10-15. Beware of greedy taxi drivers; if they pack the cab with more than just your party, don't let them swindle you into a set individual price. Remember what the total should roughly be, and don't pay much more than that.

Most of the clubs are spread out along Poseidonos, each a few kilometers apart. The views from the clubs located along the beach are worth the trip out, even if you're just in Athens for a night or two. **Privilege, Venue, Prime,** and **Envy** are perfect places to enjoy the breezy night air and party to dance music among fashionable Athenians. Hoards of serious-looking bouncers with earpieces guard the doorways to swanky open-air bars beneath discoballs and strobe lights. You've got to dress well to get in, so avoid wearing shorts. Cover is usually €10-15. Drinks vary from €4-10, but can go as high as €100 for an individual bottle of vodka, complete with mixers, for your table. Also look for **+Soda, King Size,** and **Bedside.** Along Pergamon, look for **Camel Club.** Top 40, funk, and house play until around 2am, when Greek music (often live) takes over. Dance, drink, and eye the beautiful crowd against the backdrop of the ocean, only a few feet away.

SIGHTS

ACROPOLIS

Reach the entrance on the west side of the Acropolis either from Areopagitou to the south, by following the signs from Plaka, or by exiting the Agora to the south, following the path uphill and turning right. Not wheelchair accessible. The marble can be slippery, so wear shoes with good traction. ☎ *210 321 0219.* ***Open*** *8am-7:30pm; winter 8am-2:30pm. Admission price includes access to all of the sights below the Acropolis (including Hadrian's Arch, the Olympian Temple of Zeus, and the Agora) within a 48hr. period. €12, students €6. Tickets can be purchased at any of the sites.*

Looming majestically over the city, the Acropolis complex has served as a city center since the 5th century BC. The brilliant Parthenon at its center towers over the Aegean and the plains of Attica, the greatest

THE INSIDER'S CITY

KOLONAKI

If the rough-and-tumble lifestyle of the world adventurer is starting to wear you out, shower up, slick back your hair, and escape to the trendy neighborhood of Kolonaki to enjoy a taste of the high life. Stylish Athenians and just a few tourists meet for an afternoon *espresso* after a morning of spending money on leather shoes and Italian threads. The evening energy of Kolonaki will surely refresh you.

1. Review the latest showing of Greek culture at the **Benaki Museum.**
2. Scan the upscale boutiques on Pat. Ioakeim and pick up some lavender body lotion at **L'Occitane.**
3. At **Da Capo,** relax for an hour with a *frappé,* watch the world go by, and do as the Greeks do: judge the passersby's outfits.
4. Window shop on pedestrian-only Tsakalof. The **shoe stores,** bag maker **Longchamp,** and clothier **Zara** are popular with the locals.
5. When it's time to eat, grab some Americana on a bun at Western-themed **Jackson Hall,** Millioni 4.
6. For dessert, walk down Millioni for some divine ice cream at **Dodoni.**

achievement of Athens's Classical glory and the era's most enduring architectural contribution. Although each Greek *polis* had an acropolis ("high point of the city"), the buildings atop Athens's central peak simply outshone their imitators and continue to awe even the most jaded traveler. They stand timelessly upright and, though steel scaffolding and restoration work often embrace the ancient structures, their energy and extravagance are felt by every onlooker. Visit as early in the day as possible to avoid massive crowds and the broiling, humbling midday sun.

HISTORY

BEGINNINGS. With its view toward both land and sea, the Acropolis began as a strategically located military fortress. In recent years, evidence of a Cyclopean-walled **Mycenaean** city (p. 7) has been found on and around the hill. It was initially controlled by one ruler, who lived in a palace that doubled as a temple to a nature goddess and later to Athena. Around the 12th century BC, wealthy landowners, the city's **Aristoi,** ousted the monarch and established themselves as rulers in an aristocracy (rule of the best—in practice, the rich). They shifted government away from the Acropolis to the city's northern foothills, in an area that later became the **Agora** (see p. 99). The Acropolis became a purely religious center for worshipping Athena, whose wooden shrine celebrated both Athena Polias, goddess of crops and fertility, and Pallas Athena, loving virgin and protectress of the city.

PERICLEAN PROJECT. The Acropolis's world-famous form took shape in 507 BC, when the *Aristoi* were overthrown and Athens began its experiment with democracy. In 490 BC, the Athenians began constructing a new temple on the Acropolis, this time in marble. Ten years later, Aegean city-states banded together and formed the Delian League to protect themselves against the Persians, and **Pericles** started piling up a slush fund to beautify Athens from the taxes paid by the league. He continued this practice long after the Persian threat evaporated, lavishing money on projects like the temples of the Acropolis, the **Hephaesteion** in the Agora, and the **Temple of Poseidon** at Sounion. His program was mocked as lavish and unscrupulous; Plutarch reports that Pericles was "gilding and bedizening" the city like a "wanton woman adding precious stones to her wardrobe." Nevertheless, after delays caused by the Peloponnesian War (431-404 BC), the Periclean project was completed. Four of the buildings erected thus still stand today on the Acropolis: the **Parthenon,** the **Propylaea,** the **Temple of Athena Nike,** and the **Erechtheion.**

CAPTURE AND RESTORATION. Almost as soon as the Acropolis was completed, it fell to Sparta; ever since, its function has changed whenever it changed hands. **Byzantine Christians** added the symbolic power of the Parthenon to their faith arsenal; they turned the temple into the Church of Ag. Sophia. In 1205, **Frankish Crusaders** turned back the clock and again made the Acropolis into a fortress/palace/headquarters, this time for the Dukes de la Roche. Eventually, the Parthenon served as a Catholic church, Notre Dame d'Athènes. In the 15th century, **Ottomans** used the Parthenon as a mosque and the Erechtheion as the Ottoman commander's harem. During a 1687 siege, the Venetian attackers fired shells at the Parthenon, and the gunpowder stored on the Acropolis blew off the temple's roof. Squalor ensued as Ottoman guards and their families settled on the Acropolis. It is symbolic of the amazing workmanship that went into the Parthenon that almost all the damage to the building was inflicted in the last 600 years by human hands, not by gravity. In 1833, the newly independent Greeks reclaimed the hill, dismantling remnants of the Turkish occupation and resurrecting the Temple of Nike.

The subsequent preservation and restoration of the Acropolis has kicked up a swirl of impassioned controversy. The first wave of large-scale restoration began in 1898 and lasted almost 40 years, transforming the site by demolishing and

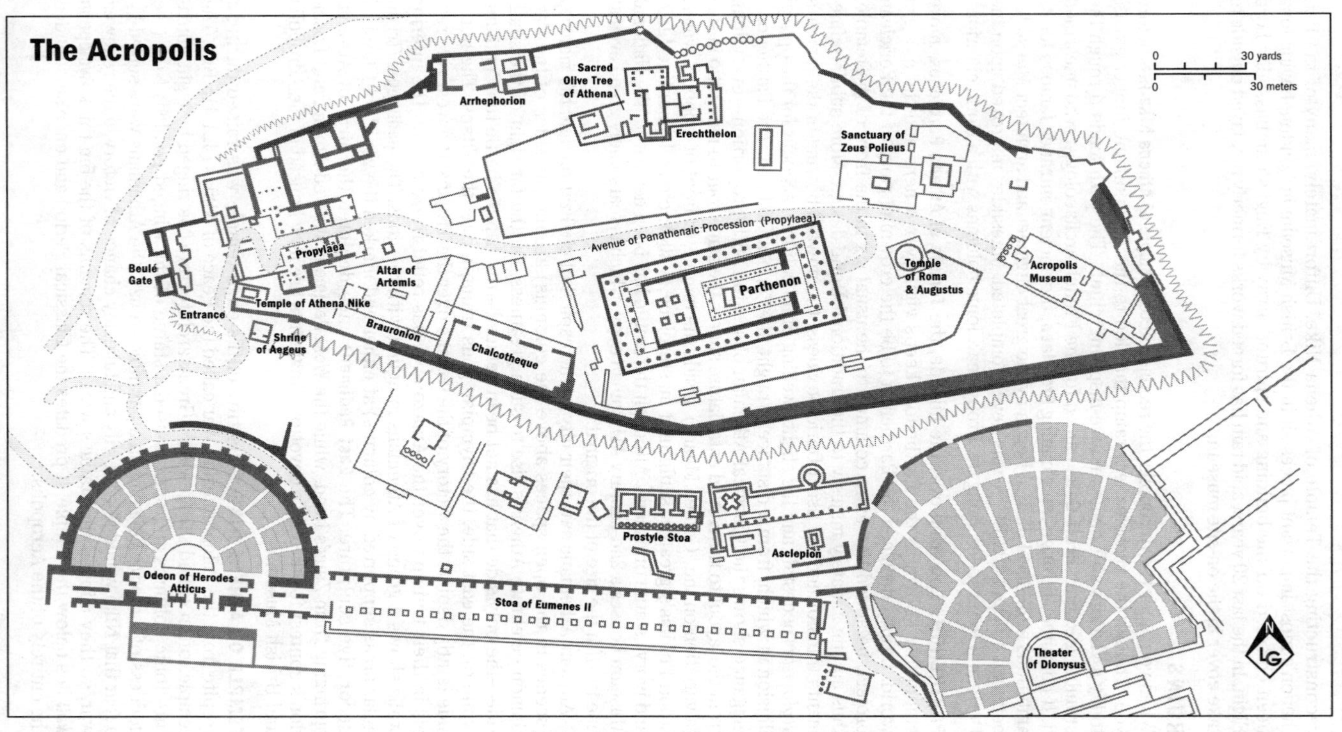
The Acropolis
0
30 yards
0
30 meters
N
LG
Arrhephorion
Sacred Olive Tree of Athena
Erechtheion
Sanctuary of Zeus Polieus
Avenue of Panathenaic Procession (Propylaea)
Propylaea
Beulé Gate
Altar of Artemis
Temple of Athena Nike
Entrance
Shrine of Aegeus
Brauronion
Chalcotheque
Parthenon
Temple of Roma & Augustus
Acropolis Museum
Prostyle Stoa
Asclepion
Odeon of Herodes Atticus
Stoa of Eumenes II
Theater of Dionysus

reconstructing the Temple of Athena Nike. Unfortunately, many of the Parthenon's most important pieces sit in the British Museum in London, having long been chiseled off the building and spirited away by English ambassador Lord Elgin. In the last 20 years, acid rain has forced works formerly displayed outside to take cover in the on-site museum.

RUINS

When you enter the Acropolis, the reconstructed **Temple of Athena Nike** lies before you. Though the Classical-era ramp that led to the Acropolis no longer exists, today's visitors still make an awe-inspiring climb. The path leads through the crumbling Roman **Beulé Gate,** named for the French archaeologist who unearthed it. It continues through the stunning **Propylaea,** the ancient entrance famous for its ambitious multi-level design. Begun by the great engineer and architect Mnesikles between 437 and 432 BC, it was never completed. Mnesikles improved upon the Doric and Ionic styles, tying the Propylaea's Ionic columns with a Doric exterior.

PARTHENON. Towering over the hillside, the **Temple of Athena Parthenos**, more commonly known as the Parthenon, keeps vigil over Athens and the modern world. Iktinos designed the Parthenon to be the crowning glory of the Periclean project; he added two extra columns to the usual six in the front of the temple, thus adding a stately majesty to the traditional Doric design. More subtle refinements transformed the usual Doric boxiness: the upward bowing of the temple's *stylobate* (pedestal) and the slight swelling of its columns account for the optical illusion in which, from a distance, straight lines appear to bend. The Parthenon's elegance shows the Classical Athenian obsession with proportion—everything from the layout to the carved entablature shares the same four-to-nine ratio in size (a variation on the "Golden Mean"). Inside the temple, in front of a pool of water, stood Phidias's greatest sculptural masterpiece, a 40-ft. chryselephantine (gold and ivory) statue of Athena. Although the statue has been destroyed, the National Museum houses a 2nd-century AD Roman copy, which is fearsomely grand even at one-twelfth the size of the original.

Ancient Athenians saw their city as the capital of civilization, and the **metopes** (scenes in the open spaces above the columns) around the sides of the Parthenon celebrate Athens's rise to such greatness. On the far right of the south side—the only side that has not been defaced—the Lapiths battle the Centaurs, while on the east side, the Olympian gods triumph over the Titans. The north side faintly depicts the victory of the Greeks over the Trojans; the west side revels in their triumph over the Amazons. A bas-relief frieze around the interior walls shows a group of Athenians mingling with the gods. The **pediments** (triangular areas supported by columns) at either end marked the zenith of Classical decorative sculpture. The **East Pediment** once depicted the birth of Athena, springing from Zeus's head, while the **West Pediment** showed Athena and Poseidon's contest for the city's devotion; fragments are now housed in the Acropolis and British Museums.

TEMPLE OF ATHENA NIKE. This tiny cliff's-edge temple was raised during a respite from the Peloponnesian War called the Peace of Nikias (421-415 BC). The temple, often called the "jewel of Greek architecture," is ringed by eight miniature Ionic columns and once housed a statue of the winged goddess Nike (the goddess of victory). One day, in a paranoid frenzy, the Athenians were seized by a fear that Nike would flee the city and take any chance of victory in the renewed war, so they clipped the statue's wings. The remains of the 5m-thick **Cyclopean wall** lies below the temple. It predates the Classical Period and once surrounded the entirety of the Acropolis.

ERECHTHEION. The Erechtheion, to the left of the Parthenon, was completed in 406 BC, just before Sparta defeated Athens in the Peloponnesian War. The building housed many gods in its time, grabbing its name from snake-bodied hero Erechtheus. Old Erechtheus couldn't stand up to Poseidon, who speared him with his trident in a battle over the city's patronage. When Poseidon struck a truce with Athena, he was allowed to share the temple with her—the east is devoted to the goddess of wisdom and the west to the god of the sea. The east porch, with its six Ionic columns, sheltered an olive wood statue of Athena; like the Temple of Athena Nike, it contrasts with the Parthenon's dignified Doric columns. The Erechtheion's south side is supported by six women frozen in stone, the Caryatids. They're actually copies—the originals are safe in the Acropolis Museum.

ACROPOLIS MUSEUM. This museum neighboring the Parthenon shelters a superb collection of sculptures, including five of the Caryatids of the Erechtheion; the sixth has been whisked off to the British Museum. The statues seem to be replicas of one another, but a close look at the folds of their drapery reveals delicately individualized detail. Compare the stylized, entranced faces and frozen poses of the Archaic Period **Moschophoros** (calf-bearer) sculpture to the more idealized, more human Classical Period **Kritias** boy for a trip through the development of Greek sculpture. *(Open M 11am-7:30pm, Tu-Su 8am-7:30pm; off season M 11am-2pm, Tu-Su 8am-2pm. Cameras without flash allowed; no posing next to the objects. English labels.)*

ELSEWHERE ON THE ACROPOLIS. The southwest corner of the Acropolis looks down over the reconstructed **Odeon of Herodes Atticus,** a functional theater dating from the Roman Period (AD 160). See the *Athens News* for a schedule of concerts and plays there. You'll also see nearby ruins of the Classical Theater of Dionysus, the Asclepion, and the Stoa of Eumenes II. *(Entrance on Dionysiou Areopagitou. ☎210 322 1459. Though the Odeon is closed for general admission, performances are held throughout the summer. Purchase tickets at the door or over the phone. Theater of Dionysus open M-Sa 8am-7pm. €2, students €1.)*

AGORA

Enter the Agora in one of three ways: off Pl. Thission, off Adrianou, or as you descend from the Acropolis. ☎210 321 0185. Open Tu-Su 8:30am-3pm. €4, students and EU seniors €2, EU students and under 18 free.

The Agora served as the city's marketplace, administrative center, and center of daily life from the 6th century BC through AD 500. The Acropolis was the showpiece of the *polis;* the Agora was the heart and the soul. Many of the debates of Athenian democracy were held in the Agora; Socrates, Aristotle, Demosthenes, Xenophon, and St. Paul all preached here. After the 6th century AD, the Agora, like the Acropolis, passed through the hands of innumerable conquerors. The ancient Agora emerged again in the 19th century, when a residential area built above it was razed for excavations. Inhabited since 3000 BC, the Agora still stands at the center of Athens. Today, visitors have free reign over the 30-acre archaeological site it has become.

HEPHAESTEION. The Hephaesteion, on a hill in the northwest corner of the Agora, is the best-preserved classical temple in Greece. The 415 BC temple still flaunts cool **friezes,** which depict Hercules's labors and Athens native Theseus's adventures. The closer you look, the more impressed you'll be.

ODEON OF AGRIPPA. The Odeon of Agrippa, a concert hall built for Roman Emperor Augustus's son-in-law and right-hand man, now stands in ruins on the left of the Agora as you walk from the museum to the Hephaesteion. When the roof collapsed in AD 150, the Odeon was rebuilt at half its former size. From then on it served as a lecture hall. The actors' dressing room was turned into a porch supported by colossal statues, three of which still guard the site.

STOA OF ATTALOS. The elongated Stoa of Attalos was a multi-purpose building filled with shops and home to informal philosophers' gatherings. Attalos II, King of Pergamon, built the Stoa in the 2nd century BC as a gift to his alma mater Athens, where he had received his education. Reconstructed between 1953 and 1956, it now houses the **Agora Museum,** which contains relics from the site. The stars of the collection are the excellent black figure paintings by Exekias and a calyx-krater depicting Trojans and Greeks quarreling over Patroclus's body. *(☎210 321 0185. Open Tu-Su 8am-7pm and M 11am-7pm.)*

STOA BASILEIOS. Plato reports that Socrates's first trial was held at the recently excavated Stoa Basileios, or **Royal Stoa.** It served as the headquarters for the King Archon, one of the leading political and religious figures in ancient Athens. As you cross the subway tracks at the Adrianou exit, it's on the left.

OTHER ANCIENT SITES

KERAMEIKOS. The Kerameikos's rigidly geometric design becomes clearly visible from above, before you enter the grounds. The site includes a large-scale cemetery and a 40m-wide boulevard that ran through the Agora and the Diplyon Gate and ended at the sanctuary of Akademos (where Plato founded his academy in the 4th century BC). **Public tombs** for state leaders, famous authors, and battle victims lined this sacred road, and worshipers began the annual Panathenaean procession along its path. The Sacred Gate arched over the Sacred Way to Eleusis, traversed in annual processions. The **Oberlaender Museum** displays finds from the burial sites; its excellent collection of highly detailed pottery and sculpture is a highlight. *(Ermou 48, northwest of the Agora. From Syndagma, walk toward Monastiraki on Ermou for 25min. ☎210 346 3552. Open Tu-Su 8:30am-3pm. €2, students and EU seniors €1, EU students and under 18 free.)*

TEMPLE OF OLYMPIAN ZEUS AND HADRIAN'S ARCH. In the middle of downtown Athens, you'll spot the final trace of the largest temple ever built in Greece. The 15 majestic Corinthian columns of the Temple of Olympian Zeus mark where the temple once stood. Started in the 6th century BC, it was completed 600 years later by the Roman emperor Hadrian. None too shy, Hadrian attached his name to the centuries-long effort by adding his arch, which marked the boundary between the ancient city of Theseus and Hadrian's new city. A tiled Roman bath borders the site. *(Vas. Olgas at Amalias, next to the National Garden. ☎210 922 6330. Open Tu-Su 8:30am-3pm. Temple admission €2, students €1, EU students and under 18 free. Arch free.)*

BYZANTINE ATHENS

Viewing hours depend on each church's priest; mornings are best. Dress appropriately: long skirts for women, long pants for men, no bare shoulders.

Like their Classical counterparts, Byzantine sanctuaries have become a part of Athens's landscape. Religious Greeks often pause before churches to pay their respects before going about their business. A little time spent in a few churches gives a glimpse of the country's modern-day culture and faith.

Athens had become a political backwater by the time of Byzantine ascendancy. Thus, Byzantine Athens is best represented by religious structures, which are all over the city. Small charming churches pepper tiny streets, squeeze between modern buildings, and hide under concrete porticos. Although many of the churches are not from Byzantine times, they mimic the style quite beautifully. There are, of course, more authentic sites to be found. Shoppers and pedestrians on Ermou will run right into **Kapnikaria Church,** which stands in the middle of the street one block beyond Aiolou. A bas-relief decorates its west wall; it escaped destruction in 1834 only by the clemency of Louis I of Bavaria. Walking down Mitropoleos from Syndagma, you may notice a tiny red church on the corner of Pentelis—it's engulfed in a modern building. You'll also pass **Agios Eleftherios** and the **Mitropoli Cathedral.** A frieze with the Attic calendar of feast days adorns the front facade. **Agia Apostoli,** a well-preserved Byzantine church, stands at the east edge of the Agora in the heart of Athens. White-walled **Metamorphosis,** in Plaka near Pritaniou, was built in the 11th century and restored in 1956. Eleventh-century Russian Orthodox **Agia Triada,** a few blocks from Pl. Syndagma at Filellinon 21, is filled with silver angel icons. If you walk down Filellinon, you'll pass the **Sotira Lykodimou,** the largest medieval building in Athens, dating to 1031. It was built as part of a Roman Catholic monastery; now it is the city's Russian Orthodox Church.

MODERN ATHENS

OLYMPIC STADIUM. The Panathenaic Stadium is wedged between the National Gardens and Pangrati, carved into a hill. The Byzantines destroyed the Classical-era stadium, but in 1895 it was restored in Panteli marble. The site of the first modern Olympic Games in 1896, the stadium lay under a cloud of disappointment in 1996, when the centennial games were held in Atlanta. Still, in 1997, the stadium held the opening ceremonies of the World Track and Field Championships and is now being refurbished for the **2004 Summer Olympics** (the new Olympic stadium sits in the northern suburb of **Marousi**—take the M1 metro line right to it). 70,000 people can pack in the stands of this marble preserve for athletes and sunbathing students; military parades and gymnastic displays are held here, and it's the finish line of the **Athens Marathon** (p. 106), which begins 42km (26.2miles) away in Marathon. Marble *steles* near the front honor Greece's gold and silver medalists. *(On Vas. Konstantinou. From Syndagma, walk up Amalias 15min. to Vas Olgas, and follow it to the left. Or take trolley #2, 4, or 11 from Syndagma. Open daily 8am-8:30pm. Free.)*

AROUND SYNDAGMA. Be sure to catch the **changing of the guard** in front of the **Parliament** building. Every hour on the hour, two *evzones* (guards) wind up like toy soldiers, kick their tasseled heels in unison, and fall backward into symmetrical little guardhouses on either side of the **Tomb of the Unknown Warrior.** Unlike the stoic British beefeaters, *evzones* are known to give a wink and a smile. Their jovial manner matches their attire—pom-pommed clogs, *foustanelas* (short pleated skirts), and tasseled hats. Sunday at 10:45am, there's a special changing of the guard, a ceremony with a band and the full guard troop. Athens's endangered species, greenery and shade, are preserved in the very pretty **National Gardens,** their natural environment. There's a duck pond and a sad little zoo. Women should avoid strolling here alone.

OUTDOOR MARKETS. Athens's two major markets attract bargain hunters and browsers alike. The **Flea Market,** adjacent to Pl. Monastiraki, has a festive bazaar atmosphere: picture a massive garage sale where old forks and teapots are sold alongside the odd family heirloom. *(Open M, W, and Sa-Su 8am-3pm; Tu and Th-F 8am-8pm; Su is the best day to go.)* If you're hankering for a **bouzouki,** seek out the master, Bill Aevorkian at Ifestou 6 (☎210 321 0024). On Sunday, a huge **food market** takes over Athinas between Evripidou and Sofokleous. Not for the faint of heart, the **meat market** overwhelms with sights and smells of livers, kidneys, and skinned rabbits. Early risers can jostle with Athenian cooks (restauranteurs and moms alike) for choice meat, fish, fruits, vegetables, breads, and cheeses. *(Open M-Sa 8am-2pm.)*

THE HIDDEN DEAL

MONASTIRAKI FLEA MARKET

Sunday at the Monastiraki flea market is not your average market day. During the week, the regular clothes, jewelry, and shoe stores in the area are open and welcome you inside. But if you're looking for something unique and a bit more exciting, head to Monastiraki on Sunday. A good starting point is the Metro stop.

Older men and women line the streets selling all sorts of faux antiques from slapdash booths and rickety card tables, aggressive vendors scream over the roar of the bustling crowd, and money changes hands all around you. You'll find just about anything on Sunday, from bird cages to old records to leather goods to coconuts to mobile phones of questionable origins. It doesn't matter what you're looking for; you'll probably find it at the Monastiraki flea market, and it will be cheap.

With every purchase, bargaining (p. 33) is a must. The first price is never accurate nor fair; don't accept it. If the price doesn't come down, express your sympathies and tell the vendor that you'll have to move on; for the most part, you'll find similar goods just a few feet away. It's a buyer's market. However, the wealth of trinkets and trivia can be distracting, and pickpockets know it. Stay alert at all times, and watch your belongings.

Open on Sundays from around 8am-1pm.

MT. LYCAVITTOS. Of Athens's seven hills, Lycavittos is the largest and most central. Try ascending at sunset, when you can catch a last glimpse of Athens's densely packed rooftops in the waning daylight and watch the city light up for the night. Take the **funicular** to the top (2min.; every 10-15min.; round-trip €4, ages 3-10 €2)—the station is a healthy walk from the peak of Ploutarchou in Kolonaki (open M-W and F-Su 8:45am-12:15am, Th 10:30am-12:15am). You can also hike up—it's a nice 15-20min. walk from any approach. Bring water, watch out for slippery rocks, and don't climb alone (especially at night, when crime, accidents, and misnavigation are most frequent). At the top you'll see the **Chapel of St. George,** where you might spy a couple tying the knot. Light a candle (with a small donation) under the ornately painted ceilings. A leisurely stroll around the church provides a view of Athens's endless panoramic expanse. Using the Acropolis as a point of reference, the neighborhoods of Monastiraki, Omonia, and Exarhia are on your right. Continuing clockwise, you will see Areos Park behind a small circular patch of green—that's Strefi, another hill. The flashy lights and music of the Lycavittos Theatre are 180° from the Acropolis. The eastern view looks out on more parks, Mt. Hymettus, and a glimpse of the Panathenaic Olympic Stadium, the National Garden, and the Temple of Olympian Zeus back near the Acropolis.

NATIONAL CEMETERY. The National Cemetery houses deceased politicians, actors, poets, and foreigners who died in Athens. There are currently two kinds of graves—family graves and rented graves that give up their bones to boxes after three years. Soon, space limits will allow only three-year graves; even VIPs will be moved to the Mausoleum Commons after three years in the ground. As you enter the main gate, the Greek-speaking information bureau is on your left. The first graves are larger and more elaborate than most, as the rich and famous try to take it with them. On the left side of the first courtyard, archaeologist **Heinrich Schliemann,** excavator of Troy and Mycenae, lies in a pseudo-temple. To the left of the large statue of an angel is the tomb of **Melina Mercury,** a national film icon, who starred in *Never on Sunday* before becoming the Minister of Culture. On the main path, there is a small church where ceremonies are held for the dead. *(In Pangrati. From Pl. Syndagma walk down Amalias, turn left on Ath. Diakou, and then walk down Anapavseos. ☎210 922 1621. Open daily 8:30am-5:30pm. Free. For guided tours call the Cultural Center, Akadamias 50. ☎210 361 2705 or 210 363 9671. Dress respectfully.)*

MUSEUMS

NATIONAL ARCHAEOLOGICAL MUSEUM

Patission 44. A 20min. walk from Pl. Syndagma down Stadiou to Aiolou, and right onto Patission. Take trolley #2, 4, 5, 9, 11, 15, or 18 from the uphill side of Syndagma, or trolley #3 or 13 from the north side of Vas. Sofias. Or take the subway to Victoria, leave the station, and walk straight to the 1st street, 28 Octovriou. Turn right and walk 5 blocks. ☎210 821 7717. Open Apr.-Oct. M 12:30-7pm, Tu-Su 8am-7pm; Nov.-Mar. 8am-5pm; holidays 8:30am-3pm. €6, students and EU seniors €3; free Su and holidays from Nov.-Mar. No flash photography; no posing in front of the exhibits.

The jaw-dropping collection in the **National Archaeological Museum** deserves a spot on even the most rushed itinerary. Even a few pieces from this, the world's most extensive array of Greek artifacts, would steal the show in any other museum. Check your bags (free) and grab a **free map** of the museum. Hold on to your ticket, since the museum's arrangement redirects you to the entry several times, and you'll have to pay again if you lose it.

The museum begins with prehistoric pieces (room 4), including Heinrich Schliemann's **Mycenae** excavations (p. 120). At first glance you may think the German archaeologist discovered the Midas touch: it is a world of gold, including the **Mask of Agamemnon** (the death mask of a king who lived at least 3 centuries earlier than Agamemnon himself). You'll also see samples of Bronze Age jewelry and pottery and, in the side rooms, magnificent examples of Cycladic art.

The next exhibition, made up of 29 rooms, surveys Greek **sculpture** from the 8th century BC through the 5th century AD. Naked **kouroi** (p. 20) or standing young men, allow the viewer to trace every last inch of Greek sculpture's development from early Archaic (marked by rigidity and Egyptian influences) to Classical (emphasizing movement and bodily form) to late Roman (ornate and emotional). In room 12, don't miss the detailed, rippling abs of statue 13, a lifelike 540 BC work found at Megara. Compare the massive 530 BC *Kouros* of Sounion (item 2720), in room 8, to the 520 BC *kouros* named Kroisos (item 3851), in room 13; you'll notice how smoothness and fluidity seeped into sculpture over a decade. The 460 BC **bronze of Poseidon** poised to throw his trident (item 15161) seems to move—it was an inspiration to Renaissance artists in Western Europe. In room 21, the bronze **Jockey of Atemision,** recovered from the sea and restored this century, is full of life.

Mentally reconstruct the scene depicted in room 30 by the 100 BC statue of Aphrodite and Eros squabbling with Pan. Move on to the fabulously sexy sculptures in room 32. The luscious neck, lips, and expression of the bust of **Antinous** (item 417), a favorite of the emperor Hadrian, will move you, while the suggestive pose of the sleeping *maenad* (item 261) may arouse something other than your artistic interests. Sober up from such erotic exhibitions with the finds in room 48 on the second floor. Exquisite wall paintings and other finds come from **Anotiri Thira,** a 16th-century-BC civilization buried by volcanic eruption. Resembling both Egyptian and Minoan art, these images of dolphins, reeds, and a boy holding a fish highlight early fresco work. Don't miss the glittering **Stathos Collection,** off room 41, where you can admire gold tiaras, crowns, and masks that were only recently donated to the museum from a private collection of a rich shipping family. Finally, rooms 49-56 hold an overwhelming collection of 11th- to 4th-century BC **pottery,** featuring pieces of every shape and style.

OTHER MUSEUMS

GOULANDRIS MUSEUM OF CYCLADIC & ANCIENT GREEK ART. This 15-year-old museum, established by the philanthropic Goulandris shipping family, displays a stunning collection. The high-density exhibition space shows off its famous Cycladic figurines: sleek, abstract marble works, some with painted details that may represent tattoos. Many pieces were either looted from archaeological sites about 100 years ago or found in graves in the Cyclades. The figurines may represent goddesses, guides to the Underworld called *psychopompoi* or concubines. Bronze jewelry from Skyros, a collection of vases, and Corinthian helmets share the space. Visit the extension of the Cycladic collection on the corner of Vas. Sofias and Herodotou. *(Neophytou Douka 4. A 20min. walk toward Kolonaki from Syndagma on Vas. Sofias; turn left on Neophytou Douka. It's half a block up. Accessible by trolleys #3 and 13. ☎210 722 8321. Open M and W-F 10am-4pm, Su 10am-3pm. €3.50, students €1.80, archaeologists and archaeology students free.)*

BYZANTINE MUSEUM. In an elegant Neoclassical building, the Byzantine Museum's excellent collection of Christian art spans the 4th through 19th centuries. Early Byzantine sculptures, icons from the entire period, and three reconstructed early Christian basilicas squeeze into the space. Room 4, in the back left corner of the ground floor, has a ceiling cut in the shape of the cross and mosaic-studded floor. It centers around an *omphalon* representing an eagle and a snake. Also on the ground floor, you'll find an ornately reconstructed 17th-century Kephalonian church, with the 1863 throne of the Patriarch of Constantinople. You might want to buy a guidebook (€8) as exhibits are poorly marked. *(Vas. Sofias 22. ☎210 721 1027 or 210 723 2178. Open Tu-Su 8:30am-3pm. €4; students and seniors €2; EU students, under 18, and classicists free.)*

BENAKI MUSEUM. This museum boasts an impressive collection of art and archaeological artifacts from around the world. It represents the collection of Antoine Benaki, amassed during his European and Asian travels. Check out the Greek costumes and follow the development of Greek culture through the ages. *(Vas. Sofias and 1 Koumbari in Kolonaki. ☎210 367 1000. Open M, W, F, and Sa 9am-5pm, Th 9am-midnight, Su 9am-5pm. €6, students €3.)*

NATIONAL GALLERY. The National Gallery (a.k.a. Alexander Soutzos Museum) exhibits the work of Greek artists, with periodic international displays. The permanent collection includes outstanding work by El Greco, as well as drawings, photographs, and sculpture gardens. Call to find out about current exhibits. *(Vas. Konstantinou 50. Set back from Vas. Sofias, by the Hilton. ☎210 723 5857 or 210 723 5937. Open M and W-Sa 9am-3pm, Su 10am-2pm. €6.50, students and seniors €3, under 12 free.)*

WAR MUSEUM. Canons and fighter jets mark the museum, which traces Greek armaments from Neolithic times to the present. It's cool if you're into submachine guns, 5th century BC Persian invasions, or Alexander the Great. Model tanks, bombs, and booby traps amuse your inner psycho. *(Rizari 2. Next to the Byzantine Museum, off Vas. Sofias. ☎210 729 0543. Open Tu-F 9am-2pm, Sa-Su 9:30am-2pm. Free.)*

FOLK ART MUSEUM. Exhibiting *laiki techni* (popular art) from all over Greece, the museum has embroidered textiles, costumes, puppets, ornamental church silverwork, and household pottery. Don't miss the temporary exhibits or **Theophilos's** (p. 21) paintings. *(Kydatheneon 17, in Plaka. ☎210 321 3018. Open Tu-Su 10am-2pm. €2, students €1, EU students and children free. No flash photography.)*

POPULAR MUSICAL INSTRUMENTS MUSEUM. This interactive museum displays 18th-, 19th-, and 20th-century instruments. Grab the headphones at each exhibit to hear frenetic *kementzes* (bottle-shaped lyres) or *tsamboura* (goatskin bagpipe) music from the islands. Tapping metal coins jingle as dancers frolic. *(Diogenous 1-2, in Plaka. ☎210 325 0198. Open Tu and Th-Su 10am-2pm, W noon-6pm. Free.)*

ILIAS LALOUNIS JEWELRY MUSEUM. An Athenian jeweller and goldsmith elected to the French Academie des Beaux-Artes, Ilias Lalounis's jewel-studded art is displayed here, in his former home. Over 3000 designs from a 50-year period gleam in cases, and other displays trace Greek jewelry from ancient to modern times. There's a workshop where visitors can watch the magic happen. *(Kallisperi 12, south of the Acropolis. ☎210 922 1044. Open M and Th-Su 9am-4pm, W 9am-9pm. €3, students and seniors €1.50.)*

JEWISH MUSEUM. Occupying a brand new, seven-story building, this fascinating museum charts the Jewish experience in Greece from the Hellenistic Period. The collection includes textiles, religious artifacts, and a thorough library. A reconstructed synagogue and an exhibit on the Holocaust are also here. *(Nikis 39, in Plaka. ☎/fax 210 323 1577. Open M-F 9am-2:30pm, Su 10am-2pm. Library Tu and Th 11am-1pm. €3, students €1.50.)*

CHILDREN'S MUSEUM. This museum offers a colorful, friendly, hands-on experience in the heart of Plaka, faithfully subscribing to the motto, "I hear and I forget; I see and I remember; I do and I understand." Learn about the subway system or play dress-up in yesterday's bedroom. *(Kydatheneon 14, in Plaka. ☎210 331 2995 or 210 331 2996. Open M and Th-F 9:30am-1:30pm, W 9:30am-6:30pm, Sa-Su 10am-2pm. Free.)*

THEATER MUSEUM. For those thespians who want to study up on Greek theater, this is the place to go. The museum does an admirable job of tracing the history of Greek performance and displays a collection of playbills, photos, and masks from modern stagings of classical plays. You can also wander through the reconstructed dressing rooms of famous Greek actors and actresses. *(Akadamias 50, by the Panepistimiou metro stop. ☎210 362 9430. Open M-F 9am-2pm. Free.*

DAYTRIPS FROM ATHENS

CAPE SOUNION PENINSULA Ακρωτηριο Σουνιο

*Two **orange-striped KTEL buses** travel to Cape Sounion from **Athens:** one leaves from the Mavromateon 14 bus stop near Areos Park and stops at all points on the Apollo Coast (2hr., every hr. 6:30am-6:30pm, €4.10); the other follows a less scenic inland route (2¼hr., every hr. 6am-6pm, €5.60). Get off the bus at the last stop and head up to the right (facing the water), past the cafeteria to a ticket booth. The last coastal route bus leaves Sounion at 9pm, and the last inland one at 9:30pm.*

One of the most breathtaking sights one can experience in all of Greece is to see the brilliant evening sun sink below the **Temple of Poseidon** on **Cape Sounion.** Words alone cannot nearly prepare you for the sight of that giant red orb and the shimmering blue Aegean in every direction below the 60m rocky promontory.

Gracing the highest point on the Cape, the Temple of Posiedon has been a dazzling white landmark for sailors at sea for millennia. Originally constructed around 600 BC, the fortress of Sounion was destroyed by the Persians in 480 BC and rebuilt by Pericles in 440 BC. The 16 remaining Doric columns rise above the coast. Look closely at the graffiti for Lord Byron's name (on the square column as you face away from the cafeteria). Bits of the **Temple of Athena Sounias** litter the lower hill. *(☎22320 39 363. Open daily 10am-sunset. €4, students €2, EU students free.)*

After an hour at the temple during the day, many people head down to the **beaches.** To reach the ocean, follow one of the paths from the inland side of the temple. Swarming with vacationing families, the beaches along the Apollo Coast between Piraeus and Cape Sounion have a carnival atmosphere on summer weekends. Towns often have free public beaches, and some seaside stretches along the bus route remain uncrowded. Drivers will let you off almost anywhere if you ask.

MARATHON Μαραθωνας

The bus from the Mavromateon 29 station in Athens heads to Marathon (1½hr., every hr. 5:30am-10:30pm, €2.45), look for the bus's "Marathon" label; sit in front and remind the driver of your destination, and flag the bus down on the way back. Private transportation is the best way to see the sites, however, as they are spread out.

Gasping out two words—*Νικη ημιν*, "Victory to us"—**Phidippides** announced the decisive Athenian victory over the Persians in the bloody 490 BC battle of Marathon; he collapsed and died immediately afterward. His 42km sprint to Athens remains legendary, and today runners trace his Marathon route twice annually, beginning at a commemorative plaque. With a car, you can explore nearby sights and beaches. At **Ramnous,** 15km northeast, lie the ruins of the **Temple of Nemesis,** goddess of divine retribution, and **Thetis,** goddess of law and justice. **Schinias** to the north and **Timvos Marathonas** to the south are popular **beaches.** Developers are building a channel at Schinias which will be the sight of the rowing events in the 2004 Olympic Games.

To reach the **Archaeological Museum of Marathonas,** ask the bus driver to drop you at the "Mouseion and Marathonas" sign, after Marathon Town and the beach. Follow the signs through 2km of farms, bearing right at the fork, to the end of the paved Plateion road at #114. The small museum's five packed rooms focus on **death rituals:** you'll find Neolithic grave pieces (4000-2500 BC), Geometric sepulchres (2500 BC), Cycladic funeral offerings, Athenian and Plateian tombs and remains from the battle of Marathon, and a first-century BC baby skeleton surrounded by two beehives. An **Athenian trophy** commemorates the battle with the Persians. Marble heads of Marathon's arts patron Herodes Atticus and his star pupil Polydenkion are on display, as are some Egyptian statues probably from a temple of Isis and one of Atticus's poems. *(☎22940 55 155. Open Tu-Su 8:30am-3pm. €3, students €1.50, EU students, children under 18, student classicists and archaeologists free. Cemeteries from the Neolithic and Classical periods lie 2km from the museum; the oldest site dates from around 2500 BC. Ask for more information at the museum desk.)*

THE AGONY CONTINUES The Athens Marathon, run every November, traces Phidippides's supposed path from Marathon to Athens. Despite the 19km of "gentle" hills in the middle of the course followed by 11km of quad-pounding downhill, relatively few participants collapse at the end (although many wish that the ancient herald had dropped dead somewhere around Rafina instead of making it all the way to the capital). The course record of 2:11:07 has held since 1969, but Kenyan runners, who went 1-2-3 in the November 2001 race, may be on their way to surpassing this mark. Those who don't feel up to the full-length chase can sign up for the 10km race covering the last leg of the course, but the day belongs to those replicating Phidippides's feat—albeit in sneakers instead of sandals.

PIRAEUS Πειραιας

The natural harbor of Piraeus (also Pireas or Peiraias) has been Athens's port since 493 BC, when Themistocles concocted an ambitious plan to create a naval base for the growing Athenian fleet. A hilly peninsula gridded with big, white apartment buildings, Piraeus has all the dirt and grime of a commercial hub, including a waterfront lined with junk shops, shipping offices, travel agencies, and banks bordered by grimy neighborhoods. Despite the run-down appearance, Piraeus remains one of the busiest ports in the world and has some of the best restaurants (mainly seafood) in Attica.

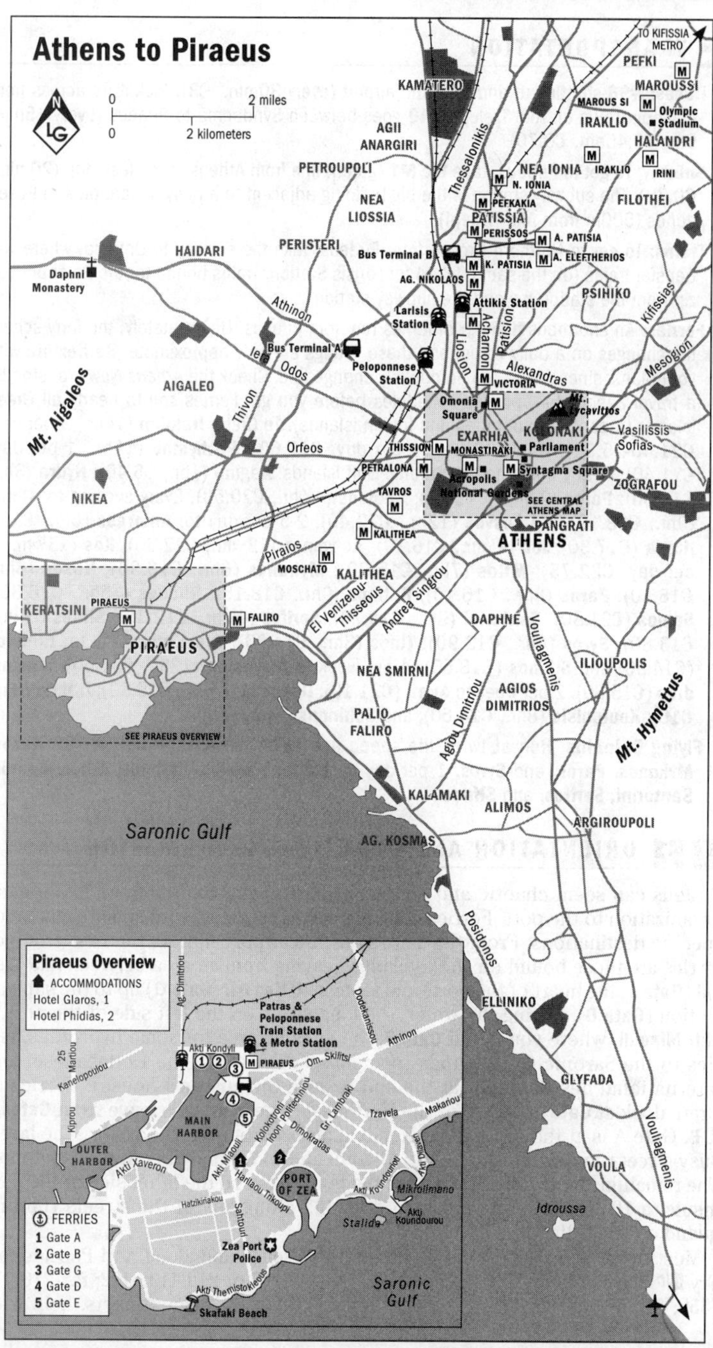
Athens to Piraeus
0
2 miles
0
2 kilometers
TO KIFISSIA METRO
PEFKI
MAROUSSI
MAROUS SI
Olympic Stadium
KAMATERO
AGII ANARGIRI
IRAKLIO
HALANDRI
PETROUPOLI
Thessalonikis
NEA IONIA
IRAKLIO
IRINI
N. IONIA
NEA LIOSSIA
PEFKAKIA
FILOTHEI
PATISSIA
PERISSOS
A. PATISIA
PERISTERI
HAIDARI
Bus Terminal B
K. PATISIA
A. ELEFTHERIOS
Daphni Monastery
AG. NIKOLAOS
PSIHIKO
Kifissias
Athinon
Attikis Station
Larisis Station
Acharnon
Patision
Liosion
Bus Terminal A
Iera Odos
Peloponnese Station
Alexandras
Mesogion
Mt. Aigaleos
AIGALEO
VICTORIA
Thivon
Omonia Square
Mt. Lycavittos
EXARHIA
KOLONAKI
Vasilissis Sofias
Orfeos
THISSION
MONASTIRAKI
Parliament
PETRALONA
Syntagma Square
Acropolis
National Gardens
ZOGRAFOU
NIKEA
TAVROS
SEE CENTRAL ATHENS MAP
PANGRATI
KALITHEA
ATHENS
Piraios
MOSCHATO
KALITHEA
KERATSINI
PIRAEUS
FALIRO
El Venizelou-Thisseous
Andrea Singrou
DAPHNE
PIRAEUS
Vouliagmenis
ILIOUPOLIS
NEA SMIRNI
AGIOS DIMITRIOS
Mt. Hymettus
PALIO FALIRO
Agiou Dimitriou
SEE PIRAEUS OVERVIEW
KALAMAKI
ALIMOS
ARGIROUPOLI
Saronic Gulf
AG. KOSMAS
Posidonos
Piraeus Overview
ACCOMMODATIONS
Hotel Glaros, 1
Hotel Phidias, 2
Ag. Dimitriou
Patras & Peloponnese Train Station & Metro Station
Dodekanissou
ELLINIKO
25 Martiou
Akti Kondyli
PIRAEUS
Athinon
Om. Skilitsi
Kanelopoulou
GLYFADA
Kolokotroni
Iroon Politechniou
Gr. Lambraki
Tzavela
Makariou
Kiprou
MAIN HARBOR
Dimokratias
OUTER HARBOR
Akti Miaouli
Akti Dilaveri
Akti Xaveron
PORT OF ZEA
Akti Koundourou
Mikrolimano
VOULA
Harilaou Trikoupi
Hatzikiriakou
Sahtouri
Akti Koundourou
Stalida
Idroussa
FERRIES
1 Gate A
2 Gate B
3 Gate G
4 Gate D
5 Gate E
Zea Port Police
Akti Themistokleous
Saronic Gulf
Skafaki Beach
Vouliagmenis

ATHENS

TRANSPORTATION

Buses: #96 shuttles to and from the airport (every 30min., €3). Pick it up across from Philippis Tours on Akti Tzelepi. **040** goes between Syndagma to Piraeus (every 15min. 5am-12:45am, €0.70).

Subway: To get to Piraeus, take the **M1** (green) line from Athens to the last stop (20min., €0.70). The subway station is the big building adjacent to a busy square on Akti Poseidonos (500m from Akti Tzelepi).

Trains: To get to Northern Greece from Piraeus, take the subway to Omonia, where you transfer trains (on the same ticket) for Larisis Station. Trains bound for the Peloponnese zip from the station beyond the subway station.

Ferries: An enormous number of ferries run from Piraeus. Unfortunately, the ferry schedule changes on a daily basis, and these listings are only approximate. **Be flexible** with your plans, since ferries are notoriously changeable. Check the *Athens News,* or stop by a travel agency for updated schedules before you go. Ferries sail to nearly all Greek islands (except the Sporades and Ionian islands). To Crete: **Iraklion** (14hr., 3 per day, €21.40-25.55); **Hania** (9½hr., 1 per day, €17.60); **Rethymno** (11hr., 1 per day, €21.40). Nearly hourly to the Saronic Gulf Islands: **Aegina** (1hr., €6.40); **Hydra** (3hr., €14.30); **Poros** (2½hr., €13.20); **Spetses** (4½hr., €20.50). Every evening to: **Chios** (9hr., €18.10) and **Lesvos** (12hr., €22.40). 2-5 per day to: **Amorgos** (6hr., €16); **Ikaria** (€17.30); **Ios** (7½hr., €16.70); **Kalymnos** (12½hr., €22.30); **Kos** (13½hr., 1 per day, €22.75); **Milos** (7hr., €15.80); **Mykonos** (6hr., €16.30); **Naxos** (6hr., €16.10); **Paros** (6hr., €16.10); **Patmos** (9hr., €18.15); **Rhodes** (15hr., €26.80); **Samos** (€21.30); **Santorini** (9hr., €18.70); **Serifos** (4½hr., €12.30); **Sifnos** (5¼hr., €13.80); **Syros** (4hr., €13.90); **Tinos** (3hr., €14.90). Every other day to: **Kimolos** (€14.30) and **Sikinos** (€18.50). 4 per week to **Astypalea** (12hr., €21.50) **Folegandros** (€15.80). 2 per week to **Anafi** (€21.10); **Donousa** (8½hr., €15.30); **Iraklia** (8hr., €15); **Koufonisia** (8hr., €14.60); and **Schinousa** (€15.50).

Flying Dolphins: Run at twice the speed and twice the cost. 2 per day to: **Naxos, Mykonos, Paros,** and **Syros.** 1 per day to: **Ikaria, Kimolos, Kythnos, Milos, Samos, Santorini, Serifos,** and **Sifnos.**

ATHENS

ORIENTATION AND PRACTICAL INFORMATION

Piraeus can seem chaotic and confusing at first glance, but there is a logical organization to the port. Ferries dock at five major gates, with specific gates for specific destinations. From the subway or the airport shuttle, the first group of ferries are those bound for the Cyclades, leaving from an area between **Akti Tzelepi** (**Gate D,** the heart of the port) and along **Akti Kondyli** (**Gate G**) up to the subway station (**Gate B**). Facing the water, the long street on the left side of the port is **Akti Miaouli,** where you'll find **Gate E,** the docking area for some hydrofoils, ferries to the Saronic Gulf Islands (some also at Gate G), the Dodecanese, and international destinations (at the end toward the customs house). Ferries to Crete dock at **Gate A;** those for the Northeast Aegean islands leave from **Gates A & B.** Gate A is at the end of Akti Kondyli, across from Ag. Dionysios. The large, busy street running alongside Akti Miaouli and Akti Kondyli is Akti Poseidonos. The remaining hydrofoils leave from the port of **Zea** on the other side of the peninsula, a 10min. walk up and then downhill along any of the streets running inland off Akti Miaouli.

Most ticket agencies can be found on Akti Tzelepi and along Akti Poseidonos. Try **Philippis Tours,** Akti Tzelepi 3 (☎210 411 2767 or 210 413 3182; fax 210 413 7359; filippistours@hotmail.com). They sell ferry and plane tickets, help with accommodations, rent cars, exchange money, and store baggage. Most **banks** along the waterfront **exchange currency. Citibank,** Akti Miaouli 47-49, has **ATMs.** (☎210 417 2153. Open M-Th 8am-2pm, F 8am-1:30pm.) There is an **American Express** office (☎210 429 5120) next door. The Piraeus **port police** (☎210 422 6000) are at Akti Zelopi; the Zea **port police** (☎210 459 3144) are along the water and under the sidewalk. For the **tourist police,** dial ☎210 429 0664. In an **emergency,** call the Athens police at ☎133, an ambulance at ☎166, and the fire station at ☎199. Stop in at **Telstar Booksellers,** just down Akti Miaouli from Citibank to grab last-minute reading for the ferry and the beaches on your island of destination. (☎210 429 3618; fax 210 429 3710; tel-star@otenet.gr. Open M-Sa 8am-8pm.) The **OTE** is at Karaoli Dimitriou 19. (Open M-F 7am-2:40pm.) To check your email, head to **Surf In Internet Cafe,** Polytexneiou 42-44 and Platonos. (☎210 42 27 478; www.surfin.gr. €3.60 per hr. Open daily 9am-9pm.) The main **post office** is off the street at the bend in the road all the way down Akti Miaouli toward the Expo Centre. (☎210 417 1584. Open M-F 7:30am-2pm.) Zea's **post office** is near their port police. (☎210 418 3380. Open M-F 7:30am-2pm.) **Postal code:** 18502 (Piraeus), 18504 (Zea).

ACCOMMODATIONS AND FOOD

Inexpensive, quality accommodations are much easier to find in Athens, but an adequate option in Piraeus is **Hotel Glaros ❸**, H. Trikoupi 4, off Akti Miaouli, toward the Expo Centre. (☎210 451 5421; fax 210 453 7889; idea@otenet.gr. Singles €36; doubles €50.) There's also luxurious **Hotel Phidias ❹,** Koundouriotou 189, near Zea off Bouboulinas (off Akti Miaouli), with spacious rooms, private baths, TVs, and A/C. (☎210 429 6160; fax 210 429 6251; phidiasgr@otenet.gr. Breakfast included. Singles €47.30; doubles €66.60.) Dockside fast food joints hawk average food for cheap. You can stock up on staples at **supermarkets** around town. There's a cute restaurant and cafe area between the buildings near Kolokotroni and Tsamadou. Dine and relax there to soft music, a welcome contrast to the jarring madness of the port. **Belle Epoque ❶** serves an incredible fruit salad (€4) with whipped cream and blackberry sauce. (Open daily 8:30am-1am.) For a more substantive meal, there's also **Brazilian ❷,** which illogically serves Greek food; try the *bekri meze* chicken. (☎210 411 4954. Open daily 6am-1:30am.) **Varoulko ❺,** Deligiorgi 14, has earned itself a prestigious Michelin Star for its wonderful seafood dishes, excellent service, and charming atmosphere. The dishes are all original and very tasty, and the prices may be the highest in Attica (entrees €25 and up).

SIGHTS

The prize possession of the **Piraeus Archaeological Museum,** H. Trikoupi 31, is the ancient **Piraeus Apollo,** a hulking hollow bronze figure with outstretched arms. Three other bronze statues of Athena and Artemis impress visitors. Found near the port in 1959, they had been shelved in a storeroom for safekeeping when Piraeus was besieged by Sulla in 86 BC. Notice their eyes—the strange spots of color are precious stones (☎210 452 1598. Open Tu-Su 8:30am-3pm. €3, students €1.50, children ages 15 and under free.) Farther south at Zea, a stroll down the ramp to the dock at Akti Themistokleous and Botassi leads to the **Hellenic Maritime Museum,** which traces the Greek navy's history using detailed ship models. Of particular note in room B is a model of an Athenian trireme used in the Persian Wars (490-480 BC). The courtyard holds torpedo tubes, naval weapons, and the top part of the World War II submarine *Papanikolis.* (☎210 451 6264; fax 210 451 6822. Open Tu-Sa 9am-2pm. €1.50, Sa free.)

RAFINA Ραφηνα

Rafina feels like a smaller, quieter version of Piraeus. It, too, is a prominent port (although recently ferry service to Rafina has lessened considerably), but there's less to do and it's easier on the eyes, ears, and lungs than its larger counterpart.

ORIENTATION AND PRACTICAL INFORMATION. The ramp up from the waterfront leads to **Pl. Plastira. Ferries** sail to: **Marmari** in Evia (1¼hr., 4-6 per day, €4); **Andros** (2hr., 2 per day, €8); **Mykonos** (5hr., 2-3 per day, €13.60); **Syros** (4 hr., Su., €11.50); and **Tinos** (4hr., 2-3 per day, €12). **Flying Dolphins** skip, at twice ferry speed for twice ferry price, daily to **Mykonos** and **Tinos** (1½hr., €25). **Nel Lines** goes to **Agios Efstratios, Limnos,** and **Kavala** (1 per week); buy tickets at the office with the red door to the left of the waterfront (☎22940 22 293). The **port authority** (☎22940 22 300 or 22940 28 888) has more info. Along the waterfront, English-speaking **Blue Star Ferries** (☎22940 23 561; fax 22940 23 350), **Rafina Tours** (☎22940 24 660 or 22940 28 518; fax 22940 26 400), or **Hellas Ferries** (☎22940 22 700; fax 22940 26 100), all open daily 6am-10pm, sell tickets for ferries and catamarans. Rafina is accessible by frequent **buses** from Athens's station at Mavromateon 29, two blocks up along Areos Park, a 15min. walk from Pl. Syndagma (1hr., every 30min. 5:40am-10pm, €1.55) or via airport shuttle (every 40min., 6am-9:20pm). Return buses leave Rafina from the ramp on the waterfront.

Both **Commercial Bank,** two blocks inland from the plateia (☎22940 25 182; open M-Th 8am-2pm, F 8am-1:30pm), and the **Alpha Bank,** one block beyond the far left corner of the plateia (☎22940 24 152; open M-Th 8am-2pm, F 8am-1:30pm), **exchange currency** and have 24hr. **ATMs. Taxis** line up in front of the plateia; call one at ☎22940 23 101. Facing inland at the dock, the **post office** is two streets to the right on El. Venizelou. (☎22940 23 777. Open M-F 7:30am-2pm.) The unmarked building that passes for an **OTE** is inland from the plateia, beside the church. (☎22940 25 182. Open M-F 7:30am-3pm.) There's a **doctor** on El. Venizelou. (☎22940 24 824 or 22940 24 135. Open daily 7:30am-noon and 6-8pm.) **Police** are available at ☎22940 22 100, and **medical emergency** service at ☎166. You can find **pharmacies** on Kyprion Agoniston and on Eth. Antistasiou, by the Alpha Bank. **Postal code:** 19009.

ACCOMMODATIONS AND FOOD. Don't stay in Rafina unless you get stuck here: it's boring and expensive. **Hotel Korali,** Pl. Plastira 11, rents standard rooms with shared baths. (☎22940 22 477. Singles €20 and up; doubles €35 and up; triples €42 and up.) Tiny inlets let you **swim** or **sunbathe** if you've got a spare hour. Head right at the top of the ramp, right again at the end of the blue fence, then follow the coast and pick your spot. If you keep walking, you'll get to a long beach with rough sand. Cafes, pizzerias, and tavernas line the plateia and waterfront. Early ferry-catchers can try **Arktopolia,** an inexpensive bakery, on the left side of the plateia when you're facing away from the water. (☎22940 26 083. Fresh bread €0.50, croissants with various fillings €1.10 and up, and yogurt €.80. Open daily 6am-11pm.) A **mini-market** sells fruits, vegetables, and toiletries off Pl. Plastira, two buildings from Arktopolia. (Open daily 8am-2pm and 5-10pm.)

PELOPONNESE
Πελοποννησος

A hand-shaped peninsula stretching its fingers into the Mediterranean, the Peloponnese is steeped in history and folklore that contribute to its otherworldly atmosphere. The remnants of ancient civilizations and their achievements mark the present-day peninsula, and its timeless natural beauty remains unchanged. The majority of Greece's best archaeological sites are here, including Olympia, Mycenae, Messene, Corinth, Mystras, and Epidavros. Uncommon landscapes, from the barren crags of the Mani to the forested peaks and flower-blanketed pastures of Arcadia, grace Pelops's former home. A world apart from the islands, the serenely beautiful and sparsely populated Peloponnese remembers 5000 years of continuous habitation, from the ancients to the traditions of village life.

HIGHLIGHTS OF THE PELOPONNESE

AN ANCIENT CITY STILL LIVES in Monemvasia, where cobbled streets and castle-like buildings line streets traversed only by donkeys and pedestrians (p. 169).

THE BYZANTINE GHOST TOWN Mystras, once the capital of the Greek part of the empire, invites you into the living architectural museum it has become (p. 162).

TAKE A BREAK FROM ANTIQUITY in the exquisite Arcadian mountain villages of mountainside Dimitsana (p. 148) and medieval Stemnitsa (p. 149).

BE A CONTENDER at ancient Olympia, where pan-Mediterranean Greek city-states squared off every four years in the original Olympic Games (p. 142).

DROP A COIN on the center stage of the acoustically marvelous theater of Epidavros, and a friend can hear it in the last row (p. 130).

PELOPONNESE

CORINTHIA Κορινθια AND ARGOLIS Αργολιδα

Argos, a monster endowed with 100 unblinking eyes, once stalked the north Peloponnese, subduing unruly satyrs and burly bulls. Corinthia and Argolis hold a lion's share of impressive archaeological sites, secluded villages, and lively cities, but, alas, the population of roving mythological beasts has declined sharply. Consider making Nafplion (p. 124) your base for exploring the region, as this charming city allows access to Mycenae, Corinth, Tiryns, and Epidavros, and Nemea, Isthmia, and Argos's Heraion.

NEW CORINTH Κορινθος

New Corinth rests on the Gulf of Corinth, just west of the canal that separates the Peloponnese from the Greek mainland. Like its ancient predecessor (7km southwest of the city), New Corinth has been rocked by several earthquakes, most recently in 1981. To prevent tectonic disasters, Corinthians have rebuilt their city with low and unimaginative, but sturdy and shockproof, buildings. The ornate dec-

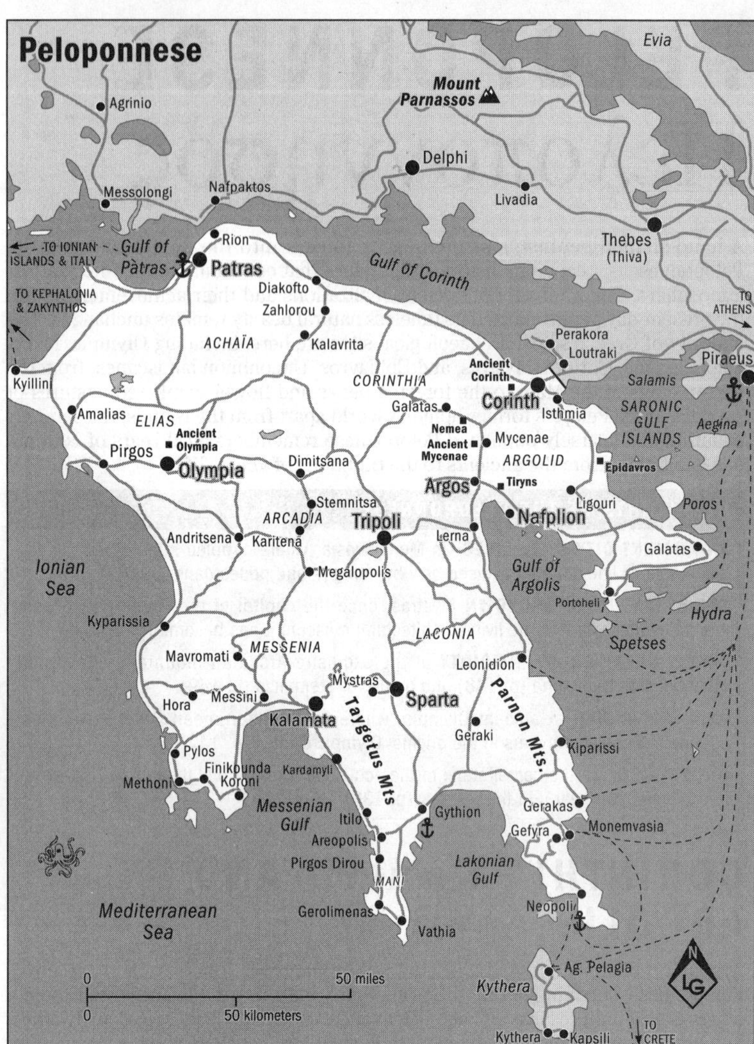

oration of ancient Corinthian architecture has not been replicated in the present. Despite an attractive harbor and a few shady cafe-lined pedestrian streets, Corinth remains fairly dirty, busy, and plain; bypass the experience by staying at out-of-town campgrounds or in nearby Loutraki (p. 117).

TRANSPORTATION

Buses deposit passengers and taxis line up at the city's central park, between Eth. Antistasis and Ermou. The train station is a few blocks southeast. To find the waterfront from the station, turn left out of the building onto Dimokratias, then take the first right onto Damaskinou.

Buses: Terminal A: past the train station on Dimokratias. To: **Athens** (1½hr., 30 per day 5:30am-9:30pm, €5.07). **Terminal B:** walking inland on Eth. Anistasis, turn right on Koliatsou, halfway through the park; the terminal is outside a bakery. To: **Ancient Corinth** (20min., 15 per day 7am-9pm, €0.80 each way). **Terminal C:** the **Argolis Station** (☎27410 24 403 for Nafplion or Mycenae, ☎27410 25 645 for Isthmia, Nemea, Loutraki) is at the intersection of Eth. Antistasis and Aratou, 1 block past the park. The station has several counters, each serving different destinations. The first counter on the right as you enter off Eth. Antistasis serves **Isthmia** (10min., 6 per day, €0.80); **Nemea** (45min., 7 per day 7:30am-5pm, €2.95); and **Loutraki** (20min., 2 per hr. 5:30am-10pm, €1.10). The counter on the left serves buses to **Mycenae** (45min., €2.40) via **Fihtia** (1.5km from the site); **Argos** (1hr., €3); and **Nafplion** (1½hr., €3.80), which leave at 7am, and then every hr. 8:30am-9:30pm. To get to **Sparta** or other points south, take the Loutraki bus to the Corinth Canal and pick up the Athens bus to Sparta, Kalamata, Koroni, or Tripoli; or depart for these destinations from a new bus station south of town, but you'll need a taxi (€3).

Trains: The **station** (☎27410 22 523) is on Dimokratias, off of Damaskinou. To: **Athens** (2hr., 14 per day, €2.60) via **Isthmia.** Two major train lines serve the Peloponnese: one travels the northern coast from Corinth to Pirgos and south to Kyparissia; the other goes south from Corinth to Tripoli and Kalamata. To: **Argos** (1hr., 6 per day, €1.18); **Diakofto** (1½hr., 8 per day, €2.10); **Kalamata** (4½hr., 4 per day, €5.60); **Kyparissia** (5hr., 6 per day, €5.60); **Patras** (2½hr., 8 per day, €3.20); **Pirgos** (4hr., 7 per day, 5.60); **Tripoli** (2hr., 4 per day, €2.19). Express trains generally cost twice as much. If you plan on using the facilities at the station, bring your own toilet paper.

Taxis: (☎27410 73 000), along the park side of Eth. Antistasis.

ORIENTATION AND PRACTICAL INFORMATION

New Corinth spreads out in a neat grid, which makes it fairly simple to navigate. The main drag, **Eth. Antistasis,** runs perpendicular to the waterfront. Both **Ermou** (on the other side of the park) and **Kolokotroni** (another block away from the park) are parallel to Eth. Antistasis. All three intersect **Damaskinou,** which borders the harbor. Two blocks inland from the shore, between Eth. Antistasis and Ermou, is the city's central park—now with peacocks. Most of the town's shops and restaurants are found on these four streets.

Tourist Police: Ermou 51 (☎27410 23 282), upstairs. Maps, brochures, and assistance. English spoken. Open daily 8am-2pm.

Banks: National Bank, Eth. Antistasis 7, 1 block up from the water, has **currency exchange** and a 24hr. **ATM.** A number of other banks with these services are also on Eth. Antistatis. Banking hours are mostly M-F 8am-2pm.

Public Toilets: Across from the park on Eth. Antistasis. Open 24hr. Toilet paper €0.30.

Police: Ermou 51 (☎100 or 27410 81 100), facing the park. Open 24hr.

Pharmacy: Many on Eth. Anastasis and Koliatsou, most open M-F 8am-2pm and 5-8pm.

Hospital (☎27410 25 711), on Athinaion; cross the train tracks and turn left. It's a long walk, so take a cab or call the hospital for an **ambulance** in an emergency. Open 24hr.

OTE: Kolokotroni 32 (☎27410 24 499). Open M-F 7:30am-1:30pm.

Internet Access: Stretto, Pinarinou 17 (☎27410 25 570), right off the first block of Eth. Antistasis. Sip coffee (€1.50) and check your email (€3 per hr., €1.50 minimum). Open M-Sa 8:30am-11pm, Su 5-11pm.

Post Office: Koliatsou 15 (☎27410 80 050), two blocks away from the park off Ermou. Open M-F 7:30am-2pm. **Postal code:** 20100.

THE 2004 GAMES

ANXIETY AND PROGRESS

To no one's surprise, the 2004 Olympic Games are on the lips of every Greek and in the pages of every publication. In every touristed town, one can buy "Athens 2004" shirts, sweatshirts, and baseball hats. Major construction projects on everything from ancient sites to city sidewalks are underway. Cities like Patras (p. 131) are making visible efforts to improve tourist services; a shiny new Info Center near the center of town and computerized kiosks scattered near transportation stations offer all manners of assistance to travelers.

Still, tourism in Greece is noticeably down this summer, and with it the hopes of restaurant owners and hotel managers that the Olympics will improve the situation. In Nafplion (p. 124), one skeptical local complained that people were pinning too much on the Olympics; he believes visitors will come to the Games and then simply return home. The Olympics-driven tourism boom, he explained, will be a huge disappointment.

In Patras, one of the four Olympic cities, many applauded the efforts made by the city to improve tourist relations but expressed concern that not enough was being done to attract and aid potential tourists. One problem is the transportation system in Greece. Not only can the trains and buses be inefficient, they can be very confusing for a first-time traveler to the country. Travelers often have to depend on the helpfulness of bus drivers or ticket sellers for information. While intrepid and seasoned travelers may be able and willing to navigate

ACCOMMODATIONS AND CAMPING

Most travelers on their way to the nearby sites don't spend much time in New Corinth, so domatia, hostels, and budget hotels are rare. New Corinth's few hotels tend to be pricey and are mostly on Eth. Antistasis and Damaskinou.

Hotel Akti, Eth. Antistasis 3 (☎27410 23 337), is your best bet for an inexpensive (but noisy) stay in New Corinth. Simple, utilitarian bedrooms have private sink (toilet and showers shared), and some have balconies with great views of the water at no extra charge. Singles €12-15; doubles €25-30. ❷

Hotel Apollon, Pirinis 18 (☎27410 22 587; fax 27410 83 875), at the intersection with Damaskinou near Dimokratias. Undergoing renovation in 2002, Apollon's clean rooms have TVs, balconies, and private baths. Singles have fans; doubles have A/C. Singles €22; doubles €35. ❷

Camping Korinth Beach (☎27410 27 920) is 3km out of town. Catch a westbound bus (toward Ancient Corinth) and get off at the signs for the campground. €3.50 per person; €2.50 per tent. ❶

Ephira Hotel, Eth. Antistasis 52 (☎27410 22 434; fax 27410 24 514), 2 blocks inland from the park. 45-room hotel has well-kept rooms with private baths, A/C, TVs, and balconies. Enjoy breakfast (€5) in a lovely, flowery courtyard. Singles €35; doubles €55; triples €70. A/C €5 extra. Prices lower in low season. ❸

Blue Dolphin (☎27410 25 766) is 1.5km beyond Camping Korinth Beach, with campsites on Lecheon beach. You can catch the Ancient Corinth-New Corinth bus back to town (the campground provides tickets) if the driver notices you waiting by the campground stop: wave if you want to snag the bus. €4.60 per person; €2.80 per small tent, €4 per large tent; €2 per car; electricity €2.80. ❶

FOOD

After 9pm, downtown New Corinth perks up a bit, as residents flock to the waterfront to dine outdoors in the balmy evening air. As in the daytime, speed seems to be a virtue in New Corinth; fast food is *de rigeur*, and waiters deftly dodge the traffic on Damaskinou to shuttle between restaurants and their outdoor seating areas across the street on the waterfront plateia.

Akhinos (Αχινος), Damaskinou 41 (☎27410 28 889), on the waterfront plateia. The colorful chairs and tablecloths add a festive touch to *al fresco* dining. Moussaka (€4.70) and feta in olive oil (€2.35) are among the many Greek specialty dishes. One of the few tavernas open for breakfast (omelette €3.60). Open daily 10am-2am. ❶

24 Oro, Ag. Nicholou 19, 1 block toward the waterfront from Damaskinou, on the right past Axinos and the museum. This taverna serves classic staples; ask to see a menu or just look in the kitchen and point to what you would like. Cucumber and tomato salad €2.50, *pastitsio* €4.50, *orzo* in clay bowl €6. ❶

Taverna Anaxagoras, Ag. Nikolaou 31 (☎27410 26 933), on the opposite side of the waterfront plateia from 24 Oro. An out-of-the-way local favorite, this large taverna offers a huge selection of Greek dishes, including seafood. Appetizers €2.30-3, entrees €8. Seafood dishes €8-28. Open daily from noon. ❷

Nekkas Bakery, at the corner of Eth. Anistatis and Adimantou, by the central park. Satiate your sweet tooth with delicious pastries such as baklava and almond cookies (€2.90 per kg) and fresh bread (€0.50-0.90). Open daily from 6am. ❶

NIGHTLIFE

New Corinth lets down its hair at night, when motorcycle-mounted teens head west of the city to **Kalami Beach.** To reach Kalami without a motorcycle, walk four blocks past the park along Eth. Anistasis, turn right, and walk ten blocks. As the neighborhood is disconcertingly dark and empty at night, women may prefer taking a taxi from the park (€1.50); tell the driver "Kalami" or "*thalassa*" (the sea). Kalami's strip has something for everyone. Mixed crowds of older couples, teens and families with small children take to the beachfront late at night. On the waterfront street, overlooking the sparkling lights of Loutraki, an assembly of cafes and clubs strut their stuff, each with thumping bass and expansive umbrellas. **Pizza Ami** marks the middle of the strip; it's a local late-night favorite for its delicious pasta (€3.50-4.90) and pizza (€5.70-10). To the left of Pizza Ami, lies a string of clubs including **Pregio** and **Unique.** You'll find Corinth's hip young things sipping beer (€3) and mixed drinks (€5-6), mingling, and listening to American dance tunes over the sounds of the crashing waves. To the right of Pizza Ami huddle restaurants, such as **Cafe Mon Ami,** and more clubs and bars, such as **Club Loft** and **Freedom.** If you'd rather hang downtown, try **Pinarinou** (Πιναρινου), right off the first block of Eth. Antistasis, as an alternative to the beach. Past the intersection with Koloktroni, the street fills with outdoor tables of cafes, pubs, and small restaurants. The typical and trendy **Saloon Giorgo** pumps bass through its doors to (relatively) quieter tables outside.

the intricacies of the bus and ferry-routes, many of those attending the Olympics may end up too frustrated to bother. Partly in response to concerns such as these, the Greek National Tourism bureau has established *Estia 2002*, an information line that travelers can call to lodge a complaint or get information. By dialing ☎171, a tourist can reach the office, which will employ people who speak English, most Western European, and some Eastern European languages.

Younger Greeks in particular seem eager to receive so many visitors and look forward to showing off the fun and beauty of their country. People in towns near large tourist attractions, be they famous beaches or ruined temples, are expecting record numbers of visitors. Many are making special arrangements: the Achaia Clauss Winery near Patras plans to bottle and sell a limited number of liters of Mavrodaphne wine from 1896, the first year that the modern Olympics were held. All in all, though opinions about the potential benefits of and preparedness for the 2004 Olympic Games may vary from enthusiastic to scornful, everyone looks to them with interest.

DAYTRIPS FROM CORINTH

ANCIENT CORINTH Αρχαια Κορινθος

7km southwest of New Corinth. Buses from Corinth city leave from outside the bakery on Koliatsou (20min.; every hr. 7:10am-10:10pm, return buses leave at half past the hour; €0.80). ☎ 27410 31 207. Open daily 8am-7pm; off season 8am-5pm. Guidebooks €6-7. Museum and site €6, students €3, EU students free.

Strategically located on the isthmus between the Corinthian and Saronic Gulfs, Ancient Corinth was once a powerful commercial center and one of the most influential cities in ancient Greece; its opulent wealth attracted *hetairai* (courtesans) as well as merchants, earning it a reputation as a sinful (but fun) city. At its height in the 5th century BC, Corinth joined forces with southern neighbor Sparta against the naval muscle of Athens—a power struggle that led to the Peloponnesian Wars (p. 10). While the war won dominance for Sparta, the long struggle weakened Corinth considerably. After the Romans sacked and virtually razed the city in 146 BC, Corinth remained deserted until Julius Caesar rebuilt it in 44 BC.

ANCIENT SITE. The remains of the ancient Roman city stand at the base of the **Acrocorinth** (a fortress atop a large mountain). Past the exit of the museum, the archaeological site is down the stairs to your left. Its bleached columns reconstructed from the 6th-century BC **Temple of Apollo** contrast strikingly with the vivid blue sky. Columns, engraved friezes, and pediments lie around the courtyard in majestic chaos. As you pick your way through the rubble, an unparalleled view of New Corinth and the Gulf stretches out below. Facing the entrance of the museum, the Corinthian columns on your left make up the facade of a Roman shrine. Behind the museum is the **Fountain of Glauke,** named after Jason's second wife, who was consumed by flames from an enchanted robe given to her by Medea, the jilted first wife of Jason (of Argonaut fame). From the Temple of Apollo and facing the mountainous Acrocorinth, the remains of the forum, the center of Roman civil life, lie in front of you. Walk down the middle of the row of central shops and you'll see the **Julian Basilica.**

To the left, near the exit at the edge of the site farthest from the museum, a broad stone stairway descends into the **Peirene Fountain,** perhaps the most impressive structure on the site. Although smoothed and patinated by the water that still flows today, the columns and fresco-covered tunnels inside the fountain have survived the centuries unharmed. Peirene was the daughter of the river god Asopus; when one of her sons (by Poseidon, no less) was accidentally killed, she shed "endless tears" and was turned into the spring. Just past the fountain is the **Perivolos of Apollo,** an open-air court surrounded by still more columns. On the uphill edge of the site, on the side farthest from the museum, somewhat ragged sheds cover the mosaic floors of a Roman villa. Unfortunately, you'll have to peer through a rusted chain link fence, as entry is not permitted.

ARCHAEOLOGICAL MUSEUM. In 2000, nearly 285 objects stolen from the museum in 1990 were returned after being found in Miami. With these valuables back in Corinth, the Archaeological Museum proudly displays its restored collection of impressive statues, well-preserved mosaics, tiny clay figurines, and pottery, tracing Corinth's history through Greek, Roman, and Byzantine rule. The Roman frescoes and mosaics date from the same period as Pompeii, and changes in pottery technique showcase Greece's evolution from Neolithic to Byzantine times. The museum's collections of sarcophagi (including one with a skeleton under glass) and headless statues in the open-air courtyard are morbidly appealing. While the exhibits are noteworthy, there isn't much explanation of their history or relationship to the site, so it's worthwhile to purchase a guidebook (€7).

FORTRESS AND ACROCORINTH. Hiking to the fortress at the top of Acrocorinth is a strenuous 2hr. climb, and only for the truly dedicated. Taxis are an easy alternative. The hike down, on the other hand, is a pleasant hour of amazing views. At the summit, the Temple to Aphrodite, once served by "sacred courtesans" who initiated diligent disciples into the "mysteries of love," remains largely intact. The relatively empty fortress contains acres of towers, mosques, gates, and walls. *(To get there from the archaeological site, grab a taxi (☎27410 31 464; €6) outside the site's exit. It will wait for an hour and drive you back down for €9.)*

ISTHMIA Ισθμια

At Terminal C, catch the bus from Corinth to Isthmia (10min., 6per day, €0.80). Ask to be let off at the green museum (☎27460 37 244). Open M-Sa 8:30am-3pm, Su and off season 9:30am-2:30pm. €3, students €2, EU students free.

Like Olympia, Isthmia was the site of prestigious athletic contests every four years. An excellent museum complements the remains of the ancient complex, displaying carefully diagrammed exhibits of finds from the Temple of Poseidon and the sites of the Isthmian games. Of particular interest are the glass *opus sectile* (mosaic panels), which survived the earthquake of AD 375 to be discovered at nearby Kenchreai. The entrance to the ruins lies to the right of the museum. All that remains of the **Temple of Poseidon** is its foundation. The **theater** is below and to the right of the temple; caves that were home to Archaic revelry lie above it.

NEMEA Νεμυα

4km from modern Nemea; coming by bus from Corinth (1hr., 7 per day, €2.80), ask to be let off at the ancient site. ☎27460 22 739. Site and museum open Tu-Su 8am-2:30pm; call to confirm. €3, students €2, EU students free.

The temple of **Nemean Zeus** had dwindled to three columns, but in 1984 reconstruction on two of the north columns began, and today one stands anew. The picturesque site includes a glass-encased grave with skeleton, a stadium (500m down the road to Corinth), and well-preserved baths. Nemea's stadium and athletic center hosted biennial games in their heyday. The airy museum has a collection of tools, coins, and statues, as well as reconstructions and drawings of the site, with excellent explanatory notes in English.

PELOPONNESE

LOUTRAKI Λουτρακι

The pebbled beach of Loutraki, just over the Isthmus of Corinth on the mainland, has attracted vacationers since ancient times. Visitors still come to soak in the natural springs for their reputed healing powers. This potent stuff is also bottled and sold all over Greece. Although hotels dominate the streets and waterfront and tourists crowd the beach, Loutraki's vacation atmosphere and beautiful surroundings allow for a pleasant overnight stay on the way to nearby sites.

TRANSPORTATION. To get to Loutraki from Isthmia, cross the canal bridge and find the bus stop next to a railroad station sign. Stay on the bus until the last stop, a triangular road island where **El. Venizelou,** the main street, meets **Periandrou** and **Eth. Antistasis.** Running parallel to the water, El. Venizelou curves away from Corinth at the northern end of the strip and becomes **Giorgiou Lekka.** The change from Venizelou to G. Lekka marks the central square of Loutraki, but the beach and most of the tourist activity are along the boardwalk and on Venizelou. **Buses** also leave the station on El. Venizelou for **Corinth** (20min.; 2 per hr. 6am-10:30pm, service reduced Su; €1.10) and **Athens** (1¼hr.; 9 per day 6:05am-9pm, service reduced Sa-Su; €5.70). Boat excursions are available at the dock past the park. Cruises sail to **Lake Vouliagmeni** and down the **Corinth Canal.** Times and prices vary; see listings posted on the pier or contact the tourism office for more information. For a **taxi,** call ☎27440 61 000 or 27440 65 000, or stop by the stand next to the Tourist Info center on El. Venizelou. For **moped rentals,** visit **Moto-Rent** (near the bus station), one of three moped rental shops. (☎27440 67 277. 50cc bike €18 per day.)

PRACTICAL INFORMATION. Loutraki has no lack of tourist information. There are two **tourist information center** kiosks: one is located on El. Venizelou one block south (Corinth-bound) from the bus station; the other is after the curve at the central square on G. Lekka, right at the end of the town park. (Both open daily 8am-2pm and 7-9pm.) The pretentiously-named **Municipal Enterprise for Touristic Development** office, in the central square, is a wonderful resource for any and all adventures in Loutraki: water parks, scuba-diving, hang-gliding, and other tours or cruises. (☎27440 26 001 or 27440 26 325; fax 27440 21 124; loutraki@kor.forthnet.gr. Open M-F 7:30am-3pm.) To get to the **National Bank,** follow El. Venizelou to the central square. (☎27440 22 220; fax 27440 64 945. 24hr. **ATM** available. Open M-Th 8am-2pm, F 8am-1:30pm.) Periandrou, the first side street on the right across from the bus station's road island, is home to **Laundry Self-Service** (on the first block on your left), which provides wash and dry (€10) and ironing. (☎27440 67 367. Open M, W, Sa 8:30am-2pm; Tu, Th, F 8:30-2pm and 5:30-9pm.) The **police,** El. Venizelou 7 (☎27440 63 000; open 24hr.), are in the same building as the **tourist police** (☎27440 65 678; open 24hr.), 2km from downtown Loutraki, on El. Venizelou as it heads south toward Corinth. The **health center** is roughly 5km from the center of town; walk five blocks up from El. Venizelou, follow the signs and turn right, and continue straight. (☎27440 26 666. Open 24hr.) One of several **pharmacies** is at El. Venizelou 21 (☎27440 21 787). Head toward Corinth just past the information kiosk on El. Venizelou to find **Las Vegas Internet Cafe.** (☎27440 69 397. €4 per hr., 15min. minimum. Open daily 8am-2am.) The **OTE** is at El. Venizelou 10. (☎27440 61 999. Open M-F 7am-2:40pm.) From the bus station, walk down El. Venizelou with the water to your left to find the **post office,** 28 Octovriou 4, a block down. (Open M-F 7:30am-2pm.) **Postal code:** 20300.

ACCOMMODATIONS. Loutraki draws a near-constant stream of moneyed vacationers, so there are many hotel options. Those on a budget can try the hotels in the center of town, where El. Venizelou becomes G. Lekka, while those looking to splurge should head to the waterfront, particularly the quieter stretch past the park. Most hotels on El. Venizelou offer A/C and private baths in room. To reach **Le Petit France ❸,** M. Botsari 3, from the bus station, take El. Venizelou in the direction you face upon exiting the station building; M. Botsari is your third right. The friendly owners of this blue-shuttered hotel extend their hospitality in every way. There is a lovely garden in back, and rooms come with balconies, ceiling fans, and baths. (☎27440 22 401; www.geocities.com/lepetitfrance. Breakfast €3. Singles €25; doubles €30-35; larger, family-style rooms available. A/C €5 extra. Call ahead for reservations in summer.) Nearly on the beach, **Hotel Marko ❹,** on Eth. Antistasis, has been recently renovated and has lovely yellow rooms with new bathrooms, TVs, A/C, fridges, and balconies. Lie on your bed and stare at the sky-painted ceiling. (☎27440 63 542. Breakfast included. Singles €35-50; doubles €44-65; suite for 3-5 people €65-88.) For domatia, call ☎27440 22 456 or consult the tourist office in the central square. **Camping ❶** is available 16km away at stunning Lake Vouliagmeni (☎27410 91 230 or 27410 91 229) and at Isthmia Beach (☎27410 37 447 or 27410 37 720). Transportation takes some effort. Consider a taxi, or take the bus and walk the rest of the way to the campsites.

FOOD AND NIGHTLIFE. The waterfront holds a good crop of fish tavernas and cafes, and restaurants lurk in hotels, on El. Venizelou, and the streets running to the water off it. There is certainly no shortage of places to eat, though prices tend to be inflated. Supermarkets are on El. Venizelou; try **Dia Discount Supermarket,** just past the National Bank toward the park. (Open M-F 8:30am-9pm, Sa 8:30am-6pm.) **Taverna Astoria ❷** opens from the back of Hotel Achillion (on El. Venizelou near the OTE) and offers scrumptious and inexpensive dinners both *à la carte* (chicken *yiouvetsi* €4.80, *tzatziki* €2.20) and *prix fixe* (3-course meal €7). For a taste of the divine, head to **Horiatiki Taverna ❹,** El. Venizelou 70, far down the street toward Corinth, near the Pepsi-Co. bottling plant. The oldest restaurant in town, Horiatiki has been in business for 40 years, drawing crowds with its elegant, vine-bedecked garden seating area and fresh seafood (fish around €15; a full meal with wine and salad €35-40). Tiny **Il Guosto Pizza ❶,** 3 blocks past the bus station on El. Venizelou toward Corinth, has an impressive variety of pizzas (€5.50-7) and Italian dishes. (☎27440 69 200. Open daily 24hr.)

Nightlife is a balance between eating and dancing. Waterfront restaurants swell in summer, staying full far beyond midnight. From the park toward Corinth, **Cafe Coral, Jamaica,** and **El Niño** pump music for steady crowds. After midnight, taxis transport the footloose to discos on the fringe of the city. **CoCoon,** at the Corinth end of the boardwalk, is a space-age venue serving food by day and partying all night long. (Beer €4, mixed drinks €5.50-6. Open daily 10am-3am.)

WATER FUN. Those seeking solace in Loutraki's healing waters can indulge in sauna treatments, whirlpool baths, hydromassage, and more at **Therma: Hydrotherapy Thermal Spa,** G. Lekka 26, past the central square along Venizelou/G. Lekka, across from the park. Four-, five-, six-, and ten-day programs are offered; call for prices and group discounts. The spa cures rheumatoid and spondylitic arthritic problems and "chronic gynecological diseases," or so the signs promise. (☎/fax 27440 22 215. Open daily 8am-1pm; in winter M-F.) At the carefully maintained **waterfalls,** a 12min. walk from the central square on G. Lekka, watch the water flow from fountains at the base of the cliff. (Open daily 10am-3am.) There's also a **water park** between Loutraki and Corinth on beautiful Lake Vouliagmeni. With Loutraki's many **beaches**, don't be confined to the boardwalk area.

PELOPONNESE

MYCENAE Μυκηνες

Excavations of ancient Mycenae have continued for 127 years, since Heinrich Schliemann first turned a spade here (see p. 121). Mycenae's famed Lion's Gate and Tomb of Agamemnon attract bus loads of bustling tour groups everyday. Most travelers make Mycenae a daytrip from Athens or Nafplion, but the tourist-friendly modern village can be a pleasant place to spend the night.

ORIENTATION AND PRACTICAL INFORMATION. The only direct **buses** to **Mycenae** are from **Nafplion** (45min., 4 per day, €1.90) via **Argos** (20min., €0.80). The site is on the Corinth-Argos road; follow the signs to Mycenae from the town of Fihtia. Four buses make the return trip to **Argos** and **Nafplion,** stopping in the town of **Mycenae** (in front of the Hotel Belle Helene) and at the **site** (a 20min. walk from the town). **Trains** (5 per day) run from **Athens** to Fihtia via Corinth. Mycenae has no bank, but a mobile **post office** booth at the site offers **currency exchange.** (Open from mid-Mar. to Oct. M-Sa 9:30am-4pm.) **Postal code:** 21200.

ACCOMMODATIONS AND FOOD. Mycenae is short on cheap accommodations—if campgrounds aren't your thing, browse the signs off the main road for well-priced domatia. Because of the lack of a nearby ATM, all establishments and shops accept most major credit cards and traveler's checks. The quiet **Hotel Belle Helene ❸,** on the main road to the site, opened its doors in 1862; Heinrich Schliemann and crew promptly moved in for two years in the 1870s. In the lobby you can examine photos of the hotel guest book, with signatures from Virginia Woolf, Claude Debussy, William Faulkner, Agatha Christie, Hans Himmler, Joseph Goebbels, and Allen Ginsberg. Grab room #3, where Schliemann stayed; it has an iron bed and period furniture. Other rooms are modern and carpeted with shared baths. (☎27510 76 225; fax 27510 76 179. Breakfast included. Singles €25; doubles €40; triples €50.) More luxurious (albeit less historic) lodgings are available next door to Belle Helen, at **Dassis Rent Rooms ❸.** This gorgeous domatia boasts spacious rooms with balconies, baths, A/C, and even some bathtubs. (☎27510 76 123. Breakfast €4. Singles €25; doubles €50.) **Camping Mykines ❶,** shaded by pine trees in the middle of town across from Dassis Rooms, offers laundry facilities (€3), free hot showers, and a nicely-priced taverna. Breakfast €5. (☎27510 76 121. €5.20 per person, €3.45 per child; €3.85 per car; €4.30 per small tent, €5 per large tent. Electricity €4.28. 10% off in low season or if you inquire about a reduction.)

A few good restaurants hide among the overpriced multitude of tour-bus troughs bearing the name of unfortunate members of the Atreus family, ancient Mycenae's infamous ruling family of legend. Inexpensive local favorite **Spiros Restaurant and Taverna ❶** is the best source of tasty food at a reasonable cost. (☎27510 76 115. Omelettes €2-2.50; grilled meats starting at €4.50; souvlaki €1.20.) Across the street and with a vast dining area that seats 500, **Achilleus Restaurant ❶** (☎27510 76 027) doesn't sacrifice quality for quantity as it serves tasty traditional Greek fare to lunch crowds of hungry sightseers; entrees run €1.50-7.

PELOPONNESE

ANCIENT MYCENAE

Walk 20 min. uphill from the town, or take the bus to where it stops at the end of the asphalt road; the ruins are on the right. Open Apr.-Sept. daily 8am-7pm; Oct.-Mar. 8am-5pm. €6, students €3, EU students free. Keep your ticket after the main site for Agamemnon's Tomb, or pay twice. Bring a flashlight for the tombs and cistern.

Excavated ancient Mycenae rests on a rocky knoll between Mt. Ag. Elias to the north and Mt. Zara to the south. Gargantuan **Cyclopean walls,** 13m high and 10m

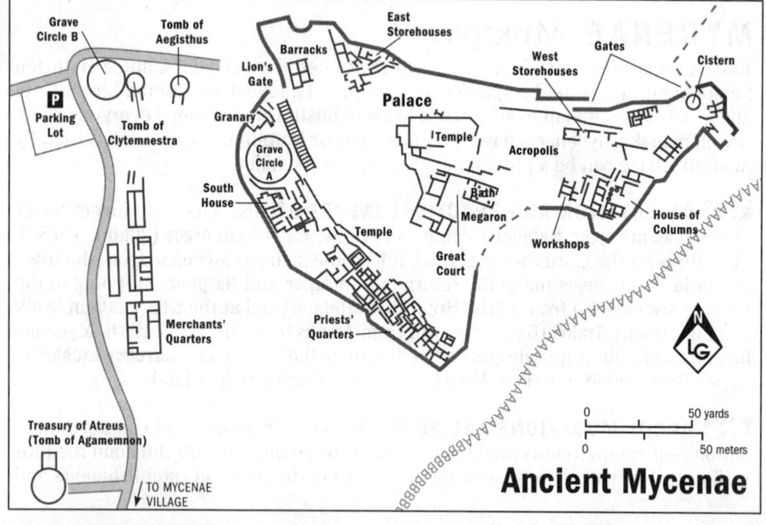

thick, surround the site; they get their name from ancients who believed that Perseus and his descendants (the city's founders) could only have lifted such stones with the help of a superhuman Cyclops. Outside the central fortified city, several *tholoi*—most notably the so-called **Treasury of Atreus**—stand guard. The bulk of the ruins left standing today date from 1280 BC, when the city was the center of a far-flung Mycenaean empire. Many of the unearthed relics number among the most celebrated archaeological discoveries in modern history and are housed in the National Museum in Athens. A guidebook can add to the experience: S.E. Iakovidis' guide to Mycenae and Epidavros, which includes a map and is well worth the €7.50. Another by George E. Mylonas, director of the excavation, takes a more scholarly approach and focuses on Mycenae (€5). For info on other nearby ruins, try *The Peloponnese*, by E. Karpodini-Dimitriadi (€9).

HISTORY

Mycenae's origins, interactions with other Near Eastern civilizations, and decline have long puzzled historians. Settled as early as 2700 BC by a colonizing tribe from the Cyclades, Mycenae (along with other nearby cities like Pylos) remained under the control of the Minoan capital Knossos for centuries. It wasn't until the cataclysmic collapse of Minoan civilization in the mid-15th century BC that Mycenae surged to the head of the Greek world (see p. 7). Mycenaean culture flourished for centuries until the warrior Dorians attacked from the north in the 12th century BC, burning and looting anything in their path. The Dorians conquered Greece, and Mycenae lost its hold on the Greek culture it had helped to create. Mycenae was inhabited through the Roman period, but Byzantine times saw it swallowed up by the earth and forgotten.

In 1874, the German businessman, classicist and amateur archaeologist **Heinrich Schliemann** burst into Mycenae. Fresh from his successful dig at Troy and eager to further establish the historical validity of Homeric epics, he went looking for Agamemnon's city. To his delight, he found massive walls and elaborate tombs laden with dazzling artifacts, fitting Homer's description of a "well-built citadel... rich in gold." Schliemann began his dig just inside the citadel walls at the spot where several ancient authors described royal graves. Discovering 15 skeletons "literally covered with gold and jewels," Schliemann decked his new 17-year-old Greek bride with the baubles and had her pose for photographs. Believing he had unearthed the skeletons of Agamemnon and his followers, he sent a telegram to the Greek king that read, "Have gazed on face of Agamemnon." Moments after he removed its mask, the "face" underneath disintegrated. Shedding a tear at such reckless excavation, modern archaeologists now date the tombs to four centuries before the Trojan War.

RUINS

LION'S GATE AND GRAVE CIRCLE A. Uphill from the entrance booth, you'll spot the imposing **Lion's Gate,** the portal into the ancient city, with two lions carved in relief above the lintel (estimated to weigh some 20 tons). They symbolized the house of Atreus, and their heads—now missing—bore eyes of precious gems. The sculpture is one of the earliest known examples of statuary incorporated into a structure's support system. Schliemann found most of his artifacts in **Grave Circle A,** a large hollow area to the right, just outside the city walls, which contains six 16th-century BC shaft graves. The barracks are up the stairs to your left just after the gate. The gate and the walls of the upper citadel date from the 13th century BC.

BUILDINGS. The ruins on the hillside are the remnants of various homes, businesses, and shrines. The **palace** and the **royal apartments** are at the highest part of the citadel on the right. The open spaces here include guard rooms, private areas, and public rooms; look for the **megaron,** or royal chamber, with its round hearth framed by the bases of four pillars. To the left of the citadel sit the remaining stones of a Hellenistic **Temple of Athena.** At the far end of the city, between the palace and the **postern gate,** is the underground **cistern,** silently offering solitude and complete darkness. A flashlight is essential to explore its depths. Be careful if you make the descent: the steps are worn and slippery, and drop off suddenly.

ROYAL TOMBS. Follow the asphalt road 150m back toward the town of Mycenae to the **Tomb of Agamemnon** (a.k.a. the Treasury of Atreus), the largest and most impressive *tholos*, named by Schliemann for the king he desperately wanted to discover here. On your way, stop at two often-overlooked *tholoi*, the **tomb of Aegistheus** and the more interesting **tomb of Clytemnestra,** both located outside the Lion's gate on the site of the town. Take the paths on your left and hang on to your flashlight. Once you get to the main event, head down a 40m passage cut into the hillside that leads to Agamemnon's resting place, looking up at the 120-ton lintel stones above you. The dim, quiet interior of the *tholos* conveys a ghostly majesty befitting the grave of such a famous and tragic figure, but the tomb was found empty, having lost its valuables to grave robbers.

ARGOS Αργος

PELOPONNESE

According to Homer, Argos was the kingdom of the hero Diomedes and claimed allegiance to Mycenae's powerful king, Agamemnon. Later, Dorians invaded and captured the city in the 12th century BC, using it as their base for control of the Argolid Peninsula. Argos remained the most powerful state in the Peloponnese through the 7th century BC, defeating even Kleomenes and the Spartans, who, in the famous 494 BC battle, were unable to penetrate the city walls. Later Argos stood with Corinth and dominant Sparta as the pillars of the Peloponnesian League. As with other Greek cities, over time Argos laid new foundations over the old. The modern city is built almost entirely on top of previous layers of habitation, and, despite a healthy ribbon of archaeological red tape, it has managed to grow into a crowded, lively city. Argos may not be the most picturesque city that the Peloponnese has to offer, but the excellent museum and the ruins of the ancient theater, agora, and Roman baths on the southeast edge of town are worth seeing if you're in the area.

ORIENTATION AND PRACTICAL INFORMATION

Argos has few landmarks and can be tough to navigate, so pick up a **map** (try a bookstore or ask at hotels) for in-depth exploring. Most amenities, hotels, and restaurants are in or around the plateia, marked by the large **Church of St. Peter.** If you ride the bus into town, go right out of the station, turn left at the first intersection onto Danaou. The plateia will be on your left and a small park on your right.

Buses: The **Argolida** station (☎27510 67 324) is on Kapodistriou, which runs parallel to and 1 block beyond the side of the plateia with Hotel Morfeas. Buses to: **Athens** via **Corinth** (2½hr., 15 per day 5am-9pm, €7.40); **Mycenae** (30min., 5 per day, €0.95); **Nafplion** (20min., every 30min., €0.85); **Nemea** (1hr., 2 per day, €1.90); **Tripoli** (1hr., 4 per day, €3.50).

Trains: (☎27510 67 212), 1km from the plateia. Walk down Nikitara past the OTE and follow the signs to Nafplion from the 5-point intersection. Follow signs for the police station until you reach the intersection with 25 Martiou. The train station is directly ahead. To: **Athens** (3hr., 6 per day, €3.50) via **Fihtia** (€0.60), **Nemea** (20min., €0.70), **Corinth** (1hr., €1.80); **Kalamata** (4hr., 4 per day, €4.40) via **Tripoli** (1hr., €2).

Bank: National Bank (☎27510 29 911), on Nikitara, off the plateia behind the small park, has **currency exchange** and an **ATM.** Open M-Th 8am-2pm, F 8am-1:30pm.

Hospital: (☎27510 24 455), opposite St. Nicholas Church. Open 24hr.

Police: (☎27510 67 222), on the corner of Inaxou and Papaoikonomou; head out from Vas. Sofias or follow the signs from the train station. Some English spoken. Open 24hr.

OTE: Nikitara 8 (☎27510 67 599). Facing the park from the main plateia, take the street along the left side of the park past the National Bank. Open M-F 7am-2pm.

Internet: Cafe Net (☎27510 29 677), around the corner to the right from the supermarket, off the plateia. Free Internet access with the order of a drink on Su afternoons. €3 per hr., €1.50 minimum. Open daily 9am-1am.

Post Office: (☎27510 67 366). Follow the signs from Hotel Morfeas in the plateia; it's three blocks down from the bus station. Open M-F 7:30am-2pm. **Postal code:** 21200.

ACCOMMODATIONS AND FOOD

It's a good idea to make Argos and Mycenae a daytrip from Nafplion since the sights can be seen in a day, and Argos has few accommodations. If you stay overnight, try the **Hotel Apollon ❷,** Papaflessa 13; to get there, take Vas. Sofias past the Palladion, turn right at the Alpha Bank, then left onto Papaflessa. Recently renovated spacious rooms have large shared baths, TVs, balconies, and ceiling fans. (☎27510 68 065; fax 27510 61 182. Singles €17-20; doubles €23.80-26.50; triples €29.40-35. Prices vary with private bath and A/C.) The **Hotel Palladion ❷,** Vas. Sofias 5, just off the plateia, is convenient, and has private baths, TV, and A/C. (☎27510 67 807. Singles €20; doubles €35; triples €50.) The brand-new **Hotel Morfeas ❷,** Danaou 2, has modern and sunny rooms with roomy private baths, A/C, TV, and balconies with a view of St. Peter's church. (☎27510 68 317; fax 27510 66 249. Singles €22; doubles €30.) Argos has the Peloponnese's largest **open-air market** in the empty parking lot across from the museum; vendors sell everything from olives to used clothing (W and Sa). The well-stocked **Dia Discount Supermarket,** to the right as you face the National Bank, provides quick meals. (Open M-F 9am-2pm and 5:30-8:30pm, Sa 8:30am-6pm.) Next to the Hotel Mycenae, the **Cafe Retro Pizzeria ❶** is discordantly decorated with chrome and wicker. (Pizzas €4.50-10.50.) At night, the cafes on the plateia serve middling Greek standards.

SIGHTS

ARCHAEOLOGICAL MUSEUM. Argos's superb archaeological museum has a large Mycenaean collection, Roman sculptures, and weaponry from many periods, as well as a garden courtyard with more sculpture and notable mosaics. In the most striking of the mosaics, 12 figures personify the months of the year in their dress, expressions, and accoutrements. On the ground floor of the museum, a detailed shard of *krater* from the 7th century BC depicts Odysseus putting out the eye of Polyphemus. In the same room, the well-preserved helmet and breastplate from the Geometric period also deserve perusal. *(Off the plateia on Vas. Olgas. ☎27510 68 819. Open Tu-Su 8:30am-3pm. €2, students and seniors €1, EU students and children free.)*

ANCIENT ARGOS. Archaeologists hope to uncover a large part of the ancient city of Argos, but at this point, most of it remains buried beneath the modern version. Major excavations have taken place on the city's western fringe at the site of the ancient agora. With a seating capacity of 20,000, the 5th century BC **theater** was the largest of its time in the Greek world, although now it's not as well preserved as its famous counterpart in Epidavros. Across from the theater are the remains of the extensive **Roman bath complex,** whose remaining walls convey the magnitude of the structure. Many of the original wall-to-wall floor mosaics are intricate, colorful, and intact. The **Roman Odeum,** 30m from the baths, survives mostly as an outline, as the rows dissolve into the hillside. Across the street are the scattered remains of the agora, built in the 5th century BC and destroyed by Alaric's Visigoths in AD 395. *(From Kapodistriou, walk about 5 blocks down Danaou away from the plateia, turn right and walk to the end of Theatron. Open daily 8am-3pm. Free.)*

THE FORTRESS OF LARISA. In medieval times, Franks, Venetians, and Ottomans in turn captured and ruled Argos. As a result, the fortress is an architectural hodgepodge, combining these disparate medieval elements with Classical and Byzantine foundations. The ruins, which lie among overgrown weeds, are mainly of interest to scholars. The Cyclopean walls are nearly 4000 years old. *(Walk along Vas. Konstantinou for roughly 1hr., or climb the foot path from the ruins of the ancient theater.)*

OTHER SIGHTS. The **Argive Heraion,** 4km northeast of Argos, dedicated to Hera, goddess of the Argives, was built in the 5th century BC. It prospered well into the 2nd century AD, hosting the celebrations that followed the official ending of the Heraia Games (archery contests held at Argos in the second year after each Olympiad) and other annual festivals. Nearby **Prosimni,** past the Heraion, is home to a series of prehistoric graves. A few kilometers east of Agias Trias are the remains of the city of **Dendra,** where tombs yielded the preserved suit of bronze armor now in the Nafplion museum (p. 129).

NAFPLION Ναυπλιο

Beautiful old Nafplion glories in its Venetian architecture, fortresses, pebble beach, and hillside stairways. Though it's the perfect base for exploring the ancient sites of the Argolid, Nafplion may entice you to spend a few days away from the ruins. A delightful central park links the two sides over shady flower-lined paths and a large children's playground. Before the Venetians built Nafplion—named for Poseidon's son Nafplius—on a swamp in the 15th century, the city consisted entirely of the two hilltop fortresses. Nafplion has vastly expanded, swallowing neighboring villages and acquiring chain stores. The charming Old Town is a maze of bougainvillea-trellised alleys packed with tavernas and craft shops—certainly worth a day of wandering.

TRANSPORTATION

The bus terminal is on **Syngrou,** near the base of the Palamidi fortress. To reach **Bouboulinas,** the waterfront promenade, from the bus station, go left as you exit it and follow Syngrou to the harbor—the **Old Town** is on your left. If you come by ferry, Bouboulinas is in front of you across the parking lot, parallel to the dock.

Buses: (☎27520 28 555), on Syngrou, off Pl. Kapodistrias. To: **Argos** (20min., 2 per hr. 5am-10:30pm, €.85); **Athens** (3hr., every hr. 5am-8pm, €8.50) via **Corinth** (2hr., €3.80); **Epidavros** (45min., 4 per day 10:15am-7:30pm, €1.90); **Mycenae** (45min., 3 per day, €1.90); **Tripoli** (1½hr., 4 per day, €3.50); **Tolo** (20min., every hr. 7am-9:30pm, €.85).

Taxis: (☎27520 24 120 or 27520 24 720), on Syngrou across from the bus station.

Moped Rental: Motortraffic Rent-A-Moto, Sidiras 15 (☎27520 22 702), on Sidiras Merarhias past the post office, away from the Old Town. 50-250cc mopeds €13.50-40 per day, includes helmet and insurance. Open daily 8:30am-10:30pm.

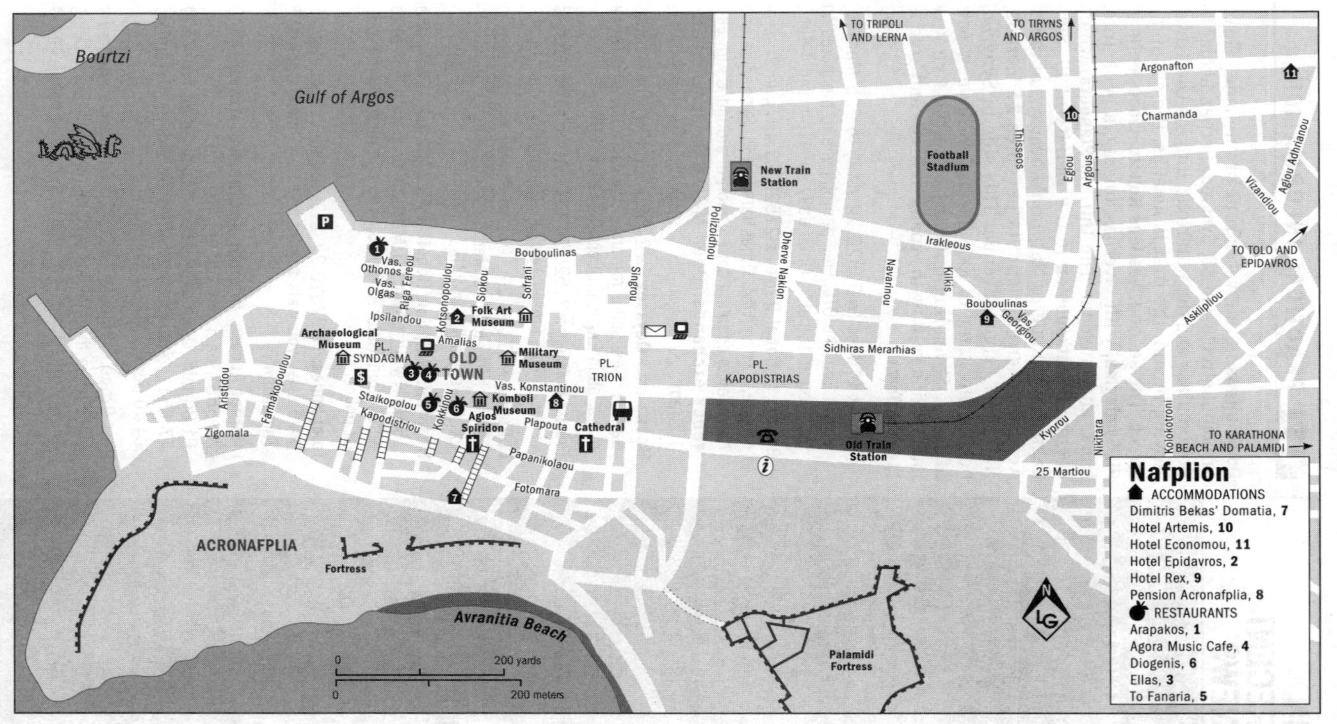

PELOPONNESE

IN RECENT NEWS

AN EMBARRASSMENT OF RICHES

The Peloponnese is rife with ancient and medieval sites: tombs, fortresses, acropolises, statues, fountains, walls, and so much more. Many of these sites are well-maintained and carefully excavated, but unfortunately many are neglected, ignored, and destroyed. As one local phrased it, "We see all of this every day, so it means nothing to us. Not like those who come to see it."

Carelessness was a hallmark of some of the first excavations of ancient sites like Mycenae and Tiryns. Heinrich Schliemann, in his single-minded search for hard proof of the Trojan Wars, often unintentionally destroyed artifacts and remnants of the cities. Schliemann's haphazard quest is at least partly responsible for the ruination of the steep road beyond the Lion's Gate in Mycenae (p. 120).

Neglect is a larger problem today. In Argos, the fortress of Larissa was allowed to fall into disrepair. Even worse, most of the remains of ancient Argos lie permanently trapped beneath the modern city, while the stunning ruins of the ancient theater and Roman bath house lie largely ignored by all but the archaeologists on the site behind a chain-link fence on the outskirts of town.

Nafplion's fortress, Palamidi, is famous, heavily touristed and well-maintained, but the same certainly cannot be said for the ancient acropolis of the town. In the 20th century, huge hotels were built on the hilltop on the site of the Acronafplia, alongside the ancient ruins. In recent years, the city seized the land out of private

PRACTICAL INFORMATION

Bouboulinas is the waterfront promenade. Three principal streets run off **Syngrou,** perpendicular to Bouboulinas and the waterfont, into the Old Town. Moving inland, the first is **Amalias,** the shopping street. The second, **Vasileos Konstandinou,** ends in **Pl. Syndagma,** with tavernas aplenty, a bookstore, bank, and museum. The third is **Plapouta,** which becomes **Staikopoulou** in the vicinity of Pl. Syndagma; it's home to Nafplion's best restaurants. Across Syngrou, Plapouta becomes **25 Martiou,** Nafplion's largest avenue. This side of Syngrou, behind the statue of Kapodistrias, is the new part of town. Spreading outward from the five-way intersection split by the roads to Argos and Tolo is the **New Town.**

Tourist Office: (☎27520 24 444), on 25 Martiou, across from the OTE. Free pamphlets and brochures on Nafplion and vicinity. Open daily 9am-1pm and 4-8pm.

Banks: National Bank (☎27520 23 497), in Pl. Syndagma, has an **ATM.** Other banks in Pl. Syndagma and on Amalias charge a commission of around €3 for **currency exchange.** Open M-Th 8am-2pm, F 8am-1:30pm.

Bookstore: Odyssey (☎27520 23 430), in Pl. Syndagma. Best-seller romance novels, sci-fi, and Greek plays, all in English. Open daily 8am-11pm.

Tourist Police: (☎27520 28 131). At the same address as the police. English spoken. Open daily 7am-10pm.

Police: (☎ 27520 22 100) on Pavlou Kountourioti, a 15min. hike along 25 Martiou from the bus station. Follow the signs. Open 24hr.

Hospital: Nafplion Hospital (☎27520 27 309) is a 15min. walk down 25 Martiou and then left onto Kolokotroni (later Asklipiou). You can also call the tourist police.

Telephones: (☎27520 22 139), on the left side of 25 Martiou as you walk toward the New Town. Open M-F 7am-10pm.

Internet Access: Internet Box, Amalias 18 (☎27520 25 556), past the Military Museum. €3.60 per hr., €1.80 min. Open daily 11am-11pm. **Filion** (☎27520 27 651), past the post office on Sidiras Merarhias. €4.40 per hr.; €1.50 minimum.

Post Office: Argous 49 (☎27520 24 855), a temporary office while the building on Sidiras Merarhias is being renovated. Open M-F 7:30am-2pm. **Postal code:** 21100.

ACCOMMODATIONS

Rooms in the Old Town are charming and beautifully situated, but those in the New Town have more amenities. Pricier options with good locations and more perks lie on Bouboulinas and in the Old Town near the waterfront.

NEW TOWN

Hotel Economou (☎27520 23 955), on Argonafton, off the road to Argos and a 15min. walk from the bus station. With an air-conditioned lobby and sparse, but bright, doubles and dorms, the hotel is also brimming with dusty backpackers. Dorms €8; doubles with private bath €20-25. ❶

Hotel Rex, Bouboulinas 21 (☎27520 26 907, 27520 26 917; fax 27520 28 106), three blocks away from Old Town. If you're craving to be catered to, this might be worth the splurge. The Rex boasts air-conditioned, mini-bar-equipped rooms with TV, private baths, and room service. Relax in the rooftop garden or lobby bar. Singles €53; doubles €80; triples €97. Reservations recommended. Wheelchair accessible. ❹

Hotel Artemis (☎27520 27 862 or 27520 28 338), on the road to Argos. Large, immaculate rooms with balconies and baths. Singles €26.40; doubles €32.30; triples €38.80. Prices lower in off season. ❸

OLD TOWN

Dimitris Bekas' Domatia (☎27520 24 594). Turn up the stairs onto Kokkinou, following the sign for rooms off Staikopoulou. Climb to the top, turn left, then go up another 50 steps. An evening on the roof, with its wonderful view of ocean and Palamidi, is well worth the climb. Small rooms with shared baths and fridges, some with balconies. Singles €13-16; doubles €18-20. Prices vary with room size. ❷

Hotel Epidavros, Kokkinou 2 (☎27520 27 541), just off Amalias, right past the Military Museum. Hardwood floors, inviting beds, and private baths. Mere steps from the Nafplion nightlife. Singles €30; doubles €45; triples €50. ❸

Pension Acronafplia, Vasileos Konstandinou 23 (☎27520 24 481). If it's full, brothers George and Dimitris can show you one of their 3 other charming, conveniently-located buildings, all with traditionally-furnished rooms. Singles €25-32; doubles €33-60. Prices vary with A/C and private baths. ❸

hands, seeking to protect the historical site, but in the end private interests won out. The city acquiesced and is allowing the hotels to be renovated and new ones to be built. Another opportunity to protect a wonderful site has been lost. A similar fate temporarily befell the island fortress of Bourtzi in the Nafplion harbor; the Venetian fort was a hotel for some years until the town reclaimed it as a historical site.

With the 2004 Olympic games approaching, some attempts are being made to further excavate and even restore sites that have seen little activity in the past decades. Hopefully, the lesser-known ancient sites will also benefit from this newfound interest in history.

FOOD AND NIGHTLIFE

The food in Nafplion is excellent and plentiful. The beautiful alleys of the Old Town hold an endless number of romantic tavernas, lit by soft flood lights and strewn with plants, balconies, and people. The waterfront is lined with fish restaurants that charge as much as €40 per entree. The best dining options are on Staikopoulou, the street inland from Pl. Syndagma, behind the National Bank. **Marinopoulos,** an excellent modern supermarket, is behind the Filion Internet cafe.

To Fanaria, a street above the plateia on Staikopoulou. The trellised alleyway provides an intimate atmosphere in which to enjoy tantalizing entrees. Soups €2.50-3, spaghetti bolognese €4.50, and fish dishes €6-8. ❶

Ellas (☎27520 27 278), in Pl. Syndagma. Refreshingly inexpensive, with cheerful staff and seating facing the action in the plateia. Veal with potatoes €6, pasta dishes €4. ❶

Diogenis, Staikopoulou 28 (☎27520 29 519). Old Town's first and only "fast food" enterprise, Diogenis' small menu focuses on the souvlaki and gyros food groups. Delicious pork or chicken souvlaki €1.50; french fries €2. The truly ravenous can devour a mixed grill plate (€5.50). ❶

Arapakos, Bouboulinas 81 (☎27520 27 675), toward the parking lot. This waterfront taverna serves only local fish, prepared in the traditional Greek style. Typical taverna fare comes at reasonable prices (appetizers €2-3.50), or treat yourself to a fish specialty (€26-45). The view and the selection are hard to beat. ❸

Agora Music Cafe, Vas. Konstandinou 17 (☎27520 26 016), is perfect for an evening cocktail or ice cream. Decorated with traditional household and farm implements. International and Greek pop play inside. Drinks €4-5, beer €2.20, huge ice cream sundaes €3. ❶

Although similar trendy cafes strung along the waterfront and Pl. Syndagma bustle far into the night, the search for spicier nightlife may land you in a taxi (€7) for the 15min. ride to **Tolo,** a packed beach resort where locals find themselves far outnumbered. You can also take a **minicruise** of the harbor and get a close-up view of the Bourtzi. Small *caïques* leave from the end of the dock.

SIGHTS AND BEACHES

The Old Town's architectural diversity is a historical sight in itself. Pl. Syndagma alone boasts a Venetian mansion, a Turkish mosque, and a Byzantine church, while the alleyways are home to Ottoman fountains, cannons, monuments, and statues. After passing from the Venetians to the Ottomans and back again, in 1821 Nafplion served as headquarters for the Greek revolutionary government and later as Greece's first capital (1821-1834). President John Kapodistrias was assassinated here in Ag. Spyridon Church; the bullet hole is still visible in the church wall. The city's three fortresses stand as testaments to Nafplion's politically checkered past.

PALAMIDI FORTRESS. The grueling 999 steps (though travelers attest that there are fewer: around 860) that once provided the only access to the 18th-century fort have since been supplemented by a 3km road (taxis €3). If you opt for the steps, they begin on Plizoidhou, across the park from the bus station; bring water and try to go in the morning when the steps are shaded. There are spectacular views of the town, gulf, and much of the Argolid at the top of the fortress. Years ago there were eight working cisterns at the site; today you can tour the cool interiors of the two remaining underground reservoirs. During the last 10 days in June, the fortress hosts concerts every night. *(☎27520 28 036. Open M-Su 8am-6:45pm; off season 8:30am-5:45pm. €4, students and seniors €2, EU students and children free.)*

ACRONAFPLIA. The fortress walls of the Acronafplia were fortified by three successive generations of conquerors—Byzantines, Franks, and Venetians. To reach the fort, take the tunnel that runs into the hill from Zigomala to the Xenia Hotel elevator, or follow the signs from the bus station. The views of the Palimidi Fortress, the Gulf, and the Old Town are fantastic. Ludwig I, King of Bavaria, had the huge Bavarian Lion carved out of a monstrous rock to guard the graves of the men who died in an epidemic in 1833-34. Today the lion guards only a small park.

MUSEUMS. Nafplion's **Folklore Museum,** is exemplary and is housed in a lovely yellow building in the heart of the Old Town on Sofrani. The award-winning collection includes an exhibit devoted to fashion. *(☎27520 28 379. Open W-M 9am-3pm. €4, students and children €2.)* The **Archaeological Museum,** in the former Venetian armory in Pl. Syndagma, has a small but esteemed collection of pottery and idols from Mycenaean sites, plus a Mycenaean suit of bronze armor. *(☎27520 27 502. Open Tu-Su 8:30am-3pm. €2, students and seniors €1, EU students and children free.)* The fascinating **Komboloi Museum,** Staikopoulou 25, in the heart of the Old Town, allows visitors to explore all facets of the famous Greek *komboloi*, or worry beads. Hundreds are on display and for sale. *(☎/fax 27520 21 618. Open Tu-Su 9am-4pm. Free.)* The **Military Museum,** toward the New Town from Syndagma on Amalias, displays artifacts and black-and-white photos from the burning of Smyrna, the population exchanges of the 1920s, and World War I and II. *(☎27520 25 591. Open Tu-Su 9am-2pm. Free.)*

BEACHES. **Arvanitia,** Nafplion's tiny, pebbly beach is along the road that curves around the left-hand side of Palamidi. On hot days the shore is packed, and pop music blares over the noise of the sun-drenched crowd. For a cleaner, more serene alternative, take the footpath that runs along the water from the Arvanitia parking lot. The scenic 45min. walk will reveal three quiet, rocky **coves.** If you're desperate for a long, sandy beach, try the mostly undeveloped **Karathona** beach, a 3km hike along the coast from Avranita, or head to **Tolo,** where you can rent watersport equipment (€8-15). Buses head there from Nafplion hourly (€0.85).

PELOPONNESE

DAYTRIPS FROM NAFPLION: TIRYNS Τιρυνθα

Take the Argos bus from Nafplion (10min., 2 per hr. 5am-10:30pm, €0.80). ☎27520 22 657. Open daily 8am-7pm; off season until 3pm. €3, students €2, EU students free. Guidebooks (€5) outline the history of the city.

About 4km northwest of Nafplion on the road to Argos lie the Mycenaean ruins of Tiryns, or **Tiryntha,** birthplace of Hercules. Heinrich Schliemann's excavation of the site began in 1875 and has been continued by the German Archaeological Institute ever since. The site is now one of the finer ones in the northern Peloponnese. Perched atop a 25m high hill that provides a 360-degree view of the Argolid, Tiryns was nearly impregnable during ancient times, until its stunning capture and destruction by the Argives in 468 BC. Parts of the stronghold date as far back as 2600 BC, but most of what remains (including the walls) was built 1000 years later, in the Mycenaean era. Standing 8m high, the massive walls surrounding the site are evidence of the immensity of the original fortifications; on the eastern and southern slopes of the ancient acropolis, they reach a width of 20m. Vaulted galleries are concealcd within these structures. While gems like the palace's frescoes have been taken to the National Archaeological Museum in Athens, a huge limestone block remains to form a bathroom floor. The walls are currently unstable, and, until 2004, access is restricted to the very top of the site. Follow the signs left from the site to a well-preserved Mycenaean-era *tholos* tomb in a hillside.

EPIDAVROS Επιδαυρος

Buses travel to and from Nafplion (45min., 4 per day, €1.90). A snack bar and cafe serve the site, but visitors may want to bring lunch. Museum ☎27530 22 009. Open daily 8am-7pm. Ticket office open daily 7:30am-7pm, F-Sa until 9pm during festival season. Ticket includes museum entrance and small map of the ruins; €6, students €3, EU students and children free. For a detailed explanation of the ruins, visitors may want to purchase a guidebook (€4-7). Plan on spending at least 2hr. among the theater, ruins, and museum.

Like Olympia and Delphi, Epidavros was once both a town and a sanctuary—first to an ancient deity Maleatas, then to Apollo, who assumed the former patron's name and aspects of his identity, and finally to the healer Asclepius, Apollo's son by Koronis. Under the patronage of Asclepius, Epidavros became famous across the ancient world as a center of medicine, reaching its height in the early fourth century BC, when the sick would travel across the Mediterranean for medical and mystical cures. Recent finds indicate that both surgeries and direct deity intervention took place in the sanctuary—diagnoses were made by the god (or by one his sacred creatures, the dog and the snake) in dream visitations. Over the centuries, the complex became increasingly grand with the benefactions of former patients, growing to include temples to Themis, Aphrodite, and Artemis. Operating until AD 426, the sanctuary complex was closed along with all other non-Christian sanctuaries by Byzantine emperor Theodosius II.

The theater, built in the early 2nd century BC, is the grandest structure at the site. Initially constructed to accommodate 6,000 people, its capacity was expanded to 14,000 later in the same century. Despite severe earthquakes in AD 522 and 551, the theater has survived the centuries almost perfectly intact. Happily, Greece's most famous ancient theater has come alive again after centuries of silence: from mid-June through August it hosts the **Epidavros Theater Festival.**

THEATER. Built into a lovely hillside, the 55 tiers of the Theater of Epidavros face half-forested, half-flaxen mountains so pretty they almost distract from the tragedies played out on the stage. Though it is often said that the theater was designed by Polykleitos, architect of an even larger companion theater at Argos, it is not old enough to have been his work. The theater's acoustics are legendary, as yelling, singing, coin-dropping, whispering, and even match-lighting tourists from all nations enthusiastically demonstrate from the stage area—every sound can be heard, even in the last row. The secret to the theater's acoustic perfection is its symmetrical architecture; the entire amphitheater, down to its seating arrangement, was built in proportion to the **Fibonacci sequence** (the natural importance of which has only recently been discovered by modern man).

FESTIVAL. The modern sets and electric lights that adorn the theater in summer may annoy those visiting the theater for its history alone, but they redeem themselves at the Friday and Saturday night shows. From mid-June to mid-August, the National Theater of Greece and visiting companies perform classical Greek plays translated into modern Greek. Performances begin at 9pm, and tickets can be purchased at the site. (*€12, students and children €6; children under six prohibited.*) You can also buy tickets in advance at the Athens Festival Box Office (☎*210 322 1459*) or Nafplion's bus station. On performance nights, KTEL buses make a round-trip from Nafplion (*7:30pm, €3.80*).

MUSEUM. The museum lies between the theater and the ruins. Most of the museum's finest pieces have been under restoration and hidden from visitors for years. Fortunately, the three open rooms contain well-preserved if ill-explained pieces. The first room holds a marble pillar inscribed with a hymn to Apollo and an array of ancient medical implements. The second room is filled with elaborately decorated architectural reconstructions and a parade of statuary. In the third room are the intricately carved **entablature** from the temple of Asclepius and the *tholos;* most of the *tholos's* beautiful decorative elements have been removed and replaced temporarily with plaster copies. Authentic and impressive, however, is the perfectly preserved Corinthian capital. It is thought to be the architect's prototype for all of the capitals of the temple of Asclepius. Archaeologists found it buried in the ground away from the site, apparently unconnected to any ruin.

SANCTUARY OF ASCLEPIUS AND THOLOS. The extensive ruins of the sanctuary, currently undergoing restoration, can be confusing. Walking from the museum, you will pass the **Xenon,** an ancient hotel, now a maze of foundations. The gymnasium containing the remains of a Roman Odeon is the first structure of the more concentrated complex of ruins. To the left is a stadium, of which only a few tiers of seats and the athletes' starting blocks survive. Two of the most important structures of the ancient sanctuary, the **Temple of Asclepius** and the famous *tholos*, are in front and to the left as you approach the ruins from the museum area. The **tholos,** thought to have been built by Polykleitos the Younger in the mid-4th century BC, is an architectural masterpiece, richly decorated with carvings. Beside the *tholos* are the remains of the **abaton,** where the sick would rest, hoping to have the correct therapy revealed in their dreams by the god. Farther from the *tholos*, along the path on the eastern edge of the site, lie the ruins of 2nd-century AD Roman baths. Visitors are restricted from going near ruins that are currently being restored, including the *tholos* and Roman odeon.

ELIAS Ηλειας AND ACHAIA Αχαια

In rural Elias and Achaia, tomatoes and beachgoers alike redden beneath the blazing sun. Corn fields, golden beaches, and occasional ruins stud the road between their capitals, Pirgos and Patras. First settled by Achaians from the Argolid, the region was later ruled by Romans. Afterward Franks, Ottomans, and Venetians all violently disputed over this land and left their legacies behind.

PELOPONNESE

PATRAS Πατρα

Patras, Greece's third-largest city, unfolds from its harbor in a mixture of urban and classical, Greek and international styles. Location, location, location—on the northwestern tip of the Peloponnese—makes Patras a busy transportation hub. Island-bound tourists often see Patras as a stopover, never looking beyond the tourist agencies and cafes. Patras's noisy exuberance makes for a lively social life; cafe-lined plateias and pedestrian-only streets overflow every night. From mid-January to Ash Wednesday, Patras breaks out with pre-Lenten Carnival madness—music, food, and an all-night festival. The port transforms into one vast dance floor, and for once the people stand a chance against speeding vehicles. The peaceful upper city invites afternoon strolls amid elegant garden-terraced homes turned toward the turquoise gulf below.

TRANSPORTATION

If you're coming from Athens by car, choose between the **New National Road,** which runs inland along the Gulf of Corinth, and the slower, scenic **Old National Road,** which hugs the coast. From the north, take a ferry from **Antirio** across to **Rion** on the Peloponnese (30min.; every 15min. 7am-11pm; €1 per person, €5.50 per car), then hop on **bus #6** (30min., €0.85) from Rion to the stop at **Kanakari** and **Aratou,** four blocks uphill from the main station.

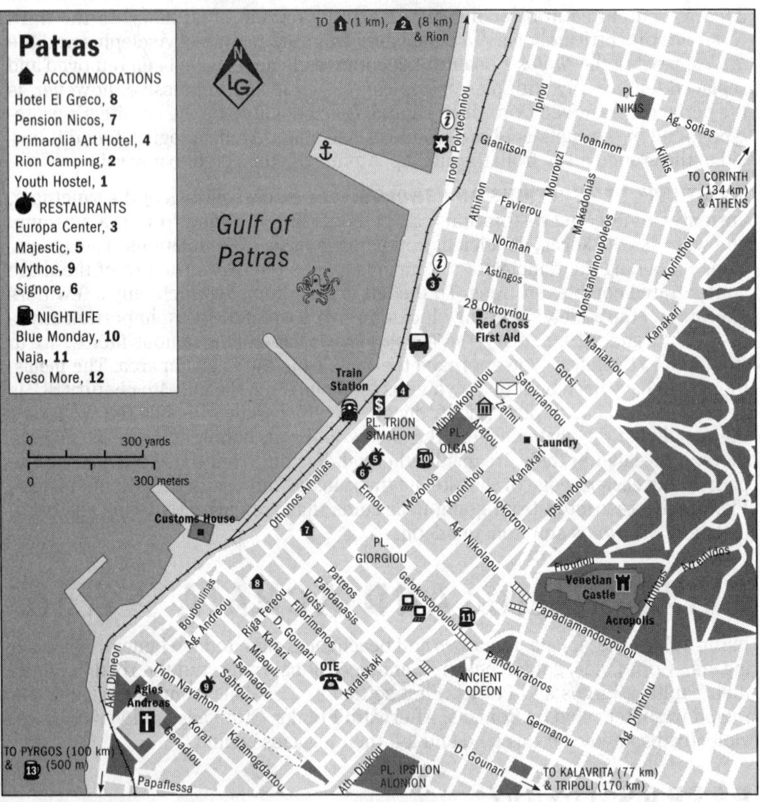

Ferries: From Patras, boats reach **Kephalonia, Ithaka,** and **Corfu** in Greece, and **Brindisi, Trieste, Bari, Ancona,** and **Venice** in **Italy.** Most ferries to Italy leave at night. Daily ferries go to **Vathy** on Ithaka (3½hr., €11) via **Sami** on Kephalonia (3hr., €10); and to **Corfu** (6-8hr., €19-22). Deck passage to **Brindisi** is €27-30 including port tax. Several ferry lines make the trip, so check the travel offices along Iroön Polytechniou and Othonas Amalias; discounts are available for those under 25. If you have a **railpass,** it will not work for domestic ferries, and it may or may not work for international ones; make sure you check with more than one line. The folks at **Manolopoulos,** Oth. Amalias 35, sell both domestic and foreign ferry tickets. (☎2610 223 621. Open M-F 9am-8pm, Sa 10am-3pm, Su 5-8pm.) For info on ferry departures, call the Port Authority (☎2610 341 002) or contact the Info Center or tourist police (see below).

Buses: KTEL (☎2610 623 886, 887 or 888), on Oth. Amalias between Aratou and Zaïmi. Buses go to: **Athens** (3hr., 33 per day 2:30am-9:45pm, €12.25); **Egio** (17 per day 7am-10pm, €2.40); **Ioannina** (4hr., 4 per day 8:15am-5:30pm, €14.55); **Kalamata** (4hr.; 8am, 2:30pm; €14); **Kalavrita** (2hr., 4 per day 5:30am-4:45pm, €5.10); **Pirgos** (2hr., 10 per day 5:30am-8:30pm, €6.15); **Thessaloniki** (8hr.; 8:30am, 3, 9pm; €28.25); **Tripoli** (4hr.; 7:15am, 2pm; €10.45); **Volos** (5½hr., 2:30pm except Sa, €17.05). The **blue buses** you'll see around town are city buses. Buy tickets at the many white kiosks; there's one in Pl. Giorgiou. Tell the kiosk man or woman your desired bus number and your destination, and make sure to get a ticket for the return trip. Ask at the Info Center for more information.

Trains: Oth. Amalias 47, (☎2610 639 108 or 109 for info, 2610 639 110 for tickets abroad). To: **Athens** (8 per day 7:06am-2:26am; slow 5hr., €5.50; express 3½hr., €10); **Egio** (slow €1.25, express €4); **Kalamata** (5½hr.; 7:03am, 2:23pm; €5); **Pirgos,** where you can catch a bus to **Olympia** (1½hr.; 8 per day 7:03am-9:51pm; slow €3, express €6). The trains to Athens are packed, so reserve seats even if you have a railpass. **Ticket booth** open daily 6:30am-3am.

Car Rental: Many along Ag. Andreou. **Thrifty/Auto Union** (☎2610 623 200), at the end of Ag. Andreou on Ag. Dionysiou, has fair rates. Open M-F 9am-9pm, Sa-Su 9am-2pm.

Taxis: (☎2610 346 700 or 2610 425 201). Line up in plateias and by the bus station. Respond to calls 24hr.

PRACTICAL INFORMATION

Patras is arranged in a grid; most hotels, restaurants and shops are in the heart of the lower city. **Iroön Polytechniou** runs parallel to the water. As you walk south with the water on your right, the road curves just before the train station and becomes **Othonos Amalias.** Just beyond the train station, it runs past the palm trees, cafes, and kiosks of **Pl. Trion Simahon.** Car-free **Ag. Nikolaou,** full of hotels and cafes, runs inland from the plateia and intersects the major east-west streets of the city. From the corner of Ag. Nikolaou and **Mezonos,** walk three blocks from the water and turn right to find **Pl. Giorgiou** and its sculpted fountains near the waterfront. The heart of New Patras lies between Pl. Giorgiou and **Pl. Olgas,** 3 blocks to the north.

Tourist Office: The brand-new **Info Center** (☎2610 461 740 or 741; infopatras@hol.gr), on Oth. Amalias between 28 Octovriou and Astingos, provides information about Patras and the area. Transportation info, **free maps,** brochures, and general information are readily available. Open daily 7:30am-12:30am. The **Greek National Tourist Agency** (☎2610 430 915) is on the water at the customs entrance. Staff hands out bus and ferry schedules, lodging advice, and maps. Open M-F 8am-8pm.

Banks: National Bank (☎2610 278 042), in Pl. Trion Simahon on the waterfront, has a 24hr. **ATM,** as do other banks on the plateia and all over the lower city. Open M-Th 8am-2pm, F 8am-1:30pm.

Luggage Storage: Europa Center (see **Food** below) will store your bags for free.

International Bookstore: Lexis Bookshop, Patreos 90 (☎2610 274 831). Useful selection for travelers: language dictionaries and various books about Greek history and culture. Open M-Sa 8:30am-2pm.

Laundromat: Zaïmi 49 (☎2610 620 119), past Korinthou. Self-service wash and dry €7. Open M-F 9am-3pm and 5-8:30pm, Sa 9am-3pm.

Tourist Police: (☎2610 451 833), in the customs complex. Offers the same services as the tourist office. Open daily 8am-9:30pm. For the **police** in an **emergency,** dial ☎109.

Hospital: Red Cross First Aid (☎2610 227 386), on the corner of 28 Octovriou and Ag. Dionysiou. Open daily 8am-8pm. **Rio Hospital of Patras University** (☎2610 999 111) is 5km away, accessible by taxi or bus #6.

OTE: at the corner of D. Gounari and Kanakari. Open M-F 7am-2:40pm.

Internet Access: There's no lack of Internet cafes in Patras. In Pl. Giorgiou, facing the upper city, **Pl@teia** (Πλ@τεια; ☎2610 277 828) will be on the right. €3 per hr., 15 min. minimum. Open daily 9am-midnight. Heading toward the upper city on Gerokostopoulou from Pl. Giorgiou, **Plazanet** (☎2610 222 190) is on your right. Have a drink in the roomy cafe while checking your email. €3.50 per hr., €1.50 minimum. Open daily 8am-1am. Just up the street is the quiet **Joy@Net.** €3 per hr. Open daily 8:30am-1am.

Post Office: (☎2610 223 864 or 2610 224 703), on Mezonos at the corner of Zaïmi. Open M-F 7:30am-8pm, Sa 7:30am-2pm. **Postal code:** 26001.

THE BIG SPLURGE

PRIMAROLIA ART HOTEL

Staying at the **Primarolia Art Hotel** will leave you feeling like you have wandered into a beautiful modern art museum. The robin's egg blue facade of the building stands out on the waterfront among the dull facades around it. Gossamer curtains separate the all-white dining room from the wonderfully eclectic and playful art deco sitting room on the first floor of this incredibly unique hotel. The lobby bar serves fine wines, and the restaurant is nothing short of gourmet. If you don't want to leave the lushness of your room, room service is available.

A glass elevator carries you to one of the 14 rooms; each one has been carefully decorated and aptly named. The "White Suite" shimmers in shades of ivory and snow, "Safari" features animal prints and fuzzy warmth, and "Just Married" is a cozy suite with a plush double bed. Though the names are wild, none of the rooms is over the top: the decor is tasteful and inventive. The rooms do share an impressive list of amenities, including private baths, A/C, water massagers, and a slew of electronic toys like TVs, CD players, fax machines, Internet hookups, and videophones.

The rooms and the open spaces in the hotel feature works of art from Greek artists like Takis, Kaniaris, and Gravalos, while the furniture is the work of designers Arne Jacobsen, Mies Van De Rohe, and others.

Oth. Amalias 33. ☎2610 624 900; fax 2610 623 559; www.arthotel.gr. Singles and doubles with a city view €118; doubles with a sea view €147; largest room €177.

ACCOMMODATIONS AND CAMPING

Most of the hotels in Patras are on Ag. Andreou, to the left of Pl. Trion Simahon as you face inland, or on Ag. Nikolaou. Very few inexpensive options exist, and the hotels you'll see are often budget in appearance, but not in price.

Pension Nicos, Patreos 3 (☎2610 623 757), 2 blocks off the waterfront. The best bet in Patras, cheery and conveniently located. Wood-paneled rooms with fans have large, modern shared baths with tubs. Bar and roof terrace with perfect sunset harbor views. Singles €20; doubles €25. ❷

Youth Hostel, Iroön Polytechniou 68 (☎2610 427 278). From the port, walk away from town with the water on your left for about 1.5km. The slightly remote hostel occupies a creaky turn-of-the-century mansion that sat empty for 40 years after being used by occupying Germans in WWII. Minimalism is the key word here, but the location near the water and the relative quiet make for a pleasant atmosphere. Free hot showers 24hr. You can leave valuables at the reception desk. Check out time 10:30am. Dorms €9. ❶

Hotel El Greco, Ag. Andreou 145 (☎2610 272 931; fax 2610 272 932). Walking along Andreou with the water on your right, it's 4 blocks past Pl. Trion Simahon. Clean, cute rooms have baths, TVs, and A/C for less than you'll pay for similar rooms in town. Singles €38; doubles €54. ❸

Rion Camping (☎2610 991 585 or 2610 991 450), 8km east in Rion, a beach-and-club suburb of Patras. Catch bus #6 at the corner of Aratou and Kamakari, get off at the port in Rion, and follow signs. €4.10 per person, €2.05 per child; €3.52 per tent; €2.05 per car. Electricity €2.34. ❶

FOOD

Patras has an overwhelming abundance of fast food joints and cafes, while more typical restaurants and tavernas are a bit harder to come by. Many establishments along the waterfront and in the plateias serve lunch to hungry travelers by day and drinks to revelers at night. **Supermarkets** can be found throughout town (most open daily 8am-3pm).

Europa Center (☎2610 437 006), on Oth. Amalias between the customs exit and bus station. This friendly cafeteria-style eatery is run by Greek-Americans ready to assist weary backpackers stumbling off ferries. In addition to tasty, low-priced dishes with large portions, they provide services such as free luggage storage, maps, book exchange, Internet access, and valuable local information. Entrees €3-5.50, including many vegetarian options. ❶

Mythos (☎2610 329 984), on the corner of Riga Ferou and Trion Navarhon. This whimsical eatery sells itself as a cafe, but they do have a food menu with a good selection of Greek entrees and pastas (€5-8.50). The draw is the amazing outdoor and indoor decor: bright pots of flowers and shrubs are adorned with pinwheels, lanterns, and lights. Open daily 8:30pm-late. ❷

Majestic, Ag. Nikolaou 2 (☎2610 272 243). This small restaurant serves standard Greek dishes and lots of vegetable plates amidst the hubbub of cafes. The excellent wine list features Achaia Clauss wines. Entrees €3.50-8.50. Open 8pm-late. ❸

Signore (☎2610 222 212), on Ag. Andreou near Ag. Nikolaou. This quasi-Italian sit-down or takeout place serves everything from calzones (€2-3) and pizza (€1.75 per slice) to sweet and savory crepes (€2.50-3.50). Delivery available. Open 24hr. ❶

SIGHTS

ACHAIA CLAUSS WINERY. A narrow road meanders uphill through grapevines and shaded countryside to the strangely castle-like, internationally-renowned Achaia Clauss winery, 8km southeast of Patras. Founded in 1861 by German-born Baron von Clauss, its weathered stone buildings have aged well, as has the wine. Try a complimentary sample of their famous Mavrodaphne, a superb dessert wine named for the black eyes of Clauss's ill-fated fiancée Daphne. Not only is the wine amazing, but the staff is friendly and incredibly knowledgeable about the winery. Be sure to take a tour of the old wine cellars to see and learn how Mavrodaphne is made and stored. *(☎2610 368 100. Take bus #7 (30min. €0.85) from the intersection of Kolokotroni and Kanakari; it stops at the main gate to the winery at the base of the hill. Free English tours every hour from noon-5pm in summer, 10am-3pm in winter. Open 11am-8pm May-Sept., 9am-8pm Oct.-Apr.)*

VENETIAN CASTLE. Continuously in use from the 6th century until World War II, the castle is more a tribute to the various influences that shaped it than to purely Venetian style. At the main entrance there is a map showing which parts of the castle are Venetian, Turkish, Byzantine, and so on. Built atop ruins of an ancient acropolis and a temple to Athena, Patras's castle has an incredible view of the entire city and waterfront. At the castle's center is a verdant courtyard with chirping birds, bright flowers, and olive and orange trees that lend the site a cheerfully medieval feel. *(☎2610 623 390. Walk to the upper city from Ag. Nikolaou. If the nearest entrance through the playground is closed, walk around to the main entrance at the opposite side of the castle, along Athinas. Open Tu-F 8am-7pm, Su 8am-3pm. Free.)*

ANCIENT ODEUM. West of the castle in the upper city, this ancient Roman theater was built before AD 160 and used until the 3rd century. Ancient travel writer Pausanias described it as the second most impressive in Greece, after Athens's Theater of Herodes Atticus. Excavated in 1889, the theater was restored after World War II. Check out the stone sarcophagi and the mosaics on the grounds around the theater. *(☎2610 220 829. Open Tu-Su 8:30am-2pm. Free.)* The theater hosts the **Patras International Festival,** where Greek and international music groups play nightly. *(Every summer June-Aug.; check at Info Center for performance times and prices.)*

AGIOS ANDREAS. The largest Orthodox cathedral in Greece, it is dedicated to St. Andrew, a Patras native martyred here on an X-shaped crucifix (he felt unworthy of dying on a cross like Jesus's). A decade ago, the Catholic Church presented the Bishop of Patras with the über-relic, St. Andrew's holy head. The crown of the head is visible through its reliquary, an ornate silver replica of the cathedral around it. The cathedral's frescoes, gold mosaics, and delicately latticed windows enhance its otherworldly beauty. To the right of the cathedral is the equally beautiful **Church of St. Andrew,** with shining silver icons and chandeliers, as well as a small well allegedly built by the saint himself. Spy the well through a doorway to the right of the church. Legend holds that anyone who drinks from it will return to Patras again. *(Walk along the waterfront or Ag. Andreou with the water to your right until you reach the cathedral, roughly 1.5km from the port. Open daily 9am-dusk. Dress modestly.)*

ARCHAEOLOGICAL MUSEUM. This small museum's most striking pieces are Roman, particularly the delicate and colorful glass vases and lamps. Make sure to see the two cases containing amazingly intact delicate gold jewelry, including a pair of earrings shaped like birds. The mosaics and statuary are also worthwhile. *(☎2610 220 829. Mezonos 42, next to Pl. Olgas at the corner of Mezonos and Aratou. Open Tu-Su 8:30am-3pm. Free.)*

CARNIVAL SEASON. From mid-January to Ash Wednesday (Apr. 23 in 2003), *karnavali* sweeps the entire town up in an indescribable energy. The weeks are packed with hidden treasure games, children-led theater, balls, parades of floats, and fantastic exhibitions. Creative, wild, and unique, Patras's Carnival is a wonderful expression of culture and always includes something new. A 7hr. parade takes to the streets the last Sunday of Carnival. The final night climaxes in the burning of King Carnival's effigy and an all-night harborside party. The festivities draw up to 300,000 people, filling every hotel room within a 100km radius, so reserve ahead.

NIGHTLIFE

PELOPONNESE

At night, the wall of cafes and pubs swells with patrons of all tastes: hardcore beer-swillers rub elbows with spiked-*frappé* sippers. All gesticulate with cigarettes and jabber into cell phones. The two main plateias, Ag. Nikolaou, Radinou (a pedestrian-only alley one block south of Pl. Olgas), and the upper part of Gerokostopoulou (extending uphill from Pl. Giorgiou) are especially dense with cafe umbrellas. **Blue Monday,** along Radinou, is a veritable shrine to 1950s America, playing a mix of soul and American and British rock. (Beer €2-3, mixed drinks €4.50-6. Serves sandwiches during the day. Open daily 10am-3am.) At the base of the steps to the upper city on Gerokostopoulou, **Naja** resembles a cave; candles and low voices give it a mellow atmosphere. (☎2610 624 140. Beer and mixed drinks €3-4. Open daily 10pm-3:30am.)

For a relaxed night out, head along the waterfront with the water on your right. Walk about 10min. past Agios Andreas Cathedral and you'll come to the entertainment complex **Veso Mare.** Featuring a bowling alley, eight movie theaters, a plethora of eating and drinking options, and live music shows, the complex is very popular with Greek families and teens alike. (☎2610 362 000 for movie times.)

Though Patras itself has much to offer in the way of bars and cafes, the wildest party-goers head out of town. **Rion,** a beach satellite 8km to the northeast, accommodates Patras's club junkies with a summertime stretch of bars, clubs, restaurants, and discos. Decor is a big deal at the beach bars—the most exciting resemble theme parks. To get to Rion, take bus #6 from Kanakari and Aratou (30min., €0.85) all the way to the port, past the beach. Get off the bus just after the port, before it turns left to head back to Patras; the strip is ahead as you walk with the water on your right. Buses to Rion only run until 11pm, so count on taking a cab (€3-5) home. The highlights of the strip, running from the bus stop, include **Sea Through,** which really plays out the pun with white decor and expanses of glass. **GAZ Club** is difficult to miss with its silver and metallic blue scaffolding, dance platforms, and lion-fountain entrance. **KU** will take you into another world—designed to look like a pyramid, KU is covered with vines, adding a primal feel to the Rion club scene. (Beer €2-3; cocktails €4.50-5 along the strip.)

DIAKOFTO Διακοφτο

Halfway between Corinth and Patras, at the base of precipitous mountains, Diakofto is famous for its rack-railway trains, which rumble past waterfalls and over steep cliffs through the mountains to Kalavrita. The long empty beach of colorful pebbles, with craggy peaks just visible across the turquoise water, stridently advertises the potential for tourism in the town. Still, the streets are quiet, lined with houses planted between citrus trees and shaded by bougainvillea. Accommodations are better in Kalavrita (p. 138), but if you plan to catch an early train toward Athens or Patras, Diakofto is a charming place to spend the night.

ORIENTATION AND PRACTICAL INFORMATION. The **train station** (☎26910 43 206) intersects Diakofto's main road about 10min. from the beach. As the town's social center, it is flanked by cafes and stores. Tiny **rack-railway trains** to **Kalavrita** make for an exhilarating ride (1hr., 4 per day, €3.80); halfway rides to **Zahlorou** (30min., €1.90) are also available. Trains to **Patras** (40min.; 9 per day 9:43am-1:17am; €1.80, express €4) and **Athens** (3hr.; 8 per day 7:53am-3:22am; €3.80, express €9.70) via **Corinth** (1hr.; €2.10, express €4.70) leave from the opposite side of the tracks. The station also offers **luggage storage** (€3.20 per item, €1.60 if traveling by train. Open daily 6am-10pm). Walk down the main road toward the sea to pass through a picturesque residential area and end up at the harbor and public beach. If you walk inland on the winding main road toward the mountains, you will see a **pharmacy** (☎26910 41 811; open M-Sa 8am-1pm and 5-9pm) and the **National Bank,** which offers **currency exchange** and 24hr. **ATM** (open M-Th 8:45am-12:45pm, F 8:45am-12:15pm). The nearest **hospital** is a 20min. drive away in Ayion. The **post office** is on the left side of the road, as you walk inland from the train station. (☎26910 41 343. Open M-F 7:30am-2pm.) **Postal code:** 25003.

ACCOMMODATIONS. Domatia are nonexistent, and hotels are nearly so in Diakofto. **Hotel Lemonies ❸,** halfway between the train station and the beach on the main road, offers decent, clean rooms that are a little faded at the edges with baths, balconies, TVs, and A/C. Downstairs is a mellow taverna, and the surrounding residential neighborhood is lovely and quiet. (☎26910 41 820. Singles €21-25; doubles €30-36.) For a bit more money, you can stay at the **Chris Paul Hotel ❸,** located a block inland from the train station, left off the main road. Rooms are carpeted and offer A/C, TVs, balconies, and baths; the hotel also has the benefits of an upscale dining room, private pool, and handicapped access. (☎26910 41 715 or 26910 41 855; fax 26910 42 128. Breakfast €4. Singles €31; doubles €56; triples €67.) A ½hr. stroll along the beach with the water on your right brings you to **Camping Eleon Beach ❶,** which sports a small playground, washing machines, kitchen, restaurant, beach bar, mini-market, and nearby disco. (☎26910 41 539. €3.50 per person; €2 per tent. Electricity €2.10. Ask about student rates.)

FOOD AND ENTERTAINMENT. Cafes and bars dot the shoreline and cluster around the train station and the main street inland from the station. On the beach at the end of the main road, **Taverna Kohuli ❶** (Κοχυλι) sits beside a docking area for small boats and serves a perfect *tzatziki* (€1.65), huge grilled meatballs (€5), and excellent grilled chicken (€4.50). For cheap but good grilled food, head inland on the main road to the **taverna ❶** with the red and white sign, just past the National Bank on the right. Make a meal out of a big tomato salad (€1.75) and a hot gyro (€1.20) or souvlaki (€1). Next door, **Fuego** is the place for an evening drink under stars and large straw umbrellas (beer and ouzo €2, mixed drinks €4). Its fashionable counterparts on the main drag are **Mess Cafe Bar,** right across from the National Bank, adorned with framed, old-fashioned travel posters (ouzo and *mezedes* for €1.80). Opposite the train station on the inland side, **Relax Place** lives up to its unpretentious name; the shaded outdoor seating and mellow tunes complement well-made *frappés* (€1.50). The local outdoor **cinema,** on the roof of a building on the mainland road just before the bank, screens American movies nightly. Check posters in town.

GREAT CAVE MONASTERY Μονη Μεγαλου Σπηλαιου

Located 26km inland from Diakofto, the famous monastery is accessible only by a combination of 19th-century rack-railway and hiking. Getting there is half the fun: the 30min. railway ride winds into smoke-blackened tunnels, through spectacular canyons and gorges created by the Vouraikos River, and over old bridges, offering rollercoaster-esque excitement (€1.90). For the monastery, get off at the **Zahlorou,** the midway point on the line.

The small mountain village conjures up stock images of mining or timber towns in the old American West. A few well-shaded, rustic buildings cluster around the tracks where they pass over the river. From Zahlorou you can either hike up to the monastery or drive (taxis are not abundant). If you decide to hike, be prepared for a challenging walk with loose ground under foot; this is not recommended for elderly people or small children. The path that leads to the monastery is marked in English. Don't forget a water bottle, long-sleeved shirt, and sturdy shoes. After about 75min. of walking, you should reach a paved road; turn left and follow the road to the sign for Megalou Spilaiou on your right. Stairs in front of the monastery lead to the main entrance. A monk will lead you to the upstairs museum with gold-encased relics and beautiful icons, such as an illustrated Bible from the 9th century. Photographs show the destruction of the centuries-old monastery by an explosion of stored gunpowder in 1934. The new monastery is built up against the cliff wall. One of the cliff's caves is accessible from the second floor of the building—peer into the darkness in search of the cave's miraculous icon, a painting of the Virgin Mary supposedly done by St. Luke.

KALAVRITA Καλαβρυτα

In a small valley at the end of the rack-railway line, Kalavrita is a close-knit mountain village that caters more to winter skiers than to summer visitors. The green mountain vistas and shaded, quiet streets do make the warmer months a pleasant time to visit, however. With cozy domatia, mountain hikes, and a sobering WWII site, Kalavrita is the perfect place for a peaceful, contemplative stay.

PRACTICAL INFORMATION. Kalavrita is accesible by a tiny and fun-to-ride rack-railway line from **Diakofto** (1hr.; 8am-3:45pm from Diakofto, 9:15am-5pm return; €3.80). The two roads perpendicular to the train station that lead to the plateia are **Konstantinou** (later called **Ag. Alexiou**) to the left and **Syngrou** (later called **25 Martiou**), initially pedestrian only, to the right. A **bus station** (☎26920 22 224) has service to: **Athens** (3hr., 9am, €10.50); **Patras** (2hr., 5 per day 6:15am-4:45pm, €5.10); and **Tripoli** (2hr., 9:30am, €5.50). To get there, take your first right off Syngrou onto Kapota, walking away from the train station. Walk several blocks until the road merges; the bus station will be on your left. **Taxis** (☎26920 22 127) line up along the side of the plateia closest to the train station. The **National Bank of Greece,** 25 Martiou 4, offers **currency exchange** and a 24hr. **ATM.** (☎26920 22 212. Open M-Th 8am-2pm, F 8am-1:30pm.) The **police,** Fotina 7, are to the right off of Ag. Alexiou, three blocks beyond the OTE, walking from the train station. (☎26920 23 333. Open 24hr.) **Pharmacies** are sprinkled throughout the town; find one a block up Syngrou from the train station. (☎26920 22 131. Open M-F 8am-2pm.) A **hospital** (☎26920 22 734) is a three-block walk away from the post office, to the right. The **OTE** is at Ag. Alexiou 10. **Internet access** at the fun **CyberNet,** Ag. Alexiou 17. (☎26920 23 555. €2.20 per hr. Open daily 9am-midnight.) The **post office,** on 25 Martiou, is to the right of the town hall, in the corner of the plateia coming up from the train station. (☎26920 22 224. Open M-F 8am-2pm.) **Postal code:** 25001.

ACCOMMODATIONS. Hotels in Kalavrita are pleasant but expensive, especially during ski season. Fortunately, affordable, well-appointed domatia abound; numerous signs near the train station will lead you to them. **Domatia Hrysa ❸** (Χρησα) is easy to find; just cross the tracks behind the train station and go straight down the road running perpendicular to the tracks. Comfortable ground-floor singles with TVs and baths open onto a fragrant garden; more luxurious rooms are on the 3rd floor. (☎26920 22 443. Singles €25-30; doubles €40-50.) With your back to the rail station, turn right and walk three blocks. Turn right immediately after the hospital and then continue two blocks to reach **Mitsopoulos Rooms ❸**. The spacious rooms with baths, TVs, majestic mountain views, and a common kitchen with free coffee are run by a friendly older woman. (☎26920 22 481. Singles €25; doubles €50.) **Anesis Hotel ❹,** just off Ag. Alexiou facing the plateia, is a lovely stone hotel featuring three types of rooms: plain ones, ones with a fireplace, and fancier third-floor rooms with wooden ceilings and balconies. All rooms have TVs and phones and are large and well-furnished with big comfy beds. (☎26920 23 070. Breakfast included. In summer, singles €35; doubles €45. In winter, singles €45; doubles €53-82.) One block up Syngrou from the train station, **Hotel Maria ❸** has rooms with TVs, telephones, balconies, and a colorful decor. (☎26920 22 296; fax 26920 22 686. Breakfast included. In summer, singles €25; doubles €45; triples €70. In winter, singles €45; doubles €65; triples €90.)

FOOD AND NIGHTLIFE. A collection of similar tavernas line Ag. Alexiou and Syngrou/25 Martiou. Centrally-located **Taverna Stani ❷** offers delicious fare displayed for your choosing and served by a friendly staff in a huge stone and wood dining room (crisp tomato and cucumber salad €2.50, veal in red sauce €6). **Taverna Aistralos ❷,** part of the Anesis Hotel, just off Ag. Alexiou facing the plateia, serves tasty dishes including spicy sausage (€4.40) and lamb with vegetables (€5.60). Right next door is **Tzaki Taverna ❷,** opposite the church, with good prices for Greek classics. (Tzatziki €1.80, moussaka €5, stuffed tomatoes €4.20.) For a wild night, the **Tehni Music Club** (TEXNH) offers some fun in town. Facing the plateia, turn right at the post office and walk one block. The cafes on the pedestrian block of 25 Martiou serve coffee and beer into the late hours.

SIGHTS AND THE OUTDOORS. One of the few sights in Kalavrita is a moving memorial to the Kalavritan men who were killed on December 13, 1943. In retaliation for the murder of one of their troopers, the occupying Nazis gathered all of the town's men and boys over age 15 on a hill outside of town under the pretext of giving them a stern reprimand for the murder. Instead, at 2:34pm, from the trees above the hill, lurking troopers opened fire on command and then burned the town itself. Today the clock of the town's church is set permanently to 2:34, and an extensive memorial stands alongside a hanging oil lamp shrine, symbolizing the anticipated resurrection of the murdered men. To reach the memorial, follow Ag. Alexiou from the train station. Signs in English point the way.

To make an afternoon of the beautiful countryside, continue walking past the memorial on the road winding up the mountain beyond. After about an hour and a half you will see signs pointing to the **Kalavrita Castle,** which appears to be an old chapel built high up on the hillside. Wear good shoes and take plenty of water. There are also several summer **hikes** around Mt. Helmos; ask around for information or a guide. In the winter months, travel to the nearby **Mt. Helmos** for fantastic **skiing.** One of the town's many ski stores and offices, the **Ski Centre,** on 25 Martiou, provides information and rentals. (☎26920 22 175. Open Dec.-Apr. daily 8:30am-3:30pm.) Not immediately accessible in Kalavrita, but definitely worth the trip if you have transportation, is the **Cave of Lakes,** 16km away. Signs in English direct the way from up the winding mountain road behind the memorial.

KYLLINI Κυλληνη

For a port town that handles almost all the tourist traffic to Zakynthos, Kyllini is surprisingly underdeveloped; the town has almost no bus service, few accommodations, and very little to occupy the passing traveler besides an overabundance of cafes and bars (crowded with bored and/or drunk travelers). If you find yourself stuck here, make the best of it by spending the afternoon at the wide sandy beach in the center of town. To bypass Kyllini entirely, take a direct bus from Zakynthos Town to any of the stops on the Patras-Athens route (p. 131).

PRACTICAL INFORMATION. To leave Kyllini, take the **bus** from the kiosk near the port gate to **Pirgos** (1½hr., 3 per day until 4:30pm, €3.35). Once in Pirgos, catch a bus to **Olympia** (40min., 16 per day, €1.40) or a train to **Athens, Patras, Kalamata,** or **Tripoli.** For all other bus connections you will have to spend €10 on a **taxi** (☎26230 71 764) to **Lehena,** the nearest town on the main Patras-Pirgos highway. **Ferries** sail from Kyllini to: **Argostoli,** Kephalonia (2hr., 3 per day, €9.40), **Poros,** Kephalonia (1½hr.; 6:30, 10:30pm; €6.30), and **Zakynthos** (1hr., 7 per day 8:30am-10pm, €4.70). Buy tickets from one of the two kiosks on the dock; the kiosk on the right sells tickets to Zakynthos, and the one on the left sells tickets to Kephalonia. The **port police** are on the dock. (☎26230 92 211. Open 24hr.) The path to town leads to the **police.** (☎26230 92 202.) The **post office** is a few blocks farther down, on a side street leading inland. (Open M-F 7:30am-2pm.) **Postal code:** 27068.

ACCOMMODATIONS AND FOOD. **Sea Garden Domatia ❸,** above the Sea Garden Restaurant two blocks inland from the port, is nothing fancy but has pleasant rooms with ceiling fans, TVs, balconies, and some private baths. (☎26230 92 165. Singles €25-30; doubles €55.) **Hotel Ionion ❸,** across the tracks and down the beach, rents large, unimaginative rooms with A/C, TVs, and private baths. (☎26230 92 318. Singles €40; doubles €50; triples with mini-fridges €66.) **Stivas ❷** (☎26230 92 045), down the street from the port gate, facing the entrance to the Sea Garden domatia, serves divine dishes cooked in a tiny, family-run kitchen. Eat under a vine-laden trellis on the side patio. Dishes change daily, but standbys like moussaka (€4) and *tzatziki* (€2) are always available. A full meal with wine costs €7-9.

PELOPONNESE

OLYMPIA Ολυμπια

Set among meadows and shaded by cypress and olive trees, modern Olympia is a friendly and attractive town which serves as a sleeping-and-eating stopover for visitors to the ancient Olympic arena. Intense tourism has inspired vigorous customer-luring tactics amongst the locals who hock their wares.

ORIENTATION AND PRACTICAL INFORMATION

Olympia consists primarily of a 1km main street called **Kondili;** buses stop in front of the tourist office on this street. Head out of town on the main road with the tourist office on your right for a 5min. walk to the Olympia ruins and archaeological museum. The road curves left just outside town; follow the signs to the site. The side road that intersects Kondili in a fork near the youth hostel has the train station, convenience store, and pricey tavernas.

Buses: Across from the tourist info shack's posted schedule. To: **Pirgos** (40min., 16 per day 6:30am-10pm, €1.40); **Tripoli** (4hr.; 8:45am, 12:30, 5:30pm; €7.80); **Dimitsana** (M, F 8:45am; €4.30); **Lala** (30min., 12:30pm, €1.50). Service reduced Sa-Su.

Tourist Office: (☎26240 23 100; fax 26240 23 125), on Kondili, toward the ruins. Helpful staff, photocopier, and free **maps.** Open M-F 8am-3pm, Sa at varying times.

Bank: National Bank (☎26240 22 501), on Kondili next to the tourist office, has an **ATM** and **exchanges currency.** Open M-Th 8am-2pm, F 8am-1:30pm.

Police: Em. Kountsa 1 (☎26240 22 100), 1 block up from Kondili, right behind the tourist office. Open daily 9am-9pm; someone is there 24hr. Also serve as **Tourist Police.**

Health Center: (☎26240 22 222; Pirgos hospital ☎26210 22 222). Olympia uses Pirgos's hospital, but has its own health center. Walk from the ruins down Kondili and turn left before the church on your left. Continue straight as the road winds right and then left, and then take a left. Open M-F 8:30am-2pm.

OTE: (☎26240 22 163) is on Kondili by the post office. Open M-F 7:30am-2pm.

Internet Access: Olympia's **Internet Cafe** (☎26240 22 578 or 26240 23 841) is a hip and spacious cafe-bar, blaring American and British tunes late into the night. Turn off Kondili with the youth hostel on your right and walk uphill two blocks; Pension Achilles is on the same street. €4.50 per hr., €1.50 minimum. Open daily 9:30am-3am.

Post Office: (☎26240 22 578), on a nameless uphill side street just past the tourist office. Open M-F 7:30am-2pm. **Postal code:** 27065.

ACCOMMODATIONS AND CAMPING

Most of Olympia's hotels offer private baths and balconies. Still, there is a great deal of price diversity: you can pay anywhere from €15-40 for a single and €20-70 for a double, depending on whether you desire A/C or a central location.

Zounis Rooms. Ask at the Anesi Cafe-Tavern, 13 Avgerinou and Spiliopoulou (☎26240 22 644). Turn off Kondili facing uphill; it's 2 blocks up the road (away from the tourist office). Pleasant rooms with balconies, nice beds, and private baths. Shared fridge available. Singles €15; doubles €25; triples €30. ❷

Pension Poseidon (☎26240 22 567), on the same street as the Internet Cafe. Turn off Kondili with the youth hostel on your right, or follow the signs. Large, clean rooms with nice curtains and private baths. Singles €20-25; doubles €30-35; triples €35-40. ❸

Youth Hostel, Kondili 18 (☎26240 22 580). The rooms may not be spotless, but beds are clean and the owner is friendly. In a good location, this hostel definitely has the cheapest rooms in town. Breakfast €2.50. Free hot showers. Sheets €1. Check-out 10:30am; rooms must be vacated between 10:30am and 12:30pm. Dorms €7. Separate male and female rooms. Private rooms available for an additional €3. ❶

Olympia Palace, Kondili 2 (☎26240 23 101; fax 26240 22 525; www.olympia-palace.gr). On Kondili, as close to Ancient Olympia as you can get, the Palace smacks of luxury through and through, right down to the price. Features shops, a cafe, a restaurant, and a gorgeous marble lobby. Rooms are no less elegant or modern, with A/C, TVs, private baths with large bathtubs, Internet connection, and huge balconies. Doubles €100-120. Breakfast included. ❺

Hotel Ilis (☎26240 22 547 or 26240 22 112), past the road to the Sports Museum on Kondili, towards Pirgos. Frighteningly cheerful sorbet-orange walls in clean rooms with A/C, TVs, private baths, phones, mini-bars, and balconies. Same management runs **New Olympia** (☎26240 22 506), on the road to the train station, with nearly identical rooms and prices. Singles €45; doubles €70; triples €90. ❹

Camping Diana (☎26240 22 314), uphill from the Sports Museum. Has hot water, helpful info (schedules and maps), a clean pool, a market, and a restaurant ❶ serving ouzo, snacks, and breakfast (€4.50). €5 per person, children €3.50; €3.50 per small tent; €5 per large tent; €3.50 per car. Electricity €3.50. 10% student discounts. ❶

FOOD

Along Kondili, numerous **mini-markets** sell picnic fixings, and fast food joints fight for your attention with large signs. Most eateries on Kondili are overpriced, but a walk toward the railroad station or up the hill leads to enticing, inexpensive tavernas. Most restaurants are open from 8am to 1am.

Ambrosia (☎26240 23 414), as you face the train station, around to the right. Don't be fooled—another Ambrosia is on the road between Kondili and the train station. Exceptionally delicious food in an elegant setting overlooking a cypress-lined meadow. Satisfying *mezedes* plate €8.30, veal with red sauce and pasta €6, stuffed vine leaves €4.80. A meal with starter, salad, entree and wine should cost about €10-12. ❷

Taverna Olympia, on the road to the train station. Relaxed feel, away from the crowds. Salads €2-2.50, Greek entrees €3.30-5.20, pastas €2.50-3, and *prix fixe* €6.80-8. ❷

Pension Poseidon (☎26240 22 567), 2 blocks uphill from the Youth Hostel. George, the cheerful owner, serves *retsina* made from the grapes that hang on the lattices overhead (€3 per liter) and generous portions made by his wife and mother. Moussaka €5.50, souvlaki with potatoes €6, omelettes €2.50, and *prix fixe* €7.50-8.50. ❷

SIGHTS

At the top of the hill, on the side of town toward Pirgos, the **Museum of the Olympic Games,** or the **Sports Museum,** on Angerinou, two blocks uphill from Kondili, tells the recent history of the Olympics and has paraphernalia from each of the modern games, including medals, posters, and photographs of athletes. (☎26240 22 544. Open M-Sa 8am-3:30pm, Su 9am-4:30pm. €2, children and EU students free.)

PELOPONNESE

ANCIENT OLYMPIA

***Site:** ☎26240 22 517. Open in summer daily 8am-7pm. **Museum:** through the parking lot opposite the ancient site. ☎16140 22 742. Open M noon-3pm, Tu-Su 8am-7pm. Cameras with flash prohibited. Museum and site €9, seniors and non-EU students €5; museum or site only €6, EU students and children under 18 free. A guidebook and map are vital, as the ruins are practically unmarked. Several guides are available at the site—try* Olympia: Complete Guide *(€5) by Spiros Photinos, or* The Blue Guide to the Museum and Sanctuary *by A. and N. Yalouris (€7.50). Maps €2-4.*

A green tract between the rivers Kladeo and Alphios, Olympia was one of the most important cultural centers of the Greek world for a millennium. Here, participants from Sicily, Asia Minor, North Africa, Macedonia, and Greece convened to worship, compete, and get cultured among poets, musicians, and masterpieces of art and architecture. Every four years, warring city-states would call truces and travel to Olympia for the most splendid pan-Hellenic assembly of the ancient world.

Olympia was settled in the 3rd millennium BC, when it was dedicated to **Gaia,** the Earth Mother, who had an oracle at the site. The first athletic games commenced in Zeus's honor, only to be forgotten again until 884 BC. The first Olympic revival took place on the Oracle of Delphi's orders to Iphtos, King of Elias; prophecy held that the games would save Greece from civil war and plague. The first recorded Olympiad was in 776 BC, with **Koroibos of Elias** emerging victorious. Every four years thereafter, another champion added his name to the illustrious list, which became the first accurate chronology of Greek history. Initially, a footrace of 192m (the stadium's length) was the only event, but longer races, wrestling, boxing, the pentathlon (long jump, discus, javelin, running, wrestling), the hoplite race (in full bronze regalia), and equestrian events eventually joined the

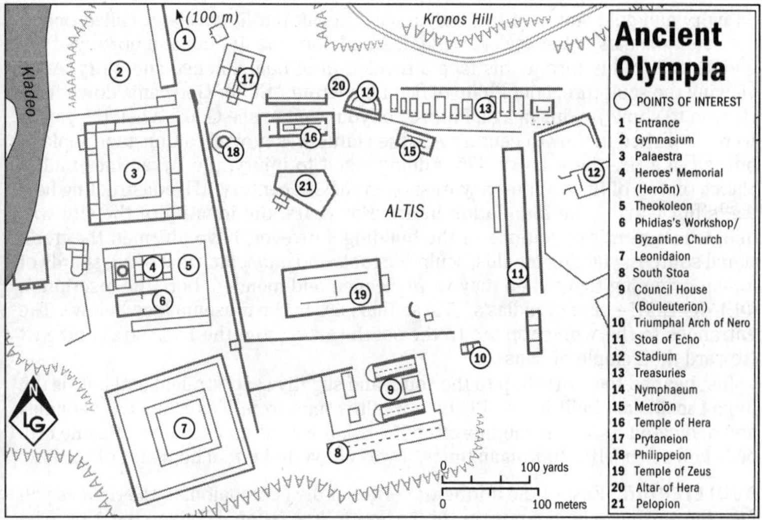

roster. Under Roman rule, Olympia mostly thrived, and the games were allowed to continue and often were actively supported. The games were celebrated through the 4th century AD; Emperor Theodosius eventually abolished the use of heathen sanctuaries and, with this decree, the games themselves. Earthquakes in AD 522 and 551 destroyed much of the Olympic site.

SIGHTS AND RUINS

The central sanctuary of the Olympic complex, which was eventually walled and dedicated to Zeus, was called the **Altis.** Over the centuries, it held temples, treasuries, and a number of monuments to the gods. The complex was surrounded by various facilities for participants and administrators, including the stadium on the far east side. **Pausanias,** a traveler who wrote in the 2nd century AD, mentions a whopping 69 monuments built by victors to thank the gods. Although the ruins are not especially well-preserved, few sections are corded off; you can climb up the steps of the Temple of Zeus and wander in Phidias's workshop as you please.

TRAINING GROUNDS. As you enter the site, facing south, the 2nd-century BC Gymnasium's thigh-high remains lie to your right as you follow the path, which veers slightly to the left. The **Gymnasium** was an open-air quadrangle surrounded by Doric columns used by runners and pentathlon athletes for training. If you continue straight (south) through the Gymnasium, you will come to the re-erected columns of the square **Palaestra,** or wrestling school, built in the 3rd century BC. Always more than just an athletic facility, the Palaestra had an educational function as philosophical as it was athletic. Young men trained their minds and bodies, wrestling one moment and studying metaphysics the next.

PHIDIAS'S WORKSHOP. As you continue south and slightly west (out the far right corner of the Palaestra), the next group of structures includes a walled-in building that is surprisingly intact. This is the workshop of **Phidias,** the marvelous sculptor who came to Olympia after his banishment from Athens under a cloud of scandal (it concerned the statue of Athena he had created for the Parthenon; use your imagination). Commissioned to sculpt for the Temple of Zeus, he produced an ivory-and-gold statue of the god so magnificent that it was later called one of the **seven wonders of the ancient world.** It stood about 12.4m tall and portrayed the god seated on his throne, his face a revelation of benevolence and glory. After viewing the sculpture, poet Philip of Salonika wrote, "Either God came down from Heaven to show you his image, Phidias, or you went to see God." When the games were abolished in the 4th century AD, the statue was moved to Constantinople; it burned in a fire there in AD 475. Adding insult to injury, the Byzantines built a **church** on top of the sculptor's workshop in the 5th century AD, constructing new walls but leaving the foundation intact. For years, the identity of the site was debated. Recent excavations of the building, however, have affirmed the traditional sources, yielding moulds, sculpting tools and, most amazing of all, shards of a plain wine jug that, when they were cleaned and mended, bore the inscription ΦΕΙΔΙΟ ΕΙΜΙ—"I am Phidias's." These finds are in the museum (see below). The entrances to the workshop are to the south (away from the Palaestra) and east (toward the Temple of Zeus).

Just beyond the workshop to the south and slightly east (straight and left) is the huge **Leonidaion,** built in 330 BC by a wealthy man from Naxos named Leonidas and dedicated to Zeus sometime after 350 BC. It was often used to host game officials and other VIPs. In Roman times, it was converted into a home for officials.

BOULETERION. East of the northeast corner of the Leonidaion, to the right as you face the entrance, lie the remains of the South Processional Gate to the Altis. The procession of athletes and trainers entered the sacred area on their way to the Bouleuterion (to the right of the Gate), where the Olympic council met. Each athlete was required to make a sacrifice to Zeus and take the sacred oath, swearing their eligibility and intent to abide by the rules of the Games.

TEMPLE OF ZEUS. To the north of the Bouleterion (toward the entrance) are the ruins of the once-gigantic Temple of Zeus, the centerpiece of the Altis after its completion in 456 BC. Home to Phidias's awe-inspiring statue of Zeus (see above), the 27m-long temple was the largest completed on the Greek mainland before the Parthenon. The temple's elegant facade, impressive Doric columns, and accurately modeled pedimental sculpture exemplified the Classical design that evolved before the Persians invaded Greece. Toppled in segments, the tremendous columns lie as they fell in a 6th-century AD earthquake.

STADIUM. Continuing east past the temple (to the right as you face the entrance), you will reach the remains of the **Stoa of Echo,** which was used for the competitions between trumpeters and heralds, whose musical prowess was no doubt enhanced by the seven-fold echo the Stoa is said to have had. At the northern edge of the Stoa (toward the hill) is the **Krypte,** the official entrance to the stadium (farther to right and east) used by athletes and judges. This domed passageway (of which only one arch survives) and the stadium as it stands today are products of the Hellenistic period, built over the remains of the earlier, similarly positioned stadium. Despite the efforts of powerful earthquakes, the stadium appears today much as it did 2300 years ago. The judges' stand and the start and finish lines are still in place, and the stadium's grassy banks can still seat nearly 40,000 spectators. Take a lap, and bond with Olympians of millennia past. As you leave the passageway to the stadium, the remains of treasuries erected by distant states to house votive offerings are in a row on the north hillside to your right. Continuing west, or left as you face the hill, beyond the treasuries, you'll see the remains of the **nymphaeum** and the **metroön,** an elegant 4th-century BC temple dedicated to Rhea, the mother of gods, and built in the Doric style. Along the terrace of the treasuries stand the remains of the bases of 16 bronze statues of Zeus, built with money from fines collected from cheating athletes.

HERA'S TEMPLE. Westward (to the left facing the hill) past the metroön and the nymphaeum are the dignified remains of the **Temple of Hera.** Erected around 600 BC, the temple is the oldest building at Olympia, the oldest Doric temple in Greece, and the best-preserved structure at the site. Originally built for both Zeus and Hera, it was devoted solely to the goddess when Zeus moved to grander quarters in 457 BC. The *cella* of the Temple is where the magnificent Hermes of Praxiteles was unearthed during excavations; you can see the statue in the museum. This temple figured prominently in the Heraia, a women's foot-race held every four years. Today, the Olympic flame is lit at the Altar of Hera, at the northeast corner of the temple. From here, it is borne to Athens by runners who each travel 1km, then pass it from hand to hand to the site of the modern games, which can involve thousands of runners, or draw upon more modern methods of transportation like boats, planes, or even laser beam (as in the unique case of the 1976 Montreal Games). The Prytaneion is northwest (toward the entrance) of the Temple of Hera and contains a sacred hearth, the Altar of Hestia. The spirit of the Games reached its culmination here with the celebratory feasts on behalf of the victors and official guests that expressed a collective appreciation for the virtues of discipline and honor that they embodied.

MUSEUM. Many find the gleaming new **Archaeological Museum** a greater attraction than the ancient site itself. A team of French archaeologists began unearthing the site from 1400 years of silt in 1829; the systematic excavations that continue today commenced in 1875. Most of what has been extracted in these 128 years resides in the museum. Since military victors from across the Greek world sent spoils and pieces of their own equipment to Olympia as offerings to the gods, the new museum doubles as a museum of Greek military history, with entire rooms filled with helmets, cuirasses, greaves, swords, spear points, and other military paraphernalia. The most spectacular military offering is a common **Corinthian helmet** (490 BC), partially destroyed by oxidation. While richer, better preserved headgear can be found elsewhere in the museum, the helmet's attraction is the faint inscription on the chin guard, which reads ΜΙΛΤΙΔΕΣ ΑΝΕΘΕΚΕΝ ΤΟΙ ΔΙΙ—"Miltiades dedicated this to Zeus." The victor of one of the most famous battles in all antiquity, **Miltiades** led the outnumbered Greeks to victory over the Persians at Marathon in 479 BC; he may have worn the helmet in the battle. Beside it is another headpiece, the inscription on which reveals it to be from the Persian side of the same battle. The museum's awesome array of sculpture includes some of the greatest extant pieces in the world. Gape at the graceful perfection of the **Hermes of Praxiteles** (340-330 BC) and the **Rape of Ganymede** (470 BC), and see how the **Nike of Paionios** (421 BC) seems to float. The pedimental sculptures and metopes depicting the 12 labors of Hercules from the Temple of Zeus are in the main room. Even the lesser-known objects astound—every case holds objects that would be highlights of a lesser collection.

ARCADIA Αρκαδια

Beyond the noisy bustle of Tripoli, mountainous Arcadia is heavily forested and lightly speckled with red-roofed villages and lonely monasteries. The region's lush mountain landscapes and undisturbed serenity ushered it into mythology and literature as the pastoral archetype, home to Pan, Dionysus, and the nymphs, satyrs, and lucky mortals who cavorted with them. While few foreign tourists make it to Arcadia's pristine outer reaches, those who do are accompanied on solitary walks by the tin bells of grazing mountain goats atop precipitous slopes.

TRIPOLI Τριπολη

The transportation hub of Arcadia, Tripoli is crowded and fast-paced, and initially feels like any other modern Greek city. But the many plateias and a huge city park, with lovely gardens and fountains, belie the fact that Tripoli has worked to beautify its urban landscape. Cars chug through the narrow shop-lined streets while cafes and tavernas brim with energy at the park's edge. Bide your time with a *frappé* in the park and watch children wreak havoc speeding on bikes and playing football, or join the adolescent nightlife of blaring bars along Deligianni.

ORIENTATION AND PRACTICAL INFORMATION

Think of Tripoli as a cross. At the center joint is **Pl. Ag. Vasiliou,** marked by the Church of Ag. Vasiliou. Four other plateias form the ends of the cross, at the ends of the four roads that branch out from Ag. Vasiliou. Most buses arrive at Arcadia station in **Pl. Kolokotronis,** to the east of the center. From the station, **Giorgiou,** to the left as you face the National Bank, takes you to Pl. Ag. Vasiliou from behind the church. Facing the church in Pl. Ag. Vasiliou, turn left and head north on **Eth. Antistasis** to reach **Pl. Petrinou,** recognizable by the large, neoclassical Maliaropouli Theater. Along with Pl. Kolokotronis, Pl. Petrinou sees most of the city's activity. Continue on Eth. Antistasis, the main shopping boulevard, past pedestrian-only **Deligianni,** which runs perpendicular to Eth. Antistasis. Travel farther up Eth. Antistasis and the city park will be on your right. At the center of the park is **Pl. Areus,** with a 5m-tall statue of War for Independence hero Kolokotronis.

Buses: Tripoli has 2 bus stations: 1 is in Pl. Kolokotronis; the other is farther southeast, outside the center of town. The **KTEL Arcadias Station** (☎2710 222 560), in Pl. Kolokotronis, runs buses to: **Andritsena** (2hr.; 11:45am, 7:30pm; €5.10); **Athens** (3hr., 14 per day 5am-9:15pm, €15.50); **Dimitsana** (1hr.; M-F 1:30 and 6:30pm, 8:30am M, F only, Sa-Su 1:30pm; €4.30); **Megalopolis** (45min., 10per day 4:45am-10:15pm, €2.20); **Nafplion** via **Argos** (1hr., 4 per day 7am-4:20pm, €3.50); and **Pirgos** (3½hr.; M-F 8:30am and 6:30pm, Sa-Su 11am; €9.30). **Blue buses** leave from Arcadias Station for **Tegea** and **Mantinea** (1 hr., every 15min., €0.90). The **KTEL Messenia and Laconia** depot (☎2710 242 086) is across from the train station. From Arcadias Station turn right onto Lagorati, which runs 1 block behind the eastern side of Pl. Koloktroni; follow it past the curve near Atlantik Supermarket until it ends at the train station—the depot is on the left. Buses go to: **Kalamata** (1½hr., 12 per day 6am-11pm, €5.20); **Patras** (3hr., 2 per day, €10.45); **Pylos** (3hr., 2 per day, €8.35); and **Sparta** (1hr., 10 per day 9:15am-10:15pm, €3.40).

Trains: (☎2710 241 213), across from the Messenia and Laconia bus depot. Trains to: **Argos** (1½hr., 3 per day, €1.30); **Athens** (4hr., 4 per day, €8); **Corinth** (2½hr., 3 per day, €4.50); and **Kalamata** (2½hr., 4 per day, €4.50).

Bank: National Banks, in Pl. Kolokotronis (☎2710 371 110) and another on Eth. Antistasis, 1 block from Pl. Agios Vasiliou (☎2710 234 878). Both **exchange currency** and have a 24hr. **ATM.** Both open M-Th 8am-2pm, F 8am-1:30pm.

Police: (☎2710 224 847), on Eth. Antistasis, in Pl. Petrinou. Open 24hr.

Hospital: (☎2710 238 542), on Panargadon road. Walk due west from Pl. Agios Vasiliou; the road becomes E. Stavrou, which intersects with Panargadon after 500m. At the intersection, turn left. After 300m, look right, and you'll see the hospital.

OTE: 28 Octovriou 29 (☎2710 226 399). From Pl. Agios Vasiliou, take Eth. Antistasis and bear left on 28 Octovriou. Open M-Sa 7am-5pm.

Internet Access: Concept Cafe (☎2710 235 600), on Dareioutou off Eth. Antistasis, before Deligianni. €3 per hr., €1.20 minimum. Open 9am-2pm. **Forth Net** (☎2710 226 407) is on Deligianni, inside Cinema Club and upstairs. €3.50 per hr. Open late.

Post Office: (☎2710 222 565). With your back to the church in Pl. Ag. Vasiliou, cross the plateia and pass the Galaxy Hotel on either side; the post office is 1 block behind it. Open M-F 7:30am-2pm. **Postal Code:** 22100.

ACCOMMODATIONS

Tripoli presents numerous bloated, mid-range hotels, better suited to business conventions than to budget travelers. Expect to pay €40-45 for a double. **Hotel Alex ❸,** Vas. Georgios 26, is between Pl. Kolokotronis and Pl. Ag. Vasiliou. The polished granite lobby of the recently renovated hotel reflects the modern style of the spacious, spotless rooms. Rooms and private baths are newly painted and tiled in soft pinks, greens, and blues with sleek new fixtures and furniture. A/C, TVs, phones, and balconies complete the feeling of luxury at the best price in town. (☎2710 223 465; fax 2710 223 466; alexhotel@icn.gr. Singles €30; doubles €50; triples €60. Suites available.) In Pl. Kolokotronis, **Arcadia Hotel ❸** offers old-fashioned rooms with private baths, A/C, and TVs. Each room features a different dramatic wallpaper pattern. (☎2710 225 551. Singles €36; doubles €62; triples €74.) **Galaxy Hotel ❸,** in Pl. Ag. Vasiliou, has the best location in town. Standard rooms with A/C, TVs, balconies, and baths at the typical Tripoli prices. (☎2710 225 195; fax 2710 225 197. Singles €35; doubles €50.)

FOOD

The restaurants in Tripoli will not wow you in general, but there are a few good options bordering the park. Sandwich shops on Eth. Antistasis and Giorgiou pile baguettes with meat and cheese (around €2). **Atlantik Supermarket,** on Lagorati, is well-stocked. (Open M-F 8am-9pm, Sa 8am-6pm.)

Klimataria (☎2710 222 058), on Eth. Antistasis, 4 blocks past the park as you walk from Pl. Petriou. The restaurant is run by two charming brothers who inherited it from their father. Popular with regulars and visitors alike. Garden seating with fountains and overhead grape vines accent the delicious, well-priced traditional fare. Try the goat with mushrooms in egg and lemon sauce (€8.20) or local beef with fresh tomatoes and onions (€5.50). A full meal with starter, entree, wine, and dessert will cost €10-12. ❸

H Gonia Taverna (η γωνια) (☎2710 227 904) in Pl. Ag. Vasiliou. No fancy decor, but cheap and filling food. *Tzatziki* €1.80. Greek salad €3.20, grilled chicken €3.20, and, the favorite of the owner's son, pork souvlaki €0.80. ❶

Alea (☎2710 225 533), in Pl. Areus, facing the park. Cafe atmosphere, but serves tasty fare like their rigatoni special (€4.50) and feta cheese (€1.80). ❶

SIGHTS AND ENTERTAINMENT

The **Archaeological Museum** is on Evangelistrias, in a pink building surrounded by roses and sculpture. Walking from Pl. Kolokotronis to Pl. Ag. Vasiliou, take the first left and then turn left again. The museum has an especially large prehistoric collection, with room after room of pottery, jewelry, and weaponry from the Neolithic to the Mycenaean periods. Among the later pieces is a Hellenistic relief showing a figure with a scroll in hand: it's one of the few surviving artistic depictions of the predecessor to modern books. For an ironic diversion, walk down a hall lined with marble heads to a room dominated by three headless statues. (☎2710 242 148. Open Tu-Su 8:30am-2:45pm. €2, seniors €1, students and children free.) Walk to the left of the Galaxy Hotel in Pl. Ag. Vasiliou to find the **War Museum.** The small but nicely presented collection of photographs, swords, guns, and uniforms covers the 1821 War for Independence through the Second World War. (Open Tu-Sa 9am-2pm, Su 9:30am-2pm. Free.) The large **Church of Ag. Vasiliou** is in the plateia of the same name; the basement shop has interesting religious art.

In summer, posters advertise dance groups, choirs, and plays performed in the city's main plateias and nearby villages. Traveling companies and local performance groups stage Greek shows in the attractive and recently renovated **Maliaropoulio Theater.** The **Lera Panigyris** is a 10-day **theater festival** beginning August 15.

At night you can rub shoulders with Tripoli's high school students at the downtown hot spot, pedestrian-only Deligianni. Especially popular is the **Cinema Classic Billiards Club,** to the right of Deligianni from Pl. Petrinou. With a big TV, A/C, and (most importantly) cheap drinks, this place fills up every night. (Beer €1.50; cocktails €3. Pool €4.50 per hr.) Numerous cafes such as **Faces** and **Metro** crowd the narrow area around Deligianni and Eth. Antistasis. **The American Music Bar,** found below a "Mobile" sign near the Billiards Club, is one of the loudest places in town.

DIMITSANA Δημητσανα

About 60km west of Tripoli lies the quintessential Arcadian village of Dimitsana, clinging to a steep, pine-covered mountainside with a view of the plain of Megalopolis and the Lousios River. Built on the ruins of ancient Teuthis, Dimitsana has been a center of Greek learning and revolutionary activity since the 16th century, producing several notable church fathers during the War for Independence. Greek city dwellers seeking a simpler life have begun to resettle in Dimitsana, bringing the money and energy to keep the town's historic buildings in good repair. Every turn in the road presents a breathtaking vista, and the scent of fresh-baked bread wafts from the open windows of stone homes.

ORIENTATION AND PRACTICAL INFORMATION. Transportation can be tricky in the mountains, and locals are roughly indifferent to the passage of time. When planning connections, keep in mind that the two taxi drivers in some towns might siesta all afternoon. There is no bus station, bus kiosk, or posted schedule. **Buses** are supposed to run to **Olympia** (1hr., at least 1 per day, €4.30) and **Tripoli** (2 per day, at approximately 10am and 7:30pm, €3.60). There is a morning bus (7am) that connects Dimitsana to the nearby mountain village of **Stemnitsa.** Schedules for all buses are erratic. Some travelers have been known to take the first bus that comes through, get off at **Karkalou** (or take a 20min., €5 taxi ride), then thumb down one of the more frequent buses to **Tripoli, Pirgos,** or **Olympia** from there.

In Dimitsana, the bus deposits you on **Labardopoulou** (the main street), near the taxi stand, about 30m downhill from the center of town. Walking uphill into the center of town, you will pass restaurants and the **police station** (☎27950 31 205; open 24hr.) to the left, followed by a small grocery store just before the turn in the road. Opposite this road is an alley leading to rooms and a museum. Continue around the corner to the **National Bank,** with an **ATM,** on your left. (☎27950 31 503. Open M-Th 8am-2pm, F 8am-1:30pm.) The **health center** (☎27950 31 401 or 27950 31 402; open 24 hr.) is a 10min. walk along the road towards Karaklou, and a **pharmacy** is on your right as you walk uphill from the bus stop. The **post office** is past the bank. (☎27950 31 234. Open M-F 7:30am-2pm.) **Postal code:** 22100.

ACCOMMODATIONS AND FOOD. Widespread, though pricey, **domatia** are really the only option, but most establishments are beautifully furnished and more like bed and breakfasts than the boxlike rooms often found elsewhere. Perhaps the best deal in town are the rooms to let above the **grocery store** ❸ in the main plateia. They include hardwood floors, great views, private baths, TV, comfortable beds, and kitchenettes complete with breakfast fixings. (☎27950 31 084 or 27950 31 562. Singles €30; doubles €38; apartment-style €70.) The home of **Vasilis Tsiapa** ❸ is set back from the road with a fragrant garden, mountain views, and gracious owners. As you walk up the main road from the bus stop, take the last right before the road bends. Gorgeous rooms have big beds, hardwood floors, TVs, and kitchenettes. (☎27950 31 583. Breakfast included. Singles €30-38; doubles €50.)

The ouzo flows freely in the cafes lining Labardopoulou, but there are fewer tavernas serving full meals. **Barougadiko ❸** (☎27950 31 629; ΜΠΑΡΟΥΓΑΔΙΚΟ), down the main street by the bus stop, is in a castle-like building with low arched doorways and small stone rooms. They serve skillfully prepared traditional Greek dishes like pork in wine sauce with potatoes (€5.50). Salads start at €2.50. **Barougadiko Bar** is to the right of the main street as you walk uphill from the restaurant. It's the only real bar in town, so you'll be sure to find the night owls there.

SIGHTS. Two small museums commemorate the town's ecclesiastic, scholarly, and revolutionary heritage. The **Historical Museum** shares its building with a small school. The museum displays an eclectic collection including vintage War of Independence pistols, two 15th-century illuminated psalters, and a handful of Italian edition Greek-Latin **incunabula** of various church fathers and ancient authors. To find the museum and library, walk up the alley next to the police station and look for the courtyard with the statue in it near a large church. (☎27950 31 219. Open Tu-Sa 9am-2pm. Free.) Walking up from the bus station, the **Icon Museum,** housed in an old mansion, is just off the main road on the last right before the bend; the same road also leads to Vasilis Tsiapa Rooms. (☎27950 31 465. Open F-Tu 10am-1:30pm and 5-7pm. Free.)

The Lousios River attracts both adventurers and those seeking more serene forms of entertainment. To reach the river, ask a local for directions, or follow the paths off the road to Stemnitsa. Strolling the banks and swimming are popular in the summer. Rafting (sometimes of the white water variety) and river tours are available and are especially popular in fall and winter months.

STEMNITSA Στεμνιτσα

From Dimitsana, walk an easy, scenic 11km (about 2hr.) along the winding road, or pay €4 for a taxi to Stemnitsa, where narrow, irregular cobbled streets betray medieval roots. With its unspoiled mountain scenery and an abundance of flowers, greenery, and hidden courtyards, it is easy to see why this town has been called one of the most beautiful in Greece. There are **buses** that come through Stemnitsa, but as with Dimitsana, they are not necessarily regular or on time. Allegedly, there are 7:30am buses to **Tripoli** and 2pm buses to **Dimitsana** on weekdays. The people in the **town hall** in the plateia are extremely friendly and helpful, and they speak English. (☎27950 81 280. Open M-F 8am-3pm.) **Postal code:** 22024.

Fortunately, the only hotel in town offers outstanding quality at a reasonable price. The splendid **Hotel Triokolonion ❸** is on the left side of the main road as you head away from Dimitsana, with an inviting terrace that offers a relaxing place to unwind after a day hiking the mountain paths. Its spacious rooms have hardwood floors, private baths, and amazing views. (☎27950 81 297; fax 27950 81 483. Buffet breakfast included. Singles €25-30; doubles €40; triples €53. Call ahead.) Consider tiny **Taverna Klinitsa ❶**, just out of the plateia on the way to Dimitsana, for an inexpensive meal. The special fried bread is particularly tasty. Entrees €3-5.

Between Dimitsana and Stemnitsa there are several monasteries, some built right into the mountain face. Some of the roads and paths leading to them are unsuitable for cars and are best attempted on foot. A loop from Dimitsana to a monastery and then to Stemnitsa could be up to 30km. The **Monastery of Ag. Ioannis Prodromos,** 10km from Stemnitsa and 16km from Dimitsana, is still inhabited by 12 monks. You can see icons painted on the bare stone walls and gravity-defying monastic cells that seem to hang off the mountain. Follow the road as it goes from asphalt to dirt and finally becomes a footpath. (☎27950 81 385. Open dawn-dusk. Modest dress required. Free.)

MESSENIA Μεσσηνια

Messenia is an oasis in the arid Peloponnese. World-renowned olives, figs, and grapes spring from the rich soil on the region's rocky coastline, which remains largely tourist-free. Most Messenians live at the head of the gulf around sprawling Kalamata, though visitors may prefer to stay in the sleepy coastal towns of Pylos, Methoni, Koroni, Kardamyli, or Finikounda, which luxuriate in clean, nearly empty beaches and quiet streets perfumed with the scent of fragrant blossoms.

KALAMATA Καλαματα

Kalamata, the second-largest Peloponnesian city, flourishes as a port and beach resort. The town played a key role in igniting the War of Independence, when, on March 23, 1821, two days before a Greek revolt was to begin, a group of impatient Kalamatans massacred local Ottomans in their sleep. A yearly reenactment of the grisly Greek victory is followed by parades and dancing. Fast-growing Kalamata has all the aspects of any other large city, some of which—grime, noise, and urban sprawl—may detract from its vacation appeal. For such a city, however, Kalamata exudes a pleasant, summery feel with flowers, open air cafes, and a clean, if crowded, 4km-long beach.

TRANSPORTATION

Trains: (☎27210 95 056), where Sideromikou Stathmou dead ends at Frantzi. As you walk away from the Old Town and toward the waterfront in Pl. Giorgiou, turn right on Frantzi at the far end of the plateia and walk a few blocks. To: **Argos** (4hr., €4.40); **Athens** (6½hr., 4 per day, €7) via **Tripoli** (2½hr., €2.80); **Corinth** (5¼hr., €5.60); **Patras** (5½hr., 4 per day, €5) via **Kyparissia** (2hr., €1.90); **Pirgos** (3¼hr., €2.80).

KTEL buses: Leave from the station on Artemidos (☎27210 22 851; open 7am-10pm), inland from Pl. Giorgiou and across the river from Aristomenous. To get to the waterfront from the bus station, take a taxi (€3), or walk down Artemidos and eventually cross to parallel Aristomenous, which leads to Pl. Giorgiou. Buses go to: **Athens** (4hr., 11 per day 4:45am-10:45pm, €14) via **Megalopolis** (1hr., €4); **Finikounda** (2½hr., 4 per day 5am-6pm, €4.40); **Koroni** (1½hr., 8 per day 5am-7pm, €2.95); **Mavromati** and **Ancient Messene** (1hr.; 5:40am, 2pm; €1.50); **Methoni** (1¾hr., 6 per day 5am-7:45pm, €3.65); **Patras** (4hr.; 8:30am, 2:30pm; €13.40) via **Pirgos** (2hr., €7.80); **Pylos** (1½hr., 9 per day 5am-7:45pm, €2.90); **Sparta** (2hr.; 9:15am, 12:45pm; €2.90) via **Artemisia** (30min., €1.60); **Tripoli** (2hr., €4.40). To get to **Areopolis** (15min., €0.80) and **Gythion** (1½hr., €2.40), go to **Itilo** (2hr., 4 per day, €4.40) and change buses. The bus stops in **Kardamyli** (€2.20) and **Stoupa** (€2.20) before Itilo.

City buses: Unfortunately for the traveler without a vehicle, the local city bus system (€0.70 per ride) is limited. City buses depart from near Pl. 25 Martiou in the Old Town; look for the large street off Aristomenous. **Bus #1** goes down Pl. Aristomenous to the water and then runs along the water. (Open 8am-10pm.) Buy your ticket on the bus.

Taxis: ☎27210 22 522, 27210 23 434, or 27210 27 366.

Moped Rental: At **Alpha Rental** (☎27210 93 423 or 27210 94 571), on Vyronos near the waterfront. 1-person mopeds €15 per day; 2-person mopeds €20. Price includes map, helmet, and insurance. Open daily 8:30am-8pm.

ORIENTATION AND PRACTICAL INFORMATION

Kalamata surges inland from its long beachfront, with a frustratingly spread-out plan. The city is divided into three sections. Closest to the water is a **residential sec-**

PELOPONNESE

tion, distinguished by the municipal park; most of the hotels and restaurants are here, clustered by the water. Heading inland, the next is **Pl. Giorgiou,** home to the train station and most amenities, like stores, banks, and the post office. The **Old Town,** with the castle, market, and bus station, is farthest inland. Navigating from one end to the other can be confusing. Use a map; they're available at the **D.E.T.A.K. tourist office** near the bus station and the waterfront **Tourist Police.** The **bus station** and **post office** are on **Artemidos.** With your back to the bus station turn left, follow this street for about 500m, and cross the "river" on your left at the third crossing to **Aristomenous,** Kalamata's main street. Eventually Aristomenous meets and runs along the left side of Pl. Giorgiou (coming from the bus station). Cross the river at the first crossing and head directly away from the bus station to get to the Old Town and castle. To get to the waterfront from the Old Town, follow Aristomenous all the way along the left side of Pl. Giorgiou until it runs into the back of the Customs and Tourist Police area.

Tourist Information: Tourist Police (☎27210 95 555), on Miaouli in the port, on the 3rd fl. of a yellow building to the right of the post office. **Free maps.** Open daily 8am-2pm. More extensive tourist info and free maps are available near the Old Town at **D.E.T.A.K.,** Poliviou 6 (☎27210 21 700), just off Aristomenous. Open M-F 7am-2:30pm.

Bank: National Bank (☎27210 28 047), on Aristomenous off the north end of Pl. Giorgiou and smaller branches in the plateia and on Akrita at the waterfront. All have 24hr. **ATMs** and **currency exchange.** Open M-Th 8am-2pm and F 8am-1:30pm.

Police: (☎27210 22 622), on Aristomenous, south of Pl. Giorgiou. Open 24hr.

Port police: (☎27210 22 218), on the harbor near the tourist police in a blue building.

Hospital: (☎27210 46 000), on Athinou. Call for **medical emergencies.**

OTE: in Pl. Giorgiou, opposite National Bank. Open M-Th 8am-1:30pm, F 8am-1pm.

Internet Access: Diktyo Internet Cafe, Nedontos 75 (☎27210 97 282), just off Aristomenous and close to the OTE. €3 per hr., €1.50 minimum. Open daily 10am-midnight. If you're staying closer to the waterfront, try **Matrix,** on Faron about 5 blocks up from the waterfront. €3 per hr., €1.50 minimum. Open daily 9:30am-1:30am.

Post Office: Iatropolou 4 (☎27210 22 810). Follow this street from the south end of Pl. Giorgiou. There's another branch on the waterfront next to the tourist police. Open M-F 7:30am-7pm. **Postal code:** 24100.

PELOPONNESE

ACCOMMODATIONS AND CAMPING

Most of Kalamata's hotels are expensive, loaded with amenities, and on the waterfront. Rooms to let and budget accommodations are uncommon here.

Hotel George (☎27210 27 225), near the train station. The entrance is on Dagre, but it's visible on Frantzi as you walk from the waterfront end of Pl. Giorgiou. Very convenient, clean, and comfortable with spacious, whitewashed rooms complete with TVs, balconies, and private baths. Singles €20; doubles €26. ❷

Hotel Nevada, Santa Rosa 9 (☎27210 82 429), off Faron, 1 block up from the water. Heading inland on Faron, take the 1st left, or take bus #1 from town and get off as soon as it turns left along the water. Rooms are large, comfortable, and wildly decorated with an assortment of kitschy posters, figurines, and artificial flowers. Shared bath and kitchen. Singles €10.56-13.50; doubles €15.55-19.37; triples €18.66-23.24. ❷

Hotel Byzantino, S. Stathmou 13 (☎27210 86 824 or 27210 83 251; fax 27210 22 924), 1 block from the train station, in the center of town. Carpeted, nicely furnished, modern rooms with TVs, phones, private baths, and balconies in the center of town. Singles €25-35; doubles €30-42. Extra fee for A/C. ❸

Camping Maria's Sea and Sun (☎27210 41 060). Take bus #1 east to the Filoxenia hotel, then walk along the road or beach for about 200m. Hot showers, mini-market, restaurant. €5 per person, children €3.50; €3.50 per small tent; €4 per large tent; €3.50 per car. Electricity €3.50. ❶

FOOD

Before leaving town, you must sample the famous Kalamata olives and figs. The immense **New Market,** just across the bridge from the bus station, is a collection of meat, cheese, and fruit shops, as well as a daily farmer's market. Great sit-down meals can be found along the waterfront. Mellow harborside dining under a thatched roof, a cheerful staff, and delicious bread make **To Petrino** ❷ stand out from the crowd. Dishes range from the traditional to the exotic. Ostrich anyone? (Excellent moussaka €4; those famous Kalamata olives €1.50. Entrees €4-7.) Strikingly different, **Obre** ❷ (☎27210 86 168) offers Mexican food in a huge outdoor seating area along the waterfront, away from town in the cluster of cafes after To Petrino. Tasty tacos (€4.90) and chili (€6) are always on the menu. Though drab and unexciting from the exterior, **Exociko Kentro** ❶ (☎27210 20 985) shines when it comes to a hearty meal with a savory lamb and potatoes (€4.80).

SIGHTS AND ENTERTAINMENT

CASTLE OF THE VILLEHARDOUINS. The survivor of a violent history, the Castle of the Villehardouins crowns a hill above the old city. Built by the Franks in 1208, it was blown up by the Ottomans in 1685 and restored by the Venetians a decade later. The restoration process following the 1986 earthquake continues to today. The castle encircles an open-air theater, which hosts "Cultural Summer of Kalamata" in July and August, featuring jazz, rock, and Greek drama. *(From Pl. 25 Martiou, walk up Ipapandis past the church on the right and take the first left. Open until dusk. Free.)*

CHURCHES. Near the castle in the old town you'll find the **Convent of Ag. Konstantinos and Ag. Elena,** where nuns sell handmade linen and lacework. Closer to the new town is the 14th-century **Church of the Ag. Apostoloi** (Holy Apostles), site of the first Greek revolt against the Turks on March 23, 1821. A doe-eyed icon of the Virgin Mary was found here; the name of the city (*kala mata* means good eyes) echoes the miraculous icon's appearance. *(Times are not standard, but most churches are open 7am-noon and 5-7pm.)*

ARTS. The Old City's **Benakeion Museum** presents its small collection more artfully and professionally than most Greek museums. Highlighted by an exceptionally well-preserved mosaic floor from a ruined Roman villa nearby, the collection is enlivened by lengthy, informative placards in English. *(☎27210 26 209. Open Tu-Sa 8am-2:30pm, Su 8:30am-3pm. Free.)* Just off the waterfront, Kalamata's **School of Fine Arts** exhibits work by Greek artists. *(Faron 221. Open M-Sa 9am-1pm and 6-10pm.)* Kalamata also supports two professional **theaters** and **cinemas;** ask the tourist police for info on events in the **Pantazopoulion Cultural Center** on Aristomenon. *(☎27210 94 819, or call the municipality with any questions at ☎27210 28 000.)*

NIGHTLIFE. Nightlife in Kalamata revolves around the beach. The strip (1km east of the port) lacks some of the over-the-top fun you can overdose on in other towns, as there are only three clubs in town, all of which are grouped in a clump. **Palladium,** Kalamata's most bizarre night hangout, offers umbrella-topped seating, a lit-up fountain accompanied by a Disney-inspired mural of "Snow White and the Seven Dwarves," and a ball-filled play area, supposedly for "the tykes"—or for the kid in you. (Beer €2.20; cocktails €4.) Pricier and offering a more typical club atmosphere are **Must,** ultramodern with lots of glass and steel framing, and similar **Heaven,** done up in red and white; both are just beyond Palladium. For a more relaxed evening out, try any one of the bars along the waterfront. For reasons unknown, many feature bright green lighting and southwestern US decor.

OUTDOORS. Shady trees arch over lovely **Train Park's** cafes, performance space, duck pond, restaurant, and ice cream parlor, which occupies a converted old train station. Antique trains repose on the tracks. It's at the waterfront end of Aristomenous. Kalamata's gravelly **beaches** empty of sunbathers as you go eastward, but Pylos, Methoni, and other southern beach towns are still a much better bet.

DAYTRIP FROM KALAMATA: ANCIENT MESSENE

*Take the bus to Mavromati (1hr.; leaves M-Sa 5:30am and 2pm, returns 2:30pm; €1.50). Taxis €16. If you rent a **moped,** you'll need 50ccs to handle the steep hills. ☎27240 51 046. Open all day. Free.*

Excavations on **Mt. Ithomi** over the last two decades have yielded one of the most impressive ancient archaeological sites in Greece, which dates back 2300 years. When the battle of Leuctra in 371 BC ended Spartan domination of the Peloponnese, Theban general and statesman **Epaminodas** built Messene, naming the town for the region's first queen. While the remains of a theater, stadium, gymnasium, public baths, and nine different temples have been uncovered, it is the city's **defensive walls** that usually receive the most attention. The 3m-thick walls circle 9km and represent the massive heft of 3rd- and 4th-century BC military architecture. Originally, huge gates reinforced with two-story towers and battlements interrupted the circuit, taking their names from the roads that they barricaded. Of the four surviving, the Arcadian gate is the best preserved, and the stone-slab road that stems from it still bears the traces of chariot wheels. A **museum** at the site houses statues and other objects. Also outside Mavromati, the 17th-century **Monastery of the Vourkan** was a staging point for rebels in the War of Independence. Its library harbors several priceless manuscripts.

KARDAMYLI Καρδαμυλη

The sleepy, one-road town of **Kardamyli** is the first major bus stop south of Kalamata near Taygetus. The flower-scented streets of this seaside town possess a few stone houses and restaurants, but its gorgeous white-pebble beach and views of the surrounding mountains captivate an increasing number of foreign visitors.

ORIENTATION AND PRACTICAL INFORMATION. Four buses run from Kalamata every day, dropping off near the *periptero* off the main plateia. All bus times are posted inside the cafe across from the plateia. **Buses** go to **Athens** (6hr., 10:30am, €18.60), **Kalamata** (1hr., 5 per day 7:20am-8pm, €2.40), and **Itilo** (30min., 4 per day 6am-6pm, €2.40), where you can switch to the **Areopolis** bus (20min., €0.80). Through the main plateia, on the road to Itilo, are the **post office** (open M-F 7:30am-2pm), a **bank** (open M and Th 9:30am-1pm) with 24hr. **ATM,** and a **pharmacy** (☎27210 73 512, open daily 8am-2pm and 5-9pm) that sits across from the post office. The **book shop** two doors down from the post office offers a large selection of best-sellers in English. To get to the **police station,** take a 5min. walk along the road to Kalamata and over the bridge; the station will be on a street to the left—look for signs. (☎27210 73 209. Open 24hr.) Walking toward Itilo, turn right two blocks past the post office to **Cafe Internet Kourearos,** next to Olympia Domatia. (☎27210 73 148. Open 5pm-1am. €5 per hr., €3 per 30min.)

THE BIG SPLURGE

KARALIS BEACH HOTEL

Aching for that secluded-island feel on the Peloponnese? Walk all the way out of town along the waterfront with the sea to your right, and you'll happen upon **Karalis Beach Hotel,** perched at the foot of Neocastro on the edge of the water.

Expensive but wonderfully decorated rooms with balconies overlook the ocean, with views of Pylos, the isle of Sfakteria (of Peloponnesian War fame), and the endless sea and sky. For a substantial cut in price, you can get a smaller room with no view and no balcony but still enjoy the rooftop dining and views from the lounge and deck. Muted pastel purples, blues, and yellows color the walls, and tasteful furniture fills the balconies. All rooms come with A/C, private bathrooms, and phones.

The road-weary traveler can choose between relaxing in a hot bath or collapsing onto a comfy veranda chair to watch the waves break on the rocks at the foot of the hotel. Just far enough out of town to avoid the noise from the plateia but close enough to stroll down the hill for a taverna meal, Karalis Beach Hotel is an island of luxury.

☎27230 22 980 or 27230 23 022; fax 27230 22 970. Ocean-view rooms include balcony and bathtub. Singles and doubles €50-80; triples €80-100. Prices vary with view.

ACCOMMODATIONS AND FOOD. Domatia are everywhere, but start with the excellent, cheap rooms let by **Olympia Domatia ❷.** Turn right off the main road, across from the post office and follow the side street. Pleasant rooms are clean and spacious, most have baths, and there is a shared kitchen for all. Olympia herself is a whirlwind of hospitality, fixing coffee for tenants at any time and handing out helpful information about the area. (☎27210 73 623. Singles €17; doubles €24; triples €30.) Across the way are equally comfortable and similarly priced rooms let by **Stratis Bravakos ❷** at Yvolvere. (☎27210 73 326. Singles €20; doubles €24; triples €30. No singles in high season.) If you plan a long stay and want it to be luxurious, head to **Hotel Anniska ❹,** at the end of the street to the right of the bank. You'll have a choice of two buildings: the studios and apartments in the old hotel have ceiling fans and easy beach access, while those in the new hotel boast A/C and pool access. Both have lovely dining areas and book exchanges. Rooms are decorated in various shades of blue, and all have balconies, small kitchens, TVs, phones, and private baths. (Old hotel: ☎27210 73 601; fax 27210 73 000. Studios €52.50-67.50; apartments €62.50-91.50. New hotel: ☎27210 73 600; fax 27210 73 000. Studios €58.50-67.50; apartments €68.50-91.50.) If you want beachfront (rental) property, walk toward Kalamata, turn left at the signs for **Camping Melitsana ❶,** and walk 1.5km down the main beach. (☎27210 73 461. €4.10 per person, €2.65 per child; €3.50 per small tent; €3.80 per large tent; €2.30 per car.)

When you get hungry, walk past the plateia toward Kalamata to find two large **supermarkets.** For delicious traditional food with a waterfront view, try the daily special menu at family-run **Taverna Kiki ❶,** downhill from the main plateia. Menu changes daily, rotating through delicious entrees like goat and *stifado.* (☎27210 73 148. Entrees €4.20-5.50.) **Kourmaristria ❸** (☎27210 73 250), next to the new Anniska Hotel, has a few unique dishes. No moussaka, but it does have minced pork stuffed with cheese and tomatoes (€5.50) or the special tzatziki, made with local greens (€2). A crowd can be found at convivial **Cafe Aman ❷** throughout the day. Walk past Olympia Domatia to the waterfront and turn right; it is about 20m ahead. If you're tired of toast for breakfast, try the avocado salad (€4.40). At night, jazz music plays, and the drinks flow. (Beer €2.40-3; cocktails €4.40.)

SIGHTS AND BEACHES. Beaches are Kardamyli's main attraction, but there are a few other things to see. A short stroll up the road to Itilo will bring you to the small but interesting ruins of the **Old**

Town (across from the supermarkets). Nearby, the frescoed **Monastery of Dekoulo** and the 17th-century Ottoman fortress are poised on a hill. One kilometer along the waterfront toward Kalamata, you'll spot the magnificent **Ritsa beach.** On an enormous natural bay encircled by barren mountains, the white-pebble shore is ideal for swimming. The roads that wind through the mountains from Kalamata to Aeropolis offer stunning vistas of the small villages and aquamarine harbors of Messenia and the Mani, including tiny **Limani,** the old harbor of Areopolis and home to the **Castle of Potrombei.**

DAYTRIP FROM KARDAMYLI: TAYGETUS MOUNTAINS. Competing with beautiful beaches as Kardamyli's main draw is the superb **hiking** that surrounds the village. Southeast of Kalamata, the limestone mountain range of the Taygetus divides Messenia and Laconia, running from Megalopolis down through the Taenarian promontory. Sacred to Apollo and Artemis, the mountains were named after **Taygete,** daughter of Atlas, mother of Lacedaemon, and lover of Zeus. Long glorified for their size, the Taygetus Mountains were dubbed "Perimiketon" ("the long one") by Homer, while Lampito declares in Aristophanes's *Lysistrata*, "I would climb as high as the peak of Taygetus, if thus I could find peace." The mountain is home to unusual amphibians, 23 species of endemic plants, the rare *testudo marninata* turtle, and adventurous paragliders, hikers, mountain bikers, and climbers, many of whom try to reach the highest peak, Profitis Ilia (2407m). Carry lots of water, wear good shoes, and be prepared—know your route and its approximate length. It's best to hike in the spring, as summer heat and aridity make the strenuous terrain rather exhausting to navigate for more than an hour or two. **Brochures** and **maps** with suggested routes are available in tourist shops and bookstores, and also in many of Kardamyli's accommodations. There are many possible day-hikes on any number of **color-coded trails.** One popular 1½hr. trail is marked in black and yellow and begins from Kardamyli, heads to Old Kardamyli, Agia Sophia, and Petrovouni.

PELOPONNESE

PYLOS Πυλος

With its delightful beaches, Ottoman fortress, museum, and splendid views of Navarino, the Peloponnese's largest natural bay, the town of Pylos is wonderfully and mystifyingly untouristed. Flower-bedecked buildings line the track of narrow streets and steep stairways that cut from the waterfront up to the residential town.

ORIENTATION AND PRACTICAL INFORMATION. Most of the town's businesses line the plateia and the roads leading uphill to Methoni and Hora. The tiny **beaches,** one sand and one pebble, lie to the right of the waterfront as you face inland, as does the 16th-century Ottoman **Neocastro** on a forested hill. **Buses** (☎27230 22 230) go to: **Athens** (6½hr.; 9:30am, 7:30pm; €17.45); **Finikounda** (1hr.; 11am, 2:15, and 7:15pm; €1); **Kalamata** (1½hr., 9 per day 6:30am-8pm, €3); and **Methoni** (15min., 6 per day 6am-9pm, €0.80). No buses travel directly to **Koroni,** but you can go through Finikounda and take a bus to **Horokorio,** the stop nearest Koroni. Buses leave for **Kyparissia** (1½hr., 5 per day 6:30am-7:30pm, €3.65), stopping at **Nestor's Palace** (30min., €1) and **Hora** (45min., €1.20); service is reduced on weekends. Tickets are sold and schedules are posted at the tiny KTEL office in the back right corner of the plateia as you face inland; buses leave from the back of the plateia. **Rent-A-Bike,** 100m off the back left of the plateia on the road running by the police station, has a moped monopoly. (☎27230 22 707. €16-25 per day. Open daily 9am-1pm and 5:30-8:30pm.) **Taxis** (☎27230 22 555) line the left side of the plateia. A **National Bank** with an **ATM** is in the plateia. The **police** are on the second floor of a building on the left side of the waterfront, on a road going uphill. (☎27230 22 316. Open 24hr.) The **tourist police** are in the same building. (☎27230 23

733. Open daily, mornings only.) Continue around the curve of the waterfront road with the water on the right to reach the **port police** (☎27230 22 225). (Open M-Th 8am-2pm, F 8am-1:30pm.) To get to the **hospital,** take the road right from the plateia. (☎27230 22 315. Open 24hr.) For the **OTE,** pass the post office and take your 1st left, then your 2nd right. (Open M-F 7:30am-3pm.) The **post office** is on the road toward Hora and Kiparissia, uphill to the left (as you face the water) from the bus station. (☎27230 22 247. Open M-F 7:30am-2pm.) **Postal code:** 24001.

ACCOMMODATIONS AND FOOD. There are several **Rooms to Let** signs as the bus descends into town from Kalamata. In general, expect to pay €15-20 for singles, €20-35 for doubles, €25-37 for triples. Perhaps the cheapest accommodation in town is the **Pension ❷,** just before the OTE, which has basic high-ceilinged rooms with private baths and A/C. (☎27230 22 748. Singles €20; doubles €25; triples €29.) **Hotel Nilefs ❸,** Rene Pyot 4, has big rooms with baths and balconies, as well as A/C and TVs. It's on the road uphill from the waterfront on the right side of the plateia, facing inland. (☎27230 22 518. Singles €25-29; doubles €32-38; triples €40-45.) **Navarino Beach Camping ❶** is 6km north at **Yialova Beach** (☎27230 22 761. €4 per person, €2.40 per child; €4 per large tent; €2.40 per car. Electricity €2.40.)

Many waterfront restaurants cook up taverna staples served alongside sunset views over the waterfront. The road leading uphill from the left of the plateia is also packed with excellent options. The best of four eating establishments with the same name, the **Navarino ❷,** around the corner from the port police, on the waterfront, has good, cheap meals. (Entrees €3.30-8.60.) At delicious **Tessera Epohes** (Τεσσερα Εποχες) **❶,** the last taverna on the water to the right of town (facing inland), everything is large, cheap, and well-prepared. (☎27230 22 739. Potatoes €1.20; lamb chops €4.50.) Opposite the police station, **La Piazza ❷** prepares wonderful pasta and pizza. Try the "Vesuvio" pizza (€5.30-6.30), made with hot peppers and hot salami. (Entrees €3-4.80. Open daily 6pm-1am.) The classy **1930 Restaurant ❷,** on the road into town from Kalamata, is accented by wood paneling, antique fishing paraphernalia, and a seafood menu with grilled octopus (€7.35).

SIGHTS AND BEACHES. Fortresses guard both sides of Navarino Bay. **Neocastro,** to the south, is easily accessible from the town; walk up the road to Methoni and turn right at the sign reading Φρουριο. The well-preserved walls enclose a fast-decaying church (originally a mosque), along with a citadel and a lovely little museum. Take a look at the pictures of the Peloponnese as it was a hundred years ago. The restored hexagonal courtyard, up the hill to your right after entering the castle, contains a series of photographs detailing its restoration. (☎27230 22 010. Open Tu-Su 8:30am-3pm. €3, seniors and students €2, EU students and children free.) The slight **Archaeological Museum,** on the road to Methoni, shows the contents of Mycenaean and Hellenistic tombs. A Mycenaean battle helmet made of boar's tusks catches the eye, while three richly colored glass vessels highlight the Hellenistic period. (☎27230 22 448. Open Tu-Su 8:30am-3pm. €2, seniors and students €1, EU students and children free.)

Just offshore is the island of **Sfakteria,** famed as the site of a rare Spartan defeat during the Peloponnesian War (p. 10). To see the isle up close, you can take a **boat tour** from the port. They stop at various monuments to the allied sailors of the Battle of Navarino and show a sunken Ottoman ship. Inquire at the small booth on the waterfront around the corner from the port police. (1½hr., €30 for 4 people. July-Aug. only.) A few small **beaches** surround the town. Although the sand is devoured by the ocean when the tide is in, the clear, choppy water makes splashing around fun. The long, sandy, and much wider **Yialova Beach** is 6km north of town; sunken ships poke out from its shallow waters. Buses to Athens and Kyparissia pass by, but you may want to use your own transportation. The **Navarino fortress** lies at the end of the beach.

DAYTRIP FROM PYLOS: NESTOR'S PALACE. In the Mycenaean world, Pylos was second only to Mycenae in wealth and artistic development. The centerpiece of the archaeological site is the **palace** where, according to Homer, Nestor met Telemachus, Odysseus's son. The palace is thought to have been built in the 13th century BC by Nestor's father Neleus, the founder of the Neleid dynasty. It was destroyed by fire around 1200 BC. Still under excavation, the thigh-high remains of the site comprise three buildings. The main building, possibly the king's residence, originally had a second floor with official and residential quarters and storerooms. Archaeologists think an older, smaller palace stood to the southeast. To the northeast lie the ruins of a complex of isolated workshops and storerooms. Archaeologists have turned up pottery, jewelry, various bronze and ivory objects, and a cache of **Linear B tablets** explaining some of the palace's administrative operations. Most finds are displayed at the National Archaeological Museum in Athens, some pottery and surviving fragments of wall paintings are at the Hora **museum,** 5km away. For €5 you can supplement your tour with the *University of Cincinnati's Guide to Nestor's Palace.* **Buses** from Pylos run through **Kyparissia** (1½hr., 5 per day, €3.60) and stop at **Nestor's Palace** (30min., €1); service is reduced on weekends. The last bus returns at 5:30pm. (☎27230 31 437 or 31 358. Open daily 8:30am-3pm. €2, seniors and non-EU students €1, EU students and children free.) A **Mycenaean tholos tomb** is across from the lower parking lot; look for signs.

METHONI Μεθωνη

With hibiscus-lined streets and a relaxed atmosphere, Methoni is a restorative reprieve from the bustle of Kalamata and Tripoli. Valued for millennia, Methoni was used as bait by Agamemnon to lure the sulking Achilles back to war in *The Iliad.* A spectacular 15th-century castle, nearly as large as the town itself, shoots its stone walkways onto the Turkish *bourtzi* in the bay. In this castle, Miguel de Cervantes penned romances while imprisoned under Ottoman guard.

ORIENTATION AND PRACTICAL INFORMATION. The town's two main streets form a Y where the Pylos-Finikounda buses stop. Facing the fork, the lower road is on the left and leads to the beach and the castle. There's no **bus** station and no posted schedule. Buses go to **Pylos** (15min., 7 per day, €0.80) and **Finikounda** (30min., 4 per day, €1), with a reduced schedule Saturday and Sunday. There are also daily buses to **Kalamata** (2hr., €3.65) and two buses to **Athens** (6hr., €15.40). Your best bet is to ask at hotels or the *periptero* just before the fork about bus schedules and frequency. The main town **beach** is a few blocks to the left end of the lower street, beside a little beachfront plateia. The campgrounds and several beach bars are on the road bordering the lengthy beach. There's also a stone walkway perfect for evening strolls by the water. The **police** are near the bus station on the upper street, just past the bank. (☎23530 31 203. Open 24hr.) The **National Bank** with a 24hr. **ATM** is 40m down the right fork. (☎23530 31 295. Open M-Th 8am-2pm, F 8am-1:30pm.) The **OTE** is in a poorly marked cream-colored building with blue shutters; go down the lower fork and turn left, toward the beachside plateia. (☎23530 31 121. Open M-F 7:30am-3:10pm.) **Internet access** is available at **Modon** on the lower road, just past the gas station. The shop also offers fax and photocopy services and buys and sells used books in several languages. (☎23530 28 707. €7 per hr., €3 minimum. Trade used books for €2; buy one for €3.) The **post office** is two blocks down the lower street on the left side. (☎23530 31 266. Open M-F 7:30am-2pm.) **Postal code:** 24006.

ACCOMMODATIONS AND CAMPING. Since Methoni receives a fair amount of August tourism, rooms can be pricey in summer. Several **Rooms to Let** signs hang along both forks of the road. Although the rooms usually lack hotel amenities, their prices are a bit cheaper. Near the end of the lower road, make a left at the small plateia with a fountain to find the unassuming **Hotel Galini ❸,** which has rooms (with A/C, fridges, and private baths) similar in quality to its flashier counterparts but at cheaper prices. (☎23530 31 467. Singles €20-34; doubles €33-44.) **Hotel Giota ❸,** in the beachfront plateia, has modern rooms with A/C, balconies, and private baths. (☎23530 31 290; fax 23530 31 212. Singles €25-30; doubles €30-45.) Giota's owners also run nearby **Hotel Alex ❸.** (☎23530 31 219; fax 23530 31 291.) Away from the noise of the plateia, **Achilles Hotel ❹,** the gleaming white building on the lower road past the cafe, provides modern rooms with all the amenities. Some have views of the ocean and the fortress. (☎23530 31 819; fax 23530 28 739. Singles €30-44; doubles €44-60. Ask about discounts for longer stays.) **Seaside Camping Methoni ❶** is a 5min. walk down the beach to the right of the plateia. (☎23530 31 228. €3.40 per person, €2.05 per child; €2.35 per small tent; €2.65 per large tent; €2.05 per car. Electricity €2.35. Prices lower May-June and Sept.-Oct.)

FOOD. Several excellent tavernas and restaurants pepper Methoni. In the waterfront plateia, the multilingual proprietor of **Meltemi ❸** serves excellent traditional entrees. (Greek salad €3, moussaka and *pastitsio* €4.) Humble **Oraia Methoni ❷** accents its simple atmosphere with high quality and low prices. Walking from the bus stop, turn left one block down the lower road and continue 30m. (*Tzatziki* €1.80, baked pork or chicken €9 per kg, gyros €1.) **Nikos ❷,** on the road closest and parallel to the castle, near the waterfront plateia, serves club sandwiches and other non-traditional fare to crowds of younger locals. (Sandwiches and entrees €4-7. Open for lunch and dinner.)

SIGHTS. No visitor to the southwest Peloponnese should miss Methoni's **Venetian fortress,** a 13th-century mini-city. To get to the castle, follow the upper or lower street to its end. Walk to the right along the path outside the castle for a great view of the open sea and fortified back wall. Venture behind the fortified gate of the fortress to wander paths above overgrown fields strewn with bright wildflowers and crumbling walls. Frankish foundations, Venetian battlements, and Turkish steam baths testify to the castle's varied history. In the center of the site stands the small church of Agia Sophia, built in 1830 and still in use today. At the tip of the peninsula, a narrow bridge connects an islet and its fortified Ottoman *bourtzi*, formerly a prison and execution site, to the main structure with interesting medieval defensive architecture. (Open M-Sa 8:30am-7pm, Su 9am-7pm. Free.) The main town **beach** is a few blocks to the left of the end of the lower street, beside a little beachfront plateia.

FINIKOUNDA Φοινικουντα

The tiny **beach** hamlet of Finikounda lies just south of Pylos and Methoni and is quickly becoming the tourist attraction of the area, outstripping its larger neighbors. Fortunately, its secluded location still prevents overcrowding. Although the town has no bank, police station, or post office, it does offer several large hotels, a smattering of domatia, many lovely campsites, and a vast array of bars, cafes, and tavernas along the beachfront road that comprises the center of town. **Buses** head to **Kalamata** (2½hr., €3.80) and **Pylos** (45min., €1) 3-4 times per day via **Methoni** (30min., €1). The bus drops off and picks up at the plateia one block up from the waterfront, outside the Hotel Finikounda. A booth by the water offers currency exchange. Should you opt to stay in Finikounda, try to find a domatia or head to

Hotel Finissia ❸, at the far right of the waterfront as you face inland. Nicely furnished rooms with shiny clean floors include A/C, TVs, phones, and private baths. (☎27230 71 457. Singles €24-36; doubles €36-47.) The closest to town of three campsites, **Camping Anemomilos ❶**, on the beach just north of town, lies among flowering shrubs and has easy beach access. Internet and massages available. To reach the campsite, walk out of town via the road past Hotel Finikounda, then walk 5min. toward Methoni, turning left at its signs. (☎27230 71 360. €5 per person, €3 per child; €3 per small tent; €3 per car. Electricity €2.50.) Restaurants are by no means hard to find, but, if you're after a view, walk to the left end of the waterfront (as you face inland) to the enormous taverna **Elena ❷** (☎27230 71 235). A little pricier than the other options in town, this popular establishment serves traditional entrees and seafood to tables hovering over the town. (Entrees €5.50-8.80; salads €2.50.) You'll find some of the **best beaches** in the Mediterranean within easy walking distance of Finikounda. Grab a towel and some sunscreen, and find one to your liking. Ask around town for directions to the top beaches of the moment. **Postal code:** 24006

LACONIA Λακωνια

Laconia, the territory of the ancient Spartans, has long prided itself on its minimalist aesthetic. The Spartans were ferocious to their enemies, simple in lifestyle, and terse in speech, hence the adjective, "laconic." This attitude seems reflected in the landscape, with the stark, imposing Taygetus Mountains and nearly nothing else beyond row after row of ancient olive trees. Although Laconia boasts one of the region's most popular sites, Mystras, the region as a whole offers a peaceful break from the more touristed urban hustle of other Peloponnesian towns.

SPARTA Σπαρτη

Citizens of today's quiet Sparta make olive oil, not war. Built directly on top of the ancient warrior city, modern Sparta offers meager ruins to occupy tourists. Still, it's by far the best base for exploring the ruins of Byzantine Mystras, 6km away. Reluctant warrior Sparta dominated the Peloponnese with its legendary sense of discipline and invincible armies. Spartans traced their austere daily regimens back to 8th-century law-giver **Lykurgus,** who demanded plain dress, simple food, and strict training for all citizens from a young age. Men and women were educated differently, but with equal severity. The Spartans produced almost no literature, art, or architecture, as they preferred to expend their creative energy in the art of war. Finally capturing upstart Athens in 404 BC to end the 28-year Peloponnesian War (see p. 10), Sparta won its greatest victory and effectively ruled Greece. Though its historical place as the military giant of Greece was assured, Sparta's hold on Classical power declined following challenges from the Thebans and the Macedonians in the 4th century BC. Earthquakes and slave revolts didn't help matters, and further losses in 222 and 195 BC to the Macedonians and the Romans, respectively, sapped the city's strength. Sparta slipped slowly into obscurity, where it remained, until the modern city was founded in 1843.

ORIENTATION AND PRACTICAL INFORMATION

Sparta is built in a grid. The main streets, **Paleologou** (named for the family of Byzantine emperors) and **Lykourgou** (named for Lykurgus), hold the necessary amenities and intersect in the center of town. From this intersection, the town plateia is one block west, away from the bus station, on Lykougrou. To reach the center of town from the bus station, walk about 10 blocks west slightly uphill on Lykourgou. The **bus station** is crowded and not particularly tourist-friendly. There are often confusing and unmentioned transfers on the bus routes, but if you pay attention to the drivers and ask questions, you'll end up where you want to be. Make your life easier and find a Greek traveler heading to your destination; follow him or her to ensure that you end up on the right bus. If you ask enough people, someone will lend a hand to point out your stop or connecting bus.

Buses: (☎27310 26 441). Walk downhill on Lykourgou away from the plateia or toward the Archaeological Museum, continuing past a small forested area on your right; the station will be on your right, 10 blocks from the center of town. Buses go to: **Areopolis** (1½hr.; 9am, 5:45pm; €4.80); **Athens** (3½hr., 9 per day 5:45am-8pm, €12.65) via **Corinth** (2½hr., €7.60) and **Tripoli** (1hr., €3.40); **Gerolimenas** (2hr.; 10:15am, 5:45pm; €6.20); **Gythion** (1hr., 5 per day 9am-9:15pm, €2.60); **Kalamata** (1hr.; 9am, 2:30pm; €2); **Monemvasia** (2hr.; 11:30am, 1:30, 8:10pm; €6.15); **Neapoli** (3½hr., 4 per day 7:15am-8:30pm, €8.65); **Pirgos Dirou** (1½hr., 9am, €5). Buses to **Mystras** (20min., 9 per day 6:50am-8:40pm, €0.80) also stop at the corner of Lykourgou and Leonidou on the left, 2 blocks past the plateia away from the main bus station.

Tourist Office: (☎27310 24 852 or 27310 26 545), to the left of the town hall in the plateia. English spoken. Bus schedules, hotels, and information are available on specific request. Purchase a map (€2.20) at a nearby photo store. Open daily 8am-2pm.

Banks: National Bank (☎27310 26 200), on Paleologou 3 blocks north (toward Ancient Sparta) from Lykourgou and the town center, has a 24hr. **ATM** and **currency exchange** (and long lines). Open M-Th 8am-2pm, F 8am-1:30pm.

Emergency: Dial ☎27310 29 106.

Police: Hilonos 8 (☎27310 26 229), on a side street off Lykourgou, a block past the museum heading toward the bus station. Open 24hr. Earnestly helpful, English-speaking **tourist police** (☎27310 20 492) in the same building. Open daily 8am-9pm.

Hospital: (☎27310 28 671 or 27310 28 675) on Nosokomeio, 1km to the north of Sparta. **Buses** run to the hospital (10 per day). Open 24hr.

Pharmacies: Many on Lykourgou and Paleologou.

OTE: Kleomvritou 3 (☎27310 23 799), accessible from Lykourgou, across from the museum. Open M-F 8am-1pm.

Internet: Aerodromi (☎27310 29 268) on Lykourgou between the bus station and the Archaeological Museum. Check email and play darts, pool, or ping pong. €2 per 30min., €0.50 minimum. Open daily 10am-late. **Hellas Internet Cafe,** Paleologou 34 (☎27310 21 500), south of Lykourgou, away from Ancient Sparta. €2 per 30min., €1 minimum. Open M-Sa 8am-11pm, Su 11am-11pm.

Post Office: (☎27310 26 565), on Archidamou off Lykourgou. Open M-F 7:30am-2pm. **Postal code:** 23100.

PELOPONNESE

ACCOMMODATIONS AND CAMPING

A bargain is hard to find among the numerous mid-range hotels on Paleologou, but TVs and private baths are plentiful.

Hotel Cecil, Paleologou 125 (☎27310 24 980; fax 27310 81 318), 5 blocks north of Lykourgou toward Ancient Sparta, on the corner of Paleologou and Thermopilion. The Cecil, with its pale yellow facade and pleasant, warm rooms, is a popular place to stay. TV, A/C, phones, private baths, and plenty of light. Singles €30; doubles €38. ❸

Hotel Maniatis (☎27310 22 665; fax 27310 29 994), right at the intersection of Paleologou and Lykourgou. This thoroughly modern hotel offers carpeted blue-and-gold rooms with sleek furniture featuring TV, A/C, private bath with bathtub, and phone. Large and comfortable couches dot the lobby and restaurant lounge. Breakfast €7.50. Singles €45; doubles €60; triples €67.50. ❹

Hotel Apollon, Thermopilion 84 (☎27310 22 491; fax 27310 23 936). Across Paleologou from Hotel Cecil at a fork in the road. Flashy, mirrored lobby with a sky mural above the bar hint at the colorful, patterned rooms. Each has its own personality with wacky bedspreads and wallpaper. TVs, private baths, phones, and A/C. Breakfast €4.50. Singles €25-30; doubles €35-44. ❸

Camping Castle View (☎27310 83 303; fax 27310 20 028; spiros@panafonet.gr), near Mystras. Take the Mystras bus and get off at the signs. Pool, modern showers, toilets, and a well-stocked market. €4.70 per person, €2.70 per child; €2.70 per car, €3 per small tent, €3.80 per large tent. Electricity €2.80. ❶

Hotel Laconia (☎27310 28 952), on Paleologou on the 1st block north (toward Ancient Sparta) from Lykourgou. With dark-wood furniture and shutters that are difficult to open, rooms in Laconia are perfect for the vampirish or those who want maximum rest from the sun. Rooms have TVs, A/C, carpeting, clean private baths. Breakfast €6. Singles €25; doubles €35. ❸

FOOD AND NIGHTLIFE

Sparta's restaurants provide standard menus at pretty reasonable prices. **Supermarkets** and **bakeries** fill the side streets of Paleologou, while cheap fast food joints hedge the main plateia. **Diethnes ❷,** on Paleologou, a few blocks north of the main intersection, serves tasty Greek food in a vibrant garden with orange trees, grape vines, and flowers. Ask the waiters for suggestions. (☎27310 28 636. Lamb and pork entrees €5.30-6; moussaka and traditional dishes €4.50.) A large selection and unusual specials spice up **Elyssé Restaurant ❷,** on Paleologou just past Diethnes, which specializes in local dishes like Greek sausage with orange peel (€2.80) and chicken *bardouniotiko* (€5.80). **Menelaion Restaurant ❷,** in the Menelaion Hotel on Paleologou, two blocks north of Lykourgou toward Ancient Sparta, has an elegant poolside setting and excellent meals with surprisingly low prices. (☎27360 22 161. Pork in wine and orange peel €5.29. Entrees €5-9.) At night, the side of the plateia near the town hall fills with young people who while away the hours at outdoor cafes. Head indoors for clubbing. **The Imago,** a hip, artsy bar, is in the alley behind the town hall. (Beer €4.50; cocktails €6. Open daily 9:30pm-3am.) **Caprice,** another popular club, is also behind town hall. (Beer €4.50; cocktails €6. Open daily 11pm-late.) Outside of the plateia, stop in for a drink at the always-packed **Ministry Music Hall,** on Paleologou one block north of intersection with Lykourgou. (*Frappés* €3; beer €4.50. Open daily noon-late.)

PELOPONNESE

SIGHTS

What little remains of **Ancient Sparta** lies in an olive grove 1km north of the town plateia down Paleologou. At the north end of Paleologou stands an enormous statue of **Leonidas,** the famous warrior king who fell at the Battle of Thermopylae (see p. 196) in 480 BC. The Spartans built a large, vacant tomb for their leader, but his body was never found. The tomb is in a public park, left of the road heading up to the ruins. The ruins consist of the outline and lower rows of one of the larger theaters of antiquity, along with a few fragments of the acropolis. To get there from the bus station on Lykourgou, turn right onto Paleologou and walk to the end of the downtown. At the statue of Leonidas, turn left and then right at the signs for the ruins 50m from the statue; the ruins are about 400m from there.

A HARD-KNOCK LIFE A young Spartan's training for a life of war began early—before conception. Lykurgus believed two fit parents produced stronger offspring, so he ordered all Spartan women to undergo the same rigorous training endured by men. Furthermore, newlyweds were permitted only an occasional tryst on the theory that the heightened (desperate?) desire of the parents would produce more robust children. If they weren't winnowed out as weak or deformed, seven-year-old boys began a severe regimen of training under an adult, away from their parents. They were forced to walk barefoot to toughen their feet, and wore only a single, simple garment in all seasons to expose them to drastic weather changes. The Spartan creed dictated that young men be guarded against temptations of any kind, so strict laws forbade everything from drinking to pederasty. Moreover, young Spartans were given the plainest and simplest foods for fear that rich delicacies would stunt their growth. One visitor to Sparta, upon sampling the fare, allegedly quipped, "Now I know why they do not fear death."

Sparta's **Archaeological Museum,** on Lykourgou across from the OTE, lies in a beautiful, well-kept park with a fountain and assorted ancient statuary. The varied collection is worth an hour; it includes spooky votive masks used in ritual dances at the sanctuary of Artemis Orthia, a large marble statue of a warrior thought to be Leonidas, and various representations of the Dioskouri—the brothers Castor and Pollux—locally revered as symbols of brotherly love and honor. One room is devoted to prehistoric pottery, weaponry, and jewelry. Especially impressive are the "unpublished" mosaics from the Roman period. (☎27310 28 575. Open Tu-Sa 8:30am-3pm, Su 9:30am-2:30pm. €2, students and seniors €1, EU students and children free.) The **National Art Gallery,** Paleologou 123, near Hotel Cecil, has a small collection of 19th-century French and Dutch paintings, mostly still-lifes and portraits, including one attributed to Gustave Courbet. Upstairs is a more contemporary exhibit by modern Greek artists, with a number of watercolor landscapes. (☎27310 81 557. Open Tu-Sa 9am-3pm, Su 10am-2pm. Free.)

For history buffs, finding the various ruins surrounding Sparta is worth the challenge. Ask the tourist police for a map before heading out. Three remaining platforms of the **Shrine to Menelaus and Helen** are 5km away. The remains of a **Shrine to Apollo** are south on the road to Gythion. From the northeast corner of town, near Hotel Apollon, a short walk east along the Evrotas River leads to the **Sanctuary of Artemis Orthia,** where Spartan youths proved their courage by enduring floggings.

DAYTRIP FROM SPARTA: MYSTRAS

Buses *that leave from* ***Sparta's*** *main station (see above; 20min., 9 per day, €0.80) drop off* ***twice:*** *once at the restaurant near the main entrance and once at the Castro entrance, near the top of the city. Ask your driver if the bus goes to the Castro. If you get off at the lower stop, you're in for a 45min. uphill walk to the castle. Buses pick up at the restaurant beneath the lower entrance. It gets hot—go early, bring water and wear good hiking shoes. Plan 3hr. to see the sights. Consider* Guidebook Mystras *by Manolis Chatzidakis (€6) to supplement your exploration. The monasteries request modest dress: wear long pants or a skirt; aprons are lent to forgetful guests. ☎27310 83 377. Open daily 8am-7pm; off season daily 8:30am-3pm. €5, EU students and children free.*

Mystras was once the religious center of all Byzantium and the locus of Constantinople's rule over the Peloponnese. Its extraordinary ruins are the remains of a city of Byzantine churches, chapels, and monasteries. Mystras was founded by French crusader **Guillume de Villehardouin** in 1249 with the building of a central castle. After the final attempt to establish Frankish sovereignty over the Peloponnese failed, Mystras was ceded to the Greeks in 1262, giving them an important military base and cultural center. In the following centuries it grew from a village to a city, draining Sparta of its inhabitants as they sought protection in the city's fortress. By the early 15th century, Mystras was an intellectual center with a thriving silk industry. Unhappy under the thumb of repressive feudal lords and clergy, restless country folk surged into town, set up schools, and created an early bourgeoisie. The glory days ended when Turks invaded in 1460. Over the next few centuries, the city crumbled to ruin. When King Otto founded modern Sparta in 1834, Mystras's fate was sealed with a table-turning exodus to its revived neighbor.

An intricate network of paths traces through three tiers of ruins, descending from royalty to nobility to commoners. Although less well preserved than many of the religious edifices that encircle it—they're almost completely intact, if a bit faded at the frescoes—the dramatic castle delivers a breathtaking view of the site and the surrounding countryside. Most people choose to take the bus to the upper entrance, climb to the castle, then work their way down through the rest of the site. Particularly beautiful is the **Metropolis of Ag. Demetrios** on the lower tier, with its detailed frescoes, flowery courtyard, and small museum of architectural fragments, clothing, and jewelry. Also on the lower tier are the two churches of the fortified monastery of **Vrontochion.** The first, **Aphentiko,** glows with magnificent two-story frescoes; **Ag. Theodoros** is its neighbor. Slightly higher up in the center of the site is the **Pantanassa,** a convent with an elaborately ornamented facade, frescoes, and a miracle-working icon of Mary. Finally, quietly tucked away in the far corner of the lower tier, every centimeter of the awe-inspiring **Church of Peribleptos** is bathed in exquisitely detailed and colorful religious paintings. Though many of the church's treasures were vandalized by the Ottomans, who dug the eyes out of saints and saviors alike, this remains Mystras's most stunning relic. At the top of it all is the **Castle,** with incredible views of the valley below and cliffs behind.

PELOPONNESE

MANI Μανη

The name of the province of Mani comes from the Greek word *manis*, meaning wrath or fury. Sparsely settled and encircling the unforgiving Taygetus Mountains (p. 155), the region juts out into the surrounding sea unprotected. In Roman times, Mani founded the league of Free Laconians and broke free of Spartan domination. Ever since, Maniots have ferociously resisted foreign rule, boasting even today that nary an Ottoman set foot on their soil. While historically fierce and still proud of that history, Maniots today are warm hosts to those who visit their villages and their unique grey stone tower houses.

GYTHION Γυθειο

Gythion has a much livelier, more Mediterranean feel than the desolate landscapes to the south. Bright fishing boats hustle in and out of the port, where dockside restaurants hang strings of octopi out to dry. A short causeway connects Gythion to the tiny island of Marathonisi, where Paris and Helen consummated their ill-fated love, and beautiful sand and stone beaches are a short ride (but long walk) away. For those who'd like to explore the Mani on their own, Gythion is the only city in the area that rents motorbikes.

ORIENTATION AND PRACTICAL INFORMATION

As you head south from the bus station along the main harbor road with the water on your left, most of the hotels are on your right. The small **Pl. Mavromichali,** consisting mostly of cafe seating, appears as the road curves and continues to the dock. The bus stop is on the far right of the waterfront as you face inland. A number of other stores and offices crowd around the inland plateia by the bus station.

Buses: The **station** (☎27330 22 228) is on the north end of the waterfront, opposite a park. To: **Areopolis** (1hr., 4 per day 5am-6:45pm, €1.70), via the campgrounds (€0.80); **Athens** (4hr., 6 per day 7:30am-7pm, €15.10) via **Sparta** (1hr., €2.60), **Tripoli** (2hr., €6), and **Corinth** (3hr., €10.95); **Gerolimenas** (2hr.; 5am, 1pm, 6:45pm; €3.70); **Kalamata** (2 hr.; 7:30am, noon; €6.20) via **Itilo** (1hr., €2.60); **Pirgos Dirou** (1¼hr., 10:15am, €2.30).

Ferries: To **Diakofti** on Kythera (2½hr., 5 per week, €8.50) and on to **Kasteli** on Crete (7hr., 2 per week, €18).

Taxis: (☎27330 23 423, 27330 23 492 or 27330 22 755). Available 24hr.

Moped Rental: Moto Makis Rent-A-Moped (☎27330 25 111), on the waterfront, between the plateia and the causeway. €20 per day including tax, insurance, a map, a helmet, and 80km; each additional km is €0.25. Open daily 8:30am-8:30pm.

Tourist Office: EOT (☎27330 24 484). Facing the bus station, go around the left corner and walk straight along a small plateia to the right. Archaiou Theatrou will head to the right; continue straight for 200m, the EOT will be on your right. Open M-F 8am-2:30pm.

Travel Agency: Rozakis (☎27330 22 650), on the waterfront near the police station, is the most convenient place in town to buy ferry tickets. Open daily 8am-2pm and 5-9pm.

Banks: National Bank (☎27330 22 313), just beyond the bus stop toward the water, has **currency exchange** and a 24hr. **ATM.** Open M-Th 8am-2pm, F 8am-1:30pm.

Police: (☎27330 22 100), on the waterfront, halfway between the bus station and Pl. Mavromichali. Open 24hr.

Port Police: (☎27330 22 262), before the causeway, past the plateia.

Pharmacies: Abound; try the one across from the bus station.

Health clinic: (☎27330 22 001, 002, or 003), on the water just past Saga toward the causeway.

OTE: (☎27330 22 799), corner of Herakles and Kapsali. As you face the bus station, take a sharp right around the left-hand side of the station onto Herakles. Open M-F 7:45am-1:30pm.

Internet: Escape Cafe (☎27330 25 177), on Kapsali, at the corner 1 block behind the National Bank from the bus station. €4.50 per hr., €2 minimum. Open daily 10am-1am. Behind Pl. Mavromichali, **Internet Cafe** is more convenient from hotels and domatia. €4.50 per hr. Open daily 5pm-2am.

Post Office: (☎27330 22 285), on Ermou. As you face the bus station, go around the left hand corner and follow the plateia to the road that intersects it. Follow this road, Archaiou Theatrou, right two blocks. Open M-F 7:30am-2:30pm. **Postal code:** 23200.

PELOPONNESE

ACCOMMODATIONS

While seaside accommodations are prohibitively expensive, you can find a few cheap, charming options farther inland. Gythion's campgrounds are a pleasant (and more interesting) alternative to city lodging—all are about 4km south of town toward Areopolis and can be reached by city bus (4 per day, round-trip); taxis cost about €3. If you stay in Gythion, get some wheels for easy beach access.

Xenia Karlaftis Rooms (☎27330 22 719), on the water 20m north of the causeway toward town. Voula and her mother have been letting cheap, spacious rooms for over 20 years. Their experience shows in their gracious hospitality. Kitchen with free coffee, fridges on every floor, and laundry. Clean, standard rooms with private baths. Singles €15; doubles €22; triples and quads €30. ❷

Kontogiannis Domatia (☎27330 22 518; fax 27330 24 195), off the waterfront near the police station, above Gregori Jewelry Shop, has large, white rooms with TVs, private baths, and some have lovely views of the water. Singles €20; doubles €35-40; triples and quads €39-48. ❷

Hotel Aktaion, (☎27330 23 500; fax 27330 22 294), the first hotel on the waterfront as you walk away from the bus station. Lovely traditional building with clean and cozy modern rooms. TV, A/C, phones, private baths, and balconies with water views. Singles €40-45; doubles €55-60; triples €63-70. ❹

Meltemi Camping (☎27330 22 833), 4km south on the road toward Areopolis. Hot showers, cooking area, washing machines, market, restaurant, and pool. €4.05 per person, €3.10 per child; €3 per car, €4 per small tent. Electricity €3.50. ❶

Gythion Bay Campgrounds (☎27330 22 522), 5km south on the road toward Areopolis. Laundry, mini-market, restaurant, and showers. €5.28 per adult, €2.23 per child; €3.23 per car; €3.23 per tent. Electricity €2.64. ❶

Mani Beach (☎27330 23 450), 5km south on the road toward Areopolis. Washing machine, mini-market, cooking area, playground, showers, and restaurant. €4.69 per person, €2.15 per child; €2.30 per car; €3.15 per small tent. Electricity €2.90. ❶

FOOD

Virtually identical waterfront tavernas serve up fresh seafood and lovely views at moderate prices. A **fruit store** and **bakery** are across the street from Masouleri Kokkalis, and a **supermarket** is behind the bus station.

Taverna To Nisi (☎27330 23 830), on Marathonisi, at the end of the causeway. This charming outdoor taverna is a favorite with locals and has a great view of Gythion's unique architecture. *Tzatziki* €1.80, entrees €2.80-5.50. ❶

Saga (☎27330 23 220), on the water between the causeway and the plateia. This slightly fancier restaurant serves delicious food served on tables pulled right up to the water. Crispy grilled and seasoned bread, cheap vegetarian salads (starting at €2.90). Fish €30-50 per kg. For a real treat, try the shrimp *saganaki* (€12). ❹

H Gonia or **The Corner** (☎27330 22 122), at the bend in the waterfront just past the plateia heading toward the causeway. The waterfront tables are constantly packed with people and food. Moussaka and traditional dishes €4.50; octopus €5.50. ❷

Masouleri Kokkalis, behind the plateia. Specializes in greasy fast food and does it well. Gyros and souvlaki €1. ❶

SIGHTS AND BEACHES

ANCIENT THEATER. The compact, masterfully built, 240° theater of Gythion has endured the centuries remarkably well. Even its class distinctions remain: note the differences between the seats for dignitaries in front and the simpler seats farther back. Arrive early in the evening to join the soldiers getting their nightly pep talk; any other time of day, it will most likely be deserted. Crumbling Roman walls are scattered up the hill. *(Heading away from the bus station, walk past the post office on Archaiou Theatrou until it dead ends at the theater entrance. Open daily 8am-noon and 5-8pm.)*

PALIATZOURES ANTIQUE SHOP: SIC TRANSIT GLORIA MUNDI. The last of its kind in the Peloponnese, this antique shop has furnished a number of museums in its day, as owner Costas will gladly tell you. The majority of the collection consists of 19th-century household items, artwork, furniture, coins, and assorted trinkets, but he claims to have a few medieval and even ancient items interspersed. By

PELOPONNESE

Greek law, foreigners may export only items made after the fall of Constantinople in 1453, but unless you plan on spending a *lot* of money, this won't be a concern. *(#25 on the waterfront, near the police. ☎27330 22 944. Open daily 11am-2pm and 6-9pm.)*

ON THE ROAD TO AEROPOLIS. When traveling from Gythion to Areopolis, look for the Frankish **Castle of Pasava** on the right. The road is rough and dangerous; check to see if it has been improved or try calling the local consulate at ☎27330 22 210 (roughly 10km down the road; taxi €5.50; tours available). Farther along, the **Castle of Kelefa** looks out to sea (taxi €6; open all day).

BEACHES. There is a disappointing **public beach** just north of the bus station, but better beaches lie outside of town. Four kilometers south, near the campgrounds, is the wide, pebble and sand beach of **Mavrovouni,** with a high surf and a number of bars (mixed drinks €3-4.50, beer €2-3.50). You can get there from Areopolis by bus (4 per day), by a €3 taxi ride, or through 50min. of walking. Three kilometers north is rocky **Selinitsa,** known for its incredibly clear water—look for signs. You can walk or take a €3 taxi. **Vathy** is 15km away on the road to Areopolis, and has fewer people, a lovely stretch of sand, and a quiet cove for topless sunbathing (around to the left as you face inland, after the river).

AREOPOLIS Αρεοπολη

Areopolis neighbors both the sea and the mountains, yet the incredible buildings of the town dominate the scenery: stone tower houses and cobbled streets just wide enough for donkey carts are framed by the dramatic purple peaks of the Taygetus. Tourists flocking to nearby coastal towns often pass right through Areopolis, leaving plenty of romantic accommodations available in the traditional tower houses that once defended the insular, suspicious clans of the Mani. Close by you'll find the caves at Pirgos Dirou alongside the beautiful beach at Limenas (which doubles as Areopolis's port), quiet and sternly beautiful Itilo, and lively Gythion, the harbor town on the opposite side of the peninsula.

ORIENTATION AND PRACTICAL INFORMATION

All local services can be found in the plateia or off **Kapetan Matapan,** the main road running into the Old Town from the plateia. The **bus "station"** (☎27330 51 229) is next to the Romeo Pub and Europa Grill, on the eastern edge of the plateia, opposite the Hotel Kouris. The road running perpendicular from the bus station is Kapetan Matapan. Follow it along the plateia, past the statue, and into the Old Town. Buses from Areopolis go to: **Athens** (6hr., 4 per day 8am-6pm, €19.80) via **Gythion** (30min., €1.70) and **Sparta** (2hr., €6.30); **Itilo** (20min.; 9am, 1:45pm; €0.80). From Itilo, you can catch a bus to **Kalamata.** A bus running into the Mani takes you to the **Vlihada Lake Caves** (leaves 11am, returns 12:45pm; €0.80) and **Vatheia** (1hr.; noon, 1:45, 7:30pm; €2.60) via **Gerolimenas** (40min., €1.55). Very limited service on Sundays and holidays. To find the **National Bank** (☎27330 51 293; open M-F 9am-noon) and its 24hr. **ATM,** walk down Kapetan Matapan, turn right at the first small church, and continue up the street. The **police** are 1km out of town toward Pirgos in the same building as the new town hall. (☎27330 51 209. Open 24hr.) A **pharmacy** is on Kapetan Matapan. A 24hr. **health center** (☎27330 51 242) is 50m down a street that starts in the main plateia and runs away from the ocean. Opposite the health center is the **OTE** (☎27330 51 299). For **Internet access,** walk 1km on the road to Pirgos Dirou, just past the police station, to find **Matrix.** (Open daily 11am-late. €4.50 per hr.) The **post office** (☎27330 51 230; open M-F 7:30am-2pm) is on the same street as the National Bank, across from the Hotel Mani. The post office **exchanges currency** and **traveler's checks** for a hefty fee. **Postal code:** 23062.

ACCOMMODATIONS AND FOOD

Staying at either Tsimova's Rooms or the Pension across from it may amount to taking sides in what appears to be a long-standing feud. The proprietors spend their days staring menacingly at the other's doors, but they are very friendly to travelers; choose at your own risk. To find these establishments, turn left at the end of Kapetan Matapan. **Tsimova ❷** rents narrow rooms with tiny doors and windows typical of tower houses—Kolokotronis supposedly slept here—and the living room displays rifles, swords, and uniforms passed down through the owner's family from the War for Independence. The war memorabilia, religious pictures, and various knickknacks give each room in the 300 year-old house its own personality. Shared baths may require a trip downstairs past the sleeping owner—try for a room with a private one. Continental breakfast €3. (☎27330 51 301. Singles €20; doubles €40; triples €55; quads €58.) Tsimova's neighbor and rival, friendly **Pierros Bozagregos Pension ❹,** lets large, modern rooms with private baths in a classic stonework building. (☎27330 51 354. Breakfast included. Doubles €45; triples €50; quads €72.) Offering spacious, generic rooms and a newly added wing, **Hotel Mani ❸** has rooms with private baths, balconies, and TVs across from the post office and near the National Bank. Walk 50m from the bus station on Kapetan Matapan, turn right at the first small church, and walk another 200m. (☎27330 51 190; fax 27330 51 269. Singles €30-38; doubles €35-50.)

A simple sign reading "Taverna" hangs in front of the splendid **Oinomageireio ❷** (☎27330 51 205), the yellow building on the left of Kapetan Matapan as you walk from the plateia. The taverna boasts intimate garden seating and first-class cooking by its internationally-recognized chef and owner. Walk into the kitchen to see and choose your meal. Try the mixed vegetables (€4) or the chicken with rice (€6). In the plateia, **Nicola's Place ❶** (☎27330 51 366) also serves rotating specials, including tasty overstuffed tomatoes (€4), accompanied by grilled, seasoned bread (€0.60). You can also head to the **supermarket** just off the plateia.

PELOPONNESE

DAYTRIP FROM AREOPOLIS

PIRGOS DIROU CAVES Σπηλαιο Πυργος Διρυου

11km from ***Areopolis,*** *the caves are an easy bus ride away. (Buses leave Areopolis 11am, return 12:45pm; €0.80.) Some tour guides speak only Greek, so you may want to purchase the guidebook* Caverns of Mani *(€5) at the souvenir shop by the cave entrance. ☎27230 52 222. Open all year 8am-3pm. Ticket includes boat tour. €14; students, seniors, and children €7.*

Part of a subterranean river, the unusual **Vlihada Cave** (Spilia Dirou or Pirgos Dirou) is cool, quiet, and strung with tiny crystalline stalactites. Vermillion stalagmites slice the 30m-deep water's surface. Discovered at the end of the 19th century, it was opened to the public in 1971 and has yet to be fully explored. Experts speculate that the cave is 70km long and may extend all the way to Sparta. The 1200m boat ride through the cave lasts about 30min.; the tiny boats guided only by a small oar rock their way through the narrow—and incredibly low—channels of the cave, forcing passengers to duck at times to avoid low-hanging stalactites. The close quarters and hollow echo of dripping water create an eerie calm. Lights floating in styrofoam rings illuminate the tour, but unlit recesses branch off on each side. Don't miss **Poseidon's Foot,** a striking hanging formation resembling (lo and behold!) a giant foot.

GEFYRA Γεφυρα

Byzantine enthusiasts on the way to their paradise, Monemvasia, may be puzzled when the bus drops them off in the unabashedly modern—albeit pleasant—coastal town of Gefyra ("bridge"). Just beyond the breaking waves off Gefyra's shore lies an impressive island, dominated by spectacular vertical cliffs. "The Rock," as it is known, looks uninhabited from the mainland; only after crossing the causeway and walking along the main road for 15min. does Monemvasia appear. Before you cross, however, it's wise to take care of your needs in cheaper Gefyra.

ORIENTATION AND PRACTICAL INFORMATION. During late July and August, an **orange bus** runs between the causeway and Monemvasia gate all day long (every 15min. 8am-midnight, €0.30). In Gefyra, the main thoroughfares form a fork, the tail of which leads to the causeway connecting Monemvasia to the mainland. The main branch of this fork, **23 Iouliou,** runs inland from the causeway, later becoming **Spartis.** With the causeway before you, the harbor is to the right, and a pebbled beach to the left. On 23 Iouliou is the **bus station,** located in the helpful **Malvasia Travel Agency,** where superwomen Eva and Mary provide a multitude of services, including **moped rental** (€15 per day), **currency exchange** (€3.50 commission), and **all tickets for Flying Dolphins and ferries.** (☎27320 61 752; fax 27320 61 432. Open M-Sa 7-7:15am, 8am-2:30pm, and 6-9pm, Su noon-2:30pm). All **buses** connect or stop in **Molai.** Daily buses at 4:10, 7:15am, and 2:15pm leave for: **Athens** (6hr., €18.65) via **Molai** (20min., €1.70); **Corinth** (5hr., €14); **Sparta** (2½hr., €6.15); and **Tripoli** (4hr., €9.70). On Monday and Friday there is an additional bus at 8:30am. Twice daily **Flying Dolphins** go to **Piraeus** (€29.80) via **Spetses** (€12), **Portoheli** (€14), and **Hydra** (€15). **Taxis** (☎27320 61 274) line up across from the police. Across from the bus station, the **National Bank** has a 24hr. **ATM.** (☎27320 61 201. Open M-F 9am-1:30pm; open 1-2 days per week in the off season.) The **police** and **tourist police** are on 23 Iouliou. (☎27320 61 210. Open 24hr.) **Internet access** available at the **Baywatch Cafe,** on the beachfront road. (€4 per hr., €2 minimum. Open daily 10am-late.) The **post office** is next door to the National Bank. (☎27320 61 231. Open M-F 7:30am-2pm.) **Postal code:** 23070.

PELOPONNESE

ACCOMMODATIONS AND FOOD. As Gefyra's hotels tend to be expensive (expect to pay at least €30 for a single and €40 for a double), the waterfront **domatia** are your best bet (doubles €15-30). A room in one of Monemvasia's traditional hotels will cost even more (doubles €50 and up). **Hotel Akrogiali ❷,** right across from Malvasia Travel on 23 Iouliou, is a diamond in the rough with its glowing white rooms with private baths, TV, and shared fridge. (☎27320 61 260. Singles €20-23; doubles €26-33.) The rooms of **Hotel Aktaion ❸,** just before the causeway, have an unimaginative decor but offer balconies with harbor views, private bath, and TV. (Singles €22-26; doubles €27-35; triples €40-45.) Beachfront rooms are available at **Hotel Pranataris ❹,** a short walk down the beachfront road away from the causeway. Large, bright rooms with private baths, balconies, mini-fridge, TV, and A/C. (☎27320 61 833; fax 27320 61 075; hotelpr@hol.gr. Breakfast €4.40. Singles €29.35-41.08; doubles €35.22-52.82.) **Camping Paradise ❶,** 4km along the water on the mainland, offers free hot showers, a restaurant, and mini-market. (☎27320 61 123. €4.35 per person, €3 per child; €2.65 per car; €2.80 per small tent; €4.05 per large tent; discounts for stays longer than three days.) The many harbor-front tavernas of Gefyra are the best option for dining in the area. **To Limanaki ❶** (☎27320 61 619), offering waterside seating on the mainland between the causeway and the harbor, serves exceptional Greek food, including the best *pastitsio* (€4) and stuffed tomatoes (€3.50) you'll find in the area. **Pipinellis Taverna ❷,** 2km from Monemvasia on the road to Camping Paradise, has featured home-grown produce for the past 25 years and is a favorite with locals. (☎27320 61 004. Entrees €5-7.) For lighter meals, try one of the town's bakeries, or follow the road forking off 23 Iouliou to find the large **Lekakis Supermarket.** (Open daily 8am-9pm. Fresh fruit and deli.) If you choose to dine in old Monemvasia, try **Restaurant Matoila ❸.** The first taverna you come to in the town, Matoila offers an ocean view from the outdoor garden. The menu includes favorites like *dolmas* (€5.50) and more decadent veal and seafood entrees (€10-15). (Open daily until midnight.)

DAYTRIPS FROM GEFYRA: MONEMVASIA. This ancient town deserves the constant attention it gets; an undeniable other-worldliness pervades the old city. Entering through the single gateway (hence the town's name, which means "one way") into old Monemvasia, you feel as though you've passed into a city frozen in time. No cars or bikes are allowed through the gate, so packhorses bearing groceries and cases of beer are led back and forth to restaurants. The winding cobbled street that passes the town's tourist shops and restaurants appears immediately upon entering the gate, and it continues to the central plateia. Scramble down the nearby alleys toward the ocean to take a stroll along the fortified sea wall. Back in the plateia, the church of **Christos Elkomenos** (Christ in Chains) is on the left as you face the ocean. On the right, a small but well-labeled (and nicely air-conditioned) **Archaeological Museum** holds a single room full of masonry, pottery, and ecclesiastical sculpture attesting to Monemvasia's 13th-century prominence. (☎27320 61 403. Open M noon-7pm, Tu-Su 8am-7pm. Free.) To get to the often-photographed 12th-century **Agia Sofia,** balanced on the edge of the rock cliffs, head through the tunnel across from Matoila and work your way through the maze of narrow streets—with hidden stairways, child-sized doorways, flowered courtyards, and the occasional cactus—to the edge of town farthest from the sea at the base of the mountain. There, a slippery path climbs the cliffside to the tip of the rock; you'll find the church on the far side of the rock. Although the faded frescoes were badly vandalized by invading Turks, the structure is still hauntingly beautiful. The top of the rock, scattered with castle ruins, offers fine views of the town and sea below.

NEAPOLI Νεαπολις

A necessary and sunny stop on the path between Kythera and the southeastern Peloponnese, Neapoli is a little coastal town with lots of waterfront restaurants, a few luxury hotels, and an increasing number of Greek and foreign tourists. The pebble and dark sand beaches are an uncrowded and refreshing break from the towel-to-towel sunbathers of more popular vacation spots, and grilled octopi are available nearly around the clock. Though there's not much other than Neapoli's waterfront to keep visitors occupied, you may be convinced by the sea, the sun, and the convivial locals to spend a day and catch a later boat or bus out of town.

Ferries go to **Kythera** (1hr.; W-Su 4 per day, M-Tu 3 per day July-Aug.; 2 per day Sept.-June; €4.80). The **bus station** (☎27340 23 222), is on a street off the right side of the waterfront as you face inland, two blocks from the pier. **Buses:** leave at 8:15am, 1:30, and 5pm for **Athens** (6hr., €21.10) via **Ag. Nikolaos** (20min., €0.80); **Molai** (1hr., €4.15); and **Sparta** (2½hr., €8.65).

To the left of the pier as you face inland, a blue and white hut on the water's edge doles out **info** and posts ferry schedules. Schedules and tickets can also be obtained at the **ticket agency** on Ag. Triados, the street one block to the right of the pier as you face inland. The agency is up a small flight of stairs on the right side of the street. (☎27340 23 980 or 27340 23 981. Open daily 8am until after the last ferry.) The **National Bank** is on the waterfront across from the pier. (Open M-Th 8am-2pm, F 8am-1:30pm.) The **port police** (☎27340 22 228) is one block from the

National Bank. The **post office** is one block inland on Dimokratias on the left of the waterfront as you face inland, past the bridge. (Open M-F 7:30am-2pm.) If you decide to stay in Neapoli overnight, scour the streets for domatia, or stay at **Hotel Arsenakos ❸,** run by a friendly ex-New Yorker and his wife, a 5min. walk from town with the water on your left. A cheery lobby with a large aquarium leads to spacious, clean, brightly painted rooms with A/C, TV, phones, private baths, balconies, and fridges. (☎27340 22 991 or 27340 22691; arsenakos@yahoo.com. Singles €18-30; doubles €22-35. Prices vary by season, highest in August.)

KYTHERA Κυθηρα

According to ancient myth, the island of Kythera rose from the waters where Zeus cast his father Kronos's severed head into the sea after castrating him. Springing from Kronos's foamy misfortune, Aphrodite washed up onto Kythera's shores and made it her homeland. In antiquity, the island supported a large temple to the goddess, where she was worshipped as Aphrodite Urania, goddess of chaste love. Though one might not associate the island's barren, mountainous landscape with the fertility for which Aphrodite is known and worshiped, its flowering shrubs, sandy beaches, and secluded villages hold a potent beauty. Like the other Ionian Islands, Kythera passed through the hands of the Venetians and the French before ending up as a British possession, yet it remains distinct in its extremely rugged scenery—desert-like in places—and its untouristed feel. Only about 3000 people live on Kythera, but improved ferry schedules (see below) have made it a more convenient destination for budget travelers. The two main island ports are northern **Agia Pelagia** and the newer, less accessible eastern port of **Diakofti.** Bus service is nearly nonexistent, making some sort of vehicle virtually essential to taking full advantage of all the island has to offer.

PELOPONNESE

AGIA PELAGIA Αγια Πελαγια

If you plan a short stay on the island and especially if you're catching a ferry, Agia Pelagia is a good place to set up camp to avoid paying for an overpriced cab or dealing with infrequent buses. The town is smaller and less picturesque than southerly Hora or Kapsali, but accommodations and moped rentals are cheaper, and its long, convenient stretch of beaches offer up both sand and pebbles.

ORIENTATION AND PRACTICAL INFORMATION. The island's main road runs between Agia Pelagia and **Kapsali** in the south, with small villages connected by subsidiary roads. This road also passes through **Potamos** (the island's largest town), **Livadi,** and **Kythera Town** (**Hora**). **Ferries** leave from Agia Pelagia for **Neapoli** (1hr., daily, €4.50) and from **Diakofti** to **Gythion** (2½hr., 5 per week, €8.50) and **Kasteli** on Crete (7hr., 2 per week, €18). **Flying Dolphins** leave Diakofti for **Piraeus** (5hr., 1 per day, €32) via **Monemvasia** (1hr., €16.60). In Agia Pelagia, a cottage to the left of the dock as you face inland is a **Volunteer Tourist Office,** where friendly staffers provide information about accommodations and sights. (☎27360 33 815. Open July-Aug. daily 8am-9pm.) A daily **bus** runs between Agia Pelagia and Kapsali in late July and August (leaves 9:30am, returns noon; €0.90). The nearest **bank, hospital, pharmacy,** and **post office** are all in Potamos. **Easy Rider,** to the right of Agia Pelagia, rents mopeds. (☎27360 33 486. Must be 21 and have a license for motorbikes. €14.80 per day for 50-100cc; €17.70 for 125cc). Ferry tickets are also available at the two tiny shacks at the end of the pier when ferries are docking and from the **port police** (☎27360 33 280).

ACCOMMODATIONS AND FOOD. The tourist office has a list of the few domatia owners in town and can put you in contact with them. Otherwise, blue-and-white **Hotel Kythereia ❸,** beside the ferry pier, has rooms with private baths, A/C, and lovely views (of either mountains or sea) for good prices. It's run by an extremely hospitable Greek-Australian family who serve a cozy continental breakfast for €3. (☎27360 33 321; fax 27360 33 825. Singles €25; doubles €30-60.) Out of town, along the waterfront toward Potamos, **Maneas Domatia ❸** lets rooms with private baths, kitchens, and phones in a large apartment-like building on the water. (☎27360 33 895. Doubles €28-35.) The other hotels in town are more luxurious (and expensive). The **Vernados Hotel ❹** has a score of amenities, among them A/C, TV, free laundry, and a tasty buffet breakfast. The hotel is just 50m inland on the road opposite the Volunteer Tourist Office cottage. (☎27360 34 205 or 27360 34 206. Singles €42.74-66.12; doubles €60.33-77.08; triples €73.44-90.27.)

Taverna Faros ❸, the first taverna to the right of the pier, has plenty of waterfront seating, decent prices, and good food. Try the stuffed eggplant (€4.50) or the delicious fish (€4-35 per kg). Farther north (right as you face inland) on the waterfront, **Restaurant Kaleris ❷** is popular with locals and visitors alike. Children play amid diners enjoying the tasty meals. Agia Pelagia has a **supermarket** opposite the beach, beside the fruit market.

BEACHES. In addition to its convenience as a port town, Agia Pelagia is the only town on Kythera that boasts six beaches all within convenient walking distance of the town center. Starting from the town's main beach, continue south, toward Potamos, with the water on your left, to five more beaches. The road is initially paved as you pass the second, dark sand beach, and turns to dirt after the Aphrodite Pelagia Hotel. Each beach offers its own unique combination of coves, sand, and pebbles; the most distant beach is only a 45min. walk away. A local favorite is small, secluded **Lorenzo** beach, just past the hill with the monastery.

PELOPONNESE

AROUND KYTHERA

The pint-size island has a lion's share of sights, enough to keep any visitor occupied. The peaceful beach town of **Kapsili,** east of Hora, has clear waters and a long shore. At Paleohora, in the east, are the ruins of the former fortified capital of the island, **Agios Dimitrios,** built during Byzantine rule. The town was destroyed by pirates led by the notorious Barbarossa in 1537. Even more compelling are the island's natural wonders, including the **Cave of Agia Sofia** (open Tu-Su 10am-2:30pm), near the village of Milopotamos on the western side of the island. The most impressive of the island's several caves, Agia Sofia also has beautiful **frescoes** painted on the cave walls, and is an easy walk or taxi ride away from Milopotamos. Kythera's **beaches** are gorgeous, with the ocean's variety of blues contrasting with the rocky brown landscape. The best beaches are a bit difficult to reach, accessible only by bumpy dirt roads that are perilous for mopeds (a car is safer). On the eastern coast, a steep staircase leads down to spectacular **Kaladi** beach, with sparkling coves and striking rock formations. **Halkos,** near Kalamos on the southern coast, is another out-of-the-way beach; its quiet beauty makes it worth the trip.

POTAMOS Ποταμας

Potamos is on a hill 9km south of Agia Pelagia on the main road, with narrow streets bedecked with flowers and an abundance of fresh fruit markets. Accommodations are scarce here. It's worth a visit, however, to stroll through the streets and admire the traditional Kytherean architecture, as well as to take advantage of the services in the small central plateia. There's an **Olympic Airlines** office, although the airport is a taxi ride away on the eastern half of Kythera. (☎27360 33 362. Open M-F 8am-4pm.) Olympic runs **flights** to and from Athens (1 per day, €41). The **National Bank** and its 24hr. **ATM** are also in the plateia. (Open M-Th 8am-2pm, F 8am-1pm.) The **police station** is behind the National Bank, tucked in a lemon-tree-lined corner. (☎27360 33 222.) The **hospital** is on the road to Hora. (☎27360 33 325. English spoken.) **Taxis** (☎27360 33 255 or 27360 33 720) park in the plateia. **Selana Cafe,** in the plateia, has **Internet access.** (€5 per hr.) The **post office** is uphill from the plateia (Open M-F 7:30am-2pm.) **Postal code:** 80200.

HORA Χωρα

The whitewashed plaster houses of the island's southerly capital, Hora (also called **Kythera Town**), gleam in the bright sun. Hora hosts many of the island's visitors. This plateia holds a **National Bank** with a 24hr. **ATM.** Facing the water, Hora's main street begins in the plateia's lower left-hand corner; along it you'll find the **police** (☎27360 31 206) and **tourist police** (open mornings only), 50m down toward the water. **Kithira Travel** has **Flying Dolphin** schedules, **currency exchange,** and is the island's main **Olympic Airways** office. (☎27360 31 390. Open daily 9am-2pm and 7-10pm.) The **OTE** is up the stairs to the left of Kithira Travel. (☎27360 31 299. Open 7:30am-2pm.) The nearest **hospital** is in Potamos. If you're catching a ferry in Diafkoto, a **taxi** (☎27360 31 720) from Hora will cost about €18. To reach **Pension Pises ❸,** head downhill and turn left off the main road on Ag. Elesis. It's the place for great views, shared baths, and creative decor. (☎27360 31 070. Doubles €25.) **Camping Avlemonas ❶,** near the town of Diakofti, offers a great location (across from the sea) and free hot showers. (☎27360 33 742. €3.50 per adult, €2.10 per child.) At the end of the main road, wildflowers have sprouted around the remains of the town's **castle,** where the wind-swept plateau offers intoxicating views of nearby Kapsali's harbor. The small, under-funded **Archaeological Museum,** on Kythera's highway just before the turn-off for Hora, has pottery, sculpture, and coins from the Classical to Byzantine periods. It also has gravestones, which are all that remain of the island's 19th-century English military base. (Open Tu-Su 8:45am-3pm. Free.) The **post office** is the plateia. **Postal code:** 81200.

EXTRA VIRGIN OLIVE OIL

A Day In the Fields

Picking olives in December is a national tradition and an annual rite. All over Greece, men and women can be found spreading large tarmacs and nets below olive trees, thwacking at the branches with sticks, climbing into olive groves, shaking trees, and raking leaves with short plastic "combs." More sophisticated olive pickers buy machines that sort the olives from the leaves. When a friend suggested I join him to shed his 40 trees of their olives, I took him up on the offer. We left Athens in the early morning, drove along the national highway, and arrived at his plot near Corinth, next to the sea. The water was calm and in the grayish light looked thick as mercury.

We were joined by two of his cousins from nearby Ellinohori, two men from northern Epirus, and a Greek-Russian. Our most important companion was his Aunt Tasia, who'd been picking olives since the age of 10. A brawny, attractive woman in her late forties, she wore sweatpants and a sweatshirt. She surveyed the eight stremmata (two acres) with a knowing eye, walked up to a few trees, plucked an olive, and bit into it. "Two thousand kilos worth of olives on these trees," she said. "I estimate 180 kilos of olive oil. A little ripe, but you'll be able to smell the olive oil in your salad, and that's what counts."

I beat a branch laden with black and yellow olives with a long six-foot wooden rod. The olives rattled onto the ground like heavy rain. When the ripest ones had been dislodged, we had to get to the ones that were harder to remove. Using ladders we climbed into the trees and combed the branches with small plastic rakes, sending a second school of olives to the ground. From inside the tree itself, I could uncover new bunches of olives, and these too soon joined their brethren on the ground.

When I stood back to admire a whole section of a tree that I'd combed of all its fruits, satisfied that no twig had remained untouched, eagle-eyed Tasia shouted at me, "No, no! You've left enough olives on there to feed an army! There, can't you see? Are you blind? Look, up there!"

By midday my jeans were graced with two knee spots of olive oil, and my sweatshirt was full of shavings from the saw and a heaviness of oil. My shoes were slippery from stepping on raw olives. We stopped at two o'clock for a lunch of kokkineli wine, feta cheese, pastitsio prepared by Tasia, and large chunks of bread. Slightly drunk, we were back at it by 3pm, less jubilant, more serious, and determined to finish before sunset. With only two hours of light remaining, the clouds began to huddle above our heads. Suddenly it started to rain, a light drizzle. Tasia quickly cleaned the remaining piles of olives; we covered the bags with branches and soon walked around in mud. There were only three trees left. My friend would return in a week, when the weather cleared up.

A small lorry came, and we piled the bags into it. We went to the olive press and left the bags of olives inside a small warehouse. This was a new olive press, which Tasia said didn't carry with it the smell and age of the old ones. "The old presses," she explained, "made even sour olives taste good." Within a few hours the olives had been pressed and poured into large tins. My friend poured some oil into a plate. It was still clouded, of a light green color. We dipped our fingers into it. Extra virgin olive oil.

Driving back to Athens, I recalled the day. At one point, I stood on the ladder, my body thrust up through the top of the tree like some sort of Christmas decoration. To my left, the wind rippled along the sea's surface, leaving its familiar treads. To my right, the impressive Corinthian landscape jutted into the sky, raw and ragged, dotted with patches of dark green cypress trees. Cottony clouds drifted above with serene nobility. And on the earth, Tasia, the cousins, and the emigrant workers: four Greeks, two Albanians, and one Russian, cutting, pruning, gathering, collecting, and laughing.

Nicholas Papandreou is the author of two novels, A Crowded Heart *(Picador) and* Kleptomnemon: The Thief of Memories. *He is currently an advisor to the Ministry of the Aegean, where a major effort is underway to preserve the architectural integrity of the area. His articles appear in newspapers and magazines throughout Greece.*

CENTRAL GREECE

Under 19th-century Ottoman rule, Thessaly and Sterea Ellada acquired a Byzantine aura; seek it along forgotten mountain-goat paths that lead to the treasures of this era. Along the way, you'll encounter glorious mountain-top vistas that look out over silvery olive groves, fruit-laden trees, and patchwork farmland.

STEREA ELLADA Στερεα Ελλαδα

Small mountainside villages, monumental ruins, the country's finest honey, and superb ski slopes make up Sterea Ellada (the "Greek Continent"), the only section of the mainland to join the new Greek state after the War of Independence (see p. 12). For thousands of years, pilgrimages from all over the Mediterranean and Asia Minor led to the Delphic Oracle, where ponderous questions met cryp-

HIGHLIGHTS OF CENTRAL GREECE

ASCEND to cloud-swept Meteora monasteries as the Byzantine saints did (p. 211).

MARVEL at the frescoes and gold mosaics at the Monastery of Osios Loukas (p. 176), an oasis of Byzantine decorative art.

ABANDON PSYCHIC HOTLINES for the real deal–Apollo's oracle at Delphi (p. 183).

FORGET YOUR TROUBLES at the springs of Krya: *Lethe* and *Mnemosyne* (p. 184).

HIT THE SLOPES on Mt. Parnassos, Greece's premier ski mountain (p. 177).

tic replies. The 10th-century Monastery of Osios Loukas, a modern religious center near Delphi, displays the Byzantines' architectural mastery. Be kind to strangers you meet on the road below the monastery: at the crossroads, an unknowing Oedipus met and murdered his father on the way to Thebes, where he married his mother.

THEBES (THIVA) Θηβα

Buried beneath the low-rise apartment buildings and lazy tavernas of modern Thebes lies its claim to fame—its illustrious (and notorious) past. History has literally surfaced in scattered spots throughout the city, as past attempts at construction often revealed the buried edifices of ancient Thebes. While other Greek cities boast streets named after fatcat philanthropists or minor local heroes, Theban buildings grace the avenues of **Cadmus** (the city's legendary first king), **Oedipus** (exiled king and originator of the Complex), and **Epaminonda** (the general who ended Spartan dominance). Rising to prominence in the heyday of the Greek *polis* (600-400 BC), Thebes capitalized on its fertile plains and strategic location between northern Greece and the Peloponnese. Alexander the Great's army cut this prosperity short around 335 BC, when it maliciously reduced the city to rubble and spared only temples and Pindar's ancestral home. It seems that Thebes is still attempting to recover from that blow; it now warrants a brief daytrip.

TRANSPORTATION. From Terminal B, Platform 4 at Liossion 260 in Athens, take the **bus** to Thebes (1½hr., every hr. 6am-8pm, €5.25). Buy tickets inside the station from the desk labeled ΘΗΒΑ (Thebes). The main **bus station** is in the valley below Thebes, on Estias (☎22620 27 512). If you ask nicely upon your arrival, the bus driver might let you off in the center of town. Otherwise, to get to town from the station, cross the parking lot with your back to the station and turn right, following the first road uphill. Follow Eteokleous up the hill to a plateia where first Pindarou and then Epaminonda veer off to the right. Turn right onto Epaminonda to find hotels, tavernas, and other comforts.

From Thebes, buses depart from the station for **Athens.** To travel to **Halkida,** take the Athens bus to the Skimatari stop (30min., €1.95); across the street from the stop, catch the Athens-Halkida (10min., every 30min., €1.10). A direct bus runs between Thebes and Halkida twice a day (7:20 and 10am). Regular buses run to **Livadia** (45min., every hr. 6:30am-9:30pm, €2.95) from a stop about 2km out of town; walk all the way down Pindarou, past the Archaeological Museum, and go down the steps. First take the left fork, and then the right onto Laiou (ΛΑΙΟΥ). Take a left onto St. Athanasiou, and follow the blue signs to ΛΕΙΒΑΔΕΙΑ (Livadia) to the small bus shelter just before the Shell gas station, on your right. Buy your ticket on board. For **taxis** call ☎22620 27 077.

ORIENTATION AND PRACTICAL INFORMATION. Thebes is built on a high hill with two parallel main streets, **Epaminonda** and **Pindarou,** running from the top of the hill into the valley below. Epaminonda hosts a variety of cafes and shops; Pindarou is lined with **banks** and **pharmacies.** The **National Bank,** Pindarou 94, has a 24hr. **ATM.** (☎22620 23 331 or 22620 25 144. Open M-Th 8am-2pm, F 8am-1:30pm.) The **hospital,** Pindarou 105 (☎22620 24 444), is between the church and archaeological museum—look for Greek and Red Cross flags. An **OTE,** 14 Vourdouba, is off Epaminonda (open M-F 7:45am-1pm). For **Internet access,** go to **Internet Cafe**, Pindarou 44. (€4 per hr. Open 10:30am-midnight.) The **post office,** Drakou 17, lies on a sidestreet between Pindarou and Epaminonda. (☎22620 27 810. Open M-F 7:30am-2:30pm.) **Postal code:** 32200.

ACCOMMODATIONS AND FOOD. If you decide to spend the night in Thebes, there are only two options in town. Both have high rates, so try negotiating. The English-speaking staff at **Hotel Niobi ❸,** Epaminonda 63, offers rooms with TVs and beautifully-tiled private baths. (☎22620 29 888. Breakfast €3. Singles €30; doubles €35; triples €41.) The rooms at **Hotel Meletiou ❸,** across the street, feature the same amenities (TVs, private baths) with a less polished decor. (☎22620 22 111. Singles €30; doubles €35; triples €44.) By evening, people of all ages fill the pedestrian-only sections of Epaminonda as tavernas move tables into the street. A multitude of tavernas tumble across Epaminonda, and its side streets to Pindarou offer similar fare at similar prices (€3-6). **Dionysos ❶,** on Epimanononda just before the main plateia, has been serving the traditional kitchen fare longer than the others, first opening its doors in 1922. Bakeries, fruit stands, and gyro and souvlaki restaurants scattered among the tavernas provide cheaper eats (€1-3).

SIGHTS AND ENTERTAINMENT. Thebes's antiquities are its main attraction. The **Archaeological Museum** at the end of Pindarou has an extensive collection of Mycenaean artifacts, including jewelry and pottery from the era of the *Iliad* and *Odyssey*, marble statuary of well-formed women and men, and intricate funerary boxes lamenting those trapped inside. The museum also displays Boeotian statuary from the 5th and 4th centuries BC and pottery galore. Especially notable are the Geometric style vases (*larnakes*), dating from 900 to 700 BC, before black-figure vase painting became commonplace (p. 19). Mosaics and funerary steles accent the courtyard, where more than half the museum's collection is simply lying about. (☎22620 27 913. Open M noon-7pm, Tu-Su 8am-7pm. €2, seniors €1, children and EU students free.)

Peer into the open **excavation pits**—the source of the museum's collection—sprinkled between buildings throughout the central city. Tantalizing segments of a Mycenaean palace and acropolis (dated to 1400 BC) are partially visible. The largest of these, the **House of Cadmus,** shows its ancient palace walls; it is along the way to the museum on Pindarou, just between the church and the hospital. Also nearby are unimpressive ancient **Mycenaean Chamber Tombs** (take Vourdouba downhill from Pindarou, passing the remains of **Proetides Gate,** turn left on Avlidos, and right on Katsina before the high school).

DAYTRIP FROM THEBES: LIVADIA (Λειβαδεια). Livadia's treasures cluster around the sacred river **Herkina,** which flows below the **Oracle of Trophonius.** Tree-shaded stone bridges crisscross Herkina, which bubbles up from the dual **springs of Krya,** called *Lethe* (forgetfulness) and *Mnemosyne* (memory). Pilgrims bathed in these waters to empty their minds of everything but the oracle's instruction just before their visit. It's a peaceful spot to relax, and park benches and cafes line the river. Across from the oracle, a now-graffitied 14th-century **Frankish castle** emerges from the mountain face overhead. Though the castle permits no visitors, a smooth stone path through the hills beyond the castle is open to all. Two tiny, whitewashed chapels, accessible by zig-zagging stairs carved into the mountain face, are perched high in the cliffs to the sides of the trail. The hike up the path and the stairs takes about an hour and provides a splendid view of the countryside.

The bus stop is in front of a school on D. Papaspyrou at its intersection with G. Sefari. With the school on your right, head down Papaspyrou through the intersection where it becomes Boufidou. Follow Boufidou until it ends in a large plateia. Follow signs to Koutsopetalou which becomes El. Venizelou. With the stream on your right, follow El. Venizelou until it deadends on Katsiotou. Turn right and cross the bridge; turn left on the other side of the stream. The oracle and streams are just ahead on the left, and the castle is on the right. Along an uphill path, a modern amphitheater is on the left; a small shrine and stone arch mark the base of the stairs to the chapels. Take a bus via Thebes (2hr., every hr. 6am-8pm, €7.50) or from Terminal B in Athens (p. 76). Buses run to Athens (every hr. 6am-6pm) and Arahova (30min.; M-F 6:15am, 12:10, 3:40pm; Sa 12:10, 3:40pm; Su 3:40pm).

PARNASSOS Παρνασσος AND ARAHOVA Αραχωβα

Winter is peak season on Mt. Parnassos (2455m), as Apollo and the muses share their abode with ski buffs and bunnies flocking to the best slopes in Greece. By night, the frostbitten masses thaw out in the village of Arahova, the country's largest ski resort, thanks to its prime location (24km away from Parnassos). In the summer months, the crowds desert both mountain and village, all the more reason to discover their off-season appeal. Outdoor enthusiasts will adore Parnassos regardless of season, and summer trekkers can hike the broad slopes undisturbed. Peaceful Arahova offers local delights like delicious unresinated red wine, Boeotian honey, and that peculiar grape-seed brandy called *tsipouro* (see **Moonshine,** p. 189) and an overwhelming view of the valley below. A three-day **festival** in April commemorates Arahova's role as the site of a pivotal victory over the Turks during the Ottoman War in 1821. In honor of St. George, the renowned dragon-slayer and the town's patron saint, the festival consists of athletic competitions, dances, and general merrymaking; during the festivities, residents don their best costumes.

ORIENTATION AND PRACTICAL INFORMATION. From **Terminal B** in Athens (see p. 76), take the Delphi bus to **Arahova** (2hr., 6 per day, €10.30). The bus stops at the end of town closest to Delphi, next to the kiosk in front of the main plateia. There is no bus station—ask at the information office for bus schedules. From the bus stop, buses make the run from Arahova to: **Delphi** (20min., 6 per day 6am-10pm, €.80); **Livadia** (30min.; M-F 3 per day 7am-8pm, Sa-Su 7am, 8pm; €2.50); and **Athens** (2hr.; 6 per day M-Sa 5:45am-6:15pm, Su 7:45am-9:15pm; €10.30). Getting from Arahova to Parnassos is slightly easier during the ski season, when a **bus** leaves in the morning and returns in the afternoon at the main plateia (8am, 3pm). During the summer months go by **car;** those without cars can hire a **taxi.** (☎22670 31 566. Round-trip €32-40.) Arahova centers on a single road, **Delphon,** which points downhill toward Delphi and has all a tourist could want. Three main plateias lie in town; directions assume you are heading into town from Delphi.

An **information office** with English-speaking staff is just to the right off the main plateia (☎22670 29 170; detpa@internet.gr; open 8am-10pm). For the **police,** call

☎22670 31 333. Several **pharmacies** offer balm for bruises and blisters; there's one in the second plateia, beside the big taverna, and another just past it down an alley to the right. A little past the post office, on the left, lies the **National Bank,** with a 24hr. **ATM.** (Open M-Th 8am-2pm, F 8am-1:30pm.) **Alpha Bank,** in the second plateia of cafes on the right, **exchanges money.** (Open M-Th 8am-2pm, F 8am-1:30pm.) Cafe Kivernio, next to the bus station, offers the only **Internet access** in town. (€6 per hr., €3 minimum. Open daily 8am-2am.) Turning right on the cross-street in the main plateia, uphill and on the right, you'll find the **post office.** (Open M-F 7:30am-1:30pm.) **Postal code:** 32004.

ACCOMMODATIONS. Several hotels, pensions, and domatia cluster near the first plateia, and more are scattered along Delphon and at the other end of town. The low-end prices listed refer to summer prices; high-end prices refer to ski season rates. **Pension Petrino ❷** (Πετρινο), down the first small alley on the right after the main plateia, offers gorgeous rooms with private baths, some balconies, and high wooden ceilings. (☎22670 31 384; fax 22670 32 663. 50% discount M-F in ski season, 10% off for stays longer than 3 days in summer. Breakfast included. Singles €15-55; doubles €25-71. Let the generous owner know you use *Let's Go.*) Spend a hard day's night at **Pension Nostos ❸,** located down the road to the right off the main plateia. Its cozy, well-appointed rooms (fridge, TV, private bath, balcony) once hosted the Beatles. (☎22670 31 385; fax 22670 31 765; nostospension@in.gr. Singles €25-75; doubles €35-75; triples €50-90. Breakfast included. €20 discount on weekdays in winter. Open 8 days a week.) Down the road past the center of town, **Hotel Apollon ❷,** Delphi 20, has comfortable rooms with shared hall bathrooms. Some rooms have balconies with uninterrupted views of the surrounding mountains. The friendly, English-speaking owner is glad to be of service. (☎22670 31 057. Breakfast €4.40 at 7:30 and 9:30am. Singles €15; doubles €20; triples €25.)

FOOD. The bakeries along the road to Delphi sell fresh bread and savory pastries (€0.50-2). Tavernas are indistinct and can be found along the main road; the best ones close for the summer. The usually moderate prices, like everything else, go up in winter. **Pizzaria** (Πιτσαρια) **Kellaria ❶,** on the right past the second plateia, serves a variety of pizza and calzones (€5-7.50) from its **brick oven,** as well as savory and sweet crepes (€3.50-4.50). **Taverna Karathanassi ❷** (Καραθανασηη), up from the second plateia on, serves the usual kitchen fare as well as a variety of grilled meats (€3-6.50) and features roof terrace dining.

SKIING, HIKING, AND THE OUTDOORS. Winter activities at Parnassos are accessible at either of its two main **ski centers, Kelaria** (☎22340 22 689 or 22340 22 624) or **Terolaka** (☎22340 22 693). There are tavernas, equipment rental shops, and child care service at each one. The ski season runs from December 15 to May 1. (Lifts: weekends €20 per day; weekdays €15 per day; full week €80; ask about discounts for students and children, as well as family passes.) There are 14 lifts servicing the 20 slopes, which have a combined length of 14,000m. Though more goats than tourists frequent Parnassos in the summer months, it's a peaceful spot for hiking and rock climbing, with literally breathtaking views: the air becomes noticeably thinner higher up. Ski centers on the mountain provide free parking and an easy starting destination for most trips; Kellaria is the best starting point for a climb to the summit. Consult the **Greek Alpine Club** in Athens (☎210 321 2429) or the **Skiing and Mountain Climbing Association of Amfissa** (☎22650 28 577 or 22650 29 201) about routes and refuges for climbers. In most cases, the hike will take no more than three hours. Summer hikers should note that trails are poorly marked and usually deserted (goats aside). Be sure to take water and sunscreen along, and be aware of the thin air and rocky paths.

OSIOS LOUKAS Οσιος Λουκας

Bus travel between Arahova and Osios Loukas is virtually non-existent; as a result, the monastery is difficult to reach. Without a car, you'll need to hire a taxi (☎22670 31 566; €15-20 each way). Monastery ☎22670 22 797. Open May 3-Sept. 15 daily 8am-2pm and 4-7pm; Sept. 16-May 2 8am-5pm. Dress modestly (long skirts for women, long pants for men, no bare shoulders). €3, seniors €2, under 18 and students with ID free.

Osios Loukas delights the eye with its mountain vistas and stunning Byzantine architecture. The exquisite monastery, built in the 10th and 11th centuries and still in use today, overlooks the fruit orchards and vineyards of Boeotia and Phokis from the green slopes of Mt. Elikon, more than 500m above sea level. Gold-laden mosaics, vibrant frescoes, and intricate brick- and stonework adorn Osios Loukas, the most famous and perhaps the most gorgeous monastery in Greece.

HISTORY. Ironically, Christian saint Osios Loukas was born in AD 896 in Delphi (p. 180), the former religious center of the Olympian gods. Inclined to an ascetic life from early on, he became a monk at the age of 14. In AD 946, Osios Loukas settled at the lush and enchanting site of the monastery that now bears his name, building a cell, a small church, and a garden. Rumors that his relic worked miracles brought believers to his church, which led to an expansion of the grounds and the beginning of a monastery. With aid from fellow hermits and money from admirers, Osios Loukas began construction of two churches. The first, the **Church of the Panagia** (Church of the Virgin Mary), was finished soon after the saint's death in 953. The larger **Katholikon of Osios Loukas,** built in 1011, became the site of his reliquary. Osios Loukas was famed as a miracle worker during his lifetime; since his death, thousands have found cures at his tomb. Unfortunately, the monastery still bears the damage from 13th-century Frankish occupation and, more recently, from German bombing in World War II.

MONASTERY. Today, the monastery consists of the two churches, a crypt, a bell-tower, and monks' cells. Also on the grounds are an archaeology museum and several tourist shops. The archaeology museum, on the right after the arched stone gate, sells tickets for entrance into the monastery. The museum holds a few relics from the monastery's architectural past (chunks of molding and such) and merits little more than a quick look.

The **Katholikon,** on the right after the museum, is the most impressive piece of the monastery. Built on the classic "Greek cross" basilica plan, the church is resplendent with brilliant frescoes and mosaics. The mosaics, crafted from minute pieces of stone, enamel, and gold, depict scenes of Christian lore: the birth, baptism, and crucifixion of Christ, and **Christ Pantokrator** (Christ in heaven, reigning in glory), which gazes down from the dome.

A small passageway in the Katholikon's northwest corner links it to the smaller **Church of Panagia.** In this passageway is the monastery's most prized relic: the desiccated body of the saint himself, lying in state in a transparent glass coffin. Orthodox pilgrims come here to pray at Osios Loukas's velvet-slippered feet. Some have been even bolder: Loukas's left hand, which protrudes from his habit to hold a rosary, has lost a few fingers to relic-seekers. The Church of Panagia down the passage features extremely fine exterior brickwork and an inlaid mosaic floor.

Between the museum and the churches and accessible by an entrance in the southern exterior of the Katholikon is the **crypt;** its stunning frescoes should not be missed. Protected from the elements, the frescoes retain their original brilliance, giving us an idea of what the churches looked like originally.

DELPHI Δελφοι

As any Delphinian will proudly attest, this town of 2500 marks the *omphalos* (belly button) of the earth. According to the ancient myth, Zeus discovered this fact by simultaneously releasing two eagles, one toward the east and one toward the west. They collided, impaling each other with their beaks, directly over Delphi. A sacred stone marks the spot. Nearby stood the most important oracle of the ancient Mediterranean. The oracle was initially devoted to Gaia (Mother Earth). Gaia was overthrown by the Olympian gods around 800 BC, when Apollo defeated the Python, Gaia's snaky, underworldly son and ruler of the site. The Apollonian oracle drew pilgrims from far and wide who sought guidance from the Pythia, the priestess of the oracle. The temples and treasury building of the ancient oracle have mostly crumbled to rubble, but Delphi remains a place of pilgrimage—for tourists. Jewelry stores, expensive restaurants, "Greek Art" trinket shops, and hotels litter the present-day town. Beyond the touristy glitter, the town's mountainside perch and its beautiful ruins make Ancient Delphi a must-see daytrip.

ORIENTATION AND PRACTICAL INFORMATION

Delphi's main street, **Friderikis-Pavlou,** runs east-west through town. **Apollonas** runs uphill from and parallel to Friderikis-Pavlou. The **bus station** (☎22650 82 317, open daily 8am-10:30pm) is at the western end of town, on Pavlou. The oracle and museum are on Pavlou at the opposite end of town, toward Athens.

Buses: From **Terminal B** in Athens (see p. 76), take a bus to **Delphi** (3hr., 6 per day, €10.20). Buy your ticket at the booth labeled Δελφοι (Delphi). From Delphi, buses leave for: **Amphissa** (30min., 3 per day 7am-10:15pm, €1.40); **Itea** (30min., 3 per day 7am-10:15pm, €1.25); **Lamia** (2hr., 3 per day, €5.90); **Nafpaktos** (2½hr., 3 per day, €6.95) via **Galaxidi** (1hr., €2.35); **Patras** (3hr., 1 per day, €8.50); **Thessaloniki** (5hr.; M-Th, Sa 10:15am, F and Su 3:15pm; €22.50) via **Volos, Larisa,** and **Katerini.**

Taxi Stand (☎22650 82 000), at the eastern end of Pavlou.

Tourist Office: Friderikis 12 or Apollonas 11 (☎22650 82 900), housed in the town hall. From Friderikis, the office is up a flight of stairs, in a stucco courtyard to your left as you walk toward Athens, marked by an "Information" sign. Incredibly helpful, quadrilingual **Efi Tsiropoulou** will assist you with bus schedules and accommodations. Open M-F 8am-2:30pm. If the office is closed, the bus station can provide directions and bus information. (Open 7:30am-10:30pm.)

THE WAY TO BYRON'S HEART Though **Messolongi,** a stop on the Athens-Delphi-Astakos bus route, may not walk in beauty like the night, it does hold **Lord Byron**'s heart–literally. The city has the sad distinction of being the place Lord Byron caught fever and met his end in 1824, while leading the local troops in the War of Independence (see p. 12). A small **War of Independence Museum** in the old town hall at the center of the plateia includes an unexceptional collection of Byron memorabilia. A Byron pilgrim's trail points to the large statue of the poet dressed in Greek garb, in front of the Hotel Liberty, just before the entrance to the Garden of Heroes. The park consists mainly of crumbling busts and other poorly maintained monuments to national war heroes; **Byron's heart** is buried beneath his statue. The noise and dirt of modern Messolongi may be tragically unromantic, but Byron would be content that the city is indeed free.

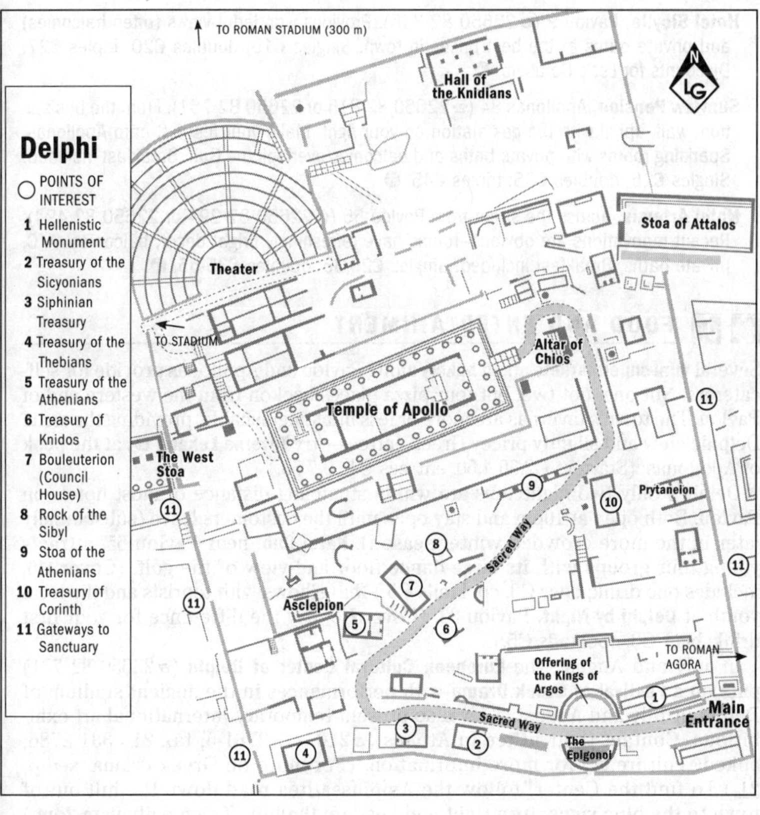

Police (☎22650 82 222), directly behind the church at the peak of Apollonas.

National Bank: Pavlou 16 (☎22650 82 622), has a 24hr. **ATM.** Open M-Th 8am-2pm, F 8am-1:30pm.

Public Toilets: At the eastern end of Pavlou behind the taxi stand.

OTE: In the town hall. Open M-Th 7:30am-1pm, F 7:30am-12:30pm.

Internet Access: At **Cafe Delfikon**, on the right side of Pavlou past Hotel Syvilla as you walk towards Athens. (€4.50 per hr., €2 minimum. Open daily 9am-midnight.)

Post Office: (☎22650 82 376) at Pavlou 25. Open M-F 7:30am-2pm. **Postal code:** 33054.

ACCOMMODATIONS AND CAMPING

Delphi is full of hotels; most are expensive. Almost all of the many hotels can be found on Apollonas or Pavlou. Prices tend to rise during the ski season. Camping is available on the road heading west from Delphi: The bus can drop you at **Delphi Camping ❶**, 4km out of town (☎22650 82 745; €4-4.55 per person; €3 per tent; €2.50 per car); or **Chrissa Camping ❶**, 10km out of town (☎22650 82 050; €5 per person; prices vary by season). Both sites have pools.

Hotel Sibylla, Pavlou 9 (☎22650 82 335). Provides wonderful views (often balconies) and private baths at the best prices in town. Singles €15; doubles €20; triples €27. Discounts for *Let's Go* users. ❷

Sunview Pension, Apollonas 84 (☎22650 82 815 or 22650 82 751). From the bus station, walk uphill with the gas station on your right. Make your first left onto Apollonas. Sparkling rooms with private baths and balconies overlook the Gulf. Breakfast included. Singles €25; doubles €35; triples €45. ❸

Hotel Artemis, across the street from Pavlou 55 (☎22650 82 294 or 22650 82 494). Recent renovations are obvious–rooms have refreshingly bright decor, balconies, A/C, private baths. Breakfast included. Singles €25-35; doubles €35-55. ❸

FOOD AND ENTERTAINMENT

Several **mini-supermarkets** and a **bakery** along Pavlou and Apollonas provide for self-caterers. Not one, not two, but four pizza places beckon from the western end of Pavlou. The town's tavernas are more or less indistinguishable, providing the same Delphic view and slightly pricey Greek entrees—try **Taverna Lekaria ❷,** at the peak of Apollonas. (Starters €2.50-4.50, entrees €4.59-7.50.)

Delphi's only two nightclubs are within stumbling distance of most hotels on Pavlou. Both open at 10pm and stay open until the customers leave (substantially later in the more crowded winter season). **Katoi Cub,** near Pavlou 65, attracts young tour groups with its large dance floor and view of the gulf. (Cover €6, includes one drink; beer €3, cocktails €5.) Rub elbows with tourists and the local youth at **Delphi by Night,** Pavlou 33. (Cover €3, pay the difference for your first drink; beer €3, cocktails €5.)

In July and August, the **European Cultural Center of Delphi** (☎22650 82 731) puts on a **Festival of Greek Drama** with performances in the ancient stadium of Delphi in July and August. They also present temporary international art exhibitions. Contact their office in Athens (☎210 331 2781-5; fax 210 331 2786; epked@culture.gr) for more information. (For more on Greek drama, see p. 21.) To find the Center, follow the Amphissa/Itea road down the hill out of town to the blue signs, turn right and head up the hill. (Open daily 9am-2pm.) Delphi is home to several other summer **festivals,** so ask around and keep a sharp eye out for posters.

KNOW THYSELF (OR ELSE) The Delphic Oracle was known for giving obscure, deceptive, metaphorical answers to pilgrims' questions. Many a suppliant went home more confused than he or she had come, having failed to draw meaning from the answer, or–worse still–having drawn the *wrong* meaning. **Croesus of Sardis,** ruler of a vast territory encompassing most of Asia Minor and the richest man in the ancient world, came to the oracle in the 6th century BC to ask about the Persian threat to his kingdom. The oracle's answer: "A great empire will be destroyed." The king returned to Sardis thinking that he would lay the smackdown on the Persians, whose empire was as large as his own. Croesus found out the hard way that the oracle had meant his own great empire would crash, as he watched his home fall to Persian invaders. Athenian leader **Themistocles** fared better when he asked the oracle how to prepare for another war with ever-pesky Persia. He was told to "build wooden walls." Most interpreted this as an order to enclose Athens in wooden walls, but Themistocles set to work building a fleet of ships. Only after Athens' decisive victory in the First Persian War at the naval battle of Salamis did the Athenians realize their leader's smarts.

ORACLE OF DELPHI

Head out of town toward Athens, following the highway until you see the paved path on the left, which leads to the ruins and museum. ☎ *22650 82 312. Museum and site €9, students and seniors €5, EU students free; museum or site only €6, students and seniors €3, EU students free.*

A sacred site from 1500 BC or earlier, the Oracle of Delphi became the most important source of sacred wisdom in the ancient world from around the 7th century BC until the advent of Orthodox Christianity after the 4th century AD. Pilgrims ventured to the Delphic oracle from all over Greece and the Near East (where Alexander the Great had brought Greek culture). After all, the Delphic oracle foretold **Cadmus's** founding of Thebes and prophesied the horrific fate of **Oedipus**—to kill his father and marry his mother. The oracle's authority extended beyond religious matters and personal fortune-telling; Delphic approval sanctioned many political decisions, including the reforms that led to democracy in Athens. The oracle's pronouncements altered nations and set off (or extinguished) military conflicts. Hoping to make powerful friends, city-states from all over the Greek world erected treasuries and donated immense sums in respect to the oracle.

ARCHAEOLOGICAL SITE. The inscription "Know thyself" (Γνοθι σεαυτον) has long crumbled from the portal of the ancient temple, but still governs the meditative atmosphere of peaceful, windswept ancient Delphi. Cut into the steep mountainside, the ancient oracle reigns over the brush-dotted valley below and overlooks eagles that fly below the lofty temple. Now, as then, the **Temple of Apollo** is the centerpiece of the oracle site. A largely wooden incarnation of the temple was burned in 548 BC. It was again shattered, this time by an earthquake, in 373 BC, and it still lies in ruin today. Ancient proclamations etched along the stone base are still visible. To reach the Temple of Apollo, visitors follow the **Sacred Way,** which winds up the site in the footsteps of ancient pilgrims. To the left, the treasuries of the supplicant cities line the Sacred Way, including the reconstructed **Treasury of the Athenians,** excavated in the early 20th century. Past the Temple of Apollo, the **theater,** with its geometric perfection and amazing acoustics, is no less impressive. For a taste of ancient Delphi as a Roman site, make your way up the slick steps to the **stadium** at the very top of the hill. Through the archway at the entrance, you'll see the golden brown and green dappled mountains framed before you. Take a break from the thin air to sit among Roman ghosts in the stadium's seats; then before you go, take a few laps around the stadium and imagine the turning posts and cheering crowds. *(Open 7:30am-6:45pm.)*

ARCHAEOLOGY MUSEUM. The museum contains many precious artifacts mined from the site: the frieze and two *kouroi* (see p. 20) from the Siphian Treasury, the haunting bronze **Charioteer of Delphi,** the altar from the temple of Athena Pronaia, enormous 7th-century bronze shields, and many ornaments and figurines in gold, silver, and ivory offered to the oracle. Nearly all of the collection was unearthed in 1939 by the **Ecole Française d'Athens.** Most labels are written in French and English as well as Greek, but a guidebook (€3.50-12) is still helpful. *(Open M-F 7:30am-6:45pm; Sa, Su and holidays 8:30am-2:45pm.)*

OTHER SITES. Before calling upon the oracle, pilgrims cleansed themselves both physically and spiritually in the **Kastalian Spring,** 300m past the main ruins along the road to Athens. The remains were covered by rocks until the beginning of this century, when a clever archaeologist cleared them out of the lush ravine. You can still see the niches carved into the rock for votive offerings. Drinking from the spring is said to confer the gift of eloquence. Just past the spring are the remains of an ancient **gymnasium.** About 200m farther down the road, the **Temple of Athena Pronaia** served as a lounge for pilgrims before they entered the sanctuary. The three remaining Doric columns of the **Tholos,** a round building used for an unknown purpose, are the sole evidence of its architectural mastery.

GALAXIDI Γαλαξιδι

The town shares its name with a drink made of *gala* (milk) and *xithi* (vinegar), which may be an allusion to the bittersweet existence of a seaman's wife—Galaxidi used to be a prominent naval base. In its modern incarnation, seafaring has evolved into pleasure boating, as locals lead tours for vacationing Swedes and Germans. Quiet during most of the year, Galaxidi delights visitors with its peaceful waterfront, pebble beaches, and gorgeous view of the surrounding mountains.

PRACTICAL INFORMATION. Galaxidi's main street, **Nik. Mama,** leads from the sole town plateia (and the **bus station**) to the cheapest hotel in town, Hotel Poseidon, and down to the harbor. **Buses** run from Galaxidi to Nafpaktos (1hr., 3 per day noon-5pm, €4.50) and to Itea, where you can transfer to Delphi (1hr.; M-F 5 per day 7:30am-8pm, Sa-Su 4 per day; €1.20). The **National Bank** is several blocks farther down Nik. Mama, past the Hotel Poseidon on the left. (24hr. **ATM.** Open M-Th 8:30am-2pm, F 8:30am-1:30pm). **Public toilets** and **showers** are across the harbor from Nik. Mama before the forest on the right. Find the **police** (☎22650 41 222) in the main plateia across from the bus station. The **pharmacy** is one block to the right of the bus station up Nik. Mama on the left. (☎22650 41 122. Open M-Sa 8:30am-1pm and 6-9pm.) Galaxidi's **post office** is next to the bank on Nik. Mama. (Open daily 7:30am-2pm.) **Postal code:** 33052.

ACCOMMODATIONS AND FOOD. From the bus stop, turn right and head down Nik. Mama to find **Hotel Poseidon ❸**, a breezy old home-turned-hotel blessed with an ultra-friendly manager, Costas, who just may break open a bottle of ouzo on the evening of your arrival. Rooms have A/C and TV; some have private baths. (☎22650 41 426. Breakfast included. Singles €25-40; doubles €35-50; triples €50-60.) Several **domatia** can also be found on sidestreets off Nik. Mama and above the restaurants along the waterfront.

To Perasma ❶, across from the National Bank, sells old standbys for typical prices (gyros €1.50, souvlaki €1). On Kon. Satha to the left of Nik. Mama before the Hotel Poseidon, **Taverna Albatross ❶** is a cheap, sit-down alternative (starters €1-6, entrees €4-5). If you're splurging, head to one of the tavernas along the harbor for a great view and tasty seafood. **O Tasos ❸** leads the pack, with a constant crowd vying for their fresh fish (€12-44 per kg) and grilled dishes (€5-6). For the best deal, head to the bakeries on Nik. Mama (€0.50 and up).

SIGHTS AND ENTERTAINMENT. On Kon. Satha, off Nik. Mama, the **Church of Agios Nikolaos** houses many fine mosaics. The 13th-century **Monastery of the Metamorphosis,** with sublime centuries-old wood carvings and a great view of town, is 6km from Galaxidi on the uphill road outside of town. Though the unshaded, uphill trip takes an hour by foot, on a cool day the views make it a perfect hike; follow K. Papapetrou out of town past the school, beneath the highway, and follow the signs through the terraced orange orchards.

In the early spring, Galaxidi shakes off its sleepiness with the Bacchanalian frenzy that is **Pre-Lenten Carnival.** Ouzo bottles are emptied by the hundreds as fantastically costumed people come from miles around for extraordinary once-a-year carousing. Revelers gyrate around a fire in traditional dances and throw brightly

CENTRAL GREECE

HEY, HEY, WE'RE THE MONKS Over the last two years a band of musical monks have been working their way onto the Greek pop scene using "the same tools as the devil" to spread their religious message. In their efforts to save young people from the temptation of the modern world, they have secured chart topping success–their first two CDs have sold more 110,000 copies, which constitutes platinum sales in Greece. The 12 members of the unlikely pop band hail from the monastery of Saint Augustine and Seraphim Safof in the village of Trikorfo, not far from Nafpaktos. Their catchy tunes have had young Greeks tapping their feet to songs addressing a myriad of issues: loneliness, depression, drug abuse, politics, and globalization (to name a few). However, their deviation from traditional monastic practices has earned them a few frowns from Orthodox bishops, who have condemned their unique approach to preaching as scandalous. The monks, unperturbed by such sharp reprimands, have stepped forward onto the international stage, holding concerts in Chicago, New York and Boston, the proceeds of which will be donated toward legal fees for death row inmates of Greek descent.

colored pigments at each other. If you want to keep your costume clean, stick to the dances by the town's children; they'll be in traditional garb.

Rocky shoreline stretches out past the docks on the forest side of the harbor; small, pebbly **beaches** are scattered throughout. Walk Nik. Mama to the waterfront, then follow the harbor toward the forest to your left until you find a resting place that suits you. Several tiny islands are within easy swimming distance, ideal for solitary tanning or snoozing.

NAFPAKTOS Ναυπακτος

Nafpaktos has something for the whole family, from *paidi* to *pappou*, but shows no signs of becoming the generic resort town that tends to cater exclusively to such a crowd. Vacationing urbanites and Greek children sunbathe side by side on the city's long, pebbly beaches, which stretch out on both sides of the picturesque Old Port. The tree-lined waterfront avenues are packed with cafes, tavernas, and playground equipment, and are mercifully closed to traffic—you might even see a 14-year-old riding a bicycle instead of a souped-up moped.

ORIENTATION AND PRACTICAL INFORMATION. Buses from points east drop off on **Athinon** (which becomes **Tzavella** and ultimately converges with Mesologgiou at the Old Port) at the base of the main town plateia. One block toward the water from Athinon is **Mesologgiou** which runs one way in the opposite direction to Athinon (away from the Old Port). There are **two bus stations** in town, both near the church one street below the main plateia on Athinon. The **first station** is located across the street and just around the corner from the front of the church, and it serves **Delphi** (2hr., 5 per day, €7) and **Larisa** (5 hr., 8:45am, €19.30). The **second station,** across from the side of the church on the street farthest from the plateia, serves all other destinations. Buses leave for **Athens** (3½hr., 1 per hr. 10am-5pm, €12.85); **Lamia** (3hr.; 11:45am, 3:15pm; €9.40); and **Thessaloniki** (8 hr.; 11:45am, 3:15pm; €24.95). Take a bus to **Antirrio** (15min., 2 per hr. 6am-10pm, €0.95) to catch the ferry that serves the Peloponnese. **Taxis** (☎26340 27 792 or 26340 27 678) are next to the main plateia, as are phones for calling them. In case of emergency, call the **police** (☎26340 27 258). The **National Bank** and **Alpha Bank,** both on Athinon just off the main plateia, exchange travelers checks and have 24hr. **ATMs.** (Both open M-Th 8am-2pm, F 8am-1:30pm.) There are **pharmacies** around the plateia and down Athinon, all with varying hours; if one's closed, there should be a sign indicating which others are open. You can get yourself connected (to the **Internet,** that is) at the **Krisi Akti Cafe,** below the hotel of the same name, on Psani beach, past the Old Port. (☎26340 21 444. €4 per hr., €2 minimum.) The **post office** is several blocks down Athinon from the banks, on the right side of the street. (☎26340 27 232. Open M-F 7:30am-2pm.) **Postal code:** 30300.

ACCOMMODATIONS AND FOOD. **Hotel Diethnes** (ΔΙΕΘΝΕΣ) ❷, on Odos Messologgiou, has hardwood floors, balconies, and blindingly white private baths. Look for the purple shutters just past the Old Port plateia. (☎26340 27 342. Singles €18; doubles €25-30; triples €30-35.) **Pension Aphrodite ❷,** on Apokaykou two blocks down from the bus stop on Gribovo beach, has it all: private baths, TV, A/C, phones, and a view, at a great price. (☎26340 27 370. Singles €20; doubles €30; triples €40. Be sure to specify pension and not hotel.) Beachfront digs at **Lepanto Beach Hotel ❸,** a short walk down Gribovo past Aphrodite, are equipped with A/C, phone, TV, balcony, and a bathtub to relax in after a tough day on the pebbly shores of Nafpaktos. (☎26340 23 931. Breakfast €5. Singles €35-50; doubles €40-70; triples €48-84.)

Bakeries, souvlaki stands, and fast food restaurants jumble together near the central plateia and Old Port. Head to the waterfront along Gribovo beach (just a few blocks down from the main plateia) for tavernas; veer left for the best prices. The first of the bunch, **O Stavros ❷,** offers a variety of succulent dishes and a great view. Not sure what you want? Go back to the kitchen and point at one of the many dishes being cooked, and it will be on your plate in a jiffy. (☎26340 27 473. Entrees €3-8. Open daily 11am-1am.) If you find yourself near Psani Beach, **Kristakis ❷,** a couple hundred meters down walking away from the Old Port, offers similar fare at great prices. (☎26340 29 446. Entrees €3-7. Open daily 10am-midnight.) The Old Port is brimming with cafes that become lively after 10pm.

SIGHTS AND ENTERTAINMENT. The **Venetian Castle,** one of the most important examples of fortress architecture in Greece, dominates the picturesque town. Besides having the best vista around, the citadel also encloses the tiny **Church of the Prophet Elias,** the remains of a **Byzantine bath** and **church,** and a large **cistern** to help the fortress weather sieges. Its walls, which reach down to the port, formed five zones of fortification, and are now woven into the construction of modern houses on the hill. Footpaths wind around the walls, past fountains, and through century-old gates. One begins off Athinon just past the post office. A leisurely walk will take about 30min. When you hit the road just below the main fortifications, follow it uphill about 1km to reach the **citadel.** Alternatively, drive to the citadel by following Athinon-Tzavella past the Old Port where it becomes Mesologgiou; veer right on Thermou and follow the signs for ΚΑΣΤΡΟ.

The **Old Port,** enclosed by parapets and watchtowers, is the sight of the town's hottest cafes and forms a romantic backdrop for any outing. Plaques on the walls commemorate the October 7, 1571 **Battle of Lepanto** and its hero, **Miguel de Cervantes Saavedra.** Both the castle and the Old Port are lit up spectacularly at night.

Most leisure time around Nafpaktos is spent on the town's beaches; many locals take a break every afternoon to relax on the beach and swim. Nafpaktos's beaches form a large crescent with the Old Port at its center. Facing the water at the Old Port, **Gribovo beach** is to the left and **Psani beach,** the better of the two, to the right. Families dominate Psani beach; small amenities, like playgrounds and a few **public showers,** add to the experience. Cafes and *ouzeria* along Psani beach and in the Old Port are filled with customers from 8:30 until 11:30pm, when families hit the hay and everyone else hits the clubs.

Club Cinema, featuring a large dance floor and pulsing DJ mixes, is conveniently located one block off Gribovo beach on Apokaykou. (☎26340 26 026. Open F and Sa 11pm until late.) Down Apokaykou, walking away from the Old Port by Pension Aphrodite is ultra-hip **Club Aman,** whose fluorescent blue disco lights illuminate the beachfront long into the night. (☎26340 26 400. Cover €3; beer €4; drinks €6. Open daily midnight-late.) **The Blue Lake** (☎26340 51 900) claims to be open "all day, everyday" and features live, traditional Greek music on Friday, Saturday, and Sunday nights. You'll need a taxi to get there. Many other clubs open only in the summer—watch out for posters around town. On the roof of Club Cinema is the outdoor movie theatre **Ciné-REX,** which features American movies and an incredible vista. (Movies at 9 and 11pm, except for long movies which show only once. €6.) Nafpaktos's week-long **Pre-Lenten carnival celebration** is a fun time for all (though some townsfolk migrate to **Patras's** larger scale festivities), with music everywhere, dancing, free wine, and free souvlaki in the Old Port.

EVRITANIA Ευριτανια

Often called the "Switzerland of Greece," this mountainous land was once a refuge for Greeks escaping Ottoman rule. Since then it has evolved into a wildlife sanctuary where hikers and adventurers can explore clean air, green forests of fir and walnut, and trails that wander past tiny mountain villages to the highest peaks of the Louchi Mountains. Old churches and shrines dot the mountains and overlook steep gorges where water enthusiasts hop in their rafts, canoes, and kayaks and try to tame the rushing Karpenisiotis, Krikelopotamos, and Tavropos Rivers.

The best way to explore Evritania is by foot. Take a stroll up and down the sunny streets of an unhurried hillside town or hike to the peak of the closest mountain for a breathtaking change of perspective. A car, however, is the most sensible (and frequently the only) option for reaching the more remote villages. Bus service is sporadic and mostly unavailable after 1pm. There's no place to rent a car or moped in Karpenisi; the nearest rental office is **Hillco Rent-a-Car** (☎22310 37 086) in Lamia (p. 192), where cars cost €15-20 per day (prices higher July-Sept.).

In winter, backpackers can contact the **Hellenic Alpine Club (EOS),** which runs several mountain refuge huts throughout Evritania. (Karpenisi Office: ☎22370 23 051; Lamia Office: ☎22310 26 786.) The adventurous can outfit themselves at **Trekking Hellas,** past the Karpenisi plateia down Zinopoulou on the right (☎22370 25 940), which offers kayak, rafting, and ski packages. A map of the region is on sale at the *periptero* in the plateia in Karpenisi and is well worth the €3 for hiking routes, a topographical key, and an invaluable guide to the area's history.

KARPENISI Καρπενησι

Karpenisi (pop. 10,000), at the tip of a long stretch of hairpinned roadway, is Evritania's relaxed capital and the perfect base for outdoor explorations in the surrounding countryside and villages. Founded when five agrarian settlements in the foothills of Mt. Timfristos merged early in the era of Ottoman rule, Karpenisi suffered for years as an economic backwater, weakened by emigration and unemployment. However, in recent years a thriving tourism industry has breathed new life into the city, bringing increased prosperity as more Greek and foreign outdoor enthusiasts discover the region's extraordinary beauty. In the broad main plateia, where old men occasionally strum guitars and join in melancholy sing-alongs, a floor mosaic spells out the names of the region's old towns. South of Karpenisi, the streets give way to rolling pastures and the Karpenisiotis River gorge.

TRANSPORTATION. Buses run to **Agrinio** (3½hr.; Sa-Th 1 per day 8:45am, F 3:30pm; €6.50); **Athens** (5hr.; 9am, noon; €16.50); **Koryshades** (10min., M-Sa 7:20am, €2.80); **Lamia** (1¾ hr., 4 per day 6:30am-3:30pm, €4.40); **Mikro Horio** and **Megalo Horio** (20min.; 7am, 1pm; €0.80); **Proussos** (M and F 5:30am, 1:30pm; €2). Ask at the bus station about bus service to smaller villages. In winter, buses to the **Velouchi Ski Center** (12km) can be arranged for larger groups. **Taxis** (☎22370 22 666 or 22370 22 100) line up at the stand just downhill from the bus station.

ORIENTATION AND PRACTICAL INFORMATION. Karpenisi sits at the foot of Mt. Velouchi, which rises up about 70km west of Lamia in central Sterea Ellada. Everything of importance is within a 5min. walk from the **bus station.** From the station, **Tsamboula** leads downhill to the spacious plateia, where it changes its name to **Zinopoulou.** After passing the plateia, the road splits in a V, with **Karpenisioti** heading down to the right and Zinopoulou continuing on the left. Most of the town's shops are on these two streets. The other main road, **Eth. Antistaseos,** forks off to the right from Zinopoulou at the top end of the plateia. As Eth. Antistaseos passes the plateia, **Grigoriou Tsitsara** branches off to the left, running roughly parallel to Zinopoulou and Karpenisioti. The largest **church** and the **town hall** are on the north end of the plateia, near a **monument** to Greek soldiers who died in 20th-century wars. Above the bus station, the town climbs up the hillside in a tangle of steep, winding streets and narrow stairways.

Directly across the street from the taxi stand, the **tourist office** is behind an inconspicuous door, beneath a green sign. The friendly English-speaking staff offers regional maps, brochures, and ideas for excursions into the Evritanian countryside, including hiking, rafting, camping, canyoning, and parachuting. (☎/fax 22370 21 016. Open M-Sa 10am-2pm and 5-8pm, Su 10am-2pm.) A map of Karpenisi and the surrounding villages, including extensive hiking trails, can be purchased at the *periptero* across the street (€3). There are a number of 24hr. **ATMs,** including one at the **National Bank** in the plateia. (Open M-Th 8am-2pm, F 8am-1:30pm.) The **police station** (☎22370 89 160 or 22370 22 966; open 24hr.) and the **OTE** (open 7am-10pm) are on Eth. Antistaseos. The **hospital** (☎22370 80 680) is a 10min. walk past the police station. For fast **Internet access,** head down Karpenisioti and turn left at the first street for the Anzonopoulos computer shop (€3 per hr.). Free Internet access is available from the **library** (M-F 4:30-9pm). The **post office** is at the bottom of Karpenisioti. (Open M-F 7:30am-2pm.) **Postal code:** 36100.

ACCOMMODATIONS. Thought there is no shortage of hotels in Karpenisi, prices aren't budget friendly, particularly on weekends and during the winter high season. The cheapest option is one of the local domatia. The tourist office lists rooms and prices. Friendly former Boston resident **Konstandinos Kousigos** ❸ offers rooms at his house at the top of a flight of stone steps behind the taxi stand. A view, private bath, and comfy beds make it feel like home. (☎22370 21 400. Doubles €30.) **Hotel Elvetia ❸,** Zinopoulou 17, has pleasant rooms with TVs, radios, phones, balconies, and a lounge area. A 4th-floor room at the front of the hotel has the best view of the mountains. (☎22370 80 111; fax 22370 80 112. Singles €25; doubles €35; family suite €52.) **Hotel Galini ❷,** Riga Feriou 3, is set back on a quiet side street; to reach it, walk down G. Tsitsara from Eth. Antistaseos and take the second right. True to its name ("serenity"), it offers quiet, comfortable rooms with balconies, TVs, phones, and private baths at very cheap rates. (☎22370 22 914; fax 22370 25 623. Singles €20; doubles €30; triples €40.)

FOOD. **Klimatria ❷**, Kosmai Etolou 25 (☎22370 22 230), 100m downhill from the top of Eth. Antistaseos, is decorated with antique local handicrafts, but a 1953 Rock-Ola American jukebox vaults the restaurant into the 20th century. The gregarious owner, whose family has owned the restaurant for over a century, will happily translate the menu for you. Excellent seasonal dishes (€4.50-7), including rabbit and rooster, are all made from local ingredients. Look for a large yellow awning. A short walk beyond Hotel Galini away from the plateia, **Taverna Panorama ❷** serves meat dishes *tisoras* (charcoal grilled) under a thick canopy of leafy vines. (Entrees €4-7.50.) Directly off the plateia, **Kitsios ❶**, Zinopoulou 13 (☎22370 25 504), soothes the sweet tooth with fresh Greek pastries (€1-1.50). To scrounge up your own meal, visit the **bakery** and large **supermarket** on Karpenisioti.

NIGHTLIFE AND ENTERTAINMENT. The afternoon and evening blend seamlessly in Karpenisi as the small cafes where young Karpenisians chat over iced coffee slowly evolve into crowded bars with hopping music. Three doors down from the plateia, mild-mannered **Peros** sheds its cafe image around midnight, serving beer with marvelous speed and efficiency. (☎22370 22 382. Beer €3; *frappé* €2. Open daily 9am-2am.) Later, head down the street to **Byzantio,** the late-night bar of choice for most young Karpenisians; pulsing beats give way to more melodic Greek songs as the night wears on. (Open daily 10pm-3am. €3 cover includes one drink.) Just past the police station (be on your best behavior) on Eth. Antiostaseos, a number of bars draw revelers out into the night. The most popular is the recently opened **Cinema Cafe.** Its breezy summer bar has great mountain views nearer the plateia. **De Facto,** has an all-Greek jukebox and outdoor seating. (☎22370 24 455. Drinks €3-3.50. Open 9am-3am.) About 1.5km south of town on the road to Koryshades, two clubs fill up on weekends with dancers who migrate down from the slopes of the city. At Karpenisi's most popular club, **Nemesis,** tourists and Karpenisians alike groove to house and trance until 2:30am. After that, it's strictly Greek music until dawn. (Drinks €3-6. €5 cover includes one drink. Open F-Sa midnight-6am.) Down the road from Nemesis, a replica stagecoach indicates the American-themed **Saloon,** where stereos blare country music, patrons slug Jack Daniel's, and dancing begins on the floor and ends up on the tables. (☎22370 24 606. Drinks €3-5.50. Open daily 10am-6am.) For live traditional Greek music, head to **Musikes Epafes,** Kosma Aitovou 17, a door down from the Klimataria restaurant, above the billiard parlor. (☎22370 25 555. Open F-Sa.) Throughout the summer, saints' days are celebrated with religious services in the mornings and revelry at night. In mid-July, the town hosts a 15-day *Yiortes Dassous* ("Celebration of the Forest") replete with exhibitions, food, and music.

MOONSHINE Ask many a taverna owner in Evritania for a taste of *tsipouro* and he'll give you a knowing wink, disappear into the back, and reappear with a chilled bottle of clear Greek moonshine. Regular old legal wine is distilled all over Evritania, using local grapes. When the grapes have been pressed, however, the farmers don't throw them away. Instead, they boil down the leftovers for a couple of days before distilling the residue in clear river water. The result is a fiery transparent alcohol that will clear your sinuses and burn your throat with a vengeance. The Greeks aren't much for rules: despite being illegal, *tsipouro* can be found at most tavernas in Evritania. Beware, though: it packs a powerful punch, and tastes a bit like wine-flavored tequila mixed with lighter fluid.

NEAR KARPENISI

Outside Karpenisi, small villages and traditional settlements beckon visitors to gorgeous rural views and hikes; old-fashioned stone houses rest on the shores of lakes while herds of goats snooze on hillsides. Hotels can be expensive in the area; domatia offer much better deals. Camping is illegal and could provoke a fine. The map of Evritania (€3.50) available at the *periptero* in Karpenisi's plateia is crucial for navigating the area.

Closed in by ominous peaks on three sides, **Koryshades** (5km southwest of Karpenisi) is a traditional, perfectly preserved Evritanian village. To get there, take the early bus from Karpenisi or hire a taxi for the short ride. Bright stone houses outfitted with elaborate wooden balconies, red slate roofs, and terraced gardens dot the hillsides. The National Council convened in 1944 in the schoolhouse in Koryshades; the site has been turned into a small **museum.** The only hotel and restaurant in the village, named simply **Koryshades** ❹ (☎22370 25 102; fax 22370 23 456) offers spectacular but expensive rooms (singles start at €40) and are happy to provide information on nearby hikes and outdoor activities. West of Karpenisi lies the village of **Klafsion** (8km away), the name of which—derived from the Greek verb "to cry"—is a tribute to the hardships endured by the townspeople when they survived a 279 BC disaster caused by Galates. The church dates from the 5th century and features an ancient mosaic floor. Most of the homes in Klafsion are inhabited by vacationing Greeks for two to three months a year. Beyond lie **East** and **West Frangista** (40km from Karpenisi), home of a fresco-covered church well worth a visit. A hometown Greek feast awaits at the village tavernas where local trout, traditional sausages, *katiki* cheese, and scrumptious country bread satisfy hungry patrons. The **Monastery of Tatarnas,** west of Frangista and 70km from Karpenisi, served as a refuge for rebels against the Turks. The extensive Byzantine art collection includes an icon of "The Lord of Glory," painted in 1350. Backpackers can take the **Trans-European Footpath E4** where it passes through Evritania on a two-day hike from Karpenisi, through the village of **Krikelo,** all the way to **Mount Oxia** in the southwestern extreme of Evritania.

MIKRO HORIO

Fifteen kilometers down the road from Karpenisi and accessible by bus (15min., €0.80) are the new and old "Little Villages," Neo and Paleo Mikro Horio. **Paleo Mikro Horio** was largely destroyed by a landslide in 1962; only a 19th-century church and the village square, consisting of five old water fountains, survived. The cool, shaded plateia overlooks terraced farmland rising from the gorge below. After the disaster, the population relocated down the hill to **Neo Mikro Horio** (pop. 250) on the slopes of **Mt. Helidona.** But they couldn't shake their bad luck: bombs scarred the new village, and occupying Nazis executed the town's 13 leading dignitaries in 1944. The route to the top of the mountain (about 3hr.) starts near the bus stop; a view of the river valleys and Kremaston Lake is the reward for the uphill trek. Lodgings range from simple, cheap domatia to expensive ski lodge-style hotels. **Taverna Nyonia** ❹ has white-walled, tiled rooms to let, with bathrooms and a small communal kitchen. (☎22370 41 393. Doubles €60). A small, narrow pathway leads through beautiful farm gardens to an outdoor taverna patio where a small menu of mostly grilled meats and salads is offered. (Entrees €5-6.) Just as you enter the village from the main road, **Horiatiko** ❸ offers good deals on rooms during low season. Colorful flowers pave the way to beautifully furnished, spacious rooms with large balconies facing out onto the mountains. Guest houses are also available to rent and are ideal for families or small groups who'd like to live in a comfortable, cozy setting. (Singles start at €30.)

MEGALO HORIO

Megalo Horio (pop. 200) is not so much a village as a handful of stone houses tossed haphazardly down an Evritanean hillside. It is an M. C. Escher utopia precariously tilted to 45 degrees. Houses are turned at improbable angles, leaning on the mountain and each other for support. Roads turn into staircases and back to roads again. As you stroll from the top of the village down, tin-roofed weather-torn huts gradually develop into sparkling mountain vacation homes. Perched midway up the hillside, the *kafeneion* tables on the plateia overlook the breathtaking gorge of the Karpenisiotis River. An enormous gnarled plane tree shades the plateia and a semi-circle of lime trees tint the summer air with the delicate scent of their blossoms. A few meters above the plateia, the main road in Megalo Horio splits in two. From the left branch begins the trail for the 3hr. climb up Mount Kaliakouda, marked clearly to the top with red blazes. The right branch curves quickly downhill and meanders past gorgeous homes where flowers fill every unused space. Take the same road to the **Folk Art Museum,** whose collection houses traditional farming equipment, a shepherd's goat-wool coat, a Revolution-era rifle, and a still for brewing *tsipouro.* (☎22370 41 502. Open F-Su 10am-2pm. Free.)

Reach Megalo Horio by the bus (7am and 1pm, €0.80) that runs from Karpenisi and through Mikro Horio. Like the rest of Evritania, Megalo Horio has a number of rooms to let scattered around the village. Cheap rooms can be hard to find during high season, however, so look around before settling somewhere. The rooms at **Petrino** ❸ are beautifully furnished with local crafts, have TVs and fireplaces, and can be economical if shared with someone else. (☎22370 41 187. Doubles €35.) The **taverna** ❷ downstairs has a wide selection of meat dishes as well as a few vegetarian options. Ask for **Maria Mahalioti** at the store (☎22370 41 263) just below the plateia, and she'll display her selection of homemade sweets, jams, honey, and sweet, fruit flavored syrup shots. Enjoy the clean mountain air, the shade of a twisted old tree, and the view of a river gorge at **Antigoni** ❷ (☎22370 41 395) in the plateia. Its staff serves sandwiches, omelettes, and Greek coffee all day.

PROUSSOS

Though small and easy to miss, Proussos is a picturesque little town, and has some of the most breathtaking views of gorges and mountainside in the Evritania region.

TRANSPORTATION. Getting to **Proussos,** 15km past Megalo Horio, is an adventure in itself; enjoy the roadside scenery and admire the KTEL driver's uncanny ability to maintain control of his vehicle as it swerves alongside steep ravines past intermittent, flimsy guardrails and shrines to drivers killed on the road. From Karpenisi, buses run Monday and Friday (5:30am, 1:30pm; €2). To catch the bus as it heads by Megalo or Mikro Horio, you'll need to walk back down to the main road or to the tiny hamlet of **Gavros.** The village climbs upward from a central plateia, which overlooks the gasp-inducing gorge below. The afternoon return bus to Karpenisi leaves Proussos at about 4pm.

ACCOMMODATIONS AND FOOD. Proussos has no hotels, but like most of the villages in Evritania, has many homes that offer domatia for fairly inexpensive prices; most are on the road through the main village. The plateia in Proussos sports many local tavernas, most of which overlook the gorge and the river below. **Proussiotissa** (☎22370 80 768) has the best location of them all, with balcony tables hanging over the valley and looking out on the monastery and clock tower. The owner cooks up local specialties like roast goat with tomato sauce (€5).

SIGHTS. Just before reaching the village, a road leads down from the statue of Karaiskakis to the serene **Monastery of the Virgin of Proussiotissa** that clings spectacularly to the cliffside. The monastery's innermost sanctuary is blasted out of the stone itself and contains a miracle-working icon of the Madonna, said to have been painted by St. Luke the Evangelist. Dress modestly (long skirt or pants, shoulders covered) to visit the monastery, where a monk will hospitably offer you a piece of *loukoumi*, a Turkish jellied candy covered in powdered sugar. In the evenings, monks' chants mingle with the sound of rushing water from the Karpenisiotis River echoing through the ravine. Above, Proussos's clock tower belts out the hour from its precarious hilltop perch. The **Castle of Karaiskakis** is a small stone fortress near the monastery; more of a crumbling tower than a castle, it now emanates an air of mystery. The dark **Black Cave,** allegedly an ancient oracle and a hideout for Greek women and children during the War for Independence, can be found along a trail that begins on the far side of Proussos, near a bridge. Bring a flashlight if you're in the mood to explore.

LAMIA Λαμια

Too busy to be concerned with its own aesthetic appeal, rarely-touristed Lamia conceals a certain charm beneath its drab appearance. The city's heart, with four central plateias connected by criss-crossing pedestrian streets, brims with energy: slickly dressed teenagers speed by on motorcycles, throngs spend their way from boutique to bakery to fast-food joint, and honking drivers do their best to slow everyone else down. But look in the shadier spots, where old Greek men argue for hours, and you'll discover that not everyone moves at such a breakneck pace—different lifestyles coexist easily in the city.

Now a jumping off point for travelers bound for northern or central Greece, Lamia was a key strategic town during the War of Independence and became the border gateway for the newly independent Greece in 1884. A snappy archaeological museum high up within the *kastro* walls, a nightlife scene that never seems to go to bed, and the beautifully tended gardens of Agios Loukas make a brief stop in Lamia worthwhile.

TRANSPORTATION

With five intercity bus stations and one local station, Lamia is a singularly inconvenient transportation hub. Directions to the bustling heart of the city depend on where your bus or train pulls in. The local **train station** is on **Kostantinopoulos;** head east (left as you face the tracks) and turn left on **Satovriandou,** which runs north-west to **Pl. Parkou,** one of the city's four central plateias (the southeast corner of the quadrangle they form). From the **bus station** serving Karpenisi on **Botsari** head east (right facing away from station) half a block to Satovriandou and turn left. If arriving from Athens or Thessaloniki, Satovriandou is just to your left as you face away from the station; turn right to the city center. Buses from Delphi pull in on the west side of **Thermopylon** while those from Larisa, Patras, Trikala, or Halkida stop just off Thermopylon on the east side. Walk uphill on Thermopylon, crossing the railroad tracks, until it dead-ends into **Kapodistriou,** where a left brings you to Pl. Parkou. Buses from Volos, Agia Marina, and Raches pull in on **Rozaki Angeli,** to the east of the city center. Facing away from the station, cross the miniscule triangular park and turn right on Kapodistriou.

Buses: From the largest station (☎22310 51 345 or 22310 51 346), south of the town center and left off Satovriandou at Papakiriazi 27, buses run to **Athens** (3hr., every hr. 5am-9pm, €13.30) and **Thessaloniki** (4hr.; 9am, 3:15pm; €18.80). Take the Athens bus and ask to be let off at **Agios Kostantinos** (45min., €3.10) for the nearest ferry hub for the Sporades. The station for buses to **Karpenisi** (1½hr., 5 per day 7am-9pm, €4.55) and the Evritania region is at Botsari 3 (☎22310 28 955), right off of Satovriandou. At the end of Satovriandou, heading south, is the local station (☎22310 51 348) at Konstantinopoulos 2, which runs buses to **Thermopylae** (15min., 5 per day 8:30am-4:35pm, €1.30), among other small locales. The station for **Delphi** (2hr., 3 per day 10:40am-7pm, €5.90) is at Thermopylon 58 (☎22310 35 494); head along Kapodistriou from Pl. Parkou and turn right on Thermopylon. The Thessaly station (☎22310 22 802) is a little farther down Thermopylon and to the left at its intersection with Nikopoleos. To: **Halkida** (2½hr.; 12:45, 7:45pm; €9.95); **Larisa** (2hr., 3 per day 11am-6pm, €8.80); **Patras** (4hr.; 12:30, 7:30pm; €11.85); **Trikala** (2hr., 6 per day 9:45am-7:45pm, €6.20). The Volos station, Rosaki Angeli 69 (☎22310 22 627), down Kapodistriou, runs buses to: the beaches of **Agia Marina** (20min.; every hr. 8am-9pm; €0.90); **Raches** (5min., 7 per day 9am-10pm, €2.10); and **Volos** (2hr.; Su-F 9am, 3pm, Sa 9am; €8.30).

Local buses: Buses marked "Stavros" (Σταυρος) also make stops at **Lionokladi**, departing frequently at the corner of Drosopolou and Hatzopolou streets at Pl. Parkou.

Trains: Trains run to **Athens** (6am, 5:25pm) from the town station, Konstantinopoulos 1 (☎22310 22 990), across from the local buses. **Lionokladi Station** (☎22310 06 161) runs trains to **Thessaloniki** (3¾hr., 8 per day 9:28am-3am, €9.25) and **Athens** (3½hr., 7 per day 10:15am-7:20pm, €6.90). Take the local bus (10min., 13 per day 9:10am-7:10pm, €1.20) from the OTE office, Averof 28. Walk down E. Venizelou from the southwest corner of Pl. Parkou to the 3rd right onto Averof.

ORIENTATION AND PRACTICAL INFORMATION

Just inland off the Maliakos Gulf and 160km north of Athens, Lamia's tangle of streets climbs gently to a northwesterly ridge, crowned by the **Kastro** in the north. The city sprawls outward from the roughly rectangular arrangement of its four central plateias. Southeastern **Pl. Parkou** is broad, crowded, and lined with banks. Maps of Lamia are posted at its northern edge. From Pl. Parkou's northeast corner, past the National Bank, **Kolokotroni** leads north to leafy and mellow **Pl. Laou,** filled with *kafeneia* and currently torn up by construction. West from Pl. Parkou up **Karagiannopolou** is sleepy, spacious **Pl. Diakou.** Head up Riga Feriaou in the northwest corner of Pl. Parkou to reach pulsing **Pl. Eleftherias,** home to Lamia's trendiest nightlife. Pl. Eleftherias connects with Pl. Diakou via **Diakou** on its south side and with Pl. Laou via **Kounoupi** on the east. On the north side of Pl. Eleftherias, Lamia's largest **church** and the **regional prefecture** (town hall) face each other on the corner of **Ipsilandon.** A network of small streets including **Rozaki Angeli** and **Karaiskaki** interlace the squares and burst with small cafes, shops, and bakeries.

Tourist office: Pl. Laou 3 (☎22310 30 065; fax 22310 30 066), next to the Hotel Neon Astron. The friendly, English-speaking staff can provide you with an excellent map of the city. Open M-F 7am-2:30pm.

Banks: Pl. Parkou teems with banks, including the **National Bank** on the corner of Kapodistriou with a 24hr. **ATM.** Open M-Th 8am-2pm, F 8am-1:30pm.

Police: (☎22310 22 331), on Patroklou, one street below Pl. Parkou off Satovriandou. Little English spoken. Open 24hr.

THE HIDDEN DEAL

ZIOGAS BAKERY

In a city where cheap eats from hamburgers to souvlaki sticks can be found on every corner, one establishment leads the budget-friendly (if not diet-friendly) pack. **Ziogas Bakery** offers quality snacks at the lowest prices in town, and they've been doing it longer than anyone else. The bakery opened its doors for the first time in 1918, and the Ziogas family took over in 1932. Now it can claim three generations of experience. Nick Ziogas, the current owner, has not betrayed his family legacy; his father and grandfather sold the same variety of savory breads and pastries at the same low prices (from €0.30 up).

If you're looking for something different, opt for one of the establishment's more recent innovations, a tasty mini-pizza complete with ham, cheese, and just the right amount of sauce. If that's not enough to meet the needs of your stomach, go for a piece of cheese pie (€0.60). The bakery isn't just the place to go during the evening pre-party–the chocolate croissants (€0.90) are the perfect treats to brighten up the morning or send you to bed with a satisfied sweet-tooth.

Look for the bright yellow signs on Kounoupi, between Pl. Elethrias and Pl. Laou. ☎22310 22 204. Open all day.

Hospital: (☎22310 56 100 or 22310 56 200). North of the city. Open 24hr.

OTE: On the west side of Pl. Eleftherias. Open daily 7am-2:40pm, 5:30-9:30pm.

Internet Access: Internet Cafe, Ipsilandon 6 (☎22310 46 315), just north of Pl. Eleftherias. €4.40 per hr.; *frappé* €2.50. Open 9am-3am.

Post office: (☎22310 23 237; fax 22310 33 727), on Pl. Diakou. Offers Poste Restante. Open M-F 7:30am-8pm. **Postal Code:** 35100.

ACCOMMODATIONS

Few tourists or budget travelers see more than the bus station on their way through Lamia, so hotels are scarce and expensive. **Thermopylae Hotel ❸,** Rozaki Angeli 36, two blocks east of Pl. Laou, has 15 rooms that are small but clean and comfortable, including TV, phone, A/C, and private bath. (☎22310 26 393 or 22310 21 366. Singles €25; doubles €33; triples €40.) **Hotel Athena ❸,** Rozaki Angeli 41, has cozy rooms featuring wooden floors, private baths, TV, A/C and balconies. (☎22310 20 700 or 22310 27 700. Singles €25; doubles €35; triples €40.) The rooms at **Hotel Elena ❸,** Thermopylon 6, are more spacious and have it all—private baths, TVs, A/C, phones and balconies. (☎22310 25 025 or 22310 27 175. Breakfast €5. Singles €35; doubles €42; triples €50.) If you're truly strapped for cash, **Hotel Neon Astron ❷** has the cheapest digs in town, but be prepared for dirty rooms close to the noisy street. (☎22310 22 246. Singles €19.25; doubles €25.30.)

FOOD

Lamia is a diner's paradise: virtually every street and side alley is crammed with pizza joints, stands hawking souvlaki and gyros, *ouzeria*, tavernas, pastry shops, and coffee bars. For fresh fruits and veggies, head to the **markets** along Rozaki Angeli and Othonos, both off Pl. Laou. **Ouzo Melathron ❶,** off Pl. Laou on Aristoteli (the stairs on the north side), offers up a variety of grilled specialties in a romantic courtyard away from the bustle of the plateias. The *pilino*, pork with ham, cheese, mushrooms, and tomato sauce (€4.70), is worth a try. (☎22310 31 502. Entrees €4-7. Open daily 1-5pm, 9pm-1am.) **Aman Aman ❷,** on Androutsou (the alley to the right on Kounoupi coming from Pl. Laou), serves tasty *mezedes* (€3-6.50). "Aman," which means "mercy" in Turkish, is the opening wail to many of the *rembetika* that the local intellectual crowd gathers to hear. (Open 9am-12:30am.)

SIGHTS

KASTRO. The imposing remains of the Kastro fortifications loom eerily over the city in nighttime illumination. Built in the Classical period, it has undergone many renovations under Greece's various rulers, including the Romans, Franks, Catalans, and Ottomans. Before Greece's 1884 annexation of Thessaly and Domokos, Lamia's Kastro served as the core of the country's border defenses. The barracks building, built by King Otto in 1880, was used until World War II. It now serves as a spacious and well-organized **Archaeological Museum** displaying finds from the Neolithic to Roman periods found in tombs outside Lamia. Aside from the numerous ceramic figurines and amphoras, highlights include the earliest preserved vase depicting a naval battle, a large engraving depicting a woman offering thanks to Artemis after safely giving birth, and a fearsome collection of rusty weaponry. *(To reach the Kastro, head east out of Pl. Parkou on Kapodistriou and make the 2nd left onto Amalias. Walk up the hill and cross Eklision when Amalias dead-ends to walk up a stone stairpath. Turn right and follow the road at the top of the stairs, with the Kastro on your left. ☎22310 29 992. Castle open Tu-Su 8:30am-2:30pm during the summer. Museum Tu-Su 8:30am-3pm. €2, students with ID and under 18 free.)*

GARDENS OF AGIOS LOUKAS. The way to the Gardens of Agios Loukas (atop Agios Loukas hill) begins at the top of Pl. Diakou behind a gloriously posed **Statue of Athanasios Diakos,** his sword broken in battle. A War of Independence hero, he was burned to death in Lamia by the Turks in 1821. Continue up the steps behind Athanasios and you'll reach the gardens. Cool hilltop breezes and the shade of mulberry trees provide welcome relief after the steep ascent; plunk yourself down on a bench for a breather or take a short stroll down stone paths lined with rosebushes. On occasional summer evenings, live music fills the gardens.

NIGHTLIFE AND ENTERTAINMENT

Young people from the Lamia area congregate around Pl. Eleftherias every night, zooming in on motorbikes and crowding around the bars and cheap gyro stands. For those looking to dance, there are plenty of clubs; for a more sedentary night out, find a table at one of the bars in northeast Pl. Eleftherias. On summer nights, most intrepid partygoers head to the seashore at **Raches** or **Agia Marina** in the countryside. These clubs are best reached by private vehicle—a taxi to the most popular clubs, **Bojo** at Raches or **Hakuna Matata** at Agia Marina, will cost €10-20 until midnight, when the rates double. Slightly closer to Lamia, but still requiring a taxi, are **Vorio, Caramela,** and **Paradise.** The **Municipal Theatre** (☎22310 33 325) on Ipsilandon, past the Internet Cafe, offers a year-long program of plays, music, and movies. Visit their offices in the **movie theater** across the street.

Venezia (☎22310 46 525), on Dikou between Pl. Diakou and Pl. Eleftherias, is *the* place to see and be seen among Lamia's cosmopolitan youth. Put on your flashiest garb and make your way through the clutter of motorbikes on the curb. Beer €3.50, drinks €5. Open 9am-late.

Aroma Musicafe (☎22310 36 808), next door to Venezia, vies fiercely with its neighbor for the title of Best in Show. Beer is €5 and cocktails are €7, but if you really want to turn some heads, drop the €100 for the Dom Perignon.

Splendid (☎22310 52 726), on Ipsilandon, off Pl. Eleftherias. This ultra-trendy night spot serves beer (€3.50) and drinks (€4.50) to the hip and hot until 3am.

DAYTRIP FROM LAMIA

THERMOPYLAE Θερμοπυλες

Take the bus from Lamia's local station (40min., 6 per day 8:30am-4:30pm, €1.30) and ask to be let off at the baths (BAN-yo), not the village of Thermopylae. To return, walk 1.5km to the village and catch the bus there.

More a highway roadstop than a destination in itself, Thermopylae (18km south of Lamia) is richer in history than anything else. As the gateway to southern Greece, Thermopylae's strategic location has made it a prime target for invading armies for thousands of years. **Leonidas** and his army of 300 Spartans fought to their heroic deaths here in 480 BC, holding back Xerxes's vast Persian army—estimated by the exaggeration-prone Herodotus to be five million strong—long enough for the united city-states to consolidate their power for victories at Salamis and Plataea. More recently, both the Ottomans and the Nazis launched fierce attacks at the straits. Sulfurous **hot springs** originate in the mountains above and attract visitors suffering from many different ailments, including rheumatism, arthritis, gynecological complaints, and respiratory illnesses. There is both a small swimming pool (€4) and numerous private bathtubs (€4) that are filled with the 42-44°C waters. (☎22310 30 065. Open daily 6am-1:30pm.) Legend holds that the healing power of Thermopylae's waters once helped Hercules regain his strength.

From the hot springs parking lot, walk down the dirt path lined with eucalyptus and oleanders, swarming with pale yellow butterflies in summer. Continue through a highway underpass and follow the path, turning right on a paved road that crosses the stream of spring water. The road leads to a highway rest stop consisting of a **plaque** commemorating the battles in Greece and Crete during World War II, the **Monument to the Thespians,** and the **Statue of Leonidas.** The defiant inscription on the statue reads *"Molon Labe"* ("Come and get it"). Across the highway from the statue is the **Archaeological Site,** where you can scramble around a network of trails, see the ruins of a Classical-era wall, and catch the view from craggy outlook points. Just beyond the Leonidas monument a dirt road runs between an olive grove and the highway to Thermopylae village, consisting of a deserted square with a bone-dry fountain and some crumbling benches. Flag down one of the frequent buses to **Lamia** (€1.30) here at the rusty **bus stop.**

AGIOS KONSTANTINOS Αγιος Κωνσταντινος

Agios Kostantinos is situated at the meeting point of the mountainous mainland and the Aegean. As the closest port to Athens with ferries to the Sporades, it serves as a gateway for foreigners and Greeks taking to the sea. It may not warrant a long stay, but the small town's charms, from its cafe-lined plateia to the tile-roofed Church of Agios Konstantinos, make the wait for ferry or bus easy to bear.

PRACTICAL INFORMATION. Arriving by ferry, the **bus station** (☎22350 32 223) is about 150m to the left along the waterfront. **Buses** go to: **Athens** (2½hr., 15 per day 5:45am-10pm, €10.20); **Lamia** (45min., every hr. 7:30am-7:30pm and 8:45-11:45pm, €3.10); and **Thessaloniki** (4hr.; 7am, 2pm; €21.85). The pier, immediately seaward of the plateia, serves both **ferries** and Flying Dolphins (☎22350 31 874). Buy your tickets at the right side of the plateia (facing inland). Two high speed ferries (prices and schedules vary depending on the season) leave daily for **Skiathos** (2hr., €20.20) and **Skopelos** (3hr., €26.90). Two ferries leave each week for **Alonnisos** (5½hr., €13.40). One to five **Flying Dolphins** go daily to: **Alonnisos** (2¾hr.,

€26.90); **Skiathos** (1½hr., €20.30); and **Skopelos** (2½hr., €26.80). Check departure times posted outside of the ticket offices or call ahead (☎22350 32 444 or 22350 32 445; fax 22350 32 234). **Taxis** line up on the opposite side of the church from the water (☎22350 31 850). The **port police** (☎22350 31 920), along the harbor, can help with ferry schedules. Facing seaward from the plateia, a right-hand turn toward the bus station takes you past the National Bank, with a 24hr. **ATM.** (Open M-Th 8am-2pm, F 8am-1:30pm.) A left turn from the plateia takes you past the **OTE** (open M-F 8am-3:10pm) and a sign for the **post office,** 20m inland on a street just parallel to the park. (Open M-F 7:30am-2pm.) **Postal code:** 35006.

ACCOMMODATIONS AND FOOD. Accommodations in Agios Kostantinos are somewhat limited. The first in the strip of hotels along the water to the right of the plateia (facing inland), **Hotel Olga** is both classy and reasonably priced. Rooms have A/C, phones, TVs, and views from private balconies. (☎22350 32 266. Singles €21-24; doubles €30-36; triples €36-43. ❷) In the center of town, **Hotel Poulia,** on Thermopylon to the right of the plateia facing inland, features small rooms with varying levels of amenities, from spartan singles to the works: TVs, A/C, and private baths. (☎22350 31 663. Singles €15-20; doubles €20-30; triples €35. ❷) You can devour toothsome souvlaki (€1-1.50), play backgammon, and do some quality people-watching just past the main plateia. In the morning, warm bread and pastries from **Aggelozumoton Asteriou,** the *artopolia* next door to Hotel Poulia, ease the pain of early-morning ferry departures. ❶

THESSALY Θεσσαλια

Thessaly provides travelers with a rare mix of the mundane and the ethereal. The region is the earthly anchor to the transcendent Meteora monasteries; at the same time, it harbors some of Greece's drabber cities. Medea supposedly dropped her witch's potions in Thessaly after returning here with Jason from Colchis (modern Georgia), and the legend won the region a reputation for sorcery and magical plants in ancient times. Thessaly's plains were once home to farmers who tended sheep and goats in summer before returning home to fish from the waters of the Pinios River. Though traditional farming has given way to modern methods, you can still buy a field guide and gather herbs off the mountain slopes or buy them in villages. In these out-of-the-way places to the north of Karpenisi and in the green Pelion Peninsula, you'll find little English and much genuine hospitality, folk songs, and reverence for all things *hiropitios* (hand-made; "poetry of the hands").

VOLOS Βολος

Volos looms large in some of ancient Greece's best-loved myths. **Jason and the Argonauts** set sail from Volos on their quest for the Golden Fleece, a legend the city won't let its visitors forget: two important streets and half a dozen hotels are named after the voyaging Argonauts. A century ago, Volos was a quiet hamlet on the Pagasitic Gulf. But after the 1922 population exchange (see p. 12), ethnic Greek refugees from Turkey invigorated the port town with their love for carousing: Volos quickly became famous for the *ouzeria* that popped up all over town. Volos is a fast-growing industrial center and transportation hub, but on the short waterfront walk eastward from the bus station toward the beach, the cranes and oil tankers quickly become a memory. Two of the four main roads running parallel through the city are pedestrian avenues. Come nightfall, strolling couples fill the harborside, fruit vendors hawk their sweet produce, and dozens of cafes and seafood restaurants push tables up to the water.

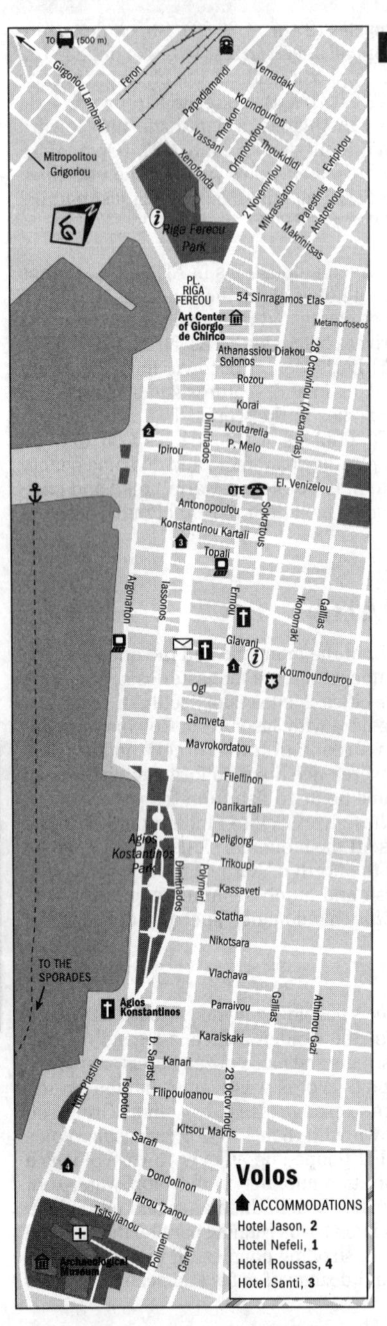

TRANSPORTATION

Ferries: To: **Alonnisos** (5hr., 1 per day, €12.30); **Glossa** (3hr., 1 per day, €10.30); **Skiathos** (2¼hr., 2-3 per day, €9.20); **Skopleos** (3½hr., 1-2 per day, €11.30). Ferries for the more distant islands of **Tinos, Paros, Santorini,** and **Crete (Iraklion)** are less frequent. Several waterfront agencies sell tickets; **Falcon Tours** (☎24210 21 626 or 24210 25 688), which also sells Flying Dolphin tickets, is by the docks.

Flying Dolphins: 3 per day to: **Alonnisos** (2¾hr.; 9:30am, 1:15, 7:30pm; €24.60) via **Glossa** (1½hr., €20.60); **Skiathos** (1¼hr., €12.30); **Skopelos** (2½hr., €22.50). Tickets available at any of the ticket agencies near the ferry pier.

Buses: The **bus station** (☎24210 33 254 or 24210 25 527), is in the Old Town, all the way at the end of Lambraki. To: **Athens** (4½hr., 11 per day 6am-10pm, €17.75); **Larisa** (1hr., 14 per day 6am-9:30pm, €3.65); **Thessaloniki** (3hr., 7per day 5:15am-8:30pm, €11.90); and **Trikala** (2½hr., 5 per day 6:30am-9:30pm, €8.90). Buses to Mt. Pelion Peninsula run to: **Makrynitsa** via **Portaria** (45min., M-F 10 per day 6:15am-9:30pm, €0.95); **Milies** (1hr., 6 per day 6am-7:30pm, €1.65); **Tsagarada** (1½hr., 3 per day 5am-3:30pm, €2.90); and other destinations. Inquire at the bus station or tourist office; most villages have daily service and can be reached in less than 3hr. Service is reduced on weekends and in winter.

Trains: The **station** (☎24210 24 056 or 24210 28 555) is 1 block west of the tourist office. From town, turn right at the first street past the tourist office. Walk 2-3min. down the road parallel to the track. To: **Larisa** (1hr., 13 per day 5:45am-9:10pm, €2.15). For **Athens** and **Thessaloniki,** passengers must travel to Larisa and change trains.

Taxis: ☎24210 27 777.

Car Rental: Avis, Argonafton 41 (☎24210 20 849; fax 24210 22 849), rents mopeds from €18 per day and cars from €55 per day. **European Car Rental,** Iasonos 83 (☎24210 36 238; fax 24210 24 192). Rentals from €50 per day.

ORIENTATION AND PRACTICAL INFORMATION

Volos's **bus station** lies west of town on **Lambraki,** an easy 15min. walk from the city and the waterfront. This main road, which leads from the bus station to town, runs past the train station and **Riga Fariou Park.** Lambraki splits at a fountain to become **Dimitriados** on the left and **Iasonos** on the right; both run parallel to **Argonafton** on the waterfront. The intersecting roads leading away from the harbor are lined with various hotels and other services like banks, pharmacies, and the post office. A walk along the waterfront, about 10min. from the ferry docks past a long park, brings you to the large **Church of Agios Konstantinos,** easily visible jutting out into the harbor. Here, Argonafton and Dimitriados join to become **Nik. Plastira,** which leads to the hospital, the archaeological museum, and various restaurants before ending at the **beach. Ermou,** the next street inland after Dimitriados and running parallel through the city, is a pedestrian street lined with shops selling women's clothes, shoes, and the occasional icon. Ermou leads to an open plateia containing the **Church of Agios Nikolaos.**

Tourist Office: Koumoundourou 31, (☎24210 20 273). Walk east along Ermou with the sea on your right and take a left onto Koumoundourou; it's on the left. Ask for information about Volos and the Pelion Peninsula. Maps available. Open M-F 8am-2:30pm.

Banks: All major banks, including **National Bank** (☎24210 23 382), **Agricultural Bank** (☎24210 23 411 or 24210 54 030), and **Bank of Greece** (☎24210 23 442) on Iasonos. Most offer **currency exchange** (M-Th 8am-2pm, F 8am-1:30pm) and **ATMs.** There's also a **Citibank** on the corner of Argonafton and El. Venizelou with a 24hr. **ATM.**

Police: (☎24210 39 061). Open 24hr.

Tourist Police: 28 Octovriou 179 (☎24210 39 057). Locals still call the street by its former name, "Alexandras." Open daily 8am-9pm.

Hospital: ☎24210 27 531, next to the museum on the eastern waterfront. Open 24hr.

Telephone: OTE, on the corner of El. Venizelou and Sokratous, across from the fruit market. Open 7:30am-3pm

Internet Access: Magic Cafe, Argonafton 56 (☎24210 20 992), in a game arcade, has 25 terminals and a printer. €3.50 per hr.; printing €0.29 per page for black-and-white, €0.88 for color. **Diavlos Info Cafe,** Topali 14 (☎24210 25 363), off Dimitriados, offers cheaper, slower access. €1.50 per hr. Open 10am-3pm and 5-10pm.

Post Office: At the intersection of Dimitria and Ag. Nikolau. Open M-F 7:30am-8pm. Poste Restante available. **Postal code:** 38001.

ACCOMMODATIONS

Volos' hotels vary little in size, location, appeal, or amenities, and almost all are quite expensive for the financially constrained traveler. Most of the cheaper options are clustered along the waterfront or on the small streets that lead away from the harbor. Wave a student ID in the air and ask for a simple room *(aplo domatio)* for a small discount.

Hotel Jason, P. Melo 1 (☎24210 26 075; fax 24210 26 975), easy to find on the waterfront, across from the ferry dock. Most of the gleaming, white rooms are filled with light and have balconies overlooking the waterfront. All have phones, baths, fans, and TVs. Singles €23; doubles €35; triples €45. ❷

Hotel Nefeli, Koumoundourou 10 (☎24210 30 211 or 24210 30 213; fax 24240 35 313; ababis@kentavros.gr). Very nice rooms with smooth wood flooring, yellow walls and wood furniture. A/C, TVs, phones, balconies, and spotless baths with tubs. Singles €33; doubles €44; triples €50. ❸

Hotel Roussas, Iatrou Tzanou 1 (☎24210 21 732; fax 24210 22 987), on the corner of Plastira and Iatrou Tzanou, midway between Church of Ag. Konstantinos and the beach. Look for the purple balconies. In a quieter area of town, the hotel features rooms with neat blue trim, baths, phone, A/C, and TV. Singles €25; doubles €32; triples €38. ❸

Hotel Santi, Topali 13 (☎24210 33 341; fax 24210 33 343), off Argonafton. Basic, dimly-lit rooms with green linoleum floors and pink walls. All rooms come with baths, TVs, phones, A/C, and tiny balconies. Singles €27; doubles €45; triples €52. ❸

FOOD

A **supermarket** on Iasonos, one block up from the ferry dock, and a **farmer's market** along Lambraki, on the way to the bus station, can provide provisions for a seaside picnic. The plentiful *ouzeria* and *tsipouradika* along Volos's waterfront are the town's saving grace. They specialize in fresh seafood and *spetsofai* (spicy sausages) and are packed with locals by mid-afternoon.

Klasico (☎24210 32 891), on Argonafton by the ferry docks, specializes in seafood but offers up more exotic options like fried octopus and goat soup. If you're especially daring, try the squid stuffed with cheese. Pricey but worth it. Entrees €4.50-14. ❸

Rotonda, Plastira 15 (☎24210 34 973), past the Church of Ag. Konstantinos on the eastern edge of town near Hotel Roussas. Specializing in fresh fish, served whole, Rotonda offers delicious calamari *psito* and swordfish souvlaki. Walk into the kitchen to pick your critter, which they'll grill up fresh. Entrees €5.50-9. ❷

Ristorante La Gondola (☎24210 39 139), next to Goody's on the waterfront. Serves up delicious pastas and pizzas as well as other Italian favorites. Entrees €5-13.50. ❷

SIGHTS

The **Archaeological Museum,** Athonassaki 1, a 20min. walk along the water from the ferry docks, houses tidbits from the later Paleolithic era through the Roman period in a lovely Neoclassical mansion. Check out the painted grave *steles* from ancient Demetrias in Room 4 and the rather morbid reconstructed tombs in Room 6. The panoply of miniature Neolithic objects in Room 3 includes collections of figurines, seals, spindle wheels, bits of jewelry, carbonized seeds, and small tools of bone and stone. (☎24210 25 285. Open Tu-Su 8:30am-3pm. €2, students and seniors €1, EU students free.) Inquire here to pick up English pamphlets with information on the nearby archaeological sites at **Dimini** and **Sesklo.** Sesklo is the oldest known settlement in Thessaly, with the oldest acropolis in Greece; the sites represent two of the oldest sites in the region: Dimini dates from 4000 BC, and Sesklo from 6500 BC. The **Art Center of Giorgio de Chirico,** Metamorphoseos 3, around the corner from Hotel Ialkos, showcases Greek landscape painting, accompanied by the racket of violins from the music school next door. The center features a collection of monotypes, lithographs, and copper prints reaching back to the Ottomans. The works of adopted Italian native and surrealist Giorgio de Chirico are upstairs, in a special collection only accessible in the morning. (☎24210 31 701. Open M-F 10am-1pm and 6-9pm, Sa 10am-1pm, Su 6-9pm. Free.) The **Kitsos Makris Museum,** in Kitsos's own home at Afendoli 50 (a.k.a. Kitsos Makris 50), includes works by folk painters **Theophilos** (see p. 21) and **Christopoulos,** as well as Byzantine icons, pottery, and wood carvings. (☎24210 37 119. Open M-F 8:30am-2pm, Su 10am-2pm. Free.)

NIGHTLIFE AND ENTERTAINMENT

The waterfront turns into a hive of activity at night, with cafes spilling revelers into the streets. In the quiet morning or afternoon, you'll wonder how the thousands of tables that stretch for half a kilometer down the waterfront are ever as packed as they are at night. The young crowd congregates at **Cafe Memory** and **Cafe Magic,** side by side on Argonafton, chatting over the loud music and pings of arcade games. A few doors down, **Lirikon** is a little more mellow; the focus here is sports on the two big screen TVs. By the museum and the beach, east-side bars thump with pounding disco beats and lots of tight black pants. **Ammos** and **Yiousouri,** side by side on the beachfront across from Rotonda, alternate between pulsing pop, house, and disco. (Beers €3-4; cocktails €4. Open nightly.) Some weekend night-spots in Volos, including **Psigeia,** are near the bus station. In late July and August, Volos hosts a **festival** in Riga Feriou Park with concerts and theater.

MOUNT PELION PENINSULA Ορος Πηλιο

Way back before propriety, the Pelion Peninsula was home to a group of rather rowdy centaurs. These mythical half-men, half-horses, well known for their enormous sex drives, had their way with whatever hot, young nymphette they could find. Chiron, a healer and tutor to Achilles, settled in Pelion despite its citizens; its abundant supply of over 1700 medicinal herbs lured him to the region. This plant variety stems from the peninsula's cool, moist climate, appreciated today by tourists tired of the scorching sun. Over the years, the mountains of Pelion have protected the area from invasion. While the rest of Greece groaned under Ottoman rule, the peninsula was a virtually autonomous center of Greek nationalism.

MAKRYNITSA Μακρυνιτσα

In Makrynitsa, one of Pelion's most beautiful villages, a wide flagstoned path bends around well preserved *archondika* (mansions) to one stunning lookout point after another. Thanks to its designation by the European Community as a protected traditional settlement, the town's roads are closed to cars. While this may bring peace and quiet within the town, the outskirts are left in traffic and tour bus gridlock. On the plateia, five immense, age-old trees form a dome of green overhead, keeping the square in perpetual shade. Nicknamed "the balcony of Pelion," the town overlooks the Pagasitic Gulf like a box seat in a giant opera house. At nightfall, the valley fills with deep indigo, broken only by the shimmer of city lights from Volos far below.

ORIENTATION AND PRACTICAL INFORMATION. Makrynitsa is accessible by daily buses from **Volos** (45min., 9 per day 6:15am-8:45pm), which twist their way up the mountainside and through the neighboring village of **Portaria.** From the bus turn-around, take a short walk up the hill to the town parking lot, where a low road (17 Martiou) and a high road lead to the plateia. The low road passes various shops purveying both tourist kitsch and local medicinal and kitchen herbs. The high road begins with a steep flight of stone steps and runs past the village **clock tower** and the **Kimisi Theotokou church.** In Portaria one can catch buses to other Pelion destinations, including the beaches at **Agios Yiannis** and **Milopotamos.** A **tourist information booth** (☎24280 90 150), on the side of the road leading to the village just after the bus stop, offers helpful maps and advice on touring the area. (Open Sa-Su only.) A **mailbox** and **payphones** are readily available in the plateia. 24hr. **ATMs,** a **post office,** and a **police station** (☎24280 99 105) can also be found in Portaria, a 20min. walk from the parking lot along the mountain road.

ACCOMMODATIONS AND FOOD. Since Makrynitsa has been designated a traditional settlement, staying here will cost an arm and a leg. The financially constrained should stay in Volos and save by making Makrynitsa a daytrip, or stay in the neighboring town of Portaria, where several homes offer domatia that won't clean out your wallet. **Hotel Achilles ❸**, on the right just before you reach the plateia via the low road, has wood-panelled walls and red-tiled floors covered with colorful mats. Rooms have TVs, phones, and basic bathrooms; some have balconies. (☎24280 99 177; fax 24280 99 986. Singles €30; doubles €40; triples €50.) On the north side of Portaria's plateia, two adjacent accommodations, **Hotel Pelia ❸** (☎24280 99 290; singles €40; doubles €50) and **Hotel Filoxenia ❸** (☎24280 99 160; singles €35; doubles €45), offer rooms perched atop the immense flower-filled patio below. Both hotels have TVs, baths, and include breakfast in the room price.

In Makrynitsa, a number of small restaurants offer outdoor dining and spectacular views from elevated verandas. Most notable is **Galini ❷**, which overlooks the plateia from the north end, next to the large fountain. (☎24280 99 256. Open 9am-midnight.) Here sentimental Greek tunes inundate the ears while patrons feast on *spetsofai* (spicy sausage) and rabbit stew. Across the way, **Pantheon ❷** (☎24280 99 143) monopolizes the spectacular view of the Pagasitic Gulf. Tables for two against the railing provide a romantic setting to sip a *frappé* and while away an afternoon. For dinner, the *moschari* and *kotopoulo kokkonisto* (braised veal and chicken, respectively) are equally delicious. (Entrees €4-7.)

SIGHTS. Makrynitsa's **Museum of Folk Art and the History of Pelion** lies down a path that begins to the left of the church in the plateia. Follow the signs about 75m down the windy path. The curator conducts tours of the authentic clothes, scabbards, and folk art. Housed in a converted 1844 mansion with a gorgeous view down the mountainside, the museum highlights old *tsipouro* stills, a collection of 16th- and 17th-century Bibles, and paintings by **Christopoulos,** all of which depict ships, gorgons, and sundry sea-related subjects. (☎24280 99 505. Open Tu-Su 10am-2pm and 6-10pm. €2.) In the plateia, cafe **O Theophilos** contains a somewhat dim wall mural painted by folk artist Theophilos himself (see p. 21). Remarkable **churches** include the one-room **Church of Agios Yiannis the Baptist** in the main plateia and the peaceful, still-functioning church of **Kimisi Theotokou,** which once housed the *krifto skolio*, a secret school that taught the forbidden Greek language during the Ottoman era. If you've ever wondered what it must be like to live inside a tree trunk, Makrynitsa is well equipped to give you some idea. Just by the door or the main church in the plateia stands a tall, leafy tree with a hollowed out trunk and a handy opening that lets you slip in and out.

The town's churches remain open at the whim of their caretakers; early to mid-morning and evenings are your most likely opportunities for a visit. From the main parking lot, the narrow road leads steeply uphill to the **Monastery of Agios Gerasimos** (a 20min. walk). The view alone is worth the trip. (Open 7am-noon and 4-6pm.) Sneak a peek at the town's old houses—stained glass lanterns, false painted windows, and symbols to protect against evil spirits festoon the outer walls.

LARISA Λαρισα

Seemingly uninterested in tourism, Larisa receives very few foreign visitors each year; its many hotels are mostly occupied by wedding parties, business conventions, and farmers' unions taking advantage of the town's central location. Nonetheless, Larisa is a pleasant place to get stranded in while traveling through central Greece. The town invites you to stroll through the elegant, tree-lined central plateias and their pedestrian sidestreets to find chic cafes and bars. Window shop at trendy boutiques, explore the partially excavated ancient theater, or dance the transit-hub blues away at one of the packed discos outside of town. Bearing the dubious distinction of being Greece's hottest city (temperature-wise), Larisa is a ghost town on steamy summer Sundays when folks head east to the beach; on these days you can hear backgammon pieces shuffle in the *kafeneia* as you walk down the empty sidewalks.

TRANSPORTATION

Buses: (☎2410 537 777). The main **station** is 150m north of Pl. Laou at Olympou and Georgiadou. Buses to: **Athens** (4¼hr., 6 per day 7am-midnight, €20.35); **Thessaloniki** (2hr.; 13 per day 6am-7:30pm, fewer Sa-Su; €10.50); **Volos** (1hr.; 14 per day M-F 6am-9:30pm, €3.65); **Kastoria** (4hr., 3 per day 7am-1pm, €12.50); **Ioannina** (4hr., 2 per day 9:30am and 3pm, €12.05). 2 counters at either end of the terminal sell tickets for different destinations. Buses for **Trikala** (1hr., 20 per day 5:45am-8:30pm, €4.05) and **Karditsa** (4hr., 11 per day 6am-8:15pm, €4.20) leave from a second station on Iroön Polytechniou (☎2410 610 214); to get there, head south on Olympou to Plateia Laou, where Panagouli begins. Continue south on Panagouli and turn right at the 5-way intersection. Walk 600m to the gas station/bus stop on your left.

Trains: (☎2410 236 250), at the end of Paleologou: head south on Panagouli and make a soft left (*not* sharp left) onto Paleologou at the 5-way intersection. The station is on the south side of the small park. **Intercity** express trains run to: **Athens** (4hr., 7 per day 7:45am-7:45pm, €18.80); **Thessaloniki** (2hr., 4 per day noon-10pm, €10); **Volos** (45min., 2 per day 3am and 8pm, €5.90). Regular *(aplo)* service to: **Athens** (5hr., 5 per day 10:15am-2am, €10); **Thessaloniki** (2½hr., 6 per day 4:15am-11:20pm, €4.70); **Volos** (1hr., 11 per day 6:30am-10pm, €2.10).

ORIENTATION AND PRACTICAL INFORMATION

Surrounded by miles of fertile corn and wheat fields, Larisa is directly southeast of the **Pinios River**, in the middle of eastern Thessaly. The bus station in the north and the train station in the south mark the boundaries of the city's main commercial district, which is laid out in a grid. From the bus station, **Olympou** heads south to **Pl. Laou,** one of Larisa's three main plateias. **A. Panagouli** begins here and heads to the bottom of the city where it crosses **Iroön Polytechniou** at a five-way intersection. On the way, Panagouli marks the eastern border of **Pl. Ethnarhou Makariou** (a.k.a. Pl. Tahydromiou, "Post Office Square"), which is the town's *kentro*, or center. The north edge of this plateia is formed by **Papakyriazi,** which can be taken west three blocks to **Papanastasiou.** From here, Papanastasiou runs north to **Pl. Mikhali Sapka,** and south past the post office and tourist office. Street maps can be very helpful and are available at magazine stores, *periptera* and some hotels.

Tourist Office, (☎2410 250 919), on Ipirou, near intersection with Botsari. Doles out city maps, pamphlets on Larisa, and advice in broken English. Open M-F 7am-2:30pm.

Banks: There is a 24hr. **Commercial Bank ATM** at the train station. Banks with 24hr. **ATMs** can be found all along Pl. Tahydromiou and Iroön Polytechniou.

Police: (☎2410 683 171), on Papanastasiou, 7 blocks south of Papakryiazi.

Hospital: (☎2410 230 031), on Georgiadou, east of the main bus station. Open 24hr.

Internet Access: Interspot, Skarlatou Soutsou 17 (☎2410 549 886), is a favorite among local computer gamers. Walk along Papkyriazi to the west and continue for 5 blocks before taking a right on Skarlatou Soutsou. €3 per hr.; *frappé* €1.50. Open 8am-2am. Just off Pl. Ethn. Markariou, next to Hotel Metropol, **Yahoo.gr** has over 20 speedy terminals and a full bar. €2 per hr. 9am-3pm; €2.50 per hr. 3pm-3am. **Arcade parlors** along pedestrian Roozvelt, running south off Pl. Tahydromiou, also offer Internet access.

OTE: (☎2410 995 376 or 2410 622 999), on Filellinion. Take Papanastasiou north and turn right on Kyprou. The OTE is down the 1st block on the left. Open M-F 7:30am-9pm.

Post Office (☎2410 532 312), on the corner of Papanastasiou and Diakou, a block north of the tourist office. Open M-F 7:30am-8pm. Poste Restante and **currency exchange. Postal code:** 41001.

ACCOMMODATIONS

Midrange to upper-level hotels can be found among the side streets that connect the three main plateias. The cheapest options are near the train station and not too far from the Trikala bus, but they're a 1.5km hike south from the main bus station.

Hotel Pantheon ❷, on Paleologou near the train station, sits atop a small taverna. Its cheap, serviceable rooms have TVs and phones—ask for one with a balcony. (☎2410 234 810. Singles €20, with bath and A/C €30; doubles €35.) **Hotel Neon ❷,** is 5 doors down from Pantheon. This hotel has only 7 small rooms, each sparsely furnished with beds and a sink. The cheery pink wall-papered rooms, however, are peaceful and spotless. (All rooms €20.) Centrally located **Hotel Doma ❸,** Skarlatou Soutsou 1, offers spacious, carpeted rooms with basic baths, A/C, TVs, phones, and small balconies. (☎2410 535 025. Singles €25; doubles €38; triples €50.)

FOOD

Most of Larisa's cafes, bars, and tavernas are centered around Pl. Tahydromiou and its adjacent pedestrian streets, where eating establishments blend into one never-ending series of chairs, tables, and blaring TVs. Dissatisfied *frappé* and Nescafe drinkers who yearn for the fresh-ground stuff will find it at various *kafekopteia* (coffee sellers), including one just north of Pl. Laou on the corner of Olympou and a very good one on Skarlatou Soutsou. Overpoweringly rich aromas pervade these old-fashioned stores, which also sell imported foodstuffs, candies, nuts, dried fruit, and herbs. If you prefer your groceries in neat straight aisles, head to the southern end of Panagouli, where you'll find a large **supermarket.**

Restaurants in Larisa are surprisingly rare, but tempting scents will entice you toward the *psistaria* grills on Panos, north of Kyprou one block east of the OTE, where whole chickens and bits of lamb slowly turn on spits in the window of each restaurant. On the south side of the plateia, **To Sidrivani ❷** (☎2410 535 933) offers old favorites like *pastitsio* and *moschari* for reasonable prices (entrees €4.50-8). Vegetarians will enjoy the rice-stuffed tomatoes, green peppers, and palate-pleasing string beans. On the opposite side of the plateia, you can find an excellent moussaka and other Greek classics (and the occasional free glass of ouzo) at the quieter **Ta Dio Fengaria ❷** ("The Two Moons"), on Asklipiou, which runs north-south from the center of Pl. Tahydromiou. The main roads of Larisa are teeming with very good *zaccharoplasteia.*

SIGHTS

Larisa's most famous archaeological site is its **ancient theater,** fenced off in the northwest corner of town at the end of Papanastasiou and currently being excavated and rebuilt. Just to the north are the unspectacular remains of the ancient **acropolis** (completely overgrown with weeds), the **Temple of Pallas Athena,** and the **Frourio,** the city's former fortress. A somewhat upscale restaurant bearing the same name now occupies the *frourio*, circling the still-standing Ottoman **Bedesten** (covered marketplace), built in the 15th-century by leader Türhanoğlu Omar Bey. Continue north east and you'll come to the **Pinios River** (a mere trickle in summer) and shady **Alcazar Park,** without a doubt the most serene spot in the city. Even the graffiti here is a bit more decorative. Modern art museum **Pinakothiki,** at Roozvelt 59, has one of the better 20th-century art collections in Greece. (☎2410 621 205. Open W-Su 10am-2:30pm and 6-8pm. €1.) The **Museum of Folk Art,** Mandilara 74, features rotating temporary exhibits and a permanent collection of men's and women's traditional dress, a setup of the precursor to the farmhouse kitchen, and a selection of 19th-century weapons. The exhibit captions are in both Greek and English. (☎2410 287 516 or 2410 287 493. Open Su-F 10am-2pm. Free.)

NIGHTLIFE

For after-dinner entertainment, the lively bars of Larisa will not disappoint. Hip joints like **Cafe del Mar** (☎2410 252 464) and **Ermes** (☎2410 621 022), on the corner of Roozvelt and Mandilara, blare until 3am. After drinks, check out some of Larisa's dynamic discos. **Venga** (☎2410 288 845), a €3 taxi ride from downtown, is an enormous open-air nightclub boasting a row of towering fountains, ten bars, and a mini club-within-a-club called **Planet Babe.** The crowd usually starts to arrive around 1am, but the top-of-the-table exhibitionism doesn't start until at least 4am. A €5-6 taxi ride in the other direction brings you to **Kika,** Larisa's most popular club, on the outskirts of town. Packed crowds gyrate nightly to American and Greek favorites under the enormous Thessalian night sky. Nearby, about 500m toward town, is bouzouki-bar **Romeo,** open weekends only. All clubs have a €6 cover, which includes one drink.

TRIKALA Τρικαλα

Greeks may snicker when they hear you've visited Trikala—many consider it a provincial knock-off of Larisa. Trikala, however, is much more pleasant than either Larisa or Volos and is wonderful for late afternoon strolls. The lazy Letheos River, named for the ancient Underworld's river of forgetfulness, carves Trikala in half; acacias, chestnuts, plane trees, and pedestrian-friendly footbridges lend the town aesthetic appeal. The striking remains of a mosque designed by Ottoman-era master architect Sinan, breezy views from the *frourio* (fortress), the labyrinthine old quarter, and the Folk Art Museum will keep you from twiddling your thumbs at the bus station. At night, young people fill the streets, strutting down the broad pedestrian arcades and dancing the night away in packed clubs outside town. Devotees of Asclepius, the god of healing who was born in Trikala (then known as Trikkis), can make a pilgrimage to his all-but-decimated sanctuary. According to ancient belief, a nap in the sanctuary (or maybe in a nearby hotel room) brings a dream-visit from Asclepius himself, who reveals the cure for whatever ails you.

ORIENTATION AND PRACTICAL INFORMATION

Trikala lies 70km west of Larisa. The curvaceous Letheos River bisects the town roughly northwest to southeast, and the two main plateias lie directly across the river from each other: **Pl. Riga Feriou** in the south and the rectangular **Pl. Iroön Polytechniou** in the north. The latter is home to a charming statue of a boy perpetually relieving himself into a small pond. The bus station is on **Othonos,** on the south bank of the river, to the east of Pl. Riga Feriou. **Asklipiou,** Trikala's main road, runs south from Pl. Riga Feriou, where it begins as a broad pedestrian arcade designed for glamorous strutting and coy ogling. It turns into a regular car-laden street after Kapodistriou, on its way to the train station south of town. **Vyronos** and **Garivaldi** cut diagonally across Asklipiou in succession. On the north bank, **Sarafi** leads west out of Pl. Iroön Polytechniou to **Varousi,** the old Turkish quarter, and the remains of the fortress in the northwest.

Buses: On the river's south bank, the **bus station** (☎24310 73 130) is at the corner of **Othonos** and **Garivaldi** streets, about 150m east of Pl. Riga Feriou. After crossing the bridge to the south bank, veer slightly left onto Apollonos. With Goodies fast food restaurant on your left, continue straight, looking for the bus station entrance on your left. Buses depart for: **Athens** (4½hr., 7 per day 7am-8:30pm, €18.20); **Ioannina** (3½hr., 2 per day 8:30am-3pm, €9.30); **Kalambaka** (30min., 20 per day 5:15am-9pm, €1.45); **Larisa** (1¼hr., 21 per day 5:45am-8:30pm, €4.05); **Pyli** (30min., 13 per day 5:45am-9pm, €1.25); **Thessaloniki** (3¼hr., 5 per day 7:30am-8pm, €12.15); **Volos** (2½hr., 4 per day 7am-7pm, €8.90).

Trains: The **train station** (☎24310 27 214) is located at the far southern end of Asklepiou, about 700m south of Pl. Riga Feriou. Keep walking straight along Asklepiou, away from the river, until the small yellow building comes into view. The station was recently renovated and has a modern ticket counter and electronic departure boards. Trains leave daily for: **Athens** (5½hr., 9:55am, €10); **Kalambaka** (20min., 4 per day 8:10am-8:20pm, €1.05); **Larisa** (3 per day 9:55am-9pm, €3.20). **Express trains** to Athens leave 3 times daily (4½hr.; 7:25am, 2:55, 5:40pm; €16.50).

Taxis: (☎24310 22 022), available in Pl. Iroön Polytechniou.

Banks: A National Bank with **ATM** is located right on the north side of Pl. I. Polytechniou. Open M-Th 8am-2pm, F 8am-1:30pm. There's also a 24hr. ATM on Asklepiou just south of Pl. Riga Feriou.

Police: The **station** (☎24310 27 401) is about 500m from the town center on the corner of Iannitson and Farmaki.

Hospital: (☎24310 22 222), on the main road to Kardista. Open 24hr.

Internet Access: Turn left on Vyronos 1 block down Asklepiou from Pl. Riga Feriou. **Neos Kosmos** (☎24310 72 591) has 9 terminals, a printer, and a full bar. Internet access €3 per hr. Open 8am-3am.

OTE: 25 Martiou (☎24310 95 328; manager 24310 95 315). Martiou runs parallel to Sarafi, 2 blocks away from the river; turn left after Pl. I. Polytechniou.

Post Office: The main **post office,** Sarafi 15 (☎24310 27 615), provides exchange and Poste Restante. Open M-F 7:30am-2pm. Walk across the bridge from Pl. Riga Feriou and turn left on the street directly in front of you (Sarafi). A smaller post office, Asklipiou 44 (☎24310 27 415), sells stamps and offers mail-related services only. Open M-F 7:30am-1pm. **Postal code:** 42100.

ACCOMMODATIONS AND FOOD

The most affordable digs in town are at the **Hotel Palladion ❷,** Vyronos 4, along the riverbank, and one street west of Pl. Riga Feriou. All types of travelers amble across the marble floors of these spacious, comfortable, colorful rooms. Phones, sinks, and TVs that receive more than 20 channels. (☎24310 28 091 or 24310 37 260. Shared baths. Singles €21; doubles €30; triples €36.) Other hotels are readily available, but often expensive. **Hotel Dinas ❸,** two blocks down Asklepiou, is right above the hippest cafes in town (the sign reads *Hotel Ntina)*. The brightly painted rooms have bathrooms, TVs, and A/C and are moderately priced for Trikala hotels. (☎24310 74 777; fax 24310 29 490. Singles €35; doubles €50; triples €60.) **Hotel Achilleion ❹,** easy to spot just south of the main bridge on Pl. Riga Feriou, offers cozy, carpeted rooms with large beds and wooden furniture. Rooms have TVs, phones, A/C, and simple baths. (☎24310 28 192 or 24310 28 192; fax 24310 74 858. Breakfast included. Singles €45; doubles €75; triples €85.)

Katzinetrou, one block west of Pl. Iroön Polytechniou off Martinou, is a lively spot for an evening meal. Tavernas line the streets, their colorful outdoor tables wrapping around the street corners. Join crowds of chatty locals at **Taverna Thea**

Atremis ❷, Ypsilandou 4, three blocks north of Martinou. The taverna offers a large selection of Greek wines to complement its traditional menu. The food is excellent, but bring a dictionary: neither the menu nor the owner can offer any hints in English. (☎24310 77 533. Entrees €4.70-7.70.) A few blocks further south, **To Dipylo ❷** serves up an assortment of souvlakis, filets, and schnitzels, as well as the "Drunkard's Delicacy" (€4.40), a spicy pork dish. (☎24310 72 722. Entrees €4.10-8.80.) Riga Feriou harbors hordes of souvlaki and pizza places, including **Jimmy's ❶**, Asklepiou 22, which offers five varieties of gyros (€1.70-4.40) in addition to sandwiches, salads, fresh desserts, and crepes. (Open 8am-1am.) A **supermarket** on Vyronos, next door to Palladion Hotel, sells mini-icons of the *Panagia* (Virgin), in addition to average foodstuffs. (Open M-F 8am-9pm, Sa 8am-6pm.)

SIGHTS AND NIGHTLIFE

Looming above Varousi are the grand stone walls and bell tower of **Fort Trikkis,** first constructed in the 4th century BC and dedicated to Artemis. The fountain-decked park and cafe in the lower half of the fort is an ideal setting for a cool *frappé* with a view (€2.50). The upper half contains the bell tower and a small garden; from mid-June to mid-September, an open-air theater shows movies in English with Greek subtitles. (10pm nightly. €5, students €3).

Pl. Riga Feriou and Asklipiou are packed with loud cafes blasting dance music and serving drinks until just shy of daybreak. In the afternoons and early evenings, the chairs are lined up like cinema seats facing the pedestrian street—prime positioning for people-watching. Just off Pl. Riga Feriou on Asklepiou is **Chaplin.** Always crowded, this cafe and bar has rows of comfortable lounge chairs outside and art-deco furniture inside. Anything from disco, to reggae, to Greek techno is blasted from the innumerable speakers. (☎24310 75 440. Beer €3; cocktails €5. Open 9am-3am.) **Il Senso,** directly across the street, has a bit more light and slightly softer music for laid-back drinking and nonchalant coolness. (☎24310 39 309. Beer €3; cocktails €5. Open 10am-3:30am.) For a cool drink any time of the day, take a taxi to nearby Pyli for **Neromylos,** a 17th-century water mill converted to a cafe and meticulously landscaped by its owner. Water flows out of numerous fountains, cascading off of the patios, turning waterwheels, and ends up coiling through a little stream at your feet on its way to the river. (☎24340 22 085. Open 10am-2am. *Frappé* €2.50; beer €3.)

KALAMBAKA Καλαμπακα

Kalambaka sits directly at the base of the Meteora rocks: all good etymologists know its name is derived from the Turkish phrase for "the rock with the cowls of monks." The lone main road channels countless package-tour buses past the town, to the rocks' summit. Though Kalambaka itself doesn't offer much beyond access to the famed monasteries, it makes a quiet, convenient base.

TRANSPORTATION

Buses: Main station downhill from the local bus station on the left, past the taxi stand. To: **Athens** (5hr., 3 per day 9am-7:15pm, €19.65) via **Lamia** (2½hr., €7.65); **Ioannina** (3½hr.; 8:45am, 3:20pm; €7.90) via **Metsovo** (1½hr., €4.50); **Patras** (6hr., Tu and Th 9am, €17.50); **Trikala** (30min.; every hr. 7am-12:30pm; €1.45); and **Volos** (3hr., 2 per day, €10.25). Buses bound for **Meteora** (20min., 2 per day, €0.80) and **Kastraki** (5min., 24 per day 6:40am-9:40pm, €0.70) pick up passengers in front of the **central plateia** at the foot of the large fountain. The 9am bus to Meteora allows you time to hike around the monasteries. Most people walk back to Kalambaka (6km downhill), visiting monasteries along the way, but you can also take a bus back from **Grand Meteoron** at 1:30pm.

Trains: The station (☎24320 22 451), on the corner of Pindou and Kondyli, is brand new and provides service to: **Athens** (4hr., 3 per day 7am-5:15pm, €19.10); **Thessaloniki** (5hr., 3 per day 9:35am-8:45pm, €10.50) via **Larisa** (1½hr., €3.15). From the bus station, walk downhill 1 block and turn left on Pindou.

Taxis: (☎23420 22 310 or 24320 22 822) congregate at a small kiosk across from the central plateia. Taxi to Meteora €4-5. Available 6:30am-midnight.

ORIENTATION AND PRACTICAL INFORMATION

Kalambaka is in the northwestern corner of Thessaly, 30km north of Trikala, near the border with Epirus. The town's central plateia is uphill from the bus station at the intersection of the town's major thoroughfares. Standing in this plateia with your back to the fountain and the Meteora cliffs, **Vlahava** is straight behind you, and **Ioanninon** runs downhill to the right toward the police station. **Patriarchou Dimitriou** goes off to your right, while **Trikalon** leads left to the sunny **Pl. Riga Fariou,** home of various banks and restaurants. A horde of cafes and bars can be found open at all hours on **Dimalou,** two blocks downhill from Pl. Riga Fariou.

Tourist Office: Vlahava 1 (☎24320 77 734), right on the central plateia underneath the town hall. The tourist office offers maps, bus schedules, lists of hotels and rooms to let, and information on the monasteries–most in English. Open M-F 9am-1:30pm and 4-9pm, Sa-Su 9am-1pm and 5-9pm. The **kiosk** by the taxi stand also provides maps of the town and of Meteora.

Banks: Both the National Bank in Pl. Riga Fariou and the Ionian Bank near the central plateia have 24hr. **ATMs.**

Police and Tourist Police: (☎24230 76 100), on the road to Ioannina, about a 10min. walk from the center of town. Open 24hr.

Health Center: (☎24230 22 222), 1km from town, on the road to Ioannina. Open 24hr.

OTE: (☎24230 22 121), down Ioanninon. Open M-F 7:30am-2pm.

Internet Access: Cafe Hollywood, Trikalon 67 (☎24230 24 964), a few blocks past Pl. Riga Fariou. €1 per 15min. for use of 1 of its 7 coin-operated, snail-paced terminals. Open 9am-2am. **Koktel** (☎24230 22 370), a block down Dimoula off Trikalon, has 4 reliable terminals in the back of the well-lit cafe.

Post Office: (☎24230 22 467), between the 2 plateias on Trikalon. Poste Restante available. Open M-F 7:30am-2pm. **Postal code:** 42200.

ACCOMMODATIONS AND CAMPING

Think carefully before you accept domatia offers from the dock hawks; some have been known to lure travelers with promises of good prices only to change their rates or add surcharges when it comes time to pay. Be skeptical when someone tells you that the place you're going has raised its rates or is closed, and make sure you agree on a rate before you agree to spend the night. Many moderately priced hotels are at the end of Trikalon; budget options are northeast of the city's center, closer to the base of the cliffs. A number of **campsites** line the roads around Kalambaka and Kastraki; many also rent rooms at cheap prices. **Kalambaka,** about 1km down the road to Trikala, is the closest. (☎24230 22 309. €2 per tent, €4 per car.) **Vrachos** is about as far away in the opposite direction, in nearby Kastraki, and has a swimming pool, bar, and restaurant. (☎24230 22 293 or 24230 23 134. €5 per person, €4 per car.)

Koka Roka (☎24230 24 554; kokaroka@yahoo.com). A 15min. walk from the central plateia; follow Vlachara until it ends, then bear left, following the signs to Kanari. On a quiet side street at the base of the footpath to the rocks, Koka Roka offers large, airy rooms with beautiful views of Meteora. Internet access available (€3 per hr.). Singles without bath €15; doubles €27, with bath €32; triples with bath €42. ❷

Alsos Rooms (☎24230 24 097 or mobile 6970 660 929), on Kanari before Koka Roka. Well-decorated, recently renovated rooms with TVs and clean, tiled bathrooms. Access to fully stocked communal kitchen. Laundry service available, and the owner expects to offer Internet access in the near future. Singles €20; doubles €30; triples €40. Discounts available to students staying more than one night. ❷

Hotel Antonadis, Trikalon 148 (☎24230 24 387; antoniadas@kmp.forthnet.gr), at the edge of the commercial district, set amongst a cluster of similar, mid-level hotels. Rooms here are a bit narrow but have TVs, A/C, phones, radios, and fridges. The hotel offers breakfast in the lobby and a swimming pool on the 6th fl. Singles €35; doubles €50; triples €65. ❸

FOOD AND NIGHTLIFE

To save some cash or to slap together a picnic lunch to take to monasteries, there's a **supermarket** just off of Trikalon on Dimoula and various **fruit stands** on Vlachara. On Fridays, Vlachara and its main intersector Kondyli turn into a full-scale **marketplace** for fresh produce and sundry household goods. Most of Kalambaka's fast food places and a few cheap tavernas are on Trikalon, south of Riga Feriou; good restaurants lean against the edge of the cliffs on the road to Karditsa.

Restaurant Panellinio (☎24230 24 735). Perched on a cobblestone platform right next to the fountain, Panellinio pretty much *is* the central plateia, and very popular at night. Mrs. Soula cooks up a mean moussaka as well as many grilled meat and vegetable dishes. Be sure to take a quick peek at their folk art display. Entrees €4.50-6. ❷

Koka Roka Taverna (☎24230 24 554), inside its namesake hotel. Ideally located with spectacular views of the towering cliffs. Entrees €3.20-5.10. ❶

Taverna Vakhos (☎24230 24 678), up a hill at the end of Patriarchou Dimitriou, has a large, fun-filled patio right under the Meteora rocks. Have a drink and soak up the view from the deck. Fish, veal, pork, and lamb dishes are served up at intimate tables. Open noon-midnight. Entrees €5-8.50. ❷

The nightlife mainly centers on **Trikalon,** south of Pl. Riga Feriou, where motorcycles, cheap fast food joints, and neon signs line the streets. There's hipper atmosphere on Dimoula, home to entertaining but indistinguishable bars, most offering beers for €4 and drinks for €5.50. **Mateus** (☎24230 75 195), Dimalou 3, has a beach bar atmosphere with palm trees, grass umbrellas, and plenty of room for dancing. (Open 10am-3am.)

SIGHTS

In the land of monasteries, it comes as no surprise that Kalambaka's foremost attraction is the Byzantine **Church of the Assumption of the Virgin,** once the seat of the bishop of Kalambaka and Trikala. Follow the signs in the central plateia; after several blocks you'll spy the graceful bell tower of the old church. Built in the 11th century on the ruins of a 5th-century basilica, the main structure was remodeled in 1573. Unfortunately, many of the interior frescoes, painted by the Cretan monk **Neophytos** and priest **Kiriazis,** have been blackened by centuries of candle and incense burning. Of particular interest is the church's marble *amdo* (pulpit), located in the center of the nave. (Dress modestly: long pants or skirts and no bare shoulders. €1.50. Open 8am-1pm and 4-6pm.) Uphill toward the end of Patriarchou Dimitriou, the **Center of Contemporary Art** displays a rotation collection of Greek modern art. Upwards of 80 pieces are housed in the newly opened museum. Guided tours are given in English during quieter periods. (€2, students and children free. Open daily 9am-3pm and 5-9pm.) In late July, the town honors its patron saint with a **glendi** (celebration) of music, dance, and food. Nearby Kastraki holds a three-day **wine festival** with free samples in late August.

METEORA Μετεορα

Buses leave for Meteora from the Kalambaka fountain M-F 9am and 1:20pm, Sa-Su 8:20am and 1:20pm. Tickets (€0.80) can be bought on the bus. Each monastery closes for 1 day of the week, and their opening hours vary slightly. All are open Apr.-Sept. Sa-Su and W 10am-12:30pm and 3:30-5pm. €2 per monastery, children under 12 free. Dress modestly: long skirts for women, long pants for men. No bare shoulders, or you will not be admitted. Wraps and shawls are available for the forgetful. Men with long hair may be asked to wrap it in a bun (as the monks do). Photography and filming are forbidden inside most of the monasteries; pack a picnic for the mid-day closing hours.

No one knows how the majestic, iron-gray pinnacles of the Meteora (meh-TEH-o-rah; "rocks of the sky") formations were created, but they're probably the remains of large salt deposits from a primordial sea. Whatever their origin, the Meteora tower over the plains of Thessaly and yield startling views of fields, forests, mountains, and monolithic stone; they'd be a must-see even without the 24 gravity-defying, frescoed Byzantine monasteries that cling to them. Six of these monasteries are still inhabited by religious orders and are open to the public. The largest monasteries, Grand Meteoron and Varlaam, have the most spectacular displays and attract hordes of tourists. The other monasteries are quieter and more intimate; if you're lucky, you might even meet one of the reclusive monks. Meteora requires a full day's visit, and it's well worth the time and the walk.

HISTORY

The origins of the settlements perched atop the Meteora rocks are unknown: one likely story holds that the first recluse was a monk named **Barnabas,** who founded the *skite* of the Holy Ghost in the mid-10th century. By the 11th century, hermits and ascetics followed his example, moving to the wind-beaten pinnacles and crevices of the Meteora, worshiping in a church dedicated to the **Theotokos** (Mother of God), which can still be seen below the Agios Nikolaos monastery. As religious persecution at the hands of Serbian marauders increased in the 12th century, devout Christians scurried to the summits of these impregnable columns of rock.

In 1344, the region's first monastic community was founded when the monk **Athanasios,** his spiritual father **Gregorios,** and 14 fellow mountain-climbing monks began to build Grand Meteoron. Athanasios was a highly educated monk whose journeys brought him from his native Patras to Constantinople, Crete, and finally Mt. Athos, which he fled to avoid Turkish invasions. He preferred to occupy his time weaving baskets in a nearby cave, referring to women as "the sling" (that vaults the stones of sin into men's hearts) or as "the affliction" (addicting men to the sinful pleasures of the flesh). When the Ottomans ruled most of Greece, Meteora served as an outpost of Christianity along with Mount Athos (see p. 256), growing in the 16th century into a robust, rich community of 24 monasteries, each embellished by the age's finest artists. In the late 1700s, when donations fell off and the popularity of monastic life waned, the Greeks sold off many treasured manuscripts and books to foreign visitors for a fraction of their actual worth. A small brotherhood still exists at **Grand Meteoron, Varlaam, Agia Triada,** and **Agios Nikolaos,** while **Agios Stephanos** and **Roussanou** are now convents.

WALKING THE MONASTERIES

The first ascetics scaled the sheer cliffs of the Meteora by wedging timbers into the rock crevices to construct small platforms; traces of these platforms can still be seen along the Meteora walls. After the monasteries were completed, visitors usually arrived by means of extremely long rope ladders. Once these were pulled up, the summit became virtually inaccessible. Visitors who were either too weak or too timid to climb the ladders were hoisted up in free-swinging rope nets. Motorized winches have since replaced rope-spool cranes, and today only provisions, not pilgrims, are yanked up by rope, though monks can be seen riding miniature cable cars over the chasms. In 1922, steps were carved into the rocks and bridges built between the pillars, so even the vertigo-prone could feel secure.

It's best to begin your walking tour from **Grand Meteoron,** the uppermost monastery, and then to visit the others on your way down. From Grand Meteoron, a road leads down about 200m, where there is a turn-off for Varlaam. Another 700m beyond this point, the road splits in two. The right fork leads to **Roussanou, Agios Nikolaos,** and eventually the village of Kastraki, after a series of switchbacks down the hillside. The left fork leads to **Agia Triada** and **Agios Stephanos** and back to the village of **Kalambaka.** Large signs at every intersection make navigation easy. There is approximately a 20-30min. walk between each monastery, but the curved road between the rocks has dazzling views of the monasteries and photo opportunities.

GRAND METEORON. The **Monastery of the Transfiguration,** known as Grand Meteoron (Μεγαλου Μετεορου), is the oldest, largest, most important, and most touristed monastery in the area. Built in the late 14th century on the most imposing of the inhabited stone columns, **Platys Lithos,** the Grand Meteoron complex, looms 613m above Thessaly's plain. It reached its peak in the 16th century, when it was visited by the reigning patriarch and accorded the same privileges as the autonomous Mt. Athos. Around this time the **Church of the Transfiguration** *(Metamorphosis)* was built, to be capped by an exalted dome with a *Pantokrator* (a central image of Christ). The monastery is filled with sounds of chanting monks—unfortunately emanating from a stereo in the **folk museum,** which exhibits holy books, religious ornaments, and the traditional monastic garb. Other rooms are preserved with historical accuracy, including a dining hall, kitchen, mausoleum, and a wine cellar with the largest barrel you will ever see (15,000L). The monks here keep mostly to their private quarters on the eastern side of the monastery. *(Open W-M 10am-5pm. €2.)*

VARLAAM MONASTERY. Some 800m downhill from Grand Meteoron stands Varlaam, the second-largest Meteora monastery. Varlaam was founded in the 14th century by a contemporary of Athanasios who, in a show of monkish humility, named the monastery after himself. The 16th-century frescoes of the *katholikon* depict desert hermits, martyrs, an apocalyptic sea serpent swallowing doomed sinners, as well as St. Sisoes looking pitifully upon Alexander the Great's skeleton (symbolic of the vanity of worldly achievements). The monastery also has an extensive **library** containing 290 manuscripts, including a miniature Bible from 960 that belonged to Emperor Constantine Porfitogenitou. Varlaam also has every third-grade science teacher's dream—an extensive **net and pulley system,** now used for supplies, which shows how earlier visitors were hoisted. Recently the monastery has gotten a face-lift, adding new walkways, handrails (thankfully), and a clock tower. *(Open F-W 9am-2pm and 3:20-5pm. €2.)*

ROUSSANOU. Bear right at the fork in the road to reach Roussanou. Visible from most of the valley, it is one of the most spectacularly situated monasteries in the area. With its steep sides, three of which overlook the sheer drop to the valley below, Roussanou feels less like a creation of man than a natural continuation of the boulders. Despite continuous renovation, the interior—which includes paintings of the criminal in paradise and a portrait of Constantine the Great—can't match the heavenly exterior, accessible without a ticket. Still, the *katholikon*, illuminated by stained glass, is beautiful. Roussanou celebrated its greatest moment when it housed Greek refugees fleeing the Turks in 1757 and 1897. Today, the monastery is home to an order of nuns. *(Open daily 9am-6pm. €2.)*

AGIOS NIKALAOS. Farther down the road lies the 16th-century Monastery of Agios Nikolaos Anapafsas, only 2½km from Kastraki. Situated on a very narrow boulder, Agios Nikolaos grew vertically rather than horizontally; it is now the second tallest of the monasteries, next to Grand Meteoron. Excellent views open from the rooftop and the small balcony beneath it. Visitors are admitted only in small groups; wait at the top of the steps for the door to open. Allow a good 30min. for the walk past Roussanou to the next monastery, Agia Triada. *(Open Sa-Th 9am-5:30pm; closed in winter. €2.)*

AGIA TRIADA. A shortcut from Roussanou bypasses a large section of road on the way to Agia Triada. Standing on the metal bridge into Roussanou, face away from the monastery, get out your walking stick, and take the (mostly) paved path uphill on the right. When the path hits the road, bear right and keep bearing right to find Agia Triada ("Trinity"); movie buffs will recognize it from the James Bond flick *For Your Eyes Only*. Looming above Kalambaka, the peak of Agia Triada gives a soul-searing view of the red-roofed town and the distant, snow-capped Pindos Mountains. Ambitious monk Dometius built the monastery in 1438, but most of the **wall paintings** weren't added for another 200 years. Sadly, most of the monastery's prized manuscripts and heirlooms were lost in WWII. Triada is now one of the least-touristed and most intimate monasteries. To get to **Kalambaka** from Agia Triada, take the (unmarked) 2km footpath leading from the bottom of the monastery's stone staircase. At the base of the cliff and with your back to the monastery, walk a few meters to your left, and then descend on the small left-hand fork in the path. The narrow, overgrown trail soon evolves into a cement-paved stone path. *(Open F-W 9am-12:30pm and 3-5pm. €2.)*

AGIOS STEPHANOS. At the end of the road, past Agia Triada, is Agios Stephanos. According to an 18th-century report, it was originally a convent; it became a monastery in the early 15th century. Today it is once again home to a large, active community of nuns. Of its two churches, only the more modern **Agios Haralambos,** built in 1798, is open to the public. The **museum** displays well-preserved icons, manuscripts, liturgical vestments, and crosses. Its wooden *iconostasis* is intricately carved into figures of birds, animals, and people. The peaceful garden out back offers spectacular views of the entire valley. *(Open Tu-Su 9am-1pm and 3:20-6pm; in winter Tu-Su 9:30am-1pm and 3-5pm. €2.)*

NORTHERN GREECE

Northern Greece rarely finds its way into package tours, but not for lack of appeal. Robust and pretension-free, the region draws adventurous travelers looking to flee the packed plateias and bikini-filled beaches of the islands. From the peaks of Mt. Olympus to the depths of Vikos Gorge, the diverse landscape holds countless opportunities to commune with nature, while ancient monasteries offer access to the gods of your choice. In ancient times, snide Athenians regarded the residents of Macedonia and Thrace as primitive barbarians. Today, the northern reaches of Greece vary greatly in their connection with modern life; Thessaloniki's trendsetting residents are constantly ahead of the curve, while the people of the Zagorohoria barely test the waters of the 19th century.

HIGHLIGHTS OF NORTHERN GREECE

SIDESTEP SCORPIONS while trekking through Vikos Gorge (p. 253), the world's steepest canyon.

GENUFLECT in reverence to Agios Dimitrios, Thessaloniki's oldest church, before being floored by the ancient mosaics inside (p. 223).

GET LOST IN THE CLOUDS atop Mt. Olympus; the gods await your ascent (p. 230).

ABIDE by 10th-century monastic doctrine at Mt. Athos's monasteries (p. 256).

FLIRT WITH FATE amid the rustling leaves of Dodoni's oracular oak (p. 248).

MACEDONIA Μακεδονια

Some of the most captivating Greek landscapes and sights belong to Macedonia, including the sublime Olympian hiking trails, millions of sparkling mosaic *tessarae* from Thessaloniki's Byzantine churches, Karala's Ottoman *imaret*, the Royal Tombs from Vergina, the austere monasteries of Mt. Athos, and the surf and sand of Halkidiki's two peninsulas. Greece's largest province tops the mainland like an ancient gold-wrought crown. You'll encounter the region's symbol, a 16-pointed star, on everything: the sidewalk at the OTE, bumper stickers saying "Macedonia is Greece," and even Philip II's gold casket in Vergina. Though rarely touristed, it's far from a backwater: hip, lively Thessaloniki, Greece's second-largest city, keeps the whole region on its toes.

THESSALONIKI Θεσσαλονικη

Thessaloniki, a jumble of Byzantine, European, Turkish, Balkan, and Greek cultural and historical debris, fans out from its hilltop fortress toward the Thermaic Gulf. From its peak, the fortress oversees the Old Town's placid streets stretching down to the city's long, congested avenues. Among glitzy and lackluster concrete facades, fashion-conscious young Salonicans rub shoulders with old women in black mourning clothes and long-bearded monks. Golden mosaics, frescoes, and floating domes still gleam in the industrial city's Byzantine churches.

TRAVEL ADVISORY. On May 21, 2002, the US State Department reissued a travel warning advising American citizens against all travel to the **Former Yugoslav Republic of Macedonia.** All US citizens in the nation of Macedonia at the time were urged to depart in July 2001 due to rising anti-foreign sentiment and increased acts of intimidation and violence against American citizens in the country. The situation in Macedonia is still unsettled and potentially dangerous as a result of armed clashes between Macedonian security forces and ethnic Albanian extremists. The unrest has resulted in periodic closures of the border between Macedonia and Kosovo. Travel restrictions on private American citizens are subject to change at short notice; see **Travel Advisories** on the US State Department website (http://travel.state.gov) for updates.

Macedonia's capital and Greece's second city, Thessaloniki was founded in 316 BC when Cassander (the ruler of Macedon) needed a new city to name after his wife. He selected a spot on the Thermaic Gulf shore and transplanted the citizens of 26 pre-existing towns to his new Salonica. Despite frequent and bloody raids by Goths, Avars, Slavs, Bulgars, and Latin Crusaders, Salonica rose to become the Byzantine Empire's second-most important city, after Constantinople. The Turks ended these glory days, conquering the city by siege in 1421 and ruling until 1912. Throughout the centuries of Ottoman rule, Thessaloniki remained a cultural and intellectual center, dominated by its population of Sephardic Jews. Although the city began the 20th century with a population more European than Hellenic, the population exchange (see p. 12) and the death of many of the city's 50,000 Jews during the Holocaust have left Thessaloniki almost homogeneously Greek.

TRANSPORTATION

BY BUS

KTEL buses connect Thessaloniki with most major Greek cities; with the exception of the bus to Halkidiki, all leave from one central, dome-shaped bus station west of the city center. **Bus #1** is a shuttle service between the train station and bus station throughout the day (buses leave every 15 min. €0.44). **Bus #78** connects the bus station to the airport (every 30 min, €0.44).

International buses (☎2310 599 100) leave from the **main train station** (☎2310 517 517), on Monastiriou in the city's western part; take any bus down Egnatia to get there (€0.44). Buses go to: **Istanbul, Turkey** (12hr., 2:30am, €72); **Koritsa, Albania** (6hr., 8am and midnight, €20); **Sofia, Bulgaria** (6hr., 4 per day 7am-10pm, €17).

DESTINATION	TIME	FREQUENCY	PRICE	TELEPHONE
Athens	6hr.	11 per day 6:45am-11:45pm	€28	☎2310 595 495
Alexandropoulis	5hr.	7 per day 8am-11pm	€19.75	☎2310 595 439
Corinth	7½hr.	11:30pm	€32	☎2310 595 405
Drama	2¼hr.	every hr. 7am-9pm	€8.60	☎2310 595 420
Edessa	2hr.	6 per day 6am-8pm	€5.50	☎2310 595 435
Florina	3hr.	7 per day 7:30am-9pm	€10.20	☎2310 595 418
Grevena	3hr.	4 per day 8:30am-6pm	€10.70	☎2310 595 485
Igoumenitsa	7 hr.	9am and 8pm	€26.40	☎2310 595 444
Ioannina	7hr.	4 per day 7:30am-9:30pm	€26.40	☎2310 595 485
Karditsa	3¼hr.	5 per day 8am-8pm	€12.40	☎2310 595 440

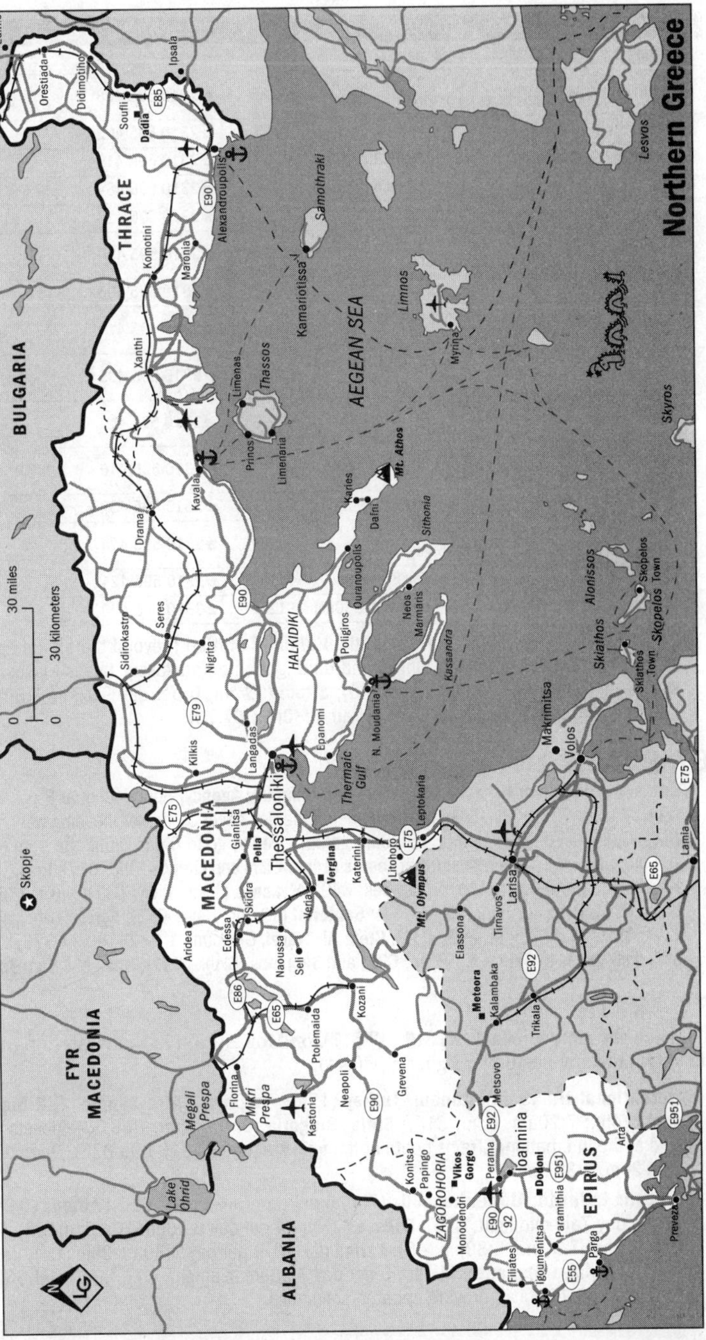

Northern Greece

DESTINATION	TIME	FREQUENCY	PRICE	TELEPHONE
Kastoria	3½hr.	7 per day 7:30am-8pm	€12.30	☎2310 595 440
Katerini	2½hr.	Every 30min. 6:30am-10:30pm	€4.35	☎2310 595 428
Kavala	2½hr.	Every hr. 6am-8pm	€9.70	☎2310 595 422
Komotini	4hr.	7 per day 8:30am-1am	€15.10	☎2310 595 419
Kozani	2¼hr.	Every hr. 6am-8:30pm	€7.80	☎2310 595 484
Lamia	4hr.	9am and 3:15pm	€18.80	☎2310 595 416
Larisa	2hr.	Every hr. 8:30am-9:45pm	€10.50	☎2310 595 430
Parga	9hr.	10am	€31.70	☎2310 595 406
Patras	7hr.	3 per day 8:15am-8:30pm	€32.55	☎2310 595 419
Ancient Pella	40min.	Every 45 min. 6:30am-10pm	€2.15	☎2310 595 435
Pirgos	14hr.	10:30am Sa-Th (F 3:30pm)	€32.55	☎2310 595 419
Serrona	1½hr.	Every 30 min. 6am-10pm	€5.25	☎2310 595 446
Trikala	3hr.	6 per day 8am-9pm	€12.50	☎2310 595 432
Veria	55min.	Every hr. 5:45am-9:15pm	€4.40	☎2310 595 424
Volos	3hr.	6 per day 8am-8pm	€11.90	☎2310 595 424
Xanthi	3hr.	8 per day 8am-1:30am	€12	☎2310 595 423

In addition, domestic buses leave from the **Halkidiki Station** (beyond the end of Egnatia—walk down Kanari for two blocks and turn right onto Karakassi). Buses to **Kassandra** (90min, every hr. 8am-9pm, €5.80); **Sitonia** (2½hr, 6 per day 9:15am-6:30pm, €8); and **Ouranoupolis** (7 per day 6:15am-6:30pm; €7.70).

BY BOAT

Ferries: Buy tickets at **Karacharisis Travel and Shipping Agency,** Koundouriotou 8 (☎2310 524 544; fax 2310 532 289), on the corner of the first street on the left heading west from Nikis. Open M-F 8:30am-8pm, Sa 8:30am-2:30pm. Ferries go to **Chios** (20hr., Sa 1am (and Tu 5pm July-Aug.), €27) with stops at **Lesvos** (14hr., €27) and **Limnos** (8hr., €17); **Ios** (20hr., F 7pm, €31); **Iraklion** (24hr., 5 per week, €40); **Mykonos** (15hr., daily, €31); **Naxos** (16hr., daily, €29); **Paros** (17½hr., daily, €31); **Santorini** (19½hr., daily, €33); **Syros** (10hr., daily, €28); **Tinos** (12hr., 3 per week, €30). **Crete Air Travel,** Dragoumi 1 (☎2310 534 376) operates daily ferries to **Skiathos** (4½hr., €31) and **Skopelos** (5½hr., €31). Open M-F 8am-9pm.

BY TRAIN

To reach the **main terminal** (☎2310 517 517), on Monastiriou in the western part of the city, take any bus down Egnatia (€0.44).

International trains to: **Istanbul, Turkey** (12hr., 7:25am, €40); **Skopje, FYR Macedonia** (4hr.; 7:20am, 6pm; €14); **Sofia, Bulgaria** (8hr., 10pm, €18.50). Tickets are sold at the International Trains booth at the train station (☎2310 599 033). Open daily 7am-2pm, 3:30-9pm.

Domestic trains to: **Alexandroupolis** (7hr., 5 per day 7am-11pm, €10); **Athens** (6-8hr., 10 per day 7am-midnight, €15); **Edessa** (2½hr., 4 per day 6:10am-10:15pm, €3); **Florina** (3½hr.; 7:30am, 6:30pm; €5); **Larisa** (2½hr., 9 per day 7:30am-2am, €4); **Volos** (4hr., 7:20pm, €6); **Xanthi** (4½hr., 5 per day 7:28am-midnight, €7). The **Travel Office** (☎2310 598 112) can provide updated schedules.

BY PLANE

The **airport** (☎2310 473 234), 16km east of town, can be reached by **bus #78** (€0.44) from the train station or Pl. Aristotelous, or by **taxi** (€10). There's an **EOT** tourist office branch (☎2310 985 215) at the airport.

Olympic Airways: office at Koundouriotou 3 (☎2310 368 311; fax 2310 229 725), is open M-Sa 8am-3:45pm. Call for reservations (☎2310 368 666) M-Sa 7am-5pm. To: **Athens** (55min., 10 per day, €75); **Cyprus** (2½hr.; Tu, Th, Sa, Su; €90); **Hania** (2hr., W and Sa, €92); **Iraklion** (2hr.; M, F, Sa; €85); **Ioannina** (50min.; M, W, F, Su; €39); **Limnos** (50min.; M, W, Th, Sa; €44); **Rhodes** (3hr., daily, €84). Also to: **Chios, Corfu, Lesvos** and **Samos** (2-3 per week).

LOCAL TRANSPORTATION

Thessaloniki and its suburbs are connected by an extensive public transportation network. **Local buses** cost €0.44 and run throughout the city. An **office** across from the train station provides limited schedules, and maps posted at many of the bus stops show the city routes. Buses #10, #11, and #31 run up and down Egnatia. Buy tickets at *periptera* (kiosks) or the ticket booths at major stations.

ORIENTATION

Thessaloniki stretches out along the waterfront of the Thermaic Gulf's north shore. Its rough grid layout—established after the Great Fire of 1917—and the orienting presence of the sea make it nearly impossible to get lost, but street signs are haphazard, so a map can be helpful. **Egnatia,** the city's busiest (and noisiest) street, cuts through the center of town. (The road was originally part of a highway from Rome to Byzantium.) From Egnatia, running parallel to the water, the main streets are **Ermou, Tsimiski,** and **Mitropoleos;** these make up Thessaloniki's central shopping area. **Nikis** runs along the seafront and is home to many bars and cafes. East of Nikis, the **White Tower,** Thessaloniki's most prominent monument, shadows the harbor like an oversized chess piece. Intersecting all these streets and leading from the water into town are **I. Dragoumi, El. Venizelou, Aristotelous, Ag. Sophias,** and **Eth. Aminis.** Inland from Egnatia is **Ag. Dimitriou** and the **Old City.** The roads north of Ag. Dimitriou grow increasingly tiny and steep towards the Old City's ancient fortress walls, panoramic views, and cheap tavernas. Between Tsimiski and the Arch of Galerius, **Pl. Navarinou,** with its Roman ruins, is a meeting ground for Thessaloniki's youth. Facing inland, head left on Mitropoleos past **Pl. Elefterias** to reach **Ladadika,** a former red-light district restored into a lovely pocket of turn-of-the-century cafes, bars, and tavernas.

PRACTICAL INFORMATION

Tourist Offices: EOT (☎2310 271 888, 2310 222 935 or 2310 265 507; fax 2310 265 504), Pl. Aristotelous, one block from the water, has **free maps,** hotel listings, transportation schedules and prices, and festival information. Open M-Sa 7:30am-3pm. Another EOT office (☎2310 985 215) is at the **airport. UTS,** Mitropoleos 28 (☎2310 286 756; fax 2310 283 156), is near Pl. Aristotelous; ring the bell by the door labeled "28" and go to the 7th floor. Ask for English-speaking Liza (make sure you're carrying *Let's Go*). Open M-F 9am-5pm.

Permits for Mt. Athos: Visit the **Holy Executive of the Holy Mt. Athos Pilgrims' Bureau,** Kou. Karamanli 14, 1st fl., opposite a Harley Davidson motorcycle shop (☎2310 861 611; fax 2310 861 811). Letter of recommendation not needed, but make sure you bring your passport. Only men are allowed to visit Mt. Athos (p. 256). Karamanli is the eastern extension of Egnatia; take **bus #12** from Mitropoleos at Pl. Aristotelous and ask to be let off at Papafio. English spoken. Open M-F 9am-2pm, Sa 10am-12pm.

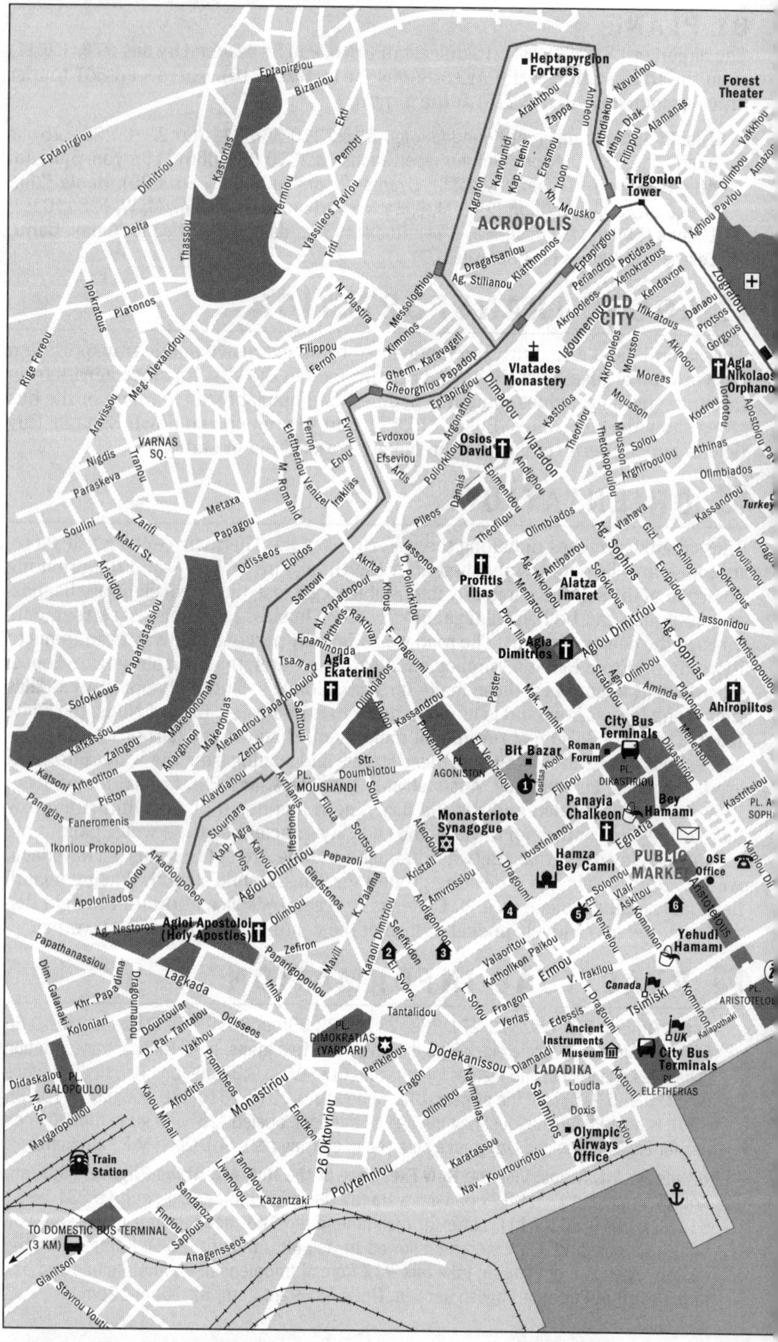
Heptapyrgion Fortress
Forest Theater
Trigonion Tower
ACROPOLIS
OLD CITY
Vlatades Monastery
Agia Nikolaos Orphano
Osios David
Profitis Ilias
Alatza Imaret
Agia Dimitrios
Agia Ekaterini
Ahiropiitos
City Bus Terminals
Bit Bazar
Roman Forum
PL. DIKASTIRIOU
PL. AGONISTON
PL. MOUSHANDI
Panayia Chalkeon
Bey Hamami
Monasteriote Synagogue
Hamza Bey Camii
PUBLIC MARKET
OSE Office
Yehudi Hamami
Agioi Apostoloi (Holy Apostles)
PL. DIMOKRATIAS (VARDARI)
Canada
UK
Ancient Instruments Museum
City Bus Terminals
PL. ELEFTHERIAS
LADADIKA
Olympic Airways Office
PL. ARISTOTELOU
PL. GALOPOULOU
Train Station
TO DOMESTIC BUS TERMINAL (3 KM)
VARNAS SQ.
Turkey
Eptapirgiou
Bizaniou
Ekti
Pembti
Kastorias
Vermiou
Vassileos Pavlou
Triti
Thassou
Dimitriou
Delta
Ipokratous
Platonos
Rige Fereou
Meg. Alexandrou
Aravissou
Nigdis
Paraskeva
Tranou
Soulini
Zarifi
Makri St.
Aristidou
Papanastassiou
Sofokleous
Kafkassou
Zalogou
L. Katsoni
Arheotiton
Piston
Panagias
Faneromenis
Ikoniou
Prokopiou
Borou
Arkadioupoleos
Apoloniados
Ag. Nestoros
Papathanassiou
Dim. Galanaki
Khr. Papadima
Dragoumanou
Koloniari
Dountoular
D. Par. Tantalou
Vakhou
Odisseos
Promitheos
Afroditis
Kalou Mihali
Didaskalou
N.S.G.
Margaropoulou
Monastiriou
Enotikon
Tandalou
Livanovou
Sandaroza
Fintiou
Sapfous
Anagensseos
Gianitson
Stavrou Voutira
Kazantzaki
26 Oktovriou
Polytehniou
Nav. Kourtouriotou
Karatassou
Olimpiou
Navmanias
Salaminos
Doxis
Loudia
Katouni
Axiou
Dodekanissou
Diamandi
Fragon
Perikleous
Tantalidou
Frangon
Verias
Edessis
I. Dragoumi
Tsimiski
V. Irakliou
Kominon
Kalapothaki
Ermou
Katholikon Paikou
Valaoritou
L. Sofou
El. Svoro
Seleftidon
Karaoli Dimitriou
K. Palama
Mavili
Paparigopoulou
Ininis
Zefiron
Olimbou
Gladstonos
Agiou Dimitriou
Dios
Kalvou
Kap. Agra
Stournara
Ifestionos
Filota
Soutsou
Papazoli
Kristalli
Afendouli
Andigonidon
Amvrossiou
Ioustinianou
Egnatia
Solomou
Vlair
Askitou
Komninon
Aristotelous
Karolou Diehl
Kastritsiou
Filipou
Tositsa Kbola
El. Venizelou
Proxenou
Kassandrou
Antion
Olimbiados
Str. Doumbiotou
Souri
Avrilianis
Klavdianou
Zentzi
Alexandrou Papadopoulou
Makedonias
Anaghiron
Makedonomaho
Sahtouri
Tsamad
Epaminonda
Pitheos
Raktivan
Al. Papadopoul
Akrita
Klious
D. Poliorkitou
F. Dragoumi
Iassonos
Pileos
Danais
Theofilou
Epimenidou
Andighou
Vlatadon
Dimadou
Argonafton
Poliorkitou
Artis
Evdoxou
Efseviou
Enou
Evrou
Irakliias
Ferron
Eleftheriou Venizel
M. Romanid
Metaxa
Papagou
Odisseos
Elpidos
Filippou
Kimonos
Gherm. Karavageli
Gheorghiou Papadop
Eptapirgiou
Messologhiou
N. Plastira
Dragatsaniou
Ag. Stilianou
Kiafthmonos
Agrafon
Karvounidi
Kap. Elenis
Erasmou
Iroon
Kh. Mousko
Arakhthou
Zappa
Antheon
Athdiakou
Athan. Diak
Filippou
Alamanas
Navarinou
Olimbou
Vakhou
Amazon
Aghiou Pavlou
Zografou
Danaou
Protsos
Gorgous
Kendavron
Ifikratous
Akinoou
Moreas
Mousson
Akropoleos
Igoumenou
Periandrou
Potideas
Xenokratous
Kastoros
Theofilou
Thetokopoulou
Solou
Arghiroudou
Athinas
Kodrou
Iordotou
Apostolou Pa
Olimbiados
Kassandrou
Iouliano
Sokratous
Iassonidou
Khristopoulou
Eshilou
Evripidou
Gizi
Vlahava
Ag. Sophias
Olimbiados
Antipatrou
Ag. Nikolaou
Meniatou
Prof. Ilia
Sofokleous
Agiou Dimitriou
Stratiotou
Agn. Olimbou
Aminda
Platonos
Menelaou
Dikastiriou
Mak. Aminis
Paster
El. Venizelou

Thessaloniki
ACCOMMODATIONS
Hotel Amalia, 6
Hotel Augustos, 2
Hotel Emporikon, 4
Hotel Ilios, 3
Youth Hostel, 8
BUS STATIONS
Halkidiki, 10
RESTAURANTS
Cafe Extrablatt, 9
Omorfi Thessaloniki, 7
Ouzeri Melathron, 5
Zithos K Yvesis, 1
ARISTOTLE UNIVERSITY
INTERNATIONAL TRADE FAIRGROUNDS
MESSEGELANDE
Kaftatzoglelo Stadium
Museum of Contemporary Art
Museum of Byzantine Culture
Archaeological Museum
Garden Theater
Vassiliko Theatro
White Tower
State Theater of Northern Greece
Octagon Building
Palace
Agia Panteleimon
Arch of Galerius
Rotunda
Agia Ioannis Prodomos
Museum of the Macedonian Struggle
Mt. Athos Pilgrims Office
TO KARAKASSI & 10 (750 m)
Cemetery
France
US
Cyprus
Gulf of Thessaloniki
Egnatia
Agiou Dimitriou
Lissikratous
3 Septemvriou
Kaftantzoglou
Megalou Alexandrou
Nikis
Tsimiski
Ethnikis Aminis
Vas. Georgiou A
Leof. Stratou
PL. SINTRIVANIOU
PL. H.A.N.TH
PL. NAVARINOU
PL. FANARIOTON
LEFKOS PIRGOS
300 yards
300 meters

Consulates: Canada: Tsimiski 17 (☎2310 256 350). Open M-F 9am-12pm. **Cyprus:** L. Nikis 37 (☎2310 260 611). Open M-F 9am-1pm. **Turkey:** Ag. Dimitriou 151 (☎2310 248 452). Open M-F 9am-2pm. **United Kingdom:** Venizelou 8 (☎2310 278 006). Open M-F 8am-1pm. **United States:** Tsimiski 43 (☎2310 242 900). Open M, W, F 9am-noon.

Banks: Banks with currency exchange and 24hr. **ATMs** line Tsimiski, including **National Bank,** Tsimiski 11 (☎2310 230 783). Open M-Th 8am-2pm, F 8am-1:30pm.

Work Opportunities: Cafe Extrablatt, see **Food,** p. 221. Will consider foreign applicants for part-time waitstaff and kitchen help. Good level of Greek needed. Contact the manager upon arrival. Pay negotiable.

International Bookstores: Molchos Books, Tsimiski 10 (☎2310 275 271), across from the National Bank, has an excellent selection of English, Classical, religious, and art history books, plus international daily newspapers. Open M, W, Sa 8:30am-3pm; Tu, Th, F 8:30am-2pm and 5:30-9pm. Two branches of **Prometheus International Bookstore,** Ermou 75 (☎2310 243 564) and Vironos 4 (☎2310 263 786), have a few shelves of novels. Open M, W 8am-2:30pm; Tu, F-Sa 8am-2pm and 5:30-8:30pm. The **Newsstand,** Ag. Sofias 37 (☎2310 287 072) offers a wide selection of international newspapers and magazines.

Laundromat: Bianca, L. Antoniadou 3 (☎2310 209 602), behind the church to the right, facing the Arch of Galerius. €5.50 for wash and dry. Open M, W, Sa 8am-3pm; Tu and Th 8am-8:30pm.

Tourist Police: Dodekanissou 4, 5th fl. (☎2310 554 870). Free maps and brochures. Open 24hr. For the **local police,** call ☎2310 553 800 or 100. There are also police booths at the train station.

Hospital: At both **Ahepa Hospital,** Kiriakidi 1 (☎2310 993 111) and **Ippokration Public Hospital,** Konstantinoupoleos 49 (☎2310 892 000), some doctors speak English. On weekends call ☎106 to find out which hospitals provide emergency treatment.

Telephones: OTE, Karolou Diehl 27 (☎134), at the corner of Ermou, 1 block east of Aristotelous. Open M-F 7:10am-1pm.

Internet Access: There are several small Internet cafes along the western end of Egnatia. **E-Global,** Egnatia 105, one block east Arch of Galerius, sports over 50 fast terminals. €2-3 per hr., open 24hr. **Meganet Internet Cafe,** 5 Place Navarinou (☎2310 269 591) offers games, videos and funky tunes. €1.50-2 per hr., open 24hr. The **British Council,** Eth. Aminis 9 (☎2310 378 300), has **free access.** Open M-F 9am-1pm.

Post Office: On Aristotelous, just below Egnatia. Open M-F 7:30am-8pm, Sa 7:30am-2pm, Su 9am-1:30pm. A **branch** office (☎2310 229 324), on Eth. Aminis near the White Tower, is open M-F 7am-8pm. Both offer Poste Restante. **Postal code:** 54101.

ACCOMMODATIONS

Welcome to the big city—don't expect to find comfort and cleanliness all at one low price. Thessaloniki's less expensive hotels are along the western end of **Egnatia,** between **Pl. Dimokratias** (500m east of the train station) and **Aristotelous.** Most are a bit gritty, ranging from ramshackle sleaze to merely cheerless, but all are easy to locate, with signs stretching from rooftop to pavement. Egnatia is loud at all hours, but rooms on the street have balconies (read: air circulation), while quieter back rooms have just a window. For more comfortable options, head toward the waterfront area two blocks west of Aristotelous. Most hotels in this area come with a hefty price tag—you may pay upwards of €150 for a double.

KIOSK PARADISE It won't take long for any visitor to Greece to realize that when it comes to sidewalk kiosks (or *periptero* (sing.), *periptera* (pl.)), Greece has the rest of the world beat. You'll find kiosks in every village, on most city blocks, and in plateias throughout the country. These sprawling, extensive structures do much more than sell cigarettes and newspapers. Greek kiosks have milk, eggs, juices, cookies, chocolate, soda, beer, and many other foodstuffs. One could easily survive for weeks living solely on kiosk food (though *Let's Go* does not recommend a kiosk diet—it's *very* unhealthy). You can also find bus tickets, phone cards, pay-phones, and souvenirs. The kiosk workers are very knowledgeable and often speak English: they are a great resource for directions and advice. The Greeks find *periptera* equally as valuable. The local kiosk is a morning or evening meeting place, where you'll find Greeks of all ages chatting and gossiping. All in all, kiosks do great business; the better located ones in Athens and Thessaloniki routinely earn revenues of over €1 million a year.

Hotel Augustos, Elenis Svoronou 4 (☎2310 522 955; ☎/fax 2310 522 500). From Egnatia, turn north at the Argo Hotel; Augustos is straight ahead. Cozy rooms with wooden floors, rugs, and high, painted ceilings. Rooms vary; ask for a balcony. Doubles and triples with bath have A/C and TVs; all rooms have phones. Singles with bath €18; doubles €25, with bath €38; triples with bath €48. ❷

Youth Hostel, Alex. Svolou 44 (☎2310 225 946; fax 2310 262 208). Take bus #8, 10, 11, or 31 west down Egnatia and get off at the Arch of Galerius (Kamara stop); or walk toward the water and turn left onto Svolou after 2 blocks. Ten rooms with six bunks each. Hot, high-pressure showers available during reception hours (9-11am and 7-11pm). €8 per person. ❶

Hotel Emporikon, Singrou 14 (☎2310 525 560 or 2310 514 431), at Egnatia. Simple, clean rooms with bright balconies overlooking leafy, tranquil Singrou. Newly-tiled bathrooms, fridges, and high ceilings. A little quieter than most other hotels on Egnatia. Singles €20; doubles €43; triples €40. ❷

Hotel Ilios, Egnatia 27 (☎2310 512 620). Comfortable, high-priced modern rooms with big windows, A/C, televisions, phones, fridges, and gleaming white baths. Some rooms have armchairs. Ask for a place away from the noisy street. Singles €32; doubles €46; triples €55.20. ❸

Hotel Amalia, Ermou 33 (☎2310 268 321; fax 2310 233 356). From Egnatia, turn right at Aristotelous and right again at Ermou. Comfortable, bright rooms with TV, A/C, bathroom and large balcony. Triples can be a bit cramped. Bar on the first floor (drinks €3-4.50); breakfast €5. Singles €50; doubles €68; triples €81.60. ❹

FOOD

Tucked along tiny sidestreets all over the city (and clustered along Aristotelous), Thessaloniki's *ouzeri* tables are mini altars of *mezedes*, upon which are placed offerings to the gods of good cheap food. Innovative places a block down from Egnatia between **Dragoumi** and **El. Venizelou** cater to a younger clientele and are open late. The most pleasant setting is under the trees on **Komninon** between Tsimiski and the flower market, where Thessaloniki's busiest sidewalks melt into a languid calm. Tables teem around 3:30pm and again around 11pm.

The maze of alleyways one block south of Egnatia and east of Aristotelous has an *ouzeri* on every corner. Roaming musicians squeeze their way through the tightly packed tables and strum a tune for your dinner (and for theirs). The **Aretsou** area, along the bay about 4km toward the airport, has excellent seafood. The **Old Town** brims with tavernas; restaurants near the **fortress** have sweeping views of the gulf. Those with fast food cravings can find gyro vendors on every block.

Ouzeri Melathron, in an alleyway at 23 El. Venizelou. From Egnatia, walk past the Ottoman Bedesten on El. Venizelou and make a right into the passageway between storefronts. Witty, 4ft.-long subtitled menus feature a spicy meat dish called "Lonely Nights" ("No nookie with this on your breath") and snails ("for friends of the hermaphrodite"). Also serves lamb, octopus and a variety of cheese dishes. Entrees €3.50-12. ❷

Zithos K Yvesis (☎2310 268 746), hidden away near the intersection of El Venizelou and Filipou. Head up Tositsa and look for an alleyway entrance between two tall buildings. Laughter and loud conversation continue well into the night in the triangular "Bit Bazar" area where this taverna is located. Delicious meat and vegetarian dishes are served by friendly, English-speaking waiters. Entrees €2.50-€6. ❶

Mesogeios, Balanou 38 (☎2310 288 460), east of Aristotelous, 1 block south of Egnatia. The largest *ouzeri* in the area—on the corner of the main intersection in the district. A popular spot among locals, Mesogeios serves large portions of meat and seafood in a festive atmosphere. Mediterranean style entrees €3.50-7. ❷

Omorfi Thessaloniki, Pl. Navarion 6 (☎2310 270 714). A popular spot that serves light seafood snacks and salads. Have a taste of complimentary (and highly potent) *tsipouro* before your meal. Entrees €2.50-6. ❷

Cafe Extrablatt, Alex Svolou 46 (☎2310 256 900), next to the youth hostel. This cheerful, family-run restaurant offers a rare blend of German and Greek cuisine. Crepes, pasta, and sausage and mushroom dishes make up the eclectic menu. Wash your meal down with one of over 50 beer options. Entrees €6-12. ❹

SIGHTS

WHITE TOWER. The White Tower presides over the eastern part of Thessaloniki's seafront and is the city's most easily recognized sight. Originally part of a 15th century seawall, the tower later became the Ottoman Death Row where **Janissaries**—an elite corps of Ottoman soldiers recruited from the Greek populace—carried out notoriously gruesome executions. Blood was so often seen seeping from the tower's stone walls that locals began calling it the **Bloody Tower.** In 1890, a prisoner whitewashed the whole building and inaugurated the current name. *(At the far eastern end of Nikis. ☎2310 267 832. Open M 12:30-7pm, Tu-Su 8am-7pm. Free.)*

OTHER SIGHTS. The Ottomans ruled Thessaloniki for almost 500 years, leaving an indelible imprint on the city's landscape. **Bey Hamami,** a 15th-century bathhouse once featured a labyrinthine interior, with a cool antechamber leading to a "tepid" room and the immense domed sauna beyond. The bathhouse is now used to exhibit a small collection of artwork. *(On Egnatia, east of Aristotelous. Open daily 9am-9pm. Free.)* Built by a *bey's* daughter in 1467-68 as a *mesçid* (a hall of worship minus the minarets), **Hazma Bey Camii** gained a minaret and official mosque status in the late 16th century; today it is the largest mosque in Greece. *(On Egnatia, just past Venizelou.)* A late 15th-century covered marketplace and craftsmen's workshop, the Ottoman **Bedesten** was said to emit delicious perfumes of musk and amber. Inscriptions carved into the domes in French, Greek, Southern Slav, and Turkish evoke the variegated ethnicity of Thessaloniki in its cosmopolitan heyday. The market has lost a lot of its bustle, but the interior still houses merchants selling fabrics and sewing supplies. *(On Venizelou, one block south of Egnatia.)*

WALKING TOURS

Just below the surface of modern, bustling Thessaloniki lies a tangle of Roman, Byzantine, Ottoman, Sephardic, and Bulgarian legacies. Temples and baths became churches, churches were transformed into mosques, and minarets were toppled to make churches again, all in a layered pile. *Wandering Byzantine Thessaloniki*, a guide available at the White Tower for a pricey €18, will satisfy the most discriminating history buff.

WALKING TOUR: BYZANTINE CHURCHES

To reach Agia Sophia, walk northwest from the White Tower up Pavlou Mela to Agia Sophia Square.

During the Byzantine Empire, Salonica was graced with enough churches to keep devout old women crossing themselves at an aerobic rate all day. Over the centuries, earthquakes, fire, and Muslim appropriations have severely damaged most of Salonica's 90 original churches, but many—such as Agios Dimitrios and Panagia Acheiropoietos—have been beautifully restored and deserve a visit. Apart from Agios Dimitrios, most churches open early (6-7am), close sometime between noon and 2pm, and reopen for a few hours in the evening (usually around 5-8pm). Come in the morning and dress modestly. Although there's usually no admission fee, donations are looked upon kindly.

Sunk into the ground at the eastern end of Ermou, the magnificent, domed 7th-century **Agia Sophia** offers a brilliant introduction to the splendor of Byzantine churches. Gold *tesserae* gleam on the dome's 9th-century circular mosaic of the Ascension, where the awestruck Apostles, angels, and Virgin witness a truncated Christ ascending in a blue globe. *(Open daily 7am-1pm and 5-7pm).*

Follow Ag. Sophias road north past Egnatia until you arrive at **Panagia Acheiropoietos** to your right, once the city's official mosque. On the underside of the church's arches you will see mosaics portraying heavenly delights—glittering fruits, birds, vases of water and fish. *(Open daily 8am-1pm and 6-9pm.)* Continue north along Ag. Sophias; turn left three streets later onto Agiou Dimitriou and the awe-inspiring **Agios Dimitrios** will appear on your right. The city's oldest and most famous church is named for the city's patron saint, a Christian Roman officer who was speared to death in the Roman bath complex that once occupied the site. Although two fires in 620 and 1917 decimated the church, the surviving fragments of the mosaics that once covered the inner sides of the colonnades are absolutely stunning. The **crypt,** down a flight of stairs on the east side, contains the shell of the original tiny church and the fountain where Dimitrios was killed. *(Open daily 8am-8pm. Crypt hours reduced Su-M. Holy Liturgy held in the crypt every F 9:30-11pm.)*

Trudge piously along Prof. Ilia (the first street on your right, west of Agios Dimitrious) until you reach the quieter, less-touristed **Profitis Ilias.** This domed 14th-century church's uniqueness lies in its architectural layout: a cross-in-square with side choruses, a style invented in 1000 by the founder of Megistis Lavras, the oldest monastery on Mt. Athos. *(Open daily 6:30-11:30am and 5-7pm.)*

For the truly devout, the final short, steep climb past Profitis Ilias will bring you to the tiny church of **Ossios David.** Head east along Olimbiados and turn left onto Ag. Sophias, then follow the signs from Dimadou Vlatadon. Perched upon a hillside with spectacular views across the gulf, Ossios David houses a brilliant mosaic of Jesus sitting on a rainbow, flanked by an angel, eagle, lion and calf with the prophets Ezekiel and Habakkuk in the corners and fish swimming in the river Jordan below. Beautiful 12th-century frescos of the nativity and baptism decorate the arches at the entrance. *(Open daily 9am-noon and 6-8pm. €1.)*

WALKING TOUR: ROMAN REMNANTS

To reach the acropolis, take bus #23 (€0.44) or walk north along Ethnikis Aminis from the white tower and follow the remains of the ancient wall to the top (a 30min. walk).

The **Heptapyrgion,** a 5th-century Byzantine fortress, is the main attraction of the city's modest acropolis. From 1890 to 1989, it replaced the White Tower as the city's prison; modern prison buildings remain both inside and outside the fortress ramparts. *(Open M 12:30-7pm, Tu-Su 8am-7pm.)* A **museum** which details the history of Heptapyrgion is open daily 10:30am-5pm. From Egnatia, turn left at D. Gounari to see the most dramatic reminder of Salonica's Roman heritage: the enormous cylindrical **Rotunda,** today surrounded by a bustling street market. Inside, beautiful mosaics of angels' heads still decorate the dome; bring a pair of binoculars to check out the intricate detail. Originally built as part of egotistical emperor Galerius's palace, the Pantheon-inspired Rotunda later became a church. The walls were once plastered with some of the city's most lavish and gleaming mosaics. An estimated 36 million *tesserae* were assembled to represent gilded facades, birds, fruits and saints; very little has survived. *(Open Tu-Su 8am-7pm.)*

From the entrance of the Rotunda, walk around to the opposite side and continue straight down towards the **Arch of Galerius.** A colonnaded processional led south from the Rotunda to the Arch and the **Palace of Galerius,** once the three components of an enormous complex. Galerius built the arch to commemorate his victory over the Persians in AD 305, covering it with **relief sculptures** detailing his triumphs. It was once paralleled by a similar structure to the east; together they formed a huge gateway commemorating the Persian defeat. The Palace of Galerius, south of the Arch on Dragoumi near Pl. Navarino, has been partially excavated to reveal a marvelous mosaic sidewalk. The centerpiece of the palace was the partially preserved **octagonal hall.**

From the Palace, retrace your steps to Egnatia and continue east towards Aristotelous. Head towards the city bus terminals on Filipou and watch for the **Roman Forum** just across the road. Considering it's not in Rome, it's not surprising that this Roman Forum is not terribly spectacular. During the 2nd and 3rd centuries, it included a public records archive, mint, odeon, *boulaterion*, and library; today it offers a restored version of the **theater.** On the south side of the Agora's lower square was once the **colonnade** that held eight caryatid statues of mythological women. Known in Ladino, the language of the Sephardic Jews, as *las Incantadas* ("the enchanted women"), they were thought to have been magically turned to stone. When the portico was demolished in 1865, the statues were moved to the Louvre. All of the excavations at the Roman Forum are described in detail at the Archaeological Museum.

WALKING TOUR: OLD CITY

To reach the Old City, take bus #22 from Pl. Eleftherias.

North of Ag. Dimitriou you'll find the streets of the Old City. **Agios Nikolaos Orphanos,** off Apostelou Pavlou, has splendid 14th-century wall paintings; some of the illustrated Biblical narratives are the most important in all of Macedonia and Serbia. From the White Tower, follow the remains of the ancient wall north along Ipodromiou, past Ag. Dimitriou, to reach the 15th-century **Trigonion Tower.** It was built as a guard post and observation point on the city's fortifications. The top of the tower is closed to the public. The **fortifications** were originally erected by the Byzantines and later refurbished by the Ottomans to strengthen and prepare them for the new technologies of artillery warfare. Continue up through the crooked sprawl of the Old Town to reach the ruins of the **Eptapirgion Walls** ("Seven Gates"), erected during the reign of Theodosius the Great.

MUSEUMS

ARCHAEOLOGICAL MUSEUM. The treasures from Vergina's royal Macedonian tombs, once the highlight of Thessaloniki's collection, were returned to Vergina (p. 227) in 1998, but the museum still shelters many jewels, including a permanent exhibit on Macedonian gold. Sculptures of a famously erotic Aphrodite and parts of an enormous statue of Athena share space with a grand mosaic depicting Dionysus with Ariadne, Apollo stalking Daphne, and Ganymede in Zeus's eagle talons. There are also finds from 121 graves at Sindos, including gold death masks and jewelry, soldiers' swords and helmets, and figurines. The museum is an ideal starting point for exploring the local Roman Forum, and the nearby sites of Vergina and Pella. *(At the western end of Tsimiski, across from the International Helexpo Fairgrounds. ☎2310 830 538. Open M 12:30-7pm, Tu-Su 8am-7pm; hours reduced in winter. €4, students and seniors €2, EU students and under 18 free.)*

MUSEUM OF BYZANTINE CULTURE. The Byzantine Museum's massive brick building, informative wall texts, and displays tracing the evolution of early Christian art and life complement its neighbor, the Archaeological Museum. The museum, which is divided between Early and Middle Byzantine artifacts, creates an impression of everyday Byzantine life with displays of fish-hooks, embroidery, toiletries, belt-buckles and dice. The second half of the museum focuses on the pilgrimages, castles, and emperors of the Middle Byzantine era, including an exhibit of early Christian iconography recently relocated from the White Tower. *(Behind the archaeological museum, across Septemvriou 3. Fully wheelchair accessible. ☎2310 868 570 or 2310 868 571. Open M 12:30-7pm, Tu-Su 8am-7pm; hours reduced in winter. €4, students and seniors €2, EU students and under 18 free.)*

MUSEUM OF THE MACEDONIAN STRUGGLE. Through extensive artifacts and reconstructed scenes, this museum tells the tale of Macedonia's guerrilla war for independence from both Turkey and Bulgaria, leading up to and including both **Balkan Wars.** The exhibits include personal artifacts of the rebel leader **Pavlou Melas** (including the bullet that killed him) as well as captured war booty like Turkish and Bulgarian arms and treasure. The museum is happy to provide English pamphlets with facts about the collection and an historical overview of the Macedonian war. *(Koromila 23, 1 block from the water, halfway between the White Tower and Pl. Aristotelous. ☎2310 229 778. Open Tu-Sa 10am-2pm and 6-9pm, Su 10am-2pm. Free.)*

ATATÜRK'S HOUSE. If you've just come from Turkey and miss the ubiquitous statues, streets, and museums dedicated to the creator of the modern Turkish state, here's a chance to get your fix. The three-story house, which was the birthplace and childhood home of Atatürk, now displays various relics from his life. Pictures of the leader adorn all the walls, and many items of clothing (including his bathrobe) are also on view. Display signs are in Turkish and Greek. *(Apostolou Pavlou 17. Open daily 10am-5pm. Free. To visit, you must present your passport next door at the Turkish consulate, Ag. Dimitriou 151.)*

MUSEUM OF ANCIENT, BYZANTINE, AND POST-BYZANTINE MUSICAL INSTRUMENTS. Three floors display replications of ancient musical instruments, tracing their evolution from 2800BC to the early 20th century. The museum's concert hall hosts a series of Byzantine music performances throughout the year—details are advertised in local newspapers and on the radio. *(Katouni 12-14, at the western end of Tsimiski near the Ladadika district. ☎2310 555 2663. Open M 9am-3pm, Tu-Su 9am-3pm and 5-10pm. Adults €4.40, students and children €2.20.)*

ENTERTAINMENT

Summer visitors looking for live *rembetika* music should spend a weekend night at **Iyoklima,** on tiny Axiou south of Nikis near the port, or **Palios Stathmos** (Old Station), Voutira 2 (☎2310 521 892). **Alexandros,** at Eth. Aminis and Nikis by the White Tower, is an indoor movie theater, but when skies are clear, head outside to waterfront **Natali Cinema,** Vas. Olgas 3 (☎2310 829 457), five minutes past the White Tower, or **Ellinis** at Pl. Chanth (☎2310 292 304), across from the archaeological museum. (Films 9 and 11pm. €6.) You can't miss the posters plastered all over town for the theater, music, and dance performances at venues like the **Dhasous Theater** (☎2310 218 092), **Kipou Theater** (☎2310 256 775), **Damari Theater,** and **Kratiko and Vassiliko Theaters** (☎2310 223 785 for both). The **International Fairgrounds,** across from the Archaeological and Byzantine Museums, holds festivals throughout the year, including the **Wine Festival** (August), **International Trade Fair and Song Festival** (Sept.), the **Dimitria Festival** (Oct.), the internationally revered **Thessaloniki Film Festival** (Nov.; www.filmfestival.gr), and the new **Documentary Festival** (Mar.).

NIGHTLIFE

There are three main hubs for late-night fun in Thessaloniki: the bars and cafes of the **Ladadika** district (once the city's red-light strip), the bustling **waterfront,** and the big, open-air discos that throb in the area around the **airport** (a €8-9 taxi ride from the center). Most of the clubs around the airport feature live modern or traditional Greek music (€9 cover includes a drink). Call ahead and dress well. Although the clubs boom until dawn, summer nightlife in the city doesn't amount to much by Salonican standards—most head to the beaches of Halkidiki (p. 255).

Decadence, by the airport, 11km east along the main highway. One of the most popular spots in town, Decadence is a booming outdoor nightclub with deafening music. The party doesn't really get started until about 3am and continues way past sunrise. Cover €10, but expect to drop a few more euros when internationally renowned DJs visit.

Podon (☎2310 424 058), 11km east of the city along the main highway, across from Decadence. For Greek music addicts only. The most sophisticated club in Thessaloniki has an equally sophisticated cover (€10, includes 1 drink). Rub elbows with Thessaloniki's hip and moneyed in the club's amphitheatric bowl, or join the crowd on stage with the live Greek pop band. The music blasts until 4:30am.

Mousis (☎2310 476 106), across the main road with a large red neon sign. The best club in Thessaloniki for live Greek music, Mousis has an enormous glass ceiling accented by blue neon lights shining over 5 bars, a compact stage, 100 tables, and plenty of room to move. Cover (€10) includes 1 drink. Open daily midnight-5am.

Kouva, Orvilou 7 (☎2310 531 944). A 2-story hotspot, with a split-level dance floor complete with catwalks and bumpin' Greek tunes. Cover (€3.50) includes 1 drink.

Stala, L. Nikis 3 (☎2310 228 237), right at the western end of the waterfront, by the port. Cool, breezy tables outside; deafening rock music in the cavernous interior. A great place to sip a drink and people-watch before heading to the clubs of Ladadika, 2 blocks away. Cocktails €5.50-6.50.

Mylos, Andreou Georgiou 56 (☎2310 525 968), in the far west of the city; take bus #31 or a taxi. Once an old mill, now an entertainment center with art exhibits, a restaurant, and bars. Live shows include jazz and groups like Massive Attack and Patti Smith.

DAYTRIPS FROM THESSALONIKI

ANCIENT VERGINA Βεργινα

***Buses** run from Thessaloniki (55min., every hr. 5:45am-9:15pm, €4.40) to Veria. From Veria take the bus to Vergina (20min., 11 per day 6:30am-8pm, €0.95). You'll be dropped off in the Vergina plateia; follow the signs to the archaeological sights. Buses run out of Vergina for Veria (20min., 10 per day 7:20am-8:20pm, €0.95) but are less reliable. Open M noon-7pm, Tu-Su 8am-7pm; winter Tu-Su 8am-7pm. An €8 ticket will grant admission to all of Vergina's sights. Students €4, EU students free.*

Unearthing the ancient Vergina ruins was an archaeological watershed—among the enlightening finds were Greek inscriptions that proved the ancient Macedonians were a Greek tribe. The findings in the tombs display such superb artistry that scholars believe they could have belonged only to the royal Macedonian family of Philip II, father of Alexander the Great; it's likely, too, since the tombs date to 350-325 BC, during Philip's rule. The ruins at Pella, discovered in 1957 by a farmer with archaeological instincts, date back to a time when the Aegean covered the surrounding fields, and Pella served as a Thermaic Gulf port and the capital of the Macedonian Empire.

MUSEUM. At once uncannily morbid and dazzlingly beautiful, Vergina's museum will no doubt be the highlight of your visit. Visitors enter the **Great Tumulus,** itself a massive burial mound more than 12m high and 110m in diameter, the largest in Greece. The Tumulus was built before the mid-3rd century BC and housed the graves of Vergina's average citizens in addition to the massive royal tombs. The atmospherically-lit museum displays artifacts found in the Great Tumulus including Attic vases, clay and ivory figurines, gold jewelry, and the carved funerary *steles* of the commoners' graves.

Four of the majestic **royal tombs** lie in their original locations. The designs of all four are similar: each has an anterior Ionic or Doric colonnade decorated with mythological scenes. The large room behind the colonnade contains the remains of the deceased and various items to accompany him or her into the afterlife. Tombs I and IV belong to unknown royal family members. Tomb IV, looted in antiquity, stored unusually beautiful and well-preserved **frescoes,** possibly the work of master artist **Nikomachus.** The most intact depicts an anguished Persephone being abducted by a grim Hades, while Demeter watches with cold sorrow.

The **Tomb of the Prince** probably belongs to Alexander IV, son of Alexander the Great; he was murdered along with his mother at age 13 by his not-so-close relative, Cassander of Amphipolis. The silver hydra containing his bones and his spectacular leaf-mimicking gold myrtle wreath are on display, along with other artifacts. The grand **Tomb of Philip II** is accompanied by a magnificent gold chest and exquisite myrtle wreath, and by fragments of his chryselephantine couch, decorated with miniature figures made of gold, glass, and wood. A huge glass case displays the charred remains of the bountiful offerings thrown on Philip's funeral pyre; they include animal offerings, figurines, and all his treasured possessions. The flames of the pyre acted as transformative agents, sending these items into the next world with the deceased. Philip's tomb also contained the remains of a woman, probably **Cleopatra,** one of his seven consorts. Her gold couch remains, as do shreds of the gold-embroidered purple cloth that wrapped her bones.

OTHER VERGINA RUINS. To get to the **Palace of Palatitsa,** turn right as you exit the museum and follow the road as it veers to the left. A short-cut through the bus parking lot followed by an uphill walk will get you to the ruins in about 20min.

What remains of the 3rd-century BC palace is now little more than a collection of toppled columns and ancient rubble; as of summer 2002, the mosaic on the south side of the palace floor was undergoing conservation work and could not be viewed. *(Open M noon-7pm, Tu-Su 8am-7pm.)*

On the walk up to Palatitsa, you'll encounter the **Rhomaios Tomb,** containing a stately marble throne; its occupant remains a mystery. The tomb itself is locked, but you can climb down the stone staircase and peer through the gates at the intact inner chamber. Next to it (but still undergoing restoration) is the **Tomb of Evridiki,** with a fresco of Persephone and Hades in the underworld rivaling that of Tomb IV. Farther up the road, a sign off to the left past a prickly meadow indicates the site of the **Ancient Theater.** It was here that Philip II was assassinated while celebrating the marriage of his daughter, Cleopatra.

ANCIENT PELLA Πελλα

Along the main Edessa-Thessaloniki highway, 38km west of Thessaloniki. ***Buses*** *to Pella (40 min., every 45 min. 6:30am-10pm, €2.75). Make sure you are let off at "Ancient Pella," not "New Pella." You should see the archaeological site off to the right. Buses to* ***Thessaloniki*** *(2-3 per hr.) pass the site; the bus stop is across from the small cafe by the archaeological site.* *☎23820 31 160. Open Apr.-Oct. M noon-7pm, Tu-Su 8am-7pm; Nov.-Mar. Tu-Su 8:30am-2:30pm. Site and museum €6, students €3, EU students free.*

As the remains of 26 Neolithic settlements indicate, the area around Pella was heavily inhabited in prehistoric times. Around 400 BC, King Archelaus opted to move his capital here from Aigai (Vergina), taking advantage of his new position to simultaneously foster eastern trade and cultivate a rapport with southern Greece. Later the birthplace of Philip II, the capital prospered under his reign. The construction of a splendid new palace attracted great minds and talents from the entire Hellenic world to the court. By the mid-4th century BC, however, the recession of the sea had made Pella a less than convenient port—its glory days came to an end in 168 BC when the city was ransacked by Roman general Aemilius Paulus.

MUSEUM. Pella only takes an hour to see, but the museum alone makes the trip worthwhile. Its treasures include gold-leaf jewelry, terra-cotta figurines, glazed and unglazed Macedonian pottery, and unusual molded pottery depicting some rather racy episodes. The collection's important objects are the exquisite **mosaics** of Dionysus riding a spotted panther, a lion hunt, and a gryphon devouring a deer, highlighted by grisly splashes of blood. The mosaics are composed of small sea pebbles outlined with thin lead strips; the missing eyes were likely semi-precious stones. They're the earliest-known mosaics to mimic a three-dimensional look.

RUINS. Directly across the highway from the museum is Pella's vast archaeological site, still under excavation by budding young go-getters from the University of Thessaloniki. At the heart of the site are the remains of the **agora,** the commercial center of the city in ancient times, and a few grand houses. To the left, the **House of Dionysos** and the **House of the Abduction of Helen** both have expansive, well-preserved mosaic floors. The beautifully-executed scenes in the mosaics seem to breathe, with subtle muscle gradations and shadows in the stag-hunting scene, and the swirling skirts and rearing horses in Helen's abduction. The **House of Plaster** has no mosaics, but it does have a splendid rectangular Ionic colonnade. North of the houses and the agora are the **acropolis** and **palace** (off-limits to visitors). The palace, built in 10 stages, is a makeshift blend of architectural styles. Expanded by Philip, it fell with the rest of Pella at the hands of Aemilius Paulus.

LITOHORO Λιτοχωρο

For most hikers, the gateway to **Mount Olympus** is the charming village of Litohoro, which caters to both fearless mountain climbers and beach-loving hedonists, who come for the sands and nightclubs of nearby Plaka. Twisting cobblestone paths lead down to the central plateia, where friendly locals relax in the shadows of enormous mountains. It's also possible to make the ascent from the western side of Olympus, beginning in Kokkinopilos village, but this route can't compare to the spectacular trails that originate in Litohoro.

ORIENTATION AND PRACTICAL INFORMATION. Litohoro lies 90km southwest of Thessaloniki, with rolling hills to the west and the Aegean Sea to the east. **Ag. Nikolaou** runs east to west and leads to a fountain at the central plateia about 500m after the entrance to the town. Down Ag. Nikolaou near the police station, you'll find the town's **tourist office** by the park, providing free maps of the town and a €3 map of the mountain. (☎23520 83 100. Open July-Nov. 8:30am-2:30pm and 5-9pm.) **Buses** (☎23520 81 271) from Litohoro's KTEL station, under the blue awning opposite the tourist office, travel to: **Athens** (5½hr., 3 per day 9:30am-midnight, €24.70); **Larisa** (2hr., 8 per day 6am-7:45pm, €5) via **Katerini; Plaka** (10min., every hr. 10:15am-7:15pm, €1); and **Thessaloniki** (1½hr., 17 per day 6:15am-8:45pm, €5.90) via **Katerini** (€1.50). **Trains** (☎23520 22 522) stop at **Litohoro** on the **Thessaloniki-Volos** and **Thessaloniki-Athens** lines. Buses run from the bus station to the train station every hour (6:15am-9:50pm, €1). Get off at the Health Center stop. **Trains** from Litohoro's station run to: **Athens** (6hr., 4 per day 9:10am-11:30pm, €15); **Larisa** (1½hr., 6 per day 7:10am-8:40pm, €3.65); and **Thessaloniki** (1½hr., 4 per day 8am-7:50pm, €3). Call the Katerini station (☎23510 23 709) or the Litohoro tourist office for more information. A **taxi** from the train station should cost around €6. There's a **National Bank** (☎23520 81 025) with a 24hr. **ATM** in the main plateia. The **police station** is just below the plateia, on the left as you walk downhill. (☎23520 81 100 or 23520 81 111. Open 24hr.) The **health center** (☎23520 22 222) is about 5km outside of town, by the beach, and has 24hr. **emergency** facilities. **Internet access** is available at **Cafe Artio,** toward the bottom of town across from Hotel Park. (☎23520 84 038. €3 per hr.) From the plateia, cobblestoned **28 Octovriou** leads left, up to the **post office** (open M-F 7:30am-2pm). The **OTE** sits across from the tourist booth, farther down the main street. (Open 7:30am-3:10pm.) **Postal code:** 60200.

ACCOMMODATIONS AND FOOD. The most affordable hotel in town is the **Hotel Park ❷**, Ag. Nikolaou 23, down Ag. Nikolaou from the plateia and past the long park; the tight but comfortable rooms have baths, TVs, fridges, and A/C. (☎23520 81 252. Singles €20; doubles €30; triples €40.) The pleasant **Hotel Aphrodite ❸,** next to the plateia and behind the bank, offers attractive rooms with TVs, fridges, and A/C. There's a large, comfortable family lounge downstairs, an outdoor terrace, and beautiful views of the mountain. (☎23520 81 415; fax 23520 83 646. Singles €25; doubles €40; triples €30.) Opposite the entrance to Hotel Aphrodite, **Hotel Enipeas ❸** provides clean, spacious rooms with phones, A/C, balconies, and baths. Ask for a room with a view of the mountains. There's a lovely balcony upstairs looking down to the plateia, and a communal kitchen is available in the basement. (☎23520 84 328; fax 23520 81 328. Singles €30; doubles €38; triples €45; quads €50.) Behind the plateia on a road that veers off to the left, **Papa Nikolau ❸** has tidy, well-maintained rooms looking out over Litohoro's red roofs. Each room is equipped with a kitchenette, TV, fridge, and fan. Beautiful flower gardens line the entrance to this family-run domatia. (☎23520 81 236; fax 23520 84 246. Doubles €35; triples €45.) The **beach,** 5km from town, is full of **campgrounds,** of which **Olym-**

pus Zeus ❶ (☎23520 22 115) and **Olympus Beach** ❶ (☎23520 22 112 or 23520 22 113) are the largest and best situated. Due to their waterfront location, expect to pay at least €8 for a site. Avoid freelance camping on the north side of the road between the town and the highway; it's an army training ground.

For a final feast before you head for the hills, try **Restaurant Erato** ❷, just off the plateia near the church. They serve up a menu of pizzas and pastas as well as the usual Greek favorites in a lovely, shaded setting. (☎23520 83 346. Entrees €3.30-9.) **Fistaria Dias** ❷, under a yellow awning on the left as you walk toward the plateia, is another local favorite. Try the grilled chicken (€5) or one of the fish, octopus, or meat dishes. (☎23520 82 225. Entrees €3.50-6.50.) On the street that forks right at the police station, **Ta Mezedakia** ❷ cooks up a range of tasty Greek classics. (☎23520 82 853. Entrees €3.50-7.)

NIGHTLIFE. If you want to party before (or instead of) hiking, the evening begins in the **bars** around the bottom of Ag. Nikolaou and moves over to Plaka by midnight. In Litohoro, **Bolero** and **Maskes** are popular for their selective American tunes. House-booming **Status** and metal-loving **Garage** see a younger and hipper crowd. At **Plaka,** techno-blasting **On the Rocks** and **Kavadimo,** right on the beautiful clear water, are popular, but the hottest spot of them all is **White Shark,** where the sleekest and trendiest Litohorians get down with their black-clad selves all night long. A taxi to Plaka costs around €4-5. Partying in Plaka can get expensive: covers are around €8, beer is also €8, and cocktails can be as much as €10.

MOUNT OLYMPUS Ολυμπος Ορος

The charm of Olympus does not lie in its natural beauty; nor its physical magnitude; the beauty of Olympus is spiritual, it is divine.

—Boissonade

Erupting out of the Thermaic Gulf, the 3000m height and formidable slopes of Mt. Olympus so awed the ancients that they believed it to be the divine dwelling place of their immortal pantheon. The sharp peaks saw no successful mortal ascent until 1913, when Christos Kakalos, a Litohorian hunter, guided two Swiss adventurers up to Mytikas's zenith. Since then, Olympus has been harnessed by a network of well-maintained hiking trails that make the summit accessible to just about anyone with sturdy legs, a head for heights, and a taste for adventure; the climb is a strenuous but fantastic must-do. As you ascend, you'll pass leafy green woodlands and shadowy pine forests before emerging above the treeline to truly spectacular views. Today some 20 mules make a daily trip up Olympus, carrying everything from cocoa to olive oil, to keep the mountain refuges freshly stocked.

Mt. Olympus has eight peaks. **Kalogeros** (2701m), **Toumba** (2785m), **Profitis Ilias** (2803m), and **Antonius** (2817m) are dwarfed by the summits of **Skala** (2866m), **Skolio** (2911m), **Stefani** (also called "The Throne of Zeus," 2909m), and **Mytikas** (or "The Pantheon," 2919m). The entire region became Greece's first national park in 1938, and the mountain is said to contain all the climates of Europe, from the Mediterranean climate of Litohoro to the rocky tundra at the summit.

LOGISTICS OF THE CLIMB

You'll find the most reliable resources for all aspects of hiking—updates on weather and trail conditions, advice on itineraries and routes, and reservations for any of the **Greek Alpine Club** (EOS) refuges—from **EOS refuge Spilios Agapitos,** or "Refuge A." (☎23520 81 800. See **Refuges** below.) The staff has years of experience and is happy to distribute information over the phone in fluent English. In Lito-

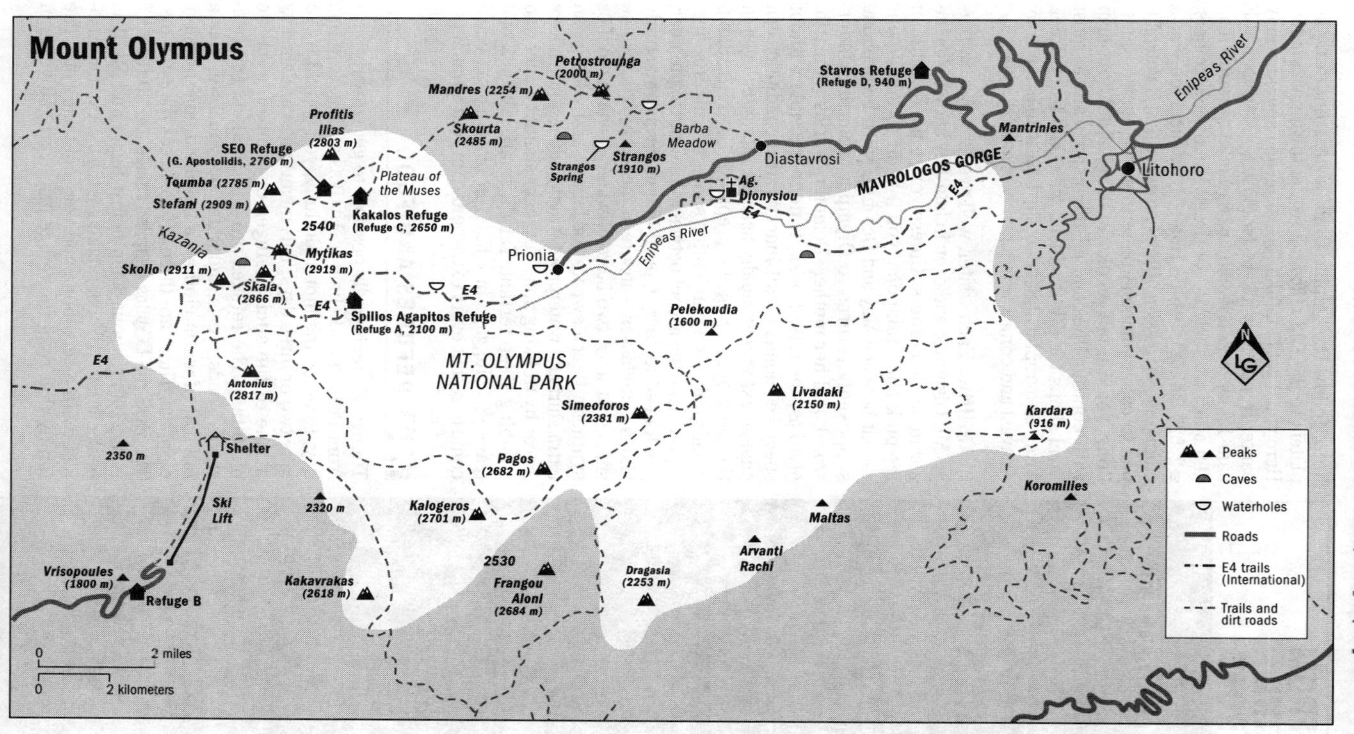

NORTHERN GREECE

FROM THE ROAD

GIMME SHELTER

It was shortly before 2pm when I finally arrived, gasping and panting, at Spillos Agapitos refuge. Gulping the last swigs of water from my plastic bottle, I stumbled toward the refuge door, serenaded by a small assembly of mules with clanging bells strapped to their necks. I stepped closer and was greeted by a chorus of friendly, German-sounding "Hullos" from a hiking group that had gathered by the entrance.

"So how long did it take you, a fit, young man like yourself?" one asked.

"About two hours," I lied. They eyed me suspiciously. "But I took a taxi to Prionia," I hastily added, admitting that I had reduced the eight-hour grueling slog to a fourth of the time.

"That's cheating!" someone remarked in a tone of mock disgust.

It seemed I was dealing with professionals. I might have guessed by the neat row of walking poles lining the refuge wall and the sensible yet fashionable hiking attire. A merry brigade of hearty Europeans, possibly raised yodelling at the foot of the Alps, all of them a good deal older (and fitter) than me.

The mountain refuge is more than a handy pit-stop. It's a place where those on the way up have the very good fortune of meeting those on the way down. My welcoming party bore beaming smiles of success, having recently conquered Olympus, and they were now happily doling out advice to those who had yet to make the climb. A well-meaning man took me to one side and led me to a map of the trails that had been hammered

horo, follow the "Alpine Club" signs from near the plateia to the **EOS office** below the town parking lot. Here you'll get helpful information and some friendly banter from fellow hikers. (☎23520 84 544. Open M-F 9am-12:30pm and 6-8:30pm, Sa-Su 9am-noon.) The **SEO office** (Association of Greek Mountain Climbers; ☎23520 83 262), behind Hotel Myrto, acts more as a clubhouse than as an official resource, but if you happen to catch someone there they can answer questions. You can buy a colorful bilingual fold-out map with contour lines and all the major trails at most local shops for €3. Produced with data from Greek Army Geographical Service, the best map is made by Anavasi and comes with a handy plastic sleeve.

PLANNING. Each winter, well over 2m of snow buries Mt. Olympus, and even in late July snowfields linger in shady corners. Unless you're handy with an ice-pick and crampons, you'll want to make your ascent between May and October, when Persephone supposedly returns to Olympus from the Underworld, and her mother, Demeter, warms the earth. Mytikas, the tallest peak, is not accessible without special equipment until June. **Weather** conditions can change extremely rapidly near the summits; even in the peak of summer, be prepared for chilly, damp clouds, rain, and unrelenting sun above the tree line. If you make the ascent between June and September, you'll need to carry typical hiking **equipment:** sturdy shoes, sunglasses, sunscreen, head covering, some snacks, at least two liters of water, a warm wool or synthetic fleece sweater or jacket, and, ideally, an extra shirt and waterproof windbreaker. Some hikers swear by trekking poles for maintaining balance and climbing steep terrain. Take a small day-pack and leave your luggage in a hotel in Litohoro, as you'll come to resent every extra pound on your shoulders.

REFUGES AND FOOD

Though it's technically possible to get an early start from Prionia and climb to Mytikas and back in one day, to enjoy the mountain fully, you should try to take two or three days. This means an overnight stay in one of the social refuges or campsites on the mountain. The refuges provide blankets (no bedsheets), beds, meals, and water, but you'll still want a full suit of warm clothes, a flashlight, and possibly earplugs. There are three refuges near the summits. The EOS-run **Spilos Agapitos refuge,** or "Refuge A," is at 2100m, about 800m below Skala and Mytikas peaks. It has 110 beds, making it the largest and cushiest, with a telephone and very cold showers. The family that runs the refuge has nearly 50 years of experience and takes great pride in the refuge's cleanliness. The **kitchen** serves meals until 9pm, with salads running around €2.20 and meat dishes around €5. (☎23520 81 800. Open mid-May to late Oct.; meals served 6am-9pm; doors close and lights go out at 10pm. €10 per bed; €8 for members of any mountain club; €4.20 to tent nearby and use facilities.) On the other side, the other EOS refuge, **Kakalos,** "Refuge C" (Γ), at 2650m, has 22 beds, no phone, and charges the same prices as Agapitos. Make reservations through Agapitos. (Open June-Sept. 15. Meals served 6am-9pm. Doors open all night.) Fifteen minutes from Kakalos, beneath Stefani and Profitis Ilias, **G. Apostolidis** (better known as **SEO Refuge;** 2760m) sleeps 90 and can accommodate extras and late-comers in its glass-walled porch or living room. The friendly proprietor will cook up a delicious meal for €5. (Open June-Sept. Meals served 9am-9:30pm. Doors open all night. €10 per bed; €8 with any mountain club membership.) Make reservations through the **Thessaloniki SEO,** which runs the refuge. (☎2310 244 710. Open M-F 8-10pm; leave a message for a reservation.) Although Kakalos is smaller than the other refuges, it boasts the best views of dawn rising above the clouds.

All of the refuges, particularly the very popular Refuge A, tend to fill up on weekends in June-Oct. Call at least a few weeks in advance for **reservations.** Otherwise, call one to two days ahead and try your luck. Meals tend to run about €2.50-3.50 for soups and salads, €2.80-5.30 for pasta and meat dishes, €3 for breakfast. Bring a **flashlight** to navigate your way to the bathroom after the generator is shut down in the evenings. The refuge managers are also prepared to handle emergency rescues if needed.

TRAILS: THE HIKE TO THE HEAVENS

There are three ways to take on Olympus: all three originate at **Litohoro** (elev. 340m). Two involve heading straight to the trailheads, and one involves an alternate hike. The first and most popular trailhead begins at **Prionia** (elev. 1100m), 18km from the village. The second trailhead is at **Diastavrosi** (also called **Gortsia;** elev. 1300m), 14km away. There are no buses to Prionia or Diastavrosi, so walk, drive, or take a taxi (Prionia €20; Diastavrosi €8) along the asphalt road (eventually a dusty, unpaved path) that winds upward starting next to the police station in Litohoro, just below the plateia. The third route is more challenging and involves hiking to Prionia via a trail along the **Enipeas Gorge;** you begin in Litohoro and eventually arrive at the Pronia trailhead. After spending the night at the Agapitos refuge, you'll

into the refuge walls.

"You have a number of options," he began, and a detailed trail tutorial ensued. He traced a pencil along the various routes, pausing only to recount any particularly relevant horror stories. He smiled paternally and added, "I hope you're not afraid of heights." Laughing, he slapped me on the back and returned to the group.

At 10pm, the strictly observed time for lights-out, the generator switched off and plunged the room into darkness. One sock on, one sock off, toothbrush still clenched between teeth, I groped around for my flashlight, knocking over plastic bottles and other blinded hikers as I went. One resourceful fellow, having forgotten his flashlight, improvised with the flickering flame of his cigarette lighter. Holding it proudly at arm's length, like the Olympic torch, he ambled downstairs to the bathroom, humming along the way.

It was a very long night. Loud snores, coughing fits and competitive nose-blowing disturbed my sweet dreams of deep ravines. Morning eventually came and electricity was restored. Packing up my gear and obediently folding my blankets, I joined the ranks of bleary-eyed hikers, silently clutching steaming mugs of coffee. The bravest of the bunch, wanting to look her best for Zeus, returned shivering but clean from an icy cold shower.

"Right," she said. "The fog's closing in. Time we made tracks."

A hike to the heavens and back—and we lived to tell the tale.

—Gary Cooney

wind to the summit the next day and head around to the SEO and Kakalos refuges. Hikers can stay another night there and walk down the next day to Diastavrosi (about 3-4hr., depending on how you fare going downhill), or pass the refuges and arrive at Diastavrosi in late afternoon. All of the trails are easy to follow, and most are marked with red blazes.

ASCENDING MT. OLYMPUS (ENIPEAS GORGE ROUTE)

The fairly strenuous but beautiful trail from Litohoro to Prionia runs along an **E4 trail** through the **Mavrologos Gorge** by the Enipeas River. Wonderful stretches punctuate the 18km climb, but it's a difficult 5hr. hike with many steep ups and downs. **Bring water.** To find the **trailhead,** walk uphill from Litohoro's main plateia past the Hotel Aphrodite, and follow signs to Mili (Μυλοι), past the town cemetery, to the Restaurant Mili. There is drinking water at the trailhead. Continue past the restaurant to the left. When you reach the concrete walkway, make a right and walk along it a short distance. At a fork in the trail, follow the yellow diamond markers marked "E4" up the left side of the Mavrologos Gorge. Keep following yellow diamonds, red blazes, spray-painted numbers, and orange-and-white plastic strips tied on trees, crossing over the river at the newly built bridges. Parts of the trail have views down into the gorge. When the trail descends to the river, lovely, clear green pools abound. After three hours you'll reach the tiny **Chapel of Agios Spileo,** built at the source of a small spring inside a gaping cave. About 20min. farther, after a bridge crossing, follow the dirt road for 60m before turning left up the hill to see the charred shell of the **Monastery of Agios Dionysiou,** which gave refuge to Greek partisans during World War II until the Nazis bombed it. A solitary monk lives there now, and there are a few beds he may allow you to use if you ask. You can fill your water bottle and leave a small donation here for the restoration of the large and beautifully situated monastery. Follow the outside wall of the monastery to a fork in the road and continue straight. You'll reach a second fork after 15min. Take the left for the **falls of Perivoli** and the right to reach **Prionia** in an hour's walk.

ASCENDING FROM PRIONIA. The most popular route toward the refuges begins at Prionia, where you'll find drinking **water, toilets,** and a small **restaurant.** From here, a 2½hr. walk uphill takes you to the Spilios Agapitos refuge ("Refuge A," elev. 2100m). The trail is well marked, and is part of the **European E4 path** from Spain to Greece. There's one last chance for water before the refuge, about 45min. up from Prionia, but don't count on it as the spout is often dry. As you approach the tree line, you'll be encouraged by the brilliantly colored masses of wildflowers. Just below the refuge, the trail climbs past a steep gorge lined with dead trees uprooted by winter avalanches. This hike can take just one day up and back, if you take the €20 **taxi** ride to Prionia from Litohoro.

ASCENDING FROM DIASTAVROSI. Another approach to the peaks begins at Diastavrosi, 14km from Litohoro. This longer but more picturesque route climaxes in a stunning ridge walk with dazzling views of Poseidon's Aegean, the Macedonian plain, and Thessaloniki's smog layer. It reaches the SEO and Kakalos refuges in about 6hr. Begin at the parking lot (take the right hand turn off the gravel road halfway between Litohoro and Priona) by taking the uphill path on the left, and follow the red blazes, striped plastic strips on trees, and signs of the mule caravan that uses this route. In about an hour, you'll pass through the Barba meadow, and in about 2hr. you'll reach a cement water tank with an unhelpful painted map off to the left. Go straight here, not left, and the path leads up and up to Petrostrounga (1800m), about 2½hr. from the trailhead. Continue on; 4hr. from the trailhead you'll begin approaching the tree line, reaching Skourta Hill in another 30min. or so. The beautiful Lemos ridge (meaning "neck") leads you gently toward the peaks. About 5½hr. from the beginning of the hike you'll reach the Plateau of the Muses (Οροπεδιο Μουσον), a sweeping expanse of green under the Stefani, Toumba, and Profitis Ilias peaks. Take the clearly marked fork left for the Kakalos shelter (2650m) or right for the SEO shelter (2760m). There's also a trail up to the top of Profitis Ilias, where there's a tiny stone church. You can usually find water in two places along the Diastavrosi trail: at the turnoff between Barba and Spilla (1½hr. from the trailhead, marked on the trail), and at Stragos spring. However, don't depend on the springs, as they run dry in very warm weather.

SUMMITS

ASCENDING MYTIKAS. Up at the summit, Mytikas (2919m) has the highest elevation of the Mt. Olympus peaks and is climbed by about 60% of hikers. There are two trails to Mytikas, both of which are considered moderately dangerous and are prone to rock slides and avalanches. It's an extremely bad idea to lug a large pack along the route or to attempt the climb in very wet weather. Both trails have stretches that run quite close to **sheer drops** and should only be taken on by hikers who are comfortable with heights.

The nearly vertical, rockslide-prone **Louki** trail, on the east face of the peak, makes for an arduous climb straight up 300m. Dotted with small plaques to honor those who fell to Hades trying to make this ascent, Louki is the more dangerous route, especially due to the risk of loose rock falling on hikers below. This trail begins 45min. south of the SEO refuge and is the quickest way to ascend to Mytikas from the Muses Plateau. The other trail runs along the south side of Mytikas by way of **Skala** peak (2860m), through a series of ups and downs that involves rock climbing by handhold and foothold. The Louki path should only be tackled by enthusiastic and fit hikers, and used only for the ascent. Both of the paths are marked with red dots of spraypaint. Get an early start, as clouds often hover around the peaks by mid-afternoon.

To reach Mytikas from Refuge A, walk uphill. After about 45min., you'll find a **map** at a fork in the road. The left takes you along the E4 trail to Skala and Skolio peaks; the right leads to the Louki ascent and the **Zonaria** trail, which leads to the SEO and Kakalos refuges. If you're going via **Skala,** 50m beyond the signpost you'll find an unmarked fork. Make a right and continue ascending for about an hour along exposed terrain until you reach Skala peak and the beginning of the **Kaki Skala** (Bad Ladder) trail to Mytikas, marked with paint blazes. The last 100m or so to the highest peak involves a fair amount of scrambling upward. The **Kazania** (Cauldron), named for the clouds of mist that usually steam up from it, drops 500m down sharply on your left. It's about a 3hr. hike from Refuge A to Mytikas's summit via the Skala route.

Back at the signpost, a right turn will take you on a 40min. walk toward Louki, the base of the ascent. Look for the short stone wall and red blazes going straight up. From there, it's about an hour of rock climbing to the summit. A slightly more dangerous trail goes up to **Stefani** peak a little farther along, marked by a bent, rusted signpost. Past this, a 20min. walk along a stony trail leads to the SEO refuge and Plateau of the Muses. The bowl-shaped slopes are known as the **Throne of Zeus.** The god of gods rested his enormous cranium on the Stefani (crown) peak above. Approaching the peaks from the Plateau of the Muses, it's about 90min. up to Mytikas via Louki, or 4hr. by the Skala route.

ASCENDING SKOLIO. If you decide not to tempt the gods by ascending Mytikas, take the 20min. hike from Skala to Skolio, the second highest peak (2911m; 6m shorter than Mytikas). The best view of Olympus's sheer western face looks out from here. It takes about 2½hr. to reach the Skolio summit from the Agapitos refuge. From Skolio, a 1hr. walk south along the ridge takes you to Aghios Antonis summit and a path descending to Refuge A.

EDESSA Εδεσσα

Edessa rests on the brink of a cliff in the foothills of Mt. Vermion, shadowing the vast, rolling plains below. Here, the city's sidestreets are lined with numerous trickling streams channeled through stone waterways; they lead out under Edessa's arched bridges to form the country's only notable waterfalls, cascading 70m to the valley floor. Most summer tourists opt for a shorter stay in the "town of the waters," stopping just long enough to admire the beautiful views over the orchard-laden plains below.

TRANSPORTATION

Edessa's main bus station (☎23810 23 511) is at the corner of Filippou and Pavlou Mela, near the center of town. **Buses** to: **Athens** (7hr., 3 per day 8am-8pm, €29.95) via **Litohoro** (3hr., €8.15) and **Larisa** (4½hr., €11.15); **Thessaloniki** (2hr., 14 per day 6am-8pm, €5.45); and **Veria** (1¼hr., 6 per day 8am-4pm, €3.05). Buses to **Florina** (2hr.; 8:45am, 11:45am; €5.25); **Kastoria** (2 hr., 4 per day 11:15am-5:15pm, €6.75); and **Kozani** (2hr., 6 per day 10am-8:45pm, €7.04) leave from a stop outside a small fast food joint next to the fruit market on Filippou, one block past the main bus station towards the city center; look for schedules on the *stasi* (stop) sign above the storefront.

From the **train station** (☎23810 23 581), at the end of 18 Octovriou, trains run to: **Athens** (7hr., €28.30); **Florina** (1½hr., €2.40); **Kozani** (2 hr., €2.80); and **Thessaloniki** (2 hr., €2.79) via **Veria** and **Naoussa. Taxis** (☎23810 23 392 or 23810 22 904) congregate on Dimokratias near the National Bank in Pl. Megalou Alexandrou.

ORIENTATION AND PRACTICAL INFORMATION

With your back to the bus station, facing the kiosk across the street, **Pavlou Mela** stretches ahead of you and leads to the town's main thoroughfares—**Egnatia** where it breaks left and **Dimokratias** where it branches to the right. A right turn on Dimokratias brings you past the cafe and playground of **Pl. Megalou Alexandrou** and leads to an intersection near the stadium, marked by a large, leafy park full of bars and cafes. The right fork, **25 Martiou,** leads to waterfalls, while the left, **28 Octovriou,** leads to the train station. **Filippou** runs parallel to Dimokratias, then merges with it near the stadium at triangular **Pl. Timendon.** Street maps are posted at many of the city's major intersections.

The **Tourist Information Office,** to the right of the waterfalls, provides maps and brochures with information in English about sights, hotels, and transportation for Edessa, the prefecture of Pella, and much of northern Greece. (☎23810 20 300. Open M-F 10am-8pm, Sa-Su 9am-9pm.) The **National Bank,** on the corner of Arch. Penteleiminos 2, has an **ATM,** as do many other banks scattered throughout town. To find the **police station,** follow Dimokratias toward the waterfalls and turn left on Iroön Polytechniou; the station is at the intersection with Arhelaou. (☎23810 23 333. Open 24hr.) The **OTE** is a blue and white building facing the Byzantine clock tower on Ag. Dimitriou (open 7am-2:40pm). **Internet access** is available at **Net Cafe** at Filellinon 17, on the street that flanks the stadium (☎23810 29 629; open 8:30am-1am; €2.35 per hr.). Edessa's **post office** is on Pavlou Mela one block up from the bus station; the larger post office on Dimokratias closed last year. **Poste Restante** and **currency exchange** are offered. (Open 7:30am-2pm.) **Postal code:** 58200.

ACCOMMODATIONS AND FOOD

There are a few good deals among Edessa's handful of hotels. The most comfortable option, **Hotel Xenia ❹,** Filippou 35, offers nicely-furnished, air-conditioned rooms with baths, TVs, fridges, and spectacular views of the valley below. The hotel's pool is open to the public for €2-3 per person. (☎23810 29 706 or 23810 29 707, fax 23810 29 708. Singles €53; doubles €75; triples €90; quads €112.) **Hotel Alfa ❸,** Egnatia 28, is conveniently located for bus-riders, a block uphill along Pavlou Mela from the station. Bare but colorful rooms have baths, TVs, A/C, and phones. Internet access and **free maps** available at reception. (☎23810 22 221 or 23810 22 231; fax 23810 24 777; hotel-@otenet.gr. Singles €28; doubles €45; triples €60.). **Hotel Pella ❷,** next to Hotel Alfa, is a cheaper alternative. Basic rooms have small balconies, TVs, and baths. (☎23810 23 541. Singles €20; doubles €30; triples €40.) **Olympia Rented Rooms ❸,** 28 Octovriou 51, is near the train station with the green neon sign. Gleaming white-tiled rooms contain baths and TVs; some have balconies. (☎23810 23 544. Doubles €25.)

Edessa suffers no shortage of fast food options—cheese pies, rotisserie chickens and gyro stands crop up on every street. Inexpensive restaurants are easy to find near the waterfall park. The largest and most popular restaurant in town is the **Public Waterfall Center Restaurant ❷,** at the top of the falls. It serves local and traditional specialties like *stamnato* (€5.68), a concoction of pork, potatoes, vine leaves, and cheese. The *tsoblex* (€5.68) is also delicious: a potato and eggplant pie filled with juicy chunks of veal. (☎23810 26 810. Entrees €4.50-8.)

ENTERTAINMENT

The most picturesque and popular of Edessa's cafes is the **Cafe High Rock** (Psilos Brahos), M. Alexandrou 2, in the southwest corner of town on—surprise, surprise—a high rock perched over the cliff. (☎23810 26 793. Coffee €2; beer €2. Open 9am-2am.) You'll find the complete night—dinner, drinks, and dancing—at **Kanavourgeio,** at the bottom of the glass elevator inside the old mill from which it derives its name. The disco blasts American and Greek music every Saturday and Sunday night. Be careful not to mistake the giant rope-twisting machines for go-go poles. (☎23810 20 070 or 23810 20 102. Entrees €3.50-8. Cover €5, includes one drink.) In the town center, the heart of nightlife is a shady park off Dimokratias just before a Goody's fast food restaurant, where eight similar cafe-bars draw masses of people into tight clusters on the sidewalks. Other bars popular with the young, restless, and fashionable are **Saloon** and **River,** both off Dimokratias.

SIGHTS

WATERFALLS AND ENVIRONS. Edessa's best sights revolve around the *katarrakton* (waterfall), where the town's rivers spill over into the valley below. Walk down Dimokratias past the stadium, where it becomes 25 Martiou, and watch for the large waterfall signs—they'll tell you when to turn right. The descending concrete terraces let you survey the falls and the agricultural plain below while catching a little spray on your face. Look out for the marble column ruins of the ancient city near a convent to the right of the valley.

The area at the edge of the cliffs once supported a collection of water mills and textile factories. The entire area has been redesigned and reconstructed as Edessa's open air **Water Museum,** featuring pre-industrial mills and tanneries, modern textile factories, the wool mill, and the cannabis factory (**Kannavourgio**), which produced rope. Water still runs through the chutes alongside each mill, and plans are in the works to return them to working condition. The tourist office has a great free brochure showing the mill locations. One of the mills has recently been converted into a small aquarium, displaying all the amphibians and freshwater fish of Edessa's rivers. *(Open W-M 10am-2pm and 5-9pm. €1.50.)* To

HOT COALS, HOLY SOULS Visitors to Northern Greece in the off season may witness some unique rural festivals. On May 21, the residents of **Langades,** north of Thessaloniki, celebrate the feast day of Saints Constantine and Helen with **fire-dancing,** which began back in the frenzied days of Dionysian worship. Orthodox Greeks imported the fire dance from Turkish Thrace during the population exchanges (p. 12). It revolves around the **Anastenarides,** a religious brotherhood of men "possessed by the saint." On the feast day, a procession carries the sacred icons of Constantine and Helen through the village, accompanied by music and drumming. The Anastenarides begin to dance around a great bonfire–slowly at first, then faster as the music accelerates, gasping and sighing all the while (*anastenazo* means "to sigh"). They enter a sort of trance, leap into the flames, and dance barefoot, calling out: "Make your vows to the Saint!" and "Restore justice lest the Saint shall destroy you!" Those who dance without damaging the feet qualify to enter the brotherhood.

reach the Kannavourgio, you can follow the steps down along the waterfalls, but a more unconventional mode of transport is Edessa's **glass elevator.** Though the elevators are short, the view overlooking the plain is still striking. The path to the elevator begins to the right of the tourist office in the little park; the Kannavourgiou restaurant-nightclub complex is a convenient resting place near the second elevator.

VAROSI DISTRICT. The old church-dotted town, which retained a Christian population during Ottoman occupation, rests along the cliff's edge, beginning to the right of the waterfall park and continuing on behind the walls of the stadium. Examples of traditional architecture abound: upper stories miraculously protrude out on creaky old wooden beams over stone bases. The quarter's convenient location near the "safe escape" of the lowlands made it a popular spot for World War II resistance fighters—much of the area was burned by the Nazis in 1944. The new **Museum of Traditional and Folk Life** is housed in one of the old buildings on the side of the drop, a block down from the intersection of Arch. Panteleimonos and Megalou Alexandrou (ignore the big yellow "museum" sign and go left, away from Cafe High Rock). In addition to regional costumes and the run-of-the-mill bread-making, weaving, and farming tools, the museum showcases paraphernalia from Edessa's old silk mill, old geography textbooks and a Quran, colorful woven rugs, and children's toys. Ring the bell if the door is locked. *(☎23810 28 787. Open Tu-Su 10am-6pm. €1.47.)*

SITES. Below the town, about 3km to the southwest, you'll find the ruins of the ancient city of **Loggos.** Though little remains of the 4th-century BC city, a few columns along the main avenue still stand, including one from a temple devoted to **Mas,** the goddess of fertility. Try going in the evening, when the dying light makes the columns glow with celestial beauty. The fastest way to the ruins begins at the landing between the two elevators. Walk to the right on the sandy path over the little mound to find a windy path. Follow it downhill (don't go through the gates on the left) and go straight; you'll reach the city in 15min.

The **Byzantine Clock Tower** occupies a block in the upstream direction from Dimokratias at Pl. Megalou Alexandriou. The very dilapidated, neglected remains of a 19th-century **Ottoman mosque** sink down on a side street: walk along Dimokratias a few blocks away from the city center, turn right after the Alpha Credit Bank, and veer left when the mosque's dome and de-crowned minaret come into view. To see Edessa's rivers united, follow any of the tributaries upstream until you hit the **Byzantine Bridge.** The bridge arches over the main stream that eventually splits off to form the town's countless rivulets and narrow channels.

EPIRUS Ηπειρος

If you came in search of idyllic isolation, consider roaming Greece's northwest coast. The postcard-worthy towns and beaches of Parga see their share of visitors, but the mountains and timeless villages of Zagorohoria near the Vikos Gorge remain undisturbed. Epirus links itself to a living past—the old Latin dialect of Vlachika is still spoken in the mountain towns, and the almost perfectly preserved mosques of the once dreaded Ali Pasha still grace the city of Ioannina. The region's mountains draw international hikers for some of Greece's best outdoor rambles.

THE PINDOS MOUNTAINS

Those who enjoy exhilaratingly fresh natural air and quality hiking will delight in the beauty of the Pindos Mountains Region. Rushing rivers and waterfalls, towering mountains, steep ravines, fertile forests, and blossoming wildflowers constitute the breathtaking scenery that provides a refreshing change from the typical Greek tourist attractions. The **European E6** path and national **O1** and **O3 routes** run through the area near Ioannina (p. 243), a good base city from which to explore the mountains. The O3 brings hikers through the Vikos Gorge and past an array of mountaintops and villages known to offer some of the best hiking in Greece. The tourist office in Ioannina has an informative, Greek-only contour map that marks all the trails. Rock climbers can scale the faces of **Eamila, Tsouka Rossa,** and **Pirgos Astraka,** and avid spelunkers can attempt the **Provatihas Cave,** the second-deepest cave in the world at 407m. Most of these expeditions are best undertaken with an experienced guide or after consulting an outdoors agency in Ioannina, as maps of the region tend to be unreliable. The **Hellenic Mountaineering Club** (EOS) supplies information and leads weekend trips throughout the region. (☎26510 22 138. Open M-Sa 7-9pm.) The **Paddler Kayaking and Rafting School** (☎26550 23 777 or 26550 23 101) in Konitsa gives lessons and oversees outings to local rivers. For alpine flowers, April through June is the best hiking season; colored foliage flares brilliantly in the dry autumns.

IGOUMENITSA Ηγουμενιτσα

For many, Igoumenitsa is the first glimpse of the Greek mainland. Greece's third-largest port and consummate transportation hub, the city links Central and Northern Greece, the Ionian islands, and Italy. Tourist agencies line the streets, harried backpackers scurry about in search of their ships, loitering old men keep an eye on all the comings and goings, and everyone seems in a desperate hurry. Though you may prefer to avoid staying the night in Igoumenitsa, the prevalence of early morning ferries makes this easier said than done.

TRANSPORTATION

Ferries: Igoumenitsa's endlessly long **port** currently has 3 subdivisions, though work is continuing on a 4th. **Old Port,** on the waterfront's north edge (to the right facing the water), mostly sends boats to Italy. **Corfu Port** is in the middle of the 3. **New Port,** beyond the Corfu Port, sends boats to both Italy and Corfu. Tickets to **Corfu** (1½hr., every 30min. 4:30am-10pm, €5) can be purchased at the Corfu Port, in one of several white kiosks. For tickets to **Italy,** shop around at the waterfront agencies. Some have student rates, and some accept Eurail and Inter-Rail passes; bargain before you buy.

Destinations include: **Ancona** (15hr., 4 per day, €40-50); **Bari** (9½hr., 2 per day, €30-35); **Brindisi** (8hr., 2 per day, €28-33); and **Venice** (21hr., 1 per day, €44-57). Prices do not include port duties. Most boats depart before noon or late in the evening.

Buses: Kipou 17 (☎26650 22 309). To: **Athens** (8hr., 5 per day 8:30am-8:15pm, €28.45); **Ioannina** (2hr., 9 per day 6:30am-8pm, €6.10); **Parga** (1hr., 4 per day 5:45am-5:15pm, €3.80; **Preveza** (2hr.; 11:45am, 3:30pm; €7.05); and **Thessaloniki** (7hr.; 10:30am, 7pm; €26.40). To reach the **bus station** from the ports, walk up Zalogo (past the Ionian Bank). When you reach the town plateia, turn left and walk 2 blocks to the **ticket office,** behind a cafe on the left marked with a blue KTEL sign.

Taxis: (☎26650 23 200 or 26650 23 500), beside Corfu Port.

ORIENTATION AND PRACTICAL INFORMATION

Igoumenitsa is on the westernmost corner of mainland Greece, about 20km from the Albanian border. **Eth. Antistaseos,** which becomes **Ag. Apostolon,** runs along the waterfront and teems with travel agencies. To the north, after it divides, the tree-lined inland side of the street is bordered by an array of cafes and bars. Igoumenitsa's main shopping area is on **Grigariou Lamprari,** the first pedestrian street parallel to the waterfront. To reach the uninspiring central plateia, walk four blocks inland on **Zalogo,** which begins across from Corfu Port.

Tourist Office: (☎26650 22 227), in the old port. Helps with transportation and accommodations. Free maps. Open daily 8am-2pm.

Banks: National Bank (☎26650 22 415), across the road from the Old Port in a string of banks with 24hr. **ATM. Exchanges currency.**

American Express: Eth. Antistaseos 14 (☎26650 22 406 or 26650 24 333). Will **change money,** cash all travelers checks without commission, and give you cash from an AmEx card. Open M-F 7:30am-2pm and 4-11pm, Sa 4-11pm.

Police: Ag. Apostolon 5 (☎26650 22 100), across from Corfu Port. Available 24hr.

Port Police: In a Corfu Port booth, near customs and passport control.

Medical Center: (☎26650 24 420). Basic health care. If necessary, they will help you get to the **hospital** (☎26640 22 203) 15min. away. Open 24hr.

OTE: (☎26650 22 499 or 899), at the end of the pedestrian street Grigariou. Open 7am-2:30pm. The new port also has an OTE (☎26650 27 757). Open 7am-10pm.

Internet Access: Netronio, on the north end of the waterfront in the cafe strip. 4 terminals at €3 per hr. Beer €2; *frappé* €1.75. Open 8am-2pm.

Post Office: Tzavelenas 2 (☎46 100), 1km north along the waterfront on the corner of a large playground. Poste Restante. Open 7:30am-2pm. **Postal code:** 46100.

ACCOMMODATIONS

Hotel Acropolis ❷, on the waterfront in Old Port, has spotless, homey rooms with wooden floors, shared baths, and phones along thick-carpeted hallways. The smiles radiated from the family that owns the hotel are contagious. (☎26650 28 346. Shared fridge and water cooler. Singles €18; doubles €30; triples €35.) Look for **Hotel Egnatia's ❸** in the central plateia's far right corner. Simple rooms have baths, TVs, phones, and A/C. (☎26650 23 455. Singles €30; doubles €40; triples €45.) Looking out over the Old Port, **Jolly Hotel ❸** makes for a more comfortable alternative with its spacious, carpeted rooms and marble-tiled hallways. All rooms have baths, A/C, TVs, and phones. (☎26650 23 971; fax 26650 23 007; jolligm@otenet.gr. Singles €40; doubles €55; triples €65.)

FOOD AND NIGHTLIFE

The best—and most locally popular—among the city's restaurants are on the north edge of the **waterfront,** past the ports and junk shops. Dozens of bakeries and small markets line the pedestrian street just inland from the harbor. Igoumenitsa's bland nightlife centers on a strip of bars along the waterfront. **Traffic** (☎26650 23 505), a few doors down from Taverna Aleko, pumps American and Greek tunes all night on the weekends. (Beer €2; cocktails €4. Open until 5am. €3 cover includes a drink.) A short distance outside the city center, **Clik** and **Ostria** attract a young, trendy local crowd. (Beer €2; cocktails €4. €3 cover includes a drink.) Buses run every hour from the center (€0.80). There's also a **cinema,** next to Taverna Aleko, that shows movies at 9:30 and 11:15pm for €5.

Mykonos (☎26650 27 567), at the beginning of the waterfront strip, north of the ports, with a vine-hung patio full of loquacious Greeks. Boasts a varied menu that includes pizza, pasta, Greek menu mainstays, and a few fish specialties. Try the feta-stuffed souvlaki (€4.40) for a stimulating and inexpensive change of pace. ❷

Alekos (☎26650 23 708), next door to Mykonos. Traditional Greek fare. Specializes in fish, big and small, fetched from the pristine harbor waters. Entrees €4.20-5.60. ❷

Strada Marina (☎26650 23 549), opposite the police station. A multilingual menu of Greek favorites between the Old Port and Corfu Port. Entrees €6-12. ❸

PARGA Παργα

Attached to the mainland by an arc of green mountains, Parga looks and feels like a Greek island town. With its luxurious beaches and bustling waterfront, Parga draws the fun- and sun-loving crowd; its streets are packed with overpriced jewelry shops, effervescent nightlife spots, T-shirt vendors, and dozens of fuschia-nosed Scandinavian children wielding inflatable alligators. The town's narrow, curling streets, Neoclassical buildings, and bougainvillea bushes create a pleasant and romantic mood that seems to have infected even the pastel pink supermarket.

ORIENTATION AND PRACTICAL INFORMATION. Parga is organized around its waterfront. The main waterfront road, which brims with tavernas, bars, and tourist agencies, has three different names: from west to east, they are **Lambraki, Anexartissias,** and **Athanassiou.** At **Krioneri Beach,** which runs alongside Athanassiou, the road forks: its uphill branch is **R. Feraiou.** Running inland from the waterfront is **Al. Baga,** which leads uphill to most of Parga's municipal buildings. Al. Baga meets **Sp. Livada** at the town's main intersection. Running parallel to the waterfront and having the highest density of tourist shops, **V.E. Vasila** leads up to the **Venetian castle** at the far southwest corner of town. From here, a stone path leads down the other side to **Valtos Beach.**

Ferries run to **Corfu Town** (2hr., Su and Th 8:30am, €25-35). **Buses** run from Parga to: **Athens** (8½hr., 3 per day 7am-5:45pm, €26.55); **Igoumenitsa** (1¼hr., 4 per day 7:15am-6:30pm, €3.80); **Preveza** (1½hr., 5 per day 7am-9:15pm, €4.60), and **Thessaloniki** (8½hr., 7am, €30.70). The **bus station** (☎26840 31 218) is a small booth next to the Chinese restaurant, at the top of Sp. Livada.

The **municipal tourist office,** across from the ferry dock, offers **maps** of the area, **currency exchange,** and information about renting boats, cars, and mopeds. (☎26840 32 107; fax 26840 32 511. Open 8am-11pm.) **Tourist agencies** pack the streets around the waterfront, ready to help you find rooms and arrange daytrips; they're generally open M-Sa 9am-2pm and 5:30-10pm. Try **ITS,** beyond the ferry dock next door to a pharmacy. (☎26840 31 833. Open 9am-1:30pm and 6:50-10pm.)

With the **OTE** building (☎26840 31 699; open M-F 7am-2:40pm) on your left and the shore behind you, the **police station** (☎26840 31 222; open 24hr.) and **post office**

(☎26840 31 295; open M-F 7:30am-2pm) are straight ahead. To the left is the **National Bank** with a 24hr. **ATM** (open M-Th 8am-2pm, F 8am-1:30pm); 100m down the road is the **health center** (☎26840 31 233; open 24hr.); going right will bring you to a junction with the main road and the bus stop. For **emergencies** you can also call the **port police** (☎26840 31 227). **Internet access** is available at **Cafe Terra,** on the waterfront, halfway between the dock and the beach. (€2 per 15min. Open 8am-3am.) **Postal code:** 48060.

ACCOMMODATIONS AND FOOD. Parga's hotels are expensive, and prices spike in the summer months. For a cheaper bed, look around the south end of the town and the top of the hill for **rooms to let.** Just below the entrance to the fortress, above a small bakery in a bright yellow building, **Kostas and Martha Christou** ❷ rent clean, simple rooms with private baths and balconies, only a 5min. walk to the pebbly shores of Valtos Beach. (☎26840 31 942. Singles €15; doubles €25; triples €35.) **Thomas House** ❷, on Tzabela, has bright rooms with shared bath and a large, full kitchen. From the bus station, walk downhill and turn left at the OTE. Follow this road as it curves right and becomes V.E. Vasila. Make another right just before the Blue Bar onto Tzabela: the rooms are 20m straight ahead. (☎26840 31 211. Singles €20; doubles €25; triples €28.) About 50m beyond the end of Krinoeri Beach, **Pavlos Vergas** ❹ is a good deal for doubles and triples. Comfortable, airy rooms are well decorated and come with small kitchen units, fridges, TVs, and balconies. Enjoy a drink on their beautiful marble patio. (☎26840 31 617. Doubles €58; triples €63.) Budget travelers can skip Parga's high-priced lodging by camping on nearby beaches. The closest is **Parga Beach Camping** ❶ (☎26840 31 161; €4.30-4.80 per tent, €3.60 per car), but **Valtos Camping** ❶, by neighboring Valtos beach, is a bit cheaper (€4.50 per person, €4 per tent, €2.70 per car).

Although there are outright tourist traps among Parga's waterfront-centered restaurants, some spots offer memorable food at decent prices. Perched on the hilltop just below the entrance to the fortress, **Kastro Entasis** ❷, with its soft, lilting music and sea blue tablecloths serves up superb food (salads €3-8, entrees €6.50-12.50). It's hard to tell whether the cuisine or the atmosphere is the stronger aphrodisiac. A few doors beyond the ferry dock as you head toward Krioneri Beach, **To Souli** ❷ cooks up lamb and feta *kleftiko* (€5), salads, and fresh fish by the kilogram (€23 per kg.) By Krioneri Beach, **Restaurant Ionio** ❷ (☎26840 31 402) has a *prix fixe* three-course menu that's a steal at €6.75. If you're looking to splurge, swank **Rudis** ❹ serves creative Greek and Italian cuisine at the end of the dock.

NIGHTLIFE AND ENTERTAINMENT. Scuttling waiters and rambunctious children run willy-nilly through crowds of jovially inebriated northern Europeans at Parga's many waterfront bars and cafes. **Caravel,** near the ferry dock, is one of the town's most popular cafes, with an upstairs balcony. Tourists fill the seats all day sipping either a morning orange juice, an afternoon *frappé*, or an evening cocktail. (☎26840 31 359. Drinks €3.50-4.50.) The more removed **Blue Bar** (☎26840 32 067), on the road leading to the castle, is a hipper choice, with stunning views of the sea and Art Deco blue-light and mirror decorations to go with the 93 cocktails mixed up by the bartenders. Try the Happy Company (€18)—served in a massive ceramic jug, it packs a punch powerful enough to floor you and three of your friends. Though the tourists here are of the family ilk, there are a couple of discos, which don't really fill up until around 2am. The biggest scenes are **Camares** (☎26840 32 000), behind Caravel, and **Arena,** down behind the beach. Camares teems with newly tanned northern Europeans, impressing each other with drunken dance moves. Arena caters to the young, hip, beautiful set behind its mirrored facade. **Factory,** whose neon signs point up side streets from near the ferry dock, is slightly less packed but made funky nonetheless by furniture transformed from the original factory machinery. Clubs stay open until 4am on weekdays and at least 6am on weekends; the cover is usually €3, which includes one drink.

SIGHTS AND BEACHES. Looking down on Parga, the massive **fortress,** or Kastro, was built by the Normans but was controlled by the Venetians from 1401 to 1797. In its glory days, the castle held 500 homes and 5000 Pargiotes. A surprising number of walls still stand; the cannons, however, which lined their tops, have long since fallen and are now strewn about the cobblestone enclosure. Although under reconstruction, the castle remains a perfect spot for a shady picnic, stroll, or dramatic re-enactment of a Venetian-Ottoman battle. It's 5min. from the water; follow the steps from the harbor up the hill. (Open 7am-10pm.)

Krioneri Beach, Parga's little waterfront, is very family-oriented; if that's not your scene, brave the 100m swim to the islet that holds the small **Church of the Panagia. Piso Krioneri Beach** is a 5min. walk around the rocky outcropping, but is a bit more secluded. Vastly nicer is long **Valtos Beach,** on the other side of the castle: a voluptuous crescent of sole-tickling pebbles turns to sand near the middle. Endless hordes of sun-worshipers sidle up to the rim of clear turquoise water. Here you can rent anything from a beach ball to a paragliding trip, or enjoy revelry at the packed **pool club.** Boats travel to the smaller beaches, including the more secluded **Lichnos Beach** (2km), accessible by car or boat (€3.40 round trip).

Tour companies along the waterfront and on the ferry dock book a variety of prepackaged excursions to more remote beaches, most of which include cheery stops at the **River Acheron**—better known as the River Styx, mythical gateway to the Underworld—and the **Necromanteion,** the Oracle of the Dead, excavated in 1958. It was here that Odysseus supposedly conversed with the Shades, who spoke to him only after drinking offerings of blood. (Open 8:30am-3pm. €2, students €1.) Both are about a 20min. drive from Parga, but trips by **boat** (€7.30) are more frequent and significantly cheaper than by bus.

IOANNINA Ιωαννινα

On the shores of Lake Pamvotis, 96km east of Igoumenitsa, lies Epirus's capital, largest city, and transportation hub. Ioannina itself might not detain you for long, but the surrounding mountains and calm lake below deliver scenic views and an uplifting breeziness to the city. Likewise, the city's post-World War II architecture is redeemed by the narrow cobblestone streets and the magnificent fortress of the Old City. No visitor to Ioannina can escape the foreboding, half-legendary Ali Pasha, the "Lion of Ioannina" (see p. 247). The Albanian-born Pasha of Trikala seized Ioannina in 1788 and built himself a sumptuous palace. Intending to make the city the capital of his Greek-Albanian empire, Ali ruled with an iron fist, alternately fighting with and serving the Ottoman Sultan, who was theoretically his ruler. Ali has certainly left his imprint on the city: his immense fortress and private Xanadu are here, and he died on nearby Nisi Island in 1822.

ORIENTATION AND PRACTICAL INFORMATION

Ioannina is at the center of Epirus, at the edge of steely Lake Pamvotis, and circled by the peaks of Pindos. Not far into the lake is a small, hilly island simply called Nisi or Nissaki ("the island" or "the islet"). The **city center** is a major intersection near the **clock tower** in Litharitses park. **G. Averof,** lined with jewelry stores and souvlaki stands, is a broad avenue that runs from the main gate of the old city to the city center. To reach the city center from the main **bus station,** walk uphill about 20m from the station to an intersection, where you'll see an **Agricultural Bank.** Facing the bank, walk uphill along the street on the left, which begins as **Dagli** but becomes **M. Botsari** after a block—the enormous Hotel Egnatia sign makes a useful landmark. You'll pass the **post office** (the **OTE** is behind it, but not visible from Botsari) and emerge next to the **Ionian Bank** on Averof, facing the park. On your right, past the long building labeled "Νομαρχιον Ιωαννινων" ("Prefecture of Ioannina"), the road splits. The right side (*not* the sharp right) is **Napoleonda Zerva,** to the left is **Leoforos Dodoni.** At the set of streetlights before the Prefecture building, a road leads downhill to the smaller of the two intercity bus stations. To reach the **Frourio** (fortress) and the **waterfront,** follow the signs from the city center to Averof's opposite end, and veer left at the Frourio walls. You will now be on **Karamanli,** which passes the main gate of the Frourio to the dock and waterfront.

Flights: daily to **Athens** (50min.; 10:45am and 9:30pm; €79) and **Thessaloniki** (40min.; M and W 4:05pm, F and Su 3:20pm; €60). **Olympic Airways** (☎26510 26 218; reservations ☎26510 23 120), where G. Averoff splits into Napoleonda Zerva and Leoforos Dodoni, above the city center. Open M-F 9am-3pm.

Buses: There are two terminals in town.

Main terminal, Zosimadon 4 (☎26510 27 442). To: **Athens** (6½hr., 11 per day 7:15am-midnight, €24.85); **Igoumenitsa** (2hr., 9 per day 5am-7:30pm, €6.10); **Konitsa** (1¼hr., 7 per day 5am-7:30pm, €4); **Metsovo** (1½hr., 3 per day 5am-2pm, €3.70); **Parga** (2½hr., 8:30am, €8); and **Thessaloniki** (7hr., 6 per day 7:30am-10:30pm, €20.45) via **Larisa** (4hr., €12).

Smaller station: Bizaniou 21 (☎26510 25 014). To: **Agrinio** (3hr., 6 per day 5:30am-7:15pm, €9.70); **Arta** (1½hr., 10 per day 5:45am-8pm, €4.40); **Dodoni** (30min.; M, W, F 6:30am and 3:30pm; €1.35); **Patras** (4hr., 4 per day 9am-5:30pm, €14.55); and **Preveza** (2hr., 10 per day 6am-8pm, €6.60).

Taxis: (☎26510 46 777, 778, or 779) also in the city center and at the bus station.

Tourist Office: EOT office (☎26510 46 662; fax 26510 49 139), about 500m down Leoforos Dodoni on the left immediately after the playground. Has **maps** and Ioannina prefecture propaganda, with a list of **Rooms to Let** in the province. Worth the 10min. walk from the city center. Open M-F 7:30am-2:30pm. Hours extended July-Sept. M-F 5-8:30pm, Sa 9am-1pm.

Banks: There are a number of banks with 24hr. **ATMs,** including **National Bank,** on Averof, just after the archaeological museum as you walk toward the waterfront. Open M-Th 8am-2pm, F 8am-1:30pm.

Alternatives To Tourism: Trekking Hellas (☎26510 71 703; www.trekkinghellas.gr), on a small side street opposite a Kodak Express shop off Napoleonda. Zerva provides information about outdoor activities and ecotourism in the Epirus region and beyond. Open M-F 10am-4pm.

Police: (☎26510 65 934). Walk along Botsari to the post office—the police and the tourist police are just around the corner on 28 Octovriou. Open 8am-10pm, but available 24hr.

Tourist Police: With the police. **Free maps** and other info available. Open 8am-10pm.

Hospital: Two hospitals, each about 5km from the center of town. One handles emergencies on even dates (☎26510 80 111); the other on odd dates (☎26510 99 111).

OTE: (☎26510 22 350 or 26510 42 777), on 28 Octovriou, next to the post office. Open M-F 7:30am-2pm.

Internet Access: Online i-cafe on Pirsinella, the last street on your right as you walk south along Averof, away from the waterfront. Highly stylish with 75 speedy terminals, shiny floors, and chessboard-patterned chairs. *Frappé* €2. Open 24hr. €2.20 per hr. noon-midnight, €2 per hr. midnight-noon. Down Pirsinella, **The Web** (☎26510 26 813) is a cheaper alternative. *Frappé* €0.75. Open 24hr. €1.50-2.50 per hr.

Post Office: (☎26510 25 498), at the intersection of 28 Octovriou and Botsari. Open M-F 7:30am-8pm. **Postal code:** 45110.

ACCOMMODATIONS

Hotel Metropolis, Kristali 2 (☎26510 26 207), on the corner to your left as you walk down Averof toward the waterfront. Look for the red and yellow sign. Spacious, comfortable, colorful rooms, but street noise continues late into the night. Conveniently located, Metropolis is a 5min. walk from anywhere in the city. Singles €20; doubles €25; triples €35. ❷

Hotel Olympic, Melandis 2 (☎26510 22 233; fax 26510 22 041; www.hotelolymp.gr). Take your 2nd left off Averoff as you walk toward the waterfront and look for the light blue sign. Beautifully decorated, spacious rooms with red carpets. Fully equipped with A/C, TVs, phones, balconies, safes, and sparkling bathrooms. Singles €50; doubles €70; triples €80. ❹

Hotel Ermis (☎26510 75 992), across from the main bus station on Sina. Bare, cell-block rooms with sinks, shared baths, and lots of street noise—but cheap and convenient for anyone just passing through. Singles €18; doubles €25; triples €33. ❷

Hotel Bretania (☎26510 23 396; fax 26510 33 589), on G. Averoff across from the clock tower. Bare but clean rooms with private baths, desks, TVs, and A/C. Singles €32; doubles €40; triples €50. ❸

FOOD AND NIGHTLIFE

Several souvlaki stands are at the end of Averof near the Frourio (and elsewhere). Seafood restaurants circle the north side of the **waterfront.**

Filippas (☎26510 31 170), on the waterfront; look out for the yellow tablecloths. Many of the delicious specials here are given the suffix "Filippas" to help keep the patrons oriented. The chicken with honey and yogurt (€6.50) is a real treat. Entrees €4.50-7. ❷

Stin Ithaki (☎26510 73 012), just beyond Filippas. This local favorite specializes in fish and serves typical Greek fare at quiet waterfront tables. Entrees €3.50-7. ❷

Oasis (☎26510 75 400), opposite Alpha Bank on Averof. An enormous, open-air restaurant serving generous portions of good food at low prices. Majestic mountain views from its sprawling patio. Classic Greek entrees like *kokoretsi* (lamb liver) and feta-stuffed beef are €4-8.50. English menu posted at the gate. Open 24hr. ❷

To Rempetiou, just beyond Averof toward the waterfront. Grilled meats galore and a good selection of salads. Entrees €3.50-6. ❷

Nousias (☎26510 25 075), Karamanli 1. Take the street that passes the main gate of the Frourio toward the dock and the waterfront; a little sweetshop, brimming with confections, pastries, chocolates, and crispy delights all baked fresh in the back. 32 different flavors of ice cream are whipped up daily (€1 per scoop). Open 9am-1am. ❶

Most of Ioannina's bars are on the waterfront in two separate clusters, both at the base of the Frourio walls: cafes to the north and late-night bars to the south. **Kura Frosuni** (☎26510 73 984) is right outside the fort, on the northwest corner of the peninsula. Always crowded with young people, the cafe has the closest tables to the water and a great view of Nisi island. To the south, **Ev. Ioanninos** (☎26510 21 669) takes up three sides of a small square, serving drinks from its outdoor bar from 9pm to 5am—*the* place to see and be seen. **Skala** (☎26510 37 676) is on the fourth side, churning loud music for pierced wannabe rock stars. **Monopolio** is Ioannina's biggest disco; locals dance to Greek or Latin tunes nightly. It's at the end of town, past seafood restaurants. (☎26510 35 985. Drinks €1.50; cover €3.)

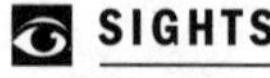

SIGHTS

FROURIO (OLD CITY)

The town's fortress, the Frourio (a.k.a. the **Kastro** or **Old City**) presides regally over the shore, a slender minaret at each end. Its massive, overgrown stone walls enclose a placid neighborhood of narrow streets and old Turkish-style homes. Like any self-respecting fortress, the Frourio's main entrance on Karamanli has several sharp turns, making invasion tricky. Just outside this entrance is the shrine to **St. George the Neomartyr,** Ioannina's patron saint, whose Turkish overlords tortured and hanged him in 1838 for marrying a Christian.

Most of the castle was built in the 14th century by **Thomas Preljubovic,** the Serbian ruler of Ioannina who was also known as **Albanitoktonos** ("Albanian-killer"). In order to secure the city's bloodless surrender in 1430, the Turks assured the Greeks that they could remain in their houses within the walls. After a failed 1611 Greek insurrection led by **Skilosofos,** the fanatical Bishop of Trikala, however, the Turks cracked down. One Sunday, when all the Greeks were in church, the sneaky Turks seized their houses and moved right in. Skilosofos, the rebellious bishop, was captured and skinned alive. When Ali Pasha came to power in 1795, he forced his Greek subjects to rebuild the pre-existing Byzantine walls on a grander scale to fortify the capital of his dreamed-of empire.

GOING OUT WITH(OUT) A BANG When Ali Pasha heard that the Sultan had finally tired of his rebellious, empire-dreaming antics, he decided to make a grand exit. Holing up on Nisi, he gave orders to Selim, his most trusted servant, to stand guard over the castle's immense casks of gunpowder with a lighted torch. If Selim heard gunshots from the island, he was to blow himself, the castle, and the city with all its inhabitants clear into Lake Pamvotis. If anyone arrived bearing Ali's rosary, all was well and he could put out the torch. The sultan's envoys, however, managed to convince Ali's Greek wife Vasilikis to betray Ali's instructions, telling her it was her duty as a Greek to save the town from destruction. Vasilikis stole Ali's rosary as he slept, and presented it to the Turks, who immediately used it to convince Selim to put out his torch. When the gun battle began on Nisi the next day, Ali waited in vain for the explosion from the mainland before discovering his rosary had vanished. Before he could order revenge against his wife, he was killed by shots fired through the floor. For her part, Vasilikis retired to the coast of Turkey, where she lived with the captain of the force sent to kill her husband.

ITŞ KALE. To reach the Itş Kale from the main entrance, walk forward, veering left, following the signs. The small ruined buildings on both sides as you enter the walls were guard posts, and the cafe on the left was originally a kitchen. Over to the immediate right along the wall are the remnants of Ali Pasha's **hamam** (baths). Around what is now the Silverworks gallery, the *serai* once housed Ali, his harem, and his ornately decorated audience chambers. Ali Pasha held most of his notorious tortures and executions at the plane tree near the *serai*, running the gory gamut from skinning to impaling and suspending on hooks hung from the tree's branches. Independence War hero **Katsandonis** is said to have sung patriotic hymns while being brutally hammered to death here, a scene re-enacted frequently in Greek folk shadow puppet theater. The ruins on the right of the complex are partially preserved, and are well worth a scramble. *(Open 8am-10pm.)*

The **Byzantine Museum** in the Itş Kale has a small collection of intricately carved wooden sanctuary doors, stone carvings, calligraphic manuscripts, and post-Byzantine icons. English-language wall plaques chronicle the history of Epirus and Ioannina. *(☎26510 27 761 or 26510 39 580. Open Tu-Su 8am-7pm, M 12:30-7pm. €3, students €2.)* The **Fethiye Camii** (Victory Mosque) next to the museum is the third mosque in its location, a space once occupied by a 13th-century church. The current mosque was rebuilt in 1795 by Ali Pasha himself. In front of the mosque, weeds and rubble obscure the **Tomb of Ali Pasha,** a sarcophagus that contains his headless body; from the neck up, he's buried in Istanbul. The tomb was originally decorated with a gilded cage that was looted by Nazis in 1943, but it was recently replaced by a green iron approximation. Ioaninna is the silversmithing capital of Greece, and at the **Silverworks Gallery,** you'll find snuffboxes, tea services, and belt buckles to prove it. An etching beside the desk depicts the Frourio's former glory. *(☎26510 25 989. Show your Byzantine Museum ticket for admission to the gallery.)*

MUNICIPAL MUSEUM. The smaller of the Frourio's walled inner areas is a little farther to the left of Itş Kale—follow signs through the crooked streets to the museum housed in the lovely **Aslan Pasha Camii.** On the left as you enter is the long, rectangular former *medrasa* (school for Quranic study). The tombstones engraved in Arabic are the remains of an **Ottoman cemetery,** and the small building behind the mosque is Aslan Pasha's mausoleum. In 1618, following Bishop Skilosofos's rebellion, the Turks destroyed the former church of St. John Prodromus and replaced it with this elegant mosque. The Municipal Museum focuses on Ioannina's diverse ethnic past and is divided into Jewish, Greek, and Muslim exhibits.

Highlights include a sword that belonged to War of Independence hero Karaiskaki and a golden dress worn by Ali Pasha's wife, Lady Vasilikis. *(☎26510 26 356. Open June-Sept. 8am-8pm; Oct.-May 8am-3pm. €2, students €1.)*

ARCHAEOLOGICAL MUSEUM. Aside from local finds, Paleolithic to Roman, the museum's highlights are the **lead tablets** used by puzzled ancients to inscribe their questions to the oracle to Zeus in nearby **Dodoni** (p. 248). Questions range from petty suspicions ("Has Pistos stolen the wool from the mattress?") to love advice ("Am I her children's father?"), and much angst has surrounded the dilemma of which deity to honor for which cause. Check out the **copper statues** from the oracle, which would speak the words of Zeus through batons they held in their hands. *(The museum is on a small road off Averoff near the city center, across from the yellow town hall building. ☎26510 33 357 or 26510 25 490. Open Tu-Su 8:30am-3pm. €2, students free.)*

NISI (THE ISLAND). Wandering chickens, cheap silver shops, a tiny whitewashed village, and five deteriorating monasteries cover Ioannina's peaceful island, a 10min. ferry ride from the harbor. Ali Pasha met his death on Nisi after falling out of the sultan's favor in a big way. Discovered and trapped in the second story of the island's **St. Pantaleemon monastery,** he was killed by shots fired up through the floorboards—you can still see the bullet holes. The victors hung Ali's severed head out for public viewing for several days before transporting it on horseback all the way to the sultan in Constantinople. The monastery now houses the **Ali Pasha Museum,** which displays Ali Pasha's enormous *nargileh*, from which he happily puffs in almost every portrait, and a large painting of the sultan ceremoniously receiving the head of his fearsome ex-governor. What goes around comes around. *(Open daily 8am-10pm. €0.75.)*

Signs point the way to St. Pantaleemon and the other four monasteries. A short walk from the museum, the **frescoes** of St. Nicholas Philanthropinos, painted by Katelanou in 1542, depict saints, the life of Jesus, and seven ancient sages (including Plato, Aristotle and Plutarch, just inside the door on the left) who were said to have proclaimed the coming of Jesus. If the monastery is locked, ask politely at the house next door for a tour. At the nearby *krifto scholio* ("secret school"), the forbidden Greek language was kept alive during the Ottoman reign. The monastery of **St. John Prodromos** has a crypt leading to a secret exit and path to the lake. *(☎26510 25 885. Take one of the little ferries (10min.; every hr. 6:30-11:30am and every 30min. 11:30am-11pm; in winter every hr. 7am-9pm; €1) from Ioannina's waterfront.)*

NORTHERN GREECE

DAYTRIPS FROM IOANNINA

DODONI Δωδωνη

Buses to Dodoni run from Ioannina's smaller station (30min.; M, W, F 6:30am and 3:30pm; €1.35). Ask to be let off at the theater. The return bus passes by at about 4:45pm—however, this doesn't leave you with much time to view the site. Alternatively, you can hire a taxi (at least €15 round-trip). ☎26510 82 287. Open 8am-5pm; €2, students and seniors €1, EU students free.

Ancient Dodoni, the site of mainland Greece's oldest oracle, hugs the base of a mountain 22km southeast of Ioannina. The name Dodoni originates from the Linear B language and may mean "great mother of civilization;" Dodoni was probably the deity worshipped there before being supplanted by Zeus. Excavations suggest that the oracle was used from the Bronze Age (2600-1100 BC) through Christianity's arrival in the late 4th century AD. Worship of Zeus at Dodoni was well established by Homer's time: Odysseus himself came to the oracle at "wintry Dodona" for advice on ridding his house of Penelope's suitors. At its height, Dodoni was one of the ancient world's greatest oracles and home of the **Naia festival,** a series of athletic and dramatic contests held every four years in Zeus's honor.

The large **amphitheater** near the entrance to the site was built in the third century AD. The original design seated 18,000 before the Romans expanded it and improved the drainage system to accommodate their blood sports. The annual ancient **theater festival** may have been revived, but the theater is in dire need of restoration. Beyond the amphitheater are the ruins of the oracle itself, where Zeus would answer queries through a still-standing oak tree. A clan of priests called the **Hellopes, Helloi,** or **Selloi** interpreted the wind's effect on the oak tree leaves' rustling, the flight of doves in its branches, and the sound of wooden batons held by a bronze statue of a boy striking a row of copper cauldrons. Using their sonic data, the priests made prophecies; trying to absorb the god's messages through the soil, they walked barefoot. Wild priestesses prone to divine frenzy eventually replaced the male *Selloi*. Little remains today of the original building that housed the tree and its horde of pilgrims. Additional buildings, now almost totally vanished, once surrounded the oracle: a 5th-century BC temple and the 350 BC *bouleuterion* and *prytaneion*. Following the Aetolian sack in 219 BC, a larger Ionic temple to Zeus was built in 168-167 BC, and the great amphitheater in the early 3rd century AD.

PERAMA CAVES

Take local bus #8 from the park behind the city center (15min., every 20min., €1.20 round-trip). At Perama, follow the signs for ΣΠΗΛΑΙΟ ("cave"). ☎26510 81 251 or 26510 81 440. Open 8am-8pm; in winter 8am-5pm; tours every 25min. €5, students €2.50.

A 163-step stairway leads through the spectrally lit, glimmering yellow Perama Caves, among the largest in the Balkans. Excavations have turned up bears' teeth and bones in the almost two million-year-old stalagmites and stalactites, as well as **paintings** devoted to the ancient worship of Hades and Persephone. The path leads from narrow passageways to immense **caverns** hanging with eerie rock formations. The 45min. Greek-only guided tour mainly introduces selected stalagmites that have been named after other objects they uncannily resemble: "Tower of Pisa," "Egyptian Sphinx," and so on. Always a comfortable 17°C/62°F inside, the cave makes for a great excursion during the scorching Greek afternoons.

METSOVO Μετσοβο

On a forested mountainside below the Pindos Mountains' 1690m high Katara Pass, Metsovo is almost painfully quaint: think ski town meets intimate village. Once upon a time, Marc Antony used to send his wife to Metsovo when he wanted to carry on more freely with Cleopatra. Now, daytripping tour buses of all nations frequent this officially designated "traditional" settlement. There's a booming trade in postcards and handmade wooden trinkets, but despite its kitschiness Metsovo makes an excellent base for hiking, exploring Metsovo Lake, and trekking the nearby European E6 trail. Visitors in mid- and late July will receive a full dose of Metsovan culture as festivals and traditional weddings kick off.

ORIENTATION AND PRACTICAL INFORMATION. Metsovo is about 100km inland in eastern Epirus, halfway between Kalambaka and Ioannina. On a stone wall in the main plateia a large, nearly illegible English-language **town map** lists hotels, sights, monasteries, restaurants, discos, and a 24-hr. "sanitary station" (☎26560 41 111) for **medical emergencies.** From the main plateia, **buses** depart for Ioannina (1½hr., 3 per day 6:15am-3:15pm, €3.50) and to Trikala via Kalambaka

(2hr.; 9am, 3pm; €4). Buses to Thessaloniki stop at the main highway above town (about 5 times per day). For **schedule info,** check any of the cafes near the bus stops. Some six or seven unlabeled streets are off the large, open plateia. Standing with your back to the big town map, the street on the left side of the souvenir shop leads slightly downhill to the municipal **police** (☎26560 41 233; open 24hr.) and the **OTE** (☎26560 42 199; open 8am-1pm). Following the path around to your right will bring you to Hotel Apollon where **Internet access** is available for a pricey €5 per hour. The main road is on your left, choked with souvenir stands and tavernas; it leads uphill to the path to the Tositsas Museum and the **post office.** (☎26560 44 200. Open M-F 7:30am-2pm.) The **town hall,** on the second floor of the large yellow building where the main road meets the plateia, can provide you with a few glossy brochures of the area. (☎26560 41 207. Open 7:30am-2pm; walk around to the building's back entrance.) On your right, a road runs downhill to Hotel Athens and Agios Nikolaos monastery; another wraps around the plateia past a **National Bank** with 24hr. **ATM,** and the art museum. **Postal code:** 44200.

ACCOMMODATIONS. Room prices peak during the two high seasons: from mid-July to early September, and from December to March for ski season. It's best to call ahead. Domatia offer the cheapest rates—most are found by veering left before the OTE, past the super market. **John Xaralabapoulos's Rooms ❷** are large and comfortable, all with TVs and phones and some with fridges and stoves. Many of the rooms have glass encased religious icons in the corners of the ceiling. An oval, handpainted sign labeled "Domatia-Rooms" marks the entrance, just past the basketball court. (☎26560 42 086. Singles €20; doubles €30; triples €40; prices rise in high season.) The **Hotel Athens ❷** is just below the main plateia, immediately to your right with your back to the town map. Family run since 1925, the hotel offers comfortable rooms with private baths, meticulously made beds, and TVs. (☎26560 41 725. Singles €15; doubles €20.) Hikers and campers are welcome to store their gear free of charge during visits to Pindos Mountain, regardless of where they're staying. The owners can also suggest hiking routes and are your best source of information in Metsovo. **Hotel Olympic ❸,** located just behind John Xaralabapoulos's Rooms, has spacious, carpeted rooms with high ceilings and wood paneling. All rooms have bath, TV, and phone. (☎26560 41 337; fax 26560 41 837. Singles €30; doubles €36; triples €42.)

FOOD AND ENTERTAINMENT. Many of the restaurants in Metsovo are very similar and cater to large groups of tourists. The restaurant in **Hotel Athens ❶** serves Greek specialties on their leafy, shady patio. Mrs. Markias's specialties include a selection of tasty grilled meats, as well as pasta and vegetarian options, which are less expensive than most restaurants in the plateia (entrees €2.50-3.50). The house wine (€2.50) is excellent and made in Athens' own wine cellar. If you'd like to eat in the plateia, try local favorite **Krifi Folia ❷** for its grilled meats, like *kokoretsi* (€6) and *kontosoufli* (€5.50). Also on the plateia is **Kria Vrisi ❷,** which specializes in *hilopittes fournou* (a pasta), and **Galaxias ❷,** on the patio atop the grassy hill overlooking the plateia. Galaxias has Metsovo's largest selection of dishes, all cooked within a traditional, ivy-covered mansion. Metsovo has little nightlife, but if you need a drink or three after dinner, head to **Tositsas** street, leading uphill from the plateia. There's little difference between bars; all charge €2-3.50 for drinks and calm down by midnight.

SIGHTS. Thanks to the generosity of Baron Tositsas, a Metsovo-born Swiss baron who donated his fortune to the town, and Evangelos Averoff-Tositsas, Metsovo has far more sights than you'd expect of a 3500-person town. The **Tositsas Museum,** in a stone and timber *arhontiko* (mansion) to the left of the main road, honors the generosity of the town benefactors. In the museum's rooms you'll find the beds, sofas, rugs, jewelry, clothing, and kitchen utensils used by the Tositsas clan from 1661 until 1950. In addition, there's also a collection of local folk art and dress. (Open F-W 9:30am-1:30pm and 4-6pm. €3. Visitors are admitted only in small groups; wait at the museum's door for the guide, who appears every 30min.)

Off the main plateia, the spacious **E. Averoff Gallery** exhibits 19th- and 20th-century Greek art labeled in English and Greek, including the private collection of Averoff-Tositsas. Highlights of the museum's 200-plus paintings include impressionistic landscapes by Pantazis (1849-84), the *Burning of the Turkish Flagship* by Lytras (1832-1904), and the postmodern *Erotic* by Gravvalos. Green clay dinosaurs gaze amiably upon visitors in the colorful **children's art room** downstairs, where dried-bean collages and delightful tempera paintings complement their oily counterparts above. (☎26560 41 210. Open W-M 10am-7pm. €2, students €1.) Next door in the conference center (Diaselo), there's an exhibition of letters, postcards, and newspaper clippings from the Balkan War, as well as a small but interesting collection of seashells. (Open Tu-F and Su 11am-2pm, Sa 10am-1pm. Free.)

A 30min. walk from the plateia is the **Agios Nikolaos Monastery;** signs point the way. Built in the 14th century and subsequently abandoned, the crumbling chapel was a refuge for itinerant shepherds for years. The smoke from their fires completely covered the luminous frescoes painted in 1702 by noted saint biographer Efsiat Chios, perfectly preserving their colors until they were rediscovered in 1950 by Averoff-Tositsas. A Greek woman now lives in and cares for the monastery, so politely knock to be admitted and wander among the chickens and cats. For information about outdoor activities in Metsovo and **Valiakalda National Park,** contact the town hall (☎26560 41 207) or the owners of Hotel Athens (☎26560 41 725).

ZAGOROHORIA Ζαγοροχωρια

The Zagorohoria is a collection of 46 villages north of Ioannina, not far from the Albanian border. According to Zagori custom, all buildings must be crafted from the gray stone slate of the surrounding mountains. From a distance, the villages appear as oddly geometric rock formations poking humbly out of the green hills. Recently, some of the larger villages have become popular as quiet getaways for Greek and European tourists seeking crisp mountain air, a relaxing rural environment, and extraordinary hiking. However, most villages in the Zagorohoria receive little more than a handful of visitors each year and remain as tranquil and pristine as they have for centuries.

HIKING AND THE OUTDOORS. Although the villages themselves are well worth a day or two, most tourists come to this rugged region for what lies in the hinterlands—rough-riding rivers, stark peaks, and the renowned **Vikos Gorge.** Outdoor enthusiasts of every skill level will find more than enough to satisfy them in the Zagorohoria and the surrounding **Vikos-Aoös National Park.** For more information, contact Mario at **Pension Monodendri** (☎26530 71 300) or Nikos at **Koulis Restaurant,** both in Megalo Papingo (☎26530 41 138). Rafting and kayaking trips can be arranged in spring through **Konitsa's Paddler School** (☎26550 24 536 or 26550 24 500). The best times for hiking are late May, early June, and September. Make sure to get good maps (available through the EOS) and good directions through reliable sources before heading out. *Periptera*, in each of the Zagorohoria villages, sell excellent maps (€4.40), marking all of the major trails.

THE GREAT ESCAPE Tucked away discreetly in the far-flung corners of Greece's northern hills, the unassuming villages of Zagori have long been the perfect getaway for Greeks on the run. The seclusion of these stone villages has allowed them to prosper free from external influences and has left them largely unscathed by Greece's tumultuous past. In 1430, conquering Turks, perhaps daunted by the region's inaccessibility (or its hungry wolves and bears), chose not to add Zagori to the Ottoman Empire in the usual manner. Instead, they opted for a treaty whereby the natives paid taxes to the Turks in exchange for retaining their autonomy. The wise Zagorian diplomats also managed to haggle another clause into the deal that prevented Turks from entering the region entirely. All of Zagori's Greek traditions remained intact throughout the Ottoman Era, unaffected by the growing Turkish presence that influenced the rest of the country. Village populations grew too, as more and more Greeks flocked to the mountains, fleeing persecution. Today, Zagorians see their peaceful homeland as a different kind of refuge. Stressed out city dwellers now follow the same journeys fugitives once took, escaping high-pressured jobs for a relaxing weekend away from it all.

MONODENDRI Μονοδενδρι

Many an enchanted traveler has tripped dreamily through Monodendri's cobbled maze, illuminated only by twinkling stars and the summertime multitudes of fireflies. Despite a few hikers, skiers, and city-escapees in summer and winter, the village remains peaceful and perfect. Its natural and architectural beauty, in addition to the inexpensive yet beautiful hotels, makes it a pleasant base for hikers.

ORIENTATION AND PRACTICAL INFORMATION. The single paved road in Monodendri runs through the upper end of the village; the bus stop, all of the hotels, and most of the restaurants cluster there. Buses go to **Ioannina** (1hr.; 7am, 5pm; €2.35), where the nearest **hospital** is. The town plateia is accessible via a footpath descending to the right as you leave the bus stop; follow the path downhill and turn left when the road forks. The plateia is bare, save for a **phone** and **post box,** but signposts for all the trailheads begin here. The narrow cobblestone paths of Monodendri can be a disorienting maze of gray rock, but most paths meander in one way or another toward the plateia. There is **no bank,** but some hotels may be able to cash traveler's checks or **exchange money** in a pinch.

ACCOMMODATIONS. Monodendri's plentiful accommodations are generally high in quality and low in price, making it one of the most affordable villages in the Zagorohoria. On the left as you walk up from the bus station, **Zarkada Hotel ❷** offers colorful, comfortable rooms with modern baths, TVs, phones, and wide stone balconies. (☎26530 71 305. Breakfast €5. Singles €20; doubles €35; triples €45.) A bit farther up the road, **Pension Monodendri ❷** has bright, cheerful rooms with colorful wool rugs and wall hangings. The owner's English-speaking son Mario is full of info on trekking in the area and can arrange to pick you up from Vikos village or Megali Papingo after your day hike for €30. His parents, Dimitris and Katerina Daskalopoulou, can provide a lunch (€3) to take on the trail. (☎26530 71 300 or 26530 71 410. Breakfast €5. Singles €20; doubles €30; triples €40.) Close to the bus station is **Ladia ❸,** a castle-like structure at the entrance to the village offering comfy, modern rooms with private baths, TVs, rugs, and the occasional fireplace. (☎26530 71 483. Singles €25; doubles €33; triples €35.)

FOOD. A few tavernas are interspersed among these pensions on the main road. The friendliest is **Katerina's ❶**, at the porch of Pension Monodendri, where Mrs. Daskalopoulou prepares an ever-changing menu, including an array of delicious traditional Zagori pies. (Entrees €3-5.50.) Usually the most crowded, **Restaurant Vikos Gorge ❶**, just above Pension Monodendri, has a spectacular view from its wide porch. An array of local wines complement the stuffed tomatoes (€3.50) and *kotopita* (€4). **Restaurant Zarkadas ❷**, below the hotel, serves up a limited selection of salads and meat dishes. (Open daily 8am-midnight.)

SIGHTS. There isn't much to see or do in Monodendri beyond admiring the architecture, breathing the mountain air, and stocking up for a foray into Vikos Gorge. Those unwilling to tackle Vikos head-on, however, can enjoy breathtaking, unparalleled views of the entire gorge at the must-see natural overlook, about a 1½hr. walk on the main road uphill from the village. A large section of the road can be bypassed by following a red-blazed trail that begins behind Pension Monodendri. The road eventually ends and gives way to a small footpath, leading to a vantage point for gazing down on the gorge's three main chasms. The sunset glow is spectacular. The abandoned Monastery of Agia Paraskevi, about 600m from the plateia, also has impressive views. From the monastery, a treacherous path skirts along the edge of the canyon and leads to a small cave, preceded by a 100m drop. Signs from the plateia point the way to Megali Spilia, another nearby cave where Zagorians used to stock food and water and hide from Albanian marauders.

VIKOS GORGE Χαραδρα Βικου

According to the *Guinness Book of World Records*, the Vikos Gorge, whose walls are 900m deep but only 1100m apart, is the steepest canyon on earth. This "Greek Grand Canyon" stretches from the village of Kipi in the south to Megalo Papingo at its northernmost tip, winding its way through the center of the Zagorohoria. In spring, the river that has taken millions of years to form its eponymous gorge rushes along the 15km stretch of canyon floor. By summertime this mighty force is reduced to a feeble trickle crawling through the massive white boulders in a bone-dry riverbed. Rusted iron deposits in the gorge's sedimentary rock leave an orange-pink tint on the walls suggestive of the last gleamings of sunset. Even more colorful are the spring wildflowers, summer butterflies, autumn foliage, and views of the bright-green spring running below Vikos village. When night falls, listen for the shrill chirping of crickets and watch fireflies dance among the trees. The long hike through the gorge is stunning: the nearly vertical canyon sides, softened by hundreds of stubborn trees, tower hundreds of meters overhead.

THE HIKE. The well-marked Vikos trail is part of the **Greek National O3 route,** which runs from the Aoös River near Konitsa all the way to Kipi. Before you go, be sure to get a **map.** The *periptero* on the main road through Monodendri sells detailed maps of all the trails in Zaghoria for €4.40. If you get confused, just look for the red diamonds on white square backgrounds with "O3" stenciled on them, which consistently mark the path. Most enter the gorge from **Monodendri,** the highest of the villages, but it can also be accessed from **Kipi,** the **Papingo** villages, and from **Vikos** village. It takes 4½hr. to walk between Vikos village and Monodendri and 6hr. between the Papingos and Monodendri.

To reach the gorge from Monodendri, take the marked path from the plateia. After about 40min. along the steep descending trail, you'll reach a fork in the path. Go left to enter the canyon's dry riverbed of smooth rocks and head toward the far-off villages of Papingo and Vikos. To the right, about an hour away, lies the village of Kipi with its trademark stone bridges. Take the left fork as it climbs above the left bank of the riverbed. The path continues for some time, fairly level and pleasant, through a mossy, shady woodland along the riverbank. Be careful when crossing the deceptively treacherous screes (long, narrow cascades of loose rock that stretch up the canyon walls). After about 2hr., there will be a sign for a **water tap** where you can fill your bottle—this is the halfway point. Continuing straight on the trail after the water tap, you'll pass some open groves mowed clean by grazing horses. Eventually you'll emerge in very bare, exposed, sunny terrain. Around this area (about 4-5hr. from Monodendri), the path will veer off in two directions at a poorly marked **major crossroads.**

Continue on the path uphill, on the left bank, to reach **Vikos** village, about 45min. farther away. Vikos has only one accommodation: small rooms rented by **Sotiris Karpouzis ❸.** (☎26530 41 176. €35.) For the **Papingo** villages, make a right and go down the slope to the inviting springs, which lie beneath a large, flat camping area. Cross over the riverbed (on the right where it's still dry) and head uphill. The green, shady springs are the perfect place for a swim, if you have the time; at least wade and refill your water bottle. From here, an arduous 1½hr. ascent brings you to the twin villages of **Megalo Papingo** and **Mikro Papingo.** The trail along this stretch becomes a bit more difficult to follow, so keep an eye out for those trusty red and white O3 blazes. You'll find another small stream, but just before it a sign in Greek points the way: Megalo Papingo to the left, Mikro Papingo to the right.

MEGALO PAPINGO Μεγαλο Παπινγο

The two Papingo villages are the most developed of the Zagorohoria. Their position at the end of the Vikos Gorge ensures their popularity with backpackers and independent travelers. In recent years, Megalo Papingo, the larger of the two, has also become a favorite spot for wealthy vacationing Greek families seeking a retreat from Thessaloniki and Ioannina. These villages boast 22 separate lodging choices, while most of their 44 Zagori cohorts don't have 22 full-time residents. Luckily, the influx of visitors hasn't diminished the villages' peaceful, rural seclusion and peculiar, stony beauty.

ORIENTATION AND PRACTICAL INFORMATION. The large, austere stone church and its attendant bell tower stand at the entrance to the village, at the end of the road to the outside world, and next to the bus stop. From here, one cobblestone main street snakes around the town, containing most of the pensions and restaurants. The road to Mikro Papingo is clearly marked to the right of the clock tower; the trailhead for Vikos Gorge is 20m down this road on the right. Buses go to **Ioannina** (1½hr.; M, W, F 6:30am and 4:30pm, W service mid-June to mid-Sept. only; €3.65). Megalo Papingo has a **phone** and a **mailbox,** both on its main street. For information on all outdoor activities, ask for Nikos at Koulis Cafe (☎26530 41 115). To find him, walk uphill, to the left when facing the clock tower from the main road, and quickly take another left at the wrought-iron fence.

ACCOMMODATIONS AND FOOD. Though lodging in Papingo is generally quite expensive, there are a few deals to be found. **Vasiliki Nikolaus ❷,** a kind-hearted, energetic lady offers simple, spacious rooms in her stone-roofed farmhouse with its communal bathroom, fridge, and washing machine. Expect to be woken by the rooster at dawn. Standing where the smooth main road meets cobblestone, facing the church, take the first right heading uphill. Fifty meters farther, go left up a small lane. The first left off this laneway takes you on a small path that leads directly to the farmhouse door. (Singles €20; doubles €28.) Along the main road, 50m uphill from the church, **Enoikiazomena Domatia ❸** (☎26530 41 087) has cheerful, colorful rooms with wooden ceilings, rugs, TVs, and private baths. (Singles €25; doubles €30; triples €36.) The beautifully furnished rooms at **Pension Koulis ❸,** with fireplaces, wooden floors, TVs, and baths, are a good deal for groups of two or three. Facing the village from where the surfaced road ends, continue along the main road and take the first left after the church. The pension is on the corner of the next crossroads to the left. (☎26530 41 138. Singles €30; doubles €40; triples €50.) Behind its beautiful entranceway of hanging grape vines, the 120-year-old **Astraka ❸**, on the other end of the main road, offers comfortable, pleasantly decorated rooms with baths, fireplaces, and TVs, plus a cozy living room. (☎26530 41 693. Singles €35; doubles €45; triples €50; quads €60.) Downhill to the right of the main road, the subtly named **Estiatorio ❷** has the best views of the gorge's craggy outcrops. Choose from a selection of Zagori pies, pork, and veal dishes. (☎26530 42 108. Entrees €5-7.) **Restaurant Papingo ❸**, to the right of the belltower in the Papingo Pension, is a popular choice among visitors to the village and serves a small selection of meat dishes and salads. (Entrees €7.50-12.)

HALKIDIKI Χαλκιδικη

The fingers of Halkidiki peninsula point south into the Aegean, sporting spectacular scenery and some of the finer beaches in Greece. Tourists with money and suntan lotion swarm to the middle and western fingers, **Sithonia** and **Kassandra,** where natural beauty tempers tourist gloss. On the eastern prong is **Mt. Athos,** a monastic community that has been the home of Orthodox asceticism for over a thousand years. Visits to Mt. Athos are strictly regulated; men must obtain permits, and women are excluded entirely. Reservations for serious pilgrims should be made up to six months in advance, both for permits and for accommodations (see p. 217). Visitors to Kassandra and Sithonia have no hoops to jump through, other than the Halkidiki public transportation system. Frequent buses run between the Karakassi 68 station in Thessaloniki (☎231 924 444) and the three peninsulas, but bus service does not run from finger to finger; you'll have to return to Thessaloniki. Moped rental allows for splendid cruises along Halkidiki's quiet, beautiful roads to your own private beach just around the corner.

SITHONIA PENINSULA Σιθονια

Tranquility persists on the isolated beaches on the south and southwest coasts of Sithonia, though (like Kassandra), the peninsula has gradually sold its soul to tourism, plunging into the plastic world of souvenirs and tour buses. There are two back roads through Sithonia: west via Neos Marmaras and east via Vourvourou.

NEOS MARMARAS Νεος Μαρμαρας

Once a quiet fishing village, Neos Marmaras has become a popular tourist hub. The beaches, however, remain gorgeous, and sunset views from Neos Marmaras' north end of town continue to amaze.

PRACTICAL INFORMATION. You can get to Neos Marmaras by bus or boat. **Buses** run to **Thessaloniki** (2½hr., 4 per day 7:30am-6:30pm, €8.05) and nearby small towns, including **Nea Moudania** (6 per day 6am-7:30pm, €3); timetables are posted outside of Dionysios's next door. **Taxis** (☎23750 71 500) group by the beach. The nearest **ferry** service to the Sporades runs from Nea Moudania. The English-speaking staff at **Marmaris Tours,** next to the bus stop, recommends rooms, **exchanges currency,** and books excursions. (☎23750 72 010. Open daily 9am-2pm and 6-11pm.) The **National Bank,** with 24hr. **ATM,** is on the main street and offers **currency exchange** on Saturdays. (☎23750 72 793. Open M-Th 8am-2pm, F 8am-1:30pm, Sa 9am-1pm.) The **police station,** open 24hr., is 3 doors up from the National Bank. (☎23750 51 111) **Internet access**

is available at **Stadium**, opposite the small church. From Maramaris Tours, turn right and walk about 300m; it's on the left. (☎23750 72 823. €3 per hr. *Frappé* €2.50; beer €3. Open 8am-2am.) The town **post office** is in the second plateia, to the left of La Plazza. (☎23750 71 334. Open M-F 7:30am-2pm.) **Postal code:** 61381.

ACCOMMODATIONS AND CAMPING. Even with an astounding 104 proprietors in town, vacancies are scarce on midsummer weekends. A sign with a map by the beach lists every domatia; most singles run €30, and anything below €25 will take a little haggling. **Domatia Pella ❸** has exceptionally clean rooms with balconies, baths, fridges, TVs, and small shared kitchens. Walk from the plateia between the two banks; the rooms are 20m uphill on the left. (☎23750 71 226. Singles and doubles €25; triples €35.) **Hotel Glaros ❸,** across the road from Maramis Tours, has small, comfortable rooms with phones and private baths. Inquire at the *ouzeri* below. (☎23750 71 205; fax 23750 72 340. Singles €35; doubles €35; triples €45.) **Alkano Rooms ❹,** in the second plateia above Alkano Grill, offers bright, colorful, rooms with A/C, TVs, fridges, and sparkling clean bathrooms. (☎23750 71 944. Doubles €40; triples €45. Prices reduced in winter.)

FOOD AND NIGHTLIFE. For a tempting selection of delicious Greek classics, head to waterfront taverna **Dionysos ❷,** on the other side of the bus stop. (☎23750 71 202. Entrees €4.50-6.70.) On the left as you approach from Maramaris Tours, tree-lined taverna **Village Corner ❷** offers picturesque views of the harbor along with tasty meat and fish dishes. (Entrees €6-12.50. Open daily 6pm-late.) Popular pagoda impostor **Zoe's Little China ❸** serves a variety of Chinese dishes. (☎23750 72064. Entrees €8-14.) Nightlife in Neos Marmaras centers on the strip of bars and a pair of discos on the beach. The most happening bar in town is the centrally located, waveside **Pluton,** where tables float on a harbor pier. (€3 cover is deducted from the price of your first drink.) Next door at **Molos,** things are more laid back; Greeks and foreigners rub elbows, drink, and watch the surf. (€3 cover is deducted from your first drink.) The big disco, **Vareladiko,** is about 2km away and plays Greek music.

RURAL SITHONIA. Explore more of Sithonia by taking the **bus** around the peninsula to **Sarti** (1hr.; 11:30am, 2:30pm, 7:30pm; €3.50). The bus passes by the most deserted, unblemished turf on the peninsula. Climb the road 5km south of **Porto Carras** to a **beach** near **Agia Kiriaki,** with a small reef and an outlying island. It's a long, hard climb down, but you'll glory in the sand once you get there.

MOUNT ATHOS Αγιον Ορος

The monasteries on Mt. Athos (the "Holy Mountain"), the easternmost peninsula of Halkidiki, have been the paradigm of Orthodox asceticism for more than a millennium. The community has existed since AD 883, when Basil I issued an imperial charter to Athos preventing local military officials from interfering with the monks. Today, the Holy Community of Mount Athos is an autonomous state comprised of 20 Orthodox monasteries and countless hamlets *(skites)*, with some 1800 monks who live and work there full-time. By limiting development to the construction of a few unsurfaced roadways, the monks have preserved the peninsula's luxuriant foliage. Only the jagged marble peak of Mt. Athos itself, soaring 2033m above the waves of the Aegean, is exposed, and wildlife ranging from eagles to foxes roams all over the peninsula. Against the background of this lush sanctuary, the monks of Mt. Athos cloister themselves from the outside world, shunning material pleasures to pursue a spiritual life. Emperor Constantine's edict of 1060 forbids women and female domestic animals from setting foot on the peninsula.

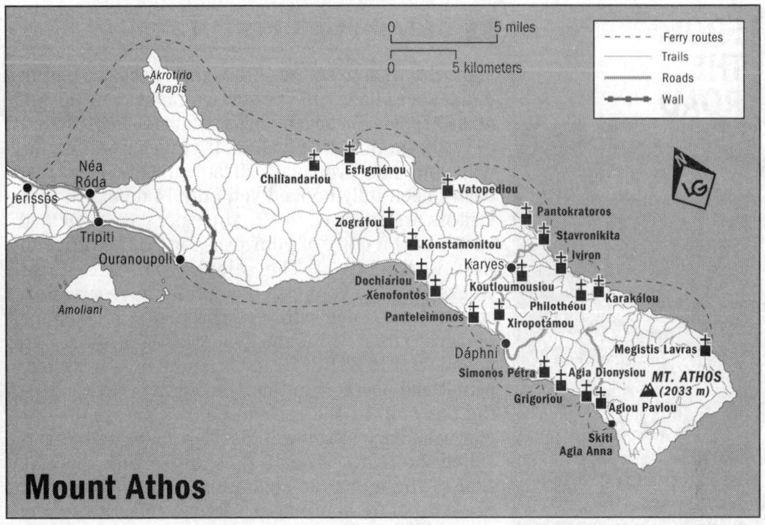

ORIENTATION AND PRACTICAL INFORMATION

Ouranoupolis, the last settlement in secular Athos, functions dually as the gateway to monastic Athos and as a hedonistic beach resort popular among Germans. With **permit** in hand, arrive here the night before your entry date into Athos, or catch the 6am bus leaving Thessaloniki for Ouranoupolis the day of your visit.

The standard approach to Athos is via Ouranoupolis, by boat to **Daphni,** then by bus to the capital city of **Karies. Buses** for Ouranoupolis leave from **Thessaloniki's** Halkidiki station (☎2310 924 444), at Karakassi 68 (2½hr., 7 per day 6:15am-6:30pm, €7.70). There is one boat per day to **Daphni** from Ouranoupolis at 9:45am (2hr., €4.60); it returns at noon to Ouranoupolis, where one or two buses to Thessaloniki will be waiting. From Daphni, you can take Athos's one **bus line** (1 per day, €2) to the capital, **Karies** (30min.), or to several of the monasteries. There is also limited (and expensive) monk-driven **taxi service** (☎23770 23 266) between monasteries. **Boats** also travel throughout the peninsula. The main boat leaves Daphni for Agia Anna daily at 12:30pm and M-Sa 8am, making short stops at Simonos Petra, Grigoriou, Dinysiou, and St. Paul. Buy your ticket on the boat (€1.60-2.90). Those without a permit can view the monasteries by boat, although the boats keep a good distance from shore. From **Ouranoupolis,** 3½hr. tours cost €12. Contact **Doucas Travel,** Venizelou 8, Thessaloniki (☎2310 269 984), or try **Avdimiotis Theophilos** in Ouranoupolis (☎23770 51 207 or 23770 51 244).

Because Athos's hikes can be long and arduous, pick up a copy of the green **Mount Athos Tourist Map** (€8) or buy a **guidebook** with a map (€4-10) in Ouranoupolis or Karies. Leave your pack in Ouranoupolis. **Karies,** the capital of Mt. Athos, has an **OTE** next to the Athonite Holy Council Building, a **post office** (open M-F 7:30am-2pm), and a hotel (€12 per person). Two restaurants in Karies also serve spartan meals, similar to those found in the monasteries (€4.40). **Postal code:** 63086.

FROM THE ROAD

DINNER IS SERVED

Having sipped ouzo and snacked on tyropita for a number of weeks, I suppose I wasn't quite prepared for the humility-inspired monastic meal-plan that I would face at Megistas Lavra. I skipped breakfast to catch an early bus to Mount Athos, only to be told that the holy fathers were fasting–a "modest" meal would be served following vespers. Even the gorgeous architecture and blissful solitude of the monastery did little to distract me from my own growling stomach.

Once the bell had sounded announcing the evening meal, I joined the hundred or so pilgrims shuffling into the dimly-lit refectory. Surrounded by faded frescoes and cold, stone tables, I was herded quickly to my seat along with my dining companions–seven elderly Orthodox Greeks with piously clasped hands and tightly shut mouths. I eyed the meal hungrily, drooling over ripe green cucumber, thinly sliced bread and a thick, brown, lumpy soup of unidentifiable contents.

The monks, in a mass of black flowing robes, positioned themselves on a small dais toward the back of the room as the faithful gathered below. The canter ambled up to the pulpit, prepared to provide the meal's entertainment by reading in a low monotone, and with a sharp, silence-inducing cough he began the prayers. The pilgrims burst to life, blessing themselves furiously before sitting down hastily to eat. I quickly learned that feeding time was strictly limited–in the time it takes for the canter to

OBTAINING A PERMIT

Men who wish to see Mt. Athos must secure a permit in advance. To get the permit, you must call the **Mt. Athos Pilgrims' Bureau** in Thessaloniki (☎/fax 2310 861 611) six months in advance. If you can be flexible with your dates, you may call later and find a day that hasn't been fully booked yet; only 14 non-Orthodox visitors are admitted to Mt. Athos per day. Then mail (don't fax) a copy of your passport to the office at Kon. Karamanli 14, Thessaloniki, 54638; call two weeks ahead of your visit to confirm the reservation, and visit the office with your passport to pick up the permit. (Open M-F 9am-2pm, Sa 10am-noon; call ahead. ☎2310 861 611.) In Ouranoupolis, **bring your permit and passport** to the Athos office, uphill from the bus stop by the gas station, by 9am on the day your visit begins. You will receive your entrance pass called the *Diamonitirion*, complete with the blue seal of the monastic community, which you must present before boarding the ferry to Mt. Athos. The Athos office in Ouranopolis opens at 8am; come early as there will be lines of men waiting to get their passes before the ferry leaves at 9:45am.

The regular permit is valid for a **four-day stay.** Passes cost €30 for foreigners and €15 for students with ISIC under age 27. You must strictly observe the **date of arrival** on your permit: if you arrive a day late, you will be turned away. You will not be admitted without your **passport**. To extend your stay, you must ask at the peninsula's capital, Karies. Unless you have an extremely compelling reason for extending your sojourn (i.e. to become a monk), your request will almost certainly be denied. Unofficial extensions are easier to come by; especially in low season, kind monks often allow considerate, genuinely interested visitors to stay longer.

ACCOMMODATIONS AND FOOD

Those staying overnight in Ouranopolis have several reasonably affordable choices. Dozens of houses offer **domatia** throughout the town, and on your arrival you will probably be greeted at the bus by offers of cheap rooms. Ask first for the location and then for the price. Any bargaining is best done before you see the room; asking for a lower price after you see the room may offend the proprietor. Most places will also store luggage while you're on Athos. **Hotel Athos ❷,** above a supermarket one street back from the waterfront, offers elegant rooms with bath. (☎23770 71 368. Singles €20.20; doubles €25; triples €35.) Those looking for a last supper before their entrance into Mt. Athos—or a triumphal reward after eating the monks' spartan cuisine—should head to the row of similar-looking tavernas on the waterfront. **Restaurant Pyrgos ❷** (☎23770 71 236) and **Restaurant Karydas ❷** (☎23770 71 280 or 23770 71 180) are two popular establishments on the strip.

MOUNT ATHOS

Derived from the name of a Thracian giant buried by Poseidon beneath the mountain, the name "Athos" predates both Christianity and Hellenism. The Christian tradition began at Mt. Athos when the **Virgin Mary,** on a sea trip from Ephesus to visit Lazarus on Cyprus, was thrown off course and led by divine sign to the Athonite coast. The peninsula, known as **Akte,** had been a notorious center of paganism; the moment Mary's foot graced its soil, the false idols disintegrated in realization of their own worthlessness. Even before Mary's time, many had tried to tame the rowdy peninsula, from Alexander the Great to Xerxes.

Although legend claims that the first monastic settlements were founded by Constantine the Great and his mother, Helen, the first record of monkish habitation does not come until the 7th century. The first monastery, **Megistis Lavras,** was built in 963 by **St. Athanasios** with the support of the Byzantine emperor, Nikephoras Phokas. Over the centuries that followed, Athos alternately flourished—at one point containing 40 settlements and 40,000 monks—and declined, as it was buffeted by natural disasters, pirate invasions, and internal squabbling. The edict banning women from the area was enacted in 1060, perhaps out of respect for the Virgin Mary, but likely because of scandalous frolicking between the monks and Vlach shepherdesses who had settled on the mountain. Unlike most of Greece, Mt. Athos retained its autonomy during the Turkish occupation by surrendering promptly to the Ottomans and accepting their rule.

During the centuries preceding the Greek liberation of 1821, Mt. Athos was supported and populated by Serbs, Bulgarians, Romanians, and Russians, who still have affiliations with particular monasteries. At the height of imperial Russia's expansionist policies, some 3000 Russian monks inhabited **Agios Panteleimon,** supplied weekly by cargo-laden ships arriving straight from Odessa.

After World War I, the Treaty of Lausanne made Mt. Athos an official part of Greece while still allowing it to retain much of its autonomy. A body of monks, elected from each of the 20 monasteries, was set up to legislate and govern the peninsula. Dwin-

recount the life of a saint, everything must be eaten in complete silence. Greedily, I tucked into the stale, dry bread, brushing off a few flies that had joined us for the feast. The soup, upon closer inspection, turned out to be a salty, lukewarm mixture of lentils. Chickpeas had never tasted so good.

I guzzled against the clock, my spoon scraping noisily against the stainless steel bowl. A severe monk-on-patrol circled our table looking for talkers, growling "Shhhh!" and pointing a gnarled finger in our direction; eight pairs of eyes dropped guiltily and focused on the food. A loud clang echoed in the hall and the pilgrims were immediately on their feet, dusting off crumbs and swallowing a last mouthful. More prayers, more chants—the flies continued feasting regardless.

The monks exited softly, with hands clasped and heads slightly bowed, and some rebellious pilgrims daringly snatched a few leftover crab apples and tucked them into their pockets. But a frowning monk was looking in my direction. The monastic vow of obedience on my mind, I abandoned the apples and I slipped out piously. After all, I would eat again...in exactly 12 hours.

—Gary Cooney

dling vocations through the 1950s threatened the stability of Mount Athos, and it soon became a prime target for greedy real estate developers. In recent years, however, Athos has been rejuvenated by hundreds of young men inspired to take vows and don the black robes and cap of Orthodox monasticism.

LIFE ON MOUNT ATHOS

Today more than 1800 predominantly Greek monks live in the 20 communal monasteries, the smaller *skites*, or alone in hermitages on the slopes of the mountain itself. Many of the monasteries were formerly idiorrhythmic communities, where each monk was allowed to keep some personal wealth to defray the immense taxes levied on the monasteries by the sultan. Today, all the monasteries are cenobitic, with communal money and duties. The last idiorrhythmic monastery, Pantokratoros, converted in 1992.

Athos retains an unsurpassed wealth of Paleologian and Late Byzantine art, manuscripts, treasure, and architecture. Each monastery houses *lipsana*, remains of dead saints that only Orthodox Christian men are allowed to see and venerate. Especially impressive are the **Hand of Mary Magdalene,** who bathed Jesus, that remains (skin intact) in **Simonos Petra,** and the **belt of the Theotokos** in **Vatopediou,** the only extant relic of the Virgin Mary. Several monasteries possess fragments of the **True Cross.** The **Gifts of the Magi,** presented to Christ at his birth, are housed in St. Paul's; five of the 28 pieces are displayed for veneration every night.

BEING A PILGRIM

Life on Mt. Athos is dedicated to building faith and devotion to God—and, as such, is likely to induce complete culture shock. The monks operate on a schedule twice removed from our own: they use the **Julian calendar** (not Gregorian), which is 13 days behind our own, and set their watches to Byzantine time, marking the sunset as midnight. At most monasteries, the morning liturgy begins at 4am (our time) and stretches until 8am. Although only the most devout pilgrims attend the beginning of the service, the ringing of bells and tapping of wooden planks called *semanitron* keep visitors turning in their beds until they too get up and go to church. Breakfast is served directly after service in fresco-covered *trapezaries* to the sound of a **chanter,** who reads the story of a different saint's life at every meal. Only the chanter talks during meals, and everyone stops eating the moment the chanter stops. Non-Orthodox pilgrims must sit at a separate table from the monks and Orthodox visitors, and at some monasteries must eat after everyone else. Breakfast and dinner both generally consist of homegrown squash or zucchini, bread, water, and fruit, with fish and other delicacies served on feast days.

Always reach the monastery where you plan to stay by 4pm, and make sure you are inside the monastery walls before the gates close at sunset. When you arrive, look for the *arhodariki*, or guest house. There, a monk will welcome you with a glass of ice-cold water, some *tsipouro*, and a jelly-like sweet as he explains the rules of the monastery. The evening *esperino* church service usually starts at 5pm and goes until 6:30pm or so, with dinner served immediately afterward. Relics are presented for veneration either before or after dinner, depending on the monastery. Both food and lodging are free at every monastery, although it is a good idea to call ahead to make a reservation if you're planning a pilgrimage for the summer.

While at the monasteries, be as courteous and cooperative as possible: always address monks by their title, *Patera*, and instead of hello and good-bye, say *evlogite* (bless us, father). Avoid talking loudly, which disturbs monks' meditation, especially during siesta and after nightfall. Also, sitting cross-legged is considered disrespectful and will earn you a few sharp frowns. Be aware of each monastery's rules: some allow non-Orthodox visitors into the church, others restrict them to the narthex, and still others forbid non-Orthodox from entering the church at all.

MONASTERIES

Athos's 20 monasteries blanket the peninsula's northern and southern coasts. Despite similar architecture, each monastery has its own distinctive character. Since visitors can stay only one night in each monastery, it's a good idea to start hiking to your next destination right after breakfast. **Hikes** through Mt. Athos's winding mountain paths, speckled by fluorescent butterflies and chirping crickets, rival any in Greece. Take along a copy of the brown **Mount Athos Tourist Map** or guidebook from Ouranoupolis or Karies, and leave your pack (and any sinful thoughts) behind in Ouranoupolis. **Paths** are narrow, overgrown, and poorly marked; furthermore, the ones on the map might unexpectedly fork in four different directions or not exist at all. When possible, keep to the dirt roads for vehicles and to seaside routes, and travel in groups. Alternatively, you can join most Greek pilgrims and hop into a monk-driven minibus for a bumpy ride back to Karies. From there, ask around for another bus that's traveling in your direction. Prices depend largely on how many pilgrims can be squashed into the taxi.

MEGISTIS LAVRAS. This monastery, on the northwestern tip of the peninsula, is the oldest, largest, and richest of the monasteries—and the only one to escape destruction by fire at some point in its history. Its monks are known to be stern and conservative. The *katholikon* architecture is in the "Athonite" style, invented here in AD 963. The huge complex houses multiple churches, chapels, and cells for monks and visitors. Though it is one of the most visited monasteries, you may find it somewhat impersonal—it certainly lacks the intimacy and friendliness of many of the smaller monasteries. It's also the most isolated: to get here, you will need to get a ride from Karies, the capital, which costs about €60. *(☎23770 23 745.)*

IVIRON. Beautifully situated near a meadow overlooking the northern coast, Iviron is rife with relics and icons such as the **Panagia Portaitissa,** the most renowned of Athos's miracle-working icons. According to legend, Athos will never fall as long as the Panagia Portaitissa remains within its borders. Founded by Georgian monks in 980, Iviron was the first non-Greek monastery on Mt. Athos and rose throughout the years to a position second only to Megistis Lavras. Today, it is completely Greek (the last Georgian monk died in 1955) and one of the most popular monasteries—you will need to call ahead for a reservation. *(☎23770 23 643.)*

VATOPEDIOU. Moated and turreted like a medieval castle, Vatopediou lies on the north coast in a beautiful, secluded bay. Built in 972 and ravaged by pirates for centuries, Vatopediou is now populated largely by Greek-Cypriot monks. It houses over 3000 priceless icons, and its treasures include the **belt of the Virgin Mary** and the largest known fragment of the **True Cross.** Vatopediou is the most visited monastery on Athos; call at least two weeks ahead for a reservation. *(☎23770 23 219.)*

PANTOKRATOROS AND STAVRONIKITA. Pantokratoros (☎23770 23 880) and nearby Stavronikita (☎23770 23 255), lie on the north coast, close to Karies and accessible by bus. Pantokratoros is one of the few monasteries that imposes no special restrictions on its non-Orthodox visitors. Home to a small community of friendly monks, it also houses the Panagia Gerontissa, the only full length icon of the Virgin Mary. Stavronikita is the smallest and "youngest" monastery, completed in 1536; it's also one of the friendliest and most peaceful, offering a more intimate atmosphere and more direct immersion in the lives of the monks than many of the larger communities.

PHILOTHEOU. Greek for "God-loving," Philotheou is one of Mount Athos's most stunningly located monasteries, sitting on a plateau over the north coast. The abbey is surrounded by orchards, gardens, and lush chestnut forests. Founded in 1015 by two ascetic monks from Megistis Lavras, Philotheou's greatest treasure is the **arm of St. John Chrystostom,** which can be venerated every night by Orthodox visitors. Philotheou is also one of the stricter monasteries: non-Orthodox guests must eat after the faithful and may not enter the church at all. *(☎23770 23 678)*

SIMONOS PETRA. Perched on the edge of a sheer cliff on the southern coast, Petra is spectacular. Dramatic, death-defying architecture and splendid **frescoes** could attract throngs of visitors, but there's only room for ten. Travelers can relax in the roomy guest quarters, which extend out on a balcony overlooking the cliff to the sea. Under constant renovation, the monastery is frequently booked; you'll need to call at least two weeks in advance to get a bed. *(☎23770 23 254.)*

GRIGORIOU. In a secluded bay just east of Simonos Petra, this is one of the more liberal monasteries, where the meals are a little tastier, the beds a little cushier, the monks a little friendlier, and the sunset views a little more poignant. Grape vines and flowers overhang the central courtyard, and guests are treated to their own private quarters just outside the monastery walls, with breeze-blown balconies paving the way to the turquoise ocean. *(☎23770 23 668.)*

KARAKALLOU. With thickly-forested hills to the north and the sparkling blue ocean to the south, Karakallou is exceptionally picturesque. Having suffered greatly throughout history at the hands of foreign pirates, today it stands fully restored with one of the most beautifully frescoed churches on Athos. Karakallou's rules for non-Orthodox visitors are particularly strict.

SLAVIC MONASTERIES. In addition to these predominantly Greek monasteries, the Slavs, not to be outdone, inhabit several abbeys. At one time, there were nearly equal numbers of Greek and Slavic monks on the mountain. However, political turmoil (notably the 1917 Russian Revolution) cut off the supply of funds and novices at the source. Today, just three Slavic monasteries remain: onion-domed Russian **St. Panteleimon,** Bulgarian **Zagrafou,** and Serbian **Hilandariou.** The collapse of Communism has reopened Russian wallets, and swelling church coffers now finance ongoing restoration of Panteleimon. Though 5000 Russians seek to enter the monastery, its population is barred from exceeding that of its nearest Greek neighbor, and a community of 50 fills its walls.

SKITES AND HERMITAGES. Many of Athos's monks choose to live as ascetic hermits, eschewing the material comforts of the monasteries in favor of caves and huts on the harsh slopes of the peak. Dozens of huts, cells, and tiny churches dot the southernmost end of the island, between Megistis Lavras and Ag. Pavlou, all occupied by monks who have given their lives to the reclusive study of sacred texts and contemplation of God. Many hermits will allow you to stay with them, but you must bring your own food and sleeping bag and be careful not to disturb their constant meditations. The barren southeastern slope of Athos, called **Karoulia** after the pulleys the monks use to bring food to their caves, is home to some of the most extreme ascetics. The **hike** around the base of the mountain is a difficult one, but it spans the most pristine areas of the peninsula.

Rougher than the monastic life is the hike to the top of Mt. Athos itself. The approach is by path from the skitic community of **Agia Anna** (☎23770 23 320), accessible by boat daily from Daphni. A five-hour climb will take you to the **Church of the Panagia,** with beds for an overnight stay, just one hour from the summit.

KAVALA Καβαλα

Be forewarned: "Kavala" stems from the Greek verb meaning "to ride" (as in "cavalry"), a word connoting the same sexual innuendo as its English equivalent—that's why people may get excited when you say you're going to vacation "in Kavala." The tree-lined avenues of the bustling town stretch from the shores of the north Aegean to the slopes of Mt. Simvolo, 160km east of Thessaloniki. Modern Kavala rests upon the ruins of ancient Neapolis (later Christopolis), where the apostle Paul once preached. In the 18th century, Mehmet Ali, a future Pasha of Egypt, was born here. Most visitors use Kavala as a handy point of departure for the nearby Northeast Aegean Islands.

TRANSPORTATION

Most ferries leave from the eastern end of the port in front of the string of restaurants. Thasos boats all leave from the western dock.

Flights: Olympic Airways (☎2510 223 622), a little west of the Thasos ferry dock on the corner of Eth. Andistassis and Kavalas. Open M-F 8am-4pm. Daily flights to **Athens** (1hr., 10 per week Su-Th, €75). A taxi to the airport from the city center is €15.

Buses: (☎2510 223 593), at the corner of Eterias and Kavalas, a block north from Vas. Pavlou and the waterfront, and a block south of the post office. To: **Athens** (9½hr., 3 per day 9:15am-7:15pm, €37.60); **Drama** (1hr., every 30min. 6am-9pm, €2.35); **Iraklitsa** (20min., every 20-30min. 6am-11pm, €1); **Philippi** (½hr., every 30min. 6am-9pm, €1); **Thessaloniki** (2¼hr., 16 per day 5:30am-8:30pm, €9.70); **Xanthi** (1hr., 11 per day 6am-2pm, €3.50). To get to **Alexandroupolis** (2hr., 7 per day 10am-1:30am, €10.35), go to **Seven-Eleven,** a fast-food restaurant located directly opposite the main entrance of the bus station. There you'll find schedules, tickets, and the bus itself.

Ferries: Nikos Milades (☎2510 220 067 or 2510 223 421), in a back corner of the main harbor, has ferry info for islands other than Thasos. Look behind the small park to the left of the row of tavernas. Open M-F 8:30am-1:30pm and 6-8pm, Sa 8:30am-1:30pm, Su 6-9pm. Ferries to: **Chios** (24hr., Su 9pm, €24.30); **Lesvos** (12hr.; Tu 11pm, Sa 4pm; €21.10); **Limnos** (5hr., 4 per week, €12.20); **Piraeus** (35hr., Su 9pm, €32). **Arsinoi Travel,** K. Dimitriou 16 (☎2510 835 671), a few doors down from Milates, sells tickets to **Samothraki** (4hr., 4-5 per week, €13.64); schedules change monthly. Open M-F 8:30am-8:30pm, Su 8:30am-3pm. Buy tickets to **Thasos** (1hr., 7 per day 8am-9pm, €2.64) at the white ticket kiosk on the Thasos ferry dock, located on the busy corner one block south and one block east of the bus station.

Flying Dolphins: Hydrofoils leave from near the Thasos ferry dock for **Thasos** (40min., 4 per day 7:10am-2pm, €7.04) and **Samothraki;** buy your ticket on the boat.

Taxis: (☎2510 232 001), in Pl. 28 Octovriou. Available 24hr.

ORIENTATION AND PRACTICAL INFORMATION

The city's main attraction, the **Panagia District,** is southeast of the port on its own peninsula, hemmed in by ancient walls under the turrets of the Byzantine fortress. The entrance is on **Poulidou** at the end of **El. Venizelou** and **Erithrou Stavrou,** two main streets that run parallel to the waterfront. On the waterfront itself is **Eth. Andistasis,** which begins at the Thasos ferry dock and runs west past the Archaeological Museum and the municipal park. A detailed **map** of Kavala can be found next to the small port police kiosk, at the Thasos ferry dock.

Tourist Office: Discovery Travel (☎2510 839 556), directly opposite the entrance to the Old City at Poulidou; look for a green and white flag. Very friendly English-speakers have information on excursions and local sights. Open M, W, Sa 8:30am-2:30pm; Tu, Th, F 8:30am-2:30pm and 5:30-9pm.

Police Station: Omonias 119 (☎2510 622 273 or 2510 622 274), 4 blocks north of the port. **Port police** (☎2510 223 716) at both ports. Open 24hr.

Tourist Police: (☎2510 622 246), on the police station ground floor. Open 8am-3pm.

Bank: The **National Bank** (☎2510 222 163), on the corner of Omonias and Pavlou Mela, has a 24hr. **ATM** and **currency exchange.** M-Th 8am-2pm, F 8am-1:30pm. Smaller banks and several ATMs can be found closer to the harbor on El. Venizelou.

Hospital: Stavrou 113 (☎2510 228 517). Call ahead.

OTE: (☎2510 222 699), on the east side of Pl. 28 Octovriou, near El. Venizelou. Open M, W 7:30am-2:30pm; Tu, Th, F 7:30am-8:30pm; Sa 8:30am-2pm.

Internet Access: **Cyber Club,** El Venizelou 56. Over 50 high-speed terminals at €1.50 per hr. *Frappés* €1.50, beer €1.80. Open 24hr.

Post Office: Main branch (☎2510 833 330), at Kavalas and Stavrou, 1 block north of the bus station. **Exchanges currency.** Open M-F 7:30am-8pm. **Postal code:** 65110.

ACCOMMODATIONS AND CAMPING

Domatia are scarce, hotels aren't cheap, and many of Kavala's rooms overlook the port (the shipping industry doesn't shut down when you do). There's a **GNTO campground** ❶ with a supermarket in **Batis,** 3km outside of Kavala. (☎2510 243 051. €3 per person; €7 per large tent; €3 per small tent; €1 to swim in the pool.) Blue bus #8 goes to Batis from Kavala every 30min.

George Alvanos Rented Rooms, Anthemiou 35 (☎2510 221 781 or 2510 228 412). Enter the Panagia District on Poulidou, bear left uphill on Mehmet Ali, and make a sharp left on Anathemiou. A centuries-old house in the heart of the scenic Panagia District has large rooms with fans for the lowest prices in town, far from the noise and fumes of the port. Many of the spacious, homey rooms look out over the sea; all have free use of a laundry machine and full kitchen. Singles €15; doubles €22. ❷

Oceanis Hotel, Erythrou Stavrou 32 (☎2510 221 981, fax 2510 225 270). At the intersection of Dagli and Erythrou Stavrou. Colorful, spacious rooms fully equipped with TV, A/C, telephone, large balconies, and sparkling clean bathrooms. Great views from the bar and swimming pool on the 8th fl. Singles €40; doubles €60; triples €70. ❹

Hotel Acropolis, El. Venizelou 29 (☎2510 224 205; fax 2510 830 752), from the bus station walk 2 blocks away from the water and turn right on El. Venizelou. It's 1 block ahead on your right. Bare but clean rooms have high ceilings and TV; some have views of the bay. Singles €28; doubles €33, with bath €44. ❸

Hotel Panorama (☎2510 224 205), across from Hotel Acropolis. Basic rooms with small balconies, TVs, and colorful drapes. Singles €26; doubles €34; triples €40. ❸

FOOD AND NIGHTLIFE

Tavernas line the water and Poulidou in the Panagia District. After hours, Kavala remains relatively calm, but a few lively Cafe-bars line the waterfront. **Megaron** (☎2510 232 164) is a popular choice, with outdoor tables and Greek music. (Open until 2am.) Otherwise, take a taxi to nearby **Palio** (€5) or the beach at **Iraklitsa.**

Mikros Mylos Bakery (☎2510 228 132), on the corner of El. Venizelou and Dangli, a block south of the Municipal Museum. This first-rate bakery makes it all. Try the *pasta flora* (marzipan and fruit tart) for €1.50. ❶

Oraya Mytilini (Οραια Μυτιληνη; ☎2510 224 749), by the port under the Old City, among a row of similar tavernas. Friendly, English-speaking staff is happy to give you a guided tour of the kitchen. Tastefully decorated with hanging cloves of garlic and a clothesline of gutted fish, the restaurant serves up delicious seafood entrees (€4-8). ❷

To Tarepnaki (☎251 226 535) About halfway up Poulidou on the left as you face uphill. The small, friendly taverna serves a good selection of seafood and meat dishes. Entrees €3.50-8. ❷

SIGHTS

CASTRO. Follow signs from the entrance to the Panagia. Originally built in the 5th century BC, the castle and its surrounding walls were later augmented by the Byzantines and the Ottomans. The well-preserved, turreted walls survey the wide panorama of the city and the island of Thasos to the south. The small **amphitheater** hosts occasional musical and cultural performances. In the **Eleftheria Festival** in late June, students celebrate Kavala's liberation from the Ottomans by performing dances at the castle. *(Open daily 8:30am-1:30pm and 5-8:30pm. Free.)*

MUNICIPAL FOLK MUSEUM. The ground floor of Kavala's small Municipal Museum houses works by famed Thassian sculptor Polygnotos Vagis (see p. 389). The marble, stone, and wooden pieces blend archaic Greek styles with modern influences like Chagall and Matisse, seen in the roughly chiseled faces of **The Moons.** Upstairs, a standard collection of traditional clothes, carpets, and farm tools stand alongside a bizarre taxidermy display featuring some ragged stuffed vultures. *(Filippou 4; take Venizelou west from the old town and turn away from the water onto Mitropelous. ☎2510 222 706. Open daily 9am-1:30pm. Free.)*

BEACHES. Kavala's waterfront is home to three beaches. Although it's not an arduous walk from town, the best bet is an intercity bus—get off on impulse, or consult the tourist office. The sandy beach of **Perigali,** northwest of the city beyond the Panagia district, is a favorite. The closest beach is near the city of **Kalamitsa,** 1500m east of the city center. The resort town of **Nea Iraklitsa,** 20km southwest of Kavala, luxuriates in long, golden beaches and some of the area's hottest nightlife.

DAYTRIP FROM KAVALA: PHILIPPI

Take the bus from Kavala (every 30min. 6am-9pm, €1). Make sure to tell the driver you want the archaeological site.

Roughly 15km north of Kavala, the once-proud city of **Philippi** lies in splendid ruins. Philip of Macedon founded Philippi to protect Thasian goldminers from Thracian attacks and named it all by himself. A 42 BC Roman Civil War battle made it famous: here, Octavian (later Augustus) and Antony defeated Cassius and Brutus, the assassins of Julius Caesar. In AD 50, missionaries St. Paul and St. Silas arrived from Anatolia to preach Christianity, in the process baptizing a woman named **Lydia,** the first European Christian. The **Cell of Paul** is the apostle's own budget accommodation: shut the door and peek at the Roman **latrines,** where most of the 42 marble seats are intact, and all the lids have been left up. (☎2510 516 470. Open daily 8am-7pm. €3, students and seniors €2, EU students free.)

THRACE Θρακη

Thrace is sliced into halves by the Evros River—Greece holds the west, Turkey the east. Ruled by the Ottomans until 1913, the region fell under Allied control during World War I but did not join the Greek state until 1919. The area was split by the 1923 Treaty of Lausanne, which granted the eastern part of Thrace to Turkey. The scarring 1922 population exchange (see p. 12) relocated Greeks in Turkish territory to Greece, and Turks in Greek territory to Turkey. Although most Muslim Greeks were shipped off to Turkey, some stayed in Thrace. Seventy-five years later, many remain there. This cultural and religious entanglement distinguishes the region from more homogenous Greek cities to the south.

XANTHI Ξανθη

Xanthi, Thrace's most charismatic city, may be the most pleasant place to experience the slightly edgy phenomenon of Greek multiculturalism. Strolling the sidewalks you'll see Muslims (about 10% of Xanthi's population), Christians, Gypsies, and occasional Pomaks, who descend from 16th-century Slavs. Getting lost in the cobbled streets of Xanthi's old town threads you through neighborhoods of Ottoman houses and elegant old mansions, the bounty of a tobacco industry that still buoys much of the town's economy. A student population from Xanthi's University of Thrace gives the modern city a smart, sophisticated feel year-round. As of late, more and more tourists are finding Xanthi a convenient and pleasant pit stop on a return journey from the islands.

TRANSPORTATION. Trains go to: **Athens** (14hr., 2 per day 4:20pm and midnight, €21); **Komotini** (45min., 2 per day 6:30 and 9pm, €1.50); and **Thessaloniki** (4hr., 3 per day, €7). A faster, cooler, and pricier intercity train leaves for Athens at 8:30am daily (11hr., €30). Tickets are sold at the train station and the **OSE Office** in the Agora Nousi shopping area on Tsaldari, just east of the central plateia. (☎25410 22 277 or 25410 27 840. Open M-F 10am-2:30pm 6-9pm.) Xanthi's **train station** (☎25410 22 581) is about 2km southeast of the central plateia. To get there, head down Karaoli, go right at the rotary of Pl. Baltati, and then left onto Kapnergaton (a.k.a. Kondili). You will see signs 100m past the stadium and the tennis courts. You can also take a taxi from the central plateia for €2. From the **bus station,** Dimokritou 6 (☎25410 22 684), buses go to: **Athens** (11hr., 9:30am and 7pm, €40.40); **Drama** (2hr., 6 per day 8am-6:45pm, €5.65); **Kavala** (1hr., every hr. 6am-11pm, €3.50); **Komotini** (45min., 16 per day 6:30am-8:15pm, €3.45); and **Thessaloniki** (3½hr., 8 per day 6am-7pm, €12). **Taxis** (☎25410 25 900 or 25410 22 702) wait in Pl. Dimokratias and Pl. Baltsazi.

ORIENTATION AND PRACTICAL INFORMATION. Xanthi is Thrace's westernmost city, about 50km northeast of Kavala. Its central plateia is **Pl. Kentriki,** also known as **Pl. Dimokratias,** easily recognizable by the clock tower in the center. From the bus station, standing at the door in front of the seating area, take **Dimokritou** on your left past **Pl. Balsazi,** a small traffic circle. Dimokritou becomes **Karaoli** and leads into the central plateia. From here, streets run off like the spokes of a wheel. The main street, **28 Octovriou,** runs south to **Pl. Eleftherias,** parallel to Karaoli, and **Vas. Konstantinou** runs north to the Old Town, across from the clock tower.

Xanthi has no tourist office, but the **town hall** (☎25410 24 444), on the upper end of Vas. Konstantinou, provides a **city map.** Walk 100m up Konstantinou from the plateia and take a right at the blue restaurant. The **National Bank,** which has a 24hr. **ATM** and four imposing white columns, is north of the main plateia. Take the first right off Konstantinou as you head toward the Old City. (Open M-Th 8am-2pm, F 8am-1pm.) Two blocks southeast of Pl. Baltsazi is the **hospital.** (☎25410 47 100 and 25410 47 200. Open 24hr.) The **police** (☎25410 23 800) are at Neston 2, north of Karaoli near the bus station. Check your e-mail in the comfortable, air-conditioned **InfoCafe,** on a small sidestreet at the entrance to the Old City, opposite a cluster of tavernas. (☎25410 67 871. Open 10am-6am. €2.80 per hr.; coffee €2; beer €3.) The **post office** (☎25410 21 224; open M-F 7:30am-2pm) is located just beyond the clock tower on Georgiou, a small street separating Klimataria restaurant and Mikros Mylos Bakery. The **OTE** (☎25410 56 199; open 8am-2pm) is left of the central plateia as you face the big, white courthouse. **Postal code:** 67100.

ACCOMMODATIONS. Neither tourists nor budget hotels have yet discovered Xanthi, and accommodations are scarce and expensive—singles generally cost around €40. If you have good bargaining skills, this is the time to use them. If you don't, this is the time to learn them. Your best bet is the comfortable, modern **Hotel Orfeas ❸,** Karaoli 40, which has carpeted rooms with A/C, mini-fridges, TVs, phones, and private baths; there's also an ice-cold drinking fountain on each floor. (☎25410 20 121 or 25410 20 122; fax 25410 20 998. Singles €32; doubles €45; triples €52.) A slightly more luxurious option is **Hotel Democritus ❹,** 28 Octovriou 41, just below the central plateia. Spacious, carpeted bedrooms lead out onto large balconies. All rooms have TVs, A/C and phones. Singles €41; doubles €58, triples €70.

FOOD. A strongly Turkish flavor pervades much of Xanthi's cuisine, with culinary specialties like syrupy *kariokes* and *soutzouk-lokum*. Restaurants, cafes, and bars concentrate in the central plateia and on Vas. Konstantinou. A **covered market,** off 28 Octovriou just south of the main plateia, is the perfect place to stock up on fruit, vegetables, and baked goods, as well as fish and immense slabs of meat—whole goat, anyone? (Open daily until 3pm.) Just north of the plateia on a sidestreet that leads to the National Bank is **Midos Taverna ❷,** Stavrou 18, serving a delicious range of Greek classics in a quiet, flagstoned courtyard. Try the "Midos Special Chicken," a closely-guarded family recipe (€5.28). **Klimataria ❶,** packed with locals under the shadow of the clock tower in the main plateia, has a big, tasty, inexpensive menu, specializing in local pork and goat dishes. (☎25410 22 408. Entrees €3.50-7.) **Palo Meraki ❶,** at the entrance to the old town on Konstantinou, sits in the midst of the busiest cafes. (☎25410 76 581. Entrees €4.40-6.50.)

SIGHTS. On these quiet little streets you'll find stately mansions, churches, and old homes, many of them bristling with balcony satellite dishes to tune into the latest news from Turkey. Orthodox priests mingle with veiled Muslim women, and the corner stores sell a variety of Greek and Turkish newspapers. Xanthi's museums are in the Old Town, behind the Town Hall. The **Folklore Museum** houses a small, standard collection of folk clothing and farm equipment. (Open Tu-Su

8am-2:30pm. Free.) **Christos Pavlides Painting Gallery,** across the way, houses a collection of 20 brilliantly colored paintings by local luminary Christos Pavlides. (☎25410 76 363. Open M-F 10:30am-1:30pm and 7-9pm. Free). In the hills northeast of town, vivid frescoes adorn the walls of **Panagia Archangeliotissa** convent. Ask if an English-speaking nun can show you around. (Open 7am-7pm.) Farther down, the **Panagia Kalamou** church is most notable for its views of the town below. (Open 8am-1pm, 4-8pm.)

NIGHTLIFE. Considering its large student population, Xanthi's nightlife is surprisingly tame. Most of the action centers on the intersection of Sophias and Edras, just below the entrance to the Old City, where young people gather for an evening's *frappé*-sipping and people-watching. **Cafe-Bar Pyxida**, below Roma Pizza, is a popular choice, blaring pop tunes until 2am. (☎25410 63 418. Coffee €2; beer €3; shots €4.) A few doors down, **Cafe-Bar Exo** has a suave interior with wicker tables and cushioned chairs that attracts a slightly older crowd. (☎25410 65 292. Greek music after 1am. Coffee €2; beer €3; shots €4. Open 9:30am-3am.)

KOMOTINI Κομοτηνη

Forty kilometers east of Xanthi, the broad Thracian plain begins to rise into the eastern Rodopi Mountains at rarely touristed Komotini. Komotini's population is about 15% Turkish (or Greek Muslim, as the Greek authorities call them), and their influence is visible in the crooked streets of the Old Town and in the graceful minarets poking up from the forest of whitewashed apartments and church domes.

TRANSPORTATION. Komotini's **train station** (☎25310 22 650) is at the far southwest corner of the city, a 20min. walk from the city center. Standing on Zoidi with your back to the main plateia, turn right and follow Zoidi as it curves to the left and heads southwest toward the station. Once you've passed the stadium, you're halfway there. There is an **OSE office** in town on Zoidou. (☎25310 26 804. Open M-F 8am-3pm.) **Trains** go to: **Athens** (12hr., 3 per day 8:20am-midnight, €22.30); **Thessaloniki** (5hr., 5 per day 8:20am-6:30pm, €8) via **Xanthi** (30min., €1.50); and **Istanbul, Turkey** (10hr., noon, €19). Trains at 8:20am are intercity express, where a 30% higher fare gets you there 30% faster in icy A/C. Call ahead. The **bus station,** G. Mameli 1 (☎25310 22 912 or 25310 26 111), is on the corner of **Tsounta.** To get to the city center, turn right from the bus station door, and then left at the first intersection; follow this road all the way to the central plateia. **Buses** go to: **Alexandroupolis** (1hr., 13 per day 6am-8pm, €4.50); **Athens** (11hr., 8:30am and 6:30pm, €43); **Kavala** (1½hr., 8 per day 5:30am-7pm, €6.50); **Thessaloniki** (4hr., 7 per day 5:30am-6:30pm, €15.10); and **Xanthi** (45min., 16 per day 6:30am-8pm, €3.50). **Taxis** (☎25310 35 911) are available 24hr.

ORIENTATION AND PRACTICAL INFORMATION. Pl. Eirinis is in the very center of town. **Orfeos** runs east-west directly above it and **Zoidi** runs east-west a few blocks below it. To the north, in the Turkish part of town, is the smaller **Pl. Ifestou,** amid a maze of narrow pedestrian streets. Following Orfeos east takes you to **Pl. Vizinou,** where you'll find a large white obelisk and a wooded city park. Komotini has no tourist office, but the **police** (☎25310 34 444), one block south of the obelisk, give out free **maps** and answer questions. The **National Bank,** Thisauis 1, north of Pl. Eirinis at the east end of Orfeos, has an **ATM.** (Open M-Th 8am-2pm, F 8am-1:30pm.) The local **hospital** (☎25310 22 222 or 25310 24 601) is on Sismanoglou in the southeast part of town; follow Georgiou east out of Pl. Eirinis. The **OTE**

(☎25310 37 799; open M-F 7:30am-1pm) is on Parasiou, a side street of Pl. Eirinis. Find **Internet access** at **Cafe Zita,** A Souzou 14 (☎25310 37 972. €2.50 per hr. Open 9am-3am.) The **post office** (☎25310 22 344; open M-F 7:30am-2pm) is next to the OTE on Parasiou. **Postal code:** 69100.

ACCOMMODATIONS. Discriminating travelers take heed: Komotini's hotels are scattered, and it takes some ambling to find a decently priced room. The cheapest option is **Hotel Hellas ❷,** Dimokritou 31, a tidy building bereft of balconies on a large intersection just north of the Archaeological Museum. Well-maintained, minimally furnished rooms with shared baths are off hallways adorned with the paintings and ceramics of the manager's artistic wife. (☎25310 22 055. Singles €18; doubles €25; triples €30.) **Olympus Hotel ❷,** Orfeas 37, west of Pl. Eirinis, offers sparkling clean rooms with a homey feel. Rooms have TVs, fridges and A/C. (☎25310 37 690; fax 25310 37 693. Singles €23, with bath €35; doubles €30, with bath €47; triples with bath €56.) **Hotel Orpheus ❸,** Parassion 1, is on Pl. Eirinis across from the OTE. Cheerful rooms with TVs, fridges, A/C, baths, and balconies. (☎25310 37 180; fax 25310 28 271. Singles €36; doubles €47; triples €53.)

FOOD AND NIGHTLIFE. The center for both dining and nightlife is the area around **Pl. Eirinis.** In the pre-midnight hours, the plateia becomes a playground for local kids as their parents relax in the cafes that flank the square; when the families head home, the bars hop until 3am. **To Kouti ❷,** Orfeus 44, just south of the Pl. Eirinis, has a mouth-watering menu and mind-easing setting in a serene ivy courtyard. The reasonably priced dishes are imaginative offshoots of Greek favorites. Try the *loukarikos* (€5.28), a baked sausage dish covered in cheese and tomatoes. (☎25310 25 774. Entrees €6-10.) Just below the white obelisk, classy **Restaurant Dimokritos ❷** serves shrimp dishes and classic *spetzofai* (spicy meatballs) in a pink decor. (Entrees €4.70-8. Open daily noon-midnight.) Directly opposite Hotel Orpheus, the balcony tables at **Oivo's ❸** let you survey the plateia from on high. A tasty menu offers meat dishes, salads, and a few American favorites. (☎25310 36 082. Entrees €7-13.50.) **Le Cafe,** near Oivo's, is a comfortable place for *frappé*-sipping to the sounds of Western pop. (Tempting chocolate cakes €2.50; coffee €2.50; beer €3.50. Open 8am-3am.) For a more lively night, head across the plateia to **Bo,** where thumping pop tunes attract a young and sharply-dressed crowd. (Coffee €2; beer €3. Open 8am-2am.)

SIGHTS. To reach Komotini's enthralling **Archaeological Museum,** follow Zoidi westward and bear right onto the cement footpath at the park. Arranged in meticulous chronological order with helpful explanations in English, the museum's artifacts are gleaned from archaeological sites from all over Thrace, including nearby Dikaia, Mesemuria, Meronia, and the banks of the Lissos River. Highlights include archaic funerary statues of lions and men, an impressive collection of ancient coins, a painted terra-cotta sarcophagus, a golden bust of the Roman Emperor Septimius Severus, and the 2500-year-old soles of military sandals. (☎25310 22 411. Open daily 9am-6pm. Free.) The converted mansion that houses the **Museum of Folk Life and History,** Ag. Georgiou 13, has household utensils, costumes, and manuscripts depicting Greek village life. (☎25310 27 344 or 25310 25 975. Open M-Sa 10am-1pm. Free.) A 30min. taxi ride from Komotini brings you to the side-by-side beaches of **Maronia** and **Fanari,** which is popular for its strip of beach bars. Maronia has a few seldom-visited archaeological sites, including an ancient theater.

ALEXANDROUPOLIS Αλεξανδρουπολις

Travelers often rush through Alexandroupolis on their way to Turkey, the Northeast Aegean Islands, and the hinterlands of northern Thrace. But in the haste to get somewhere else, don't overlook the charms of Thrace's most bustling city. Rows of fashionable stores, cobblestone streets, and a lovely wooded waterfront make Alexandroupolis worth a visit.

TRANSPORTATION

Trains: The station (☎25510 26 395) is about 400m east of the lighthouse along Alexandron, in front of Pl. Eleftherias. Open daily 6am-10:30pm. Four trains per day to: **Athens** (16hr., €24) via **Thessaloniki** (7½hr., €10), **Komotini** (1hr., €2) and **Xanthi** (2hr., €3). There's also a faster intercity train with A/C to these four cities (leaves 7:15am), but it costs twice as much. Trains run daily to **Istanbul** (7hr., 1pm, €21).

Buses: The bus station (☎25510 26 479) is at the corner of El. Venizelou and 14 Maiou, 500m from the docks. To: **Athens** (11hr., 6:15pm, €43.15); **Didimotiho** (1½hr., 18 per day 4:15am-8:45pm, €5.55) via **Soufli** (1hr., €3.85); **Kipi** (45min., 5 per day 6:50am-7:30pm, €2.50); **Komotini** (1hr., 14 per day 6:10am-8pm, €4.05); and **Thessaloniki** (5hr., 7 per day 8am-10pm, €19.75) via **Kavala** (2hr., €10.35) and **Xanthi** (1½hr., €7.25).

Ferries: The two main ferry lines are **Saos** and **Kikon Tours.** Saos (☎25510 26 721 or 25510 23 512) is on Kyprou, a few doors up from the waterfront and sends ferries to **Samothraki** (2½hr., 2-3 per day, €7.50, students €5.25). Open M-Sa 8am-9pm. Kikon Tours, Venizelou 68 (☎25510 25 455), sends one ferry per week (W 4:30pm) to: **Chios** (18hr., €22); **Kos** (14hr., €30); **Lesvos** (10hr., €17); **Rhodes** (24hr., €38) via **Limnos** (4hr., €12); **Samos** (20hr., €23). Open M-F 8:30am-2:30pm and 6:30-9:30pm, Sa 8:30am-2:30pm.

Flying Dolphins: Saos runs hydrofoils to **Samothraki** (1hr., 2-3 per day, €15.25).

Taxis: (☎25510 22 000 or 25510 27 700). Available 24hr.

ORIENTATION AND PRACTICAL INFORMATION

Though it's a large city, everything the traveler needs or wants is within 10min. of the waterfront center, marked by a lighthouse. Standing at the lighthouse facing inland, the waterfront road, **Megalou Alexandrou,** stretches left to the row of cafes and right toward the **train station.** Halfway between the lighthouse and the train station, **Kypron** leads inland to small, leafy **Pl. Iroön Polytechniou.** The three main streets running parallel to Alexandrou—**L. Dimokratias, El. Venizelou,** and **Paleologou**—lie about three blocks inland, linked by a row of narrow cobblestone streets.

Tourist Office: See the **Tourist Police,** Karaisaki 6 (☎25510 37 411), for maps and information. Open M-F 7:30am-2pm.

Banks: L. Dimokratias is one long string of banks with 24hr. **ATMs.**

Police: (☎25510 37 424), with the Tourist Police, 2 blocks inland from the water, just before the lighthouse. Open 24hr.

Hospital: Dimitras 19 (☎25510 25 772). Open 24hr.

Internet Access: Planet Games, Xarilaou Trikouri 2 (☎25510 29 751). Head west along Dimokratias until the road splits; take the left fork onto Trikouri. €3 per hr.

Post Office: (☎25510 23 122), on the water, 20m west of the lighthouse. Open M-F 7:30am-2pm. **Postal code:** 68100.

ACCOMMODATIONS AND CAMPING

Alexandroupolis offers something in everyone's price range. Inexpensive choices cluster near the bus and train stations. Call ahead, especially for weekends.

Hotel Lido, Paleologou 15 (☎25510 28 808), behind the bus station. Functional, if bare, rooms come with well-kept shared baths. Some rooms have TVs. Singles €21.13, with bath €26.41; doubles €27, with bath €33.74; triples with bath €40.05. ❷

Hotel Vergina, Karaoli 74 (☎25510 23 025), directly across the street from the train station. Ten clean, well-furnished rooms around a large, social lounge. Private showers, TVs, and phones. Singles €20; doubles €30; triples €45. ❷

Hotel Alex, Dimokratias 294 (☎25510 26 302, fax 25510 27 417), 1 block south of the bus station. Small but comfortable rooms with baths, balconies, TVs, phones and ceiling fans. Singles €29.50; doubles €40; triples €48. ❸

Camping Alexandroupolis (☎25510 28 735), 2km west of town center on the water. €4.40 per person, €3.20 per tent. ❶

FOOD AND NIGHTLIFE

Plenty of cheap fast food can be found on the waterfront and on Dimokratias, while a number of good seafood restaurants have tables along the shore. The modest nightlife in Alexandroupolis centers almost exclusively around the waterfront, where the street closes to traffic and locals stroll past cafes.

Taverna Mylos (☎25510 35 519), across from the post office—look for the windmill. Delicious fresh seafood served at tables overlooking the North Aegean. Plunge into the impressive *ouzo* and *tsipouro* selection. Entrees €3.50-12. Open until midnight. ❷

Neraida (☎25510 22 827), diagonal from I. Klimataria on Pl. Polytechniou. Popular with locals. Listen for strains of the schmaltzy live music from next door as you bite into octopus pasta (€3.82). Entrees €3-7.50. ❷

Methistaris (☎25510 82 645), 5 minutes east of the lighthouse on the waterfront. Patrons flock here for the impressive fish selection. Entrees €5-15. ❸

SIGHTS

Alexandroupolis's **Ecclesiastic Art Museum** is housed within the Cathedral of Ag. Nikolaos, two blocks inland from the National Bank. An 18th-century icon of Christ, portraying Jesus with his legs forming a heart, is the highlight of a collection of icons and church frescoes. If you can, get an English-speaking priest to give you a tour. (☎25510 37 205. Open M-Sa 8am-1pm. Donation €1.)

DAYTRIPS FROM ALEXANDROUPOLIS: DADIA

Take the ***bus*** *from Alexandroupolis to Didimotiho; it stops in* ***Soufli*** *(1hr., 18 per day 4:15am-8:45pm, €3.85). From Soufli, catch the bus to Dadia. Get maps about the Reserve at the* ***Ecotourist Center,*** *across the road from the bus stop; they also rent mountain bikes for €3 per hr. ☎25540 32 463. Open daily June-Aug. 8:30am-8:30pm; Sept.-May 9am-7pm.*

The lush green expanse of the Dadia Forest Reserve lies 40km northeast of Alexandroupolis, covering 7300 hectares of thickly-wooded hills spread near the Turkish border. Created as a protected reserve in 1980, the forest serves as a home and breeding ground for hundreds of endangered **raptors.** Of the 38 European species of these huge hunters, 36 are found only in Dadia. A well-maintained network of clearly marked **hiking trails** runs throughout the sanctuary. Blazes light the way along rugged ridges that break up the golden, untouristed Thracian plain.

From the Ecotourist Center, a main trail leads up a hill to a **bird hide,** complete with free binoculars, where you can cringe as raptors, vultures, and other early birds catch worms in the valley opposite. Just follow the orange blazes uphill from the Center for about an hour along the clearly-marked hike. The center also runs a frequent **bus** to the bird hide (10min., every 20min., €1.50). From the hide, trails extend in all directions, with most leading back to the center. To head straight back down to the Center, take the trail marked with yellow blazes.

TRAGEDY AND TRADITION

Long before "diversity" became a sought-after attribute for companies and colleges, the city of Ioannina (p. 243) was a multicultural mix of nationalities and religions, and each made its mark within the confines of the kastro. The Turks who ruled Ioannina from 1430 to 1913 left behind two mosques-cum museums, and Greek Orthodox Christians still attend the chapel of the Agioi Anargyri. But there's another fascinating house of worship within the Kastro—the still-functioning Kahal Kadosh Yashan synagogue. The current building, which dates back to the early 1800s, is a historic artifact of the vibrant Jewish community that was a substantial part of Ioannina's population before World War II. But it is also a spiritual center for the tiny group of Greek Jews who still live in Ioannina, and for the descendants of Ioanniote Jews in the diaspora.

A self-described "minority within a minority," the Jews of Ioannina are Romaniote Jews, a community that has existed in Greece since the first century A.D. Legend holds that they were sent to Rome in slave ships after the destruction of the Second Temple in 70 A.D., but a fateful storm forced them to land in Greece. Regardless of how they traveled, Romaniotes arrived in Greece over 2,300 years ago, and many settled in the thriving commercial center of Ioannina. They communicated in Greek and hybrid Judeo-Greek, and preserved their unique culture and language even after tens of thousands of Judeo-Español-speaking Sephardic Jews, who were expelled from Spain and Sicily, arrived in Greece in the late 15th-century.

By 1904, the Romaniotes in Ioannina had established two synagogues and a Jewish school, the Alliance Israelite Universelle. That year there were about 4000 Jews in Ioannina, but economic depression, the Greek war for independence in the region, and surges of anti-Semitic activity prompted many to emigrate to Palestine or to America. The number of Romaniotes had dwindled to 1,950 by September 1943, when the city came under the control of the German forces. Ioannina's Jews knew that 48,674 Jews from Thessaloniki had been deported between March and August 1943, but occupying Germans assured Sabethai Cabilli, a prominent Romaniote businessman, that his community would not be harmed. Cabilli urged total cooperation with the Germans, only to realize his fatal error on March 25th, 1944, when the Jews were rounded up for deportation, and he cried, "I have sinned." Upon arrival at Auschwitz, the elderly Cabilli was among the first group sent to the gas chambers.

Elsewhere in Greece, some Jews did manage to escape the Holocaust. The Greek Orthodox Archbishop Damaskinos and Evangelos Evert, the Chief of Police, issued false identity cards to Athenian Jews, saving two-thirds of the community. The 275 Jews on Zakynthos were unharmed after the Germans requested a list of Jews and the mayor and local bishop gave him only two names: their own.

Most Greek Jews were not so lucky: about 87% died in the Holocaust, with the number of Jews in Greece dwindling from 78,000 to about 10,000 after the war. Only 163 returned to Ioannina, many to homes inhabited by squatters. The returnees built an apartment building on the site of the dilapidated second synagogue. These apartments are now home to much of the surviving community, about fifty inhabitants.

Due to emigration and intermarriage, the number of Romaniotes in Ioannina continues to dwindle. But although it is a small community struggling to survive, it is also a far-reaching one. The Ioanniote Jews are working to refurbish the Ioannina's Jewish cemetery and to turn the women's gallery of the Kahal Kadosh Yashan into a museum. Assisting them are the members of the only Romaniote synagogue and museum in the Western Hemisphere, the Kehila Kedosha Janina in New York (280 Broome St., ☎212-431-1619, www.kehila-kedosha-janina.org). As Rose Eskononts, the president of the Sisterhood of the Kehila Kedosha Janina says, "We all think of Ioannina as our home."

To visit the cemetery or synagogue, contact the Jewish Community of Ioannina office (18B Josef Eliya St., ☎26510 25 195). For more information, read *The Jews of Ioannina*, by Rae Dalven, or visit the Jewish Museum of Greece (p. 105).

Eleni N. Gage, a former researcher-writer and editor of Let's Go: Greece and Turkey, *is the author of* North of Ithaka, *a travel memoir about Northern Greece to be published by the Free Press in Spring 2004.*

IONIAN ISLANDS

Νησια Του Ιονιου

Just to the west of mainland Greece, the Ionian Islands have an air of the mysterious etched into their rugged mountains, patchwork farmland, shimmering olive groves, and pristine beaches, all surrounded by an endless expanse of green or blue sea. Covetous invaders have conquered and re-conquered these isles: Venetians, British, French, and Russians have all left cultural and architectural fingerprints behind. Today the islands are a favorite among Western Europeans and ferry-hopping backpackers heading to Italy. Multicultural for millennia, each of the Ionian Islands possesses a unique identity and singular beauty.

HIGHLIGHTS OF THE IONIAN ISLANDS

SWIM WITH SEA TURTLES in the brilliant blue waters off Zakynthos (p. 303).

PARK YOUR YACHT and stroll past the rainbow array of neoclassical buildings of Fiskardo on Kephalonia (p. 302).

SUBMIT TO THE MATING RITUALS of party animals at Corfu's Pink Palace (p. 286).

WASH ASHORE on the beaches of Ithaka, Odysseus's kingdom (p. 292).

CORFU Κερκυρα

Homer first sang Corfu's praise, writing of its "honied fig," "unctuous olive," and "boisterous waves"; since then, Goethe, Wilde, the Durrell brothers, Sisley, and Lear have all thrown in their two cents about Corfu's perfection. Handed down from the Franks to the Venetians to the British to today's tourist hordes, Corfu (also called Kerkyra) has captivated them all. As in most of Greece's beautiful places, those who stray from the beaten path encounter unspoiled, uncrowded beaches. Try the less frenetic resorts at Pelekas, Kalami, or Agios Stefanos, or make Corfu Town your daytripping base. Even party-central Corfu holds hidden mountain villages and traditional coastal towns, where olive groves blanket the hills and you can hear the leaves rustle in the absence of rumbling tour buses.

CORFU TOWN Κερκυρα

With a substantial population year-round, Corfu Town flutters with activity day and night. Laundry lines stretch from ornate iron balconies, and the loveliness of n yellow-rose Venetian buildings and green-shuttered alleyways persists. Colorful flags and cascades of flowers create a festive note that pervades courtyards and thronged thoroughfares, amplified at nightfall by flocks of swallows inscribing circles on the evening sky. As dusk settles, people wander the winding streets of Old Corfu and sit in cafes along the Spianada, eating and chatting the night away.

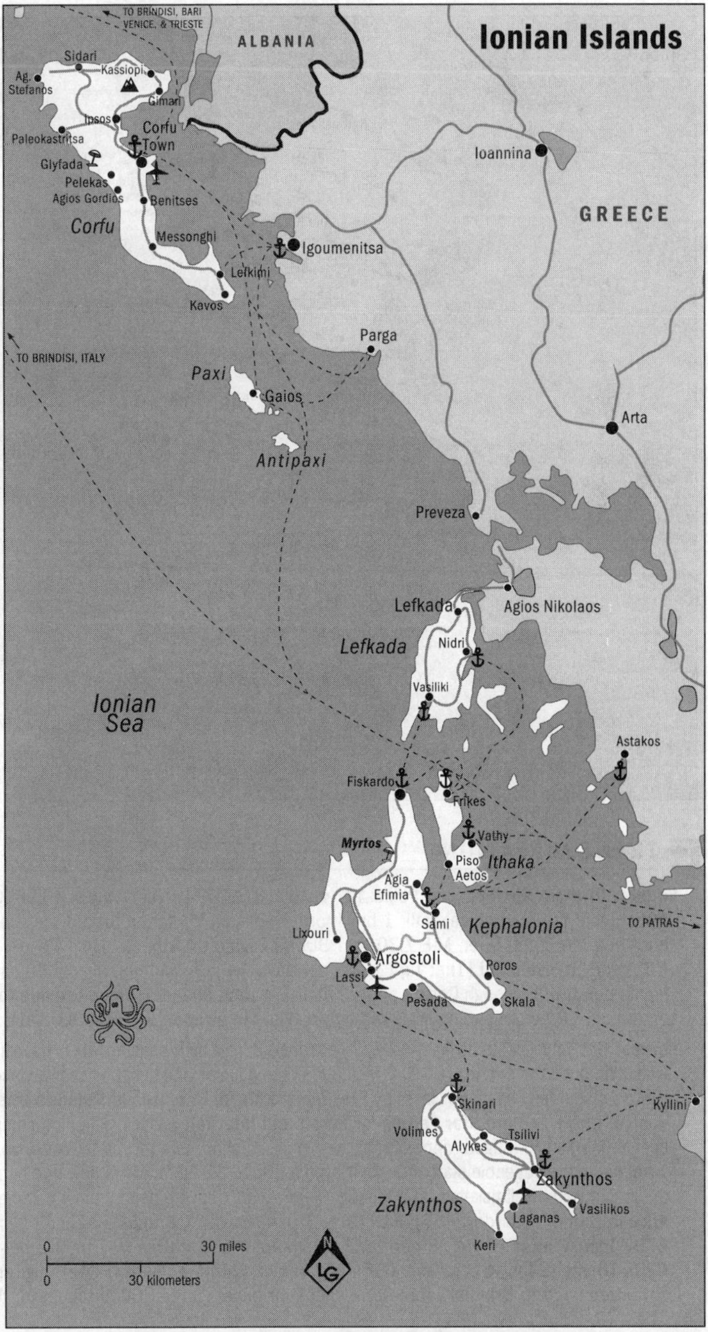

Ionian Islands

TO BRINDISI, BARI VENICE, & TRIESTE
ALBANIA
GREECE
Sidari
Kassiopi
Ag. Stefanos
Gimari
Ipsos
Corfu Town
Paleokastritsa
Glyfada
Pelekas
Agios Gordios
Benitses
Corfu
Messonghi
Igoumenitsa
Lefkimi
Kavos
Ioannina
Parga
TO BRINDISI, ITALY
Paxi
Gaios
Antipaxi
Arta
Preveza
Lefkada
Agios Nikolaos
Lefkada
Nidri
Vasiliki
Ionian Sea
Astakos
Fiskardo
Frikes
Vathy
Myrtos
Piso Aetos
Ithaka
Agia Efimia
Sami
Kephalonia
TO PATRAS
Lixouri
Argostoli
Lassi
Poros
Pesada
Skala
Skinari
Kyllini
Volimes
Tsilivi
Alykes
Zakynthos
Zakynthos
Vasilikos
Laganas
Keri
0 30 miles
0 30 kilometers
N
LG

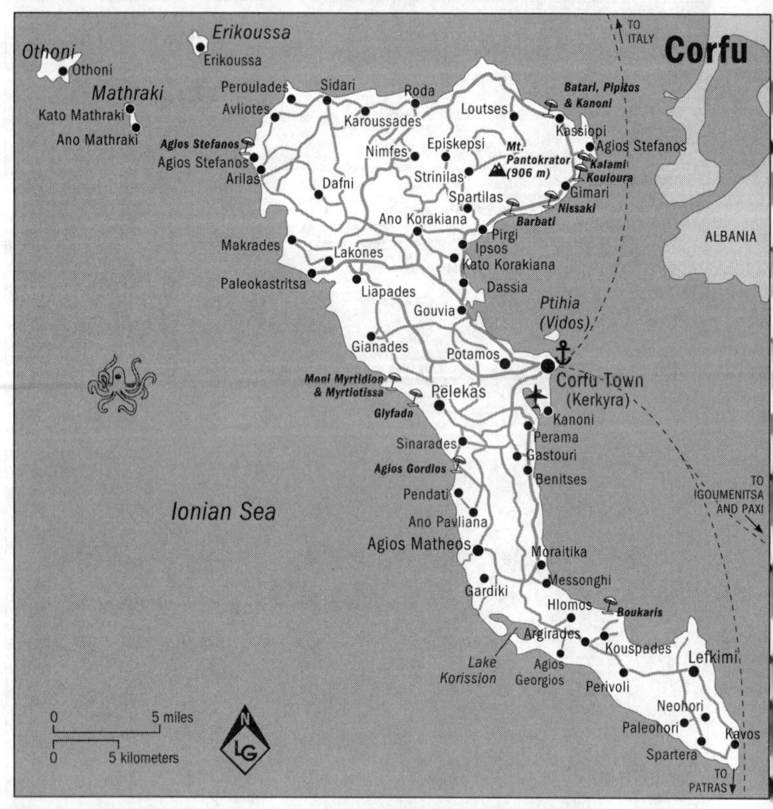

TRANSPORTATION

Flights: Olympic Airways, Iak. Polila 11 (☎26610 38 694; reservations ☎26610 38 695). From the post office, walk 1 block on Rizopaston Voulefton toward the Old City and then turn right. Open M-F 7:30am-7:30pm. Flights to: **Athens** (1hr., 4-5 per day, €95) and **Thessaloniki** (1hr.; Tu, F, Su 1 per day; €80). In summer, almost 50 charter flights per day fly through Corfu's airport; book 2-3 days ahead. A 5min. taxi ride (agree on around €8 before getting in) is the only way to the **airport** (☎26610 33 811).

Ferries: Get your tickets at least a day in advance during high season; when traveling to **Italy,** find out if the port tax (€5-6) is included in the price of your ticket. Prices vary according to season, ferry line, and class. Try **Fragline** or **HML** for **Brindisi** and **Strindzis Lines** for **Venice.** Check at **Blue Star Ferries** for **Eurail** and **InterRail** passes. Shipping company agents line Xen. Stratigou, opposite the new port, so shop here for the lowest fares. The jovial and knowledgeable staff of **Corfu Mare** (☎26610 32 467), at the new port beneath the Ionian Hotel, sell tickets with a friendly *"kalo taxidi!"* (have a good journey). Ferries to: **Ancona** (20hr., 1 per day, €56); **Bari** (9hr., 1 per day, €22); **Brindisi** (6-7hr., 3 per day, €30); **Igoumenitsa** (1½hr., 8 per day 6:30am-9pm, €5); **Patras** (6-7hr., 1-2 per day, €20); **Trieste** (24hr., 4 per week, €38); and **Venice** (24hr., 1 per day, €42). High-speed **catamarans** go to **Brindisi** (4hr.; 9am; check for prices, up to 30% discount for those under 26) and **Kephalonia** (3hr., W and Sa 9am, €62 round-trip). Schedules vary by season, and some routes run only in high season, so check before planning your trip.

Buses: 2 main lines serve the island: **green KTEL buses** (☎26610 39 862), between I. Theotoki and the New Fortress (accessible from I. Theotoki or Xen. Stratigou) and **blue municipal buses** (☎26610 37 595) at Pl. San Rocco. For a detailed green bus schedule with return times and prices, ask at the white info kiosk at the station (open 6am-8pm); equally detailed blue bus schedules are available at the ticket kiosk window in Pl. San Rocco (open 6:30am-10pm).

Green buses head to: **Agios Gordios** (45min., 7 per day 8:15am-8pm, €1.25); **Agios Stefanos** (1½hr., 6 per day 5:30am-7:30pm, €2.60); **Barbati** (45min.; 9am, 10:15am, 5pm; €1.30); **Glyfada** (45min., 10 per day 6:45am-8pm, €1.25); **Ipsos** and **Pirgi** (30min., 7 per day 7am-8pm, €1); **Kassiopi** (1hr., 7 per day 5:45am-4pm, €2.20); **Kavos** (1½hr., 11 per day 5am-7:30pm, €2.70); **Messonghi** (45min., 7 per day 9am-5:30pm, €1.50); **Paleokastritsa** (45min., 9 per day 8:30am-6pm, €1.50); **Sidari** (1hr., 9 per day 5:30am-7:30pm, €2.05). Buy tickets on board. Reduced schedules on weekends. **KTEL** also runs buses to: **Athens** (9hr.; 8:45am, 1:45, 7:15pm; €27.90) and **Thessaloniki** (9hr.; 6:45am, 7:15pm; €27); prices include ferry. Buy tickets at green bus station.

Blue buses: #10 to **Achilleon** (30min., 6 per day 7:45am-8pm, €0.75); **#6** to **Benitses** (25min., 13 per day 6:45am-10pm, €0.75); **#8** to **Ioannis** and **Aqualand** (30min., 7 per day 6:15am-1:15pm, €0.75); **#2** to **Kanoni** (1 per hr., €0.55); **#11** to **Pelekas** (30min., 7 per day 7am-8:30pm, €0.75). Buy tickets at the kiosk.

Taxis: (☎26610 33 811), at the old port, the Spianada, Pl. San Rocco, and G. Theotoki.

Car Rental: A small car starts at €55-60 per day, but price varies by season. Ask if price includes 20% tax, 3-party insurance, and mileage over 200km. **InterCorfu Rent a Car** (☎26610 93 607), on the water at the new port, offers reasonable rates.

Moped Rental: Get to those untouristed areas by renting from a place on Xen. Strategiou, near customs. You shouldn't have to pay more than €19 per day. Make sure the brakes work and get a helmet. Rental fee should include third-party liability and property damage insurance.

ORIENTATION AND PRACTICAL INFORMATION

Prepare to familiarize yourself with the Theotokos family, after whom four of Corfu Town's main streets are named: you may pass from N. to M. to G. to I. Theotoki without even realizing it. The city's peninsula juts northeast into the Ionian Sea. The endless **New Port** in the west and the smaller **Old Port** in the east span the northern coast of town. From the customs house at the New Port, it's about 1km to Corfu Town's central **Pl. San Rocco** (also called **Pl. G. Theotoki**). Cross the intersection at the light and walk uphill on **Avramiou,** which becomes I. Theotoki. On the way, you'll pass the driveway for the **KTEL** terminal on the left. On the east side of San Rocco (where the blue buses line up), **G. Theotoki** leads north into the Old Town, a beautiful, befuddling tangle of old alleyways. Continuing east from San Rocco or the Old Town, any reasonably straight walk will bring you to the **Spianada,** a large esplanade. The **Old Fortress** (Paleo Frourio) rises in the east. Arcaded buildings dotted with expensive cafes form **Liston** (Eleftherias), with narrow **Kapodistriou** running behind it. Kapodistriou curves along the waterfront, becoming **Arseniou** and **El. Venizelou,** leading back to the ports. South of town, **Dimokratias** makes a fine late-afternoon stroll along Garitsa Bay, leading to ancient Paleopolis and the Mon Repos estate. At the bay's midpoint an obelisk marks the end of tree-lined **Alexandras,** which runs back to Pl. San Rocco.

Tourist Office: EOT (☎26610 37 520), at the corner of Rizopaston Voulefton and Iak. Polila. The building is marked, and a sign directs you up the first flight of stairs. **Free maps** and information. Open M-F 8am-1:30pm.

THE BIG SPLURGE

CORFU PALACE HOTEL

Shake the dust off your boots and stroll into the ornate lobby of the **Corfu Palace Hotel.** The name is nothing if not accurate; the yellow and gold colored rooms offer enough amenities to make anyone feel like royalty: large TVs, phones, A/C, full marble baths, lush carpeting, mini-bars, balconies (many with jaw-dropping views of the bay), indulgent 24hr. room service, and a king's ransom of a price tag. The beds are as comfortable as they look, and every room is pleasantly furnished with dark wood furniture and cushioned chairs.

If you can bring yourself to leave your room, you'll find the Palace grounds very pleasing. The staff offers every kind of assistance you could need, including information on tours around the island. Take a break from lounging on your balcony to swim in the enormous outdoor or heated indoor pool. The outdoor pool is particularly lovely, with poolside sun-chairs and a bar. The hotel offers a choice of restaurants and throws a fun weekly outdoor barbecue. At the very least, drag yourself down to the restaurant for breakfast, included in the room price.

Dimokratias 2. ☎26610 39 485; fax 26610 31 749; cfupalace@hol.gr; www.corfupalace.com. June-Aug., singles €112-177; doubles €152-241. Considerably lower May-Oct. Suites available starting at €323 in high season.

Banks: Banks with 24hr. **ATMs** line the larger streets and the waterfront by the ports, including **Ionian Bank** in Pl. San Rocco and **National Bank of Greece** on the corner of Alexandras and Rizopaston Voulefton across from the post office.

Work Opportunities: The Pink Palace, see **Agios Gordios**, p. 286. Hires hotel staff, nightclub staff, and DJs. Mail a letter of introduction, a resume, and a photo in advance of arrival. Minimum 2 month commitment required.

Luggage Storage: In the customs building at the new port (€2 per bag per day). Confirm what time you will be returning for your bags. Open 7am-11pm.

International Bookstore: Xenoglosso, Markora 45 (☎26610 23 923), near the public market, has classic novels, books on Greece, and language materials. Open Sa-Su 9am-1:30pm, M and W 9am-2pm, Tu and Th-F 8:30am-2pm and 6-9pm.

Laundromat: Peristeri, I. Theotoki 42 (☎26610 35 304), just past Pl. San Rocco. Wash and dry €9 per basket. Open M-Sa 8am-2pm, and Tu, Th-F 6-8pm. **New Port Laundry** (☎26610 23 923), on Eth. Antistaseos near number 12A, has dry cleaning; wash and dry €10 per load. Open M-F 8:30am-2:30pm and 6-9pm, Sa 8:30am-2pm.

Police: (☎26610 39 509), in the same building as the tourist police. Open 24hr. In an **emergency,** dial ☎100.

Tourist Police: (☎26610 30 265). Heading toward the New Port, turn right off I. Theotoki along Pl. San Rocco onto the short street that intersects Markora; they're on the 4th fl. of the police office on the left. Maps available. Open daily 7am-2pm.

Port Police: Contact the port police (☎26610 30 481), in the customs house at the new port, or the **port authority** (☎26610 32 655 or 26610 40 002) for ferry schedules.

Hospital: Corfu General Hospital (☎26610 88 200 or 26610 45 811), on I. Andreadi. The tourist office or tourist police can help find an English-speaking doctor. For an **ambulance,** call ☎166.

OTE: Mantzarou 3 (☎26610 30 099), off G. Theotoki. Open M-F 7:30am-2pm. Card **phones** on the Spianada and in white mobile buildings at the Old and New Ports.

Internet Access: Netoikos Cafe, Kalochairetou 14 (☎26610 47 479), near Ag. Spiridon church. €4.50 per hr. Open M-Sa 9am-midnight, Su 11am-midnight. **Cafe Online** (☎26610 46 266), after the McDonald's as you walk along Kapodistriou with the Old Fortress on your left. €6 per hr. Open daily 9:30am-midnight.

Post Office: (☎26610 25 544), on the corner of Alexandras and Voulefton. Poste Restante and **currency exchange** available. Open M-F 7:30am-8pm. **Postal Code:** 49100.

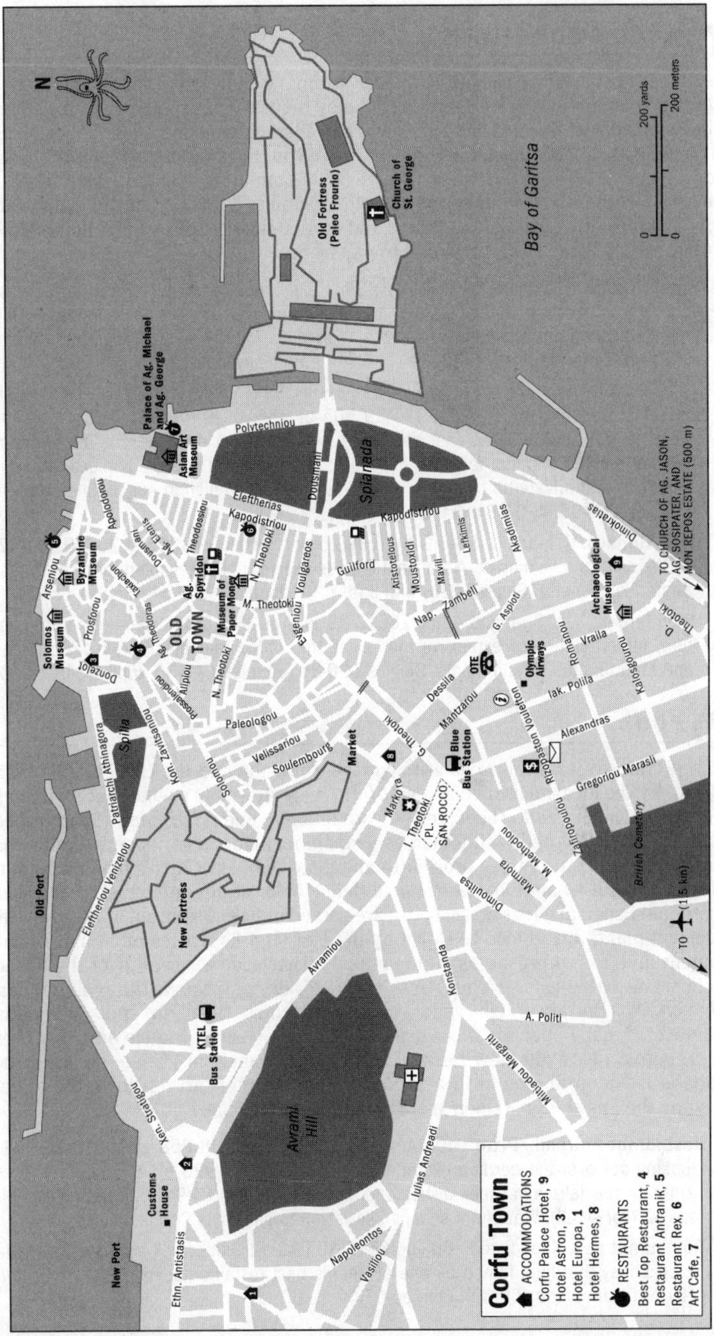

Corfu Town

ACCOMMODATIONS
Corfu Palace Hotel, 9
Hotel Astron, 3
Hotel Europa, 1
Hotel Hermes, 8

RESTAURANTS
Best Top Restaurant, 4
Restaurant Antranik, 5
Restaurant Rex, 6
Art Cafe, 7

ACCOMMODATIONS

Corfu is expensive and the pricier places lie among Dimokratias and Kapodistriou. Budget accommodations are few, and it may require extra footwork to find them. **The Association of Owners of Private Rooms and Apartments in Corfu,** Iak. Polila 24, has a complete list of rooms in Corfu and can give you the numbers of landlords to call for rooms. (☎26610 26 133. Open M-F 8:30am-2pm and 5:30-8pm.) Contact them several weeks prior to your trip to ensure availability. Consider staying outside the city in a base town with a nice beach and more domatia. Buses only run until 8 or 10pm, so you'll need to rent wheels to party-hop.

Hotel Europa, Giantsilio 10 (☎26610 39 304). From the New Port customs house, cross the main street at the light and make a sharp right onto the street that leads back from the waterfront; Giantsilio is a tiny road on the left, just where the road turns sharply left to become Napoleonta. Rooms are white and airy, with the best prices in Corfu Town. Singles €25, with bath €30; doubles €30/€35; triples €36. ❸

Hotel Astron, Donzelot 15 (☎26610 39 505 or 26610 39 986; fax 26610 33 708; Hotel_Astron@hol.gr), just past the Spilla with the water on your left. The charming building has an imperial feel, but the rooms hold all the modern amenities, including TVs, A/C, and private baths. Prices skyrocket to the listed high in Aug. Singles €40-90; doubles €50-95. A/C €6 extra. ❺

Hotel Hermes, G. Markora 14 (☎26610 39 268 or 26610 39 321; fax 26610 31 747), by the noisy public market. A leafy entry leads to basic, high-ceilinged rooms with fans. Shared kitchenette. Singles €25, with bath €30; doubles €33/€44; triples €50. ❸

Hotel Ionian, Xen. Stratigou 46 (☎26610 39 915 or 26610 30 628), right at the new port, offers relatively inexpensive rooms with full bath, balconies, the occasional fan, and unfortunate linoleum floors. Singles €30-36; doubles €42-50; triples €48-54. ❸

FOOD

The premier restaurant areas are near the Spianada and the Old Port. While in Corfu, try the local meat specialties: *sofrito* (veal stewed in a wine sauce with pepper and garlic), *stifado* (beef stewed with onions), and *pastitsada* (lamb or beef with noodles, flavored with tomatoes, cinnamon, onion, and pepper). Traditional pork *nuombolo* resembles prosciutto and is available at Corfu's famous butcher shops. Corfiot treats like *chadilia* (a dense cake of almonds, pistachios, rose water, and special citrus marmalade) are served at **bakeries** throughout town. The **kumquat** plant, introduced to Corfu by the British, fills bottles of "Koum Kouat" liqueur and jars of preserves. You can taste **homemade wines** all over the island: light white *kakotrygis*, richer white *moscato*, dry *petrokorintho* red, and dark *skopelitiko*. Bottles of light yellow *tsitsibira* (ginger beer) are another imperial holdover. A daily open-air **public market** sells inexpensive produce on Dessila, off G. Theotoki below the new fortress. (Open daily 6am-2pm.) There are **supermarkets** on I. Theotoki, one in Pl. San Rocco, and another farther down the street, beyond the bus station. (Open M-F 8am-9pm, Sa 8am-6pm.)

Restaurant Antranik/Pizza Pete, Arseniou 21 (☎26610 38 858 or 26610 23 301), looking out over the northern waterfront. Established in 1920 by Armenian refugees, Antranik specializes in Greek dishes and seafood (entrees €4-9.80). Pete's serves pizzas (€6 for small). Waterfront seating allows you to gaze over Corfiot sunsets. ❷

Restaurant Rex, Kapodistriou 66 (☎26610 39 649), 1 block back from the Spianada. A bit pricey, but long famed as one of Corfu's best restaurants. Try the savory *sofrito* (€11.20) or *stifado* (€9.80). Entrees €7.40-12.60. ❸

Best Top Restaurant, Filellinon 33 (☎26610 24 010). From the plateia at the Spilla end of Donzelot, walk up the stairs to the left. Best Top is in this second little plateia. Friendly staff serves Corfiot specialties and other dishes to the sounds of Greek music. Entrees €3.50-9. ❷

Art Cafe, in the pretty garden behind the Palace of St. Michael and St. George. Frequented only by those who stumble upon it, it's a relaxing place to enjoy an early evening ham and cheese sandwich (€2.35) and a frappé (€2). ❶

SIGHTS AND MUSEUMS

After invading Vandals and Goths destroyed ancient Corfu (Paleopolis) in the 5th and 6th centuries AD, Corfiots built a more defensible city between the twin peaks (called *Koryfes*, the probable root for "Corfu") of the Old Fortress. Wary of Ottoman raids, the Venetians strengthened this fortress, constructed the New Fortress, and built thick walls around the growing city. A series of **underground tunnels,** now closed, connected the Old and New Fortresses and all parts of Corfu Town. They later provided refuge for Corfiots after the first World War II air raids in 1940.

OLD FORTRESS. Finished in the late 14th century by the Venetians, the *Paleo Frourio* was considered impregnable—until the British blew it up in 1864 before leaving Corfu to the Greeks. Along with much of Corfu Town, the castle's imposing fortifications were restored to some semblance of their former glory for a 1994 EU summit. On the grounds are the **Church of St. George,** patron saint of infantry; a **Byzantine Gallery,** which houses works from an early Christian basilica; a library and a nearby **museum** devoted to the role of Christianity in Byzantium; and a **bell tower** that strikes the hour for all Corfu Town. Placards with maps direct you to the highlights of the fortress. *(Just east of the Spaniada. ☎26610 48 311. Open daily 8am-7pm. €4, students and seniors €2, EU students free. Tickets for the Old Fortress, Byzantine Museum, Archaeological Museum, and Museum of Asian Art can be purchased for €8 at any of the sights.)*

NEW FORTRESS. The younger, 350-year-old fort above the ferry docks opens onto panoramic views of Corfu Town ideal for sun-drenched picnics. The fort displays a small **gallery** of etchings, maps, and watercolors with nautical motifs, and an additional gallery with contemporary exhibits. Concerts and theatrical events are held here throughout the year. *(Look for signs as you walk along Velissariou from the Old Port. ☎26610 45 000. Open daily 9am-10pm. €2.)*

CHURCH OF AG. SPYRIDON. This site of pilgrimage for Orthodox Christians was built in 1590 and contains the embalmed body of St. Spyridon, Corfu's patron saint. Spyridon, born in AD 270, lived and died on Cyprus. When invading Saracens threatened his body, his preserved corpse was brought to Corfu in a burlap sack slung on the back of a donkey. Each year, the faithful give him a new pair of embroidered slippers—he wears out the old pair wandering the island doing good deeds. If the priests open the gold cover of the saint's casket during your visit, you can see Spyridon's blackened face. Above him, dozens of silver lamps swing beside gold votive offerings (most representing ships), offering thanks and prayer. Spyridon worked his latest major miracle in 1943: when the surrounding buildings were razed in an air raid, the church and the Corfiots sheltered within went unscathed. Corfiots parade the saint's remains four times a year: on Palm Sunday, the first Sunday in November (celebrating deliverance from 17th-century plagues), on Holy Saturday (for relief from a 1550 famine), and during the two-day **festival** beginning on Aug. 11 (commemorating the end of a month-long 1716 Ottoman siege). His own feast day festival is on December 12. With its lovely, colorful ceiling depicting religious scenes and hushed atmosphere, the church is the perfect place to spend a few quiet moments of peaceful reflection. *(Take Ag. Spyridon off the Spianada; it's on the left, with the rose-colored onion dome. Open daily 6am-9pm.)*

BYZANTINE MUSEUM. Housed in the 15th-century Church of the Most Holy Virgin Antivouniotissa, the museum's collection of **Cretan School** icons is worth seeing, if only for the church, with its painted "wallpaper" and wood carvings on the ceiling. The museum has remained peacefully free of tourists, an ideal spot for a calming half hour. After the fall of Rethymno in 1646, Corfu served as a pit-stop for many artists from Venetian Crete on their way to Venice. A wall chart in the museum details their movements and activities. Striking icons include St. George with a somewhat puny dragon, a gaudy St. Cyril of Alexandria, and St. Pantalemon granting mercy to the suffering; they're housed in the uniquely Corfiot three-sided exonarthex. *(☎26610 38 313. Look for signs on Arsenion as it curls downhill from the palace. Open Tu-Su 8am-3pm. €2, students and seniors €1.)*

ARCHAEOLOGICAL MUSEUM. Relics of Corfu's Mycenaean and Classical past appear in this museum's large collection. The highlight is the fantastic **Gorgon Pediment** from the Temple of Artemis in ancient Corfu, which shows the ghoulish Medusa with her children—winged Pegasus and the Chrysoar—born at the moment Perseus cut her head off. Statuettes of Artemis, a collection of coins depicting mythological figures from an ancient mint on Corfu, and funerary urns crowd the museum's halls. *(Vraila 1, on the waterfront south of Spianada. ☎26610 30 680. Open Tu-Su 8:30am-3pm. €3, students and seniors €2, children and EU students free.)*

PALACE OF SAINT MICHAEL AND SAINT GEORGE. Presiding over the stately Spaniada is the even statelier palace, built by the Lord High Commissioner Sir Thomas Maitland to house himself, the Ionian Parliament and Senate, and various public services. It now holds the unique **Museum of Asian Art,** which displays over 10,000 Oriental artifacts collected by diplomat Gregorios Manos. The extremely well-presented and explained collections includes delicate porcelain figurines., vases from the Ming Dynasty of China, Samurai armor and weapons, as well as jewelry, furniture, and clothing. *(☎26610 30 443. Open Tu-Su 8:30am-3pm. €2, students and seniors €1, EU students free.)* The **Municipal Modern Art Gallery** (**Dimotiko Pinakothiki**), around the back of the Palace through the garden, has a small but expanding collection of Corfiot paintings and rotating special exhibits. *(☎26610 48 690. Open daily 10am-6pm, but hours may vary with special exhibits. €1.50, students €1.)*

OTHER MUSEUMS. The **Solomos Museum** honors the national poet of Greece, Dionysios Solomos. Born on Zakynthos in 1798, the poet spent much of his life on Corfu. After living in Italy, Solomos dropped out of law school and began to write poetry. He was the first to use popular (Demotic) Greek in poetry, and his "Hymn to Freedom" form the lyrics to the Greek National Anthem. The museum is housed in Solomos's house, reconstructed after a German bombing, and displays copies of original manuscripts, portraits, and memorabilia. *(Look for the sign in an alleyway on Arseniou just west of the Byzantine Museum, toward the New Port. ☎26610 30 674. €1. Open M-F 9:30am-2pm.)* Fanatical capitalists will enjoy the **Museum of Paper Currency,** in the Ionian Bank Building down N. Theotoki from the Spianada, which holds, along with examples of all Greek currency that has ever existed, the first bank note printed in Greece. *(☎26610 41 552. Open M-F 10am-2pm. Free.)*

MON REPOS ESTATE. This former summer residence of the British Commissioner was given to the Greek royal family by the British government in 1864. Since the royals' exile in 1967, the lovely Neoclassical palace had fallen into disrepair, but recently the building has been totally renovated and now houses the amazing **Museum of Paleopolis.** This eclectic museum contains replicas of period rooms from the palace as well as archaeological finds from excavations around Corfu. As you wander through the rooms exhibiting plant life and pottery, you'll be kept company by soft classical music. The building alone is a treat, with polished marble floors, high ceilings, and lovely woodwork. Head up the path to the right just inside the main gate to reach the palace. *(Estate open 8am-7pm. Free. Museum open Tu-Su 8:30am-3pm. Free.)* After touring the museum you can head out into the estate to see where some of the finds came from. Paths wander in and out of the overgrown gardens, now largely a forest. From the palace, follow the path overlooking the sea with the water on your left to reach **Kardaki beach,** a tiny pebble beach, edged by the forest. It's said that anyone who drinks from its spring will remain on the island forever. To the right of the palace as you face the museum entrance, a path leads to two Doric temples, the decrepit **Temple of Hera** and the more impressive **Kardaki Temple,** possibly dedicated to Poseidon, Apollo, or Asclepius. *(Follow the waterfront south from the Old Fortress (away from the Palace) for about 35-40min. After a hotel and Mon Repos beach, the road heads inland—the estate is about 7min. further.)*

CHURCHES. On the edge of the old town in the plateia at the end of Donzelot sits the **Cathedral of Panagia Speliotissa** (Virgin of the Grotto). Built in 1577, it houses a slew of icons, including the *Demosiana* Virgin, which dates back to the 5th century. One kilometer south of Corfu Town lie the remains of several churches dating back to the 12th century. Following the waterfront south from the Old Fortress (away from the Palace) after about 20min. is a sign indicating the Church of St. Jason and Sosipater; follow it to the first church in the series, the **Church of Agios Athanassios at Anemomyios.** There is a map directing you to the remaining four churches: the **Church of St. Jason and Sosipater,** an Early Christian **Basilica,** the **Monastery of Agios Theodoros,** and the **Church of Panayia Neradziha.**

FESTIVALS. The procession of the embalmed body of St. Spyridon takes place each year during Easter celebrations, on Palm Sunday and Holy Saturday. It's a tradition for Corfiots to throw special pots full of water out of their windows at 11am on Holy Saturday—a Venetian New Year's tradition that Orthodox Greeks have appropriated to celebrate the Resurrection. The evening religious ceremonies for Holy Saturday are held in the Spaniada, and followed by music, fireworks, and a special feast including red-dyed eggs and dove-shaped breads called *colombines*. Corfu's Carnival festivities, which begin 40 days before Easter, see a mix of Greek and Venetian influence. The most striking traditions include the final Thursday's "The Gossip," a street theater performance in which women call out the latest gossip from windows across alleys in the center of the Old Town, and the last Sunday's burning of King Carnival, when the effigy "King" is tried and sentenced to death by fire for his hand in all the year's misfortunes.

NIGHTLIFE AND ENTERTAINMENT

The undisputed focus of Corfu Town's nightlife is the so-called **Disco Strip,** on Eth. Antistaseos at the waterfront, 2km west of the New Port. The many bars and clubs on the strip bustle with a multicultural crowd of locals and tourists. The typical €6 cover often includes your first drink. Beer costs €3-4.50; cocktails run €4.75-6.50. A **taxi** from Pl. San Rocco costs about €2-4. The more touristy and international clubs of the strip include **Coca Club,** on the hillside at the beginning of the strip, and **Apocalypsis,** an elaborate fusion of an ancient temple and a construction site, which plays only techno in its pool-equipped expanse. Dance music blares from **Hippodrome,** next door to Apocalypsis behind the parking lot; bright orange and silver **Privilege** plays modern club hits to a mixed crowd. The more authentic, Greek-style clubs of the strip are **Sodoma,** which blasts mostly Greek music and flashes dizzying strobes inside; **Mobile,** next door to Hippodrome and Apocalypsis; and the bona-fide hot spot of the strip, **Bouzoukia.** The club for Greeks who know how to party, Bouzoukia often has no cover, but you won't find a drink for under €6. If you're going to try and snag a table for the night, be ready to shell out up to €130. Bouzoukia's perks include live Greek music and a crowd of Corfu's most chic.

For a mellower night, head to **Liston** and the adjacent park under the big palm tree, where elegant little cafes stay lively until around 1am. By far the most popular among them is **Magnet,** at the top of Kapodistriou, where the buzz of multilingual conversations and the croaking frogs spills out into the shady plateia. The **cinemas** on G. Theotoki, a few blocks from Pl. San Rocco, and on the corner of Akadimias and G. Aspoti, screen films in English. Look for placards on G. Theotoki. (Tickets €6.) The **municipal theater** (☎26610 33 598), between Dessila and Mantzarou one block from G. Theotoki, has occasional drama, dance, and music performances, publicized on bulletin boards all over town.

DAYTRIP FROM CORFU TOWN: ACHILLION PALACE

In Gastouri. From Corfu Town, take bus #10 from 200m west of Pl. San Rocco on Methodiou (30min., 6 per day 7:45am-8pm, €0.75). ☎26610 56 210. Open daily 9am-7pm. €6, groups €3, children free.

The 1981 James Bond flick *For Your Eyes Only* was filmed in the gardens of the eccentric and ostentatious Achillion Palace, the secluded home of Empress Elizabeth of Austria from 1892 until her 1897 assassination by an Italian anarchist in Geneva. She named her home for Achilles, an obsession of hers; she, like Achilles's mother Thetis, lost two sons. Later, German Kaiser Wilhelm II summered here; he abandoned his vacations in Corfu when First World War broke out. Achillion Palace became a hospital and barracks in both World Wars; it was again reborn as the first Greek casino in 1962. It's now a museum, with the house as the subject. The rooms on the lower floor house personal items and furniture from both the Empress and the Kaiser, while the upper floors are filled with sculpture. No explanations are given; guidebooks cost €5-8. The grounds are stunning. Flowery courtyards with views down to Corfu Town lie behind the palace. Two statues of Achilles, the white "Dying Achilles" and the bronze "Achilles Triumphant," which stands eight meters tall, reside in the courtyards farthest from the palace.

WESTERN CORFU

Western Corfu is a beach lover's paradise, with wide expanses of golden sand and hidden crystal coves, majestic cliffs, and rock formations serving as a backdrop to the glimmering turquoise sea. While it sees its share of tour buses, it doesn't suffer from the same degree of over-development that mars the beautiful east and crowded south. Instead, its towering, untouched natural beauty makes it a continual delight to explore its towns and more remote beaches.

PELEKAS Πελεκας

Removed from the mass tourism of the resorts, the village of **Pelekas** sits at the top of a hill, with great views and famously beautiful sunsets. Pelekas has some of the best of what Corfu has to offer—beaches, natural beauty, great food, and fun bars—with the added benefit of being off the typical tourist path. Take **bus #11** from Pl. San Rocco in Corfu Town (30min., 7 per day 7am-8:30pm, €0.75). The long, sandy **beach** is a pleasant 30min. walk from town down a very steep road. (Plan on 1hr. back up. A free shuttle bus to and from town picks up at the left side of the beach facing inland and runs 6 times per day from 11:45am-8:30pm; signs are posted all over town.) Rooms to let are plentiful and well priced in Pelekas, but call ahead in high season to secure a spot. **Pension Tellis and Brigitte ❷,** down the hill from the bus stop, has the friendliest hosts in town and lovely rooms in a little, yellow house covered with bougainvillea. Balconies offer superb views of the surrounding countryside. (☎26610 94 326. Laundry €5. Singles €18; doubles €20-25.

Some rooms with bath.) Near the **Church of Ag. Nikolaos,** around the corner and above the bus stop, **Takis Kontis's** ❷ rooms are comfortable and airy; half have fantastic balcony views. (☎26610 94 742. All have shared baths. Singles €15; doubles €20.) On the road to the beach, next to the fork for Glyfada, the rooms at the **Pension Paradise** ❷ are a good deal and include kitchen use. (☎26610 94 530 or 26610 36 217. Showers included. Singles €15-20; doubles €22-30.) Next to the church, the well-situated **Pelekas Cafe** ❶ purees superb milkshakes (€3) from a view over the island. Just outside of town on the road to Glyfada, the **Pink Panther** ❷ restaurant and bar serves up terrific Greek and Italian food (pizzas start at €5.50; Greek entrees €5-6). If you get there early enough, the pink balcony offers great sunset views; revelry begins around midnight. **Zanzibar,** across from Pelekas Cafe, has Caffrey's and Guinness on tap. (Open 5pm-late.)

GLYFADA Γλυφαδα

Glyfada attracts more tourists than tiny Pelekas, 5km down the coast, but its seemingly endless shore accommodates the throngs admirably. Scrubby cliffs bracket both of Glyfada's remarkably shallow **beaches,** where crashing waves make swimming a bit more unpredictable. An eclectic crowd of internationals basks on the sun-speckled sand. Young sun-worshipers scope each other's tans and amuse themselves parasailing (singles €30; doubles €45), water-skiing (€18 for 10min.), or jet skiing (15min.; singles €30; doubles €45). Motorboats, kayaks, inner tubes, and paddle boats are also available. Green KTEL **buses** leave from Corfu Town at the intersection above the Grand Louis Hotel (30min., 10 per day 6:45am-8pm, €1.25), and a free bus connects Pelekas to Glyfada (10min., 6 per day 11am-8:30pm; the bus leaves from the parking lot, and schedules are posted in both towns). Budget accommodations are scarce, but it's easy to make the trip from Pelekas or Corfu Town. The nearest camping is at **Vatos Camping** ❶ (☎26610 94 505) in Vatos Village. North of Glyfada, accessible via dirt path off the main Pelekas road, lie the isolated **beaches** of **Moni Myrtidion** and **Myrtiotissa,** extolled by Lawrence Durrell as the most beautiful in the world. A section of Myrtiotissa serves as an unofficial nude beach—unless local monks complain to the police, who reluctantly bring offending nudists to court.

PALEOKASTRITSA Παλαιοκαστριτσα

Paleokastritsa **beach** rests among six small coves and sea caves that cast shadows over the blue. Although the beach is a bit narrow and can get crowded, a swim in the calm, dark-blue water encircled by cliffs, more than makes up for it. Green KTEL **buses** arrive from Corfu Town (45min., 17 per day 8:30am-6pm, €1.50). You can hire a motorboat (€8 per person; 30min. each way) or rent a pedal boat (€8.80 per hr.) or kayak (singles €3; doubles €6 per hr.) to reach the caves where, according to legend, Phaecian princess Nausicaä found the shipwrecked Odysseus washed ashore. Jutting out on a hill over the sea, bright white **Panagia Theotokos Monastery** boasts a museum with a collection of Byzantine icons, engraved bibles, and a so-called **sea monster's skeleton.** Sunlight reflects off the whitewashed walls and highlights the colors in the lovely little garden next to the courtyard; step over the railing for startlingly beautiful views. Come as early as possible—by mid-morning it's a mess of tour buses—and take a little bread with you to feed the monastery's very tame peacocks (up the little road past the vegetable garden). The paved road up the hill leads to the monastery. The 12th-century fort of **Angelokastro** sits above Paleokastritsa. A natural balcony with a magnificent view, the appropriately named **Bella Vista,** is a 1½hr. walk from Paleokastritsa. Take the road from the bus stop to the Odysseus Hotel, turn left on the path through the olive groves, and continue on the trail through a village to the fort.

GREEN THUMBS, COLD CASH Corfu has been ruled by a bevy of other nations, but Venice was the only one to take control of the island twice. During the second period of Venetian rule, which lasted 400 years from 1386-1797, the island was molded into the green, fortress-speckled Kerkyra we see today. Though they are responsible for many of the fortifications on the island, the Venetians' most significant addition to Corfu's landscape may be in terms of agriculture. Motivated by the desire to obtain a sufficient supply of olive oil (so that it would not have to imported), the Venetian government in the 17th century promised a payment of 42 gold coins to islanders for every 100 olive trees planted. As a result of this generous offer, olive cultivation boomed, and the silvery trees soon covered the island. Ironically, as a result of the olive's popularity, farmers stopped growing other basic crops, like cereal grains, which then had to be imported. Thanks to the Venetians and their love of good olive oil, Corfu is still covered with terraced olive groves.

AGIOS GORDIOS Αγιος Γορδιος

Ten kilometers south of Pelekas, Agios Gordios is highlighted by impressive rock formations and a lovely, wide **beach.** The town is host to the debauchery of the Pink Palace hotel and backpacker playground, yet all in all it remains very quiet. The main road runs uphill, perpendicular to the beach, with a short stretch of restaurants, mini-markets, and souvenir shops. The steep rock face on the southern end of the beach was once used as a lookout for pirates. Green **buses** run to Agios Gordios from the KTEL station in Corfu Town (45min., 7 per day 8:15am-8pm, €1.25). The town's accommodation is the main attraction: the infamous **Pink Palace Hotel ❷,** a favorite with American and Canadian backpackers in search of instant (and constant) gratification. Buses go to and from Athens to the Pink Palace, bypassing Patras (€38 1-way from Pink Palace; €47 1-way from Athens). Forget mingling with the locals—there's nary a word of Greek spoken at this reincarnation of MTV Spring Break. Some pseudo-Greek traditions have been appropriated to heighten the fun: toga-wrapped partiers have been known to down countless shots of ouzo as they break plates on each other's heads in a spirit of revelry that would make Dionysus proud. The Palace's impressive list of amenities makes it a self-contained party resort: there's a laundry service (€7.50); book exchange; Internet access (€3 per 30min.); a jacuzzi; basketball, volleyball, and tennis courts; an on-site nightclub; massages (€11); car rental (€18-30); clothing-optional cliff-diving (€15); boat daytrips; and various watersports. (☎26610 53 103 or 26610 53 104; fax 26610 53 025; www.thepinkpalace.com. Breakfast, dinner, and pick up/drop off at the Corfu Town ferry included. Rooms with A/C, telephones, private balconies, and baths are a bargain €25. Stuffier, dorm-style rooms €19.)

EASTERN CORFU

The east coast of Corfu is the most developed and least aesthetically pleasing part of the island. The first 20km north of Corfu Town are thoroughly Anglicized by throngs of rowdy expats, and the beaches are thin strips along a busy, clamorous coastal road. Despite its low points, Eastern Corfu *is* convenient and relatively inexpensive. Everything—beach, restaurants, hotels, nightlife—is consolidated in one strip, so you won't need to rent a moped, as you would in more remote parts of the island. It's cheaper than beautiful Corfu Town, but close enough to allow frequent trips. **Gouvia** and **Dassia,** the first two resorts north of town, thrive off package tours despite beaches stretched thin by the crowds. The visitors to notorious little **Ipsos,** a bit farther north, guzzle the day away at countless cheap bars and discos. Interchangeable souvenir stands, fast-food restaurants, and C-class hotels line the flat stretch of road across from the beach. **Pirgi,** a quieter extension of Ipsos, crawls up the base of the neighboring mountains. Hotels fill up quickly with package tour groups, so reserve ahead. There are also a few domatia and several beachside campsites in the area. Signs are posted prominently along the coastal highway for **Camping Corfu ❶.** (☎26610 93 579 or 26610 93 246. €4 per person, children €2.50. €3 per small tent; €3.50 per large tent; €2.50 per car. Electricity €3.) More beachside camping is available at **Paradise** (☎26610 93 282 or 93 552). KTEL green **buses** serve Ipsos and Pirgi (30min., 7 per day 7am-8pm, €1). **Blue** buses head to Dassia via Gouvia (every 30min. 7-9am and 3-10:30pm, every 20min. 9am-3pm; €0.75. Buy tickets on the bus.)

NORTHERN CORFU

Past Pirgi, the road begins to wind below steep cliffs. **Mt. Pantokrator,** a bare rock jutting out of the forested hills, towers 1000m above on your left, while dramatic vistas of dark, wooded Albania appear across the straits. Emperors Tiberius and Nero of Rome once vacationed here, though tourism has erased most traces of the ancient world on the north coast. The farther you get from overbuilt beach towns like Kassiopi and Sidari, the better off you'll be.

AGIOS STEFANOS Αγιος Στεφανος

The most remote northern beach town is Agios Stefanos (not to be confused with the northeastern village of the same name). A mere 15min. drive from bustling Sidari, Agios Stefanos is mercifully underdeveloped; the wide, sandy beach is set in a long curving gulf of high sandstone cliffs. The long waves roll in toward the few determined souls who have escaped Sidari and Kassiopi. The trip there is a treat in itself: the coastal road curves inland west of Sidari, past ferny hillsides of figs, olives, and cypresses, and through a picturesque mountain village. **Buses** run from Corfu Town (1½hr., 6 per day 5:30am-7:30pm, €2.60) and Kassiopi, via Sidari (4 per day 9:30am-4pm). The few who make it to town will find expensive hotels but also plenty of domatia, some at reasonable prices (€25-35); check the signs in front of tavernas along the main road to track them down. Be warned: there is **no bank or ATM** in town, so bring enough cash for your stay.

BEACHES AND THE OUTDOORS

The sheer slopes of northeastern Corfu cradle several fine **beaches** including **Barbati,** 10km north of Ipsos, nearby **Nissaki,** and the twin beaches **Kalami** and **Kouloura.** A green KTEL **bus** from Corfu Town runs to Kassiopi (1hr., 7 per day 5:45am-4pm, €2.20) and stops at most beaches along the northeastern coast; ask to be let off at less popular destinations. Kouloura and Kalami beaches are a brief walk from the main road north of Gimari village. Head down from the bus stop on the main road. Soon you'll see a yellow sign on the right marking the shortcut path to Kalami. If you're heading for Kouloura, continue down the road until you reach a fork with signs for Kouloura and Kalami. Head right down this road; blue "To the Beach" signs on the left mark the path down to Kouloura. Signs on the right side of the road point you towards Kalami.

Kalami, with its wide flat-stoned beach, was home to author **Lawrence Durrell** and his family in the 1930s. His small white house is still "set like a dice on a rock" in the southern end of town; now it houses the pleasant **Taverna White House ❷,** which serves typical Greek fare under wisteria vines with a sea view (entrees €5.50-11.50; appetizers €1.90-5.40). Super-secluded **Kouloura,** a 10min. walk along the road from Kalami, is a small, partially-shaded beach composed of mixed sand, eucalyptus leaves, and stones, with nary an umbrella or paddle boat in sight. **Taverna Kouloura** ❷ has a nice view of the marina and lots of veggie options. (Entrees €4-8; fish dishes €11-28.) It can be expensive to stay in the area overnight, and there are no accommodations in Kouloura.

To hike to the high plateau of **Mt. Pantokrator** for breathtaking views of all Corfu, start at Spartillas, a village 7km north and inland from Pirgi, along the bus route. From there, follow the same path used each summer by villagers on their way to the annual festival at Pantokrator Monastery.

LEFKADA Λευκαδα

Thucydides reports that Lefkada was part of the mainland until 427 BC, when the inhabitants dug a canal and made their home an island. A modern bridge now connects Lefkada to the mainland, just 50m away; it only recently replaced an archaic chain-operated ferry built by Emperor Augustus. Modern Lefkadians are devoted to the business of tourism. Souvenir shops and overpriced restaurants abound, especially in Nidri, which is mostly composed of tourist traps and a profusion of liquor stores. Still, miles of white-sand beaches and astonishing natural beauty remain; with a little effort, you can skirt the patches of tacky tourism and find the island's unspoiled secrets.

LEFKADA TOWN

Lefkada Town, across from the mainland, is a frenetic little city packed into a space that feels far to small to hold it. The waterfront and pedestrian streets near the main plateia are lovely and provide plenty of shopping, eating, and interaction with other tourists. If you stray into the tiny alleys off the main street, you'll discover pastel, flower-draped houses and roosters pecking in gardens—a sign that Lefkada Town retains a quiet allure beneath the busy surface.

ORIENTATION AND PRACTICAL INFORMATION. Archaeologist William Dörpfield claimed that Homer's Ithaka was really Lefkada; Lefkada Town thanked him by naming one of its main roads **Dörpfield,** a pedestrian-friendly street which runs down the middle of the peninsula that is the city's downtown. It later becomes **Strategou Mela.** Dörpfield and all the little winding streets that branch off it are for pedestrians and bikes only for the first few blocks up to the main plateia. Dörpfield also leads to the main plateia, packed with cafes and occasional traveling music acts. The entire downtown is encircled by a beltway, like a racetrack, that becomes the waterfront road to the right of Dörpfield as you face inland. This road is identified on maps as **8th Merarhias,** but on street signs it also becomes D. Golemi, I. Polytechneiou, and Ag. Sikelianou for some stretches.

From the **bus station** (☎26450 22 364)—a yellow waterfront building with a gray and yellow-striped awning, 5min. to the left of Dörpfield, as you face inland—**buses** cross the canal to **Athens** (5½hr., 5 per day 8:30am-6:30pm, €20.50) and **Aktion** (30min., 5 per day 7am-6:30pm, €1.40). **Local buses** run to: **Nidri** (30min., 20 per day 5:30am-7:45pm, €1.20); **Agios Nikitas** (20min., 6 per day 6:40am-7pm, €0.90); **Poros** (45min.; 6:05am, 1:15pm; €1.80); and **Vasiliki** (1hr., 5 per day, €2.25). Pick up a bus schedule at the station for additional routes and return times; service is reduced on Sundays. **Taxis** are available but expensive (☎26450 22 233).

Ferries leaving from **Nidri** and **Vasiliki** link Lefkada with **Ithaka** and **Kephalonia** to the south. Beware that ferry schedules change from month to month. While the duration and price of ferries are fairly stable, departure and arrival times and locations change all the time; call ahead. From **Nidri** (☎26450 31 520), ferries sail to **Frikes,** Ithaka (2hr., €4.50) and **Fiskardo** on Kephalonia (2-3hr., €3.70). From **Vasiliki,** a ferry leaves twice a day for **Fiskardo** (1hr., €3.40) and goes on to **Frikes** (2hr., €4.40). Ferries also sometimes run to **Piso Aetos** on Ithaka. Check travel offices for current schedules. **Excursion boats** leave Nidri each morning at 9:45am and return at 6pm, cruising to **Kephalonia, Ithaka, Meganisi, Skorpios,** and **Madouri.** (€20. Call ☎26450 92 658 or check at a travel agency for more information.) For other boat excursions, ask at waterfront travel offices, or read the boats' hard-to-miss signs.

There is no tourist office, but the **tourist police** can be found on 8th Merarhias. Facing the bus station, walk left and follow the road as it leads away from the water; the police building will be on your left. (☎26450 29 379. General info and island contacts for accommodations. Open 8am-10pm.) The 24hr. **police station** (☎26450 22 346) is in the same building. For detailed info about ferries, tours, or sights, try the numerous travel agencies around the bus station. There is a **National Bank** with a 24hr. **ATM** and several **pharmacies** on Str. Mela (open M-Th 8am-2pm, F 8am-1:30pm). For the **OTE,** turn right off Str. Mela onto Skiardesi, just before the National Bank. Turn left when it dead-ends into I. Marinou. (Open M-F 7:30am-1pm for purchases, until 11:30pm for information.) **Internet C@fe Lefkada,** past the police station on 8th Merarhias on the left, offers **Internet access.** (☎26450 21 507. €3 per hr. Open daily 7:30am-3am.) The **post office** is on Str. Mela past the National Bank. (☎26450 24 225. Open M-F 7:30am-2pm.) **Postal code:** 31100.

ACCOMMODATIONS AND FOOD. There are no easy-to-locate domatia in town, so if you're pinching pennies consider staying elsewhere. Hotels cluster on the waterfront near Dörpfield and on the first few blocks inland. Lefkada Town is expensive—most rooms start at €40. Advance booking and longer stays could ease the cost. Travel agencies suggest you check in **Lia**, a domatia-packed village 4km outside town; frequent buses to and from Nidri and Vasiliki pass through Lia.

One relatively affordable option is the rather deluxe **Santa Maura ❸**, off Dörpfield about three blocks from the water. Modern yellow and blue rooms have it all: A/C, TVs, full baths, phones, and fridges. (☎26450 21 309; fax 26450 26 253. Singles €30-40; doubles €45-60.) Also inland on Dörpfield is the classy but well-priced **Pirotani Pension ❹.** Beautiful rooms have tile floors, full baths, TVs, A/C, fridges, balconies, and lovely light wood furniture. (☎26450 22 270 or 26450 25 844; fax 26450 24 084. Singles and doubles €35-50.) In a higher price range is **Hotel Nirikos ❺,** at the end of Dörpfield on the waterfront. A shiny lobby and dining room give way to well-worn, simple rooms with TVs, phones, and full baths. (☎26450 24 132; fax 26450 23 756. Breakfast included. Doubles €60-73.)

By and large, dining in Lefkada town is pricey and tourist-oriented; you'll have to work a little harder to find authentic flavor. **Taverna Regantos ❶,** off the main plateia a short walk up Verigoti, is one of the classic tavernas in Lefkada. Built into an older taverna, Regentos has been passed down from generation to generation. Peek into the pots as your palate-pleasers are prepared. (☎26450 22 855. Beef in red sauce €5, stuffed peppers €3, *retsina* €2 per half-liter. Open 6pm-2am.) **Taverna Riviera ❶,** off the waterfront to the right of the bus station as you face it, has low-priced traditional dishes and draws a regular crowd of locals who while away the afternoon and much of the evening. (☎26450 21 480. Entrees €4.40-7.) For a spicier night, two clubs, **X Generation** and **Capital,** are 1km to the right, facing inland, of town. The clubs are about 500m beyond the athletic center. A taxi there should cost under €4. If you want to stay in town, head to the waterfront to the right of Dörpfield; clubs like **Excess** and **Coconut Groove** blare late into the night.

SIGHTS AND BEACHES. The **Archaeological Museum,** in a large, yellow, modern building 1km down the waterfront road, has a collection of artifacts from ancient Leukas, a prominent island city from the 7th century BC. Panels thoroughly explain the objects in English, and give interesting information about Leukas's history and culture. (☎26450 21 635. Open Tu-Su 8:30am-3pm. Free.) The **folklore museum** gives a taste of Lefkada's Italian legacy. It's off the main plateia; turn right and follow the signs. It may be temporarily closed for work on the building, so call ahead to check. (☎26450 22 473. Open M-F 11am-1pm and 6-10pm. €2.) In the second half of August, Lefkada hosts the annual **Folklore Festival,** with music and dance performances in the outdoor theater just off the plateia. While Lefkada Town has no sandy beaches, the northwest coast has miles of white pebbles and clear water. To get there, rent a **moped** (€10 per day) at **Eurocar** (☎26450 23 581) on Panagou, to the right of Hotel Nirikos, or catch a bus to the best stretch of beaches, starting at **Agios Nikitas** (6 per day, €0.90) and continuing to the sweeping view at the **Faneromenis Monastery.** (☎26450 21 105. Open 7am-10pm. Free.)

NIDRI Νιδρι

The last stop on the delightful Fiskardo-Frikes-Nidri ferry, Nidri is an anti-climactic end of the line. The waterfront, crowded with pleasure boats, has a handsome view of the dappled coves of offshore islands; the town itself is a crowded strip of tourist shops and cafes. **Ferries** go to **Frikes,** Ithaka (€4.50) via **Fiskardo** (€3.70). **Buses** from Nidri go to **Lefkada** (30min., 20 per day, €1) and **Vasiliki** (30min., 5 per day, €1.35). The **buses** stop at a small KTEL bus sign on the main street; **taxis** make the trip for €10-15.

The crowds and glitz that make Nidri unpleasant during the daytime transform it into a party zone at night, as strobe-lit clubs on the main street throw open their doors. Let the wind carry you to **Sail Inn,** far down the main street toward Lefkada Town. This snack-bar-by-day and club-by-night has a breezy atmosphere with straw umbrellas and an outdoor dance floor that opens right onto the beach. (Beer €2-2.50; cocktails €5. Cafe open 10am-8pm, club open 10:30pm-late.) **Byblos** and **Status Bar** are more mainstream dance clubs. (Beer €1.50, cocktails €3. Open 9pm-2am.) **Club Tropicana,** down the main street toward Vasiliki, is only for diehard partyers. Its doors don't even open until midnight, but, if you last long enough, you can catch the morning bus back to town.

VASILIKI Βασιλικη

Vasiliki's unique position between mountains creates distinct wind patterns that make it one of the world's premiere windsurfing towns. Despite the visitors, the town keeps a neighborly, close-knit atmosphere. Smaller than Lefkada Town and less touristy than Nidri, Vasiliki is the best Lefkada has to offer. The long beach provides a great view of multicolored windsurfing sails, while boats run to nearby beautiful pebbled coves. With an attractive waterfront of excellent restaurants and ferry connections to Kephalonia and Ithaka, Vasiliki is full of the quiet pleasures of a small beach town.

ORIENTATION AND PRACTICAL INFORMATION. Almost everything in Vasiliki lies along the waterfront or the main road running inland from the harbor, near Penguin Restaurant. **Buses** stop near the bakery on the waterfront by the road inland. Five per day (7:15am-9:45pm) run to and from **Lefkada** (1hr., €2.20) and **Nidri** (30min., €1.35). From Vasiliki, **ferries** (☎26450 31 555 or 26450 31 520) sail to **Frikes,** Ithaka (2hr., €4.40) via **Fiskardo** (1hr., €3.40); inquire at Samba Tours. Renting a **moped** or a **car** is a good idea if you plan to avoid overly touristed beach towns. **Christo's Alex's Rental,** at the intersection of the road inland with the road to Lefkada, is the cheapest. (☎26450 31 580; fax 26450 31 780. Mopeds €6 per day, motorcycle €10 per day, cars €20 and up per day.) On the left on the road inland, the incredibly helpful staff at **Samba Tours** offers a vast array of services, including **ferry and bus info,** boat excursions, faxes, car hire, flight tickets, photocopying, safety deposit, **currency exchange,** book swap, and **Internet access.** (☎26450 31 555 or 26450 31 520; fax 26450 31 522; sambatours@otenet.gr. Internet €2 per 15min. Open daily 8:30am-11:30pm.) The **National Bank** recently installed a 24hr. **ATM** on the far left of the waterfront as you face inland. The 24hr. **police station** (☎26450 31 218) is inland along the main road. For **emergencies,** contact the **health center** (☎26450 31 065); on the main road, go straight through the intersection with the road to Lefkada Town and Nidri. For **Internet access,** head along the road inland; **Star Travel** is on your right. (☎26450 31 833. €1.50 per 20min., €4 per hr. Open daily 9am-11pm.) The **post office** is up from Star Travel, just after the crossroads. (Open M-F 7:30am-2pm.) **Postal code:** 31082.

ACCOMMODATIONS. Rooms are plentiful along the waterfront, the main road, and the side streets leading off of them. With a little work, you should be able to find domatia for €15 per person or less in the off season; it's possible to get a room for as low as €20-25 in high season. The old **fruit market** ❸ (now more of a mini-market), to the right side of the waterfront when facing inland, opposite the ferry dock, lets spacious rooms with private baths, balconies, and fabulous views of the water. (☎26450 31 221. Singles €20-25; doubles €30-40.) **Hotel Lefkatas** ❸, on the left as you walk out of town on the main road, about 100m from the waterfront, has clean, comfortable rooms featuring private baths, A/C, and some ocean view balconies. (☎26450 31 801 or 26450 31 803. Call ahead. Singles €25-30; doubles €30-45.) A 1km walk along the road inland or along the beach leads to a bit of luxury at **Porto Fico** ❺. Gorgeous rooms with tiled floors, dark wood furniture, A/C, TVs, balconies, and private baths, as well as easy beach access and a swimming pool are worth the effort to get there. (☎26450 31 402; fax 26450 31 467; portofico@lantisworld.com. Breakfast included. Doubles €45-50 from Sept.-June, €55-60 from June 15-July 15, €90 from July 15-Aug. Call ahead.) **Vasiliki Beach Camping** ❶, popular among the windsurfing crowd, has superlative amenities including a great waterfront location, bar, market, laundry and shower, not to mention a clean, flowery campsite. Walk about 500m along the road inland, past the intersection with the road to Lefkada; the campsite is on the left. (☎26450 31 308; fax 26450 31 458. €6 per person; €4.50 per small tent; €5 per large tent; €4 per car.)

FOOD AND NIGHTLIFE. Nearly all the restaurants are on a short stretch of the waterfront, where full meals can be inexpensive and well-prepared. **Miramare** ❸, essentially on its own pier at the far right of the waterfront, facing inland, has friendly service and a classy feel. It specializes in pizza (€5.90-7.40) and seafood (€5-12.50). Gary and Mary will offer you a warm welcome at **Penguin Restaurant** ❷, on the waterfront at the corner of the main road running inland, which serves traditional Greek favorites (€2-7), international appetizers (€1.50-7), great vegetarian dishes (€2.50-3), and sandwiches (€2-4.50). **Stelios** ❹, next to Penguin, provides a more romantic atmosphere and fancier dishes, including a hearty lamb with oven-baked potatoes and vegetables (€10.30) and a delicious sea bass with lemon (€12.60). Save room for homemade cheesecake (€5) or another tempting dessert. (☎26450 31 581. Entrees €5.60-12.60, salads €2.50-5.90.)

After dark, try **Zeus's Bar,** on the waterfront between Penguin and Dolphin restaurants, which serves up orange juice with soda water (€1.50) to soothe the salt- and sun-weary. The place comes alive during Happy Hour (7-9pm) when cocktails are €4. **Remezzo Beach Bar,** on the beach all the way to the left of the waterfront (facing inland), offers the most popular nightlife in Vasiliki for the under-25 crowd, featuring good dance music and large indoor/outdoor bars. Doors don't even open until midnight, and the dancing doesn't end until the sun comes up again. (Cover €3 includes first beer. Beer €3, cocktails €4.)

SIGHTS. Boat tours to several of the island's beaches leave from Vasiliki. Samba Tours offers weekly trips to Lefkada's best beach, the breathtaking **Porto Katsiki** (Port of the White Goat), at the base of towering white cliffs (40-50min., round trip leaves 11am and returns 5pm, €8). The beach is also accessible by car and moped; follow the signs on the main road. A **lighthouse** built on the site of the **Temple of Lefkas Apollo** sits at the southernmost tip of the island. Worshipers exorcised evil with an annual sacrifice at the temple, in which the victim, usually a criminal or a person thought to be possessed, was launched from the cliffs into the sea. It was from these 70m cliffs that the ancient poet **Sappho,** rejected by her lady lover Phaon, leapt to her death. The best views of **Sappho's Leap** or *Kavos tis Kiras* (Cape of the Lady) are found on various **boat excursions.**

ITHAKA Ιθακη

The least touristed and perhaps the most beautiful of the Ionian Islands, Ithaka retains a close-knit feel and is happily Greek amid heavily-touristed neighbors. Those who discover Ithaka delight in the island's undeveloped pebbled beaches, rocky hillsides and terraced olive groves. Tiny villages packed with colorful homes surround the many natural harbors on the island, where the ambling pace of local

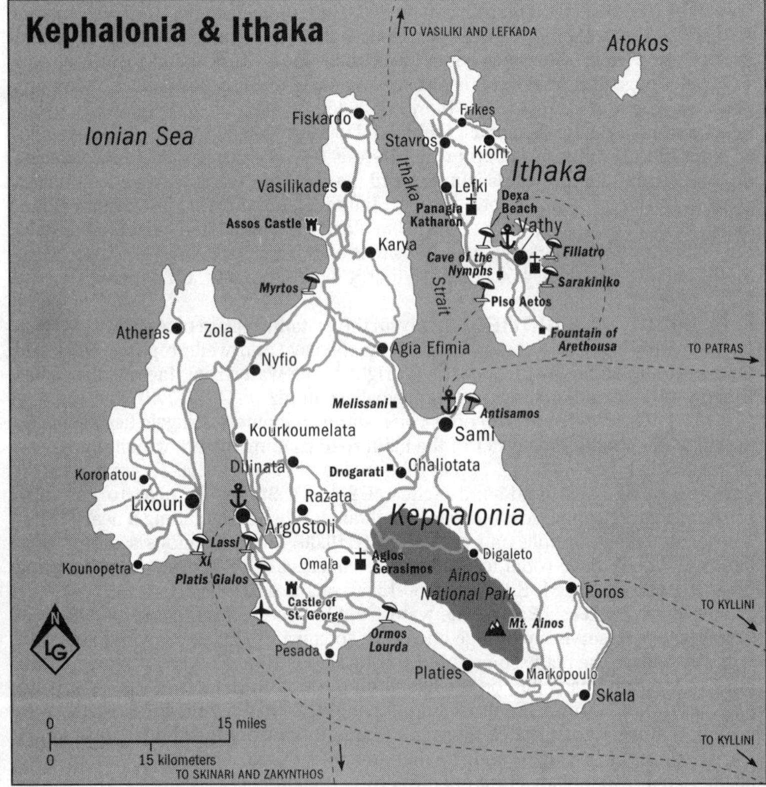

IONIAN ISLANDS

life creates a much more relaxing and quiet atmosphere than that found on nearby Kephalonia or Lefkada. Ithaka was the kingdom that **Odysseus** left behind to fight in the Trojan War (and to wander ten years on his way home). His wife Penelope faithfully waited 20 years for his return here, while crowds of suitors pressed for her hand—and Odysseus's kingdom. A glimpse of one of the isle's sparkling azure bays from the winding mountain roads makes it clear what all the fuss was about.

VATHY Βαθυ

Ithaka's lovely capital wraps around a circular bay, where garish fishing and pleasure boats bob in the water and precipitous green hillsides nudge against the water. At dusk, witness an explosion of color as the dying sun deepens the tint of the red-shingled roofs and pastel-painted houses.

ORIENTATION AND PRACTICAL INFORMATION. Facing inland, Vathy's **ferry docks** are on the far right of the waterfront, about a 4min. walk to the right of the town plateia. Depending on where you're coming from, you may need a taxi (☎26740 33 030) from **Piso Aetos** (10min., €10-12) or **Frikes** (30min., €15-20). Be sure to call ahead for a taxi, as there are not many on the island. **Ferries** connect Ithaka to Sterea Ellada (at **Astakos**), the Peloponnese (at **Patras**), and nearby **Lefkada** and **Kephalonia.** Schedules vary seasonally; check with the staff at **Delas Tours** (☎26740 32 104; fax 26740 33 031. Open daily 9am-2pm and 3:30-9:30pm), in the main plateia. Or consult **Polyctor Tours,** along the far side of the plateia as you approach from the port police. (☎26740 33 120; fax 26740 33 130. Open daily 9:30am-1:30pm and 3:30-9pm. Hours reduced Sa and Su.) Ferries depart from **Frikes,** on the northern tip of Ithaka, to **Vasiliki** on Lefkada (2½hr., 1 per day, €3.25) via **Fiskardo** on Kephalonia (1hr., €1.70). Departures from **Piso Aetos** go to **Sami** on Kephalonia (45min., 2-3 per day, €1.70). Ferries go to mainland **Patras** in the Peloponnese (4½hr.; 7am, 4:30pm; €11.50). **Rent a Scooter,** on a side street off the waterfront directly across from the port police, has standard rates of €17 per day, plus gas. (☎26740 32 840. Open 9:15am-2pm and 4:30-9pm.) For car rental, try **AGS Rent a Car,** on the waterfront about two blocks to the right of the plateia. (☎26740 32 702. €40 per day for a small car, including insurance. Open daily 8:30am-9pm.) **Taxis** (☎26740 33 030) are pricey; they line up by the water, in front of the plateia.

To reach the **police station** (☎26740 32 205) coming from the plateia, turn right on the first street after a mansion-turned-cafe and walk inland. (Open 24hr.) There is a **pharmacy** to the right of Delas Tours in the plateia. To get to the **hospital** (☎26740 32 222), walk along the waterfront with the water on your left for about 1km until you see a sign. For **laundry** service, **Polifimos** is behind the National Bank, in the far right corner of the plateia. (☎26740 32 032. €4 per kg, wash and dry. Open M-Sa 8am-1pm and 6-9pm.) The **National Bank** is in the upper left corner of the plateia, with Polyctor Tours on your left, and has a 24hr. **ATM.** (Open M-Th 8am-2pm, F 8am-1:30pm.) The **OTE** is on the waterfront, just before Hotel Mentor, coming from the plateia with the water on your left. (☎26740 32 299. Open M-F 7am-2:30pm.) **Internet access** is available at the aptly-named **Net,** on the left side of the plateia, facing inland. (€4 per hr. Open noon-midnight.) A lone computer offers Internet access at **Nirito Cafe,** in the plateia. (€6 per hr. Open daily 7am-2am.) The **post office** is in the plateia. (☎26740 32 386. Open M-F 7:30am-2pm.) **Postal code:** 28300.

ACCOMMODATIONS AND FOOD. The few hotels in town are expensive, but private **domatia** can cut you a very good deal, so they're a good way to go. Wander the streets inland from the waterfront, ask friendly locals for advice, or contact Delas Tours to see what they have available (though their offerings tend toward pricier options). Be sure to discuss price and distance before leaving the town center. A good bet is **Andriana Domatia ❸,** across from the ferry dock on the far right side of the waterfront, facing inland. Immaculate rooms include baths, TVs, and A/C, and some have pleasant waterfront views. (☎26740 32 387. Singles €25-30; doubles €40-47. Negotiate for discounts in the off season.) A short walk uphill from the plateia leads you to **Martha Maria's Rooms to Let ❷.** To find the very kind Martha, walk uphill two blocks from the plateia straight past Nikos's taverna, turn right at the T intersection, walk one block and turn left; the rooms are on your left. Odd choices of color and art fill clean, old rooms with private baths, kitchenettes, fans, and balcony access. (☎26740 32 252. Singles €20-26; doubles €26-42.) Facing inland, **Hotel Mentor ❹** is on the far left of the waterfront. The ritzy lobby leads to more basic but spacious rooms with linoleum floors. Some with stunning harbor views and bathtubs, all with baths, balconies, A/C, and TVs. (☎26740 32 433; fax 26740 32 293. Breakfast included. Singles €42-62; doubles €57-82.)

Local favorite **Taverna To Trexantiri ❶,** one block behind the post office off the plateia, dishes out huge portions. Walk inside and check out the night's dishes. (☎26740 33 066. Entrees under €6.) **Kantouni ❷** (☎26740 32 910), on the right side of the waterfront facing inland, has numerous grill selections like pork souvlaki (€5.90). Entrees run €4-6.50. **O Nikos ❷,** just down the street along the left side of the National Bank, serves traditional fare with a smile; try Nikos's famous fish soup for €7.34. (☎26740 33 039. Entrees €5-7.80.) Tiny **Lo Sputino ❷,** on the waterfront next to the port authority, offers tasty pizza, pasta, and other Italian dishes for similar prices. (Entrees and pizzas €5.50-7.)

SIGHTS. By far the best entertainment in Vathy is found outdoors on the several lovely beaches, on the water, or relaxing and sipping *frappés* in open-air cafes. But museum-lovers aren't out of luck. The airy new **Folklore and Nautical Museum,** two blocks inland from the waterfront near the plateia, houses fully assembled bedrooms, a kitchen, a sitting room from Ithaka's colonial period, photographs of the 1953 earthquake devastation, heirloom lace-trimmed clothing and linens, and a collection of nautical equipment and memorabilia. (☎26740 33 398. Open M-Sa 10am-2:30pm. €1.) The tiny **Vathy Archaeological Museum** displays finds from ongoing excavations at the **sanctuary of Apollo** at Aetos, a site that may have been Odysseus's palace. (Open Tu-Su 8:30am-3pm. Free.)

BEACHES AND THE OUTDOORS. Ithaka's beaches are beautiful, if a bit hard to reach. **Dexa,** with a long, pebbled shore and shady trees to rest under, is the closest to Vathy, a 20min. walk from town. To get there from Vathy, follow the main road out of town with the water on your right, up and over the hill with the gas station on it. On the other side of Vathy, you can visit gorgeous **Filiatro** and **Sarakiniko** beaches; walk with the water to your left, and after Hotel Mentor turn right and keep heading toward the mountain to the left of town as you face inland. Take the steep uphill road—it's about a 40min. walk. Near the village of **Agios Ioannis,** on the island's western side, are several stunning pebble beaches with views of Kephalonia. First-rate **Gidaki** is only accessible by boat (boats that make the trip dock in front of the plateia).

Fans of Homer and exercise fiends who love a great view can make the challenging hour-long, 4km **hike** up to the **Cave of the Nymphs,** where Odysseus supposedly hid the treasure the Phaeacians gave him. The cave has been under archaeological excavation in recent years and is sometimes closed to visitors. If it is closed, you can still walk around the site and view the two separate entrances (one for the gods and one for mere mortals) and perhaps chat with a few archaeologists. To get there, walk around the harbor with the water on your right on the road out of town that leads to Piso Aetos and Stavros, and then follow the signs along the road that winds up the mountain. The hike provides stunning views of Vathy; bring a flashlight for the cave. A 2hr. **hike** southeast leads to the Homeric **Arethousa Fountain,** along a steep mountain path through orchards. In summer, the fountain is dry. To find the well-marked, rocky path to the fountain, follow Evmeou St. (your first right after the Drakoulis mansion-turned-cafe when you are coming from the plateia) uphill until it becomes a dirt road. Keep an eye out for the signs.

The island's sole **bus** (45min., €1.20 to Frikes; 1hr., €1.80 to Kioni) runs north from Vathy, passing through secluded coastal villages, including the exceptionally beautiful **Frikes** and **Kioni** on the northern coast; both have small, crystal-blue harbors. The road between the two towns is peppered with lovely white pebble beaches, as is the shore around Kioni. In high season, the bus generally runs twice a day: once very early in the morning to Kioni, returning immediately, and once later in the morning, returning after a few hours (so you have time to spend in the towns). The bus also doubles as a school bus. Little **Stavros** is high in the mountains on the way to Frikes and Kioni. Follow signs in town to a small museum full of excavated items from Pilicata hill, another contender for the site of Odysseus's palace. (Hours vary. A small donation is expected.) Wander down the steep road to the small beach and harbor, or sit in a pine-shaded taverna eating *rovani*, a gooey and sweet island specialty made with rice and honey. You can also visit the **Monastery of Panagia Katharon,** on Ithaka's highest mountain, Mt. Neritos; take a taxi or moped to Anoghi and follow the signs.

PERAHORA

The small village of **Perahora** rests on the frighteningly steep mountainside 4km above Vathy. It's a town devoted to the vine; it produces the island's best wine, and hosts a **wine festival** the last Sunday in July. If you make it up to Perahora, visit the ruins of **Paleohora,** the capital of the island until it was abandoned in the early 16th century. Its stone walls crumble on the hillside next to Perahora. To get there, follow the signs in Perahora to the beginning of a footpath that leads through olive groves to the ruins. The town church ruins are the first you'll encounter; although the roof is gone and the walls have nearly fallen, frescoes still cling to the inner walls. The view of Vathy from here is unbeatable. The road leading to Perahora is on the far right of the waterfront as you face inland (opposite the road to Stavros); follow the signs. The road is extremely steep as you near the village and there is little shade, so wear good shoes and bring lots of water.

KEPHALONIA Κεφαλονια

Massive mountains, subterranean lakes and rivers, caves, dense forests, and more than 250km of sand-and-pebble coastline make Kephalonia a nature lover's paradise. Its beauty has been fought over by the Byzantine, Frankish, Ottoman, Venetian, Napoleonic, and British Empires. During World War II, after Italy had abandoned the Axis, 9000 Italian soldiers occupying the island fought their ex-allies for seven days, as Germans invaded and killed all but 33 Italians. In 1953, a disastrous earthquake forced the island to rebuild, leaving only relatively undamaged Fiskardo with the Ionian pastel neoclassical look. Today, Kephalonia's beauty draws a diverse crowd, from the upscale yachting set to budget-conscious backpackers. Inconvenient bus schedules and a number of attractions make Kephalonia perfect for a longer stay.

ARGOSTOLI Αργοστολι

The capital and by far the largest town on Kephalonia and Ithaka, Argostoli is a lively city packed with yellow and orange buildings that climb the hills from the

calm waters of the harbor. Other places on the island are more picturesque, but Argostoli has urban convenience in a fairly attractive setting. There's no shortage of hotels, restaurants, or souvenir shops, and if you're looking for true Kephalonian nightlife, the main plateia is the only place to go. Argostoli is also Kephalonia's transportation hub, so if you tire of the hubbub, hop on the first outbound vehicle you see.

TRANSPORTATION

Flights: Olympic Airways, R. Vergoti 7 (☎26710 28 808 or 26710 28 881), has 2 flights per day to Athens (€75). Open M-F 8am-3:30pm.

Ferries: Kephalonia has multiple ports for different destinations. Buses connect **Argostoli** to other ports, including **Sami,** where ferries leave for **Corfu, Ithaka, Patras,** and **Italy** July-Aug. (see p. 300). Prices and times are seasonal; inquire at a travel agency. From Argostoli boats go to **Kyllini** on the Peloponnese (1-2 per day, €9.40) and **Lixouri** in western Kephalonia (1 per hr. until 11:30pm, €1). From **Poros,** on the southeastern coast, ferries leave for Kyllini (2 per day, €6.30). Ferries head to the tiny port of **Skinari** on the northern end of Zakynthos from **Pesada,** a similarly small and inconvenient port on the southern coast of Kephalonia. Buses only head from Pesada to Argostoli in the morning. Buses from Argostoli stop at the village of Pesada; from the bus drop, it is a 1km walk downhill to the dock. You should arrange for transportation in Zakynthos as buses do not go regularly to Skinari.

Buses: The bus station (☎26710 22 281) is on the south end of the waterfront, in a light pink building all the way to the left as you face inland. Open 7am-8pm. Brochures with schedules, prices, and return times available. Buses head to: **Agios Gerasimos** (**Omala**) (10am, 12:30, 2pm; €1); **Fiskardo** (2hr.; 10am, 2pm; €3.30); **Kourkoumelata** (4 per day, €1); **Lassi** (**Platis Yialos**) (9 per day 10am-6:30pm, €1); **Pesada** (30min., 9:30am, 12:30pm; €1); **Poros** (10:30am, 2pm; €3); **Sami** (7:15am, 12, 1, 4:30pm; €2); **Skala** (10am, 2pm; €2.80). For **Travliata** you can take either the Skala or Poros buses; it should cost you about €1. Buses meet the ferry and continue on to **Athens** (1 per day, €25.50). Buses to Argostoli meet the ferry arriving in **Sami** (3-4 per day, €2). Local service is reduced Sa; none Su.

Taxis: (☎26710 28 505 or 26710 22 700). Plenty of taxis line up in the plateia; they also respond to phone calls 24hr. a day.

Rentals: Sunbird (☎26710 23 723), near the port authority, rents cars (€40) and mopeds (€13.50). Gas not included (€5-30). Open daily 8:30am-3pm and 5-8:30pm. **Thrifty,** G. Vergoti 7 (☎26710 27 461). Head inland up Vyronos for 3 blocks. Cars rent for €27-74 per day, including the first 100km (€0.17-0.36 for each km thereafter, depending on the type of car). Open 8am-2pm and 5-9pm daily.

ORIENTATION AND PRACTICAL INFORMATION

The town's cafe-packed and hotel-lined main plateia is two blocks inland from the water on **21 Maiou,** near the Port Authority and EOT. South, or left facing inland, from the plateia, **Lithostrotou** is a pedestrian shopping area with high-rent stores like Diesel and Benetton and dozens of leather, postcard, and jewelry shops.

Tourist Office: (☎26710 22 248 or 26710 24 466), beside the port authority near the ferry docks. Provides free maps, helpful information about sights and beaches, and some assistance with accommodations and restaurants. In fall, spring, and summer, open M-Sa 8am-2:30pm and some evenings in Aug.; in winter M-F 8am-2pm.

Banks: National Bank, offering **currency exchange** and 24hr. **ATM.** Open M-F 8am-2pm. Other banks and ATMs line the waterfront.

Work Opportunity: Milos Beach Bar and Cafe, Skala (☎26710 83 188; in winter ☎26710 83 231). Hires waitstaff and bartenders for tourist season; summer hiring begins in February and March. Call in advance of your arrival and ask for Joya Grouzi.

International Bookstore: Petratos Bookstore (☎26710 22 546), on Lithostrotou across from a small church, 2 blocks up from the water. English-language and foreign newspapers, magazines, and best-sellers. Open M-Sa 8am-10pm.

Laundromat: Laundry Express, Lassis 46b. Walk inland on Vyronos for 9 blocks, turning left onto Lassis. The laundry is 2 blocks farther on your right. Self-service. Bring soap. Wash and dry €5.40 per load.

Police: (☎26710 22 200), on I. Metaxa across from the tourist office. Open 24hr.

Tourist Police: (☎26710 22 815), in the police station. Advice on rooms to rent. Open daily 7am-10pm.

OTE: (☎26710 91 339), Rokou Vergoti and Georgiou Vergoti, near the Archaeological Museum. Open M-Sa 7am-2:40pm.

Internet Access: Check your email to the sounds of blasting pop music at **Traffic** (☎26710 26 261) in the main plateia. €4.40 per hr. Open daily 9am-late.

Post Office: (☎26710 23 173), 2 blocks up from the water on Lithostrotou, at the intersection of Kerkyras. Open M-F 7:30am-2pm. **Postal code:** 28100.

ACCOMMODATIONS

Private rooms are the cheapest option. Signs advertising **domatia** are all over town; for guidance, try the **Self-Catering Association of Kephalonia and Ithaka,** on the waterfront near the Port Authority. (☎26710 29 109. Open M-F 9am-3pm and 6-8pm.) Bargain hard, but in high season don't expect to find a room for much less than €25. If you plan to stay in a hotel, call ahead. Renting transportation allows you to stay in the omnipresent small town domatia and have access to the beach.

Hotel Tourist (☎26710 22 510 or 26710 23 034), on the waterfront before the port authority as you approach from the bus station. A surprisingly good deal for a hotel of considerable quality. Balconies and TVs help you forgive the name. Breakfast €4.50. Singles €24-36; doubles €37-52. ❸

Hotel Kephalonia Star (☎26710 23 180; fax 26710 23 180), farther down the street on the waterfront. Sign just says "Hotel C Star." Cheaper than similar upscale places, with extras like soundproof windows and A/C; bathrooms have tubs, and fridges are available. Breakfast €5. Singles €32-47; doubles €44-60. ❹

Ionian Plaza Hotel (☎26710 25 581), on the right side of the plateia as you face inland. Modern rooms have slate-blue wood furniture and stunning views of the town, plus all the comforts: A/C, TVs, phones, and private baths. Buffet breakfast included in room price. Singles €42-45.50; doubles €61-67. Call ahead in summer. ❹

Hotel Allegro (☎26710 28 684), up from the waterfront on Andrea Hoïda (also spelled Choïda and Xoïda), halfway between the bus station and port authority. Rooms are bare but decent, some with balconies. Singles €40, with bath €45; doubles €50, with bath €55, with bath and A/C €60. ❸

Hotel Argostoli, Vyronos 21 (☎26710 28 358), on the left as you head inland past Lithostrotou. The pretty peach building holds simple rooms with few amenities. Private baths, some with balconies. Singles €30; doubles €44. ❸

FOOD

Food is cheaper on the waterfront, but selection and quality are better in the plateia. A well-organized **farmers market** takes over the waterfront near the bus station on Saturday mornings. Permanent fruit shops, bakeries, and supermarkets line the water between the bus station and port. **Mister Grillo ❷,** near the port authority, has a constant crowd and live Greek music some evenings. The great food offerings include plenty of vegetarian options like black beans in oil (€2.64) and stuffed peppers (€4.30). Carnivores will appreciate the luscious Kephalonian meat pie (€5), octopus (€8.22), and moussaka (€4.40). If you feel like spending extra to eat in one of the plateia restaurants, try **La Gondola ❸,** with ample but often packed seating on 21 Maiou and in the plateia. Greek dishes are offered, but people come for the divine Italian food. Try the "Risotto D'Oro" (€9.20) with pumpkin and shrimp. Steeper prices get you comfortable chairs, red roses on the table, and wonderful service. (Pizza €5.60-8.70, pasta €3.90-8.90, Greek entrees €5.60-8.80. Open noon-1am.) **Taverna Anonymous ❷,** on the waterfront, offers a large menu of filling dishes. Eat right on the water or in the cozier, restaurant-side seating. (Kephalonian meat pie €5.30, pork souvlaki €6, salads €2.30-3.70.)

SIGHTS

Argostoli's requisite and worthwhile **Archaeological Museum** is housed in a lovely, brand-new building a few blocks south of the plateia, near the Municipal Theater on R. Vergoti. Pottery and jewelry from excavated sites around the island, as well as from the Melissani lake, are displayed with thorough explanations. (☎26710 28 300. Open Tu-Su 8:30am-3pm. €3, seniors and students €2, children and EU students free.) The **Historical and Folk Museum,** two blocks from the Archaeological Museum on the road to the left of the theater, is crammed with 19th-century objects ranging from household items to military medals. The French coffee cups, English top hats, and antique dolls illustrate Argostoli's history of colonialism. Of particular interest are the photographs of Argostoli during the 20th century, including shots of damage from the devastating 1953 earthquake and later reconstruction. (☎26710 28 835. Open Tu-Su 9am-2pm. €3, students €2, children free.)

DAYTRIPS FROM ARGOSTOLI

Renting a moped or car gives you the freedom to roam between sights and beaches, unrestrained by inconvenient bus schedules or pricey accommodations. You can also get to **Myrtos Beach,** on the west coast, considered one of Europe's best beaches.

CASTLE OF ST. GEORGE. The Venetian-built castle is 9km southeast of Argostoli, overlooking the village of Travliata. From its battlements, you can admire the panorama that once inspired Lord Byron. *(By moped, head toward Skala and turn when the road splits. Or take either the Poros or Skala buses (10min., €1). Open M-Sa 8am-8pm. Free.)*

LIXOURI. In the center of the western peninsula, Lixouri, former home of satirical poet Andreas Laskaratos, offers access to miles of essentially tourist-free coastline. You can rent **mopeds** at several places in Lixouri, and **buses** run to smaller villages in the area, including to **Xi,** a red sand beach surrounded by cliffs. The town itself is a smaller, quieter Argostoli, with similar conveniences. A small beach lies at the far left of the waterfront as you face inland; it's about a 5min. walk along a lovely tree-lined promenade. The cafe-filled central plateia is across from the port; restaurants fill the space between the plateia and the beach. *(Get there from Argostoli by boat (30min., every hr. on the half-hour, €1). Buy tickets on board; correct change requested.)*

SOUTH COAST BEACHES. A few beaches and interesting towns dot the area south of Argostoli. One of the best beaches is the secluded white sand beach of **Ormos Lourda,** in the middle of the south coast, but popular **Platis Yialos** is closer to Argostoli. *(Take the Lassi bus, 30min., 9 buses per day 10am-6:30pm, €1.)* Nearby **Metaza** is one of Lord Byron's adopted towns, but his house no longer exists. **Kourkoumelata** village was completely restored by a Greek tycoon after the 1953 earthquake. Check out the comfortable **Hotel Kourkoumi ❷** if you decide to stay. *(☎26710 41 645. Doubles with bath and breakfast €20.)* Outside the city in the village of **Dargoti** lies a multi-layered **Mycenaean tholos tomb,** said to have belonged to Odysseus himself; locals can thus claim that Kephalonia is the site of Homer's ancient Ithaka. **Poros,** on the southeast coast, is a modern beach town near two pebbled beaches; rooms to let are everywhere. *(Buses run from Argostoli to Poros (€3) at 10:30am and 2pm.)*

EAST OF ARGOSTOLI. The **Monastery of Ag. Gerasimos** was founded by its namesake saint; his preserved body still rests here. On the night of August 15, nearby **Omala** hosts a festival and a vigil in the saint's church, and on the saint's name days

FROM THE ROAD

I WANT MY GREEK TV

You've spent the day ogling lush landscapes, baking under the broiling sun, and hopping from crowded bus to bus. You're back in your hotel room, and you need to unwind. Flip on the TV, and take a peek at what Greece has to offer.

The Spanish soap operas are my favorite in terms of unintentional comedic value. The Spanish soaps, unlike their English-language counterparts, are dubbed into Greek. What was an overly dramatic and difficult to follow program becomes completely incomprehensible. Because they are dubbed, all of the original music and sound effects are gone. People hit tables but make no noise, silent rain pours down on dark streets, and music fades in and out at inappropriate moments.

Greek commercials are usually either funny or sexy. They often feature absurdly attractive people selling the oddest products. Ice cream and yogurt are two of the most advertised products on television. Most of the ads feature mostly naked demigods and goddesses clubbing, kissing, or flirting for 30 seconds, then eating some ice cream. It's always a fun surprise to discover what you thought was surely an ad for underwear was, in fact, an ad for a popsicle. Strong coffee drinks have the amazing ability to transform Greek geeks into studs, brawny lifeguards offer yogurt to flirtatious bathing beauties, and cell phones facilitate all manner of courtship and duplicity. Greek TV is certainly an experience in itself.

—Jen Taylor

(Oct. 20 and Aug. 16), the whole town goes wild; ask at the tourist office for info on all the fun. *(Buses run from Argostoli to Omala/Agios Gerasimos 10am, 12:30, 2pm; €1. In summer a bus leaves on Su at 8:30am and returns at 10:30am.)* **Skala** is yet another Kephalonian village with an exquisite beach; in this case, it's pebble-and-sand. The remains of a 2nd-century Roman villa are in town; almost all its structure is gone, but the mosaic floors, with geometric patterns and scenes of animals and people, are remarkably well-preserved. *(Look for the signs as you walk down the road from the bus drop towards the water. Open Tu-Su 8:30am-10pm, M 8:30am-3pm. Free.)* Every day two buses come to Skala from Argostoli and three return; the last runs at 5pm (1hr., €2.80 each way). If you must stay, ask for rooms at **Skalina Tours ❸** (open daily 9am-2pm and 5:30-8:30pm; for rooms call ☎29720 693 260) but be warned: they'll be expensive. Eat at the **Sun Rise Restaurant ❸**, all the way to the left of the beach, facing inland. It's on the expensive side, but the seafood is reasonably priced and fresh; try the seafood platter for two (€16.40). Fish entrees start at €5.40.

SAMI Σαμη

As you stroll through Sami, stunning views in all directions make it difficult to decide which is more lovely: the tempestuous blue waves crashing on the long, white-sand beach or the lush, green hills cradling the town. Reminders are everywhere that Sami served as the set for the movie *Captain Corelli's Mandolin*, based on the similarly named (and much better) novel. But despite this brush with Hollywood and heavy tourist traffic in the high season, Sami remains fairly quiet and peaceful. It's close to the natural wonders of Melissani Lake, Drograti cave and Antisamos beach, whose beauty makes it a good place to spend the afternoon and night before catching a ferry from its small but busy port.

ORIENTATION AND PRACTICAL INFORMATION. The waterfront street is lined with restaurants and cafes and intersects the main plateia. White sandy beaches lie both to the left and right of the town center. From Sami, **ferries** sail to: **Piso Aetos** on **Ithaka** (40min., 6:45, 8:45am, 3:45pm; €1.70); **Patras** (2½hr.; 8:30am, 5:45pm; €10.70); and **Astakos** (high season only 8:45am, €6.50). In summer, international ferries go to **Brindisi** in Italy (1 per day beginning in early July, €35). **Buses** leave the station on the left end of the waterfront for **Argostoli** (7:15, 8am, 3:15, 5:45pm; €2.80) and **Fiskardo** (10:15am, 1:45pm; €2.70). Buy tickets on board. **Taxis** (☎26740 22 308) line up on the waterfront beside the plateia.

Ferries land on either side of the town plateia. From the bus station, facing the water, turn left to reach the mostly asphalt plateia. You may be able to glimpse the top of the blue and white Hotel Kyma, which sits on the (unmarked) main road of Sami; this road runs parallel to the water one block inland. The plateia lies between the road and the waterfront. If you follow it with the water on your right, this main road leads to Argostoli. **Sami Star Travel,** next to the bus station on the waterfront, sells ferry tickets and offers general information. (☎26740 23 007. Open daily 9am-10pm.) Heading towards Argostoli on the main road, you'll come to the 24hr. **police station** (☎26740 22 100), three blocks from the plateia on the right. There is no official tourist office, but the police may be able to answer your questions. There are several **banks; Emporiki Trapeza** on the waterfront, to the right of the plateia as you face inland, has an **ATM.** (Open M-Th 8am-2pm, F 8am-1:30pm.) For those looking for short-time **work opportunities,** several of Sami's beach bars will consider foreign applicants during tourist season; **Melissani Restaurant and Snack Bar** hires part-time kitchen and counter help. (☎26740 22 395. Call in advance for availability.) **Pharmacies** are on the main road to Argostoli. The **OTE** is one block past Emporiki Trapeza. (Open M-F 7am-2:40pm.) For **Internet access,** try **Internet Break,** beneath Hotel Kastro, just off the waterfront. (☎26740 23 770. Open M-Sa 11am-2pm and 5:30-11pm, Su 6-11pm. €6 per hr., €2.50 minimum.) The **post office** is Argostoli road, two blocks off the right corner of the plateia. (Open M-F 7:30am-2pm.) **Postal code:** 28080.

ACCOMMODATIONS AND FOOD. Because Sami is a convenient base for travel within Kephalonia, there's a high demand for rooms, which are relatively expensive. The nearby village of **Karavomilos,** on the way to Melissani lake, offers more domatia. Try the **Hotel Kyma ❸,** in the plateia, for spectacular views, cool breezes, and decent rooms with clean, shared baths. (☎26740 22 064. Singles €17-26; doubles €30-46.) The **Riviera Restaurant ❸,** on the waterfront, lets airy rooms with double beds, private baths, and balconies. (☎26740 22 777. Singles €25-32; doubles €35-44.) At similar rates, **Hotel Melissana ❸,** two blocks inland from the port authority, on the far left of the waterfront, has small, slightly dim rooms crammed with amenities: private baths, TVs, telephones, balconies, and fridges. (☎26740 22 464. Singles €30-36; doubles €35-50.) **Karavomilos Beach Camping ❶,** a 15min. walk down a beach from town with the water on the right, is set in a huge subdivided field with shade trees and blooming bushes. There are hot showers, electricity, laundry facilities, Internet access, and a mini-market. (☎26740 22 480. €4.50, €2.50 per child; €2 per car; €2.50 per small tent; €4 per large tent. Electricity €2.50. Prices higher July-Aug.) **Taka Taka Mam ❶,** on the waterfront, has good budget fare (gyros and salads €1.50-1.75, omelets €3 and up) and friendly service. (Open daily until 1am). **Mermaid Restaurant ❷,** Taka's neighbor on the waterfront, serves more elegant meals and lots of vegetarian options (moussaka €4.10, peppers stuffed with rice and mussels €6.20).

SIGHTS AND BEACHES. Head underground in the caves of **Melissani** and Drogarati. Melissani is part of huge, underground Lake Karavomilos. To get there, walk along the beach with the water to your right until you come to a small ocean-fed "lake" with a waterwheel on the far side. Turn left after the restaurant by the lake, walk inland to the road about 30m, and turn right. Down this street you'll see signs to the cave (25-30min.). The boat tour of the cave lasts 15min. Lake guides will row you around the two large caverns flooded with sparkling water, studded with stalactites, and squirming with eels. Go when the sun is high. (Open daily 9am-7pm, in winter 10am-4pm. €5, children €2.50. A boatsman's tip is encouraged.) **Drogarati** is a large cavern full of spectacular stalactites and stalagmites 5km from Sami. To get there, head inland on the road to Argostoli and follow the signs (45min.-1hr.), or take the bus to Argostoli and ask to be let off at the fork in the road 1km from the caves. (☎26740 22 950. Open until nightfall. €3, children €1.50.) **Agia Efimia,** a pretty harbor town 10km north of Sami with few tourists and little traffic, deserves a visit. Ask the Fiskardo bus to let you off there (15min, €1). The isolated and very lovely **Antisamos** beach is a must if you are on this side of Kephalonia. The long, white pebble beach is enclosed by rolling green hills. Take a taxi to Antisamos (€4 per person), or hike (75min.) by following the waterfront left from the plateia as you face inland. Take the road between the port authority and Sami Travel. Bring plenty of water and wear good shoes.

FISKARDO Φισκαρδο

The road north ends at must-see **Fiskardo,** which escaped the 1953 earthquake and is now the only remaining example of 18th- and 19th-century Kephalonian architecture. Fiskardo's crescent-shaped waterfront is tinged with the pastel hues of the modest buildings surrounding it. At night, a romantic aura pervades the town, as jazz drifts over the harbor, which twinkles with the dim lights of boats resting in the water. Touristed largely by the wealthy, Fiskardo has avoided the garish trappings that sometimes mar other seaside towns. A splendid walk through the woods or swim from the rocks takes you to the forested tidbit of land across the harbor, where the lighthouse and ruins of a 15th-century Venetian fortress rest. For archaeology buffs, an open excavation of a 2nd-century Roman graveyard is right next door to the harbor, along the water. Fiskardo's unbeatable beach lies 500m out of town on the hilly road back to Argostoli, in a quiet cove that offers flat rocks for sunbathing.

Buses for **Argostoli** leave at 6:30am and 4:30pm from the parking lot next to the church, uphill from the town. Two **buses** per day arrive from **Sami** (1hr., €2.70) and **Argostoli** (1½-2hr., €3.40). **Ferries** go to: **Piso Aetos** on Ithaka (1hr., €2.70); **Vasiliki** (1hr., €3.40); and **Nidri** on Lefkada (2hr., €4.40). For transportation and lodging questions or helpful info, contact **Nautilus Travel Agency,** at the right end of the waterfront. (☎26740 41 440. Open daily 9am-9pm.) Rooms are not cheap in Fiskardo. Even early in summer, doubles start at €40. Although the town is brimming with excellent restaurants, most of them are on the pricey side. A charming exception is the pink-and-blue **Lagondera ❶,** just off the waterfront on the road to the right of Vassos Cafe. Though it lacks a waterfront view, it more than makes up for it with cheap and delicious salads (€2) and Greek entrees (€4-5.50).

To reach the charming lighthouse, walk all the way around the waterfront with the sea on your right to Nicholas Taverna. A path picks up where the road ends and is marked with yellow circles all the way to the lighthouse. If you need to cool off and don't want to trek all the way to the big beach, there is a smaller pebble beach in town. With the water on your left, head along the waterfront road until it turns right; the beach is on your left just past the Roman graves.

Cliffs plunge into the sea along the coastal road north from Argostoli and Sami to Fiskardo. Just off this road lies one of the best beaches in Europe, **Myrtos,** which shouldn't be missed by any visitor to Kephalonia. The pure white pebbles and clear, blue water are stunning enough, but it is perhaps the beach's location, pressed against the cliffs, that has brought Myrtos its special recognition as one of Europe's premier beaches. The **buses** from Fiskardo to Sami and Argostoli stop at the turn-off to Myrtos, 4km from the gasp-inducing beauty of the beach—hop off there and hoof it the rest of the way. Roughly 4km up the road from the Myrtos turn-off is the equally incredible Venetian castle of **Assos,** on a steep, wooded peninsula joined to the island by a narrow isthmus. Completed in the early part of the 17th century, much of the castle and most of its houses are well preserved. A good deal of the land inside the walls is privately owned and fenced—the owner's goats and chickens are penned in the crumbling shells of original castle buildings, adding or detracting from the medieval romance of the place, depending on your sensibilities. The Fiskardo buses will stop at the turnoff for Assos; it's a steep downhill 4km walk to the village and another few kilometers to the castle. On August 15, the village of **Markopoulo** in the southeast celebrates the Assumption of the Virgin Mary with a strange, spooky festival involving an all-night church liturgy. According to local belief, hundreds of small snakes with black crosses on their heads slither over the icons during the service.

ZAKYNTHOS Ζακυνθος

The varied landscapes and seascapes of Zakynthos (also known as Zante) comprise an exceptionally subtle palette of colors—white cliffs rise from turquoise water, sun-bleached wheat waves in the shadow of evergreens, and magenta flowers frame the twisting streets. Known as the greenest of the Ionian Islands, Zakynthos is home to thousands of flower and plant species, some of them unique to the island. The island is also the home of a large population of loggerhead turtles, a source of pride to the islanders. Still, in Zakynthos Town or its neighboring beaches, you'll see the sweaty backs of other tourists more than the beauty of nature. Set out for the countryside to appreciate Zakynthos's natural sights, like its famous blue caves in the north. Those who venture there will understand why the Venetians christened it *Fior di Levante*—the flower of the east.

ZAKYNTHOS TOWN

Bustling Zakynthos Town welcomes visitors with arcaded streets and whitewashed buildings. After an earthquake completely destroyed it in 1953, locals restored the city to its former state, recreating the Venetian architecture in areas such as Pl. Solomou. Head north or south of Zakynthos Town to the nearby beach communities for better nightlife and even farther for remote beaches and the serene beauty that pervades the countryside.

TRANSPORTATION

Flights: The **airport** (☎26950 28 322) is 6km south of town. Flights to **Athens** (45min., 2 per day, €74). The **Olympic Airways** office, Al. Roma 16 (☎26950 28 611), is in town. Open M-F 8am-3:30pm.

Ferries: Ferries for **Kyllini** in the Peloponnese (1½hr., 7 per day, €4.70) depart from Zakynthos Town at the southern dock, on the left side of the waterfront as you face inland. Tickets at the waterfront office for Kyllini ferries, between the police/tourist police and port police. Ferries from Pesada, **Kephalonia** (1½hr., 1-2 per day, €4) arrive in **Skinari,** north of Zakynthos Town. Be warned that both of these towns are very small and relatively inaccessible: buses in Kephalonia do not go to Pesada after noon, and there are no lodgings there; buses run to Skinari only 2 days per week (M and F), and taxis to Zakynthos Town will cost €35. Due to such difficulties, returning to Kyllini and heading to Kephalonia by ferry from there may be a better idea. Ferry tickets are available at the **boat agencies** along the waterfront. For more information, call the **port police** (☎26950 28 117 or 118).

Buses: Filita 42 (☎26950 22 255), on the corner of Pl. Eleftheriou. From Pl. Solomou, walk 6 blocks south (with the water on your left) and 1 block inland; from the police station, walk 3 blocks north (with the water on your right) and 1 block inland. To: **Athens** (6hr., 5 per day 5am-6:45pm, €21.70 including ferry) via **Patras** (3hr., €9.90 including ferry); **Thessaloniki** (10hr., 7:30am, €31.60 including ferry). Schedules for local service are posted outside the bus station; a complete list is at the info window. Local buses run to: **Alykes** (4 per day 6:50am-4:30pm, €1.05); **Argasi** (8 per day 6:45am-6pm, €0.75); **Laganas** (12 per day 7:30am-8:10pm, €0.75); **Kalamaki** (6 per day 7:15am-3:30pm, €0.75); **Keri Lake** (11am, 2:30pm; €1.20); **Tsilivi** (9 per day 6:20am-8:10pm, €0.75); **Vasiliko** (4 per day); **Porto Roma** (4 per day); **Ag. Nikolaos** (6:45am, 2:30pm; €1.05).

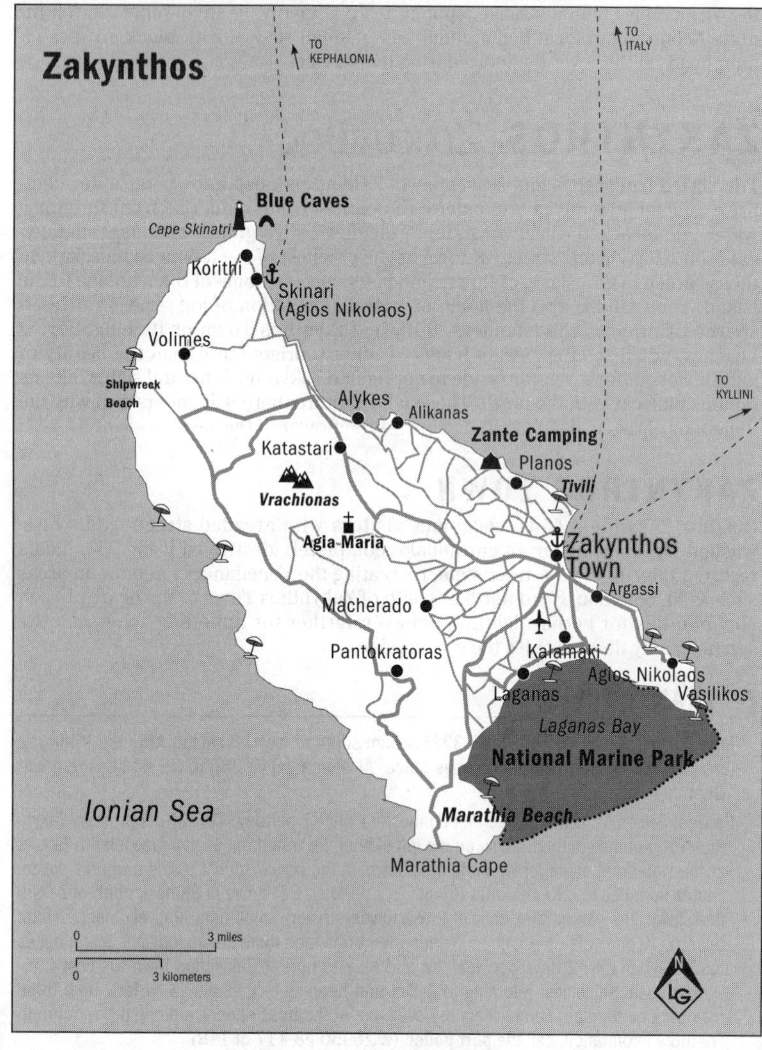

Taxis: (☎26950 48 400). Lining the side streets off the waterfront. Available 24hr.

Rentals: Pilot J., Lomvardou 78 (☎26950 28 207). Cars with unlimited mileage and full insurance from €31 per day. Must be over 21. Open daily 7am-10pm. **Hertz,** Lomvardou 38 (☎26950 45 706). Cars from €52 per day in low season, €64 in high season; prices include unlimited mileage, insurance, and tax. Must be over 21. Open daily 8am-2pm and 5:30-9:30pm. **EuroSky Rentals** (☎26950 26 278), 1 block inland on A. Makri, charges €12 per day for mopeds and €18 per day for motorcycles. License required. Must be over 23. Open daily 8am-midnight. **Spyros Rent a Scooter** (☎26950 23 963), toward the center of Lomvardou, has the cheapest moped rates: €10 per day.

ORIENTATION AND PRACTICAL INFORMATION

The waterfront runs between **Pl. Solomou** at the right end (facing inland) and **Ag. Dionysios Church** at the left end. Each end has a dock: Kyllini ferries usually dock at the left end by Ag. Dionysios; all other boats (like daily cruises) dock at the right end by Pl. Solomou. The waterfront street, **Lomvardou,** runs between the two docks and is lined with restaurants, gift shops, car and moped rental agencies, and ferry agencies. The next street inland is **Filita,** home to the bus station; Filita becomes Klavdianou toward Pl. Solomou. Behind it are, in order, **Foskolou, Alexandrou Roma** (the main shopping street), and **Tertseti.** These three streets change names or end between Martinegou and Ag. Dionysios. Three blocks inland from Pl. Solomou is **Pl. Ag. Markou,** a local gathering spot.

Banks: National Bank (☎26950 44 113), on Pl. Solomou, **exchanges currency** and has a 24hr. **ATM.** Open M-Th 8am-2pm, F 8am-1:30pm, Sa-Su 9am-1pm in high season. Other **ATMs** on Lomvardou and around Pl. Solomou.

Police: (☎26950 22 200 or 26950 24 480; emergency ☎100), at the intersection of Lomvardou and Fra. Tzoulati, roughly equidistant from Pl. Solomou and Ag. Dionysios on the waterfront. Open 24hr.

Tourist Police: (☎26950 27 367 or 26950 24 483), in the same building as the regular police. Open daily (mornings only).

Hospital: (☎26950 42 514 or 26950 42 515), uphill and less than 1km inland from the city center. Walk down Lomvardou to Ag. Eleftheriou. Follow this road inland to Kokkini, where the road heads right and becomes Ag. Spiridona. Follow the many signs from the waterfront. Open 24hr.

OTE: Dimokratias 2 (☎26950 59 301), between the 2 plateias. Open M-Th 7:30am-1pm, F 7:30am-12:30pm.

Internet Access: Top's Cafe, Filita 38. €6 per hr.

Post Office: (☎26950 42 418), on Tertseti, the 4th street inland parallel to the waterfront, near Xenou. **Exchanges currency.** Open M-F 7:30am-8pm. **Postal code:** 29100.

ACCOMMODATIONS

Rooms in Zakynthos Town tend to be expensive and scarce in July and August. Large waterfront hotels charge around €80 for a double in high season; slightly less luxurious and expensive rooms can be found in the smaller hotels just outside of town on the way to Tsilivi. Call ahead. For the best deals, look for the signs advertising domatia and bargain with the owners.

Rooms for Rent, Katrami 6 (☎26950 28 354), behind Ag. Dionysios. This small red and white domatia has clean rooms with ceiling fans, private baths, and balconies overlooking the church. Singles and doubles €17-26. ❷

Athina Marouda Rooms for Rent (☎26950 45 194), on Tzoulati and Koltoi, 3 blocks inland from the tourist police, on the left side of the street. Good prices on rooms with common bath, so they go quickly. Singles €15; doubles €35 in high season. ❷

Hotel Aegli, on Lomvardou, 2 blocks south from Pl. Solomou with the water on your left. Immaculate, if a bit pricey, rooms offer TVs, balconies, and snazzy full baths. Singles €30; doubles €45. ❸

Hotel Diana (☎26950 28 547; fax 26950 45 047), in Pl. Ag. Markou. Beautiful, spacious rooms with dark wood furniture and pastel paint jobs. A/C, TVs, private baths, and balconies. Breakfast included. Singles €40-50; doubles €52-80. ❹

FOOD

Dining in Zakynthos is a pleasure. Restaurants line the waterfront and Pl. Ag. Markou; every other establishment on Alexandrou Roma is either a cafe or a candy shop. Zakynthian specialities include *melissaki* (a nougat-almond candy) and veal in tomato sauce. Fast food is everywhere (gyros €1.20). The **Coop Supermarket,** near the police station, caters to those who cater to themselves. (Open M-F 8am-9pm, Sa 8am-6pm.)

House of Latas (Το Σπιτι του Λατα) (☎26950 41 585), 2km above the city (follow the signs to Bohalis), near the Venetian castle. Spectacular views of Zakynthos, live local music every evening. Try the grilled swordfish (€9) or veal with pasta (€8). Salads €3-6; entrees €5.50 and up. Open daily 6pm-1am. ❷

Molos Restaurant, on the waterfront. A popular joint with extremely affable owners and staff. The only restaurant in town with meat from its own farm. Try the local favorite: spicy stuffed chicken with cheese and liver (€7.40). Pizza €5.60-8.80; omelettes €2.70-3.90; English breakfast €4.50. ❷

The Garden (☎26950 48 583), next to Ag. Dionysios, in a quiet, spacious plateia removed from the hectic waterfront. Grilled octopus €8.60; moussaka €4.30. ❷

SIGHTS AND HIKES

The **Church of Agios Dionysios** is named in honor of the island's patron saint and displays a silver chest that holds the saint's relics. (Open 7am-10pm. Dress modestly.) Next door is the church museum, with murals, vestments, and beautiful engraved Bibles on display. (Open daily 9am-9pm. €1.) In Pl. Solomou, the **Byzantine Museum** houses two floors of icons from the Ionian School, a distinctive local hybrid of Byzantine and Renaissance art styles, along with elaborately carved iconostases, chalices, and miscellaneous church items. Most were rescued by devout locals who risked their lives to pluck them from the dusty rubble of area churches after the 1953 earthquake; poignant photos document the effects of the disaster. (☎26950 42 714. Open Tu-Su 8am-2:30pm. €3, students free.)

If you enjoy a hearty walk (or a nice drive), head 2km above town to the **Venetian Castle,** where 19th-century poet Dionysios Solomos wrote the poem that became the Greek National Anthem. Take Tertseti, later called N. Koluva, to the edge of town, or head inland from Pl. Ag. Markou and follow the signs uphill to Bohalis. Turn left after 1km, following the signs to the Castro. You'll find panoramas of the island and a lovely view of Zakynthos Town, particularly at night. (Open Tu-Su 8am-2:30pm.) Horse and buggy rides are available in town (€5). Look for the carriages along the waterfront near Pl. Solomou.

DAYTRIPS FROM ZAKYNTHOS TOWN

It's possible to see all of Zakynthos, including the otherwise-inaccessible **western cliffs,** by boat. Shop around for a cruise on Lomvardou. Most tours leave in the morning, usually around 9am, return around 5:30 or 6pm, and prefer a reservation the night before. Don't buy from hawkers around gift shops—they'll charge a commission (€5-9) on top of the agency's fee (usually starting around €15, although competition sometimes cuts prices). Cruises go to many of the island's best sights, including the **blue caves,** natural caves on the northeast shore past Skinari that glow blue; the **Smuggler's Wreck,** a large boat skeleton; and **Turtle Island,** so named due to its proximity to loggerhead turtle nesting grounds and the island's resemblance to a turtle. Inquire at the tourist police or agencies. To explore with far less hassle, get a **moped**—there's a rental agency at each beach (€8-15). The island is developing rapidly, so many new roads don't appear on maps. Get several road maps (€1-5) and ask directions.

4km south of Zakynthos town is the crowded sandy beach town of **Argasi.** Buses run to the village daily (20min., 8 per day 6:45am-6pm, €0.75; service reduced on weekends), but it's an easy 20-30min. walk along the main road out of town with the water on your left. Though by no means quiet or secluded, Argasi offers many of the same conveniences of Zakynthos Town without the noise. Hotels and domatia line the roads off the main street. Mopeds, car rental, and plenty of restaurants are just a few of the town's amenities. Check out the Thai, Indian, or Chinese restaurants in town. **Courser ❷,** off the main road to the right in the middle of town, is the local favorite for non-Greek cuisine. Chef Ruan Xiao serves an enormous variety of appetizers and entrees, including sesame chicken (€5.60) and beef with broccoli (€8). Fixed menus for 2-4 people available. (☎26950 42 311. Open daily 6-11:30pm; take-out until midnight.) **Internet access** is offered at **The Mouse House,** on the main road from Zakynthos Town. (☎26950 49 510. €7 per hr., €2 minimum. Open daily 9am-midnight.)

Tsilivi beach, 6km up the waterfront road with the water on your right, is nearly as close as Argasi, but walking the hilly, narrow, winding road is inadvisable. Buses run there every day (30min., 9per day, €0.75). Nearby **Planos** has plenty of domatia. **Zante Camping,** 3km past Planos, is Zakynthos's only beach campsite. It has a cafeteria and mini-market. (☎26950 61 710. €4.50 per person; €3 per car; €3.50 per small tent; €4 per large tent. Electricity €3.) For those who need to escape the crowds, nearly unscathed beaches carpet the peninsula that stretches out 16km from Zakynthos Town to **Vasilikos,** especially near **Porto Roma** and **Porto Zoro.** These beaches are pleasantly wide and sandy, with shallow, warm water full of splashing holiday-makers. Some on the western coast of the peninsula are protected areas that must be vacated in the evenings to accommodate the sea turtles that come ashore to nest. "Rooms to let" signs dot the road to Vasilikos, especially near **Agios Nikolaos Beach. Buses** leave Zakynthos Town for **Vasiliko** (M-F 6:45, 10:30am, 2:30pm; €1.05). Romantic restaurants hide among the slick tourist joints in **Alykes,** 16km from Zakynthos Town. Fringed with soft, clean sand beaches, it's nicer and less crowded than its southern counterparts. **Buses** run from Zakynthos Town to Alykes (4 per day, €1.05).

Tourists to Zakynthos should note that they share the island's beaches with a resident population of **endangered sea turtles.** Careless beachgoers can destroy hundreds of the turtles' eggs just by walking. Zakynthos is gradually making efforts to protect the turtles and their nests, including encouraging waterfront properties to cover their lights, as freshly hatched baby turtles mistake the light for reflections off the ocean and follow the twinkling inland, instead of toward the sea. Ask at tour companies about which beaches are popular spots; Gerakas, Kalamaki and Laganas all have turtle populations. **Please respect their homes!**

SKINARI Σκιναρι

At the extreme northern tip of Zakynthos, a breathtaking drive away from the bustle of busier beach towns, is tiny **Skinari,** locally known as **Agios Nikolaos.** Ferries to **Pesada** on Kephalonia depart from here. Bus service is sporadic, so incoming ferry passengers often need to arrange their own transportation to Zakynthos Town. Taxis to Zakynthos Town will cost €30-35, and Skinari has no rental agencies. All the same, if you can manage to get in and out of town without going bankrupt, Skinari is a lovely town and wonderful place to unwind for a day or to use as a peaceful base for daytrips. On the water about 200m back towards Zakynthos Town, **La Grotta** ❷ has lovely rooms with private baths and waterfront balconies. (☎26950 31 224. Singles €20; doubles €35-40.) Farther down the street away from the dock, **La Storia Restaurant** ❷ serves divine fare with the water at your feet; the seafood pasta (€7.50) is particularly good. (☎26950 31 635. Salads €3 and up; seafood entrees €6 and up; beer €2.50-3.) During the day, you can buy tickets on the waterfront for a fishing boat tour of the **blue caves** (1hr., €5), accessible only by water; for twice the price and time you can get a tour of the blue caves and the "Smuggler's Wreck" shipwreck. These tours are smaller and shorter than those that from Zakynthos Town. You can also rent canoes and boats on Skinari Beach.

SARONIC GULF ISLANDS

Τα Νησια του Σαρωνικου

When 5 million Athenians flee the city each summer in search of beaches and *pareia* (Greek for something like "food, folks, and fun"), they don't flee far. Many head to the Saronic Gulf Islands. This means two things: first, you've chosen a destination approved by discriminating Greeks; second, you're not the only one. Keep in mind that, while good times are to be had *without* 50 of your closest package tourist friends, it may require a bit of creativity to shake them, and that the islands' popularity makes them a bit of a stretch on a budget traveler's wallet. Despite their geographic proximity, each of the Gulf islands retains a distinct character: relaxed Spetses attracts Greek hipsters on summer weekends, artsy Hydra boasts pollutant-free streets, Poros holds hands with the mainland to the west, and Aegina retains shades of suburbia while catering to swarms of beach-hungry vacationers.

HIGHLIGHTS OF THE SARONIC GULF ISLANDS

BEHOLD the 360-degree view of Aegina's coastline from the 5th-century BC Temple of Aphaia (p. 315).

PUCKER UP as you pass thousands of lemon trees on your way to a picnic in the Devil's Gorge (p. 320), near Poros.

DON'T LOOK BOTH WAYS while crossing the street on vehicle-free Hydra (p. 321), but watch out for donkeys and bicycles as you wander through the art fairs.

REFRESH YOURSELF with a slice of watermelon and a dip in the sea on Spetses's stunningly colorful Xylocheriza beach (p. 325).

AEGINA Αιγινα

Bright, white-washed Aegina is an easy daytrip for city-weary Athenians, and summer weekends find the island saddled with the bustle of Greece's capital. Fortunately, Agia Marina, on the far side of the island from Aegina town, absorbs much of the beach- and booze-seeking multitude with the ease of a practiced resort town. Quieter locales play host to the island's true crown jewels. A pleasant drive through olive terraced mountains leads to the massive Church of Agios Nektarios. The clean beaches of Marathonas, a quiet hamlet an hour's walk from Aegina Town, are ideal for a late afternoon swim. The well preserved remains of the Temple of Aphaia still stand high on the west coast, a fascinating reminder of the island's ancient glory.

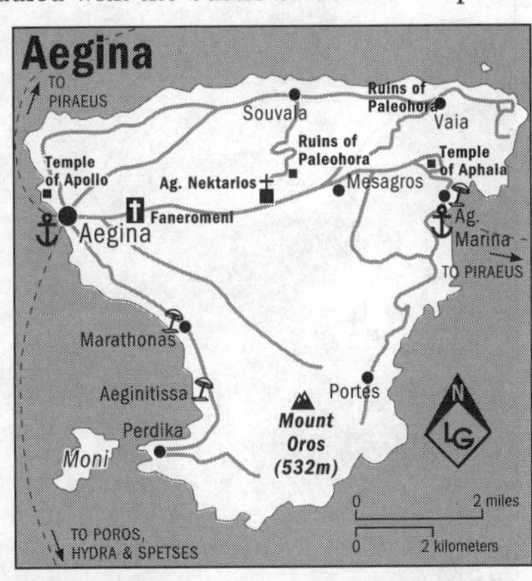

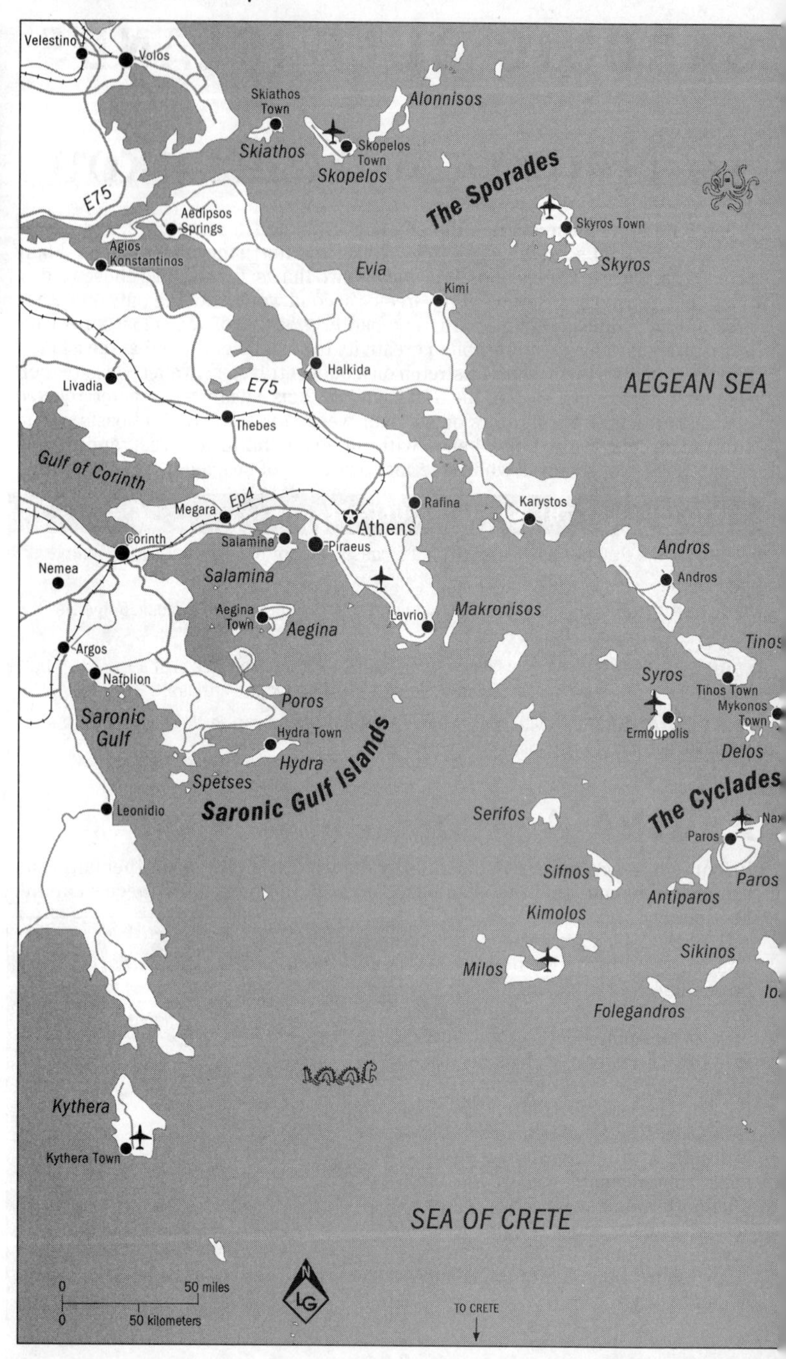
Velestino
Volos
Skiathos Town
Alonnisos
Skopelos Town
Skiathos
Skopelos
The Sporades
E75
Aedipsos Springs
Agios Konstantinos
Skyros Town
Skyros
Evia
Kimi
Halkida
AEGEAN SEA
Livadia
E75
Thebes
Gulf of Corinth
Megara
Ep4
Rafina
Karystos
Athens
Salamina
Piraeus
Corinth
Andros
Andros
Nemea
Salamina
Makronisos
Aegina Town
Aegina
Lavrio
Argos
Nafplion
Syros
Tinos Town
Poros
Mykonos Town
Saronic Gulf
Hydra Town
Ermoupolis
Delos
Hydra
Spetses
Saronic Gulf Islands
The Cyclades
Leonidio
Serifos
Paros
Sifnos
Paros
Antiparos
Kimolos
Sikinos
Milos
Folegandros
Kythera
Kythera Town
SEA OF CRETE
0
50 miles
0
50 kilometers
TO CRETE

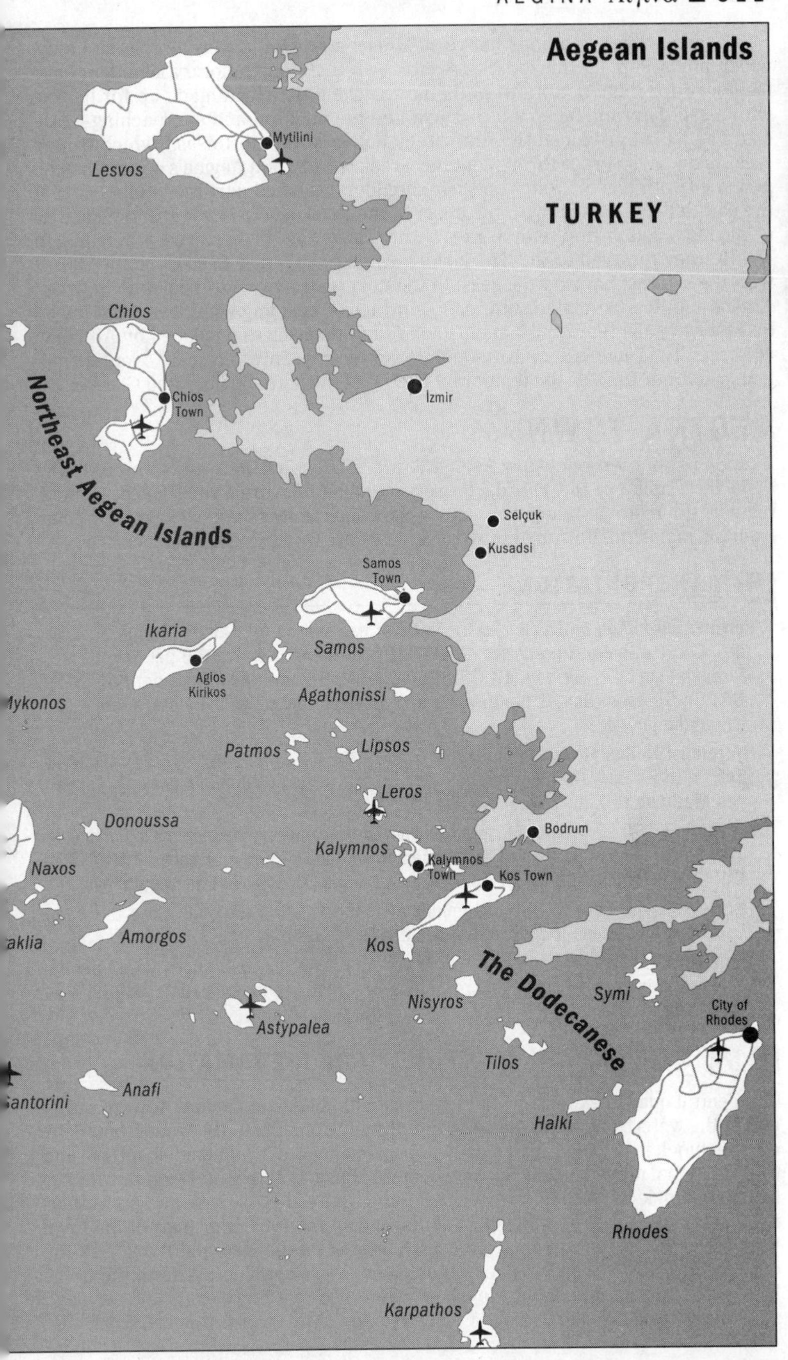

Aegean Islands
TURKEY
Mytilini
Lesvos
Chios
Chios Town
Izmir
Northeast Aegean Islands
Selçuk
Kusadsi
Samos Town
Samos
Ikaria
Agios Kirikos
Agathonissi
Patmos
Lipsos
Leros
Donoussa
Kalymnos
Kalymnos Town
Bodrum
Kos Town
Naxos
Amorgos
Kos
The Dodecanese
Symi
Nisyros
City of Rhodes
Astypalea
Tilos
Anafi
Halki
Rhodes
Karpathos

In ancient times, relations between Athens and Aegina were not so chummy, which might explain the zoo-like resort town that contemporary islanders have fashioned for their visitors from the north. The little island made up for its size with a self-determining spunk that irritated the mighty—and encroaching—Athens. The island produced the first Greek coins (silver "tortoises," which gained great financial leverage throughout the Greek world), and Aegina's sprinters, who practiced with jugs of water on their shoulders, zoomed past the competition at the pan-Hellenic games. With the onset of the Persian War in 491 BC, the citizens of Aegina sided at first with Xerxes's army, angering the besieged Athenians. In 480 BC they returned to the Greek side, winning the praise of the Delphic Oracle with the swiftest navy on the seas. In the next warring period, this time between Athens and Sparta, Aegina suffered misfortune after siding with Sparta. Trounced by Athens in 459 BC, the islanders soon found themselves displaced by Athenian colonists. The island sank into geopolitical obscurity, only to emerge over two millennia later, in 1827, as the temporary capital of the partially liberated Greece.

AEGINA TOWN

As soon as your ferry docks in Aegina Town, you'll know that you've entered "The Pistachio Capital of the World." Preserved, jellied, flavored, red, flaked, shelled, regular—there are as many ways to eat pistachios as there are package tour boats from the mainland. Fortunately, the tasty nuts are the stronger influence.

TRANSPORTATION

Ferries: Saronikos Lines (☎22970 25 951) has service to: **Agistri** (20min., 2-3 per day, €1.30); **Hydra** (2hr., 2 per day, €7.20); **Methana** (45min., 3-5 per day, €3.10); **Piraeus** (1hr., 11 per day, €4.90); **Poros** (1hr.; 3-5 per day M-F, 6 per day Sa-Su; €4.20); **Spetses** (3hr., 1 per day, €9.90). Buy your tickets at the kiosk at the inland end of the ferry dock.

Hydrofoils: Hellas Flying Dolphins has a ticket stand on the quay (☎22970 27 462). Service to **Piraeus** (35min., 12 per day, €6.70), **Poros** (40min., 1 per day, €8.40), and **Methana** (20 min., 1 per day €6.30).

Buses: (☎22970 22 787), in Ethnegarcias Park, at the corner of the waterfront left of the ferry quay. Buses run to **Agia Marina** and the **Temple of Aphaia** (30min., every hr. 6:30am-8pm, €1.50), and **Perdika** (20min., 5-6 per day 6:30am-8pm, €0.80-1.50) via **Marathonas.**

Taxis: (☎22970 22 635). Station immediately to the left of the quay along the waterfront; look for the line of grey, diesel-pumped Mercedes and Audis.

Mopeds: Moped rental places are a dime a dozen in Aegina, with prices €7-20 per day depending on bells, whistles, and paint jobs. Try **Trust,** Leonardou Lada 1 (☎22970 27 010), 1 block inland from the waterfront, on the second floor.

ORIENTATION AND PRACTICAL INFORMATION

The central quay is expensive, but tavernas and hotels get cheaper toward either end of the waterfront street, **Republic Ave.** Running parallel to the waterfront, **P. Irioti** (one block in) is lined with small shops, local markets, laid-back tavernas, and the occasional moped rental. **Sp. Rodi** becomes **Aphaias** at the intersection with **Aiakou.** Two blocks in, Aiakou runs between the National Bank and the port authority. It's home to more upscale shops, bars, and an Internet cafe. **Maps** of the town are posted on the waterfront across the street from the National Bank. Ask the congenial staff at **Pipinis Travel,** one block inland on Kanari across from the ticket kiosks, for information about the island. They also rent bicycles (€4.50 per day), mopeds (€8 and up) and cars for €35 and up. (☎22970 25 664. Open all day.)

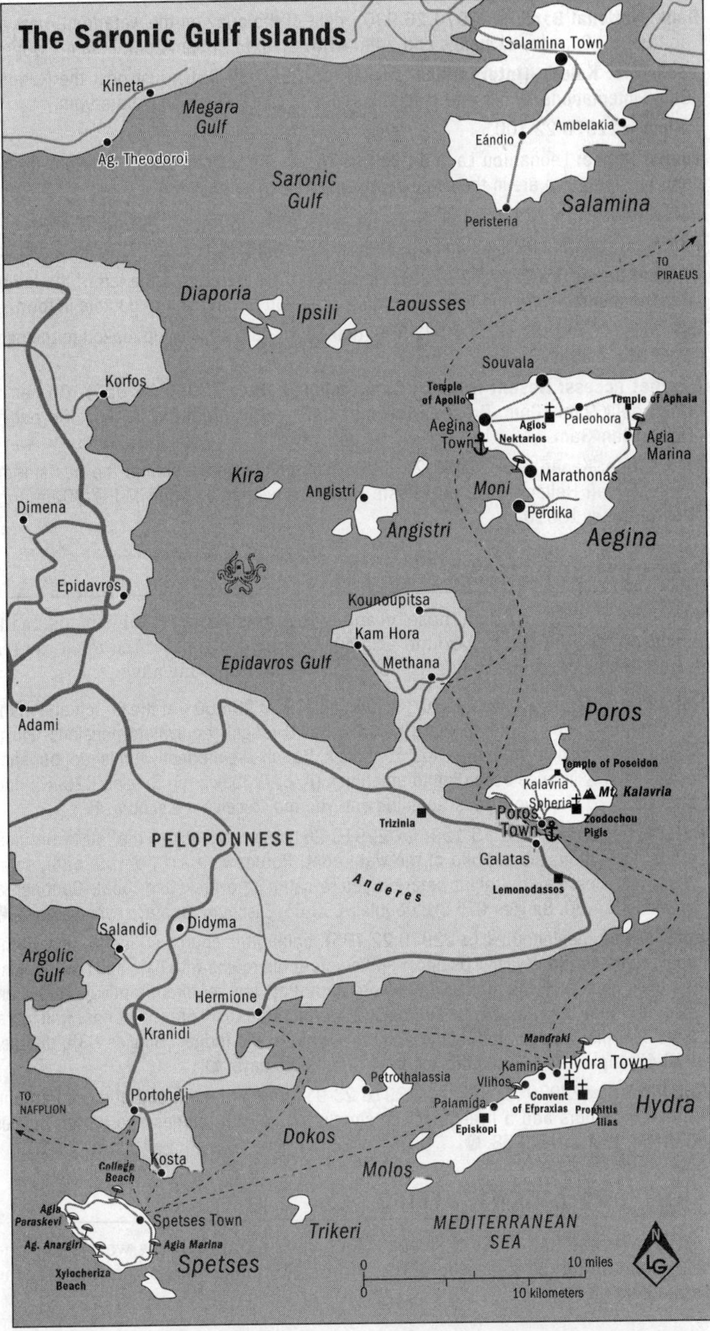
The Saronic Gulf Islands
Salamina Town
Kineta
Megara Gulf
Ambelakia
Eándio
Ag. Theodoroi
Saronic Gulf
Salamina
Peristeria
TO PIRAEUS
Diaporia
Ipsili
Laousses
Souvala
Temple of Apollo
Temple of Aphaia
Korfos
Aegina Town
Agios Nektarios
Paleohora
Agia Marina
Marathonas
Kira
Angistri
Moni
Dimena
Perdika
Angistri
Aegina
Epidavros
Kounoupitsa
Kam Hora
Epidavros Gulf
Methana
Adami
Poros
Temple of Poseidon
Kalavria
Mt. Kalavria
Spheria
Trizinia
Poros Town
Zoodochou Pigis
PELOPONNESE
Galatas
Anderes
Lemonodassos
Salandio
Didyma
Argolic Gulf
Hermione
Kranidi
Mandraki
Hydra Town
Kamina
Petrothalassia
Vlihos
Convent of Efpraxias
TO NAFPLION
Portoheli
Palamida
Prophitis Ilias
Hydra
Episkopi
Dokos
Kosta
College Beach
Molos
Agia Paraskevi
Spetses Town
Trikeri
MEDITERRANEAN SEA
Ag. Anargiri
Agia Marina
Spetses
10 miles
10 kilometers
Xylocheriza Beach
N
LG

Bank: National Bank (☎22970 26 930), right of the quay on the waterfront, past the port police. Currency exchange and 24hr. **ATM.** Open M-Th 8am-2pm, F 8am-1:30pm.

Bookstore: Kalezis (International Press) (☎22970 25 956), just past the National Bank. International books and magazines, phone cards. Open daily 9am-9pm.

Police: ☎22970 22 100.

Tourist Police: Leonardou Lada 11 (☎22970 27 777). Open daily 8am-8pm. Tourist and regular police are in the same courtyard.

Port Authority: (☎22970 22 328), on the waterfront. Ferry schedules. Open 24hr.

Pharmacy: Corner of Aiakou and Sp. Rodi (☎22970 23 714). Open 7:30am-midnight.

Medical Center: (☎22970 22 222), 2km along the waterfront to the left of the ferries. Call the tourist police and they will arrange transport or refer you to doctors in town.

OTE: Paleas Choras 6 (☎22970 22 399; dial 161 for assistance) up Aiakou to the right. Open M-F 7:30am-3pm.

Internet access: Nesant Internet Cafe, Aphaias 13 (☎22970 24 053). €6 per hr. Open daily 9am-10pm. **Prestige Internet Cafe,** at Sp. Rodi and Aiakou. €6 per hr. Open 10am-3am.

Post Office: Kanari 6 (☎22970 22 398), Pl. Ethnegersias 1 behind the bus station. Express Mail Hellenic Post and Poste Restante available. Open M-F 7:30am-2pm. **Postal Code:** 18010.

ACCOMMODATIONS

Rooms here are cheaper than those on any of the other Saronic Gulf islands. In the high season, doubles go for around €25-40. *Domatia* owners often meet the ferries, but always bargain and discuss location before following anyone.

Hotel Plaza, Kazatzaki 4 (☎22970 28 404; fax 22970 25 600), at the far left end of the waterfront. Friendly owner Michalis Kororos runs 3 roughly equivalent pensions–Plaza, Ulrica and Christina–from the Plaza front desk. Rooms are modestly furnished, but spotless, and vary in price according to amenities (A/C, TV, balcony). Singles €20-40; doubles €23-45. Show your *Let's Go* guide and you may receive a discount. ❷

Hotel Artemis (☎22970 25 195; fax 22970 28 779), set back to the left of the post office, away from the hubbub of the waterfront. Rooms with A/C, private bath; some with balconies. Pay the night before if you're catching a pre-10am boat. Continental breakfast €4.50. Singles €25-30; doubles €30-35. Discount for stays over 10 days. ❷

Hotel Pavlou, Aeginitou 21 (☎22970 22 795), behind the church on the far right of the quay. Come for the stylish 70s decor and comfortable rooms with balconies overlooking the town church. Some rooms with private bath. Payment required in advance. Owners also run the **Athina,** quietly tucked back 200m into the town on Telemonos, which features charmingly decorated rooms with private baths and fridges. Singles €35; doubles €40-47; triples €50. Discounts for stays of multiple days. ❸

Hotel Avra, (☎22970 22 303; fax 22970 23 917) at the far left end of the waterfront. Checkered floors add a lively touch to simple rooms with phones and baths. Singles €30-44; doubles €40-58. ❸

FOOD AND NIGHTLIFE

No-frills tavernas line P. Irioti street, which runs parallel to the waterfront one block inland along the right side of the harbor. For make-your-own meals, try the **supermarkets** on P. Irioti.

FRAPPÉ 101 You've seen them at every cafe, ubiquitous as small cellular phones and motor scooters—now learn to order them like a pro. *Frappés* are made-to-order blended coffee drinks. Add sugar—tell your server that you want it sweet (γλυκο)—milk (γαλα), or ice cream (παψω), and a shot of Bailey's to give it a kick.

To Patitiri (☎22970 51 520), a short walk up Aikaou, in an alley to the left. Serves marvelous, fresh Greek meals in a bougainvillea-filled courtyard. Entrees €4.20-8.20. ❷

Yacht Club/Panagakis Crêperie, on the waterfront. If you can't eat another *souvlaki,* walk upstairs to the Panagakis Cafe Bar/Crêperie. Fillings range from ice cream and strawberries to cold cuts and mayo. Crepes €3.50-8.20, cocktails €6.80. ❷

Leo Confections, Aphaias 48, just down from the Internet cafe. Mouthwatering desserts and pistachio ice cream (€1 per scoop). Open daily 8am-11pm. ❶

Zachastiki Bakery, at the intersection of Aphaias and Telemonos, will lure you in with the scent of fresh bread (€0.50) and large croissants (€0.75). A multitude of cookies go for €5.50 per kg. ❶

For a low-key evening, watch American movies out-of-doors at **Anesis,** to the right off Aiakou, 100m from the waterfront. (☎22970 24 757. Shows at 9 and 11pm; €6). Get your groove on at Aegina's dance club, **Prime,** a 10min. walk along the water to the right. (☎22970 24 570. Beer €4-5; cocktails €6-7. Cover €6, includes one drink. Open daily 10:30pm-late.) The bar **Inn on the Beach,** just before Prime, packs a serious crowd on summer weekends. (☎22970 26 440. Cover €3, includes a beer.)

SIGHTS

Aegina Town's archaeological fame teeters on the last half-column of the **Temple of Apollo.** The 8m-tall Doric column dates to 460 BC and stands on Kolonna hill, ancient Aegina's acropolis. Archaeology enthusiasts will delight in seeing the ongoing excavation of the site, now known to have been an important settlement since the Early Bronze Age (3000 BC). Now Byzantine-era cisterns and the foundations of prehistoric houses keep mute vigil with the monolithic column. The **archaeological museum** at the site features a magnificent early classical sphinx (460 BC), artifacts from the Temple of Aphaia, a statue of Hercules from the Temple of Apollo, and some neolithic pottery. (☎22970 22 248. Museum and site open Tu-Su 8:30am-3pm. €1.50.)

The underground church of **Faneromeni,** a 15min. walk inland just south of the town, houses a rare icon of the Virgin Mary. Locals say that the night before construction was to begin on a site above Faneromeni, the architect had a vision in which he was instructed to dig instead of build. Doing just that, he discovered the church and unearthed the icon.

DAYTRIPS FROM AEGINA TOWN

TEMPLE OF APHAIA. The 5th-century BC remains of the Temple of Aphaia rest 2km uphill from Agia Marina. Legend holds that Aphaia, daughter of Zeus and Karme, fled to Aegina from the amorous overtures of King Minos. There she became invisible (*aphaia*). Her temple, built on the foundation of a 6th-century BC temple, boasts a spectacular set of standing double-tiered columns. At night, peacocks roam the hills by the temple. (*A small museum opens for 15min. at 9, 11am, noon, and 1pm. The Agia Marina bus from Aegina Town stops in front. Open M-F 8:15am-7pm.)*

AGIOS NEKTARIOS. The bronze and white church of Agios Nektarios is one of the largest places of worship in the Balkans. It's part of a complex that includes Nektarios's personal residence, bed, and books. The turn-off just after Agios Nektarios leads up to **Paleohora** (about 1km), the "town of 300 churches," where locals once took refuge from pirate invasions. It's worth making the short climb to explore the 15 churches that remain and take in the spectacular view from the top of the hill. *(Take the bus from Aegina Town (15min.) and ask to be let off at Agios Nektarios. Dress appropriately: long pants for men, long skirts for women, no bare shoulders.)*

MARATHONAS. Tranquil beaches reverberate with the murmur of the Aegean in this unassuming town south of Aegina. Approaching the town on the main road, veer right onto the unpaved road after the first stand of umbrellas for the peaceful beachfront, which is lined with small tavernas and pebble beaches. **Cafe Ostria ❶** serves specialty *melizano* (eggplant) salads and calamari; juicy slices of watermelon (€1.50) accompany the perfect Aegean sunsets nicely. (☎22970 26 738. Entrees €4-6.) Family-owned **O Tassos ❶** (☎22970 24 040), accessible from the main road just before the church, is renowned for its homemade pastries, pita creations, and fresh vegetables from the family farm. (☎22970 24 040. Entrees €3-6.). Walk the 7km road from Aegina Town to see the island's cherished coastline.

AGIA MARINA. If you find yourself inexplicably yearning to see hordes of sunburned tourists, overpriced beach toys and tacky towels, then by all means swing by Agia Marina. The summer resort town is at the end of a lovely 30-minute bus trip through the island's interior, and offers some quality nightlife along with the exceedingly crowded beaches. The town is built around a main avenue, called **Aphaias,** parallel to the sea. It's lined with bars, tourist shops, and moped rentals. A multitude of hotels surround the port. Most are open only in the summer.

Hotel Myrmidon ❷, off Aphaias, sports a courtyard with a swimming pool and a lovely footbridge. The immaculate rooms have A/C, private baths, and fridges, and *Let's Go* users enjoy a 20% discount. (☎22970 32 691; fax 22970 32 558. Singles €20; doubles €35; triples €45.) **Karras Travel,** next to the bus stop, offers **currency exchange** and sells **bus** tickets. (☎22970 32 557. Open daily 9am-11pm.) Pricey waters-edge restaurants crammed with tourists mingle with cheaper gyro and fast food shops along Aphaias. A **supermarket** on Aphaias offers an alternative to eating out. You can rent paddle boats at the beach (€8 per hr.), but consider saving your money for discos like **Zorbas.** To find Zorbas, take a right on Praxitelous two blocks past the bus stop, then follow the signs (opens daily at 11pm). Summer club **Manos** lies just out of town with the water on your left.

POROS Πορος

Poros is actually two islands separated by a shallow channel: Sphaeria hugs the Peloponnesian mainland and is covered by the sprawl of tourist-heavy Poros Town, while Kalavria preserves stretches of woods and dark-watered beaches. The name Poros ("passage") refers to the channel separating it from the Peloponnese. In the 6th century BC, the seven-city Kalavrian League met in Poros to ward off hostile naval powers and ordered the building of the Temple of Poseidon. Three centuries later, the great orator Demosthenes, who improved his diction by speaking with marbles in his mouth, committed suicide beside its columns. Poros was sparsely populated until Greeks arrived from Turkey in the 1920s.

POROS TOWN

Wrapped around Sphaeria island, Poros Town centers on the waterfront that marks its perimeter. Tourist-oriented, it overflows with beach shops and tavernas that sprawl outward from the ferry dock. Quieter locations are found farther from the dock and up the hill, among the natural beauty of Kalavria.

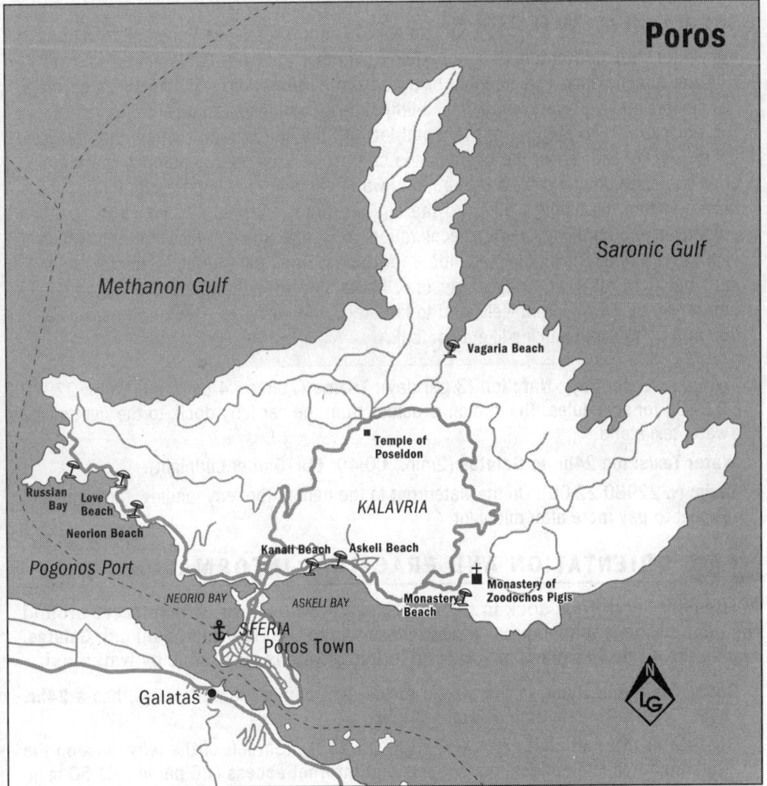

TRANSPORTATION

Ferries: Askeli Travel Agency (☎22980 24 900, 22980 24 767 or 22980 24 566), across from the hydrofoil dock, sells ferry tickets and posts schedules. 3 to 5 ferries per day to **Aegina** (1hr., €4.20) and **Piraeus** (2½hr., €7) via **Methana** (30min., €2.50). Also service to **Hydra** (1hr., 2 per day, €3.40) and **Spetses** (2½hr., 1 per day, €5.40).

Flying Dolphins: Askeli Travel sells tickets. Hydrofoils dock at the main landing in the center of town. To: **Hydra** (30min., 6-7 per day, €6); **Hermione** (1 hr., 3-5 per day, €9.10); **Piraeus** (1¼hr., 8 per day, €13.80); **Portoheli** (1½hr., 1-2 per day, €11.50); **Spetses** (1hr., 2-3 per day, €10.80).

Car Ferries: left of the main ferry docks, a few hundred meters down the waterfront. Ferries to **Poros-Galatas** (every 30min. 7am-11pm, €3.70 per car).

Port Authority: (☎22980 22 274). Marked entrance one street in from the harbor by Seven Brothers Restaurant. Up the stairs and down a long, dreary hallway. Open 24hr.

Moped Rental: Kosta's Bike Rental (☎22980 23 565), left of the waterfront past Ciné Diana. Mopeds from €7 per day (€12 for 90cc). Bikes €2.50. Open daily 9am-9pm.

Buses: Leave hourly from the main plateia, 8am until midnight. The green bus goes to the **Zoodochos Pigis** (€0.70) via **Askeli Beach.** The white bus goes to **Russian Bay** (€0.70) via **Neorion.** Buses leave **Galatas** for: **Epidavros** (3 per day); **Methana**

HELL ON WHEELS No Greek island experience is complete without the glorious (mis)adventure of a moped ride. Whether you fly past "do not enter signs" with the nonchalance of a national or putt down hillsides with white knuckles on the handlebars and a prayer on your lips, a little time on a moped can be a breezy release. But don't expect to pull out of the rental lot with the charismatic screech that island youth execute with ease; the beginning is sure to be a bit jerky. Approach the rental shop with the confidence of a veteran, and wait until later to ask the owner for a quick lesson. When choosing a bike, go the simple route–automatic, light and easy to maneuver, good braking, smooth acceleration (look for a small motor without too much kick), and a rough finish that will hide a few blows. Don't plan on being offered a helmet, but fight tooth and nail to get one. Make sure everything is explained to you before you pull away, from kickstand to kickstart. And lastly, go easy on the acceleration and try to avoid looking like a goofball.

(45min., 5 per day); **Nafplion** (3 per day); **Trizina** (20min., 4 per day). Call ☎22980 22 480 for schedules. The station is across from the car ferry dock, to the right of the water taxi stand.

Water Taxis: run 24hr. to **Galatas** (2min., €0.40; €0.70 after midnight).

Taxis: (☎22980 22 00). On the waterfront to the right of the ferry landing, facing inland. Expect to pay more after midnight.

ORIENTATION AND PRACTICAL INFORMATION

Ferries and hydrofoils dock in the center of the waterfront, which traces around the edge of the small island; the main plateia is to the right facing inland. **Galatas,** across the strait, has cheaper food and lodgings, and is accessible by water taxi.

Bank: The **Alpha Bank,** in the plateia to the right before the port police, has a **24hr. ATM.** Open M-Th 8am-2pm, F 8am-1:30pm.

Bookstore: International Press (☎22980 25 205), 25m left of the ferry dock on the waterfront has international newspapers and **Internet access** (€6 per hr., €1.50 minimum). Open daily 8am-midnight. The quiet, unassuming **Skipper & Trout International Bookshop** (☎22980 26 245), in the arcade behind Diana Cinema to the left of the main landing, is a favorite haunt of the island's expats. Buys, sells, and exchanges new and used books in many languages. Also has telephone, fax, and translation services, greeting cards, stationery, and CDs. Open M-Sa 9:45am-1:45pm.

Laundromat: Suzi's Launderette Service, left of the ferry dock in an alley just past International Press. Wash and dry €10; ironing extra. Drop-off only. 2hr. service. Open July-Aug. M-Sa 9am-2pm, 5-9pm; Sept.-June M-Sa 9am-2pm.

Police: (☎22980 22 256). From the post office in the main plateia turn right and head up the stairs to the left of Igloo Ice Cream. Turn right at the church and continue downhill past Platanos Taverna. **Tourist Police** (☎22980 22 462) are in the same building.

Pharmacy: (☎22980 25 523). Across from the ferry dock. Open daily 8:30am-2pm, 5-10pm.

Telephone: OTE (☎22980 22 199 or 22980 22 399), on the waterfront left of the main landing. Telecards and telegrams. Open M-F 7:30am-3pm.

Internet Access: International Press, left of ferry dock. €6 per hr., €1.50 minimum. **Webworld Internet Cafe,** above Coconuts Bar, in the plateia to the right of the ferry dock. €6 per hr., €1.50 minimum. Open daily 10:30am-3pm, 6:30-11pm.

Clinic: Galatas has a 24hr. clinic (☎22980 22 222), and emergencies including minor surgery can be handled at the **Naval School;** contact the tourist police.

Post Office: (☎22980 22 275; fax 22980 23 451), in the 1st plateia to the right along the water. Poste Restante (specify Poros Trinzinias). Open M-F 7:30am-2pm. **Postal code:** 18020.

ACCOMMODATIONS AND CAMPING

The best deals in Poros Town are the **domatia** advertised in almost every window; expect to pay €20-30. There's no pressing reason to stay in Poros Town, as **Galatas,** 2min. across the strait by boat (every 10-15min., 24hr., €0.40), has similar, less expensive hotel rooms.

Manos Pension (☎/fax 22980 22 000 or 697 708 0791), in Galatas. Walk left when you disembark from the small boat from Poros Town, just past the playing field. Friendly Manos and Beatrix can rent you motorbikes, tell you all about the region, and invite you to their farm for traditional Greek food and dancing. Cozy rooms will make you feel right at home. Singles €20-22; doubles €24-26; triples €30-32. ❷

Saronis Hotel (☎22980 22 356; fax 22980 25 642), across from the water taxi landing in Galatas. Simple rooms have A/C, TV, and private baths. Doubles €30. ❸

Hotel Seven Brothers (☎22980 23 412; fax 22980 23 413), to the right of the ferry dock and inland past the Alpha Bank. One of the better deals for a port side hotel. Rooms equipped with private baths, TVs, and A/C. Singles €30-40; doubles €40-50; triples €50-60. ❸

Camping Kyragelo (☎22980 24 520 or 22980 24 521), outside Galatas. Veer left onto the road running inland across from where the water taxis land and follow it 500m out of town. €3.50-4 per person; €2-3 per car or tent. ❶

FOOD

Similar restaurants line the harbor, and "charming" waiters try to convince tourists to sit down; make your choice based on the view. Several grocery stores and produce markets cluster along the waterfront to the right of the ferry dock. Cafes are open all day; more hard-core establishments open at 10:30pm.

Galatea (☎22980 23 728), in Galatas, to the left of the water taxi dock, below Hotel Galatea. Serves a wide range of well-prepared Italian pastas and pizzas at unbeatable prices (entrees €2-5). Try Chef Adonis's spaghetti and enjoy the red wine bottled on his parents' farm (Manos and Beatrix, of Pension Manos). ❶

Bobby's Taverna (Ο ΜΠΑΜΠΗΣ; ☎22980 23 629), in Galatas across from the car ferry dock. *The* place for fresh seafood and local atmosphere. Succulent seafood dishes start at €5; grilled dishes run €4-7. ❷

Igloo Ice Cream (☎22980 25 515), inland around the corner to the right of the post office. Serves breakfast, pastries, ice cream (€1 per scoop), and crepes from €2.20. ❶

Colona (☎22980 22 366), just down the waterfront to the right of the ferry dock, meets all your fast-food and gyro needs (€1.25). ❶

Taverna Poros (☎22980 25 267), one of the more relaxed waterfront restaurants, right across from the water taxi dock. Entrees €6 and up. ❷

SIGHTS AND ENTERTAINMENT

Poros isn't much of a party town, but there are several options for a night out. Check billings by the bus station for **Diana open-air cinema,** to the left of Lela Tours, where you can see American movies (9 and 11pm; €6, children €4). Fashionable locals and tourists alike head to the waterfront bars for late-night fun;

Malibu dominates the scene (☎22980 25 267, drinks €5-7). Clubs are further from town; two popular places to soothe your dance music cravings are **Sirocco,** a short cab ride to the southern point of Sphaeria on the waterfront road, and **Illusions,** in the Askeli area of Kalavria (drinks €5-6).

ARCHAEOLOGICAL MUSEUM. In Poros Town itself, the archaeological museum in the middle of the waterfront has some interesting inscriptions and photographs of the ruins at Trizina in the Peloponnese; very little of the collection is actually from Poros. *(☎22980 23 276. Open Tu-Su 8:30am-3pm. Free.)* For a pretty view of the harbor, climb the **clock tower.** The stairs are next to the library, one block inland.

MONASTERY OF ZOODOCHOS PIGIS. The 18th-century Monastery of Zoodochos Pigis (Virgin of the Life-Giving Spring) is sequestered in an overgrown glade 6km from Poros Town. Monks have been drinking blessed, curative waters here since 200 BC. The monastery once served as a meeting place for Greek naval leaders Miaoulis, Jobazis, and Apostolis, who strategized the uprising of 1821. Before hopping on the bus back, stop for delicious ice cream (€1.20 per scoop) at **Samali's,** opposite the monastic complex. If you're curious, ask nicely about the tiny church next door. Between the cafe and the small church is a fountain from the **life-giving spring,** so fill up your water bottle and be invigorated. *(To get to the monastery, take the green bus from the stop next to the main port (20min., hourly 7am-11pm, €0.70). Open sunrise to sunset, but closed 2-4:30pm in summer. Modest dress required.)* From the road below the monastery you can find the 6th-century BC **Temple of Poseidon** (take a moped–it's a few km). The ruins may be best appreciated by Greek history buffs, but the view will inspire all.

BEACHES AND THE OUTDOORS

The **white bus line** runs hourly along the shore to the beach at **Russian Bay,** where Russian ships first docked to aid the Greek rebellion. Along the way are **Neorion,** featuring a long sand beach, tavernas, and a watersports center, and the secluded blue-green waters and rocky sands of **Love Beach,** the local favorite. The tiny island near the beach was an undercover school during the Turkish occupation, when Greeks were forbidden an education. Ironically, it's now a popular sunning rock for kids playing hooky. On the way to the monastery, the **green bus** passes crowded **Askeli beach,** which has a slate of tavernas, tourist shops, and watersports.

GALATAS. If you look across a thin strait to the Peloponnesian mainland from Poros, you'll spy Galatas (Γαλατας), a working village with a different feel than tourist-frequented Poros. Surrounded by beautiful farmland and cut with flat, well-paved roads, Galatas is great for bike riding (rent them at Manos Moto) and the beaches are spared the hordes of tourists that populate Poros, though they are less picturesque. When you arrive, turn left (facing inland) to find the pleasant sand beaches of **Plaka** and **Aliki.** Plaka is about 2km from Galatas, marked by a wall that reads "Poros Marine," while livelier Aliki is 1km further, on a turn-off 200m past Plaka. Caution: only the water on the ocean side is safe for swimming. About 1.5km beyond Aliki beach is **Artemis,** where the ruins of a temple to the goddess are visible underwater. A gravel path on the right 1km past Plaka leads up through the enormous lemon grove of **Lemonodassos** ("lemon forest"). If you are riding a moped, leave it here before going up the dirt road. Walk 20 minutes up to **Kardasi Taverna** (☎22980 23 100), to get a glass of fresh lemonade (€1) and a view of windmills and 38,000 lemon trees. The beaches are quieter on the opposite side of the peninsula; try **Vlacheika.**

Fifteen kilometers from Galatas lies **Trizina,** mythical home to the hero **Theseus.** Take a bus (20min., 3 per day) there from Galatas and follow the signs up the hill out of town. Meager ruins have been unearthed near the town, but of far more interest is the lovely **Devil's Gorge,** so named for the cloven hoof footprint found in one of the rocks at the gorge's base. The shady, verdant area is a perfect picnic spot, a pleasant change of scenery from the scrubby growth of the islands. A soak in the pools of cool mountain water takes the edge off the heat. Head uphill from the bus stop in the center of town and go right, following the paved road past olive trees and fragrant citrus groves. At the fork in the road, head left and uphill (right and downhill will take you to the ruins), passing the ancient **Tower of Diateichisma.**

HYDRA Υδρα

Steep and bright, proud Hydra (EE-drah) rises out of the sea in its own bubble of smog-free, screech-free air. Even bicycles are illegal here—the steep, scaled streets only accommodate pedestrians, donkeys, and three garbage trucks. Hydra was rich long before the influx of tourist cash, first coming to prosperity as the 15th-century refuge of wealthy Greek families escaping Turkish persecution. The island then struck a deal with the Ottomans, providing the Turkish navy with the service of 30 young Hydrian men every year in return for its freedom. Hydrian youth thus learned the art of naval battle, a perk when, in 1821, Admiral Miaoulis and the Hydrian elite dedicated their fleet to the fledgling revolution. Everyone is still terribly proud of it, and the main thoroughfare is named for Miaoulis.

HYDRA TOWN

The sometimes baffling, cobbled streets of Hydra Town twist up the island's parched hills as they rise from the rich blues of the sea. Donkeys and wheelbarrow-pushing fruit vendors share the quiet alleys while the port below bustles with art students and smiling tourists during the summer months. As gorgeous as summers are, the pink-blossomed spring and salt-winded fall give the town an off season like no other. Outside Hydra Town, the island's main settlement, hidden beaches are yours for the price of a sea taxi.

PRACTICAL INFORMATION

The buildings of Hydra Town form an amphitheater around its famously picturesque harbor, with the opening facing north. Yachts and fishing boats bob in the center, accompanied by water taxis (in the southeast corner). Ferries and Flying Dolphins dock on the east edge of the harbor. Jewelry and tourist boutiques share harbor front space with pricey restaurants, bars, and cafes. **Tombazi,** in the southeast corner of the harbor, runs inland past the Internet cafe and several restaurants. **Miaouli** runs inland from the center of the harbor and **Votsi,** in the southwest corner beyond the clock tower, runs inland past the OTE, police, and medical center; you'll rarely hear locals call these alleys by name.

Ferries: Saronikos Ferries ticket office (☎22980 54 007), upstairs in the building with the gray door across from the ferry dock. Open daily 9:30am-6:30pm. 2 ferries per day to: **Aegina** (2¼hr., €7.20); **Methana** (1½hr., €5); **Piraeus** (3¼hr., €7.80) via **Poros** (1hr., €3.40). Also service to **Spetses** (1hr., 1 per day, €3.90).

Flying Dolphins: The **ticket office** (☎22980 53 813) is upstairs, on the same floor as the ferry ticket office. Open daily 6:30am-6:30pm and 8:30-10:30pm. To: **Hermione** (30min., 3 per day, €5.80); **Piraeus** (1½hr., up to 12 per day, €15.50); **Poros**

(30min., 5 per day, €6.80); **Portoheli** (45min., 4-5 per day, €9.10); **Spetses** (30min., 8 per day, €7.90).

Sea Taxis: (☎22980 53 690). Brightly-colored motorboats parked by the mule stand in the southeast corner of the harbor. Priced per boat (not per person), reflecting length of journey. Service to: **Agios Georgios** (€36); **Agios Nikolaos** (€45); **Hydra Beach** (€45); **Kamina** (€6.80); **Mandraki Beach** (€9.80); **Metohi** (€21); **Palamidas** (€14); **Vlihos** (9.80); daytrip around the island with beach stops (€98).

Bank: National Bank (☎22980 53 233), on the waterfront. 24hr. **ATM.** Open M-Th 8am-2pm, F 8am-1:30pm.

Laundry: Upstairs at the **Yachting Center,** in the southwest corner of the harbor. €12 for up to a 4kg. load, drying and folding included. Showers also available for €4. Open daily 10am-10pm.

Tourist Police: (☎22980 52 205). Follow the street to the right of the clock tower inland and go left at the fork. Look for the coat of arms, opposite the OTE. Open 24hr.

Port Police: (☎22980 52 279), upstairs in the big gray building flying the Greek nautical flag, in the northwest corner of the harbor. Open 24hr.

Pharmacy: Inland on Tombazi, just before the Amarillis Hotel. Open daily 9am-1:30pm and 5-8:30pm.

Hospital: (☎22980 53 150), inland on the street to the right of the clock tower, set back on the right, just past the tourist police. Look for a brown door with grates set in a stone wall. Open M-F 9am-1pm and by appointment; in an **emergency,** call the 24hr. nurse (☎22980 53 150) or the tourist police.

Telephones: OTE (☎22980 52 199 or 22980 52 399), facing the tourist police. Open M-F 8am-2pm. **Card phones** are just past the OTE entrance on the left.

Internet Access: Flamingo Cafe (☎22980 53 485), 20m up Tombazi on the right. €4.40 for 30 min., €8 per hr. Open daily 11am-11pm. Also offered at the **Yachting Center.** €3 for 15 min., €7 per hr. Open daily 10am-10pm.

Post Office: (☎22980 52 262), 1 block inland in the alley to the left of the Bank of Greece. Open M-F 7:30am-2pm. **Postal code:** 18040.

ACCOMMODATIONS

Hydra has the most expensive accommodations in the Saronic Gulf. Singles are practically nonexistent and doubles generally cost at least €40 during high season. Rooms in one of Hydra's famous old mansions are usually much more expensive. Weekend accommodations are almost impossible to get due to the influx of vacationing Greeks; if you can, arrive on Thursday for the weekend or call ahead. You may also be met at the ferry dock by Hydriots offering *domatia* (probably your cheapest option), but don't expect luxurious accommodations.

Hotel Amarillis (☎22980 53 611, 22980 52 249 or 22980 53 859). Walk inland on Tombazi; hang right at the fork. Rooms at this welcoming, family-run hotel have fridges, TV, and A/C. Singles €44; doubles €53; triples €60. ❹

Hydra Hotel (☎/fax 22980 52 102 or 22980 53 085; hydrahotel@aig.forthnet.gr). Looms high over the waterfront on the west side, down the street from the Koundouriotis mansion. Walk 1 block inland on Votsi, take the hard right up the stairs and around the corner, and turn right again on L. Koundouriotis (another long staircase). Wood-accented rooms have balconies with unsurpassed views and private baths. Singles €30-35; doubles €44-57; triples €52-63; quads €57-75. Discounts for longer stays. ❸

Pension Anthonios (☎22980 53 227), on Spilios J. Chasamas, across from Christina's; a 5min. walk inland on Tombazi. Bright, clean rooms off a quiet courtyard feature baths, fridges, and A/C. Doubles €50-60; triples €60-75; quads or quints €100. ❹

FOOD

Most waterfront establishments have average food, many tourists, and prices that reflect the rent. Hidden treasures compensate for location with superb food and significantly lower prices.

Barba Dima's (☎22980 52 967), a few minutes walk up Tombazi, before Xeri Elia. Shouts of "Amalia! Amalia!" can be heard as one approaches this tiny taverna. The locals are very demanding of the busy owner, but the traditional Greek cuisine she serves meets even the highest expectations. €3.50-6. Open daily 10:30am-1am. ❷

Christina's Taverna (☎22980 53 615), on Spilios Charamis just to the right of Taverna Xeri Elia. Another local favorite, this is the place for terrific home-cooking, so don't bother with the menu—just order whatever Christina has in the kitchen. Entrees €4-7. Open daily 11am-11:30pm. ❷

Taverna Xeri Elia, also known as **Douskos** (☎22980 52 886), in a trellised courtyard 5min. inland on Tombazi. With a wide range of Greek dishes and live traditional music every night, this well-known taverna attracts large crowds. €4-9. ❷

Fournos Bakery (☎22980 52 886), in the first alley to the left off Tombazi next to Vassilis Tours, delivers savory baked goods (€1.60 and down) and has a small market, all with the best prices in town. Open daily 7am-10pm. ❶

Anemoni (☎22980 53 136). Bear left uphill from the OTE. Greek pastries (€1.50) in generous portions; stop by after dinner for fresh ice cream (€2 for 2 large scoops) and almond confections. Open daily 8am-11pm. ❶

SIGHTS

HYDRA'S MERCHANT MARINERS. Despite its watery name, Hydra's land has always been too arid for prosperous agriculture. With few natural resources and a significant population of refugees from the Peloponnese, the Balkans, and Turkey, Hydra's inhabitants turned to managing the exports of others. Dodging pirates and naval blockades during the late 18th and early 19th centuries, Hydriot merchants emerged in 1821 as the financial and naval leaders in the revolt against Ottoman rule, contribut-

THE BIG SPLURGE

BRATSERA

A converted sponge factory, **Bratsera** may seem like an unlikely place to find luxurious accommodations. Indeed, a walk into the dim lobby, with its low ceiling and rough stone walls, feels more industrial than homey. But let your eyes adjust to the light, and you'll understand why Bratsera sets the standard on an island with such discerning taste. In the lobby, antique furniture and tapestries mingle easily with modern features. A quick stroll through the courtyard should be enough to convince you: a serene garden of carefully tended bougainvillea, oleander, and jacaranda provide shady sanctuary from the bustling streets of Hydra. A welcoming swimming pool lies just beyond, teasing the occasional passerby with its aqua blue waters.

The rooms themselves pamper visitors with all the amenities—TVs, A/C, full baths, telephones—and the luxury of pleasing decor. Soft colors glow in the sunlight, wood rafters give a comforting sense of space, and nautical antiques add a Hydriot touch.

The hotel's restaurant serves breakfast, lunch, and dinner. Take a seat under the wisteria-covered trellises of the courtyard and enjoy pleasant surroundings only a hop, skip and jump from your room.

Located a short walk up Tombazis. ☎22980 53 971. Doubles €94-171.

ing two-thirds of the revolution's 200-odd ships. The Venetian-built mansions of these merchants-turned-heroes dot the hills behind the harbor, and are definitely worth a look. George Koundouriotis was one of the many Hydriot leaders in the Greek War of Independence, and his grandson, Pavlos Koundouriotis, became the President of Greece in the 1920s.

The **Tombazis mansion,** on the west side of the harbor, now houses the famous **Fine Art School;** look for paint-smeared artists on the balcony. The work of Hydriot painter Periklis Byzantios, who taught at the school, and that of his son, Constantinos, is now on display in the basement of **Lazaros Koundoriotis Historical Mansion,** the yellow building high on the west side of town. Take the first hard right off Votsi and turn right again on L. Koundouriotis, then head left at the top of the long stairway. On the first and second floors, the museum exhibits an extensive array of traditional Hydriot costumes and has a brilliant view of the town. (Open Tu-Su 10am-5pm. €4, students and children 11-18 €2, children under 10 free.)

BYZANTINE SIGHTS. Those in search of peace need only check beneath the large clock tower that dominates the port. The still, white courtyard of the **Church of the Assumption of the Virgin Mary** is a striking contrast to the busy harbor streets that lie just through the alleyway. The small church is certainly worth a trip, if only for a peek at its gilded ceiling and a few wonderful moments of quiet contemplation. Before serving as a monastery, the structure was a convent, housing 18 nuns from 1648 to 1770. It is now dedicated to the *kemesis*, or ascension of Mary. The courtyard surrounds the tomb of Koundouriotis, his statue, and a statue of Miaoulis. Modest dress is required. Hidden away up the stairs are the treasures of the **Byzantine Museum.** The quality of the handiwork that went into the Byzantine icons, frescoes, gospels, and liturgical vessels is truly impressive. Especially noteworthy are the brightly colored, beautifully preserved scenes from the life of Christ produced in the 18th and 19th centuries. *(Open Tu-Su 10am-5pm. €1.50.)*

HISTORICAL ARCHIVES MUSEUM. This small museum houses old Hydriot costumes, census records, a library, naval treasures, and relics of the revolution. Don't miss the heart of Admiral Andreas Miaoulis, which is stunningly preserved in a silver and gold urn. *(To the left of the ferry building. ☎22980 52 355. Open daily 9am-4:30pm. €3, students €1.50.)*

MONASTERY HIKE. An arduous 90min. hike will take you to the **Monastery of Prophitis Ilias** and, on a lower peak overlooking the harbor, the **Convent of Efpraxia.** The monastery is the prettier of the two structures, and the monks may show you around. A donkey ride up the rocks costs about €30 and wears out the donkey—inquire at the harbor. *(Hike up A. Maiouli from the waterfront. Modest dress required. Both open daily 9am-5pm.)*

FESTIVALS. If you're in Hydra town during the **Miaoulia** (the 4th weekend in June), celebrate the feats of Admiral Andreas Miaoulis via an explosive mock battle held in the harbor. The celebration of Greek Orthodox **Easter** (April 27 in 2003) is reputedly one of the best in the land. Throngs of visitors crowd Kamini Beach on Good Friday, where men of the church, in full attire, carry the Epitaph into the sea.

ART GALLERIES. A visit to Hydra wouldn't be complete without a peek at the art that the island inspires, and it is nearly impossible to walk a few blocks in Hydra without coming upon at least one gallery. **Lagioudera,** on the northwestern corner of the harbor, and **Melina Merkouri,** on the northeastern corner, are rented out by local artists for brief shows.

NIGHTLIFE

If divine intervention is needed to turn your two left feet into a prime dancing duo, **Disco Heaven,** perched high on a cliff on the west side of town, may be the answer to your prayers. Take the white trimmed stairs just before the Sunset Restaurant. There's an indoor dance floor as well as an outdoor bar overlooking the sea. (☎22980 52 716. Cocktails €7. Cover €3. Open daily 11pm-late, summer only.) As the large contingent of artists might suggest, the Hydrian scene is about strolling the moonlit harbor, getting invited onto yachts for drinks, and wandering through the waterfront bars. The Hydriot equivalent of a pub crawl begins around 12:30am in the lounge seats of the **Pirate Bar,** tucked into the southwest corner of the harbor. (☎22980 52 711. Beer €4; cocktails €6-8. Open daily 10am-late.) It then meanders through the crowds to trendy **Nautilus** (☎22980 53 563. Cocktails €7.50. Open daily 10pm-late) and **Saronicos** (☎22980 52 589. Cocktails €7.50. Open daily 9pm-6am), both on the west side of the harbor, and ends with an early-morning swim in the deep waters off the landing past Sunset Restaurant. On a quieter night in town, enjoy the intimate setting of **Amalour,** a short walk up Tombazi (cocktails €5-7).

BEACHES

Landings and stairs cut into the rocks around the point across the harbor from the ferry dock provide access to the finest swimming on Hydra, in waters that are cool, crystal, and instantly deep. The first landing on the right is open to the public, but grab a drink at one of the cafes that serve the next few; Daiquiris at **Hydronetta** are a delicious treat (€5). A 15min. walk west along the coast takes you past the high-walled, cobbled artists' colony of Kamini. Just beyond it is a tiny, pebbly beach where the drop to the sea is less severe. Walking another 20min. brings you to slightly more populous **Vlihos Beach,** guarded by a regiment of Hawaiian-style beach umbrellas. East of town (30min. hike or 10min. water taxi) lies well-manicured **Mandraki Beach,** a genuine, if gritty, sand beach. This isn't the secluded beach of your dreams, but there are plenty of fun water toys to keep you busy. (Prices per hour: paddle boats €8, canoes €5, windsurfing €10, sailboat rental €5-15.) If you have time and money, hire a water taxi to the far side of the island; there's room for you to find a quiet beach of your own—just be sure to agree on a pickup time before getting out.

SPETSES Σπετσες

A green cloak of pine trees and rounded shoulders distinguish Spetses from its rockier neighbors. Years ago, visitors were welcomed to the island by an air of mystery: the vegetation combined with an abundance of honey to produce a sweet, magical odor. Hence the name "Spetses," which derives from the Venetian *spezzie* (aromatic or spiced). Perhaps the fact that there was something in the air can explain past Spetsiots' passionate devotion to their homeland. They played a crucial role in the War for Independence, fighting courageously and giving their fleet to the cause. Today, the island commemorates the valor of one Spetsiot captain, Kosmos Barbatsis. On September 8, 1822, the intrepid sailor piloted his explosives-laden craft directly into a Turkish flagship, destroying it and turning the tide of battle in favor of the Greek fleet. Every September 8th, Spetsiots honor his deed with the explosion of a mock Turkish ship in the harbor.

IN RECENT NEWS

PLAYING WITH MATCHES

Two years ago, a fire destroyed much of the tree cover on the southern side of Spetses, and the island is still recovering. Unfortunately, such an event is not uncommon on the Greek islands. The blazing Aegean sun dries vegetation to the point when it will burn at the slightest hint of a spark; a bottle thrown carelessly to the side of the road is enough to turn an island paradise into a barren wasteland. Islands teeter on the brink of disaster, and many show scars inflicted by past fires. The cause of the most recent fire on Spetses is not known for certain, but a few locals suspect that the fire was the result of foul play.

In Greece, it is illegal to build on forested land. This makes things difficult for real estate owners who hope to capitalize on their undeveloped holdings. The less savory characters resort to illegal means: they burn the vegetation on their property and thus ready it for development. By a strange twist of logic, the heap of rubble left in the wake of a fire is more valuable than the stand of trees that once grew in its place.

Whether it was the result of bad intentions or not, the fire on Spetses—an island known for its green slopes—was a severe blow to the local community. But Spetses has recovered from barren times before. The trees that stand today were planted by the philanthropist Sotiros Anargyrou in the early 1900s, in the hopes that he could return his beloved island to the green glory of its past.

SPETSES TOWN

The vast majority of Spetsiots live in Spetses Town, as close to the water as possible. Cafes and bars line the 4km of water, interspersed with little pebble beaches every 50m, turning the town into a round-the-clock beach club that attracts many young Greeks on the weekends. Jet-setters dock in Spetses's Old Harbor to the left (facing inland) of the ferry quay. Although topless sunbathing is technically illegal, Spetsiots know how to bend the rules.

TRANSPORTATION

Ferries: Depart once daily to: **Aegina** (3hr., €9.19); **Piraeus** (4hr., €10.80) via **Hydra** (1hr., €3.70); **Methana** (2½hr., €6.50); **Poros** (2hr., €5.40). **Alasia Travel** (☎22980 74 098), on the waterfront, sells tickets and posts schedules. Open daily 8am-9pm.

Flying Dolphins: Ticket offices: (☎22980 73 141) inland from the dock. **Hydrofoils** and **Catamarans** to: **Piraeus** (2hr., 8-12 per day, €20.40); **Hydra** (30min., 8-10 per day, €7.34); **Poros** (1hr., 1-4 per day, €9.98); **Monemvasia** (2hr., 1 per day, €13.21.)

Water Taxis: (☎22980 72 072), docked across from the Flying Dolphin ticket office, just inland of the ferry dock. To: **Agia Marina** (€18); **Anarghiri Beach** or **Paraskevi Beach** (€38); **Costa** (€12); **Emilianos** (€25); **Hinitsa** (€22); **Costoula** (€14); **Old Harbor** (€10.27); **Porto Heli** (€30); **Zogeria** (€24); and trips around the island (€50).

Buses: Schedules and prices posted at stops. To: **Ag. Anargiri Beach** (20min., 4 per day, 450dr/€1.50), from Ag. Mamas beach, 500m down the waterfront from the dock; and to **Anargyrios College** and **Lioneri Beach** from the plateia by the Hotel Poseidon (15 per day, every hr. at half past, €1).

Taxis: In front of the travel agencies to the left of the ferry dock.

Moped Rental: Several rental agencies cluster just past the Ag. Anarghiri bus stop; veer right at the kiosk. Expect to pay €15-20 per day, depending on age and engine size. **Rent-a-Bike** (☎22980 74 143), on the street running parallel to the waterfront, behind the Hotel Soleil, rents **mountain bikes.** €4 per day.

PRACTICAL INFORMATION

The waterfront road runs from the left (facing inland) of the ferry dock around the base of the town to the **Old Harbor,** past **Ag. Mama's** beach. To the right of the ferry dock are several restaurants and cafes, on the way up the hill to **Plateia Bouboulina.** The first street inland parallel to the water hosts shops, pharmacies, and tavernas. The Old Harbor, home to waterfront bars and tavernas, is a 20min. walk or €7 carriage ride; carriages wait near the ferry dock.

Tourist Agencies: Several around the corner on the left side of the boat landing. **Alasia Travel** (☎22980 74 130, 22980 74 903, or 22980 74 098; fax 22980 74 053; alasia@otenet.gr) sells ferry tickets. Open daily 8am-2:30pm and 4-9pm.

Banks: National Bank (☎22980 72 286), next to the OTE, on the waterfront to the right of the ferry docks. Open M-Th 8am-2pm, F 8am-1:30pm. 24hr. **ATM.**

Police: (☎22980 73 100). Follow signs to the Spetses Museum; 150m before the museum. Also houses the **tourist police** (☎22980 73 100) in the basement. Open 24hr.

Port Police: (☎22980 72 245), in the rear of the OTE building; walk up the street between the National Bank and the OTE and follow the signs. Open 24hr.

First Aid Station: (☎22980 72 472). Open 24hr. for **emergencies.** Call the police to reach a doctor.

Pharmacy: (☎22980 72 256), in the plateia, off the street running parallel to the waterfront. Open M-Sa 8:30am-1:30pm and 5-8:30pm; Su 10am-1:30pm and 5:00-8:30pm.

Telephone: OTE (☎22980 72 199), around to the right of the ferry dock, next to the National Bank. Open M-F 7:30am-1:30pm.

Internet Access: Delfinia Net-Cafe (☎22980 75 051; delfinianet@usa.net), left of the ferry docks, next to O Roussos, just before the beach. €4.80 per hr., €2.40 minimum. Open daily 9am-2am. Also at **Politis** (☎22980 74 519, 22980 74 652), around to the right of the ferry dock. €4.40 per hr., €2.20 minimum.

Post Office: (☎22980 72 228), left of the ferry dock on the road parallel to waterfront. Open M-F 7:30am-2pm. **Postal Code:** 18050.

ACCOMMODATIONS

Accommodations are generally expensive, with prices slightly higher on weekends and rooms scarcer. A few domatia are advertised around town; you might get picked up at the ferry dock. Be sure to bargain.

Pension Brazos (☎22980 75 152), just inland of the ferry docks. Unimpressive but convenient. Rooms have baths, fridges, fans, and balconies. Singles €20-30; doubles €25-35; triples €35-45. ❷

Hotel Faros (☎22980 72 613; fax 22980 72 614), in the plateia off the street parallel to the water. Plain rooms with fridges, A/C, private baths, and balconies. Singles €25-30; doubles €40-50; triples €55-65; quads €75-85. ❸

Hotel Klimis (☎22980 73 725 or 22980 73 334), on the waterfront to the left of the ferry docks. Baths, TVs, and A/C. Breakfast €4.20-6.80. Singles €40-50; doubles €50-55; triples €70-80. ❹

FOOD AND NIGHTLIFE

Tavernas abound in this tiny town, but they tend to be rather pricey.

Politis (☎22980 72 248), on the waterfront, just to the right of the ferry docks. Serves decadent *baklava* (€1.50), delicious waffle breakfasts with bottomless cups of coffee (€4.70-6), and a wide variety of cocktails. **Internet** access available upstairs (€4.40 per hr., €2.20 minimum). Open daily 8am-late. ❷

THE BIG SPLURGE

LITROVI

Surrender to the soothing rhythms of rocking boats and lapping tides at **Litrovi,** a paragon of fine Greek cuisine in the heart of the Old Harbor. The main seating area, a converted dock that juts out into the middle of the harbor, places customers only a few feet above the moonlit waters and several hundred yards away from the waterfront road with its buzzing mopeds. Soft candlelight and Cuban music round out the scene, but a meal here is not a mere fling with romance. The restaurant's three chefs prepare each dish with careful attention, summoning rounds of delicate flavors to satisfy the most discerning appetite.

There are few better places on the island to try the mayfish á la Spetsiotes, cooked with a delicious sauce of tomatoes, white wine, and garlic (€10). The baby veal cutlet also has special ties to the island—the tender meat is butchered at a local nunnery (€12). For those who prefer meals with less grotesque beginnings, Liotrivi also offers a range of savory pastas (€10-15) prepared with everything from parsley to pine nuts.

On the waterfront in the Old Harbor. Open all day.

O Roussos (☎22980 72 212), on the waterfront, just before the beach. Specializes in octopus, which you'll see drying on the clothesline outside. Octopus dishes around €6. Fresh seafood and traditional Greek entrees €5-9. Open daily 11am-midnight. ❷

Quarter Pizza (☎22980 72 027), in the plateia off the road running parallel to the water. Pizzas (€5.50-8.20 for regular, €6.10-9.50 for large) cooked on a wood-fire stove offer a break from the usual. Open daily 11am-midnight. ❷

Sports fans gather for Happy Hour (midnight; all cocktails €3) at **Socrates.** A younger crowd heads to **Mama's,** at Ag. Mama's beach for expensive, chic drinks (€5-7). The second inlet of the Old Harbor, around the bend from the inlet closest to Dapia, is host to many of the prime bars and clubs on the island. **Remezzo** features live traditional music on the weekends after 11pm; **Thrubie,** a relaxed ouzo bar, serves up selections of organic food. If a night on the dance floor is what you desire, head for the bumping rhythms of **Brachera;** those craving company should try **Figaro,** across the inlet, which boasts a 2000 person capacity.

SIGHTS

The **Spetses Museum** is housed in the center of town in the crumbling, late-19th-century mansion owned by Hadjiyanni Mexi, Spetses's first governor. The second floor porch provides sweeping views of Spetses Town, but stained glass windows, an old island fireplace, and carved wooden doors invite visitors to take a closer look at the imposing building itself. Its collection includes a casket of the remains of Laskarina Bouboulina (see below), coins, costumes, mastheads, folk art, and religious artifacts. (Follow the signs from between the OTE and the National Bank. ☎22980 72 994. Open Tu-Su 8:30am-2:45p.m. €3.) The **House of Laskarina Bouboulina** was home to a ship's captain who played a major role during the War of Independence. Mme. Bouboulina was a woman of unchecked patriotism and courage, and is to date the only female admiral in Greek history. Despite her valor, she did not enjoy a hero's death: an angry lover shot her in a dispute, and the bullet left a hole in the wall of her house that is shown during the tour. (Next to the park behind the National Bank and the OTE. ☎22980 72 416. Open for guided tour only; English tours run every hour and a half from 10:30am-6:00pm. €4, children €1.) The **Monastery of Agios Nikolaos** is opposite a square of traditional Spetsiot mosaics, above the old harbor. A memorial plaque to the left of the entrance commemorates Napoleon's nephew, Paul

Marie Bonaparte, who was pickled in a barrel of rum after he died in the War of Independence. The barrel was stored in a monastic cell at Agios Nikolaos from 1827 until 1832. (Dress modestly: long pants for men, long skirts for women, no bare shoulders.)

BEACHES

Spetses's warm beaches are invitingly shallow and a major draw to the island. Hop on a moped and see them all on the 24km jaunt around the island; cool off with a refreshing dip in the ocean and a frappe from the tavernas found at every beach. Big sandy **Ag. Anargiri,** on the opposite side of the island from Spetses Town, is the most popular, boasting two tavernas and a host of watersports. (Windsurfing €12 per hr.; waterskiing €15 per person, canoes €10 per hr.) In the rear of the beach's only restaurant, **Manolis,** are showers, changing rooms, and impeccable bathrooms. **Ag. Paraskevi,** about 1km to the right facing seaward, has the same blanket of pine trees and a sandy-pebbly surface without the accompanying hubbub. Midway along the Anargiri-Spetses Town bus route is the utterly peaceful **Xylocheriza.** Pure white, smooth stones contrast with the still, brightly colored waters of the bay. Refresh yourself after a swim with a hunk of watermelon big enough for two at the snack bar. Although it is most easily accessed by moped, the bus passes by the dusty road to the beach (10-15min. on foot); check with the driver about return times before you hop off. **College Beach,** in front of Anargyrios College, is home to a popular bar and tanned tourists. **Agia Marina** beach is about a 30min. walk from the far left end of the waterfront in Spetses Town, taking a right at the kiosk.

THE SPORADES AND EVIA

Circling into the azure depths of the Aegean, Evia and the Sporades form a family of enchanting sea maidens. Evia, the matriarch, nudges the coast of Central Greece, stretching from Karystos in the south, through bustling Halkida, to the warm waters of the northern coast. Her children, the Sporades, arc across the sea to the north. Sophisticated Skopelos, the eldest, quietly welcomes the moonlight to her shores with echoing jazz melodies. Wild and independent Skiathos pays homage to the sun, flaunting her beach-ringed shores for travelers from around the world. Little Alonnisos harbors pristine wilderness crossed by hiking trails and is home to *Monachus monachus* (MOM), an endangered species of seal, and its wildlife preservation organization. Austere Skyros watches from afar as a keeper of the old ways. They have beckoned visitors for millennia: 5th century BC Athenians, 2nd century BC Romans, 13th century AD Venetians, and 20th century tourists have all basked on their sun-lit shores and trod their shaded forests.

HIGHLIGHTS OF THE SPORADES AND EVIA

PEEL OFF your Fruit of the Looms on Skiathos's Little Banana beach (p. 331).

PUNK MEETS FOLK on Skopelos, home of Giorgios Xintaris, one of Greece's last great *rembetika* performers (p. 337).

PONDER POETRY by Rupert Brooke among pirate spoils in Skyros Town (p. 344).

DRINK IN a divine aphrodisiac–the view from Mt. Ohi on Evia, where Zeus and Hera fell in love (p. 351).

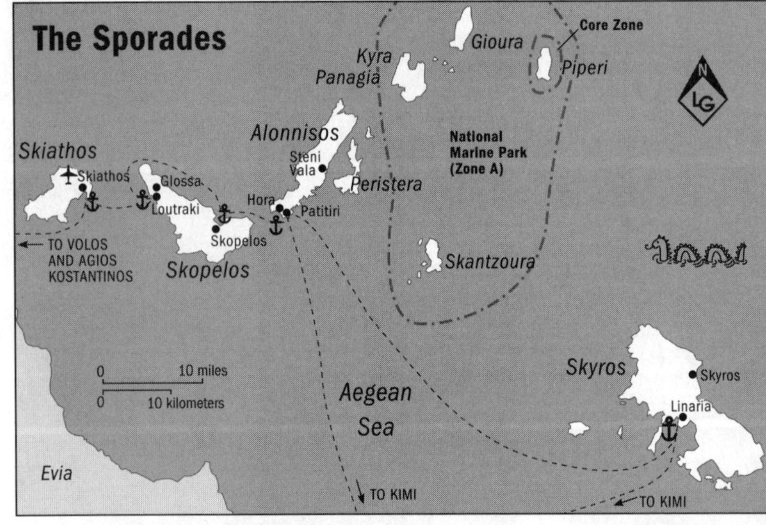

SPORADES Σποραδες

SKIATHOS Σκιαθος

Having grown up almost overnight from an innocent island daughter to a madcap dancing queen, Skiathos is the tourism (and party) hub of the Sporades. Its long waterfront, lined with travel agencies and car rental shops, gives little hint of the island's raw beauty. The traveler who escapes the tourist temptations of Skiathos Town finds majestic pine forests, ethereal beaches, and dignified monasteries.

SKIATHOS TOWN

Arriving in Skiathos Town can be a bit overwhelming: dozens of Skiathans crowd the ferry landing hawking domatia, and cafes and tavernas line every street with tacky beach shops and expensive boutiques. Yet beyond the tourist gauntlet Skiathos reveals a charming and exhilarating character. From bars packed with talkative tourists, to the picturesque backdrop of the old port, to all-night discos, Skiathos offers something for everyone. The only thing you might find lacking is a resident Greek population.

TRANSPORTATION

Ferries: Hellas Lines (☎24270 22 209), on the corner of Papadiamantis across from the ferry landing. Prices slightly higher in July-Aug. Ferries run to: **Agios Konstantinos** (3½hr., 1-3 per day, €10.10); **Alonnisos** (2hr., 1-2 per day, €6); **Glossa** (30min., 1-2 per day, €2.70); **Skopelos** (1½hr., 1-3 per day, €4.40); **Volos** (2½hr., 2-3 per day, €9.20). Some ferries are jet ferries, which have the same prices and trip durations as Flying Dolphins. To get to Skiathos from **Athens,** take the daily bus from the station at Liossion 260 to Ag. Konstantinos (2½hr., 16 per day, €10.20), and then take the ferry.

Flying Dolphins: Minoan Lines (☎24270 22 018), at the same office as Hellas. Trips to: **Agios Konstantinos** (1¼hr., 1-2 per day, €20.25); **Alonnisos** (1hr., 3-6 per day, €12); **Glossa** (15min., 3-4 per day, €5.50); **Skopelos** (35min., 3-6 per day, €8.80); **Volos** (1¼hr., 2-3 per day, €18.30).

Flights: Olympic Airways office (☎24270 22 229 or 24270 22 220), at the airport. Call 24hr. prior to takeoff to confirm flight. Open M-F 8am-4pm. Taxis from the harbor to the airport cost about €3. One flight per day to **Athens** (50min.).

Local buses: Facing inland, the **bus stop** is at the far right end of the wharf past the park. The bus to **Koukounaries Beach** (every 30min. 7:15am-1am, €1) makes stops at southern beaches along the main road. Heading out of town, sit on the driver's side for the best view. A schedule and list of stops is posted at the bus stop in Skiathos Town and at Koukounaries.

Taxis: (☎24270 24 461). Line up along the waterfront; prices are posted on a small wooden kiosk on the waterfront. Open 24hr.

Moped Rental: Prices run from €15-20 per day. **Euronet** (☎24270 24 410), **Avis** (☎24270 21 458), and **Heliotropio** (☎24270 22 430) along the waterfront include insurance in the rental price.

Charter Boats: Boats run from the Old Port. Circuits around the island, including Lalaria and Castro beaches, cost €10-12 per person and leave before 10am, returning in the afternoon. Boats to Tsougria, a small island just off the coast of Skiathos and a popular location for swimming and snorkeling, cost €8 per person and leave between 10am and noon, returning in the afternoon. Ask at the information kiosk next to the ferry dock.

ORIENTATION AND PRACTICAL INFORMATION

The midpoint of Skiathos's waterfront is marked by the **Bourtzi,** a peninsula fortified by the Venetians in the 13th century. The **main waterfront** runs to the right of the Bourtzi, facing inland, and is the location of the ferry dock, rental agencies, tavernas, cafes, and tourist shops. The **Old Port** runs perpendicular to the main waterfront from the Bourtzi. **Papadiamantis,** Skiathos Town's main drag, overflows with cafe-bars, souvenir shops and clothing stores, and intersects the main waterfront across from the ferry dock. Farther inland, **Pandra** (left at the National Bank) and **Evangelistra** (perpendicular at the post office) intersect Papadiamantis. Parallel to Papadiamantis, **Polytechniou** contains a string of bars. On the far right of the waterfront facing inland, a road winds from the bus stop up to the airport and then follows the south coast of the island all the way to **Koukounaries beach. Maps** of Skiathos and the other Sporades islands are available in shops along the waterfront for about €1.50. In the kiosk next to the ferry dock, **Vasilis Korallis,** a Skiathan with a Californian accent, can give you information on everything from lodging to beaches to how to protect local wildlife. (Open daily 9am-1pm and 6-10pm.)

Tourist Police: (☎24270 23 172). A small white building on the right side of Papadiamantis next to the school, just past where the road forks around an electronic info kiosk. Open most days 8am-9pm.

Banks: National Bank (☎24270 22 400), midway up Papadiamantis on the left side. Offers **currency exchange** and an **ATM.** Open M-Th 8am-2pm, F 8am-1:30pm.

American Express: Papadiamantis 21 (☎24270 21 463 or 24270 21 464), on the left before Evangelistra. Tourist services and **currency exchange.** Open May-Oct. daily 9am-2pm and 5-9pm.

Bookstore: A **newsstand** on the left side of Papadiamantis past the AmEx office sells international newspapers, magazines, and novels in English made for a long day on the beach. Open daily 9am-midnight.

Laundromat: Miele Laundry, about 200m up Papadiamantis on a side street across from the National Bank. €6 per load; €5.87 with their soap. Open 8am-11pm. **Snow White Laundry,** on the street parallel to and behind the waterfront. €6 per load, €2 per dryer, €1 for soap. Drying without washing costs €3.

Police: (☎24270 22 111), upstairs past where Papadiamantis forks left. Open 24hr.

Pharmacies: Several pharmacies line Papadiamantis and its side streets.

Hospital: (☎24270 22 040), on the Acropolis hill behind Skiathos Town. Open 24hr., but **emergencies** only after 1pm.

Internet Access: Internet Zone Cafe (☎24270 22 767) on Evangelistra, to the right off Papadiamantis. €3 per hr. Open daily 10am-12am.

Federal Express: (☎24270 22 006; fax 23 204), located on Simeonis, 1 block to the left of Papadiamantis before the National Bank. Open Su-F 8:30am-2:30pm and 5:30-9pm, Sa 9:30am-1pm.

Post Office: (☎24270 22 011), at the intersection of Papadiamantis and Evangelistra. Open M-F 7:30am-2pm. **Postal code:** 37002.

ACCOMMODATIONS AND CAMPING

Most tourists make prior reservations for July and August, and tour groups book most of the summer hotel rooms a year in advance. Dock hawks flock to meet the ferry and promote their domatia, which are generally the best deal in town. Be sure to **bargain.** Typical doubles run €20-30 in spring and fall and €30-50 in sum-

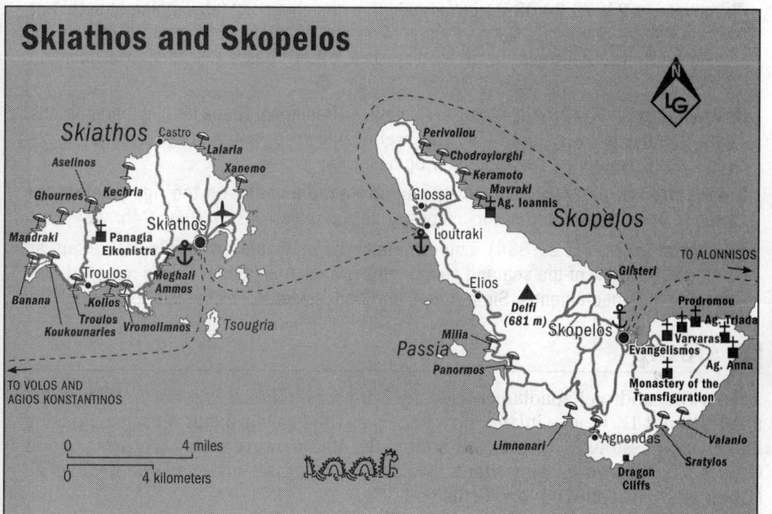

mer. Try the **Rooms to Let** office in the port's wooden kiosk, which can give you a list of rooms currently available. (☎24270 22 990. Open daily 9am-8pm.) In August, forget about finding a room, much less a cheap one—if you arrive without accommodations lined up, forgo sleep and just party the night away.

Australia Hotel (☎24270 22 488), right on Evangelistra off Papadiamantis and in an alley to the left, is convenient and equipped with a surprising range of amenities. Rooms have A/C, private baths, some kitchenettes, fridges, and balconies and are a steal before Aug. if you bargain. Singles €20; doubles €25-30; triples €36; quads €44. Prices double late July-Aug. ❷

Pension Nikolas (May-Sept. ☎24270 23 062; Oct.-Apr. ☎23940 32 756), off Polytechniou to the left past Kirki bar. Centrally located, it offers private baths and fridges. Some rooms with A/C. English spoken. Singles €20-30; doubles €30-60; triples €36-72. ❷

Pension Lazou (☎24270 22 324), on the hill overlooking the Old Port. Walk along the Old Port with the water to your left, and climb the stairs at the end. A little off the beaten track, Lazou's charming rooms have great views and private baths. Doubles €35-50. ❸

Hotel Pothos (☎24270 22 324), next to Pension Nikolas off Polytechniou. Rooms are brightly decorated, with marble floors, handcrafted furnishings, and all the amenities. Singles €35-45; doubles €45-60; triples €54-70. In August, there are no singles, and prices increase by €30. ❹

Camping Koukounaries (☎24270 49 250), on the bus route to Koukouniares; ask the driver to let you off there. Has a restaurant, mini-market, and campground a short walk from the beach. €6 per person; €3 per tent; €3 per car. ❶

FOOD

Skiathian eating establishments accommodate a wide range of tastes and wallet sizes. While traditional Greek tavernas abound, Italian, English, Chinese, and Mexican restaurants can also be found in town. Not surprisingly, more exotic food tends to be pricey; back-alley souvlaki stands and tiny tavernas off the main strip feed locals and broke backpackers. Cheap Greek food stands pack **Papadiamantis.**

Primavera (☎24270 24 086), tucked behind a church among labyrinthine streets. Turn left on Pandra before the National Bank and then left again when it intersects the end of Polytechniou. Delicious Italian food (pizza €7-9.50; pasta €5.50-8) in a romantic, Old World setting. Open daily 6:30pm-12:30am. ❷

Hellinikon (☎24270 23 225), next to Primavera. Traditional Greek fare in large portions, with live music every night. Teo, the waiter and co-owner, will accommodate any requests. Open daily 11am-3pm and 6pm-late. ❷

Crepes Krepali (☎24270 23 840), way up Papadiamantis on the right, before the school. Serves sweet and savory crepes at decent prices (€3-6). Open 24hr. ❶

To Bourtzi (☎24270 21 834), coincidentally the only cafe on the Bourtzi, offers an unparalleled view of the sea and surrounding islands from a spot quietly removed from the glitz of Papadiamantis. Sip a *frappé* and be mesmerized by the sea. Drinks only.

SIGHTS

Author Alexandros Papadiamantis's tiny 140-year-old house, set back off Papadiamantis about 1½ blocks inland, now serves as the **Papadiamantis Museum,** housing his few possessions. The museum honors the 19th-century realist who was one of Greece's best-loved prose writers. Info and short stories are available in English. (Open Tu-Su 9:30am-1pm and 6-10:30pm. €1.)

Panagia Eikonistra or **Kounistra** ("The Blessed Icon Painter") is the most important monastery on the island. The **festival** of the Presentation of the Virgin on November 21 celebrates the monastery's miracle-working icon and the island's patron saint, the Blessed Virgin. Get off the bus at **stop #18** and follow the road signs to the monastery. The **Convent of Evangelistra,** 4km north of Skiathos Town on the slopes of Karaflitzanaka, is the site where the **first Greek national flag** (a white cross on a blue background) was raised in 1807.

Ten kilometers from Skiathos Town on the north coast of the island, accessible by private vehicle or by boat, stand the ruins of a medieval walled **castle** built in the 16th century as a refuge from marauding pirates. With independence in the 19th century, the castle's occupants moved to Skiathos Town. Presently only two of Kastro's original 30 churches remain standing, notably the **Church of Christ,** which houses rare icons and frescoes and a magnificent iconostasis.

BEACHES

A single paved main road runs along the southern coast of Skiathos, between Skiathos Town and the island's most famous beach, Koukounaries. The bus makes many stops along the road, mostly at other beaches. A list of stops is available at the bus station in Skiathos and at Koukounaries. Many consider the **Koukounaries Beach and Biotrope** (stop #26) to be one of the most beautiful beaches in the Mediterranean. Plush sand arcs between blue waters and the verdant pines of the Biotrope, a protected forest area. Besides being the most revered beach on the island, it is also the most popular—expect throngs of crowds in July and August. Koukounaries offers a full slate of water sports (water skiing €20; parasailing €35) and is well-equipped with showers, bathrooms, and bars.

Banana and **Little Banana Beaches** (stop #26) are at the end of the road up the hill across from the Koukounaries bus stop. Signs lead the way. To get to curvy Little Banana from Banana, walk around the rocks on the right as you face the sea. Drop your pants on the way—both are **nude beaches. Lalaria** is accessible only by charter boat (€10-12 per person) from the Old Port in Skiathos. Boats leave by 10am.

The bus also stops at other beaches, including **Megali Ammos** (stop #5), **Nostos** (stop #12), **Vromolimnos** (stop #13), **Kolios** (stop #14). All of the beaches on the southern part of the island tend to be very crowded because of their proximity to the bus route. From the later stops, a 30min. walk through a beautiful forest of tall pines brings you to the northern beaches, where winds are stronger and beach umbrellas less prominent. **Mandraki,** one of the better ones, is up a sandy road from stop #23. If you prefer to steer clear of the bus route altogether, a 45min. walk north of town past the airport will take you to **Xanemo Beach,** frequented by locals. Private beach hunters will do well to explore the area of the coastline that stretches towards town.

NIGHTLIFE

Indulge yourself at the innumerable bars in **Pl. Papadiamantis,** on **Polytechniou,** or on **Evangelistra.** Island novelists have a tradition of writing from real life, and if you're lucky, you may be immortalized as a minor character by a latter-day Papadiamantis. Expect to pay €2-5 for beer, €5-6 for cocktails, and €3-5 cover on very popular Saturday nights. From October to May, it's a ghost town; by July it hops.

Admiral Benbow Inn (☎24270 22 980), on Polytechniou. A cozy place to begin (or end) the night, with plenty of comfy couches, a talkative crowd, and a €2-per-pint Happy Hour (9pm-midnight) most weekends. Beer €3; cocktails €4.50-5.

Kentavros (☎24270 22 980), off Papadiamantis to the right beyond the Papadiamantis museum. From British to Brazilian pop, this bar plays it all for a mixed crowd. Beer €2.50-3.50; cocktails €6.

Rock and Roll Bar (☎24270 22 944), in the old port. A relaxing place to have a drink. Yellow pillows stand in for chairs on the hill outside. Beer €3.50-5; cocktails €6.60-8.

Spartacus (☎24270 21 891), on Polytechniou. Attracts a young Scandinavian and British crowd. Stop by on "14 Beers Around the World Night" to take a shot at winning a free T-shirt. Beer €2.50-3; cocktails €5.

Party until dawn at one (or many) of the discos that line the waterfront on the right edge of the harbor, facing inland. Clubs play everything from techno to Top 40. Get your drinks beforehand, however, as beer costs about €5. **Kahlua** is one of the better venues, with both interior and exterior bars and wooden dance floors.

For more sedate entertainment, the open-air **Cinema Paradiso,** just past the Papadiamantis museum on the right, screens recent Hollywood hits in English with Greek subtitles. Schedules available on signs along the waterfront or at the AmEx office across the street. (☎24270 23 975. Tickets €6. Shows twice per night, 9 and 11:30pm.) Concerts play at the **Bourtzi,** the small peninsula jutting out next to the Flying Dolphin dock, during July and August. Ask at the information kiosk in the harbor for program schedules.

SKOPELOS Σκοπελος

Skopelos sits between the whirlwind of Skiathos and the largely untouched wilderness of Alonnisos and incorporates the best elements of both. Hikes and moped rides through shady forests of tall pine lead to numerous monasteries, bright beaches, and white cliffs that drop into a dazzlingly blue sea. By night, the waterfront strip in town closes to traffic, and crowds swarm the streets in search of the tastiest gyros and the most authentic Greek taverna. The best bars in town tend to be relaxed and appealing in unique ways, and a few quality clubs keep the kids on their feet until the wee hours of the morning.

SKOPELOS TOWN

Skopelos Town winds up the steep hills above the harbor, amphitheater to the vast stage of the Aegean. Close to the waterfront, the plethora of moped rental shops, cafes, and tavernas may deceive new arrivals. Farther up the hill, narrow streets twist among whitewashed buildings, beautiful churches peek from behind every bend, and cafes perch precariously among the sloping corridors. These alleys lie still in the night and are a joy to wander. If the silence spooks you, the lively pulse of waterfront bars and clubs are only a short stroll away.

TRANSPORTATION

Ferries and Flying Dolphins dock at the concrete landing on the left side of the harbor, facing inland. **Taxis** await near the ferry dock; the **bus station** is just down the street to the left.

Ferries: Hellas Lines (☎24240 22 767 or 24240 23 060; fax 24240 23 608), directly across from the ferry dock, runs ferries to: **Agios Konstantinos** (4hr., 1 per day every day except Wed., €13.20); **Alonnisos** (30min., 1-2 per day, €3.40); **Skiathos** (1hr., 3-4 per day, €3.10); **Thessaloniki** (2 per week, €38.87); **Volos** (4hr., 2-3 per day, €11.30). Some of the ferries are jet ferries, which have the same trip durations and prices as Flying Dolphins. Prices are slightly higher in July and August.

Flying Dolphins: Minoan Lines (☎24240 22 767 or 24240 23 060; fax 24240 23 608). Tickets also sold directly across from the ferry dock. To: **Agios Konstantinos** (2hr., 1-2 per day, €26.40); **Alonnisos** (30min., 6 per day, €6.70); **Skiathos** (45min., 6 per day, €8.80); **Volos** (2hr., 2-4 per day, €22.50).

Buses: The stop is left of the ferry dock facing inland, on the left side of the road. Bus lines run a circuit between **Stafilos, Agnondas, Panormos,** and **Milia** (12 per day, 7am-10:30pm), and another between **Elios, Glossa,** and **Loutraki** (8 per day, 7am-10:30pm). You can also request to be let off at beaches in between stops. Check the posted schedules at the stop or call **Thalpos Travel Agency** (☎24240 22 947).

Taxis: Available at the waterfront 7am-2am.

Moped and Car Rental: Shop around—most travel agencies arrange rentals. Mopeds €10-15; cars €40. Prices vary by season, amenities, sound effects, and distance.

ORIENTATION AND PRACTICAL INFORMATION

Tourist agencies, tavernas, and cafes line the waterfront. **Galatsaniou,** a fashionable street lined with souvenir and snack shops, darts upward between Cafe Cafe and Cafe Aktaion, 100m to the right of the ferry dock facing inland. **Platanos,** a small plateia brimming with souvlaki and gyro restaurants, is across from the ferry dock, with the monument on your right and the playground on your left. On the far right of the waterfront, just before the jetty, whitewashed stairs line the side of the town, passing many **churches** along the way.

Tourist Agencies: Most **exchange currency,** rent mopeds and cars, sell ferry tickets, and run trips to nearby islands. **Thalpos Travel Agency** (☎24240 22 947; fax 24240 23 057; thalpos@otenet.gr), 5m to the right of Galanatsiou along the waterfront, can advise you on everything from Flying Dolphin tickets to catching octopi and provide you with a useful map of the town and island. English spoken. Open May-Oct. 10am-2pm and 6-10pm; Oct.-May available by fax or telephone.

Banks: National Bank (☎24240 22 691), on the right side of the waterfront, has a 24hr. **ATM.** Open M-Sa 8am-2pm.

Bookstore: International Press, just off the bottom left corner of Platanos, sells international newspapers and English-language books. Open daily 8am-12am.

Emergency: For police, dial ☎100. For medical care, dial ☎24240 22 222.

Police: (☎24240 22 295), behind the National Bank.

Medical Center: (☎24240 22 222). Follow the left-hand road inland from Pl. Platanos past Ag. Ioannis to the dead end, then go right at the signs. Open M-F 9am-2pm for free walk-ins; open M-F 24hr. for **emergencies.**

OTE: (☎24240 22 139 or 24240 22 121), 100m up from the water on Galatsaniou. Open M-F 7:30am-1:30pm.

Internet access: The Internet Cafe, on the road that runs through the back of Platanos. Coming from the waterfront, take a left at the end of the plateia; the cafe is 150m down the road, on the left. Internet €4 per hr., charged by the minute. Printing €0.30 per page. Faxing to Europe €2.50 per page; US €3.50 per page. Beer €2. Open 10am-late.

Post Office: (☎24240 22 203). 50m beyond the Internet Cafe on the same road. Look for the yellow postbox. Open M-F 7:30am-1:30pm. **Postal code:** 37003.

ACCOMMODATIONS AND FOOD

In general, Skopelos's hotels cater to all-inclusive-resort tourists. Don't worry: the **Rooms and Apartments Association of Skopelos,** in the small stone building next to the town hall, around the waterfront to the right (facing inland), can provide a list of current **domatia.** (☎24240 24 567. Open 10am-2pm and 6-10pm.) Prices vary by season, but are generally €15-30 for singles and €20-40 (and up) for doubles. Dock hawks may also offer reasonable rooms.

Pension Sotos ❷, on the corner of Galatsaniou on the waterfront, is a gem, both for its fantastic location (right on the waterfront in the center of town) and its diamond-in-the-rough price. A renovated Skopelian house, the pension provides baths and fans, a common kitchen, quiet courtyard, and book exchange. (☎24240 22 549; fax 24240 23 668. Singles €17-35; doubles €24-35; triples €35-52.)

Also known as "Souvlaki Square," **Pl. Platanos** abounds with fast, cheap food. For slower-paced dining, **Taverna O Molos ❷** (☎24240 22 551), around the waterfront to the right facing inland, serves delicious traditional Greek food with a harbor view. Entrees run €4-8. Specialties include lamb kleftika (€7.20).

SIGHTS AND ENTERTAINMENT

Skopelos Town has an abundance of **churches.** Thalpos Travel (see **Orientation** above) can provide a map that pinpoints many of them. A good place to start your tour is around the harbor to the far right, where beautiful whitewashed **Panagia ston Pirgho** perches on the rocks. Follow the stairs below the church and up along the sea-edge of the city. Along the way pass tiny, simple **Evangelismos and Athanasios**—just below the Castro—the town's oldest church, built in the 11th century. Just off to the left is **Genesis tou Christou,** a larger cruciform church with a round cupola and clock tower. Continuing up the side of the city, walk over the **Castro,** originally built by King Philip of Macedon in the 4th century BC. Today it is the site of a traditional taverna featuring live Greek music. On the uphill side of the Castro, wind your way into town and head for the top of the hill, where **Spiridon** rewards tired hikers. Slightly farther into the city lies **Papameletiou,** a cruciform basilica built in 1662 with a red-tile roof and small clock tower. Closer to the waterfront, **Ag. Nikolaos,** just up Galatsaniou on the left, exhibits brightly colored icons and a marble statue of the Virgin. In **Mikhail-Sinnadon,** a stone cruciform basilica features a remarkable iconostasis. Skopelos draws international students and recognition for its **Photographic Center of Skopelos** (☎24240 24 121); call for more info. The **Folklore Museum,** 100m left past the OTE, has a dull collection of island artifacts, but the meticulously researched first-floor exhibit on popular religion is worth a look. (☎24240 23 494. Open 11am-2:30pm and 7-10:30pm. €2.)

A 10min. walk up the whitewashed stairs on the far right of the waterfront leads to **Anatoli,** the haunt of one of the world's last great *rembetika* singers, Giorgos Xintaris. Some nights (usually a little before midnight), you may be lucky enough to catch him with a group of friends singing the old songs. The sounds and setting are phenomenal. (Beer €2.50. Cocktails €5.50-6.50. Open daily 8pm-late.) For new jazz and blues, **Platanos Jazz Club,** on the far right of the harbor facing inland, near the jetty, lets you relax with a drink by candlelight under a gargantuan tree. (☎24240 23 661. Beer €3; cocktails €6.50. Open 8am-3pm.) **The Blue Bar,** two blocks up Galanatsiou in an alley on the right (just past the church of Ag. Nikolaos), plays folk, rock, and blues music that accompanies the €3 beers just fine. Skopelos's **dance clubs** cluster midway up a street off of Pl. Platanos. Chat with American painting students at **Metro.** (☎24240 24 446. Open May-Oct. daily, Oct.-May weekends only. €3 cover goes towards your first drink.) **Kounos** is Skopelos's oldest bar—nine years and counting. Top 40 and foreign hits shake the speakers. (☎24240 24 300. €3 cover goes towards your first drink.)

BEACHES

Traveling Skopelos's asphalt road by bus or car to Loutraki or Glossa gives you your pick of the lovely southern beaches. Archaeologists discovered the tomb of the ancient Cretan general **Stafylos** on a nearby hillside, along with a 15th-century BC gold-plated sword that's now in the Volos museum. Stafylos beach is crowded with families; nearby **Valanio,** over the hill to the left as you face the sea, is less full. Named for the trickling spring that was a gushing fountain in Roman times, today Valanio is advertised as the only nude beach on Skopelos. Past the small town of **Agnondas,** a paved road leads about 1km to the sparkling blue beach of **Limnonari;** ask the bus driver to let you off at the top of the road or take a water taxi. Farther along the asphalt road is the wide, deep bay of **Panormos,** the ancient forest. From here, a 5min. walk leads to the isolated **Adrina** beaches, named for the female pirate who terrorized the islands, leaping to her death in this cove after being cornered by angry islanders. Silvery **Milia,** the island's largest beach (and believed by many to be its most beautiful) is accessible by paved road and has water sports and its own little islet called **Dassia.** Closer to Loutraki, dirt paths lead to the northern beaches of **Spilia, Marraki, Keramoto,** and **Chondroyiorghi.**

HIKES FROM SKOPELOS TOWN

Due to Skopelos's predominantly dirt roads, the island is best explored by moped or on foot. The island's single, 35km-long asphalt road runs from the Skopelos bus station through Stafylos (4km), Agnondas (8km), Panormos (18km), Elios (24km), Loutraki (30km), and Glossa (32km).

Dragon Cliffs. According to local lore, a fierce dragon went on a fiery bender, eating almost everyone on Skopelos until Ag. Rigine killed it and became the island's protector. The Dragon Cliffs *(Drakondoschisma),* where the creature was hurled to its death, are now a quiet picnicking spot with a sea view and an altar portraying the dragon's grisly demise. (To find it, take the asphalt road from Skopelos Town through Stafylos and turn left down a small dirt road which disappears into the woods about 2km before Agnodas beach.)

Monasteries of Mt. Palouki. 2 paved roads leave the town from the bus depot on the right end of the waterfront. To reach the monasteries, follow the road out of the harbor to the left (facing inland)—signs mark the way to the monasteries ascending Mt. Palouki. **Evangelismos** was built in the 18th century as part of the Monastery of Xiropotamos of Athos, but its enormous altar screen—the genuine article from Constantinople—is 400 years older. Take the left-hand fork up the hot, winding mountain road for 45min.; start early in the morning before the heat and bugs intensify and in time to reach the monasteries before their 1-5pm daily closing. Up the right fork, another 45min. walk leads you to the **Monastery of the Transfiguration** (Metamorphosis). Its chapel, set in a flowered courtyard, dates from the 16th century. Another hour up the hill along the road takes you to 2 monasteries perched on precipitous ridges overlooking the sea. The first, the **Monastery of Ag. Varvaras**, was built as a fortress in 1648. Nearby **Prothromou** contains icons dating back to the 14th and 15th centuries and wall paintings. Once a functioning monastery, Prodromou is now a cloister dedicated to St. John the Baptist; its astounding setting surveys the entire coast. The dirt path that begins behind the building leads to the smaller monasteries of **Agia Triada** and **Agia Taxianches.** Farther up the road, a trail leads to the beautiful monastery of **Agia Anna.**

Monasteries of Agios Ioannis. At the end of the road on the opposite side of the island from Skopelos Town, the quiet hilltop town of **Glossa** looks down on Skopelos's second port. For a 4hr. round-trip hike from Glossa, walk the dirt track across the island to the **Monastery of Agios Ioannis,** clinging spectacularly to a boulder above the ocean. Take the main road east from Glossa and turn left on the first dirt road to Steki Taverna; it's clear sailing after that. At the road's end, a path drops to the sea, and stone steps, cut in the escarpment, lead up to the monastery. The entire road is navigable by motorbike, up to the stairs. A paved road also leads to the church from the road above Glossa, but watch out for loose gravel if you take a moped.

ALONNISOS Αλοννησος

Of the twenty-odd islands within Greece's new National Marine Park, only Alonnisos is inhabited, and its fledgling tourist industry remains friendly to those who come to explore its natural treasures. In the past, visitors to the island might have been regarded suspiciously. Until about a century ago, Alonnisos was a refuge for people hiding from the government—pirates, maligned activists, Communists, and the like. Of course, time spent on Alonnisos is more a blessing than a punishment. Hikers take to the highland trails in the north, where aromatic herbs spice the air and the coastal cliffs, awash in green pine and white sand, form an unspoiled boundary with the sea. In the south, there are beaches aplenty to satisfy less adventurous souls.

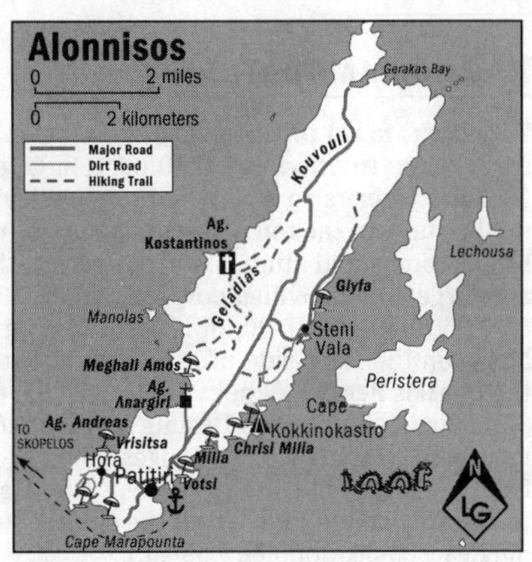

Gioura, a small island to the northeast of Alonnisos, is believed to have been the home of **Polyphemus,** the cyclops whose eye was gouged out by Odysseus' sizzling lance. Though many islands claim this distinction, Gioura hosts a rocky landscape that best fits Homer's description of Polyphemus's cavern and herds of the now-endangered brown goats with black crosses on their backs.

PATITIRI Πατητηρι

All boats dock at Patitiri, which is the only town on the island. Sharp-angled and hastily built, it's not a postcard harbor, but it serves as an easily accessible base to explore the rest of Alonnisos and the surrounding Marine Park. Work has recently been done on the port to expand the ferry dock and provide better seating areas for the waterfront cafes and tavernas.

ORIENTATION AND PRACTICAL INFORMATION

From the docks, two main parallel streets run inland: **Pelasgon** on the left, and **Ikion Dolophon** on the right. **Ferries** run to: **Agios Konstantinos** (5½hr., 2 per week, €13.40); **Skiathos** (2hr., 1-2 per day, €6); **Skopelos** (30min., 1-2 per day, €5); and **Volos** (5¼hr., 1-2 per day, €12.30). **Flying Dolphins** go to: **Agios Konstantinos** (2¾hr., 1-2 per day, €26.80); **Glossa** (35min., 3-5 per day, €10); **Skiathos** (1¼hr., 4-7 per day, €12); **Skopelos** (25min., 4-7 per day, €6.70); and **Volos** (2½hr., 2-3 per day, €24.60). Prices go up in the July-Aug. high season.

The island's **bus** runs from its waterfront stop to **Hora** (every hr. 9am-3:25pm and 7pm-midnight, €1) and to **Steni Vala** twice per day (9:20am, 2:35am). Schedules are posted at the Patitiri, Hora, and Steni Vala stops. **Taxis,** lined up along the waterfront, run until 2am; they respond to calls any time (taxi phone numbers are posted on phone booths). **Motorbikes,** the fastest way to explore Alonnisos, are available for rent at the numerous shops on Pelasgon and Ikion Dolophon. Expect to pay €8-15 for a 24hr. rental.

Alonnisos Travel, in the center of the waterfront, **exchanges currency,** finds rooms, books excursions, and sells ferry tickets. (☎24240 65 188; fax 24240 65 511. Open daily 8am-11pm.) Up Ikion Dolophon, the **Port Police** are on the corner. (☎24240 65 595. Open 24hr.) The **National Bank** with 24hr. **ATM** lies on the left. (☎24240 65 777. Open M-Th 8am-2pm, F 8am-1:30pm.) The **police** (☎24240 65 205) are on the top of the hill, near the **hospital.** (☎24240 65 208. Open daily 9am-1pm, 24hr. for emergency.) **Internet access** is available at **Il Mondo** on Ikion Dolophon, just before the post office. (☎24240 65 834. Open daily 9:30am-11pm. Internet €4 per hr., €2 minimum; printing €0.50 per page; fax €2.50 per page.) The **post office** is a 5min. walk up Ikion Dolophon. (☎24240 65 560. Open M-F 7:30am-2pm.) **Postal code:** 37005.

ACCOMMODATIONS

The **Rooms to Let Office** next to Ikos Travel can lend a hand to travelers looking for a place to stay. (☎24240 66 188. Open daily 10:30am-1:30pm and 5:30-10:30pm.) **Panorama ❷,** down the first alley on the left up Ikion Dolophon (walk up the stairs to the top of the hill and turn in at the courtyard on the right), rents bright rooms and studios with private baths, common fridges, some kitchens, and large, bougainvillea-covered common balconies with a port view. (☎24240 65 240. Singles €15-30; doubles €25-45; triples €35-50.) Inquire at Boutique Mary, on the right side of Pelasgon, about simple rooms with private baths at the **Dimakis Pension ❷** next door. (☎24240 65 294. Singles €15-32; doubles €20-32.) Magdalini and Ilias Besinis rent immaculate **Rooms and Studios ❸** with private baths, kitchens, and fridges, about 200m up Pelasgon on the left, across from I'M Motorbikes. A gorgeous stone staircase and hand-painted decor adds to the atmosphere; it's worth the splurge. (☎/fax 24240 65 451. Book exchange. Singles €25-30; doubles €35-40.)

FOOD AND NIGHTLIFE

Locals adore the little *ouzeri* **To Kamaki ❶**, on the left side of Ikion Dolophon past the National Bank. Try the delectable warm octopus salad for €5, or order the *ouzo meh mezedes* and be surprised with a sampling of local cuisine (€2.10). (☎24240 65 245. Open daily 11am-2am.) Stop by popular **To Steki ❶** (☎24240 65 816), on the corner of Pelasgon, for cheap and tasty souvlaki and gyros (€1.50). (☎24240 65 816. Open 9pm-late.) **Artolikoudies ❶**, just up from the harbor on the right of Pelasgon, serves delicious summer olive bread (€1.50) and traditional pastries (€0.90-1.40). Listen to Sting's greatest hits while you sip a cocktail (€6) under a gnarled tree and a vine-draped terrace at waterfront **Pub Dennis**, the island's oldest café-bar. **Club Enigma**, a short walk up Pelasgon, is the (only) place to boogie. (Open F-Sa June and Sept., W-Sa July and Aug.)

SIGHTS AND BEACHES

The **History and Folklore Museum** of Alonnisos, to the far left of the waterfront facing inland and up the stairs, features a wide variety of cultural artifacts from Alonnisos. Exhibits include weaponry from major conflicts from the Balkan Wars to World War II, historical maps of the Sporades and Greece, and, downstairs, an excellent series of **trade exhibits** on everything from winemaking to pack-saddle construction. (Open daily 11am-7pm. €3.)

Many **beaches** are accessible from the island's main road, which runs along the spine of the island from Patitiri to the port of Gherakas in the far north. A 90min. walk on this road from Patitiri takes you to **Votsi**, the island's other major settlement. Local boys dive off the 15-20m cliffs near Votsi beach, just outside the village. Beyond Votsi, the road passes separate turn-offs for the pine-girded beaches of **Milia** and the longer, shallower **Chrisi Milia.** The beaches are also accessible by **rented boat** from Votsi; ask at the port. Farther up the coast from Chrisi Milia is the beach and archaeological site of **Kokkinocastro**, where swimmers occasionally find ancient coins. The tiny fishing village of **Steni Vala**, 12km north of Patitiri, with a population fluctuating between 25 and 60, is the only other bus stop (20min., 2 per day, €1)—the **fantastic fish tavernas** alone are worth the trip. Sandy **Glyla** beach is along the shore, north of the village.

HIKES AND THE OUTDOORS

Only the south end of the island is inhabited, leaving stretches of mountain wilderness to the north. Though a **moped** remains the quickest way to explore—Patitiri to Gerakas takes about 45min.—it's worth **hiking.** Trails are marked at regular intervals and include terrain from paved roads to steep, rocky trails. **Blue maps**, scattered throughout the island, mark trailheads and show the trail routes, which are marked by **numerical yellow signs**, but the purchase of a good trail map (€3-5) or *Alonnisos on Foot* (€9), a walking and swimming guide, both available in Patitiri, is recommended. Numbers below refer to marked trail numbers.

AROUND ALONNISOS. The **Meghalo Nero - Ag. Anarghiri - Meghali Amos - Raches - Votsi** (**#5**, 6km, 2½hr.) trail takes you along the southeastern side of Alonnisos, to the secluded **monastery** of Ag. Anarghiri and **beach** of Meghali Amos. The trail-

THE BIG SPLURGE

TASIA'S

Good seafood restaurants aren't hard to come by in Greece, but **Tasia's** may beat them all in terms of quality control. This taverna, in the tiny village of Steni Vala, is a family operation from start to finish. Tasia Malamatenios, who inherited the business from her mother, prepares and serves the food with the help of her son and four daughters. Peter, their parrot, welcomes diners with some skillful whistling and occasional "*kalimera*," and the family's dogs provide entertainment before the meal arrives. Tasia's husband George, the family fisherman, is crucial to the taverna's distinctive appeal–instead of getting the fish from Volos, like most tavernas on Alonnisos, Tasia's is supplied exclusively by his rig. This means that while the selection is not always as wide as that of other tavernas, the fish is as fresh as it gets. You can sit down to lunch here and eat fish that was probably caught hours (and no more than a day) before.

Enjoying fresh seafood usually requires a significant financial sacrifice, and Tasia's is no exception. The seafood costs anywhere from €30-55 per kg. Nevertheless, try the lobster (€51 per kg) with spaghetti; monetary troubles will be forgotten with the first bite. For those who don't have the desire (or means) to splurge, small fried fish come in individual portions (€5) and the usual Greek fare is available as well (stuffed tomatoes €4, moussaka €5.50).

The first taverna you come to on Steni Vala's tiny harbor. Open daily noon-midnight.

head is just up the main road from Votsi. Head out Ikion Dolophon from Patitiri to get to the main road, then follow the signs to Votsi and Steni Vala. From Meghali Amos, two trails, **#7** (1½hr.) and **#8** (1½hr.) lead north to **Meghalo Chorafi,** east of the main road, the hub for hikes to **Ag. Laka beach** (**#14,** 45min.) and the church of **Ag. Kostantinos** (**#6,** 2hr.). From Ag. Kostantinos, hikes lead north to the church of **Ag. Georgios** (**#12,** 1hr.) and **Meleghakia** (**#13,** 1½hr.) in the more rugged part of the island. Hikes **#12** and **13** both bring you back to the main road. From **Steni Vala,** hike **#10** (1hr.) takes you south past the beach of **Ag. Petros** to **Isomata** and on to the main road. From Isomata, hike **#9** winds its way down to **Leftos** beach (45min.). Far north on the island, past Ag. George, a dirt road leads to the trailhead for trail **#11,** which leads down to the beach of **Ag. Dimitrios** (1hr.).

DAYTRIPS FROM PATITIRI

HORA (OLD TOWN) Χωρα

The island's only bus runs from Patitiri to Hora before continuing to Steni Vala (10min., every hr. 9am-3:25pm and 7-12am, €1). Schedules are posted at the bus stop in each town. Taxis are available (about €8 round-trip).

Set high on a hill to ward off pirates, Hora now welcomes visitors looking for the island village charm that Patitiri lacks. Its quiet, crooked alleys open suddenly onto incredible views of the island and wind their way into the dusty hills. From here, you can spy out your own private beach (see below). Tiny 12th-century **Christ Church** is run by Father Gregorias, the village priest and local legend. **Hiliadroma ❸**, up behind the church, has beautiful wood-accented rooms with stone floors, tiled private baths, and fantastic balcony views. Some rooms have kitchenettes. (☎24240 65 814. Singles €25-38; doubles €30-38; triples €35-45.) Hora is host to a variety of quaint cafes and tavernas, some perched on beautiful overlooks. From the bus stop, veer left up the hill past the old church, continuing up the stairs to reach a charming paved street with several cafes; the best views are at the end of the street. **Taverna Aloni ❷**, up the right-hand fork from the bus station at the base of an old windmill (sans blades), serves Greek food with spectacular views of the island. (Starters €2-3; entrees €5 and up.) For a similar view but different cuisine, try the pizzas and pastas at **Nappo ❷**, past the church. (Pastas €6.50; pizza €7.50. Open 7pm-midnight.)

THE BEST LAID PLANS OF MEAT AND MEN

Old villages on the Greek islands often seem designed to trap the unsuspecting tourist. The jigsaw puzzle quality of street layouts makes every casual stroll an adventure—sometimes an extremely frustrating one. Most island streets were designed in this fashion to deter pirate attacks, but Alonnisos's Hora has an unusual explanation for all the madness. Many years ago, when settlers first came to the island, they performed a goat sacrifice, beheading the animal and then cutting it into pieces. They placed the pieces of meat at potential building locations, which they had previously scouted out. Over the next few days, they checked on the meat. If a piece had kept, then they'd found a prime location for building, sheltered from sun and pests and other elements. Of course, the ancient planners weren't concerned with how easy it would be to get from one place to the next. So while street plans might seem to be the work of a one-eyed *tsipouro* fiend, take comfort in the fact that in the beginning, it was all done to give Greek cuisine its most important quality: unrivaled freshness.

HIKING TRAILS AND BEACHES. Four hiking trails lead down from Hora to beaches and overlooks in the southern part of Alonnisos. The trail to **Mikros Mourtias (#1,** 1.5km, 45min.) begins at the bus stop. Walk through town, past the church, and up the stairs to a street lined with cafés. Turn left before the street ends and walk down the narrow side street to the trailhead. A dirt road also leads down to the beach from the village. Mikros Mourtias is a small beach replete with perfectly-shaped skipping stones. The tiny inlet is perfect for a quiet evening swim. **Kalovoulos (#2,** 1.5km, 45min.) is an enchanting overlook on the rocky coast east of Hora; go here to take in the sunset. Continue on the main road past the bus stop and the trail is on the left. A miniature beach on a secluded cove, **Vrisitsa (#3,** 1km, 30min.) is accessible by trail to the right off the main road just past the bus stop in Hora. Off the main road just before the bus stop, **Patitiri (#4,** 1.5km, 35min.) connects the Old Town to the New.

NATIONAL MARINE PARK

The park islands are accessible by specially licensed boat. Most trips, advertised and sold along the Patitiri harborfront, are all-inclusive single-day trips for €40. MOM's HQ, on the corner of Ikion Dolophon, is open May-Oct. daily 10am-2pm and 6-10:30pm. (info@mom.gr; www.mom.gr.)

Surrounding Alonnisos are the 25 small, ecologically protected islets of Greece's National Marine Park. The largest and most important are **Peristera, Skantzoura, Piperi, Kyra Panagia, Jura**, and **Psatnoura.** They're strictly regulated and visited only by organized tour boats in summer. Psatnoura, Kyra Panagia, and Skantzoura are owned by nearby Mt. Athos (see p. 256) and are used in part for grazing goats. Visiting Jura and Piperi is forbidden in an effort to protect numerous rare species, including the **Mediterranean monk seal.** The monk seals number only about 500 total in the Mediterranean; a growing colony of approximately 50 monk seals is now carefully monitored by MOM, an Alonnisos-based sea patrol unit named for the Latin name of the seals, *monachus monachus*. Unless you're a MOM official, forget about seeing the monk seals. Enthusiasts *are* free to draw a **"Save the Seals"** poster for the gallery in MOM's Alonnisos ferry dock headquarters. They provide crayons, paper, and info in English about ecology and conservation efforts.

SKYROS Σκυρος

Skyros is dominated by two forces—modern tourism and local tradition—that are as diametrically opposed as the terrain found on each side of the island. But while the barren landscape of the south and the green hills of the north will always remain separate, the two influences on Skyrian life are beginning to coexist more happily. The preservation of the island's folkways has been recognized as an important priority, as well as a major draw for those travelers weary of the typical tourist-infested vacation island. The trend promises to continue, as there is no longer a link to Skyros from the other Sporades. Those who visit the island are most likely in the market for more than just a whirlwind beach and bar tour.

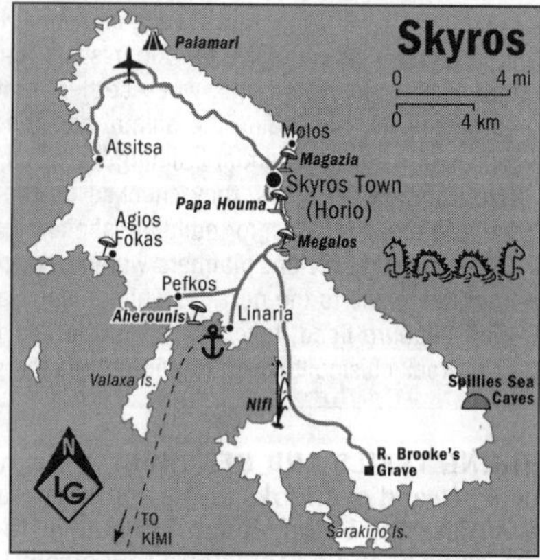

SKYROS TOWN

Like a gleaming pocket of snow, Skyros Town (Horio—"the village"—to locals) stands out in bright white contrast to the greens, yellows and browns of the hills that surround it. Beyond the requisite tavernas, cafes, and bars lie the features that give the island its distinctive character. Here, old men sew sandals by porchlight late into the evening, women embroider patterns learned from pirates, and a crazed goat-man spooks the streets at Carnival.

TRANSPORTATION

The best way to get to Skyros is to take the **bus** from **Athens** to **Kimi** on Evia (3½hr., 2 per day, €9.95), then the **ferry** to Skyros from Kimi (2 per day, €7.25). Note: buses to Kimi stop in the town, 5km from the ferry port; less frequent buses go directly to and from the ferry dock. If you land in Kimi proper, either take a **taxi** from the bus station or walk down the long winding road. No ferries run to the other Sporades. Unfortunately, hydrofoil service to the other Sporades ended in 2000, making Skyros a difficult destination to reach on an island hopping tour.

The ferry to Skyros arrives in **Linaria,** the tiny western port; a **local bus** to Skyros Town picks up when ferries arrive (20min., 3 per day, €0.80) and leaves Skyros Town about one hour prior to ferry departures; another bus runs from Skyros Town to **Molos** (10min., daily, €0.80). Skyros Travel posts schedules (see below). Buses stop in Skyros Town at the base of **Agoras,** the town's backbone road, which heads straight uphill from the stop. Veering left and downhill from the stop, the road winds around the base of the hill, passing Magazia on its way to Molos. The **military airport** (☎22220 91 607), 20km from Skyros Town on the island's northern tip, flies to **Athens** (35min., 2 per week, €33); you'll have to take a cab there (€11). **Taxis** (☎22220 91 666) wait by the central plateia or the bus stop. They aren't available late at night or during siesta hours.

ORIENTATION AND PRACTICAL INFORMATION

Shops, pharmacies, bars, and restaurants ascend the hill in Skyros Town along **Agoras.** Mazelike residential streets scatter out in every direction along the hillsides. Buildings are numbered counterintuitively, and few streets are named; when venturing off Agoras, pick out landmarks on your way. At the far end of town, **Pl. Rupert Brooke,** looking out across Molos and the sea, is dedicated to British poet Brooke and to "immortal poetry" (αθανατη την ποιησι). To reach Pl. Brooke, walk up Agoras through town until it forks left at Calypso Bar. Head left along the wall and walk up until you reach a sign pointing to "Brooke & Museums" (right) and Γιαλος (beach, left). Veer right and follow the narrow street to the plateia. At the top of the hill, before descending to the plateia, a sign points the way up marble-edged steps to the **Monastery of Ag. George** and the **castle.** Both are closed, but make the climb anyway for a great view of both the entire village and the sea. At Pl. Rupert Brooke, the stairs to the right pass the **archaeological museum** on a 15min. descent to the beach; stairs straight ahead lead to the **Faltaits Museum.**

Skyros Travel, past the central plateia on Agoras walking away from the bus station, sells **Olympic Airways** tickets; it also organizes bus and boat excursions and helps visitors find lodging. The **port office** in Linaria opens according to ferry arrivals. (☎22220 91 123 or 22220 91 600; fax 22220 92 123. Open daily 9am-2:30pm and 6:30-11pm.) The **National Bank,** just past the central plateia, has a 24hr. **ATM.** (Open M-Th 8am-2pm and F 8am-1:30pm.) The **hospital** (☎22220 92 222) is just out of town behind the Hotel Nefeli. Ask at the **police** station, beyond Nefeli across from the gas station, for **doctors** in town. (☎22220 91 274. Open 24hr., but small staff may be away on another call.) There are **pharmacies** on the right near the central plateia (☎22220 91 617; open 8:30am-1pm and 6:30-10pm) and on the right past Skyros Travel. (☎22220 91 111. Open daily 9am-2pm and 6pm-1am.) **Internet access** is available at **Meroi Cafe** on Agoras. (☎22220 91 016. €4.50 per hr., €1.50 minimum; printing €0.50 per page.) To get to the **OTE,** turn right just past Skyros Travel, walk to the end of the road, and take another right; it's on the right. (☎22220 91 399. Open M-F 7:30am-1pm.) The **post office** is across the central plateia from Agoras. (☎22220 91 208. Open M-F 7:30am-2pm.) **Postal code:** 34007.

ACCOMMODATIONS

Coming to Skyros and staying in a hotel is like coming to Greece to paddle in a pool—you've got to stay in a Skyrian house. You'll be met at the bus stop by old women offering domatia; you can also wander the narrow stairs with any sort of luggage, and you'll be asked the simple question, "Domatia?" The thick-walled houses are treasure troves, brimming with Delft ceramics, Italian linens, icons, embroidery, metalwork, and fine china bought from long-dead pirates who looted throughout the Mediterranean. Expect to pay €15-35 for a room, depending on size and season. If you decide to stay in a Skyrian house, always **bargain** over the price and look carefully for landmarks and house numbers, as the streets may be extremely confusing, and it's easy to lose your way. The aid of a travel agency will cost you an arm, a leg, and the essence of the whole experience. If you arrive during siesta, the town is dead as a doornail, and your calls for a domatia may be answered only with snores from within.

If you don't feel like searching for a room, try **Hotel Elena ❷**, on the first right off of Agoras past the bus station. The spartan but comfortable rooms have private baths, balconies, and common fridges. (☎22220 91 738 or 22220 91 070. Singles €15; doubles €30; triples €40.) **Hotel Nefeli ❹**, just before town on the main road, boasts classy, well-equipped rooms with TVs, A/C, private baths, phones, and some balconies, which look out on the swimming pool. (☎22220 91 964 or 22220 92 060. Singles €38-50; doubles € 43-69.)

FOOD AND NIGHTLIFE

After a long afternoon swim, you can't go wrong with Skyrian food. Look for the light green chairs outside the incredible **O Pappou Kai Ego** ("Grandpa and Me") ❷, toward the top of Agoras on the right. Known in town as "Pappou's", the popular spot concocts a brilliant chicken *o pappous* floating in a light cream sauce over rice, as well as many Skyrian specialties, including nanny goat au lemon. (☎22220 93 200. Entrees €4-8. Open daily 7pm-late. Get there early to avoid a long wait.) **Kristina's at Pegasus ❶,** down the alley to the left just past Skyros Travel, cooks up some delicious vegetarian entrees in a quiet courtyard. The fresh hot herb bread makes an excellent snack (€2.10). Just before Pappou's, **Obelistirio** ❶ serves up a slow-cooked, just-shy-of-healthy, incredibly delicious €1.50 gyro. (☎22220 92 205. Open daily 6pm-2am.) **Kalypso Bar,** at the top of Agoras past Pappou's, is a mellow place to sip a nightcap after a tasty Skyrian meal. (Cocktails €5-6.) For a more action-packed night, join the younger crowds at the two bars across from the central plateia, **Iroon** and **Kata Lathos** (beer €2.50-4.50, cocktails €4.50-5.50).

SIGHTS AND ENTERTAINMENT

The **Faltaits Museum,** just past Pl. Rupert Brooke, is the private collection of a Skyrian ethnologist and shouldn't be missed. Tours (available in English) guide you through the frozen-in-time ancestral home of the Faltaits family. The extensive holdings include beautiful examples of embroidery, carved furniture, pottery, costumes, copperware, rare books, and relics from the island's annual carnival—it's an excellent introduction to the island's traditional culture. The wise, friendly staff speak perfect English, affectionately calling the museum "a place where the nine muses meet." Conferences and cultural activities are held here throughout the year, including a **theater and dance festival** in late July and August; ask the staff for dates and times. (☎22220 91 232 or 22220 91 150; faltaits@otenet.gr. Open daily 10am-2pm and 6-9pm. €2.) Down the stairs to the right of Pl. Rupert Brooke, the **Archaeological Museum** holds significant island artifacts culled from on-going excavations around the island, including Bronze Age and Mycenaean relics. (☎22220 91 327. Open Tu-Su 8:30am-3pm. €2.)

Both museums have rooms decorated in the manner of traditional Skyrian homes, but if you decide to venture out onto the labyrinthine streets of the village, don't be afraid to knock on a door or two and ask to see the real thing. Most Skyrians will be proud to show you their homes, all of which are decorated with the distinctive scarves, plates and furnishings of the island. Closer to the beaten path, on Agoras after going left at Kalypso, is the "upper village," a stronghold of island tradition. In several shops in the area, jewels, sandals, and other Skyrian items are crafted and sold. The museum shop, **Argo,** can also be found here. (Open daily 9:30am-1:30pm, 6:30-10:30pm.) The shop's proprietor, Niko Sikkes, gives occasional talks on Skyros and leads walking tours of the island. Contact him to find out when (☎22220 92 707 or 22220 92 158).

Skyros is best known among Hellenes for its **Skyrian Carnival,** which runs every weekend in February, culminating on the first day of Lent. On this *Kathari Deftera,* an old man dressed in a goat mask and a costume covered with clanging sheep bells leads two young men, one dressed as a Skyrian bride and the other as a 17th-century European (with a large bell hanging from his waist), on a wild dance through town to the monastery. The festival commemorates a land dispute between shepherds and farmers and draws upon many myths and religious customs. One hypothesis holds that the transvestism alludes to Achilles, who dodged the Trojan War draft on Skyros by dressing as a girl.

HAVING HIS DAY Poet **Rupert Brooke,** known for coining the expression, "Every dog has his day," was a British national hero long before his death. Golden-haired Brooke was the empire's articulate darling, lettered and muscled, bright and impetuous. He signed up with the Hood Battalion of the Royal Naval Division in September 1914: "Well, if Armageddon's *on,* I suppose one should be there." After the disastrous Antwerp expedition, he became more patriotic and more serious, continuing to fight for his country despite presentiments of death. Brooke sailed with the British Mediterranean Expeditionary Force in February 1915, during the ill-fated Dardanelles campaign. He made it to Limnos and Egypt before dying of blood poisoning aboard a French hospital ship at Skyros on April 23, Ag. George's Day. At night, by torchlight, he was buried about a mile inland. His grave, a simple wooden cross bearing his name and dates of birth and death, is accessible from Linaria on the southwestern part of the island by car or foot. In a prophetic poem, Brooke left instructions for those who might visit his final resting place: "If I should die, think only this of me: / There is some corner of a foreign field / That is forever England."

BEACHES

The pleasant beach below town stretches along the coast through the villages of **Magazia** and **Molos,** and continues around the point. Crowded and crawling with children in July and August, it's undeniably convenient. The local nude beach, ironically named **Tou Papa to Homa** (The Sands of the Priest), remains clean and uncrowded, just south of the local beach. To get there, follow the seaside road south past Club Skyropoula and some low-ceilinged concrete structures (10-12min.); a narrow, spiky-plant-lined, slippery dirt path leads downhill along a wire fence. Be especially careful on the last 10ft. of the trail. From here, you'll have a beautiful view of the **Southern Mountain,** famous in local literature and poetry for its hourly color changes in the sloping island light. Once home to nymphs, the now-deserted **natural spring** at **Nifi,** south of Linaria, allows you to frolic solo. Scenically barren beaches and **Rupert Brooke's grave** on the southern portion of the island are accessible only by dusty paths or by boat. If you ask, buses from Linaria to Skyros Town may stop at the beaches of **Aherounis,** on the west coast, and **Mialos** on the east. Boats can explore the one-time pirate grottoes at **Spillies,** on the southeastern coast, and **Sarakino Island,** formerly Despot's Island and one of the largest pirate centers in the Aegean. During Ottoman rule, it was an important hiding-place for ships. Keep an eye out for the rare wild **Skyrian ponies.**

EVIA Ευβοια

The second-largest island in Greece, Evia is paradise to any sort of pleasure-seeker, with warm waters, forested highlands, archaeological treasures, charming villages, and therapeutic baths. Its capital, Halkida, reaches out to the mainland via a new suspension bridge. Ferries from ports near Athens connect the mainland at other locations along the western coast of the island: Aedipsos, Marmari, and Karystos. Because of this proximity to Athens, floods of Greek vacationers arrive during the summer months, but Evia absorbs the masses with ease, and its immense appeal is not threatened.

HALKIDA Χαλκιδα

Sprawling, modern Halkida (also known as Chalkida or Chalkis)—the third largest city in Greece—is the capital of Evia as well as its major transportation hub, connecting the island to the mainland. Its sparkling waterfront promenade and archaeological artifacts, nearby beaches and fresh seafood make Halkida a prime starting point for exploration of the island.

TRANSPORTATION

Halkida's main thoroughfare is tree-lined **El. Venizelou,** which runs inland perpendicular to **Voudouri** (the waterfront) for about 12 blocks before bending left into **Eikost Oktovriou.** The **Erippon Bridge,** or **Old Bridge,** connects Halkida to the mainland at the end of the waterfront to the left off El. Venizelou, and points due west, with Halkida at your back. Halkida also joins the mainland via the new **suspension bridge** on the city's south edge, now the connection point for most ground transportation. Halkida's hangar-like **bus terminal** is just off **Papanastasiou,** which intersects with El. Venizelou. **Buses** travel to: **Aedipsos Springs** (2½hr., 3 per day 10:15am-5:15pm, €5.85); **Athens** (2 per hr., €4.50); **Karystos** (3½hr., 3 per day 6am-5:30pm, €7.60); **Kimi** (1½hr., 9 per day, €5.55); **Limni** (2hr., 4 per day 8:30am-5:15pm, €5.15). **Trains** go to **Athens** (17 per day, €3.50). From the train station, cross the Old Bridge and take a left along the waterfront; Venizelou intersects it five blocks down. **Taxis** (☎22210 25 220) are available 24hr.

ORIENTATION AND PRACTICAL INFORMATION

The **port authority,** across the Old Bridge in the huge building, can help you with information about the city. (☎22210 28 888. Open daily 8am-3pm.) The **National Bank** is on El. Venizelou 2 blocks from the water, with a 24hr. **ATM** and **currency exchange.** (Open M-Th 8am-2pm, F 8am-1:30pm.) The English-speaking **tourist police** are only available in the mornings and are fairly inconvenient; their office is a 25min. walk up Venizelou and onto Oktovriou, in the same building as the regular **police.** Call instead. (☎22210 77 777. Open 24hr. except when out on call.) To get to the **hospital** (☎22210 21 901), head up Venizelou away from the water and turn left onto Arethoussas (just after Papanastasiou). Follow the street as it curves and turn left on Chatzopoulou. The hospital is two blocks down on the right. **Pl. Agios Nikolas** borders the waterfront and is host to the **public library** and the **Church of Agios Nikolas.** Dress modestly to enter the church. The **OTE** (☎22210 22 599), is at the intersection of El. Venizelou and Papanastasiou. For fast **Internet access** go to **Orionas Net Cafe,** a 15min. walk down Avanton, the street parallel to Karamourtzouni on the other side of Pl. Agios Nikolas. (☎22210 29 123. €3.60 per hr. Open daily 9:30am-midnight.) The **post office** is on Karamourtzouni between El. Venizelou and Pl. Agios Nikolas, the second left from the waterfront. (Open M-F 7:30am-2pm.) **Postal code:** 34100.

ACCOMMODATIONS

Most hotels here are of the €75-per-night variety, catering to business travelers or Athenian families, so Halkida is not an ideal place to spend the night. That said, there are two inexpensive options.

Hotel Kentrikon, the peach-colored building at Ageli Gobiou 5 (☎22210 22 375 or 22210 27 260; hotel_kentrikon@hotmail.com; www.geocities.com/hotel_kentrikon).

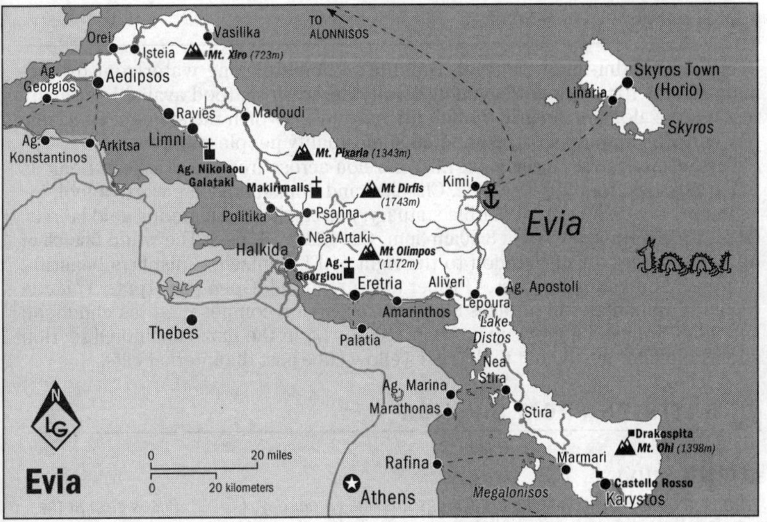

The Greek-Canadian proprietor, George Grontis, will be happy to help you make sense of the city. Spartan, functional rooms have TVs, phones, and sinks; most have shared baths. 24hr. reception. Singles €24; doubles €30; triples €34. ❷

Hotel Hara (☎22210 76 305; fax 22210 76 309), a short walk up Karoni, the street that runs uphill behind the Port Authority. Bright white rooms (TV, private bath, balconies) are a bargain for larger groups. Singles €35; doubles €53; triples €63. ❸

John's Hotel (☎22210 24 996), next to Kentrikon on the road closest to the waterfront, Comfortable, clean, carpeted rooms with baths, A/C, phones, and balconies. Singles €45-58; doubles €65-82; triples €78-98. ❹

FOOD AND NIGHTLIFE

Like hotels, restaurants in Halkida are budget-busting, though the fresh seafood available along the waterfront may justify the cost. Several bakeries hide on streets around Ag. Nikolas; fast food joints are bunched at the base of El. Venizelou and near the Old Bridge on the waterfront. Deliciously named pizzas like the "Inferno" (tomato, cheese, salami, pepper; €7) and the "Erotica" (tomato, cheese, salami, pepper; €8) emerge from the igloo-shaped oven at **La Fiamma ❷,** an Italian eatery on the waterfront. (☎22210 75 006. Entrees €4-9. Open daily 7pm-2am.) **Tsaf ❷,** on Pompastiou near the bus station, serves seafood dishes at more reasonable prices than the establishments on the waterfront. (☎22210 80 070. Entrees €4.50-10.50. Open daily 1pm-midnight.) For a traditional meal head to **Folia ❶** (Φωλια), across from the park on the Evia side of the Old Bridge. Entrees (€3-6) rotate daily; try the *dolmades* (€3.20) on Monday or the *soupies stifado* (squid with onions, €5.30) on Wednesday.

Halkida's thriving nightlife is not to be missed; follow the party-hungry hordes to one of the bars on the waterfront—**Yacht Café** and **Jam** are both packed around 1am (beer €3-5, cocktails €6; open 8:30am-late). Later on, hop a cab to the suspension bridge and take your act onto the dance floor of **Gaz** or **Mist** (cover €10).

SIGHTS

Breezy and palm-lined, **Venidou,** Halkida's kilometer-long waterfront promenade, makes for a splendid evening stroll. The fresh seafood available at many restaurants along its length, though pricey, may be worth the splurge. Or save a few euros by sipping a *frappé* and do some quality people watching.

The **Archaeological Museum,** on El. Venizelou across from the National Bank, is full of findings from the Neolithic, Classical and Roman eras. It's worth a look for its impressive collection of marble statuary, pottery, and shimmering gold laurels. (☎22210 76 131. Open Tu-Su 8:30am-3pm. €2, under 18 free.) The white **Church of Ag. Nikolas,** just off of Venidou to the right of El. Venizelou, displays beautiful paintings and vaulted arches. (Proper attire required. Open 9am-1pm.) You can trace the Halkidian life of **Nikos Skalkotas,** artist and composer, at his childhood and adult homes; he grew up at Kotsouparlou 35 in the maze behind Oktovriou street, and later moved out to the pale yellow cube past the Internet café.

DAYTRIPS FROM HALKIDA

LIMNI Λιμνι

Limni is on the Halkida-Aedipsos Springs bus line (3 per day, €5.15). Buses stop at the main intersection in town; ask before you get off when the next one comes.

If there are tourists here, they're extremely well-hidden. A 45min. bus ride south of Aedipsos takes you to the wooded cove of Limni (meaning "lake"). The fishing village remains friendly, curious about the rare outsider that stumbles upon it. The town takes a collective afternoon swim amid fishing boats and windsurfers. The splendid scenery and gorgeous setting will wow you, especially if you stay for the dazzling sunset and the star-filled night.

Limni is laid out in a "T", with the long waterfront intersecting the road upwards and outwards (to Aedipsos and Halkida). Facing inland, turn right on the waterfront for pastry shops and Pl. Eth. Antistassis, the main plateia. Turn left for most restaurants. After an afternoon dip, stop by **To Neon,** the pastry shop next to the National Bank, for a scoop of ice cream and a Greek confection. (☎22210 31 262. ❶) Before dinner, walk out on the fishing pier to watch the sunset bend hazy and fine across the distant mountains. After 10pm, you can pick from the waterfront restaurants' nightly specials. Try **Avra,** just past the plateia, for a traditional Greek meal. (☎22210 31 479. Entrees €4.25-7. ❷) If you stay for the stars, you can pick from one of two hotels in town, both on the waterfront. **Hotel Limni** is to the far right, facing inland, past the small boat dock, and has unadorned rooms with bath. (☎22210 31 316 or 31 748. Singles €11.70; doubles €21; triples €32.70. ❷) To the left, across from the bus stop, the **Plaza Hotel** has nicely furnished doubles in a renovated old house. (☎22210 31 235. Doubles €25-35. ❸)

ERETRIA Ερετρια

Eretria is accessible by ***bus*** *from Halkida. Buses going to Karystos, Kimi, and Amarinthos all swing through. (1-2 per hr. 5am-8pm, €1.40.) Buses stop 3 blocks inland and parallel to the waterfront. Facing the street from the bus station, turn left and walk to a large tree-lined avenue, Archaiou Theatrou. The waterfront is to the right, the museum and House of Mosaics to the left. At the water, Archaiou Theatrou intersects in a traffic circle with Amar. Artemidos, which runs along 1 edge of the L-shaped harbor while Archaiou Theatrou continues along the other.*

Now a popular destination for beach-bound Athenians, Eretria's former status as one of ancient Evia's most important cities has waned. Its past, however, is magnificently preserved in the archaeological excavations which today provide the best reason for a stop in Eretria. The **Archaeological Museum** is at the inland end of Archaiou Theatrou, in a courtyard brimming with marble statues, friezes, and pillars. The collection displays some quality pieces, including three large *pithoi* south of the House of the Mosaics—the remaining six are in the museum at Athens—and the mysterious six-fingered **Centaur of Lefkandi** (whose body and head were inexplicably found in separate tombs). Exhibits are in Greek and French, but you can buy an English guidebook for €6.

Museum admission lets you into the **House of the Mosaics,** a 10min. walk from the museum; just trade your passport for the keys at the front desk of the museum. Coming out of the museum, walk to the right along the main road for three blocks, turning left at the marked road. The three 4th-century BC mosaics are incredibly well-preserved and are among the oldest in existence. The Swiss School of Archaeology in Greece publishes a brochure on the house's history, available from the museum for €3. (☎22210 62 206. Open Tu-Su 8:30am-3pm. €27, students and under 18 free.) Beyond the museum is a large excavated portion of **Ancient Eretria;** highlights include the ancient theater and the ruins of the ancient city's dense residential section. Should you choose to spend the night in Eretria, inexpensive options are few and far between. Try **Pension Diamado,** on Archaiou Theatrou, past the traffic circle. The rooms are wood-panelled and feature TV, A/C, and private baths. (☎22210 62 214. Singles €26-30; doubles €32-38; triples €35-42. ❸) **Periagli,** to the left at the end of Archaiou Theatrou past the pension, offers more spacious accommodations with TV, A/C, bath, phones and balcony (☎22210 62 439. Singles €40-60; doubles €50-70; triples €60-80. ❹)

SPORADES & EVIA

KARYSTOS Καρυστος

A glowing sanctuary between mountains and sea, Karystos blooms in summer: lush trees, pink flowers, soft sands, and welcoming bars delight nature-lovers and party fiends alike. Both crowds owe thanks to Otto, the first King of Greece, who ordered German architect Bierbach to lay out the modern city's streets in a grid. It is easy to find the way from one attraction to the next within town, though your eyes may be distracted by the sparkling panorama or blurred by the haze of excessive celebration. The long bus ride from Halkida passes some unexciting strip towns, but the view of Marmari's bay more than compensates; wind-generators stand guard over the sea, while sunlight flashes from wave to wave.

PRACTICAL INFORMATION. The central plateia along the waterfront is connected by **I. Kotsika** running straight uphill to the **city hall;** the long waterfront, **Kriezotou,** is lined with tavernas and melts into beaches in both directions along the shore. Facing the water, **Kremala beach** is to the right. **Psili beach** curves around the bay on the left, past the **Bourtzi,** the stone building on the waterfront. The city hall sits on a plateia circled by **El. Amerikis,** which heads out of town to the west.

The **bus** stops one block above the central plateia on I. Kotsika; look for the KTEL sign above a restaurant on the right side of the street. Buses from Karystos travel to: **Halkida** (3hr., 2 per day, €7.60); **Marmari** (30min., 4 per day, €1.40); and **Stira** (45min., 2 per day, €2). No buses run from Karystos on Sundays. **Ferries** travel to and from **Rafina** (1½hr., 1-2 per day, €5.80). **Flying Dolphins** leave once per day for **Mykonos** (2hr., €21.20); **Paros** (2½hr., €24); **Naxos** and **Santorini** (4½hr., €23.70); and **Tinos** (1½hr., €16.50). Buy your tickets at **South Evia Tours,** on the left side of the central plateia (through Kozmos), where **Popi** and friends can help you with everything from **car rental** (€30-40 per day) to local excursions. (☎22240 26 200 or 22240 29 010; http://solmetours.tripod.com. Open daily 9am-2:30pm and 6-11pm.) **Taxis** (☎22240 26 500) are in the plateia.

FROM THE ROAD

OHI THERE

I'd been climbing Mt. Ohi for two hours when I finally spotted another soul on the mountain. The shepherd came hopping down the ridge, sandal-clad feet easily maneuvering through the loose rock, his dog following behind. Perhaps sensing that I had lost the way, he paused, pointed behind him and muttered "Ohi" before continuing on his way.

The jutting rock face was obviously the highest point for miles around; there was little doubt in my mind that it was Ohi. But the gruff gesture was reassuring nonetheless. I'd lost the trail half an hour before when a herd of goats and a dearth of trail markers convinced me to make a straight shot for the summit. The lack of tree cover on Ohi makes such stupidity less of a liability than it would be on other mountains–nearly all orienting features, from sea to ridge to village below, are visible the entire time. All the same, I paid for my decision with a fine series of scratches on my lower legs from the brambly, ankle-high brush that covers the mountain.

Veering off the path on Ohi is not likely to be the result of a conscious decision. It's well marked for the most part, but numerous side trails shoot off in every direction, making it easy to follow the wrong one. Blame it on the goats--the web-like network of trails is their doing. Ohi is a goat's mountain; be prepared for a run-in with one or two of the beasts or a rendezvous with an entire herd.

Fortunately, I only needed to take my eyes off the dusty trail to forget about the frustrations of climbing the

The **National Bank,** just uphill from the bus stop at the intersection of I. Kotsika and Karystou, has a 24hr **ATM.** (Open M-Th 8am-2pm, F 8am-1:30pm.) To find the **police** (☎22240 22 262), turn into the small alley just past the bank and climb the stairs. A **pharmacy** (☎22240 23 505) is at the head of the central plateia. The **OTE** is on Amerikis, to the right off I. Kotsika at the plateia. (☎22240 22 399. Open daily 7:45am-1pm.) **Internet access** is available for €3.50 per hour at **Cafe Kalypso,** on the left side of Kriezotou 150m past the Bourtzi. (☎22240 25 960. Open daily 10am-10pm.) The **post office** is on **Th. Kotsika,** one street over from I. Kotsika, to the left facing inland, just above El. Amerikis. (Open M-F 7:30am-2pm.) **Postal code:** 34001.

ACCOMMODATIONS. Hotel Als ❸, on the corner of Th. Kotsika and the waterfront, offers plain rooms with TV, A/C, private baths, and balconies. (☎22240 22 202; fax 22240 25 002. Singles €25-30; doubles €35-40; triples €45.) To the right of the waterfront, facing the water, **Hotel Galaxy ❸,** run by a hospitable English-speaking couple, has similar rooms with TV, A/C, and baths. (☎22240 22 600; fax 22240 22 463. Breakfast included. Singles €28; doubles €40.)

FOOD AND NIGHTLIFE. Fresh seafood abounds in the many waterfront restaurants; all have similar entrees at comparable prices. **Marino's ❷,** on the waterfront to the right as you face the water, serves typical kitchen fare and seafood, and is a bit less expensive. (☎22240 24 126. Entrees €4.50-9.) Miss McDonalds? Revive your inner teen at **Tastyland ❶** (☎22240 25 000) on the waterfront—don your disco gear and get a burger to go (€1.20).

Lazy during the day, Karystos hosts an active nightlife on weekends. Start your night at either pseudo-tropical **Archipelagos** or mellow **Ostria Bar,** on Kremala beach at the right edge of the waterfront, with a drink and a moonlit bay view. (Beer €2.50-4; cocktails €5.) Around midnight, make your way to the other end of the waterfront (100m past the Bourtzi) to popular Psili beach club **Kohyli,** which keeps the dance music—and an occasional golden oldie—thumping till late (beer €3, cocktails €4-6). Around 3am the party staggers uphill to **Barbados** disco, about 1.5km out of town to the west on Amerikis. You can catch a cab at the central plateia, though the walk might be more amusing. (Beer €3; cocktails €4 and up.) For a quieter evening, **Ciné Aura,** one block in from the waterfront on Sachtouri, shows American movies. (9 and 11pm; €5.50.)

SIGHTS. Peek into one of the holes at the back of the **Fort of Bourtzi,** the impossible-to-miss structure on the waterfront. In the 11th century, your peephole was used to pour boiling oil on attackers. Today, the fort is regularly invaded by theater-goers swarming in to watch student productions in August; ask at South Evia Tours (see above) about schedules. The **Archaeological Museum,** on Kriezotou just past the Bourtzi, houses a small collection of marble statues and inscripted tablets, as well as artifacts from the *drakospita* of Stira and Mt. Ohi. (☎22240 25 661. Open Tu-Su 8:30am-3pm. €1.50; free Su.)

DAYTRIPS FROM KARYSTOS. The widely varied terrain of the Karystos region features many spectacular daytrips. Some are most easily accessed by private vehicle. The 3hr. hike up **Mt. Ohi** affords inspiring views of southern Evia and the surrounding sea. A set of mysterious and massive **columns** appears on the side of the trail 45 minutes into the hike. The haunting ruins of the **Dragon House,** or *drakopitsa*, rest on the summit. It is believed to have been a temple dedicated to Zeus and Hera; local legend holds that it was inhabited by a dragon who terrorized the region. To get to the trailhead, take a cab to the village of **Mili** (€4), or make the 3km hike yourself by following Aiolou, one block east of the plateia, out of town.

Running from the heights of Mt. Ohi to the sea below, the **Dimosari Gorge** is a natural wonder that those with an extra day should not miss. Clear, cold water cascades down its length in pools shaded by verdant forest. The gorge is accessible by car at **Kallianou** (41km north of Karystos), or by foot—hike over the summit of Mt. Ohi and follow the gorge down the north slope of the mountain. On the slopes above Karystos is the majestic **Castello Rosso** (Kokkino Castro or Red Castle) named for the blood spilled there in the many battles for its control. From Mili, it's a 20min. hike up the hill on the left and across the stone bridge. Other interesting sites in the region include the **Roman aqueduct** past the Red Castle and the **stone church** and **cave** at **Agia Triada,** accessible by hike from **Nikasi,** where the bus can drop you off (€1.30). **Hiking maps** (€3) are available at South Evia Tours.

mountain. With no trees in the way, spectacular views can be had the entire time. It might have been the effects of building dehydration or the revelry of the night before, but the array of blues, greens, and purples was truly dizzying. I didn't think the peak could provide much more of a thrill, but the 360-degree view from the throne of South Evia was one like I'd never seen before. I'm used to mountains that fade slowly into rounded foothills. Here, mountains of comparable size dropped straight into the sea for miles around, making for a stunning contrast of landscapes.

Apparently, those who marked the trail assumed that people wouldn't want to leave such a magical place—the red arrows only point up, and most blazes are not visible from the vantage point of someone descending the mountain. I hiked down most of the mountain with no trail in sight, pursuing another circuitous route to a much less godly destination. ***—Kevin Connor***

NORTHEAST AEGEAN ISLANDS

For centuries, the northeast Aegean islands have had to protect themselves, and recent Turkish occupations have left the islanders somewhat embittered. Many islands continue to isolate themselves from the influx of tourism, hoping to preserve their authenticity. Intricate, rocky coastlines and unassuming port towns enclose thickly wooded mountains, which give way to unspoiled villages and beaches. Despite proximity to the Turkish coast and a noticeable military presence, the northeast Aegean islands dispense a taste of undiluted Greek culture.

HIGHLIGHTS OF THE NORTHEAST AEGEAN

SEEK YOUR MUSE on Lesvos (p. 370), inspiration to poetic minds from the ancient sensual lyricist Sappho to the Modernist Nobel Laureate Odysseus Elytis.

LOUNGE under rare palms on Samos (p. 358), birthplace of Pythagoras and Epicurus.

BOW before the Sanctuary of Great Gods of Anatolia on Samothraki (p. 383), where Alexander the Great's parents met, loved, wooed, and worshiped.

GAPE at the detail of the geometric designs on the houses of Pyrgi on Chios (p. 369).

IKARIA Ικαρια

Ikaria is named for reckless young Icarus, who plunged to his death off the island's coast when his wax wings—made by his father Daedalus so they could escape the Minoan Labyrinth—melted as he gleefully flew too close to the sun. Today, Ikaria provides a relaxing escape. Countless beaches lead into its clear waters along the coastline, and locals can direct you to hot springs outside of the baths at Therma that well up directly into the sea. Ikaria's residents are inexplicably nocturnal, which never ceases to amaze visitors; shops don't open and buses don't begin to run until 6 or 7pm. This all makes exploring rather difficult but no less worthwhile. Split by a rocky mountain chain, the island's odd landscape harbors around 2500 species of plant, which subtly color and scent the island. Despite being devastated by fires in 1993 and 1997, much of the landscape is surprisingly verdant.

AGIOS KIRYKOS Αγιος Κηρυκος

This lovely town's shaded plateia stretches along the giant steps leading into the sea, where fishing boats dock. The plateia is nearly deserted from noon until 6pm; then the locals begin to circulate and sip *frappés* or play football by the pier. At 2am, you'll still see small children playing energetically in front of the cafes as their parents chat and gossip.

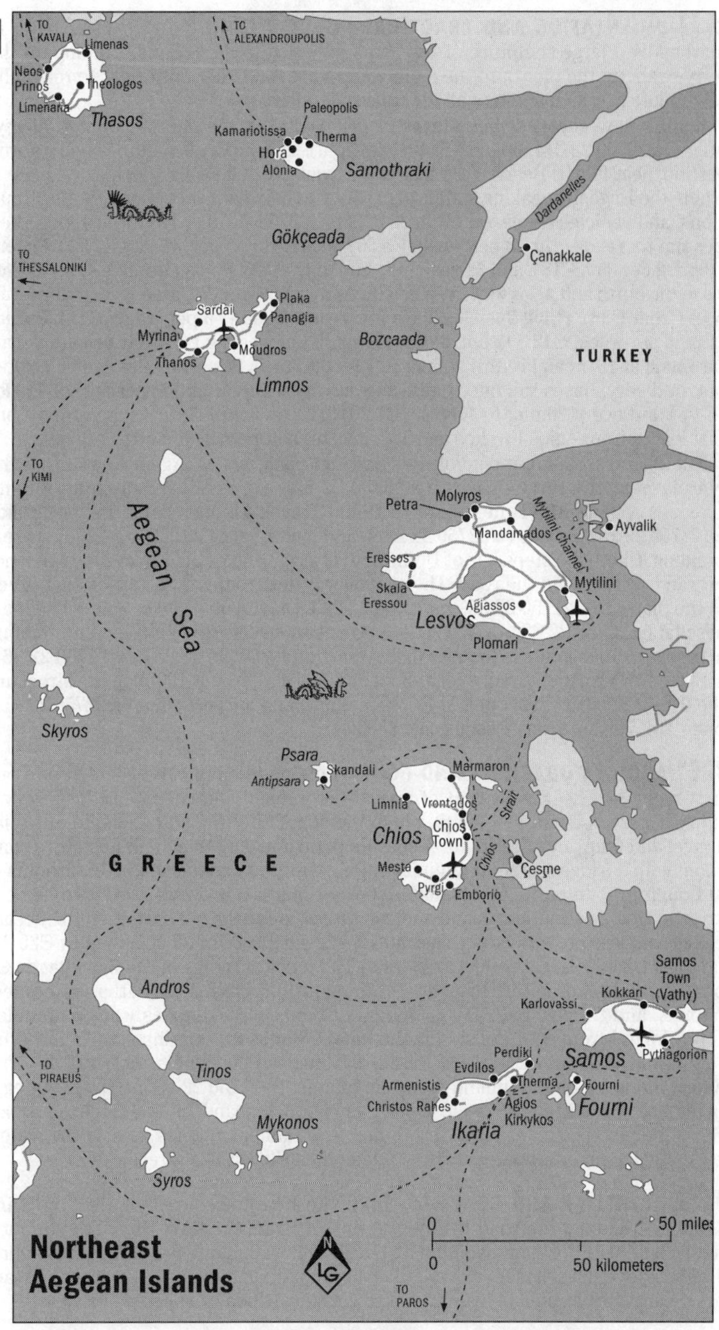

NORTHEAST AEGEAN

ORIENTATION AND PRACTICAL INFORMATION. The town's pier is marked by a large sculpture of Icarus plummeting to the ground. Coming off the ferry, walk up the pier onto the main waterfront road, then turn right to reach the town plateia, which shelters all the tourist services.

Ikaria's new **airport** serves **Athens** (1 per day, €50) through the **Olympic Airways** office (☎22750 22 214; open M-Sa 8:15am-2pm). The airport is on the island's northeast tip, near Fanari Beach. **Ferry tickets** are available at **Ikariada Travel,** in the plateia, where the English-speaking staff is also happy to help with accommodations, excursions, and vehicle rentals. (☎22750 23 322; fax 22750 23 708. Open 8am-10pm.) Ferries run to: **Fourni** (1hr., 3 per week, €5.50); **Paros** (4hr., 3 per week, €11.71); **Piraeus** (10hr., 2 per day, €18); and **Samos** (3hr., 1 per day, €12). Boats alternate stops at **Evdilos** in the north and **Agios Kirykos,** where taxis await to shuttle passengers to the other port (from €25). **Flying Dolphins** leave for: **Fourni** (30min., 5 per week, €11); **Patmos** (1hr., 5 per week, €12.30); and **Samos** (1½hr., 5 per week, €14). Daily **caïques** depart for **Fourni** at 10am and return at 6pm (€12 round-trip). **Bus** schedules can be erratic, but, in theory, buses run once daily between **Agios Kirykos** and **Armenistis** via **Evdilos** (€4-5) and every 20min. to **Therma** (€1.20). The owner of Akti Pension runs a **bus** that leaves from Agios Kirykos and Therma 2hr. before daily flights to Athens.

NORTHEAST AEGEAN

The island's banks, including the **National Bank,** are in Agios Kirykos, in the plateia near the ferry offices. (☎22750 22 553. Open M-Th 8am-2pm, F 8am-1:30pm.) A 24hr. **ATM** is next door to Dolihi Travel. All open 24hr., the **port police** (☎22750 22 207), **police** (☎22750 22 222), and **tourist police** (☎22750 22 207) share a building. Climb the steps left of Dolihi Travel at the end of the Flying Dolphin landing, and continue up the road. The **pharmacy** is next to the G.A. Ferry ticket office in the plateia. (☎22750 22 989 or 22750 22 220. Open daily 8:30am-2pm.) The local **hospital** (☎22750 22 330 or 22750 22 336) is two streets up from the pier. **Internet access** is available at the **Internet Club** to the left of Dolihi Travel. (☎22750 22 864. €1.50 per 20min. Open daily 10am-3pm and 6-11pm.) About 100m up the street are the **OTE** (☎22750 22 599; open M-F 7:30am-2pm) and the **post office** (☎22750 22 413; open M-F 7:30am-2pm). **Postal code:** 83300.

ACCOMMODATIONS AND FOOD. Finding lodging can be tough on your first night, so check your port of arrival beforehand and call ahead for reservations. To reach **Akti Pension ❷,** climb the stairs on the right-hand side of Dolihi Travel and take your first right. A seaside patio and garden and an upstairs sitting room with a fridge foster community among guests, as do the shared bathrooms—although private baths are available. Owner Marsha, a Greek-American, is very knowledgeable about the island and can direct you to the hot springs in the ocean, closer and less crowded than Therma's. (☎22750 22 694 or 23 905. Singles €20-25; doubles €25-30; larger rooms available.) The modern rooms of the **Hotel Castro ❸,** on the road leading left from the police station, have TVs, baths, balconies, phones, and fridges. (☎22750 23 480; fax 22750 23 700. Singles €30-35; doubles €40.) Inland from Akti Pension is the **Hotel O'Karras ❷,** offering simple, sky-blue rooms and spacious baths. (☎22750 22 494. Singles €20; doubles €25-40.) Taverna **Klimataria ❶** is a block inland from the plateia. (☎22750 22 686. *Briam*, an eggplant dish, €4; entrees up to €6. Open daily noon-4pm and 7pm-midnight.) **Dedalos ❶,** in the plateia, serves breakfast, lunch, and dinner to tables next to the water, perfectly located for boat-watching. (Omelettes €3, Greek entrees €3-6.)

NIGHTLIFE AND BEACHES. Like the beaches, most of the nightlife options are along the road heading to the left from the ferry dock (as you face inland), all within 20min. walking distance. The walk along the cliff road winding 10min. above the sea is lovely, and the very limited light pollution means the stars are clearly visible. Just be careful not to get sideswiped by speeding mopeds.

As you walk along the road from the dock, you'll come to **Camelot,** with a bar upstairs (open at 9pm but deserted until midnight) and a club downstairs (open at midnight but doesn't fill up until much later). The terrace overlooks the open, glistening sea. **Flik Flak,** about a 10min. walk down the road, has a fun outdoor dance floor and, occasionally, live DJs. (Cocktails €5-6. Open midnight-late.)

Beaches dot the coast along this road, and there are two **hot springs** in the ocean 30min. from town. Ask for directions, and look for greenish water and rocks (colored by the sulfur) and bathers spreading mud on their bodies. To the east of town, you can clamber down to the sandy beaches past the tourist police. **Agios Giorgios,** between Fanari and the airport, is one of the island's best beaches.

EVDILOS Ευδηλος

Heading north from Agios Kirykos, the tiny road to red-roofed Evdilos snakes along sheer cliffs through florid hill country, providing wide coastal vistas and safety risks to moped drivers. The island is very green, and the golden coast grasses against the clean blue waters paint a stunning picture. From the island's eastern heights you can see Samos, Patmos, and the Fourni Archipelago. On the way to Evdilos, the road passes a few tiny villages and beaches, many of which have limited tourist accommodations.

TRANSPORTATION AND PRACTICAL INFORMATION. **Buses** are supposed to run daily between **Agios Kirykos** and **Armenistis** via **Evdilos,** but service is unreliable at best. (€4-5; buses run mostly after 6pm.) **Taxis** may be your best bet; sharing a cab will cut costs. (☎22750 31 275. Agios Kirykos to Evdilos €25; Agios Kirykos to Armenistis €27; Armenistis to Evdilos €9.)

Blue Nice Holidays handles ferries, Flying Dolphins, excursions, flights, and car rentals, **exchanges currency,** and posts a weekly schedule for ferries serving both Evdilos and Agios Kirykos, as well as Flying Dolphins serving Agios Kirykos. (☎22750 31 990 or 22750 31 428; fax 22750 31 572. Open daily 9am-2:30pm and 7-10pm.) An **Alpha Bank** is at the port across from Blue Nice Holidays. (Open M-Th 8am-2pm, F 8am-1:30pm.) The **pharmacy** (☎22750 31 394) is between the town and the ferries' arrival dock. In case of emergency, call for **first aid** (☎22750 31 228). The **port police** (☎22750 31 007) are directly inland from the plateia, next to the pharmacy. The **post office** sits at the top of a set of white stairs that lead to the right of the plateia. (☎22750 31 225. Open M-F 7:30am-2pm.)

ACCOMMODATIONS AND FOOD. For the best view of crashing waves and a gorgeous sunset, try **Apostolos Stenos's Rooms to Rent ❸.** From the port, take the winding uphill road to the top; continue straight at the small square and then take a right. Ask for directions on the way. (☎22750 31 365. Singles €30; doubles €30; prices are flexible.) **Hambas's Rooms ❶** are easy on the budget. They're directly inland from the kiosk in the main square. (☎22750 31 523. Singles €10.) **Ioannis Spanos ❸** offers basic rooms with shared bath near the plateia at the base of the hill along the Agios Kirykos-Armenistis road. (☎22750 31 220. Doubles €25.)

Restaurants and *kafeneions* fill the plateia, each one offering distinct flavors. **Cuckoo's Nest ❶,** with tables strategically surrounding the square's central monument, serves up intriguing dishes highlighted by *mezedes.* Try the chicken in wine sauce for €4. (☎22750 31 540. Open M-Sa 7pm-late.) Catering to the late-night ferry arrivals with an array of sweets, coffees, and baked goods, **Ta Kimata ❶** (☎22750 31 952), next to Blue Nice Travel, is open 24hr.

DAYTRIPS FROM EVDILOS. Idle stone fountains hidden under the canopy of shady green leaves mark the entry to the small town of **Christos tis Rahes** (Χριστος της Ραχης; Christ's Back), the apotheosis of a traditional Ikarian village. The best time to visit is after 11pm, when the locals have finished their daily livestock care and produce gathering and are ready to run their daily errands, shopping until 3 or 4am. Visit the local baker on the main road below the plateia, where the brick-oven-baked loaves (€0.50) are left out for patrons to grab. Deposit the money in the little basket on the honor system. Ikaria's best-organized hiking trails originate from here and are marked by little orange footprints. Pick up the very handy *Guide Map and Information* or the *Round of Rahes on Foot* (€4) at any book-store or tourist shop. Highlights include the Monastery of Evangelistria.

A short distance from Agios Kyrikos on the way to the airport, **Therma** (Θερμα) makes for an ideal daytrip. It's very accessible; **buses** run every 20min., and the walk is only 2km on the path beside the police station. The village is built in a little valley with houses on the steep cliffs surrounding it. Elderly people crowd the main plateia while children clamber around the beach; people with ailments ranging from rheumatism to gynecological difficulties venture to the three springs of Therma. Each of the springs is naturally radioactive and used for different treatments. Twenty minutes in a warm bath costs a mere €1.35, so take your time.

West of Armenistis, the asphalt runs out, leaving a dirt road running to **Nas,** one of the Aegean's undiscovered gems. The inspiring beach, flanked by huge rock walls, separates an aggressive sea from a serene river. Bordered by the beach, a freshwater pool is the river's final destination. A 25min. hike south takes you to the small waterfall that forms its beginning. To reach the falls, head inland toward the wood past the pool. The hike is best accomplished by hugging the river, which may mean getting your feet wet. Approaching the final leg of the hike, notice the cavernous rock enclosure perched atop the eastern ledge. It's a favorite haunt for local goats. The smallish waterfall lies a few minutes beyond this point.

FOURNI Φουρνοι

Although few visitors stay overnight, Fourni presents rewards for both daytrippers and those willing to stay longer. Most come to the island for the fresh seafood served at waterfront restaurants, but pleasant beaches and easy hiking are also easily accessible.

The main port has more tourist facilities than one would imagine. Almost everything is either located on the waterfront or the main street that runs perpendicular to it. Weather permitting, Fourni is easily accessible by daily **caïque** from **Ikaria** (€12 round-trip). There is also limited **ferry** service three times per week from **Ikaria** (€6) and **Patmos** (€12). The **port police** (☎22750 51 207) and **police** (☎22750 51 222) share a white building at the end of the dock. The friendly, English-speaking staff answer questions about the island. To the right (facing inland), **Hotel Nectaria ❸** provides spacious rooms with baths, fridges, and fans. (☎/fax 22750 51 365. Doubles €30; triples €42.) Next door, **Toula Rooms ❸** has studios with baths, kitchens, and fans. (☎/fax 22750 51 332. Doubles €30-35.) The island's two best beaches, **Kambe** and **Psili Ammos,** are accessible from here.

SAMOS Σαμος

Lush and lovely Samos accommodates a more scholarly crowd than some of its wilder siblings in the Cyclades and Dodecanese. While short-sighted tourists see the island as little more than a necessary stepping stone on the way to Kuşadası and the ruins of Ephesus (p. 364) on the Turkish coast, this green island has been a destination in its own right for centuries. A procession of architects, sculptors, poets, philosophers, and scientists (among them Pythagoras, Epicurus, Aesop, and Aristarchus, who correctly figured that the Earth revolved around the Sun 1800 years before Copernicus) have all spent thoughtful hours on Samos's shores.

VATHY Βαθυ

Palm trees shade quiet inland streets, an engaging archaeological museum stands across from a public garden, and red roofs speckle the neighboring hillside of Vathy (also called **Samos Town**), one of the Aegean's most appealing port cities.

TRANSPORTATION

Flights: Olympic Airways (☎22730 27 237). Pass the municipal gardens and make a right after the church; the office is 20m up the street on your left. To: **Athens** (1hr., 5 per day, €73) and **Thessaloniki** (3 per week, €71). Open M-F 8:30am-3:30pm. Samos's **airport** (☎22730 61 219), past Pythagorion, is only reachable by taxi (20min., €12).

Ferries: To: **Chios** (5hr., 2 per week, €9.30); **Kos** (4hr., 1 per week, €16); **Mykonos** (6hr., 6 per week, €16); **Naxos** (6hr., 3 per week, €16.70) via **Paros** (€14.10); **Piraeus** (12hr., 1 per day, €22.10); **Rhodes** (2 per week, €30). Catamarans to **Kuşadası, Turkey,** leave from Samos Town (1¼hr.; 5 per week; €30 1-way, €44 round-trip, €8.80 Greek port tax). Turkish entrance **visas** must be purchased at the Turkish

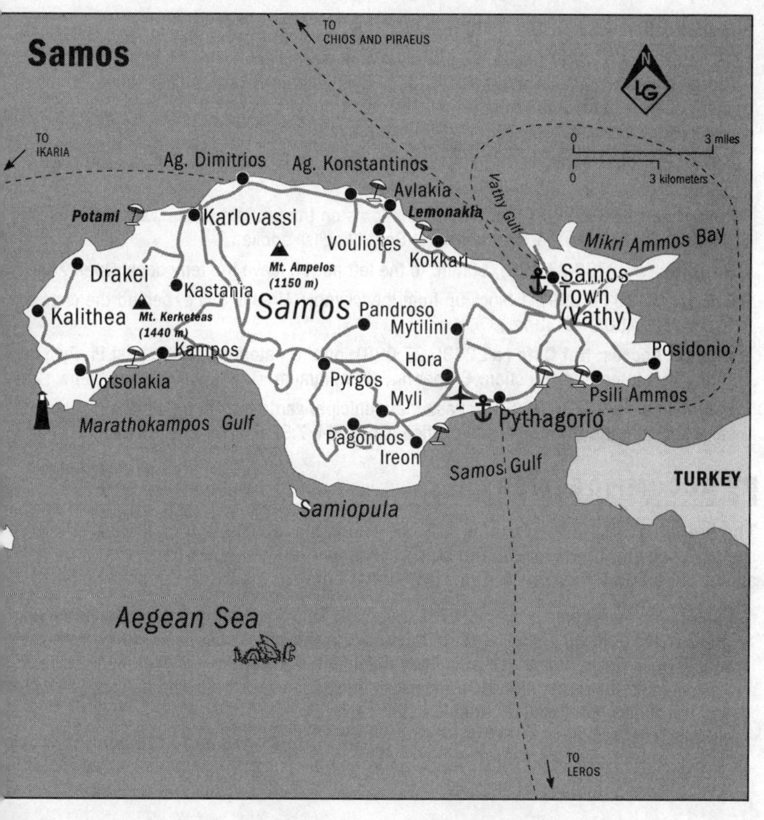

border by Americans, Australians, British, Canadians, and Irish planning to stay for more than 1 day. A visa costs US$65.

Flying Dolphins: Zip from Samos Town to **Chios, Fourni, Ikaria, Kalymnos, Kos, Lesvos,** and **Patmos,** in half the time and at twice the price.

Buses: Follow the waterfront past Pl. Pythagoras, turn left onto Lekati, and continue 1 block to the **station.** To: **Avlakia** (7 per day, €1.15) via **Agios Konstantinos; Chrissi Ammos** (3 per week); **Heraion** (3 per day, €1.51); **Marathokambos** (1-2 per day, €3.59); **Pythagorion** (12 per day, €1.08); **Tsainadon** (9 per day, €0.93) via **Kokkari** and **Lemonakia**; **Vourliotes** (3 per week).

Taxis: (☎22730 28 404). Available 24hr. in Pl. Pythagoras.

ORIENTATION AND PRACTICAL INFORMATION

Samos Town unfurls around a crescent-shaped waterfront. **Pl. Pythagoras,** identifiable by its four large palm trees, consists of cafes, taxis, and a giant lion statue; the plateia is located 250m to the right of the port (facing inland). Turn onto the side streets between the port and Pl. Pythagoras to hit the most densely packed pension neighborhood on the island. Heading along the waterfront away from the port, past Pl. Pythagoras, will take you to the **Municipal Gardens,** circled by the town's public amenities and the archaeological museum.

Tourist Office: (☎22730 28 530 or 22730 28 582), on a side street 1 block before Pl. Pythagoras. Open July-Aug. M-Sa 7am-2:30pm.

Tourist Agencies: ITSA Travel (☎22730 23 605), on the waterfront just across from the port, offers all ferry and Flying Dolphin tickets. Can also help plan excursions to Turkey. Open daily 5:30am-10pm and when boats arrive.

Banks: National Bank, on the waterfront just beyond Pl. Pythagoras, has a 24hr. **ATM.** Open M-Th 8am-2pm, F 8am-1:30pm.

Police: (☎22730 27 980), after Pl. Pythagoras on the far right of the waterfront (facing inland). Doubles as the **tourist police.** Some English spoken.

Hospital: (☎22730 27 426), 10min. to the left as you leave the ferry dock. Open 24hr.

OTE: (☎22730 28 099), 1 block up from the Olympic Airways office, behind the church. Open M-F 7:30am-1:30pm.

Internet Access: Net Cafe (☎22730 27 098), on the waterfront 200m past Pl. Pythagoras. Fast Internet connection. €4 per hr., €1 minimum. Open daily 10am-11pm.

Post Office: (☎22730 28 503). Pass the municipal gardens, turn right after the church, and left after the Olympic Airways office. Open M-F 7:30am-2pm. **Postal code:** 83100.

ACCOMMODATIONS

The limited availability of rooms in Samos makes it advisable to call ahead during the high season. If you arrive and all the beds listed below are filled, try the places around Pension Ionia (on M. Kalomiri) or get help from a travel agent.

Pension Trova, Kalomiris 26 (☎22730 27 759). Turn right at the end of the ferry dock and walk 100m along the waterfront, to take a left onto E. Stamatiadou before the Hotel Aiolis. Take the 2nd left onto Manoli Kalomiri which wraps uphill around the bend to Kalomiris. Cool, traditionally furnished rooms, some with bath and balcony, all with full hospitality. Singles €18; doubles €20. ❷

Medousa Hotel, Sofouli 25 (☎22730 23 501), on the waterfront, about halfway between the port and Pl. Pythagoras. Rooms in a prime location. Fine amenities (baths, TVs, phones). Doubles €15-30. ❸

Pension Avli, Areos 2 (☎22730 22 939). Turn right at the end of the ferry dock and walk along the waterfront until you reach Hotel Aiolis; take your next left onto Areos and proceed 2 blocks and up the stairs. An old monastery provides travelers quiet rooms around an elegant courtyard. Owner Spiros maintains a laid-back environment. Open May-Oct. Doubles €20-30; triples €30-40. ❸

Pension Dreams, Areos 9 (☎22730 24 350), just up from Pension Avli. Compulsively neat rooms with fridges, baths, TVs, and—the owners' pride and joy—coffee makers. The roof suite offers a private terrace with a view to the sea. Doubles €20-25; triples €30-35. A/C extra. ❸

FOOD AND NIGHTLIFE

Gourmands will find their time well-spent in savoring sweet Samian wine, served at all of the island's nearly indistinguishable restaurants, which otherwise offer a standard spate of traditional meals. **Gregori's** ❶ (☎22730 22 718), just past the post office, is a worthy local favorite; dishes are simple but well-prepared. (Entrees under €6. Open daily 10am-3pm and 6pm-1am.) Similarly priced and more conveniently located is **Christos** ❶, in Pl. Nikolaos behind Pl. Pythagoras, with outdoor seating for optimal people-watching in the main square. (Entrees €5-7. Open daily 11am-1am.) The markets in Vathy are also good options. There is a large **supermarket** behind the Archaeological Museum. Fruit and vegetable vendors line up in front of the OTE in the morning; pick up a fresh tomato or two for the road.

Several clubs get the party rolling on the outskirts of town, including **Cabana** and **Matrix.** Check the ubiquitous club posters for the popular theme nights on the weekends. More passive entertainment is found at the open-air **Cinema Olympia.** (☎22730 25 011. Tickets €6.) To get there, turn left at Pl. Pythagoras and right onto Katavani; the cinema is two blocks down on the left.

SIGHTS

The phenomenal **Archaeological Museum** sits behind the gardens. Its broad collection looks at Samos's past glory as a commercial and religious center for worshiping Hera. Finds from ancient Heraion, the temple of Hera, and other local digs are enshrined in two recently renovated buildings full of informative notes; you'll find more proof of Heraion's bygone splendor here than at the crumbled remains at the site. Taken together, the exhibits provide a comprehensive and interesting history of Samos. The first building houses Laconian ivory carvings of mythological notables, and awesome statues like a colossal 5m **kouros** from 56 BC. Pieces of this magnificent *kouros* were found at different times, some of them built into existing walls and cisterns. There's also the stunning Genelos group—a nearly life-size votive offering depicting a family, which is named after its sculptor and once graced ancient Heraion's Sacred Way. In the second building, an exhibit on Hera worship parades offerings made to the goddess, remarkable for their workmanship and expense. Objects from Ancient Egypt, Cyprus, and the Near East testify to the island's importance as a trade center. In the last room, a case of nightmarish, gryphon-engraved **protomes** (cauldron handles) is not to be missed. (☎22730 27 469. Open Tu-Su 8:30am-3pm. €3, seniors and students €2, EU students free.)

In late July and early August, Samos hosts a number of fine classical and jazz concerts featuring Greek artists as part of the **Manolis Kalomiris Festival.** Contact the tourist office for a schedule of events.

DAYTRIPS FROM VATHY

ANCIENT PYTHAGORION Πυθαγορειο

A bus from Vathy arrives at Pythagorion (20min., €1.08). A modern beach town of the same name now sits on the ruins of Ancient Pythagorion, 14km south of Vathy.

The ancient city of Pythagorion, once the island's capital, thrived during the second half of the 6th century BC under the reign of **Polykrates the Tyrant.** Herodotus reports that Polykrates undertook the three most daring engineering projects in the Hellenic world, among them the **Tunnel of Eupalinus,** 1500m up the hill to the north of town. The tunnel was in fact an underground aqueduct that diverted water from a natural spring to the city below. An impressive 1.3km long, it's in remarkably good condition, although only about 200m of dank cavern are open to visitors. To reach the tunnel, walk back along the road to Vathy and follow the signs. The 20min. walk to the tunnel's entrance leads past minor ancient ruins, including a Hellenistic villa and some wells; rolling hills and grazing goats fill the intervals. (☎22730 61 400. Open Tu-Su 8:45am-2:45pm, last entrance 2:15pm. €4, students €2, EU students free.) You can also check out Polykrates's second feat, the 40m deep **harbor mole,** a breakwater which supports the modern pier.

Blocks, columns, wall fragments, and entablatures are strewn throughout Pythagorion. The presentation in the small **Archaeological Museum,** located one block from the water, is no different. A little over half of the collection fits into the building; many of the pieces are haphazardly scattered on the sidewalk in front. (☎22730 61 400. Open Tu-Su 9am-2:30pm. Free.) On the south side of town are the ruins of the **Castle of Lykurgus,** built during the beginning of the 19th century by Lykurgus, a native Samian and a leader in the War for Independence. The **Church of the Transfiguration** is a pale blue variation on classic Orthodox architecture.

HERAION Ηραιον

A bus from Vathy (30min., €1.51) leaves you in Heraion Town. The temple is 1km back on the road from Vathy. ☎22730 95 277. Open Tu-Su 8:30am-3pm. €3, students €2.

Polykrates's magnum opus is in Heraion. Seven centuries worth of pilgrims had worshiped Hera on Samos when Polykrates began enlarging her temple. Eventually, 134 columns supported the 118m-long, 58m-wide 530 BC version of the **Temple of Hera.** Since a fire damaged it in 525 BC, it has been only minimally reconstructed. On the site, you'll see the lone standing column of the once-majestic colonnade and casts of the Genelos group (now in the Samos Museum). A walk along the beach brings you back to the temple at your own pace. If you can't enter through the beachside back gate, a path leads inland to the main road and the entrance, farther along the beach past two houses. Follow custom by wrapping yourself up in your best toga and carrying a jug of libations on this path, which runs close to the ancient **Iera Odos** (Sacred Way) from Pythagorion to the temple.

NORTHERN AND WESTERN SAMOS

BEACHES. The northern coast of Samos has many crowded, sandy beaches and a few rarely visited pebble beaches tucked into little coves. Most of the coast is easily accessible from the road to **Karlovassi.** On a peninsula 10km west of Samos Town, you'll find the village of **Kokkari,** skirted by white pebble shores and clear waters. **Lemonakia Beach,** 1km west of Kokkari next to Tsamadou, and the wide white beach west of **Avlakia** are both alluring. Kokkari, Lemonakia, and Avlakia are accessible from

Samos Town via the irregular KTEL **bus** service (7-9 buses per day). Infrequent buses (1-2 per day) shouldn't keep you from the splendid beaches of southwest Samos. A few kilometers west of the peaceful red-roofed hamlet of **Marathokambos** is the spacious beach at **Votsalakia.** A bit farther is an even better beach at **Psili Ammos.**

HIKES. From the village of **Agios Konstantinos,** on the northern coast of Samos, you can trek into the mountains through the Valley of the Nightingales, where songbirds regale the wooded valley just after midnight. The village of **Vourliotes,** 5km south of Avlakia, was a favorite of actress Melina Mercury, who exalted the village for years after her visit there. Several kilometers above the town, the 16th-century monastery **Moni Vrontianis** polices the behavior of the populace below. (Closed for renovations for an undetermined period of time. Consult the tourist office in Vathy for info.) 2km west of **Paleo,** a path through a pond and up a series of ropes leads to three waterfalls in the island's northwest corner.

NEAR SAMOS

SELÇUK, TURKEY

For more information on travel to Turkey from Greece, see **Daytrips to Turkey,** p. 607. Catamarans run to **Kuşadası** from Samos Town (1¼hr.; 5 per week; €30 1-way, €44 round-trip, €8.80 Greek port tax). From Kuşadası, intercity *dolmuş* (mini-buses) head to Selçuk (30min., every 20min. 7:30am-midnight, $0.90) via Ephesus (ask to be let off). Because of the instability of the Turkish lira, prices for goods and services in Turkey are listed in US dollars. Coverage of Selçuk and Ephesus was updated in July of 2001.

Selçuk serves as a base for exploring nearby Ephesus and offers a few notable archaeological sites of its own. The Selçuk castle dominates the city's skyline, along with the Basilica of Saint John, where the apostle John is buried; the İsa Bey Camii; and the ruins of the Temple of Artemis. The House of the Virgin Mary *(Meryemana)* can also be reached from Selçuk.

ORIENTATION AND PRACTICAL INFORMATION. The İzmir-Aydın road, **Atatürk,** is one of Selçuk's main drags. **Dr. Sabri Yayla,** also called **Kuşadası,** meets Atatürk from the west, and **Şahabettin Dede** meets Atatürk from the east to form the town's main crossroads. The **tourist office,** 35 Agora Çarşısı, at the intersection of Kuşadası and Atatürk, has free maps. (☎232 892 63 28; fax 232 892 69 45. Open M-F 8am-noon and 1-5pm; Apr.-Dec. also open Sa-Su 9am-5pm.) A **bank,** 17 Namık Kemal, **exchanges currency** and **traveler's checks** and has an **ATM.** (☎232 892 61 09 or 232 892 65 14. Open M-F 8:30am-5:30pm.) The **police** (☎232 892 60 16) have an office beside the bank and a booth by the *otogar* (bus station) on Atatürk.

ACCOMMODATIONS AND FOOD. At **Artemis Guest House ("Jimmy's Place")** ❶, on Atatürk, guests are greeted with a refreshing drink, shown to a carpeted room complete with bath, towels, and fans, and invited to dinner in the garden (nightly, $2.50) or to watch one of owner Jimmy's 100 movies. (☎232 892 61 91; www.artemisguesthouse.com. Internet $0.80 per hr. Laundry $2.50. Breakfast $1.60. $5 per person. 2 hotel-style rooms with A/C $30 per night.) Named after the famous Kiwi rugby squad, **All Blacks Hotel and Pension** ❶, on Atatürk, has some of the nicest rooms in the budget circuit, with immaculate tile floors and bathrooms. Ring the bell to enter. (☎232 892 36 57; www.allblacks.8m.com. Guest kitchen.

Laundry $3.75 per load. Internet $1.50 per hr. Breakfast $1.75. Singles $6; doubles $9.) For a truly zen-like dining experience, try **Karameşe Restaurant ❶**, Tarihi İsabey Camii Önü, beside İsa Bey Camii. A maze of stone paths wind through miniature waterfalls, fountains, and grass-covered gazebos. In the rear, a miniature zoo is home to swans, ostriches, and monkeys. The *ayran* ($0.40) is made with the milk from on-site cows. (☎232 892 04 66. Open daily 9am-3am.)

SIGHTS AND MUSEUMS. The stunning Selçuk mosque **İsa Bey Camii** was built in 1375 on the order of Aydınoğlu İsa Bey. It features columns taken from Ephesus, which the Ephesians, in turn, had pilfered from Aswan, Egypt. Restored in 1975, the mosque has regained much of the simple elegance that was eroded by 600 years of wear and tear. Inside the courtyard is a collection of Ottoman and Selçuk tombstones and inscriptions. The mosque's facade features Persian-influenced geometric black and white stone inlay. A few hundred meters down Dr. Sabri Yayla, walking away from town with the tourist office on your right, are the sad remains of the **Temple of Artemis.** Once the largest temple in existence and among the Seven Wonders of the Ancient World, it now consists of a lone reconstructed column twisting upwards from a bog that approximates the area of the temple's foundation. (Open daily 8:30am-5:30pm. Free.)

Directly across from the town's tourist office, Selçuk's **Efes Müzesi** (Ephesus Museum) houses a world-class collection of Hellenistic and Roman finds from Ephesus; most earlier pieces are in Vienna. The collection includes an infamous Priapus statue, Beş (Priapus) that graces postcards throughout Turkey. While this particular piece was found in the vicinity of Ephesian brothels, the image of the generously endowed demi-god wasn't a smutty novelty, but a fairly common image in the ancient world. The museum houses an excellent collection of statuary, including exquisite busts of Eros, Athena, Socrates, and emperors Tiberius, Marcus Aurelius, and Hadrian. (Open daily 8:30am-noon and 1-7pm; in winter 8:30am-noon and 1-5:30pm. $3.)

DAYTRIP FROM SELÇUK: EPHESUS. From early archaic times to the 6th century AD, Ephesus enjoyed perpetual glory and prosperity. The ruins here rank first among Turkey's ancient sites in sheer size and state of preservation; extensive marble roadways and columned avenues give an authentic impression of this ancient gateway to the eastern world. From the Selçuk otogar, take a Pamukkale-bound dolmuş to Kuşadası (5min.; Mar.-Oct. every 15min., Nov.-Apr. every 30min.; $0.60). **Taxis** run from Selçuk to Ephesus ($4) and to the House of the Virgin Mary (9km, $15 round-trip including 45min. to visit the site). Ephesus is an easy **walk** (3km, 25min.) from Selçuk along a fig tree-shaded path, beside Dr. Sabri Yayla Bul. Bring water and sunscreen. A good guidebook to Ephesus costs about $2.50 in Kuşadası souvenir shops or at the entrance to the site; it provides the history of the ruins and a more lengthy explanation of the many sights. The site is open daily 8am-7pm; the best time to visit is early in the morning.

Once you reach the site, you'll see the **Vedius Gymnasium** on the left, down the road from Dr. Sabri Yayla Bul. toward the lower entrance. It was built in AD 150 to honor then-emperor Antonius Pius and **Artemis,** the city's patron goddess. Beyond the roadside vegetation, the remains of the **stadium** open up in a horseshoe. The original Greek semi-circular theater followed the land's contours to add natural emphasis to the staged dramas. Romans plunked their own stadium right on top of the Greek theater, interpreting "drama" in another way: bloody gladiator games, wild beast hunts, and public executions. Just inside the lower entrance, a dirt path leads off to the right. On the right side of the fork, you'll find the ruins of the **Church of the Seven Councils,** where the Third Ecumenical Council met in AD 431. Beside it lies the ruined **Archbishop's Place,** destroyed by Arabs in the 6th century AD.

At the main entrance gate, a tree-lined path points to the **Arcadiane,** Ephesus's main thoroughfare. Buried under a dense swarm of tourists, the 30m by 145m **Grand Theater** is a stunning, heavily restored beast; its *cavea* (seating area), carved into the side of Mt. Pion, seats 25,000. The **Street of Curetes** begins at a slight incline. Ruts in the road are evidence of the heavy traffic between the temple and the city, and gaps between the slabs reveal glimpses of the city's **sewer system.** At the very bottom of the Street of Curetes is the **Library of Celsus,** restored by Austrian archaeologists. The large building behind the library was probably the **Temple of Serapis,** an Egyptian god of grain. Farther up the Street of Curetes, the imposing ruins of the AD 118 **Temple of Hadrian** are on your left, marked by a double-layered column construction. A little farther up the hill on the left are the ruins of the exquisite **Fountain of Trajan.**

Two pillars in the middle of the road mark the **Gate of Hercules;** farther uphill and to the left is the **Prytaneion.** Dedicated to the worship of **Vesta** (Hestia to the Greeks, and goddess of hearth and home), the Prytaneion contained an eternal flame tended by Vesta's priestesses, the **Vestal Virgins.** Vesta was vital to the Romans, and the Vestal Virgins thus gained a social standing *almost* as high as men. Immediately adjacent, the **odeon,** or *bouleterion*, remains in fine repair. The **state agora** on the right was the heart of political activity from the 1st century BC until the city's final demise. On the left lie the upper **baths.**

CHIOS Χιος

The lack of mass tourism on Chios (HEE-os) seems rather curious to those who have visited. Beautiful volcanic beaches, cypress- and pine-speckled hills, lush wide-open spaces, and charming medieval villages ought to attract travelers from around the world. Chios *is* hard to reach (ferry routes to the island are unpredictable and infrequent) and far from the rest of Greece's tourist havens. Chios's commercial value has been known, however, since ancient times, when it stood has a rich and powerful island *polis*. Ever since, human occupants have cultivated the isle's trees and exported the trees' *masticha*—a bittersweet, gummy resin used in a number of things from chewing gum to color TVs. Medieval Venetian and Genovese, among them Christopher Columbus, made themselves at home here for a while, and in 1822, Chios hosted a failed Greek nationalist rebellion. A military base and shipping center for years, it only recently has begun to attract a smattering of dedicated adventurers.

CHIOS TOWN

Merchant ships and the occasional tourist ferry dock at Chios Town. Shipping provides the lion's share of this affluent island's wealth, and tourists are the exception instead of the rule at the waterfront tavernas and trendy cafes. Inland, a crumbling medieval fortress keeps several centuries worth of island history intact within its decayed bulk. Today, visitors will find quiet residences sandwiched between long-standing tavernas and bustling markets, all in the shadow of the castle walls.

TRANSPORTATION

Ferries go to: **Alexandroupolis** (1 per week, €21.77); **Ikaria** (3 per week, €14.25); **Limnos** (2 per week, €17.40); **Mykonos** (3 per week, €12.93); **Piraeus** (8 hr., 1-2 per day, €18.91); **Psara** (3 per week, €8.15); **Rhodes** (1 per week, €26.95); **Samos** (4hr., 3 per week, €9.96); **Syros** (3 per week, €14.85); **Tinos** (3 per week, €13.46); and **Çeşme, Turkey** (45min., 1 per day, €50). Citizens of Australia, Canada, Ireland, the UK, and the US (among others) will have to purchase a **visa** if staying more than one day in

Turkey. A visa costs US$65. Ferry **tickets** are available at Hatzelenis Tourist Agency (see below). **Olympic Airways,** on the waterfront on Psychari (☎22710 23 998; open M-F 8am-4pm), sends five **flights** per day to Athens (€69). **KTEL buses** (☎22710 27 507 or 22710 24 257) leave from both sides of Pl. Vounakio, right off the municipal gardens coming from the waterfront. **Blue buses** (☎22710 23 086), in the plateia on Dimokratias, travel within the vicinity of Chios Town, making five to six daily trips to Daskalopetra, Kontari, Karfas, Karies, and Vrondados. Most trips are around €0.85; buy tickets at the station or at any kiosk. **Green buses,** on the left side of the city gardens, make trips to **Emborios beach** (3-5 per day, €2.46); **Pyrgi** (5-8 per day, €2.16); and **Volissos** (2 every other day, €3.08).

ORIENTATION AND PRACTICAL INFORMATION

Walking left from the ferry dock along the waterfront, you'll pass a bevy of cafes and restaurants. A right on **Kanari** takes you inland to **Pl. Vounakio,** the social center of town, where most services, buses, and taxis plant themselves on one side or another of the **Municipal Gardens.** Left of Vounakio lies the **market street,** where groceries and bakeries are open for business. Between the ferry dock and the Municipal Gardens, fortress walls hug the Old Town, a residential area with a few small shops and tavernas.

To reach the **tourist office,** Kanari 18, turn off the waterfront onto Kanari, walk toward the plateia, and look for the "i" sign. They provide maps and help with transportation and accommodations. (☎22710 44 344 or 22710 44 389. Open May-Oct. daily 7am-10pm, Nov.-Mar. M-F 7am-2:30pm.) **Hatzelenis Tourist Agency** lies at the end of the ferry dock and the start of town. The extremely friendly staff sells **ferry tickets** for all lines except NEL. (☎22710 26 743; mano2@otenet.gr. Open M-Sa 7am-2pm and 6-9pm, Su 7am-noon and 8-9pm.) NEL Lines has its own agency in the center of the waterfront. (☎27710 25 848. Open daily 9am-2pm and 6-10pm.) The **National Bank** is next to the OTE and offers a 24hr. **ATM** and **currency exchange.** (☎22710 22 522. Open M-Th 8am-2pm, F 8am-1:30pm.) A 24hr. **hospital** (☎22710 44 303) is 2km north of Chios. The **OTE,** Kanari 1, is up the block from the tourist office, and phones are on the waterfront. (☎22710 40 167. Open M, Th 7:30am-8pm; Tu, W, and F 7:30am-2:30pm; Sa 8:30am-3pm.) **Enter Internet Cafe,** Aigeou 98, is on the second floor of a waterfront building. (☎22710 41 058. €3.60 per hr. Open daily 9:30am-late.) To find the **post office,** follow Omirou one block inland. (☎22710 44 350. Open M-F 7:30am-2pm.) **Postal code:** 82100.

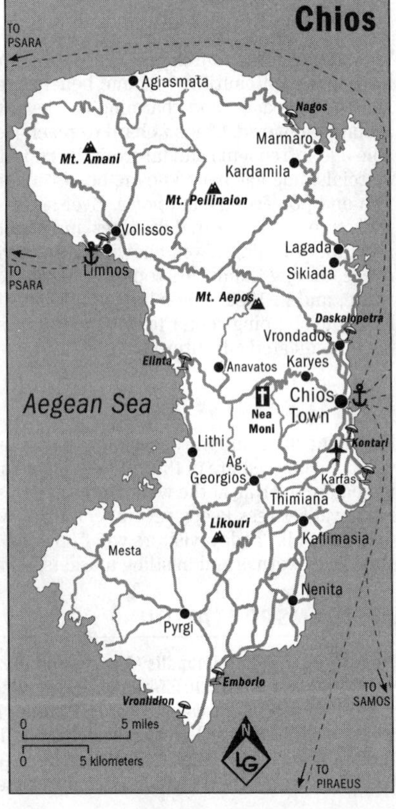

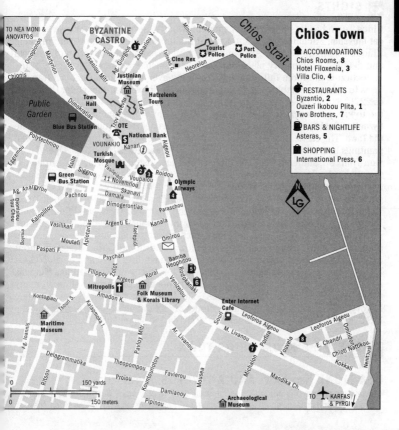

ACCOMMODATIONS

Most of Chios Town's accommodations are on the far end of the waterfront from the ferry dock, in high-ceilinged, turn-of-the-century mansions. In high season, seek help from a tourist agency to get a room. Nearby Karfas (see below) is an option if Chios Town is too crowded.

Chios Rooms, Aigeou 114 (☎22710 20 198). Hard-wood floors add a touch of class to large, well-situated rooms. The kind, helpful staff makes your stay very pleasant. Most rooms share clean baths. Singles €18-22; doubles €23-25, with bath €30; triples with bath €35. ❷

Hotel Filoxenia (☎22710 22 813), just off the waterfront on Voupalou. Rather luxurious, large rooms with A/C, TVs, private baths, and bright blue curtains. Breakfast included. Doubles €21-35; triples €35-55. ❸

Villa Clio (☎22710 43 755), on the water near the Olympic Airways office. Simple but nicely equipped rooms in a prime location. Rooms have A/C, TVs, private baths, and the occasional balcony overlooking the port. Call or inquire about rooms at the Budget Rent-A-Car office. Doubles €30-50. ❹

Chios Town

ACCOMMODATIONS
Chios Rooms, **8**
Hotel Filoxenia, **3**
Villa Clio, **4**

RESTAURANTS
Byzantio, **2**
Ouzeri Ikobou Plita, **1**
Two Brothers, **7**

BARS & NIGHTLIFE
Asteras, **5**

SHOPPING
International Press, **6**

FOOD AND NIGHTLIFE

Myriad vendors set up shop near Pl. Vounakio. For lunch on the cheap, bite into a fresh spanakopita or tyropita available in one of the many **bakeries.** Protected by the castle walls, **Ouzeri Ikobou Plita ❷,** Ag. Giorgios 20 (☎22710 23 858), conveys a sense of elegance with a beautiful, open-air seating area. The restaurant is open year-round, though the menu rotates with the seasons. Seafood, however, is a delicious constant (€7-10). Try the pumpkin pie in winter (€4). To get there, walk past Hatzelenis on Aigeou and make the fourth right. Cheap, quality taverns can be found just off the waterfront. Walking towards the Archaeological Museum from the water brings you to **Two Brothers ❶** (☎22710 21 313) on Livanou. They serve Greek favorites and much-hyped ribs with BBQ sauce (€4.40) in a garden setting. **Byzantio ❶** (☎22710 41 035), on Koulanis near Hotel Filoxenia, caters primarily to the lunch-break crowd (most entrees under €5). Chios' nightlife revolves around the innumerable cafes and arcades on the waterfront. For a game of billiards, head to **Asteras.** Besides lots of pool tables, it also has a nice selection of brand-new video games. (☎22710 43 170. Open daily 10am-3am.) Alternatively, **Cine Rex,** near the port, has evening showings of English-language films (tickets €6).

SIGHTS

Chios Town has lots of museums, most of which deserve a peek. The **Archaeological Museum,** Michalon 10, inland toward the left end of the waterfront, dissects Chios's role in the ancient Aegean world, with an extensive collection of artifacts and detailed explanatory placards. The most unusual and interesting part of the collection is the room full of tablets recording everything from financial transactions to a decree establishing democratic rule on Chios from Alexander the Great. (☎22710 82 100. Open daily 8am-7pm. €2, students €1, EU students free.) Relics of the town's past encircle Pl. Vounakio. To the right of the plateia, the walls of the **Byzantine Castro,** reconstructed by the Genovese, enclose the narrow streets of the **Old Town.** The castle houses a handful of well-restored 14th-century Byzantine wall paintings in the small and overpriced **Justinian Palace.** (☎22710 26 866. Open Tu-Su 8am-7pm. €3, students €2.) The **Ottoman Mosque,** just across from the gardens, is mostly hidden by newer buildings. If you can find the entrance, the mosque now hosts the **Byzantine Museum of Chios.** Its collection, including Jewish and Christian gravestones, is arranged like a garage sale, but it's still worth a look. (Open Tu-Su 10am-1pm. Free.) The **Folklore Museum,** on the first floor (or second floor to non-Europeans) of the **Korais Library,** is next to the **Mitropoli** cathedral. The museum presents a variety of objects, including textiles and tools; particular emphasis is placed on figurines and drawings depicting traditional Chian dress. Without explanatory placards or narration, the exhibit is a bit difficult to appreciate. (Open M-Th 8am-2pm, F 8am-2pm and 5-7:30pm, Sa 8am-12:30pm.) The **Maritime Museum,** in the southwestern portion of Chios Town, hosts depictions of ships in many media (sketches, models, photographs). The focus is not just on Greek maritime history, as the collection includes a model of Columbus's *Santa Maria* and the U.S.S. *Constitution*, among others. (☎22710 44 140. Open M-Sa 10am-1pm. Free.)

DAYTRIPS FROM CHIOS TOWN

NEA MONI Νεα Μονι AND ANAVATOS Αναβατος

Many tourist agencies around Chios run excursions to Nea Moni, but your best bet is to hop on the trips organized by the bus company. A bus excursion runs to Nea Moni, Anava-

tos, and a few other choice locations once a week (€12). Additionally, at the height of the tourist season (July and Aug.), KTEL runs a bus three times a week in the morning to Nea Moni alone (€2 round-trip). Contact the bus stations or Hatzelenis Travel for details.

On the eastern half of the island, several sites, among them Nea Moni and Anavatos, silently recall the invasion of the island by the Ottoman Turks in 1822. Pine-covered mountains 16km west of Chios Town cradle Nea Moni (New Monastery). Built in the 11th century, the **monastery** was inspired by the miraculous appearance of an icon of the Virgin Mary to three hermits. Over the centuries, the monastery complex, one of the world's most important Byzantine monuments, has been rebuilt and enlarged. An 1881 earthquake destroyed much of the complex itself, but most of its structures have been carefully restored. Before entering the main chapel, you'll pass through the inner narthex, where 11th-century gold **mosaics** are stunning despite their age. These artists were also responsible for the mosaics of Hagia Sophia in Istanbul. An adjoining chapel beside the entrance to the complex houses a **memorial**—gut-wrenchingly real with its skulls and bones—to monks and villagers massacred by the Turks in 1822, when the island's population was reduced from 118,000 to 18,000. The skeletons were once 600 priests and 3500 women and children who sought refuge in the chapel. Elsewhere on the island, 23,000 residents were killed and 47,000 sold into slavery. (Open daily 9am-1pm and 4-8pm. Free. Modest dress required.) An on-site **museum** displays church garments and religious items. (Open daily 8:30am-1pm. €2. Free Su.)

Anavatos, 15km west of Nea Moni, is a beautiful, abandoned village built into the hillside. The village's women and children threw themselves from these cliffs in resistance to the 1822 invasion. A walk among the ruins of these fortifications provides amazing views of the hills. Stop into the church near the right of the site's entrance to see a spectacular folk-art rendition of the massacre of 1822.

NORTHEAST AEGEAN

PYRGI Πυργι

You can get to Pyrgi via bus from Chios (5-8 per day, €2.16).

The villages in the southern half of the island, called *Mastichohoria*, are home to Chios's famous resin, produced by squat mastic or lentisk trees. Pyrgi, high in the hills 25km from Chios, is one of Greece's most uniquely beautiful villages, thanks to the black and white geometric designs tattooing its buildings. **Pyrgi** is also home to the 12th-century **Agioi Apostoloi** church, a replica of the Nea Moni. Located in a small alley just off the main plateia, thirteenth-century frescoes and paintings by a Cretan iconography school cover almost every inch of the interior. (Open M-F 10am-1pm. Free.)

SOUTHERN CHIOS

Only 6km south of Chios Town lies popular, sandy **Karfas,** one of the few tourist resort-like spots on the island. Many tourists take up temporary residence here, as it is convenient to both the beach and the amenities of Chios Town; Karfas is also

A FORK AND A DREAM Although it's built in the twisting alleyways of a medieval castle, little Pyrgi in southern Chios is most recognizable for its *ksista,* the unique geometric patterns that cover the walls of every house in the village. Instead of whitewashing their homes, as is common in the Cyclades, Pyrgian craftsmen first coat each house with a paint made from the gray stone at Emborio. The houses are then whitewashed, and, while the paint is still wet, the craftsmen press in geometric patterns with a fork, creating the village's trademark design. After both coats have dried, artists add splendid, colorful designs to the black-and-white geometry.

a refuge for travelers unable to find lodging in the capital. Blue **buses** run from Pl. Vournakio in Chios (every 30min., €0.85). Hatzelenis Tours in Chios Town can set you up with a double with bath and kitchen by the beach at **Villa Anatoli ❸.** (☎22710 20 002 or 22710 32 235. Doubles €35.) **Marko's Place ❷** is a haven for bargain hunters. Located in an old monastery up the hill from the beach, Marko offers small but sufficient rooms with common baths and a familial atmosphere. Enjoy a tasty breakfast in the morning, or make use of the yoga area to unwind. (☎22710 31 990. Doubles €22; triples €32.) Farther south lies pristine **Emborio,** where beige cliffs contrast with black stones and blue water below. The green **bus** from Chios Town drops off at the harbor (4 per day, €2.46). One beach is up the only road to the right (facing the water); a smaller, less crowded shore is up the stairs to the right.

NORTHERN CHIOS

Nine kilometers north of Chios Town, you'll find the pleasant, pebbly shores of **Vrondados** and **Daskalopetra.** Blue buses from Pl. Vournakio in Chios Town serve both. Heading away from Chios Town, a 2min. walk from Daskolopetra beach takes you to the **Sanctuary of Cybele.** Here, sitting on the **Stone of Homer,** where the bard is rumored to have held lectures. After Daskalopetra, the main roads wind northwest along the coast past Marmaron to **Nagos,** with its gray stone beach—perhaps a popular spot to cut Homer's classes. High in the hills toward the center of the island, the village of **Volissos,** Homer's legendary birthplace, is crowned by a Byzantine fort. **Buses** run here from Chios.

LESVOS Λεσβος

Unlike the tiny islands of the southern Aegean, Lesvos feels like its own country. Far closer to Turkey than to Athens, it remains a strong Greek influence in the politically and culturally complex north Aegean. Lesvos's cosmopolitan, off-beat culture incorporates horse breeding, ouzo, and leftist politics with equal zeal. Huge (relatively), geographically diverse, and far from the mainland, the island attracts visitors who explore its hot springs, monasteries, petrified forest, sandy

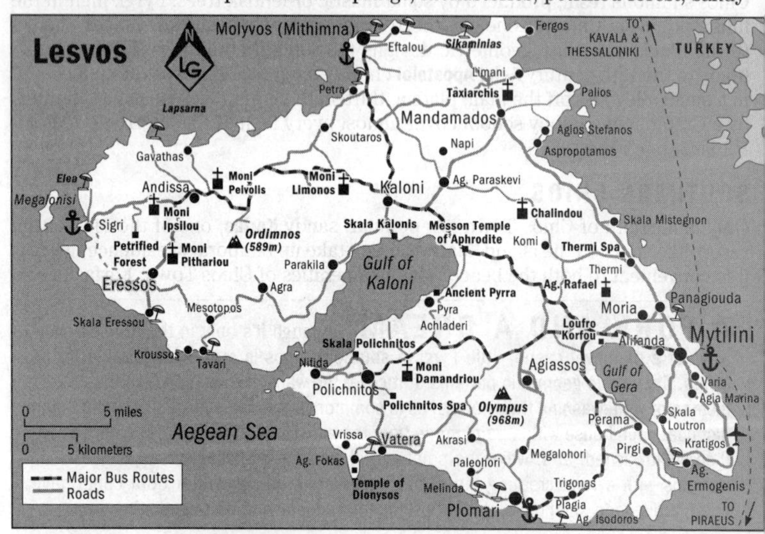

beaches, mountain villages, seaside cliffs, and art colonies. Daytrippers may be overwhelmed; you'll need four or five days to get far beyond the main harbor.

Lesvos has one of the richest cultural legacies in the Aegean. Seventh century BC poet Sappho, fablist Aesop, philosopher Aristotle, empiricist Epicurus, Nobel Prize-winning poet Odysseas Elytis, neoprimitive artist Theophilos, and art publisher and critic Tériade have all called Lesvos home. Legend also has it that Lesvos's population was once entirely female. The tale may date back to the Athenian assembly's 428 BC decision to punish the unruly residents of Mytilini by executing all adult males on Lesvos; the assembly actually repealed the sentence. Still, the idea of an Amazon isle appeals to girl-power pilgrims paying homage to Sappho and the etymological roots of the word "lesbian." Poets retrace Elytis's footsteps and Sappho's fragments. Despite the attention, Lesvos resists tourist degradations.

MYTILINI Μυτιληνη

Each morning, the wide harbor of the capital yawns into a modern, working city more reminiscent of Piraeus than of the tiny ports of nearby islands. Most come to Mytilini on business or en route to the rest of the island, and the town's residential atmosphere is a refreshing change. A walk through town will bring you to playgrounds packed with screaming children and bustling local markets—and possibly earn you a faithful crew of local canines.

TRANSPORTATION

Flights: The **airport** (☎22510 61 590 or 22510 61 490) is 6km south of Mytilini in the direction of Varia; take a **green bus** from the intercity bus station. **Olympic Airways,** Kavetsou 44 (☎22510 28 659 or 22510 28 660). Open 8am-3:30pm. Tickets for Olympic and **Aegean Airlines** flights can be purchased at nearly any travel agency in town. To: **Athens** (4 per day, €83); **Chios** (2 per week, €36); **Limnos** (5 per week, €36); **Thessaloniki** (1-2 per day, €85).

Ferries: NEL Lines, Pavlou Koundourioti 67 (☎22510 22 220; fax 28 601), on the east side of the waterfront, before the string of cafes. Open M-F 6:30am-9pm. Service to: **Chios** (3hr., 1-2 per day, 11.20.); **Kavala** (12hr., 3 per week, €21); **Limnos** (5hr., 6 per week, €15); **Piraeus** (12hr., 1-2 per day, €24); **Thessaloniki** (13hr., 1 per week, €12); **Aivali, Turkey** (1½hr., 3 per week, €45, includes Greek port tax).

Intercity Buses: Intercity buses criss-cross the island, using Mytilini as home base. Therefore, from outlying cities, you will have to head back toward Mytilini in order to get somewhere else on the island. Other convenient transfer points are **Kaloni** and the fork for **Eressos** and **Sigri.** Schedules for the entire island are available at the bus station in Mytilini (☎22510 28 873) and at most information or tourist agencies throughout Lesvos. Service to: **Agiassos** (5-6 per day, €1.90); **Molyvos** (2hr., 4-5 per day, €4.45) via **Kaloni** (€2.90) and **Petra** (€4.15); **Sigri** (2½hr., 1-2 per day, €6.80) via **Kaloni; Skala Eressou** (3hr., 2-3 per day, €6.65) via **Kaloni; Plomari** (1½hr., 3-5 per day, €2.95) via **Gera** (€1.75); **Vatera** (1½hr., 3-4 per day, €4.05) via **Polihnitos** (€3.35). Schedules reduced Sa-Su.

Local Buses: (☎22510 28 725), at the north end of the waterfront on Sappho. To: **Ag. Marina** (every 30min. 7am-8:40pm, €0.85) via **Varia** (€0.65); **Ag. Rafael** (every 30-40min. 6am-9:40pm, €1) via **Thermi** (€0.95); **Loutra** (every 1-2hr. 6:15am-8:30pm, €0.85) via **Koundourtias** (€0.50).

Taxis: Line up on the corner of Ermou and Vournazon.

Moped Rentals: N'Joy Rentals (☎ 29387 79 414), on Tenedou, next to NEL lines ticket office, off Koundourioti. Congenial Milton offers motorbikes from €15 including helmet and insurance, with discounts for longer rentals.

ORIENTATION AND PRACTICAL INFORMATION

Mytilini's harbor opens to the south. Cafes, bars, and hotels line the waterfront street **Koundourioti** (which becomes **Sappho**) on three sides. The **old market** stretches along **Ermou,** host to pharmacies, boutiques, bakeries, and a fish market. Ermou becomes **Kavetsou** at its southern end, where it intersects **Vournazon** one block inland, on the west side of the harbor.

Banks: The inner harbor has a **National Bank** with a 24hr. **ATM** on the west side next to Hotel Sappho. Open M-Th 8am-2pm, F 8am-1:30pm.

Public Toilets: In the park. Pay if you want.

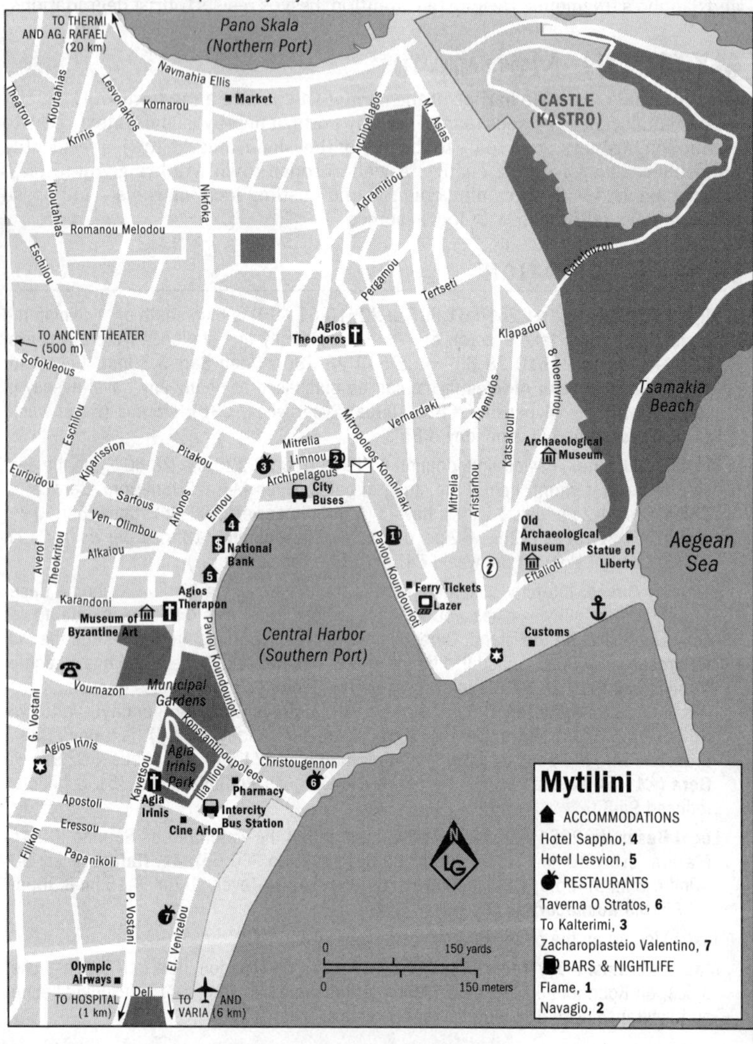

Ambulance: ☎166. **Fire:** ☎199.

Tourist Police: (☎22510 22 776), on Aristarchou near the ferry docks. Provides maps, brochures, and advice. Open 7:15am-2pm and 3-10pm.

Hospital: (☎22510 43 777), southwest of town on E. Vostani. Open 24hr.

OTE: (☎22510 24 299), on Vournazon, off Ermou on the west side of town.

Internet access: Get online at super-cheap **Laser,** on the eastern edge of the harbor, past the string of cafes. €3 per hr., no minimum. Open 8am-1am.

Post Office: (☎22510 28 836), on the northeastern corner of the waterfront. Offers currency **exchange.** Open M-F 7:30am-2pm. **Postal Code:** 81100.

ACCOMMODATIONS

Mytilini has its fair share of enterprising residents, so domatia are plentiful and well advertised. You may also be met at the ferry. Be sure to negotiate, and keep in mind that longer stays often result in lower rates. Doubles run €20-23; before July 15, don't pay more. Hotels along the waterfront are pricey. **Hotel Sappho ❸,** in the center of the western waterfront, has comfortable rooms with A/C, TVs, phones, and sparkling white private baths. (☎22510 22 888 or 22510 28 415; fax 22510 24 522. Singles €25-35; doubles €37-54; triples €44-60.) **Hotel Lesvion ❹,** on the waterfront south of Hotel Sappho, has bright rooms with A/C, TVs, phones, and private baths. (☎22510 28 177; fax 22510 42 493; lesvion@otenet.gr. Breakfast €6. Check-out noon. Singles €41; doubles €44-50; triples €53-64.)

FOOD AND NIGHTLIFE

For a typical taverna experience, head to **To Kalterimi ❶,** in the alley Thasou off Ermou, north of the port. Fresh seafood and slow-cooked grilled foods (€3.90) are the perfect complement to their wide variety of local ouzo. (☎22510 46 577. Open daily 11am-1am.) Walk seaward on the southwestern quay to find fresh fish, hearty food, and an amusing split view of the harbor and a busy children's amusement park at **Taverna O Stratos ❷.** (☎22510 21 739. Entrees €4.11-9.11. Open daily 11am-late.) **Zacharoplasteio Valentino ❶,** El. Venizelou 6, has delicious almond confections. (☎22510 23 989. Open daily 9am.)

Mytilini's nightlife centers on its gyrating waterfront. Head to the hypnotic colored lights of **Flame,** on the northeast side of the waterfront, for pulsing beats and fashionable drinks. To take full advantage of the experience, down a few shots (€2.30) and head upstairs to Flame's trippy **neon bowling alley,** where streaking lights and glow-in-the-dark bowling balls and pins make bowling cool. (☎22510 46 885; fax 22510 46 886. Cocktails €6. Bowling €3-4 per person per game, depending on time of day. Open daily until late.) On the north edge of the harbor behind the local buses, **Navagio** (☎22510 21 310) is the refuge of the moped generation and intellectual hipsters alike. Cocktails (€5.90) or big, gooey ice cream sundaes (€4.50) accompany conversations nicely.

For a more sedate evening, head to **Cine Àrion** on Smyrnis across from the inter-city bus station. Mainly American films play nightly on the theater's two screens. (☎22510 44 456. Weekly schedules at the ticket window. €6.)

SIGHTS

ARCHAEOLOGICAL MUSEUMS. Mytilini's extensive collection of archaeological relics is divided between two museums, and tickets are good for both on the same day. The amazing **new Archaeological Museum,** on 8 Noemvriou, is a delight to explore. You'll be able to walk on glass tiles atop the preserved mosaic floors from several houses of ancient Mytilini, in their original layouts. Nearly all signs are in English, and the exhibits are well-organized and beautifully displayed. *(☎22510 40 223. Open daily 8am-7pm. €3, EU students and under 18 free, all other students €2. The ticket is good for the old museum as well.)* The **old Archaeological Museum,** on Eftalioti behind the ferry dock, has a collection of Lesvian artifacts organized to give a linear history of the island. The collection includes remnants from the excavations at Thermi, as well as pottery, vases and sculpture, masks, oil lamps, lifelike figurines, and a gold-leafed crown, found and donated by fishermen. The smaller building hiding behind the main museum contains rare Aeolian tablets. *(Argiri Eftalioti 7. ☎22510 28 032. Open Tu-Su 8:30am-7pm. €3. Same ticket policy as the new museum.)*

OTHER SITES. The sprawling Gattelusi Castle stands resolute guard over the picturesque port from its perch on a pine covered hill near the museums. Originally constructed by Emperor Justinian on the site of a Byzantine castle, it bears the name of Francesco Gattelusi, who received Lesvos as dowry in 1355 after he married Justinian's daughter. Genoese, Ottomans, and Greeks have spent successive centuries maintaining the castle walls and underground tunnels. Wear good shoes for wandering the vast interior. *(☎22510 27 970. Open Tu-Su 8:30am-7pm. €1.50, EU students and children under 18 free.)*

The highest point on the north side of Mytilini is the 3rd-century BC **ancient theater,** built during the Hellenistic period, where 15,000 spectators attended performances and enjoyed near-perfect acoustics. The effect was so impressive that it inspired Pompeii to build Rome's first stone theater. *(Open Tu-Su 8:30am-7pm.)* The late 19th-century **Church of Ag. Therapon,** on the west side of the harbor, and one block inland on Ermou, is impressive for its enormous size alone *(open 9am-7pm)*. The **Byzantine Museum** is right next door. *(☎22510 28 916. Open M-Sa 9am-1pm. €2.)* The church towers over a fish market full of sardines, octopi, and small sharks. Inland and north of the harbor (one block off Ermou) is the impressive **Church of Ag. Theodoros,** housing the bones and skull of its patron saint.

VARIA. Only 4km south of Mytilini along El. Venizelou, the tiny, unassuming village of Varia (Βαρια) surprises wayfarers with the **Theophilos Museum,** featuring the work of the famous neo-primitivist Greek painter Theophilos Hadzimichali. *(☎41 644. Open May-Sept. Tu-Su 9am-2:30pm and 6-8pm. €2, students and children under 18 free.)* Next door, the **Musée Tériade** displays an excellent collection of Picasso, Miró, Léger, Chagall, and Matisse lithographs; captions are in Greek, English, and French. Tériade, a native of Lesvos (born Stratis Eleftheriadis), was a leading 20th-century publisher of graphic art in Paris. *(☎22510 23 372. Open Tu-Su 9am-2pm and 5-8pm. €2, students and children free.)* Intercity **buses** to Varia leave Mytilini every hour (20min., €0.60). Tell the driver you are going to the museum.

AGIOS RAFAEL. Twenty km into the hills above the capital is the monastery of Ag. Rafael in Thermi. The saint was particularly active in working modern-day miracles, making his chapel and grave a major place of pilgrimage. The door on the bottom level of the church, marked ΑΓΙΑΣΜΑ, leads to a source of holy water. Visitors can stay free for up to two nights, and nearby **Kafe-Estiatoriou O Fotis** offers "home cooking at fair prices." *(☎22510 71 259. Bus from Mytilini runs every hr. for €1.)*

DAYTRIP FROM MYTILINI: VATERA

Buses run to Vatera from Mytilini (1hr.; M-F 4 per day, Sa-Su 2 per day; €3.96) via Polichnitos. The bus enters via the main road, runs the length of the beachside road, and drops off and picks up anywhere along the beach.

With calm waters and 7km of wide, unbroken sands, Vatera is the premier beach on Lesvos. Don't be deceived by the lush, green hills that form its backdrop—the heat is intense here, and staying hydrated while you soak up the sun is a must. The beach is the only attraction in town, and every establishment lies just across the road, catering to sunburnt tourists.

For beachgoers too exhausted to make the trip back to Mytilini, **Hotel Aphrodite** ❹ (☎22520 61 588), 800m down the road from the main intersection, has rooms with A/C and fridges, rents **bicycles** (€6 per day), and provides **currency exchange.** (☎22520 61 588. Singles and doubles €50; triples €80. Prices double in high season.) Lavish **Camping Dionysos** ❷, 350m from the intersection and 100m from the beach, has a pantheon of amenities: hot showers, bathrooms, market, swimming pool, and bar. (☎22520 61 710 or 22520 61 151; fax 22520 61 155. Reception 8am-midnight. Seaside gate open 9am-9pm, main road gate open 24hr. €6 per person, €3 per child; €6 per tent; €6 per car.) Two supermarkets are about 50m to the left of the intersection; tavernas are along the beachside road. Candlelit **Mylos Cafe,** 100m to the left of the intersection on the beach, hosts a mixed crowd in search of a chill atmosphere. Beer (€2.30-4) and cocktails (€5) accompany the mood music. (☎22520 61 161. Open late.)

The ruins of the **Temple of Dionysus** lie to the right of the beach, facing the water. Some of the remnants of column in the site date to 300 BC, while others date to AD 100, when the temple was rebuilt. The ruins themselves are unimpressive, but amazing sunsets are visible from the beach on the other side of the point. The journey is a bit long for an evening stroll but makes for a pleasant (if strenuous) bike ride. Follow the road along the beach to the right facing the water, and veer left across the bridge at the sign for Villa Pouloudia. Bring water and avoid going during the heat of the day—the second half of the ride is hilly and taxing.

MOLYVOS Μολυβος

Hilly and cobbled, the artists' colony of Molyvos spills from the towering castle to the sea like a gingerbread village from a children's storybook. Its quaint charm and long stretches of sand make it one of the most visited spots on the island, yet the atmosphere remains serene and the prices reasonable.

ORIENTATION AND PRACTICAL INFORMATION. Molyvos has three main tiered roads: the lowest (left as you enter town from the bus station) runs along the beach past hotels and restaurants. The middle tier is the **main road,** which traces the cliff top and runs all the way to the port on the far side of town. The upper tier, veering right and uphill as you enter town, runs through the vine-covered *agora* past shops and restaurants with fantastic views.

The **bus** stops at the base of town on the main road. **Buses** run from Molyvos to **Mytilini** (1½hr., 4-5 per day, €4.45) via **Kaloni;** in summer, local buses run between Molyvos, **Petra,** and **Eftalou.** Check the bulletin board outside the tourist office for schedules and fares. Near the National Bank, **Kosmos Rentals** rents **mopeds** (€8-15 per day) and **cars** (€30-80 per day), including full insurance, tax, and unlimited mileage. (☎22510 71 710; fax 22510 71 720. Open daily 8am-1pm and 5-9pm.) **Taxis** (☎22510 71 480) stop at the intersection on the main road heading into town from the bus stop. Just into town on the left side of the main road is the **tourist information office,** where you'll find maps, schedules, and help finding rooms. (☎22510 71 347; fax 22510 72 277; mithimna@aigaio.gr. Open daily Apr.-Oct. 7:30am-4pm.) Next door, the **National Bank** offers **currency exchange** and a 24hr. **ATM.** (Open M-Th 8am-2pm and F 8am-1:30pm.) The road forks just beyond the bank; head right and uphill, and right again at the fork at the top of the hill to reach the **post office** (open M-F 7:30am-2pm). If you head left at this second fork, you'll find the local **laundry,** where €7.90 will get you one load of clean clothes. (☎22510 71 692. Open 9am-2:30pm and 5:30-11pm.) A **pharmacy** is on the same street (☎22510 71 427. Open

9am-2pm and 6-10pm.) Signs will direct you to the **police station** (☎22510 71 222). **Internet access** is available at three places on the main road: **Cinema Arion** (€4.40 per hr., €1 minimum; open daily 8am-12:30am, summer only), just up from the bus stop; **Cafe Pergola** (☎22510 71 236; pergola1@otenet.gr; €4.40 per hr., €1.50 minimum; open daily 9am-late); and **Molyvos Internet Center**. (☎22510 72 422. €4.40 per hr. Open daily 10am-2pm and 6pm-late.) **Postal code:** 81108.

ACCOMMODATIONS AND FOOD. Signs for domatia dot the town, and the tourist office will help you find a bed. Expect to pay €15-25 for a double in low season and €25-30 in high season. **Nassos Guest House ❷,** on the hill just into town, offers cheerful rooms in an old house with high ceilings, private balconies, common baths and kitchen. Owners Marcia and Betty will make you feel at home. At the cluster of motorbike rental shops on the main road, veer right uphill, and take the first switchback on the right. (☎22510 71 432 and 22510 71 421; nassosguesthouse@hotmail.com. Doubles €20-28; triples €24-34. Discounts for longer stays. Reservations recommended in Aug.) **Hotel Poseidon ❷,** on the road to the public beach, has large rooms with phones, TVs, and fridges. Tiled private baths and little balconies complete the package. (☎22510 71 981. ☎/fax 22510 71 570. Breakfast €6. Singles €20; doubles €35; triples €50.) **Camping Mithimna ❶** is 1.5km out of town on the road to Eftalou. (☎22510 71 079. €3 per person; €2 per tent.)

Tavernas clustered in the harbor, at the far end of the main road, tend to be pricier than the tavernas hidden on the steep inland roads. **Taverna O Gatos ❷,** midway up the hill before the post office, has served fresh traditional fare for over 20 years. Ask the friendly staff if you can have a rooftop seat; the view is amazing. (☎22510 71 661. Starters €1.20-5.50; entrees €4-7. Open 10am-late.) **Betty's Restaurant ❸,** past the laundry and the pharmacy on the left fork, has comparable views from its gorgeous dining rooms inside a renovated Turkish mansion, and serves up tasty seafood. (☎22510 71 661. Entrees €4-12. Open 9am-3pm and 6pm-late.) Herbivores rejoice— your prayers have been answered in the form of the **Friends Gyros Stand ❶,** on the main road. The affable owner has created a vegetarian gyro stuffed with cucumbers, french fries, and green peppers instead of meat. (☎22510 71 567. Pita €1.40-1.60.) There are several mini-markets on the main road as well.

SIGHTS AND ENTERTAINMENT. The dominant feature of the Molyvos skyline is the **Kastro,** the medieval castle. The view alone is worth a climb up, and the castle itself is superbly preserved and occasionally plays host to theatrical events; call the town hall for information (☎22510 71 313 or 22510 71 323), or keep an eye out for signs. (Castle open Tu-Su 8am-7pm. €2, students and children free.)

On summer nights, head to **Conga's Beach Club,** accessible from both the beachside and main roads, where pulsing music and tropical decor (complete with hammocks) entertain a tourist crowd. (Cover €3, includes a beer. Beer €3-5; cocktails €7. Open daily 10am-late.) **Gatelousi Bar,** on the beach-side road, is a popular place for live, traditional Greek music.

BEACHES. A long, pebbly **public beach** stretches southward toward Petra and is accessible from the first road to the left as you enter Molyvos. Beach umbrellas abound, and showers and changing rooms are available. The beautiful black sand and pebble beaches of **Eftalou** make a pleasant daytrip from Molyvos. The bus from Molyvos drops off in the middle of the main beach. Keep walking to the end of road and around the rocks to find the **thermal baths** of Eftalou, whose 46°C waters are good for rheumatism, arthritis, and skin diseases. (☎22530 71 245. €2.50 for private baths or pool. Open daily 9am-1pm and 3-7pm.) The beach continues well beyond the baths, providing ample opportunity to find a private stretch of sand.

PETRA Πετρα

Named for the monolithic rock in the center of the town, this tiny artists' beach town suns itself on a fertile plain 5km south of Molyvos. Petra's traditional village ambience and long sandy beach make it a popular daytrip from Molyvos, as well as a worthy destination in itself.

Local buses run from **Molyvos** in the summer; the **bus** stops 200m before the central plateia. Facing inland, the road straight ahead, **Theodokou,** hosts the **post office** (☎22530 41 230; open M-F 7:30am-2pm). The road parallel to the water one block inland, **Ermou,** is lined with bakeries and shops. There is no bank in town, but a 24hr. **ATM** can be found next to Supermarket Plus, on Ermou. To the right on the water is **Nirvana Travel,** providing one-stop shopping for all of your tourist needs. Friendly owner Rebecca Michealides provides info, **currency exchange,** a book exchange, excursion bookings, and help with accommodations and car rentals. (☎22530 41 991; fax 41 992; nirvanat@otenet.gr. Open daily in summer 9am-2pm and 6-10pm; available by fax, phone, and email in winter.) Next to Nirvana Travel is a **pharmacy.** (☎22530 41 319. Open 8:30am-2pm and 5:30-9:30pm.) The **OTE,** to the left of the plateia on the road to Molyvos, provides telegram services. (☎22530 41 399 or 41 199. Open M-F 7:30am-1:30pm.) **Taxis** are just a phone call away (☎22530 42 022). **Internet access** is available at **Etedra** just beyond the plateia on the waterfront (☎22530 41 170; €5 per hr.; open until midnight) and at **Reef Cafe** on the road to Molyvos, where a hearty English breakfast (€4-7) and a large selection of draft beers accompanies your surfing. (☎22530 41 488; €4.40 per hr.) **Postal code:** 81109.

The **Women's Cooperative of Petra,** upstairs in the central plateia (enter on Ermou), can help you find a room and serves up home-cooked meals in the summer. (☎22530 41 238; fax 41 309. Open daily 7am-12am. Rooms start at €20.) The beachfront is host to the usual slate of indistinguishable tavernas. If you're looking for less run-of-the-mill dinner, walk a few hundred meters up Theodakou to the cobbled streets behind the Church to find **Rigas,** the oldest taverna in town. (☎22530 41 405. Entrees €4-8. Open daily 7pm-late.) If you'd prefer to pick up something for a picnic on the beach, check out the **Agricultural Cooperative of Petra**, at the fork before town where the road to Kaloni splits off from the main road. Lesvian olive oil, honey, wine, and jams are on sale until 2pm, but fresh produce is sold in the market from 7am-11am; if you get there early, you might see the farmers come down on their fully-laden donkeys. At night, head to **Machine** bar and disco on the waterfront. (Open 10:30pm-late.) If you can peel yourself off the sand, you can watch ouzo bottling at **Ouzo Petras,** Ermou 31, an ouzo store with its own bottling equipment. (☎22530 41 231. Open daily 10:30am-1:30pm and 6:30-10:30pm.) Before downing your new bottle of anise goodness, climb up the rock in the center of town (up Theodokou past the post office) to the pretty **Church of the Holy Mary with the Sweet Kiss.** (Open daily 8:30am-9pm; modest dress required.) Also in town is the **Vareltzidaina House museum,** the opulent mansion of a former resident, with a collection of paintings and frescoes. (Open Tu-Su 8:30am-7pm.)

SKALA ERESSOU Σκαλα Ερεσου

Skala Eressou's seemingly endless beach stretches across the opposite end of Lesvos from Mytilini, completely breaking from the concrete noise of the capital. Laid-back and welcoming, Sappho's birthplace attracts an eclectic group of visitors—archaeologists, lesbian poets, and freckled families share the sand. Its western half remains one of the few legal nude beaches on the island. Perfect sunsets burn slowly down into clear nights over the mountains to the west, where the ridge forms Sappho's profile.

ORIENTATION AND PRACTICAL INFORMATION. The **main road** to Eressos and points north intersects with the long waterfront at **Pl. Anthis and Evristhenous.** To the right along the beach from the plateia are similar restaurants and cafes, while to the left (cross the bridge 1 block inland on **Kanari**) are establishments with more soul. The streets parallel to the beach on both sides of the main road have **craft shops. Buses** run between Skala Eressou and **Mytilini,** via the fork for **Sigri** and **Kaloni** (3hr., 2-3 per day, €7). The bus stops in a large parking lot on the main road two blocks from the waterfront. The incredible Joanna and the team at **Sappho Travel,** one block from the bus stop before the waterfront, can help with accommodations, **currency exchange,** information about Skala Eressou, and just about anything else. (☎22530 52 140 or 22530 53 327; fax 22530 52 000; www.lesvos.co.uk. Open daily May-Oct. 9am-11pm; Nov.-Apr. 9am-3pm.) There are **health clinics** in Eressos (☎22530 52 132; open Tu-Th) and Skala Eressou (☎22530 53 221; open M, W, F 9am-1pm), behind the Hotel Sappho. The nearest **police** are in Eressos (☎22530 53 222). In case of **emergency** call the **Health Center** in Antissa (☎22530 56 440, 442, or 444). There is **no bank** in town, but there is a 24hr. **ATM** outside Sappho Travel. **Internet access** is available at **Cybersurf Cafe,** just past the bridge on Kamari. (☎22530 52 290. €5 per hr., €2 minimum. Unlimited coffee €1.50. Open noon-10pm.) A few **card phones** are creatively hidden around town; one is alongside Hotel Sappho. The **post office** is in Eressos. **Postal code:** 81105.

ACCOMMODATIONS. Skala Eressou generally draws visitors for weeks of stunning sunsets; many come for vacation and end up staying for good. Consequently, studios and longer term accommodations are plentiful, although rooms for brief stays are also reasonably priced. Sappho Travel can help with accommodations. **Hotel Sappho ❷,** on the waterfront to the right (facing the water), is a women's-only hotel with spacious rooms, original murals, and a massage room. (☎22530 53 495 or 22530 53 233; fax 22530 53 174. Singles €20-30; doubles €30-50.) Farther down the beach to the right, **Villa Marilena ❷** has well-equipped rooms, with fridges, coffee makers, and beautifully tiled private baths, right on the beach. (☎22530 53 153 or 22530 53 094. Doubles €20-40; triples €35-45; 5-person apartment €65; discounts for longer stays.) Away from the waterfront, **Hotel Galini ❸** offers rooms with private baths, A/C, phones, and balconies in a quiet locale. From the waterfront, walk three blocks inland on the main road and go right at the sign for the hotel; it's down an alley to the left. (☎22530 53 138; fax 22530 53 137. Singles €28-33; doubles €38-50.) There is **unofficial camping** at the far end of the beach, by the nude section farthest from town, with primitive women's facilities. This camping may be tolerated but is **illegal,** so camp at your own risk.

FOOD AND ENTERTAINMENT. Food in Skala Eressou is generally very good, and the town is a vegetarian paradise by Greek standards. Eclectic **Yamas ❶** (☎22530 53 693) serves home-made wheat pancakes (€2.50) and a variety of other delectable treats (€1.50-4) all day. The longest-running bar (9 years and counting) in Skala Eressou, it has big comfy chairs perfect for viewing the breathtaking sunset over the mountains. **Sappho Restaurant ❷,** at Hotel Sappho, serves a variety of pastas, grilled dishes, and excellent meatless selections. (☎22530 53 233. Entrees €5-7.50. Open daily 9am-3pm and 7pm-midnight.) To the right along the waterfront, **Soulatso ❷** is the best Greek taverna in town and specializes in fresh fish. (☎22530 52 078. Entrees €3.50-7.40. Open daily noon-midnight.) Along the beach to the left, **Jay's Restaurant ❷** offers a diverse menu of Asian, Western, and vegetarian dishes. (Entrees €5-8. Open daily 6pm-late.) **The Tenth Muse,** in the main plateia, is a popular gay-friendly bar. (☎22530 53 287. Beer €2-4.50; cocktails €5. Open 9:30am-4am.) Revelers hang at the beachfront bars and cafes that spill onto the sand. On hot summer evenings, join the crowd for a late-night plunge in the Aegean to clear your head.

SIGHTS. Sappho fans beware: though useless trinkets and statues of the poet are easy to find in town, actual collections of her work are not. A few photographs of the landscape that inspired her work might make better souvenirs. The 5th-century mosaics once housed in the early Christian basilica of **Ag. Andreas,** three blocks north of the beach, are now in Mytilini's Archaeological Museum. Near the church is the **Tomb of Ag. Andreas.** (Open 9am-1pm.) The river, just west of Skala's center, is home to many rare and exotic birds. Peak **bird watching** season is from April to May. About 11km above Sigri on the main road is the spectacular **Ipsilou Monastery.** Situated on the peak of the Ordymnos volcanic dome, the picturesque Byzantine monastery commands an amazing view of northwestern Lesvos, and includes an ornate church and tiny museum.

DAYTRIP FROM SKALA ERESSOU. A **petrified forest** near **Sigri** is one of only two such forests in the world (the other is in the southwestern United States). The site is sprawled on a parched, rugged hillside about 10km above Sigri and is connected by 2½km of walking trails. The amazing collection of fragments and unearthed trunks of 15-20 million-year-old trees takes at least an hour and a half to appreciate fully and includes the largest fossilized tree in the world. In **Sigri,** the **Natural History Museum of Lesvos's Petrified Forest,** completed in 2001, has interesting, informative exhibits on a variety of plant fossils, both from the Lesvos site and from around the world, stretching back to the Paleozoic Era. There are also exhibits on shipbuilding and the geology of Greece. (☎22530 54 434; lesvospf@otenet.gr; www.aegean.gr/petrified_forest. Site open daily 8am-4pm. €2, children free. Museum open daily 8am-8pm. €2, children free.) The site and museum are best accessed by private vehicle, but the road that runs directly from Eressos to Sigri is not passable. Head back towards Andissa on the main road for 10km and go left at the fork for Sigri. A network of **trails** connects Eressos, the petrified forest, and Sigri. (Eressos to forest, 7½km; forest to Sigri 14km; Sigri to Eressos 16km.)

Sigri, a small fishing village, is worth a look if you make the trip to the museum. Several small tavernas cluster near the main plateia on your left as you approach the harbor on the main road. **Una Fazzia, Una Razza ❷** is an Italian eatery just around the corner from the plateia. Welcoming owners Serena and Gerado serve the cheapest lobster in the area (€35 per kg) as well as excellent pasta dishes from their native land. (☎22530 54 565. Entrees €5.50-8. Open daily 11am-4pm and 6pm-late.) For Greek cuisine, check out **Taverna Australia ❷,** just around the corner. (☎22530 54 227. Entrees €3-6. Open daily noon-late.)

Sigri's beach is signposted from the main plateia and is pleasantly sandy and calm, protected from the northern winds by the town's 18th-century Turkish castle. Wander further down the road to find less frequented beaches for a private soak in the sun. Should you decide to stay longer in Sigri to enjoy the peace and quiet, Sappho Travel, in Skala Eressou, sets up accommodations.

PLOMARI Πλομαρι

After arson destroyed Megalohori village in 1841, people resettled in the Turkish-inhabited region 12km south, now modern Plomari. From its earliest days, the town has had a split personality: it's a vacation town brimming with trinket shops and tavernas, and a crumbling fishing village ringed by the ouzo factories and olive groves at the town's outskirts.

PRACTICAL INFORMATION. Plomari is 40km by bus from Mytilini (1½hr., €2.95). The **bus** stops in the main plateia, where you'll spot a **National Bank** that has a 24hr. **ATM** and offers **currency exchange.** (Open M-Th 8am-2pm, F 8am-1:30pm.) In the top left corner of the plateia (facing inland), a road leads to **Platanos,** a charming cobbled plateia basking in the shade of an enormous tree and ringed with tavernas and food markets. **Paper Land,** in Platanos, sells **international newspapers** and books. **Taxis** (☎22520 33 331) wait in the main plateia, next to the bus stop. About 50m up the first street to the right from Platanos (running uphill behind the national bank) are a **pharmacy** (☎22520 32 381; open 9am-2pm and 6-9pm) and a **bakery.** The street immediately to the right of the bus stop (facing inland) runs past a long gauntlet of waterfront tavernas. In the same building as the Oceanis Hotel, **Dimitri's Rent-a Bike** (☎22520 32 469) rents mopeds (€20), cars (€21 plus €0.24 per km), and a few bicycles (€5). Services include: **police** (☎22520 32 222); the **24hr. Health Center of Plomari,** just outside of town (☎22520 32 151); and a **medical emergency line** ☎166. **Saloon Cafe,** to the right from the bus stop at the end of the line of tavernas, provides **Internet access.** (€5 per hr., €3 minimum. Open 9am-evening.) On the right of town on the beachside road, facing inland, are the **OTE** and the **post office,** which exchanges currency. (Open M-F 7:30am-1pm.) **Postal code:** 81200.

ACCOMMODATIONS AND FOOD. While Plomari makes a wonderful day-trip, there are places to stay should you want to relax a bit longer. **Pension Lida ❷** is housed in two adjacent buildings on the hill above Platanos: the old mansion of a Plomari manufacturer and the family home of its owner. Beautiful and diverse rooms are accented by Byzantine treasures tucked into walls and hardwood floors. Each opens onto stone terraces, balconies, or arched stone windows with views of the village. Friendly owner **Yiannis Stergellis** manufactures his own ouzo and olive oil on the premises. (☎/fax 22520 32 507. Breakfast €3. Singles €15-20; doubles €20-27; triples €30-35.) **Maki's Guest House ❷** is up the stairs to the right of Saloon Cafe; knock on the third wooden door on the left. Three pristine rooms on the waterfront have private baths, fridges, and a common balcony. (☎22520 32 536. Singles €15-20; doubles €20-30.) Rooms at **Hotel Oceanis ❷,** the large building that dominates the waterfront, have A/C, private baths, and balconies. Be sure to request a sea view—the price is the same. (☎22520 32 469. Singles €18-24; doubles €24-36.) Tavernas line Platanos and the road leading to the main plateia. **Bacchus ❷,** on the waterfront side of Hotel Oceanis, stands apart; it's the oldest taverna in Plomari. Nikos and Nikos, the friendly owners, are renowned for their souvlaki Bacchus (€5) and meatballs (€5.70), fresh from the grill. (☎22520 31 059. Entrees €4.50-6. Open daily 6:30pm-late.)

SIGHTS AND BEACHES. The local ouzo is far better than the bottled commercial variety. Try a sample at the **Barbayanni Ouzo Factory,** roughly 2km east toward Agios Isodoros on the road to Plomari. The company has been in business since 1860, and it has its very own **Ouzo Museum,** featuring the Barbayanni family's original wooden boilers. (☎22520 32 741. Ask at the factory for a free tour of the museum. Open M-F 8am-4pm.) An annual, week-long **Ouzo Festival** is held in late August and features song, dance, and, of course, free ouzo. Plomari also hosts several summertime religious celebrations and cultural events. The one-week **Festival of Benjamin,** in late June, commemorates the War of Independence leader with dancing and theatrical presentations. On August 15, the town celebrates **Panegyri** in time-honored style. Just 15km north of Plomari on the slopes of Lesvos's Mt. Olympus, you'll find the ceramic crafts center of **Agiassos.** In town, an Orthodox church treasures an icon of the Virgin Mary made by St. Lucas, originally destined for Constantinople in AD 330. When the priest transporting it heard rumors of war, he hid the icon in Agiassos's church. On August 15, Agiassos hosts **Panagia,** a local version of the Feast of the Annunciation. The village also boasts an **Ecclesiastical Museum** with Byzantine religious works (ask church officials and priests in town) and a **Folk Museum** featuring traditional costumes.

Beaches appear intermittently around Plomari. To reach small, rocky **Ammoudeli Beach,** follow the waterfront road out of town to the right from the bus stop, facing the water. Continuing straight past the beach brings you to **Ag. Nikolaos,** a church sparkling with icons spanning 400 years. About 3km east of town, the sandy, golden expanse of **Ag. Isodoros** beach draws a large, bronze-colored following.

LIMNOS Λημνος

According to a saying, everyone who visits Limnos cries twice: once when they arrive and once when they leave. Brown, remote, laced with dirt roads, and spotted with sheep, the island's solitude sinks in slowly. Limnos meets travelers on its own terms, somewhere between the two-storied capital, the flamingoes of the eastern salt lakes, and the silent military presence.

MYRINA Μυρινα

The island's capital and primary port is a well-proportioned fishing village. At night, the hilly skyline is dominated by an impressive, illuminated Venetian Castle. Each morning, Myrina is roused to the orange dawn by the harborside fishermen.

TRANSPORTATION. Ferries: Nel Lines runs to **Chios** (12hr., 2 per week, €16.90); **Kavala** (5hr., 4 per week, €12.20); **Lesvos** (6hr., 6 per week, €14.40); **Piraeus** (22hr., 3 per week, €17.70); **Rafina** (13hr., 1 per week, €18.20); and **Thessaloniki** (8hr., 2 per week, €17.70). Buy tickets at **Chrissa Karaiskaki Tours** in Pl. 8 Octovriou. (☎22540 22 460 or 22540 22 900; fax 22540 23 560. Open M-F 8am-3pm and 6:30-9:30pm, Sa 8am-3:30pm and 7:30-9:30pm, Su 7:30am-4pm and 7:30-9:30pm.) **Ferry Boat SAOS II** runs to: **Alexandroupolis** (6hr., 2 per week, €14); **Kavala** (6hr., 3 per week, €13.44); and **Samothraki** (2½hr., 2 per week, €9.33). Buy tickets at the **SAOS office,** directly across the plateia from Vayakos Tours. (☎22540 29 577. Open daily 9am-2pm and 6-10pm.) Next door, **Pravlis Travel** also sells tickets for **Olympic Airways** flights to: **Athens** (2 per day, €50 plus tax); **Lesvos** (4 per week, €30 plus tax); and **Thessaloniki** (6 per week, €50 plus tax). The **bus station** (☎22540 22 464) is in Pl. El. Venizelou, the second plateia along Kyda in the far left corner between a tourist agency and a coffee shop. Although buses serve all of the island's villages, you may get somewhere and find yourself unable to return. You'll be much better off renting a **bicycle** (€6), **moped** (€15-20), or **car** (€30); inquire on the harborfront at one of the many agencies. **Taxis** (☎22540 23 820) are at your service in the main plateia.

HEY, LADIES Though it can't claim the etymological distinction of its neighbor to the south, Limnos, like Lesvos, is rumored to have once enjoyed a period of unfettered girl power. According to myth, when Thoa was King of Limnos, the women of the island refused to worship Aphrodite. To avenge their insubordination, the goddess put a hex on the women, endowing them with a body odor so fierce that it sent their men running to Thrace to find new wives. But the Limnian women made no effort to powder and perfume their way back into the hearts of their men. Instead, they murdered them—husbands, fathers, sons, lovers—and threw them in the sea near present-day Petrassos. They headed to the fertile shores of Samothraki every once in a while to get their kicks, and the daughters conceived in the process perpetuated the civilization. Sons weren't so lucky. They probably followed the old saying about Limnos to a tee (see p. 381), shedding the expected tears upon arrival and crying again, a few moments later, when they were thrown into the sea.

ORIENTATION AND PRACTICAL INFORMATION. The city has two main waterfronts on opposite sides of the Kastro. **Romeikos,** on the northern-facing side of the Kastro, is longer, pebblier, and more popular. Once-regal Neoclassical mansions, cafes, and pricey tavernas, ideal for viewing spectacular sunsets behind Mt. Athos, line its sides. **Turkikos,** facing Turkey, is the active port, where ferries and hydrofoils dock. Its beach is sandier, shallower, and bordered by the best fish restaurants in town. To get to Romeikos from Turkikos, head inland up **Kyda** (the main artery) past most of the town, and take a left at the bridge for the waterfront.

Kyda leads inland from Pl. 8 Octovriou, past a variety of shops and into the town's central plateia where you'll find **taxis, card phones,** and the **National Bank** with 24hr. **ATM.** (☎22540 22 414. Open M-Th 8am-2pm, F 8am-1:30pm.) One block farther on Kyda, **Garofalidi** runs to the right. Here you will find the **post office** (☎22540 22 462; open M-F 7:30am-2pm) and a self-serve **laundromat** in the Hotel Astron (☎22540 24 392; priced by weight: €6.50 for 1-2kg, €8 for 5-6kg; open daily 8am-2pm and 5-9pm). Two doors down from the post office, **Joy Games** offers **Internet access.** (€3 per hr., €1 minimum. Open M-F 9am-2pm and 4-10:30pm, Sa-Su 9am-10:30pm.) There are several **pharmacies** on Kyda. Walk down Garofalidi past the post office until you come to a large intersection. The **police station** (☎22540 22 200; open 24hr.) is on the corner. Turn left and take the first right, following the signs to reach the **hospital.** (☎22540 22 222 or 22540 22 345. Open 24hr.) In case of **fire,** call ☎22 199. **Postal Code:** 84100.

ACCOMMODATIONS AND FOOD. There are many hotels in town, but they are generally quite expensive. The domatia advertised all over town are the best bet for inexpensive lodgings. **Hotel Aktaion ❷,** on the waterfront in the first plateia on the left from the ferry dock, has clean but simple rooms with fridges; most have tiny private baths. (☎22540 22 258. Singles €20; doubles €25; triples €30.) **Hotel Limnos,** at the ferry dock, offers spacious rooms with balconies and harbor views, as well as A/C, TVs, and phones. (☎22540 22 153 or 22540 24 023; fax 22540 23 329. Singles €25-35; doubles €35-45; triples €55.) The **Blue Waters Hotel ❹,** on Romeikos, offers bright rooms with A/C, private baths, fridges, and TVs. Sophia, the Greek-American receptionist, will be happy to share her knowledge of the island and its rich history. (☎22540 24 403. Doubles €55; triples €65; quads €70.)

The best fish in Myrina can be found at the *limanaki* ("little port"), on the marina near Pl. 8 Octovriou. There are several pseudo-tavernas here; **To Limanaki ❷,** on the far end, is a safe bet for some excellent seafood. Order from the glass tank near the kitchen, but remember that quality doesn't come cheap. (☎22540 23 744. Entrees from €3.80; fresh fish €17-47 per kg. Open daily 7am-late.) Souvlaki and gyros sell for €1.40-1.50 along Kyda. The restaurants along Romeikos have menus posted along the waterfront. Be sure to get a seaside table for the view of Mt. Athos. At night, cruise the cafe-bar strip at Romeikos. **Karagiozi** attracts the largest, youngest, hippest crowds with three bars, a dance floor, colorful lighting, and mixed music to match. (☎22540 24 855. Beer €3.50; cocktails €4.50. Open daily 9am-4am.) Most clubs poster in town but are found on the outskirts.

SIGHTS. The **Kastro** that pierces the skyline and divides the waterfronts also houses several dozen deer. If you don't catch sight of them, you can at least enjoy the stunning view and the ruins of the 7th-century BC fortress, reworked by Venetians in the 13th century. Many buildings are at least partially intact within the vast ruins. Wear good shoes and allow an hour to clamber through them all. Follow signs from Myrina harbor for the easiest ascent. In the middle of Romeikos, right next to Hotel Castro, the **Archaeological Museum** has well-staged exhibits accompanied by dramatic music. Informative banners throughout the building provide a comprehensive history of Limnos and explain the various artifacts, which include finds from Hephaestus, the Kabeiron, and Poliochni. Don't miss the interesting collection of ceramic siren sculptures or the skeleton of a sacrificed bull calf. (☎22540 22 990. Open daily 9am-3pm. €2, seniors €1, children under 18 free.)

Think twice about coming to Limnos if you're not comfortable on wheels—most of the island's prime attractions cannot be reached without a car or moped. Limnos is home to a number of notable **archaeological sites,** which are all on the opposite side of the island from Myrina. **Poliochni,** on the east coast, was a prehistoric settlement in the 4th and 5th millennia BC. It is considered to be one of the most complex fortified cities of its time and is credited with being the site of Europe's first parliament. **Ancient Hephaestia,** on the island's north coast, was the location of a sanctuary to the smith-god Hephaestus. Farther up the coast is the site of the 8th-century BC **Kaveiron,** or **Sanctuary of the Kaveiroi,** where the Kavirous, children of Hephaestus and Kaveros, were worshiped as gods. Here, ceremonies were held to celebrate the birth of man and the rebirth of nature. Near the sanctuary is the cave where Philoctetes, a Greek archer in the Trojan Wars, lived after he was bitten by a snake and left there by his companions; it can be explored by foot. When there is a full moon, islanders gather on the beach nearby for a night of revelry with food, drink, guitars, and good spirits—all are welcome. Other sights of interest include the longest **sand dunes** in Europe near Gomati Beach, on the north coast; the **waterfalls** near Kaspakas; and the **hot springs** at Therma. During winter and spring, the western salt plain of Lake Aliki hosts thousands of migrating flamingos.

NORTHEAST AEGEAN

BEACHES. Most of Limnos's sandy beaches are found on the coast near Myrina. The most popular beach on the island is the sandy and shallow **Riha Nera,** just north of Ranakos. Further north on the way to Kaspakas, **Avlonas** is a large, uncrowded beach with two islets of its own. To the south on the road to Kontias is **Nevgatis,** an easily accessible beach with 2km of unbroken sands.

SAMOTHRAKI Σαμοθρακη

Early on, Samothraki (also called **Samothrace**) was a place of pilgrimage for Thracian settlers who worshiped the Anatolian Great Gods who preceded the Olympian pantheon. When those first colonists arrived in the 10th century BC, they saw the same incredible vista you'll see when your ferry pulls into port: dry grassy fields spread outward from the base of the Aegean's tallest peak, the pine-blanketed 1670m Fengari (meaning "moon"). Remote, scarcely developed, and dominated by awesome wilderness, Samothraki attracts visitors who willfully choose swatting mosquitoes in a tent over clubbing until dawn. Though all kinds of people visit, there are more hiking boots than high heels, and guitars outnumber cell phones as hand-held accessories. This laid-back crowd lends the place a grungy *joie de vivre*—a change from the run-of-the-mill summer glitz of other islands.

KAMARIOTISSA Καμαριοτισσα

Even with tourist agencies along the waterfront and the busy comings and goings of buses and ferries, simple Kamariotissa retains a sleepy, untouched charm.

TRANSPORTATION

Ferries dock on the south edge of town, connecting Samothraki to: **Alexandroupolis** (2½hr., 1-4 per day, €7.50); **Kavala** (3hr., 3 per week, €13.70); and **Limnos** (3hr., 2 per week, €9.33). **Flying Dolphins** run to **Alexandroupolis** (1hr., 1-2 per day, €15.10). For tickets and schedules, ask the port police, **Saos Tours** (☎22510 41 505 or 22510 41 411;

IN RECENT NEWS

PROCEED WITH CAUTION

Careless romps on Mt. Fengari's jagged shoulders can quickly turn into life-threatening situations: accidents happen every year, and many lives have been lost along the way. In 2000, a Spanish tourist died after attempting to climb the mountain from the southeast corner of the island, near Pahia Ammos.

There are no marked walking trails in the area the man traversed. At some point during his climb, the man lost his footing, sliding down into the rough waters below. He was found 24 days later on Kypos Beach, northeast of Pahia Ammos.

According to news reports, the man decided to make a solo ascent. Despite warnings, many hikers attempt the trails alone every year, wanting to enjoy Fengari's gorgeous views in solitude.

The hike to the top appears challenging even from the ground, but the distance still allows a romantic distortion of reality. On top, clouds limit visibility, and the bright sky blinds, burns, and dehydrates. Even at dawn, when the mountain cuts a dark and ominous profile against the soft hued sky, obstacles like sharp rocks, slick surfaces, thin air, and wind make Fengari a more perilous hike than most.

Travelers are especially urged to use caution on the trails. As one local resident said, "When you come to this place, the wilderness is there for you, but you must know your limits, you must respect nature. There is nobody here to stop you, and there is nobody here to take responsibility for you."

open daily 7:30am-2pm and 6-10:30pm), or **Niki Tours** (☎25510 41 465; fax 25510 41 304; open daily 9am-2pm and 6-10:30pm). The **Hatzigiannakaidis brothers** at Niki will be happy to fill you in on the island and may tip you off to some of its hidden charms.

Buses stop on the waterfront across from Saos Tours. **Green KTEL buses** run round-trip to: **Fonias** (8 per day 6:45am-7pm, €2.50); **Hora** (7 per day 8am-6pm, €1); **Paleopolis** (8 per day 6:45am-7pm, €1); **Profitis Ilias** (4 per day 6am-3:30pm, €2); and **Therma** (8 per day 6:45am-7pm, €2). **White local buses** run to **Kypos Beach** via Paleopolis, Therma, the campsites, and Fonias; and to **Pahia Ammo Beach** via Hora, Alonia, Lakoma, and Profitis Ilias. Schedules and prices fluctuate; consult the bus drivers for more information. **Taxis** wait on the waterfront (8am-1am). Rent **mopeds** at **Pavlos Rent-A-Bike** in the flag-adorned lot on the road to Hora. (☎25510 41 035. Mopeds start at €10 per day. Bicycles €6 per day.)

ORIENTATION AND PRACTICAL INFORMATION

Everything in Kamariotissa is within a stone's throw of the waterfront. The waterfront road runs out of town to the north and the road to Hora runs east out of town just past the bus stop (at the stop sign). Facing inland, past the waterfront docks on the left, a Greek flag marks the **port police.** (☎22510 41 305. Open 24hr.) Nearby on the waterfront is the **National Bank,** which has a **24hr. ATM** and **exchanges currency.** (Open M-Th 8am-2pm, F 8am-1:30pm.) There's a **pharmacy** on the road to Hora. (☎22510 41 217 or 22510 41 376. Open M-F 9am-2pm and 6-10pm; hours reduced Sa-Su.) **Internet access** is available at **Cafe Aktaion,** on the waterfront. (☎25510 41 056. €3 per hr. Open daily 7am-2am.) The **OTE, medical clinic** (☎22510 41 217; open 24hr.), and **police station** (☎22510 41 203; open 24hr.) are in Hora. The **post office** moved from Hora to Kamariotissa in July 2002. **Postal code:** 68002.

ACCOMMODATIONS AND CAMPING

Samothraki's primary draw is its pristine wilderness; consequently, many travelers breeze through Kamariotissa on their way to **Therma** and the **campsites.** Some camp **illegally** in the surrounding area, but there's no reason to avoid the established campsites, which host guitar solos and late-night bonfires. Kamariotissa is the island's transportation hub and the only place to stay before early-morning ferries. Plentiful domatia can be found at reasonable prices, and the town is a convenient base for exploring the rest of the island.

Brisko Rooms (☎25510 41 328), set back off the road across from the ferry dock, has bright, spacious rooms with A/C, TVs, fridges, private baths, and balconies. Singles €20-25; doubles €30-35; triples €35-40. ❷

Hotel Kyma (☎25510 41 263), on the waterfront at the northern edge of town, is 10m from the stone beach and has spacious rooms with balconies overlooking the sea. A/C, private baths, and fridges. Doubles €24-42; triples and quads €28-50. ❸

Camping Platia (☎25510 98 244), 2km beyond Therma on the coast, has cold showers, baths, a mini-market, and card phones. Check-out 1 day in advance of departure. €3 per person, €1.50 per child; €2.50 per tent; €2 per car. ❶

Camping Varades (☎25510 98 291), 1km beyond Camping Platia on the coastal road, has the same amenities, but with hot showers and a cafe. €3 per person, €2 per child; €2.50-3 per tent; €2 per car. ❶

FOOD AND NIGHTLIFE

The waterfront teems with tavernas specializing in fresh seafood. Most have no need for a menu—just go inside and point at your fish of choice. **I Sinatisi ❷,** a few doors down from Niki Tours, is the best in a row of fish tavernas. Delectable seafood appetizers pave the way for perfectly grilled fresh fish, with the setting sun as a natural, gorgeous backdrop. (☎25510 41 308. Entrees €3-10. Open daily until 2am.) Another excellent spot is **I Klimataria ❶,** on the left-hand side of the waterfront, which features old standbys and some more innovative dishes, such as *yiannotiko*, pork with vegetables and cheeses. (☎25510 41 535. Entrees €3.50-6. Open daily noon-4:30pm and 7:30pm-midnight.) Head back to the kitchen to pick your cut of meat or prepared dish. **Cafe Moka** (☎25510 41 039), on the waterfront, has a variety of pastries including a melt-in-your-mouth cream pie dusted with powdered sugar and cinnamon (€1.50). Wake yourself up with a shot of Bailey's in a morning *frappé* (€3).

Nightlife in Kamariotissa is so laid-back that it's almost non-existent. Beyond a few *barakia* (little bars), the town mostly has a drink after dinner and dozes off. **Diva** on the waterfront plays an eclectic variety of music. **Cafe Aktaion** is a popular nightspot for people of all ages. Drinks at the waterfront bars are similarly priced: beer €2.50-4, cocktails €6.

BEACHES AND THE OUTDOORS

The verdant gem that is Samothraki holds a wealth of hiking trails leading to cascading waterfalls, mountain vistas, and the summit of Fengari. Trails are generally unmarked; the best way to explore is to rent a motorbike in Kamariotissa and head out to the coast or the interior. Ask locals in villages that dot the mountain's flanks for directions to nearby trails. The isle's only **sand beach** is the soft arc of **Pahia Ammo** on the south coast. Stony beaches ring the rest of the coast. Ask a bus driver to drop you off anywhere, then hunt out your own isolated stretch of shoreline. At the end of the line on the north coastal road is popular **Kypos beach.** White buses to: Pahia Ammo (3 per day) and Kypos (3 per day). Bus schedules change frequently.

The most convenient hub for outdoor activities is the town of **Therma,** which brims with dread-locked and tie-dyed alterna-types. A multitude of mini-markets and equipment stores can outfit your camping trip. Tavernas and domatia dominate the village, making it an attractive alternative to Kamariotissa, especially for stays of multiple days. **Buses** from Kamariotissa stop at the base of town, next to the refreshing **thermal springs** that give the town its name. The trail to the **summit of Fengari** is accessible from Therma. Ask around at the base of town for the best way up. Be sure to fill up your water bottles at the **fountain** at the base of town and don't hike alone. The mountain peak is usually shrouded in mist; the hike up takes 4hr. A lovely **waterfall** is also accessible from Therma. From the bus stop, head into town and take the left fork through town. Take the first right after a mini-market and follow this road past tavernas and a bakery. When the road dead-ends, turn left and follow the road; when it meets with an asphalt paved road, turn right. The road dead-ends again at Taverna Filarakia; turn right and head up the shaded road. The dirt trail to the falls follows the stream on the right side of the road; head right 20m before the Marina Hotel.

Enchanting **Fonias** will revive any tired soul slowed by the scorching Aegean sun. The easy 2km hike meanders alongside a gurgling stream and beneath gnarled trees, where dragonflies hover languidly in shafts of light. The trail ends in a sheer cliff face at a cascading **waterfall.** Shed your clothes and jump into the deep green pool at the waterfall's base carved out of the rock below. Alternatively, climb up the steep rockface to the right of the stream for a magnificent view of the falls and the mountains. The **bus** drops off at the trailhead's parking lot. (Green buses: 8 per day 6:45am-7pm, €2.50.)

DAYTRIP FROM KAMARIOTISSA: PALEOPOLIS

Paleopolis and the **Sanctuary of the Great Gods,** Samothraki's premier attractions, lie 6km east of Kamariotissa. (Open daily 8:30am-8:30pm. €3 gets you into the museum as well. Students €2; EU students free.) Before the island's 8th-century BC Aeolian colonization, the chief goddess worshiped here was **Axieros,** or the Great Mother. Three other gods completed the **Kabeiroi** group: Axiokersa, Axiokerson, and Kasmilos. These gods were assimilated into the Olympian Pantheon; Axieros was recast as the fertility goddess Demeter, while two of her consorts, believed to protect sailors, were associated with the twins Castor and Pollux.

Disclosing initiation secrets was punishable by death, so the rituals remain shrouded in mystery. It seems likely that there were two levels of membership: first, the *myesis*, then the higher *epopteia.* The first purification took place in the **Anaktoron,** at the lowest part of the temple complex. The second rite took place in the **Hieron,** a courtyard whose five reconstructed columns now form the site's central attraction. In the **palace** at the southern end, aspiring initiates donned special vestments and were given a lamp. The palace adjoins the Anaktoron, with its circular wooden platform, upon which the newly inducted were presented.

The enormous cylindrical **Arsinoëin,** given to Samothraki by Queen Arsinoë of Egypt, demonstrates the importance of circles to the site. The walls (now preserved in the museum) are decorated with rosettes and heads of oxen. They once stood at the sacrificial site. The nearby **Sacred Rock** was the original center of the cult's practices. In the center, the Doric Hieron—containing pits for sacrifices, an altar for libations, and seats for the audience—saw the final stage of initiation. Confessing their worst deeds, the candidates were purified. A scrubby hillside is all that remains of an ancient **theater.** The **Winged Victory** (or **Nike**) **of Samothrace** once stood upon a marble base near the theater. It now sits as one of the greatest treasures in the Louvre in Paris, having made a sidetrip to Turkey before being looted by a French consul in 1863. Above the sanctuary are the remains of the **ancient town** of Samothraki, where the apostle Paul lived for a year on his way to Kavala in AD 49-50.

Beside the ruins, the **Paleopolis Museum** is somewhat underwhelming. It houses gargantuan entablatures from the **Arsinoëin** and the **Hieron,** a weathered bust of the melancholy prophet **Tiresias,** and a galling cast of the Nike of Samothrace—a "gift" to Greece, courtesy of the French. The relief of dancing girls symbolizes the marriage of Cadmus and Harmonia. The dance represented the onset of winter, a time of mourning to be followed by spring's renewal of life and bursting of seed. (☎25510 41 474. Open Tu-Su 8:30am-3pm.)

THASOS Θασος

Just off the coast of Kavala (p. 263) lies Thasos, the green jewel of the North Aegean. According to legend, Thasos was founded when the devoted brother of Europa gave up pursuing his abducted sister and settled on this remote island. As an ancient exporter of gold, silver, and its famous wine, Thasos attracted the unwelcome attention of Phoenician, Athenian, and Roman conquerors. The Thasians who were not killed or sold into slavery were forced to hide, fleeing to mountain villages or caves. Along with most of northern Greece, Thasos returned to Greek rule in 1912 at the conclusion of the First Balkan War. Since then, massive forest fires have threatened the island's greenery, but the forests are slowly reviving; a sign states proudly upon your arrival, *"Welcome to Thassos, Forest is the Source of Life."* In recent years, Thasos has become quite a tourist oriented island, attracting throngs of Northern Europeans who seek a quiet place in the sun. Nonetheless, the "Green Island" still retains some of its original charm with cool, forested mountains, thriving beekeeping and jam-making industries, and an isolated southern coast that is a hiker's paradise.

LIMENAS Λιμενας ☎0593

The island's capital and tourist center is built atop the foundations of the ancient city, and ruins crowd the Old Port area. Also known as Thasos Town, Limenas sees the highest concentration of tourists yet maintains some of the best-priced accommodations on the island. The British and German tourists who pack the town in the summer find it a convenient place to rent a moped and explore the island's hundreds of secluded beaches. An important note: the arrival and departure point for ferries from Kavala is not in Limenas, but in Skala Prinos (18km west). When you arrive at Kavala, walk left to find buses for **Limenas** and **Limenaria.**

TRANSPORTATION

The village of **Skala Prinos** (18km west) is the point of arrival and departure for most ferries. Buses between Thasos's main villages of Limenas and Limenaria stop at Skala Prinos, in sync with the arrival of the ferries from Kavala.

Ferries: In Limenas, the port police building and ticket booth post schedules. Ferries go to **Keramoti** (30min., 12 per day 6am-9:30pm, €1.30). From **Skala Prinos,** ferries go to **Kavala** (1¼hr., 7 per day 6am-7pm, €2.64) and **N. Peramus** (1¼hr., 9am and 2pm, €2.50). Bus schedules between Prinos and Limenas are synchronized with the ferries. You must return to Kavala for ferry connections to other islands.

Flying Dolphins: Hydrofoils zip to **Kavala** from Limenas (45min., 5 per day 8:10am-3:45pm, €7.04), and from Limenaria, on Thasos's south coast (45min.; 8:20am, 3pm; €10.27). Schedules are posted at the port police and ticket booth, and docked boats indicate departure times with signs on board. Tickets can be bought on board.

Buses: The station (☎25930 22 162) is across from the ferry landing, on the waterfront. Open daily 7:30am-8:15pm. To: **Aliki Beach** (1hr., 3 per day 10:45am-4pm, €2.35); **Limenaria** (1hr., 8 per day 6:35am-8pm, €2.90) via **Skala Prinos** (20min., €1.30); **Panayia** (15min., 10 per day 6:30am-6pm, €0.80); **Skala Potamia** (30min., 9 per day 6:30am-6pm, €0.80); **Theologos** (1½hr., 5 per day 8:55am-4pm, €3.80); all the way around the island and back to **Limenas** (3hr., 3 per day 7:30am-4pm, €4.50). Ask at the tourist police or bus office for schedules.

Rentals: Cars and mopeds are rented all over Limenas. **Budget** (☎25930 23 150), on a street perpendicular to the waterfront. Cars €35-50 per day including 100km and damage waiver. Open 9am-2pm and 5:30-10pm. **Billy's Bikes** (☎25930 23 253 or 25930 22 490) is next door. Motorbikes €12 per day and up. Open 9am-2pm and 5-9pm.

Taxi: (☎25930 23 841), near the ports.

Water Taxi: (☎25930 22 734). Twice daily from Limenas to **Golden Beach** (leaves 10 and 11am, returns 5pm; €2 one-way) and **Makryamos** (leaves 10 and 11am, returns 10:20am and 5:40pm; €3 one-way). Schedules change frequently—call the tourist office for specific departure times.

ORIENTATION AND PRACTICAL INFORMATION

A small crossroads near the bus station and National Bank connects the waterfront road and **28 Octovriou,** a jungle of souvenir shops and souvlaki joints running parallel to the water one block inland. With your back to the water, the **Old Port,** the ancient **Agora,** and the nearest beach are on the left. The small central plateia lies about two blocks farther inland.

Tourist Agencies: Thassos Tours (☎25930 22 546), under the yellow sign, is on the waterfront. Helps with accommodations and gives advice on island tours. Also rents motorbikes (€10-15). Open daily 9am-9pm. **Thassos Tourist Services** (☎25930 22 041), on 28 Octovriou behind the row of tavernas, has maps of the ancient agora and **exchanges currency.** Open M-W and F-Su 9am-1:30pm and 6-9pm

Bank: There's a **National Bank** where 28 Octovriou meets the waterfront, with an automated 24hr. **currency exchange** and **ATM.** Open M-Th 8am-2pm, F 8am-1:30pm

Police: (☎25930 22 500), on the waterfront by the port police. Open 24hr.

Tourist Police: (☎25930 23 111 or 25930 23 580) in the same building as the police. Open daily 8am-10pm.

Port Police: (☎25930 22 355), in the white building with the light blue roof. Open daily 6am-11pm.

Health Center: (☎25930 71 100), in Prinos. Open 24hr. There is no hospital on Thasos; the nearest is in Kavala.

Telephones: The **OTE** is on 28 Octovriou, a block inland from Thassos Tourist Services. Open M-F 7:30am-3pm.

Internet Access: Millenium Net (☎25930 58 089). From the Thassos Tourist Office, turn left and continue walking past Hotel Xenia; 300m down on the left. Six computers and a pool table. Internet €3 per hr. Beer €2, coffee €1.50.

Post Office: Head inland from Thassos Tours and turn right at the fourth corner. Open M-F 7:30am-2pm. **Postal code:** 64004.

ACCOMMODATIONS

There's no need to stay in a hotel on Thasos if you're traveling on a budget—the plentiful domatia are a much better deal. The streets behind 28 Octovriou are crammed with rooms to let signs; most cost €18-20 per single; hunt around for a good price. **Hotel Athanassia** (☎25930 22 545) is closer to a domatia than an actual hotel. Walk down the waterfront with your back to the Old Port and make a left after the Hotel Xenia. On the right, at the end of a narrow lane, the hotel is swallowed up by grapevines and plane trees. Spacious rooms, some with baths, set in an unhurried countryside calm. Screened windows, a rare amenity in Greece, keep out the bugs. (Singles €15; doubles and triples €20. ❷) **Hotel Lido** (☎25930 22 929) is past the post office toward the plateia. Basic rooms in the middle of town with private bathrooms, fridges, and small balconies. Singles and doubles €22. ❷

FOOD AND NIGHTLIFE

The waterfront is packed with restaurants designed to cater to a wide range of European tastes. Multilingual menus offer "Full English Breakfasts" along with plates of schnitzel, pizza, and pasta. To hunt down a more genuinely Greek flavor, head toward the seafood tavernas along the Old Port where fresh fish and squid appetizers dominate the menus.

Simi Restaurant (☎25930 22 517), in the old port on the waterfront. One of the best-located and most popular spots in Limenas, with a laid-back atmosphere and lots of tasty fish and shellfish. Carefully prepared salads (€1.50) are all original creations. ❷

Restaurant Syrtaki (☎25930 23 353), past Simi and the old port at the end of the waterfront road. An ocean-oriented view and menu under a leafy canopy. Live Greek folk music Sa and W nights. Entrees €4-10.50. ❷

Island Café (☎25930 22 895), on the beach on Limenas's eastern edge just beyond the old port, is popular early in the night, when MTV blares and dancing moves to the sand. Serves salads and meat dishes. Entrees €4-5, beer €2.50, cocktails €4-5.50. ❶

Central Bar, under a blue neon light on 28 Octovriou, has popular tables on the 2nd fl. balcony of a jewelry store. The music is loud enough to conceal your comments on the tourists strolling unaware below you.

SIGHTS

Just past the Old Port are the ruins of the ancient **agora** and **acropolis,** built in the 5th and 6th centuries BC. The crumbled streets and toppled pillars invite you to scramble over them, and maps of the Old City are available at Thasos Tourist Services. Farther up the hill are the remains of a 4th-century BC Greek **theater.** Currently under restoration, little is visible other than a tangle of stone, dirt, and uprooted trees. To find the theater, turn right behind the old port and continue to a fork in the road, just beyond the ruins of the **Temple of Dionysus.** The middle of the three paths leads to the theater. Ringing the hills around Limenas are the well-preserved marble **city walls,** inscribed with Archaic reliefs. The **Archaeological Museum** near the old port displays mosaic floors and sculptures found on the site, including a colossal 6th-century BC statue of Apollo with a ram draped over his shoulders. The **Vagis Museum,** just outside of Potamia, displays sculptures by Thassian artist Polygnotos Vagis (1894-1965). Born in Potamia, Vagis emigrated to New York at age 14, where he studied art and began mixing Archaic forms and postures with modern movement and expression. (☎25930 61 400. Open Tu-Sa 10am-noon and 6-8pm, Su 10am-noon. Free.)

Beachgoers may have a hard time choosing among Thasos's beautiful sands. Between Panagia and Potamia, the popular golden **Chrisi Ammoudia** stretches endlessly. To the south, **Aliki**'s twin coves shelter slabs of bleached white rock and crevices ideal for snorkeling. More isolated spots can be found along the water in both directions from Limenaria—just rent a bike or head out on foot, and pick a cove. Ask at the bus station to find out which bus heads past a particular beach. For a guide to the superb **hiking** in the relatively untouched interior, pick up *Walking in Thasos* at any of the tourist agencies.

LIMENARIA Λιμεναρια

Limenaria, Thasos's thriving second town, is across the island from Limenas on a glorious curve of stony beach on the island's southern tip. Much smaller and more relaxed than its bustling counterpart, Limenaria is a haven of unhurried calm, breeze-blown waves, and long, lazy sunsets. While you won't be inundated with souvenir shops, hotels here are popular and high in quality and price.

ORIENTATION AND PRACTICAL INFORMATION. Limenaria's two main streets run parallel to the waterfront. One main crossroad, **Eth. Antistasis,** has **Speedy Rent-a-Car** (☎25930 52 700; cars €35), and beyond that, the town's **OTE.** (☎25930 513 599. Open M-F 7:30am-2pm.) The **post office** (☎29530 51 296; open M-F 7:30am-2pm) and **National Bank,** with a 24hr. **ATM,** are both on the far right edge of the waterfront, facing inland. The **bus stop** is on the waterfront, a few blocks left of the post office. Schedules and tickets are available at the *periptero* across from the bus stop. The **police** (☎25930 51 111) are on the first street inland in the center of town. **Internet access** available at Rock Cave Bar (see below). **Postal code:** 64002.

ACCOMMODATIONS AND FOOD. Hotels and rented rooms abound throughout Limenaria, but budget options are truly scarce. While perfect for families of vacationing Brits and Germans, the rooms will put a sizeable dent in a cost-conscious traveler's budget; search out domatia away from the waterfront. **Hotel Ralitsas** boasts well-decorated rooms overlooking the sea, some with A/C and TVs. (Singles €23; doubles €44; triples €50. ❷) **Hotel Molos** has bright, pleasant rooms, many with balconies overlooking the water. All have baths and shared fridges. Walk down Eth. Antistasis and turn right at the waterfront. (☎25930 51 369. Doubles €40; triples €47. ❹)

The entire waterfront in Limenaria fuses into one mega-restaurant, comprised of the town's numberless tavernas and snack bars. **Il Mare,** just opposite Eth. Antistasis, serves all kinds of seafood delicacies at the romantic tables along the water. (Entrees €4-8. ❷) At the other end of the waterfront is **Restaurant Maranos,** with a large wine cask teetering precariously over the entrance. It offers a shady environment, classic *rembetika*, and many fish choices. (Entrees €4-8. ❷)

NIGHTLIFE. Come nightfall, the wall of waterfront restaurants becomes a single long bar. **Istos Café-Bar, Nile Bar,** and **Larry's Bar** are all in a row, blaring a jumbled audio mess of Greek and American favorites. (Beer €3; cocktails €5-6.) Follow the signs two streets inland to the **Rock Cave Bar,** where the DJ spins underground rock and electronica beneath a bamboo-thatched canopy. It's quiet enough to appreciate the music while holding a conversation. Three computers with **Internet access** are available. (Beer €1.50; cocktails €4-6. Internet €3 per hr.) Popular, massive disco **Bolero,** 1.5km east of town on the road to Pefkari, booms with a different liquor promotion every night. (☎25930 52 180. Cover €3.)

CYCLADES Κυκλαδες

Happy is the man, I thought, who, before dying, has the good fortune to sail the Aegean Sea.
—Nikos Kazantzakis

When people speak longingly of the Greek islands, they are probably talking about the Cyclades. Whatever your idea of the Aegean—peaceful cobblestone streets and whitewashed houses, breathtaking sunsets, vigorous hikes, Bacchanalia—you can find it here. The archipelago derives its name from its spiral shape: the *kyklos* (cyclical) pattern around sacred Delos. Although quiet villages and untouched spots still hide in their corners, the Cyclades are known as a tourist's mecca. Santorini is the most chic and expensive, with spectacular views along its black sand beaches. Mykonos ranks a close second in sophistication (and price); it uncorks some of the wildest nightlife on earth. Beer-goggled Ios can be summed up in one word: frat party. All right, that was two words, but after a night on Ios you won't be able to count either. Paros, Naxos, and Amorgos also get their share of visitors, but they're less frantic, more pristine, and attract more families and hikers. Few non-Greek vacationers sprawl in the sand on the rest of the isles. The pint-sized Little Cyclades are isolated oases blissfully untouched by tourism.

HIGHLIGHTS OF THE CYCLADES

SPLISH, SPLASH, take a bath in hot sulfur springs while the sun sets over lava-made cliffs and smoke-colored sand on Santorini's western coast (p. 445).

DO AS DIONYSUS DID on the streets of Mykonos (p. 402), the Aegean's premier party destination.

LEND AN EAR to the clatter of electromagnetic art in Andros Town (p. 395).

LOSE YOUR MIND. Lose your pants. Party naked on Ios (p. 438).

TRAIPSE through pearly sands and stunning rock formations—products of centuries of volcanic eruptions—on Milos (p. 454).

ANDROS Ανδρος

The magnificent hour-long drive from the ferry landing at Gavrio to Andros Town winds above Andros's famous, beloved beaches. This island is *the* weekend destination for Greece's wealthy ship captains, who restrict ferry access to the island in their zeal to keep their hideaway unspoiled. Stone walls outline green and purple fields, and the island's 300 sandy beaches glow in solitude beneath the sun, each more breathtaking than the last. Andros has the distinction of being the only island in the Cyclades with a source of natural spring water. The flowing streams in the island's interior are bottled and exported for use throughout Greece. Athenians crowd in on the weekends, but Andros remains a quiet escape for those who delight in untrammeled ground and quiet nights.

BATSI Μπατσι

Humming along a stretch of golden sand, Batsi is the tourist capital of Andros, with varied food and accommodations options and the liveliest nightlife. Visitors stroll the waterfront by night, pausing for a drink at a *kafeneion*, and dance the night away in bars and clubs swelling with Athenian visitors.

ORIENTATION AND PRACTICAL INFORMATION. The main **bus stop** and the **taxi stand** are at the end of the beach in a small plateia. A single **bus** motors 4-6 times per day between **Andros Town** (€2.50); **Gavrio** (€1), Andros's port; and **Batsi** (€1). From Gavrio, **ferries** sail to: **Rafina,** (2hr., 3-4 per day 9:45am-7pm, €7.90); **Tinos** (2hr., 3 per day 9:45am-7pm, €5.80); **Mykonos** (2½hr., 3 per day 9:45am-7pm,

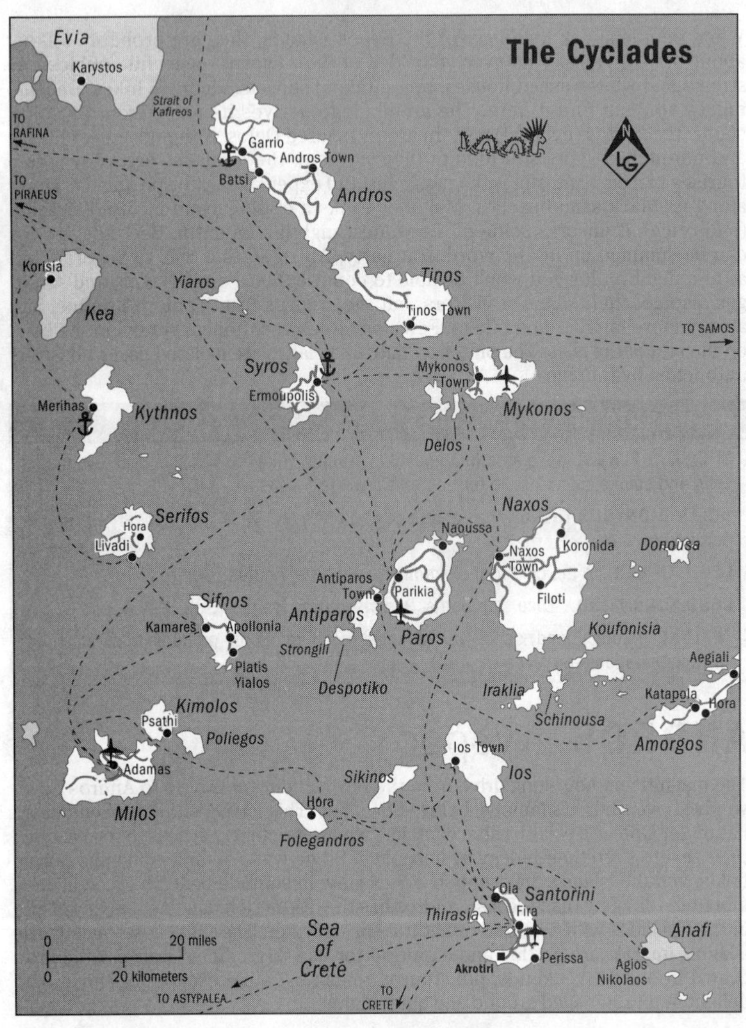

€8.10). **Flying Dolphins** skip to nearby Cycladic islands nearly daily. Check schedules and prices in Batsi at **Greek Sun Travel.** (☎22820 41 198 or 22820 41 771; fax 22820 41 239; www.travelling.gr/greeksun. Open 9am-1:30pm and 6-9pm.) You can also rent cars and find out about walking tours of the island. Greek Sun is on the right of the wharf, above an ice cream parlor. Alternatively, stop by **Andros Travel,** located past the left end of the beach. (☎22820 41 252 or 22820 41 751; fax 22820 41 608; androstr@otenet.gr. Open 8:30am-2pm and 6-10pm.) In Gavrio, **Hellas Ferries** is a good choice. Beach-bound **taxi boats** dock at the end of the wharf. (Round-trip €7.50.) Try **Dino's Rent a Bike,** behind the post office, for a **moped** (€16 and up). (☎22820 41 003. Open daily 8:30am-1pm and 5:30-9pm.)

In the square at the right side of the wharf, there's a branch of the **Alpha Bank** with a 24hr. **ATM.** A **National Bank** is farther to the right and up the hill. (Offers **cur-**

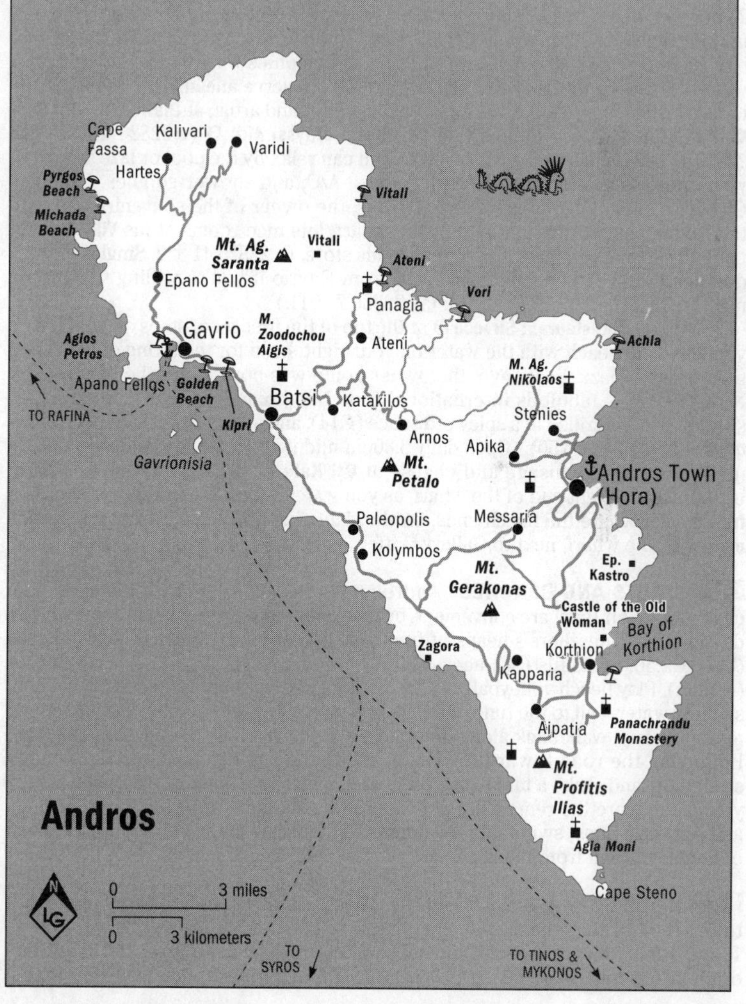

CYCLADES

rency exchange. Open Tu, W, F 8:30am-1pm.) Along the waterfront, a **kiosk** sells **international papers** and magazines. In case of an **emergency** call ☎22820 22 222 or 22820 23 333. A **pharmacy** is all the way up the hill. (Open daily 9am-1:30pm and 6:30-9pm.) To the left of the beach, behind a playground, is a **medical office.** (☎22820 41 326. Doctor available 9am-1pm.) The **dentist** is available M, W, F. (☎22820 41 450.) At the right end of the beach you'll find the **Gallery Coffee & Cocktail Bar,** which offers **Internet access** (€3 per hr.), travel info, and a terrific breakfast for €4.50. (☎22820 41 064; fax 22820 41 620.) Just before the medical office is the **post office.** (Open M-F 8:30am-2pm.) **Postal code:** 84503.

ACCOMMODATIONS AND FOOD. It's easier but generally pricier to find accommodations in Batsi than in Gavrio or elsewhere in Andros. Domatia in Batsi tend to be nicer than the hotels for comparable or lesser cost. Expect to pay €15-25 per person per night (lower if you bargain well). **Villa Aegeo** ❸ is worth the trek up four flights of stairs to the right of Batsi Gold; look for the sign. The large doubles have private baths, fridges, and breezy balconies for €30. Negotiate if you want a single. (☎22820 41 327 or 22820 41 714. Reserve ahead.) For rooms to the left of the beach, see Mike Marinakis, a bar owner and artist, at **Glari Rooms for Rent** ❸. (☎22820 41 350. Doubles €26-36.) **Hotel Chryssi Akti** ❹ (☎22820 41 236; fax 22820 41 628) is just to the left of Glari. You can relax by the pool or laze around in your spotless room complete with fridges, A/C, and shower goodies. (Doubles €41-56; triples €50-67.) Panayiotis Barous, the owner of the souvenir shop with the Kodak sign at the right end of the wharf, lets nice rooms at his **Villa Lyra** ❸. Look for signs by the taxi stop or ask in his store. (☎22820 41 322. Singles €19-25; doubles €22-30.) You can **camp** 300m from Gavrio if you're willing to skip the nightlife of Batsi. (☎22820 71 444; fax 22820 71 044.)

You'll find **Restaurant Sirocco** ❷ at the top of the first set of steps on your left as you leave the beach with the water on your right; head for the string of lights and the strains of jazz. Years ago, the owner Louie was born under the bar (really). Now he serves fabulous international food like homemade garlic bread (€1), shrimp Sirocco grilled in a spicy red sauce (€14), and a curry lover's chicken *biryani* with yogurt (€6.50). (Open daily 6:30pm-midnight.) Savor an Andros omelette made with local sausage and cheese at **Oti Kalo** ❶ (☎22820 41 287), located upstairs at the right end of the wharf, as you watch waves lap the shore. There's a **fruit market** where the beach ends, on the right side of the waterfront and a **mini-market** by the wharf, next to Gallery Coffee.

SIGHTS AND BEACHES. Andros has plenty of first-rate beaches. The clear waters off Batsi are convenient, but they tend to get crowded in summer. For daytime partying, there's heaps of fun to be had around the bar at **Golden Beach** (beer €2.50; cocktails €4), accessible by water taxi (€7.50), taxi (€6), or foot (45min.). Play beach volleyball, recline under a straw umbrella, and swim in calm, shallow water—all to the tune of top 40 pop music. If you're looking for something more low-key, walk back along the road 400m toward Batsi and descend to **Kipri.** Following the road toward Gavrio, you'll find **Agios Petros,** another secluded stretch of sand. Take a taxi to the ruins of the ancient capitol of **Paleopolis,** where you can explore the remains of a theater and a stadium, or to the **Bay of Korthion** and Andros's finest swimming. Remnants of the **Castle of the Old Woman** are north of **Korthion,** 33km from Batsi, and are accessible by car or moped.

NIGHTLIFE. Begin your evening at **Select,** a funky bar all the way up the hill to the right of the wharf (past the pharmacy). Happy Hour, every night from 6-10pm, offers fun, psychedelic cocktails replete with plenty of toys and shiny decorations for only €3. (☎22820 42 039.) About 75m to the right and up some stairs, you can sip a Heineken (€3) or do one of Andros's local shots on the patio at **Capriccio Music Bar** (☎22820 41 770). The party moves to the indoor dance floor around midnight. **On the Rocks** (☎22820 41 219), a patio bar set between the beachfront and the wharf, is a good place to find constellations, cocktails (€6), and rock and dance music. Follow the Greeks to **Nameless** (☎22820 41 698) after midnight to experience how they really party. Toss back tequila shots (€3) with orange slices with the town's plumber, travel agent, and off-duty police officers. To find it, look for the artificial flames in the back right corner of the wharf's plateia. Turn right to dance underwater at **Slammer,** where a black light shines on the blue-green walls.

ANDROS TOWN Ανδρος

Andros Town (commonly known as Hora) is built on an Aegean peninsula capped by a medieval castle. The quiet, cobbled streets lead past hotels, shops, and homes to the water, where blue waves pound the black rocks. Most tourists make Hora a daytrip from Batsi, but those who stay can relax outside with the townsfolk in one of the many candle-lit cafe-bars.

ORIENTATION AND PRACTICAL INFORMATION. The **bus** that runs between **Andros Town** (€2.50), **Gavrio** (€1), and **Batsi** (€1) drops you at a depot near a plateia where **taxis** wait (☎22820 22 171). The **bus station** is coupled with an inviting restaurant. A schedule is posted in the outdoor waiting area. Facing the white buildings with your back to the hills, walk down any lane to find the main street. **Alpha Bank** (☎22820 23 900) is on this street as you walk towards the water. The **National Bank** (☎22820 22 232) is in **Pl. Kairis,** the town's social center. The **police station** is located on the inland end of the main street. (☎22820 22 300. Open 24hr. In **medical emergencies,** dial ☎22820 22 222.) Walking seaward on this street, you'll find the **pharmacy** (☎22820 22 210; open 8am-3pm), **OTE** (open M-F 7:30am-3pm), and the **post office** (☎22820 22 260; open M-F 7:30am-2pm). **Postal code:** 84500.

ACCOMMODATIONS AND FOOD. If you visit during high season be prepared to spend, spend, spend. During the rest of the year, accommodations in Andros Town still aren't cheap. There are, however, over fifty registered domatia, which range in price from €25-35 in low season and €35-50 in high season. Keep an eye out for signs along Nimborio beach. **Hotel Egli ❸** is up the lane from Alpha Bank. Rooms have TVs, sinks, and phones; sofa lounges on each floor. Reception is next door at the hotel bar. (☎22820 22 303 or 22820 22 159; fax 22820 22 159. Private bath and breakfast extra. Singles €25-40; doubles €40-45.) **Karaoulanis Rooms ❸,** on the left corner of Nimborio Beach (as you face inland), are top of the line (kitchens, microwaves, bathrooms, A/C, TVs) and moderately priced. Management can also rent you a moped. (☎22820 24 412; riva@otenet.gr. Rooms for 2-5 people. Simple doubles €30 and up; doubles with fridges, A/C, and kitchenettes €50 and up.) If you wish to experience high society, check into **Paradise Hotel ❺** (☎22820 22 187; fax 22820 22 340), on the main road 500m before Hora. Lie by the pool and order a drink, or just take a *siesta* on your canopy bed in the tastefully decorated rooms. (Doubles €85-113; triples €106-140.) *Mezedes*, milkshakes, and pizza are among the tasty options served by friendly locals in Pl. Kairis; family-owned cafes, restaurants, and markets line the main street and Nimborio beach. Relax under the stars at the **Heaven Rock Cafe** in Pl. Kairis, or head to the Nimborio beachfront for a somewhat livelier atmosphere. **Cabo del Mar** is on the far right side of the beach on a rock outcrop. Admire the view from the jungle-like setting with thatched roof umbrellas.

SIGHTS. The **Archaeological Museum,** a large white building with a brown tile patio across from the Heaven Rock Cafe, has an excellent display on the Geometric village of Zagora and other artifacts marking Andros's ancient history, including a marvelous marble statue of Hermes. The museum patio offers a lovely view of Andros Town. (☎22820 23 664. Open Tu-Su 8am-3pm. €3, students and seniors €2, EU students free.) Turn down the lane to the left upon exiting, and travel down four sets of stairs (following the blue arrows on the left wall) to find the **Museum of Modern Art.** The building displays works by 20th-century Greek sculptor Michael Tombros. The weird noises from downstairs are not a mechanical failure—they're the clatter of the wonderful electromagnetic, kinetic art by Takis. These pieces are a fascinating must-see. Two sets of steps farther down on the right is the large space set aside for the traveling exhibitions that visit the museum every summer. (☎22820 22 444. Open W-M 10am-2pm.; June-Sept. also open M and W-Sa 6-8pm. €6, students €3.) At the end of the main road, just above the water, the **Maritime Museum of Andros** trots out intricate ship models. The guard next door will give you the key. (Open M and W-Sa 10:30am-1pm and 6-8pm, Su 10:30am-1pm. Free.) Continue on the main road for a view of the offshore Venetian turret.

BEACHES AND HIKES. Gazing at peninsular Hora from the sea, **Paraporti** beach is to the left; **Nimborio** beach is to the right. Down the rocky face at the end of the peninsula is an excellent swimming hole beneath old Venetian arch ruins. Be sure to watch out for sea urchins and a surprisingly strong undertow. North of town (and virtually inaccessible) lies **Achla,** considered to be one of Europe's most beautiful beaches. It can be reached only by moped or fishing boat. Just north of Alcha lies **Vori,** a close second, where you can swim among shipwrecks. Those yearning to see the island's more secluded spots—the many rivers, **waterfalls,** and monasteries of the island's interior—should search out **Cosmas,** who leads **hikes** on weekends or by request. (☎697 707 3088, or ask for him around Andros Town.)

TINOS Τηνος

Tinos spreads below from the summit of hulking Mt. Exobourgo. In one direction, Hora's buildings, ferries, and mystic beaches cluster together; away from the port, wildflowers, medieval dovecotes, and villages untouched by time contrast with the green mountains. The island's allure is perhaps most apparent to the thousands of pilgrims who have flocked to the Panagia Evangelistra Church in Tinos Town every year since the 1812 War of Independence. Its miracle-working Icon of the Annunciation—the *Megalohari* (Great Joy) or *Panagia Evangelistra*—was found by a nun in an underground church. Each year on the Feasts of the Annunciation (March 25) and Assumption (August 15), close to 30,000 pilgrims crawl on their knees up a red carpet from the port to the church; they then follow the icon in a 10km procession to the Kechrovouni convent.

TINOS TOWN Τηνος

A stroll past the barrage of waterfront tourist shops reveals Tinos Town's dual role as tourist and religious mecca: peddlers sell both standard tourist wares and the jugs pilgrims use to carry Panagia's sacred waters home. The town is politically significant as well: On August 15, 1940, an Italian submarine torpedoed the Greek cruiser *Elli* as it docked in the harbor for the observance of a religious holiday. Mussolini declared war two months later. The ancient Greeks believed Tinos to be the home of the wind god Aeolus; today, the cool sea breeze whispers his legacy.

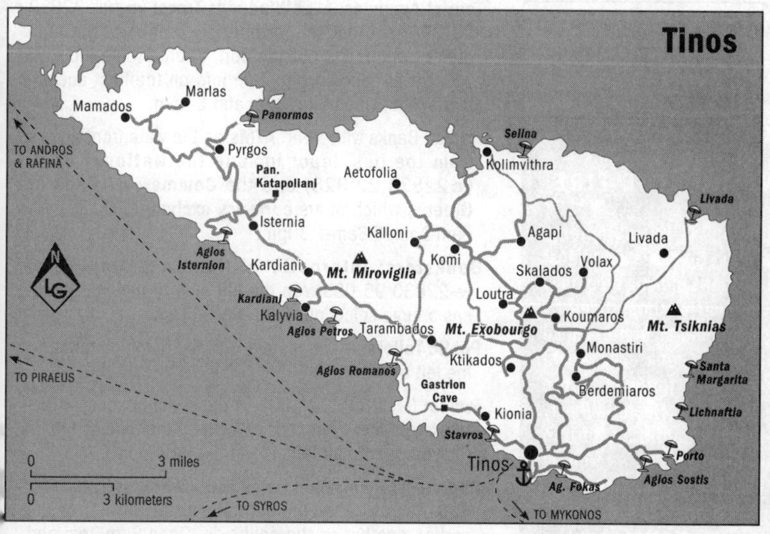

TRANSPORTATION

Ferries: Schedules vary, check with the port police (☎22830 22 348) in the central port, or **Blue Star Travel** (☎22830 24 241). Ferries run to: **Andros** (2hr., 3-4 per day, €5.80); **Naxos** (4hr., daily, €7.70); **Mykonos** (30min., 4-5 per day, €3.50); **Paros** (1hr., daily, €9.30); **Piraeus** (5½hr., 3-4 per day, €18.60); **Rafina** (4hr., 3-4 per day, €12); and **Syros** (20min., 3-4 per day 10:15am-3:15pm, €4). **Flying Dolphins** and **catamarans** run daily to **Piraeus** and **Rafina** and to many Cycladic islands nearly daily. Be aware that there are 3 ferry ports in Tinos (see below)

Buses: Leave across the street from the National Bank 3-5 times daily to: **Pyrgos** (€2.50); **Panormos** (€2.50); **Kalloni** (€2); **Steni** (€1.20); **Skalados** (€1.40); **Kionia** (€0.80); and **Porto** (€0.90). A **schedule** is posted in the KTEL ticket agency (☎22830 22 440) across from the central port, next to Blue Star Travel. Open 8am-5pm.

Taxis: (☎22830 22 470), next to Commercial Bank. Available 6am-1:30am.

Cars and Mopeds: It's worth getting your own wheels from a waterfront rental place. Try **Vidalis,** Zanaki Alavanou 16 (☎22830 23 400; vidalis@thn.forthnet.gr), on the road running inland from the right of the waterfront, across from the Commercial Bank. Mopeds €10-13; cars €27 and up. Ask the English and French-speaking staff for **free maps.** Open 8:30am-9pm.

ORIENTATION AND PRACTICAL INFORMATION

Most ferries land at the central port across from the bus depot; catamarans and hydrofoils dock at the port to the left, as you face inland. The outside port is located near a playground farther to the left. Activity centers on two main streets: sprawling **Megalochares** and parallel pedestrian street **Evangelistras** (known as "Bazaar") to the right. Both streets lead uphill to the Neoclassical facade of the **Panagia Evangelistria Church.** Many domatia are off Evangelistras and **Alavanou,** on the right of the waterfront. Hotels, tavernas, ticket agencies, and banks face the main dock. A labeled map of Tinos is posted to the left of the central port.

PUTTING OUT THE FIRE

"No Smoking" is not commonly seen nor heard in Greece. With almost half the population smoking on a daily basis (45 percent of those over 15 years old), perpetual cigarette smoke is just part of the Greek experience. But changes are on the way. In the summer of 2002, the Health Ministry began a vigorous campaign to ban smoking in public places, as well as to restrict tobacco advertising. Their efforts were successful for the most part: although the advertising ban had yet to be passed at press time, the public smoking ban was instituted in August 2002.

According to the regulations proposed by the Health Ministry, restaurants and tavernas now must designate non-smoking areas for patrons, though bars and nightclubs will be exempt. Smoking will no longer be tolerated in public transportation systems, schools, universities, airports and other transport stations, hospitals, pharmacies, and government buildings. Furthermore, the government has begun an ambitious anti-smoking awareness campaign in schools and a joint effort with the Greek Orthodox church. The goal of all these measures is to discourage tobacco use and significantly cut smoking rates, especially among Greek teenagers.

So how is the country with the most smokers per capita in Europe reacting to the new regulations? Predictably, some are outraged over governmental interference in their lives, but the ban is not as widely condemned as some may have thought.

Tourist Agencies: At **Windmills Travel** (☎/fax 22830 23 398; sharon@thn.forthnet.gr), opposite the children's park by the outside port, Sharon will handle all your travel needs. Up-to-date info on the best accommodations. Open 9am-3pm and 6-9pm.

Banks: Banks with 24hr. **ATMs** on the waterfront across from the bus depot include the **National Bank** (☎22830 22 328) and the **Commercial Bank of Greece,** which offers **currency exchange.** Open M-Th 8am-2pm, F 8am-1:30pm.

Bookstore: International News and Magazines (☎22830 95 033), on the left side of the waterfront, has a large selection. Open 8am-11pm.

Public Toilets: In the plateia with the dolphin statue, to the left of Hotel Lito.

Police: (☎22830 22 100), in the same building as the **tourist police,** 5min. out of town on the road to Kionia (leave from the far left side of the waterfront).

Pharmacy: 7 Alavanou (☎22830 23 888 or 22830 22 438), across from the central port at the left of the harbor, another on the right side. Open 8am-2pm and 6-9pm.

Medical Center: (☎22830 22 210), across from Tinos Camping. Full-time staff.

OTE: (☎22830 22 499), up Megalochares on the right. Open M-Th 7:45am-3pm, F 7:45am-12:30pm.

Post Office: (☎22830 22 247), on the far right end of the waterfront, behind the small plateia. Sells phone cards. Open M-F 7:30am-2pm. **Postal Code:** 84200.

ACCOMMODATIONS AND CAMPING

Tinos has plenty of accommodations, except during the Easter festival (which falls April 27 in 2003) and during July and August weekends when vacationing Athenians descend upon the island. Most waterfront hotels are expensive, so try bargaining with the crowd holding Rooms to Let signs as you disembark.

Dimitris-Maria Thodosis Rooms, Evangelistrias 33 (☎22830 24 809 or 6937 655 337), midway up the road to the left, on the 2nd floor. The traditional home with flower-laced balconies has a central kitchen and common bathrooms. Groups or families of 5-8 should ask about their more upscale apartments on G. Plati. Open Mar.1-Oct. 31. Doubles €30; apartments €60 for two people, €12 for each additional person. ❸

Vincenzo Rooms to Let, 25 Martiou 8-10 (☎/fax 22830 23 612; vincenzo@pigeon.gr); go up Alavanou, turn right onto 25 Martiou, and follow the signs. Simple rooms with common baths. Breakfast €4.40. Laundry facilities. Open all year. Doubles €45. 30% discount on weekdays in low season. Be sure to specify double with shared facilities, unless you wish to stay in the nicer domatia available with kitchenette and private bath (€82). Call ahead for a shuttle from the port. **Vincenzo Travel,** attached to the domatia, offers travel info, maps and **free Internet access;** car and bike rental; mountain bikes (€8); and hiking tours. ❹

Hotel Tinion (☎22830 22 261; fax 22830 24 754; kchatzi@ath.forthnet.gr), follow the main port road to the right (with your back to the water); it's on your left. If you're in the mood for high-class service at a reasonable price, call ahead to reserve one of the spacious rooms. Breakfast €8.80 per person. Double €52-68. ❹

Yannis (☎22830 25 089), at the far right end of the waterfront, to the left of the Oceanis Hotel. Offers bare, clean, hospital-style rooms in a cute blue-shuttered home. Common baths and fridges, kitchen and laundry facilities available. Garden overlooking the port. Singles €15; doubles €25; triples with bath and kitchen €35-50. ❷

Tinos Camping (☎22830 22 344; fax 22830 24 551), a 10min. walk from the waterfront to the right–signs point the way. Well-kept, with kitchen, laundry, showers, restaurant, and bar. July-Aug. €6 per person; May-June and Sept.-Oct. €4 per person. €2-3 per tent. Bungalows for 1-5 people with private baths, TVs and kitchenettes €30-45. ❶

FOOD

Tons of tavernas wait to usher you in for a bite. There's a **supermarket** two doors to the left of the post office. Small **Cafe Italia ❷,** Akti Nazou 10, behind the children's park near Windmill Travel, is a hidden jewel, serving a range of pastas (€6-8) made to the exacting standards of its Italian chef Dora. (☎22830 25 756. Open 9am-12:30am.) **Mesklies ❶,** on the left side of the waterfront above a green awning, is both a fine pastry shop, featuring ornate cakes (€1.50 per slice) and a pizza restaurant. Wrap up your meal with *tyropitakia*, the dense, cheesecake-like local specialty. (☎22830 22 151. Open 7am-3am.) **Pallada ❶,** on the little street to the right of Mesklies, is a traditional taverna where you walk in, admire the selections of the day, and pick the one you like. (☎22830 23 516. Open 11am-4pm and 6pm-midnight.) **Metaxumas ❸,** just before Pallada, prepares pricier Greek specialities.

Restaurant owners are especially enthusiastic about the new restrictions. In some cases, restaurants had previously set up non-smoking sections in order to please their foreign customers.

The tobacco advertising ban will be particularly difficult to pass: the 2004 Olympic organizing committee is desperate for advertising money, and tobacco companies are lining up to provide it. If it is any comfort to the organizers of the Games, the 2002 World Cup in Korea and Japan was successfully executed without tobacco bucks. The Athens Olympics may have to follow suit.

Whether these bans will be effectively enforced remains to be seen. More importantly perhaps is whether the Greek people will obey. If the citizens simply refuse to stop smoking in public places, all the Health Ministry's efforts will be for naught.

SIGHTS

PANAGIA EVANGELISTRA. In 1822, the Tiniote nun Sister Pelagia had a vision of the Virgin Mary telling her about an icon buried in an uncultivated field (once a church destroyed by 10th-century pirates). A year later, amid great rejoicing, the prophesied icon was unearthed, and Panagia Evangelistria was built to house it. The church continues to draw daily visits from believers who consider it evidence of the Virgin's power and presence. The relic is said to have healing powers and is credited with ridding Tinos of cholera, saving a sinking ship, and giving a blind man sight. Gifts of gold, diamonds, and jewels, and countless *tamata*—plaques praising Mary's healing powers—cover the chapel, the "Lourdes of the Aegean."

The **Well of Sanctification** is a natural spring that appeared when the icon was unearthed. Today it flows (from one of many faucets) in the church between two sets of marble entrance stairs to the chapel; visitors scoop up a bottle of it to drink or to carry as a talisman. To the right is the mausoleum of the Greek warship *Elli*, sunk by an Italian torpedo in 1940. *(Open 7am-8pm. Free. Modest dress required.)*

ARCHAEOLOGICAL MUSEUM. Tinos's small Archaeological Museum, halfway up Megalochares on the left and uphill from the OTE, exhibits sculptures from the coastal sanctuary of Poseidon and Amphitrite at Kionia, a 5th-century BC relief from a cemetary at Xombourgo, and wonderful 7th-century BC *pitnoi* (relief pottery) showing Athena bursting from Zeus's head. *(Open Tu-Su 8:30am-3pm. €3, students €2, EU students free.)*

CYCLADES

PYRGOS. Take a bus 29km northwest of Tinos Town (1hr., 3-5 times per day, €2.50) to the artsy, picturesque town of Pyrgos, home to a School for Fine Arts and inhabited by Tinos's renowned marble sculptors. Several museums and exhibitions are dedicated to past residents, such as Giannouli Chalepas, whose *Sleeping Daughter* graces Athens's central graveyard. For classy souvenirs, head to **The Blue Trunk** (☎22830 31 870), where marble and terra-cotta statues are for sale; it's on Sardela, near a cluster of tavernas and cafes frequented by the locals.

NIGHTLIFE

Late night partyers buzz around the square to the left of the hydrofoil port. Most bars are open all day and late into the evening; clubs are open from 9pm-3am. Pop music encourages bar-top dancing under the starlight at **Koursaros Music Bar** (also known as **Corsaire**), near the water, 10m seaward from Mesklies restaurant. (☎22830 23 963. Drinks €3-6.50. Open 8am-3am.) At **Plori Cafe Yacht Club** (☎22830 24 824), a 10min. walk to the left along the beach road toward Stavros Beach, sit back and relax on your choice of indoor or outdoor lounge chairs. Those who are just raring up when the bars shut down head for the bright orange doors of **Paradise,** a 5min. walk past Plori. **The Kaktos Club,** inside a windmill behind the Panagia Evangelistria Church, opens its incredible hilltop view to lovers of American music; it also hosts special live music nights.

BEACHES

The warm, inviting sands of **Kardiani** and **Agios Petros,** situated at the base of the mountains, are among the islands' best. Rocky **Agios Romanos** and two secluded neighboring coves are bordered by shallow waters and lined with pine and palms. **Stavros** beach, a 2km walk left out of Tinos Town, hosts a multitude of tourists on its 70m stretch of sand; **Agios Fokas** (to the right out of town) is equally touristy. For the best of the best, head east to **Agios Sostis** and **Porto.** Take the KTEL **bus** or drive all the way to the end of the road that starts at the water's edge in Porto. From there, either climb left to the nudity-strewn rock beaches or head right toward the sand. The medieval-era **dove-**

cotes, 2000 in total, are built of intricate white lattices and are full of nesting birds; they've become the island's symbol. To the north, lies windswept **Kolimbithra Beach** and the small shore of lovely **Panormos Bay** (2km northeast of Pyrgos). If you rent a moped or car, the landscapes along the road from Tinos Town to Panormos Bay form inspiring views. Take the KTEL **bus** from Tinos Town (3-5 per day, €0.70) or drive left along the waterfront road to explore the ruins of the 4th-century BC **temple** of Poseidon and Amphitrite and enjoy the clear-watered, fine sand beach.

HIKING MOUNT EXOBOURGO

If you have a car or moped, the villages that ring Mt. Exobourgo (Εξοβουργο Ορος; 14km north of Tinos Town) and the site of the Venetian Fortress **Xombourgo** are great places to explore. After withstanding 11 assaults, the 13th-century island capital fell to the Ottomans in 1715, becoming their last territorial gain. For a resplendent panoramic view of all Tinos, drive up to the foot of the fortress itself. If you're feeling energetic, climb the mountain from the east foothill (near the village of Xinara or Loutra) on a trail lined with wildflowers and brilliant orange moss. At the gated entrance to Xombourgo, head left into the plateia to the little gate where the rocky trail to the top starts. The road detours to a church at a fork. Go straight to get to the fort. Strong winds buffet Exobourgo, and the fort is occasionally closed as a result; stay low to avoid getting blown off the mountain.

The delightful hike from Tinos Town to Mt. Exobourgo takes 3-4hr. Alternatively, the trip from Tinos Town to Loutra and back takes 3-4hr. and takes you over much of the central island. Other direct routes up Mt. Exobourgo don't cut through all the villages; wooden signposts mark these trails. Whatever your route, bring water, provisions, comfortable shoes, and a buddy. Stick to the trail and be prepared for extremely high winds at all times. There are signs for hikes around Tinos. Ask a travel agent about various difficulties and lengths.

Ascent to Kitikados. Begin by heading left behind the Panagia Evangelistria Church to unmarked **Agios Nikolaos** (ask if you can't find it). Follow this road straight up and to the left, where the asphalt gives way to a broad cobblestone path that takes you past two white chapels within 45min. Along the ascent, look behind you to see the ferries coming into port. Past the 2nd white chapel is a small stone bridge with an arch; either go over the bridge for a 15min. visit to the unremarkable village of **Kitikados,** or continue on the main trail up to the island's main asphalt road and turn left. Continue across the road until you see a small trail marked with a wooden sign bearing a hiker and the word "Ksinara." Follow this path up to the right of the windmill. Once you pass the windmill, there is another trail marker on your right. Written in Greek, it indicates a direct ascent up to Mt. Exobourgo, looming in the distance, topped by a cross revealing the **fortress** Xombourgo. **Ksinara** is straight ahead, and **Tripotamos** is behind you. You can ascend Exobourgo from here or continue 1½hr. through the quiet town of Ksinara.

Loutra to Xombourgo. Follow the road through town until the church plateia and then head left to the narrow dirt-and-stone trail. This pathway begins your descent to the village of **Loutra** (2hr.); to get there, turn right when you hit the asphalt road. Continue on the asphalt past Loutra to Skalados; turn right to find a nice hillside taverna. From the taverna, head up and right on a street with steps to another asphalt road. Walk to the right about 15min. until you see the blue sign pointing toward **Volax.** It's worth stopping here to meander through the narrow, low-arched streets and to peek into one of the many basket-weaving workshops in town. Retrace your steps to the blue Volax sign and turn left onto the road. At **Koumaros,** look for the **Association Lounge** offering hospitality and dirt-cheap drinks and snacks. Once through Koumaros, the road turns into a stone stair trail that will take you up the northeast side of Mt. Exobourgo. At the foot of **Sacred Heart,** an impressive Catholic monastery, go diagonally through the plateia to the little gate on the left. Ascend 20min. to the Xombourgo fort for a view of the island.

MYKONOS Μυκονος

Mykonos has long been the object of envy and desire. In ancient times, merchants vied with each other to supply pilgrims en route to the holy island of Delos. By the Byzantine and Ottoman eras, with the pilgrim trade gone, pirates patrolled the seas eager for the rich plunder to be found in the nearby waters. In the 70s, Mykonos's gay scene and wild nightlife secured the island's place among the premier resorts of the Mediterranean. Today, the island is the playground of the sleek and chic—sophisticates the Greeks call *kosmopolitikoi*. Though Mykonos's gay scene has lost its former preeminence, it's anything but dead, and Mykonosian nightlife still commands the attention of hard-core hedonists the world over.

MYKONOS TOWN Μυκονος

Mykonos Town owes its labyrinthine streets (closed to motor traffic in the afternoon and evening) to Mediterranean pirates. The maze-city was planned expressly to disconcert and disorient marauders; the plan has a similar effect on tourists. Despite the influx of visitors, the town has resisted large hotel complexes. The drag queens and high fashion models seem to complement, not corrupt, the fishing boats in the harbor, the basket-laden donkeys, and roaming pelicans.

TRANSPORTATION

Flights: Olympic Airways (☎22890 22 490 or 22890 22 495; airport ☎22890 22 327). Flights to: **Athens** (40min., 6-7 per day, €76); **Rhodes** (1hr., 2 per week, €90); **Santorini** (30min., 4 per week, €65); **Thessaloniki** (3 per week, €99). A taxi from Mykonos Town is the only way to the airport (€6).

Ferries: To: **Andros** (3hr., 1 per day, €8.10); **Naxos** (3hr., 1-2 per day, €6.30); **Piraeus** (6hr., 2-3 per day, €17); **Rafina** (5hr., 1-2 per day, €13.60); **Samos** (2 per week, €16.70); **Santorini** (6hr., 3 per week, €11); **Syros** (2½hr., 1-3 per day, €5); **Tinos** (45min., 3 per day, €3.50).

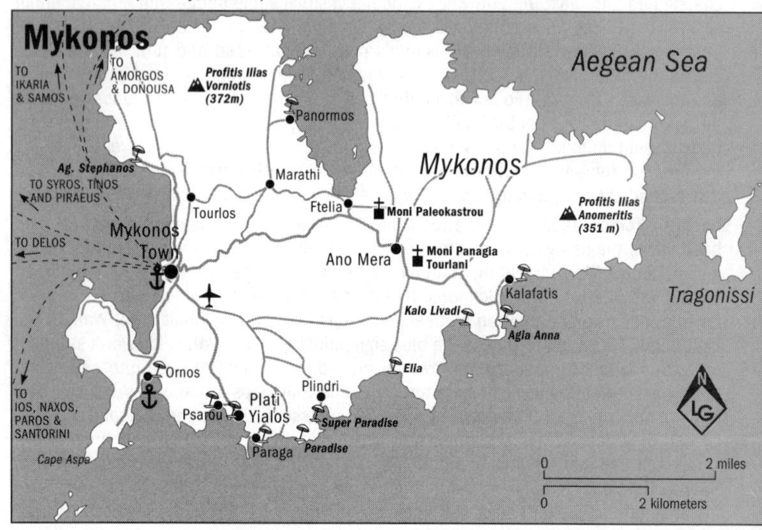

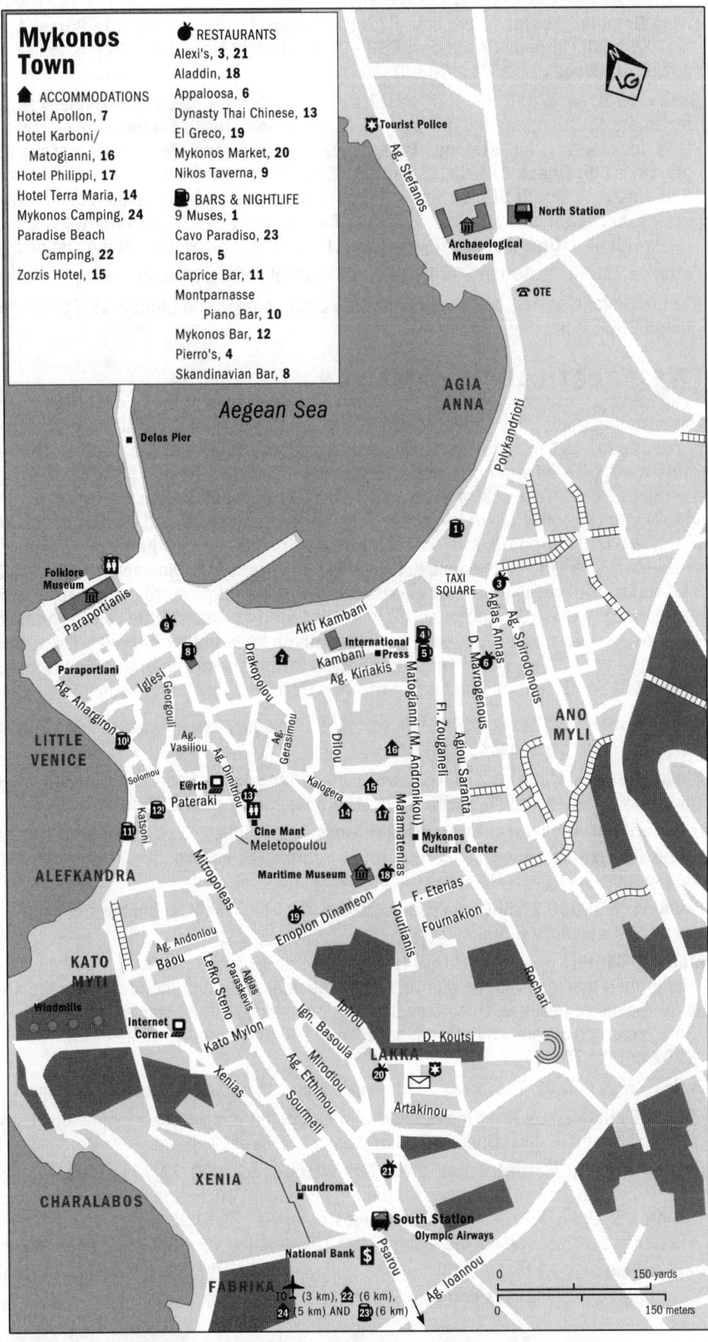
Mykonos Town
ACCOMMODATIONS
Hotel Apollon, 7
Hotel Karboni/ Matogianni, 16
Hotel Philippi, 17
Hotel Terra Maria, 14
Mykonos Camping, 24
Paradise Beach Camping, 22
Zorzis Hotel, 15
RESTAURANTS
Alexi's, 3, 21
Aladdin, 18
Appaloosa, 6
Dynasty Thai Chinese, 13
El Greco, 19
Mykonos Market, 20
Nikos Taverna, 9
BARS & NIGHTLIFE
9 Muses, 1
Cavo Paradiso, 23
Icaros, 5
Caprice Bar, 11
Montparnasse Piano Bar, 10
Mykonos Bar, 12
Pierro's, 4
Skandinavian Bar, 8
Tourist Police
Ag. Stefanos
North Station
Archaeological Museum
OTE
Aegean Sea
AGIA ANNA
Delos Pier
Polykandrioti
Folklore Museum
Paraportianis
TAXI SQUARE
Agias Annas
Ag. Spirodonous
Akti Kambani
International Press
Kambani
Ag. Kiriakis
Drakopolou
Matogianni (M. Andronikou)
D. Mavrogenous
Paraportiani
Iglesi
Georgouli
Ag. Anargiron
Fl. Zouganeli
Agiou Saranta
ANO MYLI
LITTLE VENICE
Ag. Vasiliou
Ag. Gerasimou
Dilou
Solomou
Ag. Dimitriou
E@rth
Pateraki
Kalogera
Malamatenias
Katsoni
Cine Mant
Meletopoulou
Mykonos Cultural Center
ALEFKANDRA
Maritime Museum
Mitropoleas
F. Eterias
Enoplon Dinameon
Tourlianis
Fournakion
Ag. Andoniou
Baou
KATO MYLI
Lefko Steno
Agias Paraskevis
Rochari
Windmills
Internet Corner
Ipirou
Ign. Basoula
Kato Mylon
D. Koutsi
LAKKA
Mirodiou
Ag. Efthimiou
Xenias
Sourmeli
Artakinou
XENIA
Laundromat
CHARALABOS
South Station
Olympic Airways
National Bank
Psarou
Ag. Ioannou
FABRIKA
TO (3 km), 22 (6 km), 24 (5 km) AND 23 (6 km)
0
150 yards
0
150 meters

Flying Dolphins: To: **Ios** (1 per day, €22.40); **Naxos** (1 per day, €12.60); **Paros** (1 per day, €11.20); **Piraeus** (1 per day, €33.40); **Santorini** (1 per day, €22); **Syros** (2 per day, €10); **Tinos** (2 per day, €6.90).

Buses: KTEL (☎22890 23 360) has 2 stations in town. Unless noted otherwise, all buses are €0.80 during the day and €1 after midnight. **North Station,** uphill from the ferry dock, serves: **Ag. Stefanos Beach** (every 30min.); **Ano Mera** and **Kalafatis** (10 per day); **Elia Beach** (30min., 8 per day, €1); **Psarou Beach** (15min., every 30min. 8:15am-2am). **South Station,** uphill from the windmills at the opposite edge of town, serves: **Ag. Ioannis** (every hr.); **Paradise Beach** (every 30min.); **Plati Yialos Beach** (every 30min.); **Ornos Beach** (every 30min.). Schedules are posted at the stations.

Taxis: (☎22890 22 400 or 22890 23 700). Available at "Taxi Square," along the water.

Rentals: Agencies ring both bus stops. Be sure to bargain. **Mopeds** €15-25 per day. **Jeeps** €35-50 per day.

PRACTICAL INFORMATION

CYCLADES

If you're facing inland, incoming boats dock at a pier on the far left of the waterfront. One road leads to the right along the water, past the beach to the center of town. Another road, parallel and north of the first, heads uphill to the **North Station** bus depot, and wraps around the back of Mykonos Town to the **South Station.** A turnoff on the road to South Station leads to the **airport.** The action centers around the **waterfront,** but much of the real shopping, fine dining, and partying goes on in the narrow, winding **back streets** (especially **Matogianni, Kalogera, Mitropoleas,** and **E. Dinameon**). On the right side of the waterfront is a pier for excursion boats headed primarily to nearby Delos. Past the pier is a series of churches, a lovely part of town called **Little Venice** (home to the islands' classiest bars and cafes), and a small hill lined with windmills. The town's necessities—post office, police, markets, and so forth—mostly lie in the **inland** vicinity of Lakka and South Station and can be reached by following Mitropoleas.

Tourist Police: (☎22890 22 482), in an office at the ferry landing. Very helpful English-speaking staff. Open daily 8am-11pm.

Banks: National Bank (☎22890 22 932), around the corner from South Station, offers **currency exchange** and an **ATM.** Open M-Th 8am-2pm, F 8am-1:30pm.

International Bookstore: International Press (☎22890 23 316), in a small plateia opposite Pierro's; follow signs from the waterfront. Eclectic books, magazines, and newspapers in English. Open daily noon-midnight.

Laundry: (☎22890 27 600), on Psarou, toward the windmills from the bus terminal. Full load €9. Open daily 8:30am-10pm.

Medical Center: (☎22890 23 994, 995, 996, or 997; fax 22890 27 407), on the higher road leading from the port to South Station, just beyond the turn-off for the hospital. Extensive facilities. Open May-Oct. 8:30am-midnight; Nov.-Mar. 8:30am-9pm. For 24hr. **emergency** care, call an ambulance at ☎166 or the medical center at ☎694 433 8292 or 697 765 4737.

Police: (☎22890 22 716 or 22 215), in Lakka past the South Station. Open 24hr.

OTE: (☎22890 22 699), at the left end of waterfront in a big white building, uphill and to the right of the dock. Open M-Th 8am-1pm and F 8am-12:30pm.

Internet Access: E@rth Internet Club, Zani Pitaraki (☎22890 22 791), gets you connected by Little Venice at a steep €9 per hr., although if you pre-pay for an hr. the price is only €5. Open daily 9am-3am. **Internet Corner** (☎22890 22 902), near the windmills, offers a more reasonable price. (Open 10am-11pm. €1 per 10min. under an hr.)

Post Office: (☎22890 22 238), around the corner from the police in Lakka, behind South Station. **Exchanges currency.** Open M-F 7:30am-4pm. **Postal code:** 84600.

ACCOMMODATIONS AND CAMPING

While Mykonos is one of the most expensive of the Greek islands, affordable accommodations aren't impossible to find, especially if you're willing to stay outside town. Most budget travelers find their niche in Mykonos's festive campsites, which offer a myriad of sleeping options beyond the standard plot of grass. The information offices on the dock are numbered according to accommodation type: 1 for **hotels** (☎22890 24 540; open 9am-midnight), 2 for **rooms to let** (☎22890 24 860; open 9am-11pm), and 3 for **camping** (☎22890 23 567; open 9am-midnight).

Hotel Philippi, Kalogera 25 (☎22890 22 294; fax 22890 24 680; chriko@otenet.gr), next to Zorzis Hotel. Cheerful rooms around a bountiful garden provide an escape from the busy streets. Half the rooms have private baths. Internet €5.80 per hr. Open Apr.-Oct. Singles €25-35; doubles €35-67; triples €42-67. ❷

Hotel Apollon (☎22890 22 223), on the waterfront. The oldest hotel in town is an antique-laden house overlooking the harbor. The owner is helpful and cheerful. Singles and doubles €42-50, with bath €50-65; triples with bath €56-65. ❹

Hotel Terra Maria, Kalogera 33 (☎22890 24 212, off season 22890 22 957; tertaxma@otenet.gr). Don't confuse it with Chez Maria or the nearby Marios Hotel. A/C, private baths, fridges, TVs, minibars, and balconies. Central location, but on a quiet side street next to the public gardens. Breakfast €6. Doubles €46-82; triples €55-99. ❺

Hotel Karboni/Matogianni (☎22890 22 217; fax 22890 23 264), on Matogianni, inland from the waterfront. This complex actually consists of two hotels owned by the same family. They have different amenities, so inquire about the kind of room you would like. All rooms have A/C and TVs. Doubles €40-100; triples €63-100. ❹

Paradise Beach Camping (☎22890 22 852 or 22890 22 129; for reservations paradise@paradise.myk.forthnet.gr), on the beach 6km from the port; the round-trip bus costs €0.80. The liveliest place in town, this enormous complex includes every imaginable type of accommodation, eatery, and entertainment. Chaos reigns at times, especially in the peak season, but you can't beat the location, directly on lovely Paradise Beach. Luggage storage €1. Internet access €3 per 15min. €5-7 per person; €2.50-3 per small tent; €2.50-3.50 per large tent; 2-person beach cabin €20-45; 4-person beach cabin €40-90. ❶

THE BIG SPLURGE

ZORZIS HOTEL

Mykonos is expensive, but the nightlife, the inviting beaches, and the ancient site of Delos make the trip well worth the cost. **Zorzis Hotel,** in the heart of Mykonos Town, is expensive even by Mykonosian standards, but if you've got the euros to shell out you won't regret a stay in this wonderfully maintained establishment. The proprietor is a native Australian and a former decorator, who has poured his heart and his skills into his hotel. Given the understated luxury of Zorzis, his efforts have paid off. The rooms are smartly decorated in a traditional style, and the furnishings often have a whole history themselves. According to the owner, some of the more impressive pieces can be traced to the Tsar's palaces in Russia and the Palace in London. Small details, such as down pillows and canopy beds contribute to this royal atmosphere.

The owners are happy to help with travel planning around Mykonos and beyond and will lend an ear for a chat over breakfast. Though located in a safe area on a safe island, the hotel looks out for its guests with security cameras and other protective measures. And the rooms are scrubbed to a shine everyday. From comfort to hospitality, Zorzis sets the standard for upscale accommodations.

N. Kalogera 30. ☎22890 22 167 or 22890 24 168; fax 22890 24 169; www.zorzis.com. Breakfast €5. From July 15-Sept. 15, singles €80; doubles €100; two-bedroom suites €150. Prices considerably lower during the rest of the year.

Mykonos Camping (☎22890 25 915 or 22890 25 916; fax 22890 24 578; mycamp@hotmail.com), on Paraga Beach. On the bus route to Paradise Beach. Free pick-up and drop-off at the port and airport. Smaller and quieter than Paradise Beach but still very animated. €4.70-7 per person; €2.60-3.50 per tent; €5.30-7.50 tent rental; 2-person bungalow €20-30. ❶

FOOD

Most choose to eat out on Mykonos, but budget travelers would do well to put together a picnic from the fruit stands that surround South Station. **Mykonos Market,** a short distance from the post office, offers bread, snacks, and more. (☎22890 24 897. Open 8am-12:30am.) Cheap creperies and souvlaki joints crowd nearly all of Mykonos's streets. Otherwise, it's possible to lounge the day away (off the beach) at the unremarkable cafes that line the waterfront and serve Greek staples.

Appaloosa (☎22890 27 086), one block from Taxi Square on Mavrogeneous. This classy restaurant has an eclectic mix of food, but the Mexican selections are the best. The owners know their Mexican; they stock both red and green Tabasco sauce. Delicious burritos €9.50; Mexican chicken salad €10.80. Open daily year-round 8pm-1:30am. ❸

El Greco (☎22890 22 024), on E. Dinameon. Take your pick from over 70 wines before digging into a meal of Greek favorites and Mediterranean hybrids. Very professional service. Octopus salad €7; grilled salmon €9. Open 1pm-1am. ❷

Dynasty Thai Chinese Restaurant (☎22890 24 194), in Pl. Lymni, by the cinema on Meletopoulou. If you are looking for good Asian food, Greece isn't the place for you. But Dynasty does a fairly good job of satisfying the void of Asian cuisine. Curries €9.40. The owner recommends the Peking duck (€16.50). Open daily 6:30pm-12:45am. ❸

Alexi's, at the back of Taxi Square and near South Station (2 locations). The oldest greasy spoon in Mykonos and one of the best places for a cheap meal. Alexi's has all the favorites, including gyros (€1.50) and a hearty souvlaki plate (€5.50). Breakfast €5.50. Open daily 10am-7am. ❶

Nikos Taverna (☎22890 24 320), in a cluster of restaurants inland from the excursion boat docks. This popular taverna has a mess hall feel, but the food is cheap (relatively) and pretty good. Lasagna with salmon €8; lamb *kleftiko* €8. Open daily noon-2am. ❷

Aladdin (☎22890 24 783), on E. Dinameon near Malamatenias. Offers many unusual varieties of baklava (€1.50), including tiramisu and apple. Also serves other interesting pastry creations and many coffees. Open daily 10am-1pm. ❶

SIGHTS

The prime daytime activities on Mykonos are tanning and shopping, but you don't need to blow all your money. Losing yourself in the colorful alleyways of Mykonos Town at dawn or dusk is one of the easiest, cheapest, and most exhilarating experiences the island has to offer. A stroll to the **Kastro** area—behind the Delos ferry pier, at the far left of the port if you're facing the sea—will take you to the **Paraportiani.** You'll recognize this cluster of white churches from postcards. From there, walk through **Little Venice,** where the turquoise waters of the eager Aegean lap at the legs of cafe tables and chairs. The line of stalwart **windmills** farther south along the waterfront also offers prime sunset seating.

Although cultural enrichment may not be Mykonos's primary draw, several museums on the island are worth a look. The **Archaeological Museum,** on the paved road between the ferry dock and the center of town seems to specialize in jars, including an impressive 7th-century BC *pithos* with relief scenes from the Trojan War. (☎22890 22 325. Open Tu-Su 8am-3pm. €2, students and seniors €1, EU students free.) The **Aegean Maritime Museum,** around the corner from the inland end of Matogianni, thrills with a beautifully manicured garden that houses immense nautical instruments, including ancient grave *steles* and a lighthouse. (☎22890 22 700. Open Apr.-Oct. 10:30am-1pm and 6:30-9pm. €2, students €1.) **Lena's House,** part of the town's **Folklore Museum,** is a 18th-century home with 19th-century furniture. It remains exactly as its owner left it, except for the glass cases over her jewelry and the captions on her belongings. (☎22890 22 591. Both open daily Apr.-Oct. M-Sa 5:30-8:30pm and Su 6:30-8:30pm. Free.) The **Cultural Center of Mykonos** hosts a rotating exhibition of art shows, often from up-and-coming Greek artists. (Hours vary by show, but are generally 11am-2pm and 7pm-2am.)

NIGHTLIFE

There's a good time to be had on Mykonos—perhaps the best in Greece. Come nightfall, the young and beautiful mix with mere mortals to bask in the warm embrace of chic cafes, buzzing nightclubs, and a handful of pubs. After 11pm, the bars get packed. The most popular watering holes are around Little Venice and Taxi Square. If you tire of dancing, head to **Cine Mant,** in Pl. Lymni off Meletopoulou, which shows English-language films. (☎22890 27 109. 2 shows per day. €6.)

Skandinavian Bar, near Niko's Taverna and the waterfront. There's something for everyone in this 2-building party complex which includes a disco, two bars, and a cafe-type seating area. Large enough to accommodate the massive crowds that pass through but intimate enough to contain the energy of the night. Beer and shots €3-3.50, cocktails €6 and up. Open Su-F 8:30pm-3am, Sa until 4am.

Pierro's, on Matogianni. Pierro's is the oldest gay bar in Mykonos and still *the* place to go for a good time. Spontaneous theme nights (e.g. glitter night, drag shows) keep the crowd on their toes. The upstairs portion of the bar is packed with guys of all ages and has a more techno/trance slant. Beer €5, cocktails €6-7.

Icaros, next door and upstairs from Pierro's. Shares customers, atmosphere, and a nightly drag show with its downstairs neighbor. Beer €5. Open daily 11:30pm-4am.

Cavo Paradiso, located on Paradise Beach. Considered one of the top dance clubs in the world, Paradiso hosts internationally renowned DJs and clubbers. The cover is usually very steep (around €20), but free bus service is provided to and from Mykonos Town every hr. Open F-Su 3am-11am.

9 Muses, right on the waterfront near Taxi Square. Fashion is a priority at this chic club, and only the hottest threads will do. Some dancing, but most of the crowd is focused on checking each other out. Open daily 10pm-3am.

Caprice Bar, on the water in Little Venice. Popular but unpackaged post-beach hangout with breathtaking sunsets, funky music, and lively company. Cocktails €7. Open Su-Th 6:30pm-3:30am, F-Sa until 4:30am.

Montparnasse Piano Bar, Ag. Anargyron 24. Savor the good life with a cocktail by the bay, while being serenaded by cabaret tunes from a live piano. Groovy and mostly gay. Beer €5; cocktails €7. Open daily 7pm-3am.

Mykonos Bar, in Little Venice, next to inland side of the Caprice Bar. Mykonos, on the route between Caprice and Skandanavian, attracts some of both the dancing and drinking crowd. Cover €3 and up. Beer €3.50, cocktails €5 and up. Open daily 10pm-4am.

BEACHES

Mykonos has a beach to please everyone. Although all the beaches on Mykonos are **nude,** the degree of nudity depends on where you go. To avoid the unspectacular Mykonos Town beach, get on a bus and head out of the city (see **Transportation** above). Small **Ag. Stefanos Beach** is an easy bus ride from the North Station, but it's close to the busy roadway leading to the airport, and its sands are often littered. The clear, shallow water of little **Ornos Beach** is a short hop away from South Station, as is crowded **Psarou Beach.** Buses run from South Station to **Plati Yialos,** where you can catch a **caïque** (around €1.50) to Paradise Beach, Super Paradise Beach, and Elia. You can take the bus directly to **Elia** from North Station or to **Paradise** from South Station. While **Super Paradise Beach** has the craziest reputation among Mykonos's beaches, contemplative naked people while away the daylight hours at the far reaches of Elia's quiet shores, where broad sand beaches are divided by sections of craggy rock. Majestic and remote **Kalo Livadi Beach** is about a 5km walk back along the road to Mykonos from Elia. The bus to Elia stops at the turn-off, so ask the driver to let you off at Kalo Livadi to shorten your trek.

DELOS Δηλος

Apollo wher'er thou strayest, far or near,
Delos is still of all thy haunts most dear

—Homeric Hymn to Apollo

An excursion to Delos—the sacred navel around which the Cyclades whirl—is a must-see, even for those who take little interest in mythology or history. Delos claims the most important Temple of Apollo, built to commemorate the birthplace of the god and his twin sister, Artemis. A site of religious pilgrimage in the ancient world, today Delos is something of a giant, island-wide museum.

A DRIFTING ISLAND GROWS ROOTS. After getting **Leto** pregnant with Artemis and Apollo, womanizing **Zeus** kicked her out, afraid of his wife Hera's wrath. Desperately searching for a place to give birth, Leto wandered the Aegean, only to be rebuffed by island after island, who also feared Hera's ire. At last she came upon a rocky, floating island shrouded in mist. Frightened, the little island bobbed about furtively until Leto swore by the river Styx that it would come to no harm and that her unborn child would live there forever, casting light upon its birthplace. The reassured island stopped drifting, but Leto's trials were far from over: Hera conned the goddess of childbirth, Eilythia, into prolonging Leto's labor for nine days, at which point the other gods bribed Eilythia into having mercy. Leto collapsed and gave birth beside the island's Sacred Lake. Upon the children's birth, the mist disappeared, and the island was bathed in radiance; because it could now be clearly seen, its name was changed from Adelos ("invisible") to Delos ("visible"). Grateful Leto made the island the seat of her son's worship. With Apollo's sanctuary attracting pilgrims and money, Delos was transformed into a major religious and commercial center.

HISTORY OF DELOS. With a central position among the Aegean islands, Delos's role as a maritime and political powerhouse is hardly surprising. The 5km-long island is paired with larger **Rheneia,** whose inhabitants are also called Delians. Although first settled in the 3rd millennium BC, it was during the Mycenaean Period (1580-1200 BC) that Delos began to flourish. Mycenaean rule ended around 1100 BC, and a century later the Ionians dedicated the island to worshipping Leto.

By the 7th century BC, Delos had become the political and mercantile center of the Aegean League of Islands, starting off three centuries of struggle for power between the Delians and the Athenians. The Delians put up a good fight, but slowly bled power to the mainlanders. During these years, the Athenians ordered at least two "purifications" of the island, in honor of Apollo. The second, in 426 BC, decreed that no one should give birth or die on its sacred grounds, meaning that all graves had to be exhumed, and the bodies within moved to a "purification pit" on nearby Rheneia. After the **Persian Wars,** Delos served as the treasury and the seat of the **Delian League,** supposedly an alliance of independent polises but in fact the *de facto* Athenian empire.

After Sparta defeated Athens in the **Peloponnesian War** (see p. 10), Delos enjoyed independence and wealth. Sweet prosperity soured during the Roman occupation in the 2nd century BC, when prestigious Delos was reduced to the slave-trading center of Greece. By the end of the second century AD, after successive sackings, the island was left virtually deserted. Today, its only residents are legions of leaping lizards and members of the French School of Archaeology, who have been excavating here since 1873.

DELOS ARCHAEOLOGICAL SITE

Most accessible as a daytrip from Mykonos Town. ***Excursion boats*** *leave from the dock near Mykonos Town (35min.; 3 boats per day in each direction 9:30-11:30am, returns 12:20-3pm; round-trip €6). Most trips only let you explore the site for 3hr., but each boat line has several return trips in the afternoon, so you have some flexibility. Expensive* ***guided tours*** *are offered by each excursion boat company (€26, including admission to the ruins). A more affordable option is to buy the* ***guidebook*** *by Photini Zaphiropoulou (in town or at the entrance to the site), which includes info, color pictures, and a map of the site (€5-15). Freelance guides offer their services on the island (€10 per person). Tinos, Naxos, Paros, and other islands offer joint trips to Mykonos and Delos but allow less time to explore. Open Tu-Su 8:30am-3pm. €5, students and EU seniors €2, EU students free.*

Occupying almost an entire square mile of the small island, the archaeological site includes, in the center of the ancient city, the Temple of Apollo and the agora, the outlying parts of the city, Mt. Kythnos, and the theater quarter. While it takes several days to explore the ruins completely, you can see the highlights in approximately three hours. Most of your fellow ferry passengers will follow a similar route when they disembark; reverse the route if you want some privacy. As always, bring a hat, good shoes, sunblock, and a water bottle. There is an exorbitantly priced cafeteria beside the museum, so it's wiser to bring snacks.

SACRED ROAD. The path beyond the admission booth points you toward the **Agora of the Competaliasts,** where Roman guilds built their shop-shrines. Continue on in the same direction and turn left onto the wide Sacred Road. Decorating your walk are two parallel **stoas,** the more impressive of which (on the left) was built by Phillip of Macedon in 210 BC and dedicated to Apollo. Bear right and follow this road around to the **Sanctuary of Apollo,** a collection of temples built in the god's honor that date from Mycenaean times to the 4th century BC. The sanctuary begins when you reach the **Propylees.** The biggest and most important of the temples is on the right. The famous **Great Temple of Apollo,** or **Temple of the Delians,** was completed at the end of the 4th century BC. Its immense, partially hollow hexagonal pedestal once supported an 8m-high marble statue of the god of light.

Following the direction of the Sacred Road north, 50m past its end, leads to the **Terrace of the Lions.** In the 7th century BC, at least nine marble lions looked onto the sacred lake from the terrace. Only four remain standing on Delos, and the body of a fifth, pirated by the Venetians, guards the entrance to the arsenal in Venice.

SACRED LAKE AND ENVIRONS. Proceed up the small crest left of the terrace to the **House of the Hill.** Because the building was planted deep into the earth, this archetypal Roman house is still firmly intact. Downhill lies the **House of the Lake,** with a well-preserved mosaic decorating its atrium, and the desecrated **Sacred Lake,** drained in 1925 to protect against malaria. The round form of the former lake today appears as a leafy oasis with a lone palm tree at its center (honoring Apollo's birth). On the lake's south side is the expansive Roman **agora.**

AROUND MOUNT KYTHNOS. From the museum you can hike up the path to the summit of **Mt. Kythnos** (112m). Its peak offers such a sprawling view of the island that Zeus chose it to spy on the birth of Apollo and Artemis. Although the climb is not too difficult, wear sturdy, comfortable shoes—the trail can be steep and some of the rocks dislodge easily. Ascending the mountain coming from the direction of Temple of Apollo, you will pass temples dedicated to Egyptian gods. Arguably the most spectacular antiquity on the island, the elegant bust in the **Temple of Isis** depicts the sun. The immense building blocks of the nearby **Grotto of Herakles** scream Mycenaean, but some experts suggest that it's a Hellenic knock-off of Mycenaean architecture.

Coming down the mountain, bear left away from the museum to reach the **House of the Dolphins** and **House of the Masks,** which contain intricate, well-preserved, eye-popping mosaics of dolphins and *Dionysus Riding a Panther.* Continue on to the **ancient theater,** which has a sophisticated cistern (as cisterns go) called **Dexamene,** with nine arched compartments. As you weave down the rough path back towards the entrance, explore the maze of rooms as you pass the theater: farther along, the **House of the Trident,** graced by a mosaic of a dolphin twisted around a trident; the **House of Dionysus,** containing another mosaic of Dionysus and a panther; and the **House of Cleopatra.** The famous statue of Cleopatra and Dioscourides is sheltered in the museum.

SYROS Συρος

Syros is the capital of the Cycladic islands and, despite its small size, is also home to almost half of the Cyclades's permanent residents. Syros first rose to commercial power as a Phoenician seaport; the 13th-century Venetians turned it into the trading capital of the Cyclades until team-powered ships and the rise of Piraeus as the national port finally ended Syros's glory days. In the last 20 years, the island has regained its footing, largely due to the shipbuilding that now keeps it afloat. Internationals ship in and out of town, and windsurfing has become a favorite pastime. Escape the madness of the port town Ermoupolis by following legions of Greek families to a seaside village or beach or by heading to the medieval settlement of Ano Syros, high above Ermoupolis on one of Syros's two peaks. Bold hikers will find uncharted terrain; everyone else can rely on the public bus system.

ERMOUPOLIS Ερμουπολις

Bustling Ermoupolis, the Cyclades's largest city and capital, is the city of the winged messenger Hermes, god of commerce and travel. Elegant Neoclassical buildings of Greek, Italian, and Bavarian design in Pl. Miaouli and Dellagrazia give the island an international appearance and offer a peek at the city's opulent past. They also explain its former nicknames—the "Manchester of Greece" and "Little Milan." Though the city's roles in government and shipping make tourism a secondary concern, its vitality makes Syros an exciting, lively island. Athenian vacationers jam Ermoupolis's hotels from mid-July to September; you'll probably want to head for the island's countryside.

TRANSPORTATION

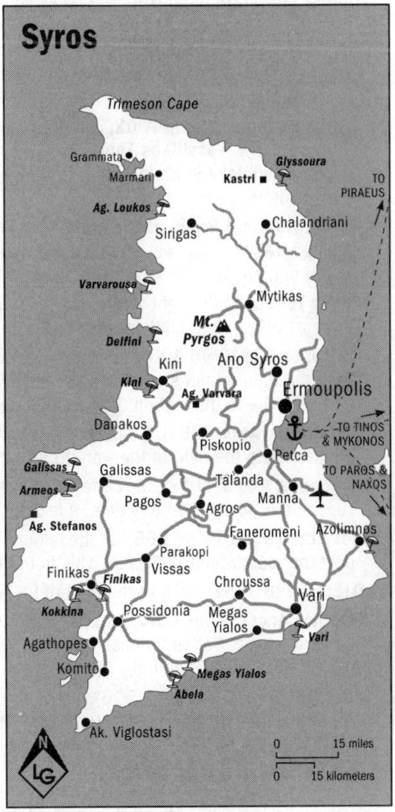

Flights: There are 1-2 flights per day to Athens, except Sa (€56.25). You must take a bus or a taxi to the airport, southeast of Ermoupolis (☎22810 81 900).

Ferries: To: **Piraeus** (4½hr., 5-7 per day, €18); **Tinos** (45min., 4-6 per day, €4); **Mykonos** (2hr., 4-6 per day, €6); **Paros** (1hr., 2 per week, €7); **Naxos** (2½hr., 2 per week, €9); **Ios** (4hr., 4per week, €11); **Santorini** (5hr., 4per week, €17); **Crete** (10hr., 1 per week, €25); and the more westerly Cyclades (2 times per week). Most boats depart from the right side of the harbor. **Flying Dolphins** depart daily for **Piraeus** and **Rafina** (2hr., €22) and several times per week to **Mykonos, Naxos, Paros,** and **Tinos.** Schedules vary; check with a travel agency.

Buses: (☎22810 22 575). Green **KTEL** buses leave from the depot near the ferry dock. One beach loop runs 13-18 times per day, passing through **Azolimnos** (45min., €1); **Galissas** (15min., €1); **Finikas, Komito,** and **Megas Yialos** (€1.30 each). Another leaves 5 times per day for the interior towns of **Episkopio** (€0.80); **Parakopi** (€1.30); **Posidonia** (€1.30); **Manna** (€1.30). 3 to 5 shuttle buses per day go to: **Ano Syros** (€0.80); **Dili** (€0.80); **Vrontado** (€0.80).

Taxis: (☎22810 86 222). Meet them by the statue of Hermes to the right of the port.

Rental Cars and Bikes: On the waterfront. Try **Enjoy Your Holidays Rent a Car,** Akti Paeidou 6 (☎22810 87 070 or 22810 81 336; fax 22810 82 739), on the waterfront by the central port. Cars, motorcycles, and scooters. Prices depend on season, model, and duration of rental; expect a range of €10-15 (scooters) to €35 and up (cars). You can also buy ferry tickets here. Open daily 8am-9pm.

ORIENTATION AND PRACTICAL INFORMATION

Facing inland when you get off the ferry, head right and walk down the waterfront for 3min. to **El. Venizelou,** the town's main street, beginning at the winged **statue of Hermes.** Venizelou runs inland to **Pl. Miaouli,** a large marble plaza marked by the Neoclassical town hall. Social life centers on this plaza, and along the right side of the harborfront. Hotels and domatia can be found all along the waterfront and the surrounding streets. A labeled map of Ermoupolis and a listing of domatia are posted on two large signs at the bus depot.

Tourist Information: Look for the "i" as you head right off the ferry—the booth is behind a statue wearing the helmet of Hermes. Free, helpful info on accommodations, good maps (€1), and books on the island. Open daily 10am-1:30pm and 3-6pm, high season only. The **Greek Tourist Board's** Office of the Cyclades, Dodecanisou 10, offers free information and maps.

Tourist Agencies: Team Work, 30 Eth. Antistasis (☎22810 83 400), at the left end of the waterfront. **Vassilikos Tours** (☎22810 84 444), on the port across from the bus depot. Open daily 8:30am-11pm. Both agencies provide schedules and prices and sell ferry, hydrofoil, and flight tickets.

Banks: National Bank, at the end of the first main street on the right off El. Venizelou (going away from the waterfront), **exchanges currency. Piraeus Bank** at the left of the waterfront, has a 24hr. **ATM.** Both open M-Th 8am-2pm, F 8am-1:30pm.

Public Toilet: On the right side of the first alley off the street with the National Bank and the post office on it. Look for the "WC" sign.

Police: (☎22810 96 100), behind the theater off the upper right corner of Pl. Miaouli. Take the right inland street from the far right corner of Pl. Miaouli, go right at the fork and continue to the station. Very helpful. **Emergency:** ☎100; **fire** ☎199.

Port Authority: (☎22810 88 888 or 22810 82 690). The office is at the end of the dock all the way to the right of the waterfront, with a Greek flag in front.

Pharmacy: A total of 18 are scattered throughout the city. Most open M-F 8am-2pm and Tu, Th-Su 5:30-9pm. At any time, a few are open.

Hospital: (☎22810 86 666), at the left end of the waterfront (facing inland) at Pl. Iroön past the roundabout, a 20min. walk from Pl. Miaouli.

OTE: (☎22810 82 799), at the right of Pl. Miaouli. Open M-Sa 7am-2:40pm.

Internet Access: Net Cafe, (☎22810 85 330), in Pl. Miaouli, to the left of the town hall's staircase. Coffee, drinks, ice cream, and erotic cartoon monitor wallpaper. €6 per hr.; €2 minimum. Open daily 9:30am-1am.

Post Office: (☎22810 82 596), down the street from the National Bank. Offers **currency exchange.** Open M-F 7:30am-2pm. **Postal Code:** 84100.

CYCLADES

ACCOMMODATIONS

Cheap domatia rooms abound, but you have to find them (look around for "Rooms to Let" signs). Off-season prices are generally 20-40% cheaper. There's a large map with names and phone numbers of hotels at the ferry dock.

Hotel Aktaion (☎22810 88 200 or 22810 88 201; fax 22810 82 675; romana@otenet.gr). Look for the rooftop sign at the right end of the waterfront. Location is only the 1st of Aktaion's attractive qualities: study-like wood-and-brick rooms have TVs, A/C, telephones, as well as complimentary goodies including candy and soap. Free Internet station for guests in reception area. Singles €40; doubles €53. ❹

Villa Votsalo, Parou 21 (☎22810 87 334 or 693 830 0557; fax 22810 86 760). Walk inland on Hiou (to the left of Venizelou); Parou is the first left off Hiou. Have a drink above this cozy traditional-house-turned-hotel, on the sunny roof garden bar, which has a full view of the harbor. Fridges. Doubles €25 and up. ❸

Hotel Almi (☎22810 82 812), on the left side of the alleyway across from the bus depot and port. Look for the dark wooden doors. A charming owner offers nice rooms with TVs. Doubles €20-45. ❸

Ariadni Rooms to Let, Nikolaou Filini 9 (☎22810 81 307 or 22810 80 245), near the ferry dock. Turn left at the kiosk before the Hermes statue and head up the stairs (look for signs). A dose of luxury, the hotel prides itself on its well-deserved class "A" rating. Private baths, TVs, telephones, and A/C. Doubles €30-56; triples €36-68. ❹

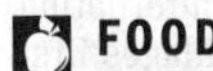

FOOD

For groceries, head to the **mini-market** halfway up from Hiou's plateia. (☎22810 81 008. Open 8am-9pm.) **Hiou** hosts fruit and seafood stalls and aromatic bakeries.

To Archontariki, Em. Roidi 8 (☎22810 81 744). On the 2nd street over from corner of Pl. Miaouli. Lose yourself in this local legend's authentic Greek atmosphere and the lively music wafting in from the more touristy restaurants around the corner. Try the pork in white wine sauce (€8). ❷

Restaurant Bakhos (Βακχος), (☎22810 84 597). Walking along Hiou, turn left on Peloponnisou; the restaurant is at the end under a leafy awning. Built in 1843, the building was a functioning pottery factory until 1922. Today, it spins out seafood, pasta, and Greek specialties. Open daily 10:30am-2am. ❷

Kechayia Sweet Shop (☎22810 84 100), on the waterfront corner of El. Venizelou. Fabulous renditions of traditional local specialties such as *chalvathopita*, a sweet concoction of almond paste, nuts, and chocolate (€1.35), and *loukoumi* (€1.50). ❶

Mavros (☎22810 82 244), in the center of the ocean end of Pl. Miaouli. Serenading accordion or guitar and the big outdoor TV will entertain as you explore the incredibly broad menu. Open daily 6am-2am. ❷

SIGHTS

At the **Church of the Assumption** *(Kimisis Theotokou)*, on Ag. Proiou to the right of the plateia facing the town hall, you can contemplate a 1562 painting by a 20-year-old Domenikos Theotokopoulos before he was known as **El Greco.** Ascend the steps at the far left of Pl. Miaouli to **Ano Syros,** a medieval Venetian settlement which Syros's Catholics still call home (20min.) or take the bus from the waterfront. Continue past the summit church through labyrinthine streets to the lofty Church of Ag. George above, and look over Ermoupolis and the coast below. The town hall's **Archaeological Museum** has a small collection of Cycladic art. (☎22810 28 487. Open Tu-Su 8:30am-3pm. Free. No cameras permitted.)

NIGHTLIFE

At night, the waterfront and Pl. Miaouli buzz with cafes, restaurants, dance clubs, and bars. If you can score a table, drink up at **Liquid** or **Cocoon.** On the right-hand strip of the waterfront, the **Cotton Club** is a hopping cafe/bar; just next to it, **Kimbara** is packed with wall-to-wall bodies and Madonna tunes. For dancing, bounce on over to **Arxaion**—it opens at 9am as a cafe and closes at 4am as a dance club. If you want some high rollin', try your luck at **Kazino Eyeou**—Aegean Casino—the only sin palace around. Men must wear pants (sorry, guys), and visitors must leave their passport and €9 at the door. (☎22810 84 400. Gambling starts at 2pm.)

BEACHES

The closest beach is sedate **Agios Nikolaos.** To get there, walk up El. Venizelou through Pl. Miaouli to the right of the Archaeological Museum. Head right and pass through Pl. Vardakas up to the right of the church of Agios Nikolau. Continue on the street until you see an archway and a stone stairway leading down to the beach. The main beach at **Galissas,** a village to the west of Ermoupolis, is beyond crowded; as *the* place to be, every inch of sand is full of sun-lovin' life. Climb past the chapel of Agia Pakou on the left side (facing the water) to discover nudist paradise: tiny, beautiful **Armeos beach.**

From Ermoupolis, **buses** travel to Galissas (13-18 per day, €1), alternating between a direct 15min. route and a 45min. route that stops in other villages first (take the longer bus for a glimpse of the island). Taking the scenic route to Galissas allows you to see the rest of Syros's southern beaches. **Finikas** and **Komito** are ideal for watersports like windsurfing. **Megas Yialos** and **Azolimnos** (featuring a large metal waterslide) are more peaceful. The beach resort of **Vari** is popular with families and package tour groups because of its shallow waters and relaxed atmosphere. North of Galissas is the tiny, quiet fishing village of **Kini,** ideal for the quintessential romantic sunset. If you happen to be in this hamlet on June 29th, the **Church of Ag. Peter** invites you and every other living thing within earshot to an all-night festival. *Bouzouki* accompanies plentiful *kakavia* (fish soup).

NAXOS Ναξος

The gleaming marble Portara, the lone remaining arch of the grandest Greek temple to Apollo, serves as the portal into diverse and splendid Naxos. The island is the largest of the Cyclades; olive groves, wineries, small villages, and chalky white ruins fill its interior, and sandy beaches line its shores. The ancients believed it to be the island home of Dionysus, but even without mythology Naxos has had a colorful history. Prosperous since ancient times, the island has wielded greater

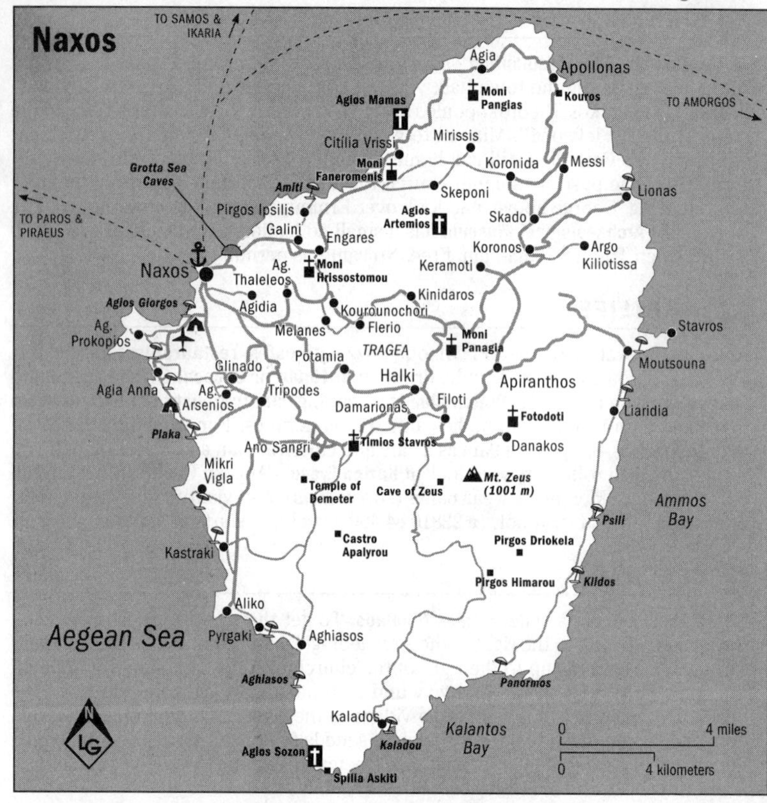

power than its small size would suggest. When the Venetians conquered the region in 1207, they made Naxos the capital of their Aegean empire.

To properly experience Naxos, it's essential to escape the clutter of Naxos Town and get to the interior. Mopeds are invaluable for combining trips to the beaches south of town and the inland sights and villages. Just be wary of the serpentine roads that aren't always well-paved. The villages and hikes of the **Tragea** highland valley (a vastly green olive grove) make up Naxos's most exhilarating features. Would-be hikers should stop by the tourist office to pick up any number of the 33 walking tour maps (€0.50 each), a detailed map of the island (€4.50), or a copy of *Walking Tours on Naxos* by Christian Ucke (€15).

NAXOS TOWN Ναξος

Naxos's capital reaches out to you before you've stepped off the ferry: as you drift into the harbor, the Portara juts out into the sea on a peninsula, and the Chapel of Myrditiotissa floats on an island. Once inside Naxos Town, both the twisting historic quarter and the hard-nosed modern area step forward. Tightly-packed on the hill leading up to the Venetian castle, Old Naxos snoozes behind the waterfront shops. Low stone archways and trellises of flowers drape the homes that crowd the labyrinthine streets descending from the castle. Hip bars and clubs near Agios Giorgios beach call you to cut loose after a day exploring the island.

TRANSPORTATION

All **ferries** to Naxos dock in Naxos Town. There are two docks at the left end of town; the larger for large ferries, the other for smaller ferries and daily cruises. Mopeds are the easiest (and most hazardous) way to get around the island.

Flights: An **Olympic Airways** desk is housed in **Naxos Tours** (☎22850 22 095 or 22850 24 000), at the left end of the waterfront. One flight per day to **Athens** (€70).

Buses: (☎22850 22 291; fax 22850 22 999), in front of the ferry dock. Check the **schedules** at the tourist office and the bus station across the street and to the left (facing inland). Buses to **Apollonas** (2hr., 4 per day, €3.80) and **Filoti** (30min., 5 per day, €1.50) are often packed. Buses also run to: **Plaka beach** (15min., every 30min. 8am-midnight, €1.10) via **Ag. Prokopios beach** and **Ag. Anna beach; Apiranthos** (1hr., 5 per day 10am-3pm, €2.10); **Engares** (1 per day, €0.80); **Halki** (30min., 5 per day, €1.10); **Pyrgaki beach** (1hr., 2 per day 11am-2pm, €1.70) via **Tripodes** (€0.80); **Melanes** (2 per day, €0.80); **Koronos** (3 per day, €2.50).

Ferries: To: **Amorgos** (2½hr., 6 per week, €7.80); **Crete** (7hr., 4 per week, €16.30); **Donousa** (4hr., 1 per day, €5.20) via **Iraklia** (1hr., €4.50), **Schinousa** (2hr., €4.80) and **Koufonisia** (3hr., €5.50); **Ios** (1hr., 3 per week, €6.90); **Kos** (7hr., 1 per week, €14.13); **Mykonos** (3hr., 3 per week, €6.30); **Piraeus** (6hr., 2 per day, €16.80); **Paros** (1hr., 2 per day, €4.50); **Rhodes** (13hr., 1 per week, €19.07); **Santorini** (3hr., 2 per day, €9.40); **Syros** (2½hr., 1 per day, €7.10); **Thessaloniki** (14hr., 3 per week, €28.90); **Tinos** (4hr., 2 per week, €9.50).

Flying Dolphins: To **Astypalea, Donousa, Folegandros, Crete, Ios, Koufonisia, Mykonos, Paros, Piraeus, Santorini, Schinousa, Syros,** and **Tinos.**

Taxis: (☎22850 22 444), on the waterfront, next to the bus depot.

Rentals: Fun Cars (☎22850 26 084) is inland and right from the roundabout. In Pl. Protodikiou, try **Rental Center** (☎22850 23 396). Friendly staff, good rental rates, and lots of info on Naxos. Also has **Internet access** for €4 per hr. Open 8:30am-11pm.

ORIENTATION AND PRACTICAL INFORMATION

Avoid the dock hawks and make your way to the waterfront tourist information office (look for the "i") to find a suitable rooming situation. The waterfront to the right of the harbor, along main road **Protopapadakis,** is lined with cafes, tavernas, and clubs. After 500m the road forks inland; follow it up 70m and turn right to find the roundabout of the central square. The Old Town lies behind this main road, accessible via any of the alleyways running inland.

Tourist Office: (☎22850 24 358 or 22850 25 201; fax 22850 25 200; chateau-zevgoli@nax.forthnet.gr), 300m from the dock, by the bus depot. Accommodation assis-

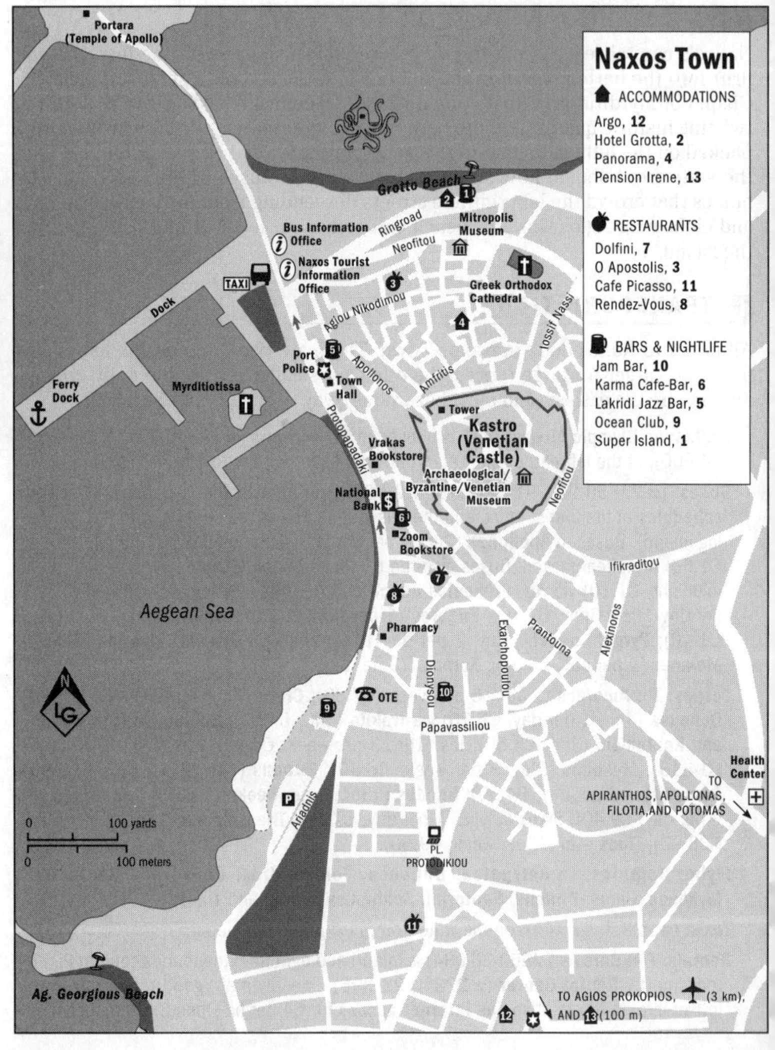

tance, bus and ferry schedules, car rental, **currency exchange,** international telephone, **luggage storage** (€1.50), safety deposit (€1.50), **laundry service** (€7.50). English speakers **Despina and Stavros** are marvelous. Open daily 8am-11pm.

Tourist Agency: Zas Travel (☎/fax 22850 22 236; naxostours@naxos-island.com), along the waterfront. **Car rental** and ferry and plane tickets. Open daily 8am-11pm.

Bank: The **National Bank** (☎22850 23 053) is one of many on the waterfront offering **currency exchange** and an **ATM.** Open M-Th 8am-2pm, F 8am-1:30pm.

International Bookstore: Vrakas (☎22850 23 039 or 22850 22 226), behind a jewelry shop. Look for signs reading "gold-silver used books." Vrakas buys at half the original price, sells for €2-10. Open 9:30am-11:30pm. **Zoom** (☎22850 23 675), to the right of the National Bank, offers international magazines. Open daily 7:30am-midnight.

Public Toilets and Showers: Behind Grotta Tours on the street parallel to the waterfront. Turn left by the dock after Zas Travel and turn left again. Toilets €0.40; showers €3. Open daily 6am-midnight.

Police: (☎22850 22 100). On the main road heading toward Ag. Giorgios beach from Pl. Protodikiou, 1km out of town. Open 24hr.

Port Police: (☎22850 22 300), on Protopapadakis, across from the small port dock.

Health Center: (☎22850 23 333). Turn inland at the fork in the road past the OTE, at the right end of the waterfront. Follow that road for about 500m; the center will be on your left. Helicopter to Athens available for emergencies. Open 24hr.

OTE: Left of the fork in the road to the right of the waterfront, inland from Cream nightclub. Open M-F 7:30am-3pm.

Internet Access: At almost every corner. Rental Center is in Pl. Protodikiou (see **Rentals**). **Veporia Play Room** (☎22850 22 003), one block toward Ag. Giorgios beach from Pl. Protodikou. Satellite TV, video games, pool. €3 per hr. Open daily 10am-late.

Post Office: Walk down the waterfront with the water on your right, and continue just beyond the main street that turns left. Pass a long playground on the right, and the post office will be on your left, up one floor. Open M-F 7:30am-2pm. **Postal code:** 84300.

ACCOMMODATIONS AND CAMPING

Most hotels on Naxos fill to capacity in late summer. Accommodations of all types can be arranged through the tourist office. Prices vary according to season. If you're looking for a unique experience, ask the tourist agency about renting century-old houses in the Old Town, but be prepared to spend quite a bit of money. Naxos has three roughly equivalent **beach camping** options, and their representatives wait eagerly at the dock. All of the sites are complete with mini-markets, restaurant, Internet access, moped rental, and laundry facilities. Prices are roughly equivalent. Inquire at the booth on the dock (camping €4-6 not including tent). **Naxos Camping ❶,** 1500m to the right along Ag. Giorgios beach, has a swimming pool. (☎22850 23 500; fax 22850 23 501.) **Maragas Camping ❶,** on Ag. Anna (a 15min. drive from Naxos Town) has studios and apartments as well as a campsite. (☎22850 42 552 or 22850 42 599. Doubles €16-29.) **Plaka Camping ❶** (☎22850 42 700), by Plaka beach, has studio/apartment options.

Pension Irene (☎22850 23 169), with two facilities, both located 100m from Ag. Giorgios. Very reasonably priced, well-equipped rooms with A/C, TVs, and showers are not far from the center of Naxos Town. One site has a swimming pool. Port shuttle available. Singles €15; doubles €20-30; triples €25-35. ❷

Panorama (☎22850 22 330), in Old Naxos. Enjoy the calm of the town in your breezy room with fan and fridge. Doubles from €25 in low season, from €30 in high season. ❸

Hotel Grotta (☎22850 22 215, 22850 22 101; fax 22850 22 000; www.hotel-grotta.gr), in Grotta, 500m northwest of Hora. For a little luxury, check into this hotel situated on a bluff overlooking the Aegean. Rooms have fridges, A/C, balconies, hair dryers, and laundry service. Doubles €40-60. ❹

Argo (☎22850 25 330 or 22850 23 059; argohotel@hellasnet.gr), 150m from Ag. Giorgios and 400m from the square; call for a port shuttle. Multilingual owners offer rooms with private baths, phones, and A/C. Rooms for 1-5 people €24-50. ❸

FOOD

Wade through the sea of waterfront tables, and grab a seat at one of the many new cafes. In Old Naxos, you'll stumble upon tucked-away moussaka havens. **Supermarkets** and fruit and grocery stands are everywhere.

O Apostolis (☎22850 26 777), on Old Market St. This traditional Greek restaurant is hidden at the foot of the old town among whitewashed walls and overhanging flowers. The cook prepares exceptional dishes for incredible prices. For starters, try the *dolmades*, a specialty with zucchini flower and rice (€3.50). Open 6:30am-2am. ❶

Dolfini (☎22850 24 320), up the steps from Ergo Bank. A slice of India (via Britain), in a lush garden. The self-proclaimed Mystic Fire Priest of Naxos challenges patrons to down their spicy dishes (curries and Thai dishes €7-10)–soothe your fiery belly with a cocktail. Open 8:30am-2am. Kitchen closes at midnight. ❷

Cafe Picasso Mexican Bistro (☎22850 25 408), one block toward Ag. Giorgios beach from the main square. A rare taste of Mexico in Greece, from tasty nachos (€5) to quesadillas (€4.50-5.50). Ease the spicy salsa with a glass of sangria (€2) or a frozen margarita (€4.50). Open 7pm-2am; kitchen closes at midnight. ❷

Rendez-Vous (☎22850 23 858). This bright pink waterfront palace concocts delicious pastries; particularly good are the *loukamades* (honey doughnuts; €2.50). Ice cream and fruit bowls are served with sparklers. Breakfast served. Open 6am-2am. ❶

SIGHTS

Naxos Town is crowned by the **Kastro,** an old Venetian castle. Of the 12 original houses within its walls, only one remains entirely intact. The Domus Della Rocca-Barozzi, vacated by its owners in 1999, is now a **Venetian museum** that showcases furniture, decorations, and household goods from past generations of inhabitants of the castle. A "Venetian Evening" is held monthly; candles light the castle as guests revel in singing, dancing and traditional drinks. A series of "Sunset Concerts" feature traditional Greek shadow theater *(karaghiozis)* and traditional or contemporary music with renowned artists and dancing. Run by local Naxians, the Kastro is a refreshing dose of culture and history. (☎22850 22 387; fax 22850 24 879. Open daily 10am-4pm and 7-11pm. Multilingual 30min. tours throughout the day. €5; €3 for students and seniors.) The **Byzantine Museum,** just around the corner, features artifacts from the 8th-10th centuries found on Naxos and surrounding Cycladic islands. (Open M-Sa 8am-2pm. Free.) Also inside the Kastro sits the **Archaeological Museum,** located in the former Collège Français where Nikos Kazantzakis (see p. 21), author of *The Last Temptation of Christ* and *Zorba the Greek*, studied. There's a significant collection of Cycladic figurines and Mycenean vessels; tucked away in one of the rooms is the island's historical archive. (Open Tu-Su 8:30am-2pm. €3, students €2.) The impressive **Catholic Church** is just around the corner (opens 10am; free). The **Mitropolis Museum,** on the left side of town next to the historical Orthodox Church, is an architectural achievement in itself. Elevated walkways lead you through the reconstructed buildings of a 13th century BC settlement. (☎22850 24 151. Open Tu-Su 8:30am-3pm. Free.) Stop by **Vallindras** and **Promobos** distilleries to sample **Citron,** a liqueur unique to the island.

THE LOCAL FLAVOR. Everyone who visits Greece is familiar with ouzo, the anise-flavored specialty drink. But only those who venture to Naxos have the opportunity to take a sip or knock back a shot of *Citron*. Distilleries on the island have been producing this unique liqueur for over a century, and the origins date back several centuries. The potent leaves of the citron fruit are crushed and then boiled with sugar, water, and alcohol to create the three different varieties that differ in alcoholic content. If you're ready for a shock, try the yellow-tinted version (colored by saffron) with 36% alcohol. If you're not up for that, try the slightly more forgiving green *Citron*. The drink is available only on Naxos and in a few areas of Syros, as the citron fruit is not grown in large quantities. It's well worth a trip to one of the two local distilleries to see the preparation in action (and to try a free sample, of course).

From the waterfront, you can see the white chapel of **Myrditiotissa** floating in the harbor on a man-made islet and the marble **Portara** archway, on its own peninsula. Climb up to it and view the unfinished beginnings of an ambitious temple dedicated to Apollo, begun on the orders of the tyrant Lydamis in the 6th century BC. With no admission and no guards, open 24 hours, the temple is an ideal place to catch romantic sunsets or star gaze deep into the night.

CYCLADES

NIGHTLIFE

After-hours Naxos serenades evening wanderers with music from cafes and clubs. Take advantage of half-price Happy Hour, then relax all night, or get ready to join the masses at the waterfront clubs. Mobilize around 11pm. Alternatively, spend a low-key evening under the stars at **Cine Astra** (☎22850 25 381), on the road to Agia Anna from Pl. Protodikiou; it's a 15min. walk from the waterfront. (Movies in English shown at 9 and 11pm. Open daily May-Oct. €6.)

Super Island Bar and Club (☎694 693 7462), on the water along the paved road next to the bus depot. All of Naxos comes here to be seen and to dance to the adrenaline-pumping Euro beats. Open 11pm-late.

Ocean Club (☎22850 30 285), facing the water at the right end of the harborfront. Ocean churns enough to make its namesake proud. Do your best Ricky Martin impression atop the go-go box; you're sure to hear something you like. Open late.

Lakridi Jazz Bar, in Old Naxos on Old Market, close to the Captain's Cafe. Chill to the sounds of Billie Holliday in the hot Naxian night. Open 8pm-3:30am.

Karma Cafe-Bar (☎22850 24 885), right in the center of the waterfront. Start your evening here grooving to the wide variety of music in this uniquely constructed building with marble walls and a view of the port. Open 9pm to late.

Jam Bar (☎22850 24 306), first left after Klik Cafe. Sit back and experience the wide variety of music while sipping on an exotic concoction such as the Naxos Butterfly. You may even get a chance to hear a bit of live music if the owner Nikos is in the mood to put on a show. Open late.

BEACHES

North of Naxos Town, you can snorkel among caves in search of rocks and sea urchins. You'll have to head south, however, for Naxos's busiest beach life, with hotels, rooms to let, bars, tavernas, discos, and creperies. The most remote, uncrowded beaches with the clearest waters are the farthest from town. There, youthful, scantily clad bathers frolic among visiting windsurfers who come to Naxos from everywhere. Near town, **Agios Giorgios, Agios Prokopios, Agia Anna,** and long and sandy **Plaka** border crystal-blue water. Beware—you may have to vie for your share of sand. On Plaka, stunning nude sunbathers stud the shore. Naxos is overflowing with opportunities for athletes. You can sign up for windsurfing lessons, rent a mountain bike, or go for a sail in a catamaran at **Naxos Surf** (☎ 22850 29 170; fax 22850 29 171; info@naxos-surf.com) and **Flisvos Sport Club** (☎/fax 22850 24 308; flisbos@otenet.gr) on Ag. Giorgios, or **Plaka Watersports** (☎22850 41 264; kpigos@otenet.gr) at Plaka and Ag. Anna. A **bus** goes from the port to the beaches every half-hour (€1.10). Desert meets sea at the more secluded beaches of **Mikri Vigla, Abram, Aliko, Moutsouna,** and **Pyrgaki,** where scrub pines, prickly pear, and century plants grow on the dunes. All are accessible by bus from Naxos Town. There is a small nudist beach on the southern protuberance of **Kastraki beach.** If you're tired of the water, you can explore the island on horseback through the **Stamatis Riding Center** (☎22850 41 879).

DAYTRIPS FROM NAXOS TOWN

APOLLONAS AND NORTHERN NAXOS

From Naxos Town, catch the ***bus*** *to Apollonas for an exhilarating ride on a beautiful coastal road (2hr., €3.50). This bus service can be used easily to make a round trip (in either direction) of the central Naxian villages and the islands' northern coast; the bus travels on an interior and an alternate coastal route. The coast is lined with secluded, sandy beaches; those on moped can pick their spot and hike down along the goat trails.*

CYCLADES

On the road to Apollonas you'll pass the secluded beach at **Amiti** on your left, down the road from Galini, and, farther on, the monastery of **Faneromenis** (the Virgin Revealer). The main attraction of Apollonas, one of the more famous *kouroi* of Naxos, is just a short walk from the harbor. While this **kouros** is nearly 11m tall, it's not as completely sculpted as the one in Flerio (see below). From the Apollonas bus stop, walk back along the main road uphill to the fork in the road. Take a sharp right and walk up until you see the stairs at the Προς Κουρο sign.

CENTRAL NAXOS AND THE TRAGEA

Buses run from Naxos Town to Halki (17km, 15-20min.) Look for the turn-off to ***Ano Sangri,*** *an isolated town of winding flagstone streets 1km west of the road. You can get off the bus at the turn-off and hike 1½hr. the entire way.*

If you're up for the 30min. amble south of Ano Sangri, you can see the 6th-century BC **Temple of Demeter** being reconstructed with original fragments and new Naxian marble. If you have a motorbike or car, an alternate route takes you from Naxos Town through Melanes to **Flerio,** where another magnificent Naxian **kouros** sleeps in a garden. This one was probably abandoned in its marble quarry because it broke before completion. Its owner runs a small *kafeneion* in the garden. From Flerio, backtrack and follow a road through three charming villages in a river valley—**Kato Potamia, Mesi Potamia,** and, upstream, **Ano Potamia**—before reaching Halki. Maps available at the tourist office in Naxos Town (€4.50 for a large map; €0.50 each for maps of individual hikes).

Halki, a placid village surrounded by Venetian towers, marks the beginning of the magnificent **Tragea,** an enormous, peaceful Arcadian olive grove. Restoration work in the **Panagia Protothonis,** across from the bus stop, has uncovered frescoes from the 11th through 13th centuries. The priest can let you in if it is closed.

A 30min. walk northwest of Halki takes you to the village of Moni, where you can admire the **Panagia Drosiani**, which houses frescos dating back to the 7th century. Southwest of Halki you will reach Filoti (20min. walk), a village at the far end of the Tragea valley. Footpaths off the main road will lead you into the dense **olive**

grove. It is easy to get delightfully lost wandering among the scattered churches and tranquil scenery of the Tragea. If you do, take note of the sun and head west to return to the main road. Naxos's largest celebration, the **Feast of the Assumption of Panagia** (the Virgin Mary) is held in Filoti from August 14 to 16.

The slopes of **Mt. Zeus** near Filoti offer superb views extending to Poros and the sea beyond. Serious hikers may want to check out the **Cave of Zeus,** the spot where an eagle gave the king of the gods the power to hurl thunderbolts. This 150m-deep cave is a good 1½hr. trek uphill from Filoti. Determined mythologists, or those simply looking for a good hike with excellent views, should bring a flashlight to fully appreciate the cave. Head up the road to Apiranthos for 20-30min. until a sign points to the right for Mt. Zeus. Follow this road to its end, passing through a gate, just before a clearing with a potable **spring water fountain.** From there, keep going, staying on the left (uphill) whenever possible. Look for red arrows on stones. After 45min. you'll reach the cave's mouth, marked with a simple sign that reads "cave." The grotto itself is large, cool, rather slimy, and fun to explore.

APIRANTHOS

Buses run from Naxos Town and Filoti (15min.).

The small town of Apiranthos houses an **Archaeological Museum** with many Cycladic artifacts in a white building on the right side of the main street. Also in Apiranthos are a modest **folk art museum,** a **natural history museum** (near the bus stop), and a **geological museum** (beside a large church). All four are "officially" open from 10am to 1:30pm, but it all depends on tourist traffic; many of the owners moonlight as goat herders. (Single ticket to all four €1.) Many Apiranthos homes are 300 to 400 years old, and lie in the shadow of the two Venetian castles that preside over the town. The Zergolis family, who live in the castle by the square, may allow you to look around. The mountain views from the edges of the town are stunning, and locals are cordial to the few tourists who come this way. More information is available at the unofficial **info center** inside the pricey Yasou Snack Bar, on the right past the Geological Museum. The road, from Apiranthos through **Koronos** and **Koronida,** a 1hr. drive, snakes through interior mountain ranges. Near Koronos, once famous as the mining center of the island, you'll find the newly restored loading station and cable for the emery mines where you can catch a glimpse into the beginnings of the industrial history of the island.

LITTLE CYCLADES

These tiny Cycladic isles provide the perfect opportunity to escape their increasingly crowded larger counterparts. Jumping off the beaten island-hopping track lets you pursue perfect isolation and meditation in this island group where goats outnumber human inhabitants. Peaceful walks, refreshing solitude, and a breathtaking nighttime sky await the adventurous traveler.

KOUFONISIA Κουφονησια

The smallest of the inhabited Little Cyclades (and the most popular), Koufonisia surrounds itself with a sparkling selection of beaches on the southeast side of the island, **Ano Koufonisia.** The name, meaning "hollow," refers to the caves perforating its surface; the small town of **Hora** serves as its capital. Tales of serene beaches and Cycladic relics lure visitors off of Ano Koufonisia to neighboring **Kato Koufonisia** and rocky **Keros.** There may be few alternatives to the well-worn path from beach to taverna, but Koufonisia's total simplicity makes it totally relaxing.

ORIENTATION AND PRACTICAL INFORMATION. Koufonisia's commercial center consists of two main streets. One runs inland from just beyond the port to the left of the mini-market; the other springs from its left side, about 100m inland and parallel to the beach. The **ferry ticket office,** up the second road parallel to the beach and a few buildings past the blue-domed church, posts a ferry schedule on its door. (☎22850 71 438. Open 9am-2pm and 6-10pm.) There are two **ferry** lines: one runs M, W, Th and Sa at 9:30am to **Naxos** (2½hr., €5.50) via **Schinousa** (30min., €3.50) and **Iraklia** (1hr., €3.50); the other runs daily to **Aegiali** (2hr., €5.50) and **Katapola** (3hr., €5.50) via **Donousa** (1½hr., €5.50). Head straight off the ferry dock toward the tiny white village and the winding lanes of Hora. The heart of Hora can be reached by turning left at the second road, just past the card phone. Be sure to bring enough money, as there is **no bank** on the island. **Currency exchange** is available at the **post office,** on the first road veering parallel to the beach at the mini-market. (☎22850 74 214. Open 8:30-noon and 6:30-11pm.) The **OTE** is on a parallel road across from Pension Melissa. (☎22850 22 392. Open 8am-2pm and 5-10pm.) **Internet access** is available at **Kohili** and **Kalamia Music Cafe** (see **Food and Entertainment**). The **medical center** (☎22850 71 370) is on the inland road to Hora near the **police.** A few **mini-markets** are on the main road. **Postal code:** 84300.

ACCOMMODATIONS AND CAMPING. The small pensions around town fill up fast, so it's best to call ahead for accommodations. Many homes with rooms to let are along the main road; prices for doubles run for €20-30 in low season and start at €40-55 in high season. **Pension Melissa ❸** is attached to the taverna 70m along the parallel street from the inland road to Hora, just up to the left from Katerina in the center of town. (☎22850 71 454. Doubles €40 in the summer.) You'll find several well-equipped pensions, including **Maria Prasinou ❷** (☎22850 71 436) and **Akgrogiali ❷** (☎22850 71 685), clustered along the road across the beach. **Harakorou Camping ❶** is a fine site affiliated with the taverna of the same name on Finikas beach. (☎22850 71 601. Around €8 for 2 people.) **Keros Hotel ❸** provides an excellent view of the harbor from its comfy rooms. (☎22850 71 601; fax 22850 71 961. Doubles €37-43; triples €42-49.)

FOOD AND ENTERTAINMENT. Throughout town you'll find good tavernas: seafood and standard Greek fare are the unanimous favorites (entrees €5-8.50). Their quality is uniform, and they're cheap. **Kohili ❶** is the perfect spot for a croissant sandwich and a view of the harbor. (☎22850 74 279. Open 8:30am-late. Internet access €3 per hr.) **Kalamia Music Cafe ❶,** 150m along the inland road by the public phones, provides drinks, sweets and an unique music blend. (☎22850 71 741. Open 8am-late. Cocktails €4.50-6. Internet access free for customers.) The artistically inclined can wander up to **Elkazein,** a new art gallery featuring the paintings and photographs of its owners. For late-night dancing set sail for **Emplo,** a word signifying the beginning of a sea voyage. Walk up the hill path to the left of the port and listen for Greek music.

BEACHES. Koufonisia's beaches spool out in a continuous ribbon along the southern coast. **Amos beach** is closest to Hora, just to the right of the ferry dock (facing inland); here you can spot nearby fishing boats and watch spirited kids' soccer games. Continuing 10min. down the road behind the sand leads you to family-packed **Finikas,** with a convenient taverna beside it. Just on the other side of the ridge from Finikas waits much quieter **Fanos.** The farther you walk, the fewer people (and clothes) you'll see. A 30min. walk from Hora brings you to **Pori beach,** the best on the island, with water and sand that is magnificent even by Greek island standards. If the sand gets too busy or begins to broil, head for the shaded rocks behind the beach to a bay that is perfect for snorkeling. Regular boats also make trips to Pori from the dock at Hora; check the posted schedule. For those who hate sharing the sand, there is always the daily ferry to Kato Koufonisia, where peace can be yours.

CYCLADES

DONOUSA Δονουσα

A trip to Donousa will give you a dose of traditional life in the rural Cyclades. Lacking banks, public transportation, and a reliable tourist office, Donousa beckons those eager to abandon modern conveniences.

The **tourist office** is across from the ferry dock; it sells ferry tickets and exchanges currency during its unreliable hours of operation. (☎22850 51 648; fax 22850 51 649. Open 8am-2pm and 5-11pm.) If it's closed during your visit, you can buy your ticket on the boat. **Ferries** travel to Amorgos, Koufonisia, Naxos and Schinousa four times per week at 8am. Travel to other islands is more sporadic. **To Kima,** the island's main hangout, also sells phone cards and some groceries; it's right beside the dock. (☎22850 51 566. Open 6am-4pm and 5pm-midnight.) Up the hill is the island's **public phone.** You can call the **doctor** at ☎22850 51 506. Vacationers often stay in the limited domatia across the bay from the main port; rooms go for about €20-45 for a double. Try **Christos Sigalas ❷** (☎22850 51 570) at the "Rooms to Let" sign or **Dimitris Prasino ❷** (☎22850 51 570) just above it. The rooms of **Venetsanou Eleftherie ❷** (☎22850 51 609), in the first complex at the right of the beach, are also a good choice. Catch a ride with the owners when you come ashore. Camping is permitted only on **Kedros Beach,** over the hill to the right of the domatia. Some of the island's tastiest food comes from the **bakery ❶** (☎22850 51 567) above the tourist office. Bear to the right from the dock to find the **mini-market** (☎22850 51 582). There are several tavernas, all visible from the dock, all serving similar Greek food (entrees €3.50-6.50).

The town beach allows children to splash under the watchful eyes of parents sipping Mythos beer. **Kedros** beach, a much nicer piece of shore, stretches out just over the ridge. Follow the road to the right of the white sign on the town beach to get to the tent-lined sand. Down this road lies even more pristine **Livadi** beach.

IRAKLIA Ιρακλια

Visitors to Iraklia tend to return: this underpopulated hideaway is magical; its scenery breathtaking. Whether exploring its caves, basking on its beaches, or sipping coffee under the starlight in a cafe, Iraklia's charms will envelop you.

ORIENTATION AND PRACTICAL INFORMATION. Ferries run every M, W, Th, and Sa to: **Amorgos** (3½hr., €6.80); **Donousa** (2hr., €5.58); **Koufonisia** (45min., €3.60); **Naxos** (1½hr., €5); and **Schinousa** (15min., €3.50). Ferries also travel 3-4 times a week to: **Paros** (€7.70); **Piraeus** (€15.50); and **Syros** (€8.70). Schedules are posted around the harbor, or consult a travel agent. **Agiazi Travel** (☎22850 74 236), at the left of the beach, sells **ferry tickets.** Rent **mopeds** from **Iraklia Rent a Scooter** (☎22850 71 564; €16 per day). From the **port,** head right past the town beach of Agios Giorgios to get to Hora. This main road splits at **Perigali,** a good place to score an island map (€0.90), at the bottom of the ravine that runs through town. Two roads run alongside the ravine and merge at the top. The **medical center** (☎22850 71 388 or 697 667 7833) is just above Perigali. Along the right-hand road is all-purpose **Melissa ❷,** a general store, ferry ticketer, telephone operator, post office, and domatia. (☎22850 71 539. Doubles with common bath €15-25.) The island's only card phone is just outside. **Postal code:** 84300.

ACCOMMODATIONS AND FOOD. In July and August, call ahead to reserve accommodations—in most cases, your hosts will pick you up at the port. **Anna's Place ❸,** near the top of Hora, looks out over the port from its spacious balconies. The rooms are comfortable and pristine with fridges and showers. (☎22850 71 145. Doubles €25-40; studios for 3 €40-65.) **Alexandra ❸,** at the top of Hora just beyond Anna's, has four breezy rooms with baths and fridges, a shared

THE 2004 GAMES

BUMBLING TO THE BLOCKS

A brief visit to Athens will quickly reveal the extensive preparations currently underway in anticipation of the 2004 Olympics Games. Cranes tower over the city, and scaffolding blankets buildings everywhere. The endless projects visible throughout the city give the appearance that all is running smoothly. However, beneath this facade lies the reality that the clock is ticking, and funds are quickly evaporating. Gianna Angelopoulos-Daskalaki, the president of the Organizing Committee (ATHOC) announced in July 2002 that budget cuts are being implemented in order to decrease construction time and costs.

When Athens won the bid for the Olympics in 1997, the city and the IOC allotted a budget of €2.5 billion. As of August 2002, the budget had increased to €4.4 billion. As a result, ATHOC is facing a series of challenges and plans on cutting back spending by cancelling the construction of facilities that will have the least pertinence in the aftermath of the games. The remodeling of the Olympic Stadium has already exceeded the original estimate by €119 million, a truly troubling total. Pressure to complete the new football stadium before the Olympic matches weighs upon the committee. Plans to build the stadium have been all but dropped, and the committee is currently searching for an alternative venue for this important and popular event. Despite the ambiguity of the situation, ATHOC remains adamant that Athens will be prepared for this long-awaited event.

kitchen, and verandas. (☎22850 71 482. Doubles €20-35.) **Maria's** ❸ (☎22850 71 485), across the road, has similar rates and amenities.

Ten minutes down the road to Livadi, you'll find a delicious variety of grilled fish and Greek specialties at **Giorgios Gavalas' Place.** Dance late into the night with his sons, or ask Giorgios if you can participate in the next all-male Miss Iraklia contest. Rave about your exploits to the folks back home at their **Internet** station (€4 per hr.) or **international telephone.** (☎22850 29 034 or 22850 71 226. Traveler's checks accepted.) **Maistrali,** up the hill just before Alexandra, sells postcards, foreign papers, and books, has an **international telephone** and offers **Internet access** (€3 per hr.); an attached **restaurant** ❶ serves good Greek food. (☎22850 71 807; maistralinick@hotmail.com. Open 7am-late.) Across the road **O Pevkos** ❶ (☎22850 71 568) sells fresh fish. For a more energized hangout try **Bar Aki Music-Dance** (☎22850 71 487) near Maistrali, the most raucous club on the island.

SIGHTS AND BEACHES. The shallow, clear waters of **Livadi beach** echo the serenity of everything else on the island. Wade out and look at the ruins of the **Venetian Castle** overhead. The water taxi *Anemos* will take you to **Karvounlakos** or **Alimia** beaches (every day in high season, departing 11am and returning 4pm, €6); buy tickets at Perigali. To step into the Greece of 40 years ago, continue along the main road past Livadi to the town of **Panagia** (45min. from Hora), where you'll find a small taverna, a church, some cows, and not much else. The taverna **To Steki** (☎22850 71 579) also serves as a general store, bakery, and the only "gas station" on the island—fill up from a canister.

THE OUTDOORS. The stalactite- and stalagmite-scattered **Agios Ioannis Cave,** with its tiny waterways you can crawl around in, will fascinate the adventurous. There is a rough but helpful map of the path on the back of the Iraklia map available in Perigali. Bring a flashlight, candles, matches, and a walking stick if possible (and get ready to get filthy). The steep, 1½hr. **hike** begins in Panagia, where a red arrow and the word "cave" are scrawled on a barn (go through the stone doorway on the left at the beginning of town)—if you don't see it, ask in To Steki. After 20min. along the stone wall-lined dirt path, you'll reach a wooden fence and another painted arrow pointing you through it. Follow the stone wall on your right until it meets another stone wall. The beaten path of the ascent becomes difficult to follow; just stay near this wall. After your climb, another wooden door stands at the intersection of two fences. Go through this door and follow the stone piles until you reach a more clearly defined pathway that marks the beginning of a 30min. descent along the back side of **Mt. Pappas** toward the two cave entrances. Crawling through the small entrance (marked by a hanging bell) brings you into the caves. You'll need the flashlight right away; leaving lighted candles along the way will help mark your path. To the left as you enter is an icon of St. John, who is celebrated in an August **festival** at the cave. There are said to be 15 rooms inside the cave. Be careful: the rocks are slippery, and daylight vanishes quickly.

SCHINOUSA Σχινουσα

A multitude of isolated yet accessible beaches line the coast of the untouched isle of Schinousa, all but guaranteeing a peaceful communion with nature. The island is best enjoyed on foot exploring its hide-away beaches and donkey-patrolled interior and getting to know the affable population—250 at last count.

ORIENTATION AND PRACTICAL INFORMATION. All boats dock at the tiny port of **Mersini,** with **Hora** a 10-15min. walk uphill. Call ahead for accommodations and you'll be picked up from the ferry, or grab a ride with a pension owner at the dock. **Flying Dolphins** or **ferries** go daily to: **Amorgos** (3 hr., €7) via **Koufonisia** (30 min., €3.50) and, 5 times per week, **Donousa** (1½hr., €6); **Iraklia** (15min., €3.50); **Naxos**(1½hr., €5). They also go to **Piraeus** twice per week (€16.50). Check the posted schedules for daily routes. Nearly everything you'll need in Hora can be found on the main road, a 5min. walk from end to end. Halfway along the main road you'll see a sign pointing to Tsigouri beach. Following this road leads to **Giorgios Grispos,** the town's travel guru, who offers one-stop tourist shopping at his **travel agency,** taverna, and domatia (with A/C) at a beachside location. (☎22850 71 930. Open daily in the summer 9am-2pm and 6-9pm.) Buy **ferry tickets** here or at the port and **exchange money** at poor rates. Note that there is **no bank** in town. Maps and phone cards are available at the mini-markets lining the main road. Off the main road, heading left, you'll find a street marked by signs for **Agnantema bakery.** The **doctor** (☎22850 71 385) is on the same road, in a clearly marked white building. Two public **card phones** are down at the port and in the plateia of Hora. The **post office** is on the main road in what seems to be a private home. **Postal code:** 84300.

ACCOMMODATIONS AND FOOD. Nearly every restaurant or general store in town offers several rooms to rent in addition to moussaka and Fanta. Centrally located **Anesis ❸** has large, clean rooms with fridges, private baths, and panoramic balcony views. (☎22850 71 180. Doubles €28-40. Be sure to bargain.) **Agnantema ❸** is in a new building with a prime location right above the bakery and restaurant. The rooms overlook a rocky terrace with tables and a gazebo. (☎22850 71 987; fax 22850 74 077. Doubles €20-50; studios for 4 people €30-60. Cafe open 8am-11:30pm. Reserve in advance during high season.) **Sunset Hotel ❸** (☎22850 71 161) and **Anna Rooms ❸** (☎22850 71 948), down the road to the left, are run by a mother and daughter and offer simple rooms with balconies, fridge, and private bath. (Singles €25-32; doubles €32-48; triples €36-55.) Enjoy traditional music and good food with a crowd of locals at **Loza Pizzeria ❶**, off the main plateia. (☎22850 74 004. Open 9am-2am.) Alternatively, gaze off the balcony as you wait for your moussaka at **Panorama ❶**, a few meters past the beach turn-off on the main road.

NIGHTLIFE AND BEACHES. A 10min. walk down a rocky path at the beginning of Hora, off the main road, leads to **Ostria Cafe,** an outdoor beach bar and restaurant, where you can spin music with the five brothers (Manolis, Agilos, Dimitris, Christos, and Antonis) who own the joint.

Schinousa's dirt roads love pedestrians as much as they hate cars. Grab a bottle of water, glance at a map, and walk until a particularly alluring cove catches your eye. **Tsigouri beach,** 450m down a dusty road, invites you to splash in its waves, play a round of beach volleyball, and rent kayaks or waterskis. **Livadi** is farther along the main road through Hora to the dirt tracks leading to the water; **Psili Ammos** sprawls on the other side of the island, about 30min. past the bakery.

PAROS Παρος

Paros's enduring legacy has always been its opaque, pure marble. Many of the great statues and buildings of the ancient and more modern world have shone because of Parian rock: the Venus de Milo, the Nike of Samothrace, and parts of Napoleon's mausoleum in Paris. A late bloomer in the tourism business, Paros had 20 donkeys for each car as recently as 15 years ago. But not even the headstrong residents of Paros could resist the call of tourism dollars, and the island has now embraced its destiny as a popular traveler destination. As the population inflates to 10 times its off-season levels in the heart of the summer, the isle welcomes its visitors with tall mountains, long beaches, and a healthy serving of hospitality.

PARIKIA Παροικια

Behind Parikia's commercial facade, flower-filled streets wend through archways, past whitewashed houses, and by one of the most treasured basilicas of the Orthodox faith. Wander through the agora to find trendy clothing, snappy jewelry, local art, homemade goods, and the outdoor terraces of coffeehouses. While the beaches aren't much to write home about, this transportation hub is a convenient base for reaching almost any spot on the island.

TRANSPORTATION

Flights: Olympic Airways (☎22840 21 900), in the plateia by National Bank. Open M-F 8am-3pm. To **Athens** (around 2 per day, €74). Taxi to airport €6.50.

Ferries: To: **Amorgos** (3hr., 1-2 per day, €9.10); **Crete** (8hr., 5 per week, €20.13); **Ikaria** (4hr., 5 per week, €11.40); **Ios** (2½hr., 7-9 per day, €7.90); **Kos** (1 per week, €14.43); **Piraeus** (5-6hr., 5-8 per day, €16.80); **Naxos** (1hr., 5-10 per day, €4.50); **Rhodes** (16hr., 1 per week, €22.95); **Samos** (6hr., 6 per week, €14.13); **Santorini** (3½hr., 7-9 per day, €10.10); **Sikinos** (3hr., 2 per week, €5.80); **Syros** (1hr., 3-6 per day, €5.19).

Flying Dolphins: To: **Crete** (3½hr., June-Sept. 6 per week, €40.30); **Ios** (2½hr.; 2-3 per day, €15.33); **Mykonos** (50min., 2-4 per day, €11.15); **Naxos** (1hr., 4-7 per day, €8.90); **Piraeus** (3hr., daily, €33.10); **Rafina** (3hr., 8 per week, €27.60); **Santorini** (1¾hr., 3-4 per day, €20.30); **Sikinos** (3hr., 2 per week, €10); **Syros** (45min., 3-4 per day, €10.20); and **Tinos** (1½hr., 4-5 per day, €15.54).

Buses: (☎22840 21 395 or 22840 21 133). Schedule posted a few blocks to the left of the windmill (facing inland). Buses run to: **Aliki** and the **airport** (30min., 10 per day, €1.10) via the **Valley of the Butterflies** (€0.80); **Chrisi Akti** (50min., 2 per day, €1.80); **Marpissa** (35min., 15 per day, €1.25); **Drios** (1hr., 12 per day, €1.80); **Kamares** (20min., 2 per day, €0.80); **Lefkes** (25min., 8 per day, €0.95); **Naoussa** (15min., 33 per day, €0.95); **Piso Livadi** (40min., 15 per day, €1.50); **Pounda** (15min., 15 per day, €1.50).

Taxis: (☎22840 21 500), inland and to the right of the windmill.

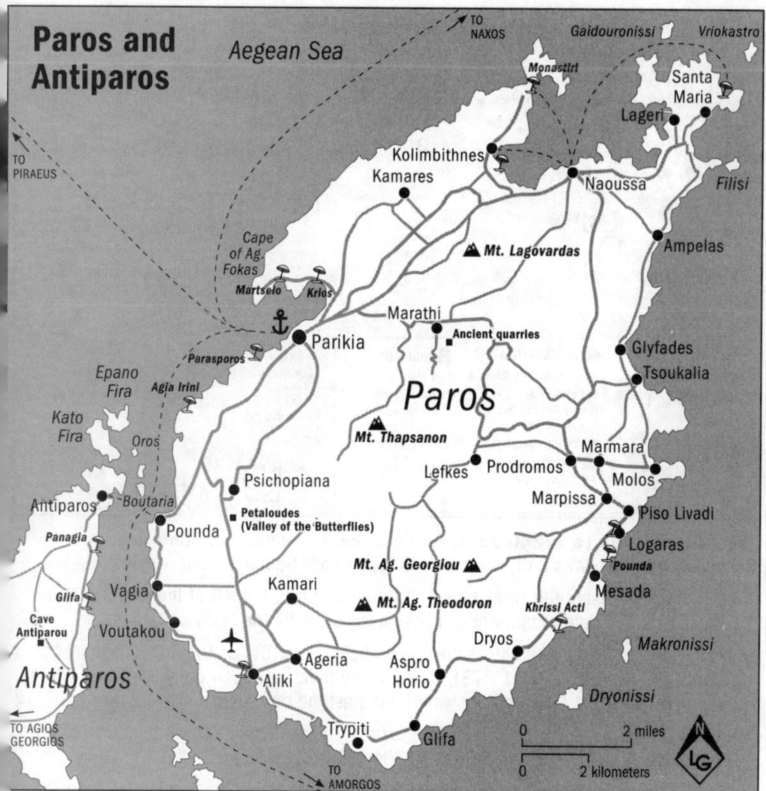

ORIENTATION AND PRACTICAL INFORMATION

Cheap hotels, tourist-related offices, and the town beach lie to the left of the ferry dock. The plateia is straight ahead, past the windmill and the tourist offices. To the right, a whitewashed labyrinth brims with shops, restaurants, and cafes. To the far right around the bend, the island's party district awaits.

Tourist Office: (☎22840 22 861) just behind the windmill to the right. Has a small selection of **maps** and some limited information about accommodations. **Luggage storage** (€3 per piece). Open daily 9:30am-1am. George from Rena Rooms is also happy to answer questions (☎22840 21 427).

Travel Agency: Polos Tours (☎22840 22 092; fax 22840 21 983), next to the OTE. Has up-to-the-minute transportation schedules and rental services. Cars €24-41 per day. Open daily 8am-midnight.

Banks: National Bank (☎22840 21 298). From the windmill, head inland to the plateia and to the right. It's in the fortress-like building at the far corner, past the playground. 24hr. **ATM** and **currency exchange** machine. Open M-Th 8am-2pm, F 8am-1:30pm.

Luggage Storage: Agencies around the port charge €3 per piece per day.

Laundromat: Top (☎22840 23 424). Pass the bus station and turn right after the ancient cemetary. Wash, dry, and fold €9. Open daily 9am-3pm and 5-9pm.

Public Toilets: Beside the small blue and white church to the left of the windmill. More toilets are to the right of the windmill beside the signs for the Frankish Castle.

Police: (☎22840 23 333), across the plateia behind the OTE, on the 2nd fl. Open 24hr. **Tourist police** (☎22840 21 673), in the same building. Open daily 8am-2pm. **Port Police** (☎22840 21 240), off the waterfront, past the bus station. Open 24hr.

Medical Clinic: (☎22840 22 500). Across from the small blue and white church to the left of the windmill. Open M-F 8:30am-2:30pm. **Emergency** care 24hr.

OTE: (☎22840 21 399). 1 block to the right of the windmill (facing inland). Open M-F 7am-2:40pm.

Internet Access: Internet cafes are all over Parikia. **Cybercookies** (☎/fax 22840 21 610), on Market St., charges €4.80 per hr. 20min. free with 1 order of food, 40min. with 2 orders. Open daily 8am-1am. **Memphis Cafe** is left of the windmills on the waterfront, past the bus station. €5 per hr. Open daily 9:30am-midnight.

Post Office: (☎22840 21 236), on the left side of the waterfront, 2 blocks past the bus stop. Open M-F 7:30am-2pm. **Postal code:** 84400.

ACCOMMODATIONS AND CAMPING

There are many hotels and domatia along the waterfront and in the Old Town; a slew of new, inexpensive pensions have opened behind the town beach to the left of the plateia. Dock hawks are known to offer good deals in Naoussa, Piso Livadi, and Antiparos, among other places; remember to insist on seeing rooms before you pay. The **Room Association** (☎22840 24 528) can help you hunt.

Rena Rooms (☎/fax 22840 22 220). Turn left from the dock and take a right after the cemetery ruins, or call ahead for a port shuttle. George, the owner, and his wife, Rena, are both friendly and ready to help; George is a Parian native and knows the island like the back of his hand. They offer bright, clean rooms with fridges, ceiling fans, baths, and balconies. Open year-round. Free luggage deposit. Doubles €18-39; triples €27-45. 20% discount for *Let's Go* readers. ❸

Festos Pension (☎22840 21 635; fax 22840 24 193). From the dock, walk to the left of the windmill, and take a right toward the Church of 100 Gates; take another right at the end of the road. Simplicity is the rule here; bare rooms come with basic private bath. Inexpensive and well-located. Laundry €3-5. Luggage storage €1. Breakfast included. 4-bed dorm €10; singles €20; doubles €30. ❷

Pelagos Studios (☎22840 22 725; fax 22840 22 708). Find Vassilis, the owner, in the port, or call and get picked up. Furnished rooms with kitchens, baths, TVs, and radios. Barbecues on the patio contribute to familial atmosphere. Convenient to Pariokia's nightlife, despite its peaceful setting. Breakfast €3. Doubles €30-50; triples €58. ❹

Parian Village (☎22840 23 187; inter@otenet.gr), about 1km north of the port; public buses run past the site on the way to Krios beach. A bit out of the way, but almost every room has a spectacular view of the city. A/C, phones, fridges, and Parian marble decoration come standard. Cafe has simple dishes and breakfast (€1.50-4). Singles €36-65; doubles €44-77; triples €59-103. ❹

Parasporos Camping (☎22840 22 268 or 22840 21 100), 1.5km south of the port; shuttle service available. Away from the bustle, beside Delphini beach. Showers, laundry, and kitchen. €6 per person; €3 per tent, €4.50 tent rental. ❶

Koula Camping (☎22840 22 081; fax 22840 22 740), 400m north of the dock, across the street from the pebbly town beach. A bustling vibe makes this site a fun place to hang out. Market, laundry, and kitchen. €5 per person; €3.50 per tent rental. ❶

CYCLADES

FOOD

Happy Green Cow (☎22840 24 691), a block inland off the plateia in the narrow walkway behind the National Bank. Vegetarian food in a psychedelic setting designed by the artist-owners. The Cow's Orgasms (pastries with cheese and peppers; €9.50) probably won't have the desired effect on cows, but they are delicious. Seafood options are also available. Open daily 7pm-midnight. ❸

Nick's Hamburgers (☎22840 21 434). Walk right from the port; it's tucked away in one of the plateias. Paros's first hamburger joint, established in 1977, serves enormous burgers and a variety of other non-Greek dishes (hot dogs, fish and chips). Nikfeast (2 burgers, chips, and salad) €3.80, fish and chips €3.25. Open daily 11am-2am. ❶

Porphyra (☎22840 23 410), next to the ancient cemetary on the right side of the waterfront. Serving seafood exclusively, Porphyra definitely offers some dishes you've never heard of, including the namesake *porphyra* (the inhabitant of a conch shell; €8.50). Also offers the closest thing to a raw bar that you'll find in Greece (raw oysters €6; raw clams €7). Open Mar.-Oct. 6:30am-12:30am. ❷

Ephesus (☎22840 21 491), behind the hospital. Combining Anatolian and Greek cooking, Ephesus serves up unique dishes you won't find at the generic taverna. The stuffed pitas (€5-6.50) loaded with toppings are deliciously messy. Kebabs with a variety of sauces are also available (€5.50-7.50). Open 10am-midnight. ❷

Apollon Garden Restaurant (☎22840 21 875). Follow Market St. away from the main plateias and keep an eye out for the signs. It's not cheap, but the enthralling garden and food are worth it. Most dishes are rotated each season, but the favorites are kept throughout the year. Chicken with mango €12.50; catch-of-the-day €6 for 1, €11 for 2. Open daily 6pm-1am. ❸

SIGHTS AND MUSEUMS

PANAGIA EKATONTAPILIANI. The **Church of Our Lady of 100 Gates** looms over Parikia's plateia in the shape of an imperfect Greek cross. Tradition holds that only 99 of the church's 100 doors can be counted—when the 100th appears, Constantinople will once again belong to the Greeks (conversely, if a door disappears, the 2004 Olympics move to Ankara). The Ekatontapiliani was supposedly conceived in the 4th century AD when **St. Helen,** the mother of Constantine, stopped here on her way to the Holy Land. While praying, Helen saw the True Cross and vowed to build a church befitting the site of her vision. She died before she could fulfill her promise, but in the 6th century, the Emperor Justinian commissioned young Ignatius, student of Isidorus of Miletus, to build her church. According to legend, the church's beauty drove Isidorus to a fit of jealousy, and both men died in the scuffle that ensued. The repentant architects can be seen bemoaning their fate on the sculpted bases of the columns across the courtyard. The main structure of the complex is the mammoth **Church of the Assumption.** The **Church of Agios Nikolaos** (the oldest of the three) and the **baptistry** flank this centerpiece to the north and south, respectively. A **museum** displays 17th century religious icons. Dress modestly: long pants for men, long skirts for women, and no bare shoulders. *(Church open daily 7am-11pm, free. Museum open daily 8:30am-10:30pm, €1.50.)*

CYCLADES

OTHER SIGHTS. The collection at the **Parikia Archaeological Museum** contains more prized pieces than your average antiquities museum, including a 5th-century BC statue of wingless Nike, a large gryphon sculpture, and a piece of the marble **Parian Chronicle,** a history of Greece up to 264 BC. *(Behind the church next to the schoolyard. ☎22840 21 231. Open Tu-Su 8:30am-2:45pm. €2, students €1, EU students free.)* A ramble through the Old Town will inevitably lead you past the lone remaining wall of the Venetian **Frankish Castle,** where you can see sections of marble and columns removed from the ancient Temple of Athena.

NIGHTLIFE AND ENTERTAINMENT

The waterfront is the home of pulsing Parian nightlife. Throngs assemble on the sidewalk or the beach, sharing booze and singing songs. Toward midnight, the tourist traffic forms a stream flowing toward the thicket of clubs that sit at the edge of town. **Pirate Blues and Jazz,** tucked away in the Old Town, anchors several mellow cafes where you'll find eclectic music offerings. (Beer €3, cocktails €7, wine €3. Open daily 7pm-3am.) The cafes are away from the dock, along the waterfront. **Saloon D'Or,** a popular cafe playing the greatest hits of the 70s and 80s, fills nightly with travelers. The **Parian Experience** consists of a sweaty, pulsating party complex that rounds out any night on Paros. Follow the spotlight and crowds to the far end of the harbor where **The Dubliner, Down Under, Comma Club,** and the **Paros Rock Cafe** all sit under one roof. Sit around or dance to any of the four simultaneously playing tunes. (Beer €2-3, cocktails €5. €3 cover subtracted from your first drink.) The subtle **Fun Club** next door offers a similar environment. If a night of boozing doesn't thrill you, outdoor **Cine Rex,** to the left of the dock along the waterfront, and **Cine Paros,** two blocks past the post office, show American movies; check signs in the plateia (2 showings per evening, €6).

BEACHES

Paros is a small place, so almost every beach on the island can be reached in under an hour's drive. In the immediate area of Parikia, though, there are some outstanding and easily accessible beaches. **Parasporos** lies a couple kilometers to the south and attracts only the occasional guest from a nearby resort (take the bus to Pounda, every hour). **Krios** beach lies across the harbor from Parikia. The sand is less pebbly and more welcoming than the beaches in town. It is accessible by bus (3 per day) and taxi boat (every 30min. from 9:30am-7pm, round-trip ticket €2).

DAYTRIPS FROM PARIKIA

MARATHI

Buses run to Marathi, on the way to several destinations, every other hour. From the bus stop, signs will direct you to the quarries.

Five kilometers from Parikia in the center of the island, Marathi is home to Paros's idle marble quarries. Still considered to be among the finest in the world, Parian marble is translucent up to 3mm-thick, with one-third the opacity of most other marble. A visit to the quarries is a serious undertaking: bring a flashlight, strong shoes, and don't go alone. Nearby **Lefkes,** 5km from Marathi, was the largest village on the island through the 19th century, as Parians moved inland to escape plundering coastal pirates. Today, it's a quiet village of 400 inhabitants with classic Cycladic architecture, the most attractive and unspoiled town in Paros's interior.

VALLEY OF THE BUTTERFLIES

Take the bus from Parikia to Aliki (10min., 8 per day, €0.80) and ask to be dropped off at Petaloudes. Follow the signs up the steep winding road 2km to the entrance. Open M-Sa 9am-8pm. €1.50.

Just 10km south of town is the cool, spring-fed Valley of the Butterflies, or **Petaloudes,** where the rare (and tongue-twisting) *Panaxiaquadripunctaria* moth congregates in massive numbers during its mating season, from June to late September. Every summer the moths return to mate, sleeping on the bushes during the day, and getting busy at night. The moths do not eat for their entire mating season, so they can ill afford to expend energy entertaining photo-hungry guests. Be respectful: don't clap or talk loudly, and don't shake the bushes.

CYCLADES

NAOUSSA Ναουσσα

Naoussa is Paros's second port, a natural harbor cradled by long, sandy beaches in the shape of crab claws. Persian, Greek, Roman, Venetian, Ottoman, and Russian fleets have anchored here over the years, and the tradition continues today as visitors from all over the world converge on Naoussa's beaches.

ORIENTATION AND PRACTICAL INFORMATION. Naoussa is easy to navigate. From the bus stop facing the water, the main road out of town is to the left and leads to the beaches of **Kolimbithres** and **Monastiri.** Buses go to the nude beach at **Laggeri.** Walking away from the water past the bus station takes you along a street with a river (more a stream) by it. To the right is a busy commercial street with Old Town just beyond it.

Buses run continuously between **Parikia** and Naoussa (15min., every 30min., €0.95). There are also buses from Naoussa to: **Ampelas** (4 per day, €0.80); **Drios** (15 per day, €1.50); and **Santa Maria** (4 per day, €0.80). Check the schedule at the bus stop booth. **Taxi boats** leave Naoussa for nearby beaches. The blue booth across from the cafes on the waterfront sells round-trip tickets to: **Kolimbithres** (12min., every 30min. 10am-8pm, €2.50); **Laggeri** (20min., every 40min., €3.50); **Monastiri** (15min., every 30min., €33); and **Santa Maria** (40min., 1 per day, €7). **Taxis** (☎22840 53 490) are available next to the bus stop.

Naoussa's **tourist office,** across from the bus stop by the bridge, offers general information on the town and its accommodations. (☎22840 52 158. Open May-Sept. 15 10:30am-6:30pm.) For more specific advice about where to stay and how to get around in Naoussa and Paros, pop into **Free Spirit Travel Agency.** For equiphiles, the agency can arrange beachside **horseback riding.** (☎22840 52 251 or 22840 53 391; fax 22840 52 294; frspirit@hellasnet.gr.) A **National Bank** is along the marina. (☎22840 51 438. Open M-Th 8:30am-2pm, F 8:30am-1:30pm.) Past the bus stop on the main road is the **General Bookstore,** selling international magazines and some books in English. (☎22840 51 532. Open daily 10am-midnight.) To find the 24hr. **police** station (☎22840 51 202), walk along the main road out of town and turn left up a large set of stairs across from the beach. The station is on the road at the top of the stairs. The **pharmacy** is on the main street inland. (☎22840 51 550; **emergencies** ☎22840 51 004. Open daily 8:30am-2pm and 5-11pm.) A **medical center** is near the bus stop on the main road (☎22840 52 304); the doctor is available 9am-10pm. The **OTE** is at the bottom of the stairs by the police station. (Open M-F 7:30am-3pm.) The **post office** is 400m past the bookstore, just beyond the Santa Maria turn-off. (☎22840 21 236. Open M-F 7:30am-2pm.) **Postal code:** 84401.

CYCLADES

ACCOMMODATIONS. For a small town, Naoussa has many places to sleep, but package-tour groups book most hotels months in advance. Rooms to let cost roughly €25-40 for doubles and €30-45 for triples; ask at the tourist office for help. **Villa Galini** ❸ is inland past the bus stop and 700m to the right. Signs mark the way. Airy rooms with private baths, phones, and fridges make your stay comfortable; the gregarious owner makes it quite pleasant. Call several days in advance for a free shuttle from the port at Parikia. (☎22840 53 335; fax 22840 53 336. Open Apr.-Sept. Doubles €20-40.) To the right of the waterfront with your back to the water lie a number of upscale pensions with spectacular views of the harbor. To reach **Pension Hara** ❹, walk along the main road out of town 300m past the port and climb the stairs that lead to the police station. You'll find impeccably clean rooms with balconies, TVs, and fridges, only 150m away from the beach. (☎22840 51 011. Doubles €40-60.) Around the corner to the right and up the hill a short distance is **Sakis Rooms** ❹, with luxurious lodgings including private baths, TVs, A/C, fridges, and balconies overlooking the sea. (☎22840 52 171; fax 22840 24 365; www.paros-online.com. Doubles €30-60; 5-person apartments €50-130.) The upscale **Atlantis Hotel** ❹ sits just around the corner from the bus station on the road out of town. Rooms are equipped with the works (A/C, phones, baths, fridges) and are complemented by a pool and jacuzzi in the pleasant garden area. (☎22840 51 340. Doubles €40-70; triples €45-85.) **Camping Naoussa** ❶ is on the road to Kolimbithres. Call for the port shuttle. (☎22840 51 595. €5 per person; €4 per tent; €6 per tent rental.) **Camping Surfing beach** ❶, 4km toward Santa Maria, offers watersports. (☎22840 51 013 or 22840 51 491; fax 22840 51 937. €6.75 per person; €3.25 per tent; €5.25 tent rental; €2 per car, €1.50 per bike.)

FOOD AND ENTERTAINMENT. Naoussan kitchens cook up famously delicious seafood; their local specialty is the fish plate called *gouna*. **Diamantis** ❷, behind the church on the commerce road about 300m from the bus station, is an excellent choice for Greek fare. Feast on the restaurant's specialty, lamb *Diamantis*, stuffed with feta cheese, tomatoes, peppers, and onions (€6.50). **Pervolaria** ❷ is a garden restaurant offering peaceful seclusion, about 200m inland on the road along the stream. (☎22840 52 490. Open daily 7pm until late. Calamari *al pesto* €5.50, avocado with shrimp €6.50.) Right across from the pretty little fishing boats on the water, **Moufagio** ❷ is a seafood-and-potatoes type taverna. Sitting under a fragrant hanging octopus, you'll enjoy a variety of seafood coming in from the boats across the way. (☎22840 51 405. Crab €5, fish egg salad €2. Open 9am-midnight.) For unbeatable *loukamades* (€2), turn left off the commercial street at the Naoussa pastry shop, and continue past the white church to **To Paradosiako** ❶ (open 5:30pm-1am).

There are several laid-back cafes and bars mixed in with the tavernas—look for dimmed lights and listen for the beat. Up the road with a stream a bit, a number of dance clubs grind away late into the night. **Varelathiko** is a huge wooden disco that draws crowds to its fun outdoor deck. Reminiscent of an old-fashioned barn, the place is decorated with wine barrels and lanterns hanging from the ceiling. (Cocktails €6. Cover €1.) Neigh-boring **Privilege** and **Nostos** share dance-hungry patrons. The **Aqua Paros** water park at Kolimbithres is a pricey option for water-slide aficionados (☎22840 53 271). On the first or second Sunday in July, eat, drink, and be merry as you cruise around Naoussa's harbor and watch traditional dancing at the **Wine and Fish Festival;** call the tourist office for details.

EASTERN COAST OF PAROS

Road meets sea at **Piso Livadi,** 11km from Lefkes. If Parikia's nightlife is not your bag, Piso Livadi is close to Paros's nicest beaches (from **Logara** to **Krissi Akti**), which will warm your heart and roast your skin. There isn't much in terms of Parian culture to find around here, but the water is fine. **Perantinos Travel & Tourism,** across from the bus stop, provides information on accommodations as well as an international phone. (☎/fax 22840 41 135. Open daily 9am-10pm.) In general, doubles run from €35-50, depending on the season and quality. Up the street from the bus stop toward Parikia are two simple hotels. **Hotel Piso Livadi ❸** (☎22840 41 387) offers doubles with bath for €36-49 and triples with bath for €41-59. The **Londos Hotel ❹** has doubles and triples. (☎22840 41 218. Doubles €45.)

CYCLADES

ANTIPAROS Αντιπαρος

Literally "opposite Paros," Antiparos is so close to its neighbor that, according to local lore, travelers once signaled the ferryman on Paros by opening the door of a chapel on Antiparos. The small island is mostly undeveloped, with a modest population to match Antiparos's size. Most travelers encounter Antiparos as a daytrip to see the caves, but it's easy to find a place to stay in the quiet capital or near the beaches of this tiny island, which makes even peaceful Paros look frenetic.

ANTIPAROS TOWN Αντιπαρος

Virtually all of the island's 900 inhabitants live in town, where the ferry docks and most accommodations are found.

ORIENTATION AND PRACTICAL INFORMATION. You'll arrive in Antiparos Town by ferry; a few waterfront restaurants and several hotels and pensions are at the harbor. Tourist shops, tavernas, and bakeries line the street leading from the dock to the tree-shaded central plateia, where a cluster of bars and cafes have opened. Go through the stone archway to the right of the plateia to reach the **Castle of Antiparos,** a village built in the 15th century. Take a direct **ferry** from **Parikia** (30min., 15 per day, €2) or a bus to **Pounta** (15min., 15 per day, €0.80), followed by a boat to Antiparos (10min., 30 per day, €0.55). The only **bus** service on the island goes to the stalactite caves.

Waterfront **Oliaros Tours** assists with finding rooms and has boat and bus schedules, **Internet access** (€6 per hr.), and **currency exchange.** (☎22840 61 231 or, in off season, 22840 61 189. Open M-Sa 9am-10:30pm, Su 9am-2pm and 5:30-9pm.) The **National Bank** is open only in high season (M-F 9am-1pm). The self-service **laundry** is behind the windmill. (Open 10am-2pm and 5-8pm. Wash, dry, and soap €8.) Call the **police** at ☎22840 61 202 or a **doctor** at ☎22840 61 219. The **post office** is on the left side of the street leading from the waterfront to the plateia. (Open M-F 7:30am-12:30pm.) **Postal code** 84007.

ACCOMMODATIONS AND CAMPING. The **Mantalena Hotel ❹,** to the right of the dock when facing inland, has recently renovated rooms with private baths, fridges, A/C, and balconies, some of which afford a fantastic sea view. A family-owned establishment for 37 years, the hotel welcomes guests with island savvy and tasty *kourabiethes*, almond cookies. (☎22840 61 206; fax 22840 61 550. Doubles €35-60; triples €42-72.) At **Hotel Antiparos ❸,** the rooms come with a fine selection of amenities (A/C, kitchens, balconies, phones) and are a great bargain. (☎22840 61 358; fax 22840 61 340. Breakfast €4. Doubles €20-30; triples €24-36.) To the right of the harbor facing inland, around the bend on the road to Camping Antiparos, **Theologos Rooms to Let ❸** offers sunny rooms with gleaming bathrooms and balconies. (☎22840 61 244; fax 22840 61 045. Breakfast €2.50. Doubles €20-40; triples €35-55.) **Camping Antiparos ❶** is 800m northwest of town, on the well-marked way to Ag. Yiannis Theologos beach. The beachside site, adjacent to the nightclub, has its own mini-market and restaurant. (☎22840 61 221. Open May-Sept. €3.75 per person.)

FOOD AND ENTERTAINMENT. The restaurants of Antiparos Town serve fresh fish pulled from the same sea that you'll gaze at while eating. Inside town, **Taverna Klimataria ❶** trades in the sea view for an idyllic garden setting, roofed with blazing pink azaleas. The meat and many of the other ingredients come from the proprietor's farm, providing customers with fresh, cheap food. Head down the main street and turn left down the alley next to the bookstore. (☎22840 61 298. Most entrees under €5. Open June-Sept. 5pm-1am.) Open for all-day service on the waterfront, **O Spyros ❷** and **Amargyros ❷** turn the catch of the day into traditional dishes. (Entrees €6-7.) For a post-meal, pre-pub stop, **The Shipwreck ❶,** just past the post office, has a variety of intriguing desserts and gentle tunes on the stereo. (☎22840 61 012. Frappes €2.10, crepes €2-4. Open 9am-3am.) Following the lead of neighboring islands, Antiparos's plateia is packed with rock-and-roll watering holes. Late night, choose your favorite from among **Time Pub, The Stones, The Doors,** and others which may or may not be named after drug-addled bands (beer €2-3). **Cafe Yam,** on the alley next to the bookstore, is badly named but still a trendy spot to sip a cocktail. (Beer €3, cocktails €5. Open daily 10pm-2am.)

SIGHTS AND BEACHES. The cool, wet stalactite **caves** at the south end of the island are Antiparos's main attraction. (Open daily 10am-3:30pm. €3.) Names of famous visitors are written on the walls with their years of entry. Unfortunately, some of the stalactites were broken off by Russian naval officers in the 18th century and "borrowed" on behalf of a St. Petersburg museum, while still more were destroyed by Italians during World War II. Despite all this defilement, the caves, which plunge 100m into the earth, are simply beautiful. The site doesn't offer any postings about its peculiar history. Ask the ticket vendor to tell stories; he will if he's in the mood. Excursion **buses** (20min., round-trip €3.50) run from Antiparos Town's port every hour from morning through early afternoon. **Psaraliki beach,** just to the south of town, is a pleasant place to bathe, as is **Glifa,** to the east.

AMORGOS Αμοργος

Much of Amorgos resembles its most enduring symbol, the Hozoviotissas Monastery, which burrows into the cliffs near Hora. The steep cliffs and clear waters were captured 20 years ago in the film *The Big Blue (Le Grand Bleu);* they remain just as startlingly big and blue now. King Minos of Crete was said to rule a kingdom on Amorgos in ancient times; a 1985 discovery of artifacts atop Mt. Moudoulia affirmed the legend of Minoan rule. Despite the recent growth of tourism,

Amorgos's relative inaccessability and a local community unwilling to commercialize have preserved the pervasive peace. Infrequent ferry connections generally stop at Amorgos's two ports in succession—**Aegiali** in the northeast and the larger **Katapola** in the southwest. Be sure to disembark at the right port.

KATAPOLA Καταπολα

The island's central port waves to visitors with its windmill arms. Whitewashed houses, narrow streets, and the overhanging Venetian castle make up little Katapola. It's free of the bustle of many other Cycladic port towns, and, even as Amorgos grows more touristed, the town retains a serene, communal atmosphere: the whole town might spend the night gathered together in front of a football game or sipping ouzo and listening to traditional Greek music.

ORIENTATION AND PRACTICAL INFORMATION. **Ferries** from both ports of Amorgos go to: **Astypalea** (3hr., 3 per week, €9.26); **Donousa** (1½hr., 5 per week, €4.50); **Koufonisia** (5 per week, €5.20); **Mykonos** (2 per week, €9.50); **Naxos** (3-6hr., 1 per day, €7.70); **Paros** (4hr., 1 per day, €8.50); **Piraeus** (10hr., 1 per day, €17); **Schinousa** (5 per week, €6.80); **Syros** (4½hr., 4 per week, €11.20); and **Tinos** (3½hr., 2 per week, €9.50). A **hydrofoil** zooms to **Rafina** once a week (3hr., €32). Frequent **buses** connect villages in summer, running from Katapola to: **Aegiali** (45min., 6 per day, €1.50); **Agia Anna** (25min., every hr., €0.80); **Hora** (15min., 1 per hr., €0.80); **Hozoviotissas Monastery** (20min., €0.80), and to several beaches (around €0.80). For **taxis,** call ☎22850 71 255.

The town surrounds the ferry dock in a horseshoe shape, with restaurants, bars, and accommodations on either side. The large port rests at the center; most tourist services are between the ferry dock and the road to Hora. Across from the ferry dock is **Synodinos Tours,** which **exchanges currency,** has an international **telephone, sells tickets** to ferries and hydrofoils, and **rents cars.** (☎22850 71 201 or 22850 71 747; fax 22850 71 278. Open daily 8am-2pm and 6-10pm in low season, 8am-10pm in high season.) Since there is a limited **post office** (open M, W, F 10am-1pm) and **no OTE** in Katapola, Synodinos Tours sells stamps and phone cards and handles registered mail. **Agricultural Bank,** across from the ferries, has a 24hr. **ATM.** (M-Th 8am-2pm, F 8am-1:30pm.) The **police** (☎22850 71 210) and **port police** (☎22850 71 259; open 24hr.) are on the right on a side street heading inland from the main plateia. The nearest **pharmacy** is in Hora. The **medical center** is at the far left end of the waterfront, in the white building behind the two statues. For **medical emergencies** dial ☎22850 71 805. There is a **laundromat** inland at the left of the waterfront. (☎22850 71 723. Open M-Sa 8:30am-2:30pm and 6-10pm.) **Public toilets** are at the start of the town beach across from **Amorgos Motor Center. Internet access** can be found in a cafe in the central plateia. **Postal code:** 84008.

ACCOMMODATIONS AND FOOD. Katapola is a small town with few hotels and many pensions. **Pension Amorgos ❹,** at the left of the plateia above the cafes, is close to the water and has a rooftop veranda with a view. (☎22850 71 013 or 22850 71 350. Doubles €50 or studios €55; 15-20% less in low season.) To reach **Big Blue Pension ❸** from the ferry dock, walk toward town, turn right after the plateia and follow signs. The pension, one of many establishments cashing in on the popularity of the French film *The Big Blue*, is indeed big, with blue windows and doors. Private bath, fridges and port shuttle available. (☎/fax 22850 71 094. Double rooms for around €30.) **Titika Rooms ❸** sits under grape and flower trellises at the far right end of the beach. Port shuttle and rooms with private bath. (☎/fax 22850 71 660. Doubles €40; triples €47.)

CYCLADES

Like the island itself, Katapola's nightlife is calm and soothing. Cafes and bars are open all day, dispensing ouzo and beer amidst cool sea breezes. Dining options tend toward simple, high-quality tavernas that are easy on the wallet. **Aigaion Cafe ❶,** in the center of the main plateia, serves fruit juices, crepes, omelettes, and homemade sweets during the day and stays open to serve coffee and drinks at night. (☎22850 71 549. Open daily 8am-late in summer; off season 9am-midnight.) **Mourayio ❶,** across from the bus stop, crowds early and empties late. The restaurant stuffs smiling diners with local specialties like octopus (€5.50) and *fava* with veggies and potatoes (€3.50). (☎22850 71 011. Live Greek folk music. Open daily noon-2am.) As always, the farther from the dock, the less touristy the eatery, so be sure to follow the road around to the restaurants opposite the port.

SIGHTS AND BEACHES. In front of Katapola's main church, a sign points to a 40min. hike to the ancient town of **Minoa,** inhabited between the 10th and 4th centuries BC. Look for the base of the temple among the ruins and the bust of a statue rising from within—the barely distinguishable acropolis once stood on the plateau above the temple. Various nude **beaches** provide sand and sun outside of town, opposite the dock. Smooth-stoned, bare-skinned **Plakes** and **Agios Panteleimonas** are quiet, yet easily accessible by foot or boat.

DAYTRIP FROM KATAPOLA. A trip to Amorgos is incomplete without a visit to otherworldly **Hozoviotissas Monastery**—one of the most exhilarating spectacles in all of Greece and an inspiration to Le Corbusier, among others. Built into the sheer face of the cliff, the 11th-century Byzantine edifice looks like a whitewashed epiphyte. Legend has it that attempts to build the monastery on the shore were thwarted; when the workers discovered their tools inexplicably hanging from the cliff, they figured it was an omen and started construction there. If you complete the hike (up 350 stairs), the monks may treat you to cold water, *raki*, and *loukoumi* (Greek sweets). To see more of the building, come in November when the entire island celebrates the **feast** of Panagia Hozoviotissa at the monastery. If you miss the bus back, take the stone stairway (10m uphill from the fork in the road leading away from the monastery). A 15min. climb up the stairs will lead you back to Hora. The road from the monastery also takes you to the crystal waters of **Agia Anna** and its two beaches; from the bus stop, one is at the end of the path through the clearing, the other at the bottom of the central steps. Catch a bus from Katapola to the monastery. (☎22850 71 274. Open daily 8am-1pm and 5-7pm. Dress modestly: skirts for women, long pants for men, no bare shoulders.)

HORA Χωρα

Katapola means "below the town"—the town is Hora. Also known as Amorgos Town, the island's capital lies 6km from the harbor along the island's only significant paved road. A fine example of Byzantine village planning, Hora's winding streets were constructed to deter and confuse raiding pirates; they now allow visitors to meander along the cafe-lined walk to **Pl. Loza,** at the far end of town. Sights include a 14th-century Venetian **fortress,** a row of retired windmills perched on the mountain ledge above town, Byzantine churches, and the first secondary school in Greece, built in 1829 (on your left as you head up to OTE).

Hora is home to Amorgos's main **post office,** tucked in a corner up from Pl. Loza (☎22850 71 250; open M-F 7:30am-2pm), and its main **OTE,** on the right at the top of town (☎22850 71 339 or 22850 71 099; open M-F 8am-2pm). The **police** are in the main plateia with the big church, next to Cafe Loza. (☎22850 71 210. Open 8am-midnight.) The **medical center** is on the main road into Hora from Katapola. (☎22850 71 207. Open 24hr.) If you decide to spend the night, you can strike a deal with the domatia owners that meet your boat, or look for "Rooms to Let" signs in town. **Maria Economidou ❹** has beautifully furnished rooms with balconies. (☎22850 71 111; kstp@otenet.gr. Private baths and kitchenettes. Doubles €38-45.) **Pension Kastanis ❹,** located next door, offers similar lodging. (☎22850 71 277. €35-45.) Both establishments offer a shuttle from the port if you call ahead.

Liotrivi ❶ (☎22850 71 700; most entrees €6), below the bus station, prepares delicious twists on Greek standards—*kalogiros* (eggplant with veal, cheese, and tomato) and *exohiko* (lamb and vegetables in pastry shell) are the house specialities. **Zygos ❶** (☎22850 71 350) serves peerless apple pie (€2) and often has live music and dancing until 5am. **Vegara** is an eclectic cafe-bar accented by *kargiosi* (shadow theater figures) on the walls and world music on the speakers. (☎22850 74 017. Open daily 9am-3am.) The newly renovated **Bayoko,** right by the bus station, is a good place to catch the sunset over the bay below, sip an ouzo or two, and, once the moon is out, dance the night away to Greek and international pop hits. For a bit of history, drop by the **archaeological museum,** downhill from the large church. Peer into a giant vase encasing skeletal fragments, or check out the remnants of Amorgos's Minoan civilization. (Open 9am-1pm and 5-7pm. Free.)

HIKE FROM HORA. Rugged mountains and a placid coast run alongside the road from Hora to Aegiali. The 4hr. hike begins behind Hora and stretches up the mountains to the village of Potamos. Forty minutes into the hike, you'll find the crumbling Byzantine church of **Christososmas** (The Body of Christ), hewn out of a small cave that was once a hermit dwelling. The trail ascends past a series of monasteries before descending to views of miniature **Nikouria** island, which swimmers can reach from the beach by the main road. Lonely and deserted **Ag. Mammas** church is the last significant marker before Potamos appears.

AEGIALI Αιγιαλη

Aegiali, the island's other port, is as close as Amorgos comes to feeling touristy. As a result, the locals seem a little wearier of travelers than on other parts of the island. With a town beach and numerous rooming and camping opportunities, leisurely Aegiali serves as a base for exploring the island's northern parts.

ORIENTATION AND PRACTICAL INFORMATION. Aegiali is built up the slope of the mountain foothills. Most tourist facilities are along the waterfront. Facing inland, clubs are to the left along the beach, cafes are to the right. **Nautilus Travel** handles all ferries, **currency exchange,** and other travel services. Across the street, **Aegialis Tours** (☎22850 73 394; fax 22850 73 395) handles accommodations, car rental, bus and boat excursions, and stores luggage. Both agencies are just inland from the waterfront. For **ferry** and **Flying Dolphin** schedules, see the listings for Katapola (p. 435). **Buses** run between: **Aegiali-Hora-Katapola** (3 per day, €1.50); **Meria-Hora-Katapola** (2 per day, €0.80); **Ormos-Lagada** (6 per day, €0.80); and **Tholaria** (4 per day, €0.80). Note that there is **no bank** or reliable **post office** in Aegiali. The **police** (☎22850 73 320) are located in Langada; the **port police** are active in Aegiali during the summer. A **first aid station** is above the town, near the road to Potamos. (☎22850 73 222. Open 9am-1:30pm; available 24hr. for emergencies.) A **pharmacy** (☎22850 73 173) is up the road by the Island Market, on the right; **phones** are next door. **Taxis** (☎22850 73 003 or 22850 73 570) wait at the end of the beach.

ACCOMMODATIONS AND CAMPING. Lakki Village ❹, at the left side of the beach, has rooms and apartments with private baths, balconies, and phones; some include A/C and television. The hotel, owned by the Gavala family, exudes a friendly, resort-like atmosphere. (☎22850 73 253; fax 22850 73 244; lakki@aigialis.com. Breakfast included; laundry service and port shuttle available. Singles €29 and up; doubles €38-55.) **Camping Aegiali ❶** (☎22850 73 500; fax 22850 73 244) is just outside town, near the road to Tholaria. It is a 10min. walk from the port and beach but provides free port pickup and drop-off. The site boasts laundry and cooking facilities, safety deposit boxes, showers, a restaurant, and a bar. (☎22850 73 500. €3.50 per person; tent rental €2.) You can also look for "Rooms for Rent" signs going up the paths in the middle of town. **Pension Christina ❹** (☎22850 73 263; fax 22850 73 109) and **Poseidon Studies ❹** (☎22850 73 007) are both up the main pathway and to the right. At these establishments, you'll find clean rooms with balconies and private baths (doubles €45-55).

FOOD AND NIGHTLIFE. **Lakki Village Restaurant ❶** (☎22850 73 253) offers delicious homegrown vegetables and souvlaki (€5) grilled in the open air. **To Steki ❷,** at the edge of the beach, serves Greek dinners for €9-11 and some expensive fish specialties for €30 and up. (☎22850 73 003. Open daily 6am-2am.) Follow the signs (and your nose) uphill from the waterfront to the aromatic **Artopio Bakery ❶** (☎22850 73 225), serving yummy and sticky pastries. Cut loose under the stars at **Delear** (☎22850 73 205), a club just down the beach from To Steki. You can relax by the port at **To Nimani** (☎22850 73 269), where, under flowery trees in the summer, you can feast on simple but quite tasty lamb and potatoes (€4.80).

IOS Ιος

If you're not drunk when you arrive, you will be when you leave. On Ios, beers go down and clothes come off faster than you can say "Opa!" You'll see everything your mother warned you about—wine being swilled from the bottle at 3pm, drinking games all day along the beach, men and women dancing madly in the streets, people swimming less than 30min. after they've eaten, and so much more. The island has settled down a bit in the past few years, making a sincere and successful effort to bring families and the older set to enjoy its more peaceful side. Of its 36 beaches, only three have been fully developed for tourism, so there's plenty of unexplored territory. Those in search of quieter pleasures stay in **Yialos** (the port), while the party animals cavort in **Hora.** Still, visitors to this mecca should prepare for loud music, hangovers, and the lustful stares of the inebriated.

TRANSPORTATION

Ferries: To: **Anafi** (3hr., 2 per week, €8.92); **Folegandros** (1hr., 5 per week, €5.13); **Mykonos** (4hr., daily, €11.64); **Naxos** (1¾hr., at least 3 per day, €7.32); **Paros** (3hr., at least 3 per day, €8.32); **Piraeus** (8hr., at least 3 per day, €17.92); **Santorini** (1¼hr., 3 per day, €5.62); **Sifnos** (3 per week, €10.02); **Sikinos** (30min., 2 per week, €10.02); **Syros** (4hr., 5 per week, €15.03). Once a week, ferries go to **Iraklion** on Crete (6hr., €15.50); **Skiathos** (€28.10); **Skopelos** (€27.58); **Thessaloniki** (22hr., €31.06); **Tinos** (€12.66).

Flying Dolphins: Catamarans are twice the speed and twice the price of ferries. To: **Iraklion** on Crete (2½hr., 3 per week); **Milos** (4hr., 1 per week); **Mykonos** (2hr., daily, €22.82); **Naxos** (45min., daily, €14.12); **Paros** (1½hr., 4 per week, €16.22); **Rafina** (3½hr., 5 per week); **Santorini** (45min., daily, €10.92); **Tinos** (2hr., 4 per week).

Rentals: Jacob's Moto Rent (☎/fax 22860 91 047), by the bus stop at the port. Bikes €12; small cars €38. **Ios Rent-A-Car** (☎22860 92 300), located in Acteon Travel in the port, offers similar rates. Other agencies are scattered about.

PRACTICAL INFORMATION

The action goes down around three locations, each 20min. apart along the island's paved road. The **port,** or **Yialos** (Γιαλος), is at one end; the **village,** or **Hora** (Χωρα), sits above it on a hill; frenzied **Mylopotas beach** is 3km farther. During the day, the winding streets behind the church are filled with charming wares and postcard pushers; as the sun sets, they become the focus of nocturnal activity. Buses shuttle between port, village and beach (every 10-20min. 7am-midnight, €0.80).

Tourist Information: Acteon Travel (☎22860 91 343; fax 22860 91 088). The main office is adjacent to the bus stop, but booths are set up all over the island. Sells **ferry tickets,** offers info on accommodations, and has **currency exchange,** vehicle rental, luggage storage and safety deposit boxes.

Banks: In the village, **National Bank** (☎22860 91 565), next to the main church, has an **ATM** and handles all your MasterCard needs. Open M-Th 8am-2pm, F 8am-1:30pm. The **Commercial Bank** (☎22860 91 474), by the main plateia next to the Lemon Club, has 24hr. **ATM.** There is an **ATM** at the port, to your left as you disembark from the ferry, and at Mylopotas beach, in the Acteon Travel office.

Laundry: Sweet Irish Dream Laundry (☎22860 91 584), next to the club of the same name. Wash and dry full load €8; half load €6. Drop-off laundry services also available at **Far Out Beach Club.**

Police: (☎22860 91 222), on the road to Kolitsani beach, past the OTE. Open 24hr.

Port Authority: (☎22860 91 264), at far end of the harbor by Camping Ios. Open 24hr.

Medical Center: (☎22860 91 227), in new facilities at the port, 100m from the dock. Specializes in drunken mishaps. Open daily 9am-1pm and 6-7pm. In Hora, reach 3 different **doctors** at ☎22860 92 545, 22860 91 137, or 22860 92 227. All 3 have offices in a row next to the **pharmacy** (☎22860 91 562 or 22860 92 112; open daily 9am-2:30pm and 5-10:30pm).

Internet Access: Located all over the port and village. At the port, **Acteon Travel** charges €6 per hr., with a €1.50 minimum. Open daily 7:30am-midnight. In the village, **Francesco's** (€1.50 per 15min.) and **Hotel Sunrise** (€0.10 per min.) have Internet access. On Mylopotas beach, **Far Out Beach Club** offers access for €0.10 per min.

Gym: Ios Gym, by the basketball courts. €6 per day; €25 per week. **Postal code:** 84001.

LIVING DAY TO DAY

D.C.-native Beatrice Robbins is a receptionist and bartender at Francesco's in Hora. She spoke with Let's Go on June 15, 2002.

Q: You've spent 5 years on Ios now. You must have some great stories.

A: Yeah. Well, we had this one Swedish regular who got stopped at customs on his way here. They opened his bag, and they took out 3 clown wigs, 2 Super Soakers, and a pair of handcuffs. He might have had a pair of shorts in there, too. They looked at him with an "are-you-a-child-molester" look. He said, "But I'm going to Ios."

Q: So there's no dress code?

A: You can do whatever you want. People ask, and we suggest they wear shoes. You can go out in board shorts and flip flops, or you can go out in a ball gown. One guest used to always dress as a preacher.

Q: Is it ever just too much?

A: It gets pretty stressful in August when the younger people come. Lots of boys show up and try to pick fights, so it gets tough. But after that the regulars return. It even gets a bit lonely. The tragedy is everybody leaves, and the greater tragedy is that they're all instantly replaced.

Q: So do you plan on returning next year, or is this it?

A: As Maria, Francesco's wife, says, it's been *avrio* (tomorrow) for 4 years now. You know, it's Greek time. We'll see. I'll probably be back.

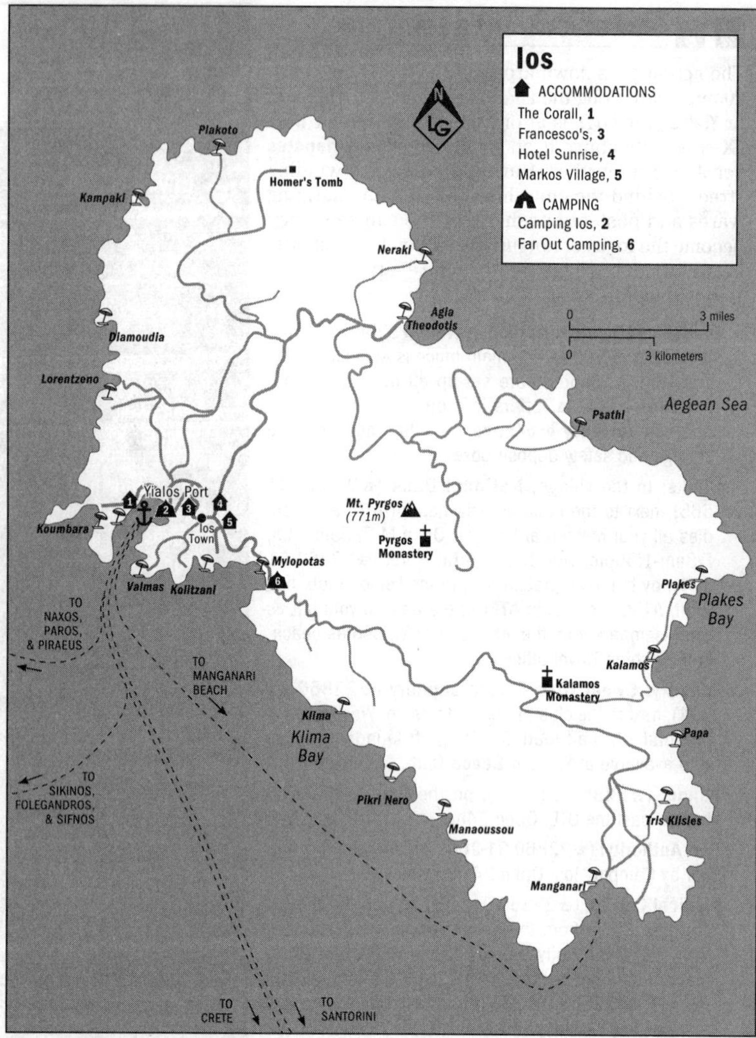

ACCOMMODATIONS AND CAMPING

Affordable accommodations can be found in the frenetic village or in the quiet port. Each area has its own personality, so weigh your interests before making your bed (and sleeping in it). A tent, bungalow, or room on Mylopotas beach lets you roll hazily from blanket to beach, foregoing coffee for a tequila sunrise.

HOTELS AND HOSTELS

Francesco's (☎22860 91 706; fax 22860 91 223; fragesco@otenet.gr), in the village. With your back to the bank, take the steps up from the left corner of the plateia, then take the first left. The Godfather of accommodations in Ios, Francesco oversees a family of hotels. Standard rooms (some with private baths) sit atop a convivial terrace bar. Dorms €7-15; rooms for 2-4 people €10-25. Additional fee for A/C. ❶

Markos Village (☎22860 91 059 or 22860 92 260; fax 22860 91 060); marcovlg@otenet.gr), at the end of the village, uphill and to the left of the bus stop. Markos, the cheerful owner, knows how to entertain. Chill by the poolside bar and sip frozen daiquiris while admiring the view. Dorms €8-12; doubles €20-45. ❶

Hotel Sunrise (☎22860 91 074 or 22860 91 527; fax 22860 91 664), just beyond Markos Village. Fine amenities including swimming pool and restaurant/bar (open 9am-midnight). Breakfast served all day. Doubles €30-78; also has triples and quads. ❸

The Corali (☎22860 91 272; fax 22860 91 552; coraliht@otenet.gr), on the peaceful port beach where umbrellas and beach volleyball spill onto the sand. At this family oriented hotel, chill figuratively in the flowered garden and literally in A/C-equipped rooms. Doubles €58 in high season. ❹

CAMPING

Far Out Camping (☎22860 92 301 or 22860 92 302; fax 22860 92 303; camping@faroutclub.com; www.faroutclub.com), at the center of Mylopotas beach. A luxurious, Club-Med-like campsite at rock-bottom prices, with a restaurant, bar, mini-market, volleyball court, swimming pool, bungee jumping, movies, showers, laundry, Internet access, live music, and nightly Happy Hours. Just about every visitor to the island congregates here during the day. Open Apr.-Sept. €4-7.50 per tent; tent rental €1.50; cabins €5 and up; bungalows €7-18. Hotel rooms available. ❶

Camping Ios (☎22860 92 035 or 22860 92 036; fax 22860 92 101). For those who want affordability and similar amenities to Far Out Camping without the nonstop action. Open June-Sept. €6 per person. ❶

FOOD

Most eating on Ios coincides with boozing, peaking in the middle of the night at cheap gyro joints. More discerning palates will find several inexpensive restaurants interspersed among the ubiquitous bars and discos in Ios village, at the port, and on the beach. There's also **Ios Market** (☎22860 91 035), across from the bus stop in Hora, and the **supermarket** in the main plateia.

Ali Baba's ❷ is next to Ios Gym; it's tough to find but worth the trip. Occasional live bands entertain in the newly renovated garden, and generous portions of Asian and international food will fill you to the brim. (☎22860 91 558. Delicious pad thai €8.50.) **Lord Byron's** ❸, around the corner from the church, serves a unique blend of Greek foods. Savory specialities will undoubtedly satisfy your appetite (entrees €12-15). **Waves Indian Restaurant and International Cuisine** ❷, to the left of the waterfront road as you disembark from the ferries, is run by a Welsh windsurfer couple who serve hearty curries and tasty stir-fries. (☎22860 92 145. Veggie curry €6.50. Takeout available. Opens daily at 10am for breakfast.) **Polydoros** ❷, 2km north (left, facing inland) of the port on Koubara beach, is the hideout of many of Ios's residents, who delight in dishes prepared with the freshest ingredients. (Shrimp *saganaki* with tomato sauce and feta €6.50).

SIGHTS AND BEACHES

Pay a visit to the new Ios **Archaeological Museum,** in the town hall across from the bus stop, and bring a smile to the lonely faces of those at the door. (Open Tu-Su 8am-2pm. Free.) According to legend, Homer died and was buried on Ios. The supposed site of **Homer's tomb** has been worn to rubble, but the site still draws a few dedicated tourists. To repent the previous night's excess at the solitary monastery, walk toward the windmills above the village to the path near the top of the hill. There's an **Open Theatre Festival Program** every summer, held above the windmills on the island—inquire at a travel agency for more information.

Beyond that, **beaches** are the place to be. Most spend their days at **Mylopotas beach,** a 20min. walk downhill from Ios town. The beach of Mylopotas, like the town, has music blasting everywhere. The farther you go, the fewer clothes you will see (or wear). Alternatively, buses (25min., 2 per day, €5) make the winding journey to the more secluded **Manganari,** the island's most beautiful stretch of sand. **Yialos** (the port beach), **Mylopotas,** and **Manganari** all offer watersports, from tubing (€12-22) to wakeboarding to windsurfing (€14-40). Continuing uphill from the OTE, look for the path leading to the secluded beach and crystal pool of water at the little bay of **Kolitsani** (a 15min. walk from Hora). Secluded, nudist **Psathi** on the eastern coast, is accessible by moped.

NIGHTLIFE

Most of Ios's extraordinary number of bars are packed into the old village area. Larger and louder discos line the main road, which is, in turn, lined with revelers. Bacchantes warm up at beachside bars, swill liquor from the bottle in the main plateia at sunset, hit the village before 1am, then migrate to the discos and to more private liaisons before sunrise.

CYCLADES

Dubliner (☎22860 92 070), near the basketball courts, is a good place to start the night. This Aussie-Kiwi bar serves big drinks at pub prices—or get your money's worth by entering the nightly drinking challenge-cum-kamikaze mission. On Thursday nights €25 buys you pizza, cover immunity, a drink, and the chance to get wasted at games held at the 5 bars comprising the ultimate pub crawl. Open daily 2pm-late.

Disco 69 (☎22860 91 064; disco69@club.com), on the main bar street, blares its mainstream dance music, inviting all comers to get smashed and dance on the bar.

The Slammer Bar, in the left inland corner of the main plateia in the village. Have the bartender whack your helmeted head before you get hammered in a different way, downing the tequila slammer (tequila, Tia Maria, and Sprite; €3).

Red Bull (☎22860 91 019), in the main plateia in the village. Kick-start the night (shots €2.40) to the tune of 90s rock before heading out to tackle the rest of the scene. Get plastered on the Red Bull and vodka energy special (€4.50).

Scorpion Disco, on the edge of town, en route to the beach. This crazy techno emporium, and the island's largest club, is strategically located for those heading to Mylopotas after they get sloshed. Cover after 1am.

Sweet Irish Dream, in a large building near the "donkey steps." Come here after you get pissed (or after 2am) to dance on tables—most save it as the night's last stop. No cover before 1am. Beer €2.50.

Q Club, on the edge of town. Showcase your breakdancing skills to the hip hop and house spun by visiting international DJs—then go ahead and get soused.

FOLEGANDROS Φολεγανδρος

Named after the son of King Minos, who according to legend made the first footprints on the island's shores, Folegandros was secluded from outside influence for many centuries due to its high, rocky cliffs and inaccessible port. The dry, steep hills are terraced with low, snaking stone walls worn by centuries of fierce wind—the only tumultuous presence on the island.

HORA Χωρα

The main town and the capital of Folegandros, cliffside Hora is friendly and beautiful, the perfect place to stay during your time on the island.

ORIENTATION AND PRACTICAL INFORMATION. After disembarking from the ferry, you can board the **bus** that runs from the port **Kararostassi** to the Hora. Buses head to the port 45min. before each ferry and then return with new arrivals (€0.80). The **post office** will be on your left as you enter town (open M-F 8:30am-2pm). From the post office, follow the heliport sign toward town to **Sottovento Travel Center** for **maps** (€2.10), ferry and bus schedules, **currency exchange,** and general information. (☎22860 41 444; fax 22860 41 430. Open 9am-1pm and 6-10pm.) At the other end of town, **Maraki Travel** offers similar services as well as **Internet access** for €6 per hour, with a €1.50 minimum charge. (☎22860 41 158; fax 22860 41 159. Open daily 9:30am-1pm and 5-9:30pm.) Irregular **ferries** run to: **Ios** (1½hr., 4 per week, €4.70); **Kimolos** (1½hr., 2 per week, €4.70); **Milos** (2½hr., 2 per week, €5.70); **Naxos** (3hr., 2 per week, €7.70); **Paros** (4hr., 2 per week, €6.30); **Piraeus** (10-12hr., 1 per day, €16.50); **Santorini** (1½hr., 6 per week, €5.60); **Serifos** (5hr., 2 per week, €8.90); **Sifnos** (4hr., 4 per week, €6.90); and **Sikinos** (1hr., 4 per week, €3.70). Several times per week, **hydrofoils** zip to **Amorgos** (3 per week, €17.70), **Milos, Santorini,** and **Sifnos** for double the price in half the time. **Taxis** can be reached at ☎694 693 957. There is an **ATM** in Pl. Kontarini, the main square in town. **Moped rental** is cheaper at the port (try **Jimmy's,** ☎22860 41 448) than in town. Past Maraki Travel, head straight past the next two tree-filled plateias, cut across to the right, then head left. A sharp right before the **market** leads to the **police** (☎22860 41 249). Call the **medical center** at ☎22860 41 222. The **pharmacy** is on the road to the port, about 50m out of town. **Postal code:** 84011.

CYCLADES

ACCOMMODATIONS AND CAMPING. Folegandros's increasing popularity has created a minor shortage of space, so be sure to reserve ahead of time. Most housing is pricey, but welcome relief can be found at **Pavlo's Rooms ❶.** About 200m from the post office, Pavlo's has simple rooms (some private baths) in a charming converted stable. (☎/fax 22860 41 232. Laundry services (€6), breakfast, and port shuttle available. Doubles €10-25, with bath €25-50; triples €30-56; quads €40-62. You can sleep on the roof for €6.) **Hotel Polikandia ❹,** near Marakis Travel, harbors rooms with breezy balconies surrounded by a pretty flagstone garden. (☎22860 41 322; fax 22860 41 323. Buffet breakfast €6. Singles €17-50; doubles €23-56; triples €29-62.) **Rooms to Let Embati ❹,** right next to Hotel Polikandia, offers simple rooms with private baths and fridges. (☎22860 41 006; fax 22860 41 469. Doubles €20-53.) **Livadi Camping ❶** is another option; call for a port shuttle. (☎22860 41 204 or 22860 41 478. €5 per person; €2.50 per tent.)

FOOD AND NIGHTLIFE. Fresh fruit and bread **markets** line the road from Kararostassi through Hora. At **Folegandros Snack Bar ❶,** across from Maraki Travel, owner Michailidia makes what could be the best cappuccino outside of Italy. He also provides vegetarian food, 40 varieties of tea, games, books, maps, and info about the island. (☎22860 41 226. Open Apr.-Oct.) **Kritikos ❷** (☎22860 41 219) serves the freshest meat on the island. Savor the grilled lamb (€5.80). **To Sik ❶** (☎22860 41 515) puts a twist on traditional Greek dishes; try their vegetarian specialities, such as stuffed aubergine (€4.40) or vegetarian pastitsio (€4.50). Pause to appreciate the prime location of **Piatsa ❶** (☎22860 41 274), in the center of Kontarini square, as you wait for a delicious traditional Greek meal. Try the island speciality, *matzata* (pasta with rabbit or chicken).

In summer, when the island's permanent population of 650 triples with the influx of tourists, Hora starts to rock. **El Greco,** on the path past Sottovento, is a bohemian cafe-bar adorned with artistic lighting and paintings. (☎22860 41 456. Cocktails €6. Open daily Apr.-Oct. 10am-3pm and 6pm-4am.) **Avissos,** the only dance club in town, plays a mixture of top 40 and Greek tracks to keep things moving at the outdoor bar. (☎22860 41 100. "Brazilian Night" cocktail €6; beer €4. Open daily 10pm-late.) **Carajo** has a lively atmosphere accented by a mix of funk and Latin music. (☎22860 41 463. Open daily 10pm-late. Cocktails-€6.) **Kellari Wine Bar,** in Pl. Pounta next to the medical center, boasts an amazing selection of Greek wines in a small stone-walled room reminiscent of a castle wine cellar. Ask the hostess for the perfect selection: her expertise will prove satisfactory. (☎22860 41 119. €3-6 per glass. Open daily 7:30am-late.)

SIGHTS. The **Church of Panagia,** above the town on Paleocastro Hill, is an excellent place to watch the sunset or photograph whitewashed domes against the mountains and sea. (Open daily 6-8pm in summer; in winter open only for religious festivals.) A demanding hike across Paleocastro Hill leads to **Chryssospilia** (Golden Cave), once a refuge for islanders during pirate invasions. Local lore insists that there is a secret tunnel connecting this unchartered cave to Panagia.

HIKES. The hike from Hora to **Agali** and **Agios Nikolaos** takes about an hour to Agali and another 30min. to Ag. Nikolaos beach. Start from Hora and take the road toward Ano Meria. There's about 20-30min. of asphalt before you hit one of two dirt paths leading left off the road and down to the beaches and terraced countryside. Across from one of several small white churches, you'll see the trail snaking down toward Agali. From here, you'll traverse rocky terraces and pass olive trees down the main dirt track (hang left) that heads straight to Agali. In Agali, you'll find a few tavernas, domatia, and several tents if you climb up past the first tavernas on the right to the rocky trail that leads to Ag. Nikolaos beach. Between the two beaches are small, rocky coves and beaches perfect for a cool, quiet swim. Bypass the hike by taking the bus from Agali; from the bus stop, it's a 10-15min. walk to sun, sea, and sand.

ANO MERIA

Ano Meria has many footpaths leading to secluded **beaches,** including **Livadaki,** the island's best. The steep, winding trails—the only access to these beaches—take at least an hour each; there is no taverna at the end. The Sottovento tourist office heads day-long boat tours around the island that stop at several beaches; inquire upon arrival. For a superb glance into Ottoman life, check out the **Folklore Museum** in Ano Meria. On an island whose history is empty of epoch-defining events, the olive presses, looms, and fishing nets detail the perpetual struggle against infertile soil and stormy harbors. Take the bus to Ano Meria and ask the driver to let you off there. (Open June-Aug. daily 5-8pm. Guidebook €6.)

Those planning an extended stay in Folegandros or who want a more intimate acquaintance with island culture should look into **The Cycladic School** (☎22860 41 137; fax 22860 41 472), run by Anne and Fotis Papadopoulous. The school leads six- to twelve-day courses that focus on drawing and painting, as well as theater, music, sailing, diving, history, and philosophy. A day at the school includes a lecture, practice time, and excursions around the island. For more information, contact Anne and Fotis Papadopoulous, GR-84011, Folegandros, Greece.

SANTORINI Σαντορινη

Whitewashed towns balanced on plunging cliffs, burning black-sand beaches, and deeply scarred hills make Santorini's landscape nearly as dramatic as the volcanic cataclysm that created it. This eruptive past—and startling beauty—has led some to believe that Santorini is the lost continent of Atlantis. According to Greek mythology, Santorini arose from a clod of earth given by the sea god Triton to the Argonauts. The island, then called Thira, was an outpost of Minoan society by 2000 BC. Around the turn of the 17th century BC, an earthquake destroyed the wealthy maritime settlement of Akrotiri, and all hope of recovery vanished when a massive volcanic eruption spread lava and pumice across the island around 1625 BC. The destruction of Santorini heralded the fall of Minoan prominence; it is thought that the volcanic eruption led to a tidal wave that wreaked havoc on Crete as well.

Natural disaster continues to threaten the safety of Santorini's residents: as recently as 1956, an earthquake caused serious damage to much of the island. But the volcanoes have enriched the soil, making Santorini a green oasis among the mostly barren Cyclades. Modern Santorini is the eastern crescent of what was once a circular island, originally called Strongili (round). The ancient eruption left a crust of volcanic ash over the hollow center of the island, which later caved in to create the caldera (basin) that now forms Santorini's harbors and western rim.

Santorini is an easily accessible mob-scene. It's one of the most beautiful islands in the world; tourists pour in from all over the world to see for themselves. The coastline, neighboring islands, and volcano make it a popular site for weddings and honeymoons. It's tempting to explore via moped, but inexperienced riders and poor bikes are a dangerous combination; traveling by foot or the excellent bus service may be a better option. The prices on the island tend to be steep, mostly due to the cost of importing water and, of course, its tourist popularity.

FIRA Φηρα

The island's activity centers in the capital, Fira (FEE-rah). Atop a hill and far from the black sand beaches, the congested assemblage of glitzy shops, whizzing mopeds, and scads of hyperactive tourists can be overwhelming to newcomers. Tourist traffic has made it almost too easy to find a hamburger or wiener schnitzel, but Fira's pristine beauty and classic Greek food still prevail. The city is perched on a cliff, and the short walk to the caldera, at the town's western edge, reveals a stunning view of the harbor. Huddled hotels fearlessly peer over the sheer cliffs and defy the seismically active island to send them tumbling into the sea. All the kitsch and overcrowding still can't negate the pleasure of wandering the tiny cobbled streets and arriving at the western edge of town in time to watch the sunset.

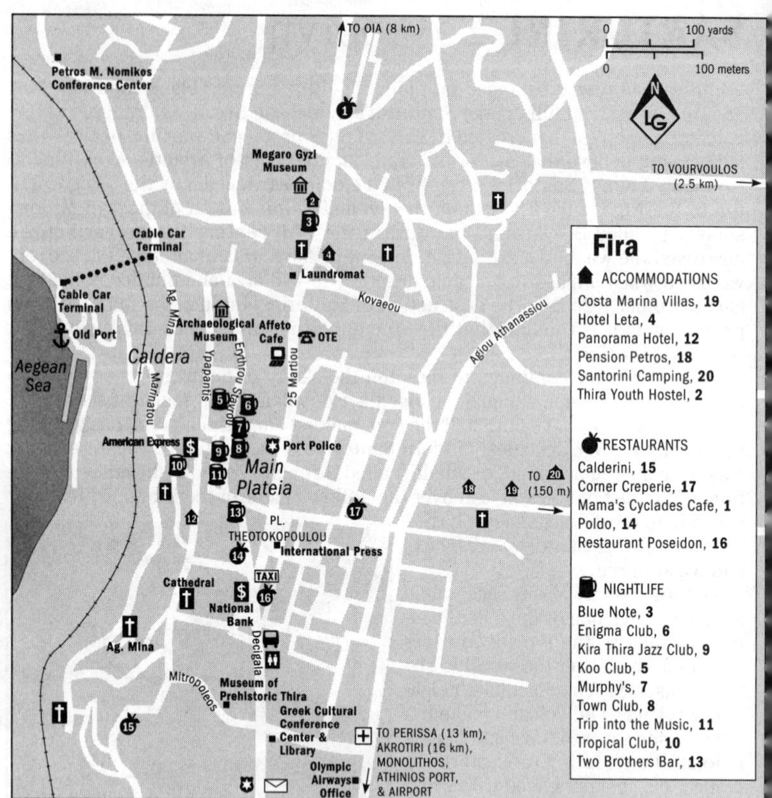

CYCLADES

TRANSPORTATION

Boats dock at one of three ports: Athinios, Fira, or Oia. Athinios is the most trafficked and has frequent buses to Fira and Perissa beach (30min., at least 20 per day, €1.50). Be aware that, even if your ferry ticket says "Fira," you may be landing in the town of **Athinios.** The **port** of Fira is down a 587-step footpath from the town; you can take a **cable car** (every 20min. 6:40am-10pm; €3, children €1.50, luggage €1.50) or hire a **mule** (€3). Both methods of transportation are fun and scenic. Santorini's **buses** run frequently and can take you anywhere you want to go, but be warned that their convenience leads to overcrowding. Arrive at the station 10 minutes early to make your bus. The estimated journey lengths below are based on ideal circumstances; busy buses often move much slower.

Flights: Olympic Airways (☎22860 22 493) flies daily to: **Athens** (€82.05); **Iraklion** (€65.05); **Mykonos** (€65.05); **Rhodes** (€90.05); **Thessaloniki** (€112.05). From the bus depot, turn left on the main street and left again at the next road. Walk to the end of the road, and head right by the hospital. Open M-Sa 8am-8pm, Su 8:30am-3:30pm.

Ferries: To: **Anafi** (2hr., 2 per week, €6.16); **Folegandros** (1½hr., 3 per week, €6.16); **Ios** (1½hr., 3-5 per day, €5.76); **Iraklion** (4hr., 1 per day, €12.60); **Mykonos** (7hr., 2 per week, €11.20); **Naxos** (4hr., 4-8 per day, €9.96); **Paros** (4½hr., 3-5 per day,

€12.10); **Piraeus** (9hr., 4-8 per day, €20.16); **Sikinos** (4½hr., 2 per week, €6.06); **Skiathos** (12hr., 1 per week, €26.80); **Syros** (8hr., 3 per week, €14.36); **Thessaloniki** (15hr., 5 per week, €33.60). **Flying Dolphins** go to similar places in half the time and at twice the price.

Buses: To: **Akrotiri** (30min., 16 per day, €1.20); **Athinios** (25min., 11 per day, €1.50); **Kamari** (20min., 35 per day, €0.80); **Monolithos** via the **airport** (30min., 25 per day, €0.80); **Oia** (30min., 30 per day, €0.85); **Perissa** (15min., 30 per day, €1.40).

Taxis: (☎22860 22 555) in Pl. Theotokopoulou beside the bus station.

Moped Rental: Marcos Rental (☎22860 23 877), 50m north of the plateia. €15 per day, discounts for extended rentals. Helmets included. Open daily 8am-7pm.

ORIENTATION AND PRACTICAL INFORMATION

From the bus station, walk uphill (north) to **Pl. Theotokopoulou,** which is full of travel agencies, banks, and cafes. At the fork in the road, the street on the right with the large National Bank building is **25 Martiou,** the main paved road. It leads from the plateia north toward Oia and hosts accommodations, including the youth hostel. Head onto the left branch of the fork and turn onto any westbound street to find back streets with many of the best bars, stores, and discos. Farther west is the caldera, bordered by **Ypapantis,** where expensive restaurants and art galleries are overshadowed by the spectacular view.

Banks: National Bank (☎22860 22 662), on the road branching off 25 Martiou south of the plateia. **Currency exchange.** 24hr. **ATM.** Open M-Th 8am-2pm, F 8am-1:30pm.

American Express: In the office of **X-Ray Kilo Travel and Shipping Agency** (☎22860 25 025), on the caldera. All AmEx services. Open daily 8am-8:30pm.

International Bookstore: International Press (☎22860 25 301), in the plateia. Many magazines and a selection of popular reading books. Open daily 7:30am-11:30pm.

Library: The Greek Cultural Conference Center and Library (☎22860 24 960), off 25 Martiou, on the side street before the post office. The island's only library, with info about island events. Open M-Sa 9am-2pm and 6-9pm; Su 10am-2pm.

Public Toilets: On 25 Martiou, beside the bus depot.

Medical Center: (☎22860 22 237). Go downhill (south) from the bus station, take the first left, and look for an unmarked building (except for an ambulance in front) at the end of the street on the left. Open for routine problems daily 8:30am-2:30pm. **Emergency** care 24hr.

OTE: (☎22860 22 135), off the plateia on 25 Martiou. Open daily 7:30am-3:10pm.

Internet Access: Internet cafes abound in Fira, and there is a surprising degree of price diversity among them. **Affeto Cafe** (☎22860 22 207) has the best prices (€2.50 per hr.) and an energetic bar atmosphere. It's located across from the OTE, about 75m before the Youth Hostel. Open daily 8:30am-1:30am.

Post Office: (☎22860 22 238), 50m downhill (south) from the bus stop. Open daily M-F 7:30am-2pm. **Postal code:** 84700.

ACCOMMODATIONS

In summer, the pensions and hotels fill up quickly and prices skyrocket out of budget range. The cheapest options are the quality **youth hostels** in Fira, Perissa beach, and Oia. Call ahead. You can find substantially cheaper places in **Karterados,** 2km south of Fira, or in the small inland towns along the main bus routes (try Messaria, Pyrgos, or Emborio). Hostels and many pensions will pick you up at the port.

Thira Youth Hostel (☎22860 22 387 or 22860 23 864), on the left roughly 300m north of the plateia, set back 25m from the road to Oia. Lonely travelers join the happy throng in the courtyard of this old monastery neighboring Fira's caldera. Quiet dorm rooms and pension-quality private rooms with baths. Quiet after 11pm. No smoking in dorms. Open Apr.-Oct. Dorms €7.50-10; doubles €20-40. ❶

Pension Petros (☎22860 22 573; fax 22860 22 615). From the bus station, go 1 block up 25 Martiou and make a right. Make a left at the bottom of the hill, then take your first right. One in a line of new and nearly identical pensions. The owner Petros shares stories and bottles of homemade wine with travelers. All rooms have baths, TV, and fridges; some have A/C. Free port shuttle. Doubles €20-53; triples €26-62. ❸

Hotel Leta (☎22860 22 540; fax 22860 23 903). Just 100m from the plateia: walking up the main road, follow signs to the right after the laundromat. This colorful building hidden in the alleyways of Fira is another popular spot for budget-conscious travelers. Downstairs rooms with bath €12 per person. Upstairs rooms with A/C, TVs, baths, and fridges. Doubles €17.50-50; triples €25-55. ❹

Panorama Hotel, (☎22860 22 271), on Ypapantis, overlooking the caldera. Pricey, but relatively reasonable for a nice caldera view. The rooms are fully stocked (A/C, TVs, balconies, fridges), as is the hotel (sauna, fitness center, jacuzzi). Breakfast included. Singles €78; doubles €135; triples €175. ❺

Costa Marina Villas (☎22860 28 923), 2 doors down from Pension Petros. Costa Marina consists of a beautiful building with impressive rooms in an unfortunate location—overlooking construction and development. Still, many of the rooms have a view of the ocean. The wrought-iron beds add a touch of class to rooms with A/C, TVs, fridges, and, often, bathtubs. Kitchens are also available. Breakfast included. Singles €56-77; doubles €72-97; triples €90-120. ❹

Santorini Camping (☎22860 22 944 or 22860 25 062; fax 22860 25 065). Follow the blue signs leading east of the plateia. This shady campsite is the most festive spot in town, with a pool, poolside bar, cafe, and mini-market on the premises. 24hr. hot showers. Washing machine €4 (soap included). Internet access €2 for 30min., €3 for 31-60min. Quiet hours midnight-8am. Open Apr.-Oct. €6 per person; €3 per tent; €6 per tent rental; €2.60 per car; €1.70 per motorbike. ❶

CYCLADES

FOOD

Inexpensive restaurants are hard to find in Fira, but the few that exist are crammed between shops on the tiny streets sandwiched between the plateia and the caldera. The caldera is lined with fine dining options that impose a hefty fee for their priceless views. Generic but convenient snack shops dot the plateia.

Mama's Cyclades Cafe (☎22860 23 032). Head north on the road to Oia; it's on the right side. Advertised as the best American breakfast in Greece, and they're not kidding. Mama is chatty, loud, and wants to feed all her "babies" generously. Her breakfast special speaks volumes as well: pancakes, 2 eggs, bacon, hash browns, and OJ all for €6. Greek specialties and original dishes (*kontosouvli*, pork stuffed with garlic, €6.50) complement the menu. Open daily 7am-midnight. Free glass of wine for *Let's Go* bearers. ❷

Calderini, (☎22860 23 050), on the caldera, behind Hotel Atlantis. One of the more reasonably priced options in the area. Enjoy pizzas (€8.50-12) and pasta dishes (€7-11) while checking out the sunset. Rooftop seating provides fabulous views of the town and water. Open daily noon-midnight. ❷

Poldo, up the street from the National Bank. Take-out includes vegetarian entrees like falafel (€3.50), tabouli (€2), and hummus (€2.50). The long line is for the tasty gyros (small €1.50, large €3.80). Open 24hr. ❶

Restaurant Poseidon, (☎22860 25 480) in a garden down the stairs next to the plateia taxi stand. Excellent *tzatziki* (€2) and enormous entrees. Try the Santorini dishes: *tomatoklefdes,* tomatoes breaded with cinnamon-flavored fried dough (€3.85), or the specialty *potmapavia*—beef with lemon sauce (€7.05). Open daily 7am-1am. ❷

Corner Creperie, (☎22860 25 512). Walk away from the caldera on the north side of the main plateia. A wide selection of crepes (€4-6) and omelettes; you can choose your ingredients from a lengthy list. Many ice cream treats. Open 8am-2am. ❶

SIGHTS AND BEACHES

The **Petros M. Nomikos Conference Center,** north of the cable car station, houses an exhibition center that currently displays life-size reproductions of the magnificent **wall paintings** of Ancient Thira; the originals are some of the most prized pieces at the National Archaeological Museum in Athens. Brightly colored and intricately detailed murals hint at the quotidian existence and imaginative life of Santorini's ancient Minoan culture, as well as an unhealthy infatuation with blue monkeys. (☎22860 23 016. Open daily May-Oct. 10am-9pm. €3, seniors and students €1.50, children under 18 free; audio tour €3.) Just steps away from the cable cars you'll find Fira's **Archaeological Museum,** which holds an impressive array of vases, figurines, and statues from the site of Ancient Thira. (☎22860 22 217. Open Tu-Su 8:30am-3pm. €3, students and EU seniors €2, EU students free.) Also interesting is the **Museum of Prehistoric Thira,** not far from the bus station, which attempts to unravel the mystery of Santorini's pre-volcanic eruption civilization. (Open Tu-Su 8:30am-3pm. Free.) The private **Megaro Gyzi Museum,** just northwest of Thira Youth Hostel, has an engrossing collection of old maps, engravings, and Greek island photographs spanning the 15th-19th centuries.

Reigning over the island from its lofty height, Fira is a convenient base for exploring beaches in neighboring towns. The closet beach is **Vourvoulou,** about an hour's walk north of town (follow the signs). It is one of Santorini's most secluded (though pebbly) black sand beaches. The black sand is hot, so bring **sandals.**

CYCLADES

OUTDOOR ACTIVITIES

When the hum of mopeds becomes a grating roar, hop on a boat and flee to the little islands along Santorini's caldera rim. The most popular boat excursion goes to the still active volcano, with a 30min. hike up the black lava rocks to see the crater. Most boats make a swim-stop afterward in nearby waters that are warmed in patches by hot sulphur springs. Be prepared to swim through cold, cold water to get there. A longer excursion goes to the inhabited island of Thirasia; on the standard daytrip, you'll only have two hours to wander the island. Built along Thirasia's upper ridge, the villages of **Manolas** and **Potamos** have spine-tingling views of Santorini's western coast. Tour groups dock at **Korfos** or **Reeva.** From Korfos, you'll have to pant up 300 steep steps, or you can hail a donkey (€3) to get to the villages; Reeva provides a paved road. **Boat tours** can be arranged through agencies all over Santorini. (Volcano and springs €12, with Thirisia €17.)

NIGHTLIFE

Fira is host to one of the hippest late night scenes in Greece. The clubs on the north end gear up around 2am. Unfortunately, exorbitant covers make a club-crawl a pricey venture. Clubs generally share drink prices and covers, which vary according to the season: beer is around €3-3.50, cocktails around €4-6, and covers start at €5 (soaring to upwards of €10 in the high season). A typical night begins at **The Blue Note,** a club/

bar with techno music next to the Youth Hostel. Then onto the dance clubs: the hippest are **Koo Club** and **Enigma** (facing each other on 25 Martiou), both of which crank into the wee hours. Chill on the outdoor decks and watch the steam rise on the dance floors inside. **Trip into the Music,** next door to Kira Thira Jazz Club, keeps its dance floor crowded with a variety of tunes, including new British rock. At **Murphy's,** next to Enigma, a consistently full house assures energetic techno-dancing and lots of chatter all night long. **Town Club,** next to Murphy's, pumps techno through a small room with a castle motif. To start or end the night off right, try one of these bars:

Tropical Club. High up on the caldera, a native Californian mixes signature cocktails as tasty as they are creative (around €6.50). "Sunset coffees" like the Bob Marley *frappé* (dark rum, Kahlua, iced coffee, and cream) go well with sunset views over the caldera. Arrive by 8pm for prime balcony seating. Open daily noon-4am.

Kira Thira Jazz Club, across from Nikolas Taverna, on a side street parallel to the main road out of town. Mellow out to jazz while sipping a gin fizz or piña colada (€6). Brass hangs from the ceiling, and the regulars kiss the DJ good night. Live jazz nightly in August. Open daily 9pm-3am.

Two Brothers Bar, next to Poldo up the street from the banks. Hidden behind a medieval prison, a relaxed crowd of locals congregates to listen to Greek music. Try a watermelon shot with your complimentary one-free-shot card. €1.50 cover goes toward the cost of your first drink. Beer €2.50. Open daily 9pm-3am.

CYCLADES

DAYTRIPS FROM FIRA

AKROTIRI. The volcanic eruption that rocked Santorini in the 17th century BC blanketed Akrotiri with lava that, despite destroying the island, preserved the maritime city of Akrotiri more completely than almost any other Minoan site. In 1967, the paved streets of Akrotiri, lined with fascinating houses and a sophisticated central drainage system, were uncovered by Professor Spyridon Marinatos. He was later killed by a fall at the site in 1974. Each house had at least one room decorated with wall paintings, some of which are the most advanced in Greece; the originals are at the National Archaeological Museum in Athens. Since no skeletons were found in the city, the theory goes that everyone escaped before the 1625 BC eruption devastated the area. Signs guide you through the excavation. (*Take the bus (16 per day, €1.20) from Fira.* ☎ *22860 81 366. Open Tu-Su 8:30am-3pm. €5, students €3.)*

Near Ancient Akrotiri is the small modern village of Akrotiri. For sustenance and a fabulous sea view, head down the road to the right of the archaeological site to reach the **Dolphins Fish Restaurant ❷,** open for lunch and until late-night for dinner; the name is based on the popular icon in Minoan wall paintings, not your lunch. For a swim, continue heading away from the ancient site and past the Dolphin Fish Restaurant to the **Red Beach,** a 20min. walk from the Akrotiri bus stop. Though Santorini is famed for its black beaches, this ruddy beach is prized for its remote location and smooth sand.

PYRGOS AND ANCIENT THIRA. Once a Venetian fortress, the lofty town of Pyrgos is girded by medieval walls. Twenty five blue- and green-domed churches highlighting the horizon are the legacy of Ottoman occupation through 1828. One of these colorful sanctuaries (near the top of town) houses the **Museum of Icons and Liturgical Objects.** *(Open Tu-Su 8am-1pm. Free.)* The fortress and museum are near one another. To find them in the maze of alleyways leading up the hill, follow the signs for adjacent Kafe Kasteli. Continuing through the town on the main road, a 40min. hike takes you to the **Profitis Ilias Monastery.** Built in 1711, it graciously shares its site with a radar station installed by the Greek military, thinking that the station would be safe from attack alongside this ancient monastery. *(Open daily 8am-1pm.)* On July 20, the monastery hosts the **Festival of Profitis Ilias.**

From Profitis Ilias, it's approximately a 1½hr. hike to the ruins of **Ancient Thira.** *(Open Tu-Su 8am-2pm)* This trek leads along the mountain that separates Kamari and Perissa and leads to fantastic views of all Santorini. Be warned that the way is poorly marked, with narrow gravel paths on the mountainside, so shoes with good traction are a must. The ancient theater, church, and forum of the island's old capital are still visible, though less spectacular than the Akrotiri excavations. *(To reach Pyrgos, take the bus from Fira to Perissa (15min., 30 per day, €1.40), and ask the driver to let you off at Pyrgos. Ancient Thira can be reached as a hike from Pyrgos. Or take a bus from Fira to Kamari (20min., 2-3 per hr., €0.80) and climb the mountain beside the water to reach the ruins.)*

MONOLITHOS. More popular with locals than with tourists, small Monolithos beach is easily accessible due to its proximity to the airport (15 buses per day, €0.80). The black sand is much finer than at many of Santorini's other beaches, though this means the winds can whip up quite a sandstorm at times. If you want a bite to eat, the fish taverna **Skaramagas** ❷ is the least expensive on the strip. Many locals come here for lunch several times a week to enjoy calamari (€5.50), Greek salads (€3), and its famed *kakavia*, fish soup (€8). The owners catch the fresh seafood, keep what they need for the restaurant, and sell the rest to other takers. *(Open Apr.-Oct. daily 8am-midnight.)*

CYCLADES

PERISSA Περισσα

Perissa is charismatically demure—nothing is overly flashy, but the town's smooth beaches, youth hostel, nearby camping, and casual nightlife scene make it popular with student travelers. To get there, take the bus from Fira (15min., 30 per day, €1.40). If black sand seems passé, take the ferry to **Red Beach** at Akrotiri. (☎22860 82 093. Leaves 11am; returns 4pm. €6 each way.)

ACCOMMODATIONS AND CAMPING. Youthful, energetic **Stelio's Place** ❷ is a 7min. walk from the plateia. From the road leading out of town, turn left after passing Cafe Del Mar on your right; it's 50m down on your left. Stelio's has 21 rooms with private baths, fridges, A/C, a pool, an adjacent bar (beer €1.50), easy beach access, and a free airport or seaport shuttle. (☎22860 81 860; splace@otenet.gr. Reservations recommended. Breakfast €3-4.50. Singles €10-20.) If the one minute walk to the beach from Stelio's doesn't suit you, **Ostria** ❸ is located right on the waterfront. Walking away from the main square, turn left about 250m down the road after a small gravel clearing; then turn right on the beach road. The rooms are actually large studios with A/C, TVs, and kitchens. (☎22860 82 607. Doubles €35-40; triples €42-48.) **Youth Hostel Perissa-Anna** ❶ is 50m before the first bus stop heading into Perissa town. Alternatively, from the final stop at the main plateia by the beach, walk inland along the main street for 500m. This popular spot provides women's and co-ed dorms, private rooms, discounts on services around Perissa, use of a nearby pool, and free safety deposit boxes. The hostel is also affiliated with a travel agency and organizes discount excursions, car rental, and plane tickets. (☎22860 82 182. 20% discount at the restaurant across the street. Luggage storage €3. Linens €1. Internet access €5 per hr. 36-bed dorm €6; 10-14 bed dorm €7; rooms for 3-4 people €8.) **Perissa Camping** ❶ is adjacent to the beach in one of the few forested spots on the island. Enjoy their beach bar, mini-market, kitchen facilities, sparkling restrooms, discounted scuba diving excursions, and taverna. (☎22860 81 343 or 22860 81 686. Internet access €5 per hr. €6 per person; €3 per tent rental; €2 per car.) **Domatia** in private homes offer more privacy. Proprietors hang around the dock at Athinios, but you shouldn't agree to anything before seeing the room. Doubles run €20-35.

FOOD. Where the main road meets the plateia, **Santo Food ❶** piles greasy french fries, *tzatziki*, and onions into its tasty gyros (€1.50). Breakfast (€3-4.50) and vegetarian sandwiches are also served. (☎22860 82 893. Open 24hr.) Across the street, calzones, 10 varieties of pizza, and pasta await at **Bella Aurora ❷.** The infamous and delicious super-calzone (€6.50) is crammed with 10 toppings; finishing it can be an intimidating prospect. (Calzones €4.50-6.50. Open daily 8:30am-11:30pm.) Head back across the street to the **Full Moon Bar,** where the loquacious Canadian owner taps Guinness (€5) and other great drafts. DJs mastermind the music nightly, honing their craft for frequent theme nights; check the signs around town for details. Happy Hour lasts five hours and promises half-price cocktails. (Cocktails and mixed drinks €3-6, beer €3. Open daily 5pm-4am.)

KAMARI Καμαρι

Although renowned for its black sand, Kamari Beach is actually covered in black pebbles, and the slippery seaweed-covered rock bottom makes wading especially difficult. Still, the beach attracts a crowd of black sand enthusiasts, who come to gawk at the scenery and each other. The long, narrow beach area is covered in umbrellas (€6) and pressed against the ocean by pricey hotels, upscale shops, cafes, and nightclubs. Buses come from **Fira** (20min., 2-3 per hr., €0.80) and deposit you about a block from the south side of the waterfront. A bumpy shuttle boat scoots between Kamari and **Perissa** (every 30min. 9am-5pm, €3). The boat leaves from in front of the Hook Bar at the right end of the waterfront.

ACCOMMODATIONS. Throughout town, doubles range €30-70. **Hotel Preka Maria ❸** (☎22860 31 266) rents rooms (€29-33) and furnished 3-person apartments (€35-65), with fridges and baths. It's on the northern end of town: heading away from the mountain, take a left before the Barbeque Restaurant, and the hotel is 70m farther. Past Preka Maria, **Pension Spiridoula ❹** welcomes you with an enormous sign. The rooms are simple but provide private baths, balconies, and fridges. (☎22860 31 767. Doubles €40.) **Hotel Roussos ❺** provides a more luxurious stay on the water, with a pool and a classy bar. The rooms are well-equipped, with A/C, TVs, and fridges, and many offer fantastic views. (☎22860 31 590. Doubles €78; triples €99.) **Kamari Camping ❶** is 1km inland along the main road out of town. (☎22860 31 453. Open June-Sept. €4 per person; €3 per tent.)

FOOD AND ENTERTAINMENT. The waterfront is lined with indistinguishable tavernas. **Eanos ❷** stands out due to its unusually large selection of pizzas (€5-7) and beautiful patio area. (☎22860 31 161. Open noon-1am). For an inexpensive snack, head to **Ariston,** a bakery and grocery selling fresh bread (under €1) at the northern end of the waterfront. (Open daily 7am-11pm.) Nearby, **Mango ❶** and **Dom** serve up a sexy combination on a sprawling complex. Mango is an upscale outdoor cafe with light fare. (Pizza, pasta, and crepes €3-5. Open daily 9am-2am.) Dom is a futuristic indoor club. (☎22860 33 420. July and August bring a €7 cover which includes 1 drink; cocktails €6. Open Su-Th 11pm-3:30am, F-Sa 11pm-dawn.) For quieter entertainment, see a flick at the **Open Air Cinema Kamari** (☎22860 31 974; tickets €6 for evening shows), on the way out of town. The **Canava Roussos** winery, 1km from Kamari Camping, will wine and dine you with its red, white, and rose *bouganvilla*. The house favorite, *mavrathiko* (€3 per glass), is a sweet wine made with red grapes instead of the traditional white. The bus between Fira and Kamari can drop you there. (Open daily 10am-8pm.)

OIA Οια

Dazzling sunsets made the posh cliffside town of Oia (EE-ah) famous; the little stucco buildings on the cliffs make it breathtaking. In the aftermath of the 1956 earthquake that leveled the town (and much of the northwest tip of the island), inhabitants carved new dwellings into the cliffside among the crumbled debris of the old. Window-shopping pedestrians rule the narrow cobblestone streets at the town's many upscale boutiques; art galleries and craft shops dominate. Although the budget traveler will not survive long in Oia, it's possible to survive a pleasant day or two without too much fiscal damage. If browsing isn't your bag, hightail it to the cliffs and secure a prime sunset view. Buses run from **Fira** to Oia (25min., 30 per day, €0.85), and ferries dock at Oia before continuing to Fira or Athinios.

ACCOMMODATIONS. The Karvounis family can help meet all your tourist needs. **Karvounis Tours** (☎22860 71 290; fax 22860 71 291; mkarvounis@ote.net.gr), on the main street beside the largest church in town, answers questions about Oia and Santorini, in addition to selling ferry and airline tickets and arranging marriages—be careful not to sign your life away. To find the agency from the bus stop, walk uphill away from Fira and turn left at the 1st alleyway; it's to the right at the the end of the alleyway. The Karvounis family's **Youth Hostel Oia ❷** has impeccable rooms with baths (with large mirrors for the narcissistic), a courtyard, and a bar open for breakfast and evening drinks. This luxurious hostel makes painfully expensive Oia bearable. Get more bang for your buck during Happy Hour (7:30-8:30pm), with cheap drinks and a free sunset on the roof patio. (☎22860 71 465; fax 22860 71 291. Single sex and co-ed dorms. Laundry €7.80 per load. Free safety deposit boxes. Wheelchair accessible. Breakfast included. Open May-Oct. Dorms €14.) Short-term domatia are rare in Oia; most proprietors expect a 5-day stay.

FOOD. Dining will cost you a bit more than in Fira, but some restaurants serve exceptional food. **Petros ❷,** Oia's oldest restaurant, at the southern end of the town's main road (turn left at the main church and walk down about 300m), overlooks the sparkling sea. Try the fresh fish soup; it's one of the best of Petros's excellent seafood dishes (calamari €7). Old Greek recipes provide a pleasant alternative to the common moussaka, and Petros Jr. continues the family tradition of making homemade wines. (☎22860 71 263. Entrees €5-8. Open daily 5pm-midnight.) Petros's family extends up the street to **Thalami Taverna ❷,** where they cook up less exotic fare but offer a better view of the caldera and stay open for lunch. (☎22860 71 009. Chicken with blue cheese and mushrooms €9, Santorini salad €7. Open noon-midnight.) **Restaurant Lotza ❸,** about 100m to the north of the main church, maintains a low-key atmosphere and serves well-seasoned dishes like curried chicken (€9), *gioourtlou* (minced meat, pita bread, and yogurt; €9), and spaghetti with seafood (€10). (☎22860 71 357. Open daily 9am-midnight.) For a very special occasion, **1800 ❹** is the classiest bistro in town. Situated in a 19th century mansion with much of the original furniture still in use, this self-titled 'slow food' restaurant serves up creative Mediterranean and Greek dishes that change from year to year. To get there, walk 50m north of the main church. (☎22860 71 485. Entrees €15-30. Open 7:30pm-1am.) For a more modest meal, there is a small **grocery/bakery** near the plateia where the buses stop. Follow the signs to fresh loaves, croissants, and pitas. (€0.60-1.20. Open M-Sa 7am-9pm, Su 7am-2pm.)

BEACHES. A 20min. trip down the 252 stone stairs at the northern end of the main road (to the right of the church) leads to rocky **Ammoudi Beach,** where a few boats are moored in a startlingly deep swimming lagoon. It's worth climbing down the cliff to swim in the stunning blue water and play on the volcanic rocks. Reenergize with a meal of fresh fish at one of the three **tavernas** at the bottom of the stairs, where meals are hauled straight from the net to the table. If you're not up for the trek back, hire a **donkey** (€3 per person) to carry you.

MILOS Μηλος

Though the ghost of past achievements continues to loom large (plastic replicas of the Venus de Milo pop up everywhere from the archaeological museum to taverna bathrooms), there's much to enjoy in Milos that France hasn't stolen. Mineral deposits and volcanoes collaborate to create a wealth of breathtaking beaches. The winding streets of Trypiti and the ancient theater and catacombs deserve an evening of aimless wandering.

ADAMAS Αδαμας

This port town stuffs most of Milos's accommodations, food, and nightlife into the space of several blocks, causing congestion that is both vibrant and stifling. Though most sights are elsewhere, the centralized bus system makes it a base for exploring the rest of the island; a rented moped or car helps, too. Follow the waterfront to the right from the ferries to reach the center of Adamas.

TRANSPORTATION

Flights: Olympic Airways (☎22870 22 380, at the airport ☎22870 22 381), on 25 Martiou. Planes go once daily to **Athens** (€55). Open M-F 8am-3pm.

Ferries: From Milos, ferries follow a complex but well-posted schedule to: **Folegandros** (2hr., 4 per week, €5.70); **Ios** (1 hr., 7 per week; €17.10); **Kythnos** (2½hr., 2-3 per day, €8.50); **Piraeus** (7hr., 3 per day, €16.50); **Santorini** (4hr., 8 per week, €12.40); **Serifos** (2hr., 3 per day, €5.60); **Sifnos** (1½hr., 3 per day, €5). The small Karamitsos ferry also goes to **Kimolos** (30min., 5 per day, €1.73) from Pollonia.

Flying Dolphins: Twice as fast and roughly twice as expensive as ferries. 6 per week go to **Amorgos, Piraeus, Serifos,** and **Sifnos.** 2 per week to **Iraklion,** Crete.

Buses: (☎22870 22 219). Buses stop by the Agricultural Bank on the waterfront and travel almost hourly to **Plaka, Pollonia, Trypiti,** and other destinations for €0.80 each way. They also travel regularly to **Paleohori, Hivadolimni,** and **Provatas,** and the **campsite** (€1.05). Check the schedule posted in the bus station or in travel offices.

Taxis: (☎22870 22 219), stand along the waterfront. Available 24hr.

Moped Rental: Milos Rent a Car (☎22870 21 994; fax 22870 24 002), across from the port. Bikes €15-35 per day; cars €40-55 per day. Minimum age 19 to rent mopeds; 23 for cars.

ORIENTATION AND PRACTICAL INFORMATION

Tourist Office: (☎22870 22 445), across from the dock. Ask for brochures, maps, ferry and bus timetables, and a complete list of the island's rooms and hotels. Open daily 10am-4pm and 6-11:30pm. Pick up a free **Welcome to Milos** guide.

Tourist Agencies: Milos Travel (☎22870 22 286; fax 22870 22 396) and **RIVA Travel** (☎22870 24 024; fax 22870 28 005; rivatr@otenet.gr) are both on the waterfront. Sell ferry tickets and help with bus schedules.

Banks: National Bank (☎22870 22 077), near the post office along the waterfront with 24hr. **ATM.** There's an **Agricultural Bank** (☎22870 22 330) in the central plateia at the harbor. Both open M-Th 8am-2pm, F 8am-1:30pm.

Laundry: (☎22870 22 228). Turn left right after Internet C@fe. €8.80 for 5kg.

Police: (☎22870 21 204), by the bus stop in Plaka.

Port Authority: (☎22870 22 100). Open 24hr.

Medical Center: (☎22870 22 700, 701, or 702), in Plaka.

Internet Access: Internet C@fe (☎22870 28 011), walk uphill on the street across from the Agricultural Bank. €5.50 per hr. Open noon-3pm and 6pm-midnight.

Post Office: (☎22870 22 288). Take the waterfront road past the bus station and turn right after the Agricultural Bank; it's 100m down this road. Open M-F 9am-2pm. **Postal code:** 84801.

ACCOMMODATIONS AND CAMPING

High season prices may wound your wallet, but fear not—persistence will turn up affordable private rooms in domatia hiding in Adamas's side streets. Book far in advance to stay here.

Semiramis Hotel (☎22870 23 722; fax 22870 22 118; www.hotelsemiramis.gr). Follow the main road past the bus station, and bear left after the supermarket; it's straight ahead. Nikos and Petros tend excellent rooms with a shaded garden outside. Breakfast €3.50. If it's full, ask about its sister hotel, nearby **Dionysus,** 50m farther along the main road. Doubles €27-47; triples 20% more. Cheaper rooms downstairs with common bath €25-33. Add €6 for A/C. ❸

Kanaris Rooms to Let (☎22870 22 184), 200m from the town center–look for the "Anezina" minibus. Private baths, fridges, balconies, and ceiling fans. Doubles €20-42. If you want slightly fancier rooms with A/C and fridges, stay at the sister hotel, Anezina. Doubles €30-80, depending on room and season. Singles 20% less. ❹

Hotel Corali (☎22870 22 216; fax 22870 22 144), around the corner from Kanaris Rooms. Private baths and ceiling fans. Port shuttle available. Doubles €35-65. ❹

Camping Milos (☎22870 31 410; fax 22870 31 412), at Hivadolimni beach, 7km from port; buses pick up at the dock before 6:30pm. New and sharp, with kitchen, laundry, car/bike rental, mini-market and restaurant. €5 per person; €6 tent rental. Bungalows with fridges and baths €47-60. ❶

FOOD AND NIGHTLIFE

Large waterfront restaurants draw tourists with their beautiful views every night. There are also several cafes peppering the waterfront, where you can watch the flood of tourists drown the island every few hours. The multitude of bakeries, creperies, and sandwich shops in the main square serve quick, cheap meals. **Pitsounakia** ❶, 10m inland on the street with the Agricultural Bank, serves traditional, home-cooked meals (Greek salad €2.95, moussaka €3.50). About 250m along the waterfront road you'll find **Navayio** ❸, a popular taverna with delicious, affordable fish dishes (swordfish fillet €10). It opens at 9am for breakfast. Though there isn't much of a bar or disco scene in Adamas, there are a few places to dance to Greek tracks. Sip a drink at **Aragosta Cafe,** located both above and beside Milos Travel. The late night dancing is at the upstairs cafe. (Pina colada €7. Cafe open 8am-3am; club open 8pm-late.) Right next door, you'll find **Vipera Lebetina,** where DJs spin mainstream music into the wee hours of the night. If you're looking for some impressive man-made scenery, head to **La Costa.** With your back to the port, head left past the tourist agency and around the corner. You can't miss the massive reconstructed ship that hovers above the bar. (☎22870 24 008. Open 9pm-3am.) The real action happens next door to La Costa at **Fuego,** where you can practice your dance moves. (€8 cover includes a drink. Open 11pm-late.)

BEACHES

Milos has emerged from centuries of volcanic eruptions with stunning **beaches** covered with exceptional rock formations and unique sand. Twenty-four distinctive beaches line the island's northern and southern coasts. In the north, the pools of **Papafragas** are embraced by a stone arch and arms of white rock reaching into the sea, creating the impression of swimming next to snow-covered mountains. Take the bus to **Pollonia** and ask the driver to let you off at the beach. Seven buses per day journey to densely populated **Hivadolimni** beach (15min.). On the south side of the island, lively **Provatas** and **Paleohori** beaches sport bars, music, comfy beach chairs, and bus access from Adamas (25min., 8 per day). The real gem sits between them at **Tsigrados** beach, where natural stores of pearlite make for deep, soft sand that glimmers magnificently in the afternoon sun. Get there by moped, or make the 1½hr. trek from Provatas. Ask at the travel agencies about boat excursions that stop at several beaches on a tour around the island. (Most run 9am-6pm and cost around €18.) If you want to get a little exercise, explore the island by kayak. Call **Sea Kayak Milos** (☎22870 21 365 or 22870 23 597; www.seakayakgreece.com) to find out more details on the various trips (ranging €30-50).

CYCLADES

DAYTRIPS FROM ADAMAS

PLAKA Πλακα AND TRYPITI Τρυπητη

Buses from Adamas run to Plaka and Trypiti (15min., every 30min., €0.80).

From the bus stop, head along the paved street, down the steps, and bear right to find the large yellow **Archaeological Museum,** which houses artifacts unearthed at Fylakopi, including the mesmerizing *Lady of Fylakopi.* (☎22870 21 620. Open Tu-Su 8:30am-3pm. €3, students and seniors €2, EU students free.) For a truly spectacular view, climb upward for 15min. from the bus station to the **Panagia Thalassitra Monastery** at the top of the old castle. Six winding kilometers from Adamas, the town of Plaka rests on mountaintops. Opposite the police station, follow the signs downhill through several twisting streets to the terrace of the **Church of Panagia Korfiatissa,** which leans into a view of lush countryside and blue sea only an arm's length away. Next door, the town's **Folk Museum** displays eerie mannequins in household settings. (☎22870 21 292. Open Tu-Sa 10am-2pm and 6-9pm, Su 10am-2pm. €2, students and children €1.)

A 3min. walk from the Archaeological Museum leads to the tiny town of Trypiti. From there a paved road winds down past several sights. A sign marks the spot where the **Venus de Milo** was buried around 320 BC; she was moved to the Louvre in Paris in the 19th century after being discovered by a farmer tilling his fields. Farther off the path a well-preserved **theater** dating from the Roman occupation provides a riveting ocean view; ask at the tourist office about performances there. Last along the road and down a set of stairs lie signs for **catacombs** hewn into the cliff face, which are the oldest site of Christian worship in Greece. The open-air ruins are small and without on-site plaques, but peering into the unlit corridors of the cool catacombs sparks the imagination. Of the five chambers, only one is open to the public. (☎22870 21 625. Open Tu-Su 8am-7pm. Free.) You can also still see part of a Dorian stone wall built between 1100 and 800 BC. Archaeology buffs will want to scramble among the ruins of **Filakopi,** 3km from the fishing village of **Pollonia** (Πολλονια) toward Adamas, where British excavations unearthed 3500-year-old **frescoes** now displayed in the National Museum in Athens.

KIMOLOS Κιμωλος

Ferries run from Pollonia on Milos to Kimolos (5 per day, €1.73).

Kimolos is loveliest at sunset, when the colors are most vivid over the sea, nearby islands, and Kimolos's shining white rock. Valued for centuries, the Venetians called the island *Argentiera* after the silver sands on the southeast part of the island. Disembark at the small port of **Psathi,** and head left for Aliki Beach or continue up to Hora. Travel around the island is difficult, and information is hard to get since the information center is rarely open. The Kastro ruins, in the center of town, are just that—ruined. Wander through the alleyways and peer into the empty shells of houses, but be careful not to step on a Coke can or other litter thoughtlessly strewn about. From the Kastro, an hour's hike will take you through mountains to the beautiful beaches of the eastern shore. You can also hire a water taxi from the port.

SIFNOS Σιφνος

Sifniots are a festive bunch, dropping everything a whopping 13 times a year to celebrate religious festivals with food, drinking, dancing, and merriment that lasts for days. Even when they return to work, their zest persists in their happening nightlife, their distinctive cuisine, and their beaches, where people are as likely to be snorkeling or leaping from cliffs as bathing in the sun.

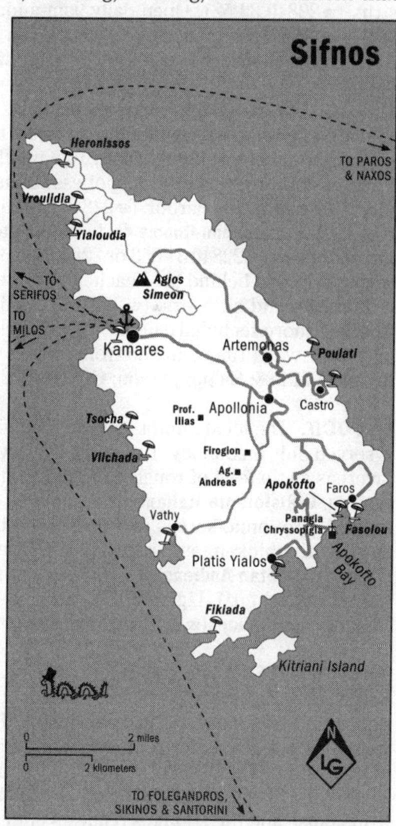

KAMARES Καμαρες

Kamares is a magnificent harbor filled with sailboats and yachts and surrounded by formidable brown cliffs in fierce contrast to the emerald sea. The town beach sweeps the harbor rim, and a few tavernas line its shallow perimeter. Kamares is an easy-going town, where the days seem to just drift away. Here you can secure a room, swim, dine, and peruse shops full of ornate local pottery; look for signs reading *keramiko* (ceramic) throughout the village.

TRANSPORTATION. From Sifnos, **ferries** head to: **Kimolos** (1hr., 1 per day, €4.70); **Kythnos** (1½hr., 1 per day, €6.30); **Ios** (2 per week, €9.60); **Milos** (1½hr., 3 per day, €5); **Piraeus** (5½hr., 3 per day, €14.40); **Santorini** (5hr., 9-12 per week, €10); **Serifos** (45min., 3 per day, €4.70);

and **Sikinos** (4½hr., 2 per week, €8.10). For roughly twice the price of ferries at twice the speed, hop on one of the **Flying Dolphins** that speed daily to: **Kythnos** (45min.); **Milos** (45min.); **Pireaus** (3hr.); **Santorini** (2½hr.); and **Serifos** (20min.). Four **buses** travel daily between a number of destinations including **Apollonia;** consult posted schedules for routes and stops. The main stop in Kamares is in front of the information office, near the port. A number of **taxis** are available on the island (☎22840 33 719, 22840 31 626, or 22840 31 347). Some of the best car rental rates are at **Niki Rent a Car.** Look for the sign past the cafes. (☎22840 33 993. Bikes €10-20; cars €38-60.)

ORIENTATION AND PRACTICAL INFORMATION. Just opposite the ferry dock, the **Information Office** helps visitors find rooms, deciphers boat and bus schedules, exchanges currency, and stores luggage. (☎/fax 22840 31 977. Open daily 9am-midnight.) The **port authority** is next door. (☎22840 33 617. Open 24hr.) Along the waterfront as you walk from the dock to town, the English-speaking staff at **Aegean Thesaurus Travel Agency** finds accommodations, exchanges currency, stores luggage, and sells tickets for ferries and Flying Dolphins. (☎22840 33 151; fax 22840 32 190; thesauras@travelling.gr. Open daily 9:30am-10pm.) **Public toilets** are next to the information office. There's an **international press** on the main strip. (☎22840 33 521. Open daily 9am-midnight.) In an **emergency,** call the **police** (☎22840 31 210) in Apollonia. A **doctor** can be reached at the clinic at ☎22840 31 315; call the **pharmacy** at ☎22840 33 541. **Postal code:** 84003.

CYCLADES

ACCOMMODATIONS AND CAMPING. During high season, you're unlikely to find a budget hotel room; inquire at **Room to Let** signs or ask at one of the many waterfront tavernas. **Hotel Kiki ❹,** 10m uphill from the main road beyond the strip of cafes and tavernas, offers spotless rooms with baths, TVs, fridges, and balconies overlooking the harbor. (☎22840 32 329; fax 22840 31 453. Doubles €45-59; triples €49-62.) **Meltemi Rooms ❸,** behind Hotel Kiki, has clean rooms with A/C and private baths. (☎22840 31 653 or 22840 33 066. Doubles €25-40.) **Maki's Camping ❶,** across the road behind the beach in Kamares, sports a taverna, laundry, and common baths and showers. (☎22840 32 366. €4.40 per person; €2 tent rental.) Another, more secluded campsite is calm, clean **Platis Yialos Camping ❶,** amid trees and stone walls 10min. inland from the bus stop; it's 30min. by bus from Kamares. (☎22840 71 286. €4 per person; €2.40 tent rental.)

FOOD. The local Sifniot specialty of chickpea soup, called *revithada* (€2.50) is served only on Sunday. There are also several **groceries** and **bakeries.** Most of the tavernas serve food of roughly the same quality and price, but some have seaside seating. **Ristorante Italiano de Claudio ❷,** on the waterfront up the main street toward Apollonia, serves up incredible pizza (€6-10) and *rigatoni delicati*, a pasta with chicken, asparagus, and cream sauce. (Open 1pm-late.) Across the street, **O Kapetan Andreas ❷** specializes in seafood—try the *astakomakaronada* (lobster spaghetti). Lights adorn the tree-filled terrace, creating a surprisingly romantic ambience. (☎22840 32 356. Open noon-midnight. Lobster €5.75 per kg.)

NIGHTLIFE. A choice sunset-watching spot is **Cafe Folie,** at the far end of the beach. It's a bit pricey (cocktails €7.50), but the colorful, funky decor, Caribbean flavor, and proximity to the water justify the hefty price tag. The **Old Captain Bar,** midway along the waterfront strip, serves coffee and fruity drinks. Tap your toes in the sand to the beat of calypso and string music. (☎22840 31 990. Open daily 11am-3am.) Farther along the road, **Mobilize** attracts a later crowd; the strobe lights pulse and the DJ takes requests until sunrise. (Open daily 10pm-6am.)

APOLLONIA Απολλωνια

The streets of Apollonia, the island's capital, meander haphazardly about the hill. Pick a landmark to get your bearings by the main road, where all of Sifnos's roads converge. A few steps from the main road, you can meander the town's narrow lanes, where you'll find a maze of shops, bars, charming houses, and all the locals and Athenians who have adopted Sifnos as their island home.

ORIENTATION AND PRACTICAL INFORMATION. All the necessities and luxuries a traveler could need can be found on the main plateia, where the **bus** from Kamares makes its first stop. Buses to **Kamares** (10min., €0.80) wait in the plateia in front of the post office, while those to villages and beaches such as **Kastro** (€0.80) and **Platis Yialos** (€1.50) stop around the corner near the Hotel Anthousa. Buses run to all three at least once every hour. An **international press** is located off the plateia next to the meat market. **Aegean Thesaurus,** near the post office, is your source for **currency exchange,** accommodation assistance, bus and ferry schedules, and their €2 island information packs. (☎22840 33 151. Open daily 10am-10pm.) The **National Bank,** up the road on the left before Hotel Anthousa, has a 24hr. **ATM.** (☎22840 31 317. Open M-Th 8am-2pm, F 8am-1:30pm.) From the other bus stop near Hotel Anthousa, head left on the road to Artemonas to find the **police station** (☎22840 31 210) in a small white building on your right and the **medical center** (☎22840 31 315) on your left. There's an **OTE** on the road back to Kamares. (☎22840 31 699 or 22840 33 499. Open daily 7:30am-2:30pm.) The **Billiard Cafe,** on the road out of Apollonia to the right, offers **Internet access**. (€5.50 per hr. Open daily 11am-midnight.) Beside the main plateia is the **post office.** (☎22840 31 329. Open M-F 7:30am-2pm.) **Postal code:** 84003.

ACCOMMODATIONS. Summer vacancies are rare in Apollonia; call well in advance for reservations. **Nikoleta Rooms ❹,** across from the Eko gas station, offers quiet, clean rooms with balconies overlooking the city and the sea. TVs and kitchenettes in room. (☎22840 71 348. Doubles €35-53.) **Sifnos Hotel ❹** has spacious rooms in the heart of the village, close to (but not too close to) the town's nightlife. (☎22840 31 624. Double €37-65.) **Hotel Sofia ❸** is just off the plateia; head up the wide paved road from the main plateia until you see it on your left above the supermarket. (☎22840 31 238. Doubles €36-42.) **Hotel Anthousa ❸,** above the pastry shop around the corner from the main plateia, offers A/C, TVs, and phones in very clean rooms. (☎22840 31 431; fax 22840 32 220. Self-service laundry €12. Singles €27-36; doubles €36-55.)

FOOD AND NIGHTLIFE. Restaurants are excellent and not as expensive as their beautiful exteriors suggest. The better tavernas are along the path across from the police. The restaurant at the **Sifnos Hotel ❶** (☎22840 31 624) serves the island specialty on Sunday—chick-peas with olive oil and lemon, cooked overnight in special ovens (€4.50). **Apostolos ❶** also ladles it up along with years of wisdom about the island. The fricassee is a classic—goat and rice covered with greens and baked in a ceramic pot (€6.50). **Vegera ❶,** on the road to Artemonas, just before the National Bank, brews strong coffee and makes crepes (€3.50-5) on an open-air veranda, a nice spot for viewing one of the island's spellbinding sunsets. Try the caramel cake—it's sinfully delicious. (☎22840 33 385. Open daily 9am-3am.) Stroll along the street behind Hotel Anthousa to tap into the Sifniot nightlife. **Isidora,** at the beginning of the street, is a local hotspot, complete with dance floor and international music. **Bodgi,** a popular cafe-bar, is likely to catch your eye and ear: candles light up both levels and the outside terrace, and the trip-hop beats your ear drum (open nightly until 4am). For a few good beers, stop by **Okiyialos,**

where they serve more than 40 kinds of ales and lagers. Live Greek music plays every night until sunrise at **Aloni,** where the Greeks are. Take the road toward Artemonas to get there. The **Camel Club,** up the road toward Platis Yialos past the Eko gas station, blares international tunes.

DAYTRIPS. Travel in Sifnos is easy with the assistance of the map available at kiosks (€1.30). Pack a picnic to nibble on as you explore Apollonia's adjacent hillside villages. The quiet but expansive village of **Artemonas,** a 10min. walk from Apollonia, has a magnificent view and several fine mansions built by refugees from Alexandria. Enchanting **Kastro** village is 3km east of Apollonia and can be reached by bus (15min., €0.80) or on foot (take a short cut via the stone pathway a few hundred meters along the paved road). This cluster of whitewashed houses and narrow streets rests on an ocean-facing mountaintop. Kastro has been inhabited constantly for 5 millennia, and the architecture has not changed since the 14th century. You may find the tiny **Archaeological Museum** while walking through the former capital's streets. (Open Tu-Su 8am-3pm. Free.) There are no hotels, but ask around for domatia. Behind Kastro and below tiny **Epta Martires** (Seven Martyrs) church is the island's best spot for **cliff diving.** Rocks form natural platforms for jumping into the deep water below. Watch the weather; foolish courage and rough seas make a dangerous duo. From Kastro, the footpath leads to the sparkling cove at **Poulati,** popular for snorkeling.

Buses run hourly to **Platis Yialos,** 12km from Apollonia, where you'll find all of the locals sipping *frappés* and enjoying the beautiful views. For a delicious meal, head to **Kalimera,** a restaurant specializing in French and Greek cuisine and sugary desserts. The Gahliatelles with smoked salmon (€9) are particularly good. (☎22840 71 365. Open 9am-midnight.) To the south, **Faros** has several popular beaches connected by footpaths. Busy **Fasolou** and **Apokof** beaches have tavernas. Farther along the path is striking **Panagia Chrysopigi Monastery,** also accessible by the Platis Yialos bus and a 10min. walk. A bridge connects the 17th-century monastery's rocky islet to the mainland. Forty days after Easter, the two-day **festival of Analipsos** is celebrated at Chrysopigi. Other renowned Sifniot festivals take place during the summer, with one in July and four in September. Inquire at the tourist office to find out when you can join in the fun.

KYTHNOS Κυθνος

Small as it may be, Kythnos has a strong personality. Whether in search of a relaxing trip to hot springs or a friendly family beach, any visitor can find a niche in Kythnos. The islanders are famously welcoming, and those few who visit their isle will delight in quiet beaches and simple small town life.

MERIHAS Μεριχας

The main port, Merihas, harbors most of the island's tourists in addition to its ferries. Making it your base of operations will help you explore the rest of Kythnos.

ORIENTATION AND PRACTICAL INFORMATION

The port town is peppered with rooms to let, a few tavernas and businesses, and several waterfront **markets. Ferries** sail to: **Folegandros** (6hr., 2 per week, €12.40); **Kea** (1½ hr., 2 per week, €5.20); **Kimolos** (3hr., 5 per week, €8.10); **Milos** (4hr., 2 per day, €8.50); **Piraeus** (3hr., 1-2 per day, €10.20); **Serifos** (1¼hr., 1-2 per day, €5.80); and **Sifnos** (2½hr., 1 per day, €6.30). Two ferries per week run to **Santorini** (8hr.,

€16.90); **Sikinos** (7hr., €13.10); and **Syros** (2½hr., €6.50). **Catamarans** skim to: **Milos** (5 per week); **Santorini** (2 per week); **Serifos** (5 per week); **Sifnos** (6 per week); and **Piraeus** (4 per week) for double ferry price in half ferry time. **Buses** stop at the waterfront and go to **Hora** (15min., 6 per day 7:15am-9:15pm); **Loutra** (30min., 6 per day 7:30am-9:30pm); and **Driopis** for €0.80-1.30; return buses follow a schedule 15min. behind this one. For a **taxi,** call ☎22810 31 272 or 407.

The **tourist office** (☎22810 32 250; open 9:30am-1:30pm, 5:15-9pm) by the dock dispenses general information, accommodation assistance, and boat schedules. Past the dock heading into town and up a flight of stairs on the left is the helpful **Milos Express** travel agency, with room information and ferry tickets. (☎22810 32 104; fax 22810 32 291. Open 9am-2pm, 5-10pm.) They also rent cars (€30-55) and mopeds (€12-18). Call the **tourist police** at ☎22810 31 201; the **port police** (☎22810 32 290) can help with ferry info. Farther along the waterfront, you'll find a representative of the **National Bank** in the supermarket with the "Bank" sign, who will **exchange currency.** The **pharmacy** is two doors left of Milos Express. (Open 9am-1pm, 6-9pm.) A **doctor** is available at ☎22810 32 234. There is no **OTE** or **post office** in Merihas. **Postal code:** 84006.

ACCOMMODATIONS AND FOOD. The few accommodations in the area surround the small pebbly beach in the town. Look up as you get off the ferry to the first white buildings at the top of the town, **Paradise Rooms ❸.** There are a mountain of stairs that lead there, but the panoramic view of the waterfront—as well as the kitchen, fan, and the private bathroom—make it worth the climb (☎22810 32 206. Doubles €25-35.) Walking with the sea on your right, turn left just before the children's playground to a series of domatia including **Panayota Rooms To Let ❸.** The spacious, clean rooms are equipped with 2-3 beds, kitchen, baths and fridges. (☎22810 32 268. €25-35.) **Kythnos Hotel ❹** is to the left of Milos Express (with your back to the water). Rooms are simple but comfortable, and there is a cafe downstairs. A/C, TVs, and fridges in room. (☎ 22810 32 247; fax 22810 32 092; kythnoshotel@in.gr. Breakfast €5. Doubles €35-50; triples €40-55.)

Sailors Restaurant ❸ (☎22810 32 056), on the central waterfront, hails you with waving flags; take your pick from its amazing selection of fresh fish—they're still flopping. Lobster spaghetti (€60 per kg), mixed fish (€15), onion pipes (€5), and fried Kythnos goat cheese (€4) are specials. Nearby **Yialos Restaurant ❸** offers similar prices and food in addition to a friendly staff. After dinner, bring the crew to the **Byzantio Club ❶** for a dish of ice cream with homemade fudge and whipped cream (€5) or an international cocktail (Long Island iced tea €8). (☎22810 32 259. Open 9am-late.) Later on, head to **Remezzo,** on the waterfront, to groove to American, British, and Greek tunes all night long. Trek uphill at the right of the harbor to **Agnanti**—you'll know it by the colored lights that illuminate the entrance. Ask the DJ to play your favorite song—chances are he'll have it. Keep walking to **Akrotiri ❶,** the only place in town with a huge outdoor dance floor. Either dance or watch the action from either of the two bars on the multi-level balconies. (☎22810 32 755. Open 6-11pm for coffee and ice cream, 11pm-late as a club. Beer €3; cocktails €8.)

BEACHES. The road that leads toward the **beaches** of Hora and Loutra also passes a turn-off for the small town of **Kolona.** After the turn-off, head left before a white building and pursue this path until you reach a long beach. As a result of protection from ocean currents, one side is warm, while the other is cool. A taverna sits above the beach, waiting to relieve your hunger or thirst. A road that heads in the other direction from Merihas takes you past little **Driopis;** stop by to check out the **Folk Museum** and the **Byzantine Museum.** (Open 10am-2pm and 7-9pm. Follow the signs from the church in the main plateia.)

SERIFOS Σεριφος

Sitting atop the crumbling Kastro, you can take in the full panorama of Serifos's charms, from the fertile arc of the port to the mining-ravaged hills and the untouched beaches. Poor roads restrict the hordes of Athenian vacationers from the port, leaving the rest of the island blissfully undiscovered. Stony Serifos got its name from Medusa. Perseus hunted her down and turned her shocking ugliness against her with a mirror; taking her head back to Polydictes, king of Serifos, he found the monarch putting the moves on his mom, Danae. Irate Perseus flashed Medusa's head at Polydictes, turning his royal court (and the island) to stone.

LIVADI Λιβαδι

Livadi, Serifos's port, keeps visitors rested and full for daytime trips throughout the island. Hora, the island's other main town, hangs above the port and is reachable by a hike (40min.) or the frequent bus (€0.80).

ORIENTATION AND PRACTICAL INFORMATION

A walk along the waterfront will take you past the services. An island map that lists useful phone numbers is available at kiosks (€1.20). Regular **ferries** from Piraeus and other western Cyclades arrive in Serifos. From Serifos, ferries travel to: **Folegandros** (5½hr.; 2 per week, €8.90); **Ios** (6 hr., M, €10.50); **Kimolos** (2½hr., 6 per week, €6.30); **Kythnos** (1¼hr., F, €5.60); **Milos** (2¼hr., 1-3 per day, €5.60); **Piraeus** (4½hr., 1-3 per day, €12.80); **Santorini** (7hr., 2 per week, €13.90); **Sifnos** (45min., 1-3 per day, €4.70); and **Sikinos** (6½hr., 2 per week, €9.90). **Catamarans** go once per day to **Milos, Kimolos, Piraeus,** and **Sifnos** in half the time and for twice the money. **Buses** travel from Livadi to **Hora** (14 per day 7:30am-11pm, €0.80); a return bus follows the same schedule with a 15min. delay. Another bus travels every Tu, Th, Sa, and Su to the beach towns of **Megalo Livadi** and **Koutalas** at 10:30am, returning from Megalo Livadi at 3:45pm and Koutalas at 4pm. Buses also go to the **monastery** (30min., daily at 3pm); they wait there for 30min. before rumbling back to Livadi. Krinas Travel rents **cars** (€30-50 per day) and **mopeds** (€12-20) at the most competitive prices on the island. For **taxis,** call ☎22810 51 245 or 22810 51 435.

Krinas Travel, (☎22810 51 488 or 22810 51 500; fax 22810 51 073; open daily 9am-midnight) at the inland end of the dock, and **Apiliotis Travel,** (☎22810 51 155; open daily 9am-2pm and 6-8:30pm) on the waterfront to the left of a supermarket, sell hydrofoil and ferry tickets and have English schedules. The **Alpha Bank,** with 24hr. **ATM,** is along the waterfront. (☎22810 51 780 or 22810 51 739. Open M-Th 8am-2pm, F 8am-1:30pm.) The **port police** (☎22810 51 470) are up the narrow steps. For **police,** dial ☎22810 51 300. The **pharmacy** is two doors to the left of Apiliotis. (☎22810 51 205. Open daily 9am-2pm and 6:30-9:30pm.) **Postal code:** 84005.

ACCOMMODATIONS AND FOOD

The small port town of Livadi is big on rooming options. **Hotel Areti ❹,** up the hill on the first left as you exit the ferry, bears blue shutters and a coat of whitewash. The hotel has a harbor view, a backyard terrace, private balconies, A/C, and fridges. (☎22810 51 479 or 22810 51 107; fax 22810 51 547. Breakfast €5. Open Apr.-Oct. Singles €30-50; doubles €46-60; elegant studios for 4 €50-88.) **Hotel Serifos Beach ❸** is a block back from the beach, under a large blue sign on the main waterfront road. Away from the main strip, rooms are quiet and comfortable. (☎22810 51 209 or 22810 51 468. Port shuttle available. Breakfast €7.50. Singles €33-41; doubles €40-50. €8 extra for A/C.) For a splurge, head to **Asteri Hotel ❺,** located right on the beach. Rooms are spacious with elegant decor. (☎22810 51 789; www.asteri.gr. Doubles €75-90; triples €65-80.) **Alexandros-Vassilias ❹,** located on Livadakia Beach, has clean rooms hidden among beautiful flowers and is perfect for families. To find it, follow the same directions given for the Coralli Camping or call for a shuttle. (☎/fax 22810 51 903. Doubles €29-56; triples €47-72; quads €53.20-65.80.) The **Coralli Campgrounds ❶,** popular with backpackers, lie 20m from Livadakia Beach and 700m left of the port. Call for a minibus, or follow uphill the first inland street right of the port, turn left one street beyond the school, and continue toward the Coralli flags. Bungalows have TVs, A/C, fridges, and private baths. A mini-market, laundry facilities, swimming pool, common kitchen, and a small restaurant are also available. (☎22810 51 500; fax 22810 51 073; www.coralli.gr. €4 per person; €3 per tent. Bungalows: singles €24-25; doubles €30-56; triples €40-65; quads €48-72.)

Restaurants and cafes spring out from hotels and line the waterfront. For an inexpensive, stick-to-your-ribs meal, head to **Stamadis ❶,** at the right end of the waterfront on the beach. The stuffed vine leaves (€3.50) and rabbit casserole with onions (€5.30) are delightful. (☎22810 51 309 or 22810 51 729. Open daily 8am-late). Visit **Vitamine C ❷,** near the Hotel Serifos Beach, for a breakfast sandwich (€5.30). The restaurant at the **Hotel Anna ❸** serves a Greek and Italian menu. (☎22810 51 666 or 22810 51 484; fax 22810 51 277. Pastas €5; meat dishes €11. Open daily 6:30am-2am.)

CYCLADES

NIGHTLIFE AND BEACHES

Karnayia, right on the waterfront, blasts classic tunes from the 70s and 80s. (Cocktails €6.50. Open 9am-late.) The **Roman** cafe, in a small shop complex by Vitamine C, has a pool table (€6 per hr.), games, and a mellow scene. (☎22810 52 242. Open late.) **Hook** is a rooftop dance club that plays a mix of American top 40 and Greek hits. Look for its red sign and large globular patio lights. (Open nightly 11pm-late).

Serifos has many secluded sandy **beaches** awaiting your lone footprints. Follow the signs at the right side of the waterfront for a 45min. walk to **Psili Amos.** In a calm bay at the base of a mountain, this quiet beach is populated by a single taverna. Follow a map along the paved and dirt roads of Northern Serifos to the unnamed beaches hiding here. For those without a vehicle or swift-footed mule, a bus travels once daily to **Mega Livadi** and **Koutalas.**

DAYTRIPS FROM LIVADI

HORA Χωρα

The dense white roofs of Hora look postcard-perfect, with whitewashed houses tumbling down the hill like a handful of white dice. The 40min. walk there from Livadi begins at a stone staircase next to the Marinos market. The footsore can catch the hourly bus from Livadi. The first stop on this route deposits you at Hora's **post office** (☎22810 51 239; open M-F 7:30am-noon) and **OTE** (☎22810 51 399), while the second drops you in front of a well-stocked **supermarket** and a few tavernas. From here you can climb up a series of steps to the small **chapel** that crowns the town. The crumbling remains of the old **Kastro** invite you to poke around them; follow the signs painted along the numerous steps up. Getting lost in Hora's maze of stony, twisty streets is even better than knowing your way around. You'll discover quiet tavernas and markets along the alleyways. The **Archaeological Museum** houses artifacts from Hora's Roman years (open daily 6-9pm, Sa-Su 10am-noon). Domatia are available in town for around €37 per double.

NORTHERN SERIFOS

Serifos's interior isn't very accessible without a car or moped, a map, and excellent driving skills. See Orientation and Practical Information *(p. 462)* *for car rental information.*

Traditional villages, scattered churches and monasteries, and traces of ruins mark the northern part of the island. With transportation, you can visit the **Monastery of the Taxiarchs,** 10km beyond Hora toward the village of Galani. Built in 1400 on a site where a Cypriot icon mysteriously appeared (and to which it returns whenever removed), the monastery also houses an Egyptian lantern and several Russian relics. Upon entering the church, notice the frescoes that have been preserved in the doorway above; there is also a 17th-century stone plate in the middle of the floor depicting the Byzantine Double Eagle. If you arrive by bus, you may meet the lone monk who has lived there for 20 years. Arrange a visit by calling ahead (☎22810 51 027). By foot, the trip takes 2hr. The monastery and town around the port have no facilities, so bring all you'll need if you choose to hike.

DODECANESE Δωδεκανησα

The Dodecanese are lean wolves and hunt in packs; waterless, eroded by the sun. They branch off every side as you coast along the shores of Anatolia. Then toward afternoon the shaggy green of Cos comes up; and then slithering out of the wintry blue the moist green flanks of Rhodes.

—Lawrence Durrell

Scattered against the coast of Turkey, the Dodecanese, or Twelve Islands, are the farthest Greek island group from the mainland. Closer to Asia Minor than to Athens, these islands have experienced more invasions than the central parts of the country. In ancient times, the Dodecanese flourished before falling to Alexander the Great. A favorite target of evangelizing biblical luminaries including St. Paul and St. John, the inhabitants of the islands were some of the first Greeks to convert to Christianity. The islands prospered in the early Byzantine years, before suffering from raids that later hurt the entire empire. Crusaders stormed through during the 14th century, building heavily fortified castles as bases for their religious wars. The Ottomans ousted them in 1522, and the lucky Dodecanese received special concessions for their proximity to Turkey. The Dodecanese ultimately joined the Greek nation in 1948 after fighting fiercely in WWII.

Eclectic architecture is the most visible legacy of all these comings and goings: Classical ruins, castles built by Crusaders, and Ottoman mosques all coexist. Travelers who venture here will find landscapes ranging from Rhodes's fertile hills to the volcanic terrain of Nisyros. Kos's hopping nightlife, the apocalyptic beauty of Patmos, the secluded beaches of Karpathos, and the hidden glory of Kalymnos are sure to entice even the most discriminating traveler.

HIGHLIGHTS OF THE DODECANESE

THINK REVELATION when visiting Patmos (p. 490), former home of visionary gospel writer St. John.

SNIFF THE SULFUR of the smoking, inactive Mandraki volcano on Nisyros (p. 505).

REJUVENATE with a bathtime scrubdown on sponge capital Kalymnos (p. 486).

STRAIN YOUR EARS for the sublime whisper of millions of bright beating wings in Rhodes's Valley of Butterflies (p. 478).

SQUEEZE into your tightest pants and strut the streets of Kos (p. 478).

RHODES Ροδος

The undisputed tourist capital of the Dodecanese, Rhodes has room for all, sheltering the centuries-old customs, natural resources, and serene escapes of the interior and smaller coastal towns. Sandy beaches stretch along the east coast, jagged cliffs skirt the west, and green mountains freckled with villages fill the interior; resort towns dominate the north. Kamiros, Ialyssos, and Lindos show the clearest evidence of the island's Classical past, while medieval fortresses slumber in Rhodes Town and in Monolithos.

RHODES TOWN

While in Rhodes, one is always dimly aware of the city's history as a busy port; perhaps it's the wind that blows persistently through the tunnel-like streets of the Old City or the boatmen sitting on neighboring barstools or working behind reception desks. The harbors continue to thrive, their bustling activity vying for attention with the New City's shops, humming cafes, and raucous nightlife.

TRANSPORTATION

Schedules for ferries, Flying Dolphins, and buses are at the EOT. Summer moped rental agencies are common throughout town. The bumpy, narrow cobblestone roads of the Old Town are dangerous on a moped: be careful.

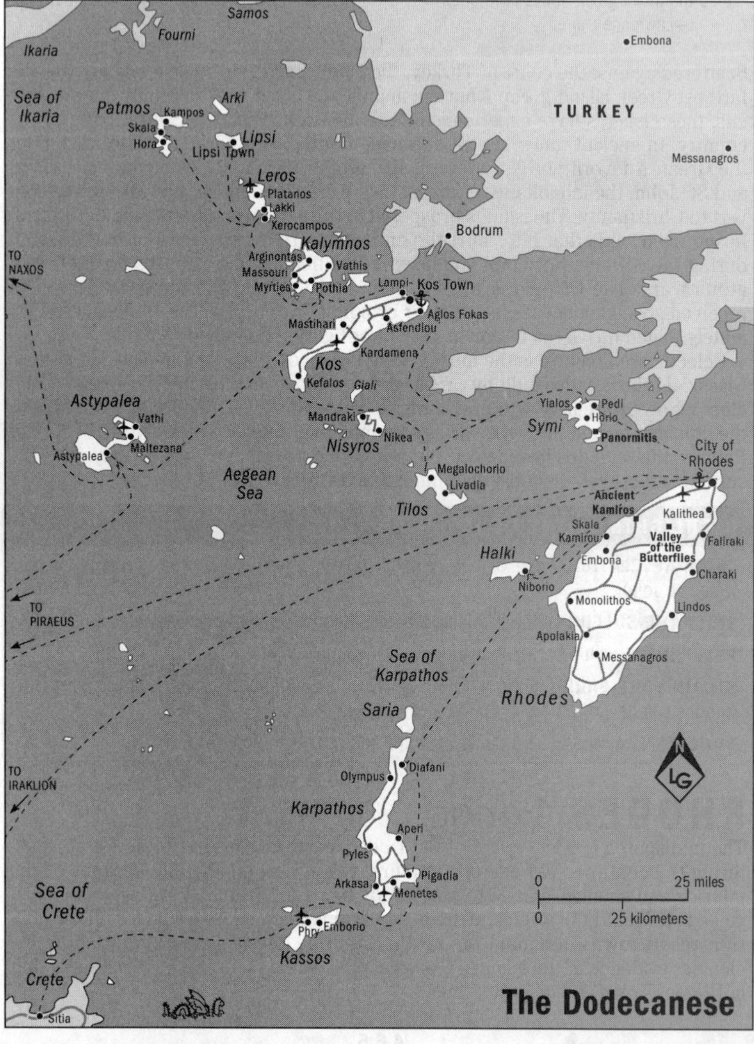

Flights: Olympic Airways, Ierou Lohou 9 (☎22410 24 571, reservations 22410 24 555), near the central EOT. Open M-F 8:30am-3:30pm. The **airport** (☎ 22410 83 406) is on the west coast, 16km from town, near Paradisi, and is accessible by public bus (5am-11pm from the west side bus station, €1.50). Flights to: **Athens** (5 per day, €90); **Iraklion,** Crete (4 per week, €87); **Karpathos** (2 per day, €28); **Kassos** (5 per week, €34); **Kastellorizo** (5 per week, €25); **Mykonos** (2 per week, €81); **Santorini** (6 per week, €80); **Thessaloniki** (1 per day, €112).

Ferries: To: **Agios Nikolaos,** Crete (3 per week, €20.30); **Astypalea** (2 per week, €16.30); **Halki** (3 per week, €6.40); **Kalymnos** (3-5 per day, €14.20); **Karpathos** (3 per week, €15); **Kassos** (3 per week, €17.50); **Kos** (1-2 per day, €11); **Leros** (1 per day, €15.20); **Milos** (3 per week, €29.10); **Patmos** (1-2 per day, €17.10); **Piraeus** (1-4 per day, €30); **Samos** (1 per week, €21.10); **Sitia,** Crete (3 per week, €19.40); **Symi** (1 per day, €6); **Thessaloniki** (1 per week, €45.80); and **Tilos** (3 per week, €9.10). Most ferries have student discounts. Daily excursions from Mandraki Port to: **Kos** (round-trip €45); **Symi** and **Panormitis Monastery** (round-trip €20).

Flying Dolphins: Hydrofoils head to Turkey and the rest of the Dodecanese. To: **Halki** (1 per day, €14); **Kalymnos** (Th, Sa, Su; €28.10); **Kos** (2 per day, €22.50); **Leros** (M and F, €30.20); **Marmaris** (1 per day, €45 including port taxes); **Nisyros** (€20); **Symi** (Su-F 1 per day, Sa 2 per day; €10); **Tilos** (1-2 per day, €18.50). Call **Zorpidis** agency for more hydrofoil information (☎22410 20 625). The **Katamaran Dodekanissos Express**

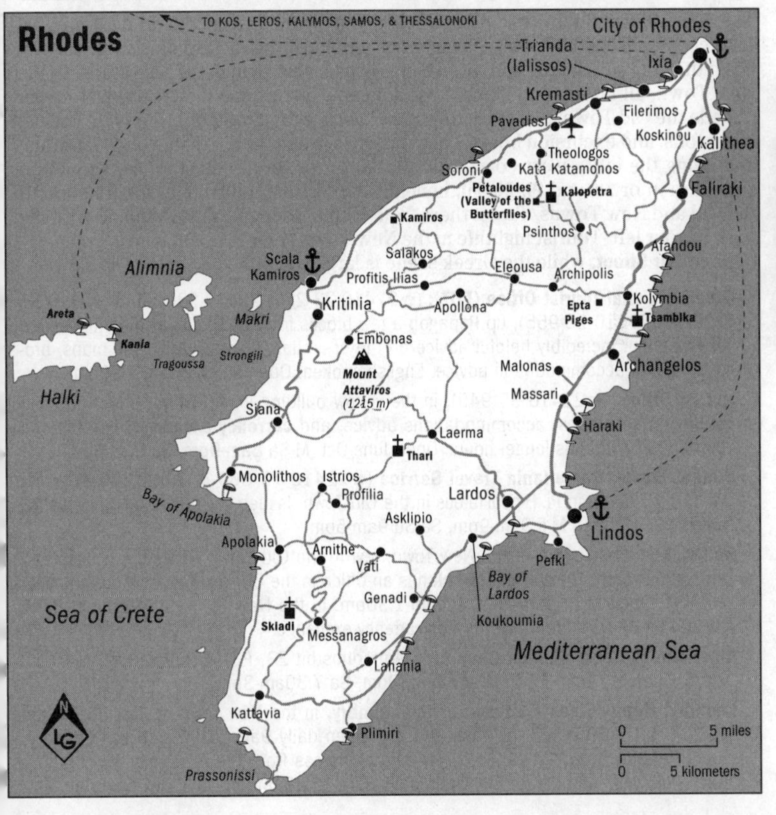

(☎22410 70 590) travels from Kolona Harbor between **Kalymnos, Leros, Kos, Halki, Nisyros, Tilos,** and **Symi** twice daily during the summer.

Buses: Stations lie on opposite sides of Papagou at Pl. Rimini.

East station is served by **KTEL** (☎22410 27 706 or 22410 75 134; fax 22410 24 268). Service east to: **Afandou** (14 per day 6:45am-11pm, €1.55); **Archangelos** (14 per day 6:45am-11pm, €2); **Faliraki** (18 per day 9am-11pm, €1.55); **Pefki** and **Gennadi** (9 per day 6:45am-7:30pm, €4.15); **Haraki** (10am, €2.45); **Kolymbia Beach** (3 per day 9am-9:15pm, €2.20); **Laerma** (M-F 1pm, €4.15); **Lindos** (14 per day 8:30am-7:30pm, €3.20); **Malona** and **Massari** (4 per day 9am-2:30pm, €2.45); **Tsambika Beach** (9am, €2.20).

West station is served by **RODA** (☎22410 26 300). Service west to: **Embona** (3 per day, €4); **Kalavarda** (8 per day 5am-9:35pm, €1.70); **Kalithea, Calypso, Kastri** (31 per day 6:30am-10:30pm, €1.55); **Kamiros** (10am, 1:30pm; €3.40); **Koskinou** (10 per day 5:50am-9:10pm, €1.55); **Kritinia** (1 per day, €3.55); **Monolithos** (M-F 1:30pm, €4.80); **Paradisi Airport** (24 per day 5am-11pm, €1.55); **Petaloudes** (9:30, 11am; €3.10); **Salakos** (5 per day 6:45am-9:30pm, €2.80); **Soroni** and **Fanes** (10 per day 5am-9:30pm, €1.70); **Pastida** and **Maritsa** (10 per day 5:40am-9:35pm, €1.55); **Damatria** (5 per day 6am-9:35pm, €1.70); **Embona** (1:45pm, €4); **Theologos** (12 per day 5am-9:30pm, €1.70).

Taxis: (☎22410 27 666), in Pl. Rimini. Radio taxis also available 24hr. (☎22410 64 712, 734, 756, 778 or 790).

ORIENTATION AND PRACTICAL INFORMATION

The city is divided into two districts. **New Town** spans the north and west and **Old Town** centers around **Sokratous,** a bustling, cobbled street descending from the castle to the commercial harbor; most Old Town streets branch off Sokratous. In the New Town, all international and most domestic ferries use the **Commercial Harbor** outside the Old Town. **Mandraki,** the New Town's waterfront, docks private yachts, hydrofoils, and excursion boats. Town beaches are to the north, beyond Mandraki, and along the city's west coast. The tourist office, both bus stations, and a taxi stand are in or around **Pl. Rimini,** beneath the fortress's turrets at the junction of the Old and New Towns. To get there from Mandraki, head a block inland with the park to your left. Tourist nightlife in the New Town centers on **Orfanidou,** popularly dubbed **Bar Street,** while the Greek scene is largely at **Militadou** in the Old Town.

Greek National Tourist Office (EOT): (☎22410 23 255, 22410 23 655, or 22410 35 226; fax 22410 26 955), up Papagou a few blocks from Pl. Rimini at the intersection of Makariou. Incredibly helpful advice on the essentials for your visit. Free maps, brochures, and accommodation advice. English spoken. Open M-F 8:30am-2:30pm.

Tourist Office: (☎22410 35 945), in the yellow building in Pl. Rimini. Bus, ferry, and excursion schedules, accommodations advice, and **currency exchange.** Less helpful than the EOT but has longer hours. Open June-Oct. M-Sa 8am-9pm, Su 8am-3pm.

Budget Travel: Castellania Travel Service (☎22410 75 860 or 22410 75 862; fax 22410 75 861), in Pl. Hippokratous in the Old Town. Issues low-priced **ISIC** and **GO25 cards** (€12). Open M-F 9am-9pm, Sa-Su 9am-5pm.

Banks: Many banks are in the New Town, few in the Old Town; **ATMs** are widespread throughout both. The **National Bank** has an office in the Old Town at Pl. Moussiou with an ATM. Open M-Th 9am-2pm, F 9am-1:30pm. In the New Town, the **National Bank** (☎22410 27 031) in Pl. Kyprou has currency exchange.

American Express: Rhodos Tours Ltd., Ammohostou 23, P.O. Box 252 (☎22410 38 217). Open M-F 9am-1:30pm and 5-8:30pm, Sa 7:30am-3pm.

Laundry: Happy Wash Express Service Laundry, in the New Town at Alex 38 Diakou (☎22410 35 693). €3 for wash and dry. Open daily 9am-11pm. **Express Laundry,** Kosti Palama 5 (☎22410 22 514), directly across from the Pl. Rimini bus station, offers full wash and dry for €3. Open daily 8am-11:30pm. The only **Old Town laundro-**

City of Rhodes

ACCOMMODATIONS
Hotel Andreas, **8**
Hotel Via Via, **13**
Mama's Pension, **5**
New Village Inn, **4**
Rhodes Youth Hostel, **6**

RESTAURANTS
L'Auberge Bistro, **9**
Da Capo, **3**
Manios, **12**
Marco Polo Cafe, **7**
Mike's Taverna, **11**
Nireas, **10**

BARS & NIGHTLIFE
Colorado Pub, **1**
Down Under, **2**

Sea of Crete
TO AQUARIUM (150 m)
TO IALISSOS, FILERIMOS & KAMIROS
PL. PSAROPOULA
NEW TOWN
OLD TOWN
Mosque of Mourad Reis
PL. KOUNDOURIOTI
Governor's Palace
Laundry
Rhodes Tours
PL. VAS. GEORGIOU
OTE
UK
Harbor Master
Fortress/Lighthouse of St. Nicolas
Hydrofoil Landing
PL. KIPROU
EOT Office & Tourist Police
PL. ELEFTHERIAS
Mandraki
Bus Terminal to West (RODA)
Bus Terminal to East (KTEL)
Windmills
Ambovaz Gate
Pili Ambovaz
PL. RIMINI
TAXI
PL. ALEXANDRIAS
Palace of the Knights of St. John
Pili Tilevolon
PL. KLEOVOULOU
TO MONTE SMITH (400 m)
Agiou Georgiou Gate
Clock Tower
Eleftherias Gate
Municipal Art Gallery
PL. SIMIS
Temple of Aphrodite
Inn of Auvergne
Museum of Decorative Arts
PL. ARGIROKASTROU
TO AKROPOLIS (500 m)
Mosque of Süleyman
Nararhiou Gate
Turkish Library
Church of St. Mary
Archaeological Museum
PL. MOUSSIOU
Inn of the Tongue of England
PL. ARIONOS
PL. HIPPOKRATOUS
Commercial Harbor
Ferry Docks
PL. ATHINAS
Laundry
PL. DORISOS
Customs House
Panagias Gate
Milon Gate
PL. EVREON MARTIRON
Agiou Athanasiou Gate
Pharmacy
Synagogue
Agiou Iannou Gate
Karetou Gate
Acandia Harbor
TO LASCALA, PARADISO & LINDOS (50 km)
0 100 yards
0 100 meters

mat, Platonos 33 (☎22410 76 047), is near Yiannis Taverna. Open daily 8am-10pm. Wash and dry €4.50.

Police: (☎22410 23 294), on Eth. Dodekanission, 1 block behind the post office. Open 24hr. **Lost and found** open M-F 8am-2pm.

Tourist Police: (☎22410 27 423 or 22410 23 329), in the EOT building. English spoken. Open 7:30am-9pm.

Port Authority: Central Harbor Master (☎22410 22 220 or 22410 28 888), on Mandraki just left of the post office. Complete boat schedules. Open 24hr.

Hospital: (☎22410 80 000; in a **medical emergency** dial ☎166), on Erithrou Stavrou, off El. Venizelou. Open for emergencies 24hr. **Visitor's clinic** open 1-3pm and 6-8pm.

OTE: Amerikis 91 (☎22410 24 599), at the corner of 25 Martiou in the New Town. Open M-Sa 7:30am-1pm.

Internet Access: Minoan Palace, Ir. Polytechniou 13 (☎22410 20 210), at corner of G. Efstathiou in the New Town. €4 per hr., €2 minimum charge. Open daily 9am-2:30am. In the Old Town, **Mango Bar,** Pl. Dorisos 3 (☎22410 24 877, 22410 28 324, or 22410 32 824). €4 per hr. Open M-Sa 10am-1am, Su 10am-midnight.

Post Office: Main branch (☎22410 30 290 or 22410 34 873), on Mandraki, along the waterfront and next to the Bank of Greece. Open M-F 7:30am-2pm. **Parcel service** and **Poste Restante** open 7:30am-2pm. Also a **mobile branch** (☎22410 35 565) in the Old Town on Orfeos, near the Palace of the Grand Master. From Pl. Museum, head down Ipoton and take a left onto Orfeos. Open M-F 7:30am-2pm. **Postal code:** 85100.

DODECANESE

ACCOMMODATIONS

OLD TOWN

Most pensions are scattered about the narrow pebbled paths between Sokratous and Omiron. Bargaining with pension owners will be worth your while; just allow wild shock to register on your face upon hearing the price and go from there. The Youth Hostel and Mama's Pension are a few steps from each other off Sokratous.

Rhodes Youth Hostel, Ergiou 12 (☎22410 30 491). Turn onto Fanouriou from Sokratous and follow the sign for the hostel. The cool, quiet courtyard of this former Turkish house almost always harbors a few talking guests, and backpackers scattered in pensions all over Rhodes gather here in the evenings for cheap drinks and food cooked in the hostel's kitchen. For a truly economical (if somewhat chilly) stay, ask about the bed on the roof (€5). Services include free luggage storage, laundry, full kitchen, book exchange. No curfew. Ask at the desk for sheets, and bring your own toilet paper. Dorms €7; doubles and triples €20. ❶

Mama's Pension, Menekleous 28 (☎22410 25 359), off Sokratous, directly above Mike's Taverna. Open-air hallways lead to bright blue-and-white rooms. Several plant-filled terraces provide views of the city. Dorms €10; doubles €25. ❶

Hotel Andreas, Omirou 28D (☎22410 34 156; fax 22410 74 285; www.hotelandreas.com). Boasts spectacular views of the city of Rhodes. Ask about rooms with their own terraces and about the "penthouse" suite with windows on all sides. Mostly shared baths. Car and motorbike rentals available. Singles, doubles, and suites €30-52. ❸

Hotel Via-Via, Pythagora 45 and Lisipon 2 (☎22410 77 027; viavia@rho.forthnet.gr). A beloved tabby cat presides over a courtyard riotous with plants and bright tablecloths. Rooms are tastefully decorated. Singles €24; doubles €30-47; triples €50.

NEW TOWN

The New Town is somewhat charmless. Expensive hotels line the coast, but affordable pensions can be found along the narrow streets of Rodiou, Dilberaki, Kathopouli, and Amarandou.

New Village Inn, Konstantopedos 10 (☎22410 34 937; www.rodosisland.gr), on a tiny side street off Kathopouli. Open-air corridors lead to modern, sparkling-clean rooms by a tile-covered courtyard. Singles €20; doubles €30-40. ❷

FOOD

The best dining options in Rhodes are concentrated in the Old Town. Two types seem to dominate: small, classy bistros run by expat chefs who make ingenious concessions to the local palate in producing their own countries' specialties, and tavernas where Rhodesians can stop for lunch and stay for the afternoon.

Nireas, Sophocleous 22 (☎22410 21 703). A surefire way to spot a good seafood restaurant is to look for sizeable populations of well-fed cats, and Nireas certainly passes the test. The fresh shellfish is a treat; try the *petalides* (sea barnacles) or *fouskes* (sea snails). Shellfish €6-8; other fish sold by the kg. Open 7:30-11pm. ❷

L'Auberge Bistro, Praxitelous 21 (☎22410 34 292). On Sokratous, go past Pl. Ippocratous toward the sea and turn right on Dimostenous. Go past Klevoulinis, take a right just before Agia Triada Church, and continue straight until you reach Praxitelous. The covert location makes this gastronomic gem even more worthwhile. Light and well-balanced French dishes are complemented by the courtyard's soft lighting and the jazz floating from indoors. Entrees €7-10. Open Tu-Su 7:30pm-midnight. ❷

Marco Polo Cafe, Ag. Fanourion 40-42 (☎22410 37 889). Excellent Greek food in a courtyard painted in blue, yellow, and earth red. The building was originally an Ottoman mansion; ask the owner to point out the harem room, which is visible from the courtyard. Internet access available. Entrees €6-9. Open 11am-3pm and 7-11pm. ❷

Manios, just around the corner from the intersection of Eschilou and Militadou. This little hole-in-the-wall snack bar is frequented by a devoted group of local men who take their lunches at the rickety tables set on the cobbled street. Delicious stuffed eggplant €4. Open 11am-5pm. ❶

Mike's Taverna, just off Sokratous on Platonos. Serves delicious grilled fish by the kg. Ask what's the freshest catch of the day. Most fish €45 per kg. Open 11am-11pm. ❸

Da Capo, G. Leontos 12 (☎22410 76 790 or 22410 37 806), in the New Town off 28 Oktovriou. Traditional Greek food (€7-8) and an extensive list of pizzas (€5-7) on its inviting patio and balcony. Efficient service. Stands out among the New Town's restaurant options. Open daily 2pm-midnight. ❷

SIGHTS

Few islands are known for a sight that no longer exists; Rhodes is one of them. One of the Seven Wonders of the Ancient World, the **Colossus of Rhodes,** a 35m bronze statue of sun god Helios near the harbor entrance of Mandraki, leaves no earthly trace today. Legend has it that the Colossus toppled in a 237 BC earthquake. Though archaeologists are skeptical that the statue actually straddled the harbor, as was long believed, two bronze deer stand on either side of the harbor entrance where a colossal foot might have crushed them.

OLD TOWN

Scattered throughout the pebbled inclines of the medieval Old Town (constructed by the **Knights of St. John**) are small bronze plaques that label historical sites and museums. Upon conquering the island, the Knights redecorated the capital city, replacing Hellenistic ruins with medieval forts. Formerly an Ottoman bazaar, shopping strip Sokratous is lined with jewelry stores, restaurants, and junkshops.

PALACE OF THE GRAND MASTER. At the top of the hill, a tall, square tower, said to be the work of Grand Master Pierre d'Aubusson, marks the entrance to the Palace of the Grand Master. With moats, drawbridges, huge watchtowers, and colossal battlements, the 300-room palace survived the long Ottoman siege of 1522, only to be devastated in 1856 by the explosion of 300-year-old ammunition in a depot across the street. After years of use as a prison by the Turks and Italians, the citadel was restored and embellished at the beginning of the 20th century by Italians determined to outdo the industrious Knights. The Italian hand can be detected in the marble paneling of the castle and in the **mosaics** brought here from Kos. The interior decoration was completed only a few months before the start of WWII; the Italians had little chance to savor the fruits of their labor. The two outstanding exhibits on the north and southwest sides of the ground floor use archaeological findings and visual aids to tell a detailed version of Rhodes's extensive history. *(☎22410 25 500. Open M 12:30-7pm, Tu-Su 8am-7pm. €6, students €3.)* For an unparalleled bird's-eye view of the entire fortified city, wait for a Tuesday or Saturday and take a **walk** along the **city walls,** but come at 2:30pm sharp—there's only a half-hour window for admittance. *(Open Tu and Sa 2:30-3pm. €6, students €3.)*

PLATEIA ARGYKASTROU. Dominating one side of the plateia with its beautiful halls and courtyards, the former **Hospital of the Knights** has been reborn as an **Archaeological Museum.** Its treasures include the small but exquisite first-century BC *Aphrodite Bathing*—also called the *Marine Venus*—a marble statue of the goddess whose fluid contours were partially created by centuries of erosion in the sea, where the statue fell during an earthquake. *(☎22410 25 500. Open Tu-Su 8:30am-7pm. €3, students €1.50.)* The cobbled **Avenue of the Knights,** or Ipoton, sloping uphill near the museum, was the main boulevard of the city 500 years ago. The **inns** of the different divisions of knights once lined this street. At the foot of Ippoton is the **Church of the Virgin of the Castle,** an 11th-century Byzantine church which the knights refashioned into a Gothic cathedral. Next to the church, the **Inn of the Tongue of England** is a 1919 copy of its 1483 predecessor, destroyed in one of many defensive battles. The Order of the Knights of St. John of Jerusalem consisted of seven different religious orders, called "tongues" because each spoke a different language. Because each tongue guarded one segment of the city wall, parts of the wall are labeled "England" or "France" on the map.

DODECANESE

PLATEIA SYMI. To the right inside Eleftherias Gate, at the base of the Mandraki, are the **Municipal Art Gallery's** contemporary paintings by local and national artists. *(Open M-Sa 8am-2pm. Free.)* Behind the ruined 3rd-century BC **Temple of Aphrodite** in the middle of the plateia stands the 16th-century **Inn of the Tongue of Auvergne,** with an Aegean-style staircase on the facade.

PLANE TREE WALK. Evidence of the city's Ottoman era is most evident in Pl. Kleovoulou. A walk down **Orfeos,** better known as the Plane Tree Walk, will take you past a large **clock tower,** which once marked the edges of the wall separating the knights' quarters from the rest of the city. The walk opens onto the highest viewpoint in the Old Town. Climbing the tower leads you to a small cafe. *(Open daily 9am-11pm.)* The **Mosque of Süleyman,** below the clock tower, dates from the early 19th century. It's distinguished by its red plaster walls, garden, and stone minaret. The original mosque was built after Sultan Süleyman the Magnificent captured Rhodes in 1522. At present, the mosque is closed to visitors.

TURKISH HORA. The **Turkish library,** built in 1793 opposite the mosque, houses 15th- and 16th-century Persian and Arabic manuscripts. *(Open daily 10am-1pm and 4-7pm. Donation expected.)* Other Old Town Ottoman-era buildings and monuments are in various states of decay, but the 250-year-old baths and the **hamam** (Turkish bath) in Pl. Arionos are worth a look.

JEWISH QUARTER. Pl. Martyron Evreon (Square of the Jewish Martyrs) lies in the heart of the old Jewish Quarter. The Jewish community was an integral part of Rhodes's history from its inception. Sephardic Jews fleeing the Spanish Inquisition, added a Spanish flair to some Old Town medieval architecture. In 1943, 2000 Jews were taken from this square to Nazi concentration camps. Today, nothing remains of the Jewish heritage in Pl. Evreon: it has been overrun by tourist cafes and shops. A few streets in the Jewish quarter's residential area, however, make up the loveliest and most peaceful parts of the Old Town. In this neighborhood, down Dossiadou, is the **Shalom Synagogue,** restored by the 50 Jewish men and women who survived the war. Oriental rugs cover the stone mosaic floor and "eternal lamps" hang overhead. *(Services are Friday at 5pm; dress modestly.)*

NEW TOWN AND MANDRAKI

You'll find stately Italian architecture throughout the modern business district. The bank, town hall, post office, and National Theater are among the Mussolini-inspired stone buildings presiding over wide Eleftherias. Opposite them is the majestic Governor's Palace and a cathedral built by the Italians in 1925. The cathedral replicates St. John's Church, leveled in an 1856 explosion. Three defunct windmills stand halfway along the harbor's pier. The **Fortress of St. Nicholas,** at the end of the pier, guarded the harbor from 1464 to the end of World War II. The **Mosque of Mourad Reis,** named after the admiral under Süleyman who died trying to capture Rhodes from the Knights of St. John in 1522, is an important remnant of the Ottoman presence. The domed building inside is his mausoleum. Turbans indicate male graves, flowers female ones. Opposite the cemetery is **Villa Kleovoulos,** which housed author Lawrence Durrell during his appointment with the Foreign Office from 1945-47. A number of Durrell's books are set in Greece, including his most celebrated: *Reflections on a Marine Venus,* which takes place on Rhodes. Rhodes Town's **aquarium,** also a marine research center for the Dodecanese, exhibits creatures of the Aegean. (☎22410 27 308 or 22410 78 320. Open daily 9am-8:30pm. €2.50.) Follow signs from the EOT to reach the **Acropolis of Rhodes.** The gusty, ruined temple is a great place to watch the sunset, and the ancient stadium below is a popular place to go running.

OUTSIDE THE CITY

Excursion boats trace the beach-filled coast from Rhodes to Lindos. Most leave the city around 9am and return to Rhodes at 6pm, making for a great escape from the crowded beaches of the western coast. The boats make several stops, including Faliraki. Schedules and prices are posted at the dock along the lower end of the Mandraki (starting at €11). Excursion boats also go to nearby islands such as Symi (round trip €22). **Waterhoppers** (☎22410 38 146) and **Dive Med Centres** (☎22410 61 115) offer **scuba diving** lessons and trips to Kalithea (lessons €45; non-diving passengers €25), as well as trips for certified divers.

NIGHTLIFE AND ENTERTAINMENT

OLD TOWN

Nightlife focuses around Militadou, off Apellou. Bars line the narrow street and music pours out from everywhere. By midnight, the boundaries between bars have completely disappeared, and there's not a bare spot to be found on the cushions scattered

WAKE UP If you hail from a country less serious about its nightlife than Greece is, it's easy to sleep through the best hours of the day–namely, 1-5am–without ever knowing what you've missed. To avoid this mistake, begin getting into the local schedule with a coffee or *frappé* at 5 or 6pm at a waterfront cafe. The caffeine will allow you to push dinner back to 9:30 or 10pm, after which you might sit somewhere quiet with a drink and bide your time. Finally, around 1am, the late-night clubs get rolling. The majority of the clientele will be standing and schmoozing until 3 or 4am, when dancers outnumber wallflowers and fill the bars until the sun comes up.

on stone benches along the street. Drink prices are comparable everywhere: wine and cocktails €5-6, beer €4. If the bartender is in a generous mood, shots may be offered to the house to down in unison—say "YAH-mas" before you throw yours back. By 2am or so, crowds tend to move to the much larger **Angel** at the head of Militadou St. for dancing. Quieter bars can be found in the plateias between Fanourion and Eschilon.

St. Francis Church (☎22410 23 605), at Dimokratias and Filellinon, echoes with sublime organ recitals Wednesday nights at 9pm; check at the EOT to verify schedule and time. In winter the **National Theater** (☎22410 29 678), off Mandraki next to the town hall, stages occasional productions, and nearby **Rodon** shows new flicks and subtitled classics (€4). **Folk Dance Theater,** on Andronikou, stages Greek dances and songs. (☎22410 29 085 or 22410 20 157. M, W, F 9:20pm.)

NEW TOWN

Nightlife here is neither shy nor tame. Although popular bars and clubs are scattered throughout the New Town, crowds flock to **Orfanidou,** widely known as Bar Street. Popular places have expensive drinks; empty bars will cut deals. The 5min. walk from end to end will give you a feel for each bar's atmosphere.

Down Under, Orfanidou 37 (☎22410 32 982). Join loud rock table-top dancers at one of the most popular bars on the strip. 90s pop music blasts until you can't hear yourself think. Drinks from €4.50, but keep an eye out for reps outside who can give you 2-for-1 drink coupons.

Colorado Pub, Orfanidou 57 (☎22410 75 120). One of the few places on Orfanidou regularly frequented by locals. Live bands until 1am. Cover €5.

La Scala, a sprawling complex southwest of town by the beachside Rodos Palace Hotel in Ixia, is the king of Rhodes's nightclubs, accompanied by covers fit for royalty. Strap on your heels and shorten your skirts if you hope to fit in. Watch for special party nights.

Paradiso (☎22410 32 003), next to Scala–almost as posh and a bit wilder on the dance floor. Eclectic music beats include house, reggae, rave, and down-home Greek. Cover €10 starting at 1am.

DODECANESE

FALIRAKI Φαλιρακη

Faliraki isn't for those looking to brush up on their Greek—English is the predominant language spoken here. Here, Anglophones in various states of undress move from the beach to the beach bars to the bars as the day passes.

ORIENTATION AND PRACTICAL INFORMATION. Faliraki is located 15km south of Rhodes City. There are two main bus stops in Faliraki, one on the Rhodes-Lindos road and one on the waterfront. **Buses** run to **Rhodes City** (17 per day, €1.90) and from the waterfront bus stop to **Lindos** (14 per day, €2.30). Faliraki is also a base for excursion boat trips to **Lindos** (round trip €11) and **Symi** (round- trip €20). Grab a **taxi** at the stand next to the waterfront bus stop, or call ☎22410 85 444 (€11 to

Rhodes). Ermou is the main thoroughfare connecting the beach to the Rhodes-Lindos highway. The **Lydia Travel Agency,** right next to the Hotel Faliro on Ermou, offers currency exchange, international phone and fax services, and car rental. (☎22410 85 483 or 22410 86 135; fax 22410 86 250. Open daily 10am-2pm and 5:30-10pm.) Directly opposite the waterfront bus stop, to the right of Ermou, is the **first-aid station** (☎22410 80 000; open 8am-6pm). Another option for emergencies is the Faliraki 24hr. **Emergency Medical Service** (☎22410 602 602). For an **ambulance,** call ☎22410 22 222. The **pharmacy** is on the main road up to the highway; look for the green cross. (☎22410 87 076. Open daily 9am-11pm.) The **Agricultural Bank,** on Ermou (open M-Th 8am-2pm, F 8am-1pm), has a 24hr. **ATM.** For **Internet access,** Antique Net Bar/Cafe is the place to go. (☎22410 86 756. Open daily noon-3am. Internet €5 per hr.)

ACCOMMODATIONS AND FOOD. Lodgings in Faliraki are difficult to find, as most places rent their rooms to British package tour companies. A few are still holding out: **Hotel Faliro ❸** is inland on Ermou, right before Ermou joins the Rhodes-Lindos road. Rooms are clean and a bit spartan, but have full baths, balconies, and pool access. (☎22410 85 483 or 399. Doubles €27-30.) **Dimitra Hotel ❹** is a fairly priced, pleasant option directly across the street from Hotel Faliro. Sparkling blue-and-white tiled hallways lead to simple, airy rooms, all with phones, baths, and balconies. (☎22410 85 309; fax 22410 85 254. Full bar and restaurant downstairs. Doubles €40.) The **Hotel Ideal ❹,** also on Ermou but closer to the sea, attracts the young and wild to its drab but clean rooms. The hotel deals with tour groups but also sets aside rooms for independent travelers. (☎22410 85 518; fax 86 530. Pool use and breakfast. Doubles €45.) Rhodes's only **campsite ❶** (☎22410 85 516 or 22410 85 358) is off the main road 1500m north of Faliraki; ask the bus driver to let you off. It has a market, hot showers, restaurant, full kitchen facilities, laundry, and an impressive pool. (€5 per person; €3 for tent rental.)

Dining in Faliraki often means inhaling a burger, greasy fries, and a soda at a fast food joint. Ermou hosts most of these establishments; the Rhodes-Lindos road has other similar options. A meal will run €6-9. For a reprieve from the typical fast-food, the Greek bakery, **Artopeio ❶,** serves up fresh fluffy loaves of bread (€0.60) and pies of all kinds (tiropita, spanakopita, and sausage-pie €1) at dirt-cheap prices. **Sarantis ❷,** on the Rhodes-Lindos where Ermou ends, is a family-run restaurant focusing on seafood. (☎22410 87 489. Entrees €5-7. Open daily 5-11:30pm.)

ENTERTAINMENT AND NIGHTLIFE. With each sunset, the sun-baked masses migrate inland from the beach toward uniformly priced beer (€3) at jubilant bars on Ermou; later there is a second exodus to a handful of popular dance clubs. **Chaplin's** (☎22410 85 662.), on Ermou by the beach, is one of the most popular 24hr. party spots: they host a handful of dawn-to-dawn beach parties during the summer—keep a lookout for their posters. **Jimmy's Pub** (☎22410 85 643), inland on Ermou, is a British bar with Guinness on tap. Additional stimuli include soul music and TVs, making Jimmy's a popular spot to watch soccer. Head up to the free-of-cover **club** above the pub. The most convenient option for Ermou indulgers is **Sinners,** a popular stop-over for house and techno music.

LINDOS Λινδος

With whitewashed houses clustered beneath a castle-capped acropolis, Lindos is perhaps the most picturesque town on Rhodes. Vines and flowers line narrow streets, and pebble mosaics carpet courtyards. The town's appeal hasn't remained a secret, however; in summer, the crowds rival those in Rhodes Town. Prices rise dramatically as rooms become scarce in late July and August; visiting Lindos outside peak season is the best option.

ORIENTATION AND PRACTICAL INFORMATION. Lindos is a pedestrian-only city: all traffic stops at **Pl. Eleftherias,** where you'll find the **bus** and **taxi** stations. Buses to and from Lindos fill quickly, so it's best to arrive early. Buses connect Lindos to: **Faliraki** (13 per day 7am-6pm, €1.90); **Kolymbia Beach** (3 per day, €2.30); **Pefkos** (8 per day, €0.90); and **Rhodes Town** (15 per day, €3.20). Check with the tourist office about recent changes and updates to the bus schedules. **Excursion boats** from Rhodes depart at 9am and return at 5pm, hitting **Rhodes Town** and **Turkey,** among other pit stops, as they travel along the coast.

Orientation in Lindos is a challenge; it's best to find your way using landmarks, as the locals do, because street signs are few and far between. From the bus station, **Acropolis** leads through town and to the acropolis; signs point to the beach after 50m or so. **Apostolou Pavlou** crosses Acropolis just past the **Church of the Assumption of Madonna.** A **tourist information booth,** located in the plateia next to the bus stop, provides bus and excursion schedules, general info on Lindos and on the Acropolis, and help with accommodations. They also sell stamps, postcards, and newspapers. (☎22410 31 900; fax 22410 31 288. Open daily 7:30am-9pm.) Next to the tourist info is a 24hr. **ATM. Public toilets** can also be found in the plateia. **Pallas Travel,** on Acropolis, **exchanges currency,** helps with accommodations, and arranges excursions. (☎22410 31 494; fax 22410 31 595. Open 8am-11pm. Closed in winter.)

Other services cluster around the intersection of Apostolou Pavlou and Acropolis. The **pharmacy** is just past Yiannis Bar. (☎22410 31 294. Open daily 9am-11pm.) Sheila Markiou, an American expat, runs the superb **Lindos Lending Library,** offering more than 7000 English, Italian, German, French, and Greek books. You can buy a book secondhand or bring an old book and trade it in. To get there, walk to Pallas Travel and bear right where the road forks; the library is up to the left. (☎22410 31 443. Open M-Sa 9am-8pm, Su 9am-1pm.) Sheila also runs a **laundry** service out of the store. The **medical clinic** is to the left before the church. (☎22410 31 224. Open M-Th 8am-2pm, F noon-2pm.) The **police** are at Ap. Pavlou 521. (☎22410 31 223. Open M-F 8am-2pm; open 24hr. for emergencies.) **Lindianet Cafe** provides cheap year-round **Internet** services. (☎/fax 22410 32 142. €5 per hr. Open daily 8am-late.) The **post office** is uphill from the donkey stand. (☎22410 31 314. Open M-F 7:30am-noon.) **Postal code:** 85107.

DODECANESE

ACCOMMODATIONS. Package tours elbow into even the tiniest pensions, making Lindos a difficult place to spend the night. One option is to arrive in the morning before the tour buses rumble in and ask the tour companies if they have any empty rooms. To reach **Pension Electra** ❹ from the main plateia, take the first left downhill after the donkey stand and follow signs for the acropolis. Electra has clean, bright, spacious rooms with A/C, fridges, and baths. Common facilities include two full kitchens, a terrace for meals, and a central garden. (☎22410 31 266. Doubles €50 per night.) **Pension Katholiki** ❹, around the corner from Electra, has clean rooms equipped with baths, kitchens, and access to a rooftop view; inquire about the few rooms with traditional Dodecanese loft beds. (☎22410 31 445. Doubles €40-50.) Nikos Kritikis, the owner of the travel agency **Village Holidays** next to Yiannis Bar, owns harbor-view rooms scattered in and around Lindos. (☎22410 31 486; fax 22410 31 344; vi-ho@otenet.gr. Doubles €35-40; quads €60.)

FOOD AND NIGHTLIFE. Creperies and snack bars on Acropolis near the plateia offer the cheapest options; crepes start at €3, yogurt and honey at €2.40. Grocery stores can also be found along the two main streets. **Agostino's** ❷ restaurant, perched slightly above the town at the opposite end from the plateia, boasts an unbeatable view of the acropolis, the harbor, and the houses of Lindos from its rooftop terrace. Clay pot moussaka, octopus, and Italian dishes range €7-10. (☎22410 31 218. Open daily 6pm-midnight.) To prepare for the climb to the acropolis or to refuel upon your descent, have some *foccaccia* or *panzerotti* (€2-3) at **Forno Bakery ❶**, around the corner from the bookstore. Ingredients are imported from Italy and food is handmade by the owner. (Open daily 8am-3pm and 6-8pm.)

Lindos municipal law requires music to stop at midnight, but revelers at many bars carry on undaunted well past this deadline. Appealing open-air nightclubs line the lantern-lit streets; the action begins at **Yiannis Bar** on Acropolis (drinks €4-6) and continues to the newer bars further down. Catch a free late-night cab to **Amphitheatre** from the plateia and dance as you overlook the acropolis and the sea. (Open daily midnight-4am.)

SIGHTS. Lindos's ancient **acropolis** stands on sheer cliffs 125m above town, caged by scaffolding and the walls of a Crusader fortress. Excavations by the Danish Archaeological School between 1902 and 1912 yielded everything from 5000-year-old Neolithic tools to a plaque inscribed by a priest of Athena in 99 BC that lists the dignitaries who visited Athena's Temple—Hercules, Helen of Troy, Menelaus, Alexander the Great, and the King of Persia. Right before the final incline, don't miss the ancient Greek *trireme*, a rectangular relief etched into rock, which the artist Pythokreitos carved into the cliffside as a symbol of Lindos's inextricable ties with the sea. Lined with staircases, the daunting 13th-century **Crusader castle** marks the entrance to the site. The arcade, built around 200 BC at the height of Rhodes's glory, originally consisted of 42 columns laid out in the shape of the Greek letter "Π." The large stone blocks arranged against the back wall served as bases for bronze statues that have been long since melted down. The remains of the **Temple of the Lindian Athena,** built by the tyrant Kleoboulos in the 6th century BC, come into view at the top of the steps. Legend has it that this area, once a tremendously important religious site, held a temple as early as 1510 BC. Kleoboulos's tomb, inscribed with Aristotle's timeless maxim, "Nothing in excess," is across the way. At the foot of the acropolis lie the remains of the **ancient theater.**

A cave called the **Voukopion,** on the north side of the rock face (visible from the path), may have been used for special sacrifices that could not be performed in the acropolis. The cave probably dates from the 9th century BC and was later transformed into a sanctuary for Athena by the Dorians. (☎22410 31 258. Open M 12:30-6:40pm, Tu-Su 8am-6:40pm. €6, students €3. Ask for the pamphlet which gives a history and explanation of the layout.)

DAYTRIPS ON RHODES

EPTA PIGES. Eleven kilometers south of Faliraki, just before Kolymbia, a road to the right leads 3km down to Epta Piges. Constructed by Italians seeking potable water for nearby Kolymbia, the aqueduct now quenches the thirst of thrill-seekers, who slide through 150m of pitch-black tunnel. Laughers and shriekers alike end up in a large, picturesque freshwater pool; if the destination sounds nicer than the journey, take the path next to the tunnel that is used to return from the pool. A decent streamside taverna (with peacocks) sits at the entrance before the tunnel. To get there, ask a Lindos/Archangelos bus driver to let you off at the tunnel. Continue inland past Epta Piges to visit the 13th- and 15th-century frescoes of the Byzantine **Church of Agios Nikolaos Fountoucli,** 3km past Eleousa. Three **buses** per day stop at Eleousa on the way to Rhodes. Villagers in **Arthipoli,** 4km away, rent rooms.

TSAMBIKAS MONASTERY. From the coast road, Tsambikas Monastery is marked by the restaurant that sits below it. A 1km road leads up to the restaurant; the Byzantine cloister and its panoramic views are 1km farther up a steep trail. The monastery takes its name from the sparks (*tsambas*) that were reportedly seen atop the hill. Upon climbing up to investigate, locals discovered a Cypriot icon of the Virgin Mary that had mysteriously appeared here, miles from home. Angry Cypriots ordered that the icon be returned, and the locals obliged, but the icon kept returning. By the third time, everyone agreed that Rhodes must be the icon's proper home. To this day, some women ascend the mountain to pray to the Virgin Mary for fertility. If the prayer works, junior should be named Tsambikos (if it's a boy) or Tsambika (if it's a girl). One bus runs to the long, flat, and sandy **Tsambika Beach,** 1km south of the turn-off for the monastery (€2.20). Any bus that passes the turn-off should let you off here for a worthwhile day in the sun.

KAMIROS. The smallest of the three ancient cities of Rhodes, Kamiros nonetheless surpasses Ialyssos and Rhodes in intricacy and preservation. The history of this ancient city has been pieced together from the evidence found in its cemeteries. After the devastating earthquake of 226 BC, the city was reconstructed with a typical Hellenistic layout and design. The cistern on the north side of the temple dates from the 5th or 6th century BC, and the stone stoa (shaped like the Greek letter Π) is from at least the 2nd century BC. Visit the precinct of Athena Kamiras on the acropolis to get a clear sense of the city's impressive chessboard layout. *(Take a bus from Rhodes to Kamiros (2 per day 10am and 1:30pm). ☎22410 40 037 or 22410 75 674. Open Tu-F 8:30am-7pm. €4, students €2.)*

You can hike to picturesque **Profitis Ilias,** where three old Italian hotels long for restoration beside gorgeous orchards. Follow dirt roads to Salakos, where a path leads straight to the peak. *(5 buses per day run from Rhodes run to Salakos, €3.)*

VALLEY OF BUTTERFLIES. Seven kilometers inland from the village of Theologos, **Petaloudes,** or the **Valley of Butterflies,** is a popular visiting spot with or without the company of its insect residents. During the summer, Jersey tiger moths flock to the valley's Styrax trees, attracted to their resin (also used in making incense) and the area's shade. While resting to live out their final days in the trees, the moths fast, living only on water and body fat to conserve energy for rigorous mating sessions. After the deed is done, they die of starvation. The valley and its many trees are worth a walk any time of year but are a particularly welcoming reprieve from summer's sun-beaten coasts. The valley is accessible from an entrance next to an old mill or from the main entrance farther uphill. The trail winds around a blue-green stream that collects in lily-covered pools and glides under bridges. Avoid clapping and stomping to incite the moths to flight, like some foolish visitors do. *(☎22410 81 801. Open daily 8:30am-sunset. €1-3.)* Hike up 300m from the end of the 1km trail to the **Monastery of Kalopetra,** home to a restored mosaic, where fresh yogurt and honey from the caretakers accompany a panoramic view of the island.

KOS Κως

Medical and literary titans have long lounged on the beaches of Kos. The island is the sacred land of **Asclepius,** god of healing, the birthplace of **Hippocrates,** father of modern medicine and the Hippocratic oath, and the home of the poet **Theocritus** and his teacher **Philetas.** In ancient times, Kos was a trading power with a population of 160,000. In Byzantine, medieval, and more recent history, its story has mirrored that of the other Dodecanese in passing through Italian, German, and British hands. Rivaling Rhodes in tourist traffic, Kos Town tends to draw a younger, louder, more intoxicated crowd, while relatively unexplored rural Kos attracts the more sedate traveler in search of stunning beaches and serene mountain villages.

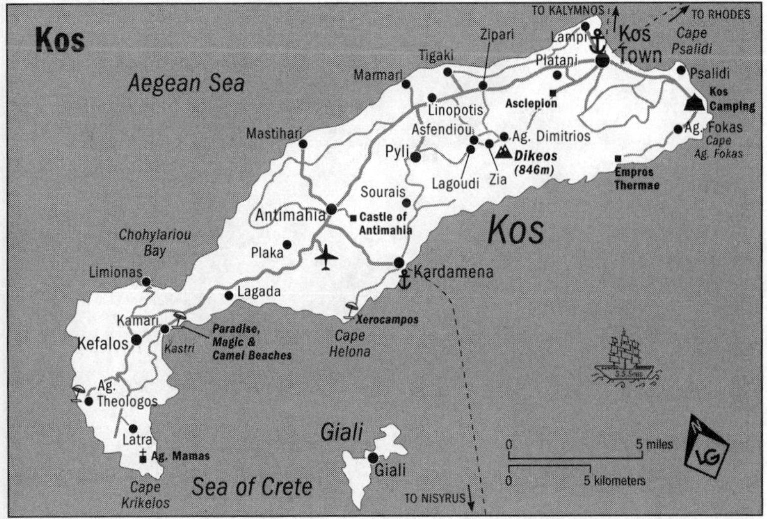

KOS TOWN

Kos Town has become a sort of amusement park for young foreigners. The waiters and bartenders at its showy nightspots are mostly temporary workers, and the patrons are more temporary still. Local culture here goes into hibernation during high season, though residents maintain their hospitality. Kos Town is a good base for exploring the island by car or moped; you can easily travel from end to end in a day, with several pauses for a swim or a long lunch at a beachside taverna.

DODECANESE

TRANSPORTATION

Flights: Olympic Airways, Vas. Pavlou 22 (☎22420 28 331 or 332), has flights to **Athens** (from €60). Open M-F 8am-2:30pm. Olympic runs a bus (€4) to the airport from their Kos Town office 2-4 times per day. Schedule posted. Taxis to the airport cost €25.

Ferries: To: **Kalymnos** (1¼hr., 1-3 per day, €5.28); **Leros** (2½hr., 1 per day, €7.34); **Patmos** (4hr., 1-2 per day, €9.41); **Piraeus** (11-15hr., 2-3 per day, €15.29); **Rhodes** (4hr., 2-3 per day, €12.35). 2 per week to: **Nisyros** (€7.40); **Symi** (€8.24); **Tilos** (€7.35). Boats run to **Bodrum, Turkey** every morning (€35-40 round-trip). Since travel is international, prices are not regulated by the Greek government.

Flying Dolphins: 1 per day to **Kalymnos** (€9.40); **Leros** (€12.65); **Patmos** (€16.76); **Samos** (€20). 2 per week to: **Agathonisi** (€18.24) and **Tilos** (€12.35). Also to: **Fourni** (3 per week, €21.47); **Lipsi** (6 per week, €12.35); **Nisyros** (3 per week, €12); **Symi** (3 per week, €15.29); **Rhodes** (1 per day, €19.96).

Buses: (☎22420 22 292; fax 22420 20 263). Leave from Kleopatras near the inland end of Pavlou behind the Olympic Airways office. M-Sa to: **Antimachia** (40min., 6 per day, €1.55); **Kardamena** (45min., 6 per day, €2); **Kefalos** (1hr., 6 per day, €2.60); **Marmari** (35min., 12 per day, €1.25); **Mastihari** (35min., 5 per day, €1.85); **Pyli** (30min., 5 per day, €1.25); **Tigaki** (30min., 12 per day, €1.25). Reduced service Su. Schedule posted by the stop; buy tickets on the bus.

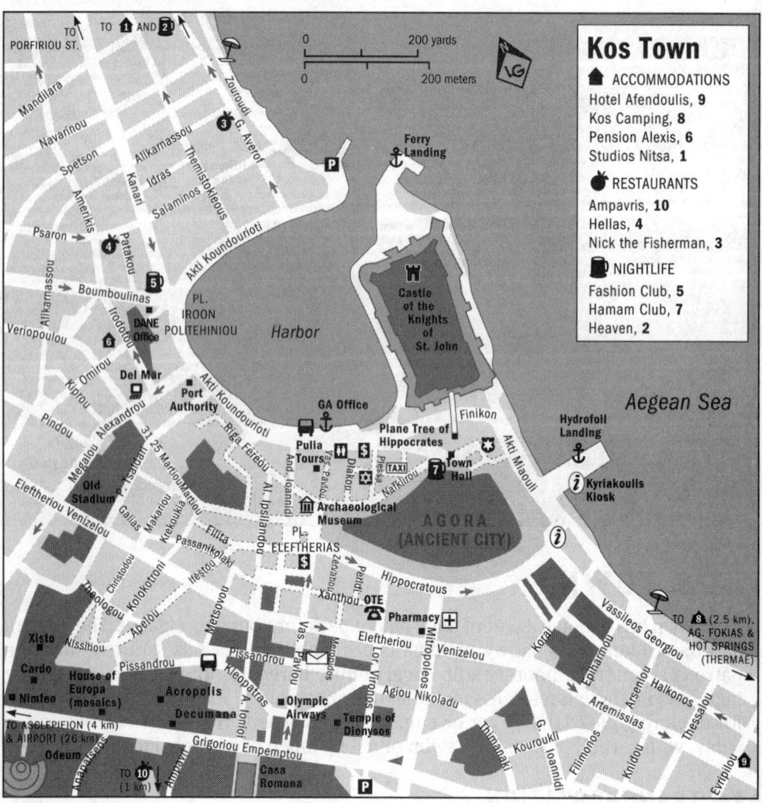

City Buses: Akti Koundouriotou 7 (☎22420 26 276), on the water. To: **Asclepion** (15min., 16 per day during visiting hours); **Agios Fokas** (50 per day); **Messaria** (9 per day); **Platani** (16 per day) and **Thermae** (20min., 9 per day). Fares €0.50-1.

Taxis: (☎22420 22 777 or 22420 22 333), near the inland end of the Avenue of Palms.

Rentals: Laws restricting rentals to those with proper motorbike licenses are more strictly enforced here than on other islands. Driving behavior does not reflect this stringency, however, and drivers should exercise caution. **Mike's** (☎22420 21 729) is at the corner of Amerikis and Psaron. Mopeds €9-15 per day. Bikes €2-4 per day. **George,** P. Tsaldari 3 (☎22420 28 480), near the port authority, rents mopeds from €9-16 per day. Bikes €2-5. Open daily 8:30am-8pm.

ORIENTATION AND PRACTICAL INFORMATION

The lamps, neon signs, and floodlit hotels that spangle the coast seem to guide ferry boats into port at night. The tourist facilities along the coastal roads (**Zouroudi** in the northwest, **Akti Koundourioti** curving around the harbor, and **Akti Miaouli** and **Vas. Georgiou** to the southeast of the harbor past the castle) are a harsh welcome; head past them to find reasonably priced bars and restaurants. Nightlife revolves around the **Dolphin Roundabout** on the harbor and the **Old Town,** just inland from the

Castle of the Knights of St. John on the far left end of the harbor. Continue past the **Plane Tree of Hippocrates** and the castle entrance by way of a bridge spanning **Finikon** to find cobblestone streets housing several bars. At the opposite end of the Old Town is **Pl. Eleftherias,** packed with banks, exchange offices, travel agencies, and cafes. From here, take **Vas. Pavlou** inland to reach **Grigoriou,** lined with ruins.

Tourist Office: EOT, Vas. Georgiou 1 (☎22420 24 460 or 22420 28 724; fax 22420 21 111; dotkos@hol.gr). Free maps and info on transportation, events, and accommodations. Open M-F 8am-8pm, Sa 8am-3pm.

Tourist Agencies: No single agency in Kos has comprehensive boat information. 3 large ferry companies, **Blue Star Ferries, DANE** and **G.A.,** and 3 hydrofoil lines, **Dodecanese Express, Kyriakoulis Maritime,** and **Laoumzis,** serve Kos and its neighbors. **Pulia Tours,** Vas. Pavlou 3 (☎22420 26 388, 22420 24 194 or 22420 21 130; fax 22420 26 388), near the waterfront end of the main road, sells hydrofoil tickets and offers rental assistance and **currency exchange.** Open daily 7am-11pm.

DANE Office: (☎22420 23 964; fax 22420 22 185), next to the Dolphin Roundabout, sells hydrofoil and ferry tickets. Open 8am-9pm.

G.A. Office: (☎22420 28 545; fax 22420 24 864), on Navarhou Ioanniou across from the National Bank, offers similar tourist services. Open 9am-10:30pm.

Banks: National Bank (☎22420 22 167), behind the Archaeological Museum, 1 block inland from the water on A.P. Ioannidi. 24hr. **ATM.** Open M-Th 8am-2pm, F 8am-1:30pm. After hours, **exchange currency** at any travel agency along the waterfront.

American Express: (☎22420 28 426). Full AmEx services at the **Credit Bank** (*Trapeza Pisteos*), Akti Kountouriotou 5, near the bus stop. Open M-Th 7:45am-2pm, F 7:45am-1:30pm.

Emergency: ☎22420 22 100. **Ambulance:** ☎22420 22 300.

Police: (☎22420 22 222), on Akti Miaouli in the big, yellow building beside the castle. Some English spoken. Open 24hr.

Tourist police: (☎22420 22 444) in the same building. Open daily 7:30am-2pm.

Hospital: Mitropoleos 13 (☎22420 28 050). Between El. Venizelou and Hippocrates. For **information** call ☎22420 28 013. Open 24hr.

Pharmacy: Around the corner from the hospital on. Open 8am-midnight. Prescriptions filled 24hr.

OTE: (☎22420 23 499), at L. Virona and Xanthou, around the corner from the post office. Open M-F 7am-2:30pm.

Internet Access: Del Mar Internet Cafe, Megalou Alexandrou 4A (☎22420 24 244), offers efficient service and modern equipment. €4.50 per hr. Open daily 9am-late.

Post Office: (☎22420 22 250), on Vas. Pavlou. From El. Venizelou, walk 1 block inland. Open M-F 7:30am-2pm. **Postal Code:** 85300.

ACCOMMODATIONS

Hotel vacancies are rare in August, so start searching for rooms early. Most inexpensive places are on the right side of town if you're facing inland. It's best to seek out your own room and avoid Kos's dock hawks, as bait-and-switch is a rampant practice. If you do choose to haggle, ask for a business card, telling them you'll check out your options and come by later; if no card is produced, move on.

Pension Alexis, Herodotou 9 (☎22420 28 798 or 22420 25 594). Take the 1st right off Megalou Alexandrou, on the back left corner of the 1st intersection. The pension is on the corner of Herodoton and Omiron. Brother and sister Alexis and Sonia preside over a beloved travel institution. The hospitable pair offer everything from help with ferry tickets

DODECANESE

to advice on touring the island to heaping platters of fresh watermelon. In the evenings, guests gravitate toward the jasmine-scented veranda. If rooms are full, the proprietor will help arrange other accommodations or cut you a deal at his elegant Hotel Afendoulis. Romantic verandas and common baths. Doubles €18-20; triples €25-30. ❷

Hotel Afendoulis, Evrilpilou 1 (☎/fax 22420 25 321 or 22420 25 797), down Vas. Georgiou. Owned by the same hospitable Alexis of Pension Alexis. All rooms have baths and balconies over the courtyard. Doubles €22-35; basement rooms €18-22. ❷

Studios Nitsa, Averof 47 (☎22420 25 810). Take Averof inland from Akti Koundourioti at the opposite end of the harbor from the castle. Nitsa will be on the left. Well-kept but small rooms come with bath and kitchenette. Convenient to most nightlife destinations. Doubles €30; triples €35-45. ❸

Kos Camping (☎22420 23 910 or 22420 23 275), 3km southeast from the center and accessible by public transport. Guests come back year after year to this family-operated campground to escape the frenzy of Kos Town. Mini-market, bar, laundry facilities, cooking room, postal service, pool, and security boxes. Buses run to and from the center every 30min. You can bring your own tent (€3) or rent one (€3.50). ❶

FOOD

The fruit and vegetable **market** in Pl. Eleftherias, on Vas. Pavlou, inside a large yellow building with a picture of grapes over the doors, caters to tourists and is not as inexpensive as it looks; mini-markets have cheaper fruit (open M-F 7am-9pm, Sa 7am-6pm, Su 10am-2pm).

Ampavris (☎22420 25 696), on Ampavris. Take E. Grigoriou and then turn onto Ampavris, the road next to Casa Romana. It's about a 1km walk up the road on your left. Father-and-son tandem cooks and waits tables. Entrees €3-5.50. ❶

Hellas, Psaron 7 (☎22420 22 609), at corner of Amerikis. Popular with locals, this unpresumptuous taverna serves good Greek food on rickety wooden tables. Lamb *kleftiko* €8, moussaka €5. Open daily 4-11pm.

Nick the Fisherman, Averof 21 (☎22420 23 098), at corner of Alikarnasou. Once a spot for locals, Nick's has been drawing more tourists as of late. Fresh seafood on a vine-covered terrace. Octopus €10, most fish €45 per kg. Open 1pm-late. ❸

DODECANESE

SIGHTS

ROMAN RUINS. The run down field of ruins bounded by Nafklirou, Hippocrates, and the waterfront was once the Agora; it's now dominated by a population of sunbathing youth. It's difficult to find good information on the ruins, but make inquiries at the Archaeological Museum (see below). Apart from the **Old Stadium,** which is somewhat removed from the other ruins along Megalou Alexandrou and might easily be mistaken for an abandoned lot, the ruins are clustered around two areas. In the **Old City,** between the castle and Hippocrates, are the meager remains of a 4th-century BC **agora** and the **Grand Stoa,** but the best ruins line Grigoriou between Pl. Tsalidari and Lourdou Vironos. Two **Roman roads,** the Decumana (running parallel to Grigoriou) and the Carda (intersecting Decumana at the Tsalidari end) are still distinctly visible. As you walk along Grigoriou from L. Vironos toward Tsalidari, you'll pass the well-preserved **Altar of Dionysus** on the right; on the left is the 3rd-century AD **Casa Romana,** uncovered by an Italian archaeologist in 1933. *(Open Tu-Su 8:30am-3pm.)* **Mosaics** under wooden shelters lie along the Decumana, including the 3rd-century AD **House of Europa,** depicting Europa's abduction by Zeus in the form of a bull. Across the street is the **Odeum,** a well-preserved Roman theater.

ARCHAEOLOGICAL MUSEUM. Good English labeling of the mostly local Hellenistic and late Roman sculptures in its collection sets this museum apart. Most of the statues, though, are more historically significant than aesthetically pleasing; their telltale crudeness only makes the discovery of the graceful sculpture in the back room, found at the Kos Odeon and presumed to be Hippocrates, all the more thrilling. A 2nd-century AD Roman mosaic in the central courtyard depicts Hippocrates and a colleague entertaining the god Asclepius. *(In Pl. Eleftherias. ☎22420 28 326. Open Tu-Su 8am-2:30pm. €3, students €2, EU students free.)*

CASTLE. The invading Knights of St. John, who built the massive 15th-century castle, came to Kos to heal the sick. The once-removable bridge that marks the entrance to the Square of Hippocrates linked the island castle to the mainland. Destroyed by an earthquake in 1495, the fortress was rebuilt by Grand Master Pierre d'Aubusson. In the 16th century, elaborate double walls and inner moats reinforced the castle to withstand Ottoman raids; now, it's one of the best-preserved examples of medieval architecture in Greece. *(Take the bridge from Pl. Platanou across Finikis. ☎22420 27 927. Ask for the helpful pamphlet available at the door. Open Tu-Su 8:30am-3pm. €3, students €2, EU students free.)*

PLANE TREE OF HIPPOCRATES. In Pl. Platanou, allegedly planted by the great physician 2400 years ago, the tree has grown to an enormous 12m in diameter, so big that metal bars now support its branches. It's alluring to envision Hippocrates teaching and writing beneath its noble foliage; it's deflating to realize that the tree is only 500 years old.

NIGHTLIFE

Clubbing is always in the air in Kos Town. Half the population spends the afternoon and evening hours on their balconies, blasting techno and hip hop while drinking Bacardi Breezers; the other half squeezes into tantalizing clothes and struts on the street below. By 11pm, watchers and watched alike congregate around **Exarhia** (a.k.a. **Bar Street**), in the Old City past Pl. Platonos, or along **Porfirou,** between Averof and Zouroundi. In both areas, beers go for €3, cocktails for €6, and the greeters standing outside the bars tend to be cheerful and cunning Anglophones who lure passersby into their establishments.

Fashion Club, Kanari 2 (☎22420 22 592), by the Dolphin Roundabout. This cavernous, red-and-chrome club is probably Kos's most ostentatious. Runway models loom like gods on enormous television screens inside the club and in the cafe out front. Club cover €8 on weekends, including your 1st drink. No cover for the cafe. Club open daily 11pm-4am.

Hamam Club (☎22420 24 938), inland from the Pl. Diagoras taxi station in the Old City. This cool and inviting stone building, a former Turkish bath, is surrounded on all sides by colorful cushions. Live DJs take over after midnight.

Heaven (☎22420 23 874), on Zouroudi opposite the beach. By day, a waterfront bar; by night, a large, popular disco. Open Su-Th 10am-4am, F-Sa 10am-dawn.

DAYTRIPS FROM KOS

ASCLEPION. The ancient sanctuary of **Asclepion** is devoted to the healer god. In the 5th century BC, **Hippocrates** founded the world's first medical school here, forever enhancing the quality of life. Combining early priests' techniques with his own, Hippocrates made Kos the foremost medical center in ancient Greece. Present-day doctors travel here to take their Hippocratic oaths.

DODECANESE

Most of the ruins at the Asclepion date from the 2nd and 3rd centuries BC. Carved into a hill overlooking Kos Town, the Aegean, and Asia Minor, the complex contained three levels. A sacred forest of cypress and pine trees still adjoins the site. If you can overlook the swarming tourists, it's easy to envision the structures as they once stood. Inside, you'll find 2nd-century AD Roman baths, complete with *natatio* (swimming pool), *tepidarium* (lukewarm pool), and *caldarium* (sauna). The three stacked levels, called *andirons*, remain fascinating. The lowest *andiron* holds a complex of 3rd-century AD Roman baths and a preserved cistern. Climb the 3rd-century BC steps to the remarkable second *andiron* and the elegant 2nd-century AD columns. The 60-step climb to the third *andiron* leads to the forested remnants of the **Main Temple of Asclepius** and an overview of the site, Kos Town, and the Turkish coast opposite. Although the site is remarkably preserved, much of its structure is gone: it was used for raw material by the Knights of Saint John in the building of the Kos Castle. *(3.5km northwest of Kos Town. Take the* ***bus*** *in summer (15min.), or a bike or moped. Follow the sign west off the main road, and go straight. Taxis are €6-7. ☎22420 28 763. Open daily Tu-Su 8am-6:30pm. €3, students €2.)*

NORTHERN KOS. The paved, flat roads of Northern Kos, most of which have bike lanes, beckon the city-weary traveler. To the east of Kos Town along the coastal road and past Kos Camping, the **Empros Thermae** (hot springs) are at the end of the road. Sandy **Lampi Beach** lies just a few km northwest of Kos Town. Along the western coast, a small road suitable for biking extends parallel to the main road. About 8km from town, the beautiful **Selveri Beach** offers clear sand, shallow water, and a panoramic view of the Turkish coast. The beach is inexplicably deserted in comparison to its built-up neighbors; walking along Selveri back towards Kos Town from the turnoff will bring you to the quietest stretches of sand.

CENTRAL KOS. Continuing to the southwest along the minor coastal road, you'll reach the tourist strips of **Tigaki** (15km from Kos Town) and **Marmari** (19km). Between the two lies a secluded nude beach and a handful of nesting sea turtles on the shore of **Aliki Salt Lake.** Each coastal village has a sister mountain village directly inland where locals working on the coast in tourist establishments make their homes. Tigaki is paired with **Zipari,** home of the ruins of the early **Christian Basilica of St. Paul;** Marmari's sister village, **Pyli,** offers 14th-century frescoes in a Byzantine church built within a castle. In the past, when the threat of piracy made coastal living a risky prospect, these present-day tourist areas were ports for their corresponding mountain villages. Further south, quieter **Mastihari,** accessible by excursion boat, is paired with inland **Antimachia,** known for its annual Honey Festival (Aug. 17). The small **Traditional House Museum** in Antimachia's central plateia has traditional loft beds lavishly hung with local tapestries.

SOUTHERN KOS. Hills, ravines, and the occasional pasture roll across Southern Kos, which is edged by the best **beaches** on the island. Get a moped to explore more freely; a private taxi will also do the trick. Heading south will land you at the most stunning beaches of the island. **Camel** is mildly busy and beautiful. **Paradise** and **Magic** offer sparkling white sands and breathtaking views of the island's southern peninsula; they are so vast and open to the sea that they hardly become crowded. The bus will let you off at any of the beaches.

A few oceanside ancient columns distinguish **Kefalos,** Kos's ancient capital. Get out of this crowded, bland town to the surrounding beaches. North of Kefalos, the beach of **Agios Stephanos** lies next to the well-preserved ruin of a basilica. Beachgoers can lie in the shade of olive trees among the crumbling walls or swim to a nearby rocky islet, on top of which perches a small blue-and-white church. On the opposite side of the peninsula is the deserted, pebbly beach of **Agios Theologos.** The superb **Taverna of Agion Theologos** ❷ overlooks the beach.

NEAR KOS

BODRUM, TURKEY

For more information on travel to Turkey from Greece, see **Daytrips to Turkey,** p. 607. Ferries run to Bodrum from Kos every morning (€35-40 round-trip). Because of the instability of the Turkish lira, prices for goods and services in Turkey are listed in US dollars. Coverage of Bodrum was updated in July of 2001.

The "Bedroom of the Mediterranean," Bodrum comes to life at night. While Bodrum's nightlife is notorious, the surrounding Acadian Peninsula is famous for its silica beaches, lush forests, secluded coves, and ancient ruins. As a multitude of visitors agree, it's easy to get sucked into Bodrum's rhythm of sun, shopping, sightseeing, and watersports—an innocent prelude to nightfall's Bacchanalian delights.

ORIENTATION AND PRACTICAL INFORMATION. Small blue signs label the streets of Bodrum; main streets radiate from the **Castle of St. Peter.** The main commercial drag, **Cumhuriyet,** runs along the beach. **Kale** runs from the left of the castle to a mosque. **Belediye Meyd,** the street to the left of the mosque, becomes **Neyzen Tevfik** along the west harbor coast. The **tourist office,** 48 Bariş Meydani, gives away free brochures and **maps** at the foot of the castle. (☎252 316 10 91; fax 316 76 94. Open daily Apr.-Oct. 8:30am-5:30pm; Nov.-Mar. M-F 8am-noon and 1-5pm.) **ATMs** pepper shopping areas. In an **emergency,** dial ☎316 12 15. The **police,** 50 Bariş Meydani, are at the foot of the castle, next to the tourist office. (☎252 316 10 04. Open 24hr.) If you need a place to sleep it off, try **Emiko Pansiyon ❶,** Atatürk, 11 Uslu Sok.; from the *otogar*, follow Cevat Çakir. toward the water, turning left onto Atatürk. After 50m, turn right down the alley marked with the pension's sign, it offers eight simple rooms with hardwood floors and bath. (☎/fax 252 316 55 60; emiko@turk.net. Guest kitchen. Breakfast $2. Laundry $3. June-July singles $7; doubles $12. Aug. singles $10; doubles $16.) Another option is the **Otel Kilavus ❷,** 25 Atatürk, near the mosque on the way to the castle. A modern hotel with a garden, pool, and bar, Kilavus has 12 rooms with large baths and phones. (☎252 316 38 92. Singles $10; doubles $16. June-Aug. singles $13; doubles $20.)

NIGHTLIFE AND ENTERTAINMENT. Cumhuriyet is the place to go for Bodrum's hottest nightlife spots: All of the following except Halikarnas are located there. On the hill at the end of Cumhuriyet, 1km from the center of town, **Halikarnas Disco** is the second-largest open-air disco in the world. This famed colosseum of rhythm juts out into the ocean, where its strobe lights reflect off the sails of nearby yachts. The club's dressed-to-be-seen clientele makes serious moves on the dance floor, while spectators gaze from above. Daily shows featuring 25 performers, great music, and a celebrity-style entrance tunnel make this club the definitive Bodrum experience. ($12 cover includes 1 drink. Foam parties Sa, July-Aug. Beer $3.) **Temple** is a popular club where edgy dancing coincides with sly socializing, as the spastic dance floor lights dart above the flicker of candlelight from the dark wooden bar. (☎252 316 17 21. Beer $2; *raki* $2; cocktails $3-6. Open daily 7pm-5am.) Next to the luminous castle, **Hadi Gari,** the oldest disco in Bodrum, fuses elegance and funkiness. Stylish customers get down under twinkling white lights on the large outdoor dance floor while others recline on plush rose and silver cushions in the softly lit interior. (☎252 313 80 97. Beer $3; *raki* $4; cocktails $7-9. Open daily 6pm-4am.) Black lights set off the neon paint at **Greenhouse,** a much-favored dance bar that extends onto the beach. Surreal interna-

DODECANESE

tional newsreels play on a big screen over the indoor bar as enthusiastic international and Turkish DJs spin from the front half of a blue bus. (☎252 313 09 11. Beer $2; *raki* $3; cocktails $3.50-6. Open daily midnight-5am.) For a riotous ride in bar craziness, join the British crowd at **Sensi,** where table dancing, karaoke, and wig-wearing 70s nights keep things lively. Drown your cares in an alcoholic fishbowl ($18), an aquatic experience best shared with friends. (☎252 316 68 45. Beer $1.80; *raki* $2; cocktails $3.60-5. Open daily 5pm-5am.)

KALYMNOS Καλυμνος

Although the first inhabitants of Kalymnos have yet to be identified, the ruins at Embrio and Vathis suggest that Phoenicians successfully colonized the island around 2000 BC. Kalymnos, however, is better known for its sponge-diving industry than its ancient history. In years past, Kalymniot men would spend five or six months of the year diving in the Libyan Sea, often working south of Muammar Al-Qaddafi's Line of Death. Sponges still lurk in warehouses, kiosks, and restaurant display cases, but sponge-diving and retail have ceased to be an important part of the Kalymniot economy (except as a performance for tourists). Now the focus is on tourism, and a big effort is being made to bring travelers to the island. The interior has remained rather barren; the rugged central mountains cascade into wide beaches and blue-green water, luring the occasional intrepid mountaineer.

POTHIA Ποθια

During the turn-of-the-century Italian occupation, Kalymniots antagonized the Italians by painting their houses blue, the color of the Greek flag. Only a few buildings, visible high above the harbor, retain the nationalistic shade, but the bright neon lights of the waterfront cafes still provide plenty of local color. This large and bustling port town (pop. 11,500) is eager to encourage tourism, but these efforts are still in early enough stages that the town offers the best of both worlds: adequate tourist facilities along with a local culture independent of the industry.

TRANSPORTATION

Flights: Olympic Airways (☎22430 31 367; fax 22430 59 800). Take the 1st left past the National Bank; it's 50m down on the left. Open M-Sa 9am-1:30pm and 5-8:30pm. No afternoon hours on W and Sa.

Ferries: To: **Astypalea** (7hr., 2 per week, €8.65); **Kos Town** (1hr., 2 per day, €4.72); **Leros** (2hr., 2 per day, €6.33); **Mastihari,** Kos (3 per day, €2.65); **Mykonos** (10hr., 2 per week, €18.65); **Nisyros** (3hr., 2 per week, €5.60); **Patmos** (3hr., 2 per day, €14.31); **Paros** (11hr., 2 per week, €19.53); **Piraeus** (12hr., 2 per day, €23.32); **Rhodes** (6hr., 2 per day, €7.35); **Symi** (4hr., 1 per week, €10); **Tilos** (4hr., 1 per week, €7.35).

Flying Dolphins: To: **Agathonisi** (3 per week, €14.65); **Astypalea** (3 per week, €16.18); **Fourni** (1 per week, €20.88); **Ikaria** (2 per week, €18.18); **Kos** (3-4 per day, €9.30); **Leros** (1 per day, €12.40); **Lipsos** (1 per day, €10.59); **Patmos** (2 per day, €16.20); **Rhodes** (2 per day, €28.10); **Samos** (2 per day, €18.07); **Symi** (2 per week, €19.96); **Tilos** (2 per week, €12.57).

Excursion Boats: To island beaches on **Pserimos** (€6) and **Vlichadi** (€8).

Buses: During the summer high season buses leave every hr. 8am-10pm (in low season every 2hr.) to: **Kastelli** (50min.) via **Hora** (10min.); **Myrties** (20min.); **Massouri** (25min.); **Panormos** (15min.). Fares €0.40-0.90. Also to: **Argos** (2 per day 7am-1:50pm, €0.60); **Emporio** (3 per day, €0.90); **Plati Yialos** (3 per day 9:15am-3pm,

€0.75); **Vilhadia** (7 per day 8am-7:30pm, €0.60). Buses to western towns leave from the town hall in the harbor center. Buses to **Vathis** (4 per day 6:30am-6pm, €0.90) depart from the northeast corner of the waterfront. Buy tickets before boarding at Themis mini-market, next to the town hall, and insert them into the automated validating box on the bus, or hand them to the driver.

Taxis: (☎22430 50 300 or 22430 50 303). Up Eleftherias, in Pl. Kyprou. Operate 24hr.

Moped Rental: Scootermania (☎22430 51 780 or 697 283 4628) is down a little alley off the waterfront between the cafes. Mopeds €8-12. Open daily 8am-9pm. Requires International or EU Driver's License.

ORIENTATION AND PRACTICAL INFORMATION

Ferries arrive at the far left end of the port (facing inland). The road leading from the dock bends around the waterfront until it runs into the large, cream-colored municipal building, a church, and the town hall. Narrow, shop-lined **Eleftherias** heads one-way inland at this point, leading to **Pl. Kyprou,** home to the **post office, telephones, police,** and **taxis.** Continue on Eleftherias to reach **Horio, Myrties,** and **Massouri.** The second most important avenue, **Venizelou,** intersects Eleftherias near **Agios Christos Church.** Follow the harbor past the town hall to access the road to Vathis. Several fish tavernas and one unparalleled sweet shop can be found here. Most streets in Pothia are unnamed, but picking out landmarks is relatively easy.

Tourist Office: The blue hut in the middle of the harbor, opposite the Neon Internet C@fe. Very helpful advice and info on accommodation, bus and boat schedules, and events in town. (☎22430 50 879. Open June-Oct. daily 9am-11pm.) A small tourist **kiosk** on the ferry dock is usually open while late boats come in and can help with accommodations.

Tourist Agencies: It's best to consult more than one travel agency to fulfill all your tourist needs. **Magos Travel** (☎22430 28 777, 22430 50 777, or 22430 28 652; fax 22430 22 608), on the waterfront near the port police, sells hydrofoil tickets and **G.A.** ferry tickets. Open daily 9am-2pm and 5-10pm. **DANE Sea Lines** (☎22430 28 200; fax 22430 29 125), near the main tourist office, sells ferry and hydrofoil tickets. Open daily 9:30am-2pm and 5-9:30pm.

Banks: A few banks on the waterfront have full services, including **National Bank** (☎22430 29 794), with an **ATM** and **currency exchange.** Open M-Th 8am-2pm, F 8am-1:30pm.

Police: (☎22430 22 100). Go up Eleftherias and take the left road inland from the taxi plateia. English-speaking help can be found in a blue and yellow Neoclassical building on the right. Open 24hr.

Port Authority: (☎22430 29 304), in the yellow building across from customs at the end of the dock. Provides ferry information. Open 24hr.

Hospital: (☎22430 23 025), on the main road to Hora, 1.5km from Pothia. Open 24hr.

OTE: (☎22430 28 956). From the taxi plateia up Eleftherias, take the inland road on the right across from the police. Open M-F 7:30am-3:10pm.

Internet: Neon Internet C@fe (☎22430 28 343) is right on the waterfront in front of the ferry deck. 6 computers and several video games. €2.50 per 30min.

Post Office: (☎22430 28 340), just past the police station on the right. Has **currency exchange.** Open M-F 7:30am-2pm. **Postal code:** 85200.

ACCOMMODATIONS

Pickings are slim in Pothia when it comes to lodgings. There are better options in Myrties or neighboring Plati Yialos, though transportation is tricky; the tourist office may help. Camping is legal on all the island's beaches, but uncommon.

Greek House (☎22430 29 559 or 22430 23 752). Rents split-level, treehouse-like rooms throughout town, many with kitchens, balconies, and views of the port. Ask at Ta Adelvia Flaskov, a *kafeneion* you'll encounter as you come from the port. Singles €18; doubles €20-25. Rooms for groups of 3 or more also available. A/C €3 extra. ❷

Pension Niki (☎22430 48 135 or 22430 28 528). Clean, quiet rooms with private baths close to town. Niki's daughter Maria will be waiting at the docks if there are any vacancies. If you don't see her, take the 1st left after the Neon Internet C@fe, a left at the wedding store, and your 1st left after that. Singles €15; doubles €15-25. ❷

Hotel Therme (☎22430 29 425 or 22430 28 891), just before the turnoff for Niki's along the waterfront road. Bright blue inside and out, Therme carries the patriotic banner for the whole city. Those who can tolerate climbing the dizzyingly monochromatic stairway will be rewarded with clean rooms and shaded balconies overlooking the sea. Singles €20; doubles €25-30. ❷

FOOD AND ENTERTAINMENT

Nightlife in Pothia is pretty tame. Most folks enjoy a few drinks in the harbor bars and tavernas before heading to the clubs in Massouri.

Xefteris (☎22430 28 642). Head inland on Eleftherias from the town hall, take the 1st right and the 1st left. Dining at Xefteris is essentially the same experience as eating in a Greek home: excellent food and no ceremony. Choose your meal from the pots on the stove. Beef *stifado* €5. Open daily 11am-11pm. ❷

Alachouzou (☎22430 29 446), past the church and along the waterfront. This pastry-lover's paradise has been making its 5 classic honey-drenched Greek desserts for over 35 years, and perfected all of them. Try the house specialty, *galaktobouriko* (custard sandwiched between *phyllo* dough and drenched in sweet syrup; €1.50). Open daily 8am-2:30pm and 6pm-midnight. ❶

Navtikos Omilos Restaurant, to the left of the port police as you face inland. Good, simple food in large portions with a relaxing view of the ocean. Spaghetti *neapolitana* €2.35. Open daily 8am-3pm and 6:30-11pm. ❷

Apothiki (☎22430 51 890), just past the town hall on the waterfront road. The sign reads "To Tzibaeri," but locals know the place as Apothiki. Pothia's trendiest nighttime haunt. Open daily 5pm-2am.

Cine Oasis, at the end of a short alleyway plastered with movie posters. Nightly shows at 8:45 and 10:45pm. €5, children €4.

DODECANESE

SIGHTS

POTHIA. The **Nautical Museum,** on the second floor a few doors down from the town hall, houses traditional island wares and explores the life and work of the island's sponge divers. Read plaques about the island's famous industry, or ask the curator, a former diver, about the experience. *(☎22430 51 361. Open M-F 8am-1:30pm, Sa-Su 10am-12:30pm. €1.50.)* Follow the blue signs from Venizelou to the **Archaeological Museum of Kalymnos,** in the former mansion of turn-of-the-century Kalymniot sponge barons Catherine and Nikolaos Vouvalis. *(☎22430 23 113. Open Tu-Su 9am-2pm. Free.)*

From the port police, take the roads to the left to reach the beach at **Therma,** 2km away. Arthritic patients once came to the sanitarium to wade in its soothing **sulphur mineral baths,** but now that the springs' reputed medicinal value has diminished, a pleasant, crowded beach has replaced the baths as the main draw. A short walk around the bend leads to a quiet swimming spot. Tranquil **Vlichadia beach**

(6km from Pothia), the island's only **scuba diving** site, lies west of Therma. Inconvenient buses keep it peaceful. Vlichadia also has a **Nautical Sponge Museum** at the port. *(Open daily 10am-10pm. €2.)* In Pothia, there is a new, sandy beach just to the left of the port police.

VATHIS VALLEY. Although most of Kalymnos sprouts grass and wildflowers, thriving mandarins, limes, and grapes cover the valley at Vathis (5½km northeast of Pothia), which begins at **Rina** village. There's no beach here, but you can swim from the pier. Within swimming range on the north side of the inlet is **Daskaleios,** a stalagmite cave. In Rina, the **Hotel Galini ❸** has decent rooms with baths and balconies. (☎22430 31 241. Doubles €25.)

WEST COAST OF KALYMNOS

HORA

The road north from Pothia is lined with villages growing gradually together; Hora, which was Kalymnos's capital until the threat of piracy made seaside living too dangerous, is the first of these. Scattered churches line the road, including the **Church of Christ Jerusalem,** after the roundabout on the road to Argos, which was built by Byzantine emperor Arcadius after he survived a storm at sea. The half-domed stone blocks with carved inscriptions are from a 4th-century BC temple to Apollo that stood on the same site. The beachside footpath leads to a quiet **cove** with strange rock formations. Bring your waterproof shoes and keep an eye out for sea urchins, which are often hidden on the undersides of ledges.

Rock climbing routes are concentrated along the west coast between Panoramos and Armeos. You'll need to bring your own equipment and there is very little organized guidance. The tourist office has a guide to hikes and climbing routes throughout the island. Many potential routes along the coast remain unexplored; use extreme caution when veering off established paths. The village of **Kantouni,** south of Panoramos and accessible by the Plati Yialos bus from Skala, is home to **Domus Restaurant and Bar ❷,** where you can watch the sunset from the rooftop and dance by the waterfront. (☎22430 47 959. Restaurant open daily 6:30pm-midnight, bar 11am-4am.) Take a left from Kantouni Beach and clamber over the rocks to find natural diving platforms of all heights. Another road from Panormos leads 2km to the sandy, flat and less crowded beach of **Plati Yialos,** one of the island's best. A stay at **Pension Plati Yialos ❷** is sure to enchant guests. Rooms overlook the coast from the cliffside. (☎22430 47 029. Doubles €20.)

MASSOURI

The mere mention of Massouri makes the faces of young Kalymniots light up; this beloved nightlife spot draws crowds from all over the island. With only one paved road running through Massouri, all the bars and clubs are within 5min. of one another on foot, and crowds in each vary from night to night. **Neon Internet C@fe** (☎22430 48 318) has a branch here where 30min. goes for €2.50. **Mariadis** taps Guinness (€2.05), hard cider (€2.35), and serves an assortment of cocktails (€5-6). **Nadir** hosts Happy Hour 8-9pm. (Open daily 6pm-late.) **Dorian Tropical** (☎697 729 5720), next to the Hotel Plaza, and **Roadhouse** both have outdoor dance floors under the stars and near the sea. (Roadhouse cover €6 on Saturday.) The last bus to Massouri is at 9pm, and a cab runs about €15 (normally €7, but prices double after midnight).

PATMOS Πατμος

Patmos has lately become a favorite destination of the rich and famous, who keep mansions hidden away in the cliffs behind Hora. The island seems to draw a slightly more diverse crowd of tourists than do its Dodecanese siblings.

In ancient times, Patmians worshipped **Artemis,** as the huntress was said to have raised the island from the sea. With the arrival of **St. John,** exiled from Ephesus, Patmos became a center of fledgling Christianity. John purportedly wrote the **Book of Revelations** here, in a grotto overlooking the main town. His words "I…was on the isle that is called Patmos, for the word of God, and for the testimony of Jesus Christ" are the island's unofficial motto. In the 4th century AD, when Christianity spread with help from the Byzantine Empire, a basilica replaced the razed Temple of Artemis. In the 11th century, the fortified Monastery of St. John was built on a hill overlooking the entire island.

SKALA Σκαλα

Built along a graceful arc of coastline, the colorful port town of Skala is mirrored in the water by the virtual city of sailing yachts that dock here. The town didn't develop until the 19th century, when the pirate threat subsided and living by the water became safe. The main administrative buildings, home to the post office and customs house, were constructed during Italian occupation (1912-1943). Skala is the most convenient place to stay on Patmos, particularly if you'll rely on the bus.

TRANSPORTATION

Ferries: Most are run by **DANE** (☎22470 31 314; fax 22470 31 685) or **G.A. Ferries** (☎22470 33 133, 22470 31 205, or 22470 32 575; fax 22470 32 180), both near the plateia. 2-3 ferries per day to: **Kalymnos** (2½hr., €6.40); **Kos** (4hr., €7.15); **Leros** (1½hr., €2.50). Daily to: **Agathonissi** (2hr., €6.35); **Lipsi** (1hr., €4.55); **Rhodes** (9hr., €21). Also to: **Nisyros** (3 per week, €10); **Piraeus** (10-12hr., 6 per week, €20); **Samos** (3 per week, €11); **Thessaloniki** (22hr., 1 per week, €37); **Tilos** (4 per week, €10.29).

Flying Dolphins: To: **Agathonissi** (40min., 2 per week, €11); **Fourni** (1hr., 4 per week, €11.31); **Ikaria** (50min., 4 per week, €12); **Kalymnos** (1½hr., 2-3 per day, €15.29); **Leros** (40min., 3-4 per day, €10.20); **Lipsi** (20min., 1 per day, €7.71); **Samos** (1hr., 3 per day, €11).

Excursion boats: To **Lipsi, Fourni,** and **Ikaria;** prices are posted on the waterfront.

Buses: Bus stop right next to the Welcome Cafe at the ferry docks. To: **Hora** (10min., 11 per day); **Grikou** (15-20min., 6 per day); **Kampos** (20min., 4 per day). All fares €0.75, except from Skala to Hora (€1). Buy tickets on the bus.

Taxis: (☎22470 31 225) Congregate in the main plateia 24hr. in summer, but are difficult to catch, especially in the post-disco flurry (3-6:30am). Taxis to Hora €3.

Car Rental: Patmos Rent-a-Car (☎22470 32 203 or 22470 32 923; fax 22470 32 203). Turn left after the post office and look for it on your right, next to the Art Cafe (2nd fl.). Cars €35 per day and up. Open daily 8:30am-1pm and 3:30-9:30pm. Discount if renting for an extended period of time.

Moped Rental: Available all over Skala. **Express Moto** (☎22470 32 088; fax 22470 32 088), left after the tourist office. New models €8-15 per day. Open daily 8am-8pm. At **Theo Giorgio** (☎22470 32 066), new models go for the same prices. Open daily 8:30am-9pm. Both also rent mountain bikes (€3-5 per day).

ORIENTATION AND PRACTICAL INFORMATION

Skala's amenities are all within a block or two of the waterfront. Excursion boats dock opposite the line of cafes and restaurants, while larger vessels park in front of the Italian building that houses the police and post office, near the main plateia. Moving inland from the post office, a street lined with shops and souvlaki stands leads to the OTE. Across from the Welcome Cafe, a parallel road is lined with pensions. Skala is on a narrow part of the island; you can walk from the water to the opposite coast in about 10 minutes.

Tourist Office: (☎22470 31 666), in the big Italian building across the dock. Maps, brochures, bus schedules, and help with accommodations. Ask for the free Patmos Summertime guide, which includes maps of Skala and the island. Open daily 7am-2:30pm and 4-9pm. **City Hall** in Hora can also provide information (☎22470 31 235 or 22470 31 058). The **Welcome Cafe,** next to the dock, is open 24hr. and has baggage storage.

Tourist Agencies: All over the waterfront, but each offers info on only the ferry lines for which they sell tickets. Consult the tourist office or the port police for schedules, and then ask where to buy your ticket. **Apollon Tourist and Shipping Agency** (☎22470 31 565; fax 22470 31 819; apollon@12net.gr) sells Flying Dolphin tickets, can help with accommodations and rentals, and is the local agent for **Olympic Airways.** Open daily 8am-10pm.

Banks: National Bank (☎22470 34 050), in the far end of the plateia. Cash advances on MC and Visa, **currency exchange,** and 24hr. **ATM.** Open M-Th 8am-2pm, F 8am-1:30pm. Exchange at **Apollon Agency** as well as most tourist agencies lining the port.

Police: (☎22470 31 303 or 22470 31 571), above the tourist office. Open 24hr.

Tourist Police: (☎22470 31 303), with the police, upstairs from the tourist office.

Port Authority: (☎22470 31 231 or 22470 34 131), to the left of the ferry dock, next to the snack bar. Information on ferries. Open 24hr.—knock loudly if it's late.

Hospital: (☎22470 31 211), on the main road to Hora, across from the monastery Apokalipsi (2km out of Skala). Open daily 8am-2pm. In an **emergency,** call the police; they know doctors' schedules and will contact them.

OTE: (☎22470 34 137 or 22470 29 333). Follow the signs in the main plateia. Open M-F 7:30am-3:10pm. The **Welcome Cafe** at the ferry dock has an international phone.

Internet Access: Millennium Internet Cafe (☎22470 29 300), past the OTE, has 4 terminals. €6 per hr., €2.50 minimum. Open M-Sa 9am-11pm.

Post Office: (☎22470 31 316), in the main plateia, next to the police. Open M-F 8am-2pm. **Postal code:** 85500.

ACCOMMODATIONS AND CAMPING

Domatia offered by locals who come to meet the boats will run €15-20 for singles and €20-30 for doubles. The street leading to the OTE, Vas. Giorgiou, is lined with pensions, but many nicer hotels can be found in the area around Pension Avgerinos and Sydney.

Pension Avgerinos (☎/fax 22470 32 118). Follow the portside road towards Meloi—past the electrical company a sign points uphill to the left. Surrounded by a jasmine-scented terrace overlooking the sea, this family-run pension has clean, spacious rooms with balconies. Doubles €20-30. ❸

Jason's Rooms (☎22470 31 832), near the OTE on the opposite side of the street. Spacious, cheery rooms run by an Italian expat. Some rooms with shared bath, most with balcony. Singles €18-30; doubles €20-35. ❸

DODECANESE

Pension Sydney (☎22470 31 689; fax 22470 32 118). Across from Pension Avgerinos. A 2min. walk to the sea on either side of the island. Free wine and water from an enormous tank in the vine-covered courtyard. Singles €18-28; doubles €20-30. ❷

Flower Stefanos Camping at Meloi (☎22470 31 821 or 22470 31 754), 2km northeast of Skala, 10ft. behind Meloi Beach. Follow the waterfront road past Apollon Travel as it wraps along the port and up the hill. Camping is to the left at the bottom–look for signs. Mini-market, laundry facilities, spotless showers, grill facilities, and shared fridges. Scooter rental (€6-15 per day). Sites €5 per person; €3 per tent rental. ❶

FOOD

Several excellent souvlaki places, fruit markets, grocery stores and sweet shops cram around the main plateia. Patmos is known for its desserts—try the *pouggia*, a ball of honey and nuts smothered in dough and powdered sugar (€0.50), or tyropita, a pastry shell filled with cheese, eggs, milk, and cinnamon (€1.20).

To Kyma (☎22470 31 192), at Meloi beach. The 2km walk from town makes for a pleasant evening stroll. Take the waterfront road around the port and go up the hill; after you start the descent look for signs for To Kyma. This simple taverna with sweet views of the ocean serves freshly prepared fish; menu depends on what the fishermen reel in during the morning. Fish €20-40 per kg. Open daily noon-midnight. ❸

Remezzo (☎22470 31 553), along the portside road to Meloi but before the hill. Greek dishes served right on the water with efficient service. Try the chicken speciality with orange and wine sauce (€8) or the classic Greek dish *domates yemistes* (stuffed tomatoes, €5). Open in summer daily noon-1am, low season 6:30pm-1am. ❷

Loukas Taverna (☎22470 32 515), right next to Jason's Rooms across from the OTE. The spit roaster out front cooks up gyros, chickens, and whole pigs. Traditional Greek food for around €5. Open 6pm-late. ❷

ENTERTAINMENT

Perhaps in deference to the island's holy element, nightlife tends to be free of the rowdy excesses found most anywhere else. The increasing number of tourists, however, ensures a standard palette of cafes and discotheques.

Art Cafe (☎22470 33 092). From the plateia, take the small footpath to the right of the post office. The sheltered roof garden and trendy downstairs bar are pleasant and cozy but offer fewer people-watching opportunities than the waterfront cafes do. *Frappés* €2, cocktails from €5. Open daily 9am-3am.

Koncolato (☎22470 32 323), a bright club and bar popular with both locals and tourists. Packed to the gills in summer. Participate in the *sfinakia* (shot) tradition–line up at the bar and go bottoms up in unison. Open daily 11pm-late.

Cafe Aman (☎22470 32 323), a chic cafe resting below the lit church of Agia Paraskevi. Draws a pre-bar crowd in the evening, but many stay all night. Open daily 10am-3am.

Lampsi Club (☎22470 32 405), near Remezzo. Patmos's best option for dancing. Cover €6. Open daily midnight-4am.

HORA Χωρα

The sleepy, tilting streets of Hora, lined with blinding, whitewashed walls, seem to absorb tourists without any disruption to their natural calm. Hora's streets are a maze, hiding sprawling gardens behind grand doors in the shelter of the monastery and making precise directions impossible. The map of Patmos at kiosks and tourist shops comes with a questionable illustration of the town; you'll need to pick **landmarks** to find your way back to where you started.

Take care of business before arriving, as a few cardphones and a mailbox at the bottom of the hill are the only links between Hora and the outside world. From the bus and taxi station, both the monastery and main plateia can be reached by walking left and following signs. Hora is 4km from Skala, a trip that you can tackle by **bus** (10min., 11 per day, €1.30), by **taxi** (€3), or by **foot,** although it's a steep hike. Hiking down might be a better option; it's easy to find your way by the footpaths and donkey paths which go slightly more directly than the main road does. The bus stops at the top of the hill outside the town, which is also the point of departure for buses from Hora to Grikou. Hora's restaurants and cafes share the spectacular view over the surrounding countryside and the whitewashed town. Post-sightseeing hunger can be sated at **Vangelis's Restaurant ❷.** To reach it, head toward the monastery and follow signs to the central plateia. The garden behind the plateia overlooks the hills below. (☎22470 31 967. Moussaka €4, entrees €4-7. Open daily 11am-2pm and 6pm-midnight.) **Cafe Stoa,** in the main plateia across from Vangelis, is the only bar in Hora proper. (☎22470 32 226. Cocktails €6, beer €3. Open daily 5pm-2am.) **Pyrgos Music Bar** overlooks the harbor along the road to Skala. (Open daily noon-3am.)

DAYTRIPS AROUND HORA

MONASTERY OF ST. JOHN THE THEOLOGIAN. The turreted walls and imposing gateway of the Monastery of St. John the Theologian make it look more like a fortress than a place of worship. At the time of its founding by St. Christodoulos in 1088, the monastery was a constant target of pirate raids. A memorial to St. John, who visited the island in the first century AD, it was transformed into a citadel with battlements and watchtowers. The courtyard and mazelike passages are skylit but completely closed to the outside, making them seem frozen in time. As you enter the courtyard, centered around the well of holy water, notice the 17th-century **frescoes** on the left that portray stories from *The Miracles and Travels of St. John the Evangelist*, written by John's disciple Prochoros. To the upper right, a fresco portrays St. John's duel of faith with a local priest of Apollo named Kynops; the saint threw the heathen into the water at Skala, where he froze into stone. The rock is still in the harbor—ask any local to point it out. Within its walls, the monastery holds ten chapels, which allow maximum prayer while respecting the Orthodox dictum limiting masses to one per day per altar. The **Chapel of the Virgin Mary** is covered with 12th-century frescoes which were hidden behind the wall faces until 1956 tremors shook things up and exposed them. The **treasury** guards icons, a copy of St. Mark's Gospel, and an 8th-century Book of Job. Look for Helkomenos, an icon painted by **El Greco,** near the end of the exhibit. (*☎22470 31 223. Monastery and treasury open daily 8am-1pm and 4-6pm Tu, Th, Su. Treasury €5, students €2.50; monastery free. Visitors to the monastery should dress modestly—pants and long skirts for men and women, respectively, no bare shoulders.)*

APOCALYPSIS MONASTERY. Between Skala and the Monastery of St. John in Hora, the Apocalypsis Monastery is built on the site where St. John stayed while on Patmos. Two kilometers from both Skala and Hora, on the winding road that connects them, you'll find the large, white complex of interconnected buildings. Most people come here to see the **Sacred Grotto of the Revelation,** adjacent to the Church of St. Anne. Though the cave is natural, it is difficult even to tell that it is a cave anymore, as the chapel was built with the cave as its back wall. Silver tokens represent the prayers of supplicants. The cave is said to be where St. John dictated the *Book of Revelation*, the last book of the New Testament, after hearing the voice of God proclaim "Now write what you see, what is to take place hereafter" (Rev. 1:19). Silver plating marks the spot upon which St. John is presumed to have slept. *(☎22470 31 223. Open daily 8am-1pm and 4-6pm Tu, Th, Su. Dress modestly.)*

RURAL PATMOS

Arriving in Skala, visitors are welcomed by a sign that reads *Patmos: Beautiful Beaches Nestled in Tradition.* As the sign attests, the island has no shortage of inviting beaches. For an amazing view of Hora and Skala, visit **Aspris Bay** at sunset. To get there, take the port side road to Meloi Beach and go uphill. Look for signs on the right towards Aspris Bay. The closest shore to Skala (besides the sandy, pleasant beaches in the harbor) is **Meloi,** a quick 2km walk north. Large trees flank the back of the sandy beach, so grilling in the sun is optional. A bit farther north, **Agriolivado** has yet another sandy beach, an alternative to more-crowded **Kambos,** a pleasant option for beachgoers that is well served by buses. Its numerous hotels help pump in the tourists; the town itself has an inviting plateia and a few waterfront restaurants.

Just over the hill from Kambos, **Vagia Beach** is a world apart—rocky, secluded, and serene. Go east along the road to Livadia, and follow the path down to an appealing, unmarked beach set against a small cliff. A bit farther east, cliff-lined **Livadia beach** and **Livadia Restaurant** share spectacular views of the string of islets just offshore. While bus service extends only as far as Kambos, hiking or biking to more secluded beaches provide you with solitude and peace. North of Kambos, the beach at **Lambi** is famed for its multicolored pebbles, which are rare (and growing rarer, as tourists pocket them for souvenirs). The strong winds that attack this part of the island make swimming difficult.

ASTYPALEA Αστυπαλια

Few travelers venture to butterfly-shaped Astypalea, the westernmost of the Dodecanese. Jagged hills and secluded orange and lemon groves make it a soothing place to unwind, but infrequent ferry service discourages intruders almost as effectively as its fort once did. For those in need of tranquility, the island's undiscovered coves are worth the effort, planning, and patience required to reach them.

ASTYPALEA TOWN

Surrounded by tawny hills, Astypalea Town is composed of Skala (or Pera Yialos) by the port, and Hora, at the top of the hill. It's the only major settlement on the island, and all of the services and amenities you'll need can be found here.

ORIENTATION AND PRACTICAL INFORMATION. **Ferries** run to: **Amorgos** (4hr., 1 per week, €9.40); **Donousa** (4hr., 1 per week, €11.40); **Kalymnos** (3hr., 4 per week, €8.50); **Kos** (3½hr., 2 per week, €10.25); **Naxos** (5½hr., 2 per week, €13.95); **Paros** (7hr., 2 per week, €18.55); **Piraeus** (10-13hr., 4 per week, €22.50); and **Rhodes** (5hr., 2 per week, €16.76). Check with a travel agency (see below) for more information. Daily excursions go to the neighboring islands of **Ag. Kyriakis, Kounoupi,** and **Syrna** (€5.50). The ever-changing **bus schedule** is chalked up where the waterfront meets the main road to Hora. **Buses** run as far as **Livadia** and **Analipsi** (€2.50); frequency varies by season. Renting a **moped** is one of the best ways to see the island from Astypalea Town; try **Moto Center Astypalea** (☎22430 61 263; fax 22430 61 540), on the waterfront near the ferry dock, or **Moto Rent Vergouli** on the main road to Hora. (☎22430 61 351. Open 8am-1:30pm and 4:30-8pm.) There is only one paved road on the island; it surrounds the island from Livadi to Analipsi. Expect high prices for rentals and insurance as much of the island has only treacherous dirt roads. Just before the town's small beach, the **police** are in a small building. (☎22430 61 207. Open 8am-7pm.) The **port police** are in a white building with a Greek flag on the waterfront between the town and the port. (☎22430 61 208. Open 8am-10pm.) In an **emergency,** call ☎22430 61 544; for a **doctor** dial ☎22430 61 222.

The **National Bank** is under the Hotel Paradissos (☎22430 61 224; open M-Th 8am-2pm, F 8am-1:30pm); the waterfront has a 24hr. **ATM.** A **tourist information** center (☎22430 61 412) operates in the Town Hall in **Hora,** directly across from the gift shop. **Astypalea Tours,** on the main road to Hora, can handle transportation, accommodation and information questions; they're also the local **Olympic Airways** agent. (☎22430 61 571 or 22430 61 572; fax 22430 61 328. Open 9am-2pm and 6-9pm.) Flights from Analypsis **airport** go to Athens. (☎22430 61 665. 40min., €53.40.) The **OTE** is above the Maistrali Restaurant. (☎22430 61 212. Open M-F 7:30am-2pm.) Several **supermarkets** (open 9am-1pm and 5-9pm), and the **post office,** offering **currency exchange**, are in this section of town. (☎22430 61 223. Open 7:30am-2pm.) **Postal code:** 85900.

ACCOMMODATIONS AND CAMPING. Rooms on the island fill with an annual influx of summering Athenians in July and August, but vacancy is the norm the rest of the year. Bargain for rooms and domatia in the offseason. **Mariakis Apartments ❸,** located in the center of Hora, has rooms with telephones, fridges and some TVs. (☎22430 61 413. Doubles €40.) **Camping Astypalea ❶,** 2.5km east of town, near Marmari, has similar rooms; a hip bar, self-service restaurant, mini-market, post, and exchange services are bonuses. Follow signs or take a bus toward Maltezana. (☎22430 61 338. €3.50 per person, €2.35 per tent.) A 10min. hike up the hill towards Hora will lead you to the elegant **Rooms Kaith ❹,** with balconies overlooking the azure bay. (☎22430 61 375. Doubles €45.) If you want to be closer to the waterfront action, **Hotel Astynea ❷,** located right by the sea, offers affordable rooms in a convenient location. (☎22430 61 040. Singles €18.)

FOOD AND ENTERTAINMENT. Restaurants cluster near the waterfront in Astypalea Town and on the square in Hora. At waterside **Albatross ❷,** tapestries and a straw roof create a cozy atmosphere for a tasty assortment of Greek, Chinese, German, and Italian foods. (☎22430 61 546. Excellent *souzoukakia* €5, souvlaki €5.90, barbecued chicken €6.50.) With tables stunningly set on the beach below Albatross, **To Akrogiali ❹** serves a local Astypalean specialty, *astakomakaronada*, which combines fresh lobster with pasta (€44 per kg), and other daily catches from €24-35 per kg. (☎22430 61 863. Open daily 8am-2am.) If you're looking for a breathtaking setting accompanied by traditional Greek music, head to **To Magazi ❷** (☎22430 61 889), up the main road across from the fifth windmill. Try one of the specialty dishes that range from the rice and meat dish *dolmadakia* (€3.80) to the delicious vegetable *briam* (€3.80). **Eva's Confectionery ❶,** 100m up the main road to Hora, delights with deliciously sticky sweets (most under €2).

SIGHTS. The **Archaeological Museum** in Astypalea Town houses a small, well-presented collection of artifacts unearthed from around the island, including stone inscriptions, early Christian sculptures, and Mycenaean grave finds. Before heading up to the castle, stop to see some of the better-preserved objects once held within the fortification. The museum is on the main road to Hora, just inland from the waterfront. (Open Tu-Su 8am-2:30pm and 6pm-12:30am, M 5-7pm. Free.) In Hora, a striking row of windmills leads to a path up to the **Castro,** originally a line of defense built by the Knights of St. John; later, the Turks moved in, leaving the island's most significant architectural presence. Much of the structure remains intact. Exploring the chamber lets you gaze out across the island and nearby islets with a clear view. From early June through mid-September every summer, a series of multi-themed concerts is held as a part of the **Astypalea Festival** (tickets €10). Ask the tourist office for details concerning the festival, which is held at the Castro or inside the holy **Portaitissa Monastery,** to the right of the entrance to the fortress.

NEAR ASTYPALEA

Head out from Hora to find good beaches. A 20min. hike southwest along the coast takes you to **Tzanaki Beach,** an uncrowded refuge for nude bathers that's much better than **Livadia,** a beach closer to town. Four kilometers farther along a dirt path, the sand and palm trees at **Agios Konstantinos** make it the western island's best beach spot. Great beaches like **Ormos Kaminakia** and **Ormos Vatses** surround the southwest part of the island past Tzamaki. From there, the hidden cave of **Spilia Negrou** is accessible by boat; it's worth the venture if you can convince a local fisherman to take you. A right turn after the sixth windmill in Hora begins a perilous 1hr. drive along a circuitous route leading past a military base to the monastery of **Agios Ioannis.** The monastery looks out over a small waterfall—perhaps the most charming sight on the island.

Northeast of Astypalea Town, the main road leads toward the other "wing" of the butterfly-shaped island, passing the campsite and several sandy beaches. Signs prohibiting nudity are the red flag for a good beach below. The road is a bus route; in addition to designated stops, a sympathetic driver may drop you off elsewhere.

Lackluster buildings and ominous construction mar the colorful gardens and gentle landscapes of the fishing village of **Maltezana** (officially known as **Analipsi**), 10km northeast of Astypalea Town. Home to miraculously intact **Roman mosaics and baths** next to the small port, Maltezana is accessible by **bus.** (4 per day, €2.50.) **Psili Amo** beach near the airport is one of the island's best and rarely sees visitors. Vathi's natural harbor divides into **Exo Vathi** and **Mesa Vathi** 2km farther; there's a decent beach nearby at **Agios Andreas.** Inland dirt roads discourage moped travel, but beaches are also accessible by boat.

KARPATHOS Καρπαθος

Midway between Rhodes and Crete, windy Karpathos often receives little more than a passing glance from the deck of an overnight ferry. Those who disembark, however, bask in a warm Karpathian hospitality that exemplifies Greece's famed welcoming spirit. Karpathos's history isn't so friendly—the island fought fiercely alongside the Spartans in the Peloponnesian War and later fell to Rhodes in 400 BC. In 42 BC, the Romans began a series of occupations and were followed by all the usual suspects: the Arabs, the Venetians, and the Ottomans. Ottoman rule ended when Italians conquered the island during the World War I; it later passed into German hands for a few years during the end of World War II. Despite its rowdy past, Karpathos has changed markedly in the last 50 years. Since a war-ravaged economy sent many Karpathians to the US, their prodigal Greek-American sons and daughters have returned to the island and invested heavily in it. As a result, Pigadia and the south have suddenly modernized. The mountainous north remains a world unto itself, steadfastly preserving its traditions, while gorgeous beaches stretch along the southeast part of the island.

PIGADIA Πηγαδια

Stretched along a single graceful sweep of shoreline, Pigadia has all the makings of an idyllic summer night: excellent, inexpensive food, a few clubs loyally frequented by locals, and a sandy beach a few minutes' walk from town where the stars are as brilliant as they would be in the middle of nowhere.

TRANSPORTATION

Schedules for ferries are available at Possi Holidays. Bus tickets are sold on board; no buses run on Sundays or local holidays.

Ferries: To: **Kassos** (1½hr., 3 per week, €6); **Piraeus** (21hr., 4 per week, €26.35); **Rhodes** (5hr., 3 per week, €15); **Santorini** (12hr., 1 per week, €25). For other Dodecanese islands, Rhodes is the connection hub. **Chrisovalandou Lines** and **Karpathos 1** run daily excursions to **Olympus** (leaves 8:30am, returns 6pm; €1). Find them near the ferry docks or book reservations at **Possi Travel.**

Buses: 1 block up Dimokratias from the town center. Serving most southern villages (€1-3); buses don't run on a regular schedule until the end of June. Check the schedule at the bus stop. Buses to: **Aperi, Volada, Othos,** and **Piles** (3 per day); **Menetes, Arkasa,** and **Finiki** (2 per day); **Amoopi** (3 per day).

Taxis: (☎22450 22 705). Taxis run 24hr. (€5-15 to nearby villages). Government-regulated taxi prices are posted at the station on Dimokratias.

Rentals: Facing inland from the bus station, walk right 2 blocks to find **Moto Carpathos** (☎22450 22 382). Fair and friendly service. Mopeds from €14-20 per day. Insurance extra. Open 8am-1pm and 5-9:30pm. **Circle Rent A Car** (☎22450 22 690), 1 block past Moto Carpathos. Cars €30-45 per day. Open 8am-12:30pm and 5-8:30pm.

ORIENTATION AND PRACTICAL INFORMATION

Karpathos Town has three main roads running parallel to one another. The first runs along the water and is lined with tavernas. The second extends one block up and inland from the dock. The police and guest houses are on the third. The bus station is on Dimokratias, running perpendicular to the other main streets.

Tourist Agencies: Possi Travel (☎22450 22 235 or 627; fax 22450 22 252), on Karpathion, sells ferry and plane tickets, books daily excursions, exchanges currency, offers bus and ferry schedules, and gives advice on accommodations and other tourist information. Open M-Sa 8:30am-1pm and 5:30-8:30pm, Su 10am-noon and 6-8pm.

Banks: National Bank (☎22450 22 409), opposite Possi Travel, has **currency exchange** and an **ATM.** Open M-Th 8am-2pm, F 8am-1:30pm.

Police: (☎22450 22 222). The corner of Eth. Antistasis, by the post office. Open 24hr.

Port Police: (☎22450 22 227), next to the ferry dock. Open 24hr.

Hospital: (☎22450 22 228); take Emboriko—the 2nd road parallel to the waterfront—straight ahead for 500m. The hospital will be on your left. English spoken. Open 24hr.

OTE: (☎22450 22 609), uphill past the post office. Open M-F 7:30am-2:30pm.

Internet Access: Internet Cafe Potpourri (☎22450 23 709). Take the 2nd road up from the seafront and walk straight ahead; the cafe is opposite Olympic Airways. Laid-back atmosphere and great music. Coffee €1.70; Internet €4 per hr., half-price in winter. Open daily 8am-2am.

Post Office: (☎22450 22 219). Go uphill from the bus station and follow the signs across from the police. Open M-F 7:30am-2pm, Sa 7:30am-1pm. **Postal code:** 85700.

DODECANESE

ACCOMMODATIONS

Camping is usually tolerated on the town beach to the north, though one should be aware that this is illegal.

Elias Rooms for Rent (☎22450 22 446; http://eliasrooms.tripod.com). From the bus station, walk up the stairs past the supermarket. Rooms are quiet but centrally located, with a beautiful, breezy terrace overlooking the gulf beyond. Warm-hearted, English-speaking Elias knows a lot about the island, especially about ways to save money. Ask about the traditional rooms with lofted bed. Singles €20; doubles €25-30. ❷

Christina's Rooms (☎22450 22 045). Rooms have balconies, kitchens, and private baths. The owner occasionally cooks large, family-style meals for all his guests. Singles €15; doubles €20-25. ❷

Harry's Rooms to Rent (☎22450 22 188). Facing inland at the bus station, turn right and take the first left. Very clean, economical rooms with balcony and shared bath. Kind owner will try to feed you at every opportunity. Singles €12-15; doubles €15-20. ❷

FOOD AND ENTERTAINMENT

The best dinner options lie along the waterfront; nightlife tends to pick up around 1:30am after the waiters from the local tavernas and cafes close up shop and head to the clubs.

Kali Karthia, across from the Miramare Hotel toward the far right end of town as you face inland, offers one of the cheapest seafood options in town: the *sipia,* served like souvlaki and cooked on the coals (€5). Open daily 8am-11pm. ❷

Ideal, between the National Bank and the church on the waterfront. One of the few waterfront tavernas with cheap, tasty options serves up all the Greek basics. Gyros €1.50. Open daily 6-10:30pm. ❶

Edem Music Cafe-Bar (☎22450 23 681), uphill from the post office. Completely packed by 10:30pm, this hot spot spins rock, reggae, and the latest Greek hits as the background for matchmaking potential. Free shuttle to Paradiso Club (see below) leaves at 2am every night.

Paradiso Club (☎22450 23 342), 2km out of town on the road heading for the airport. *The* place to be for late-night grooving. Hops all day and night during the summer. Live music by Greek pop stars is an occasional treat. No cover.

Oxygen Club, on the waterfront road, is populated by 1am every evening with locals who dance (or nod their heads) to techno music. Drinks €2.50-4. Open until 4am.

OLYMPUS

Isolation and insularity are the defining characteristics of Olympus, where living, centuries-old customs keep ethnographers and linguists in a tizzy. Eighty families seeking to escape attacking pirates founded the village in the 11th century, atop Mt. Profitis Ilias, 1750m above sea level. Each family built one windmill, one house, and one church. Olympus supported itself by shipping its men off to do migrant work; because women took control of the household while their husbands were away, property is inherited matrilineally. Plaster-sculpted nymphs, angels, eagles, and Venetian lions adorn house exteriors; the interiors are filled with hand-embroidered linens and ceramic plates. Tourist interest has led Olympians to preserve and, in some cases, rekindle craft traditions.

ORIENTATION AND PRACTICAL INFORMATION. Between Olympus and **Diafani,** take a **taxi** or the small **bus** that leaves Diafani (when the boat from Karpathos Town arrives; bus fare is included in the excursion ticket) and Olympus daily. A dusty **hike** along the valley floor is another alternative if you have the time, energy, and drinking water—it's a long, hot, uphill trip. **Minas,** at the village mayor's office, is a great resource on what the area has to offer. His perfect English and fascination with the Internet and his hometown yield a lot of information for those interested in Olympus or Karpathos.

ACCOMMODATIONS AND FOOD. Some of the best accommodations in Olympus are at **Hotel Aphrodite ❸,** where big rooms, all outfitted with their own baths and balconies, offer breathtaking views of the ocean below. If no one's around, go to the **Parthenonos Taverna** and ask for Nikos—he owns both establishments. (☎22450 51 307 or 22450 51 454. Call ahead for reservations. Doubles €35;

triples €40.) **Pension Olympos ❷,** around to the left of the bus stop near the start of the village, rents rooms with beautiful hand-carved beds, private baths, and peaceful balconies with mountain views. (☎22450 51 009. Singles €12; doubles €24.) The best food in town is served at the **Milos Tavern ❶** (☎22450 51 333), in the windmill above the museum. The pasta-like *makarounes*, a village specialty, are served with cheese and oil and sprinkled with garlic (€4). Open daily 7am-10pm.

SIGHTS. Olympus itself constitutes the main sight of the region. If you want more, check out the two working **windmills** overlooking the western cliffs where Olympian women grind the flour that they later bake in huge, stone ovens. While

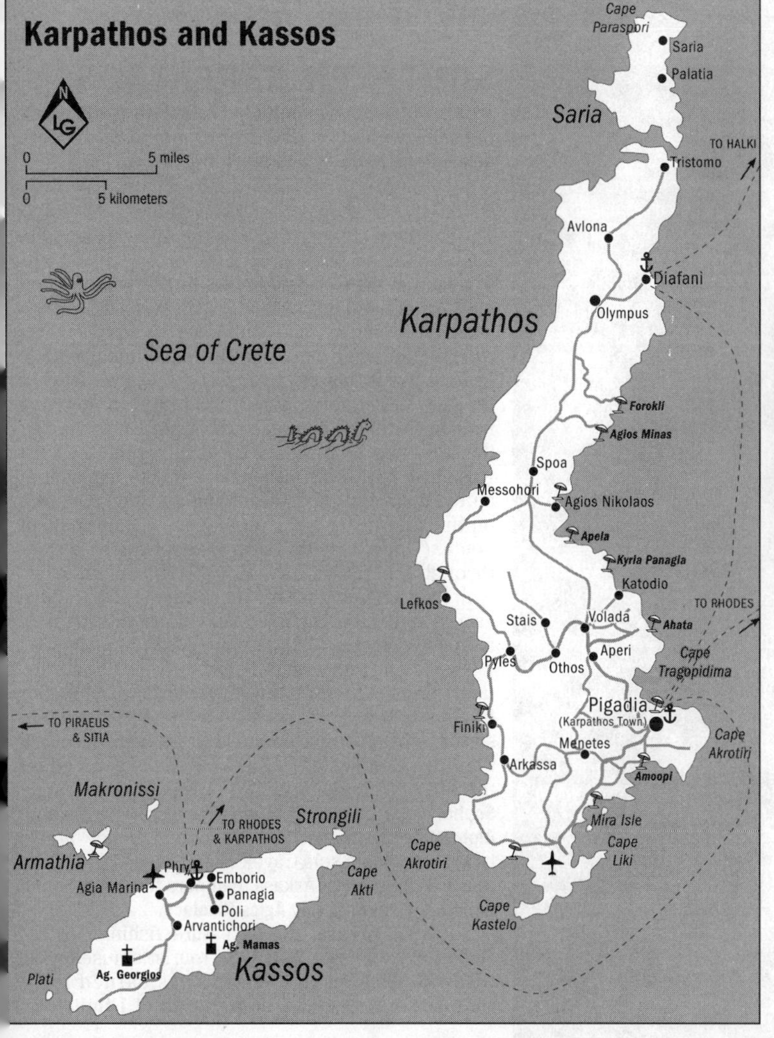

THE INDUSTRY

Theodoros Kapsalakis owns a sponge shop on Symi. This interview took place on July 11, 2002.

Q: What led to the decline in the sponge trade?
A: Artificial sponges created a problem, because they were cheaper, and they were available in every supermarket and store. They say the artificial sponges were invented in America by a Symiot who was taking a bath....The water was too hot and so he put plastic over it to let it cool, and the plastic melted into the holes of a natural sponge. I don't know if it happened that way, though.

Also, the Symiot women early this century revolted against the diving equipment, because so many men were dying.
Q: Where did the fleet of sponge boats go when they went to work?
A: First they went to Panormitis [Monastery] to be blessed. There was one big boat and four or five little boats that would use it as a base. They were paid by the gram—each diver had his corner with his sponges. The divers were obliged to the captains. They borrowed money at the beginning of the season to leave with their families, and they had to pay it back. For six months, there were only women on the island.
Q: Did everyone dive?
A: Yes, they trained from very young. You maybe couldn't even get married if you didn't dive—the family would say, "What can you do, how will you bring money in?"

you're there, brave the tiny ladder inside the windmill and watch it whirl from behind the scenes. If you're willing to bound over stone walls, visit the three oldest chapels on Karpathos, **Agia Triada.** The trio of chapels is easily visible from the town above: look down to the right of the bus stop for earthy red-arched roofs. Inside, 13th- or 14th-century **frescoes** represent birds and fish. Just past Parthenos Taverna, near the windmill, is the lavishly decorated **Kimisi tis Theotokou.** Gold foil blankets its altar, and breathtaking, hand-painted biblical scenes adorn the walls. If the priest isn't around, ask at the restaurant for a key.

SOUTHERN KARPATHOS

West of Pigadia, winding roads climb toward charming villages and cloud-covered mountains before descending to the beach-laden west coast.

APERI

The southern city of Aperi was the island's capital in medieval times, when Arab raids forced Karpathians to abandon their coastal homes in 1892. Although it has surrendered this official status, it remains at the heart of Karpathos. The church here holds a **Panagia** (Virgin Mary) icon revered throughout Karpathos. Legend has it that the icon was discovered when a monk was chopping wood; blood began spurting from one of the logs, tipping the monk off to the fact that this was no ordinary tree. Each time the icon was moved, it would disappear—only to reappear in an old church in Aperi. Building a bishop's church on the spot in 1886, the monk gave it a permanent home. (Open daily 8-11am.) West of Aperi, a walk through the last of Kato Horia's villages in **Pyles,** with its enchanting narrow alleyways, leads to olive groves and charming tavernas that serve the town's famous honey.

Two kilometers west of Pyles, the road hits Karpathos's stunning west coast. From Pigadia, a number of coastal towns are accessible by bus. The windswept remains of five parallel Cyclopean walls mark the town of **Arkasa,** whose acropolis is perched on the hill of Paleokastro. The mosaic floors of **Agia Sophia** are good reason to visit this part of the island. **Alpha Hotel,** at the north end, is one of the few hotels to accommodate solo travelers. (☎22450 61 352. Doubles €35.) South of Arkasa, campers find shelter in a beach cove near sandy **Agios Nikolaos.**

North of Arkasa, the miniature fishing port of **Finiki** today consists mostly of tourist amusements. **Dimitrios Fisherman's Taverna** has earned local renown for its careful preparation of Dimitrios's daily catch. (☎22450 61 294 or 22450 61 365. Open M-Sa 7:30am-2:30pm and 5-10pm.) The taverna also offers some of the town's very few rooms. (Doubles €25.) Continuing north along the coast, you'll come to the small beach town of **Lefkos,** where those willing to trade sandy beaches for a rocky cove will have a gorgeous stretch of coast to call their own. Inland, forested hiking terrain is shared only with the goats.

For the island's best beaches, take the unmarked dirt roads off the Pigadia-Airport mainway (use good walking shoes or private transportation). Those seeking a full-fledged tan will adore the little stretch of sand called the **River of Birds.** Take the first dirt road headed to beautiful but sometimes crowded **Amoopi** beach and take a left as the road begins to hug the coast. Deep green-blue waves reaching for the shores across from Mira Isle can be reached by taking the first left before the built-up area preceding the airport. Long coves line the bay between Cape Kastelo and **Cape Akrotiri.** Follow the dirt road from the airport toward Arkasa.

KASSOS Κασσος

The spare, rocky landscape of Kassos is billed as "tranquil," but outside the August tourist influx, "comatose" may be a better word. Kassos is a world apart from its crazier Dodecanese siblings. Peace and quiet are its main attractions, along with a few remote beaches, intriguing caves, and modest archaeological sites. Clusters of homes dot the arid hillside above Phry and Emporio 1km to the east. On the other side of the hill (not visible from the ferry), the villages of Kathistres and Chroussoulas lead the way to the island's caves. You can walk the entire loop in an hour.

PHRY Φρυ

The small port town of Phry is a somewhat generic Greek village, but it's the biggest and best that Kassos has to offer.

TRANSPORTATION. Transportation on and off the island is difficult. **Ferries** run to: **Agios Nikolaos,** Crete (5hr., 4 per week, €10.29); **Karpathos** (1½hr., 4 per week, €5.50); **Piraeus** (17hr., 4 per week, €24); **Rhodes** (6½hr., 3 per week, €16.50); and **Sitia,** Crete (3½hr., 4 per week, €7.35). **Flights** run to and from **Karpathos** (8 per week, €24) and **Rhodes** (5 per week, €45). There is no island bus service, so **taxis** are the most common way to get around. (☎6977 904 632 or 6945 427 308. €3-5 between villages.) **Moto Kasso,** on the main street in Phry, rents motorbikes. (☎22450 41 746. Mopeds from €11 per day. Open daily 9am-1pm and 3-8pm.)

ORIENTATION AND PRACTICAL INFORMATION. All of Kassos's tourist services are in Phry. **Kassos Maritime and Tourist Agency** (☎22450 41 323; fax 22450 41 036), behind the church in Pl. Iroön Kasou, provides maps, friendly advice, and timetables. The **Olympic Airways** office is next door. (☎22450 41 555. Open M-F 8am-3pm.) The **police station** is on the airport road. (☎22450 22 222. Open 24hr.) The **port police** are on the road to Emporio. (☎22450 41 288. Open 24hr.) A **National Bank** representative offers **currency exchange** in the supermarket next to the Anesis Hotel. (☎22450 41 234. Open M-F 8am-noon.) There is a 24hr. **ATM** in Pl. Iroön Kasou. The **hospital** is on Kriti, past the bus stop. (☎22450 41 333. Open M-F 8am-3pm.) The **OTE** is a few blocks inland (open M-F 7:30am-2:30pm). There is no public **Internet access** on Kassos; try the OTE in a pinch. (☎22450 41 323 or 22450 41 495; fax 22450 41 306. Open M-Sa 7:30am-2:30pm and 5-10pm.) The **post office** is off Pl. Iroön Kasou. (☎22450 41 225. Open M-F 7:30am-2:30pm.) **Postal code:** 85800.

ACCOMMODATIONS AND FOOD. Outside of August, Kassos's hotels usually have plenty of vacancies. **Anagenesis ❷,** in Pl. Iroön Kasou next to the travel agency, along the waterfront to the left of the port, has baths, sea-view balconies, and kind management; inquire at the travel agency. (☎22450 41 495 or 22450 41 323; fax 22450 41 730; kassos@kassos-island.gr. Singles €20; doubles €25-30.) **Anesis ❷,** on the main street, offers simple rooms with balconies; inquire at the supermarket below. (☎22450 41 201; fax 22450 41 730. Doubles €20.) Rooms to let, advertised by signs along the main road toward Emporio and the villages, charge €15-20 for basic singles. Restaurants set up front-row seats for the island's big daily event: the arrival of boats at the port. Across from Anagenisis, **O Milos ❷** serves delicious *dolmades* and traditional island macaroni (with onions and sheep's milk cheese) on a balcony overlooking the port. (Entrees €4-8.) The beach **taverna ❷** to the left of town as you face inland also serves excellent Kassiot macaroni and cheese. (Entrees €5-8.)

SIGHTS AND THE OUTDOORS. Leisurely excursions to the residential villages above Phry give insight into island agricultural life. Maneuver through road-side sheep herds to reach **Panagia** and the showy homes left behind by Kassiot sea-captains. Athenians and former Kassiots who summer here are gradually refurbishing these once-proud edifices. Ten minutes beyond the village of Kathistres, the entrance to the small cave of **Ellinokamara** is partially sealed. Inside, spelunkers can clamber over slimy stones. Trek down the 1.5km footpath beyond Ellinokamara, where the cave of **Selai** bristles with stalactites and stalagmites.

From **Poli,** the 40min. **hike** to **Agios Mamas Monastery** (6km from Phry) brings you to scenic overlooks of the southeast coast. The boulders you see from the monastery are reputed to be the hulls of three ships, turned to stone by vengeful monks. The one-time monastery of **Agios Giorgios at Hadies** also merits a visit, not only for the magnificent views, but also for the gorgeous **Helatros beach** below. The older families of the village of Phry still have cells at the monastery which they inhabit once a year for the festival of St. George.

SYMI Συμη

Visitors beware: Symiots say that travelers who daytrip here from Rhodes often end up staying for months. Symi's three main villages of Yialos, Horio, and Pedhi strike a delicate balance between quiet island life and the lively evening scene that tourist traffic fosters. The island's Panormitis Monastery rests at Symi's southern end, separated from the northern port of Yialos by an uninhabited, hiker-friendly mountain range. Indeed, until the 19th century, monasteries were the only dwellings on the island's steep, barren shores. Shipbuilding, sponge-diving, and fishing moved in later, as Symi received special treatment from the Ottoman sultans, eventually becoming the capital of the Dodecanese. Spice-growing and tourism have taken precedence in recent years, giving the island a measure of financial stability. A growing population of foreign residents gives the island a slightly cosmopolitan flair to contrast the pastel mosaic of houses that brighten its port.

SYMI TOWN

Symi Town, where all public boats to the island arrive, is divided into two sections: Yialos, the port area, and Horio, the village up a flight of 250 stairs where most permanent residents make their homes. The town was constructed in the Middle Ages as a fortification against pirate raids, and much construction has gone on in the last 30 years to accommodate travelers.

TRANSPORTATION

Ferries: 1 per week to: **Kalymnos** (€11); **Nisyros** (€7.65); **Tilos** (€5.60). 2 per week to: **Kos** (€8); **Piraeus** (€27.65); **Rhodes** (€9). There are ferry ticket offices at the dock, another just after the footbridge, and 1 on the next block.

Flying Dolphins: 4 per week to **Rhodes** (€10). 3 per week to: **Kalymnos** (€21.18) and **Kos** (€15.30). 2 per week to: **Leros** (€27); **Lipsi** (€26); **Patmos** (€31).

Excursion Boats: Daily to **Rhodes,** stopping at Panormitis Monastery. Book tickets at the travel agency. €11 one way.

Bus: A green van stops at Pl. Ikonomou, across the harbor from the ferry dock. Every hr. on the hr. to: **Horio** (5min., €0.70) and **Pedhi** (10min., €0.70).

Taxis: Congregate near the bus stop on the east waterfront, but the island's 4 taxis can be reached at their mobile phones (get the numbers from the travel agency).

PRACTICAL INFORMATION

The stairs leading to Horio are behind To Vapori Bar and Kaledoukias Travel; from the ferry port, head into town and take the last street going inland before the waterfront road curves. To reach Pedhi, a 30min. walk from Yialos, climb up to Horio and take the main road going down the other side.

Travel Agency: Symi Tours (☎22460 71 307 or 689), a block inland from the gold shop on the waterfront. Sells ferry, hydrofoil, and plane tickets, handles **currency exchange,** and helps find accommodations. Open summer 8:30am-1:30pm and 5-10pm; winter 9am-12:30pm and 5:30-9pm. **Kaledoukias Travel** (☎22460 71 077), behind To Vapori to the left of the steps to Horio, sells hydrofoil tickets and provides **currency exchange.** In emergencies, they may be able to arrange cash advances on credit cards. Open daily 9am-1pm and 5-9pm.

Banks: Alpha Bank, on the waterfront straight ahead toward town as you get off the ferries. 24hr. **ATM,** but it may have trouble with some foreign cash cards–inquire at the bank. Open M-Th 8am-2pm, F 8am-1:30pm.

Police: (☎22460 71 111), next to the Yialos clock tower, in a big white building on the waterfront. English spoken. Open 24hr.

Medical Center: (☎22460 71 290), next to the church, directly opposite Hotel Kokona. Open M-F 8am-2:30pm; after hours, call the police.

OTE: (☎22460 71 399), inland along the left side of the park in the middle of the harbor; follow signs from Neraida restaurant. Open M-F 7:30am-3:10pm.

Internet Access: Roloi (☎22460 71 597), over the footbridge, set back about 50m from the corner on the east side of the harbor. Open daily 9am-late. €4 per hr.

Post Office: (☎22460 71 315), in the same building as the police, up the flight of stairs on the left. Open M-F 7:20am-1:30pm. **Postal Code:** 85600.

ACCOMMODATIONS

Most travelers don't spend the night in Symi Town, but that doesn't deter the small flock of dock hawks at the port. Luckily, list prices drop fast with persistent haggling. Prices listed are for high-season; expect a €5-8 decrease in the low season.

Hotel Kokona (☎22460 71 549; fax 22460 72 620), over the footbridge to the left of the church tower. Light breezes blow the scent of lemons through the curtains. All rooms have baths and balconies. Breakfast included. Doubles €50; triples €60. ❹

Hotel Maria (☎22460 71 311), next to Hotel Kokona. Large rooms with kitchen facilities and baths. Wood furniture and paintings lend an intimate feel to the rooms. Doubles €20-25. ❷

Pension Aigli (☎22460 41 392), behind the pharmacy and across the harbor from the ferry dock. Chrissa, the owner, will likely be waiting at the dock when the boats arrive; if not, ask for her at the pharmacy. Basic rooms are breezy and quiet. Shared baths and kitchen. Good view of the harbor from the roof. Singles €18-20; doubles €20-25. ❷

FOOD AND NIGHTLIFE

For authentic Greek food at reasonable prices, look in Horio and at the far ends of waterfront along the harbor.

Georgios' Restaurant (☎22460 71 984), at the top of the stairs to the Horio. Authentic, family-owned restaurant has no set menu. Choose your meal from the fresh fish kept on ice and the pans of stuffed vegetables. Entrees €4-7. Open daily 7pm-2am. ❷

Tholos (☎22460 72 033), at the far end of the small harbor to the right of the dock. Enjoy the cook's specialty, stuffed vegetables, at tables inches from the water. Entrees €7-14. Open 7pm-late. ❸

Jean and Tonic Pub (☎22460 71 819), in Horio, up the hill from Georgios'. Happy Hour 8-9pm; friendly conversation all night with expat owner, Jean, and the locals. Open 8pm-late.

To Vapori (☎22460 72 540). Classy little bar keeps recent foreign language newspapers clothespinned to its blue wooden chairs for customers to read. By night, it's a popular hangout. *Frappés* €2.10. Open daily 8am-late.

DODECANESE

SIGHTS

At the top of the road to Horio, signs point toward the small **Archaeological Museum,** which displays well-labeled Classical and Byzantine pieces, island costumes, and utensils. (☎22460 71 114. Open Tu-Su 8:30am-2:30pm. €2.) The Archaeological Museum is housed in the **Chatziagapitos Mansion** (one ticket covers admission to both), which displays everyday objects owned by 19th- and early 20th-century Symiots in the home of an old naval family. The mansion is just down the hill and to the right as you return to Yialos from the museum.

In Yialos, the **Naval Museum** floats in a yellow neoclassical building beyond the waterfront strip. It recounts the history of sponge-diving on the island with equipment and photographs. (☎22460 72 363. Open daily 10:30am-3:30pm. €2.) Signs also lead through a maze of streets to the ruins of the old **castle,** where little remains within the Cyclopean walls aside from the **Church of Megali Panagia.**

BEACHES

Symi's tiny coves shelter a few excellent beaches at **Agios Marina, Nanou,** and **Marathounda** on the east side of the island, accessible only by boat. Symi's excursion boats function as a sort of water taxi service connecting Yialos, Pedhi, and several beaches, including the lovely, shaded beach of **Agios Nikolaos** (also accessible by foot from Pedhi). €5 buys a ticket for boats going both ways along the coast. Look for signs by the small boats in the center of the Yialos harbor. Tiny **Nos Beach** is only a 10min. walk north along the waterfront from Yialos, past the shipyard.

DAYTRIPS AROUND SYMI: PANORMITIS MONASTERY

*4 weekly **tour buses** and 1 **tour boat** run from **Yialos;** daily tour boats from **Rhodes** stop here as well. The steep and winding road to Panormitis has recently been resurfaced but still makes for a treacherous moped ride. By foot it's a rigorous full-day hike. Open daily 10am-1pm. Dress modestly; no bare shoulders or shorts. Free toilets are to the left of the complex. Museums €2, under 12 free.*

In the southern part of the island, the whitewashed buildings of the Monastery of the Archangel Michael, the patron of travelers, stretch across an entire harbor. The imposing and unadorned faces of the buildings, presiding over a waterfront path that is nearly deserted until the boats arrive, have an almost expectant air. The monastery was built in the 15th century on the spot where a local woman happened upon an icon of Michael. As is often the way with icons, it was brought to Yialos but kept returning to Panormitis. The museums contain ecclesiastical relics, folk exhibits, and displays of silver tokens left by supplicants and beaten into shapes that represent different prayers. The highlight of the small church is an exceptional wooden altar screen, renowned for its power to grant wishes.

If you want to **hike** but think the day-long trek to Panormitis is too ambitious for you, take the red paths that mark hiking trails off the main road. They lead through a forest dedicated to **James Brown** (a British soldier who aided the Symian Island during World War II) to a remote **monastery** and isolated **beaches.**

NISYROS Νισυρος

Most visitors to Nisyros come to walk among the sulfur crystals and escaping steam in the crater of the still-active volcano. This tiny island's year-round residents number only 800—the total population of the two villages perched above the volcano craters drops to about 40 in the winter. The relatively untouristed island offers surrealistic sand and stone beaches, all of them black with volcanic rock.

MANDRAKI Μανδρακι

An unshakable calm pervades Mandraki. The ebb and flow of day-tripping tourists, who make their rounds en masse from the dock to the volcano to the waterfront tavernas and back to the dock again, does little to disrupt the more leisurely rhythms of local life. Beyond the harbor, the winding, stone-paved streets and handsome views make the city a pleasant stopover.

ORIENTATION AND PRACTICAL INFORMATION

Virtually all of Mandraki lies to the right of the port (as you face inland). The main road runs to the right from the port along the waterfront, passing a small, stony beach and leading to stairs that ascend to the monastery. Continuing on the road as it curves to the left, you'll find **Pl. Ilikiomeni** ("Old Woman Square"), a cobbled plateia nearly overwhelmed by the ancient rubber tree growing in its center.

Ferries: DANE Sea Lines has an office where ferry and hydrofoil tickets can be purchased, on the main road past the bank. (Open 9am-1pm and 6-8pm.) Daily ferries to: **Kos** (€5.29); **Rhodes** (€9.40). Also to: **Kalymnos** (2-3 per week, €5.50); **Halki** (1 per week, €9); **Kastellorizo** (2 per week, €9); **Leros** (2 per week, €6.18); **Patmos** (2 per week, €6.47); **Piraeus** (1 per week, €26); **Symi** (3 per week, €7.35); **Tilos** (4 per week, €4.40).

Flying Dolphins: To: **Halki** (1 per week, €18.53); **Kos** (6 per week, €10); **Patmos** (1 per week, €14.12); **Rhodes** (1-2 per day, €17.06); **Tilos** (1-2 per day, €9.41).

Excursion Boats: Daily to **Kos** and **Kardemena** (3:30pm, €12).

Buses: To: **Emporio** (20min., 5 per day); **Loutra** (10min., 6 per day); **Nikea** (30min., 5 per day); **Pali** (10min., 6 per day); **Volcano** (30min., 2 per day, €1.50); **White Beach** (10min., 6 per day). Daily excursion buses to the **volcano** run when the boats from Kos arrive; 1 per day €6 round-trip, includes entrance.

Taxis: From Mandraki, **Babis's** (☎22420 31 460); from Nikea, **Irini's** (☎22420 31 474). To Loutra and the White Beach €2-3; Lies Beach €10; volcano €20.

Moped Rentals: John and John (☎22420 31 670 or 297 217 6984). Scooters from €15 per day.

Tourist Office: Polyvotis Tours (☎/fax 22420 31 204), right next to the ferry dock. Provides maps and advice on transportation and accommodations. Open in summer daily 9am-3pm, off-season 10am-2pm and 6-8pm.

Travel Agency: Nisyrian Travel (☎22420 31 411; fax 22420 31 610), to the left of the ferry dock, arranges excursions, walks, accommodations, "Greek Evenings," and special boat trips. Open daily 9am-2pm and 6:30-9pm. **Enetikon Travel** (☎22420 31 180; fax 22420 31 168), on the right side of the road leading into town, on the rocks. Boat and bus schedules, excursions, accommodation advice, and **currency exchange.** Multilingual staff. Open daily 9:30am-1pm and 7-9pm.

Banks: The **Co-op Bank of the Dodecanese** (☎22420 48 900; fax 22420 48 902) is located on the waterfront road; take a right from the dock. **Currency exchange** available M-F 9am-2pm. Bring cash, as there is **no ATM** on the island.

Port Authority: (☎22420 31 222), in a white building near the dock. Open 24hr.

Police: (☎22420 31 201), in the same white building as the Port Authority.

Post Office: (☎22420 31 249), in the *same* white building. Open M-F 7:30am-2pm. **Postal code:** 85303.

ACCOMMODATIONS AND FOOD

Rooms can be scarce in Mandraki, especially during the August 15 Festival of the Panagia, so calling ahead is advisable. The **Three Brothers Hotel ❷,** right next to the ferry dock, is Mandraki's best. Its breezy terrace overlooks the sea on two sides and is cool at any hour of the day, but the best time to be out there is the evening, when the charismatic brothers themselves can usually be found pouring drinks, joking with guests, and playing *tavli* at the marble tables by the windows. Rooms have balconies and fridges. (☎22420 31 344; fax 22420 31 640. Doubles €21-36; quads with kitchens €30-60.) On the main road along the waterfront and above a cafe, **Volcano Studios ❷** has basic rooms with private baths and fridges. (☎22420 31 680. Singles €15; doubles €20.)

Wonderful cooks abound in Mandraki. To find **Papatsou ❷,** take the main road to the plateia, find the sidewalk directly next to the waterfront, and double back 10m towards the ferry dock. The proprietor, who turned her kitchen into a taverna, makes a fabulous moussaka and grilled octopus; a feast for two including *mezedes*, octopus, two entrees, and *retsina* goes for €15. (Open 7pm-late.) On the main road heading away from the waterfront, **I Fabrika ❷** serves superb *mezedes*. Nearly invisible by day, I Fabrika seems to appear out of thin air in the evening when the light emanating from its cozy basement bar beckons passersby down the stairs. (Octopus €3, beer €1.50.)

A CRUSHING DEFEAT According to local legend, the formation of Nisyros was the result of one of those heavenly skirmishes that straddle the genres of epic and slapstick. The story references the battle between the Olympians and the Titans (which led to the establishment of Olympian rule over heaven); Zeus, locked in hand-to-hand combat with the Titan Polyvotis, supposedly broke off a piece of nearby Kos and crushed his adversary beneath it. The eruptions of the volcano are said to be the trapped Titan's complaints, and the main crater is named for him.

DAYTRIPS AROUND NISYROS

MANDRAKI VOLCANO. Pyromaniacs and geologists will want to take a stroll across the active volcano craters scattered within an enormous indentation at the island's highest point; steam jets from holes in the rock and sulfur crystals line the crevices. A 10min. walk along the trail behind the snack bar leads to the smaller **Alexandros Crater,** virtually unvisited but no less spectacular. It is possible to hike back to Mandraki from here with detailed directions from someone who knows the trails; ask for information at the travel agencies. *(Municipal bus from Mandraki (30min., 2 per day, €3) stays 45min. at the site before returning. Admission €1.)*

MONASTERY OF OUR LADY SPILLANI. Twisted stone passages lead up a cliff past tiny, closed cells to a church clinging to the rock face above the sea. Silver tokens of supplicants' prayers line the walls. The monastery's sacred icon used to reside in a small cave just above Mandraki's port, but it had a habit (like many icons) of mysteriously disappearing from the sanctuary and turning up on the site of today's monastery. Monks took the hint and built a new home for the icon, making a large replica of it in 1798 to display in the new church. Recently, on the rear face of the icon of the Virgin Mary, an altar boy discovered the iconographer's hidden portrait of **Agios Nikolaos,** which had been covered with an old cloth for over two centuries. Stairs lead to the monastery at the opposite end of town from the ferry dock, a 10min. walk along the main road. *(Open 9am-3pm. Donations welcome.)*

BEACHES. There is a small, stony beach in town, but jumping from the sidewalk into the sea where the yachts dock is a better option for convenient swimming. A black pebble beach, **Holakos** is a 10min. walk from the monastery stairs along a coastal footpath. **White Beach,** on the road to Pali just past Loutra, is gradually turning black again: white dust from nearby pumice quarries once gave the beach a pale top layer, but now that the quarries are inactive, the beach's natural dark color is seeping through. **Lies Beach,** 4km west of Pali, is the island's largest, cleanest, and best sunning and swimming spot. If there is sufficient demand, Enetikon and Nisyrian Travel run boats to the beaches of nearby **Yiali.** (€7.50 round-trip.) Otherwise, the boat which ferries workers to Yiali's quarries accepts the occasional tourist passenger. (Leaves at 7am; returns at 4pm. Ask at the tourist office.)

DODECANESE

LEROS Λερος

Narrow, windy Leros was first inhabited, according to legend, by the goddess of the hunt, Artemis; hot on her heels came the Persians, the Knights of St. John, and the influential Italians, who saw the potential for an ideal naval base in Lakki's natural harbor during World War II. After the war, the Greek government chose Leros as a site for mental hospitals. An exposé of the institutions' poor treatment of patients made tourists reluctant to come to the island. The hospitals were drastically reformed and improved, and today the island's economy depends more on the health care industry than on the hospitality one. Tourist facilities exist, but they tend to be kept to mostly unobtrusive levels.

AGIA MARINA Αγια Μαρινα

The wind never stops blowing in Agia Marina's harbor; napkins and receipts from the waterfront cafes can be seen taking merrily to the skies and floating out past the yellow fishing nets and tossing boats in the sea.

PRACTICAL INFORMATION

The small town supplies most island administrative and commercial services, including the island's only Flying Dolphin service. **Flying Dolphins** depart from Agia Marina to: **Patmos, Lipsi, Agathonissi, Samos, Ikaria,** and **Fourni.** Waterfront **Kastis Antonis Travel,** right near the dock, is extremely useful for **currency exchange,** excursions, and ferry tickets. (☎22470 22 770; www.kastis.gr. Open daily 8am-4pm and 6-10pm.) An **Agricultural Bank** (open M-Th 8am-2pm, F 8am-1:30pm, **no ATM**) stands by the cafes in the port; an **Emboriki Trade Bank** 24hr. **ATM** is on the Flying Dolphin pier. A 24hr. **police station** (☎22470 22 221) and moped rental shops sit along the waterfront, alongside a burgeoning collection of boutiques and tourist shops. The **OTE** (☎22470 23 199; fax 22470 25 549) and **post office** (☎22470 22 929) are in the same building along the road to Platanos' plateia, uphill past Kastis travel.

ACCOMMODATIONS

Rooms are a bit hard to find in Agia Marina, but it's only a 20min. walk to Panteli on the opposite coast and a 10min. walk to Platanos; the three towns form a saddle over a very narrow segment of the island. To reach **Agia Marina Rooms ❸,** take a left at Kastis Travel and then another left onto the right past Marcello's Pizza; the pension is the first house on the left, with a sunny, verdant courtyard. The friendly owner speaks little English, but he can recommend other pensions in Agia Marina when his is full. Large, comfortable rooms include bath, kitchen, and balcony. (☎22470 25 091. Doubles €25; triples €35.) The pension above **Tou Kapaniri ❸** taverna, along the waterfront past the Agricultural Bank, has one wall flush with the wind-tossed sea; watching the water from the rooms' balconies is like standing on the deck of a ship. Spacious rooms have fridges and baths. (Doubles €20-30.)

FOOD AND NIGHTLIFE

The Italian occupation has had a strong effect on local cuisine. **Da Giusi Marcello's ❷,** along the road to Platonos just before Agia Marina Rooms, is run by an Italian couple who import ingredients from their native country. Everything, including the pasta, is made on the spot. (Entrees €6-10; *tiramisu* €3. ☎22470 24 888. Open daily 6pm-late.) **O Neromilos ❷** enjoys an almost impossibly beautiful setting just behind the windmill opposite the hydrofoil dock. The water laps at the walls of its terrace, which looks back on Agia Marina and the castle above. (Pasta with mussels €7. Open 11am-3pm and 7pm-late.) Next to Kastis Travel, **Ta Koupia ❶** (☎22470 24 204) makes some of the best chicken souvlaki around for a mere €1.30. When the moon rises, Agia Marina becomes naughtier and livelier than its daytime calm would suggest as all the island's young people converge on the clubs by the dock. **Apothiki,** the first building you pass on the pier as you come from the hydrofoil dock, becomes so packed in the summer that there's barely room to sway to the Greek and international dance hits. (☎22470 25 785. Open daily 11pm-dawn.) **Apocalypsi,** two doors down from Kastis Travel, plays funk, soul, and jazz. (Open daily 10pm-3am.) **Enallatiko** plays the latest English-language hits all day and night and is a popular early-evening hangout; **Internet access** is also available. (€5 per hr. ☎22470 25 746. Open daily 8am-1:30am.)

LAKKI Λακκι

Lakki, an uninviting port town and the ferry-goer's introduction to Leros, has borne the brunt of Italian efforts to redecorate the island; now, no one seems quite sure what to do with the silent neoclassical waterfront buildings and wide, deserted streets. Cabs to more inviting Agia Marina cost €5.50. (☎22470 22 550 for the Lakki taxi stand, ☎22470 23 070 for Platmos, ☎22470 23 340 for Agia Marina.)

ORIENTATION AND PRACTICAL INFORMATION. **Ferries** go 5 times per week to: **Kalymnos** (€6.40); **Kos** (€6); and **Rhodes** (€15.50). There are also 6 per week to **Patmos** (€5) and **Piraeus** (€21). Kos and Patmos connect with more comprehensive ferry service. **Kastis Travel and Shipping,** Vas. Giorgiou 9, along the waterfront, across from the taxi stand, offers ferry tickets, airline tickets, and general tourist info. (☎22470 22 500 or 22470 22 872; fax 22470 23 500. Open daily 8:30am-2pm and 5-9pm.)

Virtually all tourist services are on or just inland from the waterfront. The road to the rest of the island runs perpendicular from the rotary. The closest beach is 1km west in **Koulouki,** which makes for a scenic walk along the coast. 1.5km farther beyond Koulouki, the beach of **Merikia** is even lovelier with calm water, sand, and shady trees. A **National Bank** (☎22470 22 166) is along the waterfront, and an **Agricultural Bank** (☎22470 24 355) sits inland from the police station, to the left where the road separates (both open M-Th 8am-2pm, F 8am-1:30pm; 24hr. **ATMs**). The **police** are at the far end of the waterfront from where ferries dock (☎22470 22 222; nominally open 24hr.). To find the **port police,** head inland by the waterfront school near the ferry dock and take the first left into a seemingly abandoned building. (☎22470 22 224. Open 24hr.; you may have to ring the doorbell.) A **hospital** (☎22470 23 251 or 22470 23 554) is two blocks inland of the waterfront school and open 24hr. For a **pharmacy,** head inland at the outdoor cinema on the park and take the 2nd right. (☎22470 23 367. Open daily 8am-1pm and 5-9pm.) The **post office** is a block inland from the cinema. (☎22470 22 929. Open M-F 7:30am-2pm.) If ferry schedules necessitate an overnight stay, **Hotel Artemis,** a few blocks inland before the cinema, has clean rooms with bath, kitchen, and A/C. (☎/fax 22470 22 416. Singles €23-30; doubles €25-35.) **Postal code:** 85400.

PANDELI Πανδελι

The tiny fishing village of Pandeli, a 20min. walk or €5 taxi ride from Agia Marina on the opposite side of Platanos, is one of those coastal towns where the tavernas have been built directly onto the beach without any pier or road separating them from the sand. At night, candlelit tables perch just out of reach of the waves and the locals weave among diners, greeting each other. Like Agia Marina, Pandeli shares most tourist and municipal facilities with Platmos, a 10min. walk up the hill; there's nothing here but a few pensions and tavernas, a mini-mart, and the locals' houses. **Psaropoula ❷,** the first taverna along the water, sells fish and traditional favorites with a smile; tables are set up by the water in the evening. (Entrees around €7. Open noon-late.) **Savana Bar,** at the far left end of the harbor as you face the sea, attracts a yachting crowd; many sailboats dock in Pandeli's harbor. **Pandeli Beach** is better for swimming than the beach in Agia Marina, as the wind is much less strong on this side of the island.

CRETE Κρητη

In middle of the sable sea there lies
An isle called Crete, a ravisher of eyes,
Fruitful, and manned with many an infinite store;
Where ninety cities crown the famous shore,
Mixed with all-languaged men.
—Homer, *Odyssey*

According to a Greek saying, a Cretan's first loyalty is to his island, his second to his country. The insular Cretan mindset—shaped by centuries of bitter resistance to relentless invasion—causes the island's people to view even their fellow Greeks as foreigners. Cretans are nonetheless friendly to the outsiders that continue to vacation on their beloved home, and visitors will enjoy a healthy dose of that old Greek hospitality. Like the long-mustached men in black who sit by the harbor polishing their high boots, the island welcomes you but tends to remain aloof.

HIGHLIGHTS OF CRETE

DIZZY YOUR MIND clambering through the labyrinthine leftovers at Minoan palaces at Knossos (p. 519) and Phaistos (p. 525).

OGLE endangered gryphon vultures and golden eagles as they soar above steep Samaria Gorge (p. 543).

CREEP through the rickety Venetian lighthouse to discover Hania's spectacular inner harbor shimmering on the other side (p. 537).

DANGLE YOUR TOES over the Libyan Sea from cave-riddled cliffs at Matala (p. 524).

DARE to pass through Dante's Gate to explore the ghost town of Spinalonga (p. 551), the last leper colony to close in Europe.

Records of Cretan life reach back to 6000 BC, when neolithic inhabitants dwelled in open settlements and placed terra-cotta statuettes on mountaintops to honor their deities. When settlers arrived from Asia Minor around 3000 BC, Cretans forged a civilization that would distinguish Greece, the Mediterranean, and all of Europe. Through the next two millennia, Crete's Minoans developed unprecedented technological and artistic abilities, constructing enormous palaces which still astound archaeologists and casual observers alike. Modern excavations have turned up shards of decorated pottery, colorful frescoes, intricate jewelry, ceremonial horns, stone libation vessels, and small sculptures.

Catastrophes—earthquakes, a tidal wave from an enormous volcanic eruption on Santorini, and Mycenaean invasions—plagued Minoan society; three times, the Minoans rebuilt from the ground up. Distinct artistic styles accompanied each rebuilding period. The Early Period's iconography makes it famous: women on thrones appear repeatedly, leading to speculation that early Minoan society may have been matriarchal. The Middle Period brought a political and artistic high point, as the Palace at Knossos (see p. 519) dominated a prosperous Aegean marine empire. Later Greeks dated their own origins to the Middle Period, when Zeus was born on Mt. Ida, the mythical Minotaur munched men in the Labyrinth of Knossos, and the Athenian king Theseus wrested power from Crete's Minoans and handed it to the Achaeans of mainland Greece.

In the 8th century BC, the Dorians occupied the island, carpetbagging with their own ideas about jewelry-making, sculpture, pottery, and language. Conquering Romans later set up camp, only to find the island an unstable aristocratic hangout rife with intercity fighting. Next, Crete fell under rickety Byzantine rule, resulting in the construction of countless Byzantine churches, until the Arabs conquered Crete in AD 827. The Byzantines eventually regained the island but lost it again to Frankish crusaders in 1204. After being sold to Venice, Crete became a commercial hub, with fortified ports ringing the island, and developed an early middle class, dominated by Venetian nobles and local merchants.

Cretans look back on this period far more fondly than on the Ottoman occupation that followed. From the late 17th century until Prince George's liberation of the island in 1898, Crete was Ottoman turf. After the Balkan Wars of 1913, Crete joined the Greek state. During World War II, the island combatted German occupation with strong guerrilla resistance; the period is regarded with pride. Since then, Crete has been spared conquerors and attacks as a part of the Greek nation.

Today, Crete is divided into four main prefectures: **Hania, Rethymno, Iraklion,** and **Lasithi.** Transportation networks are based on the prefectures. It's easy to get around within a prefecture, but bus transportation between prefectures can be more complicated, so make your plans with the divisions in mind.

GETTING THERE. Olympic Airways (☎210 966 6666) and **Aegean/Cronus Airlines** (☎210 998 8300) run cheap, fast domestic flights from Athens to **Sitia** in the east, **Iraklion** in the center, and **Hania** in the west. Consult the **Practical Information** section of your destination for more information on flights. Most travelers take the **ferry** from Athens (p. 76) to Crete, landing in Iraklion, Hania, Sitia, or occasionally Rethymno or Agios Nikolaos. Boats run frequently during the summer, but often irregularly. Larger boats run more often and dependably. All prices listed are for deck-class accommodations; bring a sleeping bag to snooze on the deck.

IRAKLION PREFECTURE

Iraklion Prefecture revolves around its eponymous cosmopolitan capital. As with most of Crete, the touristed areas are pressed along the beaches in the north, while the southern half of the province and the mountains that sandwich each side host fewer visitors and sustain a more traditional life.

IRAKLION Ηρακλειο

The fifth-largest city in Greece, Iraklion is Crete's capital and primary port. The chic native population lives life in the fast lane, which translates into an urban brusqueness unique among the cities of Crete and the most diverse nightlife on the island. While architectural aesthetes find Iraklion's unplanned jumble—Venetian monuments sandwiched between Turkish houses and two-story concrete flats—utterly offensive, others find a valuable reminder of the city's impressive history in the varied buildings. The biggest bus station and port on Crete are here, making this central, capital city a convenient base for exploring the island.

INTERCITY TRANSPORTATION

BY PLANE

Flights on **Olympic Airways** and **Aegean/Cronus Airlines** zip between Iraklion and other Greek destinations. Planes fly to: **Athens** (45min., 13-15 per day, €85); **Rhodes**

(45min., 6-7 per week, €85); **Santorini** (30min., 2 per week, €60); and **Thessaloniki** (2hr., 1-2 per day, €100). Discounts for those under 25 or over 60. To get to and from the Iraklion airport, take **bus #1** to the **airport** from **Pl. Eleftherias** (every 10min., €0.60). Cabs to the airport cost €6-8. Inquire about flights at the **Olympic Airways** office, 25 Augustou 27 (☎2810 244 802; open M-F 8am-3:30pm), or the **Aegean/Cronus Airlines** office, Dimokratias 11 (☎2810 344 324; open M-F 8am-7pm).

BY BOAT

Both **ferries** and **hydrofoils** dock at Iraklion. Boat offices line 25 Augustou; most are open 9am-9pm. Boats run to: **Mykonos** (8½hr., 5 per week, €19.90); **Naxos** (7hr., 3 per week, €17.08); **Paros** (9hr., 7 per week, €20.87); **Piraeus** (14hr., 3 per day, €27.41); and **Santorini** (4hr., 2 per day, €12.60). **Hydrofoils** serve these destinations in about half the time, for twice the price.

BY BUS

If you want to head out from the city, some planning is necessary, since there are several **KTEL** bus terminals. Be sure to match the station to your destination.

Terminal A (☎2810 245 017 or 2810 245 020), between the old city walls and the harbor near the waterfront, serves: **Agios Nikolaos** (1½hr., 20 per day, €4.70); **Arhanes** (30min., 15 per day, €1.20); **Hersonissos** (45min., every 30min., €2.10); **Ierapetra** (2½hr., 7 per day, €7.05); **Lasithi** (2hr., 2 per day, €4.11); **Malia** (1hr., every 30min., €2.50); and **Sitia** (3¼hr., 4 per day, €9.60).

Hania/Rethymno Terminal (☎2810 221 765) is opposite Terminal A, beside the ferry landing. Buy tickets in the cafe building. Service to **Hania** (3hr., 17 per day, €10.50) and **Rethymno** (1½hr., 18 per day, €5.90). From Hania and Rethymno, connections may be made to Plakias, Samaria Gorge, Hora Sfakion, and Akrotiri.

Terminal B (☎2810 255 965). To reach Terminal B, which is outside the Hania Gate of the old city walls, take local bus #135 from Terminal A (€1). Buses run from Terminal B to: **Agia Galini** (2¼hr., 7 per day, €5.50); **Matala** (2hr., 5 per day, €5.10); and **Phaistos** (1½hr., 8 per day, €4.20) via **Gortys** (€3.10).

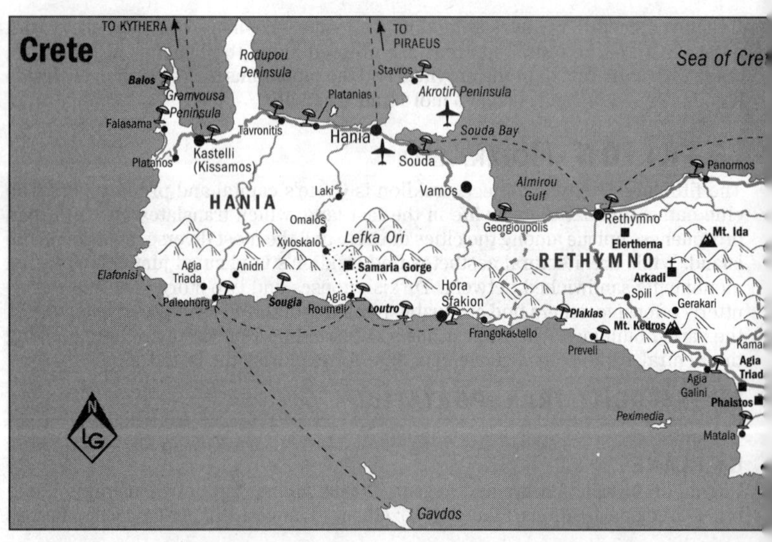

LOCAL TRANSPORTATION

Taxis: Tariff Taxi of Iraklion (☎2810 210 102 or 2810 210 168). Cabs often line up in Pl. Venizelou, across from the fountain. Open 24hr.

Car Rental: Rental car companies are scattered along 25 Augustou. Make the owners compete for your business by quoting prices from their neighbors. **Cosmos,** 25 Augustou 15 (☎2810 241 357 or 2810 346 173; fax 2810 220 379), charges €11 for a 1-day rental, plus €0.13 per km over 100km. Renting for more days reduces the price up to 30%. Open Apr.-Oct. daily 7:30am-9pm; Nov.-Mar. 8am-1pm and 5-9pm.

Moped Rental: Inexpensive rental agencies line Handakos, El Greco Park, and 25 Augustou. Check if the quoted price includes the 20% tax and insurance (50cc bikes cost around €15 per day for extended rentals, tax and liability insurance included).

ORIENTATION AND PRACTICAL INFORMATION

The city has two centers. **Pl. Venizelou** (also known to tourists as **Lion Fountain** or **Four Lion Square**), home to Morosini Fountain, is where Handakos meets Dikeosinis and 25 Augustou in the center of town. **Pl. Eleftherias** is at the intersection of Doukos Bofor and Dikeosinis on the east side of the old city. Most necessities can be found in or near these two squares. Between the two centers, a maze of streets hides a seemingly endless supply of fashionable cafes. Be warned that many of the street names contain **numbers,** so that 1866 and 25 Augustou are street names; this guide lists the address number *after* the street name.

Travel Agencies: Several agencies line 25 Augustou. **Arabatzoglou Bros. Shipping Agents Travel Bureau,** 25 Augustou 54 (☎2810 226 697 or 2810 226 698; fax 2810 222 18; www.arabatzogloubros.gr), has a knowledgeable staff when it comes to ferry schedules. Open M-Sa 8am-9pm.

Banks: The banks on 25 Augustou have 24hr. **ATMs** and **currency exchange. National Bank,** 25 Augustou 35 (☎2810 304 850), is open M-Th 8am-2pm and F 8am-1:30pm.

CRETE

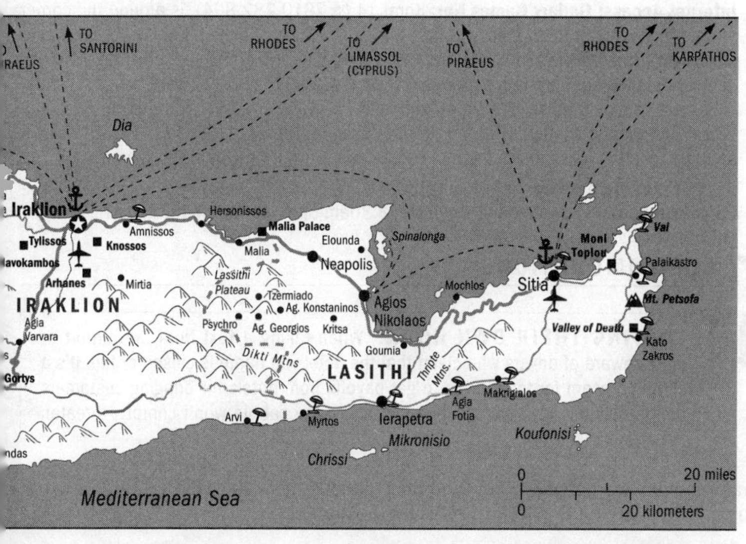

Luggage Storage: Washsalon, Handakos 18 (☎2810 280 858). €1.50 per day. Open 7:30am-10pm.

Bookstores: Planet International Bookstore, Kidonias 23 (☎2810 281 558; fax 2810 287 142), on the corner of Hortatson and Kidonias. This megastore sells books in a number of languages, with a broad selection of classics and travel literature. Some used books can be found in the back, including a nice selection of 5-year-old *Let's Go* guides. Open M-Sa 8:30am-2pm and 5-9pm.

Library: Vikelaia Municipal Library (☎2810 399 237 or 2810 399 249), across from Morosini Fountain. Limited selection in English, French, German, Italian, Russian, and Chinese. Most international books are philosophy, literature, classics, and history—peruse them in the luxurious, air-conditioned reading room on the 2nd fl. Open M-F 8am-2pm, also M and W 5-8pm.

Laundromat: Washsalon, Handakos 18 (☎2810 280 858). €6 for wash and dry, soap included. Open 7:30am-10pm.

Public Toilets: In El Greco Park, look for the underground, cage-like entrance by the swings. Also in the public gardens near Pl. Eleftherias. €0.50. Open 6am-9pm.

Emergency: ☎166.

Tourist Police: Dikeosinis 10 (☎2810 283 190), one block from the intersection with 25 Augustou. Open 8am-10pm. **Tourist information** from 8am-2pm.

Police: Pl. Venizelou 29, in a blue building among the cafes. Open 24hr. One station serves the east side of town (☎2810 284 589 or 2810 282 677); another station in the same building serves the west (☎2810 282 243). **Port Police** (☎2810 244 956 or 2810 244 912), by the harbor.

Hospitals: Venizelou Hospital (☎2810 368 000), on Knossou: take bus #2 from Pl. Venizelou for 20 min. **Panepistimiako Hospital** (☎2810 392 111): take a bus from Astoria Hotel in Pl. Eleftherias. The medical center, **Asklepieon of Crete,** Zografou 8 (☎2810 342 622), is on the southern side of Pl. Eleftherias. Open 24hr.

OTE: Minotavrou 10 (☎2810 395 316), on the left side of El Greco Park as you enter from 25 Augustou. Open 7:30am-1pm.

Internet Access: Gallery Games Net, Korai 14 (☎2810 282 804), is around the corner from the cinema at Pl. Eleftherias and down one block on Korai. €3 per hr. Open 10am-midnight. **Netc@fé** (☎2810 229 569), on 1878, logs you on for the same fee. Also has a wide-selection of Playstation games. To reach it, walk toward the waterfront on Handakos, turn left on Vistaki, and then right onto 1878. Open M-Sa 10am-3am, Su noon-3am. For a more exotic environment, **Cafe Jasmin**, Handakos 45 (☎2810 245 240), adds a touch of class to the Internet cafe scene. €3 per hr. Open 5pm-1am.

Post Office: Main office, in Pl. Daskalogianni. Open M-F 7:30am-8pm and Sa 7:30am-2pm. **Branch** in El Greco Park. Open M-F 8:30am-3pm. **Postal code:** 71001.

ACCOMMODATIONS

TOOTING THEIR OWN HORN. When taking a **taxi** from the airport or port, beware of drivers who claim that the hotel you name is closed or full. It's a common scam for taxi drivers to get payoffs from hotels for bringing customers there. Insist on your own destination, and if the cabbie won't comply, threaten to get out of the taxi.

Iraklion has many cheap hotels and hostels, most near **Handakos** at the center of town. Others are on **Evans** and **1866** near the market.

Rent a Room Hellas, Handakos 24 (☎2810 288 851), 2 blocks from El Greco Park. Large dorm rooms, with a garden bar and casual restaurant on the 4th fl. Although not technically a hostel, Hellas has a communal feel and attracts a large portion of the backpacker set. Hot water 24hr.; free luggage storage. Breakfast €2.50-4. Dorms €8; doubles €24; triples €34. ❶

Hotel Rea (☎2810 223 638; fax 2810 242 189), on Kalimeraki. From Pl. Venizelou, walk down Handakos and turn right after Rent a Room Hellas. The hospitable owners provide cool, airy rooms, hot showers, and free luggage storage. Rooms are available with common or private bath; all have fans and sinks. Breakfast €3. Singles €18, with bath €21; doubles €23/€27; triples €30/€36. ❷

Youth Hostel, Vyronos 5 (☎2810 286 281; fax 2810 222 947). From the bus station, with the water on your right, take a left onto 25 Augustou and a right on Vyronos. Midnight curfew. 24hr. hot water. Sheets €0.60. Luggage storage €3. Breakfast and dinner available (€3 per meal); beer €1.50. Check-out 10am. Dorms €8; singles €10; doubles €22; triples €22. ❶

Lato Hotel, Epimenidou 15 (☎2810 240 350), located just across the street from the Ilaria Hotel. This ultra-modern building has some of the finest rooms in the city, though it's expensive. Each room has a slightly different decorating scheme, but all have satellite TVs, A/C, and balconies. The babbling fountains in the lobby and friendly staff make checking in a pleasure. Singles €83.65; doubles €104.50; triples €131.30. ❺

Rent Rooms Verginia (☎2810 242 739), on Kalimeraki near Hotel Rea. Large windows dominate Verginia's comfortable rooms; sinks in each room and a well-maintained common bath just down the hall. A small garden sitting area is the perfect place to take in a good book. Doubles €22; triples €30. ❷

Ilaira Hotel (☎2810 227 103), at Epimenidou and Ariandis. Walking towards the water on 25 Augustou, make a right onto Epimendou, and walk about 3 blocks. Basic rooms in an ideal location. The roof garden has a fine view of the port and fortress. All rooms have private baths, telephones, and balconies. Singles €35; doubles €50. ❸

FOOD

The ritzy cafes around the **Morosini Fountain,** near El Greco Park and in Pl. Venizelou, are perfect for lounging. Bargain seekers should take a left off 1866, one block from the plateia, to reach tiny **Theodosaki** street, where 10 colorful tavernas serving big, cheap dishes (€3) are jammed side by side. Souvlaki joints abound on **25 Augustou,** and gyros are everywhere for around €2.

The best show in town is the **open-air market** on 1866, starting near Pl. Venizelou. Stalls piled high with sweets, spices, produce, cheeses, meat, and Cretan muscle shirts line both sides of the narrow street. (Open M-Sa 8am-2pm, Tu and Th-F 5-9pm.) Located in the market about halfway down 1866, **Amaltheia,** named after the goat that nursed Zeus, has cauldrons of yogurt that far eclipse the pasteurized brands found elsewhere. The store serves traditional sheep's milk yogurt (€2.70 per kg), as well as local cheeses like a special Cretan gruyère.

Tou Terzaki, Loch. Marineli 17 (☎2810 221 444), behind Agios Dimitrios chapel, off Vyronos, 1 block from 25 Augustou. Locals pack into the chic Tou Terzaki as the night grows old. It's one of the few spots in town using organic ingredients. Simple food compliments the intimate atmosphere. Fried squid €5.13; stuffed vine leaves €4.40. Open M-Sa 5pm-1am. ❷

Thraka, Platokallergon 14 (☎2810 282 355). Facing the Morosini Fountain, with your back to the street, walk about 20m to the right. Popular spot for a late-night snack. Greasy, delicious grilled ham gyros and souvlaki. Try the souvlaki with *thraka* bread crust (€2). Open M-Sa 11am-6am. ❶

Lukulos, Korai 5 (☎2810 224 435). From Pl. Eleftherias, walk past the cinema out of the square, and turn left onto Korai. Lukulos has taken standard Mediterranean dishes and tweaked them into fascinating and tasty concoctions. A great place to spoil yourself with lobster. The fine food is complimented by an extensive selection of Greek wines. Lobster medallion with spaghetti €16; veal with dried figs €18. Open noon-1am. ❹

CRETE

IT'S EL GRECO TO ME Although he made his name at the Spanish court, **Domenikos Theotokopoulos** (1541-1614) clung to his Greek heritage throughout his artistic career. Born in Iraklion, the Cretan artist melded his early Byzantine training with the teachings of the Venetian and Roman schools, where he trained with masters like Titian, Raphael, and Michelangelo. **El Greco,** as he came to be known, was a master of **Mannerism,** a painting style that places internal emotion above nature. His reputation was built on portraits and religious imagery that featured strangely elongated figures—perhaps influenced by his own fingers, which were made long and sinewy by years of disease. Although El Greco moved to Toledo, Spain, in 1576, the Spanish subjects and contexts of his work never eclipsed his feeling that he was a stranger there. Loyal to the homeland through thick and thin, El Greco continued to sign his paintings in Greek.

Lychnostatis, Ioannou Chronaki 8 (☎2810 242 117), 30m past El Greco Park on the same street as the OTE. Pace yourself during dinner because pastries, fresh fruit, and ice cold ouzo are complimentary desserts. Goat with tomatoes €4. Open noon-1am. ❶

Prassein Aloga, Handakos 21 (☎2810 283 429), between Washsalon and the Planet Bookstore. Mediterranean tastes are synthesized into a selection of unique dishes. Risotto with seafood €8. Squid with onion €6.50. Open summer M-Sa noon-midnight and Su 7pm-midnight; winter noon-4pm and 7pm-midnight. ❷

Antonios Nerantzoulis, Agiou Titou 16 (☎2810 346 236), behind the Agios Titos Church. Family-run since 1900, this bakery is famous for *oktasporo* (€6). Come early for warm pastries. Open Sa-M and W 7am-3pm, Tu and Th-F 7am-3pm and 5-8pm. ❶

SIGHTS

IRAKLION ARCHAEOLOGICAL MUSEUM

Off Pl. Eleftherias. ☎2810 226 092. Open M 12:30-7pm, Tu-Su 8am-7pm. €6; students and EU seniors €3; classicists, fine arts students, under 18, and EU students free. Illustrated guide €5-10.

Iraklion's main attraction, after Knossos (p. 519), is the superb **Archaeological Museum.** While most Cretan museums offer a hodgepodge of local finds strung across millennia, the Iraklion Museum presents a comprehensive and chronologically organized record of the Neolithic and Minoan stages of the island's history. A visit to Knossos or another Minoan palace around the island is incomplete without seeing the museum's inventory of the royal and everyday artifacts that once decorated the throne room and the woodshop. Of particular interest are the original **wall paintings of Knossos** on display here.

ROOM 3. In room 3, you'll find the most celebrated discovery from the palace of Phaistos (p. 525), the cryptic **Phaistos disc.** Scholars have been unable to decipher the 214 pictographs etched into the solid clay disc. The intricate impressions suggest that they were made by means of metal stamps, an ancient form of printing. The disk might convey a religious hymn or astrological chart. The plot thickens further: some archaeologists speculate that the disc didn't originate on Crete but still can't quite place its source.

ROOM 4. Three displays vie for top billing in room 4. Especially eye-catching are two topless **snake goddesses** clad in layered skirts, balancing cats on their heads and supporting flailing serpents on each outstretched arm. It's not known whether they're supposed to be goddesses or priestesses. The clothes are revealing in more ways than one: from the figure, you can see the cut and fashion of Minoan costume, the use of snake symbols for eternity, the high status of women in the Minoan religious hierarchy, and the way the female form was idealized in Minoan society. Nearby, the **bull head libation vase** dazzles with white mustache, tight curls of hair, and red eyes made of painted rock crystal. The vase is pierced by two holes, one for filling and one for spilling. The sacred liquid used may have been blood from a sacrificial bull. While the original wood horns have not survived, one of the eyes is still preserved in its socket. Adjacent is another stately drinking vessel, an alabaster libation vase shaped like a lioness's head. Room 4's grand finale is an **ivory acrobat,** probably leaping a bull in a Minoan ritual.

OTHER ROOMS. Look for the intricate **bee pendant** from Chryssolakkos at Malia. The pendant is composed of two bees joined delicately at their stingers, forming a cage with their antennae that encloses a golden ball and a honeycomb lying at the center—a cherished image on Crete. Room 6 stores the **Palaikastro vase,** covered with a complex pattern of spiraling tentacles that toys with your eyes. The jumble of tentacles, suction cups, seaweed, shells, and ink complement the shape of the two-headed amphora perfectly—a mix of chaos and order. In rooms 10 and 11, the **Goddess of the Poppies** stands with raised arms and opium flowers sprouting from her head. The austere power of this and other **household goddesses** shows a significant change in the Minoan concept of women from the statues in room 4.

MINOAN HALL OF FRESCOES. Upstairs is the **Minoan Hall of Frescoes,** the museum's most controversial exhibit. These are the original wall paintings found at Knossos—replicas adorn the reconstructed palace. Sir Walter Evans didn't spare these priceless finds his revisionist hand; in restoring the frescoes, he added his own ideas about the original compositions. Depicting ancient Minoan life, these frescoes capture ladies offering libations, trippy blue monkeys frolicking in palatial gardens, and Minoans in procession. They're breathtaking. But before you get too excited, check out the restoration work up close: the frescoes were reconstructed from very small original pieces, leaving room for modern day imagination. In fact, subsequent study of the **Prince of Lilies** revealed that the fragments depicted three figures: a priestess in a lily crown and two boxers flanking her.

OTHER SIGHTS

KAZANTZAKIS REMEMBERED. With views of Iraklion, the sea, and Mt. Ida to the west, the austere **Tomb of Kazantzakis** offers a peaceful break from crowded Iraklion. Because of his unorthodox beliefs, Nikos Kazantzakis, the author of *The Last Temptation of Christ*, was denied a place in a Christian cemetery and was buried alone in this tomb. The tomb is a wonderful place to watch the sun set or to contemplate the city. To reach the tomb from the city center, head down Evans until you reach the Venetian walls and the Martinengo Bastion, then turn left and walk about 100m further; the tomb is atop the city walls beside the football stadium. Alternatively, you can follow the crumbling outline of the city walls to the tomb. The village of **Varvari** outside of Iraklion is home to the **Kazantzakis Museum,** where true devotees can see many of the author's original manuscripts, as well as photos of his theatrical productions. A slide show (in English) provides historical background. *(Take a bus from Terminal A to Mirtia (€1.80) and follow the signs; make sure to check return schedules. ☎2810 741 689. Open Mar. 1-Oct. 31 daily 9am-7pm, Nov. 1-Feb. 28 Su 9am-3pm. €3, students and children €1.)*

CRETE

CHURCHES. Several majestic, ancient churches hide in the modern maze of Iraklion's streets. Magnificent **Agios Titos Church,** on 25 Augustou, is a converted mosque. Its architecture combines Muslim geometric designs and Christian regalia. The stained glass windows are all shapes rather than figures. It is lit up every night; note the *tamata* (charm-like votives) that represent the churchgoers' prayers. In Pl. Venizelou, **San Marco Church,** built in 1239, houses a changing exhibition space that features everything from 14th-century monastery frescoes to modern art. *(☎2810 399 399, ext. 228. Open 9am-8pm. Free.)* Built in 1735, the **Cathedral of Agios Minas** graces Pl. Agia Ekaternis. *(☎2810 282 402. Open 7am-11pm. Free.)* **St. Catherine's Church of Sinai,** also in the plateia, served as the first Greek university after the fall of Constantinople in 1453. The church has six icons by the Cretan master Damaskinos as well as other icons from around Crete. *(☎2810 288 825. Open M-Sa 9am-1:30pm, Tu and Th-F 5-7pm. Free.)* St. Catherine and Ag. Minas churches share their plaza with a small church building that contains the **Icons Museum,** a collection of Byzantine altarpieces and other ceremonial objects. *(☎2810 288 825. Open M-Sa 9:30am-7:30pm. €2.)* A priest gives tours of the **Armenian Church.** Head away from the town center on Kalokerianou and take a right on Lasthenous after Yiannis's store—the church is left of the bend. *(☎2810 244 337.)*

HISTORICAL MUSEUM. The collection at the undervisited Historical Museum includes a scale model of the city, Byzantine and medieval works, a folk collection, photos from the World War II Nazi invasion, displays on Kazantzakis, and perhaps the only **El Greco** painting on Crete—the 1578 work "View of Mt. Sinai and the Monastery of St. Catherine." *(On the corner of Grevenon and Kalokerianou. ☎2810 283 219. Open M-F 9am-5pm, Sa 9am-2pm. €3, students €2.20, under 12 free.)*

VENETIAN IRAKLION. As you rove the city, take in the various Venetian monuments: **Morosini Fountain,** centerpiece of Pl. Venizelou, and the nearby reconstructed **Venetian Loggia,** now a town hall. The 17th-century **Venetian Arsenal,** off Pl. Koundouriotou near the waterfront, and the **Koules Fortress** guard the old harbor. *(☎2810 246 211. Open M-F 8am-6pm, Sa-Su 10am-5pm. €2, students €1.)* For an unexpected dose of peace and beauty, walk along the olive tree-lined southeast section of the **Venetian walls.** Also accessible from Iraklion is El Greco's home village of **Fodele,** full of orange trees and history (see **It's El Greco to Me,** p. 516).

NIGHTLIFE AND ENTERTAINMENT

Trading tourist kitsch for genuine urban energy, Iraklion outdoes the resort towns with its pulsing nightlife. Day or night, the huge atrium-like **Aktarika Cafe,** across from Pl. Venizelou, brims with hip, black-clad twenty- and thirty-something Iraklionites and the people who watch them. (*Frappés* €3, cocktails €6. Open 8am-2am.) A more peaceful scene is found at **Utopia** on Handakos near Rent a Room Hellas. The high-quality hot chocolate and tea is accompanied by a selection of free pastries. (Coffee drinks €4-5. Open 9am-2am.) Around 11pm, the young and the restless of all nationalities overflow the small streets between **Pl. Venizelou** and **Pl. Eleftherias. Androgeou** becomes a veritable river of chic young Cretans drinking, smoking, and chatting. As the night proceeds, these activities merge with the rhythms of techno, pop, and Greek music along the waterfront. A walk down D. Beaufort takes you to a powerful trifecta of Iraklion dance clubs with rather intimidating names: **Privilege, Envy,** and **Diamonds and Pearls.** Each has multiple bars serving pricey drinks, while Privilege and Envy both have balconies overlooking the port. The doors of Iraklion's clubs generally demand a sharp and tidy appearance (no sneakers or sloppy jeans) and a €6 cover, which includes one drink.

Join Greeks and tourists at sites throughout the city for Iraklion's annual **summer festival** (July-Aug.), a cultural combination of plays, concerts, theater, ballet, and folk dancing. Schedules for Iraklion's **movie theaters** are posted in front of the tourist police office. (Shows begin at 9:30pm. Tickets €6; reduced student prices.)

DAYTRIPS FROM IRAKLION

KNOSSOS Κνωσσος

From Iraklion, take bus #2 (15min., every 10min., €0.85), which stops along 25 Augustou and in Pl. Eleftherias. Buy your bus tickets at a nearby kiosk in advance. ☎2810 231 940. Open daily 8am-7pm, off season 8am-5pm. €6; students and seniors €3; classicists, fine arts students, and EU students free; in winter, free on Su. Guides €5-7. Helpful tour in English (1hr.; €5). Make sure your guide is official and has the required papers.

Legend and fact are close cousins at the palace of Knossos, famous throughout the world and history as the site of King Minos's machinations, the Labyrinth and its Minotaur, and the imprisonment (and winged escape) of Daedalus and Icarus. Cretans were once ridiculed for claiming Minoan roots, but Sir Arthur Evans won them the last laugh when his excavations confirmed the Minoan's ancient presence on the island.

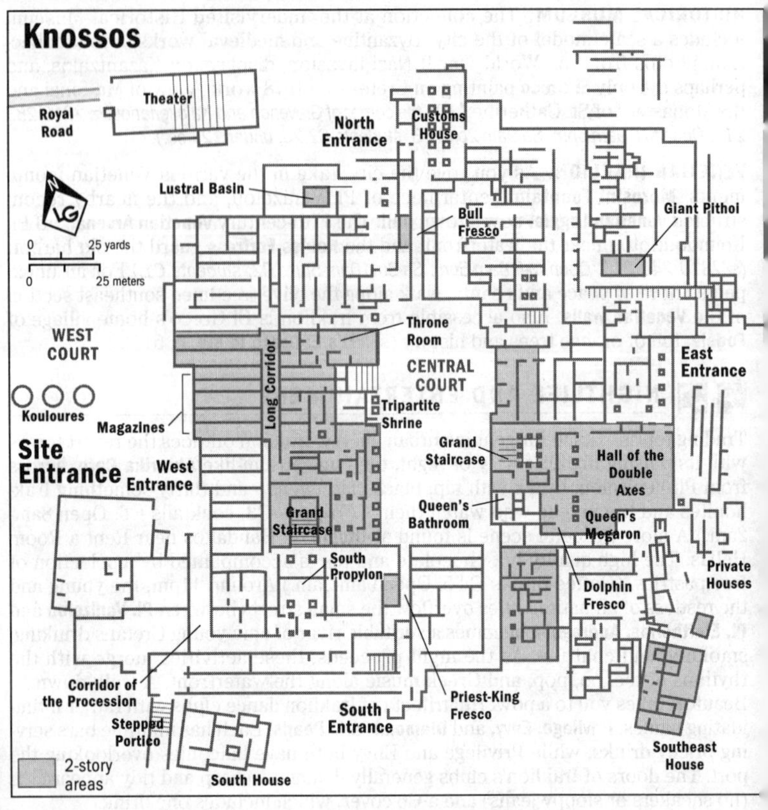

At about 150m^2, Knossos is the largest and has the most intricate architecture of Crete's **Minoan palaces.** (Phaistos (p. 525), Malia (p. 529), and Zakros (p. 561) are the locations of the others). Arthur Evans, one of Heinrich Schliemann's British cronies, purchased the hill that concealed Knossos in 1900. Evans spent 43 years and a fortune excavating it. Armed with the evidence he had unearthed, he set out to restore the palace with creativity and woeful inaccuracy. Walls, window casements, stairways, and columns were reconstructed in reinforced concrete, and some of the ruins were painted. Copies of the magnificent frescoes replaced the originals, which are now a must-see in **Iraklion's Archaeological Museum** (p. 517). Indeed, a visit to Knossos is not really complete without seeing the museum's collection of decorations and everyday objects that cluttered the palace. Visiting throngs and the brightly painted walls make the complex look like a Disney-esque "Minoanland." Knossos, however, is visitor-friendly and provides satisfying historical explanations, a factor which distinguishes it from other Minoan palaces.

THE SITE

CENTER STAGE. The gaping space in the middle of the site, the **Central Court,** was the heart of the palace and the arena for **bull-leaping.** To its left is the **Throne Room,** where the original, preserved limestone throne still sits in splendor, surrounded by paintings of gryphons. A priestess—not King Minos—probably occupied this seat. A wooden replica of the throne sits outside, erected where a pile of charred remains were found.

ROYAL QUARTERS. Leading down to the royal quarters is the grand staircase, an elegant structure that is the sturdiest part of the palace, as it was built into living rock. Because of its solid foundation, two stories below the main court survived otherwise destructive earthquakes. Don't miss the **Queen's Bathroom,** where over 3000 years ago, she took milk baths while gazing up at marvelous dolphin frescoes. The king had his quarters in the **Hall of the Double Axes.** The double axe, a sacred Minoan symbol, is carved all over the palace and into pieces in the Iraklion Museum. The double axe, *labrys*, and the tangled maze of the palace's layout (like Daedalus's maze to imprison the Minotaur) combined to form the present-day word "labyrinth."

OTHER SIGHTS. Walking north from the royal quarters, you'll stumble across the grand **pothoi**—jars so big that, according to legend, Minos's son drowned in one filled with honey. The areas painted red around each window and door were originally made of wood; they cushioned the walls from frequent seismic shock, but ultimately facilitated the palace's destruction by fire, following an uncertain disaster. One theory is that a tidal wave caused by a volcanic eruption on Santorini (p. 445) set in motion a chain of events that led to the devastation of Knossos.

ARHANES Αρχανες

Buses run from Iraklion's Terminal A (30min., 15 per day, €1.20).

A scenic suburb of Iraklion, Arhanes reveals its ancient and medieval importance in its interior old quarter and in its many sights. Once used as a burial ground by Minoans and Mycenaeans, modern Arhanes is characterized by neat pastel houses with clay tile roofs and a thriving grape export industry. Arhanes remains startlingly bereft of tourist menu billboards and harassing hosteliers.

Pleasant street ramblings aside, Arhanes's official attractions are its **Archaeology Museum** and the sites where the collection originated. To reach the museum from the bus stop, head toward the center of town, keeping an eye out for the signs. Though the collection is small, the museum provides a good understanding of the area's sites. Its one room holds relics from Phourni, Anemospilia, and the Minoan Palace at Arhanes, as well as photos of finds now in Iraklion's Archaeological Museum (p. 517). The most

A CHURCH DIVIDED

One would be hard-pressed to think of a feud that has lasted longer than that between the Orthodox Church and the Catholic Church. Their conflict has endured since the Great Schism of 1054.

But the two great branches of Christianity seem to be getting on a bit better these days. In May 2001, Pope John Paul II visited Greece and received a mostly enthusiastic welcome from Greek leaders and citizens. More recently, the Pope and Patriarch Vartholomeos signed the Declaration of Venice, a document outlining six specific recommendations for mankind to alter its behavior in order to preserve the environment. The document was the culmination of a series of joint symposia on "Religion, Science, and the Environment."

The unification of Europe through the EU is another potential catalyst to a reconciliation between the two churches. The EU is prepared to admit 10 more countries by 2004, all of which will come from Eastern Europe. This expansion will add to the EU more Catholics and many more Orthodox Christians. Catholics and Orthodox will find themselves working in close contact on many issues and surrendering sovereignty to a body that transcends religious differences.

Of course, the dogmatic and theological differences between the churches are still dramatic, and neither side wants to back down on such dividing issues. Yet, recent developments point to the potential for a rapprochement.

sensational of the Arhanes Museum's objects is the **bronze dagger** used for human sacrifice, found at the **Shrine of Anemospilia,** a 17th-century BC shrine on Mt. Iouktas outside of town. The sacrifices were most likely attempts to appease the gods, perhaps to prevent the kind of earthquake that eventually destroyed the shrine. (Open M and W-Su 8am-3pm. Free.)

The museum's artifacts come primarily from the *tholos* graves at the nearby **Minoan Cemetery,** used throughout the Palace Period (2400-1200 BC). Tholos A in the burial ground was the first unlooted royal burial site found on Crete. Most of its objects have been moved to Iraklion, but some remain in the Arhanes Museum: terra-cotta *pithoi*, child and adult sarcophagi, baby burial jars, and skeletons from Phourni. Phourni Building 4 housed a wine press and a vat for treading grapes, and an *amphora* for the wine itself. To see the cemetery after checking out its contents, follow Kapetanaki about 800m out of town and look for signs to the site; it's northwest of Arhanes. (Open Tu-Su 8am-3pm. Free.)

The town's other sights are limited to the **wine factory** and the small but charming **Church of the Panagia** (open M, Tu, Th 9am-2pm). Both are found on Kapetanaki; continue up the alleyway past the Archaeology Museum, and make a left on the large road. You'll find the clock tower 500m farther.

GORTYS Γορτυνα

From Iraklion, take the bus to either Matala or Phaistos, and ask the driver to stop at Gortyna (€3). You can also take the bus from Mires (€0.75). ☎28920 31 144. Open daily 8am-6pm; off season 8am-5pm. €2.50; students and EU seniors €1.20; under 18, classicists, fine arts students, and EU students free.

Formerly the site of a Greco-Roman city, Gortyna, 45km south of Iraklion, is a stimulating stop for the historically minded. In 67 BC, when the Romans conquered Crete, Gortys was made its capital. From Iraklion on the paved road toward Matala, the first stop is the 7th-century **Basilica of Saint Titus,** Crete's first Christian church. Built where 10 saints were executed in AD 250, the Basilica's *berma* (half dome with windows) encompasses a courtyard of fallen columns. Behind the church is the **Roman odeon,** where the famous **Law Code of Gortys** is lodged in the walls. Called the "Queen of Inscriptions," it is the most important extant source of pre-Hellenistic Greek law. Across a small wooden bridge from the odeon is the **Platanos tree,** under which distinguished brothers Minos (an early Cretan ruler), Sarpidon (a Trojan warrior), and Rodaman (the family underachiever) were born.

After you exit this part of the site, re-enter on the other side of the entrance booth to find a small, fenced-off **museum** with 13 sculpted figures. To the left of the museum is a larger-than-life **statue** of Roman emperor Antoninus Pius. If he appears somewhat nondescript, you're on to something—resourceful Romans changed the statue's head every time a new emperor came to power.

Outside the site, you have two options. The first is an expanse of ruined structures: head 50m toward Iraklion and turn right at the sign. The **Sanctuary and Sacrificial Altar of Pythian Apollo** is the first among these ruins. Nearby is the **Nymphaion,** which was the end of an aqueduct that brought spring water from Zaros. A few steps farther is the most impressive ruin at Gortys, the **Praetorium,** which was the seat of the Roman administrator. Built in the 4th century BC, the Praetorium was ahead of its time: it had a water-heating system. The 7th-century BC **acropolis** is along the other path, on the hill west of the odeon. To get there, continue 50m down the main road toward Matala, take a right after the river, and walk 200m; when you reach the corner of the fence, hike up the road for 30min. Temple ruins and pottery dedicated to Athena Poliouchos ("guardian of the city") are at the road's end.

ZAROS Ζαρος

Zaros's name has spread far and wide for its water and little else, but this small mountain town is the perfect starting point for a day spent hiking in the mountains of Iraklion prefecture. Zaros is the capital and political center of a union of villages that includes neighboring Vorisia, Kamares, and Moroni. Upon arrival, you may be alarmed to discover that the ultra-pure "Zaros" spring water originates in this gritty mountain town, but the gorgeous landscape and warm Cretan hospitality are as refreshing as its bottled export. Zaros is busiest during the spring and fall hiking seasons; in the summer, you'll have the hospitable locals all to yourself.

ORIENTATION AND PRACTICAL INFORMATION. Zaros's one main road has everything but a **bank,** which you'll find in nearby Mires. The bus stops at the downhill end of the road, near the **police station** (☎28940 31 210). You can also call the **Mires police** (☎28940 22 222). Two **buses** run daily from Zaros to Mires (40min., €1.65) and Iraklion (70min., €3.20). For **emergencies** at any hour call the hospital in Mires (☎28920 23 312). Find the **pharmacy** (☎28940 31 386; open M-F 8:30am-2pm and 5-8pm) in Zaros's downtown center. From the police station, walking to the left at the fork in the road near the gas station leads to the **medical center** (☎28940 31 206), while the flag-marked town hall (open M-F 7:30am-3pm) stands on the right fork, which also goes up to the downtown center. The **post office** is by the pharmacy. **Postal code:** 70002.

ACCOMMODATIONS AND FOOD. Lodging in Zaros is a familial experience. Expect to be invited to family meals or, at least, to a glass of *raki* or four. **Keramos Rent Studios ❷** has a comforting, homey feel. Walk uphill and turn left before the post office; it's 20m down the road on the left. The proprietor, George, makes all the wood furniture in this family-run operation by hand; his wife, Katerina, and her two daughters tend to guests with breakfasts of fresh goat cheese from their farm and homemade Cretan delights such as *pitaraki* (Christmas pastry). Most studios have kitchenettes; all have baths and central heating in winter. (☎28940 31 352. Singles €22; doubles €28; breakfast included.) **Charikleia Rent Rooms ❷,** a cottage across from the police station, has clean rooms with shared baths. Sip a *frappé* at a shaded table beneath the grape arbor. (☎28940 31 787. Singles €15; doubles €20; each additional person in a room is €10; breakfast €3.) The most upscale option is the **Idi Hotel ❹.** Idi lies on Votomos Lane, which curves to the right off the main road when walking uphill. It is about 400m up the road and well-marked. The hotel has all the amenities: sauna, indoor pool, and A/C. (☎28940 31 301 or 31 302. Doubles €49; triples €50; quads €56. All include breakfast.)

A number of tavernas take shelter in the greenery of Votomos. On your right, about 200m beyond the Idi Hotel, a 10min. walk from town, **Petrogiannakis and Ieronimakis' ❷** is renowned for outstanding fish raised on the premises. Savor perfectly cooked trout (€6.50) and salmon (€25 per kg) after touring the fish farm. (☎28940 31 071 or 31 454. Open 9am-midnight.) **Papadaki Rena ❶,** 20m past Keramos Studios, sells sweets and gifts; try the *tulta* cream cake or *baklava.* (☎28940 31 055. Most treats under €1. Open 8am-10pm.)

SIGHTS AND HIKES. Zaros has been Crete's source of life-giving **water** since the days of ancient Gortys. At the water-bottling plant just above town, you can see the fleet of trucks loading bottles to carry to the far reaches of the island. There are fountains along the main street where you can wash off and quench your thirst. Every July and August, the village celebrates its aquatic bounty in a **water festival.** Zaros also holds an annual **summer festival** every August.

Hikes and walks through gorges and up to surrounding monasteries are breathtaking; check the map in front of the police station for route suggestions. At the end of the road beyond the Idi Hotel and the Votomos tavernas is the **lake** of Votomos, popular with anglers. Take the path on the left behind the lake to reach a hike through the gorge up beyond Agios Nikolaos Church. The climb is a satisfying daytrip through the ever-changing scenery of the mountainside, but be warned that the way is often poorly marked and the path slippery with loose gravel. Another path up the mountains, starting at the nearby town of Kamares, leads to the **Monastery of Vrondisi,** where you'll find impressive frescoes said to be the work of El Greco. Every May, the annual **Paniel festival and bazaar** takes place here to commemorate the ascent of St. Thomas. Trails through the hills around the monastery lead to a cliffside sanctuary dedicated to Cretan saint **Agios Euthymios.** Shepherds keep large bottles of olive oil in the sanctuary and bring hikers into the shrines' three cave chambers to meditate before frescoes of the saint. Yet another mountain road leads to the **Kamares Cave,** where Rhea hid her infant son Zeus from his father's voracious appetite. Archaeologists have made some important finds here, including ceramics and skeletons now in the Iraklion museum. Again, your best bet is to check the route map in front of the police station for exact directions.

MATALA Ματαλα

Anyone who visited Matala 20 years ago probably has only blurry memories of a hallucinogenic trip—the caves along Matala's seaside cliffs were once full of LSD-dosed psychedelia-lovers listening to groovy music. Today's Matala is a far cry from that old hippie city. There's an admission fee and fence barring access to the caves that countercultural hedonists once called home. But the party isn't entirely over: a short hike beyond the main drag lie magnificent nude beaches, gorgeous reminders of those bygone days.

ORIENTATION AND PRACTICAL INFORMATION. Matala's single main street, where the bus stops, provides most necessities; when it hits the waterfront, the road bends to become a covered market with steps leading down to a taverna-lined waterfront. Before the covered market, a pension-filled road branches to the left, eventually heading up and over the hill to Red Beach. **Buses** go to: **Agia Galini** (45min., 3-6 per day, €2.10); **Iraklion** (1¾hr., 3-6 per day, €5.15); **Mires** (30min., 5-6 per day, €1.65); and **Phaistos** (20min., 3-5 per day, €1.10). **Monza Travel,** in the plateia, rents **mopeds** (€10-15) and cars (€25-35) and helps with accommodations. (☎28920 45 732 or 28920 45 359; fax 28920 45 763. Open daily 9am-10:30pm.) Several motorbike rental shops **exchange currency.** The **laundromat,** on the left side of town, charges €10 per wash and dry. (Open M-Sa 9am-5pm.) **Public toilets** are east of the post office, on the way to the beach. In an **emergency,** call ☎28920 22 222 for police; dial ☎28920 22 225 or 28920 23 312 for a doctor. The **police, hospital,** and **pharmacy** are in Mires, 17km northeast. **Internet access** is available at the **Kafaneio Coffee Shop,** on the right side of the road about 100m past the bus stop (€4 per hr.). The yellow **post office,** across the street from the laundromat, opens sporadically, usually weekday mornings. **Postal code:** 70200.

ACCOMMODATIONS AND CAMPING. Though hotels in the center of town tend to be pricey, don't try sleeping on the main beach or in the caves—it's illegal, and police do raid them. Instead, look outside of town for reasonable prices in a quieter setting. **Pension Matala View ❷,** on the road to Red Beach, offers cool rooms with private baths, balconies, and fridges, and a common kitchen facility. (☎28920 45 114. Singles €15-20; doubles €20-30; triples €22-32.) Walk 200m toward Phaistos and follow the blue signs to **Dimitri's Villa ❷.** The gleaming rooms have baths,

CRETE

balconies, fridges, safes, and phones. An on-site pool provides some freshwater refreshment. (☎ 28920 45 002 or 003; fax 28920 45 740; www.dimitrisvilla.gr. Singles €17; doubles €19-24.) **Bungalows Odysseas ❹**, just before Dimitri's, has simple two-room apartments with kitchenettes that can sleep four. (☎ 28920 45 777. Bungalows €50-65.) If you're set on staying in town, try **Matala Camping ❶**, just off the main road east of the post office, in a slightly wooded grove beside the beach. (☎ 28920 42 720. Showers available. €4 per person; €3 per small tent.)

FOOD AND ENTERTAINMENT. Only a few restaurants in town cater to the budget palate. On the west end of the beach, **Nikos at Plaka ❶** specializes in fresh seafood (sole with crab €7); they also serve traditional Greek foods for around €3. (☎ 28920 45 335. Open daily Apr.-Oct. 11am-11pm.) For good souvlaki and gyros, head to **Notos ❶**, between the waterfront and the covered market. (Open daily 9am-1am.) **Kantari**, on the main plateia, is a popular place to catch Latin and other world music. (☎ 28920 45 404. Open daily 9am-late. Beer €1.50; cocktails €4.50.) Tiny **Kahlua** (☎ 28920 45 253), near the end of the main road, has indoor and outdoor seating with a view of the beach and a laid-back bar atmosphere. **Giorgios** is owned and bartended by energetic Giorgios himself, who will win you over with his spunky dancing, chit-chat, and ice-cold beer. (☎ 28920 45 722. Opens daily at 6pm; the partying lasts until around 6am.)

SIGHTS AND BEACHES. Matala attracts visitors with its three tiers of spectacular **caves** beside the beach. As you sit in the damp interior, reflect on the caves' previous occupants—Nazis searching for British submarines, songwriter Joni Mitchell, and even Roman corpses. *(Open daily 11:30am-7pm. €2.)*

Matala is blessed with some of Crete's best **beaches**, many of which are spawning grounds for endangered **sea turtles**. Environmentalists run a kiosk providing info on the turtles and their habitat; if you want to support the cause, pick up a purple **Save the Turtles t-shirt** (€10.50). The main beach, a beautiful rounded cove with yellow sand and aquamarine water, captures the "here and now" spirit of Matala with a saying that is painted in block letters on the eastern side of the beach: "Today is life, tomorrow never comes." A 35min. hike past the pension-lined street and over the steep, rough trail will bring you to a magnificent strip of sand known as **Red Beach**. Bring hiking shoes, since the path is tough. Once you reach a fence, follow it to the right, and go through the goat herd gate to the shore. Cliffs surround this taverna-free nudist beach. Bring drinking water and an umbrella, as the beach has no shade, leading to speculation that it may take its name from the lobster skin-tone of unprepared visitors and not from its clay-colored sand. Five kilometers from Matala, the long, pebbly **Kommos Beach** stretches out, with one taverna and an enclave of nude bathers. Archaeologists are currently excavating a Minoan site over the beach. To get to it, take the Matala-Iraklion **bus**, ask to be let off at Kommos (€0.80), and walk a dusty 500m down to the beach.

CRETE

PHAISTOS Φαιστος

***Buses** from Phaistos go to: **Agia Galini** (25min., 6 per day, €1.35); **Iraklion** (1½hr., 8 per day, €4.30); **Mires** (8 per day, €0.90); and **Matala** (20min., 4 per day, €1.10). ☎ 28920 42 315. Open 8am-1pm. €4; students and all EU seniors €2; classics students, under 18, and EU students free.*

Seated royally on a plateau with magnificent views of the mountains, the ruins of Phaistos are one of the finest reminders of the grandeur of Minoan palace complexes. Phaistos attracts fewer tourists and has undergone less interpretive renovation than its more famous counterpart, Knossos (p. 519). Four palaces have been discovered on the site: the first, built around 1900 BC, was destroyed by the earthquake that decimated Crete around 1700 BC. The second structure was leveled by a Mysterious Cataclysm in 1450 BC; traces of two even older palaces were detected by an excavation in 1952. Since the excavations, minor reconstruction work has been done on the walls, chambers, and cisterns. Built according to the standard Minoan blueprint, the complex included a great central court surrounded by royal quarters, servant quarters, storerooms, and chambers for state occasions.

Today, visitors enter Phaistos and immediately see the **West Courtyard** and **theater area** at the lower level on their right. On the left, you'll see the intact grand staircase. At its top is the **propylaea,** consisting of a landing, portico, central column, and light well. Walk past the grand staircase and take the next left to reach the **main hall,** which contains a central fenced-off **storeroom,** where you can view goodies like *pithoi*, similar to those at Knossos.

On the perimeter of the central court, columns and boxes mark the place where sentries used to stand guard. Beyond this area, covered **royal apartments** sit to the left, with a queen's **magaron** similar to the famous queen's bathroom at Knossos and a beautiful lustral basin (covered purifying pool). In the nearby **peristyle hall,** the remains of columns can be seen lining the walls. Northeast of the central court are the narrow halls of the palace **workshops** as well as the seven-compartmented room where the renowned **Phaistos disc,** now in the Archaeological Museum in Iraklion (see p. 517), was discovered.

AGIA GALINI

Agia Galini is a standard riff on the typical Cretan beach melody, though its popular beach and hilly secrets can be hard to pinpoint through the fog of package tourists that fill them. The town's main street runs down a hill from the bus station to the harbor and contains all of the practical necessities. Off the main drag, more winding streets run so steeply that they are often composed of steps rather than pavement; most are stocked with restaurants and some accommodations. Turn left from the harbor to reach the long beach, where more tavernas await your thirst. The **bus station** has service to **Iraklion** (1½hr., 6-7 per day, €5.15); **Matala** (1hr., 2-5 per day, €2.10); **Phaistos** (30min., 5-6 per day, €1.35); and **Rethymno** (1hr., 3-4 per day, €4.20). **Ferries** run to **Paveli** and back once a day. They leave at 10am and return at 5pm (round-trip €20). Next to the bus station is a **taxi service** (☎28320 91 486). Across the street, **Monza Travel** provides info and rents mopeds and cars. (☎28320 91 004. Open daily 9am-10pm. Mopeds €10-20; cars €28-35.) The street is full of **exchange** places. Heading downhill from the bus stop you'll pass the **police station** (☎28320 91 210; open 24hr.) and a **pharmacy** (☎28320 91 168; open M-Sa 9:30am-2pm and 5-9pm). Unfortunately, there is no doctor in town so health needs can be taken care of at the hospital in Rethymno or the **health center** (☎28320 22 222) in Spili. The **laundromat** is around the corner from the Manos Hotel. (€7 per load. Open M-Sa 9am-2pm and 5-9pm) **Internet access** is available at **Cafe Alexander,** on the eastern side of the harbor. (€1.50 per 20min.; €4.10 per hr.) The **post office** (☎28320 91 393; open M-F 8am-2pm) can be found by the police station and pharmacy. **Postal code:** 74056.

Some pensions are reasonably priced and close to the beach. On the main road **Phaistos** ❸ offers rooms with private baths. (☎28320 94 352. Doubles €30.) Next door, **Manos** ❷ has rooms with shared and private baths, as well as the option of a kitchen. (☎28320 91 394. Singles €15-20; doubles €20-30.) With a nice view of the harbor, **Hotel Acteon** ❷ has rooms with A/C at good prices. To get there, walk along the harbor and turn up the street opposite a small fountain, make the first right and the hotel is at the top of the stairs. (☎28320 91 208. Singles €20; doubles €25; triples €35. Discount for students.) Large groups or beach lovers should check out **Stohos** ❹ with well-furnished rooms only 10m from the sand. (☎28320 91 433. Doubles and triples €50; apartments for 4-7 €50-70.) **Camping Agia Galini**

CRETE

No Problem ❶ has a pool, mini-market, and **taverna ❷** serving farm-fresh food, cooked on the embers of a traditional wood-stove (salad and 2 entrees €12). Call for the free minibus service; alternatively, walk along the beach until the path begins to climb a small hill and make a left. Continue for 20m down the path until it becomes paved; stay straight on the road, walk another 200m—the entrance to the camping site will be on your left. (☎28320 91 386 or 28320 91 141; fax 28320 91 239. Laundry €5. 10% discount for *Let's Go* users. €3.50-4.50 per person; tents €2-3; cars €1.50-2.50.) Getting tired of Greek food every night? Try some Italian at **Il Piatto ❶**, next to the bus stop. Using fresh ingredients to make traditional sauces, Il Piatto provides a welcome gastronomical change of pace. (☎28320 91 947. Entrees €3-5. Open Mar.-Oct. daily noon-3pm and 7pm-2am. Open on weekends only in the off season.) The small **bakery ❶**, on your right just next to Manos, has sweet treats for under €1.50. At night you can chill at a mellow waterfront bar, or check out the happening retro scene at **Juxebox,** just off the harbor across from the fountain, where the bartender is known to go to lengths to keep the party hoppin'. (☎28320 91 154. Beer €2-4; cocktails €6. Open daily 10pm-7am; €2 Happy Hour cocktails.)

HERSONISSOS Χερσονησος

With 150 bars, discos, and nightclubs around its harbor, as well as mountain villages to the south, Hersonissos (herr-SON-i-sos) becomes a playground for English and German youngsters every summer. Bungee-jumping, bumper cars, and waterslides clutter the beachfront, and Cretan culture is preserved only in a well-polished open-air museum. You don't need to know the Greek word for gin here—your bartender won't know it either.

ORIENTATION AND PRACTICAL INFORMATION

Hersonissos is just 26km east of Iraklion. The lone main road, **Eleftheriou Venizelou,** has offices, markets, and discos. Perpendicular streets lead either to the beach or to the hills. Turning right beyond the Hard Rock Cafe on your way to Iraklion puts you on **Dimokratias,** a less congested stretch of supermarkets and travel agents.

Buses: There is no bus station, just a kiosk near the Hard Rock Cafe. Bus service to: **Agios Nikolaos** (1hr., 17-20 per day, €2.50); **Ierapetra** (2hr., €4.90); **Iraklion** (45min., 4 per hr., €2.10); **Malia** (20min., 4 per hr., €0.90); **Sitia** (2½hr., €7.10).

Taxi: 24hr. station (☎28970 23 723 or 28970 22 098) on El. Venizelou beside the medical center.

Car and Motorbike Rental: Several agencies on El. Venizelou. **Autotravel,** El. Venizelou 20 (☎28970 22 761), rents cars (€45-60 per day with full insurance and tax included). Motorbikes can be found on every street for €10-20 per day.

Tourist Agencies: Mareland Travel has 5 branches; the main one is at Dimokratias 4. (☎28970 24 424; fax 28970 24 150. Open 8:30am-midnight.) **Zakros Tours,** Dimokratias 12 (☎28970 22 776; fax 28970 22 137). Open 8am-midnight. Both rent cars, sell boat and plane tickets, exchange currency, find rooms, and have maps.

Banks: Several on El. Venizelou **exchange currency** and have 24hr. **ATMs. National Bank,** El. Venizelou 106 (☎28970 22 377). Open M-Th 8am-2pm, F 8am-1:30pm.

Public Toilets: Across from the Zakros Tours office on El. Venizelou. Free.

Tourist Police: Minos 8 (☎28970 21 000). Turn toward the beach before Club 99 as you walk into town from Iraklion.

Police: Minos 8 (☎28970 22 100 or 28970 22 222).

Medical Services: Medical Emergency of Kriti (☎28970 22 063, 28970 22 600, or 28970 22 111; fax 28970 21 987), at the corner of El. Venizelou and Kassaveti, near the Hard Rock Cafe. Open 24hr. **Cretan Medicare,** El. Venizelou 19 (☎28970 25 141, 28970 25 142, or 28970 25 143), in the western outskirts of town. Open 24hr.

OTE: Eleftherias 11 (☎28970 22 299). Heading into town from Iraklion, turn right after Pelekis Jewelry. Open 7:30am-2:30pm.

Internet Access: Mouse Internet Cafe, El. Venizelou 59 (☎28970 25 292) is on your left before the public toilets (coming from the Hard Rock Cafe). €4 per hr. **Net Cafe,** El. Venizelou 109 (☎28970 22 192), is a video arcade/Internet cafe across from the National Bank. €3.50 per hr.; printing €0.30 per page.

Post Office: (☎28970 22 022). Open M-Sa 7:30am-2pm. **Postal Code:** 70014.

ACCOMMODATIONS

Hotels line El. Venizelou and offer rooms for €20-55, depending on when you arrive. Tour companies book up most of the rooms in town for the height of the tourist season, so consider making a reservation if you visit in late July or August.

Selena Pension, Em. Maragaki 13 (☎28970 25 180). Walking from the bus kiosk on the main road away from Iraklion, take a left just past Enjoy Bar. Small rooms have private bath and balcony in a convenient, relatively quiet location. The air-conditioned rooms go quickly, even early and late in high season. Doubles €25-50. ❸

Camping Caravan (☎28970 24 718), in Limenas; walk or bus 2km east toward Agios Nikolaos to Lychnostatis Museum; campsite is past the water park. Restaurant and bar. 24hr. free hot water. €4-4.60 per person, children ages 6-10 €3-3.30; tent rental €4.50; €2.30-2.50 per car; 2-person bungalow €27-31. ❶

FOOD AND ENTERTAINMENT

The Hersonissos waterfront sports the usual assortment of restaurants serving "traditional Greek food"—often code for inferior pre-packaged facsimiles. A number of sandwich and fast food places line the main road. The outskirts of town contain the most peaceful and authentic eateries.

Elli Taverna, Sanoudaki 2 (☎28970 24 758). Heading toward Iraklion, take a right after Cretan Medicare, and this modest taverna will be on your left. There's no menu, so lift the pot lids to choose from a rotating selection of Greek dishes, all cooked by the owner in olive oil that she produces herself. Entrees €4.50-7. Open noon-1am. ❶

Taverna Kavouri, Archeou Theatrou 9 (☎28970 21 161). Walk toward Iraklion, turn right before the Hard Rock Cafe onto Peace and Friendship St., and then walk left around the bend. Kavouri's 15 outdoor tables under grapevines are a pleasant escape from the waterfront. Lamb with garlic and lemon €8.90; moussaka €4.45; chicken with lemon €4.20. For dessert, try fried *tiganites* with ice cream €3.25. Open 5pm-midnight. ❶

Taverna Orion (☎28970 22 857), in the small town of Koutouloufari. Walk about 100m from the bus stop away from Iraklion and turn right onto Vasiliou. After about 1km of uphill walking, you will end up right on Orion's porch. Roof garden with wide views of the coastline and town below. Tasty food at good prices. Beef *stifado* (€6.50); stuffed tomatoes and peppers (€4.25). Open 10:30am-1am; Jul.-Aug. 3:30pm-1am. ❷

Passage to India (☎28970 23 776), on Petrakis. Just off the beach road; look for signage. Traditional Indian dishes are complemented by a continuous run of eccentric Bollywood movies in the background. The portions are modest, but they go a long way with spices the owner imports from London. Also a good pick for vegetarians. Chicken *tikka masala* (€7.20); most entrees €6-8. Open daily 6pm-midnight. ❷

NIGHTLIFE

Hersonissos's mediocre beach confirms it: you've come for the nightlife. Most venues open at dusk and close at dawn, but you'll be lonely at the clubs before 1am. You can't stray a block without encountering another bar or disco; they generally charge no cover and sell beers for €3, with cocktails around €4.50. Many clubs also have "Happy Hour All Night Long," which means with the purchase of one greatly overpriced drink, you get your second free.

Amnesia Club, at the western end of town. Walk towards Iraklion and turn right onto Eleftherias. One of the hottest clubs in town. The best dancers get a chance to strut their stuff on the elevated platforms; the masses below grind to a Top 40/rap mix.

Camelot Dancing Club, across from Amnesia, bumps until the wee hours. A diverse crowd crams the dance floor and shakes to international rave and house music.

Tiger Bar, on the beach road near Filoridon Zotou, has energetic bartenders and a fast spinning DJ to keep the party going. Don't do anything too incriminating, though, or the Tiger crew will capture it and post it on their photo board.

MALIA Μαλια

Mediterranean climate and nearby Minoan palace aside, Malia, with its pubs and Guinness taps, comes closer to evoking the pages of *Hello!* magazine than those of Homer or Kazantzakis. Young British tourists, booked months in advance on prepackaged holidays, leap to Malia's beach and club-crammed streets like salmon in a mating frenzy. Locals refer to these hordes as *barbaroi* and insist that there is more to Malia than simply partying like a rock star. Many visitors only come for a daytrip to see the palace. If you're ready for the mayhem of an overnight stay, however, bring your favorite Manchester United jersey and plenty of euros.

ORIENTATION AND PRACTICAL INFORMATION. **Buses,** which drop off on the main road, leave from a number of stops throughout the city for: Agios Nikolaos (1½hr., 2 per hr., €2.50); Iraklion (1hr., 2-4 per hr., €2.50) via **Hersonissos** (20min., €0.90); and Lassithi (1½hr.; leaves 8:30am, returns 2pm; €3.90). **Taxis** (☎28970 31 777 or 28970 33 900) idle at the intersection of El. Venizelou and the National Bank road. **Altino Travel Service** (☎28970 33 658; fax 28970 33 659), across from the old church on the way to the beach, has maps, travel advice, **currency exchange,** airline tickets, and rents **cars** (€45-55). Walking down the road to the beach, you will trip over agencies that rent **motorbikes** (€12-20 per day).

The main road from Iraklion, **Eleftheriou Venizelou,** should satisfy your practical needs with its ATMs, supermarkets, and pharmacies, while the two converging paths to the beach, full of discos and watering holes, pander to the primal. The old village (between the main road and the inland hills) has many bars and cheaper, quieter rooms; to reach its center, turn away from the beach onto 25 Martiou, about 100m past the bus stop heading towards Agios Nikolaos. A number of banks on El. Venizelou have 24hr. **ATMs.** The **National Bank** is across from the taxi station. (☎28970 31 833 or 28970 31 152. Open M-Th 8am-2pm, F 8am-1:30pm.) There are **no police** in Malia; in **emergencies,** dial ☎28970 22 222. There are two **24hr. medical centers: Medical Emergency of Kriti** (☎28970 31 594), across from the old church, and **Cretan Medicare** (☎28970 31 661). The **Internet Cafe,** Dimokratias 78, is on the right-hand side, about a 10min. walk past Altino Travel Service on the way to the beach. (☎28970 29 563. €5 per hr.) **Zorba's Net Cafe,** on 25 Maritou, also has Internet access (☎28970 32 958. €3.50 per hr). The **OTE** is in the old village; follow signs from 25 Martiou at the Bimbo Cafe. (☎28970 31 299. Open M-F 7:30am-2:30pm.) The **post office** is off El. Venizelou behind the old church. (☎29870 31 688. Open M-F 7:30am-2pm.) **Postal code:** 70007.

ACCOMMODATIONS AND FOOD. Finding reasonably priced rooms in Malia can be a challenge, where beachside spots are either booked or pricey. The affordable housing is in the old village; wander around the side streets of **25 Martiou** and look for a place that suits you. Walking away from the bus drop-off toward Agios Nikolaos, make a right onto 25 Martiou and then a left on Konstantinou to reach **Pension Aspasia ❷,** home to large rooms with balconies, common baths, and a roof for sunbathing. To find it, keep an eye out for the small sign and potted plants in front. (☎28970 31 290. Doubles and triples €20.) **Pension Menios ❷,** one door down from Aspasia, has more spartan rooms. (☎28970 31 361. Singles €15-20; doubles €18-23; triples €25-30.)

The most popular dishes in Malia are the English breakfast (€2), the steak dinner (€7), and pizza (€7). Ironically (and perhaps fittingly), the most faithful Greek food in Malia—Greek salad (€3.50) and *stifado* (€7)—is prepared by a Dutch chef, at **Petros ❷,** in the old village. (☎28970 31 887. Open 5-11pm.) On the main road, cheerful **banana vendors** sell bunches from the nearby fields for €1.50 per kg.

SIGHTS. Though few natives take much interest in the place these days, Malia was one of three great cities of Minoan Crete. Malia's **palace** lacks the labyrinthine plan of Knossos and Phaistos, but its importance as the center of Minoan power in the surrounding fertile plains is undoubted. First built around 1900 BC, the palace was destroyed in 1650 BC, rebuilt on a larger scale, and then destroyed again (by that Mysterious Cataclysm) around 1450 BC. Notice the Hall of Columns on the north side of the large central courtyard, with its six columns supporting the roof. The loggia, a raised chamber on the west side, was used for state ceremonies; west of it are the palace's living quarters and archives. Northwest of the loggia and main site is the Hypostyle Crypt, possibly a social center for Malia's learned. The plot is marked well enough to find these structures, and the admission fee includes entrance to a small gallery with a three-dimensional reconstruction of the site and extensive photographs of its excavation. Follow the road to Agios Nikolaos 3km to the east and turn left toward the sea, or walk along the length of the beach and then 1km through the rocky fields. (☎28970 31 597. Open Tu-Su 8am-3pm. €4, students and seniors €2, EU students free.)

ENTERTAINMENT. The beach road is home to many of Malia's more popular dance clubs, blaring with pop, house, international, rave, and dance music. Clubs open around 9pm, get really packed by 1am, and stay that way until 4am (weekdays) or 6am (weekends). Locals would not be caught dead partying here. Instead, all venues are filled by Northern European tourists, many of whom have decided to stay in Malia for the summer and promote the club of their choice. Most clubs have no cover but require you to buy a drink as soon as you step in (beer and drinks €3-6). Streaming right into the road, the crowd at **Malibu** blocks traffic, so you'll likely find yourself joining the party. If you don't find the club loud enough for your tastes, ask the bartenders to set off some fireworks—they'll happily oblige. The **Newcastle Bar** doesn't have much dancing, but it's a great place to observe general British debauchery. Back on the dancing scene, **Apollo** has a trance/techno focus, which is enhanced by the smoke screens and strobe lights. The crowd at **Camelot** is often out on the street, cooling off and watching the passing traffic, while at **Havana,** everyone is off their seats and dancing like mad.

At the bars toward the end of the beach road and in the Old Village, there's less dance and more chatter, with recent Hollywood movies and old British comedies playing all day and almost all night for free; Zorba's Net Cafe is one place to enjoy these films. For a quieter night of Dionysian delight, head for the smaller spots in Old Town, where a hybrid Greek-British libation is poured down willing throats every night in open-air pubs, replete with darts and grapevines.

RETHYMNO PREFECTURE

Western Crete has struggled for years to maintain its authenticity in the face of increased tourism to the region. Rethymno has been mostly successful, and each town in the area has an individual personality. Modest seaside towns fill only short sections of the shore with tavernas, leaving long stretches to the birds, waves, and hikers. The meld of Ottoman, Venetian, and Greek architecture complements the blue waters of the southwest coast and the dark mountains of the interior.

RETHYMNO Ρεθυμνο

The capital of the region, the city of Rethymno is steeped in ancient folklore and spiced with urban panache. According to Greek myth, Zeus was born of Rhea to the titan Kronos in the cave of Idaion Andron outside of Rethymno. Kronos was on the verge of eating the baby to prevent Zeus's foreseen patricide, but Cretan *kourites* (spirits) danced up a storm to distract the jealous king. Once safe from Kronos, baby Zeus nursed from the goat Amaltheia and ate honey from golden bees.

Crete's many conquerors—Venetians, Ottomans, and even Nazis—have had a profound effect in Rethymno's old city. Arabic inscriptions on the walls, a skyline full of minarets, and the Venetian fortress guarding the harbor unite into a small, distinctive cultural atmosphere that overflows the city limits like the Greek folk

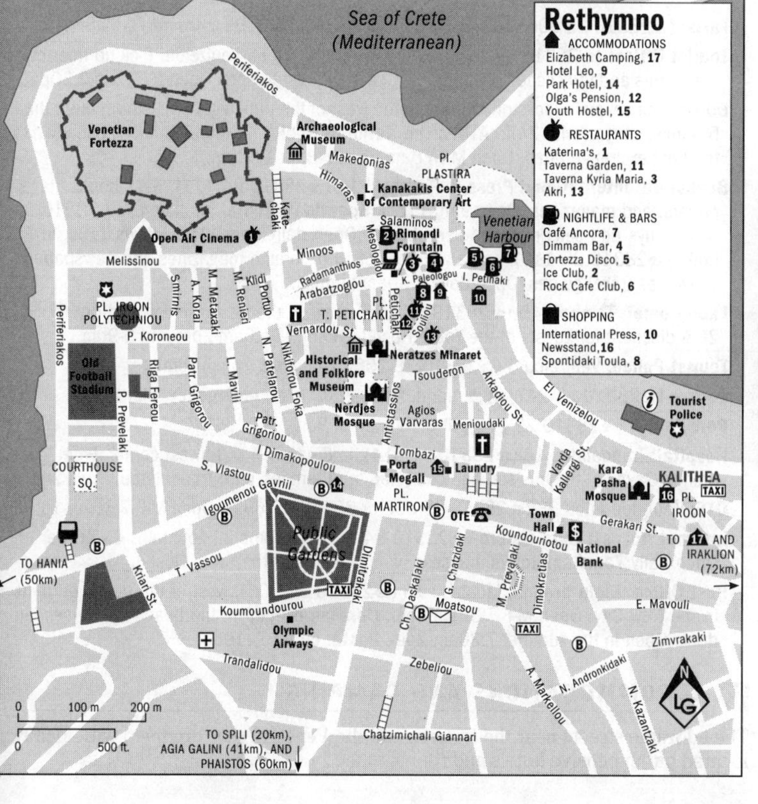

music spilling out of its cafes and garden restaurants. Even the most restless travelers may find their wanderlust inexplicably satiated as they lounge alongside contented locals, sipping *raki* into the wee hours of the morning.

ORIENTATION AND PRACTICAL INFORMATION

Pl. Martiron, between Rethymno's **Old City** to the north and **New City** to the south, is about a 15min. walk from anywhere you would want to go. To get to the plateia from the bus station, climb the stairs at the back of the station's parking lot onto **Igoumenou Gavriil** and go left; Pl. Martiron is to your left just after the **public gardens.** The **waterfront** lies at the northern edge of the old city, with a maze of ancient streets filling the space between the main thoroughfare of Igoumenou Gavriil and the water. The Venetian **Fortezza** sits at the western edge of the waterfront; the western end turns into a fine beach at the city's edge.

Flights: Olympic Airways, Koumoundorou 5 (☎28310 22 257), opposite the Public Gardens. Open M-Sa 8am-4pm.

Buses: Rethymno-Hania station (☎28310 22 212), south of the fortress on Igoumenou Gavriil. Service to: **Iraklion** (1½hr., 17 per day, €5.90); **Hania** (1hr., 16 per day, €5.55); **Agia Galini** (1½hr., 3-4 per day, €4.20); **Plakias** (1hr., 4-5 per day, €3.10); **Arkadi Monastery** (45min., 2-3 per day, €1.85).

Ferries: Buy tickets to **Piraeus** (7:30am, €23.10) at any travel office.

Taxis: (☎28310 25 000, 28310 24 316, or 28310 28 316). 24hr. at Pl. Matiron 4.

Tourist Office: (☎28310 29 148), by the waterfront on El. Venizelou. Pick up free town maps, bus and ferry schedules, info on rooms and restaurants. Open M-F 8am-2:30pm.

Banks: The several blocks of Koundouriotou west of the public gardens sprout more than 5 banks, several with 24hr. **ATMs.** The **National Bank** (on Koundouriotou) usually has the best exchange rates. Open M-Th 8am-2pm, F 8am-1:30pm.

Bookstore: International Press, I. Petichaki 15 (☎28310 24 111). Sells books, newspapers, and magazines. Open 9am-11pm. **Spontidaki Toula,** Souliou 43 (☎28310 54 307), buys and sells new and used books. Open daily 9am-11pm. **Newsstand,** in Pl. Iroön (☎28310 25 110), has a wide selection of foreign magazines and newspapers, as well as travel guides. Open daily 8:30am-midnight.

Laundromat: Tombazi 45 (☎28310 56 196), next to the hostel. Wash and dry €7.50. 20% discount for guests of the Youth Hostel. Open M-Sa 9am-2pm and 5-9pm.

Tourist Police: Venizelou 5 (☎28310 28 156). Open M-F 7am-10pm.

Police: (☎28310 25 247) in Pl. Iroön. Open 24hr. In an **emergency,** dial ☎100.

Port Police: (☎28310 22 276), at the Venetian Port.

Hospital: Trandalidou 18 (☎28310 27 814), in the town's southwest corner. From Igoumenou Gavriil at the bus station, take Kriari, and turn left onto Trandalidou. Open 24hr.

OTE: Koundouriotou 23 (☎28310 35 000 or 28310 22 699). Open M-F 7:30am-1pm.

Internet Access: Cafe Galero (☎28310 54 345), at Rimondi Fountain. €3.50 per hr. Open daily 7am-3am. Internet access also available at the Youth Hostel.

Post Office: Main branch, Moatsou 19 (☎28310 22 303), west of the public gardens in the New City. Open M-F 7:30am-8pm. **Caravan office,** on the beach by the second dock. Open in the summer 7:30am-2pm. **Postal code:** 74100.

ACCOMMODATIONS AND CAMPING

The adorable streets near the fortress and the Venetian port are lined with ideally located but expensive hotels and rooms to let.

CLICK CLACK What are those strange strands of beads that almost all Greek men are jingling in their hands? Most people guess that they are a rosary or some sort of religious object. Known as *komboloi*, these "worry beads" are secular objects, although they are not totally divorced from matters of spirit. There are a couple of schools of thought on how exactly the *komboloi* work. Some think that the physical act of working the beads simply acts as a stress reliever. The more spiritual see greater significance in the beads. Worry beads are often a gift from a loved one, and men can carry one set of *komboloi* around for life. Through all the experiences of life, the beads come to possess some life energy and power of their own. Rubbing them draws the energy back into the individual. Cheap beads (€2-3) can be found in most tourist shops, though they are often made of plastic (which everyone knows is a poor conductor of energy). Handmade beads of wood or metal can sometimes be found in smaller shops. In the city of Nafplion, the **Komboloi Museum** (p. 129) is the perfect place for those seeking more information on worry beads and perhaps a pair for the road.

Youth Hostel, Tombazi 41-45 (☎28310 22 848; www.yhrethymno.com). From the bus station, walk down Igoumenou Gavriil, take a left at the park traffic light and walk through the Guora Megali gate; Tombazi is the first right. The popular outdoor gardens and bar bustle with friendly backpackers (beer and wine €1.40-1.65). Outdoor beds available in the summer. Breakfast (€1.70) available until 11:30am. Hot showers after 10am. **Internet access** €1 per 15min. Reception 8am-noon and 5-9pm. Beds €6. ❶

Olga's Pension, Souliou 57 (☎28310 53 206; fax 28310 29 851), off Antistassios. You'll feel like part of the family with owners George, Stella, and Yiannis. Each room is carefully decorated by George with a marvelous collection of kitsch. Enjoy delicious cooking from **Stella's Kitchen** downstairs (open "early 'til late") or in the rooftop garden, lush with vegetation. All rooms with ceiling fans, some with private bath. Singles with breakfast €25, €20 without; doubles with breakfast €35, €25 without. Studios are available for extended visits. ❷

Hotel Leo (☎28310 29 958), on Vafe, just off of Souliou. Enjoy a quiet stay in a 650-year-old building. All rooms have private bath and a wood motif. Friendly service at the cafe downstairs. Doubles €30-40. ❸

Park Hotel, Igoumenou Gavriil 37 (☎28310 29 958). From the bus station, walk down Igoumenou Gavriil; the hotel is on the left, across from the entrance to the public gardens. Clean, quiet rooms make you feel like you're staying at grandma's, only better because they come equipped with TVs and A/C. Doubles €30; triples €35. ❸

Elizabeth Camping (☎28310 28 694), 3km east of town on the old road to Iraklion. Take the hotel bus from Rethymno station, and ask the driver to stop at the campsite (every 20 min. until 9pm, €0.65). Pitch your tent under a bamboo cover at this warm, family-owned campground. The owner, Elizabeth, knows the sites you'll love and how to get there. Enjoy the company of your fellow travelers at the frequent barbecues while Niko grills up meat and seafood with his famous mustard sauce. (Tu, Th, Sa; complete meal €6.80-7.50.) Self-service **taverna** open 8:30am-1am. Laundry €3.50. Open from mid-Apr. to Oct. Two adults and a tent €12.90-14. Tent rental €2.93. Free parking at reception. 10% discount with International Camping Caravan Card. ❶

FOOD AND ENTERTAINMENT

An **open-air market** next to the park, between Moatsou and Koundouriotou, opens Thursdays at 6 or 7am and closes around 1pm; selection diminishes by 10am. For affordable nighttime eats, tourists and locals head to **Pl. Petichaki.**

Taverna Garden, Souliou 37 (☎28310 28 136). Enjoy large portions of creative dishes under the lemon trees. Using a variety of unique ingredients, Taverna Garden creates a meal that you won't be able to find anywhere else. The traditional Greek dishes are quite tasty as well. Eat up, but watch out for falling lemons. Most entrees €5-15. Open daily noon-midnight. ❷

Taverna Kyria Maria, Moskovitou 20 (☎28310 29 078), to the right down the small alley behind the Rimondi fountain. Traditional Cretan food prepared by friendly Cretans, who'll treat you to a complimentary *raki* and an exquisite cheese pie. The octopus in wine sauce (€7) is a specialty. Open from mid-Mar. to Oct. daily 11am-1am. ❷

Katerina's, Melissinou 34 (☎28310 57 024). With seating beneath the Fortezza and flavored *raki* from the lovely Katerina herself, Katerina's provides a pleasant dining experience. Stuffed wine leaves are €2.65. Moussaka, Greek salad, *tzatziki*, wine and coffee for 2 costs €12. Open daily 8am-midnight. ❷

Akri, Kornarou 27 (28310 50 719). You'll find good prices on seafood at this cozy restaurant. The friendly service makes the meal quite enjoyable. Open daily 9am-1am. ❷

The bar scene in Rethymno centers around Petichaki and Nearchou near the west end of the harbor; the nightlife breaks down into two categories. One type of club caters mainly to Rethymno locals looking to meet friends and have a drink; dancing is kept to a minimum. The **Fortezza Disco Bar,** on Petichaki (☎28310 21 493), and **Ice Club,** at the intersection of Salaminos and Messologiou, are good places to check out this scene. Beware of steep covers (up to €8) and expensive drinks (beers €6). The other type of club involves more dancing and more foreigners. The popular **Rock Cafe Club,** Petichaki 8 (☎28310 31 047), is a fun place to start the night. For a more low-key evening, try **Cafe Ancora** right on the harbor; it's got a great view of the water and the passing crowds. (Open daily 9am-midnight. Beers €3-4; cocktails €5.) **Dimmam Bar,** on the second floor at the corner of Arkadiou and Paleologou, looks down on well-dressed Greeks scampering from club to club. The **open-air cinema** on Melissinou, showing Hollywood films with Greek subtitles, is also a good place to unwind after a day in the sun (tickets €6).

SIGHTS

The **Venetian Fortezza,** a fortress built in 1580, is the highest point in the city and provides magnificent views of the coast and surrounding area. Explore ruins and pretend you're defending Rethymno from invaders for a few hours. Or just play happy tourist and bring a picnic. (☎28310 28 101. Open Tu-Su 9am-6pm. €2.90, children €2.30.) Rethymno's **Archaeological Museum** occupies a former Ottoman prison adjacent to the fortress. The collection contains an eclectic mix of knives, coins, lamps, and statues from Minoan, Classical, and more modern times. The museum has enough artifacts and information to keep archeology enthusiasts occupied for an hour or so. (☎28310 54 668. Open Tu-Su 8:30am-3pm. €3, students and seniors €2.) The **L. Kanakakis Center of Contemporary Art,** Himaras 5, at the corner of Salaminos, displays 19th- and 20th-century Greek paintings and hosts temporary exhibits. (☎28310 52 530. Open Apr.-Oct. Tu-F 9am-1pm and 7-10pm, Sa 11am-3pm; Nov.-Mar. Tu-Su 10am-2pm and 6-9pm. €3, students €1.50.) The **Historical and Folklore Museum,** Vernardou 28-30, showcases artifacts of Cretan social history including farming tools, musical instruments, fabrics, and ceramics. (☎28310 23 398. Open M-Sa 9am-2pm. €3, students €1.50.)

Tattooed with graffiti and untamed by museum keepers, Rethymno's Ottoman monuments are strikingly loud. Among these eye-poppers are the **Neratzes Minaret** on Antistassios; the former Franciscan church **Nerdjes Mosque,** a block away on Fragkiskou 1 (called St. Francis on many maps); the **Kara Pasha Mosque** on Arkadiou near Pl. Iroön; and the **Valides Minaret,** which presides over the gate called **Porta Megali** at Pl. 3 Martiou. The **public gardens,** which lie at the inland end of Igoumenou, on the corner of Pl. Matiron, provide a shady retreat from the Greek sun. Romp around the playgrounds, play chess on a big board, and be nice to the sad, solitary monkey in the pen.

Rethymno's **Wine Festival** (at the end of July) is a crowded all-you-can-drink celebration, with a local dance troupe performing each evening. The city's **Renaissance Festival,** featuring theater, concerts, and exhibitions, is held in the fortress in July and August. **Carnival,** at the end of February and the beginning of March in 2003, is a major event in Rethymno, as it hosts the largest celebration in Crete. Call the tourist office for schedules and other information.

DAYTRIP FROM RETHYMNO: ARKADI MONASTERY

Take the bus the 23km from Rethymno (40min., 2-3 per day, €1.85 each way; return trips an hour later). ☎28310 83 076. Site open 8am-8pm. €2. Dress modestly.

The site of one of the most famous battles in the Greek struggle for independence from the Ottomans, **Arkadi Monastery** (Μονη Αρκαδη) became a symbol to accompany the motto *Ελευθερια η Θανατος*—"Freedom or Death." Modern Greeks refer to the event as the Holocaust of 1866. In November of that year, Greeks and Turks fought to a two-day standoff at the monastery. When Greek defenses finally gave way, the monks and *kleftes* (freedom-fighting guerrillas; literally "thieves") holding out in the monastery set off their own ammunitions supplies, sacrificing themselves to kill hundreds of Turks. The story of Arkadi inspired support for Cretan independence in Western Europe, and the original structure has since been permanently memorialized on the old 100-drachma note. Today a few monks maintain what is left of the monastery: the frame of the church and the outer complex, the roofless chamber where the ammunition was detonated, and a small museum containing a portion of the church's original decoration, including Byzantine paintings and orthodox vestments. Despite its devastation, the church is still a stunning example of 15th century Cretan Renaissance architecture.

PLAKIAS Πλακιας

Sunny and secluded, Plakias remains wonderfully underdeveloped and inexpensive compared to most Cretan beach towns. Towering surrounding mountains and steep gorges shelter the palm trees and small olive groves. Most people stay on the main street that runs along the sandy beach; stepping inland you'll find yourself among palm fronds and the sound of chirping cicadas.

ORIENTATION AND PRACTICAL INFORMATION. You'll be able to find anything you need either on the beach road or the paths that head inland from it. **Buses** drop off and pick up at the beach, and run to: Rethymno (4 per day, €3.10) and Preveli (1 per day, €1.30). **Monza Travel** (☎28320 31 433; fax 28320 31 883), on the beach road, rents cars (€28-38) and mopeds (€6-16). In an **emergency,** dial ☎100. **Police** are 20km away in Spili (☎28320 22 027). Behind Monza Travel is a **pharmacy** (☎28320 31 666; open M-Sa 9:30am-1:15pm and 5:15-8:30pm). The **hospital** (☎28310 27 814) is in Rethymno. A **doctor** (☎28320 31 770 or 697 343 4934; open M-Sa 9:30am-1pm and 5-8:30pm) can be found near the pharmacy. **Internet access** is available at Plakias Youth Hostel. The yellow **post office** trailer sits on the beach in summer (open M-F 8:30am-2pm); an office with permanent foundations is 1km north in Mirthios. Be aware that there is **no ATM** in Plakias; come prepared with plenty of cash. (€0.75 for 10min.) **Postal code:** 74060.

ACCOMMODATIONS AND CAMPING. From the bus stop, walk about 50m east (i.e. towards the sandy beach and away from the pier) and turn left at Monza Travel; turn left again at the end of the road and follow the signs pointing inland to reach the **Plakias Youth Hostel ❶**, the self-proclaimed southernmost hostel in Europe. Set in an olive grove, this happening hostel goes all-out with hot showers, good music, and cheap alcohol, making it a raved-about backpacker oasis. After one day's stay you may hear the sirens singing and never want to leave (some guests never do). Reception 9am-noon and 5-9pm. (☎28320 32 118; www.yhplakias.com. Internet access €0.75 per 10min. Open Mar.-Nov. Beds €6.) At **Pension Kyriakos ❷**, also behind Monza Travel, rooms are decked out with kitchenettes and private bathrooms. Kyriakos insists on treating all his guests to *raki*. (☎28320 31 307. Singles €20-22; doubles €25-27; apartments for 3-4 €40-42.) At the far west end of town, **On The Rocks ❸** provides rooms with amazing views of the beach and surrounding cliffs. Rooms have A/C, but there is an additional charge to activate it. (☎28320 31 023. Doubles €30; triples €35.) On the eastern outskirts of town, **Plakias Bay Hotel ❹** sits peacefully just off the beach. To get there, walk east out of town and stay on the right branch of the fork in the road for about 400m. (☎28320 31 215. Doubles €50-60 including breakfast.) To reach **Camping Apollonia ❶**, walk eastward from the bus stop and take the left fork in the road at the Old Alianthos Taverna. Follow this road 100m to a complex that includes a pool, basketball court, and snack bar. (☎28320 31 318. Laundry €4. Open Apr.-Oct.; reception 8:30am-9:30pm. €4.50 per person; €3 per tent; €3 per caravan.)

FOOD AND ENTERTAINMENT. Quiet, little **Nikos ❶**, behind Monza Travel, serves up rarely found vegetarian dishes, as well as tasty meat for the carnivorously inclined, all for dirt cheap. (☎28320 31 921. Most dishes under €5. Open daily noon-3pm and 7pm-midnight.) Try the *stifado* (€3.80) and butter beans (€2.65) at the **Old Alianthos Taverna ❶**, at the eastern end of the beach road. (☎28320 31 851. Open daily 7:30am-1am.) Head to **Ostraco ❶** for light fare and drinks. Sandwiches and omelettes are €2-3; cocktails are €5. It lies by the harbor about 100m west of the bus stop. (☎28320 31 710. Open 7:45am-2:30am.) Quiet Plakias starts to hum come nightfall, when bars light up on the outskirts of town. Ostraco is a good place to start the night. For dancing, **Meltemi,** 100m past the east end of town on the right fork, grinds nightly until 6am. If you want to dance with Greeks, don't arrive until late. (☎28320 31 305. Beers €3.)

HIKES AND BEACHES. The Plakias beach starts about 100m east of the bus stop and goes on for quite a while. The beach has fine sand and large waves, and sun-worshippers are progressively less clothed as you move east. Umbrellas and chair rental is €5. If life on the beach gets dull, Plakias has endless environments to explore. Take a walk through one of the massive gorges in the area, or trek through small villages that dot the hills around Plakias. You can take a **bus** to **Preveli Monastery,** or ask either in town or at the hostel for directions on how to complete the fantastic (but complicated) 2hr. **hike.** (Open daily 8am-1:30pm and 3:30-8pm. Modest dress required. €2; students €1; under 14 free.) From there you can reach **Preveli Beach** by walking 1km along the road to a dirt parking area; make the 1hr. climb down. Scramble up again to catch the Preveli-Plakias bus back, or take the ferry to **Plakias** (€2.95) or **Agia Galini** (€10).

HANIA PREFECTURE

Gorgeous beaches, rocky gorges, and pine-covered hills dot the western tip of Crete. Tourists flock to these natural wonders in droves, but Hania has still managed to maintain an authentic flavor, with small villages and beaches off the beaten track and awaiting exploration. If you want to party in a beachside club, look no further. If you want to flee pounding techno and foam-filled orgiastic scenes, seek out a moped, and escape will be yours.

HANIA Χανια

The island's second largest city, Hania (hahn-YAH) reacts to its yearly avalanche of summer tourism with traditional Cretan hospitality despite the port town's urban sophistication. Down by the Old Venetian Harbor, the excitement begins. Visitors meander through winding streets, listening to folk music from streetside cafes or waiting for the setting sun to silhouette the lighthouse and nearby Ottoman domes. A day in Hania is easily spent people-watching from cafes, window-shopping, or absorbing the aura of the old town by casting maps aside and blazing a route of your own.

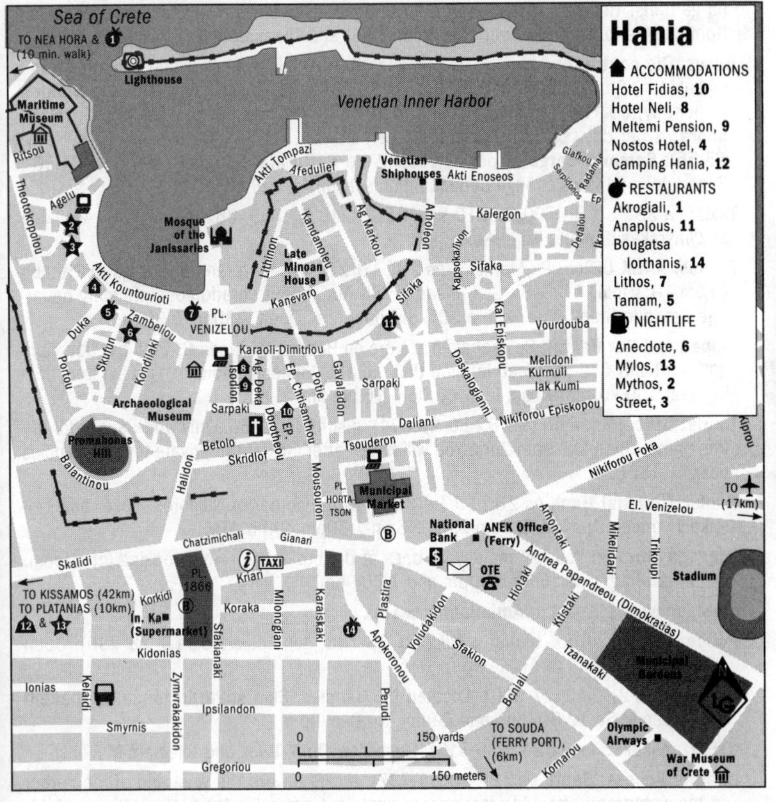

ORIENTATION AND PRACTICAL INFORMATION

To get to the city center from the bus station, turn right onto **Kydonias,** walk for one block, then turn left onto **Zymvrakakidon,** which runs along one side of a large public plaza called **Pl. 1866.** At the far end of Pl. 1866, the road becomes **Halidon** and leads to the **Old Venetian Harbor,** full of outdoor restaurants and narrow alleyways. Intersecting with Zymvrakakidon and Halidon at their meeting point is another major road, **Skalidi,** to the left (facing Halidon); to the right it becomes Chatzimichali, and then Giannari. A short distance further, Giannari forks into Tzanakaki and El. Venizelou. If you're arriving by ferry, you'll dock in the nearby port of **Souda.** Take the bus from the dock, which stops at the supermarket on Zymvrakakidon by Pl. 1866 (15min.,€0.85). Hania's business district is across from the **Municipal Market** near the intersection of **Gianari** and **Tzanakaki.** Its shops and restaurants cluster around the splendid Venetian Harbor. Sunbathers should head west of the harbor along the waterfront to find a long, thin stretch of well-populated sand at **Nea Hora.** A good starting point for all visitors is **Promahonas Hill,** on Baladinou just off of Halidon. Scaling the structure provides a magnificent overview of Hania and the mountains that frame it.

Flights: Olympic Airways, Tzanakaki 88 (☎28210 57 701, 702 or 703), near the public gardens. Tickets sold M-F 8am-3pm. Phone reservations M-F 7am-6pm, Sa 8am-3pm. Flights to **Athens** (4 per day, about €53) and **Thessaloniki** (2 per week, €120).

Buses: The **central bus station** (☎28210 93 306) fills a block within Kydonias, Zymvrakakidon, Smyrnis, and Kelaidi. Service to: **Elafonisi** (1 per day, €8); **Hora Sfakion** (3 per day, €5.10); **Iraklion** (17 per day, €10.50); **Kastelli** (14 per day, €3.25); **Paleohora** (4 per day, €5.10); **Platanias** (every 30min., €1.25); **Rethymno** (17 per day, €5.55); **Samaria Gorge** (4 per day, round-trip €10); and **Sougia** (1 per day, €4.80). Schedules and fares change depending on season, so call ahead.

Taxis: (☎28210 98 700, 28210 98 701, 28210 87 700, 28210 94 300). Available at Zymvrakakidon and Karaiskaki.

Ferries: ANEK Office, Pl. Market 2 (☎28210 27 500). *Lato* and *Lissos* go to **Piraeus** (9½hr., 8:30pm, €17.60). Call ahead in July-Aug. about an additional morning departure between 8 and 9am, with a 30% discount fare. Open 7:30am-8:30pm.

Moped and Car Rental: Several agencies are on Halidon. Mopeds €16-24 per day. Cars go for around €22-35. Keep in mind that most rentals only allow for 100 km free; driving over 100 kms may cost from €0.06-0.16 per km.

Tourist Office: Kriari 40 (☎28210 92 624), just off Pl. 1866. Only worth a visit for the free maps. Open M-F 9am-2pm. You will have better luck at the private tourist agencies near Pl. 1866.

Banks: National Bank (☎28210 28 810), on the corner of Nikiforou, Foka, and Tzanakaki streets. Open M-Th 8am-2pm, F 8am-1:30pm. 24hr. **ATM**.

Luggage storage: You can leave your bags at the bus station while looking for a room. €1.50 per bag. Open 6am-6:30pm and 7:30-9pm.

Emergency: ☎100. 24hr. **Ambulance:** ☎166.

Police: Karaiskaki 60 (tourist ☎28210 28 708, general ☎28210 28 730). Open 7:30am-8pm.

Hospital: (☎28210 27 000). Located in Mournies, 6km south of Hania. Outpatient clinic open M-Sa 12:30-2pm and 6-9pm, Su 8am-9pm.

OTE: Tzanakaki 5 (☎28210 35 519). Open 7am-3pm. Telex and telegram M-F only.

Internet Access: Sante (☎28210 94 737), a cafe toward the west end of the harbor on the waterfront, offers Internet access upstairs for free (as long as you buy a drink).

Drinks €1-4. Open 9:30am-1am. **Vranas Internet Cafe,** on Agion Deka (☎28210 58 618). €3 per hr. Open 9am-1am. **Agora Internet Cafe,** adjacent to the Municipal Market on the harbor side (☎28210 57 926). €3 per hr., drinks €1-3. Open 9:30am-11pm. **Kathodos,** Isodion 10 (☎28210 23 130). Friendly atmosphere. €3 per hr. Ouzo €1.50. Open 9:30am-12:30am.

Post Office: Tzanakaki 3 (☎28210 28 445). Open M-F 7:30am-8pm. **Postal Code:** 73100.

ACCOMMODATIONS

Inexpensive rooms are hard to come by, especially since a number of hotels and hostels have renovated their rooms and raised rates accordingly. Reasonable rates can still be found in the Old Town. Pensions in the New Town have dazzling views of the harbor and are near noisy night spots. Small hotels sprout from the beaches to the west, but expect to pay dearly for the brown sands of **Nea Kydonia** and **Agia Marina.** The private tourist agencies around Pl. 1866 can help you find a room.

Hotel Fidias, Sarpaki 6 (☎28210 52 494). Walking toward the harbor on Halidon, turn right onto Athinagora. Half a block past the cathedral on the right, Athinagora becomes Sarpaki, and the pension is on your right. Irasmos, the philosopher-owner, provides bright, comfortable rooms with balconies as well as invaluable travel tips and life advice. A renovation in the summer of 2002 promises to spruce up the external appearance of Fidias and add new amenities, such as in-room refrigerators. Free luggage deposit. Laundry downstairs. Reception 7am-10pm. Dorms €6-9; singles €12; doubles €12-18; triples/dorms €18-27. 15% senior discount in winter. ❶

Nostos Hotel, Zambeliou 42-46 (☎28210 94 743). Each room in this beautiful place is unique. Some have two levels; others have a perfect view of the harbor. All rooms have private bath, kitchen, A/C, television. The cafe downstairs serves an authentic Cretan breakfast (€5-7). Singles €35-45; doubles €50-70, triples €60-85. ❹

Hotel Neli, Isodion 21-23 (☎28210 55 533). Spacious, well-equipped rooms (including a kitchen area with fridge, A/C, and private bath) are suited for the Greek gods they are named for. Very classy decor. Doubles range from €35-50. ❹

Meltemi Pension, Agelou 2 (☎28210 92 802), at the west side of the harbor, next to the Naval Museum. High ceilings, private showers, and clear views of the harbor will brighten your day. The **Meltemi Cafe** downstairs serves *frappés* (€2.20), breakfast (€4-5), and cocktails (€4) come nightfall. Takes reservations, but no credit cards. Book early for July and Aug. Rooms range from €25-35 for two people; €5 extra for each additional person. ❸

Camping Hania, Ag. Apostoli (☎28210 31 138). Take Skalidi west out of town. A few kms down the road, take a right at the sign. For those who are put off by the noise and bustle of Hania proper, Camping Hania is a good alternative. Besides the quiet atmosphere, this site features several amenities, including laundry, pool, restaurant, and minimarket. Proximity to the beach is another plus. €5 per adult, €4.50 per large tent, €3.50 per small tent, €8 tent rental, €3.50 car parking. 10% discount for students. ❶

FOOD

You could construct a fantasy meal from the exotic foodstuffs and affordable snacks available at the open-air **Municipal Market** in cleverly named Pl. Market (Open M-W 7:30am-3pm, F-Su 8am-9pm). Wheels of cheese, fresh fish and meats (watch out for the cow's head), and homegrown vegetables accompany the many bakeries and small cafes. Inside, **Restaurant Bonne Petite** provides cooked seafood. (Open daily 8am-4pm.) For other cheap options, try the well-stocked and convenient **IN.KA Super-**

FROM THE ROAD

GETTING TO AGIA

Navigating the Greek bus system is not an easy task for any traveler, even the locals. The bus stations are chaos. The schedules are often outdated. Frustrated Greeks constantly stomp through the terminals, elbowing young backpackers out of the way. And, of course, the PA systems are muffled beyond comprehension.

There are few things more frustrating than thinking that you've heard your bus announced over the loudspeaker but not being *sure*. When this happens, your best bet is to react calmly. First, I tend to stumble around in a confused fashion. Then I try peering over someone's shoulder to ask, "Excuse me, sir, was that the Agia Galini or Agia Triada bus?" Usually, he stares back at me, his face totally blank. At this point, I sprint to find a bus station employee. When I finally lasso one, I breathlessly inquire about the PA announcements, as what may well be my bus begins to rumble to life in the lot: "Does that bus go to Agia Galini?" The helpful employee shakes his head in a non-committal fashion and points to the bus, "Agia [inaudible]." "So, it's Agia Triada then," I beg. He repeats, "Agia [inaudible]." Then I run onto the bus and ask the bus driver.

The key to getting to the correct destination, I have learned, is to ask these questions and to keep asking them. Double-checking with passengers works particularly well. Be loud and direct (but try to be polite). Being a bus traveler is like being a military officer: you have to command respect to get things done. *—Geoffrey Reed*

market (☎28210 90 558) in Pl. 1866, on the right coming from Halidon. (Open daily 8am-9pm.)

Anaplous (☎28210 41 320), on the right on Sifaka away from the harbor. This romantic open-air bistro is set in pink stone ruins; flower vines serve as the restaurant's fragrant ceiling. Brothers Angelos and Nikos claim to offer the only *pilino* (pork and lamb cooked for 6-7hr. in fresh clay) in Greece. Breaking the clay for this dish (€23.50) may also bust your wallet, but it serves 3. Traditional Hanian dishes include rabbit in white wine (€6.70) and kreatatourta, a pie with lamb and cheese (€7.50). Anaplous moves to a Venetian house across the street during winter. Open daily 10am-1am. ❷

Bougatsa Iorthanis, Apokoronou 24 (☎28210 91 345). When you walk in, the woman behind the counter will ask you "Sugar?" She needs to know how sweet you want this restaurant's sole dish *bougatsa* (goat cheese in a tasty pastry), a wonderful creation made by only one family in Hania. Portions cost €1.95. Open daily 9am-1pm. ❶

Tamam, Zambeliou 49 (☎28210 96 080). Tamam may not catch your eye among the multitude of beautiful open-air restaurants on and around Zambeliou, but the stellar food is a secret of the natives. Take a peek at the wine list; it's longer than the menu.Try stuffed peppers with cheese (€7), *hiyunkiar beyiendi* (chicken in eggplant puree, €7), or one of the many vegetarian alternatives. Open daily 1pm-12:30am. ❶

Akrogiali, Akti Papanikoli 19 (☎73 110), on the waterfront in **Nea Hora,** a 12min. walk westward along the water past the Maritime Museum. A modest, beachfront restaurant, catering mostly to Greeks, will be glad to serve you up some fresh, local seafood. During busy times, get a table right in the street. Open M-Sa 6pm-1am, Su 11am-1am. ❶

Lithos, Akti Koundourioti, on the harborfront (☎28210 74 406). Among the Americanized clones that line the harbor, Lithos stands out with its fine authentic Greek cuisine. Entrees €10-15. Open daily 10am-midnight. ❷

SIGHTS

VENETIAN INNER HARBOR. A long, hot walk to the **Venetian lighthouse,** an odd tower of stone, provides a superb view of Hania from the water. This tower guards the entrance to Hania's stunning architectural relic, the Venetian Inner Harbor. The inlet has retained its original breakwater and Venetian arsenal, and the Egyptians restored the lighthouse during their occupation of Crete in the late 1830s. On the west side of the main harbor, the **Maritime Museum** describes the tumultuous (and often ferocious) 6000 years of Crete's naval and merchant history in maps and models. The second floor houses a large exhibition on Crete's remarkable expulsion of the Nazis in 1941. (☎28210 91 875. Open daily Apr.-Oct. 10am-4pm, Nov.-Mar. 10am-2pm. €2, students €1.) In the **Venetian Shiphouse,** at the east end of the harbor where Arholeon meets Akti Enoseos, a museum is set up with ever-changing exhibitions; stop by for details and hours. The mélange of Ottoman and Venetian architecture in the **waterfront alleys** reflects the city's past. At the corner of Kandanoleu and Kanevaro, just north of Kanevaro on **Kastelli Hill,** visitors can look upon more ancient reminders of Hania's Bronze Age prosperity, including the **Late Minoan House** (c. 1450 BC) and other fenced-off and unmarked monuments.

MUNICIPAL GARDENS. Greeks of all ages flee heavily touristed streets in favor of the floral shade of the **Municipal Gardens,** *Dimotikos Kypos*, to the left as you walk down Tzanakaki from the city center. Once the property of a *muezzin* (Islamic prayer caller), the garden features an **open-air movie theater** that screens international films (☎28210 41 427) and a zoo featuring the unique combination of goats and peacocks. UNICEF sets up an annual **International Fair** in the gardens—see the tourist office for details.

ARCHAEOLOGICAL MUSEUM. The Archaeological Museum, on Halidon about 40m past the cathedral, features a broad collection of Cretan artifacts, ranging from early Minoan to Hellenistic times. Once a Venetian monastery, then the mosque of Yusuf Pasha, the high-ceilinged halls are lined with clay shards, gold jewelry, and floor mosaics. The ancient coin collection will leave you nostalgic for the pre-EU days. (☎28210 90 334. Open T-Su 8:30am-3pm. €2, students €1.) You can buy a ticket at the Archaeological Museum that will also give you access to the **Byzantine Collection** around the corner. (☎28210 96 046. Open T-Su 8:30am-3pm. Joint ticket €3, students €2.)

ENTERTAINMENT

Start off the night by cruising the many cafes along the harbor, where young Greeks pass the time by playing *tavli* (backgammon) and talking on their cell phones. When you're ready to hit the dance floor, **Mythos,** Akti Koundourioti 52, and its fraternal twin **Street** next door serve as the hip gathering places for Greeks and tourists alike, playing a rock/pop mix. Both impose a hefty cover charge (€6 and €7, respectively, including a free drink; subsequent drinks are €3-5). Doors open at 11pm, but the party doesn't really get started until 2am. **Mylos,** a must-see dance club for beach-party devotees, is only a €6 taxi ride away in Platanias (see p. 541). **Anecdote,** Zambeliou 45, an intimate, welcoming bar, serves up a self-described "ethnic rock and jazz" mix to a mostly local crowd. (Open 9pm-2am. Beer and wine €2, pitcher of *raki* €3.) For traditional music and dancing in a quiet setting, sit down and sip a drink with the older locals in **Kafe Kriti**, an outpost of Cretan culture on Kalergon on the east side of the harbor. (Open 6pm-2am.)

DAYTRIPS FROM HANIA

PLATANIAS Πλατανιας

30min. from Hania by bus (every 30min., €1.25).

Platanias (plat-AHN-yas) offers long, pretty beaches and seemingly a thousand tourists for every local. Platanias's fame sprang from a large rock island just offshore, better known as Kracken, the petrified sea monster. Perseus turned Kracken to stone with the aid of Medusa's severed head. (For a cinematic retelling, check out the special effects wizardry of *Clash of the Titans.*) Present-day Platanias's most famous phenomenon, swanky rock club **Mylos,** beats any MTV beach party for sheer numbers of gyrating hot bodies and hard, pumping beats. The converted bread mill draws nightly crowds of suavely dressed young Europeans from midnight until morning. Take the last bus from Hania, get off at the bus stop at Platanias Center, and continue walking away from Hania. After about 450m, a huge sign will alert you to the right-hand turnoff that leads past an enormous parking lot to Mylos and the **beach.** (Beer €4.40. Cover €5.86, includes one drink.) To get home, either take a cab (☎28210 68 423) for €6 or party until the 6:30am bus arrives the next morning.

AKROTIRI PENINSULA

Akrotiri Peninsula is most easily navigated by car. Using the bus, you will need two days to visit all of the sites, due to erratic bus schedules. However, it is easy to visit the peninsula's beaches ***or*** *its monasteries in one day.*

Just northeast of Hania is the sparsely populated peninsula of Akrotiri, home to herds of goats, rows of olive trees, several monasteries, and sheltered aquamarine coves. At the small white sand beach of **Kalatnos,** 16km from Hania, sunbeds with umbrellas go for €4 per day. Kalatnos lies on the route of the bus to **Stavros,** another glorious beach with a handful of cafes; the view includes a mining hill you may recognize from the movie *Zorba the Greek.* Take the bus (1hr., 4 per day, €1.40) and get off at the end of the line in front of **Christiana's Restaurant ❶** (☎28210 39 152, open daily 9am-11pm), where you can eat breakfast, lunch, or dinner for a reasonable price, enjoy the view, and listen to live traditional Greek music every Thursday night starting at 8pm. On the sand, you can rent an umbrella and a deck chair for €4 per day, or take a walk down to the rockier, though more private, end of the beach. Get more refreshments 100m inland at **Zorba's Original Tavern ❶** (☎28210 39 402, open daily 9am until it's empty).

About 6km from Kalatnos on the way to Stavros (16.5km from Hania) is the monastery of **Agia Triada** (☎28210 63 310), which was built in 1606 near ruins of a Minoan temple and has produced traditional olive oil since 1632. Enjoy a peaceful walk through the grounds and small museum, with its collection of mostly 19th-century pieces and three Byzantine paintings (1635-45). You can bottle the experience in the form of Agia Triada olive oil (€1.80 for 250ml, €2.30 for a pretty bottle). Modest dress is requested: long skirts for women, long pants for men, and no bare shoulders. (Open 8am-2pm and 5-7pm. €1.25.) Monastery buffs who just can't get enough may want to follow the road up a stubby Cretan hill (complete with wild goats and narcissus flowers) to **Gouverneto,** a similar but smaller monastery. (☎28210 63 319. Open 7am-2pm and 4-8pm.)

BALOS

Be prepared for an adventure when you set out to find this little-known lagoon on the northwestern tip of Crete; it's not easy to get there, but it's worth it. Other than chartering a boat, the only way to reach Balos is a harrowing drive across a Cretan mountain front. Most cars can probably handle the drive, but a 4x4 will make the experience much more pleasant. To get there, take Skalidi west out of Hania towards Kissamos. You will hit Kissamos after about 40km of beautiful countryside. Go through the town for about 2 more km, and look for a sign for a random phone on the side of the road. Make a right at the phone (you will also see signs for Kaliviani), and make an immediate left where there will be a sign for the Balos hotel. After about 1km, you will pass through a tiny town. Just outside the town make a right at the small sign for Balos. After 5km on this road, you should pass a small white chapel. When you finally arrive at a parking lot, take the small path with a sign and hike for 30min. through goat country to the heavenly **blue lagoon** with bright white sand and shallow waters. If you get greedy for pleasure, continue to drive down the coast through Platanos towards Kefali, and pick your spot on the breathtaking stretch of beach. Alternately, take the less travelled route southward to Elafonisi, to pass the late afternoon without the usual swarm of tourists.

SAMARIA GORGE Φαραγγι της Σαμαριας

__Buses__ for Omalos and Xyloskalo leave Hania (3 per day, €5). Early buses (6:15-8:30am) can get you to Xyloskalo in time for a day's hike; the 1:45pm bus will get you to Omalos, ready to go the next day. If you want to spend the night in Omalos, rest up at __Gigilos Hotel__ on the main road. (☎28210 67 181. Singles €12-15; doubles €20.) From __Rethymno,__ take the 6:15 or 7am buses through Hania to Omalos (€8). Early risers can take the 5:30am bus from __Iraklion__ through Rethymno and Hania to Omalos (€12). For gorge information, call the __Hania Forest Service__ (☎28210 92 287), or pick up info at the tourist offices in Hania, Rethymno, or Iraklion. Open May 1 to Oct. 15 6am-6pm. __Admission__ €3, children under 15 and organized student groups free. Hang on to your ticket; you have to give it back at the gorge's exit.

The most popular excursion on Crete is the 5-6hr. hike down the longest gorge in Europe, the Samaria Gorge, a formidable 16km pass through the **White Mountains National Park.** Sculpted by rainwater over the course of 14 million years, the gorge retains its allure despite mobs of international visitors. The rocky trail can trip you up, but try to take a look around: epiphytes peek out from sheer rock walls, wild flowers border the path, elusive *agrimi* goats clamber around one of their last natural homes, and endangered gryphon vultures and golden eagles soar overhead. Humans have settled here for centuries, as the 1379 church of **Saint Maria of Egypt,** the source of the gorge's name, attests.

Though it's possible to reach the gorge from any number of major tourist towns, **Hania** is the closest and allows for the most flexibility. The 44km, 90min. bus ride from Hania to **Xyloskalo** places you at the start of the trail and provides passengers with views of small mountain towns (and more goats). The base town boasts no more than the ticket booth, a cafeteria, a shop, and toilets—the last of their kind that you'll see for a few hours. From Xyloskalo, you begin a long descent, following a noisy but nearly dry river, and passing between cliff walls as high as 600m and as narrow as 3½m. Much of the hike is shaded by clumps of pines and by the walls of the gorge itself. The hike ends in the small beach town of **Agia Roumeli** on the south coast (see below)—from there, experienced hikers can try the hike 10hr. to **Hora Sfakion** (see below) along one of the more outstanding coastlines in the country or a path from Xyloskalo that ascends **Mt. Gigilos** to the west. If you're only interested in the dramatic tail of the gorge, you can start at Agia Roumeli; the path to the trail begins behind Hotel Livikon at the rear of the village. Known as "Samaria the Lazy Way," the climb 2hr. to the north takes you to the gorge's narrowest pass: the **Iron Gates.**

Whichever route you choose, bring water, trail snacks, and supportive shoes with good tread. The gorge is dry and dusty in summer, and well-worn stones on the path are very slippery. The altitude often makes the top of the gorge cold and rainy. If you get tired on the hike, keep an eye out for the **donkey taxis** that patrol the trail, although they can be few and far between. Be sure to bring enough **cash** to get to the gorge and home again as there are no banks on either end. Pack a bathing suit so you can cool off after a hard day at the beach in Agia Roumeli. Please observe the rules concerning litter: take all trash out with you.

AGIA ROUMELI. This town exists solely for you, the hikers, because you are tired and hungry at the end of the gorge. Here you will find nothing but a beach, restaurants, grocery store, souvenirs, and lodging. It certainly is a relief to reach these facilities, but the inflated prices are less than comforting. **Kri-Kri ❸,** on the street from the gorge, has reasonably priced rooms with A/C and refrigerators, but it gets crowded in the summer; call ahead. (☎28250 91 089. Doubles €30; triples €35.) Right on the beach, **Hotel Agia Roumeli ❸** is a good place to chill out after a day of trekking, with easy access to the sea as well as A/C. (☎28250 91 241. Doubles €30; triples €40.) **Ferries** run from Agia Roumeli regularly from April to October to **Hora Sfakion** (3-4 per day, €4.40) and to **Sougia** and **Paleohora** (1 per day, €3-6.40). From November to March, there are three ferries per week; call in advance for their times. The last **bus** from Hora Sfakion waits for the last ferry. The ferry and bus are scheduled at 6 and 7:30pm respectively, so you can make the roundtrip from Hania, Rethymno, or Iraklion in one day if you leave on a morning bus. (One-way from Hora Sfakion to Hania or Rethymno €5.10, to Iraklion €9.08.)

HORA SFAKION Χωρα Σφακιων

The extremely small port town of Hora Sfakion, often called simply Sfakion, lacks the intimacy of Plakias to the east or Paleohora to the west but serves as the transportation hub of the south coast. Its quiet streets and tavernas are a necessary resting spot following the Samaria Gorge hike, and the location makes it a convenient base for daytrips to the area's smaller gorges and lovely beaches.

ORIENTATION AND PRACTICAL INFORMATION. The town consists of one main harborfront road, which opens off a plateia 50m uphill from the ferry dock. Four **buses** per day go to: **Hania** (2hr., €5.10; last at 7pm); **Rethymno** (1½hr., €5.10; change at Vrises); and **Iraklion** (€9.08; last at 7pm; change at Vrises). Buses leave Vrises for **Rethymno** and **Iraklion** every hour on the hour. Buses also run to **Agia Galini** (2hr., €6.45). If your ferry is late, don't worry—the buses wait for the boats to arrive. Boats from Hora Sfakion travel to **Agia Roumeli** (1¼hr., 4 per day, €4.40). From April to October, most routes stop in **Loutro.** In winter, travelers go by foot or fishing boat. As always, it is a good idea to check schedules with the ticket office (☎28250 91 221). Boats also run to **Gavdos,** a sparsely populated island that is the southernmost point in Europe (€8, Sa-Su 10:30am). **Caïques** to Sweetwater Beach leave at 10:30am and return at 5:30pm every day (€1.50 each way). Walking from the plateia toward the street, you'll find the helpful travel agency **Sfakia Tours**, where you can get bus tickets and rental cars. (☎/fax 28250 91 130. Open 8am-10pm. Car rentals €40 per day). Uphill from the plateia on your right lies the flag-bedecked 24hr. **police station** (☎28250 91 205) and **port police** (☎28250 91 292) and, right nearby, the **OTE** (☎28250 91 299; open M-F 7:30am-3:15pm). Next door to Sfakia Tours is the **post office** on your left (☎28250 91 244; open M-F 7:30am-2pm). **Postal code:** 73011.

ACCOMMODATIONS AND FOOD. Hotel owners in Hora Sfakion are aware that their town is a convenient rest stop after Samaria Gorge, and their prices reflect this. If you want to cool off on the cheap, snatch up one of the cheap air-conditioned rooms at **Hotel Samaria ❷**, right on the harbor. (☎28250 91 261 or 071. Singles and doubles with breakfast are €18 and €25, respectively.) **Stavris ❷,** at the end of the back street, also offers good bargains on clean rooms with private bath. (☎28250 91 220 or 201; fax 28250 91 152. No A/C. Singles €20; doubles €22; triples €26.) The cool, grotto-like **Hotel Xenia ❸,** at the far end of the street, has pleasant and spacious rooms with refrigerators and phones. Enjoy a good breakfast for €3.50 under the flowery veranda. (☎28250 91 490; fax 28250 91 491. Doubles €28.) **Lefka Ori ❷,** on the waterfront, rents rooms with views of the harbor. (☎28250 91 209. Doubles and triples with bath €20.) The town's dining options are dominated by hotel restaurants (entrees €5-7.50). **Omprogialos ❶,** the first restaurant you will see as you walk to the harbor, is a fine choice. An open coal oven cooks up flavorful meats. (☎28250 91 204. Entrees €4-8.) The many **markets** in town may be the best bet, though, for getting a good, cheap meal.

PALEOHORA Παλαιοχωρα

Once a refuge for the embattled rear guard of the 1960s counterculture, Paleohora (pahl-eo-HOR-ah) has since retreated into a sleepier, family-friendly state of mind. The town, 77km south of Hania, is a peninsular retreat flanked by a rocky harbor on its east side and smooth beaches on its west, all set against the splendor of the Cretan mountain backdrop.

TRANSPORTATION. **Ferries** leave the modest port for: **Sougia** (2 per day, 45min., €3.80); **Agia Roumeli** (2 per day, 1½hr., €6.50); **Loutro** (3 per day, 2¼hr.,€7.90); and **Hora Skafion** (3 per day, 2½hr., €6.46). One boat per day departs Paleohora for **Elafonisi** at 10am and returns at 4pm (1hr., €4.10 each way). A boat goes to **Gavdos** three times a week (3½hr.; the post boat (M and Th 8:30am, returns 2:30pm) and the tourist boat (Tu 8:30am, returns 2:30pm); tourists may ride either boat; €9.40 each way.) More tourist boats run in summer. For information about boats and tickets, visit the friendly people at **Notos Rentals,** the right as you walk up Venizelou. (☎28230 42 110; fax 28230 41 838. Open daily 8am-1:30pm and 4:30-10:30pm.) **Syia Travel,** past the pharmacy is a general tourist office that is helpful for ferry information and tickets, as well as basic information about the region. (☎28230 41 198; fax 28230 41 535. Open daily 9am-1pm, 4-9pm.) The **bus station** is on Venizelou on the northern edge of town. Buses run to **Hania** (2hr., 3 per day, €5.10) and **Samaria** at 6am (€4.50). For a taxi, call **Paleohora Taxi Office** (☎28230 41 128 or 28230 41 061). A **car** can be hired from any of the travel agencies in Paleohora for about €30-45; mopeds go for €10-20.

ORIENTATION AND PRACTICAL INFORMATION. The restaurants and bars of Paleohora town cluster around the main thoroughfare, **Venizelou,** which runs down the center of the peninsula from north to south. Heading north on Venizelou takes you to Hania; south leads to the ruins of an old castle. Venizelou crosses **Kentekaki,** which leads west to the beach and east to the harbor. Most lodgings are located on the side streets off Venizelou.

Walking toward the center of town from the bus station, you'll find the **National Bank,** with a 24hr. **ATM** three blocks up on your right. (☎28230 41 430. Open M-Th 8am-2pm, F 8am-1:30pm.) Half a block down and also on your right is the helpful **tourist office.** (☎28230 41 507. Open W-M 10am-1pm and 6-9pm.) A block and a half farther, on your right, is the **OTE.** (☎28230 41 299. Open M-F 7:30am-3pm.) The **port police** (☎28230 41 214) are farther down the main street. Turning left toward the harbor at the OTE leads to the **police station** (☎28230 41 111. Open 24hrs.), one block down on your left. The port lies past the police station toward the harbor. Notos Rentals on the main thoroughfare (see above) runs a **laundry, exchanges money,** and has **Internet access** (€1.50 per 15 min., €2.70 per 30 min., €4.40 per hr.) All facilities are open 8am-2pm and 5-10:30pm. There is a **doctor** on Venizelou (☎28230 41 380. Open 9am-11:30pm and 5-8:30pm.), one street past the bus station heading away from town; the **public health center** (☎28230 41 211) is behind the OTE, heading away from the beach. There is a **pharmacy** on Venizelou across from the OTE. (☎28230 41 498. Open 8:30am-2pm and 5:30am-10:30pm.) To find the **post office,** head to the beach from the OTE and make a right. (☎28230 41 206. Open M-F 7:30am-2pm.) **Postal code:** 73001.

ACCOMMODATIONS AND CAMPING. Some small hotels line the road closest to the harbor. In the middle of the harbor stands a tall white building marked **Dream Rooms ❷,** run by the cordial Nikos Bubalis and his bubbly wife. Rooms with balconies look out onto the picturesque harbor and the surrounding mountains. (☎28230 41 112. Singles €12-18; doubles €15-24; triples €30-36.) Away

CRETE

from the harbor, sleepy **Savas Rooms ❸** offers simple rooms with kitchenettes and private bath. To get there, walk from the bus station 150m north on Venizelou toward Hania; Savas is on your left at the edge of town. (☎28230 41 075. Doubles €30, triples €33.) The slightly chaotic but very warm **Villa Anna ❹,** on the beach side of the southern part of town, is a fine choice for families with children. Large apartments with private bath, as well as a classically landscaped garden, provide a great alternative to the hordes of homogenous hotels. (☎28230 46 418. A 2 bedroom apartment sleeps 4-5 for €60; a 1 bedroom apartment sleeps 2-3 for €40-50.) **Camping Paleohora ❶** is a 10min., well-marked walk east of town. With its own on-site restaurant, the campsite is across the street and within earshot of Club Paleohora, the town's popular disco, and a beautiful **beach.** Walk north on Venizelou (away from town), turn right just after the bus station, take the second left on the last paved road before the beach, and walk 1km to the site. (☎28230 41 120. Open Apr.-Oct. €3.40 per person, €2.05 per child, €2.30 per tent, €4.50 per tent.)

FOOD AND ENTERTAINMENT. Markets and **tavernas** are fixtures along Venizelou and its surrounding streets; several restaurants serve traditional Greek food along the waterfront from standard tourist menus at mid-range prices (*tzatziki* €1.50-2.50, moussaka €3-4, baklava €2-2.50). The **Third Eye Vegetarian Restaurant ❶** is one of the few remaining bastions of Paleohora's counterculture days. Asian, Greek and European dishes (the family has a repertoire of over 80 vegetarian dishes, of which 20 are selected to be prepared each night) are prepared with ingredients grown on the owner's family farm. (☎28230 41 234. Entrees are under €4. Open Apr.-Oct. 8:30am-3pm and 5:30-11pm.) **Club Paleohora,** across from Camping Paleohora, is the town's popular open-air disco. Follow the directions to the campsite, or take the minibus that transports clients from **Skala** bar in front of the port to the disco every 30min. from midnight to 4am. (☎28230 42 230. Drinks €3-5. Cover F-Sa €3 includes one beer. Open Sept.-June Th-Sat 11pm-5am; July-Aug. M-Sa 11pm-5am, Su 11pm-6am.)

DAYTRIPS FROM PALEOHORA

ELAFONISI (Ελαφονισι)

CRETE

Elafonisi is a beach across from a small uninhabited island at the southwestern corner of Crete. Visitors by ferry and car start on the mainland side of the beach and proceed to wade across the shallow 100m inlet that divides the mainland from the lovely island beach. Back on the mainland side are restrooms and a taverna with prices steeper than the face of a Cretan mountain. (Open 10am-7pm. Sandwiches €2.50-3, burgers €2.50, beer €1.80.) If the sun hasn't drained all of your energy, a short walk up the road perpendicular to the beach will get you more baklava for your buck at **Panorama.** Besides the usual Greek food and good conversation, Panorama also has bungalows and apartments for rent if you miss your boat. (☎28230 61 548. Restaurant open daily 8am-midnight. Doubles €20-40).

Those tired of sun worshipping can pay homage of another sort at the cliffside monastery of **Chrisso Kalitissas,** which is operated by an order of nuns. Built from and supported by the cliffs, it's blessed with a magnificent ocean view. Reach it by walking 5km up the road from Elafonisi. The monastery will be in view on your left when you come to an unmarked but well-paved road; turn left, then make another left at the end of this road. *(Take the ferry from Paleohora along the south coast (leaves 10am, returns 4pm; €4.10 each way), or take the bus from Hania (leaves 8am, returns 4pm; €8 each way. Open daily 7am-sunset.)*

ANIDRI

Escape the crowds at Paleohora's beach at nearby Anidri Beach, which may be reached by car or on foot. Hikers should start off by taking the road out of town past Camping Paleohora for about five minutes until the road forks. The low road to the right (the 'easy' way) takes you on a long but well-established road along the coast to the beach (45min.). The high road to the left (the 'interesting' way) will take you through the mountains and up to the picturesque village of Anidri itself. To take the latter route, hike up the high road into the mountains to the village cafe (1hr.). Walk straight past its open patio (the locals can help you at this point) and onto a road with a sign pointing to a church. Follow this road to its end and make another right. You'll reach a stone road with a sign pointing back to the cafe; turn left and go down it to the dry riverbed. Follow the occasional sign and stone marker through the small gorge to the beach (40min. from town). The beautiful path is poorly marked and fairly difficult—your only company will be roaming goats. Make sure to wear sturdy walking shoes, and bring water and trail snacks.

The beaches at the bottom, especially the beach farthest to your left, are smooth, unblemished strips of pale sand surrounded by sheer cliffs and crystal clear water. No need to weigh yourself down with a bathing suit—going nude is perfectly normal here. Most visitors return along the coastal road to the west, which will return you to the right branch of the fork near Camping Paleohora.

LASITHI PREFECTURE

Lasithi Prefecture isn't much for first impressions—heavily touristed towns such as Malia may rub you the wrong way—but all hope is not lost. The road east from Iraklion eventually passes jam-packed, overpriced resort towns to arrive at the quieter, scenic inland. The smaller villages to the east, sustained not by tourism but by thriving local agriculture, provide welcome relief to the bustle-weary traveler. Heed the advice of locals who nudge you toward Crete's eastern edge, where stretches of pristine coastline fill the gaps between white villages and olive plains.

AGIOS NIKOLAOS Αγιος Νικολαος

Occupying a small peninsula on the northeast edge of Crete, Agios Nikolaos is a nouveau chic resort town where posh vacationers, most from Northern Europe, huff and puff their way up steep, boutique-lined streets, then stop in at a harborside cafe to catch their breath with a cigarette. Meander through its sparkling, hilly streets and you'll find beach-obsessed patrons, one-stop holiday-makers, and hikers on their way to more obscure destinations. There are few bargains in Agios Nikolaos or in its satellite beach towns, but the intense nightlife, diverse array of intriguingly glamorous tourists, and remnants of indigenous Cretan culture make for a lively combination. For release from the tourist scene, retire to the friendly former leper colony of Spinalonga, a few kilometers away by ferry.

TRANSPORTATION

Flights: Olympic Airways Office, Plastira 18 (☎28410 28 929), overlooking the lake. Open M-F 8am-4pm. The closest **airports** are in Iraklion and Sitia.

Buses: (☎28410 22 234), in Pl. Atlantidos, across town from the harbor. To: **Ierapetra** (1hr., 7 per day, €2.40); **Iraklion** (1½hr., 20 per day, €4.70) via **Malia** and **Hersonissos; Kritsa** (15min., 11 per day, €0.90); **Sitia** (1½hr., 5-6 per day, €5). Buses to **Elounda** (20min., 14-20 per day, €0.90) and **Plaka** (40min., 7 per day, €1.20) leave from the tourist office.

Ferries: Nostos Tours, R. Koundourou 30 (☎28410 22 819), sells tickets for departures all over Crete. Open 8am-1:30pm and 5-9pm. To: **Karpathos** (7hr., 4 per week, €17.60); **Kasos** (6hr., 4 per week, €13.80); **Piraeus** (12hr., 5 per week, €25) via **Milos** (7hr., 2 per week, €16.50); **Rhodes** (12hr., 3 per week, €20.60); **Sitia** (1hr., 5 per week, €5.90); **Spinalonga** (2 per day, €15).

Taxis: 24hr. station (☎28410 24 000 or 28410 24 001), at the bridge beside the tourist office. Taxis stand around the corner from the tourist office.

Car and Moped Rental: Shop around A. Koundourou. Car rentals €29-35 per day, motorbikes €12-22.

ORIENTATION AND PRACTICAL INFORMATION

Agios Nikolaos is easy to navigate—it's set on a small peninsula, with beaches on three sides and most services, hotels, restaurants, and discos in the center. Facing away from the water at the bus station, walk to the right onto **S. Venizelou.** Continue straight on this road until you reach **Pl. Venizelou,** a rotary. If you stay on the right, you will head down to the harbor on **Roussou Koundourou.** Don't confuse the nepotistic street names: R. Koundourou, I. Koundourou, S. Koundourou....

Tourist Office: S. Koundourou 21A (☎28410 22 357 or 28410 24 165; fax 28410 82 534). Cross the bridge at the harbor, and take a right to reach the tourist office. Assists with accommodations, sells phone cards and stamps, provides transportation schedules and **maps.** Open Apr.-Nov. 8am-9:30pm.

Banks: Several on 28 Octovriou have 24hr. **ATMs.** The **National Bank** (☎28410 28 735) on R. Koundourou is open for **currency exchange** M-Th 8am-2pm, F 8am-1:30pm.

Emergencies: For **24hr. emergencies,** go to **Cretan Medicare,** Paleologou 20 (☎28410 27 551, 552, 553, or 554; fax 28410 25 423).

Police: Stavrou 25 (☎28410 22 321). To find the station, walk up E. Stavrou, and it will be on the right. 24hr.

Tourist Police: Stavrou 25 (☎28410 26 900), in the same building as the police. Regulates hotels, registers complaints, and gives general info. Open 8am-2pm.

Medical Care: There is a hospital (☎28410 25 224) on Paleologou, at the north end of town. From the lake, walk up Paleologou, 1 block past the archaeological museum.

Pharmacies: Dr. Theodore Furakis (☎28410 24 011), in Pl. Venizelou. Open M-F 8am-2pm and 5:30-9pm.

OTE: (☎28410 95 333), on the corner of 25 Martiou and K. Sfakianaki. Open M-F 7am-2:30pm.

Internet Access: Multiplace Peripou, 28 Octovriou 25 (☎28410 24 876). €4.50 per hr. Sells CDs and books and provides funky music to accompany your web-surfing. Open daily 9:30am-1am. **Du Lac Cafe,** near the post office (☎28410 26 837). €4.50 per hr.; €6 per 2hr. Open daily 9am-2am.

Post Office: 28 Octovriou 9 (☎28410 22 062). Open M-Sa 7:30am-2pm. **Postal code:** 72100.

ACCOMMODATIONS

Many larger hotels in Agios Nikolaos fill up months in advance. There are lots of **pensions** offering clean, cheap rooms, but their rooms are also in great demand, so make a reservation. Look for cheaper accommodations inland on the east side of the harbor, although some pensions on the western waterfront are also affordable. The hotels around the bus station get less traffic and have better prices. The **tourist office** has a bulletin board with many of Agios Nikolaos's pensions and their prices. Prices listed are reduced 20-40% in the off season.

Christodoulakis Pension, Stratigou Koraka 7 (☎28410 22 525). From the tourist office, turn away from the water and turn right onto the street behind the taxi stand, then take the second left onto Stratigou Koraka. Located just above the water, the bright rooms stay cool from the sea breeze. The pension offers a common kitchen facility and large balconies for sunbathing and socializing. Singles €15. ❷

Pension Perla, Salaminos 4 (☎28410 23 379 or 26 523). Walk away from the harbor on S. Koundourou and turn right onto Salaminos. Big rooms, some with balconies and harbor views. Comfortable TV lounge and fridge space, with an assortment of stuffed animals (the taxodermic kind). Singles €14-15; doubles €15-17; triples €21. ❷

Marin (☎28410 23 830), on the waterfront past the Lipstick Night Club. Hidden in a garden courtyard away from the bustle of the waterfront cafes, Marin gives travelers quality rooms in a great location at a reasonable price. The white rooms come with private bath and ceiling fan. Singles €25; doubles €30; triples €35. Open Mar.-Nov. ❸

Hotel Panorama (☎28410 23 830), on the waterfront at Sarolidi. Claiming the "best view in the harbor, really," Panorama has a variety of well-kept rooms with varying levels of amenities (though all have phone, private bath, and balcony). New ownership promises to spice up the place with A/C and color-themed rooms. Doubles €25-50. ❸

Victoria Hotel (☎28410 22 731; fax 28410 22 266), about 1km from the harbor on S. Koundourou, near Amoudi Beach. A clean, white stucco hotel. Rooms with bath, phone, and balcony overlooking the water. Singles €27; doubles €30-37; triples €36-45. ❸

FOOD

While Agios Nikolaos's waterfront suffers from a super-chic strain of the tourist-restaurant virus, there are tasty and semi-cheap eats to be found. Supermarkets can be found throughout the city, though there is a heavier concentration near the bus stop and the archaeological museum.

Sarri's, Kuprou 15 (☎28410 28 059), from bus station, walk up Venizelou and turn right onto Kuprou at Pl. Venizelou; restaurant is on the right after 1 block. Sarri's serves freshly harvested food from the family farm. Vine-covered retreat is a rustic getaway from the nearby city center. Post-feast, enjoy the free *raki*. Soup, *tzatziki,* souvlaki, potatoes, and a glass of wine €4.50. Open 8:30am-4pm and 6pm-midnight. ❶

Loukakis Taverna, S. Koundourou 24 (☎28410 28 022), a 10min. walk past the tourist office. The business from locals hasn't slowed since this family-run taverna opened in 1952, and the tourists have only caused minimal damage to the atmosphere. Veal *stifado* €6, vegetarian dishes €3. Open 9am-midnight. ❷

Cafe-Creperie Central, R. Koundourou 6 (☎28410 22 011), near the National Bank. This sunny cafe folds up sweet and savory crepes (€2.50-2.80, additional toppings €0.30), along with a spread of baked goods (sandwiches €1.50-3). ❶

SIGHTS AND BEACHES

Around hilly Agios Nikolaos you'll find a bathtub for goddesses, goat-inhabited archaeological sites, and cheap shopping.

FESTIVALS. Every two years, the last week of June or the first of July brings **Nautical Week,** when Greek seamen race in the waters around Agios Nikolaos (the festival returns in 2004). For landlubbers, there's nightly music and dancing around town. Call the tourist office for details. For more exotic entertainment, the **Feast of All Saints** on the last weekend of June gives tourists and locals alike the chance to visit the Island of All Saints. The feast is the only time that people are allowed on the Island of All Saints due to the island's archaeological and ecological value (the Kri-Kri goats have been granted the island as their home). The island is the nearer of the two islands in view from the harbor; the other island is also uninhabited.

MARKET. You can shop for inexpensive clothes at the weekly **market,** where sundry items like paintings, knock-off Prada bags, swimming trunks (€0.90), and underwear (4 for €3) can be purchased. Watermelon, tomatoes, and Cretan honey are also sold. (On Eth. Antistassios, next to the lake. Open W 7am-1pm.)

MUSEUMS AND ARCHAEOLOGICAL SITES. Head away from the harbor on Paleologou to reach the **Archaeological Museum,** which houses an extensive collection of artifacts, including Minoan sarcophagi, a well-documented coin collection from Greek and Roman times, and art from the under-represented 7th-century Daedalic period. Two items not to miss: the "phallus-shaped idol" that greets you as you walk in and the strange bowl of knuckle bones in the last room. (☎28410 24 943. Open Tu-Su 8:30am-3pm. €3; students and seniors €2; EU students, classicists, fine arts students, and under 18 free.) Train your eye before you buy crafts at the weekly market by visiting the **Folk Museum,** next to the tourist office. Colorful tapestries, embroidered clothes, furniture, and icons from the 16th-19th centuries are lovingly displayed in this private museum by the woman who collected them. (☎28410 25 093. Open Su-F 10am-4pm. €3, under 12 free.)

One kilometer before Kritsa on the road from Agios Nikolaos, Crete's Byzantine treasure, the **Panagia Kera,** honors the Dormition of the Virgin in several narrative cycles. A patchwork of smoky 14th-century paintings adorns the central nave, while the wings bear 15th-century Byzantine frescoes. (Open 8:30am-3pm. €2.50, students and seniors €1.20.)

BEACHES. All of Agios Nikolaos's beaches are rated blue flag beaches by the EU, which means they're the cleanest of the clean. The constant sunshine and lack of rain makes these beaches perfect for sunning. Three of the more mediocre beaches are a quick walk from the main harbor, but the farther you venture, the better it gets. Lazy folks sunbathe on the concrete piers that jut out from S. Koundourou, while others head to **Ammos Beach** by the National Stadium, **Kitroplatia Beach** between Akti Panagou and the marina, or **Ammoudi Beach** farther up S. Koundourou away from town. Those with greater aspirations catch the hourly bus to Ierapetra or Sitia and get off at **Almiros Beach** (1.5km east of Agios Nikolaos), the area's best beach. Almiros is Agios Nikolaos's only natural beach, and nature abounds just up the hill, where an EU-protected **wildlife reserve** merits exploration. A river runs through the reserve and gushes cold water into the sea at Almiros; the hot springs hidden under the ocean surface mix with the cold jet for a refreshing hot/cold swim. Sandy **Kalo Horio,** 10km farther, is less crowded. Take either bus and tell the driver to let you off at the **Kavos Taverna.** Another beautiful, somewhat touristy spot is **Havania Beach,** at the Havania stop on the Elounda bus.

NIGHTLIFE AND ENTERTAINMENT

Join the happy throng at the upscale clubs around the harbor on I. Koundourou or S. Koundourou. Or take in a movie at the **open-air theater** on Kazantzaki; from October to April, flicks are also available indoors at the **Rex** theater on Lasthenos (€6).

Multiplace Peripou, 28 Octovriou 25 (☎28410 24 876). After dinner, Greek youths stream in to sip *frappés* (€2) and play or watch a game of backgammon. View of the lake. 1-stop entertainment spot with a cafe, Internet access (€4.50 per hr.), and book and music store. From Oct.-May, the club cafe hosts live music twice a week, from Greek traditional to jazz acts. Occasional cover €5-10. Open 9am-2am.

Fluffy Duck Bar (☎697 626 3342), just off the harbor on 25 Maritou. *The* place to party with rowdy Brits and shoot some pool. Good selection of beers on tap. Beer €3-4, cocktails €6. Happy hour from 6-10pm with 2-for-1 cocktails.

Rififi (☎28410 23 140). A harborside rendezvous with a large balcony for backpackers and other tourists to view the passing traffic as they down liquid caffeine (coffee drinks €2-3) and alcohol (cocktails €4-5, beer €3-4). Open 6pm-2am.

Sorrento Bar, on the harbor waterfront. A good place to begin a night of debauchery with dancing bartenders, U2 lookalikes, and lots of booze. Plays a Brit pop/retro mix. Cocktails €5, beer €2.50. Open 9pm-3am.

Lipstick Night Club (☎28410 22 377), on the waterfront; look for a pink neon sign. Join modern Bacchic frenzy with local kids. Free tequila at the door and shooters with drinks on F. Open 10pm-late. Happy Hour at the bar from 8-10:30pm.

DAYTRIPS FROM AGIOS NIKOLAOS: SPINALONGA

There are two ways to get to Spinalonga: Nostos Tours, in Agios Nikolaos, offers guided boat rides and walking tours of the island for a combined price of €15. (Note that Nostos is the only tour company that offers guiding on the island; a number of other tour companies offer guiding only on the boat trip.) Bring your bathing suit; most boats make 20min. swim stops. If you don't want a guide, you can get there slightly more cheaply by taking one of the frequent buses to Elounda (€0.90) and taking a ferry from Elounda to Spinalonga (every 30min. from 9am-4:30pm. €7). Once you arrive at Spinalonga, €2; students €1; under 18 free.

The most touted—and most disconcerting—excursion in eastern Crete is the trip to Spinalonga Island (Σπιναλογκα). A short distance across the clear sea from Plaka, the island is painted with a dichromatic scheme: robust green brush softens the harsh lines of the orange stone fortifications. This island-wide museum's simple coloring doesn't even hint at the island's long and bizarre history.

In 1204, after purchasing the entire island of Crete, the Venetians destroyed fortresses in Barba Rossa and Agios Nikolaos before investing 75 years building a third, almost impregnable, fortress on Spinalonga. When Crete gained independence in 1898, the Greeks were determined to rid the island of all outsiders, including the Turks who had overtaken Spinalonga in 1715. In a kill-two-birds-with-one-island scheme, they established a leper colony there, simultaneously frightening away the Turks and sequestering the infected, who had previously inhabited mountain caves. On October 22, 1903, the first lepers arrived at their new home. In 1957, following the development of an effective treatment for leprosy, the colony was closed, and the residents were taken to Athens and cured. Spinalonga had been the last leper colony in Europe. The island was reopened in 1970, leaving 13 years to insure the absence of bacteria for visitors' safety.

When you arrive at the island, you will enter as the lepers did, making a grim, dark procession through **Dante's Gate** and an iron-barred tunnel to **Market St.,** past reconstructed Venetian and Turkish houses. For the first nine years of the colony's existence, the lepers were not only poor but also exploited by their corrupt governor. It was only in 1913 that inhabitants began receiving social security payments of one drachma per day. When the government raised these payments to 20 drachmas a day, Greek citizens of the surrounding area protested: 20 drachmas was significantly more than the average worker's pay. The government, however, stood firm. Ever resourceful, Greeks began to provide goods and services to the now relatively wealthy lepers. Market St. in Spinalonga became a center of local trade.

At the end of the street is the **Church of Agios Pandelemonis,** founded by the Venetians in 1709 and dedicated to the Roman doctor Pandelemon, the saint of the sick in the Greek Orthodox faith. Stairs lead from the church to the **laundry,** where water was collected into tubs, heated over fires, and used to rinse bandages. The **hospital,** halfway up the hill, is identifiable by its eight-window facade. Its lofty location theoretically allowed the wind to carry away the odor of rotting flesh.

Beyond the laundry are steps to the sea; to the right of these are the modern concrete **apartment buildings** that housed the lepers. At the bottom of the steps is the original arched entrance to the **fortress.** In front is the **disinfecting room,** where everything from bedsheets to clothing to coins was sterilized. Continuing on the path around the rest of the island, you will find the small orange-roofed **Church of Agios George.** Built in 1661 by the Venetians, this is where lepers took communion. Past this church, at the top of the ramp leading back to Dante's Gate, is the cemetery and its 44 graves, left unmarked so they could be reused.

LASITHI PLATEAU Οροπεδιο Λασιθου

The inland route to Agios Nikolaos bypasses the jagged northern coastline and traverses the Lasithi Plateau, ringed by steep, crumbling mountains. This rural plain is home to 12 small, whitewashed villages full of exhausted donkeys and farmers tilling their fields. The residents of the region once harnessed the plains' persistent breezes with thousands of wind-powered water pumps; black-and-white pictures of their windmill-strewn fields adorn the walls of travel agencies across the northern coast. Since electric pumps have taken over in recent decades, a few of the windmills have been downsized, but otherwise modern life has taken the coastal road and bypassed Lasithi. Only a daytrip to Dikteon Cave for most travelers, the tranquil plain boasts sufficient natural wonders and Old World hospitality to make a longer stay worthwhile.

TRANSPORTATION. It's best to visit Lasithi on wheels (with a rental **car** or **moped**). Those who use the infrequent bus service may find themselves stranded for hours in one town or limited to the few towns within walking distance.

If you're coming from **Iraklion,** take the coastal road 8km past Gournes, and then turn right on the road to **Kastelli** (not the one on the west coast). After about 6km, the road forks right to Kastelli; stay left, heading toward **Potamies,** pausing to ogle the giant plane tree in the center of the town: it takes 12 men to wrap their arms around the trunk. Continuing on through Krassi, the main road winds around mountain ridges, cuts through the ruins of the stone windmills of the Seli Ambelou pass, and finally descends into the Lasithi Plateau.

If you're heading from **Malia,** you have two options. To reach the more manageable road, head west along the coastal road and turn left about 3km outside of town at the turn-off for **Mochos;** this road takes you onto the road that passes through Krasi, described in the directions from Iraklion. Your second option from Malia is to follow **25 Martiou** out of town and follow the signs. This road is faster than the Mochnos route, but it is largely unpopulated and involves even more hairpin turns. **Buses** run to **Iraklion** (2hr., 2 per day, €4.11) and **Malia** (1 per day, €3.90). The bus arrives first in Tzermiado, and then takes about 45min. to make its way around the whole plateau, so you can stop at any town that pleases you.

ORIENTATION AND PRACTICAL INFORMATION. All the basics can be found in Tzermiado (Dzermiado on many road signs), the capital of Lasithi and the first and only large village you pass through upon entering the plain. The bus stops at the center of the town's main plateia in front of the Kronio Restaurant. The **Agricultural Bank** has a **currency exchange** but no ATM. (☎28440 22 390. Open M-Th 8am-2pm, F 8am-1:30pm.) The **tourist police** for Lasithi Plateau are in Agios Nikolaos, but the regular police station is a few doors down from Kronio. (☎28440 22 208. Open 24hr.) The **pharmacy** is 100m from the bus stop along the road to Agios Nikolaos. (☎28440 22 310. Open daily 8am-2pm and 5:30-10pm.) The **OTE** is past the police station. (☎28440 22 299. Open M-F 8:30am-3:10pm.) The **post office** is by Kronio. (☎28440 22 248. Open M-F 7:30am-2pm.) **Postal code:** 72052.

ACCOMMODATIONS AND FOOD. In **Tzermiado,** you'll find **Hotel Kourites** ❸ by following the road with the pharmacy and the hotel beyond the gas station. If no one is at reception, check in at the hotel's other building and taverna farther along the road. The big bedrooms come with baths, balconies, and breakfast. Kourites also runs a pension with shared bathrooms. (☎28440 22 194. Singles €25; doubles €40; triples €50. Pension doubles €25.) In **Agios Konstantinos,** your only option is **Maria Vlassi Rent Rooms ❷,** behind Maria's embroidery shop on the road from Tzermiado. (☎28440 31 048. Doubles €15.) In **Agios Giorgios,** there are several good choices: **Dias Hotel ❶,** on the main road, has sunny bargain rooms with sinks and 24hr. hot water. The rooms are decorated with the friendly owner's handmade crafts; you may find her sewing when you arrive. (☎28440 31 207. Breakfast €3. Singles €8; doubles €15; triples €24. Student discount €1.50.) **Hotel Maria ❷,** on the opposite side of town, offers a hipper spin on traditional style; go to Rea Taverna on the main street to request a room. (☎28440 31 209. Singles €20; doubles €25.) For a rest stop on the way to Dikteon Cave, **Hotel Dionysos ❷** has large rooms with private bath and a taverna and sits just a few kilometers from the cave between pottery markets. (☎28440 31 672. Doubles €20; triples €25.)

Most restaurants in Lasithi Plateau are linked to hotels. An exception to the rule is the family-owned **Kronio Restaurant ❶** (☎28440 22 375), the oldest taverna in Lasithi, at the center of **Tzermiado.** There's more to this place than the delectable food (moussaka €4.50, *stifado* €5, Greek salad €3): the corner at Kronio is a convention spot for the outgoing villagers to settle utilities bills and a favorite coffee shop of the village priests. The **Kri Kri Taverna ❶,** in the center of town, lavishes tender affection on its food, though the selection is limited. Ivy-covered walls and a homey fireplace make a strange but splendid combination. (☎28440 22 170. Open 9am-11pm. Moussaka €4.80; omelette €3.) On the main road in **Agios Konstantinos,** the **Dikti Taverna ❶** has excellent moussaka (€4.50) and Greek coffee (€0.90). (Open Apr.-Nov. 8am-6pm.) In **Agios Giorgios,** the only restaurants are attached to hotels. In **Psychro,** the owner of **Taverna O Stavros ❶** delights visitors with flowers and *raki* after a meal. *Tzatziki* €2; beer €1.50. (☎28440 31 453. Open 7am-1am.)

SIGHTS. **Agios Giorgios** is home to a **folklore museum,** located in a restored 19th century house. The model people are slightly frightening, but the assortment of stuff (there is no other word to describe the holdings) makes for interesting viewing. Next door is the **El. Venizelou Museum,** a hall dedicated to the great former prime minister of Greece, who was born in Hania. (Open Apr.-Oct. 10am-4pm. Admission to both museums €2.50, students €1.50, under 12 free.)

The village of **Psychro** serves as a starting point for exploring **Dikteon Cave,** 1km away. At the turn of the century, archaeologists found hundreds of Minoan artifacts crammed into the cave's ribbed stalactites; many are now at Iraklion's Archaeological Museum. Arthur Evans, who also dug up Knossos, excavated this spot and, in a blast of misguided enthusiasm, blew apart the entrance. To get there, follow signs from Ag. Giorgios. Local members of the donkey drivers will probably offer to taxi you (€10); the uphill walk is grueling, but it should take less than an hour. (Open 8am-7pm. €4, students and seniors €2, EU students free. Parking €2.) For a nice daytrip, take the bus to Psychro, visit Dikteon Cave, and then take the 1½hr. walk across the plain to Tzermiado, and grab a bite to eat.

The **Kronion Cave** may play second fiddle to Dikteon, but it's free from Dikteon's crowds and merits a brief side trip. Clear signs outside of Tzermiado will direct you to the 2km route to the grotto, the mythical home of Zeus's parents, Kronos and Rhea. The last kilometer is badly marked and manageable only by foot. Stay on the people path (as opposed to the goat paths), and don't forget a flashlight.

If you are interested in the monastery circuit, there are a couple of monasteries on the drive to Tzermiado. Coming from Malia, the first monastery you will come upon is the **Monastery of the Panagia Kera.** Currently under restoration, the monastery has a small church and a magnificent view. (Open 8am-8pm. Donations requested.) Continuing along the road, you will see a turn-off for the **Vivandi Monastery** which has impressive ruins on site. Several other smaller monasteries, some with more to see than others, dot the road to Tzermiado.

IERAPETRA Ιεραπετρα

Although German tourists have made inroads, Ierapetra (ear-AH-peh-tra) still welcomes more Greeks than foreigners. It's touted as Europe's southernmost city, but this title is difficult to confirm. After a few days in the labyrinthine streets, you won't know which way is south anyway. After centuries of foreign rule by Arabs, Venetians, and Turks, the city's architecture reflects its worldly past, but in everyday life the traditional rural ethic shines through in the hospitality of the locals.

ORIENTATION AND PRACTICAL INFORMATION. Although not a large city, Ierapetra can be difficult to navigate because of its long, maze-like streets. It has three main plateias, connected by three roads running north-south. With your back to the **bus station,** Lasthenous 41 (☎28420 28 237), **Pl. Plastira** will be on your right. Walking straight for a block on **Lasthenous,** which then turns into **Koundouriotou,** brings you to **Pl. Eleftherias,** the central square. Keep walking in the same direction for about 100m to reach another plateia: **Pl. Kanoupaki.** South of it is the Old Town district. **Buses** run to **Iraklion** (6 per day, €7.05) via **Agios Nikolaos** (€2.40) and **Sitia** (6 per day, €4.15). Pick up a free **map** of the city from one of the travel agencies along the waterfront. The **Ierapetra Express office,** Pl. El. Venizelou 25, is helpful. (☎28420 28 673 or 28420 22 411. Open M-F 8am-2pm and 5-9pm, Sa 8am-2pm.) **Radio Taxi** (☎28420 26 600 or 28420 27 350) lines up cars in Pl. Kanoupaki. **Car and moped rental** can be arranged at **Driver's Club,** behind Ierapetra Express. (☎28420 25 583. Cars €30-35; mopeds €20.) The **National Bank,** in Pl. Eleftherias next to Ierapetra Express, **exchanges currency** and has a 24hr **ATM.** (Open M-Th 8am-2pm, F 8am-1:30pm.) The **police station** (☎28420 22 560) in Pl. Eleftherias, is in the big yellow building on the waterfront. Ierapetra is under the jurisdiction of the Agios Nikolaos **tourist police** (☎28410 26 900). The **hospital** is north of the bus station, left off Lasthenous at Kalimerake 6. (☎28420 22 488 or 28420 22 766. Open 8:30am-1:30pm; 24hr. **emergency** care.) The **OTE** is at Koraka 25. (☎28420 24 199 or 28420 80 355. Open M, W, Sa 7:30am-1pm and Tu, Th, F 7:30am-8pm.) Chic **Polycafe Orpheas,** Koundouriotou 25, just past Pl. Plastira, offers **Internet access** at €3 per 30min. (☎28420 80 462. Open M, W, Sa 9am-5pm and Tu, Th, F 9am-11pm.) The **post office** is on V. Kornarou, on the west side of the old town. (☎28420 22 271. Open M-F 7:30am-2pm.) **Postal code:** 72200.

ACCOMMODATIONS. For the most part, Ierapetra makes its beds for upscale tourists, who want only the best after a day snoozing on Chrissi Island. When bargain-hunters land in town, they avoid the mainland and knock on doors in the streets surrounding the bus station. Make a sharp right out of the bus station, and you'll see signs leading to many moderately priced pensions, including the sparkling **Cretan Villa ❸,** Lakerda 16. The 205-year-old building's white stucco-walled, brick-floored, high-ceilinged rooms hide a central garden. The owner, a University of Missouri alum, speaks fluent English. All rooms have very clean private baths and satellite TV. (☎28420 28 522; www.cretan-villa.com. Singles €26-32; doubles €32-38; triples €38-44; A/C €6 extra per night.) Bargains can also be found in the Old Town area. Walk past the taxis down Kyrva to the waterfront and make a right onto Ioanidou after passing the port police. To the right is **Hotel Coral ❷,** Ioanidou 18. It has large rooms with private bathtubs, fridges, and free luggage storage. (☎28420 22 846 or 28420 28 743. Doubles €20; triples €25; A/C €2 extra per night.) Outdoor enthusiasts can pitch a tent at **Koutsounari ❶,** 7km from Ierapetra on the coastal road to Sitia near the restaurant, bar, and beach. Take the bus to **Sitia** via **Makri Gialo** (20min., every hr., €0.80) and ask to be let off at the campgrounds. (☎28420 61 213. €4 per person; €2.10 per tent; €2.10 per car.)

FOOD. Most of Ierapetra's waterfront restaurants are identically priced. Locals and tourists of all ages and sizes frequent **Veterano ❶,** in Pl. Eleftherias opposite the Hertz office, a cafe/dessert bar with an ideal view of the palm-edged main plateia. Sip your cappuccino, spy on the bustling populace, and contemplate a second piece of *kalitsounia* (€0.70), an Ierapetrian sweet cheese tart. (Open 7:30am-midnight.) On the waterfront near the Old Town, three restaurants stand out. **Konaki ❷,** on Stratigou Samovil, offers generous portions of traditional meals and fresh catch (*giovetsi* €6) straight from the Libyan Sea.

(☎28420 24 422. Open 8am-1am.) **Napoleon ❷,** Stratigou Samovil 26, is the oldest restaurant in Ierapetra, open since 1955. Five days a week, the charismatic couple in charge cooks up seasonally priced fish, meats for €5-6, and vegetables for €3-4. (Open M-Sa noon-midnight.) The eccentric crew at **Castello ❷,** right next door to Napoleon, grills fish (€7-9) and meat (€4-6) right in the open. The owner's mother makes the appetizers fresh every day. (☎28420 24 424. Open 10:30am-1am.)

SIGHTS. It's hard to imagine that many people come to Ierapetra for the beaches. Although they receive the highest scores for cleanliness, their gravelly texture leaves a lot to be desired. Unfortunately, Ierapetra's historical sights aren't much to look at either. In the Old Town, a 19th-century **mosque** and a decaying **Ottoman fountain** *(Krini)* are covered with Greek graffiti. The 13th-century restored **Venetian fortress** *(Kales)* at the south end of the old harbor is a rather modest sight compared to some of the other fortresses in Crete, though it does provide a pleasant lookout onto the Libyan Sea. (Open Tu-Su 8:30am-3pm. Free.) The **Kervea festival,** held each summer in July and August, features music, dance, and theater performances at the fortress; call the town hall for information (☎28420 24 115). Ierapetra's **Archaeological Museum,** at Pl. Kanoupaki across from the taxi stand, has Minoan artifacts from the south coast and a worthwhile collection of Greco-Roman statues. One unique sarcophagus in the second room, adorned by hunting scenes, embodies the simple elegance of Minoan painting. The town's pride and joy, the near-mint condition Persephone Statue, is also located here. (Open Tu-Sa 8:30am-3pm. €2, EU students free.)

DAYTRIP FROM IERAPETRA: CHRISSI. Ierapetra's star attraction is Chrissi, an island 15km offshore. Free from stores and crowds, Chrissi is completely flat, adorned by green pines and surrounded by transparent green sea. Most beaches on the island are spread with very fine sand. Pack a lunch and bring water; there's nothing but a taverna near the dock, which tends to be pricey (open all day). **Ferries** depart May through October daily at 10:30am and 12:30pm, returning at 5 and 6pm, respectively (€13, including return; €5 beach chair charge).

SITIA Σητεια

A winding drive on coastal and mountain roads from Agios Nikolaos leads to the fishing and port town of Sitia. The tourism industry has made serious inroads into Sitia, but the town maintains a grittiness and authenticity. Tourists blend with locals at the harborside tavernas, and pelicans walk the streets at dawn. Sitia makes a great base for your exploration of Crete's east coast, and it's the most convenient port for departures to Rhodes.

ORIENTATION AND PRACTICAL INFORMATION

Pl. Iroön Polytechniou sits at the center of town on the waterfront; most practical necessities can be found here. With your back to the bus station, exit to the right. Make another right, then a left, and **Venizelou** will take you there.

Flights: The **airport** (☎28430 24 666) connects to Athens (3 per week, 2 per week in winter; €83). No buses to airport. Taxis cost €3 for the 1km ride.

Ferries: Port Authority (☎28430 25 555). 3 ferries per week go to: **Kassos** (4hr., €8.22); **Karpathos** (5hr., €11.15); **Rhodes** (12hr., €18.78). 5 per week go to: **Piraeus** (16hr., €23.48) via **Agios Nikolaos** (1½hr., €5.58) and **Milos** (9hr., €16.73.).

Buses: The station (☎28430 22 272) is out of town off Venizelou. To: **Agios Nikolaos** (1½hr., 4-6 per day, €5); **Ierapetra** (1½hr., 3-5 per day, €4.15); **Iraklion** (3¼hr., 3-5 per day, €9.60); **Kato Zakros** (1hr., 1-2 per day, €3.75); **Vai** (1hr., 3-5 per day, €2).

Taxis: (☎28430 22 700) in Pl. Venizelou. Usually available 24hr. on weekends.

Rentals: Porto-Belis Travel, Karamanli 34 (☎28430 22 370; fax 28430 23 830), on the east side of the waterfront past the tourist office, rents **cars** (€25-44). Open daily 9am-3:30pm and 5-8pm.

Tourist Office: (☎28430 28 300), on the waterfront. From Pl. Polytechniou, head along the water to the east; the small white building will be on your left. **Maps, currency exchange,** info on accommodations. Open M-F 9:30am-2:30pm and 5:30-8:30pm.

Banks: National Bank (☎28430 22 250 or 28430 22 218), in Pl. Venizelou. 24hr. **ATM.** Open M-Th 8am-2pm, F 8am-1:30pm.

Tourist Police: Therissou 31 (☎28430 24 200). From the plateia, follow Kapetan Sifi 2 blocks to Mysonos; go left and continue until it becomes Therissou. Open 24hr.

Police: (☎28430 22 266 or 28430 22 259), with tourist police. Open 24hr.

Hospital: (☎28430 24 311), past the youth hostel off Therissou. Open 24hr.

OTE: Kapetan Sifis 22 (☎28430 28 099). From the main plateia, head inland past the National Bank for 3 blocks. Open M-F 7:30am-1:30pm.

Internet Access: Upstairs at **Ianos Internet Cafe,** Venizelou 159, by the water. €4.40 per hr. Open 9am-5am.

Post Office: Main branch, Dimokritou 8 (☎28430 22 283; fax 28430 25 350). From the plateia on the waterfront, walk inland on Venizelou and go left on Dimokritou; it will be on your right. Open M-F 7:30am-2pm. **Postal Code:** 72300.

ACCOMMODATIONS

Call ahead for reservations in August. The youth hostel is friendly, but for more privacy, look behind the west end of the waterfront on Kornarou and Kondilaki.

Rooms to Let Apostolis, Kazantzakis 27 (☎28430 22 993 or 28430 28 172). From the main plateia, head inland on Kapetan Sifi and turn left onto Fountalidou, then right 2 blocks farther onto Kazantzakis. Bright granite stairs lead to spacious rooms with private baths and fans. A basic common kitchen area opens onto a balconied dining area. Doubles €25-30; triples €30-36. ❸

Youth Hostel, Therissou 4 (☎28430 22 693). From the bus station turn left, walk inland, and follow the signs for the main road to Iraklion and Agios Nikolaos. As you bear left, the street becomes Therissou; the hostel is 150m up. Provides a variety of accommodation types in a bug-filled atmosphere. A bit isolated from town. Reception 9am-noon and 6-9pm; if no one is around, find a bed and register later. Common kitchen. 24hr. hot water. Dorms €5; singles €8; doubles €12; triples €18. ❶

Venus Rooms to Let, Kondilaki 60 (☎28430 24 307). Walk uphill on Kapetan Sifi from the main plateia and make your 1st right after the OTE. All rooms have balconies and access to common kitchen facilities. The street-side rooms offer a heavily-flowered view out the windows. Doubles €21, with bath €30; triples €25/€36. ❷

Hotel Apollon, Kapetan Sifi 28 (☎28430 22 733 or 28430 28 155), about 3 blocks back from the main plateia. Clean, standardized rooms provide a variety of amenities including TV, private bath, fridge, and A/C. Lobby area has a cafe for breakfast as well as a lounge. Singles €29-39; doubles €35-44; triples €38-47. ❸

CRETE

AN EVENING STROLL When traveling through Greece, you may come across an interesting ritual known as the **volta,** one part constitutional, one part parade, in which, very often, all the town's residents take part. But this is not just your everyday town-wide procession; the residents get dressed up in their Sunday-best for the *volta*. Children are forced into uncomfortable shoes, women don their good jewelry, and men bring out their best set of worry beads. The result is that the *volta* takes on an added element of significance–it becomes an opportunity for residents to show off their families and their wealth.

Most Greeks insist that the *volta* is not as superficial as this sounds. They admit that there is an element of boasting in it, but they also point to the importance a ritual like the *volta* plays in maintaining a sense of community, especially as more towns are pushed to homogenize for the tourist industry.

Travelers are certainly welcome to observe a *volta* procession, though they are not always easy to locate. For most villagers, the *volta* is just a part of their daily lives, not something they would go out of their way to mention to a traveler passing through. Your best bet is to head for towns such as Sitia where the *volta* is a major event.

FOOD

The waterfront offers typical tourist fare to light *bouzouki* strumming. There's less of a view of the water but more local life at the tavernas on the inland streets.

Cretan House, K. Karamanli 10 (☎28430 25 133), right of the main plateia as you face the water, past the tourist office. Most diners eat on the waterfront, but the interior is more colorful. The Cretan appetizers offer an unique dining experience. Ask for the "Cretan viagra" to heat up your night (*staka* €2.70). Entrees €4-7. Complimentary ouzo or *raki* for Let's Go readers. Open 9am-1am. ❷

Taverna Mixos, V. Kornarou 117 (☎28430 22 416), one block up from the main plateia, with another seating area on the waterfront. Serves up an interesting variety of souvlakis including swordfish-mushroom (€5.15) and calamari (€6.20), all of which come with rice and delicious Cretan vegetables. Whet your appetite with their *dolmades* (€2.50). In winter, live music on F-Sa. 20% discount for students. ❷

Mike's Creperie, El. Venizelou 162 (☎28430 23 207), west of the main plateia. Sweet and salty crepes and friendly service. Crepes €2 and up. Open M-Sa 7pm-3am. ❶

Taverna Kali Kardia, Fountalidou 22 (☎28430 22 249), walk up Kapetan Sifi and turn left on Fountalidou. Enjoy your meal in a quiet environment off the waterfront. Ask for the *escargots* (€3.50) and a lesson on how to eat them. Stuffed vine leaves €2.50. Open 8am-3:30pm and 6pm-2am. ❷

SIGHTS

Away from the waterfront on the hill high above town, the **fortress** may not offer much protection but it does make for a fine view. (Open Tu-Su 8:30am-3pm. Free.) It hosts Sitia's **Kornareia Festival,** running from June to August, with free open-air theater and concerts of traditional and popular Greek music and dancing. Contact the tourist office for details. The **Archaeological Museum,** directly behind the bus station, is the product of the rich excavation sites around Sitia, where many prominent sanctuaries and villas were located in Minoan times. It also includes items from the palace complex at Kato Zakros. Be sure to note the Late Minoan Palaikastro *kouros* statuette—a small ivory and gold masterpiece with strong Egyptian influences. (☎28430 23 917. €2, students and seniors €1,

EU students and under 18 free. Open Tu-Su 8:30am-3pm.) Sitia's **Folk Art Museum** houses traditional 19th-century Cretan items and has a beautiful collection of fabrics and garments from the early 20th century; walk up Kapetan Sifi from the main plateia and the museum is on the right past the OTE. (☎28430 22 861. Open M-Tu, Th-Sa 9:30am-3pm and W 9:30am-3pm and 5-8pm. €1.) The town's **beach** extends 3km east toward Petra. Close to town, the beach is narrowed by a busy roadway, but the road turns inland farther down, leaving an empty expanse of sand.

NIGHTLIFE AND ENTERTAINMENT

People-watching is a favorite Sitian pastime, especially along the row of restaurants and cafes near the moonlit main plateia. A night out begins here at places like **Scala,** El. Venizelou 193, a bar with late-night DJs that draws an older Greek crowd for ouzo and gossip. (Cocktails €5. Open 5pm-3am.) **Iannos Internet Cafe,** El. Venizelou 159, becomes a frenzy of activity among young locals around 2am, with the sound track provided by an inhouse DJ. (Cocktails €4-5. Open 9am-5am.) After midnight, everyone heads to **Hot Summer,** about one kilometer down the road to Palaikastro by the beach, where a swimming pool replaces the staid dance floor. Three fully-stocked bars provide the refreshments while the über-chic talk across the pool on their cell phones. (Cocktails €6.) Around 3am, head westward several kilometers out of town to **Planetarium Disco,** where you can relax on the balcony or move your feet at one of Crete's largest clubs. (€5 cover, includes one drink. Open in summer 1am-dawn.)

DAYTRIP FROM SITIA: VAI Βαι

Buses from Sitia (1hr., 4-6 per day, €2) via Palaikastro (€0.90) stop in the parking lot in front of the beach. (Parking: cars €3; motorbikes €1.) A tourist information booth offers currency exchange. Pay bathrooms are available in the parking lot. (€0.30; €1 for shower.) First aid at the back of the parking lot. For emergencies call the police (☎28430 61 222). Chairs on the beach €3.

Not long ago, tourists headed east to Vai to get off the beaten path. Today, several buses roll into this outpost daily, depositing tourists eager to swim at a smooth, sandy **beach** and rest under the shady fronds of Europe's only indigenous **palm tree forest.** Legend has it the forest sprouted from dropped date seeds that 2nd-century BC Egyptian soldiers littered on their way to war. In the 60s and 70s, Vai became a haven for British bands like Cream and Led Zeppelin, who would camp out, smoke up, and rock out under the palms. Nowadays camping and smoking are prohibited, but rocking out is merely frowned upon. The palm trees have been mostly fenced off except for a small patch in the area immediately next to the beach.

For more secluded bathing and an umbrella-free beach, face the water and head up and over the craggy hill. Those in search of a more secluded beach experience should go left along the cliff to a perfect stretch of sand. Although camping is forbidden in the park itself, many unfurl sleeping bags in this cove to the south of the palm beach. If sandy pajamas and the possibility of arrest don't appeal to you, rent a room in quiet **Palaikastro,** 8km back toward Sitia. Although there is one **restaurant** and a **snack bar** (small sandwiches €2) in Vai, you're better off packing a **picnic** or eating in Palaikastro or Sitia. A **watersports center** offers jet-skis (€20 for 15min.; reduced prices for larger parties), and the **Vai Scuba Diving Club** organizes dives at noon and 3pm. (☎28430 71 543. €15 per session.) Try a banana grown on a local plantation, or buy a bunch from the stand in the parking lot (€1.80 per kg.).

PALAIKASTRO Παλαικαστρο

Sitting at the crossroads between major tourist attractions, Palaikastro relishes its gatekeeper status and its role as guardian of the excellent beaches in the periphery of town. The slow pace of life serves as a pleasant contrast to a day's excitement at eastern Crete's more popular sights.

ORIENTATION AND PRACTICAL INFORMATION

Palaikastro is a stop on two bus routes, running from Sitia to Vai and Kato Zakros. **Buses** leave from the main plateia for: **Sitia** (30min., 3-4 per day, €1.50); **Vai** (15min., 3-4 per day, €0.90); and **Kato Zakros** (30min., 1-2 per day, €2.10). Buy tickets on the bus. For **taxis** call ☎28430 61 380 or 28430 61 271, or inquire at the tourist office. The village has the bare necessities in its main plateia. **Lion Car Rental,** in the plateia across from the church, rents **cars** for around €25 per day. (☎28430 61 482 or 697 771 7344; fax 28430 61 482. Open 9am-1pm and 6-9:30pm.) The extremely helpful **tourist information office,** 100m down the road to Sitia on your right, has an **ATM, currency exchange,** room and restaurant info, and **maps** of local trails. (☎28430 61 546; fax 28430 61 547; www.photoart.gr/itanos. Open daily 9am-10pm.) Across the street and a few doors down is the **police station** (☎28430 61 222), one flight upstairs in a building marked by Greek flags. Nearby is a **pharmacy.** (Open 9am-2pm and 5-11pm.) A **doctor** (☎28430 61 204) visits the village three times per week, seeing patients in the mayor's building, down the road immediately left of the tourist office. The **OTE** (☎28430 61 546) is in the same building as the tourist office. **Internet access** is available at the **Argo Bookstore,** opposite the church's entrance; Argo also has used English-language books. (☎28430 29 640. Open M-Sa 9am-10pm. €1.50 per 20min.)

ACCOMMODATIONS AND FOOD

You can find rooms and hospitality in the home of **Yiannis Perakis ❷.** From the bus, take the right fork of the main road away from Sitia and continue for 200m to Pegasos Taverna on your left. Take the small gravel road to the left immediately before Pegasos, and follow it around a bend to the left. Inquire for rooms at the first door to your left. Lemon trees and bougainvillea invite you into bright rooms with shared baths and balconies. (☎28430 61 310. Singles €10; doubles €15; triples €20.) On the same path as Yiannis, **Pegasos Rooms ❷,** above Pegasos Taverna, offers balconies, fridges, and private baths. (☎28430 61 479. Doubles €23.50, with A/C €29.50; triples €29.50, with A/C €32.50; 5-person apartments €50.)

For the basics, visit the village's **mini-market** and **bakery** opposite the church entrance, 20m down the road to Vai. **Restaurant Mythos ❷,** in the plateia, is a local favorite with good prices. (Traditional dishes such as moussaka and *stifado* €3.10-6, vegetables €2. Open 11am-1am.) **Hotel Hellas ❶** serves all the standards and has the best view of the plateia. (☎28430 61 455. Greek salad €2.65, chicken with lemon sauce €4.50. Open 8am-1am.) Choose your feast at **Vaios ❶,** a family restaurant 300m past Pegasos in the next village, Agathias. (Entrees with vegetables €2-4. Open summer 6-11pm.)

BEACHES

If you're looking for activities outside of Palaikastro, take the bus headed for Kato Zakros and ask the driver to let you off at **Chochlakes.** From this village, you can walk through the valley to the secluded beach and bay of **Karoumes.** Follow the signs along the road east from Palaikastro to the tiny village of **Agathias,** beyond which lie many of Crete's most scenic and least visited beaches. Past Agathias, the road forks: its right branch leads to the **Minoan Palace** at **Roussolakos;** the left branch leads to **Hiona Beach.**

DAYTRIP FROM PALAIKASTRO

VALLEY OF DEATH AND ZAKROS

Buses travel from Sitia to Kato Zakros, stopping in Palaikastro and Zakros (1hr., 2 per day, €3.75). Ask the bus driver to drop you at the gorge's entrance, 2km down the road from Zakros's main plateia. The 11am bus from Sitia allows enough time to hike the gorge, visit the ruins, grab a bite to eat, take a swim, and make the 4pm return bus. Zakros's bus stop is in the main plateia, with taxis and police station (☎28430 93 323).

Those seeking a physical challenge should hike (4km, 90min.) through the **Valley of Death** (or **Death's Gorge,** so named for the tendency of Minoans to bury their dead in the caves that frame the valley), leading from the quiet village of Zakros to the beach enclave Kato Zakros. Although Samaria is larger, Death's Gorge equals it in beauty and far surpasses it in tranquility. The wildlife includes the usual goats, as well a selection of snakes and scorpions that slither right under your feet. Although it's impossible to wander too far astray in a gorge, the path is poorly and sporadically marked with crude red arrows. Bring along plenty of water and trail snacks, good hiking shoes, and long pants to protect against brambles; people with bee allergies may want to proceed with caution given that bees are prevalent among the bright flowers on the trail. Keep an eye out for **phaskomilo,** a tea plant with small, fuzzy, green leaves. Its scent is naturally refreshing, a pleasant change from the odor of the onion plants (identified by their small purple flowers) that also inhabit the valley.

At the end of the gorge, turn left on the dirt path—and look for the sign that leads you to the coast and the **Minoan Palace** (☎28430 93 105) of **Kato Zakros.** Destroyed in 1450 BC, the royal rubble extends up a hill and is still undergoing excavation. The palace is thought to have been one of the centers of the Minoan navy, which controlled the eastern Mediterranean seas. Royalty once bathed in pools near the bottom of the hill, now home to many turtles. (☎28430 93 105. Open 8am-5pm, last entrance 4:30pm. €3, students and seniors €2, EU students free.)

Continue along the path away from the palace to Kato Zakros and its wheelchair-accessible beach. The waterfront is largely free from clutter, and the beach is pleasant, if pebbly. Restaurant **Nikos Platanias** ❷ has exceptionally friendly, multilingual waiters who serve up fish from the Mediterranean and vegetables from the owner's farm. (☎28430 26 887. Entrees around €4-6. Open Apr.-Oct. 9am-midnight.) For lodging, head to **George's Villa** ❸ (800m up the road), or inquire at his taverna. George treats his guests to his own good humor in rooms that overlook the sea and an unspoiled beach. (☎28430 26 883. Doubles €25-30; triples €30-35.)

CYPRUS Κυπρος

From the ancient temples and Roman mosaics scattered on its shores to the Green Line that runs through its capital city, Cyprus is an island of ancient harmonies and modern tensions. After enduring a succession of conquerors that reads like a Who's Who list of historical peoples (the Phoenicians, Greeks, Persians, Ptolemies, Romans, Arabs, Crusaders, Ottomans, and Britons have all passed through), the island now exists independently, although uneasily. Contrasting landscapes—sandy beaches, cool Troodos mountain air, developing industrial cities—mean that a change of pace is just a short bus ride away. Times are changing, too: flashy signs aimed at tourists have replaced the scrawled graffiti that once proclaimed the unification of Cyprus, yet conversations with elder Cypriots can yield nostalgic ruminations well worth a night at a small *kafeneion*. Although visiting Cyprus can be expensive, more and more tourists seem convinced that the trip is worthwhile.

HIGHLIGHTS OF CYPRUS

STAY OVERNIGHT AT A MOSQUE-TURNED-HOSTEL, sup with poets at an art cafe, and stare into the foundations of one of the world's oldest cities at Larnaka (p. 569).

FROLIC on the fabulous beaches of frenetic Agia Napa (p. 576).

CROSS THE GREEN LINE to Turkish-occupied territory in Lefkosia, the world's last divided city (p. 593).

DIP YOUR TOES in Aphrodite's Divine Tub of Love and Beauty (p. 588).

HIKE the Troodos Mountains, where French poet Arthur Rimbaud once hid (p. 589).

HISTORY AND POLITICS

ANCIENT AND MEDIEVAL CYPRUS

The remains of round stone and mud dwellings date settlement on Cyprus back to roughly 7000 BC. Millennia later, Cyprus's wealth of copper and ore made it the most popular island around, leading to an increase in Cypriot trade and cultural exchange during the Bronze Age (2500-1050 BC). Linguists are unsure whether *Kypros,* from which the word "copper" is derived, first referred to the island or the metal itself. In the midst of all the copper-working, **Mycenaean** (see p. 7) traders from the Peloponnese swung through, initiating a long-lasting Hellenic influence in Cyprus. The arrival of strongwilled **Phoenician** traders in the first millennium BC forced the Greeks to share political control until the **Assyrians** arrived in the 7th century BC; the Assyrians dominated the island for a century until the **Egyptians** briefly seized control. They were soon overthrown by the **Persian** king. Pro-Hellenic **Evagoras I** forced the Persians out of Salamis and spread the Greek language throughout his kingdom, initiating the most significant Cypriot resistance to Persian rule. As Persian expansion stagnated, **Alexander the Great** (see p. 10) absorbed Cyprus into his growing empire. Following Alexander's death, the island would pass hands back to Egypt before being annexed by Rome in 58 BC.

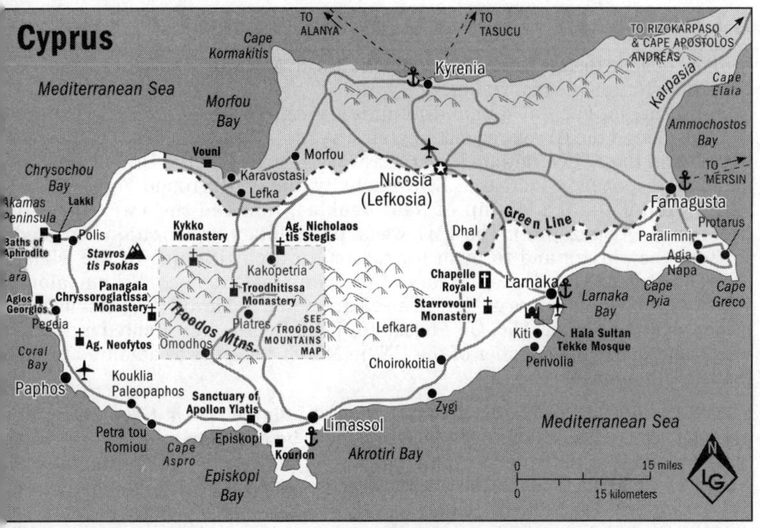

BYZANTINE TO OTTOMAN RULE

After Constantinople was proclaimed capital of the eastern half of the divided Roman empire (see p. 11), Roman civic thought, Greek philosophy, and Greek Orthodoxy were synthesized on Cyprus. Despite the advances in civilization, these centuries were bad times for the Cypriots: devastating earthquakes hit in AD 332 and 342, followed by a 40-year drought, and fierce Arab raids in the 7th century. In 1191, **Richard the Lionheart,** en route to the Crusades in Jerusalem, overran the island; he took provisions for the Christian armies and robbed the island of its treasures. Unable to carry the island around, he sold it to the **Knights Templar.** In turn, they passed responsibility on to **Guy de Lusignan,** a minor French noble who had been involved in the Crusades.

THE OTTOMAN PERIOD. The feudal system of the **Lusignan Dynasty** (1192-1489) oppressed the lower classes and suppressed Cypriot traditions and religion but bestowed Gothic churches, cathedrals, and castles upon the area. The Crusaders were forced to retreat after losing battles in Palestine, so the Lusignans invited Crusader families to bide their time in Cyprus. As a result, in the late 13th century Cyprus became the wealthiest island in the eastern Mediterranean. Profiting from the Lusignans' dynastic intrigues, the **Venetians** annexed the island in 1489. Even with strengthened Cypriot military defenses, however, the island was no match for the encroaching Ottomans. In 1570, following a two-month siege, Lefkosia surrendered to the Turks under Lala Mustafa. The fall of Famagusta one year later marked the beginning of the **Ottoman period** in Cyprus, as well as the introduction of a brand new ethnic element to the island. In the 19th century, Great Britain defended the Ottoman territories against Russian expansion in an effort to defend its own colonies. Landing at Larnaka in July of 1878, British forces assumed control of Cyprus as a **military base.** Although Cypriots received no political freedom under the British, as a consolation prize they gained many public works including roads, railways, schools, and hospitals.

CYPRUS IN THE 20TH CENTURY

In 1955, **General George Grivas,** in conjunction with **Archbishop Makarios,** founded the **EOKA** (National Organization of Cypriot Fighters), an underground *enosis* (pro-union) movement demanding union with Greece. When the United Nations vetoed the Greek request to grant Cyprus self-government, an enraged Grivas and the EOKA initiated guerrilla warfare aimed at the British government. In response to increased EOKA activity, the underground *Volkan* (Volcano), under the leadership of **Rauf Denktaş,** founded the **TMT** (Turkish Resistance Organization). The TMT was a paramilitary organization designed to fight the *enosis* and to push for **taksim,** or a partitioning of the island between Greece and Turkey. Weary of the perpetual violence, Britain, along with the foreign ministers of Greece and Turkey, agreed in 1959 to establish an **independent Cypriot republic.** On August 16, 1960, Cyprus was granted independence and became a member of the UN; in March 1961, it was admitted to the British Commonwealth.

A LINE IN THE SAND. The new **constitution** stipulated that a Greek Cypriot president and a Turkish Cypriot vice president be appointed through popular election and that the Greek-to-Turkish ratio in the House of Representatives would be 70:30. In 1959, **Archbishop Makarios** became the mixed republic's first president, and **Fazıl Küçük,** leader of the Turkish Cypriot community, was elected to the vice presidency unopposed. In 1963, Makarios proposed 13 amendments to the constitution intended to make bicommunal life easier, including the abolition of the president's and vice-president's veto power and the introduction of majority rule (in a country where the Greek Cypriots are the huge majority). When the unenthusiastic Turkish government threatened to use military force if these amendments were implemented, renewed violence broke out between the EOKA and the TMT, resulting in the division of Nicosia along the **Green Line** (p. 594). In February 1964, the UN dispatched a "temporary" peacekeeping force that has been renewed indefinitely and remains in place today.

BREAKING UP IS HARD TO DO. In 1968, Makarios and Küçük were both re-elected by an overwhelming majority, although in the years following they were subject to several coup attempts. In 1971, General Grivas snuck back into Cyprus to found the militant EOKA-B and to revitalize the call for *enosis*. The violence exploded into an international affair in 1974, when the Greek Cypriot National Guard (sans General Grivas, who died in Limassol the same year), assisted by the military junta in Greece, overthrew Archbishop Makarios and replaced him with Nikos Sampson, an EOKA member who favored immediate *enosis*. This new government lasted all of five days, ending when the Turkish army invaded Cyprus from the north to protect Turkish Cypriot interests. Early in 1975, the North declared itself the Turkish Federated State of Cyprus (TFSC), effectively partitioning the island.

RECENT YEARS

In November 1983, Turkish-occupied Cyprus proclaimed itself independent as the **Turkish Republic of North Cyprus (TRNC).** Although only Turkey has recognized the new state, the TRNC has established trade relations in Europe and with several Arab states. In 1992, the UN significantly pared down its peacekeeping mission, leaving Cypriots to resolve their situation without much international intervention. **Glafkos Clerides,** former head of the conservative **Democratic Rally (DISY),** became head of the Republic of Cyprus in 1993. Led by **Rauf Denktaş,** North Cyprus still lags behind the Republic of Cyprus economically but has retained the support of Turkish Cypriots and thousands of settlers from mainland Turkey. The two men still lead their respective halves today, and hope for cooperation is growing.

EU OR NOT EU? Greek officials are hopeful for the Republic of Cyprus's acceptance into the European Union, a prospect with uncertain implications for the political status of North Cyprus. Turkey was not a realistic candidate for admission to the EU in either the first or second round and has warned that it would seek to annex North Cyprus if the Republic of Cyprus were to join the EU. In early August 1997, Turkey and North Cyprus agreed to work toward partial defense and economic integration. The agreement came just five days before UN-sponsored talks between Greece and Turkey and incensed the Greek government. Cyprus is among six nations expected to join the EU in the next round of expansion; however, many fear that if a settlement is not reached before Cyprus becomes an EU member, the island will remain forever divided.

WE CAN WORK IT OUT. Hope for cooperation faded further in late 1997 when the Republic of Cyprus placed an order for a shipment of **S-300 missiles** from Russia. Both the Turkish government and the Turkish Cypriot government threatened that the delivery of these weapons would prompt an immediate increase in the Turkish military presence on the island. The missiles were deployed to Crete instead. In the past few years, negotiations to resolve the missile situation have progressed in fits and starts with periodic UN involvement, including the mediation efforts of the current US Ambassador to the UN, **Richard Holbrooke.** 2002 saw the most promising attempts to date to negotiate a settlement, including six months of intensive talks between Clerides and Denktaş. However, no resolution has been reached, and all parties are under increasing pressure to find an amicable solution as the country's entrance into the EU creeps nearer.

CYPRIOT SPECIAL EVENTS

Cypriots observe not only Greece's holidays (see p. 22) but their own regional and local festivities as well. Below are a few of the most significant:

Dec. 26: Boxing Day, the day after Christmas. Cypriots still celebrate this throwback to the days of British colonization.

Mar. 10, 2003: Green Monday, the beginning of Lent. In areas of more strict observance, this day initiates seven meatless weeks of Lenten fasting.

Apr. 1: Greek Cypriot National Day, commemorating the creation of the Republic.

June 16, 2003: Kataklismos, or Flood Festivals. Across Cyprus, **Pentecost** marks the beginning of days of feasting and celebration, remembering Noah's deliverance from the Flood and paying homage to Aphrodite.

Oct. 1: Cyprus Independence Day.

ESSENTIALS

GETTING THERE

Cyprus lies 64km from Turkey, 160km from Israel and Lebanon, and 480km from the nearest Greek island. **The Republic of Cyprus** (southern Cyprus) is accessible from Greece and other European and Middle Eastern countries by airplane or ferry. There are two international airports, in **Larnaka** (p. 569) and **Paphos** (p. 583); see the **Transportation** section for each city for more information on fares and

ENTRANCE REQUIREMENTS. Tourists with valid passports from Australia, Canada, Great Britain, Ireland, New Zealand, and the US do not need a **visa** to enter Southern Cyprus for stays of up to 90 days; South Africans can stay without visas for up to 30 days. Tourists wishing to stay longer should probably leave Cyprus and reenter.

YOU CAN'T GET THERE FROM HERE. Southern Cyprus is not accessible from northern Cyprus, nor is northern Cyprus accessible from southern Cyprus. If your travels originate in North Cyprus and you have a Turkish stamp in your passport, you can *never* enter the south. The quickest way to get to the south from the north is to fly somewhere else first, then hop a plane to southern Cyprus. To get to there without flying you must take a detour: catch a ferry to **Taşucu,** Turkey, a bus to **Marmaris,** a ferry to **Rhodes,** and on to southern Cyprus by plane (2 days). Ask the Turkish authorities not to stamp your passport: a **Taşucu** stamp reveals that you've been to North Cyprus.

routes. Cyprus is accessible by plane on **Olympic Airlines** (US ☎800-223-1226; Cyprus ☎24 627 950; www.olympic-airways.gr), **Cyprus Airways** (US ☎212-714-2190; Cyprus ☎22 443 054; www.cyprusair.com.cy), and many other major airlines. Roundtrip fares from Athens to Larnaka cost about US$145 (for more information on finding flights, see **Essentials,** p. 47).

CONSULATES AND EMBASSIES

CYPRIOT EMBASSIES

Australia: 30 Beale Cir., Deakin, Canberra, ACT 2600 (☎6281 0832; fax 2810 860).

Canada: 365 Bloor St. E., Suite 1010, Box #43, Toronto, ON M4W 3L4 (☎416-944-0998; fax 944-9149).

Greece: 16 Herodotou, Athens (☎210 723 2727; fax 210 453 6373).

UK: 93 Park St., London W1Y 4ET (☎0171 499 82 72 or 4; fax 491 06 91).

US: 2211 R St. NW, Washington, D.C. 20008 (☎202-462-5772; fax 483-6710).

FOREIGN EMBASSIES IN CYPRUS (LEFKOSIA)

Australia: High Commission, Annis Comninis 4 (☎22 753 001; fax 22 766 486), 500m east of Pl. Eleftherias off Stasinou. Open M-F 7:30am-12pm, 12:30-3:15pm.

Canada: Th. Dervis 15 (☎22 451 630; fax 22 459 096).

Greece: Lordou Vyronos 8 (☎22 441 880; fax 22 473 990). Open M-F 9am-noon.

UK: High Commission, PO Box 1978 Alexander Pallis (☎22 861 100 or 22 861 342 or 3; fax 22 861 150). Open M and W-F 7:30am-2pm, Tu 7:30am-1pm and 2-5:30pm.

US: PO Box 4536 Metochiou and Ploutarchou, Engomi (☎22 776 400; fax 22 720 944). Open M-F 8am-5pm, except for US and Cyprus holidays.

MONEY

The main unit of currency in the Republic of Cyprus is the **pound (£),** which is divided into 100 cents. Coins come in 1, 2, 5, 10, 20, and 50 cent denominations; bank notes in denominations of £1, 5, 10, and 20. Cyprus imposes no limit on the amount of foreign currency that may be imported but amounts in excess of US$1000 should be declared on Customs form D (NR). No more than £50 in Cypriot currency may be brought into or taken out of the country. Banks are generally open M-F 8:30am-12:30pm; see the **Practical Information** section of each city for more detailed info. The prices quoted below were effective in the summer of 2002. As inflation and exchange rates fluctuate, present prices may differ by as much as 30%. (For information on traveler's checks, ATMs, credit cards, and other financial matters, see **Money,** p. 29).

CYPRUS POUND (£)

US$1 = £0.57	**£1 = US$1.75**
CDN$1 = £0.37	**£1 = CDN$2.73**
UK£1 = £0.90	**£1 = UK£1.11**
AUS$1 = £0.31	**£1 = AUS$3.19**
NZ$1 = £0.28	**£1 = NZ$3.64**
EUR€1 = £0.58	**£1 = EUR€1.74**
TL1,000,000 = £0.35	**£1 = TL2,885,391**

GETTING AROUND

A reliable highway system serves much of Cyprus, but take caution on the winding mountain roads. **Cars** drive on the left side of the road; be prepared for British rotaries. Almost all Cypriot rental cars have manual transmission and standardized rates: the cheapest compact cars should cost £18 per day, small **motorbikes** £5, and larger motorcycles £7-8. Cypriot law requires that seatbelts be worn in front seats of cars, and an **international driver's license** or a **national driver's license** from your home country is required. A temporary Cypriot driver's license, good for six months, can be obtained from district police stations with a photo ID and £3.

There is one island-wide **bus schedule** available at tourist offices. This schedule provides all necessary information, including prices for buses and private taxi service. Bus service is less frequent in winter and is less dependable in rural areas of Cyprus. Buses run between all major cities except **Paphos,** which requires a connection in Limassol in order to reach Larnaka or Lefkosia. **Service taxis** are the most reliable form of transportation on Cyprus and are quite affordable; each taxi seats 4-7 passengers. Alternatively, **private taxis** provide a reasonable alternative. Hitchhiking is uncommon, and neither locals nor tourists are likely to offer rides. Limited bus service is available to the **Troodos Mountains.** See the **Getting There, Getting Around,** and **Practical Information** for each town or city for more information.

PRACTICAL INFORMATION

☎ **199** for ambulance, fire, or police; ☎ **112** if calling from a cell phone. ☎ **192** for queries about domestic telephone numbers; ☎ **194** for international queries.

MAIL. Post offices are open Monday through Friday from 7:30am to 1:30pm. Some have afternoon hours (4-6pm) and Saturday hours (8:30-10:30am). Poste Restante (see **Keeping in Touch,** p. 44) is available in Lefkosia, Larnaka, Paphos, and Limassol. **Airmail** is available and takes 3-4 days to travel to Europe. Faster, more expensive, courier services are also available. The cost of sending a 20g letter varies by destination: to **Europe** and **Middle East,** 31¢; **US, Australia, New Zealand** and **South Africa** 71¢. Sending a **postcard** costs 26¢ to each of the above destinations.

PHONE. Southern Cyprus has fairly reliable telephone service (administered by **CYTA**). Direct overseas calls can be made from all public phones, but you need a **phone card** to activate them even if you plan to use your own service provider. Cards are available in £3 or £5 denominations and are sold at banks and kiosks. Private phones in hotels may have a 10% surcharge. For instructions on how to call in and out of Cyprus, see **Keeping in Touch,** p. 44.

PHONE HOME	The country code for Cyprus is **357.** The international access code for Cyprus is **080.**

ACCOMMODATIONS. In general, off-season prices (Oct.-May) are about 20% lower than the high-season rates quoted in this book. Lefkosia, Paphos, and Larnaka all have HI youth hostels; expect hostels to be clean, if a bit run down, with free showers, kitchens, and common rooms. Although Cyprus has few formal campgrounds and camping in unmarked areas is illegal, some travelers still sleep on beaches and in forests. Women should not camp alone. It is generally a good idea to make reservations in advance; the Cyprus Tourism Organization (p. 568) can help travelers find rooms. For more information on **Accommodations,** see p. 41.

TIPS FOR TRAVELERS. Getting around in Cyprus is like traveling in Greece: most Cypriots speak English, and the country's main industry is tourism. There are a few additional things to be aware of when visiting this divided island. Picture taking is forbidden at the top of Mt. Olympus and at the Green Line in Lefkosia (p. 593). **Women** may feel uncomfortable traveling alone in certain urban areas; don't hesitate to go to the police if you feel you are in danger, as police take the harassment of women very seriously in Cyprus. It was only a few years ago that homosexuality was legalized in Cyprus, but **gay and lesbian travelers** shouldn't have any trouble getting around the country. A few stares and comments may be thrown your way, but as with any form of hassling, ignore it and keep moving. In general, Cypriots are known for their hospitality and truly enjoy showing travelers around their country. For more information on **Specific Concerns,** see p. 60. **Tipping** is customary in restaurants and some hotels, but *not* for taxis.

CTO OFFICES. Tourist offices in Cyprus are extremely helpful and efficient. There are offices in Limassol, Lefkosia, Larnaka, Paphos, Polis, Agia Napa, and Platres. The main office is the **Cyprus Tourism Organization (CTO),** Aristo Kyprou 11, Lefkosia 1011 (☎22 674 264; cytour@cto.org.cy). The CTO offices provide free maps and info on buses, museums, and events. A particularly helpful publication available at tourist offices is *The Cyprus Traveler's Handbook* (free). Officials generally speak English, Greek, German, and French.

Greece: 36 Voukourestiou, Athens (☎210 361 0178; fax 210 364 4798).

UK: 17 Hanover St., London W1S 14P(☎0171 569 8800; fax 499 4935; ctolon@cto-lon.demon.co.uk).

US: 13 E. 40th St., New York, NY 10016 (☎212-683-5280; fax 683-5282; gocyprus@aol.com; www.cyprustourism.org).

CYPRUS

COASTAL CYPRUS

To visit coastal Cyprus is to move among reminders of an unforgettable past. Whether swimming under a pristine white chapel at Agion Anargyroi or under satellite towers at the tip of Cape Greco, dining in view of a mosque in Larnaka or dancing in view of a monastery at Agia Napa, you will feel the presence of invaders and wanderers who have passed through before.

LARNAKA Λαρνακα

Larnaka gets its name from the ancient Greek word for coffin *(larnax)*, an allusion to the final resting place of St. Lazarus in the city's central church. Tropical Larnaka (pop. 69,000) is one of the oldest continually inhabited cities in the world. Segments of the ancient city walls and aqueducts, Bronze Age temples, and the Hala Sultan Tekke Mosque—which dates back to the first Arab invasion of Cyprus in AD 647—remind visitors of the ancient past. Alongside these enduring monuments, graffiti reading *"Hellas, Enosis, EOKA"* elicits memories of the violent movement for union with Greece a few decades ago. Quieter and cleaner than Limassol, Larnaka has lately come into its own as a leisure hotspot and a convenient base for travelers.

TRANSPORTATION

Flights: (☎24 643 000). Most flights into and out of Cyprus land at the **Larnaka Airport** located (5km) west of town. **Taxis** to the center of town cost £5 and are the easiest mode of transport. **Buses #22** and **24** run from the airport to Larnaka (Su-Tu and Th-F every hr. 6:55am-4:55pm, plus 1 bus at 5:45pm in summer, W and Sa 6:45am-12:45pm; £0.50) and from Larnaka to the airport (every hr. 6:30am-5:30pm plus one bus at 7pm in summer, W and Sa 6:45am-12:30pm; £0.50).

Buses: Intercity buses leave from Leforos Athinon by the marina on the waterfront opposite Four Lanterns Hotel. Check the bus schedule on the sandwich board where the buses stop, and double-check with the bus driver, as schedules change frequently. **Intercity Buses** (☎24 643 492) go to **Lefkosia** (M-F 5 per day 6:45am-4pm, Sa 4 per day until 1pm; £1.50) and **Limassol** (M-F 4 per day 8am-4pm, Sa 3 per day until 1pm; £1.70). **EMAN** (☎23 721 321) buses go to **Agia Napa** (M-Sa 9 per day 8:30am-5:30pm, Su 4 per day until 4:30pm; £1. Reduced schedule in the winter). **Larnaka Buses Ltd.** (☎24 657 466) bus # 6 or 7 leaves Pl. Lazarus and stops at **Ag. Helenis, Artemidos, Meneou,** and **Kiti** (13 per day M-F 6:40am-5:45pm, Sa until at 2pm, extra bus in summer M-F 7pm; £0.50).

Service Taxis: Travel & Express (☎24 661 010), main branch in Pl. Vasileos Pavlou, directly across from the CTO. All of the service taxi agencies in Larnaka have joined to form one company, Travel & Express. You might see different names on signs for taxis, such as **Kyriakos** or **Makris**–they're all the same. Taxis run to Lefkosia every 30min. 6am-7pm, Su every hr.; £2.50, Su £3. To Limassol same times; £3, £3.50.

Private Taxis: Makris' private taxi service (☎24 652 929), across from the CTO, is shamelessly expensive, but it's 24hr. **Travel & Express** (☎24 652 929, 24 655 333 or 24 652 644) also operates private taxi services, but different numbers apply to order a taxi. Standard prices for all taxis in Cyprus are £1.25 initial charge and £0.22 per km; after 8:30pm prices rise to £1.65 initial charge and £0.26 per km.

Car Rental: Phoenix Rent-A-Car, Makariou III 65 (☎24 623 407; fax 24 650 460; www.phoenix.com.cy). Prices from £15 per day. Unlimited mileage. Minimum age 25.

Moped Rental: Anemayia, Zanon Kitieos 120 (☎24 658 333 and 99 624 726; fax 24 645 571). Mopeds from £3 per day.

ORIENTATION AND PRACTICAL INFORMATION

Leoforos Athinon (a.k.a. "Palm Tree Promenade," or **Athinon**) runs along the waterfront in the heart of the tourist district and hops with various eateries and night spots. On one end of Athinon is the **Marina,** which hosts mostly foreign yachts. In front of the Marina is the **Plateia Evropi. Pl. Vasileos Pavlou** marks the city center one block in, where most practical facilities (including the post office, police station,

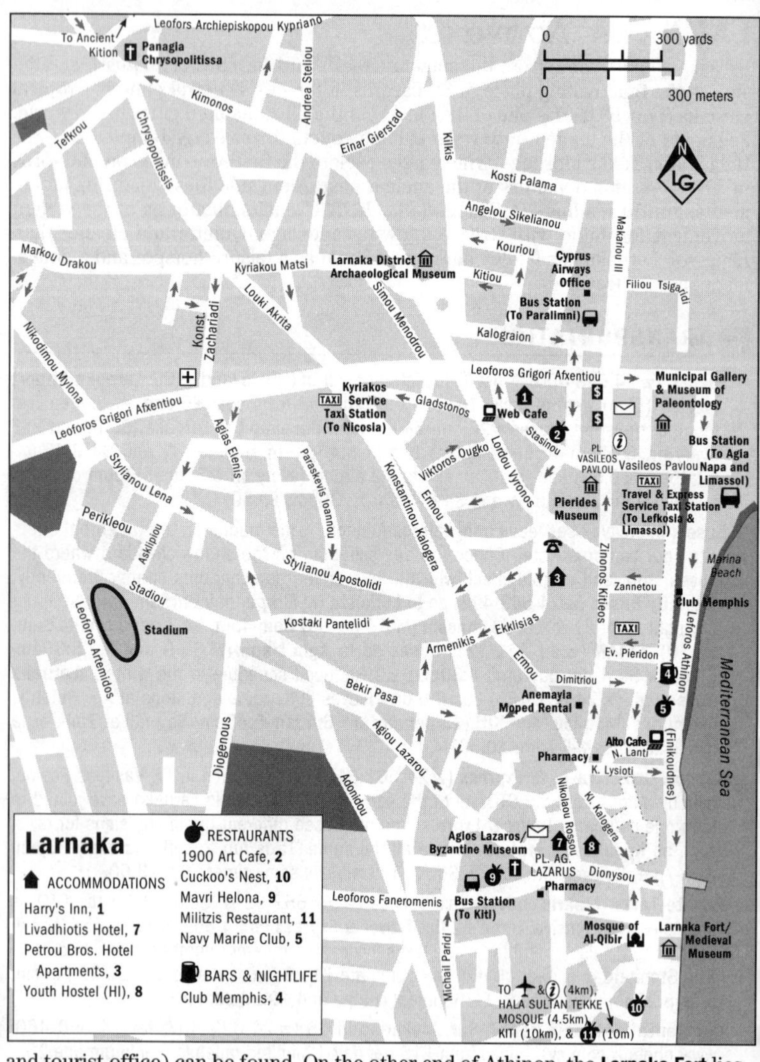

and tourist office) can be found. On the other end of Athinon, the **Larnaka Fort** lies at the juncture between Athinon and **Piyale Pasha** and between the Greek neighborhood and the old Turkish quarter.

Tourist Office: CTO (☎24 654 322), in Pl. Vasileos Pavlou. Pick up maps for all the Cypriot cities you plan to visit. Open winter M-F 8:15am-2:30pm and 3-6:15pm, Sa 8:15am-1:30pm. Open summer Th-Tu 8:15am-2:15pm and 4-6:30pm, Sa 8:15am-1:30pm. Spring and fall hours change, so check the schedule posted on its front door. The **Larnaka Airport Branch** (☎24 643 575) of CTO is open daily 8am-11pm.

Banks: The main branches of 3 major banks are in or near Pl. Vasileos Pavlou, across the street from the CTO. **Bank of Cyprus** (☎24 653 183), next to the AmEx office, has a 24hr. **ATM,** traveler's checks, and **currency exchange.** Open M-F 8:15am-12:30pm. **Popular Bank,** also called **Laiki** (☎24 814 340). Open M-F 8:15am-12:30pm. The **National Bank of Greece** and the **Hellenic Bank** have 24hr. **ATMs** throughout the city.

American Express: (☎24 843 333; fax 24 622 535), in the office of **Mantovani Plotin Travel,** across from the CTO. No traveler's checks or currency exchange. Money check forms available for those drawing funds from AmEx cards, but come before noon to draw funds, because Mantovani writes out its checks to local banks, which close at noon. Open M-F 8am-1pm and 2:30-5:30pm, Sa 9am-noon.

Police: (☎24 804 040), on the corner of Makariou III, 1 block north of the tourist office along Vasileos Pavlou, past the post office, in a building resembling a small fort. English spoken. Open 24hr.

Hospital: There is an old hospital in Larnaka with very few facilities and a new hospital outside of town that is modern and fully equipped. The **old hospital** (☎24 630 322) is on Grigori Afxentiou Ave; from the CTO cross the intersection and continue on Stasinou all the way. It's a long walk to the **new hospital** (☎24 27 999 or 24 28 111); take **bus #2** from Ermou (6:30am-5:30pm plus a 7pm bus in summer).

Copy/Fax Center: Rouvas Copy Center, Zinonos Pierides 9 (☎24 658 150; fax 24 626 659) makes copies and offers **fax** service. Helpful, efficient staff. Copies £0.05, color £0.40; faxes to Europe £1.20 per page, to the USA £1.70 per page.

CYTA: Z. Pierides 7-9 (☎24 640 257). Follow Lordou Vyronos toward the waterfront; the office is on the right, before Zinonos Kitieos. Open M-F 7:30am-5:30pm, W until 1:30pm, Sa until 1pm; off-season M-F 7:30am-1:30pm, Sa until 1pm. £3, £5, or £10 **phone cards** available at most kiosks. **Telecard phones** throughout the city.

Internet Access: Alto Cafe (☎24 659 625), on the corner of Grigori Afxentiou and Ougko, serves mainly as a trendy evening hangout but has several computers ready for web-surfers. £1 per hr., £1 minimum; printing free for a few pages, £0.10 for larger bulks. Open daily 10am-2am.

Post Office: Main branch, in Pl. Vas. Pavlou right behind the CTO (☎24 802 406). Open Sept.-June M-Tu and Th-F 7:30am-1:30pm and 4-6pm, W morning hours only, Sa 8:30-10:30am; July-Aug. M-Tu and Th-F 7:30am-1:30pm and 3-6pm, W morning hours only, Sa 8:30-10:30am. **Postal code:** 6900. **Pl. Ag. Lazarus branch** (☎24 630 182) open all year M-F 7:30am-1:30pm, also Th 3-6pm. **Postal code:** 6902.

ACCOMMODATIONS

While Larnaka is less expensive than neighboring Agia Napa, rooms are just as scarce in summer. Pricey resort hotels line the waterfront, but cheaper options can be found a few blocks inland. Prices tend to be £8-11 less in winter. For those staying in the area for more than five days, Larnaka is a good base. Flats can cost £5-10 less per person for longer stays.

Harry's Inn, Thermopylon 2 (☎24 654 453), near the tourist office. This small and cheery hotel offers clean, dim rooms and a lobby presided over by cats. Breakfast included. Singles £10; doubles £16. ❷

Youth Hostel (HI), Nikolaou Rossou 27 (☎24 621 188), near Pl. Ag. Lazarus, across the street from the Livadhiotis Hotel. The hostel is a bit dim but decently clean and efficiently run. Housed in the living quarters of a former mosque, the hostel contains 3 large rooms (female, male, coed) with at least 10 beds each, 1 room for a family, 3 full baths, and a kitchen with fridge, stove, sinks, dishware. No luggage storage, but there is a safe for valuables. Sheets £1. The hostel, but not the front desk, is open 24hr.; guests can sign in anytime. Private space may be available in the low season, but in high season it is advisable to call in advance to reserve a bed. Dorms £4 per person. ❶

Petrou Bros. Hotel Apartments, Armenikis Ekklisias 1 (☎24 650 600; fax 24 655 122; www.petrou.com.cy), 2 blocks from the waterfront. Follow Lordou Vyronos toward the waterfront; the hotel is at the corner of Ekklisias and Zinonos Pierides. Bright, modern, spacious flats with baths, phones, kitchens, and balconies. A/C available for an extra fee, as is Internet access and laundry service. Breakfast £1.50. 24hr. reception. Doubles £25; quads £35; 6-person suite £45; off-season 40% less. Cheaper prices arranged for stays two weeks and longer; mention *Let's Go* for a 10-15% discount. ❹

Livadhiotis Hotel Apartments, Nikolaou Rossou 50 (☎24 626 222; fax 24 626 406; livadhiotishotapts@cytanet.com.cy), directly across from the youth hostel, next to Pl. Ag. Lazarus. Quiet rooms within easy reach of Athinon. Private baths, TVs, fridges, and A/C; some rooms have balconies. Doubles £20; quads £22; suites (six people and up) £36. Up to 30% cheaper in winter. ❸

FOOD

Most of Larnaka's tavernas and bars are on the waterfront, where endless rows of umbrellas shelter diners from the sun. In the evening, watch young locals watch each other on Athinon. Quieter restaurants are located on Piyale Pasha.

Cuckoo's Nest, 10 Piyale Pasha (☎24 628 133). About a block away from Larnaka's Fort on Piyale Pasha; don't blink or you'll miss it. The owner, a Greek Cypriot, preserves the Greek feel with native dishes and entertaining anecdotes. Try the popular *mezedes* for 2 (£10), steak (£2.50), or the fish & chips (£3-5). Open daily 5pm-late. ❷

Navy Marine Club, Athinon 100 (☎24 627 174). Good traditional Greek food in ample portions, served before an unmatched ocean view. Open 9:15am-1am. ❷

1900 Art Cafe, Stasinou 6 (☎24 653 027), down the street from the tourist office. Van Goghs dot the walls and international music wafts out onto the balcony, where patrons sip carafes of local wine (£3-6) and coffee (£1). Serves some of the only vegetarian dishes available in the city. Most main dishes £4. Open daily 6pm-late. ❷

Mavri Helona (Black Turtle), Mehmet Ali 11 (☎24 650 661), on a small side street by the church of Ag. Lazarus. A welcoming and boisterous crowd of musicians and assorted locals carouse. Most come for the nightly live music rather than the cuisine, but no one goes hungry as *mezedes* (£7) and kebabs (£2.50) delight. ❸

Militzis Restaurant, Piyale Pasha 42 (☎24 655 867), 1 block south of Larnaka Fort on the seafront. Catch some cool sea breezes on even the most sweltering of days and relish the captivating view, spacious veranda, and excellent food. Three large clay ovens create *psita,* cooking up an assortment of fresh meat (£4) and lamb dishes (£4.25). Local wines £3-6. Open daily 12:30pm-midnight. ❷

SIGHTS

The city's major historical sights are all within walking distance of each other. The CTO offers **free walking tours,** including "Larnaka Old & New," (W 10am) beginning at the CTO (☎24 654 322) and "Skala—Its Craftsmen," (F 10am) from Larnaka Fort (☎24 630 576).

CHURCH OF AGIOS LAZARUS. This beautifully adorned 9th-century church rests on the tomb of Lazarus, a dim, low-ceilinged room often filled with incense. Legend holds that Lazarus journeyed to Cyprus after rising from the dead and became the island's first bishop, living in Kition for 30 years before dying again, and believers heap offerings on the coffin and kiss the icons in the Orthodox tradition. The church is one of the most important Orthodox pilgrimage sites, especially on the Saturday of Lazarus during Lent. Its belfry, built in the Byzantine style, was added in 1857. *(Take the first left north of the Larnaka Fort. Dress modestly: long skirts for women, pants for men, no bare shoulders. Wrap skirts provided at the door for those who are forgetful. Open 8am-12:30pm and 3:30-6:30pm in summer; in winter same morning hours and afternoon 2:30-5:30pm. Non-Orthodox visitors may attend services (8am) but should not take communion. Museum ☎24 652 498. £0.50.)*

PIERIDES FOUNDATION MUSEUM. This private museum was the home of Demetrios Pierides (1811-1895), a collector of Cypriot artifacts; his descendants still occupy the top floor of the house. Bronze Age ceramics, Roman blown glass from 54 BC, Cypriot folk wood carvings and silverware, and stone sculptures from the temple of Kition fill the rooms. The walls in the main hallway are covered in some of the earliest maps of the island. Cypriot crafts, costumes, and furnishings are also on display. *(Zinonos Kitieos 4, diagonal from the CTO. ☎24 652 495. Open M-Th 9am-4pm, F-Sa 9am-1pm, Su 11am-3pm. £1.)*

LARNAKA FORT. Built by Venetians to protect Larnaka harbor in the 15th century and rebuilt by Ottomans in 1625, the small fort served as a prison during the British occupation (1878-1959). Climb the wall for a panoramic view of the surrounding town, and peer through the same slits that the Venetians used to gaze anxiously at the sea. In summer municipal plays are put on in the refreshingly cool courtyard. There is a small museum right below the wall. Ask the guard for information on the history of the fort. *(At the southern end of Athinon and a block east of Pl. Agiou Lazarou. ☎24 630 576. Open M-F 8am-5pm, summer until 7pm. £0.75.)*

KITION. Now underground, the temple complex of the ancient city forms the substratum of Larnaka. It was settled in the early 13th century BC by refugees from the Peloponnese. The four main small temples at the site were damaged in 4th-century BC wars with the Phoenicians and Egyptians, and were later leveled by earthquake and fire in 280 BC. Part of the ancient Cyclopean wall and the **Temple of Astarte,** the Phoenician God of fertility, still remain. *(The entrance to the site is hard to find; watch small street signs carefully when following directions. About a 20min. walk from Athinon in Larnaka; going on a moped may be a better option. Walk north from the archaeological museum on Kilkis with the museum on your left. Turn left on Leontious Machaira, and left again on Ioanni Paskirati; entrance is at the end of the road. Open M-F 9am-2:30pm.)*

TORNARITIS-PIERIDES MUSEUM OF PALEONTOLOGY AND MUNICIPAL GALLERY. Five colonial-style warehouses house the Paleontology Museum and Municipal Gallery. The Paleontology Museum is two rooms filled with wood, fossilized fish, and the bones of pygmy elephants and hippopotami who once mysteriously migrated to Cyprus. Pieces date back over 490 million years to the Cambrian period. The Municipal Gallery's small but impressive set of modern abstract works and rotated featured collections address Cypriot politics and culture. Each month brings a different exhibit; the CTO has info on exhibit listings. The curator is eager to expound on the art and to refer aesthetes to private galleries throughout the island. *(Pl. Evropis, in the old customs warehouse at the end of Athinon opposite the Marina. Call a day in advance to arrange a tour. Gallery ☎24 628 587, Paleontology ☎24 658 848. Open Tu-F 10am-1pm and 5-7pm, Sa-Su 10am-1pm; off-season daily 4-6pm. Free.)*

OTHER SIGHTS. The **Larnaka District Archaeological Museum** has two main rooms, one dedicated to ceramic artifacts from the prehistoric period to the middle Bronze Age, and the other full of findings from ancient Kition. *(Follow the signs and head west on Leoforos Grigori Afxentiou; turn right on Klimonos. It's at the intersection of Kilkis and Klimonos. ☎24 630 169. Open M-F 9am-2:30pm. £0.75, Cypriot citizens free.)* Muslims still use the medieval **Mosque of Al-Qibir** as a place of worship. *(Across the street from the Larnaka Fort.)*

NIGHTLIFE AND BEACHES

The area around the **Hard Rock Cafe** shimmies with fun, teen-centered nightlife. **Stone Age Pub** (☎24 624 526), **Hard Rock Cafe** (☎24 624 292), and the **Camel** form a triangle. Walk down Athinon toward the fort and take a right onto a small footpath (officially called Watkins St.) in between the Chicago Bar and the Navy Marine Club. Join the teenage locals for a cocktail at the Stone Age (£2.50-3.50), some snacks at the Hard Rock (£2-3), or a few beers at the Camel (£1-3). **Club Memphis,** on Athinon next to the Times Cafe, hosts infamous foam parties. A dubious entrance leads to an underground throng of intense dancers moving to a range of tunes from Britney Spears to Nirvana until the wee hours of the morning. (Cover £5, one drink included. Open nightly 10pm-late.)

If you prefer your fun in the sun, check out the marina area for watersports, although you'll do better to explore beaches out of town. Pretty, less-crowded white sand **beaches** are situated to the northeast, on the way to Agia Napa (EMAN buses 8:30am-5pm, £1). You can also try a **Larnaka-Napa Sea Cruise** day trip organized by a private company; see **Mr. Karotsakis,** who oversees watersports and sea cruises. (☎24 656 949; larnaka.napa.sea.cruises@cytanet.com.cy.) Otherwise, you're left with the bustling beach—a dismal mixture of packed dirt and cigarette butts crammed with baking vacationers.

DAYTRIPS FROM LARNAKA

HALA SULTAN TEKKE MOSQUE & PANAGIA ANGELOKTISI

By moped, a trip to both sites and back to the center of Larnaca will take 3hr. Alternatively, take bus # 6 or 7 from Ag. Lazarus. Tell the driver "Tekke"; after you're dropped off, walk the paved road for 1km; pick up the same bus to proceed to Panagia Angeloktisi. Buses (£0.50) run every hr. 6:40am-7pm, Sa until 1pm. Panagia open M-F 8am-4pm, Sa 10am-4pm, Su 9am-noon. Modest dress required: long skirts for women, pants for men, no bare shoulders. Donations welcome.

The must-see Hala Sultan Tekke Mosque hangs over the edge of the Salt Lake, which dries up completely in summer. Before the lake dries, flamingoes combine with the palm trees to create a peculiarly tropical backdrop. Also called the **Tekke of Umm Haram,** it was constructed in AD 1550 during the Arab invasion of Cyprus and rebuilt in 1816 over the site where Umm Haram (Muhammed's maternal aunt) fell from a mule and broke her neck around AD 649. The mosque is one of the most sacred pilgrimage sights for Muslims after Mecca, Medina, and Jerusalem. It also houses the tomb of King Hussein's great-grandmother, who died in exile in Cyprus in 1929. Note the prevalence of the color green, symbolic of paradise in the Muslim tradition. The church "built by the angels," **Panagia Angeloktisti** lies in Kiti, a little residential village. Much of the church was built in the 11th century, atop (and incorporating) the 5th-century ruin of a prior sanctuary. A spectacular 6th-century **mosaic** in the central apse depicting the Virgin Mary with Christ is the oldest Cypriot mosaic still in its original setting. The church's narthex was built in the 14th century by the Gibelets, a Roman noble family prominent in medieval Cyprus.

STAVROVOUNI MONASTERY

Open daily 7:30am-noon and 3-5pm. No photography or video. Free. Note: women are only allowed to enter the church at the foot of the entrance, not the monastery itself. Dress modestly. No public transportation to the monastery is available; be careful driving, as the roads tend to be rocky.

Panoramic views of Cyprus's countryside, from Larnaka to Lefkosia and beyond, spread out below "Cross Mountain" monastery's 700m peak, which is just 40km outside Larnaka. This 4th-century monastery was founded by Constantine the Great's mom and Saint Helen—the woman responsible for his conversion. Stavrovouni was erected atop the ruins of an ancient temple dedicated to Aphrodite. On the way home from Jerusalem, Helen is said to have left a fragment of the True Cross there, following a dream's instructions. Despite adhering to a strict regimen, the devout monks find the time to be eminent icon painters and produce some of the island's best honey and cheese. At the foot of the rocky cliff is the small 18th-century monastery of Agia Varvara, also noted for its monks' icon painting. Ask one of the helpful guides to tell you the story of the founding of the monastery.

LEFKARA

Take the Lefkara bus from Pl. Ag. Lazarus (1 per day M-Sa 1pm, returns to Larnaka 7am.) The bus goes to Pano Lefkara and Kato Lefkara; get off at Pano Lefkara.

The narrow stone streets of Lefkara hearken back to an older Cyprus. Tour a restored 400-year-old Cypriot home at **Jacki's Art Studio** in the Greek section, visit the famous 11th century church of **Timo Stavron,** and hike the 3km trail to the **Chapel of the Transfiguration,** where there is a 360° view of the surrounding area (ask at the village for directions, or pick up a trail map at the CTO). If you are traveling by bus, the trip requires an overnight stay; spend it at the **Hotel Agora ❹,** where you can watch swallows dive to drink from the swimming pool in the sunny courtyard. (☎24 342 901. Singles £24; doubles £32.)

DHERYNIA & CAPE GRECO

By car, these two destinations are a pleasant day or overnight trip from Larnaka or Agia Napa. By moped or bicycle, it's best to leave from Agia Napa. There are often bike paths on busier roads; ask at the rental place. The Paralimni-Dherynia Bus Co. (☎24 821 318) in Paralimni sends a bus to Larnaka which passes through Dheryni and Frenaros. In summer, buses (£1) run 2 per day M-Sa; in winter 2 per day M-F and 3 per day Sa.

Several tourist lookouts in Dherynia, now the home of many refugees from Turkish-occupied **Famagusta** (Ammochostos) provide a view of the empty city. At the **Cultural Center for Occupied Ammochostos,** you may meet people who remember being forced out of their city in 1974. The UN has declared Famagusta a closed area, and no one is allowed in or out. Virtually a ghost town, the hotels loom desolate and trees overgrow streets frozen in time. At night the coastline is pitch black, except for four lights in the distance from military station points.

East of Agia Napa on **Kyrou Nerou,** resort hotels give way to an empty coast preserved as Kavo Greco National Forest. Several rough surface roads connect mainland Cyprus to the sea; the mostly unmarked hiking trail, 8km from town, leads to **Cape Greco,** a solitary—and breathtaking—communion with Cyprus's southeast coast. Maps of hiking trails can be obtained from the **CTO** and are quite helpful. Alternatively, follow the signs for Cape Greco by car, moped, or bike and pick up the trail anywhere along the coast. The cape has remained undeveloped because of a military radar installation, giving aspiring secret agents the chance to swim beneath two space-age radar dishes.

On Kyrou Nerou, the main road, signs point to **Agiou Anargyroi,** a small church that stands in splendid isolation over the sea. Next to the church, stairs descend to **sea caves** large enough to wander inside—a flashlight is helpful. The church commemorates two saints who lived in the cave. For a sandy beach, head further up the coast to Konnoi Beach, where local families relax on the weekend. A few hotels can be found here; try **Konnos Bay Apartments ❹,** Kavo Groko-Paralimni Rd. (☎24 831 632), just above the beach. Many rooms have spectacular views of the sea. Doubles £26-33.

FROM THE ROAD

HIGHWAY TO HEAVEN

There is nothing quite like driving to a remote Cypriot monastery to put one in a religious frame of mind. The road hazards are many and almost ingeniously varied, and if one's car inspires no more confidence than my tiny, white, diesel hatchback did (with its slightly bald tires and the puzzling discrepancy between the maker's marks on the steering wheel and on the body—Hyundai the former, Toyota the latter), the danger only seems more vivid.

The drive from tiny Pano Lafkara to Stavrovouni Monastery was a particular test of my mettle and of my faith. I began badly, by taking a wrong turn out of Lefkara's rat-maze of tiny, one-way streets. Still, I thought my chances were probably better being on the road to some unknown village. At least on the highway, matrons sitting in the doorways of their houses on both sides of the street would not be in constant danger of having their lace-work brushed from their laps by my sideview mirrors. So I took to the relatively open road, zig-zagging around mountains with aplomb, until I was dealt a fresh blow: the paved road that I had been following so trustingly turned suddenly to a dirt track. Bulldozers snoozed on the hill above to the right, as if to coyly suggest the possibility of improvements.

So I turned around. Lefkara's matrons were perhaps the better option. Halfway there I changed my mind again, feeling suitably absurd, and drove back over the stretch of road like a pro. When the paved road

AGIA NAPA ΑγιαΝαπα

Thirty years ago, most tourists flocked to **Famagusta,** 16km to the north, allowing Agia Napa's ruined monastery and white sandy beaches to lie peacefully vacant. When Turkish forces occupied Famagusta in 1974, Agia Napa was transformed almost overnight into a glitzy, brassy tourist resort. By day, colorful beach umbrellas shelter young visitors on the sand; by night, the sounds of American hip-hop and revving motorbikes fill the air. Through it all, the courtyard of the town's monastery remains miraculously quiet.

ORIENTATION AND PRACTICAL INFORMATION. EMAN Travel and Tours, Makarios 32a (☎24 721 321; fax 24 722 190; www.emantravel.com) can book flights, organize tours, and provide bus tickets and schedules. **Buses** run to: **Agia Napa, Protaras,** and **Paralimni** (M-Sa every hr. 9am-8pm, Su every hr. 9am-8pm; £0.50); **Larnaka** (M-Sa every 30min. 8am-5:30pm, Su 9am-4:30pm; £1.20); **Nicosia** (M-Sa 8am, £2); and **Paralimni** via **Protaras** (M-Sa 20 per day 9am-8pm, Su 5 per day 9am-6pm; in winter M-Sa 8 per day 9am-5pm; £0.50). Expensive but effective **Agia Napa Taxi** (☎99 404 704 at night, 99 402 350 during the day), across the street from the monastery on Makarios, offers 24hr. service and negotiable rates. **Bikes and mopeds** are ideal transportation in Agia Napa. To reach **Ham-Yam's Car, Motorcycle & Bicycle Rentals,** take a right on Nissi from Makarios. Daily scooter rentals start at £7.50. (☎24 721 825. Open daily 8am-8pm, off-season and Su closes at 1pm.)

Trying to navigate Agia Napa by addresses and street signs is an exercise in futility. Instead, establish landmarks using a map. The town centers on the **Agia Napa Monastery** and the bar and taverna-laden streets that wind up the hill from it to the plateia. **Makarios,** the main road, leads straight down to the harbor, where quieter restaurants and bars can be found. Uphill, Makarios becomes **Dimokratias,** which leads north to Paralimni. Toward the sea, **Leoforos Nissi** heads west of Makarios to Larnaka and Nissi beach. A free **map** will help; get one from the **CTO,** Kyrou Nyrou 12, just off Makarios. (☎24 721 796. Open 8:30am-2:15pm with afternoon hours 3:15-6pm M and Th.) **Bank Kaiki,** across from the cyber cafe on Dionysiou Solomou, has a 24hr. **ATM.** For **Internet access** head to **Intercity.** (☎24 722 233. Open 24 hr. £2.20 per hr.) The **police** (☎24 803 200) are north of town on the road to Paralimni. The closest **hospital** (☎24 821 211) is 7 km north in Paralimni. The **post office** is at D. Liperti 1A. (☎24 721 550. Open M-F 7:30am-1:30pm, Th 3-6pm, Sa 8:30-10:30am.) **Postal code:** 5330.

ACCOMMODATIONS AND FOOD. Inexpensive rooms are always elusive in Agia Napa, and in August they're nearly nonexistent—many tour groups book entire hotels so **call ahead** for reservations. To get to **Paul Marie Hotel Apartments ❹**, take Dimokratias all the way out to the road to Paralimini; the hotel is just before the turn. The spot offers currency exchange, a pool table, two bars, a rooftop pool, and 24hr. service. Rooms are clean and spacious, with fridges, A/C, and balconies. (☎24 722 481; fax 24 722 706. Studio £26; 1 bedroom £34.) More convenient to the plateia, **Chrissipos Hotel Apartments ❸** has spacious, decently clean rooms with balconies; ask to be located away from the pool unless you enjoy music blasting below your window long into the night. (Singles £16; doubles £28.) The **Leros Hotel ❹**, clean and quiet with ocean views, is located on Makarios near the harbor. (☎24 721 126; fax 24 721 127. Breakfast included. Call ahead for reservations. Singles £17.50; doubles £28.)

Good, cheap food is also hard to find in Agia Napa: try the supermarkets and 24hr. takeout shops, which serve the same food as restaurants at cheaper prices. **Esperia,** at the end of Makarios, has a patio with a lovely harbor view. (☎24 721 635. Entrees £6-11. Open 8am-1am.) **Napa House Restaurant Taverna ❷**, Dimokratias 4, on the road up to Paralimni on your right, serves decent American dishes laced with a Greek touch. (☎24 722 174. Main dishes £3-6. Local wines £5-7. Open 2pm-midnight.) The **Kebab House ❶**, D. Solomou, near Napa House, offers the cheapest and tastiest take-out in town. (☎24 723 757. Vegetarian dish £1.60, gyro plate £2. Open 11am-1am.) **Jasmin's Inn ❷**, D. Solomou 1, provides variety, large portions, and entertainment. The fearsome "Viagra cocktail" (£5 for 2 people; £10 for 4) stimulates table-top dancing and karaoke after 11pm. (☎24 721 731. Open daily 8am-2am, closed in the off season. Main dishes £3-5.)

SIGHTS. Amid the frenzied pace of the town, the 16th-century Venetian **Monastery of Agia Napa** stands as a tranquil reminder of the town's Christian roots. Just outside the walls a 600-year-old sycamore tree spreads its thick branches to encompass shade-seekers. Cypress and olive trees shade the courtyard. In the small chapel, a few icons hang, and the well of the **Miracle of Panagia**—the inspiration for the monastery—rests in the corner, small and un-ornamented. According to Christian belief, the Virgin Mary appeared here to save a group of Christians from pirate attacks. Destitute and dehydrated, the Christians would likely have perished had not the Virgin Mary directed them to the corner spring. (Open daily

ended again, the bargain-making with God began. I felt every protruding stone I failed to skirt as acutely as it struck me, rather than the car, in the underbelly, and I tried to cushion the tires from impact by sheer force of will and wishing.

But just as self-doubt started to set in, something miraculous happened: asphalt appeared on the horizon. It was then that I learned the first of many valuable lessons about mountain driving: it's the middle of the road, not the end, that's unpaved, as that's where the long arm of no municipality will reach to make improvements.

Driving the paved road up the mountain seemed like child's play, and I wasn't of a mind to complain that my car couldn't manage more than 30km/hr. I even created a few thrills for myself by wondering what I could possibly do if I ran out of gas. All in all, I was suitably reverent when I reached the monastery. If I was a hermit, Stavrouni is the place where I would likely take up residence, if not for the spectacular view, then to postpone the onerous trip back down.

—Emily Ogden

9am-10pm. Greek Orthodox services no longer performed in the monastery. Anglican services Su 11am; Catholic services Su 5pm.)

NIGHTLIFE. Agia Napa's thriving nightlife is the major draw for visitors and sets the pace of the city. After sundown, people gather near the plateia to sample drink specials at such pubs as **Volcano** (☎24 721 049), **Minos,** and **Mariella.** Around 10pm, DJs and club dancers begin coaxing the crowds to their feet, and at 1am or so, the party moves to dance clubs like **Gas,** on Makariou, which can cram 2000 people into its cavernous interior, and **Rise,** further up Makariou, which plays techno classics and house. Open 1-4am. While the pubs have no cover, the clubs often charge £5 (£3 or less with the flyer handed out in the plateia); women may get a break on the cover.

LIMASSOL Λεμεσος

This bustling port city is Cyprus's industrial center. Huge cargo ships anchor almost within swimming distance of the city's long, stony beach, which is separated from the noisy streets by a shady park where locals picnic on Saturdays. Quieter, sandier beaches lie to the north and south within 10km. Limassol also provides a base for exploring the famous ruins of Kourion and the ruined castles which testify to the sway the Knights Templar and the Hospitalliers had over the area in the time of the Crusades.

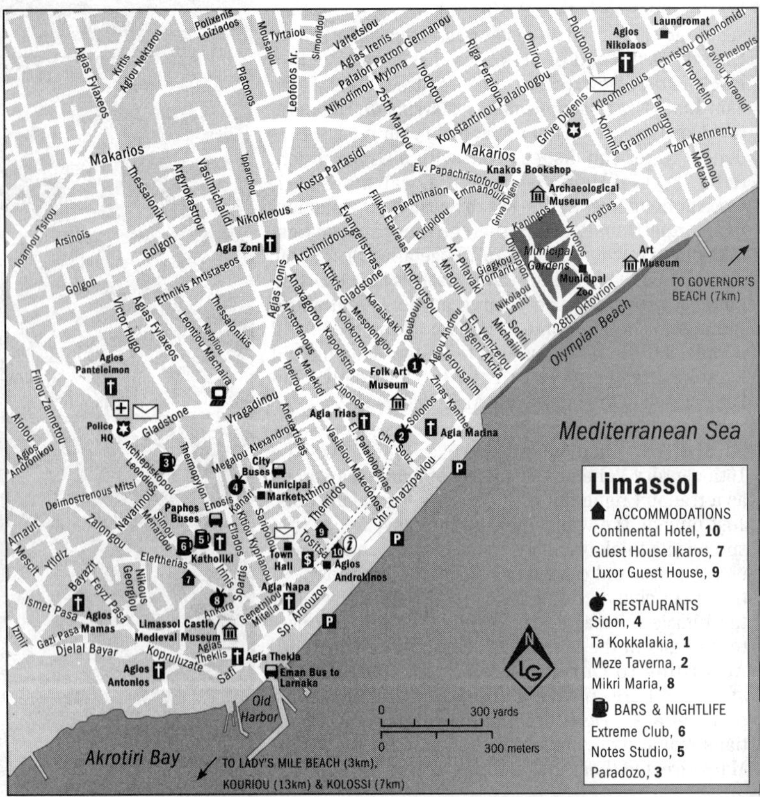

TRANSPORTATION

Most intra-Limassol buses run up and down the main sea-side road and come every ten minutes; buses stop all along the road and can drop you off anywhere. **Bus #1** runs to the port from the station near the Anexartisias market, and **bus #30** runs from the **new port** to downtown Limassol (every 10min., Sa every 30min., £0.35). For more information on intracity bus schedules, call ☎25 370 592.

Buses: Check times with the CTO. **Intercity Buses** (☎26 643 492) and **Nea Amoroza Bus Service** (☎26 936 822) both go to **Lefkosia.** Both depart from the Old Port on the seafront road (6 per day M-F 6am-6pm, Sa 7am, noon; £1.50.) **Intercity** also goes to **Larnaka** (4 per day M-F 8am-4pm, Sa 3 per day; £1.70). Nea Amorza goes to **Paphos** (M-Sa 9:30am, £2) from the Old Port; **Alepa** (☎99 625 027) buses to Paphos (M, T, Th, F 5pm and W, Sa 2pm) leave from the Panikos kiosk on the seafront. To reach the **Troodos Mountains,** contact **Travel & Express,** Thessalonikis 21 (☎25 362 061), which serves **Platres** (6 per week; M-Sa 11:15am, return 7am; £2). Buses to **Polis** are via Paphos; buses to **Agia Napa, Paralimni,** and **Protaras** are via Larnaka. The **Episkopi Village** and **Kourion archaeological site bus** stops at the Limassol Castle (every hr. 9am-1pm; returns 11:50am, 2:50, 4:50pm.; £0.80).

Service Taxis: Run 6am-6:30pm to **Lefkosia** (£3.50), **Larnaka** (£3), and **Paphos** (£2.75). Contact **Travel and Express** (☎25 364 114). Free port pickup.

Private Taxis: New Faithful Taxis (☎25 354 444).

Bike and Moped Rentals: Agencies cluster on the shore road, near the luxury hotels. Try **MikeMar** on Ag. Georgiou A, next to Pizza Hut (☎25 327 611; open M-F 8:30am-7pm, Sa 8:30am-1pm). £10 for a 50cc scooter, £3 for a mountain bike. For longer rentals, you'll find lower rates in Polis.

ORIENTATION AND PRACTICAL INFORMATION

Centrally located on the south coast, Limassol is a maximum of 2hr. from the other major cities of Cyprus. The **Castle and Medieval Museum** are situated at the **Old Port;** from there, palm-lined **Sp. Araouzou** runs along the sea. **Agiou Araouzou,** the pedestrian street, is parallel to Sp. Araouzou one block away from the coast. Restaurants, hotels, and tourist facilities are concentrated on these streets. Six kilometers east of the town center, a row of resort hotels lines the waterfront.

Tourist Office: CTO, Spiro Araouzos 115a (☎25 362 756; fax 25 746 596), on the waterfront 1 block east of the old port along the main beach road. Open M, T, Th, F 8:15am-2:30pm and 3-6:15pm, W 8:15am-2:30pm, Sa 8:15am-1:30pm. Office at the **New Port** (☎25 571 868) opens immediately following arrivals. Another office in **Dassoudi Beach,** Yermassoyias 35 (☎25 323 211), opposite the Park Beach Hotel and a few houses down (open same hours as Limassol office except closed Sa).

Tourist Agencies: Salamis Tours (☎25 860 000; www.salamis-tours.com), 28 Octovriou, offers package tours, ferry and airplane tickets, and cruises. Open M-Sa 8am-1pm and 3-6pm.

Banks: All 3 major banks are in the town center around Agia Napa church. Open M-F 8:15am-12:30pm with 24hr. **ATM** service. **Popular Bank,** one block from the Old Port CTO, has a convenient ATM for travelers waiting for the bus.

Bookstores: Kyriakos Bookshop, Panayides Building 3, Grivas Dighenis (☎25 747 555), at the roundabout near the Museum of Archaeology. The largest selection of paperbacks, dictionaries, educational books, and magazines in the city. Open M-Sa 8am-1pm, and 4-7:30pm except W and Sa.

Laundromat: Quick Service, Grive Digenis 175a (☎25 587 056), past the roundabout. Self-service or drop-off £2. Open M-F 7am-7pm, Sa 7am-3pm.

Police: (☎25 805 050), on Gladstone and Eirinis next to the hospital. Open 24hr.

Hospital: Government General Hospital, (☎25 305 777) outside of Limassol near the village Polemidia. Take the #15 bus, which stops near the Municipal Market.

CYTA: On the corner of Markos Botsaris and Athinon.

Internet Access: C&P Computer Center, 286C and 288A Agiou Andreou beyond the footpath (☎25 746 210). A bit expensive, but worth the convenience. High speed modems and the closest Internet to the center of town: £3 per hr., minimum £2. Printing available. Open M-Sa 8am-3pm. **World Explorer Net Cafe,** Gladstonos 37 (☎25 347 795), 5 blocks in from the beach front road. £2 per hr., £0.50 minimum charge. Open daily 1pm-1am.

Post Office: The main office (☎25 802 259) is next to the central police station on Gladstone. Open May-Sept. M-Tu and Th-F 7:30am-1:30pm and 4-6pm, W 7:30am-1:30pm, Sa 9-11am. Oct.-June daily 3-5pm except W. **Postal Code:** 3900.

ACCOMMODATIONS

Quirky, friendly guest houses around the town center are Limassol's budget best since the town has no youth hostel. Those craving more than the absolute basics, however, may prefer the more upscale hotels on the waterfront.

Luxor Guest House, Ag. Andreou 101 (☎25 362 265), 1 block in from the CTO and to the left on the footpath. Convenient to the town's attractions. Spartan but clean rooms. Some private baths, most shared. Full kitchen available. 2 rooms have balconies. Singles £6; doubles £12. Open year-round. ❶

Guest House Ikaros, Eleftherias 61 (☎25 354 348), off Eirinis 4 blocks from the seafront. Tapestries, fish tanks, animal skins, and a porcelain collie adorn the lobby. Spacious rooms with shared bath. Call for reservations. Singles £5; doubles £10. ❶

Continental Hotel, Spiro Araouzos 137 (☎25 362 530; fax 25 373 030), right next to the CTO on the main seaside road. Well priced for a seaside hotel; affords privacy and convenience. Private baths, phones, TVs, balconies. Breakfast included. Singles £15; doubles £25; triples £35; quads for families £40; A/C £2 extra. Discounts for children, rates decrease by £5 in winter. ❸

FOOD

There are tavernas, small kebab houses, and cafes throughout the city. The best option for the health and wealth-conscious traveler is the **Municipal Market,** in a huge warehouse on the corner of Saripolou and Kanari. A lunch of fruits, veggies, bread, and cheese costs less than £1. (Open M-F 6am-1pm.)

Meze Taverna, Ag. Androu 209 (☎25 367 333). The food at this breezy, tiled taverna is a cut above the usual fare. The chicken tandori (£5) is particularly tender and tasty. Open M-Sa 10am-11:30pm. ❷

Sidon, Saripolou 71-73 (☎25 871 614). Sample Lebanese cuisine in a beautiful setting–soft lights, open air rooms with twining flowering vines. Main dishes £5.50-12. Open Tu-Sa 7-11pm, Su by reservation only. ❸

Ta Kokkalakia, Ag. Andreou 239 (☎25 340 015), past the footpath and before the Folk Art Museum. The zebra hides aren't likely to win points with animal rights activists, but the exotic garden and bar will please even the toughest critic. Eclectic menu including ostrich steak and South African sausage, and an impressive South African wine selection. Try the Kokkalakia mixed grill, touted by the owner as a dish for the truly gutsy (and those willing to risk a heart attack). Main dishes £5-11. Open M-Sa 7pm-2am. ❸

Mikri Maria, Agkyros 3 (☎25 357 676). Endearingly unpretentious, serving exquisite food cooked over hot coals. Try the delicious grilled *lountza* and *halloumi* or the refreshing *tzatziki*. Live music in winter. Main dishes £3-5.50. Open M-Sa until 10:30pm. ❷

SIGHTS

CASTLES. The **Limassol Castle,** where Richard King of England married Queen Berengaria in 1191, was built on the site of a Byzantine fort, of which only the western wall remains. Richard gained possession of Cyprus after defeating Cypriot Isaac Commenus. In the early 14th century, the Knights Templar fortified the castle's walls and covered the Gothic windows. Later, the Knights of St. John converted the great Western Hall into a Gothic church and turned the chapel into a series of prison cells. The Ottomans claimed the castle in 1570, and the spacious West Hall was used as a prison under the British regime until 1940. Today, it is the **Cyprus Medieval Museum,** home to a scattered collection of medieval armor, stone coats of arms, and gravestones—don't miss the gravestone of the pregnant woman. *(☎25 305 419. Open M-Sa 9am-5pm, Su 10am-1pm. £1.)* The **Kolossi Castle** played a crucial role during the Crusades, when both the Knights Templar and the Knights of the Order of St. John Hospitalliers briefly made it their headquarters. The extensive ruin includes the remnants of a sugar factory built by the Hospitalliers. An excellent guidebook to the ruin with both historical and archaeological information can be purchased at the site for £1. *(9km west of Limassol; take bus #16 (every 20min., £0.40). ☎25 234 907. Open daily 9am-7:30pm. £0.75.)*

SIGHTS. The **Archaeological Museum,** on the corner of Kaningos and Vyronos, offers a collection of funerary *steles*, jewelry, statues, and terra-cotta figurines from the Greek bronze age—an impressive and informative collection worth the visit. *(☎25 305 157. Open M-F 9am-5pm and Sa 10am-1pm. £0.75.)* The attractive **Municipal Gardens,** on the waterfront between Olympion and Vyronos, are home to Cyprus's largest zoo and the **Municipal Open Air Theatre,** which hosts concerts and local theatrical performances. *(Check with the CTO for upcoming performances, and keep your eyes open around the city for posters advertising about events.)*

BEACHES. The city's long stone beach might be a little too rocky and too near the busy port for the discerning beach-goer, but a new breakwater past the town center has made the area more pleasant for swimming. **Dassoudi Beach,** 3km east of Limassol, is slightly better. *(Take bus #6 (every 15min., £0.50) from the Kanaris market.)* Further east about 7km beyond Dassoudi beach, surprisingly uncrowded **Governor's Beach** is perhaps the best bet near Limassol: sand, clean waters, and quiet. A bus leaves the Old Port at 9:50am each morning *(£2 round-trip; children under 10 free. By car, take A-1 north in the direction of Larnaka and Lefkosia and take the Governor's Beach exit.).* **Ladies Mile Beach**—so named because the wife of the British Governor of Limassol used to ride her horse along the mile-long beach—just west of the new port, is popular with locals and tourists alike. Clear blue seas preside over light grainy sand. *(Take bus #1.)* Beautiful **Kourion Beach,** which lies directly below the ruins, is long enough to hold even large weekend crowds without feeling packed. *(Outside Episkopi Village; follow the signs for Kourian (Curium) Beach.)*

FESTIVALS. Limassol hosts many special events throughout the year; pamphlets with details are available at the CTO. At summer's end, Limassol's gardens are transformed into a tribute to Dionysus for the Limassol **wine festival,** where participants fill bottles with as much of the local wine as they can guzzle. The general intoxication is enlivened by music, dance, and theater. (Admission £1.50.) From May to August, Limassol's cultural selection of activities is centered at **Kourion.** People flock from around the world for **Shakespeare Nights** at the theater of ancient Kourion. Performers from Cyprus and abroad work year-round to produce weekend shows. **Carnival,** 50 days before Orthodox Easter (usually in February), is celebrated with more vim and vigor in Limassol than anywhere else in Cyprus.

NIGHTLIFE

Local bars and cafes are sparse near the center of Limassol, but a few can be found on Ag. Andreou and near the castle. **Paradozo,** Irinis 140, is an open-air bar where you can find plenty of nooks for conversation after you battle your way through the wave of cologne and perfume. (Open 8pm-2am, weekends until 3-4am.) **Extreme Club** and **Notes Studio,** both near the castle on the corner of Eleftherias and Eirinis, fill up after 11:30pm.

Dance clubs and bars are at the edge of town in the tourist district. Taxis are probably the safest bet—just tell the taxi driver "tourist area" (£3-5). For disco dance clubs, **The Hippodrome,** on Georgiou, is the place to get down as the neighboring bars die down after 1am. Music includes popular dance hits and house, punk, R&B—you'll know it's time to break it down when the glowsticks start flashing. **The Basement Club,** a few bars down from the Hippodrome on Georgiou, hosts a diverse crew of merrymakers and is one of the last clubs to close down. Ladies can march in free of charge with a flyer.

DAYTRIP FROM LIMASSOL: KOURION

12km west of Limassol. ***Buses*** *leave Limassol Castle bound for ancient Kourion every hr. on the hr. 10am-1pm, returning at 11:50am, 2:50, and 4:50pm (£0.80). Kourion is just past Episkopi on the B-2 from Limassol. There are no signs for Kourion until you're within about 2km of the site, so a map is essential. Open year-round 8am-7:15pm. £1. Guidebook (£3) available at reception area. Handicap accessible.*

First settled during the Neolithic period, Kourion was colonized during the 14th and 13th centuries BC by Achaeans from Argos; it would become famous for its 8th-century BC **Sanctuary of Apollo Hylates** (3km west from main road; £0.75) and its 2nd-century AD **Stadium** (1km west of the main settlement and the basilica). In the 4th century AD, an earthquake destroyed several Cypriot cities, leveling Kourion. The city was rebuilt in the 5th century, only to burn in a 7th-century Arab raid. As a result, the **Temple of Apollo** and other parts of the Sanctuary of Apollo are largely reconstructed. A photo of the pre-reconstruction sanctuary hangs in the office.

The majestic 2nd-century Roman **amphitheater** opens to a splendid view of the sea. It is used for **Shakespeare Nights** in June (see **Festivals,** p. 581), occasional summer concerts and theatrical productions, and weekend theater in September. The oldest structure on the site, the theater was used for dramatic performances during Greek and Roman times, but by AD 300, Circus Maximus-style entertainment was the more popular option.

Adjacent to the amphitheater lie the **Baths and Annex of Eustoios,** built in AD 360 with exquisite mosaic floors dating to the 5th century. Look for the finely detailed round mosaics of a pheasant and a fish, the best preserved of all the floors. Across the road from the basilica lie a group of ruins under excavation. In the northwest corner are the remains of the **House of Gladiators** and its mosaic gladiator pin-ups. The **House of Achilles,** next to the ancient theatre, has mosaic floors depicting the Rape of Ganymede and Achilles's revelation to Odysseus.

PAPHOS Παφος

Paphos—the favorite city of Aphrodite—was made the capital city of Cyprus under the Ptolemies of Egypt. The city grew fabulously wealthy, developing into a cosmopolitan commercial center and remaining so under later Roman conquerors. When a 4th century BC earthquake ended its supremacy, the capital—and the political and social prestige—moved to Salamis (near modern Famagusta), and Paphos dwindled. As the upper half of the city goes about its business largely without regard for tourism, the lower half operates on a rhythm dictated by visitors.

TRANSPORTATION

Flights: CTO (☎26 932 841). Most flights arrive in Larnaka, but **Paphos International Airport** receives various European airlines and chartered flights. Get there by private taxi from the city center or Kato Paphos (£7-8).

Buses: Nea Amoroza Co., Pallikaridi 79 (☎26 236 822 or 26 236 740), in Pl. Kennedy goes to **Polis** (11 per day M-F 6:20am-7pm, Sa 6 per day 9am-4pm; £1); some continue on to **Pomos Village** (2 per day M-F 11am and 4pm, 3 per day Sa; £1.10). Service to **Limassol** (M-F 2:30pm, Sa 1pm; £2).

City Buses: ALEPA Bus (☎26 934 410 and 26 934 455) runs the municipal bus #11 between Ktima Paphos and Kato Paphos (every 15min., £0.50). Catch one in Ktima

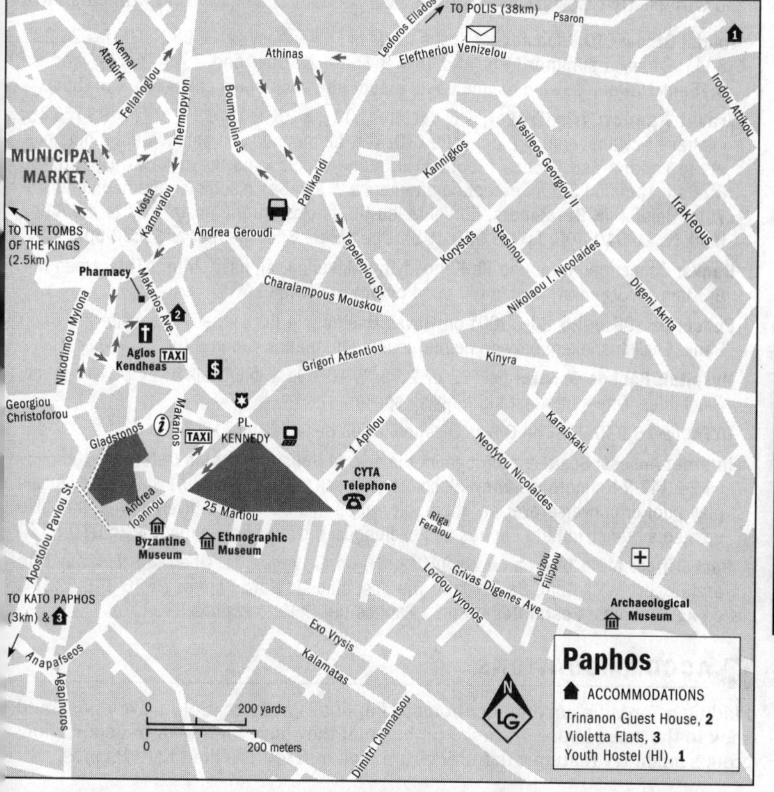

CYPRUS

Paphos, up the road from the post office at the market, or in Kato Paphos at any of the yellow benches on the road to town. ALEPA bus #10 goes to **Coral Bay** (20 per day, £0.50) along the coastal road. Bus #2 starts at **Geroskipou Beach** with stops along the coastal road (every 15-20min. 6am-7pm). Schedules available in the tourist office.

Service Taxis: Contact **Travel & Express** on Eagorou (☎26 933 181). To **Limassol** (every 30min. M-Sa 6am-6pm, Su 7am-5am; £2.75).

Moped Rental: There are several shops in Kato and Ktima Paphos and along Apostolos Pavlou, the coastal road. Cheaper options lie along Ap. Pavlou. Rent early in the day; rentals often run out during peak seasons. £3-8 per day. **4U Car & Bike rentals** (☎26 944 085 or 99 466 026) is on Tomb of the Kings Ave. Mountain bikes £3, scooters £7 per day. **Pentaras Rentals,** Ag. Antoniou 5 (☎26 941 965 or 99 603 838), in Kato Paphos, has a few cheap cars and bikes (£5-15 per day). Call ahead. Open M-F 8am-1pm and 2:30-7:30pm, Sa-Su 8am-1pm.

ORIENTATION AND PRACTICAL INFORMATION

Paphos is divided into two sections. **Ktima Paphos** (the upper section, referred to simply as "Paphos") is centered on **Pl. Kennedy,** where you'll find the shops, budget hotels, and services. **Kato Paphos** (the lower section) lies roughly 3km south, hosting luxury hotels and most of the city's nightlife. **Leoforos Apostolos Pavlou** runs south from Ktima to Kato Paphos. **Vasileon** runs up the coast to Coral Bay and is lined with costly resorts. Unless noted, everything listed below is in Ktima Paphos.

Tourist Office: CTO, Gladstone 3, just outside of Pl. Kennedy (☎26 932 841; fax 26 932 841). Open in summer M-Tu and Th-F 8:15am-2:30pm and 2:45-7pm, W and Sa 8:15am-1:30pm. In winter same hours except afternoon hours change to 3-6:15pm.

Travel Agency: Iris Travel, Gladstone 10A (☎26 948 933 or 26 937 585; iris.travel@cytanet.com.cy), opposite CTO. Very helpful and competent staff. Airline tickets to London and Greece (about £40, student discounts up to 40%). Open M-Sa 8:30am-1pm and 3-6pm except no afternoons W and Sa; in summer afternoon hours 4-7pm. Helpful **VK Developers,** El. Venizelou 56, is close to the hostel next to the Alpha Bank (☎26 910 400; fax 26 910 195). Open M-Sa 8:30am-1pm and 3:30-6pm.

Banks: Concentrated around Pl. Kennedy on Makariou. All have 24hr. **ATMs.** Open M-F 8:30am-12:30pm. ATMs can be found on any major road.

Police: (☎199 or 26 806 060) on Grivas Digenes, in Pl. Kennedy, opposite the Coop Bank. English spoken; provide helpful tourist information. Open 24hr.

Hospital: Paphos General (☎112 or 26 803 100) is a long walk away on Neophytos Nicolaides. Offers free first aid. English spoken.

CYTA: (☎26 930 228) on Grivas Digenes. Open daily 7:30am-1:30pm.

Internet Access: Scattered throughout the city. **Maroushia Fashion Cafe,** 6 Pl. Kennedy (☎26 947 240; maroushia@cylink.com.cy). Check email (£2 per hr.) while young locals play pool or converse over an afternoon *frappé.* Maroushia, the lively owner, has also opened a branch in Kato Paphos on Poseidonos, the main beach road (☎26 910 657).

Post Office: Main branch (☎26 940 223), on El. Venizelou. Open M-F 7:30am-1pm and (except W) 3-6pm, Sa 8-10am. The post office in **Kato Paphos** (☎26 940 226) is on Ag. Antoniou. **Postal Code:** Ktima Paphos 8900; Kato Paphos 8903.

ACCOMMODATIONS

Finding affordable accommodations in Paphos is a chore. Solo travelers should stick to the guest house or the youth hostel if they have their own transportation; groups might try renting a flat. Prices are higher in tourist-filled Kato Paphos.

Trianon Hotel Guest House, Makarios 99 (☎26 232 193), from Pl. Kennedy Makarios is the narrow road directly to the left as you face Pallikaridi. Airy, high-ceilinged rooms, a common living room with kitchen access, TV, and an owner very glad to help out with any queries about the town make this ideally-located budget option a brilliant choice. Shared bath. Singles £5; doubles £8-12. ❶

Violetta Flats, Dionissiou 7 (☎26 934 109; fax 26 220 734), in Kato Paphos. 7 flats with kitchen, TV, and private bath. Rooms are large, with small personal touches that warm them up. Well situated for enjoying the nightlife, poorly situated for avoiding it. Singles £18-20; doubles £22-25. A/C £2 extra. ❸

Youth Hostel (HI), El. Venizelou 45 (☎26 932 588). Walk 15min. from the plateia on Pallikaridi to Venizelou, then turn right. Out of the way, but clean and cheap. 2 single-sex rooms with 8 beds each, 1 co-ed room, and 1 family room available. Kitchen and laundry facilities. No curfew, but lights out around 11pm. £5 per bed for the 1st night, £4 per night thereafter. ❶

FOOD AND NIGHTLIFE

Restaurants in Kato Paphos are geared to money-laden foreigners, while in Ktima Paphos local tavernas are hidden among the winding streets. **Vasano Kebab House ❶,** Agapinoros 25 in Kato Paphos, has only the basics, but every morsel is prepared to perfection, and the locals know it—no evening passes without a full house. On the road down from Ktima to Kato Paphos, take a left onto Pinelopis and a right onto Agapinoros. (☎26 242 635. Main dishes £1-2.) **Athens ❶,** Pallikaridi 47, is the place for anyone who remotely likes sugar. Traditional pastries, cookies, and *pites* are freshly baked every morning. (Pastries £0.40 and under.)

Virtually all of the area's nightlife centers on Ag. Napas and Ag. Antoniou, a couple of blocks inland from the waterfront in Kato Paphos. **Club 12,** on Ag. Andreou, draws all the crowds after 1am with heavy bass and the latest techno tunes—be prepared for wild dancing on the bars and tables. (Cover £5.) **Summer Cinema** (☎26 247 747 or 99 632 229), on the waterfront, is a trendy open-air club just far enough from package hotels for the locals to call it their own. **Bubbles,** on Ag. Antoniou, hops from 10pm till late (3-4am). Every Thursday, "Carwash Night Back in Time" turns back the clock with 70s and 80s hits. A more laid-back atmosphere is found at **Different** (☎26 934 668), farther down on Ag. Antoniou. Relax and throw back a Strawberry Kiss, a must-try cocktail.

SIGHTS

TOMBS OF THE KINGS. Apostolou Pavlou St., connecting Ktima and Kato Paphos, is lined with monuments to the Roman, early Christian, Byzantine, and Venetian periods of Cypriot history. About 2km before Kato Paphos, a sign directs you to Paleokastra's **Tombs of the Kings.** Although those interred in the stone tombs were local aristocracy, not kings, the 2nd century remnants bear a strong resemblance to Egyptian peristyle court tombs. The larger tombs consist of an open court encircled by burial chambers, with Doric columns carved out of the underground rock and stairways leading to the interiors. These Hellenistic and Roman tombs were used as hideouts by Christians fleeing persecution. The most impressive are tombs three, four, five, and eight, which have underground passages to wander through. *(☎26 940 295. Open 8:30am-7:30pm; off season 8am-5pm. £0.75.)*

MOSAICS OF KATO PAPHOS. Over 2000 sq. m of mosaic floors from the **House of Dionysus,** the **House of Theseus,** and the **House of Aion** lie under weather protection tents adjacent to the ruins of the houses they were originally kept in. Some of the city's (and the Eastern Mediterranean's) most extensive ancient relics were discovered accidentally by a farmer plowing his fields. In 1962, they were excavated by a Polish expedition that found largely intact mosaics covering 14 rooms of the expansive Roman House of Dionysus. The mosaics are not unique for their time period, but are amazingly well preserved (and thus rare) examples of the norm for aristocratic decor during the Roman Period. The floors depict scenes from Greek mythology and daily life using the naturally occurring hues of the stones. The House of Theseus, toward the water, dates from the 2nd to 6th centuries AD. These ruins reveal what was once a decadent building with marble statues, columns, and mosaic floors. The most famous mosaic, now housed in the warehouse, comes from the House of Theseus and is a vibrant, circular representation of the clash between Achilles and Theseus. *(Enter through the gate at the start of the pedestrian way past the parking lot on the Paphos Fort road. Walk up the dirt path about 200m to the reception booth. ☎26 940 217. Open daily 8am-7:30pm. £1.50. Guidebook £3.)*

MUSEUMS OF KTIMA PAPHOS. The **Archaeological Museum,** on Grivas Digenes, 1km from Pl. Kennedy, has an array of Bronze Age pottery, tools, sculpture, statues, and artifacts from the houses of Dionysus and Theseus. *(☎26 940 215. Open M-F 9am-5pm, Sa 10am-1pm. £0.75.)* The private collection at the **Ethnographic Museum,** displayed in the owner's home at Exo Vrysi 1, just outside Pl. Kennedy, takes you through different historical phases of Cypriot life, complete with traditional costumes and daily tools. The garden is the highlight of the museum, with a 3rd century BC Hellenistic tomb, Christian catacombs, and *kleftiko* ovens. *(☎26 932 010. Open M-Sa 9am-3:30pm, Su 10am-12pm. £1. Guidebooks £3.)* Across the way, the **Byzantine Museum,** Andreou Ioannou 5, has icons and religious relics from local monasteries and churches, including frescoes, vestments, and manuscripts. The main attraction is the icon of Agia Marina, the oldest in Cyprus, dating to the 7th or 8th century. *(☎26 931 393. Open M-F 9am-4pm, Sa 9:10am-1pm. £1, guidebook £3.)*

CATACOMBS OF AGIA SOLOMONI. Descend into the dark catacombs that include a chapel with deteriorating Byzantine frescoes. Dedicated to Ag. Solomoni, the chapel sits on the site of an old synagogue. A marked tree—said to cure the illnesses of those who tie a cloth to it—marks the entrance to the catacombs. St. Paul was whipped for preaching Christianity at nearby **St. Paul's Pillar,** on the site of the Catholic church. *(Tombs on Ap. Pavlou. Open 24hr. Free.)*

OTHER SIGHTS. The remnants of an agora are north of the mosaics, enclosed in Kato Paphos's archaeological park. The limestone Roman **odeon,** a small, roofed theater, is still used for dance and song performances. Pick up a schedule at the CTO. *(Open daily 8am-7:30pm. Entrance is free along with your ticket for the mosaics—the sites are side by side.)* Built in the late 7th century on a hill overlooking the harbor, the **Byzantine Castle** *(Saranda Kolones)*, named for its many granite columns, protected inhabitants from Arab pirates. An earthquake destroyed most of the castle in 1222, but part of its fort and some ruins remain. No one knows exactly when the **Paphos Fort,** at the end of the pier, was built, but some speculate that the Lusignans constructed it after *Saranda Kolones* was destroyed. *(Open 10am-5:45pm. £0.75.)*

BEACHES

The two most popular beaches stretch along **Geroskipou** to the east and **Coral Bay** to the north (big, sandy, and touristy—luxury hotels line the way). For Geroskipou, take bus #2 from Ktima Paphos (5 per day 6:25am-7pm, £0.50); to reach Coral Bay, take bus #10 from the Market in Pano Paphos (every 20min., £0.50). **Cape Lara** is host to lovely, empty beaches and some local wildlife—the beach is a nesting site for Green and Loggerhead Turtles from June until September. The **Lara Sea Turtle**

Project was conceived in 1971 to protect the turtles by ensuring that nesting continues. After traveling the Mediterranean, the turtles return to the beach where they were born to lay their eggs. Turtle nests can be viewed in the Project's hatchery enclosure. Alas, there's no public transportation to Cape Lara; your best bet is a jeep excursion or motorbike. Follow signs for **Agios Georgios** from Coral Bay to the pebbly beach that sits below the church. **Sundy Beach,** 2km down the road to Cape Lara, parades umbrellas for rent.

DAYTRIPS FROM PAPHOS: KOUKLIA

Adjacent to the modern village of Kouklia are the ruins of the great **Temple of Aphrodite** and **Paleopaphos** (Old Paphos), once the capital of a kingdom encompassing nearly half of Cyprus. The temple itself was the kingdom's religious center and a destination for pilgrims from every corner of the Roman world. Built in the 12th century BC, it thrived until the 4th century AD, when the edicts of Emperor Theodosius and a series of earthquakes reduced it to rubble. The scant remains make little sense without a guide. *A Brief History and Description of Old Paphos,* published by the Department of Antiquities, is available in the adjoining **Paleopaphos Museum.** *(☎26 432 180. Open M-F 8am-7pm, Sa-Su 9am-5pm. Admission to ruins, city, and museum £0.75. The sites are best seen from excursion buses. Renting a moped is not advisable, as the road is hazardous; service taxis are a much safer bet.)*

POLIS Πολις

Polis is the quietest and the smallest of Cyprus's major seaside towns. The town is separated from the coast by cornfields; just when it seems you'll be landlocked forever, the sea appears in the distance. Polis retains its own ways, and life goes on with a peaceful rhythm. Tourism has made just enough inroads to make for sufficient rooms, but the beauty of its natural treasures has remained unscathed.

TRANSPORTATION. **Nea Amoroza Bus Co.** (☎26 936 740) passes through Polis from Paphos (10 per day M-F 6:20am-7pm, £1). **Spirides Taxi Service** (☎26 516 161) is in the plateia. **Pegasus** (☎26 321 374), also in the plateia, rents cars, mopeds (£4 per day), mountain bikes (£3 per day), and apartments. **Andy Spyrou Rentals** (☎26 936 944) on Latsi Habor rents cars, mopeds, and motorbikes. The **Lemon Garden** (☎99 647 729), away from the plateia past the Hellenic Bank, rents and sells **sports equipment** such as jet skis, mountain bikes (£2.50-3 per day, discounts for longer rentals), and diving equipment (£5-15).

ORIENTATION AND PRACTICAL INFORMATION. Polis can be difficult to navigate, though most tourist destinations are clearly marked and consolidated in the plateia. The plateia, about 1½km inland from the shore, is home to all of the town's tourist services. The **CTO** office is the island's newest, offering enthusiastic advice for daytrips and accommodations. (☎26 322 468. Open in summer Su-Tu and Th-F 9am-1pm and 2:30-5:45pm, W and Sa 9am-1pm; in winter Su-Tu and Th-F 9am-9pm, W and Sa 9am-1:45pm.) The **police** are one block from the plateia in the direction of the beach. (☎26 321 451. Open 24hr.) Around the plateia you'll find three **banks** with 24hr. **ATMs**. (Open M-F 8:15am-noon.) Two **pharmacies** (☎26 321 253 or 26 321 167) are down the street from the post office. High speed **Internet access** can be found above **The Piazetta** at Pavlou Georgiou 3. (☎26 321 518. £2.50 for 1hr.) The **hospital** (☎26 321 431) is about a short walk from the plateia toward the campground. The **post office** is also in the plateia. (☎26 321 539. Open M-F 7:30am-2pm, Th 3-5pm.) **Postal code:** 8905.

ACCOMMODATIONS. The cheapest and most reasonable accommodations in Polis are the various **rooms to let** throughout the town. Women with rooms to let often wait at the bus stop in the hopes of winning over guests with a sales pitch. Don't commit to a room without checking it out. **Elena's Rooms to Let** ❷ are a 5min. walk from the beach, along the main road that leads uphill from the beach to the plateia. Rooms are simple but clean and have all the necessities, including refrigerators. Most have private baths, and some have balconies. (☎26 321 244 or 99 675 474. £10-15 per night. Stays must be longer than 5 days.) The **Lemon Garden** ❹ has a unique combination of quality rooms, food, and atmosphere. All rooms come with kitchenette, private bath, A/C, a view, and swimming pool access. If you arrive late ring the bell; the owner and her family live upstairs. (☎26 321 443. Doubles £28.) Other inexpensive rooms to let (£5-6 per person) on the road to Latsi and the road to the beach are clearly marked; inquire at a cafe if you get tired of looking. Campers are in luck: the **campground** ❶ (☎26 321 526), 1½km from the town center in a fragrant, seaside eucalyptus grove, is open from March-October. It has shower facilities, a playground, a mini-supermarket, and a bar that hosts beach parties every Thursday and Sunday. (£1 per person, £2 per tent, tent rental £2.)

FOOD. The plateia cafes and restaurants serve pretty uniform fare (Cypriot with an Italian flare), but a few places a bit away from the center of things provide some delectable surprises. At **Mario's Garden Cafe ❷,** located down a set of stairs beyond the Akamas Hotel, a formerly dilapidated Turkish house has become a whimsical garden cafe and bar, with statues, quirky furniture, and a central bonfire. Mario doesn't cook up a full menu every day (drinks, salads, and some snacks are always available), but he saves his best for Sunday when he stirs up a *meze*-style all-you-can-eat buffet (£5). For convenient dining, visit **Lemon Garden Taverna ❷,** right below the hotel. Try the classic *pastitsio* (£3.50) or sample their rich and extensive breakfast menu. (Main dishes £2.50-5.50. Open 8:30am-11pm.) In town, **Arsinoe ❷,** across from the church, serves a fantastic catch of the day. (Swordfish £4.50, fish *meze* £6. Open 8am-1pm and 7pm-1am.)

SIGHTS. The churches of **Agios Andronikos** and **Agia Kyriaki** in Polis were built in the 15th century. In the latter half of the 16th century, invading Ottomans converted Agios Andronikos into a mosque and plastered over its frescoes. Both of the churches are closed and no longer in use. The **Baths of Aphrodite,** carved out of limestone are the mythical site of Aphrodite's first encounter with, and later marriage to, Akamas, the son of Theseus. The goddess would come here to cleanse herself after nocturnal exploits. There's no word on modern-day naughtiness, but according to legend, all who bathe in the pool stay forever young. *(Take a bus from Polis June-Oct. M-F 10am, noon, 3pm ; £0.50.)*

HIKING THE AKAMAS PENINSULA. The easternmost home of European vegetation, the peninsula contains a remarkable array of about 600 plant species and over 160 bird species, some of which (especially the stationary varieties) are marked along the trails. Stretching to the Cape of Arnaouti, this area is a must for travelers. The two primary hiking trails, the **Aphrodite** and the **Adonis,** begin at the Baths. Both take 2-3hr., although with a side trip to **Fontana Amaroza,** the Aphrodite trail can take closer to half a day. The trails take the same path for the first 2km, leaving coastal scrub behind in favor of fragrant forest. They split at the ruins of **Pyrgos tis Rigainas,** believed to be a medieval monastery, where picnic tables and a potable well sit among huge oak trees. From here, the Adonis continues left, running along a series of placid streams and returning to the main road just east of the tourist pavilion. The Aphrodite continues to the right, ascending **Mt. Sotiras** before descending toward the coast into a field cleared by a forest fire. It then hugs the coast all the way back to the Baths. Near the coast, the turnoff for Fontana Amaroza (the Fountain of Love) leads to a shipwreck and sea caves, as well as the fountain itself. While it may have worked wonders in the past, today the *fontana* is an unimpressive stagnant pool, but the gorgeous scenery makes the journey worthwhile. The CTO has free maps of the Akamas Peninsula and a helpful booklet on the vegetation and animal life.

TROODOS MOUNTAINS Τροοδος

This ancient range, whose peaks are made of 15 million-year-old rock formations called **omolites,** boasts well-maintained trails; most are moderately difficult. The pleasant hikes wind among Byzantine churches and ancient black pines. A natural experience in June and early July can turn frustrating and costly in August, when the urban crowds descend, especially on weekends. In winter, **Mt. Olympus,** the highest point in Cyprus (1951m), plays host to hundreds of skiers.

Public transportation between villages and around the area is infrequent; scheduled stops are unreliable at best, nonexistent at worst. In the mountains, those over 17 can easily rent mopeds. Cars are available in Limassol, Paphos, or Lefkosia for those over 23. Be careful: mountain roads are steep, winding, and bumpy.

PLATRES Πλατρες

Fresh mountain air and the sound of rushing streams combine to make Platres a glorious natural escape. Devoted to eateries and accommodations, relatively cheap and accessible by public transportation, the town offers no sites of its own but evokes a relaxing communion with your surroundings. It's a great base for exploring Troodos and visiting the surrounding mountain villages, and it will offer a soothing welcome after a long, full day of hiking.

TRANSPORTATION. From Limassol, **Travel & Express** leaves for Platres at 11:30am, returning to Limassol at 7am. (☎25 354 119. M-Sa, £2.) **Kyriakos** has an

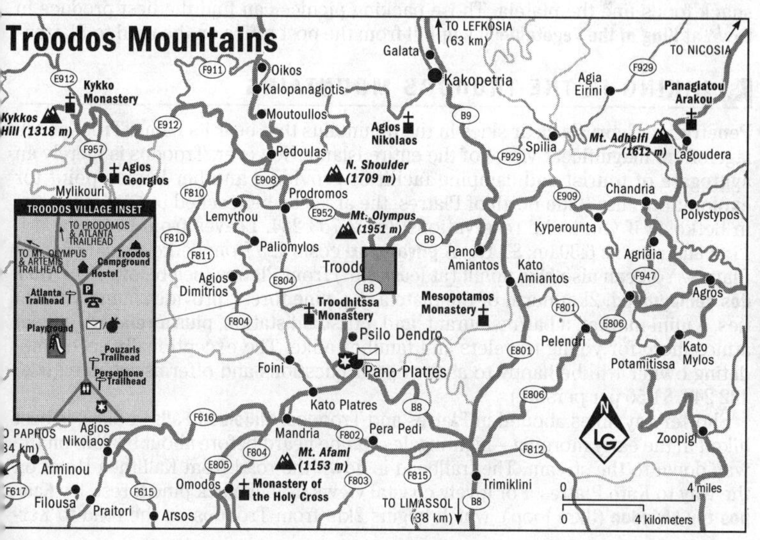

office in Platres (☎25 364 114) for transit in the area. **Pantelis Private Taxis** run within the mountain villages (☎25 423 333 or 99 429 453; ₤5 to Troodos Sq., ₤7 to Omodos). **Top Hill Souvenirs,** on the main street, down the hill from the post office, rents **mountain bikes.** There are some great bike routes in the Troodos—ask the staff for guidance. (☎25 421 729 or 99 633 752. 21-gear bikes ₤4 per day, helmets included. Open 10am-6pm.)

ORIENTATION AND PRACTICAL INFORMATION. Platres is divided into the **pano** (upper) and **kato** (lower) sections. Pano Platres contains most tourist facilities, while Kato Platres is largely residential. Hiking trails are the area's main form of entertainment. The **tourist office** is left of the parking lot in the plateia. (☎25 421 316. Open M-F 9am-3:30pm.) The **Bank of Cyprus** is opposite the tourist office, and **Popular Bank** is just up the hill. Both have a 24hr. **ATM.** The **hospital** is between Pano and Kato Platres and is no longer open 24hr. but keeps a doctor's number posted on the door for emergencies. (☎25 421 324. Open 7am-7pm.) The nearest **pharmacy** is in Kakopetria. (☎25 924 492. Open M-Sa 8:30am-1:30pm and 3:30-7:30pm.) The **police** are opposite the tourist office in a converted military chapel. (☎25 421 351. Open 24hr. English spoken.) **Top Hill Souvenirs** sells phone cards. (Open M-F 7:30am-2:30pm.) The **post office** is to the left of the tourist office. (☎25 422 624. Open M-F 3-5pm; in winter M-F 7:30am-noon and 3-5pm.) **Postal Code:** Kato 4815, Pano 4820.

ACCOMMODATIONS AND FOOD. From the post office, go down the hill and bear left to find **Kallithea Hotel ❸,** where the kind owner offers simple rooms, some with a balcony or patio. (☎25 421 746; fax 25 422 241. Breakfast included. Singles ₤15 high season, ₤12 low season.) Ask about the rooms across the street, which offer large serene balconies (₤12 per person high season; breakfast included). **To Psilo Dendro ❷,** a fish farm 2km north of Platres on the road to Troodos, serves sumptuous trout under a canopy of tall trees. (Whole trout ₤5.75. ☎25 422 050. Open 8am-5pm.) Directly below the hill from the post office is the **Petit Palais Hotel Restaurant ❸,** with a large selection of main dishes (₤3-5) and crepes (₤1-2). Try house favorites moussaka (₤4.50) or lamb (₤5). Cafes serving standard snack foods line the plateia. Those packing picnics can find the best produce in town at **King of the Vegetable**; it's uphill from the post office on the road to Platres.

HIKING IN THE TROODOS MOUNTAINS

Penetrating Cyprus's clear skies in the mountains that bear its name, Troodos village offers magnificent views of the entire island. However, Troodos is merely an aggregate of tourist and camping facilities providing another launch point for exploration. Just 10km north of Platres, the area can be reached by **Clarios Bus Co.** in Lefkosia if you make reservations. (☎22 753 234. Leaves from Lefkosia M-F 11:30am, returns 6:30am; ₤1.10.) A **private taxi** costs ₤25 from Lefkosia and ₤5 from Platres. You can also **hike** uphill (at least 2hr.) from Platres (see below). The **Troodos campground,** 2km north of the plateia in a pine forest, provides laundry facilities, a mini-market, a bar/restaurant, and a first aid station, plus a relaxed, upbeat atmosphere for young travelers and families alike. The exceptionally accommodating owner will be happy to answer your questions and offer assistance. (☎25 422 249. ₤1.50 per person.)

Shorter day hikes abound in Platres and Troodos. **Millomeri Falls** (1.3km) is best hiked in the early morning—nightingales can be heard before about 9:30am on the way down to the stream. The trailhead is down the road from Kallithea Hotel on the way to Kato Platres. For lovely coastal views from a black pine forest, try **Kampos tou Liviadon** (3km loop), which begins 2km from Troodos on the road to Karvounas. The head of the **Kaledonia Falls** trail (2 km) is to the left of To Psilo Dendro in Platres. The trail ascends to the lovely, 30ft-high Kaldonia Falls, crossing the mountain stream several times. To hike between Platres and Troodos, hike uphill from the Kaledonia Falls trailhead until it meets with the Persephone Trail, which leads to Troodos. A **map** of area trails is essential; it's available at the CTO.

Artemis Trail (7km, 2.5hr. round trip). The trailhead is on the road to Mt. Olympus from Troodos plateia. A flat, well-maintained trail with panoramic coastal views and several ancient black pines; it loops around **Mt. Olympus** about 100m below the peak.

Atlanta Trail (12km, 5hr. round trip). Similar to the Artemis trail, but at a lower altitude. Ends at the **Prodromos-Troodos road**, near the chromium mine camp. Fill your water bottle from a fresh mountain water spring 3km into the hike and enjoy views of Limassol, the Northern occupied territory, and everything in between. Consult the signs at the trailhead for the complicated directions on how to complete the loop.

Persephone Trail (3km, 2hr. out and back). Begins south of Troodos plateia, across from the police station. Gradually descends to a breathtaking lookout point at **Makria Konatarka** among huge slabs of limestone rock.

Mesa Potamos Monastery Trail (9km, 4hr. out and back). The most ambitious but least impressive Troodos hike, leading to an unremarkable monastery. The dirt track is also accessible to mountain bikes.

PLANET OF THE GRAPES The Ancient Greek god of wine, Dionysus, was always described as a joyful character: no wonder! Visit Omodos, a village renowned for its wine production, and you'll feel the same. The grapes that drape the hills of Omodos are squeezed into a wide variety of wines. The most distinctive of these is a sweet red wine called *Komandaria* drunk as an after-dinner treat. In addition to the mainstream reds and whites, hardy souls can try Greece's answer to Guinness—a thick, black wine called *Limnio* that may just leave you on knees begging old Dionysus for mercy.

KAKOPETRIA Κακοπετρια

Kakopetria is popular with urban Cypriots and foreign tourists alike. Traditional wood and stone village houses perch beside the mountain stream that flows through the center of town. According to local legend, the large rock perched on the hillside once rolled over and crushed a couple as they walked past the church, initiating a tradition in which newlyweds sit on the rock to ensure marital stability.

ORIENTATION AND PRACTICAL INFORMATION. Clarios (☎22 753 234) runs buses to **Lefkosia** from **Kakopetria** (M-F 9 per day 5am-2:30pm, Su 6am, 4:30pm; £1.20). Some buses continue to **Troodos** by reservation. **Taxis** to Lefkosia cost £12. Kakopetria consists of the main street, **Makarios,** which leads into the old section of the village, passes through the plateia, and continues to the adjoining village of Galata. The "Old Road," a steep, cobbled path, lies across the stream and can be accessed off Makarios at the Village Inn. **Hellenic Bank** (☎22 860 000, open M-F 8:30am-12:30pm), **Laiki Bank** (open M-F 8:15am-12:30pm), and **Bank of Cyprus** (M-F 8:15am-12:30pm and M 3:15-4:45pm) are in the plateia and have 24hr. **ATMs.** The **police station** is right up the hill from the Bank of Cyprus. (☎22 922 420. Open 24hr.) There is a **pharmacy** on Makarios. (☎22 924 492. Open M-F 8:30am-1:30pm and 3:30-7:30pm, Sa 9am-1:30pm and 3:30-5pm.) The **post office** is up the hill from the Bank of Cyprus. (☎22 922 422. Open M-F 7:30am-1:30pm.) **Postal Code:** 2810.

ACCOMMODATIONS AND FOOD. Kakopetria has a number of budget domatia above or behind restaurants, many along the stream with clearly visible signs. For a longer, considerably more expensive getaway, try staying in one of the **agrotourism inns,** gorgeous restored homes rented out for several days or weeks. When you arrive in Kakopetria head over to the **Serenity Coffeeshop and Inn ❸**, on the old village road, a few meters past the Linos Taverna. If you're lucky enough to secure one of their three exquisite rooms, you'll descend the hill on an ancient stone staircase to reach your quarters. Rooms have four-poster beds and balconies that overlook the mountain stream and the scattered fruit trees growing on its banks. (☎22 922 602. Singles £15; doubles £20.) The more modern **Hekali Hotel ❸**, a few blocks from the village center, has rooms equipped with TV, radio, phone, balcony, and A/C (£2 per night). The downstairs includes a full bar, dining hall, and a TV lounge. (☎22 992 501; fax 22 922 503. Handicap accessible. Singles £18.)

The Troodos area is known for its trout, and Kakopetria's **The Mill ❸** restaurant has some of the best. Ride the elevators to a spacious balcony high over the stream and watch twilight descend on the village as swallows glide through the air. (☎22 922 536. Extensive wine list; entrees £5-9. Open M-F noon-10pm, Sa noon-3:30pm. Reservations recommended.) **Linos Taverna ❷**, up the old village road, serves Cypriot food on a quiet, cobbled balcony. Try their version of *mezedes*—five main dishes of your choice in small portions for £8. Restaurants serving more mainstream fare abound in the plateia.

SIGHTS AND ENTERTAINMENT. Well-preserved village houses line the cobbled streets. Note the enormous clay jugs, once used for storage, which still rest on many doorsteps. Their bottoms are pointed to allow the last drop of oil or wine to be ladled out. Kakopetria and its smaller neighbor, **Galata,** have five Byzantine churches between them. The most notable, 11th-century **Agios Nikolaos tis Stegis,** shines 3km southwest of Kakopetria on the road to Troodos. Local buses fetch the elderly from surrounding villages for Sunday morning services. Frescoes dating back to 1320 ornament the walls, including one of the Virgin breastfeeding the Divine Child. (Open Tu-Sa 9am-4pm, Su 11am-4pm.) The monastery of **Panagia tou Arakou,** 16km southeast of Kakopetria in the village of Lagoudhera, displays elaborate 12th-century frescoes, including a dome depiction of Christ Pantokrator restored in 1968. Don't miss the portraits of the seven Cypriot saints on the semicylindrical apse wall. To get there, follow signs for Chandria; you'll see signs for the monastery. (Open 8am-5pm daily.) There is also a **hiking trail** about 1km before Laghoudera at the turnoff for Polystippos; the trail runs next to the river and passes the area's orchards. The only nightlife option in Kakopetria is the **River Bar,** on Makarios across the stream from the plateia. (Open every night 8pm-late, but weeknight hours can be irregular in the off season.)

DAYTRIP FROM KAKOPETRIA. Kykko Monastery (Μονη Κυκκο), 20km from Pedhoulas in the northwest part of the mountains, prides itself on being the wealthiest and most prestigious monastery on Cyprus. Standing strong and solitary in the depths of the Troodos Mountains, this architecturally intricate building is the result of centuries of renovation after accidental fires in AD 1365, 1541, 1751, and 1813. The most recent renovations have been underway since 1987; the building as it stands now remains true to Byzantian architecture but the actual structure is virtually modern. The priceless collection of church treasures exhibited in the monastery's museum is unrivalled in Cyprus. Vestaments, ornate ceremonial objects, and rare church documents are displayed in reverently dim rooms where Byzantine chants play softly on the stereo system. Extensive English explanations accompany the exhibits. Look for the sign telling the full legend of the monastery's founding in the 11th century by the hermit Isaiah, a story that involves a lost traveler, a golden lady, and prophetic dreams. During the Cypriot struggle for independence (p. 564), Kykko was a communication and supply center and the home of **Archbishop Makarios III.** Only 1.5km away was the secret headquarters of the first military leader of the struggle, General George Grivas. Today, the monks are very aware of their monastery's historical importance and are willing to give explanations upon request. The sanctity of the space prohibits photography in the church and museum, but a video is on sale in the giftshop.

From the Leonidou station in Lefkosia, Kambos (☎99 623 604 or 99 94 253) sends buses to Kykko Monastery (departs at noon, returns to Lefkosia 6am the next day; £0.50 each way, £2.50 with luggage). Most tourists reach Kykko by car. Rentals are available in Lefkosia (p. 593) or Limassol (p. 578). Rooms are available but are intended for pilgrims. Call ☎22 590 768 a day in advance to reserve a room. (Monastery ☎22 942 435. Open Nov.-May 10am-4pm, June-Oct. 10am-6pm.)

NICOSIA Λευκωσια

Landlocked Lefkosia, sliced in two by the barbed-wire Green Line, has the dubious distinction of being the last divided city in the world. The modern New City is separated from the Old by Venetian walls, built on top of the ancient Roman town of Ledra to defend against Ottoman invaders. In 1570, the Ottomans took only seven weeks to conquer Lefkosia, proving the uselessness of the walls. They ruled the city for several hundred years before British imperialists arrived in 1878. The British governed Cyprus until it gained independence in 1960, when Lefkosia became the capital of the island, and paved the way for present day tourism. In the aftermath of 1974, Lefkosia was split into Turkish and Greek sections and today remains under the watchful eye of the UN. Passage across the Green Line is permitted from the Lidra Palace Checkpoint.

LEFKOSIA (SOUTH NICOSIA)

Lefkosia, the name officially given to their half of Nicosia by the Greek Cypriots, is itself divided into two parts by the Venetian walls. Inside the walls lies the Old City, which caters to history buffs and politically inclined tourists. A narrow chain of public parks in varying states of upkeep surrounds the Old City; beyond these the New City is ever-expanding, full of corporate buildings and international retail chains. The New City is geared toward bureaucrats and wealthy shoppers, while most museums, restaurants, and hotels are found in the Old City. The city offers the chance to discover the island without the frills of coastal tourism, providing a poignant, intimate view of the political strife that has shaped modern Cyprus.

TRANSPORTATION

Buses: Intercity Buses (☎22 665 814), in Pl. Solomos, run to **Larnaka** (6 per day M-F 9am-6:30pm, Sa 9am, 1pm; £1.50). **Intercity Buses** and **Alepa** (☎22 625 027) both leave from Pl. Solomos and run to **Limassol** (11 per day M, T, Th, F 6am-5:45pm, 10 per day W 6am-5:45pm, 3 per day Sa 10am-2pm; £1.50). **Nea Amorza** (☎26 236 822) and **Alepa** (☎22 664 636), near Pl. Solomos, go to **Paphos** (M, T, Th, F 6:30am and 3:45pm, W 6:30am and 12:45pm, Sa 7am, £3). **PEAL Bus Co.,** Stasinou 27 (☎23 821 318), runs to **Agia Napa, Parlimni,** and **Protaras** (M-F 1:30pm, £2). **EMAN** (stops at Constanza Basiton) runs directly to Agia Napa (M-Sa 3pm, £2). **Pedoulas-Platres Bus** (☎99 618 865) runs to **Pedoulas, Platres,** and **Prodromos** (M-Sa 12:15pm, £2; no Platres stop on Sa). **Clarios** (☎22 753 234), 200m east of Pl. Eleftherias on

CROSSING THE GREEN LINE. The infamous Green Line is Nicosia's main attraction. Crossing the Green Line from the south is fairly easy—just follow the strict regulations, and don't bother trying to get information about North Nicosia on the southern side: Greek Cypriots have not crossed the line for over 20 years. You will not be permitted to cross if you are a Greek citizen or if you are of Greek descent. Head for the **Lidra Palace Checkpoint** between the Greek Cypriot and Turkish walls. This former hotel, its interior gutted and its exterior marred by bullet holes, stands on neutral territory in the buffer zone; it currently houses the UN headquarters in Cyprus. To get there from the Old City, cross through Paphos Gate and take a right on Markou Drakou immediately upon entering the New City. Continue on Markou Drakou until it is impossible to go any further. You will pass two other UN areas, the watchtower at Paphos Gate and the entrance to the UN buildings off Markous Drakou, before finally coming to the entrance to North Nicosia. You must show your passport on the Greek Cypriot side and again on the Turkish side, where you fill out a general information form in order to receive a special visitor's visa (the Turkish side once charged a border fee but no longer does; you may be asked to pay £1 at most). **Do not let them stamp your passport.** If they stamp your passport, you will not be readmitted to Greek Cyprus. They will, however, give you a form to be stamped by someone at another window. Hold on to this form—you will need it to cross back after your visit.

1. You may enter North Cyprus 8am-1pm but must return by 5pm. No exceptions. You cannot start a trip through North Cyprus by crossing the Green Line; guards will not allow you to cross with a large backpack or bag. If you remain in North Cyprus later than 5pm the easiest way for you to re-enter Southern Cyprus is to cross over to Turkey and then take a boat or plane back to the country.
2. Rental cars are not allowed across.
3. As in other areas of Lefkosia and Cyprus, do *not* take pictures of anything that has to do with the military or police.
4. You are prohibited from buying anything on the Turkish side. Any items purchased in the north will be confiscated upon your return to the south. If you wish to buy food, you must exchange your much desired Cypriot pounds for Turkish lira after you have crossed the border to Northern Cyprus.
5. If you have a problem, ask the UN soldiers (in blue berets) for help.

Costanze Bastioon, runs to **Kakopetria** (13 per day M-Sa 6:15am-7pm, Su 8am and 6pm; £1.20) and **Troodos** (M-F 11:30am, £1.50). **Kambos,** on Leonidou, runs to **Kykko Monastery** (M-Sa leaves at noon and returns 6am the next day, £2). A free route map of all the urban **Lefkosia buses** is available at the CTO (☎22 674 264).

Service Taxis: Travel & Express (☎22 777 474 or 22 730 888) runs taxis (M-Sa every 30min. 6am-6pm, Su 7am-5pm) to: **Limassol** (£3.50), **Larnaka** (£2.50), and **Paphos** (£6.25). Call ahead.

Private Taxis: Easily summoned from sidewalks and corners. Taxi stations are in Pl. Eleftherias, or call **Travel & Express** (☎22 730 888) for private service as well. Open 24hr. Private taxis are expensive, running about £1.25 initial charge and £0.22 per km daytime, or £1.65 initial charge and £0.88 per km at night.

ORIENTATION AND PRACTICAL INFORMATION

The easiest way to orient yourself in Lefkosia is to use the Venetian walls. The Green Line, running east to west at the north end of the city, divides the **Old City** into Greek and Turkish sectors. Within the walls, travelers can find most budget

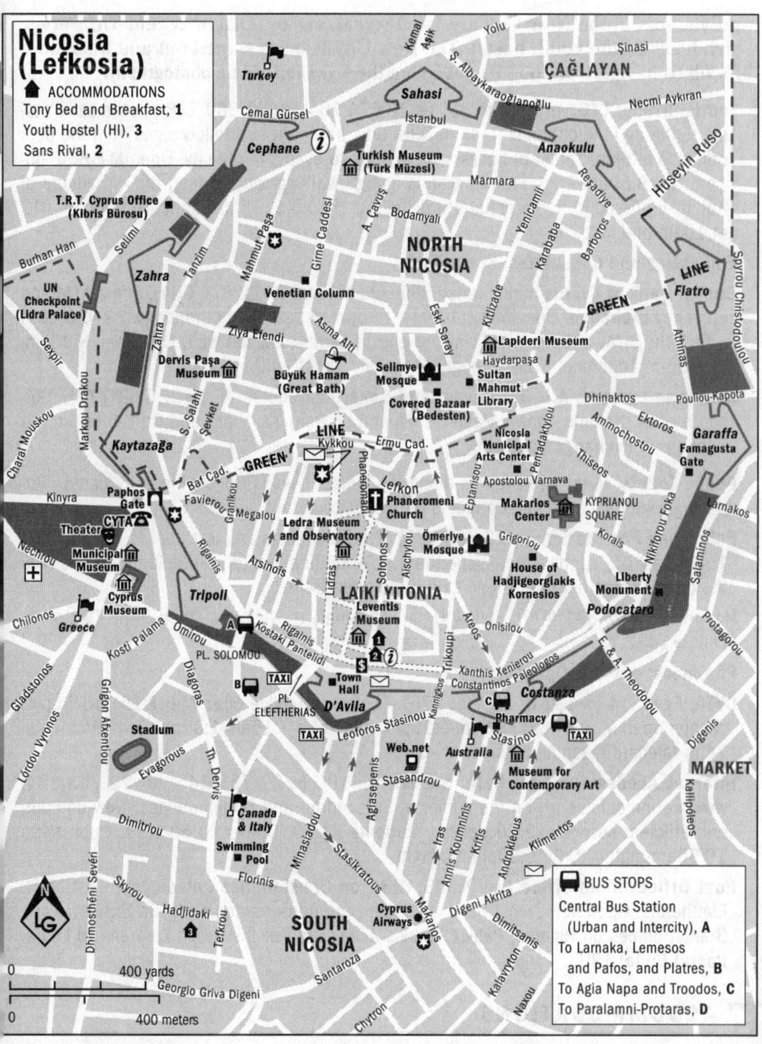

lodgings, museums, tavernas, and sights. To reach destinations within the Old City, walk along the Venetian walls and re-enter the Old City when you have come as near as you can to your destination; navigation is difficult on small back streets, and you may suddenly find yourself alone in a run-down neighborhood. Alternatively, green and yellow signs for the CTO's "Walking Tour of Medieval Lefkosia" can guide you through the city.

From **Pl. Eleftherias,** Evagoras heads southwest into the New City, while **Lidras** street, the primary pedestrian street and tourist core, runs to the north, where it intersects the Green Line. **Laiki Yitonia,** the pedestrian quarter where the CTO and many restaurants and hotels can be found, lies just to the right of Lidras. Intersecting Evagoras in the New City are Leoforos Makarios, Diagoras, and Th. Dervis, which leads to the youth hostel. The New City is quite spread out and thus more difficult to navigate on foot. **Do not ignore the signs forbidding photography.**

Tourist Office: CTO, Aristokypros 11 (☎22 674 264; fax 22 660 778), in the Laiki Yitonia. Entering Pl. Eleftherias from the New City, turn right and follow signs from the post office. Free maps, a list of buses, and a guide to events in the city. Open M-F 8:30am-4pm, Sa 8:30am-2pm. Free English-language walking tour through the old village of Kaimakli offered M, more general walking tour of Lefkosia Th; both leave from the CTO at 10am and last 2hr.

Embassies and Consulates: See p. 566.

Banks: Bank of Cyprus main branch, Phaneromeni 86 (☎22 674 064), offers **ATM** and **currency exchange.** Open M-F 8:15am-12:30pm. A convenient branch (☎22 436 161) with 24hr. **ATM** in Laiki Yitonia at the end of Ledra near the wall. Open M-F 8:30am-12:30pm. Additional ATMs throughout the city, most 24hr.

American Express: A.L. Mantovani and Sons, Agapinoras 2E (☎22 763 777), 1km south of Pl. Solomos down Makarios. Open M-F 8am-12:45pm and 2:30-5:30pm, Sa 9am-noon. **Exchanges currency.**

Public Toilets: In the parking lots along the Venetian walls (follow the W/C signs). Surprisingly sanitary, and toilet paper is blessedly abundant.

Police and Fire Station: (☎22 802 020). The 2 buildings are next door to one another, 150m east of Paphos Gate, inside the wall. Additional police station in the New City at the end of Ledra near the Green Line. Both open 24hr.

Hospital: (☎22 801 400). Follow Omirou (Homer) to Nechrou. Open 24hr. Doctor on call: ☎1432.

Pharmacy: ☎1412. Open 24hr.

CYTA: Egypt 14 (☎132 or 22 702 276). Customer service open M-F 7:15am-1:30pm; cashier open M, Tu, Th, F 7:15am-5:15pm, W and Sa 7:15am-1:30pm. Temperamental 24hr. telecard machine outside.

Internet Access: Web.net Cafe, Stasandrou 10C (☎22 753 345; fax 22 753 184; www.webnetcafe.com), on the corner of Stasandrou and Boumpoulinas. New computers, efficient service. £2.20 per hr., students £1.70. Drinks £0.60-1.30. Open M-Sa 10:30am-midnight, Su 5:30pm-midnight.

Post Office: Main office (☎22 303 123), on Constantinos Paleologos, east of Pl. Eleftherias. Open M-F 9am-1pm and 3-6pm (no afternoon hours W), Sa 8:30am-1pm. Branch offices on Riganis, Palace, Loukis Akitas, and at the Green Line end of Ledra. **Postal Code:** 1903.

ACCOMMODATIONS

Tony Bed and Breakfast, on the corner of Solon and Hippokratous (☎22 666 752 or 22 667 794; fax 22 662 225), in the Laiki Yitonia. Traditional decorations and a Victorian staircase lead to rooms of various sizes, all with radios, phones, hot water pots, fridges, A/C, and TVs. Many have sunny balconies with views of city landmarks including the mosques of North Nicosia. Guests can enjoy their breakfast on a spacious rooftop patio. Breakfast included. Singles £20; doubles £25-28; triples £30; quads £35. ❸

Youth Hostel (HI), Hadjidaki 1 (☎22 674 808 or 99 438 360), in the New City off Diagoras Dervis. An old home with a sprawling, enclosed garden. The 11pm noise curfew keeps the peace and attracts slightly older travelers. Rooms for women, men, families/couples, and 1 attic single. Full kitchen, 1 bath. Sheets £1. Dorms £4; single £6. ❶

Sans Rival, Solon 7 (☎22 669 383), in the Laiki Yitonia, a few doors down from Tony. Spacious, albeit spartan rooms. A/C in summer, full central heating in winter. Singles £17; doubles £20. ❸

FOOD

From multi-course Cypriot *mezedes* offered in Laiki Yitonia to the simpler fare served to a mostly local clientele in tavernas on Old City backroads, Lefkosia's dining options are many and varied. Consider cobbling a meal together at a **municipal market** in the New City, on the corner of Digenis Akritas and Ev. Kai Antonion Theodotou, or in the Old City at Trikoupi and Diogenous (open early morning-1pm and 4-6pm). At the Old City market there is also an open air market in the neighboring parking lot W and Sa.

Zanettos Taverna, Trikoupi 65 (☎22 765 501), near Omeriyeh Mosque in the Old City. Open since 1938, this dark, wood-paneled taverna is decidedly off the beaten path; one of a few restaurants in a neighborhood full of workshops and welding shops. Traditional Cypriot food and a local clientele. Entrees £2-3, meat *mezedes* for 2 £14. Open daily 7:30pm-midnight. ❶

Savvas, Solon 65 (☎22 668 444), in the Laiki Yitonia, serves what a Cypriot family would eat at home. Join the locals on lunch break for traditional dishes; for a true native experience try the *bambies* (baked okra stewed in a tomato, onion, and garlic sauce). All main dishes £1-2, with a glass of local wine (£0.50). Open for lunch only. ❶

Xefoto, Aeschylou 6 (☎22 666 567), in the Laiki Yitonia. Cypriot food served on a lantern-lit garden terrace. Live music on the weekends. Entrees £5-6. Open noon-11pm. ❸

SIGHTS

FAMAGUSTA GATE. Along the Venetian Walls at the end of Ammochostos street is the recently restored Famagusta Gate, the largest, best preserved, and most famous of all the gates that surround old Nicosia. The main entrance to old Lefkosia, built in 1567, it now hosts plays, concerts, exhibitions, and lectures; check the schedule at the CTO or pick one up at the Town Hall. *(Open M-F 10am-1pm, 4-7pm. Free.)* Not far down along the Venetian wall toward the Laiki Yitonia is the **Freedom Statue** (*Agalma Eleftherias*), depicting 14 Cypriots, each representing a period of the island's history, being released from the iron bars that have restrained them.

LEVENTIS MUNICIPAL MUSEUM. This museum chronicles the history and social development of Lefkosia from 3000 BC to today. Peer through the glass at your feet as you walk over an excavated portion of a medieval house from the Nicosia area. The 2nd floor consists mainly of traditional costumes, household items, and weaponry. Don't overlook the photographic chronology or the courtyard garden with its authentic Turkish baths. *(Hippocratis 17 in the Laiki Yitonia, off Solon. Open Tu-Su 10am-4:30pm. Free. Handicapped accessible.)*

PHANEROMENI CHURCH. A point of nationalist pride to Greek Cypriots, the Phaneromeni Church survived a Turkish attempt to transform it into a mosque. According to legend, **imams** of the mosque kept dying mysteriously of illness until the Turks gave up. The church was built in 1872 on the site of an ancient nunnery. *(Off Ledra street at the Green Line end. Open daily 6:30am-1pm and 3:45-7pm. Free, but donations are welcome.)*

PLATEIA ARCHBISHOPRIC KYPRIANOS. This complex of museums faces the Archbishop's palace; a statue of the Archbishop dominates the entrance. The **Makarios Cultural Center** houses several art galleries, the most impressive of which is the **Byzantine**

Museum on the first floor. The museum contains over 150 icons from the 8th to 18th centuries, many of which were collected by Makarios himself. Fragments of mosaics and frescoes from churches in areas occupied by Turkey are presented in a predictably nationalist light, and church treasures, including the Archbishop's throne and finery, round out the collection. The art galleries on the upper floors house Cypriot works from modern times and a small collection of oil paintings by European masters. *(☎22 430 008. Byzantine Museum open 9am-4:30pm and Sa 9am-1pm. £1.)* The second building of interest is **Saint John's Cathedral,** in the courtyard of the Makarios Center, built in 1662 with a single nave and five pointed arches. The tablets adorning the entrance were transferred from Venetian and Frankish buildings. *(Open M-F 9am–noon and 2-4pm, Sa 9am-noon. Free.)* Housed in a 15th-century monastery, the **Ethnographic Museum of Cyprus,** previously called the Folk Art Museum, contains Cypriot woodcarving, embroidery, pottery, basketry, and metalwork from the 18th to 20th centuries. *(On the right as you face the Makarios Center. ☎22 432 578. Open M-F 9am-4pm, Sa 10am-1pm. £1.)*

HOUSE OF HADJIGEORGIAKIS KORNESIOS. Near Pl. Kyprianos is the luxurious, 18th-century home of the famous *dragoman*, or Ottoman tax-collector and interpreter. Kornesios was actually a Greek Cypriot who, through clever strategy and knowledge of many languages, rose to the prestigious and lucrative position of tax-collector in Cyprus for the Ottoman Emperor. In 1804, the Cypriots raided his house, but the *dragoman* and his family escaped through a hidden passage. Don't miss the dark and inviting room in the very back of the second floor where a Turkish coffee set and narguile still rest on the raised floor, as though the occupants of the house were about to return and take their seats on the bank of low cushions that line the walls. *(☎22 305 316. Open M-F 8am-2pm, Sa-Su 9am-1pm. £0.75.)*

CYPRUS MUSEUM. Here you'll find the most extensive collection of ancient art and artifacts on the island, from pre-Hellenic periods through the Byzantine era. Amateur archaeologists can compare local jewelry across eras, while everyone will feel dwarfed by ancient, larger-than-life terra-cotta figures. *(Mouseiou 1, near the Paphos Gate. ☎22 865 805. Open M-Sa 9am-5pm, Su 10am-1pm. £1.50.)*

NIGHTLIFE AND ENTERTAINMENT

Lefkosia's late-night entertainment is not heavily clustered in any particular area, making bar hopping a fairly labor-intensive endeavor. Young locals tend to drive to clubs outside the city. However, many **bars** and **pubs** can be found in the Pl. Eftherias area, and some restaurants there have traditional live music and dancing late on weekend evenings. For trendier bars and clubs, try the neighborhood known as Egnomi, around Leoforou Goudia. **Sfinakia,** Th. Dervis 43 (☎22 766 661), and **Time,** on Makariou (☎22 775 427), are convenient to the Old City. Be prepared to soldier on well into the morning if it's dancing you're after; patrons will mostly sit, talk, and drink until dawn threatens. A word of caution: Women should not walk alone through the neighborhood around Pl. Eleftherias past 2am when the bars have closed and the younger crowd at surrounding cafes has thinned.

Mike & Alexander's Pub and Restaurant, Pl. Eleftherias, on Pantelidi and Laiki Yitonia (☎22 451 174). This outdoor cafe, which looks out over Pl. Eleftherias, affords excellent opportunities for people-watching, while the dark-wood interior of the restaurant mimics the Irish pub trend. Beer £1.50-2.60. Open daily 8am-2am.

Ta Kala Kathoumena, Nikokleous 21 (☎22 664 654), tucked into an alley between Ledra St. and Phaneromni Church. Lefkosia's young collegiate intellectuals gather from afternoon until evening for debate, backgammon, and drinks (£0.40-£1.20). Open M-Sa 11am-midnight, Su 6pm-midnight.

Zoo, Stasinou 15 (☎758 262). Draws a slightly older crowd. Upscale joint has a fancy restaurant upstairs and club downstairs, painted an immaculate white. Open daily 8:30am-1am, F-Su until 4am.

NORTH NICOSIA

North Nicosia is teeming with green-clad troops, who have been instructed to be kind to tourists. In contrast to the conservationism rehabilitating its southern counterpart, modernization has seized the Old City of North Nicosia. However, the glitzy highrises of the main road, Girne Caddeşi, are quickly forgotten with a walk through the crumbling and quiet back streets, where the marks that each of the city's hopeful conquerors and leaders have made on the architecture pile on top of each other like geological strata.

ORIENTATION AND PRACTICAL INFORMATION

From the south at the **Lidra Palace** crossing, a roundabout with a Turkish victory monolith in the middle is 500m up the street. Follow the city walls to **Girne Gate** (also called Cephane or Kyrenia Gate). From there, **Girne Caddeşi,** the main street, runs to the main square, where the Saray Hotel and the Venetian Column are found, and continues to the Green Line.

Because of the instability of the Turkish lira, prices for goods and services in North Nicosia are listed in US dollars. For **police,** dial ☎155; **emergency ambulance,** dial ☎112; **fire,** dial ☎199. The helpful **tourist office,** located in the Girne Gate gatehouse, is a good place to begin your tour of the city. Only **Turkey** has a full embassy in North Cyprus, at Bedrettin Demirel Cad. (☎227 23 14. Open M-F 9am-noon.) The following countries have "representative offices," offering some consular services: **Australia,** 20 Güner Türkmen Sok. (☎227 73 32; open Tu, Th 8:30am-12:30pm); **Germany,** #15 28 Kasım Sok. (☎227 51 61); **UK,** 29 Mehmet Aleif Cad. (☎228 70 51 or 228 38 61; open M, W, F 9am-1:30pm; Tu, Th 9am-1:30pm and 2:30-5pm); and **US,** 6 Saran Sok. (☎225 24 40; open M-F 8am-1pm and 2-3:30pm). Several offices along Girne Cad. offer **currency exchange** (open M-F 8am-1pm and 2-4pm). **ATMs** are near the Saray Hotel; the one outside **Türkiye İş Bankası** takes foreign cards. The **police** (☎392 22 3311) are on Girne Cad. close to Atatürk Meydanı. A **hospital** (☎392 22 8541) is 3km from the town center on the road to Girne, 700m from the Victory Monument. Look for the *Hastane* sign. **Pembe Telefon,** near the post office, has metered booths and sells phone cards. (Open M-F 7:30am-2pm and 3:30-5:30pm.)

The **Saray Hotel** (☎392 22 8315) ❸, next to the Venetian column, offers an upscale lunch and a magnificent view of the city from the hotel's top floor. The **cafe** ❸ in the former Chapter House of Agia Sophia, now the **Selimye Mosque,** serves Cypriot specialties and delicious orange juice in the shady courtyard. For takeout, seek out the Turkish kebab houses at the Green Line end of G. Caddesi.

SIGHTS

The **Büyük Hamamı** (Great Bath), was built on the ruins of the 14th-Century Church of St. George during the Ottoman era. From G. Caddesi, take a left near the Venetian column. Since the time of the building's construction, the road level has risen about 2m, leaving the *hamam* slightly subterranean. An original wooden knocker, which once served to warn bathing harem members of the coming of intruders, still hangs from the door to the steam room. (Open M-F 9am-5pm. $1. Bath, exfoliation, and massage by professional male masseur $15.)

The **Selimiye Camii** mosque, formerly **Agia Sophia Cathedral,** is a bizarre sight: two minarets have been grafted onto a 13th-century French gothic cathedral. To get there, follow G. Caddesi nearly to the Green Line end, then take a left on Arasta, the pedestrian road. The vast, high-ceilinged interior has been whitewashed and the floor carpeted with prayer rugs; a mimber (pulpit) and mihrab (altar) have been added. Saints carved in the arches above the door and flying buttresses testify to the edifice's original purpose. Refurbished by the Ottomans in 1570, the Roman Catholic cathedral was originally built in the Gothic style during the city's Lusignan period by French architects at the behest of Queen Alix of Champagne.

Beside the mosque is the 14th-century Orthodox **Cathedral of St. Nicholas,** and beyond it the **Bedensten,** a warehouse filled to overflowing with produce stands. (Open M-Sa 9am-5pm.) Behind the mosque lie several small museums. The **Library of Sultan Mahmut** no longer holds books, but a poem inscribed to Mahmut II by a Cypriot poet is engraved in the walls. ($1.20, students $0.60.) **Lusignan House,** with its ornate wooden ceilings added in the Ottoman period, offers a taste of how the other half lived in the 15th-century. If you find the door locked there or at the **Lapidary Museum,** which houses examples of stonework, inquire at the **Eaved House**—someone may be able to let you in. (Both open irregular hours M-F.) Just a dice throw away is the **Kumarcılar Hanı** (Gamblers' Inn). This 17th-century caravanserai for traveling merchants now houses the Northern Cyprus Antiquities Department (open M-F 8am-2pm).

APPENDIX

CLIMATE

The climate is fairly uniform throughout Greece; the islands are a bit milder, and higher altitude areas (especially in the north) are cooler—expect it to be much colder on mountainous hikes. **Summer** is sunny, hot, and dry. **Winter** temperatures hover around 50°F. October to March is the rainy season.

Avg. Temp. (lo/hi),	JANUARY		APRIL		JULY		OCTOBER	
Precipitation	°F	in.	°F	in.	°F	in	°F	in.
Athens	55/43	2.5	68/52	0.9	91/73	0.2	75/59	2.0
Thessaloniki	48/36	1.8	68/50	1.6	90/70	0.9	72/55	2.3
Trikala	48/32	3.4	70/46	3.2	95/66	0.8	77/54	3.2
Naxos	59/50	3.6	68/55	0.8	81/72	0.1	75/64	1.8

To convert from degrees Fahrenheit to degrees Celsius, subtract 32 and multiply by 5/9. To convert from Celsius to Fahrenheit, multiply by 9/5 and add 32.

°CELSIUS	-5	0	5	10	15	20	25	30	35	40
°FARENHEIT	23	32	41	50	59	68	77	86	95	104

METRIC CONVERSIONS

1 inch (in.) = 25.4 millimeters (mm)	1 millimeter (mm) = 0.039 in.
1 foot (ft.) = 0.30 m	1 meter (m) = 3.28 ft.
1 mile = 1.61km	1 kilometer (km) = 0.62 mi.
1 ounce (oz.) = 28.35g	1 gram (g) = 0.035 oz.
1 pound (lb.) = 0.454kg	1 kilogram (kg) = 2.202 lb.
1 fluid ounce (fl. oz.) = 29.57ml	1 milliliter (ml) = 0.034 fl. oz.
1 gallon (gal.) = 3.785L	1 liter (L) = 0.264 gal.
1 square mile (sq. mi.) = 2.59km^2	1 square kilometer (km^2) = 0.386 sq. mi.

TELEPHONE CODES

See **Keeping in Touch** (p. 44) for full information and advice about telephone calls in Greece and Cyprus, including international access.

		COUNTRY	CODES		
Australia	61	Greece	30	South Africa	27
Canada	1	Ireland	353	Spain	34
Cyprus	357	Italy	39	Turkey	90
France	33	Japan	81	UK	44
Germany	49	New Zealand	64	US	1
		CYPRUS	357		
Agia Napa	03	Limassol	05	Paphos	06
Larnaka	04	Nicosia	02	Platres	05

GLOSSARY OF USEFUL TERMS

acropolis a fortified, sacred high place atop a city
adelfos brother
adelfi sister
afto this
aftokinito car
agape love (see *erotas*)
agora the ancient city square and marketplace
alithea truth
ammos sand
amphora a two-handled vase for oil or wine storage
angouri cucumber
apse nook beyond the altar of a church
architrave lintel resting on columns and supporting the entablature, below a frieze
arni lamb
astinomeio police
astra stars
Archaic Period 700-480 BC
arnaki lamb
Asia Minor Turkey, particularly its once-Greek Aegean coast
aspro white
astakos lobster
atrium house's open interior courtyard; typically Roman
avga eggs
avgolemono egg-lemon soup
avrio tomorrow
basilica church with a saint's relic; especially holy
bouleterion meeting place of an ancient city's legislative council
bouzouki stringed instrument
Byzantine Period AD 324-1453
caïque fishing or passenger boat, usually wooden
capital decorated top of a column
castro castle or fortifications
cella inner sanctum of a classical temple
chrono year (or time, in a grandiose sense)
chryso gold
cigara, or **tsigara** cigarettes
Classical Period 480-323BC
Corinthian column ornate, leaf- or flower-engraved top (or capital) of a column
cornice top of the entablature of a temple
Cyclopian walls massive irregular-cut Minoan and Mycenaean stone walls, so called because only a Cyclops could lift such stones
demos people, citizens
dimarchio town hall
dolmades warm stuffed grape leaves with sauce of egg and lemon
dolmadakia cold stuffed grape leaves
domatia rooms to rent in private homes; rooms to let
Dorian referring to invaders of 1100 BC
Doric column cigar-shaped columns with wide fluted shafts, cushion tops (or capitals), and no bases
efimerevon 24hr. pharmacy
eleftheria freedom
eleftheri/os single, free
entablature upper parts of a temple facade, atop columns
epicremeni/os upset, sad, disappointed
erotas erotic love or sex
erotevmeni/os madly in love
etos year
exoteriko international
exedra curved recess in classical/Byzantine architecture
exonarthex outer vestibule in a Byzantine church
Faneromeni Virgin Revealer
feta soft, white, omnipresent goat-milk cheese
filaki (accent on la) kiss
filaki (accent on ki) jail
forum Roman marketplace
frappé whipped, frothy frozen coffee drink
frieze illustrated middle part of a temple exterior (in particular, the entablature); see *metopes* and *triglyph*
frourio medieval fortress or castle; often called a Castro
gaiduri donkey (masculine)
gaidara donkey (feminine)
galaktopoleio dairy shop
galaktobouriko cream pastry
ghala milk
glika sweets
gyro greasy, pita-wrapped lamb sandwich
haroumeni/os happy
Hellenistic Period 323-46 BC
heroon shrine to a demigod
hora (chora) island capital or main town in an area
iconostasis screen that displays Byzantine icons
Ionic column slender column topped with twin scrolling spirals and with a fluted base
iperastiko long distance (phone calls, transportation)
kafeneion cafe
kaimaiki specialty ice-cream with *mastika* (gum)
kalamarakia baby squid
kasseri hard yellow cheese
kastro castle or fortifications
Katharevoussa uppity "pure" Greek literary language, taken from ancient Greek
kathemera every day
kathemerino daily
katholikon monastery's main church or chapel
kato hora the lower part of a village
kefalos head
kefi feeling of exuberance
KKE Greek communist party
koine "common" Greek used before the Byzantine era
kore female statue
kotopoulo chicken
kouros male nude statue
ktapodhi octopus
KTEL inter-city bus service
ladhi oil
leoforos avenue
leoforeo bus
libation gift of food or liquor to a god
limani port
logariasmo check
magiritsa tripe soup with rice
malaka common obscenity that connotes masturbation
mastika chewing-gum or gum
mavro black
megalo big (opposite of *mikro*)
megaron large hall in a house or palace
melizanes eggplants
meltemi an unusually strong north wind in the Cyclades and Dodecanese
metopes painted or sculpted square block in a Doric frieze that contains scenes with figures; *metopes* are separated by *triglyphs*
meze, mezedes, mezedakia appetizers to go with ouzo
mikro small (opposite of *megalo*)
Minoan Period 3000-1250 BC
mitera mother
moni monastery or convent
moro/moraki baby
moschari veal
moussaka a lasagna-like dish made with layered eggplants, meat, and potatoes
moustarda mustard
Mycenean Period 1600-1100 BC
naos holy innermost part of a temple or church

narthex vestibule on the west side of a Byzantine church
nave church aisle
ne yes
Neolithic Period 3000-2000 BC
nomos Greek province
nosokomeio hospital
odeion semi-circular theater
odos road
ohi no
oikos house
omphalos belly-button
opa! much-used expression; hey!; oops!; look out!
ouzeri *ouzo* tavern serving *mezedes* and other yummy treats
ouzo national brew of Greece
omorfia beauty
ora time (hour)
OTE the Greek national telephone company
paleohora old town
palaestra classical gymnasium
Panagia the Virgin Mary
pano high or upper
panigiri local festival, often religious
Pantokrator a mosaic or fresco of Christ in a Byzantine church dome
papaki duckling (slang for moped)
pareia a group of friends
patera father
pedi child; "ela, pedia" means "come on, kids"; used to call the *pareia* at any age
pediment triangualar, sculpture decorated space in an ancient temple's facade
peplos mantle worn by ancient Greek women; Athena's nightgown
periptero street kiosk
peristyle colonnade around a building
philos buddy, friend
pima poem
piesi high blood pressure, nerves
piperi pepper
pithos ceramic storage jar
plateia town square
pleio ferry
polis city-state
portico colonnade or *stoa*
pronaos outer column-lined temple porch
propylaion sanctuary entrance flanked by columns
prytaneion administrative building
psaras fisherman
psaria fish
psomi bread
raki Cretan local liquor
retsina sharp white wine
rhyton cup shaped like an animal's head
Roman period 46 BC-AD 324
satyr lusty follower of Dionysus
simera today
skala port for an inland town
souvlaki oh-so-tender meat on a skewer (usually lamb)
spili, spilia cave, caves
stele a stone slab that marks a tomb
stoa in ancient marketplaces, an open portico lined with rows of columns
taverna restaurant or tavern
techni art
tholos Mycenean earth-covered, beehive-shaped tomb
tiri cheese
triglyph part of a Doric frieze comprised of 3 vertical grooves that alternate with *metopes*
trireme ancient ship with 3 sets of oars
tsipouro mainland bathtub liquor
tsoutsoukakia meat balls in tomato sauce
varka boat
volta evening walk
vouno mountain
voutiro butter
xechasmeni/os forgotten
xeri dry
xeri carpi nuts, dry snacks
yiayia grandmother
yialos waterside (port, beach)
zaccharoplasteio sweetshop
zakhari sugar

GREEK ALPHABET

The Greek alphabet has 24 letters; the chart below can help decipher signs. The left column gives the name of each letters in Greek, the middle column shows lower case and capital letters, and the right column shows the pronunciation.

LETTER	SYMBOL	PRONOUNCIATION	LETTER	SYMBOL	PRONOUNCIATION
alpha	α Α	*a* as in father	nu	ν Ν	*n* as in net
beta	β Β	*v* as in velvet	ksi	ξ Ξ	*x* as in mix
gamma	γ Γ	*y* as in yo or *g* as in go	omicron	ο Ο	*o* as in row
delta	δ Δ	*th* as in there	pi	π Π	*p* as in peace
epsilon	ε Ε	*e* as in jet	rho	ρ Ρ	*r* as in roll
zeta	ζ Ζ	*z* as in zebra	sigma	σ (ς) Σ	*s* as in sense
eta	η Η	*ee* as in queen	tau	τ Τ	*t* as in tent
theta	θ Θ	*th* as in health	upsilon	υ Υ	*ee* as in green
iota	ι Ι	*ee* as in tree	phi	φ (ϕ) Φ	*f* as in fog
kappa	κ Κ	*k* as in cat	xi	χ Χ	*ch (h)* as in horse
lambda	λ Λ	*l* as in land	psi	ψ Ψ	*ps* as in oops
mu	μ Μ	*m* as in moose	omega	ω Ω	*o* as in row

COMMON WORDS AND PHRASES

USEFUL PHRASES		
yes	ναι	NEH
no	οχι	OH-hee
ok	ενδαξι	en-DAX-ee
please/you're welcome	παρακαλω	pah-rah-kah-LO
thank you (very much)	ευχαριστω (πολυ)	ef-khah-ree-STO (po-LEE)
sorry/pardon me	συγνομη	sig-NO-mee
Do you speak English?	μιλας αγγλικα;	mee-LAHS ahn-glee-KAH?
I don't speak Greek	δεν μιλαω ελληνικα	dhen mee-LAHO el-leen-ee-KAH
I don't understand	δεν καταλαβαινω	dhen kah-tah-lah-VEH-no
How much?	ποπο κανει;	PO-so KAH-nee?
Leave me alone!	ασεμε!	AH-se-me
Help!	Βοητηεια!	vo-EE-thee-ah!
shit	σκατα	ska-TA
darling	λατρεια	lah-TREE-ah
maybe; I'm thinking about it	το σκεπτομε	toh SKEP-to-meh
it does (not) matter	(θεν) πειραζι	(then) peer-ADZ-ee
I love you	Σ'αγαπαω	SAH-gap-AH-o
I miss you	Μου λιπις	mou LEE-pis
I want you	Σε θελο	seh THEL-oh
GREETINGS		
good morning	καλημερα	kah-lee-MEH-rah
good evening	καλησπερα	kah-lee-SPE-rah
good night	καληνυχτα	kah-lee-NEE-khtah
hello/goodbye (polite, plural)	γεια σας	YAH-sas
hello/goodbye (familiar)	γεια σου	YAH-soo
Mr./Sir	κυριος	kee-REE-os
Ms./Madam	κυρια	kee-REE-ah
What is your name?	Πως σε λενε;	pos-se-LEH-neh?
My name is ...	Με λενε	me-LEH-neh ...
QUESTIONS AND DIRECTIONS		
why?	Για τι;	yah-TEE?
where? who? when?	που; πιος; ποτε;	POO? pYOS? POH-teh?
Where is...?	Που ειναι;	pou-EE-neh...?
Where are you going?	Που πασ	POU-pahs?
I'm going to...	Πηγαινω για	pee-YEH-no yah...
When do we leave?	Τι ωρα φευγουμε;	tee O-rah FEV-goo-meh?
stop	στασι	STA-si
I need a ticket	Χπειαζομαι εισητεριο	kree-AH-soh-meh eeseeTEERio
Can I see a room?	Μπορω να δω ενα δωματιο;	bo-RO nah-DHO E-nah dho-MAH-tee-o?
here, there	εδω, εκει	eh-DHO, eh-KEE
left	αριστερα	ah-rees-teh-RAH
right	δεξια	dhek-see-AH

I am lost	χαθηκα	HA-thee-ka
I am ill	Ειμαι αρροστος	EE-meh AH-ross-toss
airplane	αεροπλανο	ah-e-ro-PLAH-no
airport	αεροδρομειο	ah-e-ro-DHRO-mee-o
bus	λεωφορειο	leh-o-fo-REE-o
ferry	πλοιο	PLEE-o
port	λιμανι	lee-MA-nee
suitcase	βαλιστα	vah-LEE-tsah
ticket	εισιτηριο	ee-see-TEE-ree0o
train	τραινο	TREH-no
TIME		
What time is it?	Τι ωρα ειναι;	tee-O-rah EE-neh?
Monday	Δευτεπα	def-TEH-ra
Tuesday	Τριτι	TREE-tee
Wednesday	Τεταπτη	teh-TAR-ti
Thursday	Πεμπτη	PEHmp-tee
Friday	Παρασκευι	pah-rah-skeh-VEE
Saturday	Σαββατο	SAH-vah-to
Sunday	Κυριακη	kee-ree-ah-KEE
yesterday	χθες	KTHES
today	σημερα	SEE-mer-a
tomorrow	αυριο	AV-ree-o
morning	πρωι	pro-EE
evening	βραδι	VRAH-dhee
later tonight	αποψε	ah-PO-pseh
first	πρωτο	PRO-to
last	τελευταιο	teh-lef-TEH-o
SIGNS		
bank	τραπεζα	TRAH-peh-zah
church	εκκλησια	eh-klee-SEE-ah
doctor	γιατρος	yah-TROS
hospital	νοσοκομειο	no-so-ko-MEE-o
hotel	ξενοδοχειο	kse-no-dho-HEE-o
market	αγορα	ah-go-RAH
museum	μουσειο	mou-SEE-o
pharmacy	φαρμακειο	fahr-mah-KEE-o
police	αστυνομεια	as-tee-no-MEE-a
post office	ταχυδρομειο	ta-khee-dhro-MEE-o
restaurant	εστιατοριο	es-tee-ah-TO-ree-o
room	δοματιο	dho-MAH-teeo
toilet	τουλετα	twa-LE-ta
open, closed	ανοικτο, κλειστο	ah-nee-KTO, klee-STO
COMMERCE		
I need	Χρειαζομαι	khree-AH-zo-meh
I want	Θελω	THEH-lo
I would like ...	Θα ηθελα	thah EE-the-lah ...

I will buy this one	Θα αγορασω αυτο	thah ah-go-RAH-so ahf-TO
Do you have?	Εχετε;	Eh-khe-teh?
bill	λογαριασμο	lo-gahr-yah-SMO
water	νερο	ne-RO
good	καλο	kah-LO
cheap	φτηνο	ftee-NO
expensive	ακριβο	ah-kree-VO
NUMBERS		
zero	μηδεν	mee-DHEN
one	ενα	Eh-nah
two	δυο	DHEE-o
three	τρια	TREE-ah
four	τεσσερα	TES-ser-ah
five	πεντε	PEN-dheh
six	εξι	E-ksee
seven	επτα	ep-TAH
eight	οκτω	okh-TO
nine	εννια	en-YAH
ten	δεκα	DHEH-kah
eleven	ενδεκα	EN-dheh-kah
twelve	δωδεκα	DHO-dheh-kah
thirteen	δεκατρια	DHEH-kah TREE-ah
fourteen	δεκατεσσερα	DHEH-kah TES-ser-ah
fifteen	δεκαπεντε	DHEH-kah PEN-dheh
sixteen	δεκαεξι	DHEH-kah E-ksee
seventeen	δεκαεπτα	DHEH-kah ep-TAH
eighteen	δεκαοκτω	DHEH-kah okh-TO
nineteen	δεκαεννια	DHEH-kah en-YAH
twenty	εικοσι	EE-ko-see
thirty	τριαντα	tree-AN-dah
forty	σαραντα	sa-RAN-dah
fifty	πενηντα	pen-EEN-dah
sixty	εξηντα	ex-EEN-dah
seventy	εβδομηντα	ev-dho-MEEN-dah
eighty	ογδοντα	og-DHON-dah
ninety	ενενηντα	en-EEN-dah
hundred	εκατο	ek-ah-TO
thousand(s)	χιλια(δες)	hil-ee-AH(-dhes)
million	εκατομμυριο	eka-to-MEE-rio

DAYTRIPS TO TURKEY

The Turkish Aegean coast is full of chill beach towns, beautiful mosques, and ancient Greek ruins. Daytrips to Turkey are cheap and easy from several Greek islands, including Samos (p. 358), Chios (p. 365), and Kos (p. 478). To go for the day, just catch a ferry to the Aegean coast from a nearby island. Not every Turkish daytrip is accessible by direct ferry, however. If your destination is Çanakkale, Eceabat, İzmir, Ephesus (Efes), or Selçuk, you'll need to head to Bodrum, Çeşme, or Kuşadası and catch a bus to your destination. For more information on transportation, accommodations, and sites, check out *Let's Go: Turkey 2003.* Prices for goods and services in Turkey are listed throughout in US dollars, as the Turkish lira is very unstable.

PRACTICAL INFORMATION

PHONE HOME	The country code for Turkey is **90.** The international access code for Turkey is **00.**

Ferries: Boats run from **Samos, Chios,** and **Kos** to the Turkish Aegean coast.

- **Samos:** From Vathy (Samos Town) 5 per week to Kuşadası (1¼hr.; €30 1-way, €44 round-trip).
- **Chios:** From Chios Town 1 per day to **Çeşme** (45min.,€50).
- **Kos:** From Kos Town 1 per day in the morning to **Bodrum** (€35-40 round-trip).

Visas: To enter Turkey, citizens of **Australia, Canada, Ireland, the UK,** and **the US** need a visa. A visa costs US$65. Citizens of **New Zealand** and **South Africa** do not need visas to enter Turkey. New Zealanders may stay for up to 3 months with a valid passport, South Africans for up to 1 month. Visas must be purchased with foreign currency.

Tourist Offices: Aid with everything from directions to transportation to accommodations. **Selçuk:** 35 Agora Çarşısı (☎232 892 63 28; fax 232 892 69 45). **Bodrum:** 48 Barış Meydanı (☎252 316 10 91; fax 252 316 76 94). **Çeşme:** 8 İskele Meydanı (☎232 712 66 53; open 8:30am-5:30pm; also open in summer Sa-Su 9am-5pm). **İzmir:** 1/1D Gazi Osman Paşa (☎232 445 73 90; fax 232 489 92 78).

Transportation in Turkey: Buses run up and down the Aegean coast. **Selçuk** is reachable by bus from **Bodrum** (3hr., 1 per hr. 2am-6pm, $8) or **İzmir** (take a Bodrum- or Kuşadası-bound bus and ask to be let off at Selçuk; 1hr., $2). **Mini-buses** run between Kuşadası and Selçuk (20min.; every 15min. May-Sept. 6:30am-11:30pm, Oct.-Apr. 6:30am-8:30pm; $0.80). The Selçuk *otogar* (station) is at the intersection of Şahabettin Dede and Atatürk. To get to **Ephesus** (Efes), take a taxi ($4) or walk (3km, 25min.) from Selçuk. **Bodrum** is very well-connected to all major cities in western Turkey by bus. From **Selçuk,** a bus runs every hr. from 8:15am-1:15am to Bodrum (3hr., $8). From **İzmir,** there is a bus every hour from 4am-7pm (4hr., $7). The Bodrum *otogar* is on Çevat Şakir. Buses run between **Çeşme** and **İzmir** (1½hr., every 20min. 6am-10pm, $2). From İzmir, you can hop a bus to wherever you want to go. The **Çeşme** *otogar* is at the corner of A. Menderes and Çevre Yolu.

EMERGENCY NUMBERS	**Police:** ☎155	**Ambulance:** ☎112
	Fire: ☎110	**Gendarme:** ☎156

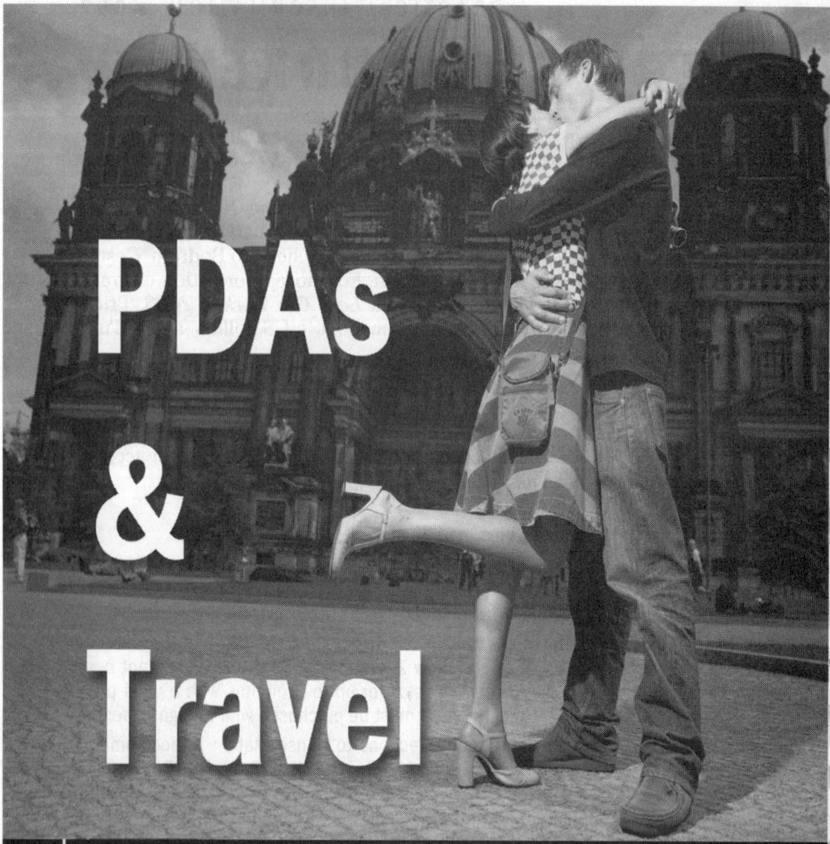

INDEX

INDEX

A

B

C

D

E

I

J

K

INDEX

INDEX

P

R

S

T

INDEX

U

V

W

X

Z

MAP INDEX

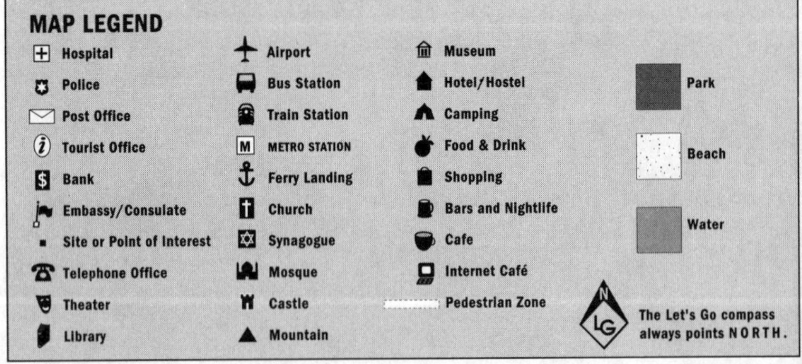

MAP LEGEND
Hospital
Police
Post Office
Tourist Office
Bank
Embassy/Consulate
Site or Point of Interest
Telephone Office
Theater
Library
Airport
Bus Station
Train Station
M
METRO STATION
Ferry Landing
Church
Synagogue
Mosque
Castle
Mountain
Museum
Hotel/Hostel
Camping
Food & Drink
Shopping
Bars and Nightlife
Cafe
Internet Café
Pedestrian Zone
Park
Beach
Water
N
LG
The Let's Go compass always points NORTH.